LET'S GO:
ITALY

is the best book for anyone traveling on a budget. Here's why:

No other guidebook has as many budget listings.

In Rome we list dozens of places to stay for less than $7 per night; in the countryside, hundreds more for much less. We tell you how to get there the cheapest way, whether by bus, train, plane, or thumb, and where to get an inexpensive and satisfying meal once you've arrived. There are hundreds of money-saving tips for everyone plus lots of information on special student discounts.

LET'S GO researchers have to make it on their own.

No expense accounts, no free hotel rooms. Our Harvard-Radcliffe student researchers travel on budgets as limited as your own.

LET'S GO is completely revised every year.

We don't just update the prices, we go back to the places. If a charming trattoria has become an overpriced tourist trap, we'll replace the listing with a new and better one.

No other budget guidebook includes all this:

Coverage of both the cities and the countryside; in-depth information on culture, history, and the people; distinctive features like rail, city, and regional maps; tips on work, study, hiking and biking, nightlife and special splurges; and much, much more.

LET'S GO is for anyone who wants to see the real Italy on an inflation-fighting budget.

LET'S GO:

The Budget Guide to

ITALY

(INCLUDING TUNISIA)

1989

Kathryn S. Moffett
Editor

Scott C. Gelormino
Assistant Editor

Written by Harvard Student Agencies, Inc.

PAN BOOKS
London, Sydney and Auckland

Helping Let's Go

If you have suggestions or corrections, or just want to share your discoveries, drop us a line. We read every piece of correspondence, whether a 10-page letter, a postcard, or, as in one case, a collage. All suggestions are passed along to our researcher/writers. Please note that mail received after June 1, 1989 will probably be too late for the 1990 book, but will be retained for the following edition. Address mail to: Let's Go: Italy, Harvard Student Agencies, Inc.; Thayer Hall-B; Harvard University; Cambridge, MA 02138; USA.

In addition to the invaluable travel advice our readers share with us, many are kind enough to offer their services as researchers. Unfortunately, the charter of Harvard Student Agencies, Inc. enables us to employ only currently enrolled Harvard students both as researchers and editorial staff.

Published in Great Britain by Pan Books Ltd
Cavaye Place, London SW10 9PG
9 8 7 6 5 4 3 2 1

Published in the United States of America
by St. Martin's Press, Inc.

ISBN: 0 330 30548 4

Let's Go: Italy is written by Harvard Student Agencies, Inc., Harvard University, Thayer Hall-B, Cambridge, Mass. 02138, USA.

Printed and bound in the United States of America.

Editor	Kathryn S. Moffett
Assistant Editor	Scott C. Gelormino
Publishing Manager	Mark D. Selwyn
Managing Editors	Alice K. Ma
	Andrea Piperakis
Production/Communications Coordinator	Nathanael Joe Hayashi
Researcher/Writers:	
Sardinia, Tunisia	Peter M. Ferren
Liguria, Piedmont, Lombardy, Trentino-Südtirol/Alto Adige, Veneto, Friuli-Venezia Giulia	Kristina Wynne Friberg
Lazio, Umbria, Abruzzo, Molise, Puglia, Basilicata, Calabria	Ellen P. Goodman
Sicily, Malta	Nathaniel Hupert
Emilia Romagna, Tuscany, Marches	Alexander Nagel
Lombardy	Heidi M.V. Sullivan
Rome, Campania	Michael Paul Ventre
Advertising Manager	Kimberley Harris
Advertising Representatives	Kelly Ann McEnaney
	Charles Emmit Ryan
Legal Counsel	Harold Rosenwald

CONTENTS

ACKNOWLEDGMENTS

What a time!
What a civilization!
—Cicero

What a time of it Scott, Alice, I, and our seven dauntless researcher/writers had compiling and recording the remains and modern extension of Cicero's raucous Roman empire! And what a reclusive, uncivilized civilization of Ring Dings, throbbing top 40, *paella* madness, and ochre/mauve sunrises we basement bunnies harbored in cantankerous, cavernous Canaday G cellar! Unlike Cicero's world, we had no room for decline; we were in the bottom of a building, receiving rock-bottom pay, with revelry and dissipation low on our long Andrea-style lists of "things to do."

And in Roman style, our glories—Food Fests, the conquering of Mike's 150-page Rome copy, Alice's breaking of the world-record for months gone without shut-eye (and my record for months gone on vacation), and the pic on the front page of *USA: TODAY*—were balanced and challenged by our temporary tragedies: Kristina's fateful fall, Scott's bouts with an ancient Japanese germ and ensuingly with the largest pile of to-be-copyedited to ever weigh down an assistant editor's desk, and the failure of our long-planned strike to come into being. Indeed, some you win, and some you lose, but this summer was an undeniable victory over time and pure paper volume.

The true troopers behind this effort were those camouflaged budget travelers who carried their pens and pads snug as guns and shot through every region of the boot with incredible celerity and efficacy. Starting from the top of this long, pointed shoe-house called Italy, Kristina Friberg, a little misstepping aside, imbued the Italian Riviera with renewed charm and color, breezed through the deluge of research for the lush Lake region, and floated through the serpentine canals of Venice's accommodations and food sections. Milan's cathedral defies gravity, and, luckily, Heidi Sullivan defied the gravity of her original OstDeutschland/Oesterreich itinerary to come south to this bastion of fashion and make sure the *duomo* and the establishments we list were still standing. Tuscan dynamo Alex Nagel rewrote village and city intros and sights sections (and what is Tuscany but one big medieval and Renaissance sights section) with the savvy of only a prospective Fine Arts Ph.D, and with the warmth and vibrance of the rust-red, mustard-yellow, and olive-green Tuscan countryside itself. Veteran Mike Ventre must have been the third little tyke after Romulus and Remus to suckle the she-wolf who nurtured the founders of Rome. He literally rediscovered and redefined Rome, digging up the newest, hippest cheap sleeps, eats, and boogies. Dealing not with an empire but with the fortified hill towns of green Umbria and Lazio, and corners farther south, Ellen Goodman's descriptions were nothing less than poetry, and her excellent research poetry to the obsolete listings. Nate (Hupert) the Great joined our battalion by a fortuitous twist of fate and pursued to move mountains the likes of Etna to update and rejuvenate Sicily and the jet-set pet, Malta. Ferocious Peter Ferren bushwhacked his way through the rugged terrain of Sardinia and withstood the desert sands of Tunisia to also know this gentle Arab land's oases.

Back at the subterranean ranch, Scott Gelormino (the King of Lucubration, Overtime, and Herculean Effort) ploughed through copy with a well-honed pick and the eye of a farmer who cares about his crop. Alice in Wonderland, ma friend, (Robo-)Ma was the unwavering guiding light when one benighted editor was in the dark about format and general editing etiquette. Any accuracy and clarity this tome may have is due to Alice's otherworldly precision. Mark ("Isn't he great??") Selwyn was the in-house shrink and miracle doctor, epitomizing equanimity and calmness, and supplying culinary comforts during those longer nights. Fallay André Flipperakis Dukakis Piperakis—whatever I may call you, you remain my model of efficiency and diligence. I hope that for many years we will share pieces of pieces. Grovier, merci beaucoup pour le squash et le coke et les Ring Dings et ton humeur bizarre. Andola Angola Spagola Schmarola Zola, I just might have to write my thesis on the derivation of that jarble I endearingly refer to you as. What would Editor's Row have been without your non-stop stand-up comedy show, Jim Mazur? Thanks for your friendship and all the times you let me ramble into your ear. Jamey Flyaplane, would have been nice if we'd met in that veritable fest o' foliage known as Currier (our mutual site of sequestration) instead of the musty cellar we all called home. JD, Jr., you scared the spooks out of Cambridge Common on too many nights when the sun was already close at hand. Thanks to Dave, my coffee-taste-test companion, for the concert and all, and Lynley, we will have to rally bigtime in the old U.K. My gratitude goes also to those others who brightened my basement life: Allen, Joe, Sue, Alex, Emily, Julianne (Navratalova), Carolla, and Jay Bobay. Kudos to those who helped a lot for a little, Ellen Rubin, typist extraordinaire, Debbie Benor and Sally Haden, impeccable proofreaders and Bill Cole, who glossed over the rather dulled glossary.

Finally, I owe much to my idols in life and Porquerolles pals, Alex Sapirstein and Betsey Schmidt, whose exuberance and love endowed me, as old, with the energy to finish this encyclopedic endeavor. I also wish to thank those patient souls who carried the weight of my burden vicariously as summer companions in Cambridge: Beccaroobee, Ello Jello and Benj (mentors, therapists, fellow chunky monkey fetish-holders), Amy (weekend wonderwoman), Heather, Frankie, Kevin, and Oona. To my mother, and to my father and Lucy, I dedicate this book, for they made (always do) everything possible.

—Kay

The journey was a success! It seems that in spite of the plagues, accidents, and computer failures, God was with Italy for '89. Special thanks go to Kay Moffett for her phenomenal editing in times of trouble; Mark Selwyn for his support and encouragement at every stage of the copy flow process; Joe Hayashi for saving us—literally—*and* sparing us lots of trouble more times than I can count; and Alice Ma, whose infamous "eye for detail" I'll never forget. The rest of the office and our devoted researchers also deserve plaudit for all their support, encouragement, and help. They propelled us—with inspiration, kindness, and spirit. Undoubtedly, this summer was one of my most satisfying and exciting. I know, though, that it's only the beginning . . .

I would also like to remember all my mentors and friends from Jersey City, The Hudson School, Regis, Harvard, and, of course, CRS. There's not enough space here to list all of you, but you know who you are—forever with me in my heart. Lastly, there are those who were with me through the storms and always brought the sun back into view: Nelson, Richard, Sue, Mr. DiMichele, Jin, Dave, Michael, Matt, Mary Ellen et al., Maryrose, Walt, Aunt Aedan, Tim, Len, and, of course, Mom. You all have my love—*always.*

—Scott

About Let's Go

In 1960, Harvard Student Agencies, a three-year-old nonprofit corporation established to provide employment opportunities to Harvard and Radcliffe students, was doing a booming business selling charter flights to Europe. One of the extras HSA offered passengers on these flights was a 20-page mimeographed pamphlet entitled *1960 European Guide,* a collection of tips on continental travel compiled by the staff at HSA. The following year, Harvard and Radcliffe students traveling to Europe made notes and researched the first full-fledged edition of *Let's Go: Europe,* a pocket-sized book with a smattering of tips on budget accommodations, irreverent write-ups of sights, and a decidedly youthful slant. The first editions proclaimed themselves to be helpmates to the "adventurous and often pecunious student." Throughout the sixties, the series reflected its era: A section of the 1968 *Let's Go: Europe* was entitled "Street Singing in Europe on No Dollars a Day"; the 1969 guide to America led off with a feature on drug-ridden Haight Ashbury.

During the seventies, *Let's Go* gradually became a large-scale operation, adding regional guides to parts of Europe and slowly expanding into North Africa and nearby Asia. In 1981, *Let's Go: USA* returned after an eight-year hiatus, and in the next year HSA joined forces with its current publisher, St. Martin's Press. Since then, the series has continually blossomed; the additions of *Let's Go: Pacific Northwest, Western Canada, and Alaska* and *Let's Go: California and Hawaii* in 1988 brought the the total numbers of titles to eleven.

Each spring, over 150 Harvard students compete for some 70 positions as *Let's Go* researcher/writers. An editorial staff of 14 carefully reads stacks of 10-page applications and conducts thorough interviews. Those hired possess a rare combination of budget travel sense, writing ability, stamina, and courage. Each researcher/writer travels on a shoestring budget for seven weeks, researching and writing seven days per week, and mailing back their copy to Cambridge—about 500 pages in six installments. Train strikes, grumpy proprietors, noisy hostels, irate tourist officials are all in a day's work, but sometimes things become more serious. The afflictions of the summer of 1988 included one tear gassing, two totaled cars, one concussion, one near-drowning, and, in the most bizarre tale to date, one researcher/writer was chased up a tree by a pack of reindeer.

Back in a cluttered basement in Harvard Yard, an editorial staff of 25 and countless typists and proofreaders spend four months poring over more than 50,000 pages of manuscript as they push the copy through 12 comprehensive stages of intensive editing. In September the collected efforts of the summer are converted from computer diskette to nine-track tapes and delivered to Com Com in Allentown, Pennsylvania, where their computerized typesetting equipment turns them into books in record time. And even before the books hit the stands, the next year's editions are well underway.

LET'S GO: ITALY

General Introduction

US $1 = 1403 lire(L)	L1000 = US $0.71
CDN $1 = L1163	L1000 = CDN $0.86
UK £1 = L2370	L1000 = UK £0.42
AUS $1 = L1125	L1000 = AUS $0.89
NZ $1 = L929	L1000 = NZ $1.08

Nationwide Emergency Numbers: 112 or 113.
Nationwide Tourist Information Number: 116.

You may have the universe if I may have Italy.
—*Giuseppe Verdi*

Metternich said, "Italy is a geographic expression," and, for centuries he was right. From the fall of Rome to the close of the nineteenth century, the Italian peninsula was a conglomeration of independent city-states, papal hierarchies, and tiny empires. Massive medieval walls still encircle most Italian cities. In addition to insulating towns and villages from the chaos of the outside world, they've encouraged the development of distinct dialects, customs, and artistic and architectural styles. Though the asphalt and steel of the twentieth century have long since broken the tough stone seal, a proud individualism persists in each region of "the boot."

Italy today mixes the high fashion of Giorgio Armani with the simple rusticity of Tuscan farmers, and the violence of Mafia gang wars with the holiness of the papacy. Among more modern elements, somber Christian churches sparkle with Byzantine frescoes in Ravenna, San Gimignano bristles with the forbidding towers of the later Middle Ages, and Florence revels in the glory of the Renaissance. Doric, Ionic, and Corinthian columns and the ideal forms of the sculpture of ancient Rome are everywhere still.

To help you explore this varied country, *Let's Go* is packed with information on transportation, lodgings, eating, and sightseeing. Our researcher/writers travel on a shoestring budget; their frank appraisals are designed to save you hours of unnecessary head-scratching—and thousands of lire. Before you go, *Let's Go* guides you through the maze of passport applications, travel arrangements, and money, health, and insurance considerations. Once there, *Let's Go* covers all 20 of Italy's provinces in depth: Sicily and Sardinia, the beaches of Liguria, the medieval villages of Tuscany, hiking trails in the Dolomites, and, in addition, Tunisia and Malta. Italy is more than just a "geographic expression," and, with *Let's Go,* you can discover this for yourself for less money than you thought possible.

Planning Your Trip

Although a detailed itinerary can be restrictive, it's always a good idea to plan ahead. Research the places you'd like to go, ways to get there, and things to do along the way. Travel is one of Italy's largest industries, and you'll be surprised how much information is available. Spend some time writing to the organizations listed in *Let's Go*'s general and regional introductions, and ask specific questions about hiking, entertainment, festivals, or anything else that interests you. And re-

AUSTRIA
HUNGARY
Zurich
SWITZERLAND
FRANCE
YUGOSLAVIA
Zagreb
Trieste
Dubrovnik
Mt. Blanc
Matterhorn
Aosta
Italian Alps
VALLE D'AOSTA
The Lakes
Como
Milan
Brescia
LOMBARDY
Pavia
Cremona
Turin
PIEDMONT
Maritime Alps
Northern Appenines
LIGURIA
Genoa
Merano
Bolzano
Adige R.
Dolomites
FRIULI-VENEZIA GIULIA
Udine
TRENTINO-ALTO ADIGE
Trent
Verona
Vicenza
VENETO
Venice
Padua
Mantua
Ferrara
Parma
Modena
EMILIA-ROMAGNA
Bologna
Rimini
San Marino
Pesaro
Ancona
La Spezia
Lucca
Pisa
Arno
Pistoia
Florence
TUSCANY
Monaco
Nice
Ligurian Sea
Arezzo
Siena
Lake Trasimeno
Perugia
Assisi
MARCHES
Adriatic Sea
Ascoli Piceno
Orvieto
Elba
Viterbo
UMBRIA
Tiber River
ABRUZZI
Pescara
L'Aquila
Termoli
Tremeti Islands
CORSICA
Citavecchia
Cerveteri
LAZIO
Tivoli
Rome
MOLISE
Southern Appenines
Gargano Massif
Foggia
Latina
CAMPANIA
Bari
PUGLIA
BASILICATA
Brindisi
Porto Torres
Olbia
Sassari
Alghero
Naples
Ischia
Capri
Sorrento
Pompeii
Salerno
Potenza
Matera
Taranto
Lecce
Metaponto
Nuoro
SARDINIA
Tyrrhenian Sea
CALABRIA
Sila Massif
Cagliari
Catanzaro
Ustica
Messina
Lipari Islands
Palermo
Reggio di Calabria
Trapani
Egadi Islands
Marsala
SICILY
Mt. Etna
Taormina
Ionian Sea
Enna
Catania
Agrigento
Syracuse
N
Tunis
TUNISIA
Mediterranean Sea
0 100 miles
0 100 kilometers

member to leave enough room in your schedule to relax. Blitzing every sight and city in Italy in two weeks won't leave you much time to slow down and talk to people. A well-placed *"Ciao!"* or *"Grazie!"* can do wonders.

A Note on Prices

The information in this book was researched during the summer of 1988. Although Italy's 1988 inflation rate hovered around 5%, prices fluctuate, and those we quote will most likely have increased by 1989. Note that prices are listed in *lire* (L) in Italy, *Maltese lire* (Lm) in Malta, and *dinars* (D) in Tunisia. The currency exchange rates we list at the beginning of each section are also from the summer of 1988.

When to Go

Ever since the Phoenicians and the Greeks started visiting, Italy has been a tourist hot spot. Each year, fifty million visitors invade this peninsula, a number almost equal to Italy's entire population. You can avoid the swarms of tourists by visiting in the off-season, when local residents have more time to help you, air fares are cheaper, and even flying standby is relatively simple. Hotels, sights, and streets will be less crowded, and you'll be able to visit fall wine harvests and festivals, the Dolomites in winter, and St. Peter's at Easter. Chances are you'll return with a more accurate picture of what life is like in Italy if you visit between September and May.

On the flip side, many hostels and hotels are closed; museums and tourist offices keep shorter hours; and the streets are less vibrant in the off-season. Venice, for instance, is much more subdued in winter. And although Italian winters are mild, the weather can foil outdoor ventures such as camping.

If you decide to travel in July and August, make reservations wherever and whenever possible (see Accommodations below). They may limit your flexibility, but they'll allow you to travel more securely. Don't forget that many businesses, restaurants, and hotels may be closed in August, when most Italians take *their* vacations. (See Life and Times below for a list of Italian festivals and holidays.)

Useful Organizations

Centro Turistico Studentesco e Giovanile, via Nazionale, 66, Rome 00184. With offices throughout Italy (see each city's Practical Information section), CTS provides travel and sight-seeing discounts, as well as information for students and young people. Sells the YIEE card.

Compagnia Italiana Turismo (CIT), 666 Fifth Ave., New York, NY 10103 (tel. (800) 223-7987 or (212) 397-9300), with branch offices in Chicago, Los Angeles, Toronto, and Montréal. A national travel agency specializing in individual and group tour packages.

Council on International Educational Exchange (CIEE/Council Travel), 205 E. 42nd St., New York, NY 10017 (tel. (212) 661-1414; for charter flights (800) 223-7402). Information on budget travel and educational, voluntary, and work opportunities throughout the world. ISIC and YIEE cards. IYHF memberships. Write for their annual *Student Travel Catalog* (US$1) or pick it up free at one of their offices. Also available are *Work, Study, Travel Abroad: The Whole World Handbook* (US$8.95, postage US$1), *Work Your Way Around the World* (US$10, postage US$1), and *Volunteer! The Comprehensive Guide to Voluntary Service in the U.S. and Abroad* (US$5.50, postage US$1). CIEE operates branch offices in Austin, Atlanta, Providence, Dallas, Chicago, San Francisco, Los Angeles, Berkeley, San Diego, Seattle, Portland, Long Beach, Amherst, and Boston. Address all mail inquiries to the N.Y. office.

Educational Travel Center, 428 N. Frances St., Madison, WI 53703 (tel. (618) 256-5551). Flight information, IYHF cards, and Eurailpasses. Write for their free pamphlet *Taking Off,* providing information on tours and flights.

Federation of International Youth Travel Organizations (FIYTO), 81 Islands Brygge, DK-2300 Copenhagen S, Denmark (tel. (01) 54 32 97). Issues the YIEE (FIYTO) card to anyone (not just students) under 26. Free annual catalogue lists over 8000 discounts available to cardholders. FIYTO also offers reduced-rate accommodations, as well as cultural activities and tours. Offices in Italy include:

ACNT, via Gallera, 92, 40050 Funo Di, Argelato, Bologna.
Instituto "Vittorio Alfieri," via Dell'Oriuolo, 20, 50122 Florence.
STS, via Zanneti, 18r. 50123 Florence.
EUROPA YSTC, via Mezzocannone, 119, 80134 Naples.
ATG, via dei Barbieri, 3A, 00186 Rome.
CTS, via Nazionale, 66, 00186 Rome.
ETLI, Youth Section, via L. Serra, 19, 00153 Rome.
CTG, via Piave, 49, 00186 Rome.
Turismo Universitario, via Aquileia, 50/3, P.O. Box 18, 33100 Udine.

Forsyth Travel Library, 9154 W. 57th St., P.O. Box 2975, Shawnee Mission, KS 66201 (tel. (913) 384-3440 or (800) FORSYTH, that's (800) 367-7984). A mail-order service that stocks a wide range of European city, area, and country maps, as well as guides for European rail and boat travel. The sole North American distributor of the Thomas Cook *European Timetables,* a compilation of train schedules for all of Europe (US$19.95, postage included). Write or phone for a free newsletter and catalog.

International Student Travel Conference (ISTC): Weimbergstrasse 31, CH-8006 Zurich, Switzerland. **USA,** CIEE/Council Travel Services (see address above). **Canada,** Travel CUTS (see address below). **U.K.,** STA Travel (see address below) and London Student Travel, 52 Grosvenor Gardens, London SW1W 0AG, Britain (tel. (01) 730 34 02). **Australia,** SSA/STA, 220 Faraday St., Carlton, Melbourne, Victoria 3053, Australia (tel. (03) 347 69 11). **New Zealand,** Student Travel, Courtenay Chambers, 2nd floor, 15 Courtenay Pl., Wellington, New Zealand (tel. (04) 850 561). Issues the International Student Identity Card (ISIC).

Italian Cultural Institute, 686 Park Ave., New York, NY 10021 (tel. (212) 879-4242). Information on Italian art, music, literature, civilization in general, and current events. Call and ask about anything that interests you in Italy—they're friendly and helpful (though very busy in summer).

Italian Government Travel Office (ENIT), 630 Fifth Ave., #1565, Rockefeller Center, New York, NY 10111 (tel. (212) 245-4822); 500 N. Michigan Ave., #1046, Chicago, IL 60611 (tel. (312) 644-0990); 360 Post St., #801, San Francisco, CA 94108 (tel. (415) 392-6206); 3, Pl. Ville Marie, 56 Plazaz, Montréal, Québec H3B 2E3 (tel. (514) 866-7667). Write for their detailed guide, *General Information for Travelers to Italy,* and for lists of local festivals and information on specific regions.

John Muir Publications, P.O. Box 613B, Sante Fe, NM 87504 (tel. (505) 982-4078). Publishes 3 books by veteran traveler Rick Steves. *Europe through the Back Door* (US$12.95) offers good advice, especially on traveling light and avoiding tourist traps. *Europe in 22 Days* (US$6.95) is an itinerary for those who want to "do" Europe. *Europe 101: History, Art and Culture for the Traveler* (US$11.95) is ingenuous, but better than nothing.

Let's Go Travel Services, Harvard Student Agencies, Inc., Thayer Hall-B, Harvard University, Cambridge, MA 02138 (tel. (617) 495-9649). ISIC and YIEE cards, American Youth Hostel memberships (valid at all IYHF hostels), Eurailpasses, travel guides (including the entire *Let's Go* series), and travel gear—all available on the spot. ISIC and YIEE cards also available by mail.

STA Travel, Priory House, 6 Wrights Lane, London W8 6TA (tel. (01) 581 10 22 for intercontinental information, (01) 581 82 33 for European information). Provides bargain flights, travel services, accommodations, tours, rail tickets, and ISICs. Exclusive charter programs to destinations across Italy.

Superintendent of Documents, U.S. Government Printing Office, Washington, DC 20402. Publishes *Your Trip Abroad* (US$1), *Key Officers of Foreign Serving Posts* (published 3 times per year, US$5 per year), *Safe Trip Abroad* (US$1), and *Health Information for International Travel.*

Travel Cuts (Canadian Universities Travel Service), 187 College St., Toronto, Ont. M5T 1P7 (tel. (416) 979-2406), with offices in Victoria, Vancouver, Halifax, Edmonton, Saskatoon, Winnepeg, Ottawa, Montréal, and London, U.K. Offers special student rates on both domestic and international travel. ISIC, YIEE, and IYHF cards and discount travel passes (e.g., Transalpino and Eurotrain), as well as Eurailpass and Eurail YouthPass. Canadian Work Abroad Program for ages 18 to 25. Their newspaper, *The Canadian Student Traveler,* is free at all offices and on campuses across Canada.

Wide World Books and Maps, 401 NE 45th St., Seattle, WA 98105. Publishes a free catalog listing the most recent guidebooks to every part of the world.

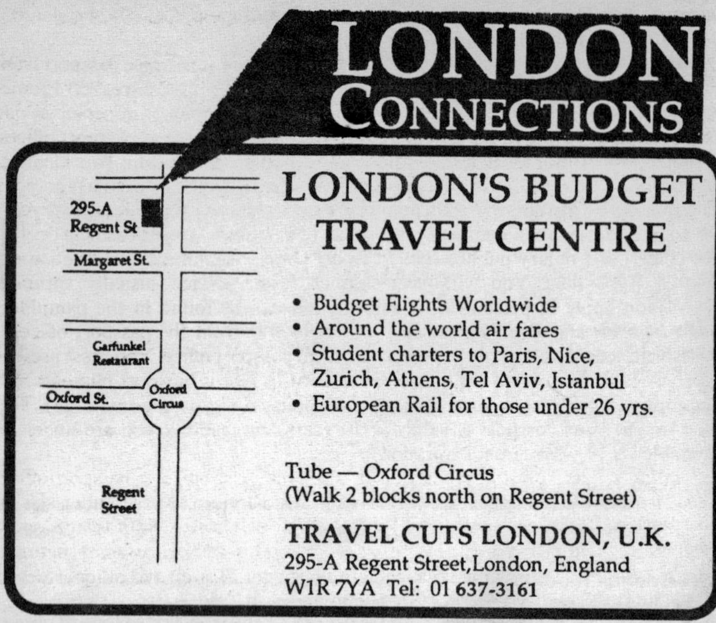

Documents and Formalities

Passports

A valid passport is necessary to enter Italy and reenter your home country. Just in case your passport is lost or stolen, you should get a photocopy of it showing its number and date and place of issue. Keep this separate from your passport. It's also wise to carry a few extra passport-type photos. If you do lose your passport, notify the local police and the nearest consulate immediately (see Once There below for a list of consulates). Consulates recommend that you carry an expired passport or an original copy of your birth certificate (essentially, you should have another issued by the Bureau of Vital Statistics of your state or province—don't take *the* original) in a separate part of your baggage. The Italian police will issue a declaration for L4000 stating that your passport has been stolen; you may use this as identification until your passport is replaced.

U.S. citizens can obtain a passport valid for 10 years (US$42) or, if they're under age 18, a passport valid for five years (US$27). Apply at any U.S. Passport Agency office or at one of the several thousand federal or state courts or post offices that accept passport applications. If this is your first U.S. passport, if your current passport is more than 12 years old, or if it was issued before your 16th birthday, you may apply by mail. Parents may apply on behalf of children under age 13. Submit a completed application, proof of U.S. citizenship (a certified copy of your birth certificate or your naturalization papers, or a previous passport not more than 8 years old), positive identification (e.g., a driver's license), and two identical passport photographs with your signature, taken not more than six months before the application date. If you renew by mail (US$35, US$20 for those under 18), your former passport will serve as both proof of citizenship and positive identification. Processing usually takes from two to three weeks if you apply in person, much longer otherwise. It's wise to apply several months in advance. If you have proof of departure within five working days (e.g., an air ticket), it is possible to obtain a passport through the Passport Agency's while-you-wait rush service; arrive in the office before 1pm. For more information, write to the Bureau of Consular Affairs, Passport Services, #386, Department of State, 425 K St., Washington, DC 20524 (tel. (202) 783-8200 or 523-1462, lines open 24 hours).

Canadian citizens may apply by mail for a five-year, non-renewable passport from the Passport Office, Department of External Affairs, Place du Centre, 200 Promenade du Portage, Hull, Québec K1A OG3 (tel. (819) 994-3500), or in person at one of 18 regional offices. Submit a completed application (available at passport offices, post offices, and travel agencies); evidence of Canadian citizenship; two identical passport photos; and CDN$25. In addition, your identity must be certified on your application by a "guarantor," someone who has known you for at least two years and who falls into one of a number of categories (e.g. mayor, lawyer, medical doctor, police officer, and notary public). The Passport Office recommends that you apply in winter, if possible. You will receive much faster service—usually within a week—if you apply in person. More information can be found in the pamphlets *Canada Passport* and *Bon Voyage, but . . .*, both free from the passport office.

British citizens should apply in person at a local passport office. You must present original copies of your birth certificate; two identical, recent passport photographs; and a copy of your marriage certificate (if it applies and you are under 18). The fee is £15 and your passport is valid for 10 years, five years if you are under 16 (extendable to 10 years upon expiration).

Australian citizens must apply in person at a local post office or passport office. The fee is AUS$66, and your passport is valid for 10 years. Those under age 18 must pay AUS$27 for a passport valid for five years. You must submit two passport photographs signed by the applicant, proof of citizenship (an old passport, naturalization or citizenship papers, or an original full birth certificate), and other evidence of notification as deemed necessary by the interviewing officer.

New Zealand citizens must visit or write the Office of Internal Affairs in Wellington (or their local district office) for an application. You must submit two passport photographs (one certified by a friend), a marriage certificate (if applicable), and a birth certificate. The fee for a 10-year passport (5 years if you are under age 10) is NZ$50; the office will provide speedy processing in emergencies. Children under age 16 may be included on a parent's passport.

A passport is probably the only document you'll need to visit Italy for up to three months. If you decide to stay longer, you should apply to local Italian authorities or the Italian Police *(questura)*. You will be allowed to stay for 90 additional days provided you can prove you are a tourist with adequate means of support. You cannot request the extension for study or employment.

Remember that your passport is a public document and may not be withheld or used as collateral without your consent.

Visas

If you plan to work, study, or travel in Italy for at least three months, the Bureau of Consular Affairs recommends you obtain a visa before departure. A visa is a stamp placed on your passport by a foreign government permitting you to visit that country for a specified purpose and period of time (usually six months, although this may be extended). Admission does not include permission to work (see Work below).

Since obtaining a visa or visa extension while in Italy is extremely difficult, you should get one before you leave. Apply well in advance at the nearest Italian embassy or consulate. To apply for a student visa, you will need a letter of acceptance from the university you will be attending and either a statement from your parents stating that they will finance you during your stay, or a letter from your bank or accountant stating that you have sufficient personal financial resources. The U.S. Department of State provides two useful pamphlets, *Visa Requirements of Foreign Governments* and *Tips for Travelers,* both free. Write to the **Bureau of Consular Affairs,** Passport Services, Department of State, #5807, Washington, DC 20524 (tel. (202) 783-8200 or 783-8170). Citizens of Great Britain, New Zealand, Canada, and

Australia have similar visa requirements. (See Once There for Italian consulate offices in the U.S. and Canada.)

Italy requires tourists with visas to register at the nearest police station within three days of arrival in the country. Hotel management is responsible for the registration of their guests, but if you aren't staying in hotels, the responsibility is technically your own.

Student Identification

The **International Student Identity Card (ISIC)** is often required for student flights, trains, and clubs. The ISIC can also get you discounts on museum admission, theater tickets, transportation, and more; get into the habit of presenting it and asking about student discounts wherever you go *(c'è un sconto studentesco?).* When issued in the U.S., the card provides sickness and accident insurance (see Insurance below). See Useful Organizations above for places that sell the ISIC. When applying for the card (US$10), you must supply the following: (1) current, dated proof of your full-time student status (a letter on school stationery, signed and sealed by the registrar, or a photocopied grade report); (2) a 1½×2 inch photo with your name printed on the back; and (3) proof of your birthdate and nationality (a photocopy of your birth certificate or passport). The card is valid for 16 months, from September 1 through the end of the following calendar year. Be sure to pick up a copy of this year's *ID Discount Guide,* listing by country some of the discounts available.

If you aren't eligible for the ISIC but are under 26, you can take advantage of the **Youth International Educational Exchange Card (YIEE)** issued by the Federation of International Youth Travel Organizations (FIYTO). Also known as the FIYTO card, the YIEE card gets you discounts on transportation (air, sea, and overland), accommodations, and cultural activities in 56 countries. See Useful Organizations for places that sell the YIEE card (US$4). You must bring your passport number and a photograph. For further information, write to FIYTO (see Useful Organizations for the address).

Hostel Membership

To stay in youth hostels affiliated with the **International Youth Hostel Federation (IYHF),** you must often become a member of IYHF. In most countries, membership cards are available while you wait from many budget travel agencies (see Useful Organizations above). The cost varies by country ($20 in the U.S.), and your membership is good through the calendar year. The IYHF affiliate in Italy is **Associazione Italiana Alberghi per la Gioventù,** via Cavour, 44, 00184 Rome. Other affiliates follow (see also Accommodations below.)

U.S.: American Youth Hostels (AYH), P.O. Box 37613, Washington, DC 20005 (tel. (202) 783-6161).

Canada: Canadian Hostelling Association (CHA), 333 River Rd., Tower A, 3rd floor, Vanier City, Ottawa, Ont., K1L 8H9 (tel. (613) 748-5638).

Britain: Youth Hostel Association (YHA), 14 Southampton St., Covent Garden, London WC2E 7HY (tel. (01) 836 85 41) and **International Youth Hostel Federation (IYHF),** Midland Bank Chambers, Howardsgate, Welwyn Garden City, Herts, England (tel. (0707) 332 487).

Australia: Australian Youth Hostel Association, 60 Mary St., Surry Hills, Sydney, New South Wales 2010 (tel. (02) 212 11 51).

New Zealand: Youth Hostel Association of New Zealand, The Arts Center of Christchurch, 28 Worcester St., P.O. Box 436, Christchurch (tel. (03) 79 99 70).

Driver's Licenses

All foreign drivers in Italy (including those renting cars) must have a valid driver's license and a translation of the license. You must also have a "green card," or **International Insurance Certificate,** available through rental agencies, travel agents, the **Canadian Automobile Association (CAA),** or the **American Automobile Association (AAA).** Contact local chapters of the AAA, or write their main office: 8111 Gatehouse Rd., Falls Church, VA 22047.) Most rental agencies include this coverage in their rates; check to see that your insurance applies abroad. If not, you can take out short-term policies.

Customs

The maximum amount of Italian currency you can export is L400,000. No other export restrictions apply, except on antiques and precious art objects.

Upon returning to your home country, you must declare all articles acquired abroad and pay a duty on the value of those articles above an allowance established by your country's customs service. Before you leave home, record the serial numbers of all valuables you take on your trip, and carry receipts for these items to prove that you did not buy them abroad. Be especially careful with items made abroad that you purchased in your home country. In addition, a customs agent at your point of departure may be able to officially stamp or certify your list of serial numbers. Keep the receipts for anything you purchase abroad to help establish its value when you return home. Keep in mind that items you buy at duty-free shops abroad are *not* exempt from duty when you return: "duty-free" means only that you didn't pay taxes in the country of purchase.

U.S. citizens may bring back US$400 worth of goods duty-free; you pay 10% on the next $1000 worth. Duty-free goods must be for personal or household use and cannot include more than 100 cigars, 200 cigarettes (1 carton), or one liter of wine or liquor (you must be 21 or older to bring liquor into the U.S.). All items included in your allowance must accompany you; they cannot be shipped separately. Exemptions of persons traveling together may be combined.

You may mail unsolicited gifts back to the U.S. duty-free if they're worth less than $50. However, these gifts may not include liquor, tobacco, or perfume. As spot checks are occasionally made on parcels, it's wise to mark the accurate price and nature of the gift on the package. If the parcel is worth over $50, the Postal Service will collect the duty and a handling charge from the recipient. If you mail home personal goods of U.S. origin, mark the package "American goods returned." For more information, write for the brochure *Know Before You Go,* available from the U.S. Customs Service, P.O. Box 7407, Washington, DC 20044 (tel. (202) 566-8195). To avoid problems when carrying prescription drugs, make sure the bottles are clearly marked, and have the prescription ready to show the customs officer.

Canadian citizens may bring back CDN$20 worth of goods after 24 hours absence, any number of times per year. After 48 hours absence, you may bring back goods to the value of CDN$100. Written declaration may be required. After seven days or more, once per calendar year, you may bring back goods to the value of CDN$300. If you are over 16, you may include 200 cigarettes, 50 cigars, and 0.91kg tobacco in your 48-hour or seven-day exemption. If you meet the age requirement of the province of your point of re-entry, you may include 1.1 liters wine or liquor or 24 (355ml) cans or bottles of beer in your 48-hour or seven-day exemption. After 48 hours, any number of times per year, you are entitled to a 20% tax rate on goods valued up to CDN$300 over and above your CDN$100 and CDN$300 exemptions. You may send gifts up to a value of $40 duty-free, but you cannot mail alcohol or tobacco. Before leaving, list the serial numbers of all valuables on a Y-38 form at a Customs Office or point of departure. For more information, write to the Canadian Department of External Affairs, Ottawa, Ont. K1A 0G2 for their booklets *I Declare,* and *Bon Voyage, but . . . ,* as well as *Canada: Travel Information.*

Australian citizens are allowed 200 cigarettes, 250g of cigars (or 250g of tobacco), and one liter of alcohol. You are allowed to bring in up to AUS$200 worth of goods duty-free; the next AUS$160 worth will be taxed at 20%. These goods may not include tobacco, alcohol, or furs, and must be carried into the country with you. If you are under 18, your allowance is AUS$100. You may mail back personal property; mark it "Australian goods returned" to avoid duty. You may not mail home unsolicited gifts duty-free. Before going, buy a departure tax stamp at any office of the Department of Immigration and Ethnic Affairs or at the passport office of the Department of Foreign Affairs. Fill out customs form B263 at a customs office or at your point of departure to list goods that you will be taking with you, so they can be re-imported duty-free. For more information, write for the brochure *Australian Customs Information—All Travelers,* available from the Australian Customs Service, Customs House, 5-11 Constitution Ave., Canberra, A.C.T. 2600.

New Zealand citizens should list valuables to be taken on the trip on a Certificate of Export to be signed by a customs officer. Upon return, you may import NZ$100 of goods duty-free. If you are over 17, you may bring in 200 cigarettes or 250g of tobacco or 50 cigars or any combination of the three not exceeding 250g. You may also bring in 4.5 liters of wine or beer and 1125ml of spirits or liqueur. Free copies of the pamphlets *New Zealand Customs Guide for Travelers, Traps for Travelers,* and *If You're Not Sure About It, Declare It,* are available at any embassy.

Money

Currency and Exchange

The Italian monetary system is based on the lira. The smallest denomination of Italian currency is the L10 coin. The smallest note is a L1000 bill. Before leaving home, buy at least US$40 worth of lire to save you time at the airport or train station, and probably some money, as exchange rates are better at home than in Italy.

When exchanging money, shop around. Banks often offer the best rates, but generally charge commissions (as much as US$3). To minimize your loss, exchange large sums at once, though never more than is safe to carry around. Remember: Every time you convert, you lose—particularly at train station offices, or worse yet, at luxury hotels or restaurants, where rates can be appallingly disadvantageous.

Traveler's Checks

No part of your trip is likely to cause you more headaches than money—even when you have it. Carrying large amounts of cash, even in a money belt, is unwise.

Traveler's checks are the safest way to carry money, since they can be replaced if lost or stolen. Although not all Italian establishments, including banks, accept traveler's checks, the occasional inconvenience is a small price to pay for safety and peace of mind. American Express is perhaps the most popular traveler's check company today.

Most banks and many agencies sell traveler's checks, usually for face value plus a 1-2% commission. Consult your bank or phone book for the nearest vendors, or call the numbers listed below. All of the following operate affiliated offices in Italy from which you can obtain replacement checks or emergency funds on the same day or on the next business day.

American Express: Call (800) 221-7282 in the U.S. and Canada; call collect (801) 968-8300 from elsewhere. Available in 8 currencies.

Bank of America: (Also known as **WorldMoney**) Call (800) 227-3460 in the U.S.; call collect (415) 624-5400 from Canada and elsewhere. Available only in U.S. dollars.

Barclays: Call (800) 221-2426 in the U.S.; call collect (415) 574-7111 from Canada and elsewhere. Available in U.S. and Canadian dollars and British pounds.

Citicorp: Call (800) 645-6556 or (800) 523-1199 in the U.S. and Canada; call collect (813) 623-1709 from Alaska and elsewhere. Available in U.S. dollars, British pounds, German marks, and Japanese yen.

MasterCard: Call (800) 223-9920 in the U.S. and Canada; call collect (212) 974-5496 from elsewhere. Available in 11 currencies.

Thomas Cook: Call (800) 223-7373 in the U.S.; call collect (212) 974-5696 from Canada and elsewhere. Available in 11 currencies.

Visa: Call (800) 227-6811 in the U.S. and Canada; call collect San Francisco (415) 574-7111 or London (01) 937-8091 from elsewhere. Available in 14 currencies.

Whether you should buy your checks in lire or your home country's currency depends largely on the current exchange situation. If your country's currency is stronger than the lira, buy checks in your own currency and exchange them in Italy as needed. If you buy your checks in lire, however, you can often use them to pay directly for hotel rooms and purchases, especially in larger cities. If you'll be visiting several countries, buy your checks in your home currency—you'll save yourself the cost of repeatedly exchanging currency. Buy most of your checks in large denominations, and buy a few in small denominations. Large notes will spare you long waits in bank lines; small notes will minimize your losses when you must settle for bad exchange rates.

In the event of theft or loss, you should expect a fair amount of red tape and delay even in the best of circumstances. As a precaution, separate your check receipts and keep them in a safe place. If you need replacement checks, receipts will speed up the process dramatically. Record check numbers as you cash them to help you identify exactly which checks are missing if some disappear. In addition, leave a list of check numbers with someone at home.

Credit Cards

Low-cost establishments rarely honor credit cards, particularly in southern Italy, but they can be invaluable in an emergency. Major credit cards such as **Visa** and **American Express** allow you to get instant cash advances as large as your remaining credit line from banks throughout Europe that honor the card. This quick transfusion of cash might be your *only* source of cash for several days, since many traveler's check vendors will not cash a personal check, and transatlantic money cables take at least 48 hours (see Sending Money below). In addition, American Express and Visa have installed Automated Teller Machines (ATMs) throughout Europe; cardholders can now get instant cash around the clock.

American Express Travel Service (tel. (800) 528-4800) provides an assortment of useful services to cardholders: Full-service offices will honor personal checks up to $1000 in any seven-day period (in cash and traveler's checks, depending on the office's funds). They will also wire to replace lost or stolen cards. Cardholders can use American Express offices as mailing addresses for free; otherwise, you must pay (or show American Express traveler's checks) to pick up mail from their offices. Perhaps the greatest bonus is Global Assist, a service which automatically provides holders of U.S. issued cards with a 24-hour help line, providing information and monetary aid in cases involving personal medical or legal emergency, visas, or inoculations. You can also send urgent, emergency medical messages home through this service. British and Canadian cardholders can subscribe to these services. Global Assist is a limited version of American Express's Europe Assist, which is available only by subscription.

The Traveler's Companion, a list of full-service offices throughout the world, is available from American Express Travel Service offices or by mail from American Express, 65 Broadway, New York, NY 10006. WorldMoney checkholders are eligible for membership in **Bank of America's Safe Travel Network.** The *International Travel Guide* is free to travelers from Visa. Write to Chase Visa, P.O. Box 5111, 1400 Union Turnpike, New Hyde Park, NY 11042. **Barclays,** Britain's largest international bank, operates over 4000 branches in 70 countries, and their card is widely accepted in Europe (tel. (212) 530-0100). Mastercard, also accepted throughout the world, offers comparable services to its cardholders.

If your income level is low, you may have difficulty acquiring an internationally recognized credit card. However, if a family member already has a card, it's easy to get an extra card. American Express will issue an extra green card for US$25 per year (or an extra gold card for US$30); bills go to your loved ones. Check with your bank for details on obtaining extra Visas and MasterCards.

Sending Money

Sending money overseas is complicated, expensive, and often extremely frustrating. Do your best to avoid it. Either carry a credit card or keep a separate stash of traveler's checks for emergencies. If, however, you need money sent to you while you're in Italy, it's quickest and cheapest to have someone **cable money** through the local office of a large Italian bank. There is less chance of delay in an in-house transaction involving a bank that has numerous branches throughout the country, since it can often reach you in a remote corner. Usually, money can be cabled within 24 hours, though it costs—commissions of 7% are common for rush orders.

Having money sent through a large commercial bank, such as Citicorp, is almost as efficient and inexpensive (US$9-22). The sender must either have an account with the bank or bring cash to one of its branches (some will not cable money for non-customers). Note that you may be charged a fee to pick up the money, which can arrive the same day, the next day, or within a week, depending on when the money was sent, what time zones it must cross, and the sophistication of the receiving banking system. The sender can sometimes specify the currency in which the money is to be disbursed. All information the sender gives, such as your passport number and the recipient bank name and address, must be exact to avoid significant delays.

Sending money through a company such as **American Express** costs about as much as sending it through a bank. Normally, the sender must have an American Express card to use American Express services, but some offices will accept a commission instead. The money is guaranteed to arrive within 72 hours at the designated overseas office, where it will be held 14 days before being returned to the sender. It costs $15 to send up to $500, and $60 to send up to the maximum of $2000. The first $200 will be disbursed in the local currency, the rest in traveler's checks. This service operates only between American Express offices proper—not their representatives.

Western Union offers convenient but expensive service. A sender in the U.S. with a Mastercard or Visa can call (tel. (800) 325-6000 or (800) 325-4176) and cable up to $2000. A sender who doesn't have a card must go to a Western Union office with cash or cashier's check (no money orders accepted). The money will arrive at the central telegram office of the city the sender designates, and you can pick it up after showing suitable identification. In Italy, you will usually get the money, which arrives in lire, in two to five business days. Money is held seven to 30 days; at the company's discretion, before being returned to the sender minus the cost of having it sent. Rates vary (US$11-45), depending on the receiving bank's own service charge.

Barclays will send **International Payment Orders** (25 pence per 100 pounds), convertable to cash upon request.

Finally, if you are an American in a life or death situation, you can have money sent to you via the State Department's **Citizen's Emergency Center,** Department of State, #4811, 2201 C St. NW, Washington, DC 20520 (tel. (202) 647-5225). For a fee of about $25, the State Department will send the money within hours, or sometimes overnight, to the nearest consular office, which will then disburse the money according to instructions. The agency prefers not to send sums greater than $500. The sender must provide his or her name and address, the name of the recipient, and the nature of the emergency. If requested, the State Department will include a message with the money. The quickest way to get the money sent is to cable the State Department money through Western Union.

Bargaining

It's standard to bargain almost everywhere in Italy except government or hotel shops. Try bargaining, for instance, in markets or for taxi fares (always *before* getting into the cab). If you speak no Italian at all, memorize the numbers. Let the merchant make the first offer and offer one-half or two-thirds of this. Never offer anything you are unwilling to pay—you are expected to buy if the merchant accepts your price.

Safety and Security

Large cities demand extra caution. In southern Italy, especially, carry all valuables in a **money belt** or a **necklace pouch** (both available at any well-stocked travel store), and carry your daypack or purse crosswise on the side away from the street—moped riders often purse-snatch. Never put valuables in the outside pocket of your daypack. Be careful of your belongings on buses, and don't check baggage on trains, especially if you're switching lines. You may want to ask the managers of your hotel or hostel for advice on specific areas to avoid, and you might feel safer staying in places with either a curfew or a night-attendant. If you are in a dormitory-style room, or if there are no locks on your door, keep all valuables on you, not just next to your bed—a trip to the shower could cost you a camera or a wallet.

While traveling, steer clear of empty train compartments, particularly at night. If you plan to sleep outside, or simply don't want to carry everything with you, store your gear in a train or bus station locker, but be aware that these are sometimes broken into. **If you are ever in a potentially dangerous situation anywhere in Italy, call the Emergency Assistance number—112 or 113.**

Don't forget to take safety precautions before you leave home as well. Stop mail and newspapers, and tell the police or a trusted neighbor when and how long you'll be gone.

Insurance

The firms listed below offer insurance against theft or loss of luggage, trip cancelation/interruption, and medical emergency. You can buy a policy directly from a firm or through a travel agent. Beware, however, of unnecessary coverage. Check to see whether your homeowner's insurance (or your family's coverage) provides against theft during travel. University term-time medical plans often cover summer travel. Homeowners' policies will generally cover theft of travel documents (passports, plane tickets, rail passes, etc.) up to $500. Buying an ISIC card in the U.S. provides you with $2000 worth of accident and sickness insurance and $100 per day up to 60 days of in-hospital sickness coverage while the card is valid. CIEE also offers an inexpensive Trip Safe plan with options covering medical treatment and hospitalization, accidents, and even charter flights missed due to illness (see Useful Organizations above).

Remember that insurance companies usually require a copy of the police report filed at the time of the theft, or evidence of having paid medical expenses (doctor statements, receipts) before they will honor your claim. Have these written in English, if possible, and make sure you return home within the time limit to file for reimbursement. ALways have proof of insurance and policy numbers on hand during the trip.

Travel Assist, 1133 15th St. NW, #400, Washington, DC 20005 (tel. (800) 821-2828). Formerly Europ Assistance Worldwide Services, Inc. Health and legal assistance, document recovery, cash advances, and insurance. Membership can be costly, depending upon the number and length of your trips; annual membership is $145 for an individual. Offices in Brussels, London, Madrid, Munich, and Paris. 24-hour hotline.

Access America, Inc., 600 Third Ave., Box 807, New York, NY 10163 (tel. (800) 851-2800). A subsidiary of Blue Cross/Blue Shield that offers travel insurance and assistance. Covers everything from luggage, trip cancelation/interruption, stolen passports, and bail money to emergency medical evacuation and on-the-spot medical payments in cash. 24-hour hotline.

The Travelers Insurance Co., 1 Tower Sq., Hartford, CT 06183-5040 (tel. (800) 243-3174; in CT call (203) 277-2318). Baggage, trip cancelation/interruption, disruption/default, accident, and emergency medical evacuation insurance. Comprehensive coverage with "Travel Insurance Pack."

Arm Coverage, Inc., 120 Mineola Blvd., P.O. Box 310, Mineola, NY 11501 (tel. (800) 645-2424 or (516) 294-0220). Their Carefree Travel Insurance package covers trip cancelation/interruption, medical, baggage, and accident coverage. Only cancelation/interruption coverage can be purchased separately. 24-hour hotline.

Travel Guard International, P.O. Box 1200, Steven's Point, WI 54481 (tel. (800) 782-5151). Offers a comprehensive "Travel Guard Plus" package. 24-hour hotline.

Edmund A. Cocco Agency, 220 Broadway, #201, P.O. Box 780, Lynnfield, MA 09140 (tel. (800) 821-2488, in MA (617) 595-0262). Their Tour Master Travel Insurance can cover travel, accident, sickness, and baggage, as well as on-the-spot payment of medical expenses. Services include legal assistance, emergency cash transfers, and medical transportation. Protection against bankruptcy or default of airline and cruise tickets is also offered. 24-hour hotline.

Healthcare Abroad, 243 Church St. W., Vienna, VA 22180 (tel. (800) 237-6615). All plans have emergency assistance. Optional trip cancelation, accidental death, and baggage protection plans are offered as well.

WorldCare Travel Assistance Association, Inc., 2000 Pennsylvania Ave., N.W. Suite 7600, Washington, DC 20006 (tel. (800) 521-4822). Membership fee can be annual or per trip. Distinctive ScholarCare program for students and faculty spending a semester or full year abroad. 24-hour hotline.

Drugs

Purchase and possession of a small amount of marijuana, hash, cocaine, and LSD for personal use is **legal** in Italy. The law, however, has never specified the precise meaning of a "small amount". Law-abiding Italians limit their purchases to about an evening's worth. Sentences for drug violations are stiff (up to 15 years and L200,000,000), and as a foreigner, you are still subject to Italian law. Your government is completely powerless in the judicial system of a foreign country. Consular officers can only visit the prisoner, provide him or her with a list of attorneys, and inform family and friends.

Travelers have been jailed for possessing as little as three grams of marijuana. Penalties can include pre-trial detention for months or even years (without bail) and lengthy prison sentences without parole. Even if you don't use drugs, beware of the person who asks you to carry a package or drive a car across the border. For more information, write to the **Bureau of Consular Affairs,** CA/PA #5807, Department of State, Washington, DC 20520 (tel. (202) 647-1488) for their pamphlet *Travel Warning on Drugs Abroad* (enclose a stamped, self-addressed envelope for a quick reply).

Health

A man who has not been in Italy is always conscious of an infirmity . . .

—Samuel Johnson

Samuel Johnson aside, you should eat well and avoid overexerting yourself. Avoid caffeine and keep your daily mileage low to prevent traveler's anxiety. Protein is an excellent source of sustained energy, and fluids are essential. Although Italian water is safe for locals, and occasionally for tourists (especially in large cities), relying on bottled mineral water is always wise. Write IAMAT (see below) for their World Climate Chart, part of which is reprinted below. Their pamphlets *How to Avoid Traveler's Diarrhea, How to Adjust to the Heat,* and *How to Adapt to Altitude* are also helpful.

Finding **toilets** is always challenging in Italy. Musty and sporting a puzzling variety of flushing mechanisms, Italian toilets severely decrease in abundance the farther south you travel, though farmers are usually more than willing to lend you their outhouses. Look in museums, your surest bet, or restaurants.

At every **drugstore** (*farmacia*) in Italy, there is a list of pharmacies open all night and on Sundays. **First Aid Service** (*Pronto Soccorso*) is available in airports, ports, and train stations. *Let's Go* lists hospitals in most cities. Before you leave home, you may want to write for a list of English-speaking physicians worldwide from the **International Association for Medical Assistance to Travelers (IAMAT),** 417 Center St., Lewiston, NY 14092 (tel. (716) 754-4883); in Canada, 40 Regal Rd., Guelph, Ont. N1K 1B5 (tel. (519) 836-0102). Membership is free (donations accepted), and doctors are on call 24 hours for IAMAT members. Also check the first-aid centers listed in *Let's Go,* as well as English-speaking embassies and consulates; American Express and Thomas Cook offices can also help you find English-speaking doctors. Otherwise, the best place to find a good doctor may be a university hospital. If all else fails, go to a hospital in the largest city possible.

It's wise to include a small **first aid kit** among your traveling accessories. It should include bandages, antiseptic soap, a thermometer in a sturdy case, a Swiss army knife (including tweezers), sunscreen, mosquito repellent, aspirin, a decongestant, something for motion sickness (e.g., Dramamine), an antihistamine, something for diarrhea (ask your family physician to recommend something), and contraceptives (remember to take time zone changes into account if you're on the pill). With the recent AIDS epidemic, condoms are also common throughout Italy. You can also buy a kit: the **American Red Cross First Aid Kit** (US$26.20) is available from local Red Cross chapters.

If you wear glasses or contact lenses, take an extra pair or a prescription with you, and make arrangements with someone at home to send you a replacement pair in an amergency. If you wear contacts, you should take along a pair of glasses to rest tired eyes, especially in Rome, where the pollution can cause discomfort and difficulty. Bring extra solutions and eye-drops.

Check your medical records to make sure your inoculations are up-to-date. Typhoid shots remain good for three years, tetanus for 10.

Write the Superintendent of Documents, U.S. Government Printing Office, Washington, DC 20402 for *Health Information for International Travel,* which includes advice and recommendations, and *Campers First Aid* (US$2.50). Richard Dawood's *How to Stay Healthy Abroad* is available from Viking Press (tel. (201) 933-1460). To order, write Attn. Direct Order, 299 Murray Hill Pkwy., East Rutherford, NJ 07073. **The Pocket Medical Encyclopedia and First-Aid Guide** might also be helpful. Write Simon and Schuster, 200 Old Tappan Rd., Old Tappan, NJ 07675, Attn: Direct Order Dept. (tel. (800) 223-2336.) The **Traveler's Medical Manual,** by Angelo Scotti, is available from Berkeley Pub, ICD 250 W. 55th St., New York, NY 10019 (tel. (212) 262-7444).

Travelers with a chronic medical condition requiring medication regularly should consult their physicians before leaving. Always carry up-to-date prescriptions and/or a statement from your doctor, especially if you will be taking insulin, syringes, or any narcotics. Carry an ample supply of all medications, since matching your prescription with a foreign equivalent may be difficult. It's a good idea to carry medication and/or syringes with you on flights, in case your baggage is misplaced. For more information, write to the **American Diabetes Association,** 1660 Duke St., Alexandria, VA 22134 (tel. (800) 232-3472). They will send you a reprint of the article "Your Turn to Fly" from their magazine, *Diabetes Forecast,* containing many travel tips. For 75¢ you can also become a member. You will receive an ID card and a copy of their information sheet which lists ways to say you're diabetic and to request help in several languages.

Travelers with medical conditions that cannot be easily recognized (e.g., diabetes, allergies to antibiotics, epilepsy, heart conditions) should consider obtaining a **Medic Alert Identification** tag. This internationally recognized tag identifies the medical problem and provides the number of Medic Alert's 24-hour hotline, through which attending medical personnel can obtain information about the member's medical history. Lifetime membership is US$20; write to Medic Alert Foundation International, P.O. Box 1009, Turlock, CA 95381-1009 (tel. (800)-IDALERT, that's (800) 432-5378).

Abortion is legal and free in Italy, though the law specifies that it cannot be used as a means of birth control. Local health units called *consultorii* counsel women on rights and procedures. In Rome, the office is **Consultorio La Famiglia,** via della Pigna, 13 (tel. 678 94 07); in Milan, **Consultorio Familiare ANCED,** corso Buenos Aires, 75 (tel. 671 05 79). There are also hospitals in most large cities that administer "morning after" contraceptives free.

Work

The employment situation in Italy is grim for natives and worse for foreigners. Visas to work in Italy are extremely difficult to obtain since you must have a promise of a job that cannot be filled by an Italian. Any openings are coveted, and competition is fierce. On the other hand, the cash-based, untaxed, underground economy—*economia sommersa* or *economia nera*—may make up as much as one-third of Italy's economy. Be forewarned: Working without a visa is illegal, and punishments can be stiff. Most foreigners do harvest work, restaurant or bar work, housework, or work in the tourism industry, where English-speakers are needed. Teaching English can also a major source of income. Local language schools, usually called "The Cambridge School" or "The Oxford School" are listed in the phone book. Some schools simply post signs in stores, hairdressers, or cafes. No more than "pidgin" Italian is usually necessary to teach conversation. For information, write to the **Interexchange Program,** William Sloane House, 2nd floor, 356 W. 34th St., New York, NY 10001 (tel. (212) 947-9533) for catalogs of work abroad programs in Italy and other European countries.

If you're convinced that you can find a legitimate job, *The Directory of Overseas Summer Jobs* (US$9.95, postage US$2) may help. It lists 50,000 volunteer and paid openings worldwide. It's available from Writer's Digest Books, 1507 Dana Ave., Cincinnati, OH 45207 (tel. (800) 543-4644; in OH (800) 551-0844). For listings of publications and organizations with information on work in Italy, check the biennial *Whole World Handbook* (US$7.95 from CIEE or in bookstores; see Useful Organizations above). The *1988 Directory of Summer Jobs Abroad* lists 30,000 vacancies in a variety of fields (£5.95). Write to Vacation Work, 9 Park End St., Oxford OX1 1HJ, England (tel. (0865) 24 19 78). It is also distributed in the U.S. by Writer's Digest Books (see above). In Italy, check the help-wanted columns in the *Daily American* and the *International Daily News,* two English-language papers. In Milan, you can place a free advertisement in the weekly *Secondamano* (also good for finding lifts); in Rome, contact *Porta Portese,* via di Porta Maggiore, 95 (tel. 77 00 41), or *Il Mercato delle Pulci,* via Prenestina, 359 (tel. 25 84 71), for free advertisements.

The magazine *AAM Terra Nuova* (Agriculture and Alternative Nutrition and Medicine) is good for jobs on the land and can be contacted at P.O. Box 2, 50038 Scarperio (tel. (055) 843 04 36). Radios will usually also broadcast free advertisements, and prospective *au pairs* should consider placing advertisements in women's magazines.

Summer positions as tour group leaders are available with **American Youth Hostels (AYH),** P.O. Box 37613, Washington, DC 20013-7613 (tel. (202) 783-6161). You must be at least 21, and you must take a weeklong leadership course (US$225, room and board included). You must also lead a group in the U.S. before taking one to Europe. The **Experiment in International Living (EIL),** Kipling Rd., Brattleboro, VT 05301 (tel. (800) 451-4465); for admissions (802) 257-7751), requires leadership ability and extensive overseas experience for similar positions. You must be at least 24.

Teaching offers another source of work in Italy. The government, in cooperation with the **Institute of International Education (IIE),** dispenses several assistantships through the Fulbright scholar program, an annual competition to graduating seniors and others with a bachelor's degree from an American university. The IIE also publishes *Teaching Abroad,* a directory of teaching opportunities in over 100 countries worldwide. To purchase a copy (US$11.95), send a check made out to IIE to: Communications Division, Box TF, Institute of International Education, 809 United Nations Plaza, New York, NY 10017 (212-883-8279). With a master's degree you may be able to find an assistantship yourself. Write to the U.S. Department of Education, Information Services, 555 New Jersey Ave., N.W., Washington, DC 20208 (800-424-6616), and International Schools Services, P.O. Box 5910, Princeton, NJ 08540 (609-452-0990). The ISS, which focuses on English-speaking schools abroad, publishes the *ISS Directory* and an *International Quarterly,* and holds recruitment conferences February of every year for active candidates only.

Long-term employment is difficult to secure unless you have skills in high-demand areas, such as medicine (including nursing), computer programming, or teaching. One useful booklet, *Employment Abroad: Facts and Fallacies,* covers the major considerations involved in seeking overseas employment and includes many sources of further information. It's available for free from Publications Fulfillment, Chamber of Commerce of the United States, 1615 H Street, N.W., Washington, DC 20062 (202-262-5652). Job-hunting strategies can be found in Eric Kocher's *International Jobs: Where They Are, How To Get Them,* published by Addison-Wesley, Reading, MA 01867 ($8.95). For jobs in private industry, contact the Italian consulate for a listing of appropriate firms, or consult *Directory of American Firms Operating in Foreign Countries,* published by World Trade Academy Press, 50 East 42nd St., New York, NY 10017.

Farmcamps are no easy ride. The pay is low (about US$30 per day if you work hard). The work is stressful and tiring, and involves long hours. In addition, it can easily be disrupted by bad weather. Ages usually range from 18 to 25, and the farms operate from June through September. Workers are paid by the amount of fruit they pick. For more information, write to **International Farm Camp,** Hall Rd., Tiptree, Colchester, Essex CO5 OQS, England (include an International Reply Coupon).

Lastly, the **Association for International Practical Training (AIPT)** is the U.S. affiliate of the International Association for the Exchange of Students for Technical Experience (IAESTE). AIPT offers on-the-job training for full-time students with more than two years of university study in engineering, computer science, math, the natural sciences, applied arts, or agriculture. Apply (US$65) to IAESTE Trainee Program, *c/o* AIPT, Park View Building, #320, 10480 Little Patuxent Parkway, Columbia, MD 21044 (tel. (301) 997-2200).

For more information on work in Italy, contact the Interexchange Program (see above).

Volunteer Work

Volunteering is a great opportunity to meet locals, as well as other students, and you may even receive room and board for your work. *Volunteer! The Comprehensive Guide to Voluntary Service in the U.S. and Abroad* (US$5.50, postage US$2.50) offers advice and listings and is available from CIEE (See Useful Organizations above).

CIEE also offers placement in international **workcamps.** Established after WWI to promote peace and understanding, over 2000 operate in Europe today. Workcamps enable volunteers from throughout the world to live and work together on a two- to four-week project (most involve manual or social work). A working knowledge of Italian is required for projects in Italy, and participants must be at least age 18. You must pay an application fee of $100, your transportation costs, and sometimes your food and lodgings losts. Write **CIEE International Voluntary Projects,** 356 W. 34th St., New York, NY 10001. You can also contact **Volunteers for Peace,** 43 Tiffany Rd., Belmont, VT 05730 (tel. (800) or (802) 259-2759) for their directory of current workcamps (US$10).

Civil Service International, Rte. 2, Box 506, Crozet, VA 22932 (tel. (312) 977-0031) runs workcamps throughout Italy. Apply well in advance.

For **YMCA positions,** write to Overseas Personnel Programs, YMCA of the USA, 101 N. Wacker Dr., Chicago, IL 60606 (tel. (800) 222-3000 or (800) 222-9873).

For information on archeological digs, write to the **Centro Camuno di Studi Preistorici,** 25044 Capo di Ponte, Valcomonica (Brescia) (tel. (0364) 420 91). A center of prehistoric research, they specialize in primordial and primitive art, offering voluntary work, tutoring, research assistantships, educational grants, and training and apprenticeship in scientific art and editing. You can also contact the **Archeological Institute of America,** 675 Commonwealth Ave., Boston, MA 02215 (tel. (617) 353-9631) for lists of field projects available, as well as a copy of the "Archeological Fieldwork Opportunities Bulletin" (US$8).

Study

To get a general picture of study-abroad opportunities, refer to the *Whole World Handbook* (US$7.95 from CIEE or bookstores), providing descriptions of various work, study, and travel opportunities worldwide. The **Institute of International Education (IIE)** publishes several annual reference books. *Basic Facts on Foreign Study* (free), and *Academic Year Abroad* (US$20) describe 1600 semester- and year-long programs. *Vacation Study Abroad* (US$20) details over 100 spring, summer, and fall study programs offered by U.S. colleges and universities and foreign and private sponsors. Order from 809 United Nations Plaza, New York, NY 10017 (tel. (212) 883-8200). Their office answers inquiries and staffs a reference library open by appointment. The **Centro Turistico Studentesco e Giovanile (CTS)** is connected with the Italian Ministry of Foreign Affairs and the Italian Ministry of Education to facilitate foreign study in Italy. Information on programs is available in CTS offices. The **American Institute for Foreign Study** (tel. (800) 243-4567) helps arrange study programs, transportation, and room and board for both term-time and summer courses at several Italian universities.

If your Italian is fluent, consider enrolling directly in an Italian university. You will find that universities are overcrowded—due to the high unemployment rates, many Italians continue their education indefinitely, but you will probably make a good number of Italian friends and develop a real feeling for the culture. To apply to an Italian university, write to the nearest Italian consulate (see Embassies and Consulates below) for a general application. In Rome, contact Segretaria Stranieri, Cittá Universitaria, piazzale delle Scienze, 2, Roma. Also ask about scholarships offered by the Italian Ministry of Foreign Affairs. All holders of B.A. degrees are eligible for these, yet few apply. Remember that visas are required of foreign students in Italy.

The **American Field Service (AFS)** offers both summer- and year-long opportunities in Italy for high school students. Write to AFS International/Intercultural Programs, 313 E. 43rd St., New York, NY 10017 (tel. (800) AFS-INFO, that's (800) 237-4636, or (212) 949-4242).

A number of student organizations in Italy can provide you with leads and advice:

Amicizia, P.O. Box 42-PG I, via Fabretti, 59, 06100 Perugia (tel. (075) 352 83). International student organization for work and study in Italy and abroad.

Ufficio Centrale Studenti Esteri in Italia (UCSEI), via Monti Parioli, 59, 00197 Rome (tel. (06) 360 44 91). National organization of foreign students in Italy, offering information to visitors about the land, its culture, and opportunities available.

Relazioni Universitarie—Associazione Italiana Per Il Turismo e Gli Scambi Universitari, via Palestro 11, 00185 Rome (tel. (06) 475 52 65). University cultural exchange information.

Graduate students can also look into the **American Academy,** via Masina, 5, Rome (tel. (06) 58 86 53), an organization for resident fellowship scholars and artists.

Another option is studying at an institute run for foreign students by an Italian university. Write to the Italian Cultural Institute for a complete list of programs (see Useful Organizations above). The following schools and organizations offer a variety of calsses.

ABC Centro di Lingua e Cultura Italiana, Borgo Pinti, 38, 50122 Firenze (tel. (55) 247 92 20). Month-long language, studio art, and art history courses.

Centro Linguistico Italiano Dante Alighieri, via dei Bardi, 12, 50125 Firenze; via B. Marliano, 4, 00162 Roma; and p. la Lizza, 10, Siena (tel. (55) 234 29 84 or (55) 234 29 86). Language classes, cultural daytrips, extracurricular activities. Write a month in advance, 2 months in summer.

Instituto di Lingua a Cultura Italiana "Michaelangelo," via Ghibellina, 88, 50122 Firenze. Italian language and civilization, teacher, and interpreter refresher courses.

Istituto per l'Arte e il Restauro, Palazzo Spinelli, Borgo S. Croce, 10, 50122 Firenze. Summer and year-long courses on Italian language, art, and art restoration.

Koinè, Centro Koinè via de' Pandolfini, 27, 50122 Firenze (tel. (055) 21 38 81 or (055) 21 69 49). Italian language school for foreigners. A teachers' cooperative. 2- to 4-week language courses. Offers several courses in various towns.

Università Italiana per Stranieri, Palazzo Gallenga, p. Fortebraccio, 4, 06100 Perugia (tel. (75) 643 44). Language classes, cultural instruction, daytrips, and extracurricular activities.

Packing

Pack light. Set out everything you think you'll need, and then pack only half of it—and leave room for gifts and souvenirs. Leave jewelry and expensive watches at home. You'll find that the less luggage you carry, the less you'll be treated like a tourist.

Decide first what type of luggage suits your needs best. You might consider a light **suitcase** if you're going to stay in one city or town for a long time. Those who wish to travel unobtrusively might choose a large **shoulder bag** that closes securely.

If you're planning to cover a lot of ground by foot or bus, a sturdy, **backpack** with several compartments is hard to beat. Packs come with either an exterior frame or an interior X- or A-shaped frame. For normal loads, when the pack functions primarily as a suitcase, an interior-frame model, less cumbersome and bulky, is preferable. A front-loading pack, rather than a top-loading model, saves you from having to dig and grope for hidden items. Don't buy a cheap pack: After mauling your shoulders, the straps are likely to rip or fray under the strain of hard traveling. A good internal frame pack usually costs anywhere between $90 and $300. Try out several models at a good camping store, since packs fit people differently. Fill the pack with weights, adjust the straps, and take it around the block a couple of times to see if walking with the pack is comfortable. To minimize tottering, pack heavy items up against the inside wall, and lighter items toward the back and top.

No matter what kind of luggage you choose, a small **daypack** is indispensable for plane flights and sightseeing. You can carry lunch, a camera, some valuables (including your *Let's Go*), and some toilet paper (supplies in Italian restrooms are scarce). You should also use a **money belt** to avoid being left with nothing if robbed. Label every piece of baggage with your name and address, and purchase a few combination locks for the baggage.

Check Climate below for an idea of what the weather will be like where and when you'll be visiting. Dark-colored clothes will not show the full wear and tear you'll be giving them, but light colors will be more comfortable in hot weather. Natural fibers or cotton blends are cooler than synthetics; they don't wrinkle and can be easily washed.

Sturdy footwear is crucial—and not the place to cut costs. Lace-up walking shoes or a pair of well-cushioned running or tennis shoes are a must. If Alpine forays are in your plans, good hiking boots are essential. Break-in your shoes before you go. Sprinkling talcum powder on your feet and inside your shoes, and wearing two pairs of socks helps prevent uncomfortable rubs and sores, while moleskin relieves any blisters that do develop.

One pocket of your backpack should be devoted to sundries—a flashlight, pocket knife, first aid kit (see Health above), and a travel alarm. Toiletries will usually be available, so you needn't start out with too many tubes of toothpaste. Laundry services in Italy especially in the big cities can be is expensive and inconvenient; consider doing your wash in your hotel sink. A mild liquid soap (available in camping stores) is great for everything from dish detergent to shampoo.

Those who'd like to use their favorite electrical appliances will need an **electric converter.** The voltage varies throughout Italy but is either 115 or 120 volts in most cities and towns. Check with your hotel before plugging in. Visitors from the U.S. and Australia will definitely need an adapter, since Italy's prongs are round, not flat. Send a stamped, self-addressed envelope to the Franzus Company, 53 W. 23rd St., New York, NY 10010 (tel. (212) 463-9393) for the pamphlet, "Foreign Electricity Is No Deep Dark Secret."

Cameras

Keep in mind that camera equipment is valuable, fragile, and heavy. The less you bring, the less you'll worry and the better your back will feel. In many small towns, film availability is limited and prices inflated; at tourist attractions the situation is even worse. Take supplies along or pick them up in larger cities. Despite disclaimers to the contrary, airport X-ray equipment often fogs film—the higher the speed, the more likely the film is to be damaged. Resist the pleas of personnel to send your camera and film through; have it hand-checked. For extra protection, purchase a lead-lined pouch and stash your rolls in it.

Climate

The climate in Italy is temperate for the most part. The north is fairly warm in the summer (70s) but rarely blistering, while the south is dry and hot. Beware of Venice in August, as the air is still and the canals stagnate a bit. If you are on the coast, however, the breeze off the sea is cool. Winter in the Alps is very cold, while Milan, Turin, and Venice are chilly and damp. Winters in the Veneto region are damp, but Tuscany fares better, with temperatures in the 40s. In the south, temperatures usually stay in the 40s and 50s during the winter.

The following information is drawn from the International Association for Medical Assistance to Travelers's *World Climate Charts.* In each monthly listing, the first two numbers represent the average daily maximum and minimum temperatures in degrees Celsius, while the numbers in parenthesis represent the same temperatures in degrees Fahrenheit.

	Jan.		April		July		Oct.	
Bologna	5/−1	(41/30)	18/10	(64/50)	30/20	(86/68)	20/12	(68/54)
Capri	11/8	(52/46)	16/12	(61/54)	27/21	(81/70)	20/16	(68/61)
Frienze	9/2	(48/36)	19/8	(66/46)	30/18	86/64	20/11	(68/52)
Genova	11/5	(52/41)	17/11	(63/52)	27/21	(81/70)	20/15	(68/59)
Milano	5/0	(41/32)	18/10	(64/50)	29/20	(84/68)	17/11	(63/52)
Napoli	12/4	(54/39)	18/9	(64/48)	29/18	(84/64)	22/12	(72/54)
Roma	11/5	(52/41)	19/10	(66/50)	30/20	(86/68)	22/13	(72/55)
Sicily (Palermo)	16/8	(61/46)	20/11	(68/52)	30/21	(86/70)	25/16	(77/61)
Venezia	6/1	(43/34)	17/10	(63/50)	27/19	(81/66)	19/11	(66/52)

Keeping in Touch

Mail

The postal system in Italy ranges from decent to notorious. Aerograms and air letters from Italy should arrive in the U.S. in a week to 10 days, while surface mail, much less expensive, takes a month or longer. Since postcards are low-priority mail, important messages should be sent by airmail letter. Letters and small parcels rarely get lost if sent *raccomandata* (registered), *espresso* (express), and *via aerea* (air mail). Stamps are available at face value in *tabacchi* (tobacco shops), but you should mail your letters from a post office to be sure they are stamped correctly.

Mail from home can be sent to a hotel where you have reservations. In some larger cities you can have mail sent to you c/o American Express offices. Most offices will give you your mail free if you have an American Express card or American Express traveler's checks; nonmembers must usually pay a small fee (see Money above).

You can also have mail sent to you Fermo Posta (general delivery) in any city or town. Letters addressed to the post office with your name and phrase "Fermo Posta" will be held at the post office for pick-up. You must claim your mail in person with your passport as identification, and you may have to pay L150 per piece of mail. In major cities, the post office handling *Fermo Posta* is usually efficient and open long hours (though closed on Sunday). Since there may be more than one post office in any city, you should be sure to write the address of the office handling *Fermo Posta.* It's also a good idea to have the sender capitalize and underline your last name to ensure proper sorting. Just to be sure, check under your first name too.

Telephones

There are three types of telephones in Italy. One uses **tokens** called *gettoni,* which cost L200 apiece and are available from machines in train and bus stations, coffee shops, and telephone booths. *Gettoni* are also accepted as L200 change, so there's no need to worry about buying too many. Many *gettoni* telephones also accept L100 and L200 coins. Instructions are posted on all phones; one *gettone* buys five minutes. You should usually deposit three or four, even if your call is local. If you don't overestimate, you may be cut off in the middle of your conversation. At the end of your call, press the return button for your extra *gettoni.* To place long distance calls, deposit six *gettoni* initially, and continue to feed them in every time you hear a beep. For intercity calls, deposit eight or more. Each city's telephone code is listed under the city's Practical Information section.

Scatti calls are made from a phone run by an operator (who may simply be the proprietor in a bar). A **meter** keeps track of the cost of your call, and you pay when you finish. Remember that the operator may tack a substantial service fee onto the cost of your call. Check with the operator before you lift the receiver. Every town has at least one bar with a *telefono a scatti,* and these can be used for international calls.

The third type of phone is relatively new, and can usually be found in large public buildings. Rather than inserting coins directly, you buy a **card** from a machine usually placed next to the phone. After inserting the card, a digital readout informs you of the number of lire on your card. After the call, remove the card if you haven't used it all up, as you can re-use it. If you happen to run out in the middle of a call, you must insert another card, so buy more than one if you're planning a long call.

Intercontinental calls cannot be made from pay phones except in Rome, Genoa, and Naples, where magnetic money cards can be used. These cards, sold in the telephone offices of major train stations, are available in denominations of L3000, L6000, and L9000, and are convenient for direct-dial calling. In other cities, international calls must be made from telephone company offices (SIP or ASST), generally found near the main post office and sometimes in major train stations, or from a *telefono a scatti.* When direct-dialing is possible, dial two zeros and then the country codes (U.S. and Canada 1, Ireland 353, Great Britain 44, Australia 61, and New Zealand 64. Calls to the U.S. cost L10,000 for three minutes and L3000 each minute thereafter. Fortunately, rates go down between 11pm and 8am on holidays, and between 2:30pm on Saturday and 8am on Monday. Some offices ask for a L10,000 deposit. To place a call, you must fill out a form at the counter, and you will be assigned to a specific booth. For the most part, it is not difficult to make long-distance calls within Europe. A person-to-person call is *con preavviso,* and a collect call is *contassa a carico del destinatario.* If you want to make a collect call to North America, you *must* dial 170 and talk to an Italian operator first. Don't call long distance from your hotel room; it will cost twice as much.

Telegraph

The surest way to get your message across the ocean without actually going yourself is by wire service, sent from the post office. **Telegrams** are sent from the post office and cost L815 per word, including the address; L370 per word up to 22 words for night letters, which unlike mailgrams in the U.S., are wired and then delivered.

Additional Concerns

Senior Travelers

Senior citizens enjoy an assortment of discounts on transportation and admission—always ask about these. The **International Youth Hostel Federation** sells memberships to those over age 59 for $10, half the regular price. (See Getting Around below for information on train ticket discounts.) A number of organizations cater to seniors, offering information, assistance, and/or discounts.

American Association of Retired Persons, Special Services Dept., 1909 K St. NW, Washington, DC 20049 (tel. (800) 227-7737). Those 50 years and older can receive benefits from AARP Travel Services and get discounts for hotels, motels, and car rental and sightseeing companies. Annual membership US$5.

Bureau of Consular Affairs, Passport Services, Department of State, Washington, DC 20524. Send a postcard requesting a free copy of *Travel Tips for Senior Citizens,* which provides information on passports, visas, health, and currency.

Elderhostel, 80 Boylston St., #400, Boston, MA 02116 (tel. (617) 426-7788). Several universities in Italy participate in this program, which offers short-term residential courses in a variety of academic fields for those over 60 and their spouses.

E.P. Dutton Publishing Co., Inc., 2 Park Ave., New York, NY 10016. Publishes *The Discount Guide for Travelers Over 55,* by Caroline and Walter Weintz (US$10).

Mature Outlook, P.O. Box 1205, Glenview, IL 60025. Provides those over 50 with special domestic and international vacation packages, reduced travel insurance, and other travel discounts. Membership US$7.50 per couple.

National Association of Mature People, P.O. Box 26792, 2212 NW 50th St., Oklahoma City, OK 73126 (tel. (405) 752-0703). Information and travel assistance. Discounts on hotels, car rentals, and group travel. Membership US$9.95.

National Council of Senior Citizens, 925 15th St., Washington, DC 20005 (tel. (202) 347-8800). Information on discounts and travel abroad.

Pilot Industries, Inc., 103 Cooper St., Babylon, NY 11702 (tel. (516) 422-2225). Publishes the *Senior Citizen's Guide to Budget Travel In Europe,* revised edition, by Page Palmer, a guide to European travel for senior citizens.

September Days Club (SDC),2751 Beford Highway, Atlanta, GA 30324 (tel. (404) 325-4000). Discounts on hotels and travel group services for those over 50. $12 membership includes spouse.

Travelers Aid Association of America (TAAA), 125 S. Wilke Rd., SUite 205, Arlington Heights, IL 60005 (tel. (312) 392-4202). Provides individual social services to fit the distinct needs of travelers, regardless of age, race, citizenship, or handicap.

Disabled Travelers

Italians are making an increased effort to meet the needs of the disabled. Write to the **Italian Government Travel Office** (see Useful Organizations above) for the *Annuario Alberghi D'Italia,* which ranks disabled accessibility in hotels.

In most train stations, a porter will help you for L500-1000 per bag. Italian law requires that all wheelchairs be transported free of charge, but since the chair gets packed with the rest of your luggage, you may need assistance boarding and leaving the train, bus, or plane. It is best to travel with a companion.

If you plan to take a seeing-eye dog into Italy, contact your veterinarian and the nearest Italian consulate. You will need an import license, a current certificate of your dog's inoculations, and a letter from your veterinarian verifying your dog's health.

When making arrangements with airlines or hotels, specify exactly what you need. If you give them time to prepare and confirm the arrangements, you should have few problems.

These organizations may also prove helpful:

American Foundation for the Blind, 15 W. 16th St., New York, NY 10011 (tel. (800) 232-5463; in NY, (212) 620-2147). Offers information, recommends travel books, and issues ID cards for discounts to the legally blind.

Directions Unlimited, 720 N. Bedford Rd., Bedford Hills, NY 10507 (tel. (800) 533-5343, (212) 829-5110, or (914) 241-1700). Schedules group trips and tours for the blind. Also assists in planning trips both in the U.S. and abroad.

Disability Press, Ltd., Applemarket House, 17 Union St., Kingston-upon-Thames, Surrey KT1 1AA, England (tel. (01) 549 63 99). Publishes the *Disabled Traveller's International Phrasebook* (£1.50 in U.K., £1.75 elsewhere, postage included), a compilation of useful phrases in 8 languages, including Italian.

Facts on File, 460 Park Ave. S., New York, NY 10016. Publishes *Access to the World* (US$16.95), a travel guide for the disabled.

Federation for the Handicapped, 211 W. 14th St., New York, NY 10011 (tel. (212) 242-9050). Plans an annual trip each summer either in the U.S. or overseas, as well as spring and fall weekend trips. Annual membership US$4.

The Guided Tour, 555 Ashbourne Road, Elkins Park, PA 19117 (tel. (215) 782-1370). Your round full-time travel program for developmentally and learning-disabled adults as well as separate tips for those with physical disabilities. All expenses included in price of tour except lunches.

Mobility International, USA, P.O. Box 3551, Eugene, OR 97403 (tel. (503) 343-1284, voice and TDD). Information and travel programs, accommodations, access guides, organized study, and more. Publishes the *Guide to International Educational Exchange* and *Community Service and Travel for Persons with Disabilities.*

Travel Information Service, Moss Rehabilitation Hospital, 12th St. at Tabor Rd., Philadelphia, PA 19141 (tel. (215) 329-5715, ext. 2468). An information clearinghouse. For US$5, they will mail a packet of information with brochures on their services.

The Society for the Advancement of Travel for the Handicapped (SATH), 26 Court St., Penthouse Suite, Brooklyn, NY 11242 (tel. (718) 858-5483). Provides several useful booklets for the disabled. Annual membership US$40, students and senior citizens US$25.

Whole Person Tours, P.O. Box 1084, Bayonne, NJ 07002-1084 (tel. (201) 858-3400). Conducts tours and publishes *The Itinerary,* a bimonthly magazine for travelers with physical disabilities.

Wings on Wheels, Evergreen Travel, 19505L 44th Ave. W., Lynnwood, WA 98036 (tel. (800) 435-2288 or (206) 776-1184). Provides travel information and plans tours all over the world for the disabled. They're the best; they've been arranging travel for the disabled for 25 years.

Gay and Lesbian Travelers

In general, the attitude of Italians, particularly in Southern Italy, may be somewhat restrictive for the gay or lesbian traveler. However, holding hands with someone of the same sex is common in Italy. *Gaia's Guide,* available in most bookstores, lists lesbian and feminist information numbers and publications, women's cultural centers and resources, bookstores, restaurants, hotels, and meeting places in Italy (as well as many other countries). The *Spartacus Guide for Gay Men* provides over 1000 pages of similar information for men, covering almost every country in the world. Contact Bruno Gmünder Verlag, Lützowstrasse 106, P.O. Box 30 13 45, D-1000, Berlin 30, West Germany, or your local bookstore. **Giovanni's Room,** 435 S. 12th St. NE, Philadelphia, PA 19107 (tel. (800) 222-6996; in PA or (215) 943-2960) is an international feminist, gay, and lesbian bookstore and mail-order house. **Ferrari Publications,** P.O. Box 35575, Phoenix, AZ 85069 (tel. (602) 863-2408), publishes *Places of Interest for Men and Women* (US$11), *Places of Interest for Men* (US$10), and *Places of Interest for Women* (US$8). Ferrari also publishes *Inn Places,* which lists international accommodations for gay and lesbian travelers.

Women Travelers

Women traveling in Italy must take extra precautions, especially if traveling alone. Memorize the emergency number (112 or 113), and keep money handy for telephone calls, as well as emergency bus or taxi rides. Should you find yourself the object of catcalls or propositions, your best answer is generally none at all. While our advice stems from real experiences, we do not mean that all Italian men should be avoided. Italian males consider flirtation both an art form and a game; most comments should not be taken too seriously. Always look, however, as though you know where you're going. Ask women and couples for directions if you feel uncomfortable and if you are simply tired of the constant attention, try donning a pair of wire-rimmed glasses; one of our female researchers found that this reduced the catcalls to a livable hum. In addition, wearing a walkman or other device with headphones signifies to anyone thinking of making a comment that you aren't listening.

Budget accommodations occasionally mean more risk than savings. Avoid small dives and city outskirts in favor of university dormitories or youth hostels. Centrally-located accommodations are usually safest and easiest to return to after dark. *Let's Go* notes individual accommodations that are particularly safe or unsafe for women, and includes, wherever possible, locations and numbers of women's centers, special accommodations for women, and rape crisis centers. Some religious organizations offer rooms for women and are also safe. For a list of these institutions, contact the archdiocese of the Italian city concerned or write to the provincial tourist office. Also helpful is the **Associazione Cattolica Internazionale Al Servizio Della Giovane,** via Urbana, 158, 00184 Rome (tel. (06) 495 19 89); in Milan corso Garibaldi, 123 (tel. 659 52 06 or 659 96 60), an organization that runs hostels for women throughout Italy (also see Accommodations below).

Traveling with Children

Planning a detailed itinerary can be especially useful for those with children. Remember that traveling with children sometimes slows your pace considerably. Avoid hassles and complaints by booking rooms ahead of time and ensure that your sightseeing plans include stops that your children will enjoy. In addition, train systems in Italy sometimes offer discounts for traveling families. Eurail offers passes for groups of three or more, and children under four usually travel free. Some families might find it cheaper and more convenient to travel by rental car (see Getting Around below). For more information, consult the following:

Hippocrene Books, Inc., 171 Madison Ave., New York, NY 10016 (tel. (212) 685-4371). Publishes *Baby Travel* (US$12, postage and handling additional).

Wilderness Press, 2440 Bancroft Way, Berkeley, CA 94704 (tel.(415) 843-8080). Distributes *Backpacking with Babies and Small Children* (US$8.95) and *Sharing Nature with Children*(US$6.95).

Dietary Concerns

Orthodox **Jewish travelers** can write the Italian Government Travel Office (see Useful Organizations above) for a list of kosher restaurants. Also useful are *The Jewish Travel Guide,* published by the Jewish Chronicle, 25 Furnival St., London EC4A 1JT and distributed in the U.S. and Canada by Sepher-Hermon Press, Inc., 1265 46th St., Brooklyn, NY 11219 (tel. (718) 972-9010).

Jewish travelers to the Catholic capital might consider picking up the pamphlet *Jewish Rome,* which lists sites of historical interest. Write to Ente Provinciale Turismo in Rome (see Rome Practical Information).

Vegetarians should write the Società Vegetariana Italiana, via de Piatti, 3, 20123 Milano, for information. *Let's Go* includes some vegetarian restaurants. You can always ask for a dish *senza carne* (without meat). For more information, contact The Vegetarian Society of the U.K., Parkdale, Dunham Rd., Altrincham; Chesire WA 14 4QG (tel. (061) 928 01 93, which publishes *The International Vegetarian Travel Guide,* listing vegetarian and health-conscious restaurants, guesthouses, societies, and health food stores throughout the world. The book is distributed by Bookspeed, 48a Harilton Place, Edinburgh EH3 5AX, England (£3.99). The North American Vegetarian Society, P.O. Box 72, Dolgeville, NY 13329 (tel. (518) 568-7970), sells the *International Vegetarian's Handbook* (US$8.95, postage included).

Getting There

From North America

By Air

It is impossible to estimate specific airfares, as prices and market conditions vary weekly, but some generalities do apply.

Off-season travelers enjoy lower fares and face much less competition for inexpensive seats, but you needn't travel in the dead of winter to save. Peak-season rates are set on either May 15 or June 1 and run until mid-September. Actual dates will vary with your destination—peak season in Italy usually ends earlier than in England. If you arrange your travel dates carefully, you can travel in summer and still save with low-season fares. You might also be able to take advantage of cheap flights within your own country to reach an advantageous point of departure. Try to keep your itinerary as flexible as possible; a flight to Brussels or Frankfurt could cost considerably less than one to Milan or Rome.

Have a knowledgeable travel agent guide you through the options outlined below. Commissions are smaller on cheaper flights, so be aware that some travel agents will be less than eager to help you find the best deal. In addition, check the travel section of the Sunday *New York Times* or another major newspaper for bargain fares. Also consult CIEE, Travel CUTS, Let's Go Travel, and other student travel organizations.

In general, **charter flights** are the most economical. You can book charters up to the last minute, but most flights at the beginning of summer fill up well before the departure date (later in the season, companies may have trouble filling their planes and either cancel or offer special prices; watch for both). One of the big advantages of charters is that you may stay abroad for as long as you like, and often to fly into one city and out of another. Charters do not, however, allow for changes

of plan. You must choose your departure and return dates when you book, and you lose most, if not all, of your money if you cancel your ticket. In addition, charters can be unreliable: Charter companies reserve the right to change the dates of your flight, add fuel surcharges after you have made final payment, or even cancel the flight. The most common problem is delays. Charter companies usually fly a single plane to and from Europe, so delays accumulate and mechanical failures become a major hassle; prepare for a long wait. Charter companies also often have messy reservations systems; have your ticket in possession as far in advance as possible, and arrive at the airport several hours before departure. In some cases, you may get a discount for early reservations.

CIEE (tel. (800) 223-7402) was among the first on the charter scene and offers service from various U.S. cities to destinations all over the world. CIEE is one of the largest U.S. charter operators and their flights are extremely popular, so reserve early. **UniTravel,** P.O. Box 16220, St. Louis, MO 63105 (tel. (314) 727-8888) also offers charter flights from New York to Rome, and some to Milan.

Airline ticket consolidators advertise prices lower than most charters and sell unused tickets on schedulaed flights. Check with **Discount Travel International,** Ives Bldg., #205, Narberth, PA 19072 (tel. (800) 824-4000); **Last Minute Travel Club,** 132 Brookline Ave., Boston, MA 02215 (tel. (800) LASTMIN, that's 527-8646, or (617) 267-9800); or **Air Hitch,** 2901 Broadway #100, New York, NY 10025 (tel. (212) 864-2000). Other companies include **Stand-Buys, Ltd.,** 311 W. Superior, 4th floor, Chicago, IL 60610 (tel. (800) 255-0200 or (312) 943-5737) or **Moment's Notice,** 40 E. 49th St., New York, NY 10017 (tel. (212) 486-0503).

If you decide to make your transatlantic crossing with a commercial airline, you'll be purchasing greater reliability, security, and flexibility—at a higher price. The major airlines offer two options for the budget traveler. The first is to fly **standby.** You can purchase standby tickets in advance, but are not guaranteed a seat on any particular flight. Seat availability is known only minutes before departure, and the system whereby standby seats are assigned varies from airline to airline. The advantage of a standby fare is its flexibility; you can come and go as you please. But you cannot fly standby into southern Europe, and the big transatlantic carriers **Pan Am, TWA,** and **British Airways** offer standby only to London. Flying standby during high season can turn into a nightmare as hordes compete for a diminishing number of seats. In addition, standby tickets are no longer budget wonders; in 1988, standby fares were more expensive than APEX and economy round-trip fares on many routes.

Your second option on a commercial airline is to fly on the **Advanced Purchase Excursion Fare (APEX).** This provides confirmed reservations and flexible ports of arrival and departure. However, your excursion must fit rigid minimum/maximum length requirements, usually seven to 60 or 90 days, and you must purchase your ticket three weeks in advance. Book APEX fares early—by June you may have difficulty getting your desired summer departure date. **Alitalia,** Italy's national airline, flies from several cities in the U.S. to Italy, but is geared to executives and well-heeled travelers so their fares are high.

Inexpensive flights from Canada are substantially higher than the lowest fares from the U.S.; it may be more economical for Canadians to leave from the States. Be sure to check with Travel CUTS (see Useful Organizations above) for information on special charters.

From Europe

Some travel agents in your home country can give you specific information on intra-European travel, but it's simpler, and usually less expensive, to make travel arrangements once you arrive on the continent. Check newspapers, travel agents, and student travel organizations. Look into the **Student Air Travel Association** and **Scandinavian Student Travel Service,** 17, Hauchsvej 1825, C, Frederiksberg (Copenhagen), Denmark (tel. (01) 21 85 00), for student and youth charter flights. Also check **Worldwide Student Travel Ltd.,** 39 Store St., London WC1E 7BZ, England (tel. 580 77 33, telex 28151), and **STA Travel,** 117 Euston Rd., London NW1 2SX, England (Tube: King's Cross; tel. (01) 388 22 61), and 74 Old Brompton Rd., London SW7 3LQ, England (Tube: S. Kensington; tel. (01) 581 10 22).

By Plane

Budget fares are frequently available on high-volume flights between northern Europe and Italy, but these are usually offered only in spring and summer. Carriers within Europe often offer student discounts. There are many good charter flights from London.

Pilgrim Air, 44 Goodge St., London W1P 2AD, England (tel. 01 580 28 31), the largest independent company offering flights and tours to Italy, advertises charter flights from England to Italy for as little as US$45. Calling themselves air brokers, they sell unsold seats on Britannia and Orion Airways, charging a 12½% commission for charter flights. They service all large Italian cities and offer low student rates.

London Student Travel, 52 Grosvenor Gardens, London SW1 (tel. (01) 730 34 02), offers competitive fares all over the continent; there's no age limit for many of their flights. **Miracle Bus,** 408 The Strand, London WC2 (tel. (01) 379 60 55), offers inexpensive flights within Europe, despite its name.

By Train

The great majority of budget travelers in Europe use the economical and efficient rail system. If you're under 26, you can to purchase BIJ tickets, which cut up to 55% off regular second-class rail fares on international runs. BIJ tickets are sold by **Transalpino** and **Eurotrain.** Both organizations have no representative in the U.S., so Americans will have to purchase tickets in Europe. Contact Eurotrain through CTS London, 33 Windmill St., London W1P 1HH (tel. (01) 580 45 54) or CTS Paris, 20, rue des Carmes (tel. (43) 25 00 76). Contact Transalpino Ltd. at 71-75 Buckingham Palace Rd., London SW1W 0QL (tel. (01) 834 96 56), or in Milan, at via Locatelli, 5 (tel. 65 92 41). When you buy a BIJ ticket, you must specify

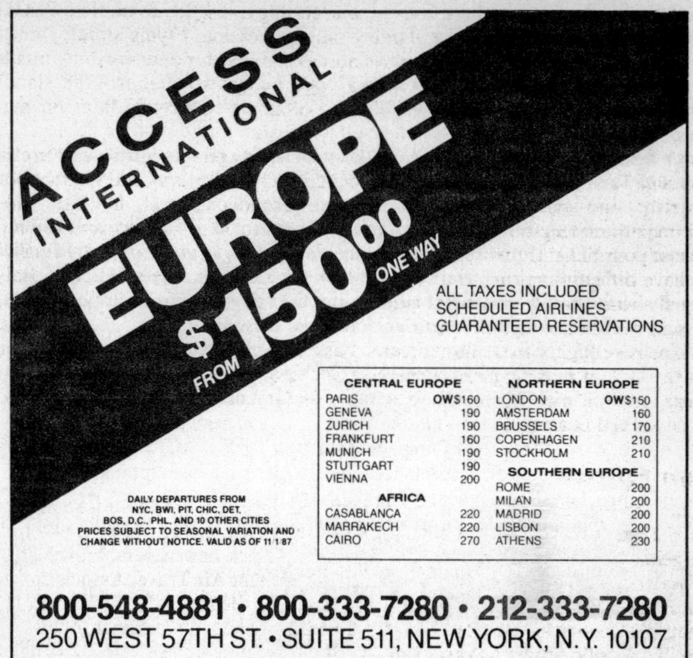

both your destination and route, and you have the option of stopping off anywhere along that particular route for up to two months. The fare between London and Venice is about US$75 one-way or US$140 round-trip; between London and Rome, about US$75 one-way and US$150 round-trip. Fares from Paris, Zurich, Frankfurt, or Brussels will be less expensive. The regular, second-class rail fare between Zurich and Milan (5-hr.) is $26 one-way; between Paris and Milan $62 (all round-trip fares are double).

On an overnight ride, you might want to purchase a **cuccetta,** the economy version of a full sleeping berth (about US$11).

Just this year, the Italian railway introduced the CARTAVERDE, available to anyone under 26 years. The card allows a discount of 20-30% on any state train fare, and, in addition, only costs L8000. It can be purchased in most train stations throughout Italy or travel agencies throughout the world.

By Bus

Few people think of buses when planning to travel to Italy, but they are available. **Magic Bus** offers cheap, direct service between many major cities in Europe. Their offices are located at 67-68 New Bond St. in London, England; Rokin 38, 1012 KT, in Amsterdam, Holland; and 20 Filellinon, Syntagma, in Athens, Greece. Information on Magic Bus is available from cooperating offices in many other cities. Magic Bus also offers cheap charter flights within Europe and bargain flights world-wide. **Magic Tour's Budget Bus** also provides reasonable service between major cities. For information on Budget Bus routes contact them at 1745 Clement, San Francisco, CA 94121; Rokin 10, Amsterdam, Holland; and 53 Stamford Hill, London N16, England. Both companies offer comparable fares. **Miracle Bus,** 408 The Strand, London WC2, England (tel. (01) 379 60 55), offers fares from London to Milan or Venice for US$55-75; from London to Florence for US$75. **International Express,** near Victoria Station at 52 Grosvenor Gardens, London SSW1W 0AU, England (tel. (01) 730 82 35), operates buses to Rome, Paris, and other points throughout Europe.

Once There

Tourist Offices

Many towns in Italy operate an office that provides information on the town and surrounding areas. These are especially useful in summer when festivals and special events abound. Tourist offices are staffed by local residents, all of whom should speak English. When the office is not crowded, the staff can give you directions and invaluable advice. Ask specific questions if possible. The **Ente Nazionale Italiano di Turismo (ENIT)** is a national tourist office with bureaus in Rome (via Marghera, 2) and abroad. In the provincial capitals, look for a branch of the **Ente Provinciale per il Turismo (EPT),** which provides information on the entire province. Many towns have an **Azienda Autonoma di Soggiorno e Turismo,** or city tourist board, which serves both tourists and visitors staying longer. The Azienda tends to be the most useful and most approachable; the EPT is less accustomed to dealing with tourists and is a more formal bureaucracy. The information the EPT provides is usually no better than the information from a more accessible Azienda. Also keep an eye out for a local branch of **Compagnia Italiana Turismo (CIT),** the government-subsidized travel agency that specializes in activities such as camping and boating, and the **Centro Turistico Studentesco e Giovanile (CTS)** (see Student Accommodations below), which provides information on student travel and in many cities runs an accommodations service. These offices are listed in the Practical Information section of each town. CTS's main branches are: Milan, via Sant' Antonio, 2, 20122 (tel. 86 38 77); Rome, via Genova, 16 (tel. 467 91); Florence, via dei Ginori, 11/R, 50100 (tel. 29 21 50); Genoa, via S. Vincenzo, 117/R (tel. 56 43 66); Turin, via Alfieri, 17, 10131 (tel. 53 59 66); Venice, Dorsoduro, Ca' Foscari, 3251 Fondamenta Tagliapietra, 30123 (tel. 70 56 60); Naples, via A. De Gasperi, 35 (tel. 32 00 74).

Embassies and Consulates

Your home country's embassy or consulate in Italy can provide you with legal advice and a list of doctors and will contact relatives in an emergency. All embassies provide consular and passport services, plus a 24-hour referral service in emergencies. Consulates are, in general, better equipped than embassies to handle travelers' problems. All nations have embassies in Rome. Many, including the U.S. and Britain, have consulates in the following cities: Florence, Genoa, Milan, Naples, Palermo, Trieste, and Venice. See the Practical Information section of these cities. Below is a partial list of Italian consulates.

California, 12400 Wilshire Blvd., #300, Los Angeles 90025 (tel. (213) 820-0822) and 2590 Webster St., San Francisco 94115 (tel. (415) 931-4924).

Florida, 2600 SW 3rd Ave., Miami 33129 (tel. (305) 854-1758).

Illinois, 500 N. Michigan Ave., Chicago 60611 (tel. (312) 943-0703).

Louisiana, 708 Cotton Exchange Bldg., 231 Carondelet St., New Orleans 70130 (tel. (504) 524-2271).

Massachusetts, 100 Boylston St., Boston 02116 (tel. (617) 542-0483). Their jurisdiction includes Maine, New Hampshire, Rhode Island, and Vermont.

Michigan, 719 Griswald St., 1 Kennedy Sq., #2305, Detroit 48226 (tel. (313) 963-8560).

New York, 320 Park Ave., New York 10021 (tel. (212) 737-9100, student office 535-1764), at 51st St.

Pennsylvania, 421 Chestnut St., Philadelphia 19103 (tel. (215) 592-7329).

Quebec, 3489 Drummond St., Montreal 109 PQ (tel. (514) 849-8351) and 3, place Ville-Marie, Montreal H3B 2E3 (tel. (514) 866-7667).

Ontario, 275 Slater St., 11th floor, Ottawa K1P 5H9 (tel. (613) 232-2402).

Emergencies

Few legal systems are as convoluted and ambiguous as Italy's. Interpretations of the law are as varied as the dialects of the land. Your consulate will find you attorneys, but remember that you will be subject to Italian law; your consulate can only advise you.

A knowledge of the Italian police system may prove useful, though you should avoid encounters with this bureaucracy. The **Carabinieri** are a police force for civilians but are actually part of the Italian Army. They usually deal with the most serious crimes, particularly political terrorism. The **Polizia Urbana,** or **pubblica Sicurezza,** are the non-military police who deal with local crime. Lastly, the **Vigili Urbani** manage less violent, less serious offenses, such as traffic violations. They also give directions to lost tourists. More specialized police groups exist; the Guardia di Finanza, for instance, enforces tax laws and guards against illegal currency export.

Accommodations

Hostels

Hostels, available to travelers of all ages, are not as abundant in Italy as in northern Europe. Italian youth hostels, *Ostelli Italiani,* are inexpensive, however, and many are situated in historic buildings and areas of great natural beauty. Hostelers meet travelers from all over the world. Curfews, daytime lock-outs, separate quarters for men and women, and often, inconvenient locations are some of their drawbacks. Security is less certain than in a locked hotel room, so be sure always to keep your valuables with you, or check them at the office. In cities with an active nightlife, or on days when the rain just won't stop pouring, the curfews and daytime shutouts are especially painful.

Hostels in Italy are run by the **Associazione Italiana Alberghi per la Gioventù (AIG),** Palazzo della Civiltà del Lavoro, Quadrato della Concordia, 00144 Rome (tel. (06) 59 31 702 or 59 31 758). To stay in their hostels, you must have an IYHF membership card, available from major hostels, student travel services (see Useful Organizations and Hostel Membership above), and various CTS and AIG offices throughout Italy.

Hostel accommodations usually consist of bunk beds, each with a mattress and blanket, in dormitory rooms. Sleeping bags can be used, as well. Hostels usually receive guests 6-11:30pm in summer and 6-10:30pm in winter (Oct.-March). Officially, you must settle your account by 9am or pay for another night. The curfew is usually midnight in summer and 11pm in winter. Rates are determined locally. Prices average L16,000 per person including breakfast; dinners are usually available for about L5500 more.

Hotels

Low-priced and centrally located, Italian hotels are great travel bargains. They are registered with a provincial board that inspects each establishment and assigns it to a class based on the level of service and amenities offered. No hotel may legally charge more than permitted for its class. You can ask to see the official card stating maximum rent in each room. Remember that showers and breakfast often cost extra.

Under this system, it is almost impossible to get ripped off by checking into the first place you find, or to find an unusual bargain by spending hours shopping around. Differences between hotels are largely a matter of location and character, rather than price or facilities. In general, the most charming places are near the historic town center, while the cheap, noisy, depressing hotels lie near the train and bus stations.

The entire industry is still in the process of changing to a regional, five-star system under which *all* accommodations will be called *hotels.* While some cities (such as Florence) have already officially switched over, many proprietors still retain their old classifications. This could cause confusion, as it's impossible to say which *pensioni* and *locande* will be named *hotels* in 1989. Under the old system, *hotels* and *alberghi* both denote first- through fourth-class hotels, though as a rule, the more expensive places call themselves *"hotels."* *Pensioni,* divided into three classes, refer to small second- through fourth-class hotels. *Locande* usually offer the least expensive rooms and sometimes cater to long-term residents.

Prices fluctuate regionally, but singles generally start at L12,000; doubles at L18,000—prices are generally higher in Rome and Florence. Rates are geared more to the number of persons than to the room: Try to find a shared room (triples or quads for somewhat less per bed). A room with a double bed is called a *matrimoniale* (though it is no longer necessary to be in the state of matrimony to make use of it). A double with separate beds is called a *camera doppia,* and a single is a *camera singola.* Few of these hotels will have showers in the room. Often there is a L1000-2500 charge for showers. Most rooms have a bidet; feel free to use it for chilling wine or washing socks. *Let's Go* indicates exactly what individual hotel prices include. Some places offer only full pension, meaning room and board (3 meals per day), or half pension, meaning room, breakfast, and one other meal.

Except in Rome, Florence, and Venice (and other popular tourist spots in July and August), you usually needn't write for reservations. In high season, however, you'll have to start looking for a room in the morning. Pick up a list of hotels and their prices from the local tourist office (addresses and hours given in each city's Practical Information section). If you will arrive late, call and ask a hotel to hold a room for you. If possible, call a few days in advance, since many small hotels accept phone reservations. A long-distance phone call anywhere in Italy shouldn't cost more than L1000.

Italian law establishes a high and low season for areas popular with tourists. Remember that off-season months are different for alpine regions and seaside resort areas. When there is a difference in high and low season dates, *Let's Go* mentions it.

Day hotels (*alberghi diurni*), usually listed separately from common ones, are good places to go when you need to clean up and don't have a room. Offering showers, barbershops, and often a place to store luggage, they're generally found in town centers and near railroad stations and are open 6am-midnight.

Student Accommodations

Student residences in Italy are inexpensive and technically open to foreign students during vacations and whenever there is room. Presently, however, these accommodations are often very difficult, if not impossible, to arrange. All university towns operate a *Casa dello Studente* to which you can apply. A useful source of information on student housing is the *Guide for Foreign Students,* which can be obtained from the **Italian Ministry of Education,** viale Trastevere, Rome (L500; enclose 2 international reply coupons). Also write to the Casa dello Studente for an application in the following towns: Bari, Bologna, Camerino, Catania, Ferrara, Florence, Genoa, Messina, Macerata, Modena, Milan, Naples, Parma, Pavia, Perugia, Pisa, Rome, Salerno, Sassari, Siena, Urbino; and to Casa Fusinato, via Marzolo, Padova; Casa del Goliardo, Palermo; and Foresteria dell'Istituto di Ca'Foscari, Venice. The EPT in university towns can also provide specific information.

The **Relazioni Universitarie** of the Associazione Italiana per il Turismo e gli Scambi Universitari operates an accommodations service for foreign students throughout the year in many of the major university towns. Prices are low. The organization also offers discount student travel services. The main office is at via Palestro, 11, 00185 Rome (tel. 47 55 265).

The **Centro Turistico Studentesco e Giovanile (CTS)** (see also Tourist Offices above) is the Italian student and youth travel organization. Their offices, located in over 65 Italian cities, will help you find accommodations in *pensioni.* They will also book accommodations for you. They have offices in London, Paris, and Athens, so if you're going to Italy from these cities, you might want to reserve a room through them for the first few nights. Their central office is on via Nazionale, 66, 00184 Rome (tel. 46 791). CTS also provides information on student dormitories.

Camping

Many campgrounds throughout Italy are beautifully situated on lakes, rivers, or by the ocean. Often you can find peaceful seclusion mere steps away from the tent area, although there's usually not much space between sites. In August, you might have to arrive well before 11am to ensure yourself a spot.

Italian campsites come with a variety of amenities. Rates average L4000-5000 per person and L2500 per tent per night. The **Touring Club Italiano** publishes an annual directory of all camping sites in Italy, *Campeggi e Villaggi Turistici in Italia* (L15,000), available in any bookstore in Italy. The Touring Club also operates alpine huts available to hikers (see Alternative Accommodations below). Other helpful resources include *Europa Camping and Caravanning* (US$11), available from **Recreational Equipment, Inc. (REI),** P.O. Box C-88126, Seattle, WA 98188 (tel. (800) 426-4840), and *How to Camp Europe by Train,* by Lenore Baken (US$13), available from **Ariel Publications,** 14417 SE 19th Pl., Bellevue, WA 98007 (tel. (206) 641-0158).

Spend some time perusing catalogs and questioning knowledgeable salespeople before buying any equipment. There are many reputable mail-order firms—use them to gauge prices and order from them if you can't do as well locally. **Campmor,** 810 Rte. 17 North, P.O. Box 999, Paramus, NJ 07653 (tel. (800) 526-4784), offers name-brand equipment at attractive prices. Twenty-four hours, 365-days-per-year, **L.L. Bean,** Freeport, ME 04033 (tel. (207) 865-3111), is a legend with plenty of its own equipment and some national-brand stuff. Lastly, **Mountain Equipment, Inc. (MEI),** 4776 E. Jensen Ave., Fresno, CA 93725 (tel. (209) 486-8211), will send a product catalog and dealer listing, although they don't sell directly. For the best deals, look around for last year's merchandise, particularly in the fall; tents don't change much, but the price may be reduced as much as 50%.

If you're just starting out, you'll need to obtain the basics. Most of the better **sleeping bags**—either of down (lighter) or synthetics (cheaper, more water resistant and durable) are rated for specific minimum temperatures. The lower the mercury, the higher the price. Anticipate the most severe conditions you may encounter, subtract a few degrees, and then buy a bag. Not only will you waste money buying one suitable for alpine winters when you'll be sleeping on beaches in Tunisia, but you'll spend more time perspiring than sleeping. Expect to pay at least $20-50 for a lightweight synthetic bag and $70-$150 for a down bag meant for use in subfreezing temperatures. **Pads** to go under your bag are around $6-10 for simple Ensolite pads and $50 for the best air mattress or a sophisticated hybrid.

Modern **tents** are remarkably clever and a far cry from the canvas contraptions scouts seem so fond of. The best tents are "self-supporting" (equipped with their own frames and suspension systems), can be set up quickly, and do not require staking, although stakes are usually used to prevent movement. Up-to-date versions of simpler designs still require staking but are made of modern materials and have effective insect netting and integral floors like the self-supporting variety. Backpackers and cyclists may wish to pay a bit more for a sophisticated lightweight tent and should get the smallest tent possible—some two-person tents weigh under 3½kg (2 pounds). Expect to pay at least $70 for a simple two-person tent, $100 for a serviceable four-person one. Be sure to buy a tent with a protective rain fly. It is sometimes possible to get a decent tent for as little as $30, but examine it carefully and make sure it's returnable.

Other basics include a battery-operated **lantern** (*never* gas) for use inside the tent, and a plastic **groundcloth** to protect the tent's floor. Some accessories can dramatically increase comfort or decrease expenses. If you will be staying in primitive campgrounds, consider purchasing **water sacks** and/or a **solar shower. Campstoves** come in all sizes, weights, and fuel types, but none are truly cheap. Also, try not to venture into the woods without some **waterproof matches;** otherwise, a spill in the lake can leave you without a fire for the night.

You may want to write to the **Automobile Association,** Fanum House, Basingstoke, Hampshire RG21 2EA, England, for their publication *Camping and Caravanning in Europe.* Contact the **National Campers and Hikers Association, Inc.,** 4804 Transit Rd., Bldg. #2, Depew, NY 14043 (tel. (716) 668-6242) for more information.

Many travelers camp illegally in Italy (on beaches, roads, or any flat, inconspicuous plot of ground big enough for their sleeping bag). If you don't make a fire or leave litter, chances are you will not be disturbed. It is, however, extremely important to respect property rights—within sight of a farmhouse, ask permission. You will usually have no trouble. Remember: Your behavior affects the reception accorded to those who come after you.

Alternative Accommodations

For an experience with an institution that has profoundly affected Italian history for over a thousand years, you can stay in the guest house of a Roman Catholic **monastery.** Guests need not attend services but are expected to make their own beds and, often, to clean up after meals. Found in rural settings, monasteries are usually peaceful, and you probably shouldn't stay in one unless you want a quiet and contemplative experience. Carrying a letter of introduction from your own priest, pastor, or rabbi (on letterhead) may facilitate matters. Many monasteries accept only Roman Catholic guests. For more information about specific regions, write to the archdiocese of the nearest large town (e.g., in Rome: Archidiocesa di Roma, Roma, Italia). National and regional tourist boards also often maintain lists of monasteries with guest houses.

For a quiet, non-religious atmosphere, stay in a **rural cottage** or **farmhouse.** Usually, you will be given a small room and asked to clean up after yourself, but you will have freedom to come and go as you please. For more information, write to the main office of Agriscambi, Foro Traiano, 1A, 00187 Rome (tel. 67 95 917).

If you plan to hike in the Alps or the Dolomites, you should contact the **Club Alpino Italiano,** via Ugo Foscolo, 3, Milan, about alpine huts available to hikers. The **Touring Club Italiano,** corso Italia, 10, Milan, publishes a number of books giving detailed hiking itineraries including stopovers in the mountain refuges.

The **Protezione della Giovane (PDG),** via Urbana, 158, Rome (tel. 46 00 56), is a religious organization that assists women in finding inexpensive accommodations in its own hostels, convents, and inexpensive *pensioni* throughout Italy. If you don't mind the occasional 10:30pm curfew, this service is extremely convenient. The PDG staffs offices in train stations of major cities and maintains centrally located bureaus in many towns.

You might also want to contact international host organizations. **Servas** is an organization devoted to promoting understanding among different cultures. Members stay free of charge in host members' homes in over 90 countries. You must contact your hosts in advance and be willing to fit into their household routine. Stays are limited to two nights, unless you are invited to stay longer. Prospective members are interviewed and asked to contribute $45 plus a refundable $15 fee (hosts receive no money). To apply, write U.S. Servas Committee, Inc., 11 John St., #706, New York, NY 10038 (tel. (212) 267-0252).

Volunteers for Peace is a work camp organization with similar goals. VFP publishes a newsletter and an annual directory to workcamps in 30 countries primarily in Eastern and Western Europe (student donation US$6). Write to VFP, Tiffany Rd., Belmont, VT 05730 (tel. (802) 259-2759). Placement is quick, and volunteers' reservations are generally confirmed within a week.

Traveler's Directory prints a semiannual registry of its members, listing names, addresses, ages, interests, and offers of hospitality to other members. You must be willing to host other members in your home. You must be in the directory for two editions before you receive a free copy (pay an additional $10 otherwise). (Annual membership US$20, outside North America US$25.) The directory's newsletter, *Vagabond Shoes,* is available to nonmembers for $10 a year and gives budget travel advice. Send a stamped, self-addressed envelope to Traveler's Directory, 1501 Wylie Dr., Modesto, CA 95355.

Pax Christi, The International Catholic Movement for Peace, has as its mission "to organize everywhere the work of Christians for peace." The movement has established centers at places where there is both a long spiritual tradition and an important tourist industry. In these houses, international groups of young people offer food and lodging to travelers of both sexes for a maximum of five days in summer. A Friends of Pax Christi card is required and can be purchased at the center.

Sleeping in European train stations is a time-honored tradition. Though free and often tolerated by local authorities, it is not especially fun or comfortable or safe. Spending the night in an urban park is also cheap; so is your life.

Getting Around

By Plane

Italy's train system is so efficient and airline prices so high that it makes little sense to fly **ATI, Alitalia,** or **Alisarda** (Italy's 3 domestic airlines) unless you need to go a long distance in speed-of-light time. These airlines offer discounts on domestic travel, especially to those 21 or younger. Inquire at any of their many offices.

By Train

Ferrovie dello Stato (FS), the Italian State Railway, is one of the last European rail systems to provide inexpensive service. The fare between Rome and Venice, one of the longer trips made in Italy, is only $29 one-way second-class. Italian trains retain the romance and convenience that American railways have lost. However, they are not always safe. Overnight travelers should know that compartments are sometimes gassed; while passengers sleep deeply, they are robbed and sometimes attacked. Be sure you open a window and thoroughly ventilate your compartment. Daytime travel, on the other hand, is usually safe.

Although the low Italian train fares do not themselves justify the expense, consider buying a **Eurailpass** if you will also be traveling outside Italy. The Eurailpass is valid for unlimited travel in 16 European countries and also entitles you to free passage or reduced fares on some ferries and buses. If you're under 26, you can purchase the **Eurail Youthpass,** valid for one or two months of second-class travel at $320 and $420 respectively. If you're 26 or older, you must purchase a first-class Eurailpass (15 days $298, 1 month $470, 2 months $650, 3 months $798.) Eurailpasses may be bought only outside of Europe and are available only to those who do not reside in Europe. For more information or to purchase a pass, contact CIEE, Travel CUTS, Let's Go Travel Services (see Useful Organizations above), or a travel agent.

If you're under 23 and planning to travel extensively, consider the **InterRail Pass,** valid for a month of second-class travel in all countries covered by the Eurailpass, as well as Morocco, Yugoslavia, Romania, Hungary, and Great Britain. It allows you to travel "free" in each of these countries except the one in which it is bought, where you get 50% off full fares. Unfortunately, InterRail Passes are officially sold only to those who have lived in Europe at least six months. InterRail Senior Passes are available to travelers over 65.

The Italian State Railway offers its own passes, valid on all train routes within Italy. The **BTLC "Go Anywhere"** train pass is available in first- or second-class. Second-class passes cost US$107 for eight days, US$130 for 15 days, US$152 for 21 days, and US$185 for 30 days. Travelers must have the dates of validity stamped on the BTLC ticket at the first station of embarkation. Unless you travel like a crazed lightning bolt, however, there's no way to make this pass worth its price—train fares in Italy are simply too cheap.

The **Italian Kilometric Ticket** is good for 20 trips or 3000km (1875 miles) of travel, whichever comes first, and can be used for two months by as many as five people. Three thousand kilometers is a long way in Italy, so it's virtually impossible for one person to break even on the Kilometric Ticket. When used by more than one person, mileage per trip is calculated by multiplying the distance by the number of users. Children under 12 are charged half of the distance traveled, and those under four travel free. A first-class Kilometric Ticket costs US$207; second-class, US$116, a little more if purchased in the U.S. When buying the ticket, be sure the sales agent stamps the date on it, or you may find yourself with a useless pass. Either pass may be bought from the Italian State Railway representative, 666 Fifth Ave., New York, NY 10113 (tel. (212) 397-2667), and in Italy at major train stations and offices of the Compagnia Italiana Turismo (CIT).

Families of four or more, or a group of up to five adults traveling together qualify for discounts on Italian railways. Men over 65 and women over 60 get a 30% discount if they buy a "silver card" (about L5000, with proof of age). The discount is not available from June 26 to August 14 and from December 18-28. These discounts apply only to tickets purchased in Italy.

The Italian rail system involves four kinds of regular trains. The *accelerato,* more colloquially (and appropriately) referred to as a *locale,* usually stops at every station along a particular line and is excruciatingly slow, sometimes taking twice as long as a faster train. Travel on a *locale* only if you need to get off at a particular stop or want to soak in the scenery. The *diretto* makes slightly fewer stops. The *espresso,* stops only in major stations. Lastly, the *rapido* (which is air-conditioned) stops only in the largest cities and is considerably faster than the *espresso.* You will be charged more for a *rapido* ticket, but this may well be worth the money on long hauls. Some *rapido* trains, however, do not have second-class compartments, placing the cost of a ticket out of the budget traveler's range. On overnight trips, consider paying extra for a *cuccette,* fold-down bunks which come six to a compartment (US$9).

In addition, *freccie* trains run directly between cities that are normally connected only through other cities. There are 14 *freccie* all together, each running once per day and covering all regions of the country.

By Bus

Regularly scheduled bus routes are seldom used in Europe for long-distance travel. They are slower than *diretto* trains and no cheaper. Many inveterate bus travelers, however, enjoy the camaraderie that often develops among passengers. Buses in Italy are cheap and run fairly frequently. Punctual and often more comfortable than trains, they usually service many points in the countryside that are inaccessible by train. Italian buses are also often very crowded. For rides over an hour, find out where the bus begins its course, and board at or near the first stop. You may also want to buy tickets ahead of time.

Europabus is run by the European Railways. Most of their service consists of guided tours which include meals and hotels, but they also offer regular bus service to some cities. Most travel agencies can book seats on Europabus; you can also write Europabus 2, *c/o* German Rail, 747 Third Ave., 33rd floor, New York, NY 10017 (tel. (212) 308-6447, 308-3107, or (800) 223-6063). Many buses in Italian cities require that you purchase a ticket before boarding and fine you if you don't. Tickets may be purchased in the U.S. through Europabus 2 or in Italy at train stations or CIT offices.

By Car

If you're pressed for time or touring with friends, traveling by car may prove the most enjoyable and practical way to see Italy. It can also cut severely into your budget. Renting a four-seater for one week will run around US$250. Gasoline cost about US$4 a gallon in 1988. If you need a car for 3 weeks or more, leasing will be less expensive than renting. Most firms lease to drivers 18 and over, while rentals usually require you to be at least 21. Many companies also require a major credit card. Some offer discounts for foreigners.

Several U.S. firms offer rental and leasing plans in Italy. Call for prices and catalogs. If you are a student or faculty member, inquire about special discounts, or contact CIEE or CTS for more information (see Useful Organizations above). Stateside reservations are usually much cheaper than renting once you've arrived. Many agencies require that you reserve the car in advance while in the U.S. Unfortunately, rental cars are not eligible for Italy's tourist gas coupons. Among the major firms renting in Italy are **Avis Rent-A-Car** (tel. (800) 331-2112); **Auto Europe** (tel. (800) 223-5555; in Canada (800) 237-2465); **Europe by Car** (tel. (800) 223-1516); **Foremost Euro Car, Inc.** (tel. (800) 423-3111; in CA 272-3299); **Frances Auto Vacances** (tel. (212) 867-2625); **Hertz Rent-A-Car** (tel. (800) 654-3131); **Kemwel Group, Inc.** (tel. (800) 678-0678); **Maiellano Tours,** 441 Lexington Ave., New York, NY 10017 (or through Alitalia; special discount if pre-paid in the U.S.); and **Nemet Auto International** (tel. (800) 221-0177). Remember that all Autostrada direction signs are marked in green; all secondary roads in blue. Road maps are essential, since traversing the Italian countryside can easily turn a pleasant afternoon into a nightmare. Small roads constantly wrap around one another and create an extensive labyrinth only navigable by locals. Its good to have more than one map, as each emphasizes different roads.

Although Italy requires only a standard driver's license with an Italian translation (which rental agencies should provide), many other European countries require an International Driver's License.

By Moped

Motorized bikes have long graced Italian roads with their flashy colors and constant buzzing. They offer an enjoyable way to tour the country, especially in coastal areas where the view demands frequent attention. Mopeds cruise at an easy 40kph and don't use much gas. However, like bicycles, they're dangerous in the rain and extremely unpredictable on rough roads or gravel. Exercise caution at all times. Keep in mind that you should never ride wearing a backpack, and always wear a helmet. If you've never been on a moped before, Italy is not the place to start. The Vespa-style motorbikes with small wheels and a center platform for your feet are particularly hazardous. Rentals are difficult to arrange in many places, but ask at bicycle and motorcycle shops.

By Bicycle

In the flat Po Valley, bicycles can be found everywhere—women and men of all ages glide around carrying everything from eggs to children. Most of Italy, on the other hand, is pitched too steeply for the casual cyclist: The High Apennine Mountains run diagonally across the country northwest-southeast; the grape-growing slopes of Tuscany, the wooded hills of Umbria, and the Seven Hills of Rome are equally discouraging. You may also have to deal with baggage limitations and getting in serious shape for long-term bicycling. However, roads are generally in good condition, and more importantly, a bicycle's pace lets you feel more a part of Italy than does a car or any means of mass transportation.

You can ship your bicycle from home, though crating it for the trip can be somewhat difficult. Check with individual airlines for restrictions and costs. Some carriers include the bike as part of your baggage allowance, but will only consider bikes of a certain size (usually under 62 inches) as baggage. Others charge a flat fee of around $75, while still others charge different rates for different destinations. The amount of disassembling and crating required also varies. Italy, home of Campagnolo and Atala, is also a great place to purchase a good bike inexpensively.

Long- and short-term rentals are widely available, and we list rental agencies in many towns. The French National Railroad (SNCF) rents bikes and has representatives in 11 countries, including Italy. With a ticket or railpass and identification, you can rent a bike for about US$3 a day and a US$20 deposit.

Getting all the necessary equipment together may be your biggest hassle. While some local bike shops can provide helpful information, the costs involved in stocking an inventory usually make their prices exorbitant. Bicycle accessories—panniers and other touring bags, lighting equipment, racks, and most other parts—are cheaper and of better quality in the U.S.; get at least panniers and racks from U.S. suppliers. Definitely buy proper equipment for touring; riding a bike with a frame pack strapped on it or your back is not quite as safe as pedaling blindfolded over ice. Fortunately, mail and telephone ordering has been perfected to a fine art in the U.S. Don't spend a penny before you scan the pages of *Bicycling* magazine for the lowest sale prices. **Bike Nashbar,** 411 Simon Rd., Youngstown, OH 44512 (tel. (800) 345-BIKE) almost always offers the lowest prices, but when they don't, they cheerfully subtract 5¢ from the best price you can find. If you call their toll-free number, the parts will usually be on their way the same day. They regularly ship anywhere in the U.S. and Canada and will also send things overseas to military addresses. Their own line of products, including complete bicycles, is the best value. The first thing you should buy is a bike helmet. At about $60 for the best, it's a lot cheaper and more pleasant than having your head fixed—there aren't many neurosurgeons in remote Dolomite villages.

Fixing a modern derailleur-equipped mount is something just about anyone can do with a few simple but specialized tools. Many books offer useful advice; *The Complete Guide to Bicycle Maintenance and Repair,* by the editors of *Bicycling Magazine,* (US$14) offers tips on buying a bicycle and accessories. Call Rodale Press (tel. (800) 441-7761).

To lessen the odds of not finding your bike where you left it, buy a U-shaped lock made by **Citadel, Master,** or **Kryptonite.** It's relatively expensive (about US$30-40), but worth it. Each company insures its locks against theft of your bike for one or two years, or up to a certain amount of money.

If you want to transport your bicycle to another part of Italy by train, go to the *ufficio bagagli* at the railroad station with a very well labeled bicycle and it should arrive within three days. If the train has a *bagagliaio* (baggage compartment), you and your bike can ride the rails together. The Touring Club Italiano publishes a helpful book (in Italian) called *Manuale Pratico di Cicloturismo.*

By Thumb

You can make good time hitchhiking from city to city in Italy and it's a good way to meet Italians. Italy has an excellent network of tollroads (*autostrada*) linking the major cities. They run east-west, between Venice, Milan, and Turin, and north-south connecting Milan, Rome, and Naples. The latter route is known as the Autostrada del Sole (Highway of the Sun). Hitching on the *autostrada* itself is illegal, and you must stand in front of the tollbooths on the entrance ramps. Tolls are expensive, and if you can, you should offer to help out. In most cases, drivers will politely refuse. If you are more intent on seeing the countryside and meeting Italians than you are on making time, you should hitch the primary road system, which is quite good and carries a large volume of short-range traffic.

Women who plan to hitchhike should be forewarned: Some men may consider you fair game for harassment or worse. Hitch with a companion. Bulletin boards at hostels may be a good way to find a hitching partner. Newspapers and university message boards also sometimes carry ads looking for passengers to share driving and costs. Women alone or in pairs should definitely refuse rides in the back of a two-door car, unless the front seats are occupied by a couple. Don't lock the door. Keep your luggage handy—don't let it be thrown in the trunk. Never fall asleep in cars unless you have a stalwart companion—some Italians consider it tantamount to a wholesale sexual invitation. If you start to feel uneasy about a ride for any reason, get out at the first opportunity or firmly demand to be let off, no matter how unfavorable the spot appears to be for further hitching. Men traveling solo are also sometimes propositioned and should take similar precautions.

The lighter you travel, the better. Stack baggage carefully in a tight pile—many drivers will whip by if your baggage seems excessive, though it does serve to make you look "legitimate." A sign with your destination written in large letters is also helpful. If long-distance traffic is scarce, or if you're planning a particularly long hitch, aim for the next large town on the road and scrawl out a new sign.

Life and Times

History

Let's Go uses the terms B.C.E. (Before Common Era) and C.E. (Common Era) rather than B.C. and A.D.

According to myth, **Romulus and Remus,** the twins suckled by a wolf, founded Rome in 753 B.C.E. The Walter Cronkheit of his time, **Livy** reports in his annals that neither of the two relished sharing power, and in the ensuing altercation, Romulus slew Remus shouting, "Thus always to anyone who will cross my walls." Thus also began the Roman legacy of bloody politics. Although this upstart city was prosperous, its population was composed almost entirely of male refugees from the surrounding area. Romulus soon foresaw that the glory of Rome would be short-lived unless they procured women to bear them descendants—quick. When Roman envoys to neighboring tribes were rejected, Romulus hit upon a scheme. He invited his new neighbors to a carnival and tour of the new city, and during the festivities, the Romans seized their neighbors' wives. This tricky move, known as the **Rape of the Sabine Women,** has since been immortalized by countless artists.

Romulus's successors were kings over an increasingly powerful Rome the next couple of centuries. Then, in 509 B.C.E., T. Superbus was impeached, bringing the monarchy to an abrupt halt. The republic was established and the word *rex* (king) became anathema to generations of Romans. The next four centuries were relatively calm and Rome resolved to grow. These expansionist tendencies would come to define the Roman nature. Enemies encountered included **Pyrrhus,** the last of the Greek military adventurers in the style of Alexander the Great; he won a Pyrrhic victory over the Romans in 280 B.C.E.

The most important battles of the republic were the Punic Wars against Carthage, a Mediterranean power in present-day Tunisia. The Carthaginian leader **Hannibal** attacked Italy by bringing his army (elephants and all) across the Alps, but was stalled by inclement weather. Rome turned the tables, and the xenophobic **Cato** urged the total destruction of Carthage. His wish came true in 146 B.C.E., when Carthage was laid waste, and the vindictive Romans sowed the ground with salt to prevent it from ever thriving again.

The century following the Punic Wars was a time of vast social upheaval and violent domestic strife. The charismatic conqueror of Gaul, **Julius Caesar,** emerged as the new leader but refused to be crowned dictator. His power was great enough, however, to worry some of his former friends, notably **Brutus,** who conspired to assassinate him on the Ides (15th) of March in 44 B.C.E. Ignoring a soothsayer's command to "Beware the Ides," Caesar was attacked by a swarm of dagger-wielding senators upon entering the senate chambers. According to Shakespeare, Caesar's ally **Mark Antony** used his funeral oration ("Friends, Romans, countrymen, lend me your ears . . . ") to turn the crowds against the assassins, who were forced to flee the city. And civil war reigned again.

Caesar's grand-nephew and adopted son, **Octavian,** took a decisive victory at Actium in 31 B.C.E. While professing to restore the republic, Octavian took on the title *Augustus* (revered one), and actually inaugurated an imperial government. His reign lasted until 14 C.E. and is generally acknowledged to be Rome's golden age. However, many of his successors were less successful. These included **Caligula** (37-41 C.E.), the much-dreaded **Domitian** (81-96 C.E.), and **Nero** (54-68 C.E.), who supposedly got his kicks from using Christians as torches for his lawn parties and reveling while Rome burned around him.

Still, the empire continued to expand until it reached its peak around 180 C.E., stretching from Britain, to Africa, and finally, to the Euphrates River. After the death of **Marcus Aurelius** in 180, however, Rome's control over its vast domain began to unravel. Weak leadership and the migration of Germanic tribes southward combined to create a state of total anarchy in the third century. Using tactics of increased brutality and repression aimed particularly at Christians, **Diocletian** secured control and established order with a heavy hand. The fortunes of Christianity took a turn for the better only when **Constantine,** Diocletian's successor, saw a huge cross in the sky along with the command, "By this sign you shall conquer." During the next day's battle, Constantine and his troops marched under the Chi Rho (still used by the Church as shorthand for *Christos*) and emerged victorious. Convinced and converted, Constantine instituted Christianity as the state religion. Episcopal cities took on the administrative structure of the decaying provincial capitals, citizens were tied to the land and vocation of their ancestors, and huge armies of barbarian mercenaries patrolled Rome and the frontiers. These measures planted the first seeds of medieval European culture, but they could not save the Roman Empire. **Alaric,** King of the Visigoths, sacked Rome in 410, and **Odoacer,** an Ostrogoth chieftain, was crowned King of Italy in 476.

The Papacy emerged from the rubble as the chief authority on the peninsula. The Pope's power was limited to spiritual matters until the arrival in Rome of the Frankish king **Charlemagne.** When he was crowned Emperor by Pope Leo III on Christmas Day, 800, the great amalgam called the **Holy Roman Empire** was born (though

Voltaire once noted that it was neither holy, nor Roman, nor an empire). Unfortunately, its fatal flaw was an ambiguous division of power between the pope and emperor. When the powerful **Frederick Barbarossa** was crowned emperor in 1155, war broke out between his backers, known as the Ghibellines, and the supporters of the Pope, the Guelphs. This schism cut across family lines within towns, causing citizens to fortify their homes and erect huge defensive towers, 13 of which still adorn the skyline of San Gimignano.

Although the Papacy eventually asserted itself, the leaders who clasped the fallen scepter in the fifteenth and sixteenth centuries were politicians of the individual city-states, not the Vatican. The city-states (also known as *communes*) were left to their own devices over these anarchic years and concentrated on furthering their own economic and territorial interests. Their leaders initiated a political fragmentation that would plague Italian history. Great ruling families, such as the Gonzaga in Mantua, the d'Este in Ferrara, and especially the Medici in Florence, gained great stature after suppressing the traditional oligarchies. Epitomized by **Lorenzo de' Medici** (and glorified by **Machiavelli** in *The Prince*), these tyrants brought about important reforms in commerce and law, and their cities flourished. Princes, bankers, and merchants utilized their increasing wealth to patronize the artists and scholars whose work defined the **Renaissance.** Unfortunately, the power-hungry princes also gave the Renaissance a gloomier side—constant warfare. Although much of the fighting was conducted by mercenaries, the cities were weakened militarily and yielded easily to the Spanish invasions of the sixteenth century.

The Spaniards brought the Counter-Reformation, the Jesuits, and the **Inquisition.** Although such intellectuals as Galileo Galilei and Giordano Bruno were persecuted, many Italians welcomed an end to the chaos of the fifteenth century. By 1600, the Papacy had once again gained firm control of the Italian state. As Spanish power waned in the two subsequent centuries, Austrian domination of Italy began to increase. A few nationalistic stirrings, however, continued to shake the divided peninsula.

Realizing that a unified Italy would be easier to rule than a fragmented one, **Napoleon** brought the southern provinces together with the Kingdom of Naples and the Roman Republic, uniting the country politically for the first time since antiquity. Napoleon further stimulated Italian patriotism by stirring up national resentment against the French presence. Although the Congress of Vienna officially unified much of the country, Italy was politically segmented upon Napoleon's fall. In subsequent decades, sentiment against foreign rule evoked a movement of nationalist "resurgence" called the **Risorgimento.** Responsibility for the success of the Risorgimento belongs primarily to three Italian heroes: **Giuseppe Mazzini,** the movement's intellectual leader; **Giuseppe Garibaldi,** the military leader and commander of the "red-shirts"; and **Camillo di Cavour,** the outstanding political figure.

Although the much-revered Garibaldi and his army of 1000 anomalies conquered the Bourbons in the south, the greatest credit for Italy's birth as a nation belongs to Cavour. In 1858, he and Napoleon III of France strengthened an alliance against the Austrians that freed Lombardy from control abroad. The alliance lent credibility to the new Kingdom of Italy, which went on to annex Romagna, Parma, Modena, and Tuscany. In 1866, the Prussians forced the Austrian Hapsburg Empire to surrender Veneto to Italy; Rome was relinquished by France on September 20th, 1870 (a date which has at least one *piazza* named after it in most cities). Once the elation of unification wore off, however, the age-old provincial differences reasserted themselves. The North wanted to protect its relative prosperity from the economic stagnation of the Mezzogiorno, the more agrarian south. The city-states of central Italy were wary of surrendering too much power to a central administration in Rome. Cavour's death in 1861 left a power vacuum that was not filled until the rise of **Fascism** in the early 1920s.

The Fascists' success stemmed from the chaos that followed World War I. Italy had joined the Allies against the Hapsburg Empire, but afterwards, overly ambitious territorial claims and a depleted economy triggered widespread dissatisfaction. The Bolsheviks had recently gained control in Russia, and **Benito Mussolini,** Il Duce, took advantage of an Italian "red scare" to destroy his domestic opposition. He also hoped to increase Italy's sphere of influence abroad, invoking the memory of Imperial Rome to support his conquest of Ethiopia.

Italy joined World War II in 1940, shortly before the fall of France, enjoying an instant victory. When the tide turned three years later and the Allies landed in Sicily, Mussolini fell. By the end of 1943, the government had changed direction, declared war on Germany, and was promptly invaded and occupied by its former ally. Some of the most savage fighting took place as the Allies struggled up the peninsula. Italy's pain was compounded by the ongoing civil war between supporters of the deposed Fascist government and its democratic replacement.

Modern Politics

Figuring out modern Italian politics is like trying to eat pasta without getting sauce on your shirt. The war ended with no one in clear control, but the **Christian Democrats** emerged as the major party. Since then, Italy's government has been in constant chaos. The country has elected 47 different governments since World War II. Most have been anchored by the Christian Democrats; nonetheless, the **Italian Communist Party** (which has distanced itself from Moscow since the days of Stalinist repression) exerts a great deal of influence, gaining 30% of the vote in most national elections.

The international view of Italian politics has been colored by the widely reported acts of terrorist groups, especially the **Red Brigades.** The tragic kidnapping and murder, in May 1978, of Aldo Moro, prime minister from 1963 to 1968 illustrates a tendency for violence that recalls the internecine warfare of the Renaissance city-states. Recently, however, the government has cracked down on terrorism, and today's political situation is not so much dangerous as it is incomprehensible.

One reason for the confusion is the lingering regionalism of the peninsula. Although the land of Italy is extremely old, the nation of Italy is yet very young, and city or regional bonds have proven stronger than national bonds. The biggest division exists between the highly industrialized, north European areas and the agrarian, south Mediterranean regions (Il Mezzogiorno). Despite the reluctance of the south to modernize, Italy's GNP recently surpassed all of Britain's, and the country became the fifth most industrialized nation in the world. Inflation is low, although unemployment is still reasonably high. Many of the unemployed are, however, actually busy in the extensive *economia nera,* the black market that may account for as much as 25% of Italy's GNP. Labor unrest still remains a problem, and summertime strikes have practically become a sacred tradition.

Recent Italian politics have not helped to clear the air. After three long years, socialist Bettino Craxi resigned from the prime minister's chair in March 1987, claiming that the Christian Democratic majority hampered him from ruling freely. Seventy-nine-year-old Armintore Fanfani stepped to the fore. Elections were held in June 1987, and the Communists suffered a major setback. Both the Socialists and the Christian Democrats subsequently took gains. In late July, President Francesco Cossiga, a Christian Democrat, asked Giovanni Goria, also a Christian Democrat, to form a five-party coalition and become the new Prime Minister. Goria, at 44 (the youngest post-war prime minister), is a noted economist and former Treasury Minister. Perhaps the most exciting candidate in the most recent election was Ilona Staller, a Hungarian-born erotic dancer who was elected to the "camera of deputies" in Viareggio. Dedicated to politics, this Radical Party candidate asked for a moment of silence from her followers to ponder the plight of all malnourished children in the world.

If this survey of modern Italian politics doesn't answer all your questions, don't hesitate to ask the views of any Italians you meet. Most will be only too happy to enlighten you with their perspectives. To stay informed, read—on a spectrum from left to right—*L'Unita, Il Corriere della Sera, La Repubblica,* or *Il Giornale.* Remember to keep political slants and tendencies toward sensationalism firmly in mind.

Language

Modern "standard" Italian was created by the influence of a great triad of writers—Dante, Petrarch, and Boccaccio—who chose to write in the Florentine dialect. However, vastly different dialects continue to exist today. Most Italians learn and speak standard Italian at school while conversing in their own dialect at home. In fact, a Venetian traveler to Sicily might have as much difficulty understanding the Sicilian dialect as an American would. All educated Italians are, however, able to communicate in the standard *Florentine* dialect, an outgrowth of medieval Latin.

Even if you don't speak Italian, a few basic terms will help you get around. Scan a phrase book (such as Berlitz's *Italian for Travelers*) beofre you go and then take it along with you. Any attempts at Italian are appreciated and encouraged, though you'll find that quite a few people in larger cities understand at least a little bit of English. If you can learn only one complete sentence, learn *"Parla inglese?"* (PAHR-lah een-GLAY-zay: Do you speak English?). Don't be rude—always ask before imposing your language on a citizen of a non-English-speaking country. Learn the numbers, if only to bargain and assure yourself you've gotten on the right train or bus. Learn the essentials of courtesy as well. *Let's Go* provides a glossary with helpful phrases at the end of the book. (See Study above for information on learning Italian in Italy.)

In addition to the spoken language, Italians are fluent in an amazing array of gesticulatory body language. Since many common gestures are obscene, *Let's Go* cautions against sophomoric imitations. However, great fun can be obtained simply by watching the show of body language, which increases the farther south one travels.

Art and Architecture

In Italy, you don't find art only in museums; in fact, you don't have to *find* it—it's all over—in churches, streets, alleys, palaces, and villas. For centuries, Italian artists and craftsmen have devoted energy and talent to beautifying their cities. Public spaces, buildings, and private residences have been sculpted to please the eye; and they, along with the art in and around them, are essential to the experience that is Italy. Wherever you go, keep your eyes open—Italian *piazze* and churches offer the opportunity to appreciate centuries of art in their intended settings.

Roman artists emulated the Greek sculpture they encountered in southern Italy and Sicily; the greater part of our present knowledge of Greek art actually comes from their faithful replicas. The Romans proved their creativity as engineers and architects in building roads, bridges, aqueducts, and large basilicas. Architectural innovations include the arch, used to vault great spaces, and the first extensive use of manufactured materials such as concrete and brick. The basic structural features of Doric Greek temples—the column, cornice, and entablature—all reappear in Roman buildings, but only for framing arched openings or embellishing blank walls. The **Colosseum** (80 C.E.) and the **Pantheon** (117-125 C.E.) in Rome are two examples of the marriage of Greek aesthetics and Roman technology.

The collapse of the Roman Empire and the rise of Christianity did not immediately inaugurate a conscious search for new aesthetic forms. The color, composition, and treatment of subjects in the Catacombs (5th-7th centuries) recalls classical Roman wall painting, though degenerate in quality and technique. Bacchic and pastoral figures from classical mythology represent Christ and the Apostles. Similarly, the early Christian church was an adaptation of the Roman basilica, a long hall divided into two aisles and ending in a semi-circular extension called an apse. In early churches, on the other hand, rows of columns support a flat roof rather than the high vaulted ceilings of the basilica: Architects probably no longer possessed the technical knowledge to raise high vaults. The Churches of Santa Maria Maggiore and Santa Sabina (5th century), and the largest of all, the Church of San Paolo Fuori le Mura (4th century), still stand, largely unaltered, in modern Rome.

The first important non-classical style introduced into Italian art was the **Byzantine style,** which favored a modified basilica form. Its emphasis on brilliantly-colored mosaics and sophisticated devices like the arch and buttress obscured classical proportions. Italian examples of Byzantine construction include the Church of San Vitale in Ravenna (547) and the Church of San Marco in Venice (1063-1073).

Foreign occupation and strong local tradition created a regionally diverse and complex **Romanesque** architecture. The rejection of structural innovations being undertaken in northern Europe in favor of a continued refinement of decorative elements still based on the classical system was one unifying point. Thus, the interior of the cathedral at Pisa (1068-1118), with its procession of classical columns, is not much different from early Christian churches. Romanesque artists were not, however, consciously classical; with their brightly colored marble bands and shimmering mosaics, they were more akin to the Byzantine than the classical spirit.

The Italian **Gothic** style (12th-14th centuries) did not develop from the Romanesque (as in France), but was introduced as a mature style. The least classical features of the design were filtered out of the Gothic in its transition to the Mediterranean: The flying buttress and coupled towers which disrupt the classical harmony between vertical and horizontal forms are notably missing in Italian Gothic churches. Lacking external support, the roof is held up directly by the walls, making impossible the lofty ceilings and stained-glass windows of the north. A colored marble facade crowned with a pediment often replaces the coupled front towers of the northern Gothic style.

In late thirteenth- and fourteenth-century painting, figures become fresher and more lifelike, preparing the way for the great aesthetic innovations of the Renaissance. The most influential exponent of the new realism in painting was *Giotto* (1267-1337), who transformed the stiff, stylized Byzantine manner into a more fluid form, replacing flat backgrounds with landscapes of sky and mountains. The architectural setting of his *Death of St. Francis* (Bardi Chapel of Santa Croce, Florence) paved the way for experiments in perspective important to Renaissance design. Heir to Giotto's technique, **Masaccio's** (1401-1428) work demonstrates a new awareness of light, as well as an effective and sober use of color. Like Giotto's, his figures have a solemnity and dignity typical of the early Renaissance.

Masaccio's painting actually benefited from a study of two of the most prominent **Early Renaissance** sculptors, **Ghiberti** (1378-1455) and **Donatello** (1386-1466). Ghiberti's *Gates of Paradise,* the bronze doors of the Florentine baptistery, contain gracefully proportioned figures arranged in a harmonious, classical composition. The construction of these doors was an important coup for Ghiberti. When the Opera del Duomo held a competition for their design in 1402, Ghiberti was up against Brunelleschi, Jacopo della Quercia, and Nicolò Lamberti. When the content narrowed to focus on Ghiberti and Brunelleschi, the former won for his elegant lines and deep perspective. Donatello employed a coarser, more vigorous technique—full of life and character. His statue of Saint George and his bronze *David* are in the Florentine Bargello.

The two most important architects of the early Renaissance are **Filippo Brunelleschi** (1377-1446) and **Leon Alberti** (1404-1472). Brunelleschi completed Santa Maria del Fiore (*duomo*) in Florence by raising the first great dome since classical antiquity. In his church designs, Alberti tried to attain a classic monumentality akin to the great open spaces of ancient Rome. The vault of Sant' Andrea in Mantua (25m across) served as a prototype for church interiors for the next two hundred years. Classical monumentality was also the aim of **Donato Bramante** (1444-1514), the leading architect of the **High Renaissance.** In his design for the new **Saint Peter's** in Rome (1503-1514), he envisioned a huge, centrally planned church crowned by a powerful dome in the manner of the Pantheon. His monumental *Last Supper* (1492-1496), executed for the rectory of the convent of Santa Maria delle Grazie in Milan, conveys deep emotion and great psychological insight. Once severely damaged, the *Last Supper* has recently been restored.

Michelangelo's genius, like da Vinci's, revolutionized the decorative arts. The formal, tranquil *Pietà* in Saint Peter's, the youthfully elegant *David* in Florence's

Academy, and the vigorously emotional Florentine *Pietà* manifest his remarkable versatility as a sculptor. Likewise, da Vinci's *Last Supper* will live on forever—no supper will ever by the same. Recently, the extensive restoration of the frescoes of the Sistine Chapel (1508-1513) has revealed a brightness hidden by years of wear and tear. While Michelangelo was working on these frescoes, the young **Raphael** di Giovanni Sanzio (already famous for his series of Virgins) was painting his great historical and allegorical frescoes for the Papal apartments in the Vatican.

When Rome was pillaged in 1527, the serene world that nurtured the Renaissance came to an abrupt end. The uncertain political atmosphere which followed encouraged the development of **mannerism.** In conscious revolt against inflexible traditions, artists adopted an exaggerated emotionalism, expressed in harsh, vivid colors and distorted human forms. Architects such as **Giulio Romano** (1499-1546) took delight in flouting the most sacred Renaissance rules, incorporating asymmetrical details and stressing imaginative, whimsical decoration.

The **baroque** style, which lasted well into the eighteenth century, was characterized at first by a reaction against the excessive stylization of the mannerists. Caravaggio (1573-1610) harked simple biblical scenes populated with ordinary people in stark settings devoid of iconography. **Tiepolo** (1696-1770) has been immortalized by his wonderfully illusionistic frescoes and canvases, which extend landscapes and pastoral scenes into an ever-extending ephemeral horizon.

The most important sculptor of the period, and in many ways the creator of the **high baroque** style (characterized by its color, opulence, and exuberant illusionism) was **Gian Lorenzo Bernini** (1598-1680), who succeeded in representing swift movement and creating a convincing three-dimensional space into which the viewer is readily drawn. It has been said that the city of Rome is a Bernini museum. Baroque buildings also exhibit a love of complex and intricate elements. The forms of their facades struggle between architecture and sculpture.

Through French influence, the more delicate **rococo** style and the sterner formalities of **neoclassicism** succeeded the Italian baroque. French artists came to the fore in the beginning of the modern period with the innovations of Monet, Cezanne, and Picasso (the latter a native of Spain). In Italy, this predominance was reflected in the work of the two foremost artists of the pre-fascist era. **Umberto Boccioni** (1882-1916) was the major exponent of the rather short-lived **Futurist** movement (1901-1916), based loosely on the tenets of Cubism in its desire to represent multiple dimensions in space and time simultaneously. Futurism focused on the principle of *velocità* (speed), claimed to be an essential feature of modern life. At the same time, **Giorgio de Chirico** took up another French inspiration, **surrealism,** and created his own form of "dream writing" using spatial ambiguities and mannequin-like figures to express the anxiety of pre-World War I Europe.

The works of a few internationally acclaimed Italian artists alive today are on exhibit in various galleries around Italy. **Sandro Chio** and **Enzo Cucci,** both neo-expressionists, have an intriguing style that manifests itself in humorous juxtapositions of subjects. **Francesco Clemente,** one of Italy's most talented new artists, paints to evoke dissatisfaction or disgust. **Marino Marini,** is a renowned figure sculptor.

To trace the current path of Italian art, visit some of the collections in the modern art galleries of Rome, Florence, Venice, Turin, Milan, Naples, and Genoa, as well as the Canova Museum at Passagno. A number of books can provide more background. Try *The Architecture of the Italian Renaissance* by Peter Murray, *Painting and Experience in Fifteenth-Century Italy* by Michael Boxandall, *Italy: A Cultural Guide* by E. O. Hauser, and Irving Stone's popular biography of Michelangelo, *The Agony and the Ecstasy.*

Music

From cradleside arias to the graveside *siciliana,* from the Genoese fisherman's *bravura aria* to the High Mass at San Marco's, the passionate lyricism of Italian music resonates through all strains of Italian life.

Perhaps because of the mellifluousness of its language, Italy has earned a position of influence in European music, particularly through its contributions to vocal music. Italian music has its roots in Dante, who set his verse to melodies. In the Trecento, the Middle Ages's last flowering, the lovely melodies and delightful rhythms of Italian song were best expressed by **Jacopo da Bologna** in the north and **Francesco Landini**—also known as Il Cieco (The Blind One)—in Florence. The slightly exotic *Ecco La Primavera* by Landini and the sensuous *Fenice Fu* by Jacopo bespeak an era steeped in the *dolce stile novo* (sweet new style). In the fifteenth century, powerful families such as the Medici in Florence and the Malatesta in Pesaro commanded the best musicians and composers from abroad to adorn their splendid courts and indigenous music thus languished.

By the sixteenth century, Italians finally took a place at the center of the music world as native pupils succeeded their northern masters in the coveted position of *maestro di cappella* (choir master) for the great cathedrals. In Venice, the Church of San Marco was not merely a place of worship but also a public showplace where the glory of the Venetian republic could be opulently displayed. The magnificent standards set by the government for its church officials necessitated religious music with rich textures, colorful use of instruments, and a lack of concern for the dictates of Rome. **Gabrielli's** works for two or three choirs, at least two organs, and a variety of instruments (all placed in different parts of the basilica), certainly produced the desired effect. **Palestrina** and his Roman colleagues, worried that the Council of Trent might banish the use of polyphony in the liturgy, eschewed the flamboyant style of Venice, opting instead for solemnity in their masses. The **madrigal** also blossomed at this time. Uniquely Italian, these free-flowing secular songs with three to six parts and a relatively serious text (often by Petrarch) still move and delight audiences today.

Born in Florence, nurtured in Venice, revered in Milan, and frowned upon by Rome, **opera** is Italy's most cherished art form. Early opera, which showcased *stile recitativo,* a singing style modeled closely on speech, was an attempt to recapture the simple, evocative singing and recitation of classical drama. **Monteverdi** and his contemporaries drew freely from history, blithely juxtaposing high drama, concocted love scenes, and bawdy humor. In Monteverdi's early jewel, *Orfeo* (1607), music and poetry are joined in perfect balance.

In seventeenth-century Rome, instrumental music began to establish itself as a legitimate genre. **Corelli** developed the concerto form with its contrasting moods and tempos. His Christmas Concerto is still often played. Most famous for the *Four Seasons* concertos, **Vivaldi** wrote over four hundred concertos while working at a home for orphaned girls in Venice. His consistent freshness and dynamism allow few rivals.

Eighteenth-century Italy was primarily a music exporter; Italian words and expression became established as musical jargon, and Italian virtuosos impressed audiences throughout Europe. **Domenico Scarlatti** wrote over five hundred sonatas for the harpsichord, and **Sammartini** experimented with the early symphony. In opera, baroque ornamentation yielded to the classical standards of moderation, simplicity, and elegance. Worshiped even more than their descendants are now, Italian opera stars knew no moderation and sometimes had superfluous arias arbitrarily inserted to showcase their skill.

To today's opera lovers, Italian opera means **Verdi, Puccini, Bellini, Donizetti,** and **Rossini**—all figures of the late nineteenth and early twentieth centuries. With plots of legendary length relying on coincidences, mistaken identities, and fate, nineteenth-century Italian opera continues to dominate modern opera houses. Bellini's *Norma* and Puccini's *Madame Butterfly* display *bel canto* (literally, beautiful song, but meaning also the traditional Italian singing style) at its best. Composed while Italy was still ruled by the Hapsburgs, Verdi's music came to symbolize Italian unity; his operas contain frequent references to political assassinations, exhortations against tyranny, and jibes at French and Austrian monarchs. His works *Aida* and *Il Trovatore* (The Troubadour) are compassionate and poignantly evocative, while *Otello* is mercilessly tragic. Rossini boasted that, like Vivaldi, he could produce music faster than copyists could reproduce it, but Rossini was such an infamous procrastinator that his agents were said to lock him up with a single plate of spaghetti until he completed his compositions. His *Barber of Seville* is a favorite with modern audiences, and everyone knows the tune, popularized by *The Lone Ranger,* of his *William Tell* overture.

Italian music continues to grow and change in the twentieth century. **Respighi,** composer of the popular *Pines of Rome* and *Fountains of Rome,* experimented with shimmering, rapidly shifting orchestral textures. **Gian Carlo Menotti,** who now lives in the U.S., has written a conglomeration of different pieces, including short, opera-like works such as *Amahl and the Night Visitors* and *The Telephone.* **Luigi Dallapiccola** worked with serialism, achieving the most success in his choral music, works such as *Canti di prigionia* (*Songs of Prison*) and *Canti di liberazione* (*Songs of Liberation*); both protest fascist rule in Italy.

Opera season runs from December to June. The music can be heard in almost every city in the country; the productions at the Teatro alla Scala in Milan, the Teatro San Carlo in Naples, and the Teatro dell' Opera in Rome are especially spectacular. Tickets are surprisingly cheap; a decent seat can be obtained for under US$10. Don't despair if you miss the season; throughout summer, you can enjoy open-air opera at the Terme di Caracalla in Rome, the Arena in Verona, and the Teatro Rossetti in Trieste, as well as at many major music festivals. The **European Association of Music Festivals,** 122, rue de Lausanne, 1202 Geneva, Switzerland, publishes the booklet *Festivals 1989,* which lists the dates and programs of major European music and theatre festivals. Don't be discouraged by some high prices; student rates are often available.

Important Italian Music Festivals:

Aosta: Organ Music in the Cathedral, July-Aug.

Bolzano: International Piano Competition, Aug.

Florence: Maggio Musicale Fiorentino, May-June.

Perugia: Sagra Musicale Umbria, Sept.

Ravello: Ravello Classical Musical Festival, July.

Ravenna: Rocca Brancaleone Outdoor Opera, July or Aug.

Siena: Settimana Musicale Senese, Aug.-Sept.

Spoleto: Festival of Two Worlds, June-July.

Literature

Latin literature is often snubbed by Hellenists who claim that it consists of mere imitations of ancient Greek literature. Although Rome's literati did borrow a great deal from their predecessors (especially in the genre of myth), they imbued it with an unmistakably Roman flavor.

Publius Virgilius Maro (*Vergil*) wrote the great Latin epic, *The Aeneid,* with the support of Augustus. *The Aeneid* follows the Trojan Aeneas through his wanderings after the destruction of his city. Since myth had it that Aeneas would father great, long-lasting progeny, the Romans were very happy to portray him as their founder. *The Aeneid* has undergone wide shifts in popularity. During the Middle Ages, when Homer was not available in Europe, Vergil was practically deified. However, the modern era has not held him in such esteem. (Ezra Pound thought him a second-rate imitator of Homer.) There are dozens of translations available; Robert Fitzgerald's is regarded as one of the best.

Lovers of the poetry of love will appreciate **Catullus, Ovid, Propertius,** and **Tibullus.** All wrote sophisticated poems on the sorrows and delights of timeless *Amore.* Ovid also wrote *The Metamorphoses,* a series of poems narrating stories of how things changed to what they are today. Ovid's poems incorporate a delightful raciness which runs counter to the conservative wishes of Augustus. Whether because of this naughtiness or his personal life, Augustus mysteriously exiled Ovid in 8 B.C.E. Another lyric poet, **Horace** expressed sentiments more amenable to the wishes of the state: "*Dulce et decorum est pro patria mori.*" ("Sweet and fitting it is to die for one's country.")

For a taste of Romans doing what they did best (i.e., politics) check out **Cicero** or **Caesar.** Though a bit dry for the casual reader, the writings of these two form the basis of many a high-schooler's Latin studies. **Plutarch's** *Lives* offer interesting, if historically questionable, portraits of Rome's leaders from the perspective of a sympathetic Greek. The literature of the pre- and post-Augustan ages is varied and generally less esteemed. **Plautus** offers some rollicking farce, **Juvenal** some biting satire, and **Petronius'** *Satyricon* a strange, uncensored look at the decadence of the age of Nero.

As Vergil is to Latin literature, so **Dante Alighieri** is to Italian literature. Author of *La Divina Commedia,* Dante is known, even today, simply as Il Poeta (The Poet). He is still revered as the father, godfather, and arbiter of Italian literature. T.S. Eliot once said, "Dante and Shakespeare divide the modern world between them. There is no third." One of the first major European literary works composed in the vernacular, *La Commedia* explores every aspect of the human experience with insight and compassion, from the depths of guilt and degradation in the Inferno to Paradiso's lofty exaltation. If you can, read Dante's own euphonic *Terza Rima,* but if English is more your speed, try Ciardi's or Mandelbaum's translation.

In a lighter vein, **Boccaccio's** *Decameron* is a series of *novelle* narrated by young Florentines traveling to escape the plague-infested city. Its tone ranges from the bawdy to the sublime, with pious maidens, licentious friars, carefree nobles, and pathetic paupers populating the sparklingly witty tales. **Francesco Petrarch** wrote poetic works strikingly modern in their sense of a constantly changing world and in their probing of human doubt and torment in spiritual and personal relationships. **Niccoló Machiavelli** achieved fame (or infamy) with his ruthless depiction of the perfect pragmatic politician in *Il Principe* (*The Prince*).

I Promessi Sposi (*The Betrothed*) by **Alessandro Manzoni** is the quintessential Italian novel—a sprawling and profoundly human epic that probes the suffering of humanity in the random course of history. Revealing most of the temperament and morality of the Risorgimento era, this work follows those of Dante, Boccaccio, and Petrarch in importance.

Twentieth-century exposure to communism, socialism, and Fascism provoked many of the anti-traditional literary achievements of the modern day. Nobel prize-winning playwright Luigi Pirandello produced philosophical and moving human dramas such as *Sei personaggi in cerca d'autore* (*Six Characters in Search of an Author*). His novels are less known but no less brilliant: *I Vecchi e I Giovani* (*The Old and the Young*) deals with socialist uprisings in Sicily, and *Uno, Nessuno, e Centomila* (*One, No One, and One Hundred Thousand*), his final novel and a bizarre, challenging work, fractures self-assurance by posing grotesquely witty questions about human existence.

A Triestino of German descent and James Joyce's model for Leopold Bloom, **Italo Svevo** produced three masterpieces of unconventional language: *Una Vita (A Life), La Coscienza di Zeno* (*The Confessions of Zeno*) and *Senilità* (*Senility*). The novels demonstrate an extraordinary grasp of Trieste's ambience, exploring the city's ordinary *borghese* psyche. Both neo-realist writers, as well as political activists, **Ignazio Silone** and **Carlo Levi,** wrote semi-autobiographical works describing their experiences with Fascism and the Second World War. Silone's *Pane e Vino* (*Bread and Wine*) paints the countryside as the unassuming masque of the Italian underground. The protagonist is a political exile searching for refuge and understanding from the Italian peasants. In Levi's *Cristo si è fermato a Eboli* (*Christ Stopped at Eboli*), the main character is exiled to an isolated village untouched by civilization, or symbolically, by Christ. Look for one of the workers' descriptions of America; it is a marvelous portrayal of the attitudes you might encounter in the tiny towns of southern Italy.

Numerous Italian poets have attained prominence in the twentieth century. The most flamboyant and controversial is **Gabrielle D'Annunzio,** whose cavalier heroics during and after World War I earned him as much fame as his eccentric verse. **Salvatore Quasimodo** and **Eugenio Montale,** both Nobel Prize winners, and **Giuseppe Ungaretti** are also noteworthy.

Particularly appealing prose works for travelers include Giorgio Bassani's *Il Giardino dei Finzi-Contini* (*The Garden of the Finzi-Continis*), Cesare Pavese's *La Luna e I Falò* (*The Moon and the Haystacks*), and Elio Vittorini's *Conversazione in Sicilia* (*Conversation in Sicily*), which deals with a return to Italy after a long sojourn in America. For a modern female writer's view of the Italian experience with Fascism, read Natalia Ginzberg's *Lessico Famigliare* (*Family Sayings*), an autobiography which provides a good indication of Italian sentiments during the war. Recently published, Italo Calvino's *Italian Folktales* and *Se una Notte d'Inverno un Viaggiatore* (*If On a Winter's Night a Traveler*) received clamorous praise in the international press. Perhaps the most delightful way to acquaint yourself with the rich sounds and deep colors of Italy's past is to read Umberto Ecco's *The Name of the Rose,* a fascinating mystery set in a fourteenth-century monastery and full of ecclesiastical pomp and peasant ingenuity.

Film

The achievements of the Romanesque period and the Renaissance might lead you to think the Italian contribution to art had faded by the late nineteenth and early twentieth centuries. You won't find the great Italian art of this century in the *piazze,* churches, or museums, however. You must go to the movies; the masterpieces there will immerse you in myriad aspects of modern-day Italian life.

Italy's silent film era was not remarkable and is merely a prologue to true Italian cinema, which began with the fall of Fascism in the mid-'40s. Inaugurated by **Luchino Visconti's** *Ossessione* (*Obsession,* 1942), a tale of restlessness and morbid love, and **Roberto Rossellini's** *Roma, Città Aperta* (*Open City,* 1946), which used actual footage of the Italian Resistance during World War II, Italian neo-realism was a revolt against Fascism's attempt to conceal the oppression and poverty of the Italian people. Partially because of the economic disarray of the post-war years, the neo-realists rejected artificial sets and, for a while, professional actors, preferring to achieve shattering social and psychological authenticity. The two greatest works of the early days of neo-realism were Visconti's *La Terra Trema* (*The Trembling Earth*), the story of a Sicilian fisherman exploited by his employers, and **Vittorio de Sica's** *Bicycle Thief,* about the solitude of a steel-worker, both made in 1948.

In the 1950s and '60s, Italian film expanded and universalized its conception of reality to include fantasy, imagination, and mysticism. As box-office receipts began to dwindle, however, the directors sought stars who could draw larger audiences. The two most famous and fruitful of the director/star collaborations were Rossellini's work with **Ingrid Bergman** in such films as *Europa 51* (1952) and *Voyage to Italy* (1953), and **Federico Fellini's** work with **Giulietta Masina** in numerous films including *La Strada* (*The Street,* 1954), *Il Bidone* (*The Cheater,* 1955), and *Juliet of the Spirits* (1965). Other important works include Fellini's *La Dolce Vita* (*The Sweet Life,* 1952), **Michelangelo Antonioni's** *Blow Up* (1966), and **Bernardo Bertolucci's** *Il Conformista* (*The Conformist,* 1970), and his major work on the Fascist era, *1900* (1976).

Because the Italian arts depend upon government funding, the modern film industry is subject to the tides of Italian politics. Although the 1970s were difficult years for Italian filmmakers, a few withstood the difficulties of dwindling funds and audiences. Fellini's *Roma* and *Amarcord* are testimony to this. Also noteworthy are Vittorio de Sica's *Il Giardino dei Finzi Contini* (*Garden of the Finzi Continis*), a portrayal of an upper-class Jewish family at the dawn of World War II, and Visconti's *Death in Venice.* The '80s began richly when **Francesco Rosi** made *Cristo si è fermato a Eboli* (*Christ Stopped at Eboli*) from Carlo Levi's book. In 1986, **Paolo** and

Vittorio Taviani adapted to the screen five stories by Pirandello in their enthralling *Kaos.*

Important Italian Film Festivals:

Florence: Festival of Documentary Films, Dec.

Messina and Taormina: Festival of the Nations, July-Aug.

Orvieto: International Film Festival on Folk Arts, Dec.

Pesaro: International New Cinema Exhibition, Sept.

Salerno: International Festival of 16 and 18mm Films, Sept.

Trieste: International Science Fiction Film Festival, July.

Venice: International Film Festival at the Venice Biennale, last week in Aug.-first week in Sept.

La Dolce Vita

Food

Though Italian cuisine stems from the Greek, Roman, and Arab cultures, the gastronomy of Italy remains unique in its eclecticism. The Italians have a way of making any food taste indigenous—the infamous tomato—believe it or not—was first introduced into Italy after Columbus "discovered" America.

While everyone agrees Italian food is *delicioso,* there are great regional differences in cuisine, which assures variety as you travel up or down "the boot." The north is known for its creamy sauces and flat, handmade egg noodles. The cuisine of central Italy is rich and spicy in comparison to the north. Romans flavor the delicate meats of the north with the heavy spices of the south. The food of the south is a bit coarser, but far less expensive than in the rest of Italy. Pizza as we know it originated in Naples. Campania is the birthplace of the most renowned "Italian" food; tomato sauces, tubular pasta, and deep-fried fish dishes dominate here, where meat is scarce. If you like fish, order a lot in Italy. The endless coastlines provide an astounding array of piscine delicacies.

Most Italians begin the morning in a *bar* (a cafe) with *caffè* (coffee) and a roll. The famous, or infamous, "continental breakfast" may leave non-European travelers, accustomed to hearty breakfasts, famished. **Lunch,** or "dinner," is the big meal of the day in Italy. Almost everything closes down from 1pm to 4pm, so you might as well enjoy it. Though more Italians are now shifting their eating patterns to conform to the "business" lunch hour, most still find time to linger over a salad or plate of pasta in a *trattoria* at midday. Restaurants stop serving around 2pm until suppertime. If you don't want a big meal, eat lunch at an inexpensive *tavola calda* (literally, hot table) or *rosticceria* (grill). You can also picnic on the banks of some lazy river or on the steps of a *piazza.* You can buy sandwich materials at a *salumeria* or an *alimentari,* both grocery stores. Fruits and vegetables are best purchased at the open markets. A fitting cap to lunch is a leisurely stroll with world-famous Italian ice cream: *gelato!*

Italian **suppers** begin considerably later and last much longer than their American counterparts. The farther south you travel, the later supper will be served. Milan eats at about 7:30pm, Florence at 8pm, and Rome at 9pm. Small towns usually dine around 8pm. Supper at an *osteria, trattoria,* or *ristorante* (in order of increasing expense) begins with an *antipasto* (appetizer), which can be as simple as *bruschetta,* a type of garlic bread, or as fancy as *prosciutto e melone,* thin strips of ham with melon. Next comes the *primo piatto* (first course), pasta or soup. The *secondo* (second course) consists of meat or fish. After dinner, have a piece of cheese or fruit and sip a *digestivo* (liqueur).

The *menù turistico* (referred to by *Let's Go* as *menù*) isn't the bargain it once was. Since the government controls what is served in order to ensure fair dealing, there are no surprises. This may be comforting to non-Italians, but it also means the food is usually rather dull. The fixed price has been rising steadily, too, though you can still find a few bargains. When selecting a restaurant in Italy, keep in mind that family-run places will be a few thousand lire cheaper than those with hired help.

The **billing** at Italian restaurants can be a bit confusing. Most *conti* (bills) include a 10-15% service charge, and some tack on a *coperto* (cover charge). Although locals often do not tip, it is customary for foreigners to leave extra change according to the quality of service (about 5-8%). Beware that in family-run establishments without hired servers, tipping may be considered offensive. In a bar there will often be a sign stating either *servizio compreso* (service included) or *servizio non compreso* (service not included). In the case of the latter, there will be a kitty on the bar. The *Ricevuta Fiscale* (receipt) is an irritating device to frustrate tax evasion. A restaurant must legally make up an R.F. and hand a copy to the client, who then must keep it until 60m from the restaurant. If the tourist is stopped (a rare occurrence) and caught without it, both customer and restaurant may be fined.

The most important thing to remember about eating in an Italian restaurant is not to let the menu intimidate you. You don't have to eat all the courses, nor do you have to eat them in the prescribed order. If there's anything in Italy besides art that you can't miss, it's the food—*mangia!*

Wine

The Greeks called Italy *Oenotria* (land of wine), and even today one-seventh of Italy's arable land is planted with grapes. Its rocky soil, warm climate, and hilly landscape give it a natural advantage. Wine is the staple beverage (served to children from the age of 6 slightly diluted), as well as an export steadily increasing in importance as its reputation as an unrefined, coarse product fades.

Wines from the north tend to be heavy and full-bodied; the hotter sun of the south produces stronger, fruitier wines. *Chianti* from Tuscany is a universal favorite, rich and similar to claret. For a Tuscan splurge, ask for *brunellodi Montalcino.* Good heavy red wines include *falerno* from Naples, *barolo* and *barbera* from Piedmont, and *valpolicella* from the Venetian district. Among the leading white wines are *soave* from Verona, *frascati* from Rome, *orvieto* from Umbria, *lacrima Cristi* (*Christ's Tear*) from Naples, as well as *tocai* and *pinot grigio* from Friuli. Italian island wines are strong and sweet: Try the Sicilian *marsala,* which resembles a light sherry, and *cannonau,* from Sardinia. Sparkling wines are common in the north, and sipping them just before dinner at dusk is meant to give you a sense of the *dolce farniente* (sweet apathy). *Asti spumante* from Piedmont and *moscato* from Lombardy are good sparkling whites, though a bit sweet. *Vecchio* means "old," and *stravecchio* means "very old." *Secco* means "dry" and *abboccato* means "sweet."

A good rule-of-thumb is asking for the local wine—it will be cheaper and best-suited to the cuisine of the region.

Festivals and Holidays

Traditional festivals are celebrated in most Italian towns. Though they come and go according to the whims of the local administration and budget, you will undoubtedly hit a few without even trying. Most of these festivals commemorate local historical or religious events, and they often include elaborate re-enactments. Following are descriptions of just a few.

Every June, Florence stages a soccer match in sixteenth-century costume in memory of a match between the Florentines and the soldiers of Charles V, who were then laying siege to the city. Another medieval legacy, the Sienese *Palio* is a bareback horse race in the town square; in late June or July the audience stands in the middle and the horses careen off mattress-padded storefronts. Gubbio's "Palio of the Archers" is a re-enactment of a medieval crossbow contest, with arms and costumes, held on the last Sunday in May. On the third Sunday in July, Venetians commemorate the end of the epidemic of 1575 with a gondola procession. Try to include a few of these in your itinerary. *Let's Go* lists other local festivals in the appropriate regions' sections. You can obtain a list of festivals from the Italian Government Travel Office, 630 Fifth Ave., #1565, Rockefeller Center, New York, NY 10111 (tel. (212) 245-4822).

There are also various festivals of music, drama, ballet, and film throughout the year (see Music and Film above). Plays are often performed at sites famous during the classical era, such as Syracuse, Paestum, and Pompeii.

Holidays, both legal and religious, are another consideration when planning your itinerary. You can either curse these days (banks, shops, and almost anything else will be closed), or get into the spirit. Officially, Italy closes on the following dates: January 1 (New Year's Day); Easter Monday; April 25 (Liberation Day); May 1 (Labor Day); August 15 (Assumption of the Virgin); November 1 (All Saints Day); December 8 (Day of the Immaculate Conception); December 25 (Christmas Day); and December 26 (Santo Stefano). Offices and shops also shut down in the following cities on the local feast days honoring their patron saints: Venice (April 25, St. Mark); Florence, Genoa, Turin (June 24, St. John the Baptist); Palermo (July 15, Santa Rosalia); Naples (Sept. 19, St. Gennaro); Bologna (Oct. 4, St. Petronio); Cagliari (Oct. 30, St. Saturnino); Trieste (Nov. 3, San Giusto); Bari (Dec. 6, St. Nicola); and Milan (Dec. 7, St. Ambrose).

Recreation

In Italy, one sport surpasses all others in popularity and enjoyment—*il calcio* (American soccer, or European football). Many Italian youth grow up playing the game, and some say that Italy's victory in the 1982 World Cup did more for national unity than any political action could have ever hoped to achieve. But *il calcio* also strengthens city loyalties since native teams are fiercely defended and rivalries between cities (notably Naples and Rome) are hot grounds for arguments.

Bicycling is also big in Italy. Besides manufacturing some of the best bikes in the world (such as Bianchis and Fiorellis), Italians host the **giro d'Italia,** a 25-day race throughout Italy in May comparable to the Tour de France. (For information on touring Italy by bike, see By Bicycle above).

Scuba diving is new in Italy and more popular with tourists than with the natives. It can be enjoyed along the many miles of Tyrrhenian, Adriatic, and Ionian coastline. Inquire at local Ente Provinciale Turismo (EPT) offices for information. Italy's Alps and Appenine Mountains attract thousands of **skiers** from December to April. **Summer skiing** is available on glaciers surrounding the resorts of Bardonecchia, Aosta, Courmayeur, Cervinia, Stelvio Pass, and others. Refer to *Let's Go* regional sections for more detailed information.

Weights and Measures

1 kilogram (kg) = 2.2 pounds
1 meter (m) = 1.09 yards
1 kilometer (km) = 5/8 mile
1 liter = 1.05 quarts

NORTHERN ITALY

Liguria (Italian Riviera)

Liguria is the narrow coastal strip that stretches 350km along the Mediterranean between the French border and Tuscany. Genoa, in the center, divides the coast into the Riviera di Levante (Rising Sun) below and to the east, and the Riviera di Ponente (Setting Sun) above and to the west. Ligurians have their own vocabulary, incomprehensible to other Italians, let alone to foreigners. This individuality, however, has not prevented Liguria from playing a leading role in the unification of the Italian peninsula. Giuseppe Mazzini and Giuseppe Garibaldi, two great heroes of the Risorgimento, were Ligurians, and the famous red-shirted army that liberated southern Italy from the Bourbon monarchy was composed of fierce Ligurian sharpshooters.

Today, the region is one of Italy's most prosperous, led by Genoa, Italy's principal port. Protected by mountains to the north, and blessed with a mild winter climate, Liguria is a popular year-round resort. The climate encourages lush vegetation, and the landscape in summer is ablaze with deep reds and purples, while the air is scented with lemons and almond blossoms. The olive trees that shade the endless rows of flower beds produce some of the best olive oil in Italy.

The character of the Italian Riviera differs from that of its French neighbor. There is neither the arrogance of Cannes or St. Tropez, nor their inescapable resort atmosphere. The palm-lined boulevards and clear turquoise water are the same, but in each Italian town these are offset by the *città vecchia* or *alta* (old or upper city), an entirely Italian maze of narrow cobblestoned streets. If you must choose between the two parts of the Italian Riviera (Ponente and Levante), you might wish to follow Dickens's advice and opt for the latter, also the favorite of Byron and Shelley. Slightly more expensive, Levante is also more inviting. Less built-up than Ponente, it harbors rocky coastlines and cool green forests. On longer stays, you might base yourself in the charming town of Santa Margherita or in the Carrara hostel. In addition to the azure waters bordering these towns, many intriguing daytrips lie nearby. If you plan to stay closer to the French border in Ponente, try Finale Ligure, a resort town with medieval ambience and infinite stretches of sandy beach. The Italian Riviera remains primarily a family resort and, except for the large port areas of Genoa and Savona, has retained most of its old-world charm.

Getting around Liguria is no problem as all the coastal towns are linked by frequent trains and boats, and the hill towns inland are accessible by adequate bus service.

Beachside accommodations can be scarce in July and especially August, but Genoa makes a convenient base for daytrips. Besides the hostels listed below in Finale Ligure and La Spezia, *pensioni* and official campgrounds will be your main recourse, as beach camping is strictly prohibited in all towns, less so between them.

Ventimiglia

Ventimiglia divides neatly into three sections: modern Ventimiglia in the center, the Roman quarter with its classical architecture to the east, and the medieval town of twisting turrets to the west. Though once a popular resort, it becomes evermore run-down, lacking the glamor of such places as Nice and Monte Carlo. Near Nice (10-15 trains per day, 40 min.) and Genoa (10-15 trains per day, 1 hr.), Ventimiglia is within reach of all the famous riviera oases. Unlike them, it is also within reach of even the thinnest of money belts. In Ventimiglia you'll find the natural splendor

0 50 miles
0 50 kilometers
AUSTRIA
Innsbruck
Brenner Pass
Zürich
SWITZERLAND
St. Moritz
Geneva
FRANCE
Ljubljana
YUGOSLAVIA
Rijeka
Zadar
JULIAN ALPS
Trieste
Aquileia
Lignano-Sabbidoro
Gulf of Venice
Adriatic Sea
Ancona
Pesaro
Rimini
FRIULI-VENEZIA GIULIA
Udine
Cortina D'Ampezzo
Belluno
Feltre
Dobbiaco
Fortezza
ALTO ADIGE
Merano
Ortisei
Bolzano
DOLOMITES
Trent
TRENTINO-
Asiago
Bassano
Vicenza
VENETO
Venice
Padua
Verona
Adige River
Ortles
Riva del Garda
Lake Garda
Salo
Sirmione
Desenzano
Mantua
Sabbioneta
Cremona
Po River
Ferrara
Modena
Bologna
EMILIA-ROMAGNA
Parma
Colico
Lake Como
Bellagio
Lecco
Lake Lugano
Como
Bergamo
Brescia
Milan
Monza
LOMBARDY
Pavia
Varese
Lake Maggiore
Verbania
Omegna
Lake D'Orte
PIEDMONT
Matterhorn
St. Bernard Pass
Mt. Blanc
Courmayeur
Aosta
Gran Paradiso
VALLE D'AOSTA
ITALIAN ALPS
Cogne
Turin
MARITIME ALPS
RIVIERA DE PONENTE
LIGURIA
Savona
Finale Ligure
Imperia
San Remo
Ventimiglia
MONACO
Nice
Genoa
Northern Appenines
Rapallo
Portofino
Sestri Levante
RIV. DE LEVANTE
La Spezia
Lerici
Ligurian Sea
TUSCANY
Arno River
Pistoia
Florence
ITALY
N

of the Mediterranean and the mountains, the cultivated lines of gardens and castles, and the delights of sun and sand—all for fantastically few lire.

Orientation and Practical Information

From the station, cross the street and walk down **via della Stazione.** The second cross-road is **via Cavour,** the third **via Roma.** Much of what you will need lurks on these two streets.

Tourist Office: Azienda Autonoma Soggiorno Turismo, via Cavour, 61 (tel. 35 11 83). Signora Angela will be most gracious if you show her your *Let's Go* book. Beware the tourist map: Streets that appear to converge may not. Bus tickets and information are next door.

Post Office: via della (corso) Repubblica, 8 (tel. 35 13 12). Open Mon.-Fri. 8:10am-1:30pm, Sat. 8:10-11:30am. Closes at noon on the last working day of each month. **Postal Code:** 18039.

Telephone Code: 0184.

Hospital: via E. Basso (tel. 35 67 35).

Police: Piazza della Libertà, (tel. 35 75 75 or 35 75 76).

Accommodations and Food

Ventimiglia *can* be a surprisingly inexpensive place to stay. Ignore the hotel ratings, as they are no indication of affordability or attractiveness.

Cavour, via Cavour, 3 (tel. 35 13 66). Doubles L21,000, with bath L31,500.

XX Settembre, via Roma, 16 (tel. 35 12 12). Singles L12,500. Doubles L22,000. Restaurant offers a L13,000 *menù* and wine at L1800 per ½-liter. Open July-May daily noon-3pm and 7:30-9:30pm.

Abbo, via Cavour, 33 (tel. 35 11 04). Small but spotless rooms in noisy environs. Helpful management. Singles L15,000. Doubles L30,000, with bath L40,000. Restaurant open daily 9am-3pm and 5-11pm. *Menù* L13,000, ½-liter wine included.

Camping Roma, via Peglia, 5 (tel. 335 80-35 76 13), 400m from the waterfront. May-Aug. L5000 per person, L5500 per tent, Sept.-April L4000 per person, L4000 per tent.

You will pay dearly for quality, sitdown meals here. Try the **Standa Supermarket,** via Roma at via Ruffini, for staples. (Open Mon.-Sat. 8:30am-7:30pm.)

Mercato dei Fiori, via della Repubblica. An open-air market with endless fresh food (except dairy products). Open daily 7am-1pm.

Caffè Mike, p. Battisti, 32 (tel. 35 77 55). The least expensive option for a "real" meal. *Menù* L12,000, wine L4500 per liter (the larger the group, the lower the price).

Sights and Entertainment

Classical antiquity will be at your feet when you visit the Roman ruins of the archeological zone along via Aurelia. (Turn left on via Cavour, and continue about 1 km.) Roman theater is in especially good condition, and soon (in Italian terms, this may mean a millennium), it will again house classical drama. A trip to the **Balzi Rossi** will take you farther down history's alleys. Take the bus from the corner of via Cavour and via Martiri della Libertà (20 min., L700) to see the remains of Cro-Magnon people and the caves they inhabited. Get off the same bus (15 min., L600) a few stops earlier to see the legacy of a more manicured way of living. The **Hanbury Gardens** (tel. 395 07) include some of the world's most exquisite and exotic flora. Sir Thomas Hanbury, a British nobleman, created this blooming heaven to adorn his castle-on-the-hill. (Admission L8500. Open in summer daily 9am-6pm; in off-season Thurs.-Tues. 10am-4pm.

Across the river in the medieval city, sinuous alleys sheak through clusters of aging masonry after branching off *via Garibaldi,* the old city's main street. It runs past the **cathedral** with its intricate Gothic portal and adjoining **baptistry.**

If the knee-deep flowers of the Hanbury Gardens aren't enough, be sure to catch a whiff of the **Battaglia dei Fiori** (Battle of the Flowers) on the second Sunday of June, when bikini-clad women on floral floats pelt onlookers with petals. From the city's past comes the **Corteo Storico e Regata dei Sestieri** (Historic Parade and Regatta of the Six Quarters), a spectacle of medieval costumes held on the second Sunday in August.

Near Ventimiglia

When the Goths sacked Ventimiglia in the fifth century, the locals fled to the hills. Although wandering warriors are unlikely to disturb your stay, a jaunt into the mountains is still a great escape. Of the many valleys fanning inland from Ventimiglia, **Val Nervia** is the most accessible. On foot, continue past the Roman theater to the Val Nervia road on your left. Rent a bicycle or a scooter from **Negri,** via Aurelia, 24 (tel. 29 43 10), in nearby Valecrosia. (Bikes L8000 per day. Open Mon.-Sat. 8am-noon and 3-7pm.) Valecrosia is accessible by a Riviera Trasporti bus that leaves from the corner of vie Cavour and Firenze (every 15 min., L600).

Riviera Trasporti also runs buses to the surrounding castle-topped hills. **Dolce Acqua** is framed by a Roman fortress whose narrow, twisting stone streets are still bustling (L1000 by bus from Ventimiglia). Note the heavy wooden doors along the road to the ruined fifteenth-century Dorian castle above. Turn right at the bottom of the old city and walk across the elliptically arched Roman bridge. Sample the excellent local wine while viewing this bridge, a small chapel, and the terraced hillside vineyards, all put to canvas by Monet. On August 15, the village celebrates its patron saint with swirling regional dances, traditional costumes, and mouth-watering local pastries. **Pigna,** farther into the valley (same bus, L1600), offers a similar experience without the crowds.

Brodighera

Known as the "City of Palms," Bordighera's claim to fame is the abundance of these jade-colored, swaying trees. In fact, the city supplies the Vatican with palms during Holy Week. Legend has it that Sant' Ampelio brought the seeds from Egypt. Bordighera is now one of the most popular resorts on the Riviera di Ponente, with lush gardens and a partly fortified old town. Ever since the British claimed this chunk of the Riviera, Bordighera has hosted an upscale crowd. Eva Perón inaugurated a park named in her honor, and once upon a time, the queen of Italy maintained a residence here. The celebrity glamor is reflected in Bordighera's prices. But if you know where to look, your tight budget can stretch a long way.

Orientation and Practical Information

The bus from Ventimiglia (15 min., L850) will drop you off along the main street, **via Vittorio Emanuel.** Most of the offices and shops are along here, while the residential area is farther inland uphill.

Tourist Office: via Roberto, 1 (tel. 26 23 22). Open Mon.-Sat. 9am-12:30pm, 3:30-6pm.

Post Office: p. della Libertà, next to the station. Open Mon.-Sat. 8am-4pm.

Bus Tickets can be purchased at the *tabacchini.*

Biblioteca Internazionale, via Romana, 52 (tel. 26 63 32). Astounding collection of English-language books. Open daily in summer 9am-1pm, in off-season 9am-noon and 2:30-6pm.

Accommodations and Food

It is difficult to find a place for just a night; most cheap hotels prefer full pension guests staying a few days.

Villa Miki, via Lagazzi, 14 (tel. 26 18 44). Small, musty rooms, but a serene setting and balconies overlooking the valleys. Singles L15,000.

Villa Loreto, via Giulio Cesare, 37 (tel. 29 43 32). A hike, but the nuns provide the lowest prices and best company around. They can select or reject potential guests. Open to youth only in summer, senior citizens in winter. Singles with bath L15,000. Doubles negotiable. Full pension L37,000, with bath L39,000. Curfew 10:30pm.

Pensione Monte Carlo, via V. Emanuele, 61 (tel. 26 04 80). They say full pension at L38,000 for several nights. The tourist office brochure adds singles L12,000, doubles L22,500. Try it.

The cheapest sit-down meals can be had at the various *trattorie* in the *città alta* (old city). Try the **mercato coperto** (p. Garibaldi, open Mon.-Sat. 7am-noon and 4-7pm) or the **Supermercato Standa** (via Libertà, 32; open Mon.-Sat. 8:30am-12:30pm and 3:45-7:45pm) for picnic lunches and dinners. **Trattoria degli Amici,** via Lunga, 2 (tel. 26 15 79), in the *città alta* serves lasagne for L7000. (Cover L4000. Open mid-Sept. to mid-June Tues. and Thurs.-Sun. noon-2pm and 6pm-1am.)

Sights and Entertainment

If you're game for an attractive if lengthy walk, head east along via Romana. The bright pink roses everywhere attest to the fact that Bordighera belongs to the Riviera dei Fiori. Fork off onto via Rossi, where the cannons still stand above an awesome expanse of deep blue sea. Take the steps down to the **Church of St. Ampeglio,** built around the grotto where the Holy Hermit lived. Knock on the door and someone might let you in.

In late July and August, Bordighera holds an international **humor festival** with its shows and exhibits. For a taste of local festivity, go to nearby **Sebborga,** where there is music, dancing, and mounds of cheap native fare two evenings a week in summer. Call the post office for information (tel. 296 14).

Sanremo

The first resort on the Italian Riviera, Sanremo once had a reputation for glitter and glamor. Today the town has the slightly squalid feel that attends the fading of a once-grand watering hole, but its elegant Edwardian hotels and colorful side streets still possess plenty of old-world charm.

Practical Information

Tourist Offices: Azienda Autonoma, largo Nuvolini, 1 (tel. 856 15 or 856 16)), to the left from the station. Help in finding a room. Open Mon.-Sat. 8am-7pm, Sun. 9am-1pm. The **Hotel Service** in the station (tel. 801 72) also locates pads, requiring a deposit but no commission. Open June-Sept. daily 7:45am-7:45pm; Oct.-May Mon.-Sat. 7:45am-7:45pm. English spoken at both places.

Post Office: via Roma, 156 (tel. 88 46 35), in the town center. Open Mon.-Sat. 8:10am-7:50pm. **Postal code:** 18038.

Telephones: SIP, via Roma, 60 (tel. 783 84), at corso Mombello. Open 8am-9:30pm. **Caffè Dogliani,** via Roma, 34 (tel. 866 23). Go right from the station. Open daily 8pm-1am. **Telephone code:** 0184.

Transportation: Most trains on the Ventimiglia-Genoa line stop at Sanremo's **station** (tel. 717 50). **Riviera Trasporti's** (tel. 707 41) blue buses run to neighboring coastal towns; tickets may be bought at Marina Viaggi, p. Colombo, 19; the *tabacchi* in the train station; and other shops with the sign *Punto vendita R.T.* The Hotel Service also sells bus tickets and organizes tours to nearby cities. A wine tour of the Three Valleys costs L13,000, a daytrip to Nice and Cannes L16,000.

English Bookstore: Rabin, via Corradi, 89 (tel. 862 18). 5 shelves' worth of used books (L3500-L7000) from Jane Austen to Jackie Collins. Open Tues. and Thurs.-Sat. 9am-12:30pm and 3:30-7:15pm.

Hospital: via G. Borea, 56 (tel. 799 21), behind the old city.

Police: Carabinieri, corso Inglesi, 403 (tel. 634 93). After hours, call 113.

Accommodations and Camping

Fifty one-star hotels speckle Sanremo, so you should easily find an affordable place to stay—except in August when everything fills to the brim. As a rule of thumb, the cheapest hotels line **via Matteotti.**

Albergo San Marino, corso Mombello, 49 (tel. 804 62), 2 flights up, near the shore. Clean rooms, a solicitous owner, and super prices. English spoken. Singles L13,000. Doubles L21,500. Open Nov.-Sept. Reserve in Aug.

Pensione Ina, via Gaudia, 12 (tel. 708 53), off corso Matteotti. Run by a sympathetic older couple who greet their guests by name. Cluttered hallways, but acceptable rooms that hold up to 4 people. Will be remodelled in 1989. Singles L16,000. Doubles L26,000. L10,000 per additional person.

Hotel Internazionale, p. Colombo, 17 (tel. 745 32), at the far end of via Matteotti. Spacious rooms overlook the *piazza,* but somewhat noisy. Singles L14,000, with bath L15,000. Doubles L23,000, with bath L27,000.

Camping: Villaggio dei Fiori, via Tiro a Vola (tel. 606 35), 2km along the coast toward Ventimiglia. Watch out: In high season the prices tower over those of most hotels.

Food

Competition keeps prices low and variety (if not necessarily quality) high in Sanremo's restaurants. At midday throngs of people scrounge for eats along via Palazzo, off p. Colombo. Treat yourself at one of the bakeries—try the generic **Panetteria-Pasticceria,** at #35. The **covered market,** off p. Eroi Sanremesi, offers produce, meats, pasta, cheese, and bread. (Open Tues.-Sat. 7am-2:30pm.)

Supermercato Standia, via Roma, 173. Open Mon.-Sat. 8:30am-12:30pm and 3:15-7:30pm.

Il Cantautore, via Corradi, 30 (tel. 88 47 01). Delicious *panini* only L2000-3000.

Pizzeria Vesurio, via Corrodi, 5 (tel. 763 10). Offers a hearty pizza for L4000-6500. Try the *calzone.* Cover L1000. Open daily noon-midnight.

Ristorante Grotta Azzura, Tel. 857 27. Their L14,000 *menù* offers a number of choices and includes everything except drinks; wine is L6000 per liter. Walk from the Azienda towards the casino; Azura's cool, quiet rooms lie on an alleyway off the uphill side of corso Imperatrice, 60, by the Hotel Paris. (Open Dec.-Sept. Tues.-Sun. noon-2pm and 7-10pm.)

Ristorante Rheingold, via A. Fratti, 3 (tel. 838 83), off corso Garibaldi. Despite the blah exterior, cuisine is aromatic and tasty. *Menù* L11,000. Cover L1500. Open Oct.-Aug. Tues.-Sun. 8am-3pm and 7:30-11:30pm.

Sights and Entertainment

Start off in **Pigna** (Sanremo's old city), climbing the steep wonderland of narrow brick walks. At the top, you can rest and enjoy the view from via Romolo Moreno. The hole in the fence here must have been carved out especially for photographing the magnificent vista. Descend the hill to **via Palazzo,** the pedestrian street. Avoid the tacky tourist shops and visit the **Tunnel dell' Arte,** via Palazzo, 9/A (tel. 74 10), where you can splurge on a painting or print by an Italian artist. (Open in summer Mon.-Sat. 9am-8pm, in off-season 10am-12:30pm and 4-7pm.) Continue down via Corradi to via Matteotti, and dream of Sanremo's glory days as you pass the Edwardian **Casino,** corso Inglesi, 18 (tel. 799 01). (Entrance fee L10,000. Must be 18. Open 2:30pm-2am.) From there, glance to your left; the scene could be right out of a Ukranian landscape. The Byzantine onion domes of the **Russian church** were built in the 1920s, when the Czarina of Russia, along with other exiled Russian nobles, frequented Sanremo in the winter. She also had planted the palm trees that line **corso Imperatrice.**

Bussana Vecchia is an old hillside village destroyed by an earthquake in 1887. Now a group of artists live in (and remodel) the buildings, leaving the outside rubble untouched. From Sanremo, take a blue "T" Riviera Trasporti trolley towards Taggia (every 20 min., L800, most easily caught at the station). At the turn-off for Bussana, just beyond the lighthouse, get off and walk uphill, following the yellow Bussana Vecchia signs (45 min.). You can also try hitching. Once there, contemplate the ruins of the church in which the entire population of the village sought shelter and died when it collapsed. Emerging onto the main road, you can proceed to the Taggia train station by the same bus or return to Sanremo.

Imperia

Imperia, port town and capital of the Riviera dei Fiori (Riviera of Flowers), lacks the resort atmosphere common to most of its neighbors. Though equipped with the obligatory promenade and an attractive beach, most of Imperia's waterfront alternates between huge olive oil storage tanks and boats of all shapes and sizes, rather than between ice cream stands and kiddie rides, as in Sanremo or Finale Ligure. Especially during August, finding a room is much easier in Imperia than in either of the other two places.

Orientation and Practical Information

The Imperio, a small stream, splits Imperia in two. The east bank is known as **Oneglia** and is the industrial and commercial sector. **Porto Maurizio,** on the west bank, is the residential area and ancient city. If your train stops only in Oneglia, buy a ticket at the newspaper stand in the station and catch orange AMAT bus #2 or 3 right outside. It will take you down to **viale Matteotti,** the main road.

Tourist Offices: Azienda Autonoma, viale Matteotti, 22 (tel. 607 30), in Porto Maurizio. Little English spoken. Open June 15-Aug. Mon.-Sat. 8am-2pm and 4-7pm; Sept.-June 14 8am-2pm. **EPT,** viale Matteotti, 54 (tel. 249 47). Go here only if referred by the Azienda.

Currency Exchange: viale Matteotti, 5 (tel. 616 18). Open Mon.-Fri. 8am-12:30pm and 3-7:15pm, Sat. 3-4:30pm.

Post Office: viale Matteotti, 55 (tel. 212 10). Open Mon.-Sat. 8:15am-8pm, Sun. 8:15am-2pm. **Postal code:** 01800.

Telephones: SIP, via Berio, 35, near the Oneglia station. Open 8am-7:30pm. After hours, go to **Caffè Vittoria,** viale Matteotti, 10 (tel. 609 06). Open June-Aug. Tues.-Sun. 7am-midnight; Sept.-May 7am-11pm. **Telephone Code:** 0183.

Hospital: Via Sant Agata (tel. 28 31 11).

Police: Carabinieri, viale Metteotti, 46 (tel. 255 34; in an emergency 21 21 21).

Accommodations

Many of the cheaper hotels cluster below the azienda near the water, although possibilities pepper the whole way to the shore.

Pensione Irene, via Pirinoli, 34b (tel. 65 03 43), off an alley between via Pirinoli and via S. Lazzaro, by the port. The efficient proprietor has 17 rooms. Singles L15,000, doubles L30,000, with *pensione completa* L34,000, with bath L38,000. In July and Aug. *pensione completa* required.

Locanda Anna, via S. Antonio, 21 (tel. 615 33). Informally run in a nondescript but newly renovated building. Homey interior and pleasant owner whose son speaks English. All rooms except one have a balcony. Singles L17,000. L17,000 per additional person. Breakfast included.

Pensione Aurora, via S. Antonio, 19 (tel. 639 45). Bright, large rooms with marble floors. L15,000 per person (slightly less in off-season).

Hotel Paola, via Rambaldo, 30 (tel. 629 96). Smallish rooms but the perfect place if you need to wash your clothes—every window has a clothesline. Singles L15,000. Doubles L30,000. Triples L45,000. Prices cut by L1000 in off-season. Breakfast L4000.

Camping: Eucaliptus, via Littardi at via D'Annunzio (tel. 615 34), in the west end of town near roads and the water. Take bus #2 or 3 from the station for 5-10 min. L4500 per person, L3000 per tent. If full, look at **La Pineta,** on via Littardi, about 200m north of Eucaliptus (tel. 614 98). Quieter and with spectacular views. L4000 per person, L2700 per tent. Hot showers L500.

Food

Hobo's Pizzeria, via Rambaldo, 40 (tel. 642 05), off via Scarincio. The ideal place for wandering hoboes to party with laughing locals. Try to eat in the *gazebo.* Pizza L4000-7000, beer L2000 a pitcher, and wine L6000 per liter. (Open in summer nightly 6pm-3am; in off-season Fri.-Wed. only.)

Trattoria Vassallo, via S. Maurizio, 12, just off via Felice Cascione. A climb but also a bargain. *Menù* L13,000 in unusually clean and elegant surroundings. Try the *calamari fritti* (fried squid). Wine L4000 per liter. Open Mon.-Sat. noon-2:30pm and 6:30-11pm.

Olio Grosso, via Parrasio, 36, opposite the newly repainted pink building, all the way up at p. Parrasio (the highest point in the old city). Totally appetizing fare includes specialties such as *penne al Windsurfer.* Meals run L10,000-12,000. Open Thurs.-Tues.

Sights and Entertainment

Unless you are a sailor or boat-lover, little will be of interest in Imperia itself. There are two harbors, one in Oneglia, one in Porto Mauririo, with vessels ranging from rowboats to Naval ships. If you'd rather not risk getting wet and are up for a climb, the **Museo Navale Internazionale** hosts some fascinating displays. (On piazza Duomo, in the old city; open in summer Wed. and Sat. 9-11pm; in off-season 5-7:30pm.) Across from the museum stands the imposing **Cathedral of San Maurizio,** wonderfully incongruous in its birthday-cake yellow and white neoclassicism. On June 6, all manner of pomp and pageantry bursts out of this birthday cake as the patron saint's name-day is celebrated. The steep paths and weathered masonry of the old city can be dull, but the view from the top tops any panorama in the region.

Imperia does not lack in festivals. The **Festeggia menti di S. Giovanni** in June and the **Festa al Parasio** in July feature local dances, comedies, and cuisine. If in town in September, don't miss the parade of historic yachts. Ask about this and the many annual sports tournaments at the tourist office.

Near Imperia

An unforgettable excursion from Imperia is the 7-km trip to the medieval village of **Dolcedo.** Across the bridge with the Cross of the Knights of Malta carved on it to the old market square, where official measuring basins from the fifteenth century are still in use. Stop for lunch at the moderately priced **Ristorante da Tunu,** the only one in town; pasta is L3500-7000. (Open Mon.-Sat. 7am-midnight.) Riviera Trasporti buses leave p. Dante in Oneglia 11-15 times per day. Buy tickets at the restaurant in the station (L1400).

Cervo, an enchanting, medieval hillside village with white houses, red roofs, and stone archways remains unspoiled—but perhaps not for long, as the town now has a train station. To get there, take the *locale* along the Ventimiglia-Genoa line. You can also take a blue Riviera Trasporti bus towards Andora. Buses leave Imperia from p. Dante or anywhere along corso Garibaldi (every 15 min., L1000). Servo hosts an international chamber music festival in July and August, held in front of the baroque **Church of San Giovanni Battista.** Be sure to go in to see the *Family of St. John,* an intricate wooden sculpture by Maragliano.

Albenga

Instead of moneyed vacationers milling in and out of chic boutiques, in Albenga you are more likely to encounter soldiers milling in and out of the city's two *caserne* (military barracks). Since the time of the Roman legionaries, Albenga has been a home for the military—a pleasant and culturally-endowed home at that. Visit the charming historic center, where various Roman legacies are sprinkled among more modern buildings.

Orientation and Practical Information

Most of the town lies east of the river Centa. Parallel to the river, a few blocks away, **viale Martiri della Liberta** forms the main drag.

Tourist Office: Ente Turistico Pro Loco, viale Martiri della Libertà, 17 (tel. 504 75). Turn left as you leave the **station** (tel. 503 00), and then right on the central road. Open Mon.-Fri. 9am-noon and 3-7pm, Sat. 9am-noon.

Money Exchange: p. Torlaro, 3 (tel. 54 30 51), on the far side of the old city.

Telephones: SIP, p. del Popolo, 12 (tel. 508 53). Phone boxes for **taxis** at p. del Popolo. **Telephone code:** 0182.

Hospital: p. del Popolo, 13 (tel. 508 92).

Police: Carabinieri, via Massone, 19 (tel. 502 05 or 502 06).

Accommodations

Albenga caters to *Torinesi* and *Milanesi* on vacation, and its one-star *pensioni* resemble two-star hotels; unfortunately, when you get your bill, you'll see how they do it. Reservations are vital in July and August.

Hotel Italia, viale Martiri della Libertà, 10 (tel. 504 05). A two-star, but worth it—central location, elegant, clean rooms, and pleasant bathrooms. No common showers for rooms without baths. Singles L21,000. Doubles L38,000, with bath L45,000. Open Nov.-Sept.

Pensione Gabbiano, via Genova, 71 (tel. 503 77). Conveniently located. Smaller, but cheaper. Space for cars in courtyard. Doubles L25,000. Triples L35,000. Quads L45,000.

Pensione Bucaniere, lungomare C. Colombo, 22 (tel. 502 20). On the water—some wonderful views if you're lucky. Walk right by the disorderly terrace to the modern and tidy interior. Don't bother getting a room with a shower; all you will find is a tiny glass cage. Singles L23,000, with shower L25,000. Doubles L35,000, with shower L38,000.

Camping: Campgrounds are plentiful along this part of the coast. **Dei Fiori,** on lungomare Colombo (tel. 523 39), offers pricey but rudimentary facilities close to the beach. In summer L5200 per person, L5200 per tent; in off-season L3800 per person, L3800 per tent.

Food

Cheap *trattorie* and *pizzerie* abound in Albenga, due to the nearby military base.

Da Franco, via Milite Ignoto, 22 (tel. 504 07), the 1st left as you walk from p. del Popolo toward the station. Yummy bargain pizza (L3000-6000) and margaritas (L2500). Spaghetti L3500. Wine about L4000 per liter. Cover L1500. Open Tues.-Sun. noon-3pm and 6pm-2am.

Il Fagiano, across the street at #5 (tel. 522 16). Slightly cheaper and a little rowdier. Similar fare. Pizza L3000- 6500. Wine from L4000 per liter. Open Tues.-Sun. 1-3:30pm and 6pm-1:30am.

Gelateria Artigiana, Tel. 503 07. Of the many *gelaterie* lining viale Martiri della Libertà, this one knocks the pants off its neighbors—26 homemade flavors and prices that will let you sample a lot of them (2 scoops L1000, 6 scoops L3000). Try the *castagna* (chestnut), *tiramisù,* or *zuppa inglese,* the latter two made with Italian liqueurs. (Open Feb.-Nov. Thurs.-Tues. 3pm-midnight.)

Sights

If you've wanted to see an old city but haven't had the stamina to climb one of those steeply angled hills, visit Albenga's *città vecchia,* built entirely on flat ground. Though the streets themselves are not as fascinating as those in neighboring towns, the central *piazza* is surrounded by impressive buildings. Take a peek inside the excessively ornate church **Santa Maria in Fontibus,** but move on rather quickly to the **Cattedrale di San Michele Arcangelo.** Built in the fifth century and reconstructed in the thirteenth, it still holds masses today. The **Baptistry,** across from the cathedral and connected to the **Ingauno Museum,** dating from the fifth century, is the most intriguing structure in town. The oldest monument in Liguria, it has an octagonal shape and an original sixth-century colored mosaic replete with the standard medieval symbolism—12 doves stand for the 12 apostles and three circles for the Holy Trinity. In the anteroom to the baptistry lies the **Albingaunum,** where the municipal committee held court through the Middle Ages. Relics of times past are collected here: ancient measures, a tomb, a well.

The only other must in Albenga is a walk along the river Centa. You'll look in vain for the Roman remains marked on the tourist office's map—they are located *below* ground. But in the early morning, you can watch fishermen throwing out their nets.

Near Albenga

Alassio, a 10-minute train ride from Albenga on the Genoa-Ventimiglia line (L600), boasts one of the best fine-grain sand beaches on the Italian Riviera. Though some choice stretches of sand are restricted, public beaches exist as well. Alassio is blessed with an enchanting church, **Sant' Ambrogio,** with paintings by Giovanni de Ferrari, and the **Palazzo Scofferi,** which displays a crucifix attributed to Giambologna. To experience *Star Wars*-like caverns with glistening pastel green, white, and rose stalagmites and stalactites, go to the village of **Toirano's** two natural caves, **Grotta della Basura** and **Grotta di Santa Lucia.** These were inhabited in Paleolithic times, and remains of both humans and animals have been excavated. Some are preserved in the nearby **Prehistoric Museum.** While the museum is largely uninteresting—especially if you have already seen the one at the Balzi Rossi—the caves are entrancing. (Caves open daily 9:30-11:30am and 2-5pm. Admission L5000, children L2500, by guided tour only.) Take a bus from p. del Popolo to Borghetto (L800; buy tickets on the bus), and change there for Toirano.

Finale Ligure

Finale Ligure is an unpretentious resort that combines luxurious nature with pauper's prices. Striped umbrellas speckle the wide, sandy beaches; flowers and tea rooms line the oceanside promenade; and the city as a whole is a bargain for the Riviera di Ponente.

Orientation and Practical Information

Finale Ligure divides three ways: Finalmarina, Finalpia, and Finalborgo, the old city. The **station** (tel. 69 27 77) is in Finalmarina, as are most places listed below.

Tourist Office: AAST, via S. Pietro, 14, near the waterfront. Open Mon.-Fri. 8am-1pm and 3-6pm, Sat. 8am-1pm. The**Associazione Alberghi,** across from the station (tel. 69 42 52), will help you find rooms.

Post Office: via Concezione, 29 (tel. 69 28 38), along the beach. Open Mon.-Fri. 8:10am-6:45pm, Sat. 8:10-11:30am.

Telephones: Bar Casanova, via Brunenghi, 75 (tel. 69 56 15). Open daily 6am-2am. Also a phone in the station. **Telephone Code:** 019.

Hospital: via della Pineta (tel. 69 07 95). Go underneath the railroad, follow via Brunenghi, then turn right on via XXV Aprile.

Police: Carabinieri, via Brunanghi, 68 (tel. 69 26 66).

Accommodations

Go to the Associazone Alberghi first—it could save you a trek.

Castello Uvillermin (IYHF): via Generale Caviglia (tel. 69 05 15), in a turreted castle overlooking the sea. From the station, turn left onto via Torino and walk until you see the Esso station. To your left, you will see 321 steps—interrupted, mercifully, by a road. You won't regret the climb to the hostel. The price is one of the lowest on the coast, and the tiny concession is stocked with the essentials—postcards (L100) and bottles of spumante (L2500). No kitchen. The grounds harbor orange trees, olive trees, and oleanders. Reservations advised; otherwise, arrive before 5pm, when reception opens. L8500 per person. Breakfast included. Open April 15-Oct. 15. Curfew in summer midnight, in winter 11:30pm.

Villa Lidia, gradinata delle Rose, 5 (tel. 69 25 54), downhill from the hostel. A garden with beautiful vines and the kind of lawn furniture that makes you look around for plastic gnomes. The interior features Persian carpets and a grandfather clock. Warm rooms—both literally and figuratively. Doubles L25,000, with breakfast L35,000, with *pensione completa* L45,000. Open May-Sept.

Camping: Eurocamping, on via Calvisio (tel. 60 12 40), is the closest to the beach and 3km from the station. The bus along via Torino leaves for Calvisio (1 per ½ hour, L600). Swimming pool, hot showers, and a bar. May, June, and Sept. L4,500 per person, L3000 per tent; July and Aug. L5500 per person, L3500 per tent.

Food

Trattorie and *pizzerie* line the streets closest to the beach: Pay less for the same food farther inland along vie Rossi and Roma.

Trattoria Beppi, a 25-min. climb up via XXV Aprile, past the hospital. A worthwhile treat at around L20,000 (including wine) with a fantastic view and superb cuisine. Try the *coniglio* (rabbit). Open March-Oct. daily noon-3pm and 7-11pm.

Spaghetteria da Michel, via A. G. Barreli, 28 (tel. 925 42), on the main pedestrian drag. Pasta dishes L4000-8000, wine about L6000 per liter, cover L1000. Try the *spaghetti al pesto.* Open Wed.-Mon. noon-7pm.

Salumeria della Chiesa, via Pertica, 13 (tel. 69 25 16), toward the station off via Rossi. Gorgeous seafood salads L1000-2500 per *etto.* Perfect place to pack a picnic lunch for the beach. They also have great pasta, stuffed peppers, and zucchini. Open daily in summer 7:30am-1pm and 4-8pm, in off-season 7:30am-1pm.

Paninoteca Pilade, via Garibaldi, 67 (tel. 69 22 20), off p. Vittorio Emanuele II. Some of the best *panini* on the Riviera (L2000-3000). If Finale had a university, students would hang out here: Rock music, old Coke posters, and cheap food. Frappe L1800, beer L1800, wine L900. Open Sept. to mid-June Thurs.-Tues. 10am-2pm and 4-8pm; mid-June to Aug. 10am-2pm and 4pm-1:30am.

Gelateria la Favola, via S. Pietro, along the beach. Heaven on earth for those with a sweet tooth. Fruit flavors galore. Open daily 10:30am-1pm and 2pm-midnight.

Sights

Otherwise a typical Ligurian *città vecchia,* **Finalborgo** is unique in that it is still dominated by the lofty **Castel San Giovanni** and surrounded by intact ancient walls. You can climb up to the castle along the old stone path, but in the words of an Italian child, there is "nothing up there." The castle is closed and the view not unusual. Many of the other buildings in Finalborgo, however, have interesting, deceptive ornamental facades—see if you can tell which reliefs are real and which *trompe l'oeil.* The overall structure of the **Basilica of San Biagio** is hideous and over-done, but amidst all the grotesque clutter hides some beautiful artwork. Try to focus on the delicate marble inlay work on the side altarpieces.

The **Basilica of Saint John the Baptist** in **Finalmarina** is a repeat of its counterpart in Finalborgo. The gaudy facade signals a painted interior verging on the rococo.

If Finale Ligure becomes too much—or too little—getting to nearby towns is easy. **S.A.R. buses** leave town towards Ventimiglia (L4400, round-trip L7600); tickets available on the bus). To take the **ACTS bus** towards Genoa (L3500, round-trip L5800), purchase a ticket at the newspaper stand in the station. (Open 6am-8pm.) **Train** connections along the Genoa-Ventimiglia line are just as simple (same price as bus).

Genoa (Genova)

If Calabria is the toe of Italy and Rome its knee, then Genoa is just about the armpit. If you visit Genoa today, you may understand why Christopher Columbus, its most famous citizen, felt the urge to get away.

Civic myth also claimed Genoa as the birthplace of another pioneering emigré to the New World—blue jeans. Originally called *le blu di Genova,* the denim slacks were allegedly first worn by the city's dockworkers. Today, the sprawling port defines Genoa—industrially robust but aesthetically effete.

There are really only two reasons to visit Genoa. The first is two major train stations, which will send you at all times of the day and night to all corners of the boot. The other concerns Genoa's propensity for fine architecture and city design; grand Renaissance palaces, manicured parks, and broad boulevards hide under centuries of grime and neglect. If you find yourself in the city, try and look beyond the sooty surface, take advantage of the city's myriad performing arts events, and then scoot out as soon as possible.

Orientation and Practical Information

Genoa, in the midst of the Italian Riviera, lies about an hour and a half south of Milan by rail (L7800), three hours north of Florence, and two hours east of the French border. Although there are a dozen train stations in the city, most travelers arrive at **Stazione Principe** (on the western edge of the city, near the port) or **Stazione Brignole** (to the northeast). Downtown lies between the two, squeezed among hills along the waterfront. Many trains from the south arrive at Brignole, and some go on to Principe. Bus #37 connects the two stations (or a 20-min. walk). Some **buses** are equipped with ticket machines, but tickets (L700) may be bought at *tabacchi* as well. Within the city, you will rarely need the bus. The two principal thoroughfares are **via XX Settembre** (from Brignole, walk down via Fiume, then turn right) and **via Balbi,** leading east from the *piazza* in front of Principe. The former ends in giant **piazza de Ferrari;** the latter culminates in the **piazza Nunziata.** A maze of smaller streets along the periphery of the **Centro Storico** (historical center) links the two. Stay mostly in this area if you value your life and your sense of direction—venturing farther south towards the docks is fruitless and potentially dangerous. Also avoid the area around and between piazze Verdi and Vittoria—even if you manage to avoid being hit by a car (crosswalks exist with little avail), you will probably get lost.

Genoa's double sequence of street numbers (red for commercial establishments, blue or black for residential or office buildings) is often difficult to decipher, particularly since the red numerals, when dirty, look black. A tip: The two colors are in different fonts and sizes—red is larger and simpler.

EPT: Main office, via Roma, 11 (tel. 58 14 07 or 58 13 71), up 2 floors, near p. Corvetto. Open Mon.-Thurs. 8am-2pm and 4-6pm, Fri.-Sat. 8am-1pm. **Stazione Principe,** Tel. 26 26 33. Open Mon.-Sat. 8am-8pm. Unhelpful and unfriendly—come only for train information or a map. Much warmer assistance can be found at the main office and **Stazione Brignole** (tel. 56 20 56). Open Mon.-Fri. 9am-noon and 3-6pm, Sat. 9am-noon. **Airport,** Tel. 26 90 47. The **Azienda Autonoma** has an office at via Porta degli Archi, 10 (tel. 54 15 41), near

p. Dante. Be sure to pick up the monthly *Agenda* for detailed information and a calendar of events.

Budget Travel: D.G. Viaggi, p. S. Matteo, 3r (tel. 29 36 21), next to the church. Tiny, trendy office; Transalpino tickets, ferry information. **Guimar Tours,** via Balbi, 192r (tel. 25 63 38 or 25 63 37), on your right as you leave Principe. More convenient and changes money, too. Open Mon.-Fri. 9am-12:30pm and 3-7pm, Sat. 9am-noon.

Consulates: U.S., p. Portello, 6 (tel. 28 27 41). Open Mon.-Fri. 9am-5:30pm. **U.K.,** via XII Ottobre, 2 (tel. 56 48 33). Open Mon.-Fri. 9am-noon and 2:30-4:30pm. **France,** via Garibaldi, 20 (tel. 20 08 79). Open Mon.-Fri. 9am-noon.

Currency Exchange: Exchange booths at the stations are open daily 7am-10pm, but charge L3000 on traveler's checks and are only for those buying tickets. In addition, there are several *cambios* on via Balbi that are open in the afternoon, and a *cambio* on XXV Aprile, 6r (tel. 29 59 08). Open Mon.-Fri. 9am-12:30pm and 3-7pm, Sat. 9am-12:30pm.

American Express: Aviomar, via E. Vernazza, 48 (tel. 59 55 51), parallel to via XX Settembre. L1000 for mail inquiry without AmEx card. Cardholders cannot buy traveler's checks with personal checks here. Open Mon.-Fri. 9am-12:30pm and 3:30-7pm.

Post Office: Main office, via Dante (tel. 161), off p. de Ferrari. Fermo Posta at window #25, stamps at #5. Open Mon.-Sat. 8:15am-7:40pm. Convenient offices (without Fermo Posta) in the Stazione Principe, across the street from the Stazione Brignole, and at largo della Zecca. Open Mon.-Fri. 8:15am-8pm, Sat. 8:15am-1pm. **Postal Code:** 16100.

Telephones: SIP, in the post office. The shortest lines are here. Open daily 8am-11:50pm. Also nearby at via XX Settembre, 139 (open 24 hours) and either train station (Brignole open daily 8:15am-9:15pm; Principale open 8am-11pm). **Telephone Code:** 010.

Airport: C. Colombo Internazionale, in Sestri Ponente (tel. 269 01). Flights to and from London and other European points. **In-town Terminal,** p. Vittoria, 32r (tel. 58 13 16), south of Brignole. Buses depart here 1 hr. before scheduled flights.

Train Stations: Stazione Principe, p. Acquaverde (tel. 26 24 55). **Stazione Brignole,** p. Verdi (tel. 58 63 50). For train information, call 28 40 81, 7am-11pm.

Buses: ATM is the municipal bus company, with an office on p. de Ferrari (tel. 599 71), where you can buy an all-day tourist pass for L1000. **Tigullio** (tel. 31 38 51) provides service along the eastern coast. Departures from p. Vittoria, across from Bar Vittoria and Wranglers jeanseria, south of Brignole.

Ferries: Major destinations are Porto Torres, Palermo, and Tunis. It's easiest to visit one of the travel agencies listed above, but here are some particulars. (All fares are one-way deck class.) **Grandi Traghetti,** Tel. 26 71 28 or 58 93 31. To Sicily (22 hr.; June 18-July 22 and Aug. 11-Sept. 30 L65,000 per person, July 23-Aug. 10 L85,000 per person. **Tirrenia,** Tel. 25 80 41. To Tunis (in summer L113,000). Boats to Sardinia and Tunis require reservations in the summer. To reach the ferry terminal (Stazione Marittima, tel. 26 14 66), go around the side of the train on via Andrea Doria and head toward the water.

Taxis: Radio Taxi, Tel. 26 96. Very cheap, frightfully fast. Good for reaching obscure destinations in the old city. L2200 plus L830 per km.

Hitching: Take bus #17, 18, 19, or 20 from Brignole to the Genova West entrance, from where you can catch a ride to points north and south.

English Bookstore: Bozzi, via Cairoli, 2/a/r (tel. 29 87 42). Classical works, Tolkien's trilogies, and a deliciously wicked sprinkling of junk à la Rona Jaffe and Harold Robbins. Open Mon.-Fri. 8:30am-7pm, Sat. to 8:30pm. Closed 1 week in Aug.

Laundromat: Sprint, via Caprera, 28r (tel. 30 25 26). At via Serra, 40, they charge by the pound.

Public Showers: Diurno, in the underpass in front of the bombed-out theater in p. de Ferrari (tel. 56 49 80). Showers L3000, bath L4500. Open Sun. 8am-noon, Mon.-Sat. 8am-6pm.

Swimming Pool: Sportiva Sturia, via V. Maggio, 2 (tel. 38 93 25), Quarto.

Pharmacies: Tel. 192 for the name of an all-night pharmacy. **Pescetto,** via Balbi, 185r (tel. 26 26 97) is open daily.

Medical Assistance: Ospedale S. Martino, viale Benedetto XV, 10 (tel. 353 51; in emergencies 38 45 24). For an **ambulance,** call 59 59 51.

Police: Questura, via Diaz (tel. 536 61).

Accommodations and Camping

Genoa swarms with cheap hotels and *pensioni;* they dot every corner of the city. Finding inexpensive accommodations that are safe and clean is another story. No matter where you arrive, make the effort to search for lodgings near Brignole; both the establishments and the neighborhood are substantially nicer and more secure than elsewhere, and prices only minimally higher. The cheapest places near the port in the old city are unpleasant at night, if not downright dangerous. In October, Genoa hosts nautical conventions; this is the one time rooms are tight.

Pensione Mirella, via Gropallo, 4 (tel. 89 37 22). From Stazione Brignole, walk along via de Amicis to your right; at the first intersection (p. Brignole), go right again, across the tracks and up via Gropallo. The large, ornate building on your left houses several *pensioni;* of these, Mirella offers the best value. The rooms are large, clean, and elegantly furnished, and the proprietor is pleasant. Singles L10,400. Doubles L17,300, with shower L20,800. Showers L4800. **Carola** (tel. 89 13 40) offers similar conditions but charges more. Singles L18,700. Doubles with bath L34,000. Showers L4000. **Valle** (tel. 88 22 57) has inexpensive doubles (L19,000, with bath L25,000) of varied quality. Some rooms are run-down; others, done in floral pastels, seem spacious and serene. **Leda** (tel. 89 24 02) offers commodious and clean rooms, which sometimes have limited electricity. Singles L13,800. Doubles L21,300, with shower L27,000. Showers L13,000. Leda and Carola close for 2 weeks in Aug.

Casa della Giovane, p. Santa Sabina, 4 (tel. 20 66 32), near p. Annunziata. Women only. Single women especially should take advantage of this clean and safe dormitory. An excellent deal. Rooms most plentiful on weekends. Meals in the restaurant only L5000. Doubles and quads L8000 per person. Showers, luxurious baths, and breakfast included. Curfew 10:30pm, plenty late for Genoa.

Pensione Carletto, via Colombo, 16 (tel. 54 64 12). From Stazione Brignole, walk out via Fiume, turn right on via Colombo, and walk through p. Colombo. Friendly environment, huge beds, and beautiful rooms. Singles L24,400, with shower L27,600. Doubles L30,000, with shower L33,800. Showers L2000, collected only if you don't have your own bath towel.

Pensione Switzerland, p. S. Brigitta, 16 (tel. 25 67 76), off via Balbi. Not prepossessing at all, but 5 min. from the station and squeaky clean. Doubles L30,000. Showers included.

Camping: The area around Genoa is rife with campgrounds, though many are booked solid during July and August. Possibilities in the city are limited, and many campgrounds unattractive; try for something on the beach. The closest camping is west of the city at **Villa Doria,** via Vespucci, 25 (tel. 68 06 13), in Pegli. Take the train, or bus #1, 2, or 3 from p. Caricamento (near the port) to Pegli, then walk or transfer to bus #93 up via Vespucci. English spoken. Up to 2 people with a small tent L11,500, L4000 per additional person. If no space, look farther east in Rapallo or farther west in Voltri.

Food

Eating in Genoa may do untold damage to your waistline, but your budget will remain unharmed. Genoa's fine cuisine is distinctive and amazingly varied. Pesto, the traditional sauce, is made from basil, garlic, and cheeses cooked in olive oil: Try it with lasagna or spaghetti. The *Genovesi* also claim that ravioli originated in their region. Known as the Scots of Italy because of their reputed cheapness, the *Genovesi* say they created ravioli so that left-over scraps of meat, vegetables, and cheese might be combined with unused bits of pasta dough to make a meal. A hearty torte called *pasqualina* (originally prepared for Easter) is stuffed with greens and eggs. *Burrida* is a delicious fish stew, and *cima* is a meat version of *pasqualina.* Some of the more characteristic dishes are *ripieni* (stuffed zucchini and peppers), *trippa* (tripe), *lumache* (snails), *farinata* (a thin bread made from chick-pea flour, oil, and water), *totani* (calamari), and the scrumptious *pansotti* (little ravioli stuffed with spinach in a sauce made from nuts). *Focaccia* is the local, crater-faced flat bread, and *pandolce* the sweetbread. For elegant yet cheap (L700-850) pastries, go to **La Forneria,** p. Colombo, 26. Try their heavenly *sfogliate di mele* (apple pastry). Many shops in the old part of the city, especially along via del Campo, have less sweet, heartier pastry. Genoa is not really an ice cream town, but you can try **Gelateria**

Tonitto, p. Dante, 31r, near p. de Ferrari. (Open Mon.-Sat. 8am-1am.) If you're a die-hard for regional authenticity, order a *frappe, frullata,* or *shaker* (all much like milkshakes but with an occasional twist of liqueur or coffee).

Bruciamonti, via Roma (tel 56 25 15). An upscale *salumeria* established in 1885, with delectable local take-out specialties. Try their snails (L3500 per *etto*) and eggplant parmesan (L2000 per *etto*). Open Thurs.-Tues. 7:10am-1:30pm and 4pm-2am.

Cucina Casalinga da Maria, vico Testa d'Oro, 14r (tel. 57 10 80), off via XXV Aprile. One of the best places to go in Genoa. Notwithstanding the bright green walls, the place is clean and comfortable (linen tablecloths, no less), and the food is tasty, abundant, and very cheap: *Menù turistico* only L7000, including *pane,* cover, and wine. Full meal a la carte L10,000-12,000. Open Sun.-Thurs. noon-2:30pm and 7-9pm, Fri. noon-2:30pm.

El Merendero, via di S. Zita, 18r (tel. 58 07 98). Walk down via Brignole from Stazione Brignole, turn left onto viale Brigata-Bisagno, then left again onto via di S. Zita. An amiable owner and excellent food. *Primi* about L3000, *secondi* with *contorno* about L7200. Be daring—try the *penne arrabbiate* (hot!). Wine L6000 per liter. Open Mon.-Sat. noon-3:30pm and 7pm-midnight.

The Hong Kong Trattoria, p. S. Carlo, 2 (tel. 20 77 36), off via Balbi. While you may feel sacrilegious eating *chop suey* instead of *spaghetti al pesto,* this is the place for a Chinese food fix. Chicken, beef, and pork dishes L4000-5000, shrimp L5500-7000. Fixed *menù* L11,500. Beer L1800. Chinese liquor L3000. Cover L1500. Open Tues.-Sun.

Self-Service Moody, largo (not via) XII Ottobre, 51 (tel. 59 54 31), near p. de Ferrari at via Ettore Vernazza. Relax on Moody's leather sofas among leisured *Genovesi.* Excellent cafeteria food. Full meals L10,000 and up. Dinner *menù* L9500. Open Mon.-Sat. noon-2:30pm and 7-10pm.

Da Guglie, via San Vincenzo, 64r (tel. 56 57 65), the 2nd right off p. Verdi from the station. Eat at the slate tables alongside the regulars or take your food out to the *piazza. Primi* L1500-3000, brick-oven *pizze* L2000-3000, wine L1000 per ¼ liter. Open Mon.-Sat. 6am-9pm.

Sâ pesta, via Giustiniani, 16r, near p. Matteotti. Everyone from dockworkers to doctors gathers here for a little tradition and lots of terrific food. Sâ pesta was established in the sixteenth century, when it sold *sale pestato* (ground salt). You can see whole eggs in the scrumptious *pasqualina* (L1300). Or try the *castagnaccio,* a chestnut concoction. Open Mon.-Fri. 11:30am-2pm and 5-8:30pm, Sat. 11:30am-2pm.

Al Veliero, via al Ponte Calvi, 10r (tel. 29 18 29), in p. Caricamento. White walls decorated with nautical paraphernalia, white tablecloths, and little kids trying to keep their white, Sunday-best outfits pristine. *Primi* L2200-6500, *secondi* L6000-12,500, *barbero or dolcetto* (local wines) L4800 per liter. Cover L1600. The *zuppa di pesce* (similar to *bouillabaise*) makes you wonder how anyone can live away from the sea. Open daily noon-2pm and 7-9pm.

Burghy's, via XX Settembre, 209; via Fiume; and several other locations. For a fast-food fix; Genoa's version of McDonalds.

Supermercato Standa, via XX Settembre, 60, 2 floors down. Open Mon. 3-7:30pm, Tues.-Sat. 9am-7:30pm.

Sights

Genoese art can compare with its Florentine and Venetian counterparts only in architecture. Still, the *Genovesi* are historically marvelous merchants and have assembled some fine collections of Oriental, Flemish, and Italian art from other regions.

Sadly enough, you may have difficulty recognizing the splendor of a facade through many years' build-up of dirt and disrepair. The *Genovesi* do not look after their one aesthetic asset too well, though the scaffolding throughout the city may indicate a change.

The city's affinity for exquisite architecture is clear from the outset: The open and airy train station, the Stazione Principe, is graced by a small square with a statue of young Christopher Columbus, a distant view of the port, and the straight, narrow **via Balbi** lined with noble Renaissance *palazzi.*

At via Balbi, 10, is the eighteenth-century **Palazzo Reale** (royal palace, designed by Bartolomeo Bianco), with a fine courtyard that once opened onto a beautiful seaside garden—now it looks out on a major road and construction cranes. If nowhere else, glance down at the black and white pebble inlaid path under your feet. Upstairs, the **Galleria d' Arte** (tel. 20 68 51) provides a window onto the lifestyles of eighteenth-century Genoese nobility, with paintings by Tintoretto, van Dyck, and Bassano. (Open daily 9am-1:15pm. Admission L2000.)

From Stazione Principe, via Balbi leads to **piazza Nunziata,** a characteristic Genoese square: small, irregular, and distinguished by formal *palazzi.* The severe neoclassical facade (1843) of the **Church of SS. Annunziata** (1591-1620) conceals an incongruously rococo interior. (Open daily 6:30am-1:30pm and 3:30-6:30pm.) From piazza Nunziata, continue east to largo Zecca then turn right on via Cairoli. Via Cairoli leads to **via Garibaldi,** one of the most beautifully planned streets in Italy, lined by an uninterrupted succession of sixteenth- and seventeenth-century palaces so perfect in form they appear to have grown out of the pavement. The facades here conceal both graceful courtyards and rooms decorated with the most lavish frescoes of the Genoese school of the seventeenth and eighteenth centuries.

The **Palazzo Bianco** (1548, rebuilt 1712) at via Garibaldi, 11 (tel. 29 18 03), now houses one of the city's most important collections of Ligurian art and also has its finest array of Dutch and Flemish paintings. The coldness and precision of the Flemish paintings intrigue viewers: Note especially G. David's *Crucifixion* and J. Provost's triptych. The wonderfully expressive faces of the two old men in Van Dyck's *Christ of the Coin* evoke another mood of the Flemish style. Other works of interest include Paolo Veronese's visibly pre-baroque *Jesus on the Cross,* Pontormo's *Florentine Gentleman,* and Lippi's painting of St. Sebastian and St. Francis. (Open Tues.-Sat. 9am-1:15pm, Sun. 9:15am-12:15am. Minimal admission fee.)

Palazzo Rosso, via Garibaldi, 18, built in the seventeenth century, is a magnificently furnished palace that preserves its character as a princely dwelling and now houses the **Galleria di Palazzo Rosso** (tel. 28 26 41). Among its collection of paintings on the first floor is Mattia Preti of the resurrected Jesus showing his wounds to incredulous apostles. Some magnificent full-length van Dyck portraits are on the second floor, along with a Dürer painting of a youth whose swarthy complexion is beautifully set against a velvety green background, and a lush portrait of *Christ Carrying the Cross* by Rubens. The small terrace commands a lovely view of the picturesque rooftops and steeples of the old city. (Open Tues.-Sat. 9am-1:15pm and 3-6pm, Sun. 9:15am-1:15pm.)

The *galleria* faces the vigorous Renaissance facade of the **Palazzo Municipale** (1564-70), whose beautiful roof gardens provide open space without destroying the continuity of the wall surfaces. The **Palazzo Podestà** (1565), via Garibaldi, 7, has a courtyard with an unusual grotto fountain and an interesting stucco decoration of a merman. **Palazzo Parodi** (1578), via Garibaldi, 3, boasts an elegant doorway whose caryatids are nose-less. Via Garibaldi ends in piazza Fontane Marose with a view of the sixteenth-century Gothic **Palazzo Spinola:** Black and white bands mark its levels and statues occupy the niches.

From here, salita di Santa Caterina takes you to **piazza Corvetto.** Spread out on the hill to your left is the **Villetta Di Negro,** where you can relax amid waterfalls, grottoes, and terraced gardens. Its summit offers a clear view of the port and an extraordinary museum of Oriental art, the **Museo D' Arte Orientale E. Chiossone** (tel. 54 22 85). On the first floor are housed some fine sculptures, of which the miniscule dog-dragon is particularly expressive. The other floors contain delicate eighteenth-century paintings and various pieces of Samurai armor. (Open Tues.-Sat. 9am-1:15pm and 3-6pm.)

From this point, return to via Garibaldi and via Cairoli for a descent into the old city. Wander into the back alleys—you may think you have inadvertently stepped into a scene from the musical *Cats.* It is difficult to say whether felines or churches are more numerous. Via S. Siro leads into **via San Luca,** the main street of the old city, where you'll find many of Genoa's most important monuments. The **Church of San Siro,** the first cathedral of Genoa (redone 1588-1613), has a rich and vast baroque interior with a splendid high altar. The **Church of San Luca** is a little, twelfth-century jewel in the shape of a Greek cross, crowned by a dome.

To the right of the entrance, a 1681 wooden sculpture of Christ reclines on what looks like a giant silken pillow more appropriate for an odalisque in a bordello. (Both open Mon.-Sat. 7am-noon and 3-7pm.) **Palazzo Spinola,** in p. di Pellicceria (follow the yellow signs), exemplifies Genoa's mercantile wealth between the sixteenth and eighteenth centuries. In the *palazzo*'s rooms, which retain most of their original decoration and furnishings, are works of art donated by the Spinola family along with others being gathered together to form the **Galleria Nazionale di Palazzo Spinola** (tel. 29 46 61). The collection includes a haunting and melancholy *Ecce Homo* by Antonello da Messina, *Portrait of a Child* by van Dyck, *Praying Madonna* by Joos Van Cleve, and *St. Jerome* by Ribera, as well as works by seventeenth-century Genoese painters. Not to be missed are portraits of the four evangelists by van Dyck in the Sala da Pranzo. (Open Tues.-Sat. 9am-6:30pm, Sun. 9am-1pm.)

Piazza Caricamento, by the port on the other side of p. Banchi, is bordered on one side by medieval arcades (Portici di Sottoripa) that give a wonderful sense of the ancient city port. The effect is spoiled by the steel colossi moored just 50m away. Across the *piazza* is the **Palazzo San Giorgio,** a part-Gothic (1260), part-Renaissance (1571) structure that was home to the famous Genoese bank of St. George.

From piazza Caricamento, via S. Lorenzo leads to piazza San Lorenzo and to the **Cathedral of San Lorenzo.** Built between the twelfth and fifteenth centuries, the cathedral is the major medieval monument of the city. Black and white marble stripes give life to an otherwise clunky facade. The lower portion of the church has the deep, rich doorways of a French Gothic church. More faithful to the ancient Romanesque construction, the sides of the church are decorated with remains of ancient sarcophagi (third and fourth centuries) and a canopied tomb from the Church of San Giovanni de Prè. The church's severe and dark interior is somewhat enlivened by the black and white decoration of the central nave and galleries and by the richly carved capitals of the columns. In the right nave is a moving crucifixion in relief (1443) and next to it the shell that, fired from an English ship on February 9, 1941, entered the church, but miraculously never exploded. The **cathedral treasury** (at the end of the left nave) displays the Sacred Basin of green crystal, which corresponds to descriptions of the Holy Grail; a casket wrought in silver with scenes from the life of St. John the Baptist; and the Cross of Zaccaria—a fine example of the art of Byzantine goldsmiths—encrusted with emeralds and rubies, and containing a small piece of the Cross. (Open Mon., Wed., and Fri.-Sat. 10am-noon and 2-5pm, Sun. 10am-noon.)

Church and state have a long history of cooperation in Italy, and Genoa is no exception. Right off piazza S. Lorenzo, site of the city's most important church, lie piazza Matteotti and the **Palazzo Ducale,** once home of the city's most powerful rulers. This grand old residence of the doges was built in the twelfth century and renovated in the fifteenth, sixteenth, and seventeenth centuries. Inside rest two beautiful courtyards, one framing an elegant seventeenth-century fountain. Diagonal to this imposing palace stands the ornate **Church of Gesù** (also known as SS. Ambrogio e Andrea; 1549-1606). Illuminated by golden light, this baroque church is filled with *trompe l'oeil* effects, false perspectives, double cupolas, and two important Rubens canvases: *The Circumcision* (1605, behind the high altar) and *St. Ignatius Healing a Woman Possessed of the Devil* (1620, 3rd chapel off left aisle). Also of note is the *Ascension* by Guido Reni.

Just a horn's bleat away from the aging splendors of piazza Matteotti lies the large and pompous center of the new city. **Piazza de Ferrari** is dominated by three elaborate French Second Empire buildings and a monstrous fountain resembling a raised hubcap. On one side of the square are the neoclassical ruins of the 1829 **Teatro Communale dell'Opera,** now being reconstructed.

Off p. de Ferrari is Genoa's most characteristic and charming square; **piazza San Matteo** is an almost private fief. It contains the houses and family chapel of the Doria family, which belonged to the medieval oligarchy that ruled Genoa. Each building has a black-and-white facade decorated with exquisite doorways, arcades, and *loggie.* The animal reliefs above the first floor are the trademarks of the masons who built the houses. At #14 and 15 are sculpted panels of San Giorgio, Genoa's protector, who perches above many of the city's doorways. The **Church of San Matteo** (1125) is engraved with descriptions of the great deeds of the family. On the left through a small door hides a lovely fourteenth-century cloister, with slim, twin columns topped by human and animal figures. A couple of eighteenth-century coffee shops, **Romanengo** and **Klainguti,** were established by the Swiss colony that once inhabited Genoa.

Centro Storico (Old City) and **Porta Soprana,** which lie south of via San Lorenzo and via Porta Soprana, are somewhat less manicured. The three straight streets (via Canneto il Lungo, via Giustiniani, and via San Bernando) of this oldest part of the city follow the lines of the old Roman settlement. Though much of the area suffered heavy bombing during World War II and yearns for reconstruction, some interesting churches remain scattered among the old tenements and medieval ruins. The **Church of Santa Maria di Castello,** a labyrinth of chapels, courtyards, cloisters, and gardens, once served as a crusader church and hostel. Originally paleochristian with twelfth-century additions, its interior juxtaposes Roman capitals and columns with medieval interpretations of the same forms. The *Crocifisso Miracoloso* is in the chapel to the left of the high altar—Jesus' beard supposedly grows longer every time crisis hits the city. **Via Canneto il Lungo** embodies the great age of the city with its twisting medieval buildings and lovely Renaissance doorways and reliefs. The medieval **Porta Soprana** embodies this part of the city. You can walk past the supposed boyhood home of Christopher Columbus (his father was the gatekeeper) and the ruins of the twelfth-century cloister of the **Church of Sant' Andrea.** This part of town should be visited only during the day; at night you will feel very much like a foreigner, perhaps an unwanted one.

Finally, the newest edition to the old city, the Genoese art museum, was created within the former monastery of Sant' Agostino. This museum attempts to represent Genoa's history through art that has survived the city's various destructions. It's most outstanding piece is the funerary monument of Margherita of Brabant, carved in 1312 by Giovanni Pisano, one of the greatest Italian sculptors. The fragments of this monument derive from various corners of the continent, and the hope is that someday it will once again be complete, as other pieces turn up.

To get a bird's-eye view of this multi-faceted city, take the funicular railway (6:30am-midnight every 15-25 min., L700—same tickets used for city buses) from Largo Della Zecca, on the eastern corner of piazza Nunziata, to **Righi.** Here, about 350m above sea level, you can enjoy a stupendous vista. It's also a good place to go for lunch or dinner. Of the restaurants with panoramic terraces, **Da Bolognese** serves pizza (open Thurs.-Tues., pizza served 7-11pm).

Entertainment

June brings the **Vivi Centro Storico,** an extensive program of late-evening concerts in the old city's streets and squares. For information, ask the EPT or call 29 24 93. During spring and summer, **Musica in Piazza** offers jazz concerts in the courtyard of the Centro Sociale, via S. Fruttuoso, 72 (across the tracks near Stazione Brignole). More performances in various media in city parks and squares throughout July and August are organized under the title **Le Sere di Genova** (Evenings in Genoa). *Il Secolo XIX,* the city paper, announces programs, as does the detailed booklet *L' Agenda,* a free monthly calendar of events available at tourist offices. The three-month opera season, held at the **Teatro Margherita,** begins at the end of January; during the rest of the year, the theater hosts dramatic and other musical performances. The box office is at via XX Settembre, 16 (tel. 58 93 29), and is open daily 10am-12:30pm and 1:30-7pm. Balcony tickets run L20,000. During July, nearby Nervi and its magnificent gardens host a prestigious **ballet festival.**

Perfect for a night stroll are the arcades of **via XX Settembre.** Here you can stop for coffee or ice cream, watch others out for their evening *passeggiata,* or listen to live piano music.

Riviera di Levante

The most stunning stretch of the Riviera is the breathtaking Riviera di Levante (Riviera of the Rising Sun), east of Genoa. Mountains rise directly from the shore, forming an enchanting coastline dotted with inlets and coves and sheltering small, gemlike fishing villages. Each town's harbor greets you with a blaze of color; lush greenery and azure water provide a backdrop for the yellows, pinks, reds, and even purples of the houses and boats. The transportation system is excellent—frequent buses, trains, and boats connect all major towns. Trains from Genoa leave from both Stazione Principe and Stazione Brignole, though more frequently from the latter. You'll have to move mountains to find a room in high season: Phone around, flaunt your *Let's Go* book, and try to make reservations, even if you call only a day in advance. Finding accommodations in off-season will pose little problem.

Camogli

Camogli, a contraction of "Casa Moglie" (roughly, "wives' house"), gets its name from the women who stayed here all day while their husbands were out fishing. The village's six-story houses were painted in bright colors so that the men could distinguish their own from the water. Weather has washed the colors into a soothing melange of pinks and ochres, siennas and ivory. The town climbs uphill, clothed in pine and olive groves and bordered by a pebble beach, which is separated from the fishing harbor by a promontory. Dickens commented that this town was "the saltiest, roughest, most piratical little place," but Camogli has mellowed into a quiet, peaceful resort. Most of its festivals, naturally enough, revolve around the sea. On the second Sunday in May, an enormous fish-fry, **La Sagra del Pesce,** is held on the quay with free fish for all. The festival was originally held to dispel Camogli's reputation as the stingiest town in Liguria, but the tourist draw is now no doubt, an incentive as well. The giant pan used in the festival (4m across, with enough room for over 2000 sardines) adorns a wall at the entrance to the town.

Reach Camogli by train from Genoa (½ hr., L1000) or from Santa Margherita (10 min., L600). **Tigullio** buses depart to nearby towns across from the station. Tickets are sold at Bar Aldo, next to the station. (To Santa Margherita, 14 per day, L1000. To Portofino, 4 per day, L800.) More expensive are the ferries. From Camogli, ferries take you around the rugged headland to San Fruttuoso, set on its own bay (in summer 7-10 per day; one way L3000, round-trip L5000). If you prefer to walk, pick up the Camogli tourist office's useful trail map, or a more elaborate version for L4500. The hike takes about three hours. The **tourist office** at via XX Settembre, 19 (tel. 77 10 66), to your right as you leave the station, will help you find a room and answer even the zaniest questions, all in broken English. They also have **telephones.** (Open July-Aug., Mon.-Thurs. and Sat. 9am-12:30pm and 3:30-6:30pm, Fri. 9am-12:30pm and 3:30-5:30pm, Sun. 9am-12:30pm; Sept.-June Mon.-Sat. only.) Camogli's **telephone code** is 0185. The **post office** is at via Cuneo, 1 (tel. 77 01 14), to the left of the station. (Open Mon.-Fri. 8:10am-6:45pm, Sat. 8:10-11:30am.) **Exchange currency** at either of the two banks that lie along via XX Settembre between the tourist office and the station. (Open Mon.-Thurs. 8:20am-1:20pm and 2:45-3:45pm, Fri. 2:45-3:30pm.)

Pensione La Camogliese, a two-star hotel, is a steal. Walk down the stairway near the train station to via Garibaldi, 55 (tel. 77 14 02), near the seafront. The clean, commodious rooms are a joy, and the proprietor was born for his job. He'll give discounts to those with *Let's Go* books. (Singles L15,000, with bath L20,000. Doubles L30,000, with bath L40,000.) If La Camogliese is full, walk left from the station past the post office to **Albergo Selane,** via Cuneo, 16 (tel. 77 01 49). (Singles L28,000. Doubles L45,000. Additional charges: balcony L10,000, TV L2500, reservations L5000.) For seafood and a wonderful view, eat at **Ristorante La Camogliese** on the shore, where fish dishes run L10,000-12,000. Try the *trofiette all Camogliese* (L5000). (Open Thurs.-Tues. for lunch and supper.) Visit **Crema e Cioccolata,** piazza Colombo, 8 (tel. 77 02 55), at the port just below the church, for dessert. Fight the five-year-olds to the counter for a massive cone or cup of *gelato* (L1500 per 2 flavors, L2000 per 3). Or taste their Sicilian *granite* for L2200-2700. (Open Thurs.-Tues. 8am-9pm.) For cookies, go across the street to **Revello,** via Garibaldi, 185 (tel. 770 77). Rave reviews in chic Milanese magazines hold true.

San Fruttuoso

The tiny fishing hamlet San Fruttuoso is set in a natural amphitheater of pines, olive trees, and green oaks that lead down to the sea. It is accessible by boat (see Camogli or S. Margherita) or by foot. Too expensive for a prolonged stay, San Fruttuoso is a wonderful daytrip.

For a great view, walk to the left of the bay to the medieval **lookout tower,** constructed by the D'Oria family. Fifteen meters offshore and 18m deep is a bronze statue with upraised arms, the *Christ of the Depths,* erected in memory of casualties at sea. The statue now serves as the protector of scuba divers, and on August 22, the town sponsors a **festival** commemorating those lost at sea. On your way back to town, you can visit the Benedictine **Abbey of San Fruttuoso di Capo di Monte.** In the eleventh-century church, a small, white, jewellike structure, you can see an exact replica of *Christ of the Depths* (for those who forgot their scuba-diving paraphernalia), as well as a musical nativity scene that sings and moves for L200. The Abbey also includes a thirteenth-century palace, a Romanesque cloister sheltering the tombs of the D'Orias, and other buildings presently undergoing renovation. For this reason, the barren rooms are not now worth the L4000 entrance fee. (Open daily 10am-1pm and 2-6pm.)

The owner of La Cantina (tel. 77 26 26), on an inlet adjacent to the abbey, will show you the succulent daily catch before he cooks it. You can eat at tables on the beach, but such luxury is dear: The *menù* is L30,000. Maybe fasting as the monks of the abbey did isn't such a bad idea. (Open Jan.-Nov. daily 9am-8pm.)

Portofino

Gorgeous Portofino was long ago discovered by the wealthy and exclusive. Today their yachts fill the harbor and their boutiques the streets, but the curve of the shore and the tiny bay may be enjoyed by paupers and princes alike. After being jostled by busloads of binocular-toting tourists, however, you may be ready to head for the hills. Portofino is surrounded by a nature reserve, through which you can trek to San Fruttuoso (2 hr.) or to Santa Margherita (3 hr.). If you choose to stay around town, escape to the coolness of the simple white **church.** A few more minutes up the road to the **castle** (open Wed.-Mon., L1000) will set you in an enchanting garden with a fairy-tale view of the clear bay and a bird's-eye slant on the ants sunning below. Look for the footpath marked "Al faro" to reach the lighthouse (20 min.) and an awesome coastline vista.

There's no train out to Portofino, but Tigullio **buses** (every ½ hr., L800; buy tickets on the bus) run along the coastline to and from Santa Margherita, making the 30-minute ride a visual delight. During summer, boat service is another option (several times per day; San Fruttuoso to Portofino one way L3500, round-trip L6000; S. Margherita to Portofino one way L3500, round-trip L5000). If you're not wearing the latest, greatest fashion, you may feel out of place, but you can still get maps and English brochures at the **tourist office,** via Roma, 35 (tel. 690 24; open June-Sept. Mon.-Sat. 9am-7pm, Sun. 9:30am-12:30pm and 3:30-7:30pm), where some English is spoken. Portofino's **telephone code** is 0185, and **telephones** are available at the tourist office.

Santa Margherita Ligure

Reasonably priced for its location near the small villages and beautiful beaches, Santa Margherita Ligure is pleasantly devoid of the hum of tourist sounds. Instead, you'll hear the buzz of bees around the white Margherita bushes that decorate the city and resemble huge snowballs when in full bloom. Blessed with the quaint and personal quality of a small town, Santa Margherita Ligure has the accessibility of a large one. Train service along the Riviera is phenomenal. (To Genoa, 4:30am-midnight 3 per hr., L1500; La Spezia, 6am-2am 2 per hr., L3500.) The trains also run to major inland cities. (To Florence, 1 per day, L10,700.)

In the morning, visit the local **fish market** on lungomare Marconi for a look at the day's catch, or come by between 4 and 6pm to catch Santa Margherita's fishing fleet bring in its haul. More exalted sights include the rococo **basilica** on p. Carrera (with some good Flemish and Italian works) and the **Church of San Siro** off corso Matteotti (sporting a bell tower, a painted ceiling, and marble floors).

Practical Information

EPT: via XXV Aprile, 26 (tel. 28 74 85). Turn right from the train station onto via Roma, then right on via XXV Aprile. Information, a free town map, an accommodations service, and currency exchange. English spoken. Open July-Sept. Mon.-Sat. 8:15-11:45am and 3:15-5:45pm Sun. 9:15-11:45am; Oct.-June Mon.-Sat. only.

Post Office: via Roma, 36 (tel. 28 65 44), to the right of the station. Open Mon.-Fri. 8:10am-6:45pm, Sat. 8:10-11:30am. **Postal code:** 16038.

Telephones: Il Fiocco, via Gramsci, 83 (tel. 28 95 92), along the waterfront. Open Thurs.-Tues. 7:30am-1am. Also at **Bar Dangliò,** via XXV Settembre, near the tourist office. Open Fri.-Wed. 5:30am-9pm. **Telephone code:** 0185.

Trains: At the summit of via Roma (tel. 28 66 30). The bag depot is open only 6am-9pm.

Buses: Tigullio buses depart from p. Martiri della Libertà. *Biglietteria* in rotonda Mare open daily 7am-10pm. Service to Camogli (L1000) and Portofino (L800).

Ferries: Tigullio also offers boat service. To Portofino (one way L3500, round-trip L5000), San Fruttuoso (one way L6000, round-trip L10,000), and Cinque Terre (one way L14,000, round-trip L20,000). Service less frequent June-Sept. 15.

Bike Rental: Motonoleggio, via Pagana, 5b. Bicycles L5000 per hr., L30,000 per week. Scooters L10,000 per hr., L60,000 per day, L200,000 per week.

Hospital: via Fratelli Arpe (tel 28 36 11), past p. Mazzini.

Police: via C. Vignolo (tel. 28 71 21).

Accommodations

Stay away from the water. You won't have a view and you'll have to walk a little, but your reward will be peace, quiet, and a L10,000 savings.

Hotel Fasce, via Luigi Bozzo, 3 (tel. 28 64 35), off corso Matteotti. You'll feel as though you're staying at the Hilton. Jean and Arry will go to any lengths for their guests and speak fluent English. Modern, stylish rooms with telephones. L20,000 per person. Washing machines, showers, and breakfast included. *Pensione completa* L41,000, ½-pensione L39,000.

Corallo, via XXV Aprile, 20 (tel. 28 67 74), about 3 blocks from the tourist office. The cheapest place in town. The owner and his son are kind; the rooms are spotless and spacious. Singles L14,000. Doubles L28,500. Triples L40,000. Showers L3500. Breakfast L5000.

Albergo Annabella, via Costasecca, 10 (tel. 28 65 31). Capacious, clean, and contemporary rooms. Singles L19,000. Doubles L32,000, with breakfast L38,000. Triples L48,000, with breakfast L57,000. Showers L2000. You can take half-pension at their restaurant, Ristorante A. Begudda, for L38,000.

Food

Supermarkets, bakeries, fruit vendors, and butcher shops line corso Matteotti. Every Friday morning from 8am to 1pm, the shops oust the cars and spill onto the *corso.* The best snacks in Santa Margherita are the ubiquitous *focacce,* a cracker-like bread filled with cheese or meat (about L700).

Pasticceria Ragi e Polli, via Cairoli, 1c (tel. 28 94 05), near p. Mazzini. Smells like a chocolate factory. Try the sinfully rich *margheritine* (L2200 per *etto*). Open 7am-1pm and 4-7:30pm.

Rosticceria Revelant, via Gramsci, 15 (tel. 28 65 00), east of p. Martiri della Libertà. Run by a father and his three gregarious adult sons. Try the lasagna (L9000 per kg). Open Mon.-Tues. and Thurs.-Sat. 7:30am-1pm and 4-8pm, Sun. 4-8pm.

Trattoria da Pezzi, via Cavour, 21 (tel. 28 53 03), parallel to via XXV Aprile. Packed with loud, jovial customers. Pizza L3000, wine L2800 per ½-liter. Cover L1000. Open Sun.-Fri. 10am-2:15pm and 5-9:15pm.

Trattoria Baicin, via Algeria, 9 (tel. 867 63), off p. Martiri della Libertà near the water. A great place for a memorable indulgence. Full meals at this family-run establishment from L15,000; *primi* L3000-5000, *secondi* L9000-10,500 (meat) or L15,000-17,000 (fish). Wine L6000 per liter. Open daily noon-4pm and 7pm-midnight.

Trattoria San Siro, corso Matteotti, 137. Farther away than you expect. *Menù* L12,700. Try the *pansotti* (small ravioli-like pasta in a walnut sauce) for L4500. Open July-Aug. Sun.-Fri. 11am-4pm and 6-11pm.

Trattoria Da Martino, p. Roccatagliata (tel. 28 81 87), off corso Matteotti. Satisfying meals. Try *lasagna al pesto* (L4000) and the *calamari* (L7500). Wine L4000 per liter. Cover L2000. Open Aug. daily 8am-5pm and 7pm-1am; Sept.-Oct. and Dec.-July Fri.-Wed. only.

Ristorante A. Begudda, via Roma and via Tripoli, 5A (tel. 28 09 86). Specialties are grilled meats and mushroom dishes. *Menù* with wine L1000. Open mid-June to Oct. 12:45-2pm and 7:30-10pm, depending on the number of guests from Albergo Annabella on half-pension (see Accommodations).

Sestri Levante

Praised in poetry by both Dante and Petrarch, the peaceful beauty of Sestri Levante is today as dead as are they. The town has fallen prey to tourism and development. Avoid stopping here unless you cannot find a place in Santa Margherita, La Spezia, or the Carrara youth hostel (see La Spezia). The **tourist office** is at via XX Settembre, 33 (tel. 414 22; open June-Sept. Mon.-Sat. 9am-12:40pm and 3:30-7pm, Sun. 10am-noon; Oct.-May usually Mon.-Fri. 9am-noon and 3:30-6pm). Sestri's **telephone code** is 0185; the **postal code** is 16039. If cruel gods strand you in Sestri, walk down to the **Baia del Silenzo,** east of p. Matteotti. The bay is no longer silent, but the colorful hamlets clustered on its shore make it a spectacular spot. Sestri's sand is silken—if you manage to shove your way to a free patch. Consider going to Lavagna, about 10 minutes to the west by train, which has miles of open beaches, or to Riva Trigoso, the same distance east. The people at **Albergo Leda** (tel. 414 01) in Sestri are affable and speak a little English, and the rooms are airy and clean. Walk down viale Roma from the station, turn left on viale Mazzini, then right to via XX Settembre, 15. (Singles L18,900. Doubles L31,300. Triples L40,000. Quads L50,000.) Slightly cheaper is **Pensione Giovanna,** via Privata Sertorio, 4 (tel. 424 42), off viale Mazzini. (Singles L16,000. Doubles L27,000. *Pensione completa* L39,000.) The nearest campground is **Cava Santa Anna** (tel. 439 24), 100m from a rocky beach. From the train station, follow the arrows north toward via Antica Roma, where you'll turn left and walk about 1.5km. (L4200 per person plus L3100 per small tent, L4700 per large tent. Hot showers L300.) Sestri's *trattorie* charge exorbitant prices. Fortunately, the town has a plethora of *pizzerie.* The old standby is **Pizzeria Rivi** at viale Rimembranza, 41. Pizzas are L5000. (Open Wed.-Mon.)

La Spezia

La Spezia possesses typical Riviera charm; its unique function is as a departure point to Corsica and as an excellent base for visiting the surrounding coast (Portovenere, Cinque Terre, and Lerici), where rooms are rare in summer. Art lovers, architects, engineers, and others will enjoy a daytrip to the marble caves of **Carrara,** where Michaelangelo went to buy blocks for his sculpture. Today, it remains the only source of white marble in Italy. There are no fixed times and no permission is needed to enter—proceed at your own risk. The **EPT** in La Spezia can provide information, as can the **tourist office** in Carrara, p. II Giugno (tel. 708 94). But be prepared to brandish your thumb or rent a car, as the quarries are a few kilometers from the station at Carrara-Avenza.

Orientation and Practical Information

The best way to reach La Spezia is the **Rome-Genoa train line** (from Pisa about 40 per day, L7000; from Genoa 30 per day, L3900), but coming from Florence you might prefer the **Lazzi bus** (7 per day, L11,400).

EPT: viale Mazzini, 47 (tel. 360 00), 3 flights up, near p. Verdi and the seafront. From the station, take via Fiume (which becomes via del Prione) through p. Mentana, and turn left onto via Mazzini. Information and informal accommodations service. Open Mon.-Tues. and Thurs.-Fri. 8am-1:30pm and 3:30-6:30pm, Wed. and Sat. 8am-1:30pm.

Post Office: p. Verdi (tel. 293 81). Stamps and Fermo Posta at window #2. Open Mon.-Fri. 8am-7:30pm, Sat. 8am-1pm. **Postal code:** 19100.

Telephone: SIP, via da Passano, 30, off via Chiodo. Open daily 8am-9:30pm. After 9:30pm go to **Albergo Venezia,** via Paleocapa, 8, near the station. **Telephone code:** 0187.

Train Station: La Spezia Centrale, via Paleocapa, at the north end of town uphill from via del Prione. Take bus #4, L, or S into town and get off at via Chiodo near the seafront, or walk (15 min.). Information office (tel. 353 73) open daily 7am-noon and 3-8pm. Exchange open daily 7:30-11:45am and 4-7pm.

Buses: ATC, p. Chiodo, 9 (tel. 50 31 23). Municipal tickets L700. Buses for Lerici (bus L) leave from the station every ½ hr., for Portovenere also every ½ hr. (L1000); grab bus P either in p. Verdi or along via Chiodo. **Lazzi,** viale Amendola, 142 (tel. 294 55). Departures to Florence from p. Chiodo, 26.

Ferries: In Tur, via Mazzini, 47 (tel. 243 24) or via Italia, 5 (tel. 390 03). Ferries from Banchina Revel for Portovenere one way L3500, round-trip L5000. Ferries operate April-Sept. **Linea Pozzale,** based at the neighboring dock, offers an inexpensive tour of the islands (2 per day, 1½ hr., L6000). Ask at the EPT for further information—a plethora of other companies will take you to a variety of places.

Laundromat: Lavanderia Automatica Bucato Lampo, via Canaletto, 377 (tel. 51 17 71).

Pool: Campo Sportivo Alberto Picco, viale Fieschi (tel. 223 08 or 223 09), north of the town center.

Public Baths: Albergo Diurno, p. Cavour (underground). Toilets L300. Showers L3500, with towel L4000. Open daily 8am-noon and 3-7pm.

Hospital: Ospedale Civile S. Andrea, via Vittorio Veneto, 197 (tel. 533 11). For an **ambulance,** call 70 21 21 (Red Cross) or 363 86 (public assistance).

Police: Questura, via XX Settembre, 4 (tel. 350 41), near p. Verdi.

Accommodations, Camping, and Food

La Spezia hosts workers from the province during the week, making rooms tight. The situation improves, however, when these folks go home for the weekend, and, certainly compared to surrounding coastal areas, La Spezia is a viable accommodations option.

The nearest **youth hostel** (IYHF), and an idyllic daytrip in itself, is in Marina di Massa, at viale delle Pinete, 89 (tel. (0585) 202 88), 33km by train (station Carrara-Avenza), plus 3km by bus. Managed by jocular brothers, the hostel grounds include a garden, accessible beach, and kitchen facilities; many of the 12 bedrooms have terraces. (L8500. Breakfast and shower included. IYHF card required. Make reservations.) If the establishments listed below are full, check around with the EPT's list.

Culinary specialties of the region are the *zuppa di datteri,* a fish soup, and *farinata,* a local pizza made with chickpea flour. Made from the grapevines visible on surrounding coastal hillsides, the two renowned local wines are the portlike **Scia che tra** and the lighter, dry **Cinque Terre** white. Follow the locals in their evening *passeggiata* down via del Prione. In morning hours, take your stomach to the **open-air market** in p. Cavour at the widening of corso Cavour (open Mon.-Sat.).

Flavia, vicolo dello Stagno, 7 (tel. 274 65). From the station, take via Fiume through p. Garibaldi to via del Prione. Turn right onto vicolo dello Stagno, a few meters past the Gelateria Caraibi sign. A charming place with charming management. Singles L10,000. Doubles L20,000, with bath L24,500.

Giglio Rosso, via Carpenino, 31 (tel. 313 74), off p. Battisti. A small place with pink walls and a personable proprietor. Be prepared: Squat toilets require some agility. Many hangers on here, so check early for a room. Singles L16,000. Doubles L23,500. Shower included.

Camping: Campeggio Maralunga, via Carpanini, 61 (tel. 96 65 89), in Lerici. For fun you can take the ferry (see listings); otherwise take bus L. The closest to La Spezia. Hot showers included and the sea is nearby, but prices are stiff: L7000 per person plus L5000 per small tent, L7000 per large one. Before June or after Sept., phone for winter hours.

Restaurant da Sandro, via del Prione, 268. One of the best in La Spezia, with full meals L11,000-13,000. The cook recommends *trittico della casa,* pasta with seafood (L6000), and *coniglio alla cacciatore* or *al forno* (rabbit, both L5500). Wine L4000 per liter. Open Fri.-Wed. at noon and 7pm.

Il Sorbetto, via del Prione, 276, virtually next door to Sandro's. Top off a meal with the excellent ice cream here. Open Mon.-Sat. 9am-12:30pm and 3pm-evening.

Portovenere and Cinque Terre

A mosaic of multicolored homes and home to hundreds of cats, Portovenere is set on and among rocks—seemingly removed from the rest of the world. At the far end of the village lies the optically intriguing **Church of San Pirtro;** the black-and-white-striped facade appears from a distance to be an extension of the steps. While the zebralike marble sections were done in 1277, the original portion, containing polychrome marble paving, dates from the sixth century. To the right of the entrance lies a marvelous rocky cove, where Byron once departed for a swim to Lerici.

Portovenere has no train station but is easily accessible from La Spezia (see La Spezia bus and ferry listings). The tiny **Pro Loco** (tourist office), p. Basteri (tel. 90 06 91), is in the center of town near the bus stops, and sells boat and bus tickets. (Open June-Sept. daily; Oct.-May Mon.-Sat.). The only reasonable lodging option in Portovenere is **Il Genio** (tel. 90 06 11; singles with bath L30,000, doubles with bath L45,500), but cheaper rooms are available in La Spezia.

The islands **Tino, Tinetto,** and **Palmaria,** famed for its **Grotta Azzurra,** are just offshore. To visit, take a ferry from La Spezia (see La Spezia Practical Information), rather than pay the L15,000 for a boat. From the docks, ferries also run to Monterosso and Verazza in the Clinque Terre area. Seasonal boats to Lerici are available through Società battellieri del golfo dei peori at the center of town one or two times per day in season (**In Tur** L10,000).

The **Cinque Terre** (Five Lands) are five villages: Monterosso (the farthest from La Spezia), Vernazza, Corniglia, Manarola, and Riomaggiore (the nearest). All perched on the rocky coast north of La Spezia, they are famous for their fine wine and picturesque surroundings. The best way to visit is by a combination of train and foot. **Monterosso** is 20 minutes from La Spezia on the local train (25 per day). The **Pro Loco,** via Fegina, 38 (tel. 81 75 06), below the train station, operates an accommodations service and a currency exchange, and will give you a free map of the coast. (Open April-Oct. Mon.-Sat. 10am-noon and 5-7pm, Sun. 10am-noon.)

Monterosso is the largest and most crowded of the five villages. The **Convento dei Cappuccini** stands on a hill between the two halves of town and houses an interesting, moving *Crucifixion* by a student of van Dyck. The southern half of town has more allure, with a free beach at the extreme southern end of the cove. Boats may be rented here for L10,000-12,000 per hour. From the town castle, you can enjoy a marvelous view. A 1½-hour hike along a narrow goat path amid splendid vineyards and olive groves brings you to **Vernazza,** perched in its entirety on a rock jutting into the sea. This village proves the old adage that some of the best things come small. **Corniglia** (a 1½-hr. uphill walk from Vernazza), though set high up on a cliff for the most part, still manages to have a long, pebbly beach. Above the beach, a wide trail leads you to **Manarola** (1 hr.), with its colorful ochre houses that hug the rockface on which they are perched. These trails offer magnificent peeks at the jagged coast and staggeringly terraced hillsides. They are much more interesting than the overrated and overcrowded **via Dell' Amore** between Manarola and **Riomaggiore** (15 min.). Along with Monterosso, the latter is the most touristed of the group, and neither of the two really measures up to their three less-frequented counterparts.

Camping in the Cinque Terre area itself is impossible. Your best option is nearby **La Mammola** (tel. 81 63 87); get off the train at Delva Merina, somewhat north of Manterosso, and look for the Arenelle section of town. In Levanto, try **Cinque Terre** (tel. 80 04 49), in the Busco section of town (open March-Oct.)

Piedmont (Piemonte)

If Jane Austen had been Italian, she would most certainly have come from Piedmont. From the elegant streets of Turin to the perfectly manicured vineyards of Asti, the entire region is as refined as nineteenth-century English prose. Behind its austere facade, however, Piedmont bubbles in a political cauldron. It is the mecca of the Unione Monarchica, which seeks to reinstate a national monarchy, and of the dialectically opposed Red Brigades, whose violent extremism grew out of the slums of Turin.

The area can be roughly divided into three zones: the Alpine, with the two stellar peaks of Monviso and Gran Paradiso; the Pianura, the beginning of the fertile Po Valley, encompassing Turin, the region's capital; and the hilly havens north and south of the Po. If you are a mountain lover, the majestic Italian Alps are more economical than their crowded Swiss and French counterparts. Piedmont is also home to many medieval towns and castles, harkening back to the times of feudal sieges and gala processions. While making your way from drawbridge to drawbridge, be sure to sample some of the famous wines of Italy. Many castles in the Monferrato area (near Turin) have their own vineyards and wine cellars. Bacchus himself would have reveled in the offerings here.

Turin (Torino)

It is hard to believe that an Italian city could give such a convincing semblance of peace and organization. Crafty urban planners have been at work here; just beyond the train station, cars drive in a neat circle around the exquisitely manicured *piazza Carlo Felice.* On the putting-green grass you will find benches filled with chic people reading their morning *La Stampa* (and police who will demand to see your passport if they catch you eating your ice cream on the grass). France has several times occupied, annexed, and "liberated" the region, leaving its mark on the capital's architecture and lifestyle. The porticos along via Roma shelter fancy shops selling silks and antiques and cafes offering rich desserts and tasty sandwiches. Indeed, the part of Turin you're likely to see is cultured and courteous. However, it cannot be an accident that the train station sends you out facing north. Employees of the Fiat auto company, a bastion in Turin live and work in the south end, a giant modern slum with an ironically pretty name: Mirafiori, birthplace of the Red Brigades. These radical crimson troopers are part of the same legacy of French revolutionary spirit that established Turin as the intellectual and moral fountainhead of Italian political unification in the eighteenth and nineteenth centuries. This turbulent Turin, the side that makes the city a capital of Italian extremism, is something you may not detect while admiring the elegant heart of the town, but will find easy to fathom if you've seen its other face.

Orientation and Practical Information

Turin lies on a broad plain on the left bank of the river Po, surrounded by the Alps on three sides. **Stazione Porta Nuova,** in the heart of the city, is the best place to disembark, as **Stazione Porta Susa,** the stop before Porta Nuova when coming from Milan, will leave you on the outskirts of town. Turin is an Italian rarity in that its streets meet at right angles. The feeling of assurance that this can provide is not to be underestimated; it's a cinch to get around either by bus or on foot. The EPT map is easy to read. The three main streets are **corso Vittorio Emanuele II,** running past the station to the river; the elegant **via Roma,** housing the principal sights and running north through p. San Carlo and p. Castello; and **via Garibaldi,** stretching from **piazza Castello** to **piazza Statuto.**

EPT: Via Roma, 226 (tel. 53 51 81), under the left arcade on p. San Carlo. Up-to-date listings of museum hours. Open Mon.-Fri. 9am-noon and 3-7pm, Sat. 9am-noon. The smaller office at the **Porta Nuova** train station (tel. 53 13 27) has longer hours but isn't as well stocked with maps and the like; however, English is spoken. Both will help you find a room free of charge.

Informa Giovani: Via Assarotti, 2 (tel. 57 65 35 76), off via Garibaldi, between p. Castello and Porta Susa. From feminist groups to flea markets to fortune tellers, they will show you dynamism with a vengeance. Youth hostel membership, ISIC, and BIJE tickets. The *Torino Giovani* guide is available in English, Italian, French, and German. English spoken. Open Wed.-Mon. 10:30am-6:30pm.

Centro Turistico Studentesco: Via Alfieri, 17 (tel. 53 59 66), past the post office on a street perpendicular to via Roma off p. San Carlo. Offers student (ages under 26) travel information and discount rail and air tickets. Exceedingly helpful. English spoken. Open 9:30am-12:30pm and 3-6:30pm, Sat. 9:30am-12:30pm.

Transalpino Representative: Franco Rosso Italia, via Roma, 69 (tel. 51 13 37). Air, sea, and land tickets of all types. English spoken. Open Tues.-Sat. 9am-12:30pm and 2:30-7pm.

Consulates: U.S., via Pomba, 23 (tel. 51 74 37), parallel to via Roma, 3 streets away.

Currency Exchange: The Ufficio Informazioni, at the railroad station. Decent rates. L3000 per traveler's check and L500 per bill exchanged. Open daily 7am-8:30pm.

American Express: Malan Viaggi, via Accademia delle Scienze, 1 (tel. 51 38 41), off p. Castello. Even if you have no AmEx card, any mail sent to you at this address will be handed over with little hassle or cost. English spoken. Car rental. Budget travel information. Britrail, Interrail, and air and sea travel. Open Mon.-Fri. 9am-12:45pm and 3-7pm, Sat. 9am-12:30pm.

VISA: Banca d'America e d'Italia, via dell'Arcivescovado, 7 (tel. 554 31). Open Mon.-Fri. 8:30am-1:30pm and 2:45-3:45pm.

Post Office: Via Alfieri, 10 (tel. 54 70 97), off p. San Carlo. Telex and telegram service. Open Mon.-Fri. 8:15am-2:20pm, Sat. 8:15am-1pm. Also at the **Porta Nuova** station. Open Mon.-Sat. 8:10am-7:20pm. **Postal code:** 10100.

Telephones: ASST, via Arsenale, 13, off via S. Teresa, around the corner from the post office. Open 24 hours. **SIP,** at the Porta Nuova station. Open daily 8am-9:30pm. Gettoni-operated phones available 24 hours at via Roma, 18. **Telephone code:** 011.

Airport: Caselle Airport, Tel. 577 83 61 6am-midnight; 577 81 midnight-6am. Flights to London, Paris, Brussels, and Frankfurt. Take a bus from the ATIV agency on corso Siccardi, 6, at via Cernaia (5:15am-11:15pm every 45 min., L2600).

Train Stations: Porta Nuova, Tel. 51 75 51 2am-11pm. The largest and most convenient. All trains from Turin originate here. To Milan (every hr., 1¾ hr., L7800), Venice (every 2 hr., 4½ hr., L20,700), Genoa (every hour, 2 hr., L8300), Aosta (every 2 hr., 2-3 hr., L6400), and Rome (every 2 hr., 9-11 hr., L32,800). **Porta Susa** and **Dora** are the other main stations, though they provide less train service and are rather inconvenient.

Bus Station: Autostazione Terminal Bus, corso Inghilterra, 3 (tel. 44 25 25). Take bus #60 from porto Nuova to the station. Or pick up outgoing buses at **Porta Susa Viaggi,** p. XVIII Dicembre, 5 (tel. 553 74), under the arcade opposite the station. Buses serve ski resorts, the Riviera, and the western valleys of Susa and Pinerolo. Service is fast and frequent to Courmayeur (8 per day, 3 hr., L10,000), Aosta (15 per day, 2 hr., L7800), Chamonix (3 per day, 3½ hr., L22,500), Milan (15 per day, 2 hr., one way L10,500, round-trip L17,500), and Geneva (L45,000). **Eurolines** leave only from the central terminal to London (1-3 per week, 22 hr., L137,000) and Paris (1-3 per week, 13 hr., L81,000).

City Buses: Tickets cost L700 and must be bought before boarding the bus—available at *tabacchi.* The system is easy to navigate but a map is helpful—available at most terminal offices. Bus #4 runs north-south on via XX Settembre parallel to via Roma. Bus #1 connects Porta Nuova to Porta Susa.

Taxi: Tel. 57 37, 57 30, 57 44, or 57 48. L3000 plus L800 per km.

Car Rental: Hertz, at the American Express office. **Avis,** at Stazione Porta Nuova.

Bicycle Rental: At via Lagrange, 12 (tel. 57 65 36 53), just off via Roma. The city of Turin loans bicycles here at no charge. For the addresses of dozens of other bike outlets, contact Informa Giovani or the EPT.

Lost Property: Ufficio Oggetti Smarriti, via Corte d'Appello, 1 (tel. 576 51).

English Bookstore: The British Bookstore, Libreria Internazionale Luxembourg, via Accademia delle Scienze, 7 (tel. 53 20 07), across from palazzo Carignano. A wide selection of French, English, Italian, and American titles. Open Mon.-Sat. 9am-12:30pm and 3-7:30pm.

Laundromat: Alba, via S. Secondo, 1 (tel. 51 73 07).

Swimming Pool: Piscina Comunale Statio Civile, corso G. Ferraris, 294 (tel. 32 25 38). Take bus #41 from corso V. Emanuele near the station. Open Sat.-Sun. 10am-12:30pm.

Day Hotel: Albergo Diurno (tel. 54 78 34), in Porto Nuova. Clean and elegant, but expensive. Showers and baths L5000, both with towels. Toilet L1000. Open daily 7am-8pm.

Hospital: Mauriziano Umberto, largo Turati, 62 (tel. 508 01).

Ambulance: Tel. 57 47.

Police: Questura, corso Vinzaglia (tel. 558 81).

Accommodations and Camping

Hotel accommodations abound but tend to reflect Turin's role as a leading commercial and university city. Prices can be steep, even for purely functional rooms. Since cheap places fill up, it is best to call in advance. Some shelter students, others house the thousands of southern Italians who come to Turin in search of employment. The newly renovated youth hostel is probably your best bet for cleanliness and facilities. Since Turin does not cater primarily to tourists, accommodations are actually easier to find in summer than during the rest of the year.

Ostello Torino, via Alby, 1 (tel. 68 37 38), a small street off via Gatti. Take bus #52 from Stazione Porta Nuova. Get off at p. Crimea, the 2nd stop after crossing the river Po. Located in a hilly residential neighborhood dotted with art nouveau mansions. Contemporary, clean, and comfortable. Most rooms with 4 beds. Members only, L10,000. Sheets and breakfast included. Meals L7000. Strict daytime lockout 9am-6pm. Curfew 11:30pm. Hostel cards for sale.

Locanda Studium, via Carlo Alberto, 47 (tel. 51 53 07), 3 blocks east of via Roma. The cheapest place to stay downtown. Nothing spectacular. Small bathrooms. Tidy, though, and full of students. Singles L16,000. Doubles L22,000. This place is affiliated with **Pensione Alfieri,** via Pomba, 7 (tel. 53 15 02). Better bathrooms, concerned owners, and cheaper. Singles L13,000. Doubles L19,000. Breakfast included.

Casa Marano Dello Studente, via Po, 27 (tel. 839 75 11). Spic-and-span, spacious doubles off a quiet courtyard. Men only. L10,000 per person. Sheets included. Showers L2000.

Pensione Roma, via Roma, 305 (tel. 51 91 13), not to be confused with the Hotel Roma in the nearby p. Carlo Felice. Lots of room, excellent location, and an eclectic decor of hardwood floors, high ceilings, marble stairwells, and Mickey Mouse posters. Singles L20,000. Doubles L28,000. Triples and quads L13,000 per bed. Showers included.

Pensione Lagrange, p. Lagrange, 1 (tel. 53 88 61), near the train station. Convenient, hospitable, and spotless. All rooms with telephone and small bathroom, most with shower. Often full, so be sure to call ahead. Singles L27,500. Doubles L49,000. Triples and quints L18,000 per person. Management might give you a L5000 discount if you stay for a few days. Breakfast L2500, lunch and dinner L10,000.

Alloggio Vanchiglia, via Vanchiglia, 2 (tel. 88 24 17), down the street from Hotel Verdi, towards p. V. Veneto. Only the prices are extraordinary. Singles L17,000. Doubles L22,000. Showers included. Call ahead.

Albergo Nuova Casa, corso Vittorio Emanuele, 67 (tel. 54 26 49), to the left of the train station. Plush red carpet in the hall and polished wood floors in the rooms. Singles L26,000. Doubles L33,000, with bath L42,000.

Camping: Campeggio Riviera sul Po, corso Moncalieri, 422 (tel. 63 87 06), on the Po River. Take bus #67. **Campeggio Villa Rey,** strada superiore Val S. Martino, 27 (tel. 87 86 70). Open mid-June to early October. Both L2500 per person, L2000 per tent.

Food

Piedmontese cuisine is a sophisticated combination of hearty Italian regional cooking and elegant French garnishings. Try *agnolotti* (ravioli stuffed with lamb and cabbage), *bagna cauda* (a wintertime dip made of garlic, anchovies, and spices fried in oil), and *bolliti misti* (steamed meats served plain or with a fine parsley sauce). For dessert, try *torta di nocciole* (hazelnut cake) and *bignole* (cream-puffs). During carnival time in February, indulge in the sinfully delicious fried sweets called *bugie* (literally, little lies). Even those not given to the demands of a sweet tooth will delight in Turin's famous chocolates, the delicate *gianduiotti.*

Turin serves delicious native pastries, including the obscenely rich *Bocca di Leone,* a donut filled with whipped cream or chocolate (about L2000). You can try them all at **Cossolo il Pasticciere,** via Roma, 68; via Gramsci, 1; and via Garibaldi, 9. Their *sospiri* (chocolate rum pastries) are as light as air and almost as cheap (L1000). Revel also in the white caps worn behind the counter here, as well as in most Turin *pasticcerie.* (Open Wed.-Mon. 7:30am-12:30pm and 2:30-11pm.)

Several trendy *gelaterie* can be found along the near side of p. Castello coming from the station. Try the spiffy **Barblù** (open Tues.-Sun. 7am-2am) or **Ra Palino** (open Tues.-Sat. 2:10-6:30pm), where you can try the bizarre flower flavors *rosa* and *viola.*

Elegant bakeries, pastry shops, produce stores, and delicatessens line the segment of **via Lagrange** that runs parallel to via Roma. More riotous and less refined is the **open-air market** at p. della Reppubblica (open Mon.-Fri. 8am-1pm). On Saturday (8am-6pm), a cornucopia of non-edibles is sold here—everything from baskets to underwear.

Quality and low prices are best combined in restaurants around the university.

Around Piazza Castello

If you want to stroll and sample assorted tidbits, try **via Garibaldi,** free of cars and lined with benches and flower beds.

Ristorante Taverna Fiorentina, via Palazzo di Città, 6 (tel. 54 24 12), just off p. Castello. Small, family-run restaurant frequented by locals. Try the *asparagi alla Bismark.* Plate of the day L5000-8000. Open Aug.-June Sun.-Fri. noon-3pm and 7-10pm.

Trattoria Amelia, via Mercanti, 6 (tel. 51 84 78), off via Garibaldi. A homey *trattoria* right in the center of town. Run by a friendly mother and son with family-style cooking. Drab interior. *Menù turistico* L10,000. Open Sun.-Fri. noon-2:30pm and 6:30-10pm.

La Grangia, via Garibaldi, 19, near via San Francesco d'Assisi. A decent self-service joint. You can eat outside. *Menù* L8,000. Open mid-Aug. to July Mon.-Sat. 8am-8pm.

Ristorante Self-Service, via Santa Teresa, 16, a street off of p. San Carlo. *Primi* L1800-2200, *secondi* L2200-2500, wine L600. Cover L400. A hub of office workers and students. Open Mon.-Sat. for lunch.

Feng Dian, via Garibaldi, 17 (tel. 54 45 22). Take-out. Wonton L2000, Cantonese rice L3500. Open Mon. and Wed.-Sat. 10:30am-2:30pm and 4-8:30pm, Sun. 3:30-8:30pm.

Near Porta Nuova

Trattoria Messico, via Bernadino Galliari, 8 (tel. 650 87 98), 2 streets north of via V. Emanuele II, near Porta Nuova. No sombreros here, just tourists afraid to stray too far from the station and locals willing to endure the orange walls. Try the terrific pasta or the *fettuccini al messico* (L4000). Wine L3000 per liter. Cover L1000. Open Mon.-Sat. noon-3pm and 7-11pm.

Cucina da Tonino, via B. Galliari, 16 (tel. 68 60 59), down the street from Messico. Bright, intimate, and full of the neighbors. Try *carne cruda in bella vista* (uncooked ground beef in a tangy lemon sauce)—another Turinese specialty—for L6500, and *rigatoni all'arrabiata* (literally "angry," actually with hot peppers) for L3500. Wine L2000 per liter. Cover L1000. Open Fri.-Wed. noon-2:30pm and 7-10pm.

Seven Up, via Andrea Doria, 4a, off via Roma. The cheap pizza will leave you and your wallet full. Margherita L3000, wine L1800 per liter, cover L500. Open Tues.-Sun. noon-2:30pm and 6:30pm-midnight.

Torino Uno, via Lagrange, 43/B (tel. 54 21 26), parallel to via Roma. Hot and dark self-service; but the mass-produced fare tastes fine. *Primi* L1600, *secondi* L2900, wine L1000 per ¼-liter. Open Mon.-Sat. 11:45am-2:30pm and 6:45-9pm.

Trattoria Toscana, via Rattazzi, 5, off corso V. Emanuele II, 2 blocks from p. Carlo Felice. (Not the only place of this name—see below.) Treat yourself. Try the deliciously spicy *spaghetti elettrici* (L4000) and their cold *rosatello* wine (L2700 per bottle). Full meals about L17,000. Cover L2000. Open Sun.-Fri.

Near the University

Trattoria Toscana, via Vanchiglia, 2 (tel. 87 69 14), off p. V. Veneto. A hit with locals. Occasionally the place rings with live banjo music. Small portions. Don't miss the *agnolotti alla piemontese* (L2500) or the *coniglio al forno* (baked rabbit). Open Sept.-July Sun.-Fri. noon-4:30pm and 7-9:30pm.

Mama Licia, via Mazzini, 50 (tel. 88 89 42), off p. Carlo Felice near the Po. A university hangout. The proprietor is an ex-boxer who travels abroad every year and displays his souvenirs on the walls. Open June-April Tues.-Sun. 12:45-2pm and 8:15-10pm.

University Mensa, via Principe Amadeo, 48, just past via Rosine. Edible cafeteria-quality food. Buy tickets (more than L13,000 each) at the Opera Universitana, corso Raffaello, 20, near Porta Nuova. Student ID required. Open Mon.-Fri. noon-2pm and 7-8:30pm.

Caffè Torino, via Roma, 204. A Turin tradition famous for its coffee and pastries. Bring a copy of *La Stampa* and buy a cappuccino at the bar (L1200). If you're in an extravagant mood, sit down and savor the solicitous service provided by tuxedo-clad waiters. Sprinkles the milk foam of their cappuccinos with a tradfemark insigna—an intricate fan.

Sights

It's hard to say which the Turinese revere more: the sooty secularism of the successful auto industry or the cultural clout of the Holy Shroud. Nonetheless, the city has much to offer those who are neither religious pilgrims nor auto buffs. Turin hosts a plethora of museums, architectural feats, and serene gardens. Ambitious types driven to "do" all of Turin's museums may be put off by the standard L3000 admission. All Italians are admitted gratis—you might see if you can go incognito.

Turin impresses visitors immediately with its dazzling **Porta Nuova** train station. Its name derives from the station's ornate *porta nuova* (new door), which was built in the nineteenth century to please Marie Christine, the young bride of Vittorio Amadeo I, upon her first trip to Italy. Designed by Alessandro Mazzuchetti in 1868, its playful geometrical patterns are the perfect complement to green piazza Carlo Felice, where benches are hard to come by any time of the day. Farther down via Roma, piazza San Carlo has all the formality and grandeur of a French *place.* The equestrian Duke Filiberto Emanuele sheathes his sword upon his pedestal at the center of this perfect rectangle. The square is elegantly complemented by its seventeenth-century buildings and by two baroque structures, the **Churches of Santa Cristina** and **San Carlo,** both designed by Filippo Juvara, one of the two great architects who designed Turin's most beautiful buildings.

Farther along, via Roma ends in **piazza Castello,** the historic center of the city, dominated by the imposing **Madama Palace** (so called because the widow of Vittorio Amadeo I, "Madama Reale," Marie Christine of France, lived here; natives often refer to it as the Palazzo Reale, however, which is a bit confusing as there is another royal palace in Turin). The colossal two-story pilasters and columns are set against a richly embellished facade designed by Filippo Juvara, creating a calm beauty in a bustling modern square. A majestic double staircase and vestibule lead from within the Madama Palace to the **Museo Civico di Arte Antica** (Museum of Ancient Art; tel. 57 65 39 18), which has a fine collection of medieval and Renaissance objets d'art. (Open Tues.-Sat. 9am-7pm, Sun. 10am-1pm and 2-7pm. Admission L3000, Fri. free.)

Though the city's glory has always risen with its political rather than pontifical leaders, unadulterated splendor blesses the **Church of San Lorenzo,** in p. Castello. The modest facade of the church (actually no facade at all, but the covering of another building) in no way prepares you for the church's opulent interior. Constructed between 1668 and 1680, it is Guarini's most original creation—just follow the moldings as they weave in and out of side chapels to see why. Or count the myriad columns, of every color, shape, size, and texture imaginable. The dome is the highlight, a multi-layered kaleidoscope of wishbones and starfish with ribs whirling about like the tails of flashing comets. Cross the courtyard to see the Royal Palace (the real Palazzo Reale; tel. 54 67 31), a rather plain building that the Princes of Savoy called home from 1660 to 1865. Its red and gold interior is a frigid Las Vegas— all the glitter with no gusto, but visit to see the state dining room, modeled after the Hall of Mirrors in Versailles, and the outstanding collection of Chinese porcelain vases. (Open Tues.-Sat. 9am-2pm. Admission L3000. Obligatory Italian tour 1 hr.) The **Cathedral of San Giovanni,** not to be missed, is down via San Giovanni. It housed Guarini's remarkable creation, the **Cappella della Santa Sindone** (Chapel of the Holy Shroud, 1668-1694). A black marble dome built of ribs in V-shaped patterns caps a somber rotunda that houses the funerary monuments of the House of Savoy as well as a silver vessel containing one of the strangest relics of Christianity, the **Holy Shroud of Turin.** This is the piece of linen in which Christ was supposedly wrapped for burial after his crucifixion. The outline of a crucified body is uncannily imprinted on the cloth. Although the claim that this is actually Christ's shroud cannot be proven, scientists have not been able to refute it. The shroud went on display for the first time in 45 years on August 26, 1978, amidst great fanfare (bullet-proof glass, electronic alarms, and special Church police with guns in hip holsters and silver crosses on their caps) to commemorate the four-hundredth anniversary of the shroud's arrival in Turin from Chambéry, France. Now an exact replica of the shroud, complete with an analysis of each fragment, lies in the sacristy. Before leaving the cathedral, don't miss Luigi Gagna's oil reproduction of Leonardo's *Last Supper* above the front door. Requested by King Carlo Felice when the original fresco started to deteriorate, the painting is considered the best copy of the Renaissance masterpiece. Turn onto via S. Tomaso from via Garibaldi. The cathedral is 2 blocks from this intersection. (Chapel open Tues.-Sat. 7:30am-noon and 3-5:30pm, Sun. 9:45am-noon. Free. Tel. 54 26 64.)

Via Accademia delle Scienze is lined with wonderful museums. The **Palazzo dell' Accademia delle Scienze,** a large black building on the corner, built as a Jesuit college by Guarini, today houses two excellent ones. Crammed into two floors to the right is the **Egyptian Museum,** via Accademia delle Scienze, 6 (tel. 53 75 81), with one of the finest collections in Europe, considered second only to that of the Cairo Museum. They have several copies of the Egyptian Books of the Dead and an intact sarcophagus of Vizier Ghemenef-Har-Bak, which stands out among the large sculptures and architectural fragments on the ground floor. You can't miss the colossal statue of the goddess Sakhmet with a lion's head. Upstairs is the fascinating Tomb of Kha, an architect from the fourteenth century B.C.E. who was buried with his wife Mirit. Theirs was one of the few tombs spared by thieves, so its contents have been wonderfully preserved: Food (bread and olives), furniture, clothing, and treasure—all the essentials for living it up in the after-life. (Museum open Tues.-Sun.

9am-2pm. Admission L3000.) The third floor houses the **Galleria Sabuada** (tel. 54 74 40). The wealth of non-Italian masters may surprise you. The Gallery is especially well known for its paintings by Flemish and Dutch artists: van Eyck's *St. Francis Receiving the Stigmata,* Memling's *Passion,* van Dyck's *Children of Charles I of England,* and Rembrandt's *Old Man Sleeping.* These are accompanied by a fine collection of Italian masterpieces, several Melozzo da Forlis, Domenico Venezianos, and an interesting Botticelli study for his *Birth of Venus.* The Sabauda also swells with mannerist and baroque paintings: There's a noteworthy Poussin, several Strozzis, and Volture's *Decapitation of John the Baptist.* (Open Tues.-Sun. 9am-2pm. Admission L3000.)

Art buffs will be pleased that there are many more museums, though many are "temporarily" closed for renovations. The **Museo di Antichità,** farther north at corso Regina Margherita, 105 (tel. 51 22 51), contains some beautiful Greek and Roman busts, a collection of Greek and Cypriot ceramics, and pieces from the treasury of Marengo. There are also several pre- and proto-historic materials from the Piedmont and Valle d'Aosta regions (closed in 1988). The **Museo Civico di Arte Antica** (Museum of Ancient Art; tel. 57 65 39 18), accessible from inside Palazzo Modano, has a fine collection of medieval and Renaissance objets d'art (closed in 1988). The **Galleria d'Arte Moderna,** via Magenta, 31 (tel. 48 83 43), off largo Vittorio Emanuele I, contains representative works of late nineteenth- and twentieth-century masters, including Chagall, Picasso, Courbet, and Renoir, in addition to works by local painters. These paintings hold the record for being "temporarily" inaccessible: three years.

For car enthusiasts and tire fanatics, Turin has a **Museo dell' Automobile Carlo Biscaretti di Ruffia,** corso Unità d'Italia, 40 (tel. 67 76 66), housed in a three-acre, ugly, modern building that makes the antique autos seem like toys from a prehistoric age. (Open Tues.-Sun. 9am-12:30pm and 3-7pm. Admission L4000.) True devotees of cylinders and pistons may also want to make the pilgrimage to Fiat's Mirafiori plant, on corso Unione Sovetica, past the Piscina Communale. Take bus #41 from corso V. Emanuele II, near the station. Tours are available on request.

Only rock climbers and Alpine fans will be interested in the **Museo Nazionale della Montagna "Duca degli Abruzzi"** (tel. 68 87 37), on the **Monte dei Cappuccini.** Besides a rather dry collection of rocks, photos of plants, and stuffed wild animals, there is an uplifting exhibit of mountain climbers in action on the second floor. (Open Tues.-Fri. 8:30am-7:15pm, Sat. 9am-12:30pm, Sun. 9am-2:45pm, and Mon. 9am-7:15pm. Admission L3000). Across from the Cathedral San Giovanni, you will find the **National Cinematograhic Museum,** piazza San Giovanni, 2 (tel. 51 03 70). You will probably be the only person in this treasure trove. The operator will give you a personal tour. Turin was the birthplace of Italian cinema; *Cabiria,* an important silent film, was shot on the banks of the Po. The museum maintains a fascinating library, and sometimes has screenings in the replica of an old theatre that has been constructed in the *palazzo.* (Museum closed in 1988.)

The **Museo Nazionale del Risorgimento Italiano,** via Accademia delle Scienze, 5 (tel. 51 11 47), is in the **Palazzo Carignano.** One of the great baroque palaces of Europe, it is a masterpiece of white marble relief and elegant statues, and in the nineteenth century housed the first Italian parliament and the birth cradle of Prince Vittorio Emanuele II. The museum today contains historic documents and other paraphernalia of national interest—go only if you have some knowledge of Italian or are prepared to fall asleep standing up. (Open Tues.-Sat. 9am-7pm, Sun. 9am-1pm. Admission L3000, Sun. free).

A walk along the banks of the Po through gorgeous gardens to the **Valentino Castle** is the cure-all for a culture-weary visitor to Turin. A medieval castle built in 1884 for a world exhibit, it looks like something from *Alice in Wonderland.* The outside world fades away as the guide takes you through room after room of enchanting objects—a sink in the shape of a castle, a throne that converts to a potty. Unfortunately, both the dungeons and towers are inaccessible.

Analogous to the Eiffel Tower or the Empire State Building, the **Mole Antonelliana,** via Montebello, 20 (tel. 839 83 14), a few blocks east of p. Castello, rises to its full height of 183m. It began, in a flurry of political intrigue, as a synagogue, but ended up as a Victorian eccentricity—a two-story Greek temple perched atop a giant glass pyramid and crowned by a lighthouse. Like so many curiosities, it has been adapted to accommodate tourists, and now has an observatory at the top. (Open Tues.-Sun. 9am-7pm. Admission L3000).

Entertainment

Turin comes alive with the sound of music, theater, and dancing shoes July 14-24 when the city invites international companies to the **Sere d'Estate** festival. For information and programs, contact the **Assesorato per la Cultura,** p. San Carlo, 161 (tel. 576 55 73). Prices run L2500-10,000. The tourist office has information on locations, schedules, and events. Classical music fans should visit Turin in September for **Settembre Musica,** a monthlong extravaganza of classical concerts given all over the city. There are two performances per day throughout the month and occasional seminars and lectures by composers. Contact the Assesorato for a program. Culture in a more formal context is available at the **Teatro Regio** in p. Castello. Concerts, ballets, and operas are staged here year-round and often draw audiences from as far away as Genoa and Milan. At least 50 tickets are offered for sale one hour before each performance. (Balcony seats about L25,000.) Buy tickets or get information from the **Biglietteria Teatro Regio,** p. Castello, 215 (tel. 54 80 00); open Tues.-Sat. 10am-noon and 3:30-7pm, Sun. 10am-noon and 2-6:30pm). The second and third weeks in April see the Mostra **Mercato dell' Antiquariato,** one of Italy's largest antique fairs, at impressive Palazzo Nervi. (Admission L5000.) Hop onto bus #73 from p. Crimea, near the youth hostel, and you'll ride past the wealthy villas in the hills of Turin along serpentine roads. The fair is theoretically held annually, but call the **Pro Mark** at 61 26 12 to be sure.

When he was a student in Turin, Erasmus said that magic pervaded the city. Ever since, Turin has cultivated its reputation as a center of the occult. Get your palm read at the Porta Pila or flirt with the world of black clothing and magenta walls at **Inferno,** via Carlo Alberto, 55 (tel. 54 56 53) and via Po, 14 (tel. 839 74 42), where local punks come to chat more than shop. (Both open Tues.-Fri. 9:30am-12:30pm and 3:30-7:30pm, Sat. 9:30am-12:30pm and 3-7pm, Mon. 3:30-7:30pm.) Visit the city's pink counter-culture at **Triangolo Rosa,** via Garibaldi, 13, a centrally-located gay nightclub. Or, if you want something totally down-to-earth, join the local football fans outside the TV shop on corso Vittorio Emanuele II, 65, in the evening to watch the daily game of *calcio.*

Near Turin

When Turin was beseiged by the French on September 6, 1706, Duke Vittorio Amadeo II made a pact with the Virgin Mary to build a magnificent cathedral in her honor if the city held out. Turin won, and the result was the magnificent **Basilica of Superaga** (tel. 89 00 83), erected on the summit of a hill 672m high. It showcases a neoclassical form with a deep porch and a magnificent dome supported by a high drum. From the spacious terrace, you can look out over the city, the Po Valley, and the Alps. Half the fun is getting there. Take tram #15 from via XX Settembre to Stazione Sassi and then board a small cable railway for a delightful 20-minute ride amid fragrant countryside. (Open daily 8am-12:30pm and 2:30-6:30pm. Free.)

Turin is about two hours from many excellent **ski slopes** in the Alps. An hour up the nearest mountain, alpine refuges beckon the budget traveler. **Sestriere** (2035m), 105km from Turin, has the most comprehensive and exclusive equipment with four cableways, 20 ski lifts, excellent runs, and a skating rink. Bus service connects the area with Oulx (on the Turin-Paris rail line) and Turin. There are 13 hotels, one *pensione,* and one camping area in town. A *Rifugio alpino* (alpine hut), called **Venini,** is located on the town's outskirts. For more information contact Sestriere's **tourist office,** piazzale G. Agnelli, 11 (tel. (0122) 760 45). Other nearby skiing areas include **Sauze D'Oulx** (1509m), only 85km from Turin. It has 23 hotels, two *pensioni,* one camping area, and **Ciao Paris,** an alpine refuge in the woods above town. The **tourist office** is at p. Assietta (tel. (0122) 850 09). **Alagna Valsesia** (1200m) is 156km from Turin and 138km from Milan. It has the second largest lift in the area, four hotels, one *pensione,* and one camping area. It is a bit more remote than the other resorts. Farther north is **Macugna** (1327m), 183km from Turin and 141km from Milan. It boasts the longest ski lift at 1540m, 16 hostels, five *pensioni,* and three moderately expensive hotels. Skiing is possible here from November to May. Ask about the snow conditions before hitting the slopes. All lifts are linked with Turin by bus and rail. For more information and a listing of accommodations, write the EPT tourist office in Turin, and request an *Annuario Alberghi* and their booklet *Orizzonte Piemonte: Dove la Neve è "Più Neve"* (Piedmont Horizon: Where the Snow is "More Snow").

Our *Let's Go* researcher/writers did not make it to Asti and the Monferrato Area in 1988. Prices and hours may have changed.

Asti and the Monferrato Area

Asti, more famous for its vineyards than medieval grandeur, is the home of many private wineries as well as the famous Italian sparkling wines *Asti Cinzano* and *Asti Spumante.* Italians claim that these sparkling wines rival the champagnes of France. Asti's economy depends mainly on agriculture—the production and processing of grapes for wine. There is an almost family spirit encouraged by the wineries and local people, many of whom work in the vineyards.

The lush fields of Asti, a province of Piedmont, are set in the rolling hills area known as Monferrato. Its boundaries are Turin to the north, Alessandria to the east, Cuneo to the west, and Savona to the south.

The Asti region also has a wealth of medieval castles and churches. There are so many in any direction you can come upon them peeking over the hills above the winding roadways. The tragic poet Vittorio Alfieri, whose name graces many a *piazza* and *via,* was an Asti native, as were the saints Don Bosco, Domenico Savio, and Giuseppe Cafasso. Paleontology storms ahead at **Cinaglio, Valleadona,** and **Villafranca d'Asti,** where remains of mastodons, rhinoceroses, and other huge land and sea animals have been found.

The modern name Asti is derived from the Roman Hasti Pompeia, which Pliny referred to as one of the most important Roman colonies in ancient Liguria. It was first recognized as a colony in 89 B.C.E. and became one of the richest and most powerful provinces in Italy by the thirteenth century. Asti then spent 500 years alternately under the reign of the House of Savoy and of Italians. Though the city was destroyed several times during its wars, the 120 thirteenth-century towers are preserved to this day.

The City of Asti

In Asti, modern and medieval architecture exist side by side. Stroll down narrow cobblestone streets lined with flowers, scurry between modern high-rises, or relax in the beautifully kept parks. Asti has a population of over 75,000, but it follows small-town rhythms. Asti is also a great launching point for daytrips to nearby vineyards and castles.

Orientation and Practical Information

Asti is easily accessible by rail from Turin (every ½ hr., 45 min., L3000) and Alessandria (every ½ hr., 20 min., L1800.) A direct train leaves daily for Milan (L15,900). The train station, in p. Stazione (tel. 503 11), is just a few short blocks south of the heart of the town, **piazza Vittorio Alfieri.** All of Asti's important sights are easily within walking distance. Piazza Vittorio Alfieri connects with **corso Vittorio Alfieri,** running east to west through the center of town. When touring the city it is best to walk down the side streets, using corso Alfieri as a guide (the *corso* itself is heavily trafficked and very noisy). Many of the hotels are located near the railroad station, with costlier ones near the center of town.

EPT: p. V. Alfieri, 34 (tel. 50 357), at the entrance to the *piazza,* coming from the train station. Help with accommodations and information on daytrips to wineries and castles. Pick up the *Guide to Asti and its Province.* English spoken. Open Mon.-Fri.

Currency Exchange: None at the train station, but the **Banco Popolare di Novara,** corso Alfieri, 313, down the *corso* in the direction of Torre Rossa, will change your money.

Post Office: corso Dante, 55 (tel. 532 82), off p. V. Alfieri. **Postal code:** 14100.

Telephones: Galleria Argenta, 6 (tel. 550 11), across from Upim on corso V. Alfieri toward the hospital. Open daily 8am-9:45pm. **Telephone code:** 0141.

Bus Station: p. Marconi (tel. 54 61), near the train station. To Castignole (4-5 per day, ½ hr., L1600) and Isola d'Asti (4-5 per day, 20 min., L1000).

Ambulance: Croce Verdi Asti, p. Libertà, 8 (tel. 53 345 or 55 154).

Hospital: Ospedale Civile, via Botallo, 4 (tel. 39 21).

Police: Questura, corso XXV Aprile, 5 (tel. 21 66 21).

Accommodations and Food

Across from the train station is **Albergo Cavour,** p. Marconi, 18 (tel. 50 22 23). Modern, stylish, and clean, Cavour is the best value in Asti. (Singles with bath L28,000. Doubles with bath L46,000. Open Sept.-July.) Near the town center, the **Hotel Reale,** p. V. Alfieri, 6 (tel. 502 40), rents singles for L25,000, with shower L35,000. Doubles are L34,200, with shower L48,700. English is spoken here. Another option is **Pensione Rosalba e Pizzeria,** corso Alfieri, 432 (tel. 532 82). Next to the church of Santa Caterina and the Red Tower, it is built in the ruins of a medieval structure. (Singles L20,000. Doubles L40,000. Open Sept.-July.) Pizza runs about L3000-6000. Cover is L1000. (*Pizzeria* open Sept.-July Wed.-Mon. 7pm-midnight.)

Camping in Asti is cheap, and, for once, the campground is actually within city limits. To reach **Campeggio Umberto Cagni** (tel. 27 12 38), turn onto via Aro from p. Alfieri, then take a left to via Valmanera, 78. Sites cost L2500 per person, ages 6 and under L1000, and L2000 per tent. (Open April-Sept.)

At the **Campo del Palio,** north of the station, which sees double-duty as a parking lot and a racetrack, everything from leather to lettuce to lampshades is sold (open Mon.-Sat. 8:30am-1pm. If one more *panino* will push you over the edge, walk across the Palio to **Trattoria Mercato Asti,** corso Enaudi, 50. A full meal with wine costs about L12,000. Try the *Milanese,* a fried, breaded steak (L5000). Open Mon.-Sat. noon-2pm and 7-9pm. **Pizzeria da Gianni,** corso Alfieri, 83, toward the hospital, has pizza from L3000, *primi* for L2500-3000, and *secondi* for L4000-8000. The house specialty is *lumache alla parigiana* (Parisian snails, L6000). (Cover L1500. Open Wed.-Mon.)

Sights

From p. Vitt. Alfieri, focal point of the town, a short walk west on via Garibaldi will take you to p. Santo Secondo, location of the eighteenth-century **Palazzo di Città** (City Hall) and the medieval **Collegiate Church of San Secondo,** patron saint of Asti. The church was built between the thirteenth and fifteenth centuries in the Romanesque-Gothic style. One block north and west on corso Alfieri, past p. Roma, lies **Palazzo Vittorio Alfieri,** birthplace and home of the poet. Today this palazzo houses the National Center for Alfierian Studies. Farther west on corso Alfieri stands the famous **Torre Rossa** (Red Tower), also known as the **Tower of S. Secondo,** because of the Saint's imprisonment there; Asti's oldest tower, it dates back to the time of Augustus. Adjoining the tower is the eighteenth-century elliptical **Church of Santa Caterina.** Visible to the south is the dome of the **Santuario della Madonna del Portone** (Sanctuary of the Madonna of the Gate). This splendid Byzantine church can be reached by going south on p. S. Caterina to via S. Anna.

North of corso Alfieri, the medieval street of via Massaia leads directly to piazza Cattedrale, dominated by the eclectic **Cathedral of Asti.** If you have time to visit only one sight in Asti, this is the one to see. Its size and grandeur make it one of the most noteworthy Gothic cathedrals in Piedmont. Most of the cathedral was built in the fourteenth century. Then, in the sixteenth and seventeenth centuries, local artists covered every inch of the walls with frescoes. Ancient Roman mosaics cover the floor of the altar. If you wander about for a few minutes, the caretaker might come out and give you a private tour of the cathedral, taking you behind the altar and explaining every fresco, stained-glass window, and even the history of the pews. If you offer him money for the tour, he will tell you to donate it to the church. Up via delle Valle from corso Alfieri (not far west of p. V. Alfieri) is the **Torre Troyana** (Troyana Tower). Built in the thirteenth century, it is the highest tower in Piedmont. Asti also has its own wine cellar, near p. V. Alfieri, which can be visited on Wednesdays. Ask at the EPT for tour information. The **Giardini Pubblici** (Public Gardens), between p. V. Alfieri and campo del Palio, are a wonderful place to relax. Go up to Asti's best gelateria **Dolce e Freddo,** corso Alfieri, 72, about a block east of the *piazza,* and get a cone (L1000, open daily 10am-11pm). At night, Asti's locals hang out along **corso Alfieri,** between corso Dante and via della Valle.

Seasonal Events

There are two main festivals in Asti. **Asti Teatro,** held during the first three weeks of July, is a series of theatrical productions from the medieval to the modern. Its location varies from production to production so be sure to cali for information. Reservations are suggested. (Teatro Alfieri, via L. Grandi, 16 (tel. 39 92 68). Open daily 3-7pm. Tickets L12,000, students and children L8000.) The theatrical hits the streets with the **Palio di Asti,** held annually on the third Sunday of September. The Palio recalls the town's liberation in 1200 C.E. with the man and mare alike draped in medieval garb. The procession commences at the cathedral, passes through the town, and ends at the campo del Palio where the horses are liberated of their costumes for the festival's racing finale. Asti's wine industry had some bad times in 1985 and 1986, when it was rumored that economy-minded vintners were pouring antifreeze into their bottles. In 1987 the industry rebounded, and Asti continues to court prospective buyers with annual Bacchanalias, each dedicated to a different fruit of the vine. Spring celebrates the **Vino Nuovo della lunadi Marzo,** during the last week of March in the Salone delle Manifestazione, p. V. Alfieri. In the fall, agricultural Asti revels in the **Douja d'or,** a month-long festival in September.

Near Asti

There are many vineyards and castles near Asti that are worth the trip. At p. Marconi you can catch a bus to **Castigliole,** home of a medieval castle and a wine cellar (*Enoteca;* open Tues.-Sun. 10am-noon and 2:30-5:30pm). Partake of a royal splurge for lunch or dinner, served at the castle Tues.-Sun. 12:30-2pm and 6:30-10pm (complete *menù* L20,000 and L30,000). (See Practical Information for bus information.)

Two other short bus rides away from Asti are **Isola d'Asti,** with its two medieval churches (the bus passes Isola d'Asti on its way to Castigliole), and **Canelli** (by train change at Nizza, L3600), which has many vineyards. If you are an epicure of medieval castles and fortresses, invest in a trip to enchanting **Alessandria,** about ½ hour by rail from Asti.

Valle d'Aosta

Our *Let's Go* researcher/writers did not make it to Valle d'Aosta in 1988. Prices and hours are likely to have changed.

Even with the opening of the Mont Blanc tunnel in 1965 and the subsequent development of a full-fledged tourist industry, the Valle d'Aosta remains relatively unspoiled and affordable. It offers unrivaled Alpine scenery, hiking, climbing, skiing, and valleys filled with hayfields and medieval castles.

Entering the Valle d'Aosta by cable car from Chamonix is dramatic but expensive (about $30). The car ride (hitching is easy here in summer) is also spectacular, even through the tunnel. The train only goes as far north as Pré-St.-Didier, but you can reach Courmayeur and other points with the thorough bus service. Although prices here are low for the Alps, they are astronomic for Italy. If you stick to the less-known villages, you will find lower prices. The Valle d'Aosta is an "autonomous region" within Italy, and many cities are officially bilingual because of their proximity to the French border.

The largest and most accessible towns in the area are Aosta and Courmayeur. Good for currency exchange and tourist offices, these Valdostan metropolises are best left to crowded tour buses.

Hiking

Hiking is the best way to see the region, but the weather vacillates at these altitudes. Trails will often bring you above 10,000 ft., so you must be adequately clothed. Hiking boots are cheaper in Milan and Turin than in Valle D'Aosta itself. Don't be tempted to wing it with sneakers or light shoes: Often the easiest trails have tricky stretches. You'll need a sweater, windbreaker, a pair of gloves (it's best to bring these from home), heavy woolen socks, and a compass. The best time of the year to hike is in July, August, and the first week of September, when all the snow has melted. The worst time is in April and May, when the thawing snow often causes avalanches. Unfortunately, not all the trails in this region are marked with numbers, so get yourself a reliable map—*Kompass* are the most accurate. Also beware of poisonous snakes, which are becoming more and more numerous as the birds that prey upon them fall victim to illegal hunting. Be especially careful on rocky tracts at low altitudes.

Rifugi alpini (mountain refuges) are not only for hikers and climbers. Some are only a cable car or a half-hour walk from main roads, and many offer half-*pensione* for L28,000-30,000. Public refuges (though generally empty shells) are free, and those run by caretakers cost L10,000-13,000 per night. For a complete list of alpine refuges and detailed information about all things mountainous, contact the **Club Alpino Italiano** in Aosta. (The L24,000 membership includes 30% refuge discounts and L5,000,000 insurance.)

Skiing

Valle d'Aosta is Italy's budgetary retort to Swiss Alpine opulence. Whistle a week away sliding down the slopes or hiking through the Nordic trails for the cost of a Swiss Army knife. While all 11 valleys are equipped with ski lifts, **Courmayeur,** with its vistas of Monte Bianco, and **Cervinia,** home of the Matterhorn, are the finest and most famous downhill ski resorts. Ski experts should head for the **Val d'Ayas** (especially **Champoluc**) and for **Val di Gressoney,** where the prices are lower and the skiing more challenging. Two of the best areas for cross-country skiing are **Cogne** in the Gran Paradiso National Park and **Brusson** in the Val d'Ayas. In winter, rooms are almost impossible to find and only affordable as part of a package deal. The whole valley participates in the *settimane bianche* (white weeks), whereby a week of skiing, room, and board is offered at a flat rate, lowest from December to April and February 14 to March 22. (Full board L260,000, half-board L240,000, bed and breakfast L190,000. All with ski passes.) In high season, prices are 10-20% higher. Make reservations by October for the winter *settimane bianche* through either the local tourist offices or hotels. For information, write to the **Ufficio Informazioni Turistiche,** p. Chanoux, 8, 11100 Aosta, and request their pamphlet *White Weeks Aosta Valley.*

In Cervinia and Courmayeur tank tops replace parkas for **summer skiing** on the nearby glacier (late June-late Sept.). In June, early July, and late September, it's possible to find room without reservations or the rigidity of *settimane bianche.* Summer package deals, similar to those available in winter, can be arranged through the Azienda in either Cervinia or Courmayeur.

Kayaking, rafting, and (for undaunted souls of Norse ancestry) swimming in the rivers of Valle d'Aosta provide inexpensive adrenalin highs. The most navigable rivers are the **Dora Baltea,** which runs through the valley; the **Dora di Veny,** which branches south from Courmayeur; the **Dora di Ferre,** which branches north from Courmayeur; the **Dora di Rhêmes,** which flows through the Val di Rhêmes; and the **Grand Eyvia,** which flows through the Val di Cogne. Seven kayaking lessons and a week of camping on the Dora Baltea cost L215,000 through the **Sevola di Canoa di Courmayeur,** Emanuele Pernasconi, Cas. Post., 11013 Courmayeur. (See Aosta Practical Information.) A daylong rafting expedition costs L63,000. (Courses offered June 29-Sept. 6.)

Aosta

Aosta is mercifully free of the saccharine-sweet chalets or sterile modern complexes that inundate other Alpine resorts. The city would be unremarkable anywhere else. The pyramid peaks of Emilius (3559m) or Becca di Nona (3142m) attest to Aosta's debt to geography. The magnificent surrounding glaciers seem to have frozen time, and the city's cobblestone streets echo the footsteps of Roman legionnaires. Aosta's prices, however, are ultra-modern.

Orientation and Practical Information

By train, Aosta is most easily reached from Turin (13 per day; 2 hr. on a *diretto,* 3 hr. on a *locale;* round-trip L10,000). From Milan change trains at Chivasso (5 hr., L11,200). Rome (L37,300), Genoa (L14,600), and Venice (L24,300) can be reached via either Milan or Turin. Buses are more reliable and more convenient, especially for excursions within Valle d'Aosta. (See Buses below for more information.)

Ufficio Informazioni Turistiche: p. Chanoux, 8 (tel. 356 55), in the center of town. Efficient and considerate, with an accommodations service that works miracles. Information on the entire region. Be sure to pick up a bus schedule. English spoken. Open June-Sept. 9am-1pm and 3-8pm; Oct.-May Mon.-Sat. 9am-1pm and 3-8pm, Sun. 9am-1pm; July 20-Aug. 23 Mon.-Sat. 9am-1pm and 3-9pm, Sun. 9am-1pm.

Club Alpino Italiano: p. Chanoux, 6 (tel. 401 94). Detailed hiking and skiing information. Ask about alpine refuges and Club Alpino membership. Open Mon. 9am-noon, Tues. 8-10pm, Fri. 9am-noon and 8-10pm.

Currency Exchange: Banco Valdostano A. Berard and C., p. Chanoux, 51. Handles Visa money withdrawals. Open Mon.-Fri. 8:20am-1:20pm and 2:50-3:50pm.

Post Office: p. Narbonne (tel. 36 22 87). Open Mon.-Fri. 8am-7pm, Sat. 8am-1:30pm. **Postal code:** 11100.

Telephones: SIP, av. Xavier de Maistre, 28A (tel. 43 997). Open Mon.-Sat. 8:45am-7:15pm, Sun. and holidays 10:30am-5:30pm. In the evenings, try **Albergo Europa,** p. Narbonne, 8 (tel. 437 73), where the buses stop. Open daily 9:30pm-8am. **Telephone code:** 0165.

Train Station: p. Manzetti (tel. 36 20 57).

Bus Station: p. Narbonne (tel. 36 20 27), in front of the train station. Buses to Turin (12 per day, 2½ hr.), Milan (4-6 per day, 4 hr.), Cogne (8 per day, 2 hr.). If you are heading for Cervinia, take the bus or train to Châtillon, where you will find 4 buses per day to Cervinia (2½ hr.; one way L5000, round-trip L7900). Also to Fenis (2 per day, 30 min., L1200), St. Pierre (2 per day, 15 min., one way L1200, round-trip L2000), Genoa (1 per day, 4½ hr., L21,300), and Courmayeur (8 per day, 1 hr., one way L2700, round-trip L4300). The EPT provides complete schedules.

Snow Conditions: Tel. 57 31, for Piedmont, Valle d'Aosta, and the French and Swiss Alps.

Hospital: viale Ginevra, 3 (tel. 30 41).

Ambulance: Tel. 30 42 11.

Police: Questura, viale G. Cartucci, 8 (tel. 32 14).

Accommodations

Although low-priced establishments are rare, you will have trouble finding a room only from late July through August and at Christmas and Easter.

Juventos, via Aubert, 33 (tel. 340 88), on the main strip. A lovely, clean establishment with an efficient proprietor. Conveniently located, but sometimes noisy. All rooms have bath. Singles L15,000. Doubles L25,000. In high season (Dec. 23-Jan. 7, Mar. 27-April 3, and July 7-Sept. 10: singles L18,000; doubles L32,000. 35% per additional bed. There is a jazzy sandwich shop and bar on the ground floor that is great for a morning cup of *cappuccino* (L900 at the bar, L11,000 at a table).

Mancuso, via Voison, 32 (tel. 345 26). From the station, take a left on via Carducci, then walk under the tracks. A fine, family-run hotel with clean and pleasant rooms, downright luxurious bathrooms, and a good restaurant downstairs (*menù turistico* L13,000). Singles L20,000. Doubles L28,000. July-Sept.: singles L24,000; doubles L40,000.

Monte Emilius, via G. Carrel, 9 (tel. 356 92), near the station. Worn rooms, but renovations scheduled. Singles L15,000. Doubles L30,000. Showers included. Breakfast L4000. *Menù* in the restaurant L13,000.

Camping: The cheapest is **Camping Ville D'Aosta** (tel. 328 78 or 58 24 79), in Les Fourches, 1km from Aosta. L3200 per person, L2500 per child, L3200 per tent. Open June-Sept. Also open for winter camping is **Camping Milleluci** (tel. 324 37), in Roppoz, also 1km from Aosta. Prices vary seasonally. L4200-4500 per person, L2800-3100 per child, L4000-4300 per tent.

Food

The economical strategy in Aosta is to get a snack or a one-dish meal at one of the inviting *brasserie* or *paninoteche* along via dei Tillier, via Aubert, via Porte Pretoriane, or via Croce di Città.

Your best choices for picnic provisions are the local cheeses, especially *toma valdostana* and *fontina,* although fresh brie is also available at a marginally lower price. Tuesday (7:30am-3pm) is market day at **piazza dei Mercati,** off via Torino. But the mass merchandizing supermarkets are easier on the wallet. The most convenient supermarket is the **Standa** on via Torino, between the train station and the bus depot. (Open Mon.-Sat. 8:30am-12:30pm and 3:30-7:30pm.)

Brasserie du Commerce, via dei Tillier, 10. Try their house omelette with ham, mushrooms, and cheese (L5000). Eat it in their leafy, lush garden. Fondue (L9000) requires reservations. Open Mon.-Sat. 10am-1pm.

Ristorante Pizzeria Ulisse, via Aubert, 58. Mediocre pizza, but a wide selection of firsts and seconds. *Primi* L6000. Full meals L12,000-14,000. Open Sat.-Thurs. noon-2pm and 7-11pm.

Grotta Azzurra, via Croce di Città, 97 (tel. 36 24 74). Go uphill where via dei Tillier merges with via Aubert. Locals tolerate fake wood paneling for the pizza, pasta, and full meals. Try the *gnocchi alla gorgonzola* (L4000). Pizza L3500-6000. Wine L2500 per ½-liter. Open Thurs.-Tues. noon-2pm and 7-11pm.

ACLI, via Salimbeni, 9, past p. della Repubblica off corso Battaglione. Green and hot like a jungle. Otherwise, a pleasant, cheap cafeteria in a workers' neighborhood. *Primi* with wine or mineral water L3500, *secondi* with drinks L4500. Full meal L6500. Open 11am-2:40pm and 6-9:30pm.

Rosticceria Angelo, via S. Anselmo, 19 (tel. 40 883), near the Porta Praetoria. Reasonably priced dishes L2000.

Sights

The ruins, which date from the time of Emperor Augustus (after whom the town was originally named Augusta Praetoria) have given Aosta its nickname of "Rome of the Alps." The original Roman walls still surround the old town. Double arches at the **Porta Praetoria** mark the eastern limits. **Via S. Anselmo,** part of the medieval city and today's main tourist drag, leads to the **Arch of Augustus.** The most impressive ruins are those of the **Roman theater,** including a reasonably intact backdrop. (Open in summer 9:30am-noon and 2:30-6:30pm; in off-season 9:30am-noon and 2-4:30pm.) From its medieval period, the town retains the **Church of St. Ursus,** constructed in an architecturally interesting mix of Gothic, Romanesque, and mountain chalet. The cloister dates from 1000 C.E. and is renowned for the carvings that cap its pillars, each of which represents a different scene from the story of Christendom. St. Ursus, who converted the first Christians in the Valle d'Aosta, is buried in the crypt below the altar. Make sure to continue on behind the church to the excavations of the fifth-century **Church of San Lorenzo,** where the archeological work has been tastefully displayed. (Open April-Sept. Mon.-Sat. 10am-noon and 3-5pm, Sun. 3-5:45pm.) The old **Roman Forum,** today a small park with a crypt, is off p. San Giovanni near the cathedral. (Open in summer daily 9:30am-noon and 2:30-6:30pm; in off-season 9:30am-noon and 2-4:30pm.)

Aosta is proud of the role it played in the World War II Resistance effort. You can hear the whole story from a solicitous gentleman at the **Istituto Storico della Resistenza nella Valle D'Aosta** at av. Xavier de Maistre, 22 (tel. 404 86; free).

Entertainment

October brings amusing grist for the postcard mill with the **Bataille de Reine** (Battle of the Queens). An ancient variation on mud-wrestling involving nymphs? No, it's none less than **cow fighting.** Every year, between 150 and 200 cows compete in an elimination tournament of head-butting. On the last Sunday of the month, a handful of mighty bovines are heralded queens of Aosta. Aosta's most ancient festival, the **Foire de Saint-Ours,** held both in the last weekend of January and during August's first week, does not have domestic animals on its guest list. But the 989th showing of the festival will invite traditional medievalist artists in tribute to the saint who brought Christianity into the valley. Aosta hosts two other important musical festivals. The **Rassegna Internazionale di Corali Polifoniche,** already in its 10th year, is a series of choral concerts performed at St. Ursus in late June and early July. Groups from both Italy and abroad participate. The **International Organ Festival** is held during the same period at the cathedral. Most events are free; the tourist office has a schedule.

During the evening, many people sip Asti while people-watching from their favorite bars in the center of town. Of the town's five cinemas, the most accessible is the **Teatro Giacosa,** via Xavier de Maistre, 15 (tel. 36 22 20), off p. Chanoux. If your boots need to boogie, try the **Meeting Club,** via Chambéry, 98A (tel. 453 33), past p. della Repubblica.

Near Aosta

You don't have to be a *Dungeons and Dragons* enthusiast to be enchanted by the castles in the valley southeast of Aosta. Go into a bookstore and leaf through the trilingual book *Castelli della Valle d'Aosta* (L5000) to choose your destination. The two finest are Fenis and Issogne. Both are accessible by bus from Aosta (see Aosta Practical Information). **Fenis** (tel. (0165) 76 42 63) may be a typical Baldostem castle, but it looks like a toy-castle with its double crenelated walls and variously shaped turrets. Built by a feudal family in 1340, the castle was used both as living quarters and as a fortress. (Open March-Nov. Wed.-Mon. 9:30am-noon and 2-5:30pm; Dec.-Feb. 9:30-11:30am and 2-4pm. Admission L2000.) Farther down the valley, 1km from Verres on the Aosta-Turin train line, at **Issogne** (tel. (0125) 92 93 73), is one of the most beautiful fortresses in northern Italy. Built in 1480 by the Lord of Verres, Giorgio de Chalant, the castle is especially famous for its charming courtyard, which still contains original fifteenth-century frescoes. On the upper floors you can visit the seigneurial apartments, which house tapestries and furniture. (Open March-Nov. Tues.-Sun. 9:30am-noon and 2-5:30pm; Dec.-Feb. 9:30-11:30am and 2-4pm.)

Two castles closer to Aosta (15 min. by bus on the Aosta-Courmayeur route; L1200) are **Saint-Pierre,** housing a naturalist museum (open May-Sept. Wed.-Mon. 9am-noon and 3-7pm; admission L2000, children L1000) and **Castle Sarriod de La Tour,** a five-minute walk across the road from St.-Pierre. The Sarriod castle contains an archeological exhibit on ancient Aosta and the surrounding valley (open May-Oct. Tues.-Sun. 9:30am-noon and 3-7pm; admission L2000).

The Valleys

For centuries, folk have been drawn to this region of emerald rivers and fecund valleys. The region offers a wealth of hiking, skiing, and picnicking sites. Cutting northward from the city, the Valle del Gran San Bernardo, home to the St. Bernard dogs immortalized in countless Walt Disney movies, and the **Valtournenche,** crowned by the spectacular Matterhorn, hem the lower edges of the Swiss Alps. Bargain-basement prices reign along the **Val d'Ayas** and neighboring **Val di Gressoney,** where a new lift complex has opened on the powdery slopes. Farther southwest on the **Val di Cogne,** compasses and battered jeans beat out lift tickets and slinky ski suits.

Valle del Gran San Bernardo

The Great **St. Bernard Valley** (2472m) links the Aosta valley with Switzerland, ending at Martigny. This pass is legendary for its **Hospice of St. Bernard,** where monks once ministered to pilgrims and mountaineers in distress. The hospice and the rescuing St. Bernard dogs have become this region's symbol. The **Festa dei Pastorelli e Bataille des Reine,** held on the third Sunday in August, is a scaled-down version of Aosta's cow contests. **Entroubles,** the valley's largest town, has a grand total of 495 inhabitants. Ski facilities are equally sparse: 13 downhill runs scattered along the valley and 7km of cross-country tracks around each town. In **Saint-Oyen,** the **Mont Velan** (tel. 782 07) offers singles for L13,000 and doubles for L26,000. **Des Alpes,** in Saint-Rhemy, charges L15,000 for singles and L30,000 for doubles. Outdoors folks should try **Camping Pineta** (tel. 781 13 or 781 14), in Saint-Oyen, which rents sites for L3000 per adult, L2500 per child, and L3000 per tent. There are no Alpine refuges in the area.

For more information, contact the tourist office in Aosta or call the Saint-Oyen/Saint-Rhemy **ski-lift office** (tel. 78 09 13 or 78 09 28). The valley is in the Aosta telephone area and uses the **telephone code** 0165.

A Great St. Bernard Tunnel was opened in 1964; the challenges once faced by travelers are today only a memory. A bus leaves Aosta daily at 8am and returns at 5:30pm (round-trip L13,000). Remember to bring your passport since the hospice is just on the other side of the Swiss border.

Valtournenche

Valtournenche is the Valdostan equivalent of Aspen, prices and all. **Cervinia-Breuil,** at the head of the valley, provides the backdrop for the mighty **Matterhorn** (in Italian, Cervino). The smaller towns that line the valley lack the glitz but maintain the profit margin. There is a cable car from Cervinia-Breuil up to **Testa Grigia** (3840m) on the Swiss border; the view is cosmic. An extraordinarily well-traveled path marks a three-hour trek up to the **Colle Superiore delle Cime Bianche** (2982m), where you can glance over the gorgeous Valle d'Ayas to the east. If you don't want to go that far, the same road takes you to **Lake Goillet,** with its eerie green color and the impressive Matterhorn in the background, in an hour and a half.

Skiing in Cervinia is prohibitively expensive unless included in the *settimane bianche* packages. **Leonardo Carrel** (tel. 94 90 77) offers the cheapest: half-board L287,000 (Dec. 14-22, Jan. 5-Feb. 7, and April 27 to the end of the season), L308,000 (Feb. 8-April 11), or L336,000 (Dec. 23-Jan. 4 and Easter). Six-day lift tickets are L124,000 year-round. Skis can be rented at many outlets; try **Top Ski** (tel. 94 93 43). The height of hedonism, summer skiing, is possible here.

Rent *rampichino* through the **Hotel President** (tel. 94 94 76). Even cosmopolitan Cervinia annually stages that pervasive contest of bovine might, the **Bataille de Reines,** held on the third Saturday in August.

You can try to beat Valdostan prices at **Albergo Serenella** (tel. 94 90 41). The management is impersonal, but the place is clean, and doubles are L43,000, with bath L46,000. The **Hotel Lac Bleu** (tel. 94 91 03), 2km out of town on the road to Valtournenche, is slightly less expensive with singles for L19,000 (off-season L16,000) and doubles for L45,000 (off-season L35,000). Also try **Hotel du Soleil** (tel. 94 95 20), which has a two-star rating and a few singles for L20,000 (off-season L16,000) and doubles for L35,000 (off-season L26,000). Roughing it pays off. **Camping Glair-Lago di Maen** charges L3100 per adult, L2500 per child, and L2800 per tent. (Open June 15-Sept. 15.) The 16 Alpine refuges in the area are a godsend for hikers. **Guide del Cerrino** (tel. 94 83 69) is at the summit of the cable car that goes up to Testa Grigorio. **Theodule** (tel. 94 94 00), is 30 minutes on foot and 10 minutes on skis from the cable car summit. (Open in winter from the 3rd week in Sept.) Both have a caretaking staff, so expect to pay L10,000-L13,000 per night, L28,000-L30,000 for half-*pensione.*

Life in Cervinia is expensive, so plan to picnic (the cheeses are wonderful). If you insist on restaurant fare, the best place is **Pizzeria Coppa Pan** (tel. 94 91 40; open Fri.-Wed.), at the head of the main street, with appetizing food and the best pizza in town (L4500-5500).

The **tourist office** can be phoned at 94 91 36 or 94 90 86. **Cervino Cableways** (tel. 94 84 24 or 94 84 21) also provides skiing and transportation information. To contact the **Società Guide** (Alpine guides' society), call 94 81 69 or 94 87 44. **Marian Tour Matterhorn,** p. Guido Rey (tel. 94 90 31 or 94 90 01), can arrange hotel bookings. Brevil Cervinia's **telephone code** is 0166.

Cervinia-Breuil is accessible by eight buses per day from Châtillon on the Aosta-Turin train line. From June 15 to September 15 and December-April, one to four direct buses arrive daily from p. Castello in Milan.

Val d'Ayas and Val di Gressoney

The less expensive ski resorts of Val d'Aosta lie in two valleys of powder snow to the east of the region: **Val d'Ayas,** overseen by the cities of Brusson and Champoluc, and **Val di Gressoney,** dominated by Gressony-St. Jean and Gressony-La Trinitè. Crisscrossed by downhill runs, **Champoluc** and **Gressoney** are now connected by the new lifts of the monolithic Monterosaski complex (Japanese sounding, but actually a catchy amalgam of "Monte Rosa Skiing"). **Brusson,** south of Champoluc, may be the best starting point for cross-country skiing.

Settimane bianche ski-packages in the area are offered at reasonable rates. The cheapest accommodations in Val d'Ayas are located in Saint Jacques, 5 minutes from Champoluc. The **Hermitage** (tel. 30 71 92) offers full board for L200,000 per week in high season (Feb. 2-March 22 and Easter) and L180,000 in low season. At **Casale** (tel. 30 76 68), a refuge in Saint Jacques, full-board is L190,000 per week and half-*pensione* is L165,000 per week. In Gressoney-La Trinitè, **Grizzetti** (tel. 35 52 19) offers the cheapest package at L210,000 for full board and L140,000 for half-board. In Gressoney-St. Jean, **Famiglia** (tel. 35 52 19) provides bed and breakfast for L91,000. White weeks in Brusson are slightly more expensive but will save cross-country *afficionados* the cost of daily commutes to the city's 45km of trails. Try **Croce Bianca** (tel. 30 03 48), which offers full board for L210,000 and half-board for L175,000. Seven-day ski passes for the entire Monterosaski area (including the 4 lifts around Brusson) are L88,000 in low season and L97,000 in high season.

Equipment and information can be obtained from **Luciano Fosson** (tel. 30 03 97). To rent skis in Brusson, go to **Frachey Sport** (tel. 30 71 65). Two trails (one 5km, the other 20km) begin from Gressoney-St. Jean; most ski trails become hiking paths in the summer. Rent hiking equipment from **Nando Laurent** (tel. 35 51 48). **Mountain bicycles** can be rented at **Sport "4"** (tel. 30 65 30), in Antagnod a few kilometers south of Champoluc on a local road, or at **David Sport** (tel. 36 61 24), in Gressoney-La Trinité.

On June 24, ethnic gear is paraded in all its splendor down the streets of Gressoney-St. Jean, in honor of the town's patron saint. In the middle of August, the costumes come out again—this time in honor of the tourists. Aosta's bovine sisters duke it out in Brusson's **Bataille de Reines,** held at the end of August. Not to fear—humans get their chance, too, in the **Coppa Consiglio Valle,** an international sporting event.

The least expensive hotel near Champoluc is the **Hermitage** (tel. 30 71 92), in Saint Jacques. In high season, singles run L12,000-15,000, with bath L15,000-18,000. Doubles are L22,000-25,000, with bath L25,000-30,000. In low season, singles cost L10,000-12,000, with bath L12,000-15,000. Doubles are L20,000, with bath L20,000-24,000. (Open Dec. 26-April and June 15-Aug.) In Brusson try **Aquila** (tel. 30 01 26), where singles are L17,000, doubles L34,000; in low season singles L15,000, doubles L30,000. (Open July-Sept. 10.) In Gressoney-St. Jean, **Famiglia** (tel. 35 52 19) offers the best deal: Singles L12,000. Doubles L20,000. (Open Dec. 20-Jan. 1 and June-Sept. 15.) Campers should try **Camping Deans** (tel. 30 02 97) in Brusson: L3500-4000 per adult, L2000-L3100 per child, and L3500-L4000 per tent. In Gressoney-St. Jean, try **Camping La Pineta** (tel. 35 53 70), where camping is L3200 per adult, L2600 per child, and L3500 per tent.

Of the 13 *rifugi Alpini* in the Ayas-Gressoney area only three are easily accessible. **Cassale** (tel. 30 76 68) is near Champoluc on the outskirts of Saint Jacques. (Open Dec.-April 4 and June 15-Sept.) Follow the Val di Gressoney road a few kilometers past Gressoney-La Trinité and take the *ovivia* (a sort of cable car) to Lago Gabiet. At the summit, walk over to the **Lys** refuge (tel. 36 60 57), 5 minutes away. (Open June 20-Sept. 15 daily; in off-season weekends only.) Or go a bit farther to **Gabiet** (tel. 36 62 46), 10 minutes away. (Open March-April and June 20-Sept. every weekend) All of the refuges are staffed, so expect to pay L10,000-13,000 per night and L28,000-30,000 for half-*pensione.*

There seems to be a **tourist office** in every hamlet in these two valleys (in Champoluc, tel. 30 71 13; in Brusson, tel. 30 02 40; in Gressoney-La Trinité, tel. 36 61 43; and in Gressoney-Saint Jean, tel. 35 51 85). The **Società Guide** can be reached through the **Casa delle Guide** (tel. 30 71 94) in Champoluc. In addition, the **Club Alpino Italiano** can be contacted in Gressoney-La Trinité through the **Studio Camisasca e Rial** (tel. 36 62 59). Tourist agencies in the area are **Evançon Vacances et Voyages** (tel. 30 76 48), in Champoluc, and **A. & A. Turismo e Viaggi,** p. Umberto (tel. 35 55 95), in Gressoney-Saint Jean. The **telephone code** for the entire area is 0125.

Reach Champoluc and Brusson by catching a bus from Aosta (6 per day, 2½ hr. to Brusson, 3 hr. to Champoluc). Or sacrifice convenience for speed and take the train to Verrès (about 20 min. on the Aosta-Turin line) and hop on the bus there (6 per day, 40 min. to Brusson, 1 hr. to Champoluc). From June 15 to September 14, a bus departs from p. Castello in Milan daily for the Val d'Ayas (3½ hr. to Brusson, 4 hr. to Champoluc).

Up among the glaciers, lifts and a 30-kilometer trail connect Champoluc to Gressoney, but along the asphalt Gressoney is serviced by buses (6 per day from Aosta, 2¼ hr.). These buses also pass through **Pont Saint Martin,** the train station nearest Gressoney, 30 minutes from Aosta on the Aosta-Turin line. From June 14 to September 16, daily buses depart from p. Castello in Milan for Gressoney (2 hr.).

Val di Cogne

Val di Cogne provides easy passage into the **Gran Paradiso National Park,** the natural highlight of the Valle d'Aosta. Originally part of the Savoy family's royal preserves, the park was given to the Italian state in 1919. It was dedicated as a park for the protection of Alpine flora and fauna, among which is the ibex, a mountain animal related to the deer, with beautiful ridged and arched horns. Chamois, often called the "kings of the alps," abound here as well.

In Cogne, 50km of **cross-country skiing** is the name of the game. Skis can be rented at several shops around town, including **Mon Sport** (tel. 743 95). Cross-country skiing, originally just a means of transportation instead of a form of entertainment, is now a popular winter sport. The big sporting event in town, though, is the **Marci Gran Paradiso,** a non-competitive, 45-kilometer foot race held on the first or second Sunday in February.

In Cogne, stay at the clean **Hotel Vallée de Cogne** (tel. 740 79) with singles for L21,500 (off-season L20,000 and doubles for L36,500. Also try **Hotel Alberta** (tel. 740 67), which rents singles with bath for L22,000 and doubles for L30,000, with bath L36,000 (off-season L24,000, with bath L30,000). The most accessible campgrounds near Cogne are in Valnontey, south of Cogne along a local road. Try **Camping Grand Paradiso** (tel. 741 05), which charges L2850 per adult, L2350 per child, and L2850 per tent. Another tactic to avoid expensive hotels is to grab the trail mix, and head for a refuge in the hills. To get to the nearest refuge from Valnontey, take the trail ("2" in a triangle) that climbs up to **Rifugio V. Sella.** This is a steep climb that takes about three hours. **Rifugio V. Sella** (2584m; open Easter and June-Sept.) is a fine refuge where you can get something to eat, spend the night, and admire gorgeous Alpine scenery. Expect to pay approximately L10,000-13,000 per night and L28,000-30,000 for half *pensione.* If you've left early enough in the morning (the 6:10am bus from Aosta) and feel fit, you might want to try the six-hour trek to **Eaux Rousses** in Valsavarenche, passing over the **Col Lauson** (3296m). It's steep, but the view from the top is extraordinary. Keep in mind that the last bus back to Aosta leaves Eaux Rousses at 5pm (July-Aug. only). Hitching is a reliable option here. If there is room (unlikely in high season), you may want to spend the night at the little **Hotel Col Lauson** (tel. 957 01), which is clean and cheap. (Singles L18,000. Doubles L36,000.) Since the food in the restaurant is especially good, try full *pensione* (L38,000).

The Società Guide operates under the guise of Cogne's **tourist office** (tel. 740 40). Seven or eight buses travel between Aosta and Cogne daily from 6am to 11pm.

Courmayeur

Courmayeur is a spruced-up mountain village set in a valley at the foot of **Monte Bianco** (Mont Blanc). On a clear day, the mountain's visage will inspire a rush of adrenalin and awe. The town has recently been turned into one of the world's newest ski capitals; the skiing is excellent, and the development profits the traveler—there are many new hotels, *pensioni,* and restaurants. All the cheap accommodations in this town are booked solid from mid-July until the end of August; reserve long beforehand.

Practical Information

Azienda di Soggiorno e Turismo: p. Monte Bianco (tel. 84 20 60), near the bus terminal. The young staff is often too swamped to regale you with local myths or give you tips on hot night spots, but they are very accommodating. English spoken. Open Mon.-Sat. 9am-12:30pm and 3-6:30pm, Sun. 9am-12:30pm.

Società Guide: p. Abbé Henry (tel. 84 20 64), in the Museo Alpino across from the church in vicolo della Chiesa. Find out everything you ever wanted to know about the Alps from a rugged staff. Get the multilingual **Mountain Huts Guide,** which lists all the refuges in the Valle d'Aosta.

Ski Club Monte Bianco: p. Monte Bianco (tel. 84 24 41), in the center of town.

Currency Exchange: p. Monte Bianco, 3 (tel. 84 13 97), in the travel agency that sells bus tickets. Open daily 7:45am-12:30pm and 2:30-7:30pm.

Post Office: p. Monte Bianco (tel. 84 20 41), behind the tourist office. Open Mon.-Fri. 8:10am-6:45pm and Sat. 8:10-11:45am. **Postal code:** 11013.

Telephone Office: p. Monte Bianco (tel. 84 32 13), next to the Mont Blanc Tour Operator. Open Mon.-Sat. 9am-12:30pm and 3-6:30pm, Sun. and holidays 9:30am-12:30pm. **Telephone code:** 0165.

Buses: First bus from Aosta 6:20am, last one back 8:35pm; one way L2700, round-trip L5200. Courmayeur is also linked by bus to other towns in the region: Turin (7 per day, L10,000), Milan (3 per day, L19,500), Chamonix (2 per day, L8000), and Geneva (2 per day, L20,500); service is frequently reduced in high season. **SAP** lines serve La Palud (in summer every 15 min., in winter every hr.; one way L1200, round-trip L2000; 15 min.) and La Thuile (via Prì St. Didier, 8 per day, L2600). Buy tickets at **Mont Blanc Tour Operator** or on the bus (after hours only).

Cable Cars and Ski-Lifts: Funivie Val Beny, strada Regionale, 47 (tel. 84 10 21), past via Roma toward Aosta. Lifts and cable cars up the mountains around Val Veny. **Funivie Monte Bianco,** La Palud (tel. 899 25). Cable cars and lifts right up to the French border at the foot of Monte Bianco. 6-day pass to both lifts L145,000 in high season, L123,000 in low season. 6-day pass valid for only the Courmayeur Cable Car, Dolonne Gondola Lift, and Val Veny Cable Car at Val Veny L67,000. 6-day pass valid for only the Monte Bianco and French Colle del Gigante facilities L100,000. 6-day pass for the Colle del Gigante lifts L45,000. Individual trips on Val Veny and Monte Bianco cable cars L10,000-23,000.

Bookstore: Libreria Buona Stampa, via Roma, 4 (tel. 84 31 34), past the church. Mountain guidebooks galore, some in English. Chat with the knowledgeable, multilingual staff. Open June-Sept. Fri.-Wed. 9am-12:30pm and 3-7:30pm.

Public Baths: In the *piazza* where the buses are parked. L1500, with towel and soap L2000. Toilets L100. Open daily 8am-8:30pm; in off-season 8am-7:30pm.

Medical Assistance: Call Dottore (Dr.) Bassi (tel. 84 24 55) for an ambulance to take you to the regional hospital.

Police: Ufficio Polizia di Frontiera di Monte Bianco (tel. 899 65) at Entrèves, 2km west of Courmayeur on the road towards Chamonix.

Accommodations

Only the early bird lands a nest from mid-July to the end of August. At other times, rooms abound in Courmayeur.

AGIP, strada Regionale, 72 (tel. 84 24 27), 1km north on via Roma. Part of a gas station and road motel franchise, but family-managed. Sterile and spotless. High season is Feb.-March, July-Aug., and major holidays. Singles L15,000 (off-season L13,000). Doubles L28,000 (off-season L25,000). Showers included. Breakfast L3500.

Bel Soggiorno, viale Monte Bianco, 63 (tel. 84 32 59), off p. Brocherel. Rooms right out of the *Sound of Music:* white-washed walls, pastel comforters, pine furniture. A quiet garden overlooking meadows and mountains. English spoken. Singles L18,000-20,000. Doubles L35,000-36,000. Showers included.

Petit Meublè, via Marguerita, 25 (tel. 84 24 26). Go left out of the main parking lot as you face the highway and pass under via Marguerita. A 5-min. walk takes you to this home of fluffy pillows and a rushing river. English spoken. Singles L23,000-25,000. Doubles L40,000-42,000. Showers included. Breakfast L4000. Restaurant serves fixed menus to smiling locals for L15,000. Open daily noon-3pm and 7:30-9:30pm.

Meublè Laurent, via Girconvallazione, 23 (tel. 84 17 97), about 2 blocks from p. Monte Bianco. Rooms and prices are good, but Bel Soggiorno and Petit Meublè win out in the post-card panorama contest. Singles L20,000. Doubles L35,000. Showers included. Breakfast L4000. Closed for 1 month after Easter.

Locanda Ferrato, via Roma, 86 (tel. 84 22 49), in the center of the city. Small bathrooms, creaky furniture. Gregarious staff. Showers of the obtrusive glass-cage variety; otherwise, showers on each floor included. Doubles L50,000 (off-season L40,000).

Camping: The nearest campground is about 6km from Courmayeur, snuggled between mountains near the church of Nôtre Dame, one of Valle d'Aosta's most moving medieval monuments. To get to **Camping Cai-Uget Monte Bianco** (tel. 892 15), take a bus headed for Val Veny and Nôtre Dame from Courmayeur (July-Sept.; one way L1200, round-trip L1800) and get off in front of the church. From the church, go left. L1500 per person, L2300 per tent. Open June 28-Sept. 6.

Alpine refuges: Of the 25 refuges in the area, only **Rifugio Torino Vecchio** (tel. 84 22 47) can be reached easily by cable car from La Palud (1 per hr.; 15 min.; one way L15,000, round-trip L20,000). A jaunt up the slope takes 2 hr. L10,000-13,000 per night, L28,000-30,000 for half-*pensione.*

Food

Even if you don't eat at the internationally renowned **Maison de Philippe** in Entrèves, you'll find the restaurant prices high. Eat at the establishments connected with the hotels—they're the cheapest. Expect to pay L10,000 or more for merely mediocre meals. Picnicking is the best alternative: Local cheeses are excellent (try the *fontina*) and *salumerie* (delicatessens) abound. At **Pastificio,** passagio del Angelo, 94, you'll find excellent cold cuts and *pâté* garnished with Alpine violets. Try their *torta di mele,* with apples and apricots, at L1300 per slice. (Closed for 2 weeks in July.) Wednesday from 8:30am to 2pm is market day. The buses that usually glut **piazza Stazione** are displaced by stalls selling produce and paraphernalia. Have someone prepare you *panini* (L1300) downtown at **Bar La Briciola,** via Roma, 3 (tel. 84 20 54), frequented by the city's youth and by every neat-looking veteran visitor under 45. Most of the inexpensive *pizzerie* and restaurants surround **piazzale Monte Bianco.** (Open Fri.-Wed. 7:30am-8:30pm.)

Le Vieux Pommier, p. Monte Bianco, 24 (tel. 84 22 81), commands a great view of the mountains and of all the Mercedes in Courmayeur's biggest parking lot. *Menù* is L18,000. (Open Tues.-Sun. noon-2pm and 7-9pm.) **Pizzeria du Tunnel,** via Circonual Lazione, 8 (tel. 84 17 05), is piney but cramped inside and pleasantly open on the patio. Pizza aromas spread all day (L4500-6500), and an a la carte meal runs about L16,000. (Open Thurs.-Tues. noon-3pm and 7pm-1am.) **La Boîte,** strada Margherita, 8 (tel. 84 37 96), past Le Pommier and under the highway, designs complex pizzas, such as the *4 stagione* (4 seasons; usually ham, artichokes, mushrooms, and olives; L6000). (Open daily noon-3pm and 7pm-midnight; in off-season Wed.-Mon.)

Sights

A town with Courmayeur's location has never needed to create beauty in man-made structures. If, however, you are in Courmayeur for the day, you might want to stop by the small **Museo Alpino,** p. Henry, 2 (tel. 84 20 64), across from the church in vicolo della Chiesa. The museum houses a collection of Alpine artifacts, including relics of famous mountain guides who were lost on the job. (Open Tues.-Sun. 9am-12:30pm and 3:30-6:30pm.)

Courmayeur is too chic for obscure folk festivals. The only notable celebration moos from nearby **La Thuile** during the traditional **Batailles des Reines,** another reverse tug-of-war between cows.

Skiing and Other Activities

For **winter skiing,** Courmayeur's glitter will cost you dearly. **Bel Soggiorno** offers a white week of full board for L315,000, half-board L266,000, B&B L154,000. Bed and breakfast is cheaper at **AGIP:** L115,000 (off-season L98,000). (See Accommodations.) **La Palud** is higher in elevation but lower in price; one hotel there, **La Quercia,** offers a week of half-board for L210,000. (See Near Courmayeur.) In Rhêmes-Nôtre Dame, the only moguls on the slopes are multimillionaires with their hot-shot pre-schoolers. **Hotel Galisia,** località Capoluago (tel. 96 10 00), offers a week of full board for L210,000 (off-season L192,000). Seven-day lift tickets are L42,000 (off-season L38,500). Contact **Pro Loco** (tel. 961 04), the local tourist office at the Hotel Grata Parei, for the lowdown on downhill fees. Approximately 6km from Courmayeur, Rhêmes-Nôtre Dame is connected only by occasional bus service in winter, so try hitchhiking.

Or forgo the crowds around the lifts altogether and enter the world of squirrels and icicles along 35km of **cross-country** trails. Downhill skis may be rented on the slopes, and cross-country skis at **Savoie Sport** (tel. 84 20 68), in Dolonne under the *autostrada* leading from Courmayeur proper.

In the **summer** (mid-June to mid-July and mid-Aug. to mid-Sept.), you can indulge in the delicious paradox of bikini-clad skiing in Courmayeur. Weeklong packages, including skipasses for the Monte Bianco area, cost L290,000 for half-board at **Hotel Joli** in La Palud and L200,000 for bed and breakfast at the **Petit Meublé** in Courmayeur. (See Near Courmayeur and Accommodations.) Afterward, doff the skis but keep the bathing suit, and take the plunge into two area swimming pools. **Plan Chécrouit,** at the summit of the Courmayeur cable car (one way L5000, round-trip L8000), and **Courba Ozeleuna,** at the summit of the Val Veny cable car (same prices), will help you cool off after a day on the slopes. (Open June 27-Sept. 13 daily 10:30am-5pm. L900 per person. Showers and saunas included.) **World Cup** ski races bring the best to Courmayeur every year.

Near Courmayeur

La Palud is the highest town in the region and the terminus of the cable car extending into France. Everyone in town speaks at least French and English. Buses climb the 4km from Courmayeur to La Palud, but should your internal time-clock not coincide with the bus company's timetable, consider hitching. You can ride to Punta Helbronner and back for L23,000; it's worth it for all the views of Monte Bianco. To get away from it all, stay in La Palud at the **Joli** (tel. 899 49), whose singles are L21,000, with bath L23,000. Doubles are L40,000. **La Quercia** (tel. 899 31) is a ski bungalow charging L40,000 for doubles with bath.

La Funivia has decent rooms without the piney primness of many other establishments. The attic hosts a hostel-like *dormitoire* frequented by hikers paying L10,000 per night and L6000 for breakfast. La Palud restaurants make those in Courmayeur look like cheap diners with the possible exception of the restaurant at the **Hotel Joli** (open daily noon-9pm). Arrive outside of the usual meal times, when you can buy a cheap *panino* rather than the taxing main course dishes. If you're up to a short hike, you might try the climb to the summit of **Mont Chetif,** right in front of Monte Bianco. For L8000 round-trip (in winter L12,000), you can take the Funivia Courmayeur (or a 2-hr. walk) up to Plan Chécrouit (1701m). At 2334m, the view is spectacular. From La Palud, cross over to **Chamonix** by cable car (one way to Punta Helbronner at the summit of Monte Bianco L17,000 and 84F (US$25-30) for the descent). *Fantastique* cannot describe the views here.

For hiking excursions in Italy, take the bus that leaves every hour from viale M. Bianco to **Combal Lake.** For a beautiful six-hour hike, follow the road up the valley past Rifugio Elisabetta to where the path (marked by a "2" in a triangle) branches off to the left and climbs up to the Chavannes Pass (2603m). The trail then runs along Mont Perce, beneath the crest, until it reaches Mont Fortin (2758m), where it descends once again to Lake Combal. The view from Mont Fortin is equally breathtaking, and the bus brings you back to Courmayeur. A map is crucial on these jaunts.

The English gentlemen who launched the first climbing expeditions of Mont Blanc sketched out the **Giro del Monte Banco** as a two- or three-day tour for "less adventurous travelers who want to avoid the difficulties and dangers of the High Alps" (John Ball, The London Alpine Club, 1863). Today, most local guides suggest that the trip be completed in at least a week. As the name suggests, the trail leads around Monte Bianco, running past Chamonix, Courmayeur, and obscure mountain passages. All along the route, refuges and hotel dormitories are spaced five or six hours apart. But you need not invest a fortnight in the wilderness; one leg of the larger trail is an ideal daytrip, and two sections make a wonderful weekend.

The best Italian guidebook for the tour is *Intorno al Monte Bianco* by Stefano Ardifo, available in Courmayeur; guidebooks in French are also available.

Lombardy (Lombardia)

For centuries Lombardy has been coveted by German emperors, French kings, and native despots and communes. Today Lombardy's industries, agriculture, and financial vitality make it a keystone of the Italian economy. Since World War II, thousands of poverty-stricken southern Italians have come to the "new Italy." The province has recently become a mecca for immigrants from even farther south: Africa and the Middle East. Tension between long-time denizens and immigrants subsides slowly, and residents of Lombardy are today among the least provincial Italians.

Beyond Milan's cesspool of couture, cartels, and clubs, life proceeds evenly in the fecund Lombardan countryside. Centuries of civilization have left a great store of art and architecture in cities such as Bergamo, Brescia, Pavia, and Cremona, each an hour or less from Milan and ideal daytrips. Outside Pavia lies a famous *certosa* (charterhouse) whose intricate façade epitomizes the best of the Lombard Renaissance. Mantua, at the eastern extreme of the region, is replete with churches and palaces from the Renaissance and from the creativity of mannerist Giulio Romano. Also within shouting distance of Milan is the verdant lake country, where northern Italy's great bodies of water lap the shores of Switzerland and passes wind through the Alps.

Milan (Milano)

Frenetically industrious, Milan is the only Italian city where skyscrapers outnumber Renaissance *palazzi*. Even the city's historical emblem, the *duomo*, is precipitously vertical and spiky, closer to a technical coup than a lyrical masterpiece. Heavily bombed during World War II, Milan was speedily rebuilt, and a large part of its historic core was replaced with steel and glass. Milan is not a city to savor meditatively; here, culture means the latest movies, the most innovative plays, and the most chic fashions.

After a period as a free commune in the ninth through thirteenth centuries, Milan was shaped by successive omnipotent families, the Viscontis and the Sforzas. Great prosperity resulted from the clout of these clans and the introduction of the silk industry. The fifteenth century witnessed Milan's Golden Age, when such geniuses as Bramante and Leonardo da Vinci granted the city status as a new Athens. The modern age arrived when French troops entered the city in 1797 and kindled a revolutionary spirit. The city soon became the crux of the Italian unification movement.

Orientation

Milan lies in the heart of northern Italy, closer to Switzerland and France than to the Mediterranean or Adriatic. It is linked by rail to all major cities in Italy and Western Europe. The city resembles a giant target, encircled by a series of ancient city walls. In the outer rings lie suburbs built during the '50s and '60s to house southern immigrants. The area around the train station is a mish-mash of skyscrapers dominated by the huge **Stazione Centrale** (1931), a frightening union of art deco and Fascist bombast, and the sleek **Pirelli Tower** (1959), one of the tallest buildings in Europe. The **duomo** and **Vittorio Emanuele II Galleria** are the bull's eye, roughly at the center of the downtown circle. Within this circle are four central squares: **piazze Largo Cairoli,** nearest Castello Sforzesco; **piazza Cordusio,** connected to Largo Cairoli by via Dante; the **duomo,** at the end of via Mercanti; and **piazza San Bibila,** a haven for clothes horses along corso V. Emanuele. Northeast and north-

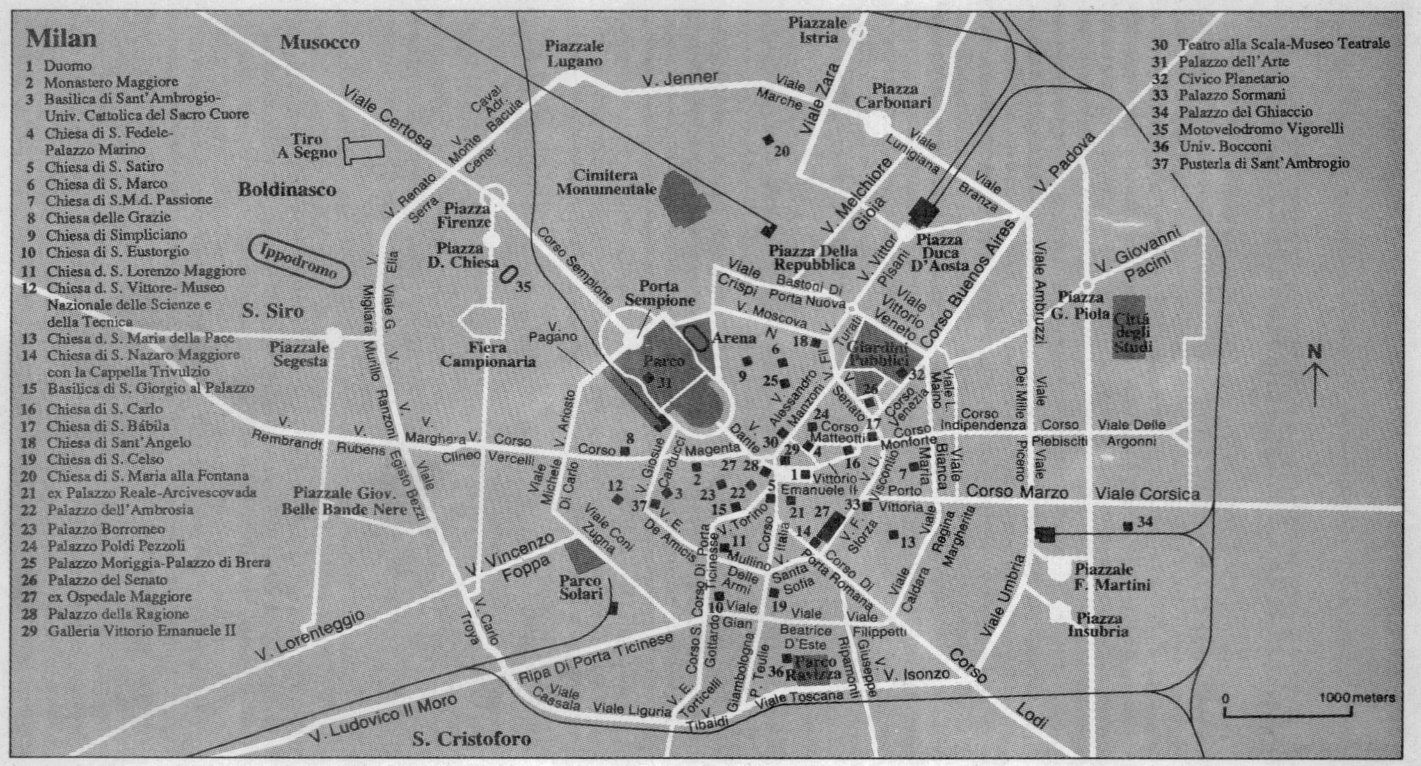
Milan
1 Duomo
2 Monastero Maggiore
3 Basilica di Sant'Ambrogio-Univ. Cattolica del Sacro Cuore
4 Chiesa di S. Fedele-Palazzo Marino
5 Chiesa di S. Satiro
6 Chiesa di S. Marco
7 Chiesa di S.M.d. Passione
8 Chiesa delle Grazie
9 Chiesa di Simpliciano
10 Chiesa di S. Eustorgio
11 Chiesa d. S. Lorenzo Maggiore
12 Chiesa d. S. Vittore- Museo Nazionale delle Scienze e della Tecnica
13 Chiesa d. S. Maria della Pace
14 Chiesa di S. Nazaro Maggiore con la Cappella Trivulzio
15 Basilica di S. Giorgio al Palazzo
16 Chiesa di S. Carlo
17 Chiesa di S. Bábila
18 Chiesa di Sant'Angelo
19 Chiesa di S. Celso
20 Chiesa di S. Maria alla Fontana
21 ex Palazzo Reale-Arcivescovada
22 Palazzo dell'Ambrosia
23 Palazzo Borromeo
24 Palazzo Poldi Pezzoli
25 Palazzo Moriggia-Palazzo di Brera
26 Palazzo del Senato
27 ex Ospedale Maggiore
28 Palazzo della Ragione
29 Galleria Vittorio Emanuele II
30 Teatro alla Scala-Museo Teatrale
31 Palazzo dell'Arte
32 Civico Planetario
33 Palazzo Sormani
34 Palazzo del Ghiaccio
35 Motovelodromo Vigorelli
36 Univ. Bocconi
37 Pusterla di Sant'Ambrogio
Musocco
Boldinasco
Tiro A Segno
Ippodromo
S. Siro
Piazzale Segesta
Piazzale Lugano
V. Jenner
Piazzale Istria
Piazza Carbonari
Cimitera Monumentale
Piazza Firenze
Piazza D. Chiesa
Fiera Campionaria
Porta Sempione
Parco
Arena
Piazza Della Repubblica
Piazza Duca D'Aosta
Giardini Pubblici
Corso Buenos Aires
Viale Vittorio Veneto
Piazza G. Piola
Città degli Studi
Corso Marzo
Viale Corsica
Piazzale F. Martini
Piazza Insubria
Piazzale Giov. Belle Bande Nere
Parco Solari
Parco Ravizza
S. Cristoforo
V. Ludovico Il Moro
V. Lorenteggio
Ripa Di Porta Ticinese
Corso Sempione
Viale Certosa
V. Padova
Viale Ambruzzi
Viale Umbria
Corso Lodi
Viale Toscana
N
0 1000 meters

west lie two large parks, the **Giardini Pubblici** and the **Parco Sempione.** Farther northeast is the **Stazione Centrale,** directly connected to the downtown core by bus #60, and **corso Buenos Aires,** where the zeroes on the clothes price tags are actually countable.

The subway (**metropolitana milanese,** abbreviated "MM") is the most useful part of Milan's extensive public transport network. **Line #1** (red line) connects the pensioni district east of Stazione Centrale to the center of town and extends as far as the youth hostel (Molino Dorino fork). **Line #2** (green line) links Milan's three train stations and crosses MM1 at Cadorno and Loreto. The metro is active from approximately 6am to midnight. Among the many useful train and bus routes, **trams** #29 and 30 travel the city's outer ring road, while the inner road is serviced by **buses** #96 and 97. Tram #1, which runs during the wee hours, also departs from Centrale and runs to p. Scala, near the *duomo.* Tickets for buses, trams, and subways must be purchased in advance at newspaper stands or from ticket machines; bring small change. A ticket (L800) is good for one subway ride or 75 minutes of surface transportation. Tourists can buy all-day passes (L3200) from the **ATM** office at the Duomo and Centrale stops.

Milan shuts down vehemently for vacation during most of August, when visitors should be prepared to encounter a half-deserted city.

Practical Information

APT: Via Marconi, 1 (tel. 80 96 62), in p. del Duomo to the right as you face the *duomo.* Everyone here speaks some English and is helpful. Information on both a local and regional level. Especially useful map. The APT will not reserve rooms but will phone to check for vacancies. Open Mon.-Fri. 9:45am-12:30pm and 1:30-6pm, Sat. 9am-12:30pm and 1:30-5pm. Branch offices at **Stazione Centrale** (tel. 669 05 32 or 669 04 32; open Mon.-Sat. 9am-12:30pm and 2:15-6pm) and **Linate Airport** (tel. 74 40 65; open Mon.-Fri. 9am-4:30pm). For hotel information and reservations, call **Hotel Reservation Milano** (tel. 70 60 95).

Municipal Information: Comune di Milano, Galleria V. Emanuele, 11 (tel. 87 05 45), at p. della Scala. A wealth of information in an office resplendent with gleaming marble and amber-colored wood. Ask for information on the city-wide programs *Milano d'Estate* (mid-June to mid-Aug.) and their paper *Qui Milano.* Some tickets may be reserved here. Some English spoken. Open Mon.-Sat. 8am-9pm.

CIT: Galleria V. Emanuele (tel. 86 66 61), under the glass dome. The most central travel agency. Also changes dough. Open Sept.-June Mon.-Fri. 9am-1pm and 2-5:50pm; July-Aug. Mon.-Fri. 9am-1pm and 2-5:50pm.

Centro Turistico Studentesco, via S. Antonio, 2 (tel. 86 38 77 or 87 63 97). Open Mon.-Fri. 9am-1pm and 2:30-6:30pm, Sat. 9:30am-12:30pm.

Transalpino Tickets: Next to the train information office in the atrium of Stazione Centrale (tel. 670 51 21). Open daily 8am-7pm. When closed, go to **Italturismo,** to your right as you leave the station, tucked under the grand drive-through. 1-month InterRail passes (L285,000, including ferries L346,500). Open July-Aug. daily 6:45am-8pm; Sept.-June Mon.-Sat. 6:45am-8pm.

Consulates: U.S., p. Carlo Donegani, 1 (tel. 65 28 41; after hours 21 41 05, code 181). Open Mon.-Fri. 9am-noon and 2-4pm. **Canada,** via Vittor Pisani, 19 (tel. 669 7451; after hours 66 98 06 00). **U.K.,** via S. Paolo, 7 (tel. 869 34 42; after hours 86 24 90). Open Mon.-Fri. 9:15am-12:15pm and 2:30-4:30pm. **Australia,** via Turati, 40 (tel. 659 87 27). Open Mon.-Thurs. 9am-noon and 2-4:30pm, Fri. 9am-noon. Call after hours only in emergency. **New Zealand** citizens should contact their consulate in Rome.

Currency Exchange: Banca Nazionale delle Comunicazioni, at the Stazione Centrale (tel. 669 02 53). Offers standard commercial rates. Open Mon.-Sat. 8am-7:30pm, Sun. 9am-2:30pm. The *ufficio cambi* there changes money 24 hours at horrendous rates. Nighttime service notoriously unreliable. In town, **Banca Cesare Ponti,** on p. del Duomo (tel. 882 11), near the Galleria, offers good rates. Open Mon.-Fri. 8:30am-1:30pm and 3-4pm, Sat. 9am-1pm. All **Banca d'America e d'Italia** branches allow cash advances on Visa cards. Avoid long lines at the head office near p. della Scala by going to the equally central branch at via San Prospero, 1, off p. Cordusio. Open Mon.-Fri. 8:30am-1:30pm and 2:45-3:45pm. At **Aeroporto Linate,** Banca Popolare di Milano (tel. 742 64 06) and Banca Popolare di Lodi (tel. 738 02 53) are open daily 8am-9pm.

American Express: Via Brera, 3 (tel. 855 71; financial services 855 72 77), at of via dell' Orso. Walk through the Galleria, across p. Scala, and up via Verdi. Holds mail free for American Express customers, otherwise L1000 per inquiry. Will accept wired money for a hefty $30 fee per $1000. Open Mon.-Fri. 9am-5:30pm, Sat. 9am-12:30pm.

Post Offices: Central Post Office, via Cordusio, 4 (tel. 160), near p. del Duomo—not the building marked "Poste" in nearby p. Cordusio. Stamp window (#30) and Fermo Posta (#34) open Mon.-Fri. 8:15am-7:40pm, Sat. 8:15am-5:40pm. **Telephones** open daily 7am-12:45am. Also at Stazione Centrale; open Mon.-Fri. 8:15am-7:35pm, Sat. 8:15am-3:35pm. **Postal Code:** 20100.

Telephones: ASST, in the post office listed above. **SIP,** in Galleria V. Emanuele. In the evenings it's a better place for learning the latest in Italian profanity than for actually making phone calls. Open 8:10am-9:30pm. **Telephone Code:** 02.

Airports: Intercontinental flights use **Malpensa Airport,** 50km from town. Buses leave in connection with specific flights from p. Luigi di Savoia, on the east side of Stazione Centrale; the **Doria** travel agency (tel. 669 08 36 or 669 11 36), just inside, posts a list of buses for the upcoming week and sells tickets (1 hr.; L7000, ages under 11 L3500). **Linate Airport** is only 7km from town and handles domestic/European flights. The bus to Linate departs Stazione Centrale 5:40am-9pm every 20 min. (L3000, children L1000). It's cheaper to take bus #73 from p. San Babila (MM1). **General Flight Information** for both Malpensa and Linate airports, tel. 74 85 22 00.

Train Stations: Stazione Centrale, p. Duca d'Aosta (tel. 675 00), on MM2. The primary station. To Genoa and Turin (both 1 per hr.; L7800, round-trip L13,400), Venice (17 direct per day, L13,200), and Florence (25 direct per day, L15,600). Open daily 7:25am-3pm and 3:25-11pm. **Porta Garibaldi,** also on MM2, handles some trains to Pavia, Monza Piacenza, and Bergamo. **Lambrate,** also on MM2, handles trains to and from Pavia, Genoa, Brescia, and Bergamo. Centrale's **Eurail Pass Central Office,** corso Magenta, 24 (tel. 677 71, ext. 6139). **Branch office,** MM: Cadorna. Open daily 8:30am-12:30pm.

Buses: ATM, in the p. del Duomo MM station (tel. 87 54 95). Municipal buses require prepurchased tickets (L800). Day passes for non-residents L3200. Open Mon.-Sat. 7:45am-1pm and 1:45-7pm. Also at **Stazione Centrale.** Open the same hours. **Intracity** buses make little sense because of the extensive train network, but **SAL, SIA, Autostradale,** and many others depart from p. Castello and the surrounding area (MM: Cairoli) for Turin (1 per hr.; one way L11,500, round-trip L19,500), the lake country, Bergamo, and points as far as Rimini and Trieste. For inquiries, try Autostradale, p. Castello, 1 (tel. 80 11 61).

Taxis: The main taxi stands are in p. Scala, p. del Duomo, and largo Cairoli. Or contact them by radio (tel. 67 67 or 83 88). The official Milan taxis are yellow and uniformly expensive, starting at L4000. A ride to Linate will cost around L20,000, to Malpensa L80,000.

Car Rental: Hertz, Galleria delle Carrozze (tel. 669 00 61; after hours 659 81 51), outside the station, to the left as you exit. Tourist rates are about 2/3 those for Italians. Open Mon.-Fri. 7:45am-8pm, Sat. 7:45am-2pm.

Bike Rental: The city of Milan and **Radio Service** (tel. 657 14 40) subsidize a cheap bike rental program. Bicycles are available at the yellow area between the *duomo* and the *galleria.* Bikes L3000 per 3 hr. Open daily 8am-8pm.

Hitching: For Bologna, Florence, and Rome, stand at the entrance to the Autostrada del Sole at p. Corvetto (tram #13 from via Mazzini near p. del Duomo). For the lake country and Turin, go to viale Certosa (tram #14 from largo Cairoli, on MM1), or pl. Kennedy (MM1: Lampugnano). For the Ligurian coast and Riviera, take the **Autostrada dei Fiori** at p. Belfanti, near the Romolo end-station of MM2. If it's summer, lines outside the **autostrada** entrances can exceed 5km. For a price, **Viaggi e Passaggi,** via Col di Lana, 14 (tel 89 40 27 63), run out of a private home on the 2nd floor, will introduce you to a driver with an empty seat. Open Mon.-Fri. 6-8pm, Sat. 9:30am-12:30pm.

English Bookstores: The American Bookshop, Via Camperio, 16 (tel. 87 09 44), at largo Cairoli. The best selection in Milan. Open Tues.-Fri. 10am-7pm, Sat. 10am-1pm and 2-7pm, Mon. 2:30-7pm. Closed 1 week in Aug. **Libreria Rizzoli,** Galleria V. Emanuele, 79 (tel. 80 73 48), near the *duomo.* 2 shelves of English books in the basement. Open Mon. 3:30-7:30pm, Tues.-Sat. 9:30am-7:30pm. Also the **English Bookshop,** on via Maschereni at via Ariosto.

United States Information Service (USIS): Via Bigli, 11A (tel. 79 50 51). Library with U.S. publications for perusal.

Synagogue: Via Guastalla, 19 (tel. 551 20 29 or 551 21 01). The largest synagogue in Milan with conservative services in Italian and safardic services in Hebrew. Services Mon.-Fri. at 7:45am and 8:45pm, Sat. at 9am, Sun. at 8:45pm.

All Saints Anglican Church: Via Solferino, 17 (tel. 655 22 58, pastor's home number). Services daily in English.

Day Hotel: Albergo Diurno, beneath p. Duca d'Aosta and reached by the escalators to the metro in front of the Stazione Centrale (tel. 669 12 32). A daytime facility for washing up or sleeping between trains. Toilets L500, with soap and towel L1000, with baths L5500, with showers L5000. Ventilated sleeping cabins L13,000 first 2 hr., L1000 each additional hr., with bath L16,000. Open daily 7am-8pm. You can also store your **luggage** here 6:50am-8:10pm. L1000 per 24 hours.

Swimming Pools: Out of a dozen, the closest to Stazione Centrale is **Cozzi,** viale Tunisia, 35 (tel. 659 97 03), off corso Buenos Aires. **Lido di Milano,** p. Lotto, 15 (tel. 36 61 00), is near the youth hostel. Open daily 10am-7pm. Admission L4000, noon-2:30pm and 5:30pm-closing L2500, children L3000.

Laundromats: Self-Service Lavanderia Automatica, via Botticelli, 7 (tel. 266 33 00). Open late Aug. to mid-July. **Aqua Secco,** via Betti, 426 (tel. 30 63 80).

All-Night Pharmacy: Though nocturnal duty rotates among Milan's pharmacies (call 192 to find out who is working the night shift), the one in Stazione Centrale never closes (tel. 669 07 35 or 669 09 35).

Medical Assistance: Tel. 77 33 for an ambulance. **Ospedale Maggiore Policlinico,** via Francesco Sforza, 35 (tel. 551 35 18 or 546 91 79), 5 min. from the *duomo* on the inner ring road.

SOS (tel. 113). Tram #1 takes you to the HQ.

Police: Questura, via Fatebenefratelli, 11 (tel. 622 61, ext. 327). English spoken.

Accommodations

Milan harbors over 60 reasonably-priced *pensioni,* but quality and location whittle the choices down dramatically. You can usually find a room east of Stazione Centrale—try p. Aspromonte, via Lulli, via Lippi, via Valazze, or via Ricordi, but the places are impersonal and several kilometers from the center of town. To reach this area, take the subway (MM1 or MM2) to Loreto, or walk east of the station. Somewhat better is the area south of Stazione Centrale between via S. Gregorio, corso Buenos Aires, viale V. Veneto, and p. della Repubblica. At night, however, this area resembles a Red Light District. It is best to find a place either in the city center or on its periphery, even if this involves crossing town from the station. The tourist offices may help you find a room, but be wary of their urgings to spend L10,000-12,000 more on a nicer place. Hotel rooms are invaded in June and July by Italian students who come from outlying areas to take exams. Believe it or not, resort areas like the Riviera and the Alps offer better bargains than "untouristed" Milan.

Hostels

Ostello Piero Rotta (IYHF), viale Salmoiraghi, 2 (tel. 36 70 95). From any train station, take MM2 (green line) to Cadorna and change to MM1 (red line) going out to Molino Derino, not Inganni. Get off at QT8—a district in the leafy outskirts. Modern hostel with 6-bed rooms and a sunny garden, but run by a stringent regime. Beware of 7:30am, 8am, 8:30am, and 9am alarms, and unbending enforcement of the daytime lockout rule. *Gettoni* telephone available. English spoken. Individuals may not make reservations, but in the summer groups should (deposit 50%). IYHF card strictly required, but foreigners can purchase it at the hostel (L15,000). L13,500. Breakfast and lockers included. Open Jan. 13-Dec. 20 7-9am and 5-11pm. Curfew 11:30pm. Depending on the management's biorhythms, lights suddenly die between 11:20pm and midnight.

Casa Famiglia (ACISJF), corso Garibaldi, 123 (tel. 659 52 06). MM2: Moscova. Pristine rooms, partitions between beds. Modern doubles overlook a garden. Run by neat nuns. Open to women travelers 29 and under. L13,000. Showers included. Reserve 2-3 days in advance. Curfew 10:30pm. Reception opens at 7am.

Near Stazione Centrale

Hotel Valley, via Soperga, 19 (tel. 669 27 77). From the station, turn left and left again under the overpass onto via Lepetit, the 2nd street. MM2: Centrale or Caiazzo. A reassuring, piney scent in the sparkling bathrooms, brand new furniture, and blue-and-white rugs, paint, and curtains. English spoken. Singles with shower L28,000, with bath L33,000. Doubles with shower L46,000, with bath 55,900. Reception open until 1am. Guests may be able to wrangle keys and stay out later.

Magic Hotel, via Copernico, 8 (tel. 68 33 82 or 688 93 28), 3 streets west of Stazione Centrale. Turn right as you exit. MM2: Centrale. Big bathrooms, smallish rooms with low lights, and a casual TV lounge with bar; everything down-to-earth. English spoken. Singles L27,000. Doubles L35,000, with bath L45,000. Showers L4000. Open daily until 1am.

Hotel Adri, via Lulli, 18 (tel. 23 56 92), off p. Aspromonte. MM2: between Loreto and Piola. Posters a la Hallmark, but fresh towels, congenial management, and tidy rooms. Singles L25,000. Doubles L32,500. Lenient on the L3000 shower charge. Curfew 2:30am.

Albergo Hotel Principe, corso Buenos Aires, 75 (tel. 669 43 77), MM1 or MM2: Loreto. Spic-and-span, spacious rooms, outspoken proprietor, and prices that reflect security and convenience. Singles L29,000. Doubles L42,500, with bath L60,000. Showers included. Curfew 1:30am.

Hotel il Palio, p. Aspromonte, 7 (tel. 23 57 45). MM2: Loreto and Piola. An ivy-covered building on a quiet *piazza.* Mercurial owner. Nearby streetside walls decorated with colorful graffiti denouncing the current regime. Singles L18,5000. Doubles L28,000. Showers L5000. Curfew 12:30am. Open Aug. 18-July 31.

Around Corso Buenos Aires

All of these hotels are near MM1: Porta Venezia.

Viale Tunisia, 6. This building houses 6 floors of budget hotels, equidistant from the station and the city center. Some English is spoken at all 3 of the following hotels. The chief appeal of **Hotel S. Tomaso** (tel. 20 97 47), on the 3rd floor, is the joyful management. Modern, clean rooms and capacious showers and baths. Singles L30,000. Doubles L50,000. Showers included. **Albergo Canna** (tel. 22 41 33 or 204 00 55), on the 5th floor, offers singles and doubles for the same prices, as well as 3-bed rooms with shower (L25,000 per person), a bar, and a TV room. Reception open until 12:30am, but night owls can get a key. **Hotel Kennedy** (tel. 20 09 34), on the 6th floor, also maintains spotless, luxurious rooms. Singles L30,000. Doubles L48,000, with shower L52,700, with bath L60,00. Triples with shower L23,000 per person. Hall showers included. Reception open until midnight, but keys available.

Pensione Aurora, corso Buenos Aires, 18 (tel. 27 89 60). Commodious rooms with huge beds. Slightly seedy on the outside, but welcoming rooms on the inside. Singles L38,000. Doubles L50,000. Showers included. 3-bed room with shower L75,000. Curfew 2am. Open Sept.-July.

Pensione Boscovich, via Boscovich, 43 (tel. 22 16 41), near the Aurora. Set back from the street, with geraniums in the windows. Rooms comfortable but beginning to fray. Curtainless showers. A haven for late arrivals: Open all night. Phone reservations accepted. Singles L26,000. Doubles L38,000. Showers included. Open Sept.-July.

West and South of the City Center

Pensione Dante, via Dante, 14 (tel. 86 64 71), near the Castello Sforzesco. MM1: Cairoli or Cordusio. Short of sacking in the *duomo,* it's impossible to get a more central location. Rooms from the sublime to the ridiculous. Lots of English-speaking clients, but no English-speaking owner. Doubles L35,000. Triples L51,000. Showers included.

Pensione Cantore, corso Genova, 25 (tel. 835 75 65), a 10-min. walk southwest of the *duomo.* MM2: Genova. Personable, in a neat neighborhood of apartments and shops. Big, tidy rooms. Singles 27,000. Doubles L40,000-41,000. Showers included. Usually closed half of Aug., but ownership will change hands in 1989.

Pensione Rovello, via Rovello, 18/A (tel. 87 39 56). Via Rovello runs parallel to via Dante. MM1: Cairoli or Cordusio. New rooms small but neat. Singles L30,000. Doubles L49,000, with bath L59,000. Triples with bath L75,000. Showers included. Flexible curfew 2am.

Albergo Alcione, via G.G. Mora, 2 (tel. 837 93 01), on a tiny street off corso Porta Ticinese. Walk down via Torino from the *duomo.* Great cafes nearby. Renovated and comfortable, but somewhat shabby—you can do better for the price. Singles with bath L40,000. Doubles with bath L60,000.

Camping

Il Bareggino, via Corbettina (tel. 901 44 17), in Bareggino. Very hard to reach without a car, though you can take an *extraurbane* bus from p. Lotto (MM1: on the Molino Dorino line). L4100 per tent, L4100 per person, L2000 per child.

Autodromo, in the park of the Villa Reale (tel. (039) 38 77 71), in Monza. Take a train or bus from Stazione Centrale to Monza, then a city bus to the campsite. A step down. L2900 per tent, L2900 per person, L1200 per child under 6. Open April-Sept.

Food

In Milan—in contrast to most Italian towns—clothing stores outnumber restaurants three to one. Yet, like the best clothing, Milanese cuisine is understated and classic. Specialties include *riso giallo* (rice with saffron), *cotoletta alla milanese* (which has become standard throughout Italy), and *cazzouela* (a mixture of pork and cabbage). *Pasticceria* (pastry) and *gelateria* (ice cream) shops crowd every block. Try the Milanese sweet bread *panettone* (made with raisins and citrons), an Easter bread that's become a year-round tradition.

Avoid the area around the train station, which is generally overpriced and unappetizing. Walk beyond viale Tunisia for some good eats. One final note: The entire city—including most restaurants—closes for vacation in August and. In order to prevent mass starvation, the city sponsors an outdoor cafeteria in the **Parco Sempione,** near the Arco della Pace. Full meals are about L8000. (Open noon-2pm and 7:30-9:30pm.) Come after 1:30pm, when the lines are shorter. The newspaper *Il Giornale Nuovo* lists all the restaurants and shops open in the city. In June, the Communist party serves local specialties in abundancy on long tables along the canale Darsena near p. XXIV Maggio. L10,000 buys a full meal, good humor, and a half-liter of wine. The largest **markets** are around via Fauché or viale Papiniano on Saturdays and Tuesdays, along via Santa Croce on Thursdays. On Saturday, the **Fiera di Sinigallia** occurs on via Calatafini—a 400-year-old extravaganza of the basic and the bizarre. The location of neighborhood daily markets is listed in city newspapers near the entertainment section.

Splurge on local pastry at **Sant' Ambroeus** (tel. 70 05 40), a culinary monument among Milanese. (Under the arcades at corso Matteotti, 7. Open Mon. 3:30-8pm, Tues.-Sat. 8am-8pm.) For supermarkets, try **Pam,** off corso Buenos Aires at via Piccinni, 2 (tel. 20 27 15), or the air conditioned store at via Piane, 38b. (Both open Mon. 2-7:30pm, Tues.-Sat. 8:30am-7:30pm.)

South of Stazione Centrale and near Corso Buenos Aires

Pizzeria del Nonno, via A. Costa, 1 (tel. 285 02 62), off p. Loreto. MM1 and MM2: Loreto. A pizza joint that's dark, cavernous, and teeming with rowdies. Enormous, delicious pizza L5000-6500. Cover L500. Open daily noon-2:30pm and 6-11:30pm.

Ristorante Lon Fon, via Lazzaretto, 10 (tel. 271 51 53), at via Palazzi. MM2: Centrale F.S. A respectable and cheap Chinese restaurant. Lanterns and garish dragons galore. Full meals as high as L20,000, but fine chicken dishes around L5000. Cover L800. Open Aug. 20-July 20 Thurs.-Tues. 11am-3pm and 7-11pm.

Moby Dick, via Porpora, 161 (tel. 23 05 91). MM1 or MM2: Loreto. Pizza with pizazz. Upscale clientele. Try the Simpatia with tomatoes, ricotta, olives, oregano, and prosciutto (L6000). Or go animal with the Moby Dick, loaded with salmon (L12,000). Pasta dishes L6000-8000. Cover L2000. Open Thurs.-Tues. 11am-3pm and 7pm-1am.

Pizzeria da Andrea, via Porpora, 14 (no phone). Short of invading a private home, the best neighborhood for pizza by the slice and pasta to go. Most dishes L1000 per **etto.** Open Mon. 7:30am-1:30pm, Tues.-Sat. 7:30am-1:30pm and 4-8pm.

Mamma Italia, via Tarra, 6 (tel 60 36 89), via Copernico 2 blocks from *stazione centrale.* If you're cornered into eating near the station. *Primi* L4000-6000, *secondi* L7000-10,000, wine L3500 per ½-liter. *Menù* L22,000. Open Sept.-Aug. 5 Mon.-Fri. 11am-3pm and 7pm-midnight, Sat. 7pm-midnight.

La Piccola Napoli, viale Monza, 13 (tel 285 33 97). MM1 or MM2: Loreto. A nest for night owls. Pizza L4500-6000. Open Sept.-July Tues.-Sun. 6pm-3am.

Ciao, corso Buenos Aires, 7 (tel 271 11 09). MM1: Porta Venezia. Classier than anything ever to pass beneath the Golden Arches, but the same standardization. Pasta L4000-4300, hamburger L4300. Extensive salad bar L2500. Wine L2200 per ½-liter. Open Sat.-Thurs. noon-3pm and 5:30-11:30pm.

Near Piazza del Duomo

Trattoria da Bruno, via Cavallotti, 15 (tel. 70 06 02), off corso Europa east of the *duomo.* MM1: Duomo or San Babila. A small place popular with locals. The food is better than you expect. *Menù* L10,000. No a la carte. Open Sept.-July Mon.-Fri. noon-2pm and 7-9pm, Sat. noon-2pm.

Ciao, corso Europa, 12 (tel. 79 11 42). MM1: Duomo or San Babila. A clone of Ciao on corso Buenos Aires, down to the number of plants in the stairwell. Open Tues.-Fri. and Sun. noon-3pm and 6:30pm-midnight, Sat. noon-12:30am.

Peck, *rosticceria* on via G. Cantù, stores at via Spadari, 9 (tel. 860 84 21, 87 17 37, or 87 53 58), and across the street. Peck is to Milan what Harrod's Food Hall is to London. Since 1883, this has been *the* place to shop. Overpriced, but don't miss it. Pizza and pastries sold by the kilo. A large portion of pizza about L3000, chocolate mousse L3000 (L25,000 per kg). Open Tues.-Sat. 8am-1pm and 3:30-7pm.

Centro Macrobiotico Italiano, via Larga, 7 (tel. 86 68 19), in a rounded building set back from the street. Take the left staircase to the 1st floor. A vegetarian restaurant. The store also sells natural, health, and beauty products. Open Tues.-Sat.

Flash, via Bergamini, 1 (tel. 890 06 78 or 890 06 76), at via Larga. MM1: Duomo, then bus #60 a few blocks. The only reasonable *pizzeria* near the *duomo* with a modicum of character. Pizza L5000-7000, wine L5000 per liter. Sandwiches at bar L2500-3000. Cover L1500. Bar open Mon.-Sat. 7am-6:30pm. Pizza Tues.-Sun. noon-2:30pm and 7pm-midnight. Closed much of Aug.

Between Largo Cairoli and Piazza Cordusio

La Birreria Uno, foro Bonaparte, 59 (tel. 86 27 59), near the Castello Sforzesco. MM1: Cairoli, or MM1 or MM2: Cadorna. A cheery cafeteria frequented by workers. *Panini* around L4000, *primi* L6000. Order simple dishes for great culinary satisfaction. Open Aug. 23-Aug. 8 Mon.-Fri. noon-2:30pm. Self-service open later.

Pizzeria Vecchia Napoli, via San Tomaso, 6 (tel. 80 07 09), at end of via Rovello, off via Dante. MM1: Cordusio. Charming hole-in-the-wall with tasty if small pizzas L4000-9000. Open Sun.-Fri. 10am-11pm. No pizza 3-7pm.

L'Ultima Follia di Califuria, via Ponte Vetero, 8 (tel. 80 56 966). MM1: Cairoli. A feast for the senses. Live jazz, salsa, or classical music, with a salad for every note in the scale. Cold cuts L5000, *tortine di verdure* (vegetable pies) L6000. Open Mon.-Sat. evenings.

Ciao, via Dante, 5 (tel. 890 03 75). MM1: Cordusio or Cairoli. A chain—see South of Stazione Centrale. Open Sat.-Thurs. noon-11pm.

Near Via Torino and Corso di Porta Ticinese

A neighborhood in the throes of gentrification: Here esoteric ambience meets homespun prices.

Exploit Birreria, viale Col di Lana, 5 (tel. 835 02 59). MM2: San Agostino, then walk down viale Papiniano and viale Annunzio to p. XXV Maggio. Buses #29 and 30 run between p. San Agostino and XXV Maggio. Black and white floor and typical *trattoria* garden in the back. Loudspeakers bring the crowd to life most evenings. *Menù* L8500 (available only Mon.-Fri. noon-2:30pm). Wine L1500 per carafe. Open Sept.-July Mon.-Fri. noon-2:30pm and 9pm-1:30am, Sat. 9pm-1:30am.

Be Bop Disco Bar, viale Col di Lana, 4 (tel. 837 69 72), across from Exploit. Same idea, same crowd. Becomes a disco at night. *Menù* L8000, wine L5000 per liter. Open Sept. to mid-Aug. Mon.-Sat. noon-2:30pm and 8pm-1am.

Mergellina, via Molino delle Armi, 48 (tel 837 07 80), off corso di Porta Ticinese. Catch bus #15 along via Torino. A place to hang out and chow down. Terrific pizzas L4500-6000. Cover L1500. Open Sept.-July Thurs.-Mon. noon-2:30pm and 7pm-1:30am, Wed. 7pm-1am.

Trattoria Artisti, corso di Porta Ticinese, 16 (tel. 837 07 02). Walking away from the *duomo,* take the left fork of via Torino (about 20 min.). MM2: S. Ambrogio or bus #15. The L10,000 lunch menu includes ¼-liter of wine or ½-liter mineral water or coffee. Wine otherwise L4000 per liter. Open Sept.-July Mon.-Sat. noon-3pm and 7-10pm.

Hippopotamus, via dei Fabbri, 1 (tel. 837 91 03), just down from Trattoria degli Artisti. Inexpensive meals served in rooms with white stucco and mustard-yellow plastic on the walls—an attempt at upscale decoration. Pizza L5000-7000. Wine L4000 per liter. Open Tues.-Sun. noon-3pm and 7pm-midnight.

Mimi, via Torino, 48 (tel. 65 25 75), within walking distance of the *duomo.* Traditonal *forno* (oven) cooks up pizza by the slice (L2000-3000). Open Tues.-Sun. 10am-11pm.

Between Via Pontaccio and Piazza XXV Aprile

Mirrors Pub, corso Garibaldi, 46 (tel. 80 00 12). MM2: Moscova. Conveniently located 10 min. from the Porta Garibaldi train station. MM2: Moscova. Modest fare, but one of the cheapest *menùs* in Milan at L8000 (available Mon.-Fri. lunch only). Open Mon.-Sat. 9am-1am; in off-season closes at midnight.

Trattoria da Carmela, via Garibaldi, 127 (tel. 65 02 37). MM2: Moscova. A neighborhood place with a standard *menù* at a rock-bottom L7000, everything included (available 7am-3pm only). Amazing food, and amiable family. Open Sept.-July Mon.-Sat. 7am-3pm and 5-7:30pm.

Pizzeria da Giuliano, via Paolo Sarpi, 60 (tel. 34 16 30), off p. Baiamonti near via Canonica. MM2: Moscova, then walk along via A. Volta, or catch bus #61. The Giuliano clan established its reputation with a pie of tomato, mozzarella, sardines, and oregano. Now an institution with 250 tables and still one type of pizza (L3800, **porzione abbondante** L4500). Impressive beer list. Open Tues.-Sun. noon-midnight.

Spaghetteria Enoteca, via Solferino, 3 (tel. 87 27 35). MM2: Moscova. An incredible place devoted entirely to the wonderful world of spaghetti. Everything is prepared *all' instante* (on the spot). *Assagini* (small portions) of 6 different types of spaghetti L1000 each. Cover L1800. Open Sept.-July Mon.-Sat. from 7:30pm.

Gelaterie

After WWII, a man named **Viel** began selling fruity gelato from a little cart outside the *duomo.* Soon a brother was opening a store of his own on one street corner, a cousin on another, and a son on a third. Now the patriarchal namesake is synonymous with exotic, fresh fruit *gelati* (L1500-2000) and *frullati* (whipped fruit drinks, L2000). One *gelato* caveat: On hot days buy this ambrosia in a cup, not a cone; otherwise you'll find it on your clothes instead of your stomach. For the freshest and fanciest, take your tastebuds to **Viel Frutti Esotici Gelati** on via Luca Beltrami (MM1: Cairoli), which specializes in fruit: fruit frappes (*frulatti di fruta*), fruit flavors, and fruit toppings. Outdoor seating is available. If you need a fix while sightseeing, try **Odeon duomo** on p. del Duomo, facing the cathedral. At **Viel Celso,** via Marconi, 3E (tel. 869 25 61), past the tourist office, you can buy a cone holding four scoops and take it to the outside tables (one of the cheapest places to sit near the *duomo*).

Gelateria Pozzi, p. Cantore, 4 (tel. 89 40 98 30). A household word in Milan. Sit under a thatched roof enclosed by hedges. Open Tues.-Sun. 8am-2am.

Grasso Gelateria, viale A. Doria, 17 (tel. 669 45 70), east of Stazione Centrale. Try their *granite,* an iced sorbet. Here the ice cream is much nicer than the part of town. Outdoor and indoor seating. Open Tues.-Sun. 8am-1am.

Toldo, via Ponte Vetero, 11 (tel. 87 25 17), in the Brera area. Sundry exotic flavors. Open Mon.-Sat. 7am-1am.

Gelateria Buenosaires, p. Oberdan. MM1: Porta Venezia. 40 flavors, cool *frappes,* and boppy music.

Jack Frost Gelateria, via Felice Casati, 25 (tel. 669 11 34), off corso Buenos Aires at via Lazzaretto. MM1: Porta Venezia. Creamy *gelato* and fairy-tale decor. Try their *bacio* (a chocolate and hazelnut "kiss"). Open Thurs.-Tues. 10am-12:30am.

Sights

Around the Duomo

The **piazza del Duomo** marks not only the center of town, but also its touristic, commercial, and social focus. The *duomo,* a huge, radically vertical Gothic creation with vague classical proportions, presides over the *piazza.* Over its 450 years of sporadic construction (beginning in 1386) have amassed 2245 statues, 135 spires, 96 gargoyles, and kilometers of tracery.

Napoleon commanded that the awkward triangular facade, overloaded with classical and Gothic windows and doors, be finished in 1805 (his statue in antique costume stands among those on the roof). The 52 columns rise to canopied niches that contain statues reaching almost the full height of the ceiling—48m. The church, a five-aisled cruciform, can seat 40,000 worshipers. Narrow side aisles end in stained glass windows said to be the largest in the world. The interior decoration, however, is swallowed by the enormous volume of the church. The imposing sixteenth-century marble tomb of Giacomo de Medici in the right transept is inspired by Michelangelo. From outside the north transept, you can climb to the top of the cathedral, where you will be surrounded by florid outbursts of turrets and spires (admission L1500, L3500 to take the elevator). This magical kingdom on the roof of the nave terminates in the central tower (1765-69) and is crowned by a gold-plated Madonna. Back on the ground, go around to see the magnificent apse windows decorated with great swirls of tracery. The family shield of the Viscontis, bigwigs in the thirteenth and fourteenth centuries, figures prominently in the central window. (Open daily June-Sept. 9am-5pm; Oct.-May 9am-4:30pm. No shorts, miniskirts, sleeveless shirts or dresses.)

The **Museo del Duomo,** p. del Duomo, 14 (tel. 86 03 58), is across the *piazza.* The newly renovated museum hosts a collection of sculpture and reliefs from the cathedral and documents the history of the cathedral's construction. Particularly interesting is the story of the *duomo*'s bronze doors, which trace the rapid changes in sculptural style before the structure's completion. (Open Tues.-Sun. 9:30am-12:30pm and 3-6pm. Admission L4000, seniors, children, and school groups L2000.)

On the north side of the *piazza* is the monumental entrance to the **Galleria Vittorio Emanuele II.** The four-story arcade of shops and office is covered by a glass barrel vault and a beautiful glass cupola, 160 ft. high. The entrance facing the *duomo* entertains the dynamic social pick-up scene.

The *galleria* is a passageway to p. della Scala. The **Teatro alla Scala** (also known as La Scala), the world's premier opera house, is a simple neoclassical building completed in 1778. It stands on the site of the Church of Santa Maria alla Scala, from which it took its name. World War II bombing demolished La Scala, but it was rebuilt by 1948. To see the many-tiered, lavish hall seating 2800 people, enter through the **Museo alla Scala** (tel. 805 34 18). Here a succession of small rooms are lined floor to ceiling with portraits of famous musicians (including Carollo Emerto, Susano Legro, Scotto Gelormino, and Giacomo Deloplano), composers, and conductors. Palm-readers can test their skills here: The collection includes plaster castings of the hands of famous conductors—plus Verdi's mythologized top-hat, pencil depictions of his last hours on earth, and photographs of opera singer Maria Callas. (Open June-Sept. Mon.-Sat. 9am-noon and 2-6pm, Sun. 9:30am-noon and 2:30-6pm; Nov.-March Mon.-Fri. 9am-noon and 2-5pm, Sat. 9am-noon and 2-4pm; Oct. Mon.-Fri. 9am-noon and 2-5pm, Sat. 9am-noon and 2-4pm, Sun. 9:30am-noon and 2:30-5pm; April Mon.-Sat. 9am-noon and 2-5pm. Admission L3000.)

Passing sixteenth-century Palazzo Marino (opposite La Scala, now the mayor's office) and the side of the church of San Fedele (1569), brings you to the strange **Casa degli Omenoni** (1565). This small Renaissance palace is embellished with eight giant Atlases, their heads bent forward by the weight they support. The street ends at **piazza Belgioioso,** a lovely square of old Milan dominated by the eighteenth-century Belgioioso *palazzo* and the picturesque house of nineteenth-century novelist

Alessandro Manzoni, the Tolstoy of Italy, who wrote **I Promessi Sposi** (The Betrothed). The **Museo Manzoniano** inside (via Morone, 1; tel. 87 10 19) is devoted to his life and works. Among the portraits of his friends is an autographed picture of Goethe. (Open Tues.-Fri. 9am-noon and 2-4pm. Free.) Continuing down via Morone brings you to **via Manzoni.** A fitting beginning for this street, medieval **Porta Nuova** is a Roman tomb sculpture and a Gothic niche containing statues of saints. At #29 stands the **Grand Hotel,** where Giuseppe Verdi spent his last days in 1901. While he was sick, the street was covered with straw so that the noise of passing carriages and horses wouldn't disturb him. The real gem of the *via* is the **Museo Poldi Pezzoli** (at #12; tel. 79 48 89), an outstanding private collection of art that was bequeathed to the city in 1879, housed in a building formerly occupied by the founder. The museum's masterpieces are hung in the Gold Saloon, which overlooks a beautiful garden (visible through a Palladian window). The paintings include a Byzantine *Virgin and Child* by Andrea Mantegna; Bellini's *Ecce Homo; St. Nicholas* by Piero della Francesca; the magical *Gray Lagoon* by Guardi; and the museum's signature piece, Antonio Pollaiolo's *Portrait of a Young Woman.* (Open Tues.-Wed. 9:30am-12:30pm and 2:30-6pm, Thurs.-Sat. 9:30am-12:30pm and 2:30-5:30pm, Sun. 9:30am-12:30pm; also Thurs. evenings 9-11pm (except Aug.). Admission L4000.)

Near Castello Sforzesco

After the cathedral, the huge, fifteenth-century **Castello Sforzesco** (tel. 62 36) is Milan's best-known monument. If you've misplaced a slipper, get to the palace by metro (MM1: Cairoli). Its majestic tower provides a light touch to an otherwise gloomy exterior. The interior is divided into three courts; the first one is so large it drowns out architectural details. In the other two, gracious Renaissance arcades occupy much of the castle interior. On the ground floor around the Ducal Court is the excellent sculpture collection renowned for Michelangelo's *Pietà Rondanini,* whose elongated forms lend new dimension to suffering. The picture gallery features paintings by Mantegna, Bellini, Lotto, and other masters of the Renaissance, as well as an outstanding *Madonna with Angels* by Lippi. There is an Egyptian collection and a tremendous display of Roman, Greek, and Etruscan artifacts in the basement. Five centuries of musical instruments are displayed on the first floor. (Open Tues.-Sun. 9:30am-12:15pm and 2:30-5:30pm. Free.)

Via Verdi, alongside La Scala leads to **via Brera,** another charming street lined with small, brightly colored palaces and art galleries a hop, skip, and a jump from the *duomo* (MM1: Cordusio; for doorstep service, catch bus #61 from MM1: Moscova). The **Pinacoteca di Brera** (Brera Art Gallery), via Brera, 28 (tel. 80 83 87), is in a seventeenth-century *palazzo* and displays a loaded collection of paintings—even for Italy. The courtyard consists of a two-storied *loggia* and a forceful statue of Napoleon as a victorious Roman Emperor. Paintings include Bellini's desperately intense *Pietà* (1460); Andrea Mantegna's foreshortened *Dead Christ* (1480) with its bitter but human expression of death; Raphael's *Marriage of the Virgin,* a Renaissance tour-de-force; Caravaggio's *Supper at Emmaus* (1606), in which Jesus looks like the carpenter he was; and Piero della Francesca's fifteenth-century *Madonna and Child with Saints* and *Duke Federico di Montefeltro.* The vibrant, animated frescoes by Bramante from the *Casa dei Panigarola* (Rm. 24) provide comic relief from the dramatic intensity of these works. A small but choice collection of modern Italian masters including Modigliani and Carlo Carra provides an even more striking contrast. (Open Tues.-Thurs. 9am-6pm, Fri.-Sat. 9am-1:30pm, Sun. 9am-12:30pm. Admission L4000.)

The **Church of Santa Maria delle Grazie,** on p. di Sta. Maria delle Grazie and corso Magenta off via Carducci (MM1: Cairoli, or take bus #21 and 24), is renowned for the splendid tribune Bramante added in 1492. Note the eccentric pilasters in the shape of candelabra that rise from a base carved with medallions representing saints. Below are set the coats of arms of the Moor and Dominican orders. Inside, the Gothic nave with its tunnel-like vaults is juxtaposed with the light and airy Bramante tribune. To the left, a door leads to Bramante's elegant square cloister. (Open daily 7am-noon and 3-7pm.)

Next to the church entrance in what was the monastery's refectory is the **Cenacolo Vinciano** (tel. 490 75 88), containing Leonardo's *Last Supper.* In spite of damage from bombing, flooding, and natural decay, it remains as riveting as ever. In late afternoon, the natural light from the windows matches the lighting in the fresco. From the far end of the room, you can see how Leonardo used converging lines to create a third dimension. The fresco captures the moment when the apostles reacted to the foreboding words of Jesus, "One of you will betray me." Look for the expression of Doubting Thomas with his raised forefinger; the sad profile of lonely Philip, who leans forward with arms folded in fear that he unknowingly is the betrayer; or Peter, partially blocked by Judas clutching his 30 pieces of silver and springing forward so fast that his right arm flails unnaturally. Although it has been partially covered with scaffolding for several years, the fresco still merits a visit. (Open Tues.-Sat. 9am-1:15pm and 2-6:15pm; Sun.-Mon. 9am-1:15pm. Admission L4000.)

If you are still in pursuit of the imagination of da Vinci, or are an all-around technology buff, explore the **Museo Nazionale della Scienza e della Tecnica "Leonardo da Vinci,"** via San Vittore, 21 (tel. 46 27 09), off via Carducci. A large section is devoted to applied physics and a huge room is filled with wooden models of Leonardo's most ingenious inventions. To arrive in appropriately high-tech fashion, take MM1 to San Ambrogio or buses #50 or 54. (Open Tues.-Sun. 9am-5pm. Admission L4000.)

The most influential medieval building in Milan, the **Church of Sant' Ambrogio** (MM1: San Ambrigio) served as a prototype for churches throughout Italy. An atrium housing remains of ancient tombstones and frescoes fronts the low-pitched facade. On either side are two towers; the one to the right is from the ninth century, the other from the twelfth. The high altar, encased in glass, retains the original ninth-century brilliant reliefs, silver and gold, enriched with enamel and gems. The crypt contains the gruesome skeletal remains of Sant' Ambrogio, the patron of the city, and two early Christian martyrs. The tiny fourth-century **Chapel of San Vittore,** with exquisite fifth-century mosaics adorning its cupola, is through the seventh chapel on the right. Leaving the church on the left, you pass under the curious **Portico della Canonica** (1492) by Bramante, the end columns of which have notches resembling those of tree trunks. Also by Bramante are the two exquisite courtyards in the adjacent **Università Cattolica,** originally the monastery of San Ambrogio.

From Corso di Porta Romana to the Navigli

This part of town lacks the grandeur of downtown Milan, but several interesting monuments warrant a visit. Be advised that distances are longer here; plan your journey and consider using public transportation.

The **Church of San Nazaro Maggiore,** on corso di Porta Romana, accessible from the *duomo* by bus #13, was constructed in medieval Lombard-Romanesque style. The Renaissance funerary chapel of the Trivulzio in front is the work of Bramante's pupil Bramantino (1512-1547). The tomb bears the famous epigraph: "Qui numquam quivit quiescit: Tasc." (He who never knew quiet now reposes: Silence.)

The **Church of San Lorenzo Maggiore,** on corso Ticinese (MM2: Porta Genova, then bus #59), the oldest church in Milan, testifies to the greatness of the city during the Paleochristian era. Its handsome interior may once have formed the principal hall of some antique baths or palace to which the sixteen Corinthian columns in front also belonged. More likely, the building started as an early Christian church in the second half of the fourth century. Although it was rebuilt later (12th-century *campanile,* 16th-century dome), it retains its original octagonal plan. On the four cardinal sides are large, semi-circular screened spaces behind which runs an ambulatory, in the manner of San Vitale at Ravenna. To the right of the church is the fourteenth-century chapel of San Aquino. Inside is a beautiful fourth-century mosaic of a young, beardless Christ among his apostles, and a carved sarcophagus from the fifth century. A staircase behind the altar leads to the remains of an early Roman amphitheater. Near the front of the church is the twelfth-century gate, **Porta Ticinese.**

An ancient edifice of fourth-century origin, the **Church of Sant' Eustorgio** stands farther down corso Ticinese (bus #15). The present building (erected in 1278) has a typical Lombard-Gothic interior of low vaults and brick ribs supported by heavy columns. The real gem of this church, and one of the great masterpieces of early Renaissance art, is the **Portinari Chapel** (1468), attributed traditionally to the Florentine Michelozzo. (L500 fee to open the gates in the back of the apse.) Similar to Brunelleschi's Pazzi Chapel in Florence, the plan of the chapel involves a square crowned by a dome with a smaller niche on one side also mounted by a dome. A *Dance of Angels* is carved around the base of the multicolored dome, and frescoes depict the life and death of Peter the Martyr. In the center of the chapel is the magnificent Gothic tomb of Saint Eustorgius, sculpted by Giovanni di Balduccio of Pisa (1339).

Through the neoclassical Arco di Porta Ticinese (1801-1814) or outside the MM2: Porta Genova station, you will find an Italian version of Amsterdam: canals, small footbridges, open air markets, picturesque alleys, and trolleys. This is the **Naviglio Grande,** part of the medieval canal system (whose original locks were designed by Leonardo) that connected the city with the lake region to the north.

South and East of the Duomo

One of the largest constructions of the early Renaissance is the **Ospedale Maggiore,** on via Festa del Perdono near p. Santo Stefano. The "General Hospital," now the University of Milan, has no fewer than nine courtyards. The inside arches are blanketed by multicolored circles and diamonds and the Gothic frames with medallions. Inside is a magnificent seventeenth-century court and a gracious smaller court attributed to Bramante.

In 1479, Bramante designed the mystical **Church of San Satiro** on via Torino, a few blocks or a few minutes ride on bus #15 from the *duomo.* Despite its modest proportions, the interior creates a marvelous illusion of space. Compare the imaginary and the real by standing at the back of the church and then behind the high altar. The octagonal baptistery, also by Bramante, contains a beautiful frieze of *putti.* In the back of the left transept, a curious Byzantine chapel has an exquisite painted terracotta *Pietà.* This chapel belonged to the original tenth-century church, and the tenth-century *campanile* was the prototype for subsequent Lombard-Romanesque bell towers.

Following via Spadari off via Torino and then making a right onto via Cantù will lead you to the minute but beautiful **Pinacoteca Ambrosiana,** p. Pio XI, 2 (tel. 80 01 46). The 14 rooms of the Ambrosiana house exquisite works from the fifteenth through seventeenth centuries, including Botticelli's *Madonna of the Canopy;* Leonardo's *Portrait of a Musician;* Raphael's cartoon for the *School of Athens;* Caravaggio's *Basket of Fruit,* the first example of still-life painting in Italy; and the two plush paintings of *Earth* and *Air* by Breughel. (Open Sun.-Fri. 9:30am-5pm. Admission L4000.)

Other museums in the city include the **Galleria d'Arte Moderna,** via Palestro, 16 (tel. 70 23 78), in the neoclassical Villa Comunale next to the Giardini Pubblici (MM2: Porta Venezia). Napoleon lived here with Josephine when Milan was capital of the Napoleonic Kingdom of Italy (1805-1814). Important modern Lombard art is displayed here, as well as works by Picasso, Matisse, Renoir, Gauguin, and Cézanne. The house and the adjacent gardens alone merit a trip. (Open Wed.-Mon. 9:30am-12:15pm and 2:30-5:30pm. Free.) The **Museo di Milano,** via Sant' Andrea, 6, shares quarters in an eighteenth-century mansion with the small **Museo di Storia Contemporanea** (Museum of Contemporary History; tel. 70 62 45; MM2: San Babila). Most of the "ologies" are on display here, from "anthro" to "zoo." View the Canadian dinosaur and a restored dodo. (Open Tues.-Sun. 9am-12:15pm and 2:30-5:30pm. Free.)

Several interesting streets lie east of the *duomo.* **Corso Vittorio Emanuele,** between p. del Duomo and p. San Babila, is the major shopping street of the city.

Except for the **Church of San Carlo al Corso** (another neoclassical building modeled after the Pantheon), the street was entirely rebuilt after the war. **Via Monte Napoleone,** off p. San Babila, the most elegant street in Milan, is lined with early nineteenth-century *palazzi* and late twentieth-century Armanis and Cardins, now used by the most exclusive of city businesses and the most exquisite of its *ateliers* (designer show rooms). The part of **corso Venezia** bordering the Giardini Pubblici is a broad boulevard with sumptuous palaces. A stroll through the **Giardini Pubblici** is ideal on a sunny afternoon, especially in summer when the yellow flowers of the *timo* trees give off a sweet fragrance. (The park also houses a small zoo and is open year-round roughly 7am-10pm.)

Shopping

Those with overstuffed luggage and understuffed money belts can easily make window shopping a portal into contemporary Italian urban culture. Milan's most elegant boutiques are found between the *duomo* and p. S. Babila, especially on the extremely chic **via Monte Napoleone.** If you can tolerate the stigma of being an entire *season* behind the trends, famous designer brands may be purchased from **blochisti** (wholesale clothing outlets). Try **Monitor** on viale Monte Nero (MM2: Porta Genova, then bus #9); **La Vela,** on via Jommelli, 22, off via Porpora (MM1 or MM2: Loreto, then bus #93; open Mon.-Fri. 3:30-7:30pm, Sat. 10:30am-12:30pm and 3-7pm); or **Il Salvagente,** on via Bronzetti off corso XXII Marzo (bus #60). **Fiorucci's** original shop is at Galleria Passarella, 1 (tel. 70 80 33), at corso V. Emanuele (MM1: San Babila). More reasonable, but still well-designed, is the clothing sold along **corso Buenos Aires,** while **via Torino,** near the *duomo,* and **via Sarpi,** near porta Garibaldi, are lined with inexpensive department stores and boutiques catering to a younger crowd. The area around corso di Porta Ticinese is fast becoming the center of *chic ma non snob* (irreverent Italian slang for *avant garde*). From MM2: Porta Genova, take bus 59. On the cutting edge of fashion is **Eliogabalo,** p. Sant' Eustorgio, 2 (tel. 837 82 93), named after a Roman Emperor renowned for his preoccupation with matters sartorial. Less unique and less pricey are the department stores, **Rinascente,** downtown across from the *duomo,* or **Upim,** at p. San Babila, 5. True Milanese bargain shoppers wait until the large street markets on Saturdays and Tuesdays to buy threads. These are on **via Fauché** (MM2: Garibaldi), **viale Papinian** (MM2: Sant' Agostino), and the four-century-old **Fiera di Sinigallia** on nearby via Calatafini (Sat. only). For used clothing try the Navigli district or corso Garibaldi. (Enough military gear is sold here to supply a platoon of U.S. Marines.) Camping equipment can often be bought reasonably at the **American Shop,** via Giambellino, 79 (tel. 47 44 10), down via B. d'Alviano (MM1: Bande Nere). Shop at the end of July and in the middle of January for the pre-Ferragosto sales wars (20-50% off). (Clothing stores are generally open Mon. 10am-noon, Tues.-Sat. 10am-noon and 2-7:30pm.)

Entertainment

Music and Theater

Emblematic of the pastiche of populism and posh that characterizes the arts scene in Milan is the **Musica in Metro** program, a series of summer concerts performed by local music students, dressed in black-tie best, in metro stations. Launched in 1987, the project enjoyed such raging success it's bound to become an annual event.

The kids playing their hearts out in subway stops probably hope to someday perform at **La Scala,** which traditionally opens its season on December 7th. Opera performances continue through late May. The summer season, primarily during June and September, offers further recitals, operas, and concerts, as well as some ballet. Though good tickets are usually sold out long in advance, gallery seats (notorious for inducing altitude sickness) go for as little as L10,000. Don't expect to see much, but your ears will smile. (Box office (tel. 80 91 26) is open Tues.-Sun. 10am-1pm and 3:30-5:30pm. On performance days tickets go on sale 5:30-9:30pm; unsold gallery seats and standing room are available 1 hr. before curtain.) The **Conservatorio,** via del Conservatorio, 12 (tel. 70 17 55 or 70 18 54), near p. Tricolore, offers more classical music, while the **Teatro Lirico,** via Rastrelli, 6 (tel. 80 00 46), south of the *duomo,* is Milan's leading dramatic stage (tickets from L20,000). Summer brings special programs of music and culture: Milano d'Estate (Milan in the Summer) in July, and Vacanze a Milano (Vacation in Milan) in August.

Now owned by the city, the **Piccolo Teatro,** via Rovello, 2 (tel. 87 23 52), near via Dante, began in the post-war years as a socialist theater. (Performances Tues.-Sun. night. Tickets L5000.) **Ciak,** via Sangallo, 33 (tel. 73 00 21), near p. Argonne east of the *duomo,* is a favorite haunt of young *milanesi* for theater, films, and sometimes cabaret. Take train #5 from Stazione Centrale to viale Argonne.

The **Teatro di Porta Romana,** corso di Porta Romana, 124 (tel. 58 24 55 or 548 35 47; bus #13 from via Marconi off p. del Duomo), is building a reputation for experimental production and first-run, mainstream plays (tickets about L16,000). In what has become an annual project, the **Teatro dell' Elfo,** via Ciro Menotti, 11 (tel. 71 67 91), sponsors the **Festival dai Festival,** bringing together the best of the many local theater festivals staged throughout Italy. (Performances throughout July. Tickets about L20,000.)

Movies and Nightlife

Milan's cinematic scene thrives. Theaters such as the **Leonardo,** on p. Leonardo da Vinci at via Villani (tel. 23 09 80), and the **Angelicum,** p. Sant' Angelo, 2, off via Moscova (tel. 66 17 12 or 63 27 48), specialize in showing films in their original languages (L3000-5000). The **Mexico,** via Savona, 57 (tel. 47 98 02), southwest of the *duomo,* shows musicals, including *Rocky Horror,* with live performers (L5500). Finally, between late June and late August, the *Cinema nel Parco* festival offers outdoor showings of recent films (L3000).

Milanese newspapers (the biggies are the left-leaning *Corriere della Sera* and the reactionary *Repubblica*) print daily listings of plays, movies, and clubs. On Thursdays both publish mini-magazine inserts devoted exclusively to entertainment. The **Navigli** area, once a haunt of prostitutes and black-marketeers, is now coming alive with entertainment and clubs. *Birrerie* (beer-halls which serve hundreds of brands) and *paninoteche* (sandwich bars) are opening up everywhere and attracting a young crowd. One central quarter that is safe and attractive lies around **via Brera;** here you'll find art galleries, small clubs and restaurants.

Rock and all that's hot: After Bologna, Milan supports the best rock scene in Italy. Among the best clubs is **Prego,** via Besenzanica, 3 (tel. 407 56 53). Open Tues. and Thurs.-Sun. until 2am. **Rolling Stone,** corso XXII Marzo, 32 (tel. 73 31 72), east of the *duomo,* is easy on hip and heavy on chic. Open Thurs.-Sun. until 2:30am. Cover L10,000. **Plastic** (officially **Il Killer Plastico**), not far away at viale Umbria, 120, verging on disco, swings between a punk/new wave and a fashionable New York crowd. Open Tues.-Sun. until 2:30am. Cover L15,000, Sat. L18,000. **Bella Epoque,** p. XXIV Maggio, 8 (tel. 832 21 60; MM2: Porta Genova, then bus #59), looks back to the golden era of rock and roll. Come here for a Beatles fix.

Jazz and Folk: Capolinea, via Ludovico il Moro, 119 (tel. 47 05 24). Walk out corso Italia towards the Navigli and Porta Ticinese, south of the *duomo.* A student crowd. Open Tues.-Sun. until 1:30am. **Le Scimmie,** via Ascanio Sforza, 49 (tel. 839 18 74), beyond the Capolinea. Milan's premier jazz spot. Open Wed.-Mon. 8pm-2am. In the Brera area, **Biblo's,** via Madonnina, 17 (tel. 805 18 60), usually has folk performers. Open Tues.-Sun. Admission L10,000.

Discos: USA, via B. Cellini, 2 (tel. 702 93 81), near corso Porta Vittoria. One of Milan's top discos, but expensive. Cover L15,000-20,000. Open Wed.-Sun. 11:30pm-3am. **American Disaster,** via Boscovich, 48 (tel. 22 57 28), near Stazione Centrale. Less happening but also less expensive. Cover L8000. Open Wed.-Sun. **No Ties,** Foro Bonaparte, 68 (tel. 87 27 80). A chic, both gay and straight place with a long line at the door. Cover L10,000-12,000, Wed. 2-for-1 admission. Open Wed.-Sun. 10pm-3am. **Nuova Idea,** via de Castillia, 30 (tel. 689 27 53; MM2: Gioia). A huge and notably gay hangout, famous throughout Italy. Cover L8000-10,000. Open Tues. and Thurs.-Sun. 9:30pm-1 or 2am. Another gay club is **Contatto,** corso Sempione, 76 (tel. 31 56 75), behind the Castello Sforzesco; take bus #57 from MM1: Cairoli.

Neither Fish nor Fowl: The African community's **Zimba** ("lion" in Swahili), via Gratosoglio, 108 (tel. 826 33 16), has shocked xenophobes by becoming one of the city's biggest hangouts.

Conga, rhythm and blues, Carribean music. Open Tues.-Sun. New bands looking for a break start out at **Magia Music Meeting,** via Salutati, 2 (tel. 481 35 53; MM2: San Agostino). Open Sun. only. The great lament of Milanese musicians is that they lack an indigenous modern musical tradition of their own. The same surely cannot be said of Milanese wines. Try any of 500 vintages at **Provera,** corso Magenta, 7 (tel. 805 05 22; bus #24 from p. Cordusio). L1500 per glass. At **Portnoy,** via de Amicis, 1 (tel. 837 86 56; bus #15 from via Torino off p. del Duomo), at corso di Porta Ticinese, writers give nightly readings of their work followed by discussion. As Portnoy would have hoped, food too—*panini* about L2500, *primi* L6000. Open Mon.-Sat. 7am-2am; in summer readings at 9:30pm, in off-season 7:30pm; no readings in Aug.

Our *Let's Go* researcher/writers did not make it to Pavia, Cremona, Mantua, Bergamo, and Brescia in 1988. Prices and hours may have changed.

Pavia

Pavia basks on the banks of the Ticino, near the river's confluence with the Po. Once an important imperial Roman town, Pavia weathered Attila in 452 and Odoacre in 476, reaching its heyday as a capital of the Gauls and Langobards, who presided from the sixth to the eighth centuries. That the city continued to thrive three centuries later as a commune is evidenced by the magnificent Romanesque churches.

The university, established in 1361, remains prestigious. The sumptuous *certosa* (Charterhouse), built in 1473, 10km north of Pavia, ensures a steady trickle of visitors. And the city's earth-toned buildings set among magnolias and its peaceful style make it a refuge from Milan's urban crush. You'll do best to limit your relaxation to the day; the city's yuppie prosperity precludes budget accomodations.

Orientation and Practical Information

Pavia lies on the train line between Milan (½ hr.) and Genoa (1½ hr.). Frequent buses from Milan are useful only if you want to visit the *certosa* on the way, as only five trains per day stop there (see Buses and Near Pavia). Buses leave from p. Castello in Milan and make Pavia an easy day's excursion. The train station lies to the west of the town, which spreads along the northern bank of the Ticino. In town, **corso Cavour/Mazzini** runs east-west, while **strada Nuova** runs north-south.

EPT: corso Garibaldi, 1A (tel. 221 56). Walk down viale V. Emanuele II, which becomes corso Cavour. After 5-10 min., turn right on strada Nuova, and keep a sharp eye out for corso Garibaldi on your left. The office is helpful, but not particularly welcoming. Open June-Aug. Mon.-Fri. 8:30am-1:30pm and 3-6pm, Sat. 9am-noon; Sept.-May Mon.-Fri. 8:30am-1pm and 3-6pm, Sat. 9am-noon.

Post Office: p. della Posta, 2 (tel. 269 19), off via Mentana. Open Mon.-Fri. 8am-7pm, Sat. 8am-1pm. **Postal code:** 27100.

Telephones: SIP, via Galliano, 8, around the corner from the post office. Open daily 8am-9:30pm. 9:45pm-8am, go to **Hotel Palaces,** viale Libertà, 89 (tel. 275 18). **Telephone code:** 0382.

Train Station: At the head of viale V. Emanuele II at the western end of town (tel. 230 00). To Genoa (one way L5900, round-trip L10,000) or Milan (one way L2000, round-trip 3400). Every 3 hr. to Cremona (one way L3700, round-trip L6200) and Mantua (one way L6900, round-trip L11,600).

Buses: SGEA depart from Bar Piavè, viale V. Emanuele II, 28 (tel. 253 71), opposite the station. To Milan (5am-10pm every hr.; 75 min. and L2600, 50 min. and L3000 direct) via the *certosa* (10 min., L1300). All of these buses may also be caught at viale Matteotti, near the Castello Visconteo.

Medical Assistance: Ospedale S. Matteo, p. Golgi, 2 (tel. 39 01). For an **ambulance,** call 241 13.

Police: Questura, p. Italia, 5 (tel. 30 12 04).

Accommodations and Camping

Albergo Regisole, p. del Duomo, 2 (tel. 247 39), across from the *duomo* in the town center. Clean, spacious, and pleasant. Singles L17,000. Doubles L30,000, with bath L35,000. Showers included. Breakfast L3500.

Albergo Moderno, viale V. Emanuele II, 45 (tel. 268 19 or 217 43), in front of the station. Run-down but huge and friendly. English spoken. Singles L22,000, with bath L28,000. Doubles L38,000, with bath L45,000. Full pension L45,000.

Hotel Splendid, via XX Settembre, 11 (tel. 247 03), off corso Cavour. Somewhat seedy. The nicest free showers in town, though. Singles L18,000. Doubles L29,000.

Camping: Lido, via Varazza (tel. 332 69). L3500 per person, L3000 per tent. Open May-Sept. **Ticino,** via Mascherpa, 10 (tel. 200 15). Equipped with a swimming pool. To get to either, walk down viale V. Emanuele II from the station, then turn right at the statue of Athena, and cross the bridge at the road's end.

Food

Coniglio (rabbit) and *rana* (frog) are specialties, and Pavia also has some excellent pastry shops and *panetterie,* especially along corso Cavour and corso Mazzini. Try the delicate *panini allo yogurt.* Don't look around for the daily **street market**—it went underground a few years ago to make way for cars. Today, it's under p. Vittoria off corso Cavour. (Open Tues.-Sat. 8am-12:30pm and 4-7:30pm.) Claustrophobes can go to the **open-air market** in p. Petrarca, behind the *duomo.* (Open Tues.-Sat. 8am-2pm.) On sultry summer Sundays, when the *pavesi* flee their city streets, most of the younger generation flees to **Pampanin,** p. Vittorio, 20 (tel. 291 67), diagonally across from the *duomo,* a *gelateria* with soft rap music and umbrella-shaded tables. (Open Thurs.-Tues. 10am-10:30pm.)

Trattoria da Andrea, via Teodolina, 23 (tel. 242 10), off p. del Duomo. A homey room full of good smells. *Menù* L12,000. Pasta L5000. Wine L1000 per ¼-liter. Despite the sign, reservations are not required. Open Sat.-Thurs. noon-3pm and 6:30-11pm.

Hosteria della Malora, via Milazzo, 79 (tel. 343 02). Cross the covered bridge and walk along the river to your left. Heartily recommended by everyone in town. In summer, eat outside in the tent. *Primi* L4000, *pesciolini fritti* (little fried fish) L5000, *rana fritta* (fried frog) L10,000. Cover L1500. Open Sept.-July Tues.-Sun. 12:30-2:30pm and 7:30-10pm.

The Insomnia Café, via Emilia Cravos, 21. Turn left onto vicolo S. Sebastiano from strada Nuova. Delicious if not hunger-busting. Coffee, drinks, pasta dishes, and often live rock. Open Tues.-Sun. nights.

Ristorante Pizzeria Capri, corso Cavour, 32 (tel. 200 67). If you had friends studying in Pavia, they would take you here for pizza. Between L3000 (for a humble *margherita*) and L5500 (for *quattro formaggi*). Open Wed.-Mon. noon-2:30pm and 6:30pm-midnight.

Medagliani, corso Cavour, 37 (tel. 227 48). Pastries and pizza. About L1000 per *etto* of either. Open Mon. 8:30am-12:30pm, Tues.-Sun. 8:30am-12:30pm and 4:30-7:30pm. Another branch of the family runs a store at corso Garibaldi, 10 (tel. 232 94).

Ristorante della Madonna, via dei Liguri, 28 (tel. 30 28 33), at via Cardano, the continuation of corso Garibaldi. A lively, elegant place. A bit pricey. Open Sept.-July Tues.-Sat. noon-2:15pm and 8pm-midnight.

Sights and Seasonal Events

It was in the **Church of San Michele** that the great medieval Lombard king Frederick Barbarossa (1123-1190) was crowned. The church's massive eleventh-century facade (made of yellow sandstone) is divided into three parts and topped with a typical Lombard-Romanesque *loggia.* Vigorously sculpted griffins, snake-tailed fish, monsters, and struggling human figures depicting the battle of Good and Evil adorn the three doorways. On the right side of the church, above a massive portal, is a frieze on which Christ gives a papyrus volume to St. Paul and the Keys of the Church to St. Peter. Decorating the chancel inside are a 1491 fresco of the Coronation of the Virgin and bas-reliefs from the fourteenth century. A silver Byzantine crucifix (12th-century) graces the chapel to the right of the presbytery. To get to San Michele, follow the directions for the EPT office, and continue along corso Garibaldi. (Open Tues.-Sat. 9-11:30am and 2:30-6:30pm, Sun. 9am-noon.)

From San Michele it's a short walk to Pavia's layered, motley-colored *duomo.* Begun in 1488 and influenced by the designs of Bramante, Macaluso, and Leonardo, it is one of the most ambitious undertakings of the Renaissance in Lombardy—much of it was not actually completed until 1895-1933. The huge interior space in the form of a Greek cross is a typical Renaissance central-plan church. (Church open 7am-noon and 2:20-10pm.) Beside the church rises the ponderous **Torre Civica** (Civic Tower, 12th-century) and the sixteenth-century **Bishops' Palace.**

The **University of Pavia** (tel. 354 91), on strada Nuova, was founded in 1361, but originated in the tenth century. Over 17,000 students currently attend classes at this institution, headquartered in the neoclassical *palazzo.* The three towers rising from the university's property on p. Leonardo da Vinci are the vestiges of the more than 100 medieval towers that once pierced the city's skyline.

Strada Nuova ends at the **Castello Visconteo** (1360), a huge medieval castle set in a park that was once the Viscontis' private hunting ground. The castle's vast courtyard is bordered on three sides by richly colored windows and elegant terra-cotta decoration. The fourth was destroyed in 1527 during the Franco-Spanish Wars. Pavia's **Civic Museum** (tel. 338 53) here houses an extensive Lombard-Romanesque sculpture collection and a picture gallery. (Admission L2000, ages under 12 L500.)

From the front grounds of the castle, you can see the low rounded forms of the **Church of San Pietro in Ciel d'Oro** (St. Peter of the Golden Sky) to the west. Access to the church is from via Griziotti, off viale Matteotti. Another exquisite example of the Lombard-Romanesque style, it was consecrated in 1132. Inside on the high altar is a magnificent marble reliquary containing the bones of that most catholic of Christians, Saint Augustine, under an ornate Gothic arch. (Open daily 7am-noon and 3-7:30pm.)

Pavia's past resurfaces each September when folklore, concerts, and parades animate the city for 15 days in the **Settembre Pavese** festival. The **Commune di Pavia** (tel. 39 91) has the most current information. If you prefer modern rites, join the rowdy masses who gather in May or June to watch the **Coppa Città di Pavia,** a national soccer tournament held in the **Campo Spartivo Frigirolo.** If you'd rather perform sun and surf rituals, visit the **Ticino** river, Pavia's center for speed boats and sedentary sun-addicts.

Near Pavia

Ten kilometers north of Pavia stands the **Certosa di Pavia** (Charterhouse of Pavia; tel. 92 56 13, ask to speak with multilingual Padre Sisto). Both buses and trains can drop you 15 minutes away. Buses leave Pavia from p. Piave opposite the station (L1300) and Milan from p. Castello (L2300). From the **bus** stop, the *certosa* stands at the end of a long road lined by trees; from the **train** station, go to the left around the outside wall of the monastic complex and turn inside to the right at the first opening. This Carthusian monastic complex and mausoleum was built for the Viscontis who ruled the area from the twelfth to fifteenth centuries. Construction began in 1396, and decoration from every period and style was added on until the late eighteenth century. The exuberant facade (late 1400s-1560) is an outburst of sculpture and inlaid marble, representing the apex of the Lombard Renaissance. The interior of the church shelters a plethora of masterworks including those of Bergognone and Amadeo. The Old Sacristy houses a Florentine triptych carved in ivory, with 99 sculptures and 66 bas-reliefs narrating the lives of Mary and Jesus.

The monument to Ludovico il Moro Visconti and his child bride Beatrice d'Este is especially remarkable. The large cloister contains 122 terra-cotta arches and is still ringed by the cottages of monks who have sworn vows of obedience, stability (they won't go out of their cottages unless their prior sends for them), and "conversion of manners" (poverty and chastity). They are often silent in order to hear God's word better. Monks lead delightful tours of the complex whenever a large enough group has gathered (usually every ½-hr.), leaving from inside the church. (Open May-Aug. Tues.-Sun. 9-11:30am and 2:30-8pm; March-April. and Sept.-Oct. Tues.-Sun. 9-11:30am and 2:30-5pm; Nov.-Feb. Tues.-Sun. 9-11:30am and 2:30-4pm. Free.)

Cremona

Situated on the left bank of the Po in the middle of the river's valley, Cremona is blessed with both agricultural prosperity and an impressive cultural heritage. The monumental architecture dates back to the city's period as a free commune (11th to 14th centuries). The greatest violin-makers in the world lived and worked here—the most renowned among them Antonio Stradivari (1644-1737) and Giuseppe Antonio Guarneri, also known as Guarneri del Gesù (1687-1745). Today, violinists from around the globe have their instruments repaired and test new violins at the International School of Violin-Making.

Orientation and Practical Information

Cremona is a 1½-hour train ride from Milan on a *diretto,* and a 2½-hour ride on a *locale.* The city is also on the Pavia-Mantua train line. From the train station, north of the center, walk straight down via Palestro, which turns into corso G. Verdi. Walk left through p. Cavour and straight onto p. del Comune in front of the *duomo* (10 min.). Or take bus #1.

EPT: p. del Comune, 8 (tel. 232 33), in front of the *duomo.* Helpful and kind staff, but English is not their forte. Be sure to pick up their guide *Cremona, Art City.* Open Mon.-Sat. 9am-12:30pm and 3-7pm, Sun. 9:30am-12:30pm.

Post Office: via Verdi, 1 (tel. 234 94). Most services open Mon.-Fri. 8am-7pm, Sat. 8am-1pm. **Postal code:** 26100.

Telephones: SIP, p. Cavour, 1. Open 9am-7:45pm. At night, go to **Albergo Bologna,** p. Risorgimento, 7 (tel. 242 58), a few blocks to the right of the train station as you exit along via Dante. **Telephone code:** 0372.

Train Station: via Dante, 68 (tel. 222 37). Ask for piazza Stazione (or resort to onomatopaeic sound effects). To Milan (11 per day; one way L4400, round-trip L7600), Venice via Brescia (one way L11,700, round-trip L20,000), Bologna via Fidenza or Piacenza (one way L7300, round-trip L12,400), Pavia (7 per day; one way L3700, round-trip L6200), and Mantua (16 per day; one way L3200, round-trip L5400).

Buses: Autostazione di via Dante. To Milan (2 per day; one way L4700, round-trip L7700) and Brescia (11 per day, L4400). Tickets at **La Pasticceria Mezzardi,** via Dante, 105.

Laundromat: Lavasecco a gettoni, corso Matteotti, off p. Libertà. L12,000 per 5kg. Open Mon.-Fri. 8:30am-12:30pm and 3:30-7pm.

Medical Assistance: Ospedale (tel. 40 51) past p. IV Novembre to the east. **Ambulances,** Tel. 434 45.

Police: Pubblica Sicurezza, via Tribunali, 6 (tel. 233 33).

Accommodations and Camping

Accommodations are quite inexpensive in Cremona. Most visitors arrive in groups, so phone ahead to discover which hotels have been invaded.

Albergo Concordia, via Pallavicino, 4. (tel. 204 12). Take viale Treato e Trieste from the station and turn right on corso Matteotti. Clean and cheery rooms. Easygoing management. Workers live here in winter. English spoken. Singles L13,000. Doubles L23,000. Triples L33,000. Ristorante Concordia, downstairs, serves meals for about L10,000.

Albergo Touring, via Palestro, 3 (tel. 213 90). From the station, walk across via Dante and straight down via Palestro. Spacious, electrically furnished rooms. Little space on weekends. Singles L18,000. Doubles L25,000, with bath L30,000. Closed 2 weeks in Aug.

Albergo Brescia, via Brescia, 7 (tel. 43 46 15). From the station, turn left down via Dante and left onto via Brescia at p. Libertà. A sunny yellow building containing pale pink or faded green rooms at low prices. More space on weekends. Singles L15,000. Doubles L25,000.

Albergo San Marco, p. Risorgimento, 16 (tel. 223 05). From the train station, go left on via Dante. Clean and pleasant, and run by a gracious old-world couple. Often full on weekdays. Rooms are a bit small but some have balconies. Singles L16,000. Doubles L25,000. Modern showers included.

Camping: Parco al Po, via lungo Po Europa (tel. 271 37), southwest of town. From p. Cavour, take corso V. Emanuele for 20 min. L3400 per person, L2500 per tent. Open May-Sept.

Food

Cremona's best known dish, *mostarda di Cremona,* evokes the sixteenth-century combination of savory fruits—cherries, figs, apricots, melons—preserved in a sweet mustard-flavored syrup and served on boiled meats. Less of an acquired taste, *torrone* is a candy (made from eggs, honey, and almonds) that comes in white bars. *Mostarda di Cremona* can be found in most local *trattorie* and some bars. *Torrone* abounds in the elegant pastry and candy shops on via Solferino. Sweet tooths prone to evening fits of sugar withdrawal will appreciate the long work days at **Lanfranchi** at #30. (Open Mon.-Sat. 8:30am-1pm and 3:30-8pm, Sun. 8:30am-1pm.) On Wednesday and Saturday from 7am to noon, food vendors hold an **open-air market** in p. Marconi, past p. Cavour on corso G. Verdi.

Italmense Agnello, via Vianello Torriani, 7 (tel. 221 19), off via Boccaccio north of the *duomo.* Popular with students and office workers. Full meals L7700. Open Mon.-Fri. noon-2pm. Closed 2 weeks in Aug.

Italmense, via Mocchino, 11 (tel. 287 61). Another *mensa* with L7700 full meals. Open Mon.-Fri.

Trattoria Bissone, via F. Pecorari, 3 (tel. 239 53), off via A. Manzoni. Cremona's oldest and most famous restaurant. Prices can be high, especially at night when there is live jazz. *Menù* L20,000. Try *cotechino con lenticchie* (sausage with lentils) or *manzo bollito* (steamed beef). Open Aug.-June Mon.-Sat. noon-3pm and 8-9:30pm.

Pizzeria allo Stagnino, corso Garibaldi, 85 (tel. 391 53), at via Oberdan. Bronzed and boisterous soccer players come here after games. Highly polished wood tables, airy garden. Family-run, and the family runs about. Pizzas L3500-5000, wine L5000 per liter. Cover L1500. Open Sept.-July Wed.-Mon. noon-3pm and 6:30pm-12:30am.

Duomo, via dei Gonfalonieri, 13 (tel. 352 42), and **Pizzeria Piedigrotta,** p. Risorgimento. Cremonese *conoscenti* prefer this family-owned franchise. Duomo is the more elegant establishment, with cool marble and smooth service. Cover L1000. Open daily noon-3pm and 6:30pm-1am. Piedigrotta is a bit funkier. Cover is higher (L1500), and hours shorter (open Tues.-Sat.). At both, pizzas L3500-7000 and wine L6000 per liter.

Trattoria Pace, p. Pace, 18 (tel. 207 06). The cheapest *trattoria* in town. Full meals up to L12,500. A lunchtime favorite of many Cremonese. Open Mon.-Sat. noon-2pm and 6-8pm.

Sights

Two and a half centuries after the death of Stradivari, violins and their production constitute the primary attraction in Cremona. Closest to the train station, the small **Museo Stradivariano,** at via Palestro, 17 (tel. 233 49), is a fascinating introduction to Stradivari's art. Also included are finished examples by such modern masters as Giuseppe Lecchi and Gaetano Sgarabotto. The museum demonstrates the versatility of Stradivari, including his plans and models for harps, lutes, mandolins, and guitars. (Open Sept.-July Tues.-Sat. 9:30am-12:15pm and 3-5:45pm, Sun. 9:30am-12:15pm. Admission L1000, includes the Museo Civico around the corner.) When school is in session, the **International School of Violin-Making** workshop in the Raimondi Palace on corso Garibaldi provides an entertaining example of artisanry in action. Compare modern tools with those of Stradivari, and note the continuing preoccupation with detail that distinguishes the school. If you really want to fiddle around, go to the second floor of **Palazzo del Comune** in p. del Comune, a plush town hall decorated with sixteenth-century Renaissance terra-cottas. Its Saletta del Violini showcases five masterpiece violins attributed to Andrea Amati (1566), his nephew Nicolo Amati (1658), A. Stradivari (1715), and G. Guarneri (1734)—most recently played by Pinchas Zukerman. Both Stradivari and del Gesù learned their trade from Andrea Amati, whose family dominated violin-making in the sixteenth and seventeenth centuries. (Open June to mid-Aug. Mon.-Sat. 9am-noon and 3-5pm, Sun. 9am-noon; mid-Sept. to May Mon.-Fri. 9am-noon and 3-5pm, Sat.-Sun. 9am-noon. Free.)

Directly across from the *palazzo* is the pink marble *duomo,* a major creation of twelfth-century, Lombard-Romanesque architecture. Its central, two-story Gothic porch shelters a statue of the Madonna and two saints (1310) above a charming frieze depicting the Labors of the Months. Though the interior is dark, the cycle of sixteenth-century frescoes by Boccaccio Boccaccino, Gianfrancesco Bembo, and others is clearly visible. (Open daily 8am-noon and 3-7pm.) The tower to the left of the cathedral is the late thirteenth-century **Torrazzo,** at 108m the tallest *campanile* in Italy. A massive brick structure lightened by an octagonal marble crown, it bears Cremona's coat-of-arms and a sixteenth-century clock. The Age of Aquarius found some roots with the sixteenth-century Cremonese: The clock of the bell tower is ornately decorated with all signs of the Zodiac. (Scale the heights mid-March to Nov. daily 9am-noon and 3-7pm; Dec. to mid-March Sun. and holidays only. Admission L2000, about L20 per stair.) The **baptistery** (1167) is a remarkable, solid brick structure whose dome rises in a perfect, unadorned octagonal pattern to a small skylight. Completing the square is the **Loggia dei Militi,** across from the baptistery. Erected in 1292 in Gothic style, it was used as a meeting place for the captains of the citizens' militia. The Gothic **Church of Sant' Agostino** (1345), near via Plasio, contains Bonifacio Bembo frescoes and the *Madonna with Saints* by Perugino (1494).

Because Cremona continued to develop as a city well into the sixteenth century, it is blessed with some fine Renaissance buildings. One of the most representative is the **Palazzo Fodri** (1499) at corso Matteotti, 17. Its elegant terra-cotta shelters a courtyard embellished with panels depicting military scenes. The columns in the courtyard bear French royal insignias in homage to Louis XII of France, who occupied the duchy of Milan in 1499. Though many of the *palazzi* have become private residences, the **Palazzo Affaitati** (1561), via Ugolani Dati, 4, sports an impressive marble grand staircase that leads to the **Museo Civico** (tel. 293 49). The collection of paintings of the Cremona school (15th to 18th centuries) includes the illustrious families of Bembo, the Campi, and Boccaccino. Caravaggio's San Francesco contemplates a *memento mori* (a skull), and the fifteenth-century codices harken to Renaisance politicking. (Hours and prices same as at Museo Stradivariano.)

The remarkable fifteenth-century **Church of San Sigismondo,** on via Marmolada, is a 20-minute walk from p. Libertà—take via Ghisleri. From p. Cavour, take bus #2 to the church. Built to commemorate the marriage of Bianca Maria Visconti, a duchess of the Milanese ruling family, to Francesco Sforza, a scion of the principal rival family, the church joined the entire city of Cremona as Bianca's dowry.

Each year, Cremona hosts **Rassegna Musical "Porta Mosa,"** a pop, rock, and jazz festival. Concerts take place throughout June and July. The **Teatro C. A. Ponchielli,** corso V. Emanuele II, 52, stages plays and concerts year-round. (Box office open daily 4-7pm. Gallery seats L10,000.)

Mantua (Mantova)

Home to the lavish Gonzaga Dynasty, Mantua became an important court in Renaissance Europe. The Gonzaga arose from peasant origins, but once they made it to the top, they spent 400 years embellishing the town center with their palaces, castles, towers, and churches. Though their *noveau riche* munificence verged on tastelessness (as in the large group of dwarfs gathered for their court), they enticed great Renaissance artists to their court. Leon Battista Alberti designed the churches of San Sebastiano and Sant' Andrea, and Andrea Mantegna covered the walls of several palace rooms with splendid frescoes.

Modern Mantua's cars and busy roads outside the historic center are an innocuous backdrop for the century-old treasures the city preserves and for the peasant flavor its ruling family sought so fiercely to repudiate. The Mantovese submersion in the inexorable march of seasons and crops is a soothing salve for visitors bruised by the song-and-dance routines of more touristed towns.

Orientation and Practical Information

Mantua is connected by direct trains to Verona, Modena, Cremona, and Milan (from Milan you can also change at Codogno). From Brescia and Parma, change at Piadena; from Bologna at Modena; and from Venice at Verona. The train station, to the southeast, is a 10-minute walk along corso V. Emanuele and corso Umberto, from Mantua's three central *piazze:* piazza Mantegna, piazza Concordia, and piazza Marconi. Mantua is surrounded on three sides by the Mincio, which then widens to form three surrounding lakes—Lago Superiore, Lago di Mezzo, and Lago Inferiore. The cheapest, worthwhile city guide is by Rita Castagna, available in local bookstores (L4000).

EPT: p. Mantegna, 6 (tel. 35 06 81), adjacent to the church of Sant' Andrea. Efficient and amiable young staff. Get both of the maps they offer. Ask about the *agriturismo* program (see Near Mantua). Information on concerts and other cultural events. Open Mon.-Sat. 8:30am-1pm and 3-6:30pm, Sun. 9am-12:30pm; Oct.-March Mon.-Sat. 9am-1pm and 3-6:30pm. There is a second office with the same hours at the Casa di Rigoletto, behind the *duomo.*

Post Office: p. Martiri Belfiore, 15 (tel. 32 64 03). Open Mon.-Fri. 8am-7pm, Sat. 8am-2pm. **Postal code:** 46100.

Telephones: SIP, via Corridoni, 17 (tel. 32 77 11), off via Roma. Open daily 8am-7:45pm. After hours, go to the **ACI di Mantova,** p. Fanteria, 13, between p. Martini Belfiore and p. Cavallotti. **Telphone code:** 0376.

Train Station: p. Don Leoni (tel. 32 16 47), at the end of corso V. Emanuele southwest of town. To Cremona (every hr.; 40 min.-1½ hr.; one way L3200, round-trip L5400), Verona (every hr.; 40 min.; one way L2000, round-trip L3400), and Milan (11 per day; 2¼ hr.; one way L7800, round-trip L13,400). In Mantua, your bags have a curfew (after all, you never know what mischief a worldly backpack might get into): **bag deposit** closed midnight-6am.

Bus Station: p. A. Mondadori (tel. 32 72 37), across and to the right as you leave the train station. Buses to Brescia (14 per day, 12/3 hr., L4800), Sabbioneta (the bus to Viadana, 7 per day, 50 min., L2700), and Parma (3 per day, 2 hr., L5300).

Bike Rental: Umberto Ferrari, via Concilazione, 6 (no phone), to the left of the bus station. Open Mon. 2:30-7pm, Tues.-Sat. 8:30am-12:30pm and 2:30-7pm.

Police: Questura, p. Sordello, 46 (tel. 32 63 41).

Hospital: Ospedale Civile, viale Alberoni, 1-3 (tel. 32 92 61).

Swimming Pool: Piscina Comunale E. Dugoni, at viale Montegrappa and viale Montello (tel. 32 77 29), near Palazzo Te. An indoor pool that's boisterous on weekdays, packed solid on weekends. Open June-Sept. 15 9:30am-7pm, ticket sales stop at 6:30pm; Sept. 15-May Sat. and Mon. 6-11pm. Lounge around in the showers until 8pm. Admission L3000, ages 5-14 L2500, under 5 free. Sun. L500 more.

Accommodations and Camping

Apart from the beautiful youth hostel, bargains are sparse in Mantua.

Ostello Sparafucile (IYHF), in the nearby hamlet of Lunetta di San Giorgio (tel. 372 24 65). From the train station, exit to your right, and walk left down corso V. Emanuele II to p. Cavallotti (5 min.); or take bus #3 or 4 then change to #2, 6, 9, or T from in front of the

UPIM in p. Cavallotti. Otherwise an easy 1½-kilometer walk from p. Sordello—take via S. Giorgio to bridgelike via Legnago, and follow it for about 500m. This lovingly restored sixteenth-century castle is, as its name implies, the supposed hangout of the thug in Verdi's *Rigoletto.* The visual charm and amiable guests are more remarkable than the services. L7500, nonmembers L10,000. Lockout 9am-6pm. Curfew 11pm. Open April-Oct. 15.

Casa della Giovane, via Trieste, 15 (tel 32 74 03). Walk along via G. Bertani from p. Mantegna, then turn right on via Pompanazzo. Run by nuns; for women only.

Locanda La Rinascita, via Concezione, 4 (tel. 32 06 07), near p. Virgiliana. From the train station, walk left on viale Pitentino (15 min.), then right on via Zappetto, which intersects with via Concezione. Reasonably clean rooms and cordial proprietor. Gossip is tossed more readily from balcony to balcony than across phone cables in this spirited neighborhood. Singles L18,000. Doubles L28,000. Showers L1500. Reserve 4 or 5 days in advance.

Albergo Roma, via Corridoni, 20 (tel. 32 21 00), off via Roma, which leads right to the historic center. Large, clean rooms with good mattresses. Management will give you a key should you desire to prowl the streets at night. Singles L17,000. Doubles L28,000. Showers included but towels L2000. Open Aug. 19-Dec. 21 and Jan. 9-July 31.

Albergo Bianchi, p. Don Leoni, 24 (tel. 32 15 04), across from the train station. Modern and comfortable. English spoken. Singles L20,000, with bath L30,000. Doubles L35,000, with bath L50,000. Curfew 1:30am.

Camping: Sparafucile, next to the youth hostel (tel. 37 24 65). L2500 per person, L1500 per tent. Shares facilities with the hostel. May be open Nov.-March 1988-89.

Food

As if to make up for the dearth of budget accommodations, Mantua offers a wealth of inexpensive eateries. A small produce **market** takes place in p. delle Erbe (Mon.-Sat. 7am-noon); on Thursday a much larger market fills the entire *centro storico* (7am-1pm). But the prices there are higher than at any one of the number of vegetable stores or supermarkets easily found 1 block away from the center. Prime picnic spots are **piazza Virgiliana,** off via Cavour and along Lago di Mezzo, and **Cippo di Belfiore,** past the train station to the right as you exit and along Lago Superiore.

Centro Ristorante Sociale, p. Virgiliana, 57 (tel. 36 45 74). From p. Sordello, take via Fratelli Cairoli to p. Virgiliana and turn left. A clean, EPT-sponsored *mensa.* Tasty full meals under L10,000. Open Mon.-Fri. noon-2pm.

Ristorante Espresso "Il Punto," via Solferino, 36 (tel. 32 75 52), to the left of the train station as you exit. Cheery yellow fittings, but unexciting fare. L9000 buys you a full lunch including bread and either wine or water. Open Mon.-Sat. noon-2pm.

Self-Service Nievo, via Ippolito Nievo, 8 (tel. 32 88 44), off via Verdi. Zero atmosphere, but cosmopolitan crowd. Full meals L8500. Open Sept.-July Mon.-Fri. 11:30am-2pm and 7:30-10pm.

Al 145, corso Garibaldi, 145 (tel. 32 15 77). Shove through the crush to get some piping hot pizza with gooey cheese. L2000 will satisfy minimum daily pizza requirements.

Trattoria al Lago, p. Arche, 5 (tel. 32 33 00), in a small square connected to p. Sordello by via Don E. Tazzoli. Dull and drab from the street, inside it teems with bustling waiters and satisfied customers. *Rane fritte* (fried frog) L6500. *Agnoli in brodo* (tortellini-like pasta in broth) L3500. *Menù* L11,000. Wine L3500 per liter.

Due Cavallini, via Salnitro, 5 (tel. 32 20 84), off corso Garibaldi. An earthy place with a never-ending well of wine. Portions are generous, and the owners enjoy their guests. The house specialty is *maccheroni con stracotto d'asino* (L4000)—the sign above the door with the two prancing horses (*"due cavallini"*) should clue you in (*asino*—donkey). Full meals about L17,000. Wine L4000 per liter. Cover L1500. Open Sept. to mid-July Wed.-Mon. noon-2:30pm and 7:30-10pm.

Al Quadrato, p. Virgiliana, 49 (tel. 32 74 31). Huge, excellent pizzas (L2800-5500) and delicately prepared food that's twice as expensive. Packed tables outside overlook peaceful park. Cover L700 for pizza, L1500 otherwise. Service 15%. Open Tues.-Sun. noon-2pm and 7:30pm-1am.

Pizzeria Marechiaro, viale Risorgimento (tel. 36 18 64), near the Palazzo Te. Tables offer a picturesque view but are noisy due to traffic. Exuberant clientele. Pizzas L3500-6000. Meals with meat about L13,000, with fish L20,000. Wine L5000 per liter. Cover L800 for pizzas, L1700 otherwise. Open Sept. 24-Aug. 26 Thurs.-Tues. noon-3pm and 7pm-2am.

Aquila Nigra, vicolo Bonacolsi, 4 (tel. 35 06 51), off p. Sordello. Mantua's finest restaurant and very expensive (full meals from L25,000), but its old-world elegance and truly outstanding food make it a superior splurge. Reservations recommended on weekends. Open Sept.-July Tues.-Sat. noon-2pm and 7:30-10pm, Sun. noon-2pm.

Sights

Cobblestone **piazza Sordello** is the center of a huge complex built by the Gonzaga, lords of Mantua from 1328 to 1707. The **Palazzo Ducale** (tel. 32 02 83) dominates the *piazza.* One of the most sumptuous palaces in Europe, it testifies to the clout of the Gonzaga. The 500 rooms and 15 courtyards were constructed over a period of 300 years (14th to 17th centuries). They now house an impressive collection of antique and Renaissance art. The **Magna Domus** and the **Captain's Palace,** two fourteenth-century Gothic structures, constitute the main part of the palace. Guided tours leave regularly from the room next to the ticket office. Though in Italian, they are the only way to see the palace's interior, and guides are very strict about keeping visitors in groups. Near the entrance is the Hall of Dukes where you'll find the ghostly frescoes (1439-44) by Antonio Pisanello representing the deeds of medieval knights. They were discovered in 1969, under thick layers of plaster. Pass through the early seventeenth-century apartment of Guastalla and the New Gallery to the Tapestry Rooms. Here hang duplicates of sixteenth-century tapestries modeled after the Raphael cartoons in the Vatican. The Gonzaga's Summer Room looks out onto a hanging garden (1579) bordered on three sides by a fine portico. The Hall of Mirrors displays paintings of mythological and allegorical scenes. Some have unusual optical effects (the arms of the figure in the 5th lunette from the left appear to follow you from one side of the room to the other). From the Paradise Chambers, so called because of their idyllic view of the lakes, you enter the Dwarfs' Apartments, tiny low rooms built as much to amuse the court as for actual dwellings.

Just as the tapestries and sixteenth-century murals begin to cloy, the tour enters the **Castello di San Giorgio** (1390-1406), the most formidable structure in the palace complex. Formerly an imposing fortress, the *castello* was converted into a wing of the palace when the Gonzaga no longer needed it in a military capacity. Andrea Mantegna's famed frescoes of the Gonzaga family (1474) in the **Camera degli Sposi** (marriage chamber) are among the first works to experiment with perspective. On the center wall, among his family and friends, sits the elder Marquis Lodocio talking to his secretary. At his side reclines the formidable Barbara of Brandenburg. The stern and haughty Nana, the court's favorite dwarf, stands at her side. (Open Tues.-Sat. 9am-6pm, Sun.-Mon. 9am-2pm. Admission L4000.)

The **cathedral** has an eighteenth-century facade but is much earlier in origin, as witnessed by its Romanesque *campanile* and the Gothic elements on its side. Its interior by Giulio Romano (1545) is late Renaissance, but the baptistery in the lower chamber of the *campanile* was frescoed in the thirteenth century. (All churches in the province open daily 8am-12:30pm and 3-7pm.)

Piazza delle Erbe opens onto the **Palazzo della Ragione** (Palace of Reason, 13th century, seat of the High Court of Justice) and the **Rotonda di San Lorenzo.** (*Palazzo* not normally open. *Rotonda* open during regular church hours.) This circular, eleventh-century Romanesque church (rebuilt early this century) is also known as the Matildica after the powerful noblewoman who, dying without heirs, left the rotunda to the pope. The rotunda was partially demolished in the sixteenth century and used as an interior courtyard for the small houses that once leaned against it.

Opposite the rotunda rises Mantua's most important Renaissance creation, Leon Battista Alberti's **Church of Sant' Andrea** (1471-1594). The unique facade combines the classical triumphal arch motif—barrel vaulted portal, flanking pilasters—with that of an antique temple front. The interior is staggering in size; it was the first monumental space constructed in classical style since imperial Rome. The plan—a vaulted church with a single aisle, flanking side chapels, and a domed crossing—served as a prototype for ecclesiastical architecture the next 200 years. The first chapel to the left houses the tomb of the painter Andrea Mantegna.

The **Palazzo d'Arco** (tel. 32 22 42), off viale Ritentino, elevates astrology to high culture. The star of the *palazzo* is the zodiac chamber, an extravaganza of ambers and ochres by Fontanello. Other rooms sport more quotidian comforts from the fifteenth to the nineteenth centuries. From p. Mantegna, follow via G. Verdi (which becomes via V. Fernelli then finally via S. Domenico) to the *palazzo.* (Open March-Oct. Tues.-Wed. and Fri. 9am-noon, Thurs., Sat., and Sun. 9am-noon and 3-5pm; Nov.-Feb. Thurs. 9am-noon, Sat.-Sun. 9am-noon and 2:30-4:30pm. Admission L2000.)

Mantua's moment of musical super-stardom arrived in 1770, courtesy of the D'Arco family. The **Teatro Accademico,** via Accademia, 47 (tel. 32 76 53), off p. Erbe, was inaugurated by a cameo performance by 14-year-old *Wunderkind* Wolfgang Amadeus Mozart. (Open Mon.-Sat. 9am-noon and 3-6pm. Admission L300.)

A contrast to luxurious palaces and padded academies is the plain, boxlike house of the artist **Mantegna** (via Acerbi, 47; tel. 36 05 06 or 32 66 85). Built in 1476, it is now used for temporary art exhibits, and between shows, visits can be arranged by phone. Opposite the house stands Alberti's **Church of San Sebastiano** (1460), whose Greek cross layout initiated the wave of centrally planned churches so important in the Renaissance.

A trek through p. V. Veneto and down largo Parri will be rewarded by the opulence of the **Palazzo Te** (tel. 32 32 66 or 36 58 86), one of the most famous of Italy's sixteenth-century villas. It was built by Giulio Romano as a suburban retreat for Francesco II Gonzaga. The rooms inside show the Renaissance fascination with absolutely anything Roman. Francesco's Banquet Hall is frescoed with idyllic murals of Psyche, noted for their vividness and eroticism. Another wing of the palace features regular shows of modern Italian artists, and there is also a collection of Egyptian art. If you are traveling with an entire tribe, reservations are necessary to see the Egyptian collection. (Open July-Aug. Tues.-Sat. 9am-12:30pm and 2:30-5:30pm, Sun. 9am-12:30pm; April-June and Sept. Tues.-Sat. 9am-12:30pm and 2:30-5:30pm; Oct.-March Tues.-Sat. 9:30am-12:30pm and 2:30-5pm. Admission L2500, students L1500.) Plans for 1989 are to stage an exhibition of *every* one of Giulio Romano's works, to be carted here from across the Boot.

The **Teatro Sociale di Mantova,** p. Cavallotti (tel. 32 38 60), off corso Vittorio Emanuele II, stages operas in October and plays from November to March. (Cheap seats around L15,000.)

Near Mantua

Sabbioneta, 33km southwest of Mantua, was founded by Vespasiano Gonzaga (1532-91) as home for his feudal court. Its importance as an art center in the late Renaissance earned it the title "Little Athens of the Gonzagas." Inside the well-preserved sixteenth-century walks of the city lie the **Ducal Palace,** the **Olympic Theater,** and the **Palazzo del Giardino,** all fascinating Renaissance structures. The best way to see the town is to take the guided walk, which enables you to see the otherwise inaccessible interiors of buildings. The 45-minute tour (L4000) leaves whenever enough eager travelers have gathered (usually every 20 min.) at the **tourist office** (tel. (0375) 520 39; open Tues.-Sat. 9:30am-12:30pm and 2:30-6pm, Sun. 2:30-6pm). So far, no tours are in English, though one of the staff members is hitting the grammar books. Around seven buses per day go to Viadanna via Sabbioneta.

Every summer Sabbioneta stages a **Festival di Musica e Danza,** and from mid-April to mid-March antique aficionados come for the vast **mercato del Antiquariato.**

A unique way of discovering the rich cultural heritage and natural beauty of the province of Mantua is to participate in the EPT's new *agriturismo* program. Starting at about L8000 per night, you can stay at one of five gorgeous, old villas in the countryside, be close to the region's less renowned artistic treasures, and take part in the daily life of a farm. Some will put you up gratis in exchange for work. For information and reservations, contact the EPT in Mantua.

Bergamo

Beautiful Bergamo has an interesting split-personality, Divided physically and spiritually into two distinct parts. The *città alta,* the hilltop Bergamo, shows its medieval origins in every rough-edged tower, winding alleyway, and ice-cold stream flowing from the ancient fountains. On the plain below lies the clean, shady, and modern *città bassa.* The two halves compliment each other perfectly—Bergamo is exceptionally beautiful and dynamic.

Orientation and Practical Information

Bergamo is an easy train ride from Milan, Brescia, and Cremona. The train station, bus station, and hotels are in Bergamo Bassa. To get to the more interesting *città alta,* take bus #1 or 3 to the *funicolare,* which ascends from viale V. Emanuele to the Mercato delle Scarpe (L500 for both), or walk up the old footpath from behind the funicular station on viale V. Emauele to the city (10-20 min).

Tourist Information: APT, p. Mercato della Scarpe (tel. 23 27 30), in the *città alta* at the top of the funicular. Helpful and modern office. Ask for *Prossimamente Bergamo,* which lists entertainment and other cultural activities in the city. Open Mon.-Sat. 9am-12:30pm and 3-6pm. The main administrative office with identical services is at viale V. Emanuele, 4 (tel. 24 22 26), in the *città bassa.* Open Mon.-Fri. 8:30am-2:30pm and 3:30-6:30pm, Sat. 9am-noon.

Centro Turistico Studentesco (CTS): via Pignolo, 43B (tel. 22 22 49). **ISICs** and **Transalpino** tickets. Open Mon.-Fri. 9:30am-12:30pm and 3-7pm, Sat. 9:30am-12:30pm.

Centro Turistico Giovanile (CTG): via Paleocapa, 4 (tel. 24 42 80). Open Mon.-Fri. 6-8pm, Sat. 5:30-7:30pm.

Currency Exchange: After hours money exchange at Hotel Excelsior San Marco, p. della Repubblica, 6 (tel. 23 21 32), off viale V. Emanuele. Also at the office on via S. Francesco d'Assisi.

Post Office: via Masone, 2A, at via Locatelli. Open Mon.-Fri. 8:30am-7:30pm, Sat. 8:30am-1pm. **Postal code:** 24100.

Telephones: SIP, largo Porta Nuova, 1, at the end of viale Papa Giovanni XXIII. Walk straight ahead from the train station to the right of the twin towers in the town center. Open daily 8:15am-9:45pm. **Telephone code:** 035.

Airport: Regular flights to Ancona-Rome only. One way to Rome L137,500. A few international charter flights. Take the airport bus from Porta Nuova.

Train Station: Tel. 24 76 24. To Milan (every hr., 1 hr., L3000) and Brescia (every 2 hr., 1 hr., L2500).

Taxi: Tel. 24 20 00 or 24 45 05.

Laundromat: Lavaggio A Secco, on via S. Francesco d'Assisi. Open Mon.-Fri. 9am-6pm.

Hospital: Ospedali Riuniti, largo Barozzi, 1 (tel. 26 91 11). **Red Cross:** Tel. 25 02 46.

Police: via Monte Bianco, 1 (tel. 24 20 40).

Accommodations

The only affordable accommodations are in the *città bassa.* The youth hostel is definitely first on the list.

Ostello EPT Bergamo (IYHF), via Galileo Ferraris, 1 (tel. 34 23 49). Walk or take bus #1 to Porta Nuova, then take #14 to località Monterosso. Outstandingly equipped—6 per room, TV lounge, and balconies. L8000 per person. Breakfast included. Take the L19,000 *pensione completa* only in case of starvation. Meals L6500. Rooms assigned at 6pm, but open 7am-12:30am.

Mamma Grande, via N. Sauro, 8 (tel. 21 84 13). Big Momma is a bit run down, but clean, with reasonably sized rooms and an outstanding location 3 min. from the *città alta* and 1 min. from the art gallery. Singles L13,000. Doubles L23,500, with bath L28,000. Reserve early for late July and Aug.

Locanda Caironi, via Torretta, 6 (tel. 24 30 83), off via Borgo Palazzo. A family-run *trattoria* and *locanda* in a quiet, unspectacular quarter not far from the *città alta.* Tidy, appealing singles under L10,000, doubles under L20,000. The excellent *trattoria* serves ample pasta dishes and fresh salads.

Valentina, via Quarenghi, 35 (tel. 23 71 77), near the station. Leaving the station turn left immediately on via G. Bonomelli. The 2nd major right is via Quarenghi. The cheerful proprietor almost always has something available. Singles L14,000. Doubles L22,000. No bathrooms, but all with clean sinks. Good restaurant downstairs. Open Sept. to mid-Aug.

Albergo S. Antonio, via Paleocapa, 1 (tel. 21 02 84). Down from the station on viale Papa Giovanni XXIII and left on via Paleocapa. Simple, clean rooms. Singles L18,500. Doubles L28,000. Triples L36,000. Showers included. Open mid-July to mid-Sept. Curfew midnight. ACLI Mensa downstairs (see below).

Hotel Leon d'Oro, via Paleocapa, 6 (tel. 21 81 51), from the Antonio. Clean rooms—insist on one with a real window and *not* one onto a corridor. Singles L16,000. Doubles L27,000. Triples L35,000. Showers included. Enter from via Novelli on Fri., when the downstairs restaurant is closed.

Hotel Commercio, via Tasso, 88 (tel. 24 36 26), off p. Matteotti. Large modern rooms and a pretty garden. Singles L17,500, with bath L26,000. Doubles L32,000, with bath L40,000. Obligatory breakfast L3000.

Food

Food is cheaper in the *città bassa,* but generally better and served in classier surroundings in the *città alta*—as long as you avoid the traps with L16,000-20,000 tourist menus. For lunches, try the excellent cheeses from the Bergamasco hinterlands, *taleggio* and *provolone.* There are a few excellent bakeries and pastry shops along via Colleoni and especially via Gambito, both in the *città alta.* Try their version of *polenta,* a sweet corn pastry.

Città Bassa

Mensa ACLI, via Paleocapa, 1, in the basement of the Hotel Sant' Antonino (see above). Two dishes, *contorno,* bread, and wine for L8000. Open Mon.-Sat. noon-2:30pm and 7-8:30pm.

Ristorante Self-Service Dany, via Taramelli, 25 (tel. 22 07 55). From the station walk down viale Papa Giovanni XXIII, turn right on via San Francesco d'Assisi, then left. *Primi* from L1700, *secondi* from L3200.

Pizzeria Gino, via Previtali, 12 (tel. 24 93 50), off via S. Bernardino. A bit out of the way, but simple, appetizing pizza cooked in a wood-burning oven. Cheery checked tablecloths out back in the garage. *Primi* under L5000, *secondi* under L9000, lunch menù under L12,000. Open Thurs.-Tues. 11am-3pm and 6-11pm.

Trattoria Casa Mia, via S. Bernardino, 20 (tel. 22 06 76), off via Zambonate. A plain, unpretentious place offering a complete meal (including wine, water, coffee, bread, and service) for under L12,000. Open Sept.-July Mon.-Sat. noon-2pm and 6:30-9:30pm.

Città Alta

Trattoria Barnabò, via Colleoni, 31 (tel. 23 76 92), past p. Vecchia. One of the best restaurants in Bergamo, with *menù* under L13,000. They serve varieties of *polenta,* combined with cheese, mushrooms, or sausage. Open Fri.-Wed. noon-2:30pm and 7pm-midnight.

Ristorante da Franco, via Colleoni, 8 (tel. 23 85 65). A pleasant place in a small inner courtyard with a steep tourist menu (L16,000), but reasonable pizza (L4000-7000). Tasty 1st courses from L4500. Open Thurs.-Tues. noon-3pm and 6pm-midnight.

Mensa Universitaria, via San Lorenzo, 11 (tel. 21 83 52), off via Colleoni. The only slightly modern-looking building around. Adequate, well-prepared filling meals L4000. Chance it straight away, or get permission from the Registrar at the University office on via Salvecchio, past p. Vecchia, off via B. Colleoni.

Birreria Bergamo Alta, via Gambito, 1/B (tel. 24 36 61), off p. Vecchia. Centrally located; an outstanding selection of beers and sandwiches.

Sights

Città Bassa

Begin a tour of the city at p. Matteoti, the center of Bergamo Bassa and a favorite meeting place for the evening *passeggiata.* In the **Church of San Bartolomeo,** at the far right of the square, is a superb altarpiece of the *Madonna and Child* by Lorenzo Lotto (1516). Via Tasso on the right of San Bartolomeo leads to the **Church of Santo Spirito.** Its fine Renaissance interior (1521) houses paintings by Lotto, Previtali, and Bergognone. **Via Pignolo** connects the lower city with the upper and goes past a succession of handsome palaces (16th to 18th centuries). Along the way is the tiny **Church of San Bernardino,** whose multicolored interior protects a 1521 altarpiece by Lotto. A right on via San Tommaso takes you to the astonishing **Galleria dell' Accademia Carrara,** one of the most important art galleries in Italy. Housed in a splendid neoclassical palace, the collection is remarkable broad. There is a wealth of seasoned landscapes and sensitive portraits of the Venetian school (1500-1700). The Florentines are equally well represented. Botticelli's *Giuliano de' Medici* is a model of pale, haughty nobility. The *San Sebastiano* by Raphael is an eerie, powerful work, with the sweet-faced saint holding one of the arrows that will soon plunge into his body. There are also fine canvasses by Mantegna, Signorelli, Fopa, Carpaccio, Titian, Tintoretto, Paolo Veronese, and Giovanni Bellini, to name a few. Foreign artists are also well represented, a rarity in Italian galleries. There is a brooding, silvery-black marching army by Dürer, a light-hearted *Rissa dei Contadini* (Fight of the Farmers) by Hans Holbein the Younger, along with works by Breugel, van Dyck, and El Greco. (Open Mon. and Wed.-Sun. 9:30am-12:30pm and 2:30-5:30pm. Admission L1000.)

Città Alta

From the Carrara gallery, a terraced walkway (via Nora) ascends from the lower city to **Porta Sant' Agostino.** This sixteenth-century gate was built by the Venetians as part of their fortifications for the city and takes its name from a nearby church, now abandoned. From the church's *piazza* there's a lovely view of the countryside. Stop in the verdant Parco Sant' Agostino for a picnic or a view from atop the walls. Via Porta Dipinta leads to the heart of Bergamo Alta, first passing the Romanesque **Church of San Michele** (12th to 13th centuries) decorated inside with colorful frescoes, and then the neoclassical **Church of Sant' Andrea,** which contains a fine altarpiece by Moretto of the *Madonna Enthroned* (right chapel). The street continues as narrow and steep via Gombito, passing a massive twelfth-century tower of the same name. Around the corner from the tower is a quiet little *piazza,* miraculously shielded from the noise and confusion. Its shaded benches are a perfect place to picnic, and at night it is the favorite hangout of young Bergamese couples.

Via Gombito ends in **piazza Vecchia,** a majestic complex of medieval and Renaissance buildings with restaurants and cafes at its fringes. On the right is the white marble **Biblioteca Civica** (1594), modeled after Venice's Sansovino Library, depository of Bergamo's rich collection of manuscripts. Across the square is the **Palazzo della Ragione** (the Palace of Justice, 1199), massive and angular with a robust arcade. This was Bergamo's former communal palace, and it retains a grand salon decorated with frescoes from the fourteenth and fifteenth centuries. Note the fine Gothic window and the lion of St. Mark which, though added recently, effectively records the Venetian domination of the city. To the right and connected to the *palazzo* by a sixteenth-century covered stairway stands the twelfth-century **Torre Civica** (Civic Tower). Its fifteenth-century clock still sounds the curfew every night at 10 o'clock.

A passage between the two buildings leads to **piazza del Duomo.** Straight ahead is the multicolor marble extravaganza facade of the **Colleoni Chapel** (1476). It was designed by G. A. Amadeo (who also did the Charterhouse of Pavia) as a tomb and chapel for Bartolomeo Colleoni, a celebrated Venetian *condottiere* (mercenary). (Open daily 9am-noon and 3-6pm.)

To the right of the chapel is the octagonal baptistery, graced by a gallery made from red marble. It is actually a reconstruction of a fourteenth-century baptistery that once stood in the **Basilica of Santa Maria Maggiore.** This basilica, which adjoins the Colleoni Chapel to the left, was constructed in the second half of the twelfth century. The exterior is sombre and Romanesque, with fascinating detail carved into its rough tan stone. Its three Romanesque entrances are particularly remarkable. The first is a colorful Lombard porch (1353), which shelters an equestrian statue of St. Alexander. In a corner of the wall a second doorway bears a charming Nativity scene, the work of Giovanni da Campione (1367).

In startling contrast to this Romanesque understatement is the interior, which appears at first sight an unrelenting baroque orgasm. Be patient, however, and finer details begin to emerge from the confusion. Lorenzo Lotto created the biblical scenes adorning the choir balustrade exclusively out of natural wood, still managing to work greens and purples into the landscapes. (Ask to have them illuminated.) Rich Flemish and Tuscan tapestries hang along many of the walls. Across from the door is an interesting fresco (dated 1347) of St. Bonaventure and his scriptural tree of life. Before leaving, take a look at the baroque confessional, so elaborate that sitting in it is itself an act of penitence, and the schmaltzy Victorian tomb of the composer Donizetti (1855). (Open 8:30am-noon and 2-5pm.) Opera lovers should pick up the brochure *Bergamo, Donizetti Places* (in English), which locates and describes a plethora of monuments, artworks, and museums devoted to the peripatetic and troubled life that produced the lyric masterpieces "Lucia di Lammermoor" and "Don Pasquale."

After exploring the culture of Bergamo, head for the **Parco Suardi,** the beautiful city park. There's ample shade for picnics, and huge grassy stretches perfect for sunbathing or frisbee. Many of Bergamo's lively inhabitants may be found strolling among the tall trees. To get there take via Pignolo down the hill from Porta S. Agostino, and hang a left on via San Giovanni. (Open April-Sept. 9am-9pm; Oct.-March 9am-8pm; Nov.-Feb. 10am-4pm.)

Seasonal Events

Home to a musical tradition that finds its greatest expression in the works of native son Gaetano Donizetti (1797-1848), the city continues to host young talent with an **International Piano Festival** in May and June. Tradition has it that the popular figures of the Commedia dell' Arte, Arlecchino and Brighella, were born in Bergamo. Whether or not this is true, the quality and originality of Bergamese entertainment are high. (See EPT for schedule.)

Brescia

For centuries Brescia was the object of fierce contention among local lords and bishops and the Milanese Torriani, Malatesta, and Visconti families. From 1426 to 1797, it was the prized possession of the Venetian Republic and a magnificent cultural center, but there are few reminders of this period of splendor. Brescia has returned to the Milanese industrial orbit and lives at the frenetic pace of a modern commercial center.

Practical Information

Brescia is only 75 minutes from Milan on the direct rail line to Venice (L3900). Bus C or a 15-minute walk up corso Martiri della Libertà and corso Palestro will get you from the train station to the *centro storico.* While most sights and establishments are concentrated in this old center, prudent use of the urban bus system will keep you from running out of steam on the longer stretches to the periphery (i.e., the train station) and back.

Tourist Office: corso Zanardelli, 34 (tel. 434 18), an office complex on a busy arcaded street in the center of town near p. Vittoria. Friendly and knowledgeable staff has complete information on transportation, local and regional sights, and a free accommodations service. Open Mon.-Thurs. 8:30am-12:30pm and 3-6:30pm, Fri. 8:30am-12:30pm and 3-5pm.

Post Office: p. Vittoria, 1, the central Mussolini-era horror. Open Mon.-Fri. 8:30am-8pm, Sat. 8:30am-1pm. **Postal codes:** Brescia 25100. Centro storico 25121.

Telephone Office: SIP, via Moretto, 46 (tel. 110 or 181), off via A. Gramsci. **Telephone code:** 030.

Buses: viale Stazione (tel. 582 37 or 440 61), near the train station. Ticket office open Mon.-Sat. 6am-8pm, Sun. 7-11am and 3-6pm.

Taxi: via Tartaglia, 31B (tel. 444 61). 24-hour service at Stazione (tel. 441 08).

Police: via Carlo Donegani (tel. 424 40).

Accommodations

Accommodations are reasonably priced in Brescia, but are often full of business-people during the week; weekends are better. In the summer your best bet is one of several dorm-type facilities for students and workers.

Servizio della Giovane (ACISJF), via Fratelli Bronzetti, 17 (tel. 553 87), 5-10 min. from the station. Take viale Stazione to p. della Repubblica and cross to via dei Mille. From here, via Bronzetti is your 1st right. Friendly nuns operate this inexpensive establishment. Women only. All ages admitted. Doubles L7000 per person. Quads L5500 per person. One of the few places with full kitchen facilities available to guests. Curfew 10pm.

Albergo Stazione, vicolo Stazioni, 17 (tel. 521 28). On the left as you exit the station (not to be confused with the expensive Albergo Igea on viale Stazione). Rooms are clean and surprisingly quiet for being so near a major thoroughfare. Singles L18,000. Doubles L27,000. Showers L2000.

Locanda San Marco, via Spalto San Marco, 15 (tel. 455 41). From the station take via Foppa, turn right on via XX Settembre, make the next left, and turn right onto via V. Emanuele II, which becomes via Spalto San Marco. Rooms are clean but due for a renovation that may raise prices. Clientele generally young and fun. Singles L15,000. Doubles L27,000. Open Sept.-July.

Franciscanum, via Callegari, 11 (tel. 28 91 11), off via Spalto S. Marco in the historic part of town. Follow the directions above. A spanking clean and modern dorm facility for both men and women. All rooms have private bath and telephone for about L12,000 per person. Check-in 7-10am. No curfew. Many vacancies June-Sept.; Oct.-May phone before coming.

Cavallino, corso Garibaldi, 31 (tel. 402 13). Similar to the San Marco but somewhat more central—on the continuation of corso G. Mameli, the main street leading from p. Loggia. Singles L12,000. Doubles L22,000.

Food

There are large **markets** daily on both p. Mercato and near p. Loggia (open 8am-noon and 3-6:30pm). Reasonably priced restaurants and several centrally located *mense* make inexpensive dining on fare other than bread, fruit, and cheese possible. Local specialties include stews, skewer meals, and *polenta* (a bread substitute with the texture of pudding). *Tocai di San Martino della Battaglia,* a dry white wine, *Groppello,* a medium red, and Botticino, a dry red of medium aging, are all local favorites.

ACLI Mensas, in several locations serving full meals with ¼-liter of wine or fruit for L6000. On via Monti, 22, near Franciscanum (tel. 481 60; open Mon.-Sat. 11:45am-2pm); on corso Zanardelli (tel. 29 05 68), next to the cinema (open Mon.-Sat. 6:45-8:45pm); or "La Rotunda," via Mazzini, 4 (tel. 492 69), behind the *duomo* (open Mon.-Sat. 6:45-8:45pm).

Ristorante Rosticceria Mameli, corso Mameli, 53 (tel. 595 02), near p. Loggia. An enticing array of prepared foods sold downstairs for take-out, and upstairs in the restaurant; what you see is what you get. *Primi* around L4000, *secondi* L8000, wine from L6000 a bottle. Open Tues.-Sun. 11am-2:30pm and 7-10:30pm.

Gastronomia al Ceppo, via Gramsci, 11 (tel. 562 32), off p. Vittoria. Tasty salads and sandwiches (L1500) and main dishes (L4000) served cafeteria-style at stand-up counters. Open Mon.-Sat. 9am-2pm and 4-8pm.

Cantina del Frate, via Musei, 25, behind p. del Duomo. Airy, vaulted rooms. Primarily serves scrumptious cold cuts. Caters mostly to locals, maintaining its exclusivity through not having a written *menù.* A unique place. Open Mon.-Sat. 11am-2pm and 5-11pm.

O viesse, corso Mameli, on the left as you leave p. Loggia. A large supermarket with discount groceries in the basement. Open Mon.-Fri. 9am-6pm, Sat. 9am-noon.

Sights

Piazza della Vittoria, in the center of town, is a brutal reminder of the Fascist period. No effort has been made to tone down the massive force of its white stone buildings, which create an uncomfortable Kafkaesque setting.

Just down the street is a far more lyrical demonstration of power, the **piazza della Loggia,** built when Venice ruled the city. On one side of the square stands the **Torre dell' Orologio,** modeled after the clock tower in p. San Marco, Venice, with two stone figures that strike the hours, and an astronomic clock. Across from the tower, the **loggia** is a gracious Renaissance building reminiscent of Palladio's basilica in Vicenza. Sansovino designed the upper part with rectangular windows and added sumptuous decoration to the columns and frieze. Underneath the portico, an elaborate door leads to a monumental staircase and a room adorned with paintings from the sixteenth century. On the south side of the *piazza* is the **Monte di Pietà** (1489) with an elegant *loggia* in Venetian style.

Across via X Giornate is the **piazza del Duomo,** nearly suffocated by its heavily manneristic *duomo nuovo* (1604-1825). The green cupola is the third highest in Italy. Next door is the old *duomo,* or **Rotonda,** a refreshingly simple Romanesque building with endearing patchwork and uneven windows scattered around its two-story circular plan. Within is a *stauroteca,* a reliquary containing fragments of the "true" Cross. (Open Wed.-Mon. 9am-noon and 3-7pm.) Behind the cathedrals, at via Mazzini, 1, is the **Queriniana Library,** with 300,000 volumes and rare medieval manuscripts. (Different rooms open at different times.) The **Broletto Palace,** next to the *duomo nuovo,* is a typical Lombard medieval town hall topped by an eleventh-century tower. Its unusual interior court is medieval on three sides and baroque on the fourth.

Down via dei Musei is the **Tempio Capitolino,** a Roman ruin impressive despite having been almost completely reconstructed. The temple was erected by the Emperor Vespasian in 73 C.E. over an older sanctuary. Upstairs is a small museum with assorted mosaics, a medieval road map, and excellent bronzes, the best of which is a life-sized **Winged Victory,** possibly a copy of a Praxiteles original. (Museum and temple open Tues. and Thurs.-Fri. 9am-noon and 2-5pm, Sat. 9am-noon, Sun. 2-5pm. Free.)

From the Tempio Capitolino it's a short walk up via Gallo to Brescia's principal attraction, the **Pinacoteca Tosio Martinengo.** The solemn 22-room *palazzo* has a good collection of Brescian masters (notably Moretto), but better still is the serene, feminine *Cristo benedicente* by Raphael. There are also first-rate works by Veneziano, Tintoretto, Clouet, Vicenzo Foppa, and Lorenzo Lotto. (Open Tues.-Thurs. 9am-noon and 2-5pm, Sat. 9am-noon, Sun. 2-5pm. Free.)

If you have more time, the *castello* on the high ground behind via dei Musei is good for laughs. This hodgepodge of architectural styles houses a sad little zoo, an observatory, the Risorgimento Museum (with mementos from seventeenth- and eighteenth-century Brescia), and the Luigi Marzoli Museum of Arms (with hundreds of armaments from every era). On the grounds are the **San Pietro in Oliveto**

Church (reconstructed in 1510), surrounded by gnarled olive trees, and, down via Piamarta, an intact Roman gate.

The Lake Country

In the eighteenth and nineteenth centuries, artists and writers from all over Europe came to the Italian lake country for inspiration and solace. Now hordes of tourists tread the lakeside paths, hike the thickly forested granite mountains, and spend exorbitant amounts of money, especially in the larger towns. More realistic for the budget traveler, and more in the spirit of the natural setting, are the humbler villages removed from the vacation centers. In some hamlets, time seems to have stood still, and even the occasional incongruous Mercedes cannot damper the peace and isolation. Try to stay just outside Como or Lecco, and sample the cool waters from there.

Restaurants are very expensive, so picnics are a good idea. Large supermarkets have not yet hit this area, so look for the smaller *alimentari.* Local cheeses include *taleggio,* with a soft tangy flavor, *robiola* (a cream cheese), *caprino* (goat cheese), and the piquant *fontale.* All cost about L800 per *etto,* enough for several sandwiches. Another specialty of the Como region is *agone,* sun-cured fish from the lake. *Brianza* is the trademark name of most local wines.

Lake Garda (Lago di Garda)

Garda is the largest and cleanest of the Italian lakes, and thus also the most popular. The balmy, yet breezy climate closely resembles that of the Mediterranean. Of the lake's major towns—Desenzano, Bardolino, Garda, Torri del Benaco, Malcesine, Riva, Gardone Riviera, and Sirmione—only the last three warrant a visit: Riva for its seclusion, reasonable prices, and splendid swimming; Gardone Riviera for the fascinating villa of Gabriele D'Annunzio, an eccentric Italian twentieth-century poet and novelist; and Sirmione for its extensive Roman ruins, beautifully situated medieval castle, and *great* beaches. If you're coming from Verona, however, the beautiful tiny bay at **Punta San Vigilio** (just past Garda) is the best place for a daytrip of swimming, sunning, and picnicing.

Desenzano lies on the Milan-Venice rail line, 2 hours from Venice, 25 minutes from Verona and Brescia, and 1 hour from Milan. Once there, it's easy to get to all the lake towns by bus or the more expensive hydrofoils and ferries. Check the schedules carefully and plan ahead. For shorter trips take the ferry—it's cheaper and you can sit on deck. The hydrofoil is pricier and reminiscent of an airplane. However, it makes the Riva-Desenzano trip in only two hours (L12,600). Official **campgrounds** surround the lake but are concentrated between Desenzano and Salò; unofficial camping is discouraged here and must be done with discretion. Many private residences rent rooms (mostly doubles) in Lake Garda's larger towns. Get a list of these rooms from the Azienda, and then head out, ready to bargain.

Sirmione

> *What delight and joy to visit you, O Sirmione, jewel of peninsulae and islands! A more beautiful place does not exist in all the transparent pools and vast reaches of the sea.*
>
> *—Catullus, XXXI*

Catullus would be heartbroken to see his beloved Sirmione today, with its crop of luxury hotels and swarms of tourists. Yet the waters are still cool and clear, and at the end of the peninsula on which the town is built lies an oasis of cypresses, olives, and Roman ruins still worthy of great poetry.

Buses run to Sirmione every half hour from Brescia and Verona, making it an easy daytrip. Buses drive out the long peninsula along via Colombare, via XXV Aprile, and finally viale Marconi in Sirmione proper. They park across the street from the helpful **tourist office** on viale Marconi, 2 (tel. 91 61 14), which has maps and camping information. (Open in summer daily 9am-8pm; in winter Mon.-Fri. 9am-12:30pm and 3-6pm, Sat. 9am-12:30pm.) The **post office** (tel. 91 61 14) is nearby on via Dante, behind the castle (open Mon.-Sat. 8:30am-12:30pm and 4-7:30pm). **Bikes** and **mopeds** may be rented (for a hefty L10,000 and L30,000 per day, respectively) from the stand near the tennis courts 10-minutes back up the road. **Motorboats** are even steeper (L35,000 per hr., with reductions for each successive hr.). Go to the harbor next to the tourist office. For **boat tours** of the lake, head for the **Sirvet travel agent** back up the main road at via Colombare, 142 (tel. 91 94 49; open Mon.-Sat. 9am-1pm and 4-8pm). The **telephone code** for Sirmione and Desenzano is 030; the **postal code** is 25019. The **hospital** for the region is in Desenzano (tel. 914 47 61).

Accommodations and Camping

A room of any sort is rare in July and August—reservations are mandatory. The tourist office has a complete list of private rooms for rent—many right on the water, centered around via Colombare, 85, above the public beach. Virtually all rooms are doubles averaging L25,000 per night, but vigorous bargaining may drop the price considerably, especially if you plan to spend more than one night. The hotels in town are very expensive and generally require you to take at least half-pension in high season. In general, the farther you walk up the main road toward the mainland, the lower the prices become.

In **Desenzano,** try the **Flora,** via Guglielmo, 3 (tel. 914 15 12), or the more conveniently located **Hotel du Lac** (tel. 914 16 12), near the bus stop. It's fastidiously kept. Unsullied and well-run. Call ahead.

Albergo Speranza, via V. Emanuele, 2 (tel. 91 61 16), right in the center of town just past the castle. One of the two cheapest places in town. Congenial singles L20,000. Doubles L30,000. Showers L3000. Open March-Oct.

Albergo Risorgimento, on via V. Emanuele (tel. 91 63 25), near the archway of the castle. Ordinary rooms but *fabulous* location. Singles L22,000. Doubles L30,000. Summer vacancies unlikely. Open April-Oct.

Albergo Regina, via Antiche Mura (tel. 91 61 47), off via V. Emanuele. Clean, central, and cheap for Sirmione. Doubles only, L29,500. Breakfast L2500.

Albergo Touring, via Colombare (tel. 91 90 24), at the corner with via Verona. The other "cheapest place in town," despite its two stars. Way out at the beginning of the peninsula (a 20-min. walk from town) and on a noisy street, but very big and likely to have space. Singles L17,000. Doubles L28,000, with bath L38,500.

Albergo Lo Zodiaco, via XXV Aprile, 18 (tel. 91 60 95), a 5-min. walk back up the road from the tourist office. Friendly place with a garden on the lake. Doubles only L27,000, with bath L34,000. Breakfast L4000. Open Feb.-Nov.

Camping: Sirmioncino, località Colombare (tel. 91 90 45). A 15-min. walk from town up via Colombare, then a left turn in front Hotel Benaco; go all the way to the water. Very crowded in summer—just down from a popular local beach. Has 700 places. L6400 per person. L6000 per tent. Open in summer. **Lugana Marina,** località Lugana (tel. 91 91 73), several km up the road towards Verona. Take the Verona bus and ask to be dropped at the campground (near the Pizzeria Lugana Marina). Has 360 places. L9500 per person with tent. Arrive before 10pm.

Food

Restaurants in this region loot the lire, so it's probably better to get supplies at the large and inexpensive supermarket near Hotel Touring or the small grocery store in town. The **Pizzeria la Roccia,** via Piana, 2, at the corner of via S. Salvatore, has excellent pizza (L4000-6500), a pleasant garden, and cases of foreign beers. (Open Fri.-Wed.) The **Pizzeria la Botte,** via Antiche Mura, 21, has cheaper but inferior pizza (about L3500-5500), and a L1000 cover charge. (Open 11:45am-2:45pm and 7:45-10:45pm.) For fuller meals, try the **Osteria al Pescatore,** via Plana, 20-22, near the Pizzeria la Roccia. Prices for full meals start around L10,000; try the excellent *trota dorata alla salvia* (trout fried in butter and sage) for L7500. (Open Jan.-Nov. Thurs.-Tues. noon-3pm and 7pm-midnight.) Sirmione's **market** is held on Fridays from 7:30am to 1pm.

Sights

Dominating the central *piazza* is the **Rocca Scaligora,** built in the thirteenth century by Mastino I della Scala. The robust, turretted structure surrounded by water served its defensive purpose well until the siege and conquest by the tourist industry. The L3000 admission entitles you to a tour of the battlements and a great view from one of the towers. (Open in summer daily 9am-8pm; in winter Mon. 9am-noon, Tues.-Sat. 9am-noon and 3-8pm.)

Walking out via G. Piana, which becomes via Catullo, the souvenir stands thin out, giving way to the tranquil woods that once clothed the entire strip of land. Follow the narrow street that branches off via Catullo, and the tourist presence vanishes. At the top of the hill is the **Church of San Pietro in Marino,** the oldest church in Sirmione. The shady area surrounding the church is a quintessential picnic site, and the thirteenth-century frescoes within still maintain their softly radiating colors.

Returning to via Catullo, you are faced with a choice. Down the hill is the nicest public beach in town. Sand is scarce, but the water is pellucid and ideal for wading. The off-shore reefs are also excellent perches for sunning. You can rent deck chairs (L12,000 per day) and pedal boats (L9000 per hr.).

To the left, via Catullo continues out to Sirmione's most spectacular area, the **Grotte di Catullo.** Though Catullus probably had nothing to do with this sumptuous vill-bath-crypt complex, it is a splendid set of ruins. (Open Tues.-Sun. 9am-6pm; L3000 admission.) Furthermore, a private beach lies directly below the ruins and the cliffs. If you wander out on the rocky lake floor, you'll be treated to a spectacular view of the site from the water. At the site, start with a tour of the little museum just inside the gate. It has a map to orient you, and fragments of mosaics and frescoes that give some idea of the former decor. The huge, chalk-white ruins are up the hill, wreathed by gnarled olives and cypresses. The cool blue waters of Lake Garda lap the rocky shore all around, providing an unforgettable backdrop to the idyllic scene.

Gardone Riviera

Gardone Riviera has the lingering aftertaste of its former life as a watering hole for the rich and famous in the late nineteenth and early twentieth centuries. Its sumptuous villas and palatial hotels have the delicious decadence of an elaborate English garden gone to seed. Business caters to an older crowd and, for the time being, the tourist throng has yet to descend on the town's elegant lakeside promenade.

Practical Information

Tourist Office: at the front of salita S. Maria, off the central corso Zanardelli (tel. 203 47). Helpful, but no hurry. Open in summer daily 9am-12:30pm and 4-7:15pm; in winter 8:30am-12:30pm and 2-5:30pm.

Post Office: via Roma, 8 (tel. 208 62), on the hill near the botanical gardens. Open Mon.-Fri. 8am-1:30pm, Sat. 8:10-11:45am. **Postal code:** 25083.

Telephone Code: 0365.

Buses: Buses run to and from Brescia (every ½ hr.) and Desenzano (2 per day Mon.-Sat., 5 on Sun.).

Hospital: p. Bresciani (tel. 403 61), in Salò, is the closest, 3km away from Gardone.

Police: corso Zanardelli, 62 (tel. 201 79), near the tourist office.

Accommodations and Food

Gardone is best seen as a daytrip. If you must, get a room at **Pensi Diana** (tel. 218 15), on the water directly in front of the tourist office. (Doubles L30,000. Breakfast included.) All rooms with shower, and if you're lucky you will get a magnificent view of the lake. Excellent homemade meals served for L13,000. (Open May-Oct.) The delicious pizza at the **pizzeria/Ristorante Emiliano** can easily feed two people (L3000-8000). Enter at corso Zanardelli, 57, or down the waterfront to the left of the tourist office (open noon-2:30pm and 7pm-1am). For *really* special food, go to the **Ristorante lo Sporting** at via Carera, 4, near the Vittoriale. Complete meals, with homemade pasta and *scrumptious* grilled meats, run L12,000.

Sights

There could not be a more fitting backdrop than Gardone to the **Vittoriale,** a relic of the Fascism of Italy in the early twentieth century. The Vittoriale is up the hill, best reached along via Roma and via dei Colli. It was the last home of Gabriele D'Annunzio, and is a reflection of both his genius and extravagance. Before moving to Gardone, D'Annunzio lived in Rome, Naples, Florence, and France, and during his tempestuous career produced what some consider the greatest poetry of this century. Visit the house early in the day, before the crowds arrive. The building is chock-full of fascinating objects that reveal the artist's eccentric lifestyle. The *Sala del Mapamondo* contains a huge globe ("mapamondo"), an Austrian machine-gun, and hundreds of art books and classics, including a giant version of Dante's *Divine Comedy.* The *Salla della Musica* is an experience in itself, with its weirdly colored lamps and intriguing decorations. The *Sala del Lebbroso* contains a coffin surrounded by leopard skins on which D'Annunzio used to lie and contemplate death. If you follow viale Aligi up the hill, you'll find the poet's mausoleum. Just down the hill, the bow of the ship *Puglia* juts out of a cypress forest. The ship's commander was killed in action related to D'Annunzio's attempt to recapture Fiume, a Yugoslav city that had been promised to Italy in pre-war agreements, but was later denied it due to the country's poor performance in the war. There is also a panorama of the lake from here. Don't miss the cool **botanical garden,** beautifully laid-out around a stately villa (halfway up the hill to the Vittoriale). (Open March-Oct. daily 8am-7pm. Admission L2000).

Riva del Garda

Riva del Garda, an endearing town set among the craggy mountains at the northern tip of Lake Garda, has a slight Austrian flavor. In fact, the town is in Trentino-Alto Adige, not Lombardy. Snow-capped peaks dip northward from the Alps. Lake Garda's azure waters frame the city's other end—that is, if you can see any water between the countless colored sails of windsurf boards and sailboats. The region is also ideal for a climb; hiking trails snake through the hills around the city. Riva has also acquired the well-groomed parks and impeccable thoroughways of a modern city. Somewhat removed from the heavily touristed southern portion of Lake Garda, Riva is able to offer less expensive accommodations (especially the youth hostel) and greater quiet, especially during weekdays. Weekends bring European families off their main route along the Brennero Autobahn.

Practical Information

Riva is easily reached by bus from Trent, Verona, Desenzano, Brescia, and Milan, and by hydrofoil from any lake town. The **train station** at Roverto has many buses daily to Riva (30 min.). For **hitchhikers,** Riva is 15km from the "Roverto Sud" exit of the Brennero Autobahn.

The Azienda Autonoma di Soggiorno (tel. 51 44 44), toward the lake from viale della Liberazione and behind the tennis courts, has plenty of information about Riva and its surroundings; it will also make free room reservations. (Open Oct.-April Mon.-Fri. 8:30am-noon and 2:30-6pm; May-Sept. Mon.-Sat. 9am-noon and 2:30-6:30pm, Sun. 9am-noon.) Those at **Budget Travel,** via Monte Oro, 14 (tel. 521 88), speak English and German. (Open Mon.-Fri. 9am-noon and 2:30-6pm, Sat. 10am-noon.) The **hospital** is at via Negrelli (tel. 55 40 04); call for **police** (tel. 55 23 26). The **telephone code** is 0464, and the **postal code** 38066.

Accommodations and Camping

From the budget traveler's perspective, Riva is one of Lake Garda's few havens.

Ostello Benacus (IYHF), p. Cavour, 9 (tel. 55 49 11), next to the church in the center of town. Will be renovated in the winter of 1988, with the possibility of dorm rooms transforming into doubles and triples. Effusive proprietor. L9000. Breakfast L2500 (request fruit or cheese). The ACLI Mensa is downstairs (see Food). Open March-Sept. Check-in after 6pm, lights out at 11pm, but doors are never really locked. In summer advance reservations (with 30% deposit) recommended. Members only.

Garni Carla, via Negrelli, 2 (tel. 55 21 40). From the Church of the Inviolata walk up viale dei Tigli, turn left on via Rosmini, and then right onto via Negrelli. A dream of a hotel—it almost feels like home. Sparkling clean rooms, cool balconies, and tables in a lush garden. An extremely courteous proprietor will greet you from the window. American-style breakfast (eggs and bacon) with the Italian touch of salami and prosciutto. L27,000 per person. Includes bath and breakfast.

Villa Minerva, viale Roma, 40 (tel. 55 30 31), near the Inviolata. More central than Garni Carla and also very attractive. *Almost* elegant rooms plus a decent restaurant and bar. They also have a dog. Singles L19,000. Doubles L30,000. Prices reduced in off-season. Reserve by April for the summer.

Locanda La Montanara, via Montanara, 18-20 (tel. 55 48 57). Central, cheery, and cheap. Singles L12,000. Doubles L20,000, with bath L22,000. Breakfast L4500. 3-night minimum stay L19,000. Also has more pleasant rooms at a not-as-pleasant price: Singles L19,000. Doubles L38,000.

Locanda Bastione, via Bastione, 19 (tel. 55 26 52), just outside the gates to the old part of town. Dubiously augmented to a two-star. Rooms spic-and-span, but no nicer than Garni Carla. 9 doubles L19,000, bath included. *Pensione completa* L52,000 for two.

Food

Lake specialties such as *polenta* (a pudding-type bread substitute) with rabbit, trout, and *Trentino* wines from the local *cantina* abound in Riva. A large **open-air market** is held every second and fourth Wednesday.

ACLI Mensa, p. Cavour, 9 (tel. 55 49 11), in the youth hostel. Full meals L6500. Open noon-1:30pm and 7-8pm.

Pizzeria Bella Napoli, via Diaz, 29 (tel. 55 21 39), off p. Cavour. Excellent pizza (L3500-5000) and a good selection of other dishes such as *truita ai ferri* (grilled trout) for L6000. Open noon-2:30pm and 5:30pm-midnight.

Ristorante Grand Bleu, in the p. 3 Novembre. Sit outside and people-watch. *Pizza* L3500-5000. *Pasta* L6500. Open daily 11:30am-3pm, 6:30-10:30pm.

Ristorante Rocco, in the castle on the lake (tel. 55 22 17). Spoil yourself with a royal feast and relief from the hot, crowded streets. Pasta L5500-7500, fish L12,000. Cover L2500. Open daily noon-2pm and 7-10:30pm.

Sights

Riva's most prominent feature is the twelfth-century **La Rocca** (castle), later enlarged by the Scala family and Venetians. The inner court houses a rather banal museum—spend the L3000 on a huge *gelato* instead. The Austrian-influenced **Church of the Inviolata** (1611) provides an unusual example of baroque construction. The octagonal exterior has three sets of finely carved wooden doors. Stucco, cherubs, and gilding predominate inside, and although the transition from an octagon to a circle is awkward, the idea is interesting. Each stucco pilaster is unique and whimsical. A steep walk goes above the town to the ruined **bastione,** a round tower built in 1508 by the Venetians. Check whether the funicular is working. If pebbles covered up with Germans are to your taste, the **beach** a few hundred feet beyond La Rocca (toward Torbole) invites a quick dip.

A nice excursion only 3km from Riva is the impressive **Cascata Varone,** near the village of the same name. Bring a picnic and enjoy the natural gorge surrounding this 100-meter-high waterfall. Buses to Varone from Riva are few and at odd hours, but you can hike or hitch. A circular hike between Riva and Lago di Ledro (round-trip 4 hr.) leaves by trails #413 and 453, returning along trails #453 and 402. Obtain a complete map from the Azienda.

Lake Como (Lago di Como)

Como is the romantic and worldly big brother of Maggiore and Garda, outshining them in wealth and refinement, if not mass appeal. The shores mingle the atmosphere of the Mediterranean and the mountains—lavish villas against a craggy backdrop, the heat of a Riviera sun relieved by lakeside breezes. The "lake" itself is actually a forked amalgam of three long lakes joined at the Centro Lago area of Bellaggio, Tremezzo, Menaggio, and Varenna. Take the boat bound for Colico and get off at the first stop that strikes you—Varenna is one of the best-preserved fishing villages on the lake. Try to catch Como when it's dozing (Nov.-March).

Lake Como has four excellent **IYHF youth hostels,** in Como and in Lecco (see both below), as well as in **Domaso,** via Case Sparse, 4 (tel. (0344) 851 92), 16km from Colico by bus (open March-Oct.; L8000 with breakfast) and in **Menaggio,** via 4 Novembre, 38 (tel. (0344) 323 56), 35km north of Como (Open April-Oct. and Dec.-Feb.; L7500 with breakfast). The latter two are the best on the lake because they are situated far from the over-developed lakeside cities.

Excellent, secluded **campsites** dot the northwest shore of the lake, between the pellucid waters and towering mountains. Walk or hitch from where the buses from Como let you off. Another option for hikers and campers is to take the bus from Menaggio to Porlezza on Lake Lugano, and then do the scenic loop through S. Bartolomeo, S. Nazzaro, and Cavargna. Here, as in the upper region of Lake Como, tents and sleeping bags are a must. The Como and Lecco tourist offices provide complete camping information.

Como is a half-hour from Milan and 40 minutes from Lecce (L2500). Check change-over times, or you may find yourself stranded in nowhereland.

Como

Orientation and Practical Information

Como lies at the tip of the southwest fork of the lake. As you leave the station, the town is straight ahead; the lake to your left.

EPT: p. Cavour, 17 (tel. 26 20 91), in the center of the old town near the lake. Go down the steps from the station and then straight. Understaffed, but extremely helpful. After-hours currency exchange. Open in summer Mon.-Sat. 9am-noon and 2:30-6pm; in off-season shorter hours.

Currency Exchange: At the EPT office.

Post Office: via Gallio, 4 (tel. 26 64 01). Open Mon.-Fri. 8:30am-8pm, Sat. 8:15am-1pm. **Postal code:** 22100.

Telephones: SIP, via Bianchi-Giovini, 41, off p. Cavour in a magnificent 15th-century palace that is worth the trip even if you don't need a phone. Open daily 8am-9:40pm. **Telephone code:** 031.

Buses: The bus station is at the curve halfway down lungo Lario Trieste. Regular service to Menaggio (L2600), Bellaggio (L2800), and Gravedona (L3800), among other destinations. **City bus** tickets (L500) can be bought at *tabacchi.*

Ferries: Tel. 27 22 78. Daily to all lake towns. Fares L4000-15,000. Leave from the piers along lungo Lario Trieste, near the EPT.

Taxi: tel. 26 02 59 or 27 14 66.

Bike Rental: Available just short of the curve in lungo Lario Trieste.

Pedal Boats: For rent at the harbor. L5000 per ½-hr., L10,000 per hr.

Medical Emergency: Tel. 113.

Police: Questura, viale Roosevelt, 7 (tel. 27 23 66).

Accommodations

Since the town's lakeshore is too polluted for swimming, and there are few palatable inexpensive hotels near the lake anyway, try the hostel-type options first.

Ostello Villa Olmo (IYHF), via Bellinzona, 6 (tel. 55 87 22), northwest of town. Take bus #1, 2, or 6 from the center of town and the station, or walk along via Borgovico (20 min.). Cheery dining and common area, excellent showers, lockers, discounts on the nearby lakeside swimming pool (L2000), and one of the friendliest managers in town. L8000. Breakfast included. Dinner L7000. Reservations recommended. No age limit but IYHF cards strictly required. Check-in from 5pm. Check-out from 7am. Strict curfew 11pm. Open Feb. 15-Dec. 15.

Protezione della Giovane, via Borgo Vico, 182 (tel. 55 84 49), on the way to the youth hostel. Take bus #1, 2, or 6. Women only. Less friendly, but with more facilities. Spotless singles and doubles, some more modern than others. A spacious building with a central courtyard and garden. Kitchen available. L7000. Washing machines L1500. Lunch at 12:30pm or dinner at 7pm L7000.

Hotel Canova, via Gallio, 5 (tel. 27 34 85), between the station and the tourist office. Simple, tidy rooms, and efficient management. Singles L21,500, with shower L31,500. Doubles L31,500, with shower L47,000.

Food

Como's hamburgers and vegetable salads are cheap and filling but nothing to write home about. Snack on the infamous *panini* and pizza sandwiches.

Trattoria Patrioti, via Coloniala, 45 (tel. 26 90 42), off p. Aleide de Gaspari at the end of lungo Lario Trieste. Excellent local specialties. Full meals L14,000. Open Fri.-Wed. until 10pm.

Ristorante Carducci, via Carducci, 4 (tel. 27 63 88), in the old part of town near the Basilica di San Fedele. An inexpensive EPT-run *mensa* in a functional room. Full meals L5500. Open Mon.-Fri. noon-2:15pm and 6:30-7:45pm, Sat. noon-1:30pm. Closed 2 weeks in Aug.

Dopolavoro Ferroviario, via Venini, 7 (tel. 26 61 05). From the train station turn right and go up the nearby stairs. Another *mensa* with tasty food in a mess hall atmosphere. Full meals L5500, *primi* L1500, *secondi* L3000. Open daily 11am-2:30pm and 6-8:30pm.

Cavour, p. Volta, 33 (tel. 27 24 60), off via Garibaldi. Well-deserved reputation for having the best pizza in town. Open Thurs.-Tues.

Sights and Seasonal Events

Como rhymes with *duomo* in the same harmonious way that the Gothic and Renaissance features of the structure mesh together. The columns and spires that rise out of its facade are strikingly Gothic, as is the huge central rose window; yet the portal and the overall outline of the facade are all Renaissance. The vigorous sculptures that animate the exterior of the church are the work of the Rodari brothers. Note especially the statues of two famous citizens of Como, Pliny the Elder and Pliny the Younger, on either side of the door. Against the *duomo* is the sturdy **Broletto,** the former communal palace, with thick pillars, colonnaded windows, and balconies in pink, gray, and white marble.

The **Church of San Fedele** will look familiar to those who have seen Ravenna's Byzantine churches since the earliest parts of the building, the altar and the blind arcade behind it, were built by the Lombards during the same period. The eleventh-century Lombard **Church of Sant' Abbondio** warrants the walk to the edge of town. The two belfries and five aisles are typical of this style. When in the nineteenth century the church was restored to its eleventh-century state, Roman inscriptions from 485 C.E. were discovered on the foundations. The original fifth-century cruciform structure had been altered in the eleventh century to accommodate the liturgy of the Benedictine monks, its new owners.

On the last Saturday of June, Como celebrates the **Sagra di San Giovanni,** a weekend of folklore and fireworks. The festivities are held in the castle on Isola Comacina.

Near Como

After visiting Como's monuments, take the *funicolare* (cable car) up to **Brunate** for excellent hiking and views. The cars leave from the far end of lungo Lario Trieste (one way L2000, round-trip L3500). If you plan to return to Como, be aware that the last car comes down from Brunate at 10:30pm, but three rough-and-ready *baite* (guesthouses) lie along the trail, providing room and board in either private accommodations or a dormitory-style room. Most serve three meals daily, but only a breakfast is included in the overnight cost (about L20,000 per person). Check with the EPT in the off-season to make sure they're open.

North of Como on the western shore sits **Villa Carlotta,** between the towns of Cadenabbia and Tremezzo, south of Menaggio. Marquis Clerici built this palace in the eighteenth century, and European aristocracy has modified it since. The design of the villa and gardens, as well as the vista, is unsurpassed. (Open March-Nov., but the flower gardens are most beautiful in April and May.)

Lecco

Less tourist-infested than the rest of Lake Como, the sounds of Lake Lecco echo in peace and quiet. Interesting towns and shores lined with granite mountains go beautifully with reasonable prices, and with Leonardo da Vinci's *Mona Lisa* (Lecco is its presumed background). Its most famous son is Alessandro Manzoni (1785-1873), a classic nineteenth-century liberal whose political and social theories were a catalyst for Italy's unification. Manzoni's novel, *I Promessi Sposi* (*The Betrothed*), is a classic of Italian narrative fiction.

Orientation and Practical Information

No main street will orient you here, but the breezes will carry you down via Cavour to the lake.

Azienda di Turismo: via N. Sauro, 6 (tel. 36 23 60), off p. Garibaldi. From the train station walk down via Cavour and turn right 1 block up from the lake. Open Mon.-Sat. 9am-12:30pm and 2:30-6pm.

Post Office: viale Dante. Open Mon.-Fri. 8:15am-7:40pm, Sat. 8:15am-1:50pm. **Postal code:** 22053.

Train Station: p. Diaz (tel. 36 41 30 or 36 13 17). Lecce is easily accessible by train from Bergamo (L2000) and Milan (L2500).

Hospital: via Ghislanzoni, 22 (tel. 49 43 43).

Telephone Code: 0341.

Accommodations and Food

Ostello del Resegone (IYHF), via Filanda, 8 (tel. 49 45 09), a little out of town up on a hill. Take bus #2, 3, or 8 from near the station on via Cavour to the hamlet of Germanedo. Run by a friendly couple who speak English and are happy to give you advice. Members only, L8600. Dinner L6500. Open April-Nov. 8am-11:30pm.

Vecchio Borgo, vicolo Granai, 4 (tel. 36 75 48), on a tiny street off p. Cermenati. Regular clients render these clean, comfortable rooms in the center of town often unavailable. Singles L18,000. Doubles L27,000. Triples L32,000.

Hotel Due Torri, via Roma, 42 (tel. 36 24 25). Less amiable. Singles L21,000. Doubles L30,800.

Hotel Croce di Malta, via Roma, 41 (tel. 36 31 34), off p. Garibaldi. Expensive but on the lake. Gregarious management. Singles L25,000, with shower and breakfast L35,000. Doubles with breakfast L43,000.

Pizzeria San Lucia, Mascari, 33 (tel. 36 50 36). Lecco's best restaurant. Try local *montevecchia* wines. Pizza L4500-5500. Full meal L19,000. Open Thurs.-Tues. noon-2:30pm and 6pm-2am.

Bar Cristallo, on p. Largo Europo. Well lit on the lakefront. Excellent *granatine* (fruit-flavored ice drinks, L1500). Open 4pm-2am.

La Bottega del Gelato, next to Bar Cristallo. An ice cream mecca. Open daily from 9am.

Sights

Manzoni maniacs may want to view **Villa Manzoni,** where the courtier spent his youth, now a museum. (Open Mon. and Wed. 2:30-5:30pm, Tues. and Thurs.-Sun. 10am-noon and 2:30-5:30pm.) Lecco's **basilica** is known for its Giottoesque frescoes dating from around 1380, depicting the Annunciation, the Deposition, and the life of San Antonio. The **Palazzotto di Don Rodrigo** is an interesting testimony to a period of Spanish domination in the sixteenth and seventeenth centuries. Lastly, the **Ponte Azzone Visconti,** built between 1336 and 1338, is the city's oldest monument. (The bridge has recently been obscured by construction work.)

Lake Maggiore (Lago Maggiore)

Far quieter than its easterly cousins, Lake Maggiore cradles the same temperate mountain waters framed by the same lush shores. An air of opulence hangs over the whole area, but between the multi-starred hotels and restaurants hide surprisingly cheap alternatives. Northern European tourists have discovered this, and descend from mid-July to mid-August. Still, there are plenty of secluded spots, and not even an army of tourists could adulterate this lake.

Stresa

Stresa retains most of the charm that brought visitors here in droves during the nineteenth and early twentieth centuries. The town is 1½ hours from Milan on the Milan-Domodossola train line. The **tourist office** (tel. 301 50) is at p. Europa, 3. From the station, go toward the lake on Duchessa di Genova, and make the second right onto via de Martini. (Open Mon.-Fri. 8:30am-12:30pm and 3-6:15pm, Sat. 8:30am-12:30pm.) The **post office,** on via Roma near p. Congressa, offers mail telegram services. (Open Mon.-Fri. 8:15am-8:30pm, Sat. 8:15-11:40am.) **Telephones** for long distance calls are available at Bar Sport, via Roma, 20, down the street from the post office (open daily 10am-10pm), as well as any bar with a yellow telephone sign. Stresa's **telephone code** is 0323.

Accommodations, Camping, and Food

Stresa's lakefront teems with magnificent hotels that cost at least an arm and a leg. The farther inland you go, however, the more reasonably priced the rooms. Food is geared towards the up-scale hotel denizens. **Locanda del Tulipano,** via R. Sanzo Carciano, 2 (tel. 302 82), is the biggie here. Carciano is a quiet suburb of Stresa; take a left from the station on via Principe di Piemonte, cross a stream, and follow the sign uphill to the left. After the second church, the *locanda* will stare you in the face. Pleasant modern matrimonial suites cost L36,000, breakfast included. (Open March-Oct.)

Hotel Mon Toc, via Duchessa di Genova, 67-69 (tel. 302 82), near the station in Stresa. Walk to your right as you exit, and turn right under the tracks. Comfortable, modest rooms. Singles L19,000, with shower L25,000. Doubles L30,000, with shower L38,000.

Hotel Primavera, via Cavour, 39 (tel. 312 86). If you're sick of dingy rooms, this deliciously extravagant hotel is worth the extra lire. Singles L35,000. Doubles L65,000. Showers and breakfast included.

Camping: In **Gignese,** at the **Sette Camini** (tel. 201 83). L3500 per person, L4500 per tent.

Taverna del Pappagallo, via Principessa Margherita, 40 (tel. 304 11), off corso Umberto I. The best pizza and Italian dishes in Stresa's uncommonly affordable L5000 range. Open Thurs.-Mon. noon-2:30pm and 7-11pm.

Osteria degli Amici, via A.M. Bolongaro (tel. 304 53). Be careful: A.M., G.F., and Luigi Bolongaro are three roads near each other. Slightly expensive, but a great selection and efficient service. Fish dishes around L10,000. Full 4-course menù L16,000. House wine L7000 per bottle.

K2, via A.N. Bolongaro, 7. The best "Italian Ice" in town. Large cone or cup L1500. Open daily 10:30am-midnight.

Sights and Seasonal Events

Stroll along the lakeside for a look at the **Regina Palace Hotel** and the **Grand Hôtel des Iles Broomées,** two imposing monuments to nineteenth-century aristocratic tourism. You may still glimpse a nanny watching the boys play tennis on the estates' front-lawn courts.

From the last week in August to the third week in September, some of the finest orchestras and soloists in the world gather in Stresa for the internationally acclaimed **Settimana Musicali di Stresa.** Tickets are generally expensive; student tickets are available on four out of 19 evenings. Write to the ticket office, Palazzo dei Congressi, via R. Bonghi, 4, 28049 Stresa, for information and programs.

Near the beach where the ferries depart (out viale Principe di Piemonte, then down viale Lido) is a *funivia* up steep **Mt. Mottarone** (1500m) for an unparalleled panorama of Lake Maggiore and its jewel-like islands (9:20am-noon and at 5:20pm, last car back at 5:50pm, 20 min. L9000).

Baveno

Baveno, about 5km north of Stresa and accessible by Stresa's Arona to Locarno ferry, any of the sightseeing boats leaving from p. Marconi (round-trip L4600), and less frequent bus service (7 per day, from the bus station at Stresa's center port, L1500). The town is more sedate and less expensive than Stresa, as well as less tourist-mobbed once you leave the lakefront. Relax in the courtyard of Baveno's fourteenth-century church; dozens of jabbering crows will replace the dozens of jabbering tourists. **Villa Fedora**'s shoddy appearance begs restoration, but the gardens remain charming and well kept, opening onto a shady public beach. The water here is clean enough for swimming. To get there, walk down via Garibaldi (the main road) away from Stresa—enter the park after crossing the bridge. (Park open in summer Mon.-Sat. 9am-12:30pm and 3-6pm, Sun. 9am-12:30pm; off season closed Sat. 9am-12:30pm and Sun.) Baveno's **tourist office** at via Garibaldi, 16 (tel. 246 32), provides a complete list of Baveno's many inexpensive lodgings. The **post office** is across the street (open Mon.-Fri. 8:15am-6:30pm, Sat. 8:15-11:40am). **Hotel Elvezia,** on via Montegrappa (tel. 241 06), near the church, has fresh-smelling well-furnished rooms, some with a view of the lake. (Singles L21,000. Doubles L30,000. Full pension L45,000. Open Easter-Oct.) **Lido Camping Bruno** (tel. 247 75) is a beautiful, shaded campsite with a beach adjacent to Fedora's. (April-June L3000 per tent, L2500 per car; July-Aug. L4000 per tent, L3500 per car.) Baveno has several stores that sell food at normal Italian prices. Otherwise, try **Piccola Napoli,** on via Garibaldi (tel. 242 86), which sells delicious pizza for about L5000.

The Borromean Isles

Harboring many seaside treasures and pleasures, these gorgeous islands won't desert you. However, the outrageous admission fees for the sights here might desert your wallet. The cheapest way to see the isles is to purchase a day ticket (L7100) from the **Navigation Offices** (tel. (0322) 466 51) at Stresa's center port (open 8am-8pm).

Isola Madre is the loveliest and quietest of the three islands. Its palace is simpler and more elegant than Isola Bella's and contains a great number of portraits of Count Vitaliano Borromeo and his family, who transformed the islands into palace residences in 1670. The gardens are organically arranged, with an aviary full of brightly colored parakeets. (Admission L6000, ages 6-15 L3000.) **Isola Bella,** the most touristed of the islands, is home to the overly decorative seventeenth-century **Palazzo e Giardino Borromeo,** a study in bad aristocratic taste. (Open March-Oct. Tues.-Sun. 9am-5pm. Admission L5000, ages 6-15 L2500.) The formal gardens are the main attraction, but their extravagant baroque decorations tend to overwhelm. Skip **Isola dei Pescatori** (Isola Superiore) as this small fishing village is a royal rip-off. If you are a garden enthusiast, disembark the ferry at the **Giardini di Villa Taranto,** the park of a large villa formerly owned by an English family (the chief caretaker will tell you the story). The park is a botanical garden, and the greenhouses shelter colorful exotic flowers. (Open daily 8:30am-6:30pm. Admission L5000, ages 14 and under L4000.)

Lake d'Orta (Lago d'Orta)

Only a fraction the size of Maggiore, Lake d'Orta is the unspoiled recluse of the Lake Country. Restaurant and hotel prices (and the solicitous treatment tourists receive) are a relief after the more commercialized lakes. Small towns rim the lakes, and Orta San Giulio juts forward with its maze of cobblestone alleys and small shops. Transportation around the lake is limited, and cars scarce. A wayward stroll into the woods may not get you anywhere, but your mind will drift to Walden Pond. Lake d'Orta lies on the Domodossola-Novara **train** line (8 per day from Novara, 1 hr. 20 min.). Get off at Orta Miasino and take the shuttle bus (L600) or walk downhill to the lakeside (15 min.). **Buses** leave for Orta from the train station in Arona (Sept.-June Mon.-Sat. 1 per day, July-Aug. 2 per day; 1 hr.) and from the main square in Stresa (July-Aug. 1 per day, 1 hr.). To get to Omegna at the northern tip of the lake, take a bus from the train station in Verbania (every 20 min.).

The **Azienda Autonoma** is in p. Motta (tel. 903 55; open Tues.-Wed., Fri.-Sat. 9am-12:30pm and 3-6:30pm, Thurs. 3-6:30pm, Sun. 9am-noon and 3-5pm). The **post office** is at p. Ragazzoni (open Mon.-Fri. 8:30am-noon and 2-6pm, Sat. 8:30-11am; the **postal code** is 28016). The **telephone code** is 0322.

Antico Agnello (tel. 902 59) off p. Motta, offers clean, comfortable rooms and the kindest service around. (Singles L18,000, with shower and breakfast L25,000. Doubles L28,000. Breakfast L2500. Full pensione L44,000.) Their **restaurant** is highly recommended with *primi* L3000, *secondi* L7000. Try their *trota al burro* for L6000. (Open Feb.-Nov. noon-3pm and 7-9pm.) **Amici Miei,** via Olina, 40 (tel. 904 44), down the street, has less personality but pleasant enough rooms. (Singles L16,000. Doubles L20,000, with shower L32,000. Open April-Oct.) Phone ahead in July and August. They also serve well-prepared *primi* (L4000), *secondi* (L8000), and a *menù* (L15,000-18,000). There is **camping** at **Cusio,** near the train station on via Vecchia Carcegna (tel. 902 90), a hillside site with a pool, tennis courts, a panorama of the lake, and two four-person trailers for rent for L30,000 per day. (L3800 per person, ages 8 and under L2800, L2900 per tent. Open Feb. 10-Jan. 10.) A good-sized **open-air market** occurs every Wednesday morning in front of the tourist office at p. Motta. *Alimentari* are scarce and expensive.

The **Palazzotto Comunale,** a frescoed building from 1582, is still almost intact. The **municipio** (town hall) down the street at #11, formerly a private home, and its small lakeside garden give you an idea of the life of past wealthy vacationers to Orta. On the more ascetic side, set high in the cool, verdant hills above town is the **Sacro Monte,** a monastic complex of 20 chapels devoted to Saint Francis of Assisi. Its chapels were built from 1591 to 1770 and vary in architectural style and merit. They are adorned with some fine frescoes and eerie, life-size polychrome terra-cotta figures. **Isola di San Giulio,** across from Orta, has an interesting Romanesque **basilica** from the twelfth century, built on fourth-century foundations. The frieze on the black marble pulpit depicts the struggle of Christianity against paganism—symbolized by a griffin and crocodile alternately triumphant over each other. (Open Tues.-Sun. 9:30am-12:30pm and 2:30-7pm, Mon. 2:30-7pm.) A circular route around the island leads through picturesque, narrow streets passing ivy-covered walls and terra-cotta roofs. To get to the island, take the launch that leaves from p. Motta in Orta San Giulio every half-hour (daily June-Sept.). Buy your round-trip ticket on board (L1500). Boats make only two runs per day in winter.

Omegna, only 15 minutes away by train, is a grim, industrial town situated at the northern tip of the lake. Visitors can usually find lodgings in one of its many pricey *locande.* It's also accessible by bus from the train station in Verbania (20 min., L1200). Stay at slightly dingy **Pensione Cusio** (tel. 622 01), with singles for L12,000 and doubles for L22,000; **Costa Azzurra** (tel. 622 17) with L15,000 singles; or **Vittoria** (tel. 622 37), which offers singles for L14,000, with bath L16,000, and doubles for L23,000, with bath L27,000. All are comfortable and have free showers. There is unadvertised camping on the beach below the **AGIP** gas station. Register in the station, and enjoy the solitude of the lake and its facilities. (L3500 per person, L3000-4500 per vehicle or tent.) The **tourist office** is at p. Mameli, 7 (tel. 64 30 01). The **telephone code** is 0323.

Trentino-Südtirol/Alto Adige

"*Grüss Gott!*" Travelers to Italy's northern reaches often hear this and fear they have tripped across the Austrian border. And they have in all but name. Trentino-Südtirol/Alto Adige, one of Italy's four autonomous regions, is split into two culturally and otherwise distinct provinces. Trentino in the south is predominantly Italian-speaking, while Südtirol (South Tirol) in the north (south of Austria, and thus the designation) is largely German-speaking, encompassing most of the mountain region known as the Dolomites. Snowcovered peaks speckle the area and narrow roads weave through green valleys and swift rivers. Originally part of the Holy Roman Empire, the provinces were conquered by Napoleon only to pass into the hands of the Austro-Hungarian Empire. At the end of World War I, however, Trentino and the Südtirol slided under Italian sovereignty. During the 1920s, Mussolini's brutal efforts to Italianize the Südtirol were curtailed by Germany, but not before he had supplied every German name in the region with an Italian equivalent (Toblach to Dobbiaco, Moos to Moso, etc.).

The Südtirol now undergoes an Austrian cultural resurgence. The advent of "complete provincial autonomy" in the last few years has meant, among other things, that the Austrian names now take precedence in all official publications. North of Bolzano, you may get better service by trying to speak German; in Trent, Italian is the ticket.

The entire region, but especially the north, experiences extreme seasons. Between Christmas and Easter and between July 15 and September 10, hotels and resort facilities run at full capacity and prices run about 20% higher. During the low seasons, all services open and close at unofficial times.

Dolomites (Dolomiti, Dolomiten)

Stunning limestone spires shoot skyward from billowing fields and pine forests. These amazing peaks—fantastic for hiking, skiing, and rock-climbing—start just west of Trent and extend north and east to the Austrian frontier.

Finding accommodations in the Dolomites is as easy as making it down a bunny slope. Least expensive are the hundreds of alpine refuges (see Hiking below) and the rooms in private homes advertised by the *zimmer/camere* signs. The complete *Südtirol Hotel Guide* is available free at the provincial office in Bolzano and in local tourist offices. These offices also provide complete listings of about 40 legal campsites in the region, but some travelers camp almost anywhere—with discretion. Keep in mind that bushwhacking at high altitudes without proper equipment borders on suicide.

The **SAD** (Società Automobilistica Dolomiti) has an armada of **buses** that covers virtually every paved road in the area with surprising frequency. If you plan to move around a bit, pick up a free *SAD Orario* (bus schedule with map) at the Bolzano/Bozen bus station. **Car rentals** run about L50,000 per day, weekend specials L100,000, gas not included. You do not need an International Driver's License, but a major credit card helps, and you must be over 21. Keep in mind that distances in this region may be short but movement on twisty mountain roads is slow.

Hiking

In the Dolomites even the least intrepid can become Alpinists. The terrain varies from wide, gentle trails to vertical cliffs. Hiking boots (*scarponi*) and rock-climbing equipment are available in Alto Adige, but are least expensive in Trent or Verona.

Over the centuries the number of **alpine refuges** has increased into the hundreds, making forays into the mountains easy and safe. All refuges are clearly marked on the *Kompass Wanderkarte* (L4300), the best map of the region, available at most newsstands or bookstores. Some refuges lie at the end of days of hiking, while others are accessible by bus or cable car.

The refuges are generally open from June to early October. Some remain open year-round, however, and at higher altitudes, some are open for much shorter periods. Willy Dondio's *I Refugi Dell' Alto Adagio* is the best of a large collection of guides in Italian and German. The provincial tourist offices in Trent and Bolzano provide information in English on their respective provinces. The Alpine desk of the office in Bolzano is run by Dr. Hannsjörg Hager, a noted Alpinist and author of several renowned Dolomites guides. He speaks English and can help you pick a suitable route and make sure the refuges are open before you get into the mountains.

Refuge prices increase with the altitude, averaging about L6000 per dormitory cot and L11,000 per bed. All refuges offer an unspectacular *menù* for L6000-10,000, depending on how high you are; carry your own food up if possible. Pick up information about *Winter Wanderwege* (winter walking paths) from the tourist office. For further information, contact the SAT on via Manci, 109 (tel. 215 22), in Trent.

Skiing

The Dolomites are excellent for downhill skiing. One caveat: Smaller towns have less crowded trails if more limited ski facilities. The **EPT** in Bolzano is a good source of information; ask for *Ski Panorama: South Tyrol* or their pamphlet for cross-country skiers. The **UPT** in Trent will supply you with *Snowy Planet* (include a few thousand lire). When you write, explain your price range and the kind of skiing that interests you, and request a specific recommendation for a ski area. Major ski centers near Trent include: **Folgaria, Brentonico, Madonna di Campiglio,** and **Monte Bondone** (especially close to the city); near Bolzano: **Alta Venosta** (around Lake Resia), **Colle Isarco,** the **Val d'Isarco** (near Bressanone), the so-called **Zona dello Sciliar,** and the **Alta Badia** (around Corvara).

One amazing deal is offered by the **Skiarena Ortler,** Rentweg 4, 39026 Prad am Stilfserjoch, around and to the east of Merano: A six-day pass good in eleven areas, on 63 lifts, costs L94,000, only L75,000 from mid-January to mid-February. One of the cheapest and most convenient ways to enjoy a skiing holiday in the Dolomites is to get a **settimana bianca (white week)** package deal from a CTS or CIT office anywhere in Italy. Prices start below L500,000, including seven days' room and board and ski passes. If you want to travel the region by bus or car, investigate the **Superski Dolomiti** pass, which allows you access to all 430 cablecars and lifts in the Dolomite area: L31,900 per day in high season and L26,500 in low season (early Dec., late Jan., and April); L169,000 per week in high season. Ski rental is about the same everywhere: L15,000 for a cross-country pair and L24,000 for a downhill set. One hour of private lessons starts at L22,000. Be warned that Christmas and early February to mid-March are considered high season, when prices are significantly higher than those quoted above. Regional passes, such as for Alta Badia only, cost considerably less.

Trent (Trento, Trient)

The Council of Trent may be a vague memory from history class. Called to discuss ways to thwart the rising tide of Lutheranism, it dragged on from 1545 to 1563, by which late date, their task ahd become impossible. Few realize that Trent today is an attractive city worth a stop on any tour of northern Italy. With its flowers and frescoed facades, Trent is a delightful surprise.

Trent was the perfect site for a summit on the challenge to Rome from beyond the Alps, for this city is a traditional site of confrontation between the Latin and German worlds. One of the most hotly contested cities of World War I, Trent was wrested from the Hapsburgs at the end of the war. One of Italy's greatest heroes, Cesare Battisti, was a *trentino.* He was martyred by the Austrians behind the Castello di Buonconsiglio; his remains now watch over the city from a simple neoclassical mausoleum. But the days of excitement are gone from Trent. What remains is a pleasant, inexpensive waystation on the Brenner Hwy. (A22), ideal for skiing or hiking.

Orientation and Practical Information

Trent lies between Verona and Bolzano on the Bologna-Brenner train line. Trent's sights, hotels, and services are concentrated in the old city, so unless you're staying at the campground, you won't need the public bus system. One more blessing: In summer Trent is practically tourist-free.

Azienda Autonoma di Turismo: via Alfieri, 4 (tel. 98 38 80), diagonally to the right across p. Dante from the station. Well-staffed. The usual maps and hotel lists. Open Mon.-Fri. 8:15am-12:30pm and 3-6pm, Sat. 9am-noon. Also on p. del Duomo (tel. 98 12 89), under the Palazzo Pretori. Open June-Aug. Tues.-Sat. 9am-noon and 3:30-6:30pm, Mon. 3:30-6:30pm, Sun. 9am-noon.

Ufficio Provinciale di Turismo: corso III Novembre, 132 (tel. 98 00 00), the continuation of via Garibaldi and via Santa Croce. A summer's worth of literature on the town. For information on the province, not the city. Refuge information on the 3rd floor. Open Mon.-Fri. 8:30am-noon and 2-4pm.

Budget Travel: Globetrotter Viaggi, via S. Pietro, 3 (tel. 98 63 44), near p. Battisti. Transalpino tickets. Large and efficient. Open Mon.-Fri. 9am-noon and 3-7pm, Sat. 9am-noon. **CTS,** via Cavour, 21 (tel. 98 15 33), near p. del Duomo. Organized outings and Transalpino tickets. Services mostly for ages under 26. Open Mon.-Fri. 9am-12:30pm and 3:30-7pm, Sat. 9am-noon.

Post Office: via Calepina, 16 (tel. 98 72 70), between the *duomo* and p. Vittoria. Open Mon.-Fri. 8:10am-7pm, Sat. 8:10am-1pm. **Postal code:** 38100.

Telephones: SIP, via Belenzani, 30, off p. Duomo. Open daily 8am-9:30pm. **Telephone code:** 0461.

Train Station: on p. Dante (tel. 345 45). To Verona (every hr., 1 hr., L4700), Bolzano (every hr., 45 min., L3000), Venice (every 2-3 hr., L10,700).

Bus Station: via Pozzo (tel. 98 47 00), next to the train station (turn right as you exit). To Riva del Garda (every hr., L3100), Madonna di Campiglio (5 per day, L4100), and Molveno (5 per day, L2700).

Taxi: Tel. 98 60 90 by day; 261 73 by night.

Hiking Equipment: Rigoni Sport, p. Battisti (tel. 851 29). Convenient. Open 9am-noon and 3:30-7:30pm. **Mountain Shop,** p. Generale Cantore, near the campground. Cheap.

Swimming Pool: via Fogazzaro, 4 (tel. 91 10 06), off corso III Novembre.

Alpine Emergency: CAI-SAT hotline, Tel. 331 66. Main office, tel. 215 22.

Hospital: Ospedale Santa Chiara, corso III Novembre (tel. 92 51 25).

Police: Questura, p. Mostra (tel. 259 73).

Accommodations and Camping

Trent teems with rooms, except in August, when most hotels are full of vacationing families. Don't hold your breath for Trent's planned youth hostel, but ask the Azienda in 1989.

Casa della Giovane, via Prepositura, 58 (tel. 343 15), to the right as you leave the station, set back from the street. From via Pozzo, turn right at via Roma, then take the 2nd left. A tidy, contemporary ACISJF hostel for women only, with a *mensa.* Doubles L15,000 per person. Singles with shower L17,000.

Centro di Accoglienza Mons. Bonomelli, via Lungo Adige S. Niccolò, 6 (tel. 234 89). From the train station, walk right on via Pozzo, right on Cavalcavia S. Lorenzo, and go over the bridge. At the highway intersection, go to the far side and down the ramp on the left. Follow the highway running along the river to the left. This is lungo Adige S. Niccolò, and the sign for the center is lit up on the right (15 min.). A committed community center that takes in down-and-out men for up to 3 consecutive nights. In the absence of a youth hostel, they accept male travelers as well. Kitchen facilities. Washing machines. Immaculate, modern doubles and triples. L500 per night. Show up 5-10pm, and they'll put you in whatever bed is free.

Albergo alla Mostra, p. Mostra, 12 (tel. 98 02 23), right under the Castello di Buon Consiglio. Take bus #4 or 9 to p. Venezia, or follow via Magnosi to the left as you leave the station. A charming, if slightly musty place, with great views. Nana's favorite. A fantastic deal for 3 or more. Singles L20,000. Doubles L32,000, with shower L40,000. Showers included. Breakfast L3000.

Albergo al Cavallino Bianco, via Cavour, 29 (tel. 315 42). From the station, walk right along via Pozzo and then take via Orfane to via Cavour. Not a bargain but fastidiously kept, safe, and cheery. Couples welcome. Singles L23,500, with shower L32,000. Doubles L39,000, with shower L52,000. Open Dec. 26-Dec. 15.

Camping: Camping Trento, on lungo Adige Braille (tel. 82 35 62), a 20-min. walk upstream along the river. Take bus #2. L6650 per site plus L4800 per person. Open until 11pm.

Food

The **market** in p. Lodron behind the *duomo* bustles every morning from 8am to noon. The afternoon hours vary according to a complicated seasonal and religious schedule. Thursday welcomes the **open-air market** to vie Maffei, Prati, Esterle, Torrione, and Borsieri, as well as piazza d'Arogno.

Mensa, at the Casa della Giovane (see above). Cheap, wholesome, and unexciting food, but a good place to meet local and foreign students. Breakfast L2000. Lunch and dinner L5500-6000. Open 7:15-7:45am, noon-1:45pm, and 7-7:30pm.

Cantinota, via S. Marco, 24 (tel. 98 03 27), the continuation of via Roma and via Manci. Not to be confused with the *vicolo* of the same name. Rather posh, but a good place to try Austro-Italian specialties or get a late-night snack under a vaulted ceiling. *Primi* from L6000 and *secondi* from L8000. Cover and service L2000. Open Aug.-June Fri.-Wed. noon-2:30pm and 7pm-2am.

Taverna Al Tino, via S. Trinità, 10 (tel. 98 41 09), near p. Vittoria. A cheerful hole-in-the-wall and local hangout. Pizza from L3000, large portions of pasta L3500-4000, and full meals under L16,000. Cover L1000. Open July 10-June 16 Mon.-Sat. noon-2pm and 7-10pm.

Tre Di, via Belenzani, 46 (tel. 363 56), near p. Duomo. Set in a small courtyard. Pizza from L3500, *primi* L3000-3800, *secondi* L6500-8500, wine L6000. Try their delicious *strangolapreti* (a blend of spinach, noodles, and dough) for L3800. Open Sat.-Thurs. noon-3pm and 6-11:30pm.

La Botte, p. del Duomo, 29 (tel. 322 10). Tourists attracted by quaint, ivory-colored entry and walled garden. Local fare in an elegant setting. Full meals about L15,000. In an elegant setting. Cover L1000. Open Mon.-Sat. noon-2pm and 7-9pm.

Self-Service, in the bus station. Decent and cheap, though open only for lunch 11am-2:30pm. Full meals L6000-9000. Expensive food store on the same floor. Open daily 7am-9pm.

Sights

The pointed dome of Trent's Gothic-Romanesque *duomo* rises in modest semblance of the encroaching Alps. Inside, two unusual, twin-arcaded staircases climb the walls of the nave, while the remains of thirteenth- and fourteenth-century frescoes decorate the transept. The famed Council's decrees were formulated in front of the huge cross in the Chapel of the Holy Crucifix. A group of fascinating "knotted" columns, masterpieces of medieval stonemasonry, support the eastern end of the building outside. (Open daily 6:30-11:50am and 2:30-8pm.) In the *piazza* also stands the twelfth-century Palazzo Pretorio, which houses the **Museo Diocesano.** This museum contains seven famous Flemish tapestries as well as the treasures of the *duomo* and memorabilia of the Council. (Open Thurs.-Tues. 9am-noon and 2-6pm. Admission L1500.) Walk out of p. del Duomo and along **via Belenzani,** a Renaissance street with intricate but apocryphal frescoes from the past century. Take a right at the end of the street onto via Roma to continue to the castle, Trent's other main sight.

The **Castello di Buonconsiglio,** once residence of the bishop-prince who ruled Trent, was built into the city's walls; its several parts were finally connected during the seventeenth century. The large round tower, part of the **Castel Vecchio,** was joined to the Renaissance **Magno Palazzo,** built in 1536 by the most benevolent of Trent's rulers, the patron-bishop Bernardo Clesio. The castle houses the **Museo Provinciale d'Arte** with frescoes by Dosso Dossi in the Sala Grande and the remarkable "frescoes of the twelve months" by an anonymous fifteenth-century artist in the **Torre dell' Aquila.** (Castle and museum open April-Sept. Tues.-Sun. 9am-noon and 2-6pm; Oct.-March Tues.-Sun. 9am-noon and 2-4:30pm. Admission L2000.)

Near Trent

Monte Bondone rises majestically over Trent, and is a pleasant spot for a daytrip or overnight excursion. Skiing is superb on all levels in this resort area (day pass for all lifts is L17,500). Check with the tourist office (tel. 471 37) in **Vaneze,** located halfway up the mountain, about accommodations and maps. **Ski School Monte Bondone** (tel. 471 37) offers lessons and rents equipment. Pick up a map at the tourist office in Trent, and then catch the cable car from Ponte di San Lorenzo, between the train tracks and the river, to **Sardagna** (7am-6:30pm, L2000). From there, a 10- to 12-kilometer hike will take you to **Malga Mezavia Campground** (tel. (0461) 474 78; L4000 per person, L6000 per tent).

Although removed from the other Dolomites, the **Dolomiti di Brenta** (or Brenta Group) are among the most spectacular. All refuge information for the Brenta group is contained in the brochure *I Rifugi della S.A.T.,* available at the Azienda in Trent. Prices run L9500-11,000 per night. The best base for exploring this area is **Molveno,** a small town that can be reached by SAD bus from Trent (see Practical Information). From here, the classic hike is the climb to **Rifugio Pedrotti** (2491m), a large Alpine refuge just beneath the Bocca di Brenta (tel. (0461) 58 60 42). From Molveno, take the chairlift to **Rifugio Pradel** and pick up trail #340. Continue on this trail until you reach **Rifugio Selvata** (1630m), where you can transfer to trail #319. This path will take you to the summit (4 hr.). Once at the top be sure to pick up #318 right away unless you have rock climbing equipment and want to tackle the world-famous **Via della Bocchette.** The other alternative from Rifugio Pedrotti is to follow #318 under the Via della Bocchette in the direction of Madonna di Campiglio. (This way Pedrotti-Madonna is 7 hr.) From Madonna di Campiglio, you can either take the bus or hitch back to Trent. The scintillating **Lago di Caldonazzo,** 5km east of Trent, is a haven for hiking, swimming, and resting. Local trains from Trent stop in villages such as San Cristoforo al Lago on the shores.

Bolzano (Bozen)

Bolzano is a truly bilingual city. Few of its residents, however, actually *speak* both Italian and German. Only the city signs, *menùs,* and public places use two tongues. The ebb and flow of ethnic tensions have not interfered with the city's rapid development as a center of industry and tourism. In spite of its smog and resort hype, Bolzano has kept heavy traffic out of the center, and spacious *piazze* and shady parks in. The town is the best place to get your bearings for a foray into the mountains and is itself a vibrant center of local culture.

Orientation and Practical Information

Bolzano is a 2½-hour ride from Verona, while the Brenner Pass and Innsbruck are 1½ hours to the north. The center of town is a triangluar area bordered on the south by the Isarco (Eisack) River, on the west by the Talvera (Talfer), and on the northeast by an excellent hiking hill, the Renon (Ritten). Bolzano has its share of tourist offices, all on **piazza Walther.** To get there, walk along via Stazione from the train station (tel. 97 42 92) or via Alto Adige from the bus station. If you intend to set out on a hiking expedition, you will need more specific information, and you should make sure to arrive on a weekday when the Provincial Tourist Office is open (see below).

Information Office: p. Walther, 8 (tel. 97 06 60 or 97 56 56). Should be your 1st stop. They'll book rooms for free, supply you with a map and list of hotels, and graciously answer any questions in English. Pick up the Bolzano/Bozen calendar. Open Mon.-Fri. 8:30am-12:30pm and 2-6pm, Sat. 9am-12:30pm.

Provincial Tourist Office for South Tyrol: p. Parrocchia/Pfarrplatz, 11-12 (tel. 99 38 08), off p. Walther. A visit to this office is essential for anyone traveling to the South Tyrol, especially the mountains, though the staff is less than forthcoming. Pick up the Hotel Guide and talk to Dr. Hannsjörg Hager at the Alpine Desk (see Hiking under Dolomites). Open Mon.-Fri. 8:30am-12:30pm and 2-5:30pm.

Club Alpino Italiano (CAI): Obstplatz, 46 (tel. 97 81 72), and **Alpenverein Südtirol (AVS),** via dei Bottai/Bindergasse, 25 (tel. 97 87 29). These are, respectively, the Italian and Austrian Südtirol Alpinist clubs. Group tours meet with Europeans. Weekend daytrips about L12,000 (CAI trips Sun. only). *Kompass Wanderkarte* for the area, billboard with notes for used ski equipment. But don't expect to hear English. CAI open Mon.-Fri. 11am-1pm and 5-7pm. AVS open Mon.-Fri. 3:30-7:30pm.

Room-Finding Service: At the train station. Charges a 10% commission, so you're better off going to the information office. Unreliably open April-Oct. daily 12:30-2pm and 4:30-9pm.

CIT: p. Walther, 11 (tel. 97 85 17), on the opposite side of the square from the information office. Student travel services and information on skiing package deals. **Currency exchange.** Open Mon.-Fri. 8:30am-12:30pm and 3-6:30pm.

Post Office: via della Posta, 1, by the *duomo.* Open Mon.-Fri. 8:15am-7:30pm, Sat. 8:15am-2pm. **Postal code:** 39100.

Telephones: SIP, p. Parrocchia, 18, near the post office. Open daily 8am-7:30pm. After hours, try the office at corso Italia, 34. **Telephone code:** 0471.

Buses: via Garibaldi, 20 (tel. 97 12 59), near the train station. **SAD** buses to Collalbo, Cortina, Alpe di Siusi, Merano, and many other mountain villages. Pick up the free *orario* at the information window. Open 7am-noon and 4-8:30pm.

Taxis: Tel. 97 01 97 or 98 11 11.

Car Rental: Avis, p. Verdi, 18 (tel. 97 14 67). **Hertz,** via Alto Adige, 30 (tel. 97 71 55). Rates are a complicated concoction of fees, taxes, and insurance. It works out to about L82,000 per day, L130,000 for Fri.-Sun.

Camping Equipment: Sportler, via dei Portici (Lauben gasse) 37A (tel. 97 81 81). Not a bargain, but extensive selection. Considered the best hiking and camping store in the Südtirol. Open Mon.-Fri. 8:30am-12:30pm and 3-7pm, Sat. 9am-12:30pm.

Laundromat: Seccoblitz, via Palermo, 35/B (tel. 91 01 63). Take bus #5. Open Mon.-Fri. 8am-noon and 3-7pm.

Hospital: Ospedale Regionale S. Maurizio, via Lorenz Böhler (tel. 90 81 11).

Police: Questura, via Druso, 8 (tel. 99 73 57). **Ufficio stranieri,** via Marconi, 33 (tel. 97 81 81).

Accommodations and Camping

Bolzano has budget deals coming out of its ears in the spring and fall; in summer and winter, however, you will have to keep your eyes peeled to find anything affordable.

Garni Casa Regina Angelorum, via Renon (Rittner Strasse), 1 (tel. 97 21 95), across from the train station. Modern, impersonal, and noisy during business hours. But you can get squeaky clean in their hot showers. A better deal for larger groups. Singles L22,000. Doubles L33,000. L16,800 per additional person. Office open 6:30am-11pm.

Kolpinghaus, via Ospedale (Spitalgasse), 1-3 (tel. 97 46 45), near the train station. Spic-and-span dormitory rooms. If there's no one to receive you in the main hall, follow the signs to **Büro.** Singles L23,000. Doubles L20,000 per person.

Albergo Klaus, via della Mostra (Kohlern), 14 (tel. 97 12 94), 1km above town. Go under the train tracks and across the river to the base station of the "Kohler-bahn" cable car. After a steep 5-min. ride, turn right up the hill. A real farmhouse with warm people. Always cool and quiet. Bring your own food or indulge in the owners' well-meant *Wienerschnitzel* (about L8000 with salad). Singles L16,000. Doubles L21,000. L5000 per additional person.

Casa della Giovane, via Castel Weinneg, 2 (tel. 312 74). Take bus #7 to the foot of via Castel Weinneg (see Practical Information). Enormous, contemporary place with 62 beds and more to come. A hike from the center. Mostly triples and quads, but they'll put men in singles if possible. L15,000 per person. Office open 8am-11pm.

Camping: Moosbauer, via S. Maurizio, 83 (tel. 91 84 92). Take bus #8 from the station (last bus around 8:30pm). First tent L10,000, L5000 per additional tent and additional person.

Food

The region's fare combines Italian and Austrian cuisine, but the latter prevails. *Rindsgulasch* is a delicious beefstew; *Speck* is tasty smoked bacon; and *Knödel* (dumplings) come in dozens of varieties. For good wine, just ask for *un vino locale.* Fall highlights the vineyards with the weeklong Südtiroler Törgelen tasting spree. Be sure to try some wines with the *Kalterer See* label from the vineyards near Bolzano. There is also a daily **market** on p. dell' Erbe. (Open Mon.-Sat. 8am-noon.)

Restaurant Weisses Rössl, via dei Bottai (Bindergasse), 6 (tel. 97 32 67), the continuation of via Laurin and via dei Grappoli, at the end of via dei Portici. A great, cheap place with Austrian atmosphere. Recommended by locals and a *Knödel* capital. Nearly 100 regional and Italian dishes listed plus numerous daily *menù* (L4500-6500). Open Aug.-June Mon.-Fri. 7am-1pm, Sat. 7am-3pm.

Ristorante Larcher, via dei Bottai (Bindergasse), 35 (tel. 97 30 10). An intimate joint with plenty of filling German food. *Menù* L10,000-15,000. Pizza L3000, L500 per additional topping. Open Aug.-June Mon.-Sat. 1-9pm.

Spaghetti Express, via Goethe, 20 (tel. 97 53 35). A noisy, fun place with a young crowd. Try any of the umpteen kinds of pasta—the one with crabmeat, cream, and brandy is great. Dishes L4500-5500. Open Mon.-Sat. noon-2:30pm and 7:30pm-midnight. Closed for renovation in 1988.

Self-Service Restaurant GTAP, across from the train station behind Garni Regina Angelorum. A favorite of local workers. Select carefully and fill up for L4000. Open Mon.-Sat.

Panificio Lemayr, via Goethe, 17. Gobs of gluttonous bread and pastry. Open Mon.-Fri. 8:30am-noon and 3-7pm, Sat. 8:30am-noon.

Sights and Entertainment

Bolzano has beautiful castles and churches, all described in the Bolzano/Bozen pamphlet available at the information office in p. Walther. The monthly calendar also lists times and places for sights, exhibits, concerts, theater, hikes, and shops. Written in only Italian and German, it's easy to decipher even if you lose your Berlitz guide. The English guidebook *Walks and Hikes* suggests two- to six-hour excursions. The *Südtiroliën* succeed in preserving their towns' charm. Piazza Walther is clean and attractive—even the McDonalds on the corner is tasteful. Inside Bozano's fourteenth-century *duomo,* which presides over the *piazza,* medieval frescoes and stonework are now complemented by angular modern altars of rose-colored marble. (Open 7am-noon and 2-6pm.) **Piazza dell' Erbe** (Obstplatz), with its Neptune fountain, is the crossroads of the old town and the location of a daily outdoor market.

The fourteenth-century **Church of the Francescani** rests in a peaceful garden off the *piazza.* (Open 6am-noon and 2:30-6pm.) **Castel Mareccio** (tel. 97 66 15), on *passeggiata* lungo Talvera, once a water castle, was built in the thirteenth century, though its five towers are later additions. (Open Mon.-Sat. 10am-noon and 3-6pm.) The former **Dominican monastery,** in p. Domenicani, shelters chapels covered with frescoes of the Giotto school and a cloister executed by Friedrich Pacher.

Across the Talvera River, the quarter around p. Gries boasts two imposing churches. The **Church of the Benedictine Abbey of Muri** (tel. 28 11 16) on the *piazza* is a mighty baroque construction (1770) graced with Martin Knoller frescoes. The **Gries Parish Church** (tel. 28 54 87), off the *piazza,* has an elaborate woodcarved altar (1471-1480) by Michael Pacher. (Open Mon.-Fri. 10am-noon and 2-4pm. You must call ahead.)

At the northern tip of town is **Castello Roncolo,** on via Sarentino (tel. 98 02 00; open in summer Tues.-Sat. 10am-5pm; in off-season call ahead). Take bus #1 from the station to the last stop and then walk the extra 200m.

In Bolzano, there are Italian and German language theaters, exhibits by local artists, and frequent expositions of regional food and crafts. The homesick may find solace in American and Australian imports. International jazz, classical, folk, and rock music events abound. Annual events include **provincial wine exhibitions** (March-April), the **F. Busoni International Piano Competition** (late Aug.-early Sept.), and the **International Fair,** an interesting combination of commercial wares and entertainment (Sept.).

Near Bolzano

The mountains around Bolzano beg to be hiked. Pick up a *Kompass Wanderkarte* (L4300) from any newsstand or tobacco shop and consult Dr. Hager at the Alpine Desk of the provincial tourist office.

To get a feel for the mountains without expending much energy, your best alternative is a daytrip to **Soprabolzano** (Oberbozen/auf dem Ritten) and **Collalbo** (Klobenstein). The **Funivia del Renon** (Renon cable car, or Rittnerbahn) climbs to scenic Soprabolzano from Bolzano's via Renon, to the right of the train station. From there, a quaint train will take you the 7km to Collalbo (every hr., round-trip L5500). Both the towns and their surroundings are perfect for a leisurely hike.

Fortunately, the **Alpe di Suisi (Seiser Alm)** and the **Catinaccio (Rosengarten)** group are close to Bolzano. These spectacular sights have the highest concentrations of refuges in the region. Four or five buses per day leave Bolzano for almost every town in the area; many are only 40 minutes away.

Entrance to the Suisi (Schlern) group is easily gained from the west at **Fie allo Scillar (Völs)** or **Tiero.** Under two hours on easy footpaths will take you to **Rifugio Bolzano di Monte Pez** (Schlernhaus; tel. (0471) 61 60 24; open late June-Oct. 5). Yet another hike (3-4 hr.) brings you to **Rifugio Bergamo** (Grasleiternhütte; tel. (0471) 64 21 03; open late June-Sept.). Both are breathtaking refuges built in the 1880s by the Alpine clubs. If you wish to cross over to the Rosengarten group, head for **Rifugio Vaiolet** (tel. (0462) 632 92; open June 15-Sept. 25) and be prepared for a stiff climb.

To get directly into the Rosengarten group from the south, catch a bus to Passo di Constalunga (Karer Pass), and get off at the Alpenrose Hotel, where there is a chairlift to **Rifugio Paolina.** (Open June-Oct. 20 and Dec. 24-Easter.) To continue toward the Suisi (Schlern) group, you can follow one of two possible routes. If you feel energetic, follow trail #550, which climbs steeply up to Passo delle Coronelle (2630m) and then descends (meeting trail #541) to Rifugio Vaiolet.

Keep in mind that the refuges mentioned are only a few out of the 20 or so packed into a relatively small area. Consult your map and local Alpinists to discover other trails. Most cost L6000-11,000 per person.

Merano, 30km northwest of Bolzano, is one of the most famous spas in Italy. Developed under the Austro-Hungarian Empire, the place is a Central European watering spot in the grand style, complete with promenades and gigantic Edwardian hotels. Its surroundings, though not part of the Dolomite range, have some of the most picturesque mountains of the region. *Pensioni* are abundant.

In Merano, the **tourist office,** corso Libertà/Freiheitsstrasse, 45 (tel. (0473) 352 23), will change money, sell bus tickets, and quickly find you a room. (Open in summer Mon.-Fri. 8am-12:30pm and 3-6:30pm, Sat. 9am-noon and 3-5pm; in off-season Mon.-Fri. only.) Insist on something cheap; there are many *pensioni* with rooms for L11,000-18,000. For local hiking information, consult the **Alpine Association,** via Galilei, 45 (tel. 371 34; open Mon.-Fri. 9am-noon), or the **CAI** office, corso Libertà, 188 (tel. 489 44). Picnicking is a good idea in Merano, since restaurant food is expensive. Visit the Super Sconto in town or the **market** (open daily 9am-noon) near corso Libertà.

North of Bolzano on the Brenner Hwy., **Bressanone/Brixen** sizzles with the religion and scenery of old Austria. The ***duomo/Dom*** has a particularly decorative transept (*Kreuzgang*). (Open daily 9am-6pm. Free.) The **Kapital Haus** next door houses church treasures. (Open April-Oct. 10am-noon and 3-5pm.) The rest of the town's religious relics, largely the possessions of eighteenth-century bishops, rest in the **Hofburg** (tel. (0472) 305 05) and its adjacent museum. (Open March-Oct. Mon.-Sat. 10am-5pm.)

Hiking and **skiing** in the region are unbeatable. On weekdays, buses serve Varna (Vahrn), Millan (Milland), Bolzano, and Brunico several times per day.

The main **tourist office,** viale Stazione/Bahnhofstrasse, 9 (tel. (0472) 224 01), provides efficient service. (Open Mon.-Fri. 8am-noon and 2:30-6pm, Sat. 9am-noon.) Hotels are cheaper outside of town and camping convenient. In Varna/Vahrn, try the **Löwenhof,** Löwenviertel, 13 (tel. (0472) 232 16), a friendly establishment with a restaurant. Their rooms run L21,000-25,000, including breakfast and showers. Camping here costs L5500 per person and L4500 per tent.

Bolzano is also the main access point for the **Badia** region to the east (see Dolomites and Cortina).

Cortina d'Ampezzo

Buried in the mountains east of Bolzano lies Cortina d'Ampezzo, site of the 1956 Winter Olympics. The setting under the peaks of Tofane, Cristallo, and Sorapis is cosmic, but so are the prices. The mountain villas of this European Beverly Hills house foreign film stars, mink coats, and sports cars. Unless you have camping equipment or massive luck, you might easily drop L60,000 a day here just on food and accommodations. (See Near Cortina for some alternatives to the lifestyles of the rich and famous.)

Orientation and Practical Information

The ubiquitous **SAD** buses (tel. 27 41) run frequently to the surrounding towns, but only in high season (Aug. and Dec.-April). Fewer than half the buses run during low season, and these are further hampered by frequent strikes. Remember that the train line to Bolzano is an easy 35-kilometer hitch away in Dobbiaco/Toblach. The train to Venice is about twice that distance south in Calazo. Both bus and train run twice per day, depending on weather conditions and local politics.

Azienda Promozione Turistica, p. S. Francesco, 8 (tel. 32 31). From the bus station, go left on via Marconi, then right and downhill at via XXIX Maggio, turn left onto corso Italia, then cut diagonally across p. Venezia to p. San Francesco. Well-supplied but understaffed. Open Mon.-Fri. 9am-12:30pm and 3-7pm. Also on p. Roma opposite the Albergo Poste. Open Mon.-Sat. 9am-12:30pm and 3-7pm, Sun. 9am-12:30pm.

Gruppo Guide Alpine Cortina, p. S. Francesco, 5 (tel. 47 40), next to the Azienda. A treasure chest of information. They organize rock-climbing daytrips for beginners and provide advice on excursions. Open July-Aug. Mon.-Sat. 8am-noon and 4-8pm, Sun. 5-8pm.

Post Office: largo delle Poste, 16. Open Mon.-Fri. 8:15am-7:30pm, Sat. 8:15-1pm. **Postal code:** 32043.

Telephones: SIP, around the corner in the covered passageway. Open daily 9:30am-8pm. **Telephone code:** 0436.

Swimming Pool: In the Guargne section of town (tel. 607 81). Indoor. L4000 per person. Open daily 2-8pm.

Ice Skating: In the Olympic Ice Stadium (tel. 34 69). L6000 for skate rental and 2 hr. of skating. Open 10:30am-12:30pm and 2:30-4:30pm.

First Aid: Tel. 20 75.

Police: corso Italia, 33 (tel. 662 20).

Accommodations and Camping

Camping is highly recommended. Listed below are the cheapest rooms available in Cortina. These places are often booked and there are none cheaper. Contact the Azienda for reservations or complete listings. The houses run by nuns are by far the best deal in Cortina, but only if you write far in advance—by January for summer. Friendly **Suore Canossiane,** Casa Regina Mundi, Crignes, 18 (tel. 26 60), will put you in a single or double for L18,000-25,000 per person, with bath L4000. Other possibilities are **Suore Francescane,** Casa S. Francesco, via Cianderies, 7 (tel. 22 79), and **Suore Missionarie,** via XXIX Maggio, 2 (tel. 46 62), both offering full pension at L48,000 per person.

Albergo Cavallino, corso Italia, 142 (tel. 26 14). From the tourist office, head up the street toward via del Castello. Spotless and snug. Wonderful proprietors. Singles L26,500. Doubles L42,000. Showers included. Cheaper in off-season and for extended stays.

Locanda Battochio, via Franchetti, 4 (tel. 24 30), near the beginning of via Roma. Pleasant rooms on a noisy street. Singles L26,000. Doubles L40,000. Showers L2500. In off-season up to L10,000 cheaper.

Camping: Campsites are clustered in the fields about a 15-min. walk from town and are frequented by motorhomes. Take bus #1, which leaves p. Roma every hr. until 8pm. **Cortina** (tel. 24 83), **Dolomiti** (tel. 24 85), and **Rocchetta** (tel. 50 63) line via Campo, along the river. Prices are L4500 per person, in low season L4000, plus L6000-9000 per tent. The Cortina also operates a *pizzeria.*

Food

You'll find the best prices on staples (still 20% higher than elsewhere) at the **Cooperativa** on corso Italia.

Self-Service Autostazione, at the bus station on via Marconi (tel. 25 76). Decent fare, and one of the cheapest *menùs* in town (from L11,000). Open Sept.-July Sun.-Fri. 11:30am-1:30pm; Aug. 11:30am-1:30pm and 7-9:30pm.

Hamburger Kenny, via Stazione (tel. 33 96). You'll probably be avoiding this place all over Italy. But its cheap. Hamburger L1800. Open Wed.-Sun. 11am-3pm and 6-10pm.

Ristorante/Pizzeria Buca dell' Inferno, via Stazione, 31 (tel. 86 62 83), near the station down a flight of steps (or up one from via Marconi). A relative bargain. Eat in a cozy, wood-lined room in winter or under a leafy canopy in summer.

Pedavera, corso Italia, 163 (tel. 24 19). English, publike interior. Tasty meals also served outdoors. Friendly service. Meals L10,000-15,000. Open Tues.-Sun.

Spaghetti Haus 2000, corso Italia, 192 (tel. 37 03). *Menù* L15,000. Wine L6500 per liter.

Near Cortina

Cortina is a mountain resort, so waste as little time as possible in town and head for the hills. In winter, **skiing** is superb in the surrounding area. Ski and boot rentals come to L18,000-24,000 per day; a ski pass for all the lifts in the area is about L30,000 per day, L140,000 per week, depending on the season. In summer, there are many **hiking** opportunities. You can easily plan your routes with the Azienda's excellent trail guide. The **Freccia del Cielo** (Arrow of the Sky) cable car goes to the summit of the **Tofana di Mezzo** (3244m; round-trip L17,500). At the other end of town, another cable car will take you to the top of the **Tondi di Falória** (2343m; round-trip L14,000). The refuges in Le Tofane are privately run by the ski resorts, so if you want to stay in the mountains and avoid the resort scene, arrive at Cortina early in the morning and hike across to the **Fanes** group (see below).

In high season, five buses per day leave for the scenic **Lago di Misurina.** Stay at the campsite here, hike to the **Rifugio Fratelli Fonda Savio CAI** (2 hr., tel. 390 36), or take the cable car to **Rifugio Col de Varda** (tel. 390 41).

Just over an hour north of Cortina by bus, **Brunico** is one of the most charming villages in the Südtirol. A combination of narrow medieval streets and broad eighteenth- and nineteenth-century *piazze,* Brunico is perhaps the best and cheapest place to get a feel for the region without the tourist hype. The efficient **tourist office,** via Europa (tel. (0474) 857 22), above the bus station, will help find rooms for under L11,000 per person and change money from 9am to noon and 3 to 6pm. The **Hotel Krone,** Oberragen, 8 (tel. 852 67), is on one of the prettiest streets in town and houses a favorite local restaurant. (Singles L18,000. Doubles L25,000.)

While hiking in the Dolomites surrounding Cortina can be an exhilarating experience, you should plan your route carefully. Either tourist office can provide an excellent free map of the footpaths near Cortina, complete with projected hiking times and degree of difficulty. Private refuges indicated by the symbol PR cost L15,000-20,000; subsidized CAI refuges cost L8000-10,000.

From either **Pedraces** or **Santo Vigilio,** you can hike through the **Alpe di Fanes** and approach Cortina from the west through pristine countryside. One particularly satisfying route is to hitch or take a bus to Pedraces and take the chairlift to the foot of the **Croce** group. Stay on trail #7 for some 6km of moderate hiking to **Rifugio Varella** (tel. (0474) 510 79; open mid-June to Oct. and Christmas-March 5). Set aside some time to spend beside the several **Alpine lakes** in this area. Pick up trail #11 to #20, and continue to **Rifugio Scotoni** (tel. (0471) 850 31; open June-Sept.). From here Cortina or any of Le Tofane are less than four hours away on easy trails.

You can reach the foot of the Tofane Group using the **Cortina-Col Drusciè** cable car (L4500), where, in an ambitious mood, you can hike to **Rifugio Giussani** (2561m). As you leave the cable car, follow the road that winds up the hill until you see the beginning of trail #405. Take the steep climb up this route to **Rifugio Duca d'Aosta** (2098m), where you can either continue on #405 until it reaches trail #403, which will lead you to Rifugio Giussani, or take the slightly more difficult, but shorter #420, which eventually leads to trail #403. No rock-climbing skills are needed on either route, but both trails are rigorous.

The **Cristallo Group** requires technical experience and equipment. If you're game, take the cable car lift from Rifugio Rio Gere, east of town, and then make your way down. The **Sorapis Group** to the south is more accessible. Take the Cortina-Tondi di Falòria cable car (above) to **Rifugio Tondi** (2327m). From here you can follow the virtually horizontal trail #213 (and later #216) to the Forcella di Cadin (2306m). Follow the beautiful descent to **Rifugio Vandelli** (1928m) and **Lake Sorapis,** at the foot of three impressive glaciers. From this point, trail #215 leads down to the Tre Croci Pass (1809m), where you can either take the bus or hitch back to Cortina.

Salubrious for both soul and wallet is exploration of the German-speaking **Alta Badia** region to the northwest of Cortina. SAD buses run from Cortina several times per day, although winter storms can disrupt the schedule, to Pedraces, Colfosco, San-Cassiano, and the two largest towns, **La Villa** and **Corvara.** Alta Badia is in the heart of the Superski Dolomiti region (see Dolomites). Novice and intermediate skiers will enjoy the lifts above Corvara, while advanced skiers can frolic on the runs near La Villa and San Cassiano. (Ski rental L16,000-22,000 per day.) Pick up the booklet *Notizie Utilie Manifestazioni/Nutzliche Hinweise und Veranstaltungen* at any hotel or information office for information and an events schedule. The region's main **tourist office** is in La Villa (tel. (0471) 84 70 37); the one in Corvara is on the main street in the town center (tel. (0471) 83 61 76). They will gladly make room reservations and provide sport information and the *Walking/Hiking Guide to Alta Badia.* Try the **Pension Raetia** (tel. (0471) 83 60 88) in Corvara at the foot of the ski slopes. A power breakfast and luxurious rooms cost L25,000 per person.

Veneto

If art and architecture are the yardsticks of civilization, then Veneto surpasses most regions on the European continent Measure for Measure (Shakespeare agreed, setting numerous plays here). Veneto was dominated by Venice in the High Renaissance. When the Turks conquered Constantinople in the late fifteenth century and forced the great trading city of Venice to turn to the mainland for its livelihood, colonization began in the hilly but fertile country to the west. Once Venetian nobles went to live in the *terra ferma,* as this new region was called, painters such as Titian and architects such as Palladio carried ideas back to Veneto from Florence and Rome, where they were then reinterpreted in the unique Venetian context. As Venetian power waned, so did its bustling productivity, but the fine architecture survives and fuels the twentieth-century Italian tourist economy. Beginning a little east of Milan, winged lions, the symbol of San Marco, and Byzantine-styled arched windows adorn public spaces, making the former satellite towns of Verona, Vicenza, and Padua among the most elegant in the world. The Alps occupy almost one-third of Veneto's territory, and northern towns are surrounded by stunning mountain vistas.

Until the twentieth century, the Venetian dialect was a distinct Romance language, actually more like Spanish than Italian; today Venetians speak a slurred jangly Italian in which the letter "g" is pronounced "z" (Giudecca becomes "Ziudecca"). The food is also different here. Rice, the staple starch, is often served with peas (*risi e bisi*) or fish (*risotto al pesce*). *Polenta,* a chewy cornbread, often replaces *panini,* and wine is strictly regional: the dry white *soave,* the light red *bardolino,* and the full-bodied *valpolicella.* Outside Venice and some of the mountain resorts, accommodations prices are reasonable and the local meat and dairy products will keep your lira-output low.

Venice (Venezia)

She is the Shakespeare of cities—unchallenged, incomparable, and beyond envy.
—John Addington Symonds

Indeed, Venice can be compared only to the western world's most influential literary figure in its superior singularity, popularity, and ability to evoke grand emotions. The dismal mudflats on which Venice is built were not a place any sane people would choose to settle. But when Atilla and his colleagues swept down from the north, the original inhabitants of the fertile Veneto had no choice but to take to the swamps. By the eleventh century, the barbarians were at bay and the mudflats made livable. Marco Polo made Venice the center of European trade with the exotic Orient, but when Vasca da Gama made a successful journey to India around the Cape of Good Hope in 1498, Venice lost its monopoly on trade with the Far East, and decline began. By the eighteenth century, Venice had become the licentious pleasure capital of a none-too-decorous continent. Operating overtly out of their own *palazzi,* Venetian *courtesans* were treated with more respect than anywhere else in Europe, but the party ended in 1797, when Napoleon came to conquer, bringing the downfall of the republic just around its thousandth birthday.

As if to commemmorate its millennium, the republic celebrated itself by becoming the world's premier tourist town. Flustered tourists who crowd piazza S. Marco, pay inflated prices in a restaurant, and leave the next day will have missed this city's magic. Give yourself time to explore the city. Note that in late July and August, Venetians on holiday evacuate the city. You may find yourself surrounded by other tourists rather than locals.

This mass exodus is not, however, merely a seasonal phenomenon. *De*population is one of the greatest problems facing modern Venice. Today there are half as many inhabitants as in the seventeenth century. Furthermore, bureaucracy impedes conservation of monuments and such modern necessities as sewage disposal and effective control of the destructive tides that flood the streets in winter.

Whatever time of year and whatever the circumstances, however, do not miss the showy splendor of Venice. Sansorino wrote that the word Venice must be derived from the Latin "*veni etiam,* that is, come again, and again, because no matter how often you come you will always see new aspects and new beauties."

Orientation

Venice is easily accessible from Milan, Florence, Rome, and all the cities of the Veneto by rail, and linked to the towns of the Dolomites by bus. The **Santa Lucia Train Station** (or simply *ferrovia*) lies on the northwestern edge of the city, linked to the mainland by a long causeway. Make sure you stay on the train at the stop marked "Mestre (Venezia)," an ugly industrial town on the mainland. The garages, car rentals, and bus terminals are just across the Grand Canal in nearby **piazzale Roma**—this is where you get off if you come by car, since Venice allows no cars. If you're in a rush to get to San Marco (and the central tourist office) from the station and piazzale Roma, take *vaporetto* #2. For a splendid introduction to the *palazzi* along the stately Canale Grande, take #1 or 34.

You won't have trouble "losing" yourself in this beautiful city, even if you're a seasoned traveler and the best navigator since Marco Polo. Your first move should be to buy a good, if expensive, map. The free one from the tourist office is helpful for locating general areas and the names of most churches and palaces, but is otherwise inadequate. The best is the one with a red cover published by Edizioni Foligraf

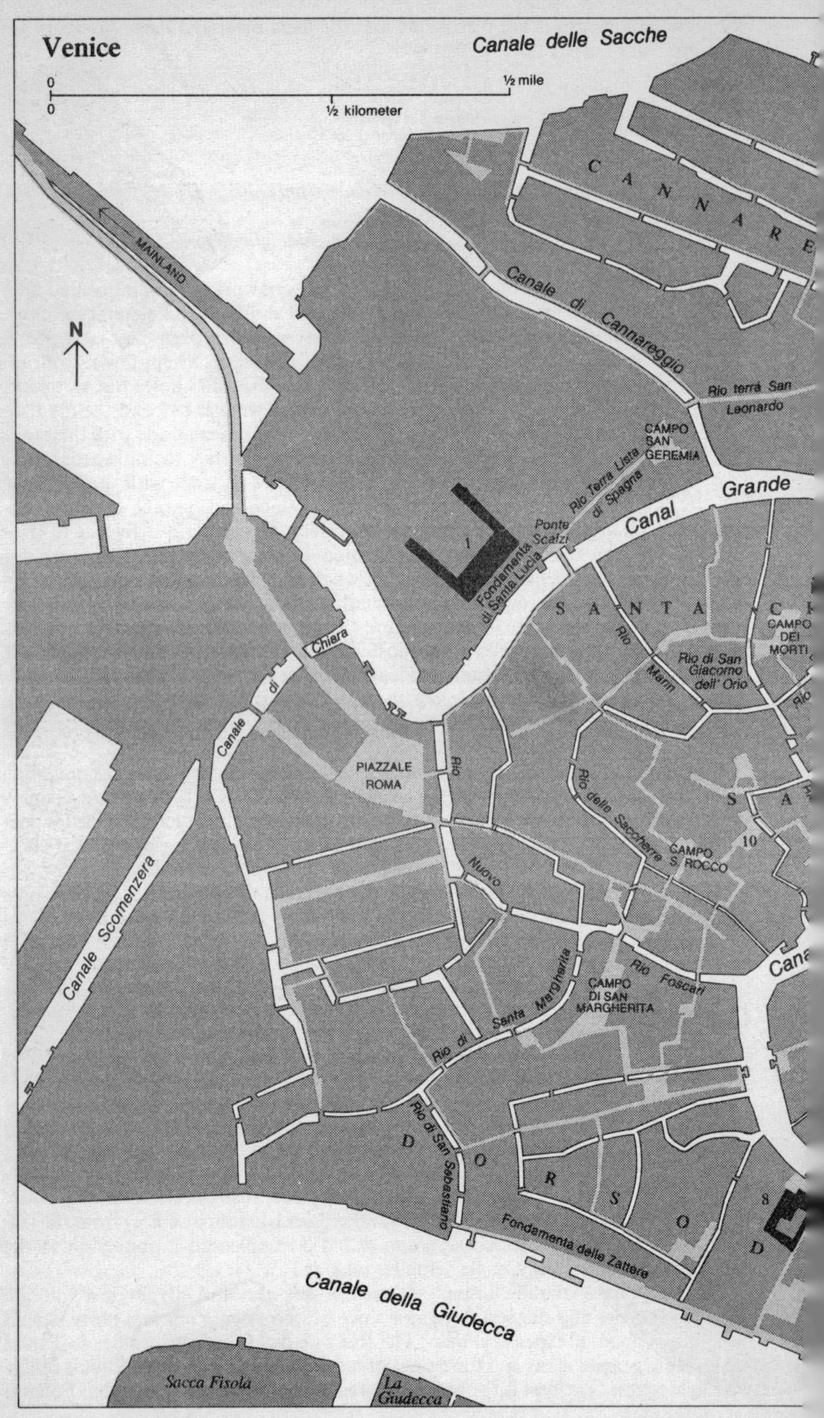
Venice
Canale delle Sacche
0
½ mile
0
½ kilometer
MAINLAND
N
CANNAREGIO
Canale di Cannareggio
Rio terrà San Leonardo
CAMPO SAN GEREMIA
Rio Terra Lista di Spagna
Canal Grande
Ponte Scalzi
Fondamenta di Santa Lucia
1
SANTA CROCE
CAMPO DEI MORTI
Rio Marin
Rio di San Giacomo dell' Orio
Chiara
Canale di
PIAZZALE ROMA
Rio
Rio delle Sacchere
CAMPO S. ROCCO
10
Nuovo
Canale Scomenzera
Rio Foscari
CAMPO DI SAN MARGHERITA
Rio di Santa Margherita
Rio di San Sebastiano
DORSODURO
8
Fondamenta delle Zattere
Canale della Giudecca
Sacca Fisola
La Giudecca

1 Train Station
2 Post Office
3 Amex
4 IYHF
5 Piazza San Marco
6 Palazzo Ducale (Doge's Palace)
7 Campo San Salvatore
8 Gallerie dell'Accademia
9 Church of S. Maria Della Salute
10 Campo dei Frari
11 Church of San Zaccaria
12 Campo S. Giorgio
13 Campo SS. Giovanni e Paolo
14 Church of S. Maria Formosa
15 Teatro Goldoni
Canale delle Navi
MURANO
Cimitero San Michele
Sacca della Misericordia
Strada
Rio di Noale
Felice
Rio di San
Rio di
Nova
CAMPO DEI S.S. APOSTOLI
Rio delle
due Torri
Rio di San Cassiano
Rio dei Mendicanti
Rio di San
Marina
Barbaria delle Tole
Ponte Rialto
Madonnetta
POLO
Grande
Rio di San Salvador
Calle dei Fabbri
Rio della Guerra
CASTELLO
Rio San Lorenzo
Rio dei Greci
Palazzo o della Paglia
CAMPO MANIN
Rio di San Luca
CAMPO SAN ANGELO
MARCO
Rio dei Barcaroli
Molo
Riva degli Schiavoni
Rio delle Ostreghe
Moise
Rio di San
Canale di S. Marco
LIDO
San Giorgio Maggiore

Mestre-Venezia (L4000). At the very least, make certain your map indicates *vaporetto* (motorboat) stops and the outlines of the six *sestieri* or sections of the city: **San Marco, Castello, San Polo, Santa Croce, Cannaregio,** and **Dorsoduro.** Within each section, there are no individual street numbers, but merely one long sequence of numbers (roughly 6000 per *sestiere*), which wind their tortuous way through the district with virtually no logic. *Let's Go* lists the *sestiere* and then the number.

The first thing to notice when you open your map is that the **Grand Canal,** the main canal of Venice, can be crossed on foot only at the **ponti** (bridges) **Scalzi, Rialto,** or **Accademia.** *Traghetti* (gondola-like ferry boats) may seem too picturesque to use practically, but in fact are a commonly used way to cross the canal in places where a bridge is nowhere in sight. You can also take a more expensive *vaporetto* across—they traverse the river many times as they travel up and down the canal. When you set out to find something, use the city's major sights and *campi* (squares) to navigate. The city is also blanketed with invaluable yellow signs to central spots such as Rialto, the Accademia, San Marco, piazzale Roma, and the *ferrovia.* Unfortunately for pedestrians, the Grand Canal is not a good reference point since it is accessible mainly by boat. Furthermore, it winds confusingly in a backward "s" curve. Once in the right neighborhood, ask directions.

The alternative to walking is taking the **vaporetti** (motorboat buses), which ply the Venetian lagoon. Though expensive, they are also convenient. Tickets cost L1000 or L1500 for the *accelerato,* L2000 for the faster *diretto,* and L300-1000 for the slower *traghetti,* which generally make ferrylike crossings between the islands or across the Canal Grande. All the principal boats run 24 hours but come only once per hour after 1am. A 24-hour *biglietto turistico,* available at any ticket office, costs L8000 and allows you unlimited travel on all boats. It is only a good deal if you're on a kamikaze tour. If you plan on a stay of more than four days on Giudecca, or plan to visit some of the outlying islands, a **Cartavenezia** is extremely valuable. With this, the *diretto* is only L600, the *accelerato* L500, and you can use it for three years. Bring L8000 and a passport photo to the ACTV ticket office in the Corte dell' Albero at the S. Angelo *vaporetto* stop (tel. 70 03 10; open Mon.-Sat. 8:30am-1pm).

Not all stations sell tickets all the time; carry extras with you and machine-validate them as you board, or buy them once on board from the conductor (L300 surcharge). Be careful, because ticket vendors habitually short-change tourists. The fine for riding the *vaporetti* without a ticket is L15,000. It is wise to listen for news of a *sciopero* (strike) of the *vaporetti,* especially if you intend to stay at the youth hostel or the nun's institution on Giudecca. Travelers working toward a scout's badge in navigation may wish to purchase the exhaustive **ACTV** timetable (L1000 at the office in p. Roma).

The major lines include:

#1: Piazzale Roma-Rialto-San Marco-Lido and back. An *accelerato* (the slow variety) makes every stop up and down the Grand Canal.

#2: Rialto-Ferrovia-p. Roma-Rio Nuovo-San Marco-Lido. A *diretto* with no intermediary stops.

#5: Circolare Destra—San Marco-Guidecca-p. Roma-Ferrovia-fondamenta Nuove-Murano; **Circolare Sinistra**—Murano-fondamenta Nuove-Ferrovia-p. Roma-Giudecca-San Marco. Take the Sinistra from the station to the youth hostel and also from San Marco to Murano to see the glass-blowers.

#8: San Marco-Giudecca. An alternative to #5 for getting to the youth hostel from San Marco.

#12: Murano-Burano-Torcello-Treporti. Leaves from fondamente Nuove. L2000 to the 1st island, L1000 between the islands.

#16: Fusina-Zattere. To the camping-hostel, leaving every 20 min. from the bank in Dorsoduro, which faces the island of Giutecca.

Traghetti: Across major canals. Riva S. Maria del Giglio to Riva di S. Gregorio daily 8am-7pm; Riva di S. Samuele to Riva di S. Barnaba (Palazzo Grassi to La' Rezzonico) Mon.-Fri.

7:30am-2pm; Riva di S. Tomà (near the Frari) to Riva di Ca' Garzoni Mon.-Sat. 7am-9pm, Sun. 8am-8pm; Riva del Vin to Riva del Carbon Mon.-Sat. 7:45am-2:30pm, Sun. 8:45am-1:30pm; Riva di S. Sofia to Riva Peschiera (the Rialto fish market) Mon.-Sat. 7am-9pm, Sun. 7am-7pm; Riva di S. Marcuola to Riva del Fontego dei Tedeschi Mon.-Sat. 7am-2pm; from in front of the train station to fondamenta S. Simeon Piccolo Mon.-Sat. 7:45am-2:30pm, Sun. 8:45am-1:30pm.

It is highly advisable to check with the tourist office to find out whether Venice is still afloat. Seriously. High tides (usually Nov.-April) cause *acque alte,* the periodic flooding that covers parts of the city, notably San Marco, in as much as three feet of water. If you don't like wet feet, check ahead and consult the signs posted at all ACTV landing stages. *Acque alte* usually last two to three hours and planks or platforms are laid out across most major thoroughfares.

Practical Information

EPT Tourist Information: Offices at the **train station** (tel. 71 50 16; open daily 8:30am-9pm) and in summer at the **bus station,** p. Roma (tel. 522 74 02; open daily 8am-7:30pm), handle accommodations services and little else. They will locate a room and collect a L10,000 deposit, which will be subtracted from your hotel bill. As friendly as might be desired but disorganized. Main Office at **San Marco,** Ascensione, 71/F (tel. 522 63 56), under the arcade at the far end of the *piazza.* More complete information, English spoken, and can also make reservations. Open Mon.-Sat. 8:30am-7pm. On the Lido, the **Azienda di Turismo** is at Gran viale, 6/A (tel. 76 57 21; open Mon.-Sat. 9am-2pm). Pick up *Un Ospite di Venezia* (A Guest in Venice), a bilingual weekly (monthly in the winter) with a wealth of information and entertainment listings. More exhaustive guides to art and entertainment in Venice are *Marco Polo* (L5000), a glossy monthly, and *Venezia In Jeans* (L1000), aimed at budget travelers.

Budget Travel: Centro Turistico Studentesco (CTS), Dorsoduro, 3252, on fondamenta Tagliapietra (tel. 70 56 60), near campiello Squellini due west of campo S. Margherita. *Vaporetto:* s. Tomà. Accommodations service, student IDs, and transportation. For **Transalpino** tickets also try **ATG,** Dorsoduro, 3856 (tel. 523 49 55 or 523 64 76), across the bridge. Both open daily 9am-12:30pm and 3:30-6:30pm (ATG until 7:30pm). **AIG,** S. Marco, 5043 (tel. 520 44 14). 15-30% discounts on tickets to IYHF cardholders.

Consulates: U.S., a representative at via dei Pellegrini, 42 (tel. (040) 91 17 80), in Trieste, but the closest full-fledged office is in Milan. **U.K.,** Dorsoduro, 1051 (tel. 522 72 07). The nearest **Canadian** and **Australian** consulates are in Milan.

Currency Exchange: Banca Cattolica del Veneto, S. Marco, 4481 (tel. 95 70 66), on calle Goldoni near campo S. Luca. One of the more honest establishments with standard bank rates from Milan and only a L500 commission. **Banca d'America e d'Italia,** S. Marco, 2216 (tel. 520 07 66), across the bridge from the American Express office. Particularly good rates but a L3000 commission. They cash credit on Visa cards here. Normal banking hours Mon.-Fri. 8:30am-1:30pm and 3-4pm. The best rates and longest lines are to be had at **Guetta Viaggi,** San Marco, 1289, just before American Express. Open Mon.-Sat. 9am-7pm, Sun. 9am-1pm.

American Express: S. Marco, 1471 (tel. 520 08 44), on salizzada S. Moisè, a few blocks west (toward the train station) of the *piazza.* Wired money accepted here, but all of the arrangements must be made at the agency or bank from which money is sent. Helpful travel information, if you catch them at a calm moment. L3500 inquiry charge on mail for non-cardholders. Open Mon.-Sat. 8am-8pm. Mail pick-up Mon.-Fri. 9am-6pm and Sat. 9am-1pm.

Post Office: Main branch, salizzada Fontego dei Tedeschi (tel. 528 93 17), near the eastern end of the Rialto bridge. Fermo Posta (L250 per letter, rarely charged) at desk #6; stamps at #11 and 12. Open Mon.-Sat. 8:15am-7pm. Another convenient office is just through the arcades at the end of p. S. Marco. Open Mon.-Fri. 8:10am-1:40pm, Sat. 8:30am-noon. Also a branch at the train station facing platform #10. Open Mon.-Fri. 1:40-7pm and Sat. 1:40-6pm. **Postal code:** 30124.

Telephones: ASST, in the same building as the main post office. Phone booths have fans to forestall the dread sweat-box effect. Open daily 8am-8pm. **SIP,** in p. Roma and along viale S. Maria Elisabetta on the Lido. Open daily 8am-9:30pm. If you dial a number the phone refuses to accept, try substituting the 1st digit in the number with "52." **Telephone code:** 041.

Airport: Aeroporto Marco Polo (tel. 66 12 62; for lost and found 66 12 66). Flights to Rome, Milan, Turin, Palermo, and major western European cities. ATVO buses leave from p. Roma to the airport (30 min., L4000). ACTV local bus #5 is cheaper and leaves from p. Roma (every ½ hr., 30 min., L500).

Train Station: Stazione di Santa Lucia (tel. 71 55 55; for lost and found 71 61 22). To Padua (30 min.; L2000, round-trip L3400), Verona (1¾ hr.; L5900, round-trip L10,000), Milan (3½ hr., L13,200), Florence (4½ hr.; L12,900, round-trip L21,800), Rome (L29,000), Bologna (2 hr.; L7800, round-trip L13,400), Vienna (10½ hr., L56,000), and Zagreb (8½ hr., L25,000). **Orient Express** to London (1 per day, US$1000). **Baggage check** L1000.

Bus Station: ACTV buses from p. Roma (tel. 528 78 86). Pick up their schedule of frequent buses to the villas on the Riviera del Brenta (Malcontenta L600, Mira L1400, Strà L2000), Padua (L2500), Mestre (L600), and Treviso (L1700). Ticket office open daily 6:15am-midnight. **ATVO** buses serve the area from p. Roma. Office at #597 (tel. 520 55 30).

Car Rental: Europcar, p. Roma, 540 (tel. 523 86 16). The best rates in Venice. Only L108,000 per weekend from Fri. 2pm to Mon. 9pm, mileage and insurance included. You must reserve in advance, be over 21, and leave a credit card or substantial deposit. Open Mon.-Fri. 8am-7:30pm, Sat. 8am-2pm, Sun. 8am-noon.

English Bookstore: Il Libraio a San Barnaba, Dorsoduro, 2835/A (tel. 522 87 37), fondamenta Gherardini, off campo S. Barnaba. Classics, Agatha Christie, and all American fiction set in Venice. Loosely open Jan.-Oct. daily 10:15am-1pm and 3:15-8pm; Nov.-Dec. Mon.-Sat.

Laundromats: Lavaget, Cannaregio, 1269 (tel. 71 59 76), on fondamenta Pescaria off rio Terrà S. Leonardo near Ponte Guglie. Self-service. Make sure laundromats don't overcharge you. L10,000 to wash and dry 3kg. Open Mon.-Fri. 8:15am-12:30pm and 3-7pm, Sat. 8:15am-12:30pm.

Public Baths: Albergo Diurno (Day Hotel), S. Marco, 1266, in the *ramo secondo* (2°), directly off the west end of S. Marco. Showers L4000, toilets L500. Some toilet stalls have showers in the corner. Open daily 9am-7:30pm.

Medical Emergencies: Ospedali Civili Riuniti di Venezia, campo SS. Giovanni e Paolo (tel. 520 56 22; for first aid 520 08 25). Boat **ambulances** are surprisingly efficient (tel. 523 00 00). To locate **late night pharmacies** check the *Ospite di Venezia* or dial 192.

Police: Questura (headquarters of the state police), on fondamenta S. Lorenzo in the Castello. **Ufficio Stranieri** (Foreigners' Office; tel. 520 07 54). **Carabinieri,** p. Roma (tel. 523 53 33).

Accommodations

Plan on spending twice as much on rooms here as elsewhere in Italy, but wallow in the disarming hospitality Venetians have perfected in their 200 years as a tourist city. There has been rumor of a prospective law disallowing anyone without hotel reservations to step onto the island—don't worry; the law doesn't really make sense and wasn't passed. Reservations, preferably written, will, however, preserve your sanity. An intelligent solution to Venice in the summer is to approach the city through one of the towns nearby. From Padua, Vicenza, or Verona you can call for reservations the afternoon or evening before you arrive in Venice. Many *locande* will hold a room until 10 or 11am. A disadvantage to using an accommodations service is that hotels must stick to their quoted, maximum price; if you go directly they will often lower their prices. If you need help, though, the **EPT** at the train or bus stations will book rooms, but the **CTS** accommodations service (see Budget Travel under Practical Information) is somewhat less harried. Singles listed below vanish in summer, so be prepared to double up. If the situation becomes desperate, try one of the campgrounds at Mestre or Padua's youth hostel (closes 11pm). Police have begun to crack down on impromptu crashing in parks and beaches. However, backpackers from around the world continue to sack out on the train station's concrete steps.

The cheapest lodgings are not in hotels, but in hostels, schools turned over to travelers in summer, and religious, charity-run dormitories. Dormitory-type accommodation is always available somewhere in Venice without reservations, even during August and September. In addition to these, Venice is packed with small one-star hotels (*locande, pensioni,* and *alberghi*). But high season prices can be as astronomical as Venice is otherworldly. Beware as well of the mandatory L10,000 breakfasts and other forms of bill-padding, keep your wits about you, and agree on what you'll pay before you hit the pillow. "San Marco" is a dateline for the rich and famous, and *pensioni* prices are set accordingly. Castello and Cannaregio establishments are still fairly central, but both prices and the number of tourists are lower. Cultured visitors consider Dorsoduro, San Polo, and Santa Croce the "wrong" side of the canal; Venetians call it home, and budget travelers may well do the same.

Hostels and Student Accommodations

Ostello Venezia (IYHF), fondamenta di Zitelle, 87 (tel. 523 82 11), on Giudecca. Take *motoscafo* #5 (*sinistra*) from the station (L1500), #5 (*destra*) or #8 from S. Zaccaria near S. Marco (L1500). Get off at Zitelle and walk to your right. In a spotless and slickly renovated *palazzo,* but with a few too many stairs and a capricious water supply. Each room has 30 beds. Call ahead. Fluent English spoken. Members only, L12,000. Breakfast included. Full meals L7000. IYHF cards L15,000. Open 7:30-9am, noon-2pm, and 6-9pm. In summer arrive by 3 or 4pm; they start admitting the throng at 6pm. Reserve in writing. Check-out 7:30-9am. Curfew 11pm.

Instituto Cannosiano, fondamenta del ponte Piccolo, 428 (tel. 522 11 57), also on Giudecca. Take boat #5 to S. Eufemia, and walk to your left as you descend. Women only. The small garden is a welcome relief. Less rambunctious than the hostel, and run by solicitous nuns. 5-bed or dorm rooms L10,000 per person. Lockout 8:30am-4pm. You can arrive at any time of day to leave your bags. Curfew 10:30pm. Check-out 6-8:30am.

Domus Civica, S. Polo, 3082 (tel. 522 71 39), on the corner of calle Chiovere and calle Campazzo, between the Frari Church and p. Roma. Along the yellow-arrow road between p. Roma and the Rialto. Women only. Great management. Singles L22,000. Doubles L36,000. Showers included. Strict curfew 11:30pm. Check-out 10am. Open June-July and Sept. to mid-Oct.

Instituto Ciliota, S. Marco, 2976 (tel. 520 48 88), in calle delle Muneghe off calle delle Botteghe and campo Morosin. *Vaporetto* #2 to S. Samuele. Unmarried couples or single men will have no problem getting rooms here. Near the biggies (San Marco, the Accademia), yet off the major thoroughfares. Courtyard complete with benches, roses, and cats. One of the friendliest of its kind. At least one of the nuns speaks English. Singles L30,000, with shower L35,000. Doubles L50,000, with shower L60,000. Breakfast included. Curfew 11pm. Open June 15-Sept. 30. Phone reservations accepted.

Foresteria Valdese, Castello, 5170 (tel. 528 67 97). Take the *vaporetto* to S. Zaccharia, a 5-min. walk from campo S. Maria Formosa. From the *campo,* take calle lunga S.M. Formosa; the building's just over the 1st bridge. The 18th-century guesthouse of Venice's biggest Protestant church. Engaging frescos and equally ebullient management. Reserve 1 month ahead for their 2 beautiful doubles (L38,000). Otherwise, dorm rooms with bunk beds for 8, 12, or 16 people at L16,000 per person. Breakfast included. Check-in 9:30am-1pm and 6-8:30pm. Lockout 10am-1pm. No curfew.

Instituto S. Giuseppe, Castello, 5402 (tel. 522 53 52). From p. dei Leoncini to the left of S. Marco, take calle dei Specchieri to campo S. Zulian, then go right on campo de la Guerra over the bridge, and turn left immediately. 5- or 6-bed rooms in the center of town, with a garden. Couples should go in separately. Reserve 1 month ahead with deposit. L18,000 per person. Curfew 11pm.

Suore Mantellate, S. Elena, calle Buccari, 10 (tel. 522 08 29). A breathtaking 40-min. walk east from S. Marco. Quite far from the station. Take *vaporetto* #1 or 2 to S. Elena, and walk across the park. This leafy neighborhood is still the domain of locals. Friendly nuns and large rooms. Doubles or triples L27,500 per person. Showers and breakfast included. Open Sept.-July.

Foresteria S. Fosca, Cannaregio, 2372 (tel. 71 57 75). From the train station, walk down lista di Spagna and rio T.S. Leonardo to campo S. Fosca, then cross the bridge. A meeting place for international youth. Open July 15-Sept. 15 10am-noon and from 6pm. Lockout 10am-6:30pm. Curfew 11pm.

Archie's House, Cannaregio, 1814/B, S. Leonardo (tel. 72 08 84), where S. Leonardo meets campiello Anconetta, on the side of the street closest to the Grand Canal. Privacy, location, and price compare favorably to the youth hostel, especially for larger groups. Archie (who speaks 12 languages) and his wife (she's from Taiwan and speaks English) loathe rowdy guests and will quote higher prices to scare them away. Refrigerator in the hall. 3-, 4-, and 5-bed rooms. L17,000 per person. Hot showers (under lock and key) L500, cold ones L300.

Hotels

Cannaregio (From the Station to the Rialto)

Alloggi Nives Ottolerghi, Cannaregio, 180 (tel. 71 52 06), on Calle del Forno off Lista di Spagna, less than 5 min. from the station. Come here first; Mama and Papa will provide a true home and warm hugs. Doubles L36,000. Triples L51,000. Quads L64,000.

Locanda Antica Casa Carettoni, Cannaregio, 130 (tel. 71 62 31), along rio Terrà Lista di Spagna, just to the left of the station. Gorgeous rooms and a homey atmosphere. Singles L22,000. Doubles L40,000. Showers included. Open March-Jan. Closed 1 week in Aug.

Locanda Rossi, Cannaregio, 262 (tel. 71 51 64), off calle della Procuratie, a sunny alley to the left a bit father down the rio Terrà Lista di Spagna. An oasis in crazed Cannaregio. Rooms are modern and sterile. Adjacent garden. Singles L28,000, with shower L39,500. Doubles L44,000, with shower L62,500. Showers L4500. Obligatory breakfast L4500 the 1st few nights. Open Feb.-Dec.

Pensione Smeraldo, Cannaregio, 1333/D (tel. 71 78 38). Located in an old palace where a *principessa* lived until 1940. Fun rooms with high ceilings; cosmically cool in summer. Singles L28,000. Doubles L45,000, with bath L60,000. Frequent discounts, e.g., for students. Also try **Rooms' Biasin,** Cannaregio, 1252 (tel. 71 72 31), nearby and under the same management. More contemporary. Same prices.

Albergo Bernardi-Semenzato, Cannaregio, 4363 (tel. 522 72 57). From strada Nuovo, walk away from the canal on calle del Duca, then turn right on calle dell' Osa. Tidy rooms. Loquacious English-speaking proprietors will share invaluable city tips. Singles L22,000. Doubles L37,000, with bath L49,000. Breakfast L3500.

Albergo Adua, Cannaregio, 233A (tel. 71 61 84), across and about 30m east of Casa Care Honi on rio Terrà Lista di Spagna. Relics of '70s tackiness; rainbow wallpaper and scarlet bead curtains at ultra-modern prices. Singles L28,000. Doubles L44,000, with bath L62,500. Showers included. Obligatory breakfast L6000.

Dorsoduro, San Polo, and Santa Croce (Across the Canal Grande from San Marco and Cannaregio)

Ca' Foscari, Dorsoduro, 3888 (tel. 522 58 17), on calle della Frescata, at the very foot of calle Crosera where it hits calle Marconi. Take the *vaporetto* to S. Tomà. Look carefully for the camouflaged sign. Family-run with pride. Tastefully decorated rooms. Singles L26,500. Doubles L42,500. Showers L1000. They accept groups March-June, so phone ahead. They will hold a room for you until noon. Open Feb.-Nov. 5.

Locanda Montin, Dorsoduro, 1147 (tel. 522 71 51). From campo S. Barnaba, go south through the passageway Casin dei Nobili, across the bridge, right on the fondamenta Lombardo, and around the corner onto fondamenta di Borgo. A great bargain worth hunting down. Modern paintings and restored antiques coexist. The **restaurant** in the backyard under a fragrant grape arbor is excellent if expensive. Singles L25,000. Doubles L40,000. Showers included. Open Feb.-Dec.

Locanda Sturion, S. Polo, 679 (tel. 523 62 43), on calle Sturion, the 4th right off fondamenta del Vin (along the Grand Canal) going south from the Rialto bridge. A classic since 1290. Its views of the Grand Canal grace many a postcard. Rooms large, clean, mock *fin de siècle* decor. Flashdancers take note: Jennifer Beals slept here. Singles L28,000. Doubles L44,000. Showers L1000. Breakfast L6500.

Locanda Stefania, S. Croce, 181/A (tel. 520 37 57), on fondamenta Tolentini off fondamenta S. Simeone Piccolo, across the Grand Canal from the station. Look for a little lantern with the name on it. An old building, complete with creaky door and shadowy stairway. Huge, tidy rooms with uncomfortable beds, many brightened by candy-colored frescos. Singles L26,000, with bath L30,000. Doubles L44,000, with bath L57,000. Showers L3000. Open Dec. 15-Nov. 15.

San Marco (From the Basilica west to the Grand Canal)

Locanda Casa Petrarca, S. Marco, 4394 (tel. 520 04 30). From campo S. Luca, go south on calle dei Fuseri, take the 2nd left and then turn right onto calle Schiavone. All is sweetness—from wicker furniture and candy-cane-colored bedspreads to the hospitality of the woman who runs the show. English spoken. Singles L28,000. Doubles L44,000, with bath L62,500. Showers L2000. Breakfast L5000.

Locanda San Samuele, S. Marco, 3358 (tel. 522 80 45). Hard to miss, on the *salizzada* of the same name, leading out of the *campo* of the same name, just beyond campo Morosini. Rooms and bathrooms are small and dark. Bright management, though, and terrific prices. Singles L26,000. Doubles L40,000, with bath L50,000. Showers L2000. Breakfast L4500.

Hotel Orion, S. Marco, 700/A (tel. 522 30 53), in calle Spadaria between campo S. Zulian and p. dei Leoncini. Commodious, clean rooms with garish orange bedspreads. Doubles L57,000. Shower and breakfast included. Reservations with deposit only.

Castello (From San Marco to the Island of Sant' Elena)

Pensione Casa Verardo, Castello, 4765 (tel. 528 61 27). Take Rimpetto la Sacrestia out of campo SS. Filippo e Giacomo across the bridge (*vaporetto:* S. Zaccaria). Absolutely *the* find in this part of town—run by a hospitable, outgoing family. English spoken with good intentions. Singles L23,000. Doubles L38,000, with bath L47,000. Triples L63,000. Quads L80,000. Showers L2000. Breakfast L4000. Open Feb.-Dec.

Locanda Silva, Castello, 4423 (tel. 522 76 43). Take calle dell' Angelo (it starts next to S. Marco), then make the 2nd right, continue across the bridge, and go left when you hit fondamenta del Rimedio. On a charming canal, this is a large and fastidiously kept place. Singles L24,000. Doubles L40,000, with bath L50,000. Shower included. Breakfast L6000.

Locanda Tiepolo, Castello, 4510 (tel. 523 13 15), just off campo SS. Filippo e Giacomo, in the tiny ramo del Spezier (*vaporetto:* S. Zaccharia). An affable owner. Huge, clean rooms, with antique furniture and ceiling frescos overlooking side canals. Singles L31,000, with bath L42,500. Doubles L42,500, with shower L64,500. Showers L3000. Breakfast included.

Locanda Corona, Castello, 4464 (tel. 522 91 74; *vaporetto:* S. Zaccharia). Head north on Sacrestia, take the 1st right, and then the 1st left onto calle Corona. Gregarious proprietors with lots of kids. Fine rooms, but limited hot water supply. Drop by the Fucina degli Angeli (Angel's Forge), next door, for a look at glass-blowing. Singles L25,000. Doubles L37,000. *Pensione completa* L48,000. Showers L2000. Breakfast L6000.

Locanda Toscana-Tofanelli, Castello, 1650 (tel. 523 57 22), a little farther, where via Garibaldi hits riva dei Sette Martiri (*vaporetto* #1 or 4 to Giardini). The seaside location makes it worth the walk. Not elegant, but reasonable. The two caring sisters prefer quiet guests and couples over 20. English spoken. Restaurant downstairs (see below). Singles L17,000. Doubles L35,000. Showers L1000 but usually included. Breakfast L3500. Curfew midnight.

Locanda Sant' Anna, Castello, 269 (tel. 528 64 66). Take via Garibaldi, which becomes fondamenta S. Anna, turn left across the bridge at calle Crociera, then right at corte del Bianco (*vaporetto* #1 or 4 to Giardini). Definitely worth the hike. The family proprietors charm, as does the lack of tourists in this far eastern end of Venice. Starched sheets, sparkling rooms. Singles L28,000. Doubles L44,000, with bath L62,500. Showers L2500. Breakfast L5000. Open Dec.-Oct.

The Outskirts of La Serenissima

Ugly and industrial Mestre on the mainland; Lido, the island of sand-seekers; and Litorale del Cavallino, to the east along the Adriatic, have the lowest prices and most frequent vacancies around Venice.

To reach Mestre, just across the lagoon (all trains out of Venice stop there), walk up via Cappucina to the left of the station and past the intersection with via Sernaglia. Hotels **Dina** (tel. 92 65 65) and **Maria Luisa** (tel. 93 14 68) are at via Parini, 2 and 4, to the left of via Cappucini. (Dina: Singles L20,000; doubles L35,000. Maria Luisa: Singles L25,000; doubles L41,000.) **Hotel Roberta** is at via Sernaglia, 21 (tel. 92 93 55), several blocks away, and its 26 one-star rooms are usually vacant and almost evenly split between singles (L25,000) and doubles (L41,000).

The **Lido,** the long, thin stretch of beach that separates the Venetian lagoon from the Adriatic, is connected to the mainland by *vaporetto* lines #1 (L1500) and 2 (L2000), among many others (departures from Riva degli Schiavoni). Should you decide to stay here, be aware that room prices fluctuate with the season. (High season is April-Nov. and late Aug. to mid-Sept.) **Villa Aurora** on Rivierà S. Nicolò, 11/A (tel. 526 05 19), a two-star hotel with prices in the one-star range, offers rooms of varying quality. (Singles L31,000, with bath L43,000. Doubles L54,500, with bath, balcony, and a gorgeous view out on the water L72,000. Take bus A to the left as you leave the boat.) You can also camp on the Lido (see Camping below).

Ridiculously cheap accommodations cluster in the less accessible region of **Litorale del Cavallino.** Take *vaporetto* #14 from S. Marco to Punia Sabbioni (40 min., L2000). Of the 14 one-star hotels, the champion price slasher is **Al Buon Pesce Da Alto,** via del Faro, 31 (tel. 96 80 64). (Singles L18,000. Doubles L30,000.) **Da Giovanni** (tel. 96 80 63), is at #35. (Singles L20,000. Doubles L35,000.)

Sleeping Bag Crashers (Saccopellisti)

A little out of the way, but the least expensive, is **La Fusina Punta Sabbioni** (tel. 96 90 55), which offers bunks with eight people per room for L8000 per person. From p. Roma, take bus #4 (L600) to Mestre and change to bus #13 (across the street from Supermarket Pam). Ride to the last stop (1 hr., last bus at 10pm). By boat it's more picturesque and convenient but also more expensive. Take *vaporetto* #5 (L1500) left to Zattere and then take #16 (L2000) for 20 minutes to Fusina. Call ahead. They speak English. Several elementary schools with kitchen facilities, usually centrally located, are sometimes open to crashers (L10,000) or to hardier types willing to go tentless in the great outdoors (L3000). (Entrance fee L2000. Lockout 9:30am-7:30pm. Open mid-June to Aug.) For information ask at any of the tourist offices, or phone the **Department of Public Education** (tel. 522 92 62 or 523 03 65).

Camping

The **Litorale del Cavallino,** on the Adriatic side of the peninsula just east of Venice, is one endless row of campsites on the beach. From S. Marco, *vaporetto* #14 winds its circuitous and scenic way to Punta Sabbioni (40 min., L2000). **Marina de Venezia,** in the Punta Sabbioni area (tel. 96 61 46), charges L5500 per person and a hefty L15,000 for pieces of turf lavishly equipped with electricity, water, and a large parking space. (Open April-Sept.) **Ca' Pasquall,** via Fausta (tel. 96 61 10), is marginally less expensive. (Open May 10-Sept. 17.)

S. Nicolo (tel. 76 74 15) on the **Lido** is a rustic site with modern showers about 45 minutes from S. Marco and 15 minutes from the beach. Take *vaporetto* #1 or 2 (L1500-2000) to the Lido and bus A (L500) to the left to the last stop.

Food

It is possible to eat decently and cheaply in Venice if you know the secret password: **bar snacks.** These are not potato chips or pretzels, but meat- and cheese-filled pastries, little tidbits of seafood, rice, meat, and fish. In addition, there are the famous Venetian sandwiches, served in *osterie* with wine on a small round bun, and *tramezzini,* triangular slices of soft white bread with every imaginable filling. You can buy Venetian bar snacks for L400-1000, depending on the ingredients.

It is becoming difficult to actually sit down to a good meal in Venice at terrestrial prices. Remember to read the fine print on every menu and beware of extras like coffee. Remember, you can stop at an *osteria* for appetizers before dinner and a bar for dessert afterwards.

If you decide to shell out for a fish dinner, cross over to one of the outlying islands or districts. *Seppie in nero* is a tasty soft squid coated with its own black ink and usually served with *polenta,* a bland cornmeal rectangle (similar to grits). A plate of *pesce fritta mista* (at least L9000) usually includes *calimari* (squid), *polpo* (small octopus), shrimp, and other shellfish—try to order it where it's made fresh.

Good places to hunt for inexpensive *trattorie* are both north and south of campo S. Margherita. *Fegato alla veneziana* is an unpretentious dish of liver and onions. Vegetarians and the less adventurous can order a plate of *pasta e fagiolo,* a mixture of pasta and beans. For dessert, try a *tiramisù* (literally "pick-me-up"), a light cake, laced with rum and topped with crumbled chocolate.

Kosher food is served inside Europe's oldest Jewish ghetto, in Cannaregio at the end of a series of Hebrew and Italian signs. Seek out the **Casa di Reposo,** 2874 (tel. 71 80 02), in the Ghetto Nuovo section.

Gastronomie, rosticcerie (bakeries that sell pizza by the slice), and *pasticcerie* (pastry shops) are halfway between dining out and eating supermarket foods. The pizza at **Cip Ciap,** Castello, 5799/A (tel. 523 66 21), off campo S. Maria Formosa, deserves to be beatified (L3500-6000, slices L2000-4000), and the *disco volante* (literally "flying saucer;" with mushrooms, eggplant, ham, and salami; L8000) will send you reeling. (Open daily 9am-9pm.) For take-out food of the deli variety, the best and most central is **Aliani Gastronomia,** S. Polo, 655 (tel. 522 49 13), on ruga Vecchia S. Giovanni, a left off ruga Orefici, the street that leads to the Rialto bridge on the S. Polo site. Amazing cheeses and cold cuts, lavish lasagne (L1100), roasted chickens (L9000), and veggies are yours for the munching. (Open mid-Aug. to July Mon.-Sat. 8am-1pm and 5-8pm. No cheese sold on Wed. afternoons.) Incorrigible sweet-tooths may decide to skip the main course altogether and subsist solely on confections.

La dolce vita thrives at **Il Golosone,** S. Marco, 5689 (tel. 528 67 38), on calle S. Lio, just south of campo S. Maria Formosa where it meets calle del Mondo Nuovo. Even the air here is delicious—and after one whiff you may find yourself hard-pressed to avoid living up to the bakery's name (glutton). Sample the *dolci dei dogi* (L3500), heavy and hearty buns stuffed with almonds and marbled with chocolate and marzipan. (Open Feb.-Dec. Tues.-Sat. 8am-7:45pm.) Or stop by **A. Rosa Salva,** S. Marco, 5020, on Marzaria S. Salvador near the Rialto bridge. Locals say it's Venice's premier bakery.

If you're shopping, avoid any fruit vendor around the train station or the Accademia; the best place to buy both fish and produce is at the large **market** every morning at the Rialto bridge (in S. Polo) or in campo S. Margherita and nearby campo S. Barnaba, where you buy right off the boats. Locals shop on the side streets near **campo Beccarie.** Less photogenic but more convenient are the **supermarkets.** Often they are unmarked or in dark streets. In Dorsoduro, go to **Mega 1** at campo S. Margherita, 3019B, an unmarked entrance between a phone booth and a caffe. (Open Thurs.-Tues. 8:30am-1pm and 4:30-8pm, Wed. 8:30am-1pm.) In Cannaregio, the **Standa,** at #3660 on the Strada Nuova, stocks a poor selection of fresh food (Open daily 9am-7:45pm.) In Castello near S. Marco, there's **Su. Ve.** on calle del Mondo Novo off campo S. Maria Formosa. (Open Mon., Tues, and Thurs.-Sat. 8:40am-1:10pm and 4:30-7:45pm, Wed. 8:40am-1:10pm.) But the best deal in town is a huge nameless place that costs 30% less than the others. It's on fondamenta Zattere, 1492, near the S. Basilio stop (*vaporetto* #5), conveniently on the way to the youth hostel or to Fusina. (Open Mon., Tues., and Thurs.-Sat. 8:30am-12:30pm and 3-7:30pm, Wed. 8:30am-12:30pm.)

Each of the three *gelaterie* listed below is a favorite hangout with locals and the sort of meeting place that is the Venetian equivalent of a *passegiata.* **Gelateria Santo Stefano,** in the northwest corner of campo Morosini (also called S. Stefano), is thought by some to have the best pistachio and *panna* (whipped cream) in the world. (Open Sat.-Thurs. 7:30am-midnight.) **Gelati Nico,** fondamenta Zattere, 922, near the *vaporetto* stop of the same name, is widely considered the best in Venice. The prices are higher than at S. Stefano's, but the portions huge. *Gianduiotto,* a slice of dense chocolate hazelnut ice cream dunked in whipped cream, is their specialty. Flashy **Il Doge,** on campo S. Margherita, 3058/A, has an assortment of flavors, tasty *granite* (flavored ices), and *frullate* (fruit shakes) that challenge *gelato*'s supremacy. (Open Feb.-Dec. daily 9am-1am.)

Near the Train and Bus Station:

Mensa DLF (tel. 71 62 42), off to your right as you leave the station. This is the railway workers' cafeteria. Portions are large, food is decent, and everyone is congenial. Pasta L2400, main courses L4500. Wine L1200 per ½-liter. Open daily 12:30-1:30pm, but the best stuff disappears early. The **pizzeria,** with a terrace, is not bad either. Open 5:30-10pm.

Al Bolognese, S. Croce, 462 (tel. 523 75 97), in seedy p. Roma, where the buses arrive. At L12,000 this and the place next door offer the cheapest *menù* in town. Pink tablecloths and A/C. Open Thurs.-Tues. 11:30am-3:30pm and 6:30-9:30pm.

Da Ezio, S. Croce, 465 (tel. 522 24 24), next door to the above. Striped-shirt cab drivers converge here. *Menù* L12,000. Open daily 6:30am-11pm.

In and near Dorsoduro (From the Frari Church to Zattere)

Trattoria Dona Onesta, Dorsoduro, 3922 (tel. 522 95 86), on the calle of the same name, off calle Crosera between campo San Pantalon and the Frari. Right along the rio della Frescada. Worth seeking out. *Antipasti* about L6000. *Primi* L3000-4500, *secondi* (meat) L6500-8000, carefully prepared fish L9000-10,000. Cover L1000, service 10%. Open Sept.-Aug. 14 Mon.-Sat. 9:30am-3:30pm and 6-11pm.

L'Incontro, Dorsoduro, 3062 (tel. 522 24 04), on rio Terrà dei Pugni between campo S. Barnaba and campo S. Margherita. Interesting inventions including cold pasta salads that are a welcome change from the old Venetian standards. Often tries to keep its clientele Italian by closing the gate to its outside tables and not printing any menu. Be brave. An epicurean splurge, from *antipasti* to dessert, around L23,000. Open Tues.-Sun. noon-3pm and 5:30-10pm.

Antica Locanda Montin, Dorsoduro, 1147 (tel. 522 71 51). Follow the directions above to the hotel. In a nice garden. The finest gourmet the city has to offer, but most customers spend well over L30,000 per person. The *spaghetti ai frutti di mare* (with seafood, L7000) is a light meal. Go animal and order the *pesce alla griglia* (grilled fish) for L17,000. Cover L2000. Open Thurs.-Mon. noon-2:30pm and 7-10pm, Tues. noon-2:30pm.

Mensa dell' Architettura, S. Croce, 2553, on rio Terrà S. Tomà facing the north side of the Frari complex. Boisterous atmosphere. Filling cafeteria meal L6000. Open mid-Sept. through June Mon.-Sat. noon-1pm and 6-8:30pm. Closed for restoration in 1988.

Frigittoria da Bruno, Dorsoduro, 2754/B (tel. 520 69 78), on calle Lunga S. Barnaba off the *campo.* A serviceable neighborhood eatery animated by gossiping pensioners. Avoid the *menù* (L12,000) and enjoy the many reasonable a la carte dishes (L4500-9000). *Seppie con polenta* L9000. Zesty house white L4000 per liter. Open Mon.-Wed. and Fri.-Sat. 1-2:30pm and 6:15-10:30pm, Thurs. 6:15-10:30pm.

Trattoria S. Tomà, S. Polo, 2864 (tel. 523 88 19), in campo S. Tomà between the Frari and the S. Tomà *vaporetto* stop. Leafy garden, fine fare, and amiable waiters. Tasty *calzone* L5500. *Menù* L15,000. Cover L1500, service 12%. Open July-Sept. daily noon-2pm and 7:30-11pm; Oct. and Jan.-April Wed.-Mon. noon-2pm and 7:30-11pm.

Near the Rialto (San Polo Side)

Cantina Do Spade, S. Polo, 860 (tel. 521 05 74), in sottoportego delle Do Spade. Tucked away under an archway before the Do Spade bridge south of the fish market. Really a winery, but serves sumptuous little sandwiches (L1200-2000). Try a dry *tocai* or any of the hundreds of Friuli and Veneto whites and reds. Especially good is *inferno,* from the Val Telina (L900 per glass). Open Sept.-July Mon.-Sat. 9am-1pm and 5-8pm.

Cantina Do Mori, S. Polo, 429 (tel. 522 54 01), down the street from the above. Venetians have been coming to this cavernous snack-and-wine bar since 1571. Open mid-Sept. to mid-Aug. Mon., Tues. and Thurs.-Sat. 8:30am-1:30pm and 5-8:30pm, Wed. 8:30am-1:30pm.

From the Rialto to San Marco:

Osteria al Mascaron, S. Marco (tel. 522 59 95), on calle longa S. Maria Formosa. Classy and classic. Pasta L5000-6000. Try the *polipi* (octopus) for only L8000. Wine L6000 per liter. Open Sept.-Aug. 15 Mon.-Sat. 11am-3pm and 6-11pm.

Vino, Vino, S. Marco, 2007/A (tel. 522 41 21), on ponte della Veste between Teatro La Fenice and via XXII Marzo. Listed in the *New York Times* for excellence. New and slick in black, white, and red. Wines galore L700-8000 per glass. Pasta L4000. Plate of the day L9000. Open Wed.-Mon. 10am-1am.

Al Volto, S. Marco, 4081 (tel. 522 89 45), in calle Cavalli off campo Manin. An *enoteca* (wine bar) with a place to sit down and eat their large hot sandwiches (L1500) and drink (many) small glasses of wine (L800-3000). Try *sangria* for L1500. Open Sept.-July daily 9-11:30am and 4:30-9pm.

Leon Bianco, S. Marco, 4153 (tel. 522 11 80), on salizzata S. Luca just off campo S. Luca. Tasty food you eat standing up at marble counters, shoulder to shoulder with business suits. Main courses L5500. *Risotto* L3200. Medium-sized sandwich L2500. Tasty fried snacks L1000-2000. Open Mon.-Sat. 9am-8pm.

S. Bartolomeo, S. Marco, 5424/A (tel. 522 35 69), in calle de la Bissa off campo S. Bartolomio. Neon lighting and tacky plastic, but all is clean and the food wholesome. Self-service and long narrow eating counters. 1-course *menù* L8000. *Calamari* L3500 per *etto.* Open Feb.-Dec. Tues.-Sun. 10am-2:25pm and 4:50-9pm.

Trattoria a la Riveta, S. Marco, 4625 (tel. 528 73 02). From p. S. Marco, weave around the building complex to the left and then right over a bridge. Take the short ruga Appollonia to campo SS. Filippo e Giacomo—the restaurant's squeezed in to the right just before you cross ponte S. Provolo. Look for the lantern. One of the only genuine and reasonable places near S. Marco. Come here to try your requisite plate of *pesce fritta mista* (large portion L9000). Open Aug.-June Tues.-Sat. 9am-11pm.

Elsewhere

Trattoria da Rino, Cannaregio, 5642 (tel. 520 69 98), at the foot of the bridge to campo SS. Apostoli under the archways. Food and prices both moderate. This and the place next door are much better values than the tourist traps around S. Marco. An adequate L15,000 *menù,* everything included. Open mid-July to mid-June daily noon-4pm and 7-10pm.

Promessi Sposi, Cannaregio, 4367, across from Albergo Bernardi-Semerzato. Young mixed crowd. *Menù* L9500. Order a *spritz*—wine, campari, and carbonated water. Open Thurs.-Tues.

Do Mori, Giudecca, 588 (tel. 522 54 52), near the S. Eufemia *vaporetto* stop. On the other side of the Giudecca canal. A view of the sunset over Venice. An impeccable *trattoria* recently opened by two of the best chefs in Venice. Pasta L4000-7000, fish L15,000, meat dishes L12,000-13,000. Cover L2000. Open Mon.-Sat.

Da Gianni, Zattere, 918 (tel. 523 72 10), near the *vaporetto* stop and Gelateria Nico. On the fondamenta Zattere. Stick to their excellent pizza (L4000-7000). Cover L1000 for pizza, L2000 a la carte; service 12%. Open Feb.-Dec. Thurs.-Tues. 7am-11pm.

Trattoria Toscana, S. Marco, 1650 (tel. 523 57 22). Walk down the river from S. Marco to the head of via Garibaldi. Average meals L15,000-18,000. Watch the sunset over S. Giorgio Maggiore. Open Thurs.-Tues. noon-2pm and 6-8am.

Sights

Let Venice's myriad canals engulf you by wandering aimlessly through them; if you try to cover everything all at once, you will wash up from the cesspool water-logged and delirious. If you like to know the lay of the land (sea) before you start, take *vaporetto* #1 down the Grand Canal for an introduction to Venetian architecture, aquatic life, and the backward "s" looping of its main waterway. But don't leave without a map. You'll soon be meandering through the city's sundry *sestieri* (quarters). The largest number of tourists are in **San Marco,** while **Rialto** is the commercial district of town. Compared to these wealthy districts, in **Cannaregio** the buildings seem plain, taller, and densely packed. **Castello,** originally separated from the rest of Venice by marshes, was once the most popular district of town, and still has the feeling of a quiet village isolated from the rest of Venice. **Dorsoduro, Santa Croce,** and **San Polo,** though they have their fair share of visitors threading their way from the train station and p. Roma to San Marco and back, also harbor some genuinely Venetian corners themselves.

Venice, A Portable Reader, edited by Toby Cole, narrates city history from Casanova to Mark Twain, touching on all the sites in between (Frontier Press, L20,000). Mary McCarthy's *Venice Observed* (Penguin, L12,500) is a trenchant, absorbing collection of essays. James Morris's *Venice* (Faber and Faber, L17,000), is an entertaining and insightful description of the art, history, and character.

In high season, explore in the early morning and you'll avoid most of the throngs. Bear in mind that churches (apart from Saint Mark's) tend to hold to the traditional timetable of 9am-12:30pm and 3-6pm.

The Patriarcato of Venice (tel. 520 03 33) offers free guided **tours** of Venice's most famous church and its most ancient. (Tours of St. Mark's Mon.-Fri. at 10:30am, 11am, 2:30pm, 3:15pm, and 4pm; Sat. at 10:30am. Tours of the Basilica on Torcello Thurs. at 10:45am, 11:45am, and 3:15pm; Sat. at 10:45am and 11:45am.)

The Grand Canal (Canal Grande)

The Grand Canal has always been the quintessential emblem of Venice. The facades of the fabulous *palazzi,* which preen along the banks, reflect the city's past; as wealth and power were shared among a relatively large oligarchy, so too the facades strike notes of reserved but immense wealth. The Venetian aristocracy, in fact, disdained all titles of rank, calling themselves simply *Nobil' Uomini* (noble men) until the Austrians conquered them in 1815 and reduced them to counts. Sit back on *vaporetto* #1 or 4 and cruise the channel. The *palazzi* all share the same structure despite the external decorative features, which reflect the styles of various historical periods. From early on, living quarters were rather cramped and didn't permit the luxury of a central courtyard. Instead, Venetian *palazzi* were constructed with axial halls running from front to back to allow for necessary air circulation and light. On the ground floor this served as an entrance hall, and on the *piano nobili* (second floor) as a reception hall. The overall effect, unlike the "closed" fortress-palaces of the Florentine Renaissance, is of an elegant invitation.

The oldest surviving palaces, from the thirteenth century, were influenced by Byzantine and early Christian art and have rounded arches in low relief, like those on the **Ca' Da Mosto.** The beautiful **Ca' D'Oro** (east bank), whose name derives from the gold leaf that used to coat the balls protruding on its facade, is a graceful example of Venetian Gothic.

The Renaissance works are the creations of three major Venetian architects: Mauro Coducci, Jacopo Sansovino, and Michele Sanmicheli. Coducci's early **Palazzo Corner-Spinelli** and **Ca' Vendramin Calergi** are both on the east bank. These buildings were the first *palazzi* to break the traditional Venetian mold. Coducci's leadership inspired Sansovino's stately **Ca' Corner** and Sanmicheli's **Palazzo Grimani,** also on the east bank.

San Marco and Castello

Piazza San Marco and environs

Piazza San Marco is the elegant, vibrant living room of Venice. Napoleon was impressed enough to call it "the most magnificent entry in the world," but it does not take a world conquerer or an art connoisseur to see why. Water and land traffic merge at the Molo and riva degli Schiavoni, from where Venice spreads in unsurpassed magnificence. The piled domes and pillars of the church confront the classical facade of Sansovino's Libreria Vecchia, and the two styles merge in the porticos of the two Procuratie that flank the large *piazza.* From the end near S. Marco and the Clock Tower, the design becomes more and more classical as you approach the *biblioteca* and the tall brick *campanile.*

The **Basilica of San Marco** (tel. 522 56 97) was begun in the ninth century, when Saint Mark's remains (now under the main altar) were stolen from Alexandria in the Middle Ages by two upwardly mobile merchants of Venice. To conceal his corpse from Arab officials, the traders ensconsed Saint Mark in pieces of pork. The heroic event is commemmorated in a mosaic to the left of the three entrance arches. The basilica's cruciform plan and bulbed domes, borrowed from the church of the Holy Apostles in Constantinople, gave it prestige intended to rival both Byzantium and Saint Peter's. It was rebuilt after a fire in the tenth century and enlarged and embellished over the next five centuries. For successive generations, the cathedral represented a vast, spiritual clubhouse, to which each privileged member paid his dues in nonspiritual currency.

The four bronze Hellenistic horses over the door, which Venice stole from Constantinople, are copies; the originals stand inside. The church bursts with mosaics of all ages—perhaps the best are those on the atrium's ceiling. Inside, latch onto a tour group for an exhaustive rundown. The basilica's main treasure is the glittering *Pala d'Oro,* a gold Byzantine bas-relief studded with precious gems. In the area behind the screen are Sansovino's bronze reliefs and his sacristy door (left, behind the main altar), with a self-portrait on the middle left. The ticket to this area will also get you into the small **treasury,** an incredible hoard of gold and relics. (Open Mon.-Sat. 9:30am-5pm, Sun. 1:30-5pm. Admission L500.) Through a door in the atrium you can also visit the **Galleria della Basilica** (tel. 522 52 05)—worth it for a better view of the mosaics on the walls and floors. The recently restored Hellenistic horses are here, too. (Open daily 9:30am-5pm. Admission L500.) Remember that, as in all Venetian churches, no shorts or sleeveless shirts are allowed. For an excellent explanation of the stories and styles of the mosaics as well as a close-up view, go next door to the Ateneo S. Basso (tel. 522 38 05) to see the widely advertised slide show *I Mosaici di San Marco.* It lasts 45 minutes, costs L2500, and is shown March through August at 10am, 11am, noon, 3pm, 4pm, and 5pm.

To the right as you come out of S. Marco stands Coducci's ornate **Torre dell' Orologio,** a pretty arrangement of sculpture and sundials. The two bronze Moors still strike the hours. From Easter to Pentecost, the three Magi join the procession of figures as the hours are struck. (Closed for restoration in 1988.) The arch below marks the beginning of the **Mercerie,** Venice's main street leading to the Rialto. To the left of the Clock Tower stretch the sixteenth-century **Procuratie Vecchie,** half of the offices of the Procuratori di San Marco, who were among the most important civic officials. The complementary **Procuratie Nuove** were built a century later.

Between S. Marco and the lagoon stands the **Palazzo Ducale** (Doge's Palace; tel. 522 49 51.) (Open daily 8:30am-7pm. Admission L5000, students and seniors L3000. Separate admission charge for frequent special exhibits; check *Un Ospite di Venezia.*) The columns on the ground floor are carved with all sorts of symbolic figures; the most interesting are the trades. At the side of S. Marco stand the *Quattro Mori,* embracing statues of four jointly ruling Roman emperors. Crusaders "borrowed" the figures from Constantinopole in 1204. Rizzo's **Scala dei Giganti,** sweeping up to the second floor in the left end of the courtyard, is crowned with Sansovino's *Mars and Neptune.* Up his famous **Golden Staircase** are the Senate Chamber and the Room of the Council of Ten (the much-feared secret police of the Republic), both covered with paintings. Come while daylight illuminates the dark Tintorettos and Veroneses. Before leaving the top floor, those feeling belligerent can visit the **armor museum.** The route then leads back to the second floor, where after passing some enormous globes, you can wander through the echoing **Grand Council Chamber.** The room contains the resplendent and huge Tintoretto *Paradiso,* which was recently restored, as well as Veronese's *Apotheosis of Venice* on the ceiling. Portraits of all the doges of Venice except Marin Falier also adorn the walls of this room. An empty frame commemorates this over-ambitious doge, who was executed for treason after his unsuccessful coup in 1355. From the balconies of the chamber there is an expansive view of the basin, at one time the vantage point from which the doges kept an eye on the entrance to their city. Notice throughout the building the little slits in the walls where secret denunciations were inserted to be investigated by the Ten.

From the Council Chamber, a series of secret passages leads across the **Bridge of Sighs,** burdened with legend and sentiment, out the back of the palace and to the prisons. Casanova, who describes crossing the bridge in his memoirs, was one of the criminals condemned by the Ten to walk across it to the jail. Though generations of romantics have issued amorous sighs during moonlight strolls over the bridge, the name alludes to the bitter groans of prisoners. The private apartments of the palace were the scene of central bureaucratic decisions, conspiracy, and an intricate system of discipline and punishment. The English translation of *Il Libro del Palazzo Ducale* can be bought at the *biglietteria.* Don't miss the descriptions of Casanova's imprisonment and impetuous escape.

Facing the Palazzo Ducale across p. S. Marco are Sansovino's most successful buildings, the elegant **Libreria** and the **Zecca** (mint). The main reading room of the **Biblioteca Marciana** (tel. 520 87 88), on the second floor, is adorned with frescoes of philosophers and allegorical figures by Veronese and his contemporaries. (Entrance at #12. Open Mon.-Fri. 9am-7pm, Sat. 9am-1pm. Prior permission required.) Venetian artists received their quota of classical erudition from the sculptures in the **Museo Archeologico** (tel. 522 59 78), next door. (Open Mon.-Sat. 9am-1:30pm, Sun. 9am-12:30pm. Admission L2000.) Close by is the structure with the finest sense of timing in Venice, the **Campanile di San Marco** (tel. 522 40 64). Built in 902, the bell tower marked its millenium in 1902 by crumbling into a pile of rubble. The stairs in the original tower were made wide enough that a noble on horseback might ascend, but modern Venice has overcome the inconvenience of the 99-meter equine climb by installing an elevator. (Open daily 9:30am-7:30pm. Admission L1500.)

There are two famous cafes in the *piazza.* In the eighteenth century, those who supported the Austrian regime controlling the city patronized **Caffè Quadri** (open Tues.-Sun. 9am-1pm); patriotic Venetians went to **Caffè Florian.** (Open Thurs.-Tues. 9am-midnight.) Henry James favored the latter. There is no more seductive way to spend a Venetian evening than to sit in the *piazza,* listening to the cafes' orchestras play in friendly competition and sipping a cappuccino (a whopping L5000 per cup).

Under the portico at the opposite end of the *piazza* from the church is the entrance to the **Museo Correr** (tel. 522 56 25). It houses a couple of Bellinis and Carpaccio's *Courtesans,* not to mention such sundry curiosities of daily Venetian life as the foot-high platform shoes once worn by sequestered noblewomen. (Open Mon. and Wed.-Sat. 10am-4pm, Sun. 9am-12:30pm. Admission L3000, students L1500.)

West of San Marco

Just around the corner from p. S. Marco, on calle Vallaresso in front of the S. Marco *vaporetto* stop, is **Harry's Bar,** "Ernesto" Hemingway's hangout. (Drinks L6000. Service 20%. Open Feb.-Dec. Tues.-Sun. 10:30am-11pm.)

The opulent restoration of the **Palazzo Grassi** contrasts with the display of modern art inside. Take *vaporetto* #2 to S. Samuele (L2000).

The Mercerie

Starting under the arch of the Torre dell' Orologio in S. Marco, the shop-filled and tourist-clogged Mercerie leads up to the **Church of San Giuliano,** commissioned by the Venetian doctor Tommaso Ragone as a monument to himself. His portrait by Sansovino sits over the door, framed by inscriptions and allegories.

The Mercerie passes by **campo S. Salvatore.** The church here resolves the architectural controversy of the square Greek cross versus the long Latin cross; it consists of three square crosses stuck together. Don't miss Giovanni Bellini's *Supper in Emmaus,* as well as the two Titians inside.

A few steps east of the *campo* along calle dell' Ovo lies the home of **Goldoni** (tel. 523 63 53), Italy's answer to Mozartian mentor Molière. The museum displays many of the original manuscripts for Goldoni's plays. (Open Mon.-Sat. 8:30am-1:30pm. Free.)

Near Piazza San Marco

North of the *piazza* stands the **Church of Santa Maria Formosa.** At the bottom of the *campanile* leers a carved head, which, to Ruskin, "embodied the type of evil spirit to which Venice was abandoned, the pestilence that came and breathed upon her beauty." Coducci's Greek cross plan, a rebuilding of an ancient church, houses Palma il Vecchio's painting of St. Barbara, the exemplar of female beauty in Renaissance Venice.

Across the bridge, a twisted alleyway leads to the haunting **Palazzo Querini-Stampalia** (tel. 520 34 33). Its intriguing aristocratic rooms house paintings from the fourteenth to the eighteenth centuries. (Open Tues.-Sun. 10am-7pm. Admission L5000.)

North of campo S. Maria Formosa, calle Lunga and calle Cicogna lead to campo **SS. Giovanni e Paolo** and the **church** of the same name (*San Zanipolo* in Venetian dialect). This grandiose Gothic structure built by the Dominican Order over a period of two centuries (mid-13th to mid-15th) looks like a brick barn, and the monuments to various doges along the sides are no improvement. Hanging over the second altar of the right-hand nave, however, is a wonderful polyptych by Giovanni Bellini, and from the left transept you can gain access to the Cappella del Rosario (Rosary Chapel), which, although damaged by a fire in 1867, still has four marvelous paintings by Veronese on the ceiling. In the *campo* stands an equestrian statue by Andrea del Verrocchio of Bartolomeo Colleoni (alias the Regian Mr. Bartholomeo), a famous Venetian *condottiere* (mercenary captain). Upon his death, Colleoni left the Senate all his loot on the condition that they erect a statue to him in p. S. Marco; the Senate claimed, however, that the exact wording of the will allowed them to raise the statue not in the center of the city, but here, in front of the **Scuola di San Marco.** (Not open to the public.) The Scuola, next to S. Zanipolo, was begun by Pietro Lombardo and his son Tullio and finished by their rival Coducci.

Nearby on calle del Squero, off calle della Testa, is one of two remaining *squeri* (shipyards), where war ships were built during the republic. If you cross the Ponte Rosso and go straight, you'll come to the Lombardos' masterpiece, the **Church of Santa Maria dei Miracoli.** Inside, the pilasters stand in a carved underbrush while *putti* peer from their leafy base.

To the east of S. Marco, off the riva degli Schiavoni, stands the unusual and beautiful **Church of San Zaccharia.** Though the body of the church dates from the fifteenth century, Coducci designed the striking facade, a blown-up version of his San Michele. Inside, the second altar on the left houses Bellini's masterpiece, *The Madonna and Saints.* Some vibrant frescoes by the Florentine Andrea del Castagno are in the San Tarasio chapel (tip L500). Around the corner, on the waterfront, is Massari's **Church of the Pietà,** with Tiepolo's celebrated frescoes on the ceiling.

For a real treat, make your way through the *calli* to the **Scuola di San Giorgio degli Schiavoni** (tel. 522 88 28). Here, from 1502 to 1511, Carpaccio decorated the ground floor with some of his finest paintings, depicting episodes from the lives of St. George, St. Jerome, and St. Trifone. (Open Tues.-Sat. 9:30am-12:30pm and 3:30-6:30pm, Sun. 10am-12:30pm. Admission L3000.) The **Museo dei Dipinti Sacri Bizantini** (tel. 522 65 81), nearby at Ponte dei Greci, displays religious paintings from the Byzantine and post-Byzantine periods. (Open Mon. and Wed.-Sat. 9am-1pm and 2-5pm, Sun. 9am-12:30pm. Admission L2000.)

For a glimpse of the city's unrivaled maritime supremacy, visit the **Museo Storico Navale** (tel. 520 02 76), on the shorefront of the Castello district where via Giuseppe Garibaldi hits riva dei Sette Martiri. (Open Mon.-Fri. 9am-1pm, Sat. 9am-noon. Admission L1000.) A bit farther down the waterfront are the mysterious and overgrown grounds of the biennial International Art Exhibition, and beyond this, across the bridge, the welcome open space of the **Parco delle Rimembranze.** If you've made it this far, take *motoscafo* #1 or 2 back to S. Marco.

Cannaregio

From the Rialto to the Ghetto

Heading north from the Rialto bridge on salizzada S. Giovanni, you reach the last of Coducci's churches, **San Giovanni Crisostomo,** a refined Greek cross. The interior contains works by Bellini, Sebastiano del Piombo, and Tullio Lombardo. Marco Polo supposedly lived just under the arch in corte Seconda del Milion.

From the Crisostomo church, head out on the only street that goes to the northwest (slightly to the left). Crossing two bridges and two small squares will take you to the **Church of SS. Apostoli,** with an amusing Tiepolo painting of S. Lucia's first communion. The church is at the foot of the expansive Strada Nova, chiseled out of crowded alleys so that Napoleon's horsemen might pass. Nearby is the **Ca' d'Oro,** where the **Galleria Giorgio Franchetti** (tel. 523 87 90) recently opened. This formerly private collection displays minor painters and two masterpieces: Titian's *Venus* and Mantegna's *St. Sebastian.* (Open Mon.-Sat. 9am-1:30pm, Sun. 9am-12:30pm. Admission L2000.) North of here is the **Church of the Gesuiti.** Set in the flowery green and white marble interior is Titian's *Martyrdom of St. Lawrence.* The painter lived next door to the church for almost 50 years. In a far-flung northern corner of Cannaregio is the **Church of Madonna dell' Orto.** Take scenic *vaporetto* #5 (*destra*) to the Madonna dell' Orto stop (L1500). Arguably the only attractive Gothic church in Venice, the church is the sacred complement of the Ca' d'Oro and a bastion of Tintoretto's works.

Between the church and the train station lies the **Jewish Ghetto,** the first in Europe. Established by ducal decree in 1516, the Ghetto Nuovo remained the enforced enclave of the Jews in Venice until Napoleon's victory over the Venetian Republic in 1797. The area still houses five synagogues, of which three are open to the public. The **Sinagoga Grande Tedesca** is less opulent and more digestible than the **Sinagoghe Spagnola** and **Levantina.** There is a small **Jewish Museum** (Tel. 71 53 59. Open March 16-Nov. 15 Mon.-Fri. 10:30am-1pm and 2:30-5pm, Sun. 10:30am-1pm; Nov. 16-March 15 Sun.-Fri. 10am-12:30pm. Admission L2000, students L1000.)

San Polo

The **Ponte Rialto,** straddling the Grand Canal, is the entrance to this commercial district. In the center of the **Erberia,** the fruit part of the open market, is the **Church of San Giacomo di Rialto,** the oldest in Venice. A stubby column with a staircase to the top stands in front of it, supported by a bent stone figure. The column was a podium from which state proclamations were issued; the statue, called *il Gobbo* (the hunchback), has served as a bulletin board for public responses since Roman times.

From the **Rialto** bridge, be carried by the crowd down the ruga degli Orefici, then turn left and follow ruga Vecchia S. Giovanni to the **Church of San Polo** (*San Apponal* in local dialect); the young Domenico Tiepolo completed the dramatic 14 stations of the Cross in the chancel. Nearby, in the great Gothic Franciscan **Basilica dei Frari** (1340-1443), Donatello's wooden *St. John the Baptist* keeps company with a later Florentine statue of the saint by Sansovino and three purely Venetian paintings: Giovanni Bellini's triptych of the *Madonna and Saints* over the sacristy, Titian's *Assumption,* and his *Madonna of Case Pesaro.* (Open Mon.-Sat. 9am-noon and 2:30-6pm, Sun. 9am-6pm. Admission L800. Sun. free.)

The *scuole* of Venice were a combination of guilds and religious fraternities. Members paid annual dues for the support of their needy fellow members and for the decoration of the *scuola*'s premises. The pride members took in their clubhouse manifested itself in the collection of first-rate paintings. One of the most famous and richest of all, the **Scuola Grande di San Rocco** (tel. 523 48 64), is across the *campo* at the end of the Frari. Note the details of the exterior, such as the crazy monsters at the bottom of the columns. Tintoretto, who set out to combine, in his words, "the color of Titian with the drawing of Michelangelo," covered the inside with 56 paintings. To see them in chronological order, start on the second floor in the Sala dell' Albergo and then go downstairs. Along the walls are strange allegorical figures, products of the seventeenth-century imagination. Their significance is explained, in Italian, on the scroll held by Mercury next to the door. Downstairs there are more Tintorettos, with violent to tranquil atmospheric effects. (Open daily in summer 9am-1pm and 3:30-6:30pm; in off-season 10am-1pm and 3:30-6pm. Admission L5000.)

A cheaper jaunt is the less embellished **Scuola dei Carmini,** nearby in campo Carmini off campo S. Margherita. (Open Mon.-Sat. 9am-noon and 3-6pm. Admission L1000.)

Dorsoduro

The Ponte dell' Accademia crosses the Grand Canal at the **Gallerie dell' Accademia** (tel. 522 22 47). The Venetian-school paintings here should top your list of things to see. Mantegna's tiny *San Giorgio* dominates the entire room containing it. Veronese's huge *Supper in the House of Levi* enraged the Inquisition with its indulgent realism—a Protestant German and a monkey did not belong at dinner with Christ, and Tintoretto was forced to change the name from the original *Last Supper.* Rounding off the collection are a number of works by Tiepolo, Canaletto, and Longhi, whose refined cityscapes are considered the height of early urban art. Be sure to examine the powerful cycle of *The Legend of St. Ursula* by Carpaccio (1490-95). (Open Mon.-Sat. 9am-7pm, Sun. 9am-2pm. Admission L4000.

The **Ca' Rezzonico** (*vaporetto* stop of the same name) is on the fondamenta Rezzonico, across a bridge from campo S. Barnaba. Designed by Longhena, this is one of the great eighteenth-century Venetian palaces. Inside, stroll around like a prince in the **Museum of the Eighteenth Century** (tel. 522 45 43), begun by the Bon family but completed by the wealthy Rezzonico family. Step out on the balcony and look out over the Grand Canal at the newly restored Palazzo Grassi across the way. The small bedrooms and boudoirs on the second floor house delightful works by Tiepolo, Guardi, and Longhi. (Open Mon.-Thurs. and Sat. 10am-3:30pm, Sun. 9am-12:30pm. Admission L3000, students, children, and seniors L1500.)

The **Collezione Peggy Guggenheim** (tel. 520 62 88), housed in the late Ms. Guggenheim's Palazzo Venier dei Leoni, near the tip of Dorsoduro, is an eclectic collection of modern art. It has rapidly become one of Venice's most popular museums, largely because of Guggenheim's eccentric personality. A tomb to all her dead dogs lies in the garden. In an interview shortly before her death, she explained that she began to collect art out of boredom and that her life became entwined with those of the artists whose works she collected. These included Brancusi, Marino Marini, Kandinsky, Rothko, Max Ernst, and Jackson Pollock. (Open Wed.-Fri. and Sun.-Mon. noon-6pm, Sat. noon-9pm. Admission L5000, seniors, children, students with ISIC L1500. Sat. 6-9pm free.)

The **Church of Santa Maria della Salute** stands at the tip of Dorsoduro and is the most theatrical piece of architecture in Venice, designed by Longhena as the scene of the dramatic Festa della Salute (Nov. 21). The church and the festival together comprised a covert deal with God that saved Venice from the plague of 1630. In the sacristy are several Titians and a Tintoretto. (Open daily 8am-noon and 3-6pm. Admission to the sacristy L500.)

A bit north of fondamenta Zattere, toward the western end of town, lies the sixteenth-century **Church of San Sebastiano.** It was here that Paolo Veronese took refuge in 1555 when he fled Verona, apparently after killing a man. By 1565 he had filled the entire church with some of his finest paintings and frescoes. On the ceiling, you'll find his breathtaking *Stories of Queen Esther.* To get a closer look at the panels, climb up to the nuns' choir. Here you'll also see the artist's moving fresco *St. Sebastian in Front of Diocletian.* Ask the custodian to turn on the lights (tip L500). Approach the church by sea from the San Basilio stop on routes of *vaporetto* #5 or 8 (L1500).

Outlying Sights

Many of Venice's most beautiful churches are a short boat ride away from S. Marco. Two of Palladio's most famous churches are visible from the *piazza.* The **Church of San Giorgio Maggiore,** just across the lagoon (take boat #5 or 8), graces the island of the same name. The church houses Tintoretto's famous *Last Supper,* which is, however, poorly hung. Be sure to look at the wonderfully carved choir benches behind the altar. The **campanile** (a later addition) may be ascended for a superb view of the main islands. (Open daily in summer 9am-12:30pm and 2-6:30pm; in off-season 9am-12:30pm and 2-3:30pm. Admission L1000.)

A bit farther out on the next island, Giudecca, is Palladio's famous **Church of Il Redentore** (the Redeemer). During the pestilence of 1576, the Venetian Senate had sworn to build a devotional church if the plague would leave the city, and to make a yearly pilgrimage there. Palladio accommodated this use by enlarging the church's tribune, which allowed the entire Senate to sit comfortably, while still keeping the building's layout unified. Take *vaporetto* #5 or 8 (L1500).

The tiny **Church of San Michele** in Isola, on its own island on the far side of the lagoon, is one of Venice's most beautiful. The pristine marble facade, with its delicate scallops, was Venice's first Renaissance structure, started by Coducci in 1469. Venice was slow to abandon its own beautiful and unique, but essentially medieval, architecture, so the ideas of Alberti and Brunelleschi took a long time to penetrate the lagoon. When they did, they were influenced by the Byzantine, to which this facade attests. The small hexagonal chapel to the left is a later addition. Take *vaporetto* #5 to the *cimitero* (cemetery) stop (L1500).

The Islands of the Lagoon

Accessible by *vaporetto* #1 and 2, the Lido was the setting for Thomas Mann's *Death in Venice* and Visconti's haunting film version, both of which give an unforgettable impression of the sensuality and mystery for which Venice is famous. Lovers of the *belle époque* will enjoy a visit to the fabled Grand Hôtel des Bains. From the *vaporetto* stop, just follow the crowd that troops daily down Gran Viale Santa Maria Elisabetta or take bus A (L500).

Boat #12 departs from fondamenta Nuove, near campo dei Gesuiti, for the islands of Murano, Burano, and Torcello. (You can walk or take boat #5 to the departure point; Murano is also serviced by the #5.) **Murano** has been famous for its glass since 1292, when Venice's artisans decided to transfer their operations there. Today, serious glass-making and tourist-oriented enterprises exist side by side, with many opportunities to watch the glass-blowing process. For a look at the most successful efforts of past masters, visit the **Museo Vetrario,** on fondamenta Giustinian, along the main canal, with a splendid collection of glass from Roman times onward. (Open in summer Mon.-Tues. and Thurs.-Sat. 10am-4pm, Sun. 9:30am-12:30pm; in off-season Mon.-Tues. and Thurs.-Sat. 10am-3pm, Sun. 9:30am-3pm. Admission L3000, seniors, students, and children L1500.) Also on Murano is the exceptionally pretty **Basilica SS. Maria e Donato,** originally built in the seventh century but owing its exterior to the twelfth.

Burano, a half-hour out of Venice, caters heavily to tourists but also remains a bona fide fishing village. It is famous for its lace, which is hawked all over Venice. If you're interested, visit the small **Scuola di Merletti di Burano,** a lace museum. (Open daily 9am-7pm. Admission L5000, children, seniors, and students with ISIC L2500.)

Today **Torcello,** the remaining island, is the most rural of the group. Of the first-time visitor to Venice, Englishman John Ruskin wrote "Let him not . . . look upon the pageantry of her palaces . . . but let him ascend the highest tier of the stern ledges that sweep round the altar of Torcello." The **Cathedral of Torcello,** founded in the seventh century and rebuilt in the eleventh, leaves much to be desired, but its interior Byzantine mosaics are so incredible that a nineteenth-century restorer took a few back to Wales with him. (Cathedral open daily 10am-12:30pm and 2-6:30pm. Admission L1000. Adjacent **museum** open Tues.-Sat. 10am-12:30pm and 2-5:30pm, Sun. 10:30am-12:30pm and 2-5:30pm. Admission L1000.)

Never too far from water, prosperous Venetians built their farming villas along the Brenta River connecting Venice with Padua and rode back and forth in the *Burchiello,* an elegant horse-pulled barge. Today a modern tourist boat makes the cruise, stopping briefly at a few of the most famous villas (April-Oct. Fare L95,000, lunch included—reserve at any travel agency).

A better way to make the same trip, pay less, and take your time at the villas, is to take the ACTV buses from p. Roma (see Practical Information). **Villa Malcontenta** (also called "Villa Foscari"), built by Palladio on a temple-like plan, is, like Villa Rotunda, one of the most influential in the world (tel. (041) 96 90 12). (Open May-Oct. Tues., Sat., and the 1st Sun. of every month 9am-noon. Admission L5000.) To get to Villa Malcontenta, take bus #16 from p. Roma (L600). To reach the two other villas, hop on the bus (not the direct line) that leaves approximately every half-hour for Padua (L1400-2000). **Mira** (also "Palazzo Foscari," "Palazzo Witmann," and "Palazzo Rezzonico"; tel. 42 35 52), one of the most attractive villas on the Brenta, is now open for tours. (Open Tues.-Sun. 9am-noon and 2-6pm. Admission L5000, seniors L2000.) **Strà** (also "Villa Pisani"; tel. (049) 50 20 74) is farther along, nearer to Padua. It is known for its grand design by Figimelica and Preti and, especially, for its interior decoration. Its many notable frescoes include works by Urbani and Tiepolo. Look for the fresco of *The Apotheosis of the Pisani Family.* (Open Tues.-Sun. 9am-1:30pm. Admission L3000.)

Entertainment

The weekly booklet, *Un Ospite di Venezia* (free at tourist offices), and the monthly **Marco Polo** (L5000) list current festivals, concerts, and gallery shows. There are concerts once or twice per week in the larger churches such as S. Marco and the Frari. The **Teatro La Fenice** (tel. 52 51 91) has an excellent summer program, featuring mostly music, with many guest artists (tickets L10,000-30,000). Its **Festival Vivaldi** takes place in early September. During the summer, Vivaldi is also featured in a concert series in the church of **Santa Maria della Pietà,** where Vivaldi was choirmaster. (He allegedly had a say in the church's design.)

Mark Twain called the **gondola** "an inky, rusty canoe," but only the gentry can afford a ride aboard one. The authorized rate starts at L40,000 for 50 minutes, but most charge at least L90,000. Haggling works well in the morning. Rides are most romantically economical if procured about 50 minutes before sunset, and just economical if shared with as many people as possible. There is, however, a sneaky way to get a cheap ride just for the experience. There are several points along the Grand Canal where many Venetians need to cross, though there is no bridge. To solve the problem, *gondole* operate a short, cross-canal service. One good ride departs from just south of campo S. Tomà; another will take you from campo del Traghetto next to campo S. Maria Zobegno over to Dorsoduro. Each trip lasts only a minute or so, but are more authentic and infinitely cheaper than the "romantic" variety. Give L500 to the gondolier as you step on. (See Practical Information.)

Surprisingly, Venice's selection of nightclubs is paltry; most people seem to prefer mingling and dancing in the city's streets. However, **El Souk** (tel. 520 03 71) is a swanky place in calle Contarini Corfù, 1056/A, near the Accademia. It's a kasbah with an aura of corruption, run like a private club. (Open 10:30pm-4am. Cover with 1st drink L15,000.) Beyond this, the Lido is your best choice; there you can visit **Club 22** (tel. 526 04 66), at lungomare Guglielmo Marconi (go right after you hit the beach).

The famed **Venice Biennale,** centered east on Canal San Marco, takes place every even-numbered year, with a gala exhibit of international art. (Tickets to all exhibits L10,000, less to see individual bits and pieces.) The **Venice International Film Festival** is held annually from late August to early September. Tickets (about L5000) are sold at the Cinema Palace on the Lido (where the main films are screened) and at other locations—some late-night, outdoor showings are free. Contact the EPT. Call the city's toll-free number (tel. 198) with questions about cinema. The **Festival of Contemporary Music** rocks the city from late September to early October.

After an absence of several centuries, Venice's famous **Carnival** was successfully revived as an annual celebration in 1979, and is the most hopping time of the year. During the 10 days preceding Ash Wednesday (Jan. 28-Feb. 7 in 1989), masked Venetians dance the streets, and there are carnival-related art exhibits, performances of all types of music, and even lectures and workshops on mask-making. Write to the EPT office in December for dates and details. Venice's most colorful festival is the **Festa del Redentore** (3rd Sun. in July). The Church of Il Redentore is connected with Zattere by a boat-bridge for the day, and one of the most magnificent fireworks displays in the world takes place between 11pm and midnight on the Saturday night before (July 15-16 in 1989). On the first Sunday in September (Sept. 3 in 1989), Venice stages its classic **regatta storica,** a pell-mell gondola race down the Grand Canal, preceded by a procession of decorated gondolas. The religious festival of **Festa della Salute** takes place on November 21 at Santa Maria della Salute, with another pontoon bridge constructed, this time over the Grand Canal.

Every year since 1954, Venice, Pisa, Genoa, and Amalfi celebrate their collective heritage as former Mediterranean maritime republics with a historical pageant and regatta. Although the pageant is designed mostly for tourists, the **Old Republics' Maritime Regatta** is taken quite seriously by the locals. The competition alternates between cities every four years. Alas, Venice's next turn isn't until 1992.

The **Vogalonga** is a recently invented and very popular boating course of 30km, threading through the islands of the lagoon. For L5000, anyone in any kind of boat can row in this all-inclusive event, which takes place the last weekend in May. The official headquarters of the race is a pastry shop (tel. 521 05 44).

If **shopping** is your first resolve, a few caveats are in order. Do not shop in piazza San Marco and around the Rialto bridge. Shops outside these areas boast products of quality and a better selection, cahrging about half the price. Venetian glass is best bought towards the Accademia bridge from San Marco, and between the Rialto and the station in Cannaregio, though for fun you may want to look in the showroom at the glass-blowers' factory behind the Basilica of San Marco.

Padua (Padova)

Dante, Petrarch, and Galileo are just three of the many cultural luminaries who've inhabited Padua, and 40,000 or so students continue to enliven this small city. For Padua's size, the town is cosmopolitan and intriguing, thanks to the 600-year-old university and many art treasures, notably the Capella degli Scrovegni, containing frescoes by Giotto.

Orientation and Practical Information

Padua is connected to nearby Venice by frequent trains on both the Venice-Milan and Venice-Bologna lines (½ hr.). When the trains are crowded, tickets are almost never collected on this stretch, but if you're caught without a ticket, you must pay double the cost. Intercity buses to Vicenza, Venice, and other towns are frequent and quite cheap (L2500). The train station is at the northern edge of town. **ACAP** city bus #3 or 8 (L600) will take you to the center of town; you can also stroll the 10 minutes down corso del Popolo.

Beware that in late July and August, the students and many *padovani* (locals) desert the city, leaving three quarters of the stores closed in their wake. But most establishments catering to tourists stay open during this time.

Azienda Promozione Turistica (APT): In the train station (tel. 875 20 77). Efficient accommodations service and information on buses to villas outside Padua. English spoken. Open Mon.-Sat. 8am-8pm, Sun. 8am-noon.

Student Travel: CTS, via S. Sofia, 94/96 (tel. 875 17 19), at via Gabelli. Student IDs and travel information. BIJ, Transalpino, and other rail tickets. Commission charged on each train ticket reservation. English spoken. Open Mon.-Fri. 9:30am-12:30pm and 3:30-7pm, Sat. 10am-noon.

American Express: via Risorgimento, 20 (tel. 66 61 33), near p. Insurrezione. Efficacious. L2000 to claim mail if you don't have an AmEx card. Open Mon.-Fri. 9am-1pm and 3-7pm.

Post Office: corso Garibaldi, 25 (tel. 65 75 29). Fermo Posta and stamps at desk #22. Open Mon.-Fri. 8:15am-7:40pm, Sat. 8:15am-12:20pm. **Postal code:** 35100.

Telephones: ASST, corso Garibaldi, 31. Open 24 hours. **SIP,** in the passageway by Caffè Pedrocchio. Open daily 8am-9:30pm. **Telephone code:** 049.

Train Station: p. Stazione (tel. 875 06 67), in the north part of town at the head of corso del Popolo, the continuation of corso Garibaldi. To Venice (every ½ hr.; ½ hr.; one way L2000, round-trip L3400; for *rapido* add L600), Verona (every hr., 1 hr.; one way L4400, round-trip L7600; for *rapido* add L1300), Vicenza (every hr., 20 min., same rates as Venice), Milan (every hr., 2½ hr.; one way L11,200, round-trip L19,200; for *rapido* add L3200). Padua is on the Venice-Milan line; from Florence and Rome, change at Bologna. Money can be changed daily at the station 7am-noon and 3-4:50pm, but beware of the L3000 commission per traveler's check.

Bus Station: ATP, via Trieste, 40 (tel. 66 47 55), near p. Boschetti, 5 min. from the train station. A convenient main transportation center with frequent buses to Bassano (6am-9pm every ½ hr., 1¼ hr., L3000), Vicenza (6am-9pm every ½ hr., 50 min., L2500), Venice (every ½ hr., 45 min., L2500), and elsewhere in Veneto. The best way to visit the villas between Padua and Venice.

Bicycles and Mopeds: A stolen bicycle (or moped) can be bought for as little as L10,000. Consult the bulletin boards at the *mensa* on via San Francesco, 122. Buying hot bikes is a Paduan institution and unlikely to get you into trouble. Once you've got one, keep an eye on it; otherwise it will be right back up on that bulletin board.

English Books: Feltrinelli, via S. Francesco, 14 (tel. 875 07 92), right by Palazzo del Bò. Everything from Jane Fonda to Hemingway. Also other languages. Open Mon.-Fri. 9am-7:30pm, Sat. 9am-1pm and 3:30-7:30pm.

Swimming Pool: Stabilimento Comunale di Nuoto "Rari Nantes Patavium," via V. Veneto (tel. 68 15 58), south of Prato della Valle off via Cavollotti. Catch bus #22 at Prato della Valle, or farther north at Riviera Ponti Romani near p. Eremitani. Open June-Aug. daily 9:30am-7pm; Sept.-May 9:30am-1pm. Ticket sales end at 6pm. Tickets L4500.

Hospital: Ospedale Civile, via Giustiniani (tel. 821 11 11), off via S. Francesco.

Police: Questura, via S. Chiara (tel. 83 31 11). **Ufficio Stranieri** (Office for Foreigners), Riviera Ruzzante, 13.

Accommodations

Cheap lodgings abound in Padua, but people are catching the drift and staying here rather than in Venice, and the town fills quickly. If you can't get into any of the places listed below, try any of the hotels near **piazza del Santo.** In summer, start looking at 7am. All are similar, with singles averaging L16,000-18,000, doubles L27,500-28,500. A godsend to late arrivals at the train station, an electronic display outside the tourist office lists two dozen hotels (including Albergo Pavia), indicating whether or not they have vacancies.

Ostello Città di Padova, via Aleardi, 30 (tel. 875 22 19), off via Camposampiero. Take bus #3, 8, or 18 from the station. Get off near the Basilica or Prato della Valle, a 10-min. walk from the hostel. Not IYHF, but run by the local Centro Turistico Giovanile. Quiet location with large, light, and immaculate, if crowded, rooms. Accommodating staff. English spoken. Yellow sidewalk arrows lead around the corner to a cheap and friendly hostel bar—the best place to meet local travelers, even if you're not staying at the hostel. L10,000. Breakfast included. Hot showers. Flexible about daytime lockout and lights out. 5-day maximum, though you can probably push it. Also offers **free bicycles,** though the supply is limited. Open daily 8-9:30am and 6-11pm. Register and drop off your stuff anytime Mon.-Fri. (no one is there during the day on weekends). **Bar** open same hours.

Casa della Famiglia (ACISJF), via Nino Bixio, 4 (tel. 875 15 54), off p. Stazione. Go right as you leave the station—it's a small street to the left. Women ages 30 and under only. An office to receive you in the station is open daily until 5pm (tel. 364 57). The good sisters reserve the right to turn away "undesirables." Modern and tidy doubles, triples, and quads L10,000 per person. Curfew 11:30pm.

Casa del Pellegrino, via Cesarotti, 21 (tel. 278 01 or 356 32), along the northern side of Sant' Antonio. Another quasi-institutional set-up. Though also a 2-star hotel, this 129-room place serves mainly pilgrims to the adjoining basilica. Ascetic rooms—crucifix-filled and painted in pink or brown. English spoken. Singles L17,500, with bath L24,000. Doubles L31,000, with bath L43,000. Meals served noon-2pm and 7-9pm (about L13,500). Flexible curfew midnight. Open Feb.-Dec. 10.

Locanda Lidia, via U. Foscolo, 12 (tel. 65 11 07), off corso del Popolo in the ugly part of town near the station. Commodious, fastidiously kept rooms. Singles L15,000. Doubles L25,000. L15,000 per additional person. Showers (often cold) included.

Albergo Pavia, via Papafava, 11 (tel. 66 15 58). Corso del Popolo, after several changes of name, becomes via Roma. Pass the department store UPIM and the ritzy cafe Pedrocchi. Go right on via Marsala and then left, 2 blocks later, on via Papafava. Cordial proprietors and spartan rooms. English spoken. Singles L18,000. Doubles L28,000. Cold showers included; hot showers L1000.

Albergo Pace, via Papafava, 3 (tel. 875 15 66), down the block from Albergo Pavia. Capacious, elegant rooms. Personable management. Rarely available singles L18,000. Doubles L28,000. Showers L1000.

Camping: The nearest campgrounds are along the *statale,* the local, potholed road from Padua to Venice.

Food

Markets are held on both sides of the Ragione, but most of the edibles are sold on the side of p. Erbe. During the academic year, student *mense* pop up all over town, so ask around. Usually you will pay more as a nonmember, but you can try slipping through incognito or waving your own student ID. If you're successful, meals are about L3000; if not, you'll still pay only L6000. The bargain-basement prices are due in part to 1987 student protests—another Paduan tradition.

Mensa Universitarià, via S. Francesco, 122. The most pleasant and convenient. Also come for the bulletin boards, especially helpful if you're looking for a used car or motorcycle. **Casa Degli Studenti,** half a block up via Marzolo from via Jappelli, operates a *mensa* and cheap bar. A student hangout. Others are on via Padovanino (Mensa Ampi) and via Leopardi. Generally open noon-2pm and 7-9pm, rarely open Sun., sometimes Sat. Some of the smaller ones close or strike during the summer.

Ristorante Vecchia Padova, via Zabarella, 41 (tel. 386 79). Avoid the pricey dinnertime table service, but at lunch, the same gourmet food can be relished cafeteria-style in the cheerful, wood, air-conditioned dining room. Generous salad bar. Full meal with wine L13,000-16,000. Open Sept. to mid-Aug. Tues.-Sun. noon-3pm and 7:30pm-midnight.

Al Pero, via S. Lucia, 38 (tel. 365 61), near via Dante. Bustling neighborhood eatery with fantastic fare. To visit Veneto without tasting *polenta* is a sacrilege. Remain unsullied by ordering the *salamini arrosti con polenta* (small roasted sausages, L4000). Meals average L11,000. *Primi* L2500-3000, *secondi* L4000-4500. Wine L3000 per liter. Cover L1200. Open Sept.-July Mon.-Sat. noon-2pm and 6:30pm-12:30am.

Gigibar, via Verdi, 18 (tel. 392 05), off p. Insurrezione. Delectable pizza and an enormous selection of hot and cold plates. As much a social center as a gastronomic one. Brusque service. Pasta L3000-4500, cold plates L2500-7500, main courses L3500-10,000. Cover L1000, service additional. Open Wed.-Mon. 10am-2pm and 6:30pm-2am.

Pizzeria Trattoria Serius, via Cavazzana, 24 (tel. 66 26 62), near the corner of via Sanmicheli and close to S. Giustina. Removed from the center, but amazing eats. Try the *scaloppine al vino, limone,* or *marsala* for L7700. Scrumdelicious pizza from L2700. Other non-meat dishes under L5000. Eat outside under a canopy of grapevines. Cover L1500. Open Sept. to mid-Aug. Wed.-Mon. 11am-3pm and 6:30pm-2am.

Alexander Bar, via S. Francesco, 38, off via del Santo, east of the *piazze* cluster Erbe, Frutti, Duomo, and Pedrocchi. You'd have to stay in Padua for months to sample every type of ice-cold beer served here. Almost as many sorts of *panini* (L2000-3000). Open Mon.-Sat. 8am-2am.

Sights

Although under the aegis of Venice for four centuries, Padua is anything but colonial. The city cherishes dearly its ancient civic identity, those parts of its character that are distinctively Paduan: the legend of its founding by Trojans; the tribute to its local saint, Sant' Antonio (the patron saint of lost objects to whom an unbelievable number of hopeful pilgrims flock annually); and even the reputation of its university. Three-hour tours of the town (L10,000), organized by the tourist office, leave from in front of the **Museo degli Eremitani** (Tues.-Sat. at 3pm, Sun. at 9:30am).

Even if begging a boon of Sant' Antonio is not high on your agenda, the **Capella Degli Scrovegni** (tel. 65 08 45), designed and filled with frescoes by Giotto, alone merits a pilgrimage to Padua. As early as the fourteenth century, it was the envy of neighboring churches, whose priests complained it was luring away members of their congregations. Giotto's famous cycle begins at the far right-hand corner, facing the interior from the entrance. It tells the apocryphal tale of Joachim and Anna (parents of the Virgin Mary), of the early life of the Virgin, and the story of the life of Christ. Each episode of the story is incredibly dense, with several events compressed into one frame. (Open April-Sept. daily 9am-7pm; Oct.-March Mon.-Sat. 9am-5:30pm, Sun. 9:30am-12:30pm. Admission L5000, groups L2000. The ticket desk closes 15 min. before closing.)

Next door, the **Church of the Eremitani** (tel. 314 10) has a beautifully carved ceiling. It also contains Mantegna's *Assumption, Martyrdom of St. Christopher* (on the right), and *Martyrdom of St. James* (on the left), in the chapel to the right of the altar. Unfortunately, only these fragments remain after the World War II bombing. (Open April-Sept. Mon.-Sat. 8:15am-noon and 3:30-6:30pm, Sun. 9am-noon and 3:30-6:30pm; Oct.-March Mon.-Sat. 8:15am-noon and 3:30-5:30pm, Sun. 9am-noon and 3:30-5:30pm. Free.)

Il Santo, as Padua's patron is familiarly called, is immortalized by a complex of buildings on p. del Santo. The **Basilica di Sant' Antonio** (tel. 66 39 44), where the saint is entombed, is an architectural potpourri of domes and towers. Built shortly after Sant' Antonio's death in 1231, the basilica was an important pilgrimage destination during the later Middle Ages, and flocks of unlucky peregrines continue to pay homage. The altar is embellished with sculpture by Donatello. Sant' Antonio's tongue and jaw are preserved in a head-shaped reliquary in the apse of the church. (Open April-Sept. daily 6:30am-7:45pm; Oct.-March daily 6:30am-7pm. Free.)

The adjoining **Oratorio di San Giorgio** houses fine examples of the Giotto-style fresco, and the **Scuola del Santo** on the corner has more excellent frescoes, including three Titians. (Both open May-Sept. daily 9am-noon and 2:30-6:30pm; Oct.-April daily 9am-noon and 2:30-6pm.) The **Museo Civico,** currently being moved from p. del Santo to p. Eremitani, houses a *pinacoteca* (art gallery) with Giorgione's *Leda and the Swan* and a Giotto crucifix.

In the center of p. del Santo sits Donatello's bronze equestrian statue of **Gattemelata,** a mercenary general remembered for his agility and ferocity in all fields (his name means "calico cat"). Conscious of the statue's historical importance as the first Renaissance bronze cast of significance, Donatello modeled it after the well-known Roman equestrian statues of Marcus Aurelius and **Marcus Selwyn.**

A verdant refuge lies a block away in the **Orto Botanico** (tel. 65 66 14), the oldest in Europe, where Goethe and others studied the sex lives of plants. (Open Nov.-Feb. Mon.-Sat. 9am-1pm, March-Oct. Mon.-Sat. 9am-1pm, Sun. 9:30am-1pm. Admission L3000.)

The **university** is scattered throughout the city but has its headquarters in Palazzo Bò (tel. 65 14 00). In Venetian dialect *bò* means steer or castrated bull. Ostensibly, the name derived from the sign of the inn that formerly occupied the *palazzo*'s site, but female students find it fertile fodder for putting into question the sexual prowess of their male colleagues. Founded in 1220, it's the second-oldest Italian university after Bologna. The **teatro anatomica** (1594), the first of its kind in Europe, saw the likes of Englishman William Harvey, who discovered the circulation of blood. Almost all Venetian noblemen got their *de rigueur* education in law and public policy in the Great Hall, and the "chair of Galileo" is preserved in the **Sala dei Quaranta,** where the physicist supposedly lectured. Grueling public oral exams (sweating, nail-biting, tears, fainting) take place at the university in June, July, and September. (*Palazzo* open Mon.-Fri. 9am-1pm and 3-5pm, Sat. 9am-1pm; Aug. Mon.-Sat. 9am-1pm. Guided tours on the hour. Free.)

Caffè Pedrocchi (tel. 755 20 20), across the street, was a hangout for nineteenth-century liberals who supported Mazzini. When it was first built, the cafe's famous neoclassical facade had no doors, since it was open 24 hours; here, every university student was entitled to a free newspaper and a glass of water. The battle between students and Austrian police here in February 1848 was a turning point in the Risorgimento. For the price of a cappuccino (L2000), you can try to recapture the days of Goethe and Byron. (Open Sun.-Fri. 7:30am-1am, Sat. 7:30am-2am.)

Entertainment

Padua's nightlife is elusive; there are no established student locales, and the social scene shifts locations quickly. Try **Lucifer Young,** on via Altinate off p. Garibaldi, with its *al grotto di Lucifer,* or **Alla Ventura,** via S. Martino e Solferino, which has long tables at which to converse with the locals about other "in" spots. The **Prato Della Valle** runs a tacky amusement park on summer evenings (rides L1000-3000) and a boisterous flea market during the day (Sat. 7am-6pm, but the hot stuff runs out early).

Check the posters around Palazzo Bò or pick up a copy of the newspaper *La Mattina* for concert and film listings. In July the city organizes the **Cinema Città Estate,** a series of open-air films shown in the Arena Romana. (Tickets L5000 1st night, L3000 2nd night. Call the Commune di Padova (city council) at 65 52 00.)

You can sample a glass or three from the nearby Colli Euganei winery district or the sparkling *lambruschi* of Emilia Romagna. Two of the most distinctive whites are produced by **Nane della Giulia,** via Santa Sofia, 1, off via S. Francesco (open Tues.-Sun. 11am-2pm and 7pm-midnight), and **Spaccio Vini Carpanese,** via del Santo, 44 (tel. 305 81; open Mon.-Sat. 9am-12:30pm). Delicious wines run L1000-2000 per glass if you stay away from the Möet.

Near Padua

The **Colli Euganei** (Eugan Hills), southwest of Padua, whip up a veritable feast for the senses. Delight your eyes with the rolling landscape, sate your appetite with sensuous fruit (especially peaches), and lift your spirit with the local wines. Padua's tourist office provides pamphlets suggesting various itineraries.

Stay in a hillside farm at **Azienda Agrituristica "Savellon Molini,"** via Savellon Molini, 35043 Monselice (tel. (0429) 734 21), about 25km from Padua, along the bus route to Monselice and 4km from the Monselice train station. Another farm that is also part of the fledgling *agriturismo* program is the **Azienda Agricola "Villa Dottori,"** via S. Andrea, 17, 35020 Lion di Albighasego (tel. (049) 716 71), 6km from Padua and accessible by bus. Both villas offer beds in doubles or triples for L15,000 per night, including breakfast and showers. Full pension is L31,500.

Bassano del Grappa

At the foot of imposing Monte Grappa, Bassano del Grappa serves as a hideaway for refined Italian and Austrian tourists. The city is a conglomeration of ancient red-tile-roofed buildings, bordering the Brenta, which is a rushing alpine torrent in winter and a refreshing green river in summer. Its seclusion in the foothills of the Italian Alps makes Bassano considerably cooler and quieter than the cities to the south.

Practical Information

Azienda Autonoma di Soggiorno e Turismo: viale delle Fosse, 9 (tel. 243 51 or 266 51). From the station, walk down via Chilesotti to viale delle Fosse and turn right. The exceptionally helpful and well-informed staff will inundate you with information and brochures on the entire Veneto area. Open Mon.-Sat. 9am-12:30pm and 3-6:45pm.

Post Office: via Verci, 31 (tel. 221 11), off p. Cadorna. Open Mon.-Fri. 8am-7:30pm, Sat. 8am-5:30pm. **Postal code:** 36061.

Telephones: Bar Danielli, p. Garibaldi. Open daily 7am-9pm. **Telephone code:** 0424.

Train Station: At the end of via Chilesotti (tel. 250 34), east of the town center. Direct trains from Padua (L2500), Venice (L3500), and Trent (L4900). From Verona (L4900), change at Vicenza and again at Cittàdella.

Bus Station: p. Trento (tel. 250 25). As you come up via Chilesotti, turn left on viale delle Fosse. More direct and more frequent than trains. Buses to villas, Maser (6 per day, L2000),

Lugo di Vicenza (every 40 min., via Thiene), Asiago (7 per day, L3000), Marostica (every hr., L1000), and Vicenza (every hr., L2500). Buy tickets in the Trevisani Ristorante in the *piazzale.*

Hospital: Ospedale Civile, viale delle Fosse, 43 (tel. 242 01, for **first aid** 21 71 11).

Police: via G. Emiliani, 35 (tel. 223 10).

Accommodations and Food

There are few cheap rooms in town and no campgrounds, but Bassano is hardly tourist-infested; if you show up by early afternoon you will find a vacant room.

Locanda Castello, p. Terraglio, 20 (tel. 234 62), back-to-back with the early 10th-century Castello degli Ezzelini. Large, comfortable rooms. Dark bar downstairs. Modern bathrooms. Singles L17,000. Doubles L28,400. Showers included.

Albergo Bassanello, via Fontana, 2 (tel. 353 47), a 10-min. walk around the station. Exit to the left, cross the tracks, and turn left again. Adequate rooms run by a proper family in a boring part of town. Singles L17,000. Doubles L28,400.

The town's most potent claim to fame is *grappa,* the potent liquor that takes its name from the nearby mountain and is distilled from the seeds and peels of grapes. Bassano also exports *funghi porcini,* an extraordinary variety of herbs and mushrooms. On Thursdays and Saturdays from 8am to noon, an **open-air market** centered in p. Garibaldi seeps its way into most of the old part of town. Pick up fresh produce and neon-pink sandals.

Paninoteca al Porton, via Gamba, 5, between p. Bonamigo and Ponte degli Alpini. A bar with great sandwiches (try asparagus, ham, and egg, L1800) and thick, juicy hamburgers (L2500). Open Mon.-Fri. 9:30am-7pm, Sat. noon-6pm. When this is closed for holidays at the end of July, try across the street at *Caffé-Bar a Saiso,* which offers a similar selection. (Open. Thurs.-Tues.)

Mensa Ferrovieri, via de Blasi, 9 (tel. 291 50), to the right as you exit the train station. A windowless cafeteria with pink table-cloths and plenty of spirit. Full meals only L7200. Open daily 11am-3pm and 6-11pm.

Trattoria Combattenti, via Gamba, 22 (tel. 267 14), near the *paninoteca.* One of the finest family-style restaurants in northern Italy. Carefully prepared dishes of Veneto's best cuisine. Try *spezzatino con polenta,* a rich stew made with cornmeal bread. Meals around L20,000. Open Tues.-Sun. noon-2pm and 7-9pm; don't be late. Closed mid-late July.

Sights and Entertainment

Bassano's charm is epitomized in the small **Ponte degli Alpini,** a covered wooden bridge dating from 1209 and last redesigned by Andrea Palladio (1568-70) to resemble a fleet of ships anchored in midstream. The **Museo del Ponte degli Alpini** will tell you everything you do (and don't) want to know about the bridge. (Open Tues. and Fri. 10am-noon and 8-10pm.) Save one or two hours to stop by the **Museo Civico,** in p. Garibaldi. The museum owes its assets to the beneficence of several wealthy inhabitants of Bassano (one of whom donated a splendid collection of early Magna Graecia ceramics) and the genius of the local Da Ponte (better known under their adopted name Bassano), one of the great painting families of the later Italian Renaissance. The most illustrious member of the family, Iacopo da Bassano (1517-1592), is represented by his luminous *Flight into Egypt* and the gentle *Saint Valentine Baptizing Saint Lucilla.* The museum also contains sculptures and chiaroscuro sketches by Antonio Canova (1757-1822), the master of neoclassicism who was the toast of Europe for most of his career. Don't miss the room devoted to the Bassano native Tito Gobbi, a legendary operatic baritone. Some of his more elaborate costumes are displayed to the musical accompaniment of the maestro singing his greatest hits. (Open Tues.-Sat. 10am-12:30pm and 2:30-6:30pm, Sun. 10am-12:30pm. Admission L1000.)

Near Bassano

In the foothills of the Dolomites on a miniature plateau above the Vicentine plain lies the resort village of **Asiago.** This is a fun and easily accessible place to catch a breath of mountain air while enjoying almost every sport imaginable. Asiago boasts a golf-course, track, swimming pool, skating rink (ice and roller), stables, and celestial slopes for hiking and skiing.

The section of town called Ekar houses an **IYHF youth hostel** on via Costa-lunga (tel. (0424) 627 77; L11,000, breakfast included; open Dec.-March and June 20-Sept. 10) Reserve early as other accommodations in Asiago are likely to be costly or booked. Just 100 yards away is **Camping Ekar** (tel. (0424) 637 52; L6000 per tent, L4000 per person).

Asiago's **tourist office** is at p. Carli, 56 (tel. (0424) 626 61 or 622 21; open Mon.-Sat. 9am-noon and 4-6pm, Sun. 10am-noon and 3:30-5pm). Buses run from Bassano (5 per day), Padua (8 per day), and Vicenza (8 per day, FTV). If you are staying at the hostel, do not get off at Asiago, but at Gallio; from here the hostel is a 1-kilometer walk.

Vicenza

Vicenza's pride in its native architect, Andrea Palladio (1508-1580), is displayed not only in its well-kept *palazzi* and civic buildings, but on practically every store-front in town—Bar Palladio, Oro logerie "da Palladio," Cinema Palladio . . . . Palladio's style is tirelessly duplicated, reverberating throughout Europe and America. The omnipresent eyes of an American army base in Vicenza are a continuing reminder that many of Vicenza's *palazzi* were destroyed by Allied bombing during the last months of World War II.

Orientation and Practical Information

Vicenza is located in the heart of Veneto, halfway between Verona and Padua. The train station is in the southern part of town. **AIM** city buses #1, 2, 5, and 7 will take you to the center of town and p. Matteotti (L500). Next to the train station is also the intercity **FTV** bus station, with connections to Bassano (L2500), Padua, and other nearby cities and villas. To walk into town, take viale Roma across the park to corso Palladio (the central street), and turn right; p. Matteotti is at the other end (10 min.).

EPT: p. Matteotti, 12 (tel. 22 89 44), next to the Teatro Olimpico. Map of the villas and information on how and when to visit them. For the disabled, a city map of wheelchair-accessible facilities. The summer staff is particularly bubbly if not savvy. English spoken in the way Byron described his command of Italian: more fluently than grammatically. Open Mon.-Sat. 9am-12:30pm and 3-6:30pm, Sun. 9am-12:30pm. Also an office at p. del Duomo, 5 (tel. 54 48 05). Open Mon.-Fri. 8:30am-12:30pm.

Travel Agency and Car Rental: AVIT, viale Roma, 17 (tel. 54 56 77), just before you reach the supermarket PAM. BIJ and Transalpino tickets. **Avis** rental cars. Open Mon.-Fri. 8:30am-12:30pm and 3-7pm, Sat. 9am-12:30pm.

Post Office: contrà Garibaldi (tel. 54 45 65), near the *duomo.* Open Mon.-Fri. 8am-7:45pm, Sat. 8am-1pm. **Postal code:** 36100.

Telephones: SIP, p. Giusti. Open daily 8am-9:30pm. At night, go to **Ristorante La Taverna,** p. dei Signori, 47 (tel. 54 73 26). Open 9:30pm-1am. **Telephone code:** 0444.

Train Station: p. Stazione (tel. 23 94 27), at the end of viale Roma. To Venice (38 per day, 50 min., L3500), Verona, Padua (40 per day, 25 min., L1800), and Milan (27 per day, 2½ hr., L9800). A convenient map stand outside the station.

Bus Station: Ferrovie e Tramvie Vicentine (FTV), viale Milano, 7 (tel. 54 43 33 or 54 48 40), to the left as you exit the train station. To Bassano (every hr., L2500), Marostica (every hr., take the bus for Bassano via Marostica, L2000), Thiene (every hr., L2000), Lugo via Thiene (5 per day, L2500), and Pojana (10 per day, L2500). Beware the L30,000 fine for riding without a stamped ticket.

Hospital: Ospedale Civile, via Rodolfi (tel. 395 55; for **first aid** and **ambulance** 23 95 55).

Police: via Muggia, 2 (tel. 50 40 44). **American Military Police,** Tel. 50 18 00.

English Radio Station: Armed Forces Radio 106FM. American top-40, country music, baseball scores, news, and American community activities for homesick Yankees.

Laundromat: Puliget, via Legione Antonini, 11 (tel. 56 37 52).

Swimming Pool: Piscina Comunale, via Forlanini (tel. 223 13), northwest of town.

Accommodations

Vicenza's bourgeois tenor does not allow for inexpensive *pensioni.* To compound the problem, many establishments close for vacation in early August, and most are packed in September during the annual architecture course.

Albergo Milano, stradella dei Servi, 7 (tel. 23 86 43). Located centrally between p. Signori and via Oratorio Servi. Bordering on elegant. Singles L20,000. Doubles L29,000, with bath L37,000. Showers L1000, free after a while.

Casa San Raffaele, viale X Giugno, 10 (tel. 23 56 19), a 10-min. walk from the station. If you're going to liberally lose lire in Vicenza, do it here. Magnificent views from the hill next to Monte Berico. Call before walking up. Singles L23,000. Doubles L37,200. Bath included.

Pensione Villa Marzia, via Mure Pallamaio, 96 (tel. 22 70 55), 5 min. from the train station. As you leave the station, turn right on viale Venezia and continue as it curves left into via Eretenio. Central and quiet. Singles L15,000. Doubles L26,000. Reception open Mon.-Sat. 8am-noon and 6-8pm.

Hotel Alpino, Borgo Casale, 33 (tel. 50 51 37), 8 min. beyond the tourist office. Not prepossessing but the cheapest place in town. Singles L15,000, with bath L19,000. Doubles L22,000, with bath L28,000.

Food

Buying food in and around **piazza delle Erbe**'s open **market** is like lending money to a thief. In general, the shops across the river offer much better value for the money. Going into or out of downtown, you can't miss **Supermercato Pam.** (Open Mon.-Tues. and Thurs.-Sat. 8:30am-1pm and 3-7:30pm, Wed. 8:30am-1pm.) *Il baccalà* is a local stew of fish, tomatoes, oil, and herbs gently simmered for at *least* 7 hours.

Gastronomia Ceppi, corso Palladio, 196 (tel. 54 44 14). Fantastic vegetable *antipasti* with mouth-watering aromas. Ham and cheese *cannelloni* L960. Open 7:45am-12:45pm and 4:30-7:30pm.

Self-service Righetti, p. del Duomo, 3 (tel. 54 31 35). A self-service restaurant. Soup and pasta L2500, main dishes L5000. Decent fare without a chain-food atmosphere. Open Mon.-Fri. noon-2:30pm and 7-9pm.

La Cantinota, strada Garofalino (tel. 23 63 94), north of corso Palladio, behind Cinema Corso. Where the young crowd goes for neighborhood-style self-service food at L14,000. Enjoyable eats in amiable company. Discount with ISIC. Open Mon.-Sat. 8:30am-1am.

Dal Bersagliere, via Pescheria, 11 (tel. 23 39 94), off p. Erbe. A boistrous neighborhood hole-in-the-wall. Simple but filling lunch *menù* L10,000. Open Mon.-Sat. 8am-2:30pm and 6pm-1am.

Antica Trattoria Tre Visi, contrà Porti, 6 (tel. 23 86 77), off corso Palladio. The regal architecture of Palladio blossoms in this rosy interior. *Antipasti* L7000, *primi piatti* L7000. Main courses around L15,000. *Baccalà alla Vicentina* L18,000. Open Tues.-Sat. 11:30am-2pm. Open late Aug. to mid-July.

Sights

Piazza dei Signori is the town center; it was the town's forum when Vicenza was Roman and the town's showpiece when it was Venetian. Palladio began and ended his architectural career in this square; the renowned **basilica** made the young architect famous. When the Gothic Palazzo della Ragione, the city's hall of justice, began to collapse in the 1490s, the city government called in the best architects of the day to redesign and restore the symbolic building. Sansovino, Serlio, Giulio Romano, and all the other architects who tried, failed to produce a structurally sound edifice that captured the humanistic tone desired by Vicenza's cultured aristocracy. But in 1546, Palladio presented his project, backed by the wealthy Giangiacomo Trissino, who had educated the young local and given him his classical name. Palladio pushed his scheme through the town council by 1549 and worked on the building from then until his death in 1580. The two *loggie,* with their Doric and Ionic columns, noble arches, and the enigmatic marble faces on their keystones, are an ingenious solution. The "Serliana" motif (straight piece, arch, straight piece) gives the illusion that the building's facade is regular, but, in fact, the pilasters in between are adjusted to hide the irregularities of the previous structure's Gothic bays. What is no illusion is the basilica's genuine stone construction, in contrast to most of Palladio's other nearby works, which are built in brick and then stuccoed over to give the illusion of masonry. The name "basilica" was given to the building by the sixteenth-century noble literati who commissioned it to be a place where justice was administered, recalling the Roman sense of a basilica. You can get a good idea of the former medieval *palazzo* by walking around under the *loggie,* and from the style of the **Torre di Piazza,** the needlelike tower next to it. The first town clock was put in the tower in 1378. (Basilica open Tues.-Sat. 9:30am-noon and 2:30-5pm, Sun. 10am-noon. Free.)

Across the *piazza,* the **Loggia del Capitano** illustrates a later Palladian style. This ornate work was begun in 1571 to commemorate the Victory of Lepanto. Palladio left the facade unfinished at his death, having completed only the three bays with grand balustraded windows and the four sets of gigantic columns.

The two symbolic columns of Venice complete the *piazza.* On top of one is the lion of San Marco, the symbol of Venice; on the other, a statue of the Redeemer. On the opposite side of the *basilica,* the fruit market on p. delle Erbe is dominated by the medieval **Torre del Tormento,** a former prison.

Behind the Loggia del Capitano, the **Palazzo del Comune** faces **corso Palladio,** Vicenza's main street. Vicenzo Scamozzi's precise design for the *palazzo* demonstrates a much sharper interpretation of classical architecture than that embodied in the buildings of Palladio, his master.

Corso Palladio, lined with Renaissance *palazzi,* runs the length of Vicenza, from Porta Castello in the east to the Teatro Olimpico on the banks of the Bacchglione River. In p. Castello, a medieval gate from the castle that once guarded the town's entrance remains. In front of it, on the left, the two bays of the **Palazzo Porto-Breganze** are an imposing fragment of the structure begun by Scamozzi to Palladio's designs. Scamozzi managed to finish the **Palazzo Bonin,** also designed by Palladio (at #13 on the right-hand corner of corso Palladio).

Contrà Vescovado leads out of the *piazza* next to Palazzo Porto-Breganze. At the end of the *contrà* is the ***duomo,*** a large Gothic structure in brick, with a graceful apse and a Palladian cupola. The **Casa Pigafetta** on nearby via Pigafetta proves that Palladio wasn't the only architect to influence Vicenza; this unique early Renaissance house successfully fuses the Gothic, Spanish, and classical styles.

Farther south, on the banks of the Retrone near ponte S. Michele, is the **Palazzo Civena,** an early Palladian house. The bridge across the river offers lovely views of the town. The only structure of note on the far side is the **Oratorio di San Nicola da Tolentino,** in *contrà* Ponte San Michele, ornately frescoed in heavy sixteenth-century Venetian style by Maffei.

North of corso Palladio, Vicenza is full of Renaissance *palazzi,* each rivaling its neighbors. For more Palladio, try the **Palazzo Valmarana-Braga,** corso Fogazzaro,

16, in which sculptured figures on the corners distinguish the *palazzo* from the rest of the street. The sixteenth-century art critic Vasari thought Palladio's unfinished **Palazzo da Porto-Festa** the most magnificent of all, but some prefer the more grandiose **Palazzo Porto-Barbaran** or the **Palazzo Thiene,** on contrà Porti, a felicitous blending of Palladio with the incredible terra-cotta corners and portals of Lorenzo da Bologna. (All 3 *palazzi* are on contrà Porti.) The **Palazzo Schio** is a refreshingly non-Palladian masterpiece.

At the far end of corso Palladio, on what was once a lawn sloping down to the river, Palladio built the villa-like **Palazzo Chiericati.** The *palazzo* now houses the **Museo Civico** (tel. 22 13 48); the ground-floor rooms on the left still bear their frescoes. The painting collection in the *pinacoteca* on the first floor includes works by Bartolomeo Montagna (*Madonna Enthroned*), some of Bassano's best endeavors, a rare and refined *Madonna* by Cima da Conegliano, Van Dyck's *Three Ages of Man,* and a Memling *Crucifixion.* (Open Tues.-Sat. 9:30am-noon and 2:30-5pm, Sun. 10am-noon. Admission L1000, Sun. free.)

The **Teatro Olimpico** (tel. 23 43 81), also at the west end of corso Palladio, embodies the same classical atmosphere that the sixteenth-century *palazzo*-building patrons created. The *Accademia Olimpica,* as the literati nobles called themselves, met in the pseudo-Roman theater for recitals of their own plays. The theater still hosts productions every year from September through June, with both local talent and excellent visiting companies. A multilingual tour guide strives to be equally spectacular. (Open March 16-Oct. 15 Mon.-Sat. 9:30am-12:20pm and 3-5:30pm, Sun. 9:30am-12:20pm; Oct. 16-March 15 Mon.-Sat. 9:30am-12:20pm and 2-4:30pm, Sun. 9:30am-12:30pm. Admission L2000, Sun. free.)

Entertainment

Pick up a copy of one of the local newspapers (*Il giornale di Vicenza* or *Il Gazzettino,* L800 each) for listings of special exhibits, concerts, and other cultural events. Besides the performances in the **Teatro Olimpico** (tickets L20,000-25,000), Vicenza now hosts an annual summer cultural festival, **Estate insieme,** with shows and performances of all kinds. (Performances run mid-July to mid-Aug.; tickets average L15,000-20,000.)

Near Vicenza

Palladian villas are scattered throughout the Vicentine countryside. But they are difficult to access, have unpredictable schedules, and often allow tours of their exteriors only. It's a good idea to phone ahead or contact the **Amministrazione Provinciale Assessorato al Turismo** in Vicenza on via Gazzolle (tel. 39 91 58). If you are making the connections yourself on public buses, keep in mind that it takes at least a half-day to see one of these fabulous country estates.

A group traveling together should consider splitting the cost of a car, since there are no moped or bike rentals in Vicenza. The EPT provides good literature on Palladio's works, but they have only written information on the villas in the immediate province. For further information, ask the APAT (above). The only complete map, *Ville Venete,* put out by the Istituto Geografico de Agostini (L8000) and available at many newsstands and most bookstores, is helpful though sometimes difficult to read. Villas are listed with public transportation in mind. (See Near Venice, and Between Bassano and Vicenza.)

Fortunately, there are some great villas close to town. The **Villa Rotonda** (also called Villa Capra; tel. (444) 22 17 93), is the brochure favorite, but nothing can prepare you for the magnificence of the estate itself. An atypical but amazing example of Palladio's country houses, it is within walking distance of town (or take bus #8 or 13 from near the station). Most of Palladio's villas were designed as working farms as well as elegant residences; the sole purpose of the Rotonda was for the pleasure and partying of a cardinal. The building is exquisitely positioned on the estate: Four columned verandas front the round central hall, providing an unparalleled vista of the surrounding countryside. Goethe considered the Villa Rotonda one of the most magnificent architectural achievements ever, and it was later a model for buildings in France, England, and the U.S., most notably Jefferson's Monticello. (Interior open Wed. only. Exterior open Tues.-Sun. 10am-noon and 3-6pm. Admission to the interior L5000, to the exterior L2000.)

Palladio's equally unusual and unfinished **Villa Thiene** (tel. 55 68 99) is stately and forlorn, despite the encroaching suburbs of Quinto Vicentino. Take city bus #10. (Open Mon., Wed., and Fri. 10am-12:30pm, Tues. and Thurs. 10am-12:30pm and 6-7pm.)

In contrast, Muttoni's **Villa Valmarana** (tel. 22 18 03), nicknamed "ai Nani" after the statues of dwarfs in its garden, is introverted. Frescoes by Gian Battista Tiepolo (with a bit of help from his son Domenico) cover the *palazzina* with scenes from classical and Renaissance poems. Those in the hall and the Iliad Room are the most vivid: The figures emerge from their painted settings into the space of the rooms. The **Foresteria** (Guest House), with its *loggia,* is decorated with Domenico's charming depictions of people and country scenes. An aristocratic Italian family still lives here, and the magnificent frescoes coexist with more modest snapshots. (Open March-April Mon.-Wed. and Fri. 2:30-5:30pm, Thurs. and Sat. 10am-noon and 2:30-5:30pm, Sun. 10am-noon; May-Sept. Mon.-Wed. and Fri. 3-6pm, Thurs. and Sat. 10am-noon and 3-6pm, Sun. 10am-noon; Oct.-Nov. Mon.-Wed. and Fri. 2-5pm, Thurs. and Sat. 10am-noon and 2-5pm, Sun. 10am-noon. Admission L4000, with ISIC L1500.)

The southern edge of Vicenza is hemmed in by the stately **Monte Berico.** As you leave the train station, go right on viale Venezia, cross ponte S. Libera, then hang a right again onto steep viale X. Giugno. At the summit perch baroque arches of the **Basilica Monte Berico.** Art pilgrims should see Veronese's vast *Feast of St. Gregory the Great,* tucked in the refectory next to the postcard-and-relic stand. Montagna frescoes decorate the sacristy. (Open in summer Mon.-Sat. 7am-noon and 2:30-7pm, Sun. 7am-noon and 2:30-6pm; in off-season closes 1 hr. earlier.)

The **IYHF youth hostel** in **Montagnana** is an hour south of Vicenza by bus, in the Castello degli Alberi (tel. (0429) 810 76; open April-Oct. 15; L6000). The **tourist office** is in p. Maggiore (tel. (0429) 813 20). Take the bus to Pojana and walk the 2 or 3km. En route, explore the **Villa Pojana** (tel. (0444) 89 85 54), whose curious front portal was the result of straying from Palladio's original plans. (Open daily 3-4pm. Free.)

Montagnana is on the Mantua-Monselice train line with access to several of the lovely Ville del Polesine, the most important of these being the **Villa Badoer** (tel. (041) 523 56 06), at Fratta Polesine (change trains at Legnano). Its beautiful proportions and elongated breadth are the work of Palladio, while its interior is decorated with grotesques by the Florentine painter Giallo. (Open Sept. 15-March Fri.-Wed. 2-5pm, Thurs. 9am-noon and 2-5pm; April 1-April 15 Mon.-Wed. and Fri.-Sat. 3:30-7pm, Thurs. 9am-noon and 3:30-7pm, Sun. 3:30-7pm; April 16-Sept. 30 also open Sun. 10am-noon.) Call the EPT in **Rovigo,** the principal town of the Polesine, for more information (tel. (0425) 36 14 81; open Mon.-Wed. and Fri. 8am-noon and 3:30-6pm, Thurs. and Sat. 8am-noon.)

Between Bassano and Vicenza: The Ville Venete

Palladio's designs also participated in the Venetian expansion to the mainland that began in the early fifteenth century. As Venice's wealth accumulated and its once-unchallenged maritime supremacy faded, the nobles began to turn their attention to acquiring property on the mainland. Here, they were ordered by the Venetian Senate to build villas, not castles, to keep them from the temptation of becoming fortified warlords in control of their own territories. The architectural consequences were magnificent: Veneto is now the home of hundreds of the most splendid villas in the world, each conceived as the heart of a working community from which the well-born farmer could supervise his crops.

The bus from Vicenza to Bassano stops at Thiene. Here, change for the tiny village of **Lugo** to see two famous Palladian villas at close range (L2500, Mon.-Sat. 5 buses per day, Sun. 2). The **Villa Godi-Valmarana** (a.k.a. "Malinveri"; tel. (0445) 86 05 61) was the architect's first. Just a few yards up the street is the more elegant **Villa Piovene.** You can trace Palladio's development from Godi-Valmarana's austere simplicity to the still-classical expansiveness of Piovene 40 years later. (The interior of the former open March 19-May and Sept.-Oct. Tues., Sat.-Sun., and holidays 2-6pm; June-Aug. Tues., Sat.-Sun., and holidays 3-7pm. Admission L3000.) Villa Piovene may be viewed only from the outside; for a closer look, pay L2000 to enter the wonderful park around it. (Open in summer daily 2:30-7pm; in off-season 2-5pm.)

That the well-educated Venetians did not sacrifice beauty for practicality is demonstrated by the justly famous **Villa Barbaro-Volpi,** at **Maser.** Built in 1560 by Palladio, the building rests on a gentle hillside covered with pines. Behind the house is the water-filled *Nymphaeum*—practical Palladio had the water flow from here into the kitchens, then down to the orchards in front of the house. Likewise, the elegant central pavilion is flanked by arcaded wings that manage to hide unglamorous necessities such as stables, while adding grandeur to the facade. Inside are Paolo Veronese's fabulous frescoes. The deities in the Hall of Olympus double as the zodiacal signs, and portraits of the Barbaro family are painted into the scene along the fake balcony. At one end of the series of doorways running through the house, Veronese left a portrait of himself, and ever since there has been speculation that the distant woman who gazes at him was his mistress. Finally, wander to the base of the hill to see the exquisite circular temple that Palladio built for the owners. The glossy, 100-page guide called *Maser,* sold at the villa, will pay in facts for its L8000 price. (Interior open June-Sept. Tues., Sat.-Sun., and civic holidays 3-6pm; Oct.-May 2-5pm. Call (0423) 56 50 02 for more information. Admission L1500.) Maser lies about 15km east of Bassano, an easy trip by bus from Bassano (6 per day, L2000), or the train-accessible town of Montebelluna.

A short train ride south from Montebelluna (or a trip from Bassano or Vicenza via Castelfranco) takes you to Fanzolo to see **Villa Emo** (tel. (0423) 48 70 40). Considered along with Maser to be one of the most typical Palladian villas, the interior frescoes balance harmoniously with the architecture and are G.B. Zelotti's masterpiece. (Open May-Sept. Sat.-Sun. and national holidays 3-6pm; Oct.-April Sat.-Sun. 2-5pm.)

If you are in this corner of the world on the second weekend in September of an even-numbered year, you must not miss the **Human Chess Game,** played in the small town of **Maróstica,** between Vicenza and Bassano. Complete with costumes and giant board, the game is a reenactment of a match played on an equally giant scale in 1454 to win the heart of a fair maiden. For information and reservations, contact Pro Loco at 36063 p. Castello (tel. (0424) 721 27).

Every summer an **entertainment series** of operas, ballets, plays, and musical concerts animates the Ville Venete. For information about concerts, inquire at the **Assessorato alla Cultura e al Turismo** in Vicenza (tel. (0444) 39 91 11). For information about plays, refer to the tourist offices of Recoavo Terme (tel. (0445) 751 58), Asiago (tel. (0424) 622 21), or Villa Verla (tel. (0445) 85 60 73). For information about the opera, call the **Ufficio Festival** (tel. (0424) 845 02).

Verona

There is no world without Verona walls,
But purgatory, torture, hell itself.
Hence banished is banish'd from the world,
And world's exile is death . . .
—*Shakespeare, Romeo and Juliet*

Shakespeare went a little overboard, but this city of romance and rose-colored marble has never incited anything less than superlatives. No one rushes and nothing bustles in this town of lounging *piazze* and luxurious *palazzi.* The canal-like River Adige loops in lazy Venetian style; in fact, Venice's Lion of San Marco ruled here for three centuries. But Verona's formative years were spent as a Roman metropolis, the birthplace of the poet Catullus. More massive columns and triumphal arches stare down the city's streets than anywhere save Rome itself, and the vast arena is still used for public performances, 19 centuries after it was built.

Orientation and Practical Information

Verona is an important rail center, where the Venice-Milan line crosses the Bologna-Brenner Pass line to Austria and Germany. Most **APT** buses (tel. 341 25) that serve the province and Lake Garda depart from the bus station at p. Cittadella; others originate from the train station and p. Isolo. **AMT** bus #2 will take you from the station north to p. Brà and p. Erbe, in the center of town (otherwise it is about a 20 min. walk to p. Brá and the center of town), as well as p. Isolo. If you walk, turn right from the station, then left past the porta Nuova gate onto corso Porta Nuova (20 min.). Bus tickets (L600) are available to tourists from the *biglietteria* outside the station, as well as at *tabbacherie;* day passes (L2500) only outside the station.

Azienda Promozionale Turismo, via Dietro Anfiteatro, 6 (tel. 59 28 28), on the street behind the arena in p. Brà. Extremely helpful but understaffed. Up-to-the-minute accommodations information but no reservations. Reasonable exchange rates (commission on traveler's checks L2500). Open Mon.-Sat. 8am-8pm, Sun 9am-2pm.

EPT: via della Valverde, 34 (tel. 300 86), in the ACI building off corso Porta Nuova between the station and p. Brà. Turn right as you exit the station. Kind staff afflicted with *la dolce far niente* (sweet apathy). Will phone hotels to check on vacancies. Open Mon.-Fri. 9am-noon and 3:30-6pm, Sat. 9am-noon.

Budget Travel: CIT, p. Brà, 2 (tel. 59 17 88). Student discounts on plane, train, and bus tickets, including Transalpino. Commission on traveler's checks L2000. Open Mon.-Fri. 8:30am-12:30pm and 3-6:30pm, Sat. 8:30am-noon.

Centro Turistico Giovanile, via Seminario, 10 (tel. 345 92), across the river off via Carducci, on the 3rd floor. The 1st student travel office in Italy. Mellow staff sells student cards, hostel cards, BIJ tickets, and Transalpino tickets. Occasionally organizes interesting tours of the city and region. Open Mon.-Fri. 8:30am-12:30pm and 2-7:30pm.

American Express: Viaggi Vertours, Galleria Pelliciai, 13 (tel. 59 49 88), between p. Erbe and via Quattro Spade. Holds mail for several years. Italian cash only for your personal check with card. Open Mon.-Fri. 9am-12:30pm and 3-7pm, Sat. 9am-12:30pm.

Post Office: p. Poste (tel. 59 09 55), also known as p. Francesco Viviani, adjacent to p. Indipendenza. Open Mon.-Fri. 8:30am-6:30pm, Sat. 8:30am-1pm. **Postal code:** 37100.

Telephones: ASST, at the station. Open 24 hours. 12:30pm-7am, ring the bell to get in. Phones operated by the *schieda* coins. **SIP,** via Leoncino, 53, behind the arena. Open daily 8am-9:30pm. **Telephone code:** 045.

Train Station: In front of p. XXV Aprile (tel. 59 06 88), linked with p. Brà by corso Porta Nuova. To Venice (37 per day; 2 hr.; one way L5900, round-trip L10,000), Milan (40 per day; 2 hr.; one way 7300, round-trip L12,400), Brennero (26 per day; 4 hr.; one way L11,700, round-trip L20,000), Rome (6 *diretti* per day; 6 hr.; L26,800), and Paris (3 *diretti* per day; L93,000). Between the bank and the information desk, money can be changed daily 7am-9:30pm. A preposterous L5000 commission is charged per traveler's check. Station open 7am-10pm.

Bus Station: p. Cittàdella, to the left of p. Brà as you walk toward the train station. Buy tickets at the bar in the center of the *piazza.* Many buses also leave from corso Porta Nuova. To Lago di Garda (L3600).

Taxis: Radiotaxi, via G. Galilei, 9 (tel. 53 26 66). Fare L1700 plus L1200 per km.

Car Rental: Hertz, at the train station (tel. 800 08 32). Be sure to ask for their "Affordable Europe Rates," which give foreigners a 30% break. Open Mon.-Fri. 8am-noon and 3-7pm, Sat. 8am-noon.

Bike Rental: Bellomi Paolo, via degli Alpini, opposite the arena off p. Brà. L3000 per hr., L16,000 per day. Open in summer 9am-11pm; in off-season 9am-7pm.

Swimming Pool: Centro Nuoto Piscina Coperta, via Col. Galliano (tel. 57 79 85 for outdoor pool; 56 76 22 or 56 78 25 for indoor pool). Take bus #7 from p. Erbe or Castelvecchio to the beginning of corso Milano and ask for further directions. Both indoor and outdoor are Olympic-sized. Open in summer daily 10am-9pm. Admission L4000, ages over 60 or under 14 L3000.

Day Hotel: Under the Barbieree Bagni sign to the far right just after you exit the station. Open Mon.-Sat. 8am-12:30pm and 3-8:30pm.

First Aid: Ospedale Civile Maggiore, borgo Trento (tel. 93 11 11). **Croce Verde** (the paramedics), lungadige Panvini, 15 (tel. 59 59 99).

Police: Tel. 59 67 77. The people at the **Ufficio Stranieri** (Foreigners Office) speak English. Open Mon.-Sat. 9am-noon and 4:30-7:30pm.

Accommodations

Verona's convenient spots bulge like many of the waists of the star singers during the opera months of July and August, so make reservations. Student-style accommodations are plentiful, cost the least, expand to take in extra people if necessary (especially the youth hostel), and none (except for Don Bosco) has an age limit or requires a hostel card.

Student Accommodations

Ostello Verona (IYHF), salita Fontana del Ferro, 15 (tel. 59 03 60), on the southern slope below Castel San Pietro. From the train station or downtown, take bus #2 across the river (on Ponte Nuovo), and get off in Isolo. Walk ahead to via Ponte Pignolo at the end of the *piazza,* turn right (you'll see the hostel sign), walk 3 blocks until the street ends, turn left here, take the 1st right, and finally the 1st left. One of the most beautiful hostels in Europe, and the only one adorned with 15th-century frescoes. The restoration of the building, the Villa Algarotti-Francescati, has been a labor of love for Prof. Fiorenzo Scarsini. Rooms are spotless and bathrooms modern. A bar, kitchens, washing machines, and meditation rooms. The young staff will put out mattresses in the chapel if more space is needed. Beds L10000. Hot showers, starched sheets, and continental breakfast included. Huge 3-course dinners L7500. A small, cheerful **campground** nearby. L6500 per person, tent and breakfast included. Rooms open at 6pm, but you can bring your pack any time to hang out or take a shower. Arrive early. Strict curfew 11pm, but if you go to the opera (you may be asked to flash your tickets), you can stay out ½-hr. after curtain call.

Casa della Studentessa, via G. Trezza, 16 (tel. 282 78), across the river and 5-10 min. from the youth hostel. Take bus #1, 2, or 8 across Ponto Nuovo and walk down via Carducci, turn right on via S. Vitale, and left on via G. Trezza. Women only in this well-maintained complex around a garden. Cozy and respectable. Singles with bath L18,000. Multi-bed rooms L11,000 per person. Showers included. Meals served in a pretty dining room 12:30-2pm and 7:30-8:30pm (L10,000). Men can eat here if a female friend is staying. Curfew 11pm, but they often stay open late, especially for operas and important concerts.

Casa del Giovane Don Bosco, via Antonio Provolo, 16 (tel. 59 13 00), by the Castelvecchio. Take bus #2 to the castle, or walk the 15 min. from the station. Head straight across p. XXV Aprile, continue on viale Luciano dal Cero to Porta Palio, turn right onto Stradone Porta Palio, then left and left again at the square onto via Provolo. A private boys' school with two dorms, one for men and one for women, each with about 50 beds. Members only. L10,000 the 1st night, L6000 per additional night. Hot showers included. Breakfast L2500. Reception opens at 6:30pm, though bags can be left at any time. Traces of high-school regimentation: wake up 7:45am, documents check 8:15am, breakfast 8:30am. Curfew 10pm, exceptions made for opera and concerts. Open July-Sept.

Casa della Giovane, via Pigna, 7 (tel. 59 68 80), off via Garibaldi, accessible via the ubiquitous bus #2. A Catholic Youth Association (ACISJF) hostel for women. Spotless rooms (mostly doubles and triples) and optimum location. Doubles or triples L12,000 per person. 8-bed dorms L10,000 per person. Somewhat flexible lockout 10am-6pm. Curfew 10:30pm, unless you have opera tickets.

Hotels

Locanda Catullo, via Catullo, 1 (tel. 800 27 86), off via Mazzini. In the 1st alley to your left. Cheerful and clean. Singles L15,000. Doubles L26,500. Showers included.

Albergo al Castello, corso Cavour, 43 (tel. 800 44 03), opposite the castle. Ideal location near p. Brà. Eager-to-please management. Singles L20,100. Doubles L30,300, with shower L34,800. Full pension L50,000.

Locanda Rosa, vicolo Raggiri, 9 (tel. 800 56 93), off via Rosa near p. delle Erbe. Pink halls recall Pepto Bismol, but well-furnished rooms are a pleasant surprise. Singles L18,500. Doubles L30,000. Triples L41,000. Showers L1000. Open Dec.-Oct.

Camping

Ostello Verona: campground at the hostel. See above.

Campeggio Castel S. Pietro, via Castel S. Pietro, 2 (tel. 59 20 37). Take bus #3 or 15, get off at the 1st stop on via Marsala, then ascend toward the castle. Leafy, terrific view and respectable facilities. Geared towards tent-toting types.

Food

Verona is famous for its *soave* (dry white) and *valpolicella* and *bardolino* (both red). This fecund area also supplies Italy with peaches and many other fruits and vegetables. Street stands offer bargains, though you may be disappointed by Verona's central **market** in p. delle Erbe where prices tend to be tourist-inflated. (Open Mon.-Sat.)

In the Center

Osteria Cucina al Cristo, p. Pescheria, 6 (tel. 305 50). Down-to-earth Italian cuisine, under the arcades of a quiet square. Meals around L10,000. Wine L2800 per liter. Open Mon.-Fri. 8am-2:30pm and 6-10pm, Sat. 8am-2:30pm.

Self-Service Bolzano, p. delle Erbe, 32 (tel. 319 44). A green, modern, and cool (in summer) cafeteria with appetizing food. Caters to locals and tourists alike. Immense *primi* L3000, *secondi* L5000. Full meal L11,000. Open Tues.-Sun. noon-3:30pm and 7-10pm. Closed much of July.

Pizzeria Corte Farina, corte Farina, 4 (tel. 59 10 32), at the end of via Pelliciai from p. delle Erbe through the Galleria. An unexpected oasis of peace and pizza (L3500-5500). Escape the orange-and-blue tartan tablecloths by eating outdoors. Open Tues.-Sun. 9am-3pm and 6pm-1am.

Gastronomia Sinico, via Leoni, 5 (tel. 800 25 81), down from p. delle Erbe near the Ponte Navi. Abundant gourmet deli. Open Mon.-Tues. and Thurs.-Sat. 8:10am-12:50pm and 4:30-7:50pm, Wed. 8:15am-12:50pm.

Bar-Pizzeria Cavour, p. Brá. Join the crowds for one of their terrific tropical drinks. Pizza L4000-7500. Open Tues.-Sun.

Across the River

This is by far the best dining area in Verona. The food is better, the prices lower, and the clientele native.

Trattoria al Cacciatore, via Seminario, 4 (tel. 59 42 91), the 4th left off via Carducci, which begins at the Ponte Nuovo. Unpretentious neighborhood place with delicious food. L10,000 *menù* includes *primo, secondo, contorni,* bread, service, *and* wine. Open Mon.-Fri. 8am-3pm and 6:30-10pm, Sat. 8am-3pm.

Trattoria Ropeton, via San Giovanni in Valle, 46 (tel. 300 40), below the youth hostel. They insist on serving full 3-course meals (around L16,000). Superb food served in a lovely courtyard. Open Wed.-Mon. noon-3pm and 7-11pm.

J.W. Wimpy, lungoadige Teodorico, 4 (tel. 59 12 03), upstream from Ponte Nuovo. Americophile name notwithstanding, Wimpy is not a sterile factory. It's a busy young hangout with tasty burgers and hot dogs (L1500-3000). Plenty of beer and a resonant stereo system. Fills up at night, especially during the academic year. If you miss loud '60s rock, you'll love it here. Open Tues.-Sun. noon-2am.

Il Grillo Parlante, vicolo seghe S. Tomaso, 10 (tel. 59 11 56), hidden in a tiny corner alley near lungadige Teodorico. Verona's vegetarian hotspot. Open Mon.-Tues. 12:15-2:15pm, Wed.-Fri. 12:15-2:15pm and 7:30-9:30pm.

Mensa Universitaria (tel. 809 81 11), just after via dell' Artigliere becomes via dell' Università, on the right. Hardly worth the walk. L6500 to outsiders. Open Sept.-June.

Antica Gelateria de Amicis, p. Isolo, 48, off via Carducci. Decked out with signature Veronese rose marble and pseudo-classical statues. Oh-so-cool during the school year. Open Tues.-Sun. 10:30am-12:30pm and 2:45pm-midnight.

Sights

Verona's tourist office offers the pamphlet *Passegiando per Verona,* which proposes several walking routes, with information on the sights along the way. The majestic pink **arena** (tel. 232 04) in **piazza Brà** is the largest in existence after the Colosseum. It was once even bigger—the fragment that soars on one edge, called the *ala* (wing), shows you the original wall. The arena's good condition is a tribute to Verona's municipal pride. In the sixteenth century, a special committee was set up to restore the amphitheater, and it has hosted events ever since. (Open in summer Tues.-Sun. 8am-6:45pm; in opera season 8am-1:30pm. Admission L3000.)

From p. Brà, via Mazzini takes you into **piazza delle Erbe,** former location of the Roman Forum. The center of the *piazza* is marked by the Madonna Verona fountain, installed by Cansignorio della Scala in 1368. San Marco's column was erected at the far end in 1523. The *piazza* is enclosed by various *palazzi* and towers dating from the eleventh through seventeenth centuries. The Gardello Tower, built in 1370, stands between the imposing neoclassical Maffei palace and two buildings with frescoed facades and spacious terraces that were once home to Verona's first families, the Scaligeri and the Mazzanti. The medieval Casa dei Mercanti (on the corner of via Palladio) with its crenelation and two-arched windows also stands out. In the center of the *piazza,* almost covered up by the awnings of the fruit vendors, is the Berlina—a marble structure once used by local officials to punish criminals. During medieval times, convicted outlaws were tied to the Berlina and pelted with rotten fruit by the populace.

The Arco della Costa, called the "Arch of the Rib" for the whale rib hung on it, separates p. delle Erbe from **piazza dei Signori.** This magnificent aristocratic *piazza* is the perfect counterpart to the mundane p. delle Erbe. The **Palazzo della Ragione** (Palace of Justice, 1193) stands on the corner, vacillating between the two *piazze.*

This densely knit brick and marble ensemble was the seat of the Scala family dynasty for centuries. The Scala were a violent and neurotic lot, as their names suggest: Cangrande (Big Dog) was the clan's head, Mastino's name means "Mastiff," and Cansignorio, "Head Dog." Yet Dante passed many months here as the guest of Cangrande, and eventually dedicated his *Paradiso* to the powerful warlord.

Through the arch at the far end of p. dei Signori are the peculiar outdoor **Tombs of the Scaligeri,** further testimony to the Scala family temperament. A copy of the statue of Cangrande sits high under a Gothic canopy. "Big Dog," naked sword in hand, sits back arrogantly on his hollow-eyed steed. (The original is in the Castelvecchio museum.) If you're in an amorous mood, visit the houses where Romeo and Juliet supposedly grew up. You are likely to be disappointed by **Casa Romeo,** for the dilapidated building is now a coffee bar populated with Veronese pensioners (around the corner from p. dei Signori at via Arche Scaligori, 2). At **Casa Capuletti,** more commonly known as **Casa Giulietta,** you will find a tall, ivy-covered wall next to a balcony where you can wait your turn in line to stand where Juliet once did. (At via Cappello, 23, tel. 383 03, toward the river from p. delle Erbe. Open Tues.-Sun. 8am-6:45pm. Admission L3000.) Juliet's "tomb" is in the middle of nowhere at via del Pontiere. From via Pallone (ponte Aleardi), go south (downstream) on Lungadige Capuletti, turn right on via Shakespeare, then left immediately and left again to the entrance. (Open 7:30am-7pm. Admission L3000.)

At the other end of via Arche Scaligeri, corso Sant' Anastasia will lead you to the **Basilica of Sant' Anastasia,** built in 1290. The Romanesque exterior is worn and was in fact never completed, but the Gothic interior bulges with art treasures. Pisanello's *St. George Freeing the Princess* (in the Giusti Chapel at the end of the left transept) is considered one of his best paintings, and there are frescoes by Altichiero and Turone as well. Most of the apse is decorated with terra-cottas by Michele da Firenze. Down via Duomo from the basilica is the *duomo,* decorated with medieval sculpture by the famous local stone carvers. The first chapel to the left features Titian's ethereal *The Assumption of the Virgin.* The arch to the left of the facade leads to a picturesque cloister where the remains of an early Christian basilica are visible. The **Biblioteca Capitolare** (tel. 59 65 16), the oldest library in Europe, has a priceless medieval manuscript collection, which you can see if you convince the priest you're serious. (Library open Mon., Wed. and Sat. 9:30am-12:30pm, Tues. and Fri. 9:30am-12:30pm and 4-6pm. Cathedral open daily 7am-noon and 3-7pm.)

Across the Adige (over the Roman Ponte Pietra) is the recently uncovered **Teatro Romano** (tel. 800 03 60), where Shakespearean plays are now performed. The theater was built during the Augustan and Flavian years at the foot of what is today called St. Peter's Hill. The site also incorporates the **archeological museum** (tel. 339 74). The Romans had a fortress on the hilltop; the castle now standing dates from the nineteenth century and was built by the French and Austrians. There's a wonderful view of Verona from up here, especially in the evening. (Complex open Tues.-Sun. 8am-6:45pm, in off-season only until 2pm. Admission L3000.)

At the bottom of the hill, the Interrato dell' Acqua Morta leads to the fifteenth-century **Church of Santa Maria in Organo.** Although Sammicheli made a significant contribution to the facade, the most delicate inlay work was completed by Giovanni da Verona. Behind the church on via S. M. in Organo lies the splendid **Giardino Giusti,** a wonderful eighteenth-century garden great for picnics. (Open daily 9am-8pm. Admission L4000.)

The della Scala fortress, the **Castelvecchio** (tel. 288 17 or 59 47 34), was carefully reconstructed after decimation during the last war. (Napoleon used the original medieval castle as a barracks.) An extensive collection of sculptures and paintings is exhibited in a well-restored interior of many levels, walkways, and parapets. Intriguing works include Pisanello's *Madonna and Child* and Luca di Leyda's *Crucifixion,* which balances passion and compositional rhythm. There are also works by Andrea Mantegna, Francesco Morone, Tintoretto, and Tiepolo. (Open Tues.-Sun. 7:30am-7:30pm. Admission L3000.) The **Scaligeri Bridge** that crosses over the Adige River from the *castello* to p. Sacco e Vanzetti is the most impressive of the 15 bridges spanning the river. **Piazza Sacco e Vanzetti** commemorates the two Italian immigrants executed in the U.S. in 1927, allegedly for murder but more likely for their anarchist sympathies.

The Renaissance came to Verona with Andrea Mantegna, who arrived from Tuscany in the mid-fifteenth century. His greatest legacy is the altarpiece in the **Church of San Zeno Maggiore.** The work has also had great appeal for thieves. Napoleon took it to Paris and left bits of it throughout France, and in 1973 it was stolen but recovered. Pay to light it up—the positioning makes it hard to see its splendid color on all but the brightest days. The church's large, simple brick Romanesque construction is beautiful, outshone only by the eleventh-century bronze doors. Interspersed in the interior's two-story apse are twelfth-century carvings with capitals from Roman temples. (Open daily 7am-noon and 3-7pm.)

Entertainment

Verona has parlayed the romance of its pervasive rosy marble and vast Roman arena into the city's premier cultural event. The not-so-ruined ruins come alive July and August in a riot of opera and ballet. In 1988 the operas *La Gioconta, Aida,* and *Turandot* and the ballet *Zorba il Greco* were staged. Ticket prices are quite high, starting at L15,000 for unreserved gallery seats. Some tickets are usually held until an hour before the performance, but reserve tickets in advance by going to the box office under arch #6 of the arena. (Open Mon.-Fri. 8:40am-12:20pm and 3-5:50pm, Sat. 8:40am-12:20pm.) You can also write with a bank draft or check to Ente Lirico, Arena di Verona, p. Brà, 28, 37100 Verona. No tickets are available by phone. (Concert tickets information tel. 235 20, 222 65, or 386 71.) For more detailed information, go to the **Ufficio Stampa,** at via Roma, off p. Brà on the second floor. (Open Mon.-Sat. 9am-12:30pm.)

The **Teatro Romano** produces Shakespeare every summer—a bit strange in Italian, but the setting is wonderful and the price right: L8000 for the cheapest seats. They also stage musical events such as jazz and ballet. Try to reserve ahead. (At arch #8. Open from mid-June Mon.-Sat. 10am-noon and 3:30-7pm. For information tel. 92 91 11, for reservations call 59 06 89; or write to Arcovolo 8 dell' Arena.) The evening *passeggiata* takes place down the Listone, in p. Brà.

Friuli-Venezia Giulia

I have always been sorry that such a beautiful Italian land has never been taken into consideration . . .
—Carlo Goldoni

This eighteenth-century dramatist's words hold true today; Friuli-Venezia Giulia is strangely underrecognized, known primarily by Trieste, its cultural and transportation center. The new resorts on the Adriatic Sea, such as Lignano Sabbiadoro and Grado, however, attract more and more tourists to their long, sandy beaches.The lush Tagliamento River Valley, between Udine and Pordenone, is a fecund area noted for its ham and dairy products. The Corniche (Carnia Alps) to the north and the Julian Alps to the east offer hiking, climbing, and skiing.

With a name befitting its complicated genealogy, Friuli-Venezia Giulia was formed after World War II from the provinces of Udine, Pordenone, Gorizia, and Trieste. After successive invasions by Romans, Goths, and Lombards had each left their mark upon the region, the local clergy unified around the Patriarchate of Aquileia and maintained autonomy from the sixth to the fifteenth centuries. The entire region was then appropriated by the Venetian Empire, only to be reabsorbed, Venetians and all, into Austria-Hungary. Tied to the culture of the Balkan Peninsula, these provinces were devastated by the two World Wars; the region suffered the savagery of Great Power politics, only to be decisively separated from its eastern neighbors.

Literature, however, has already found its place here. James Joyce lived in Trieste for 12 years, during which he wrote the bulk of *Ulysses,* and Ernest Hemingway's *A Farewell to Arms* draws its plot from the region's role in the World War I. Novelist Italo Suevo and Jewish poet Umberto Suba also hailed from these northern reaches.

Trieste

Trieste, with a long and turbulent history, experiences hard times once again. Formerly the largest port of the Adriatic and a thriving doorway to the Austro-Hungarian Empire, the city was a dynamic melting pot. Many citizens were fluent in Italian, Serbo-Croatian, German, and often Hungarian. The city is peppered with the enormous neoclassical monuments of the imperial golden age; but that era eludes memory. Today, this impersonal port is an anticlimax to the inviting countryside.

The impact of two world wars and the intervening Fascist period is more evident in Trieste's gargantuan war monuments than anywhere else in the nation. Italy's acquisition of the city during World War I was followed by brutal suppression of non-Italian culture by the Mussolini government. Despite the institution of bilingual schools and street signs, the Slovene minority still glances longingly over the Yugoslav border. World War II, which many Westerners remember as a great victory, is referred to locally as "the Disastrous Great War." Trieste has not yet adjusted to its catastrophic separation from the Austro-Hungarian Empire, and its well-being remains perilously dependent on border trade with modern Yugoslavia.

Stroll along the gray, industrialized quays to piazza Unita d'Italia, or climb to the top of the Capitoline Hill for a splendid view of the city and coastline. Trieste is an ideal place to launch an expedition down the Yugoslavian coastline. Depending on your nationality, you may need a visa to do this. Check at home first, or go to your consulate here.

Orientation and Practical Information

Trieste is a direct train ride from Venice or Udine. Five buses per day leave from just outside the station for Rijeka, Yugoslavia (Italians still insist upon calling it Fiume). From Rijeka, a ferry makes stops at virtually all the Yugoslavian ports and eventually at Corfu and Igoumenitsa in Greece. (Departures year-round Sun. at 6pm; in summer 2 additional boats: July 8-Aug. 26 Mon. at 6pm and July 3-Sept. 9 Wed. at 10:30pm.) The trip along the coast is wonderful, though the deck gets crowded in summer. Yugoslavian boats, in general, are less expensive than Italian ones. From Trieste, boats run east along the Istria Peninsula (see Near Trieste), stopping at small towns along the way and finally winding up at Pula. To reach downtown from the train station, walk along vie Cellini and Ghega and through p. Dalmazia to **piazza Oberdan.** The main drag, **Via Carducci,** runs between p. Obertan and Garibaldi in the east. Trieste's principal square is belligerently-named **piazza Unita D'Italia.**

Everything in Trieste except public services closes on Monday, except some occasional morning hours.

Azienda Autonoma di Soggiornoe Turismo: In the train station (tel. 42 01 82), in a cubbyhole on the right of the building, facing the city's major road. Helpful and gracious, if scatter-brained. Copious information on Trieste, listing of *manifestazioni* (cultural events). Yugoslavian excursions and travel to the rest of Italy. James Joyce fanatics can try to cajole the staff into digging up the last surviving copy of a Joycean walking tour, which points out most of his personal hangouts. English spoken. Open June-Sept. Mon.-Sat. 9am-1pm and 4-7pm; Oct.-May Mon.-Sat. 8am-2pm.

Travel Agency: Aurora Viaggia, via Milano, 20 (tel. 613 00 or 602 61), between corso Cavour and via Carducci. Information on transportation and lodging in Yugoslavia. Open Mon.-Fri. 9am-12:30pm and 4-7pm, Sat. 9am-noon. **CST:** p. Dalmazia (tel. 65 60 8), at the head of via Carducci. Student IDs and travel information. Open Mon.-Fri. 9am-12:30pm and 3-6pm, Sat. 9am-noon.

Consulates: The U.S. no longer has a consulate in Trieste, but it does have a representative at via dei Pellegrini, 42 (tel. 91 17 80). **U.K.,** vicolo delle Ville, 16 (tel. 30 28 84). **Yugoslavia,** Strata del Friuli, 54 (tel. 41 01 25).

Currency Exchange: Banca d'America e d'Italia, via Roma, 7 (tel. 63 19 25). Cashes Visa cards. Open Mon.-Fri. 8:20am-1:20pm and 2:45-3:45pm.

Post Office: p. Vittorio Veneto, 1 (tel. 680 78), along via Roma, the 2nd right off via Ghega coming from the train station. Ferma Posta at counter #21, stamps at #30. Open Mon.-Sat. 8:05am-7:30pm. **Postal code:** 34122.

Telephones: SIP, viale XX Settembre. Open daily 8am-9:30pm. **ASST,** via Pascoli, 9, off p. Garibaldi. Open 24 hours. Phones also at the station. **Telephone code:** 040.

Train Station: p. della Libertà (tel. 41 82 07), northwest of the center along the water. Frequent trains to Udine (1¼ hr.; one-way L4200, round-trip L7200), Venice (2½ hr.; one-way L7800, round-trip L13,400), and Latisana, the train station nearest Lignano-Sabbiadoro (1 hr.; one-way L3700, round-trip L6200).

Buses: corso Cavour (tel. 681 03), near the train station.

Ferries: Agemar, p. Duca degli Abruzzi, 1 (tel. 606 26). **Agemar Viaggi,** around the corner (tel. 690 21), is their travel agent and will arrange your trip. To Pula, Yugoslavia (early June to mid-Sept. Thurs.-Tues., March and mid-Sept. to mid-Dec. Thurs. and Sun.; L14,500), Grado (L4500), and Rovigno (L11,500). **Viatur,** via del'Orologio, 1 (tel. 778 52 05. Open Mon.-Fri. 9am-noon and 3:30-7pm, Sat. 9am-noon). To Venice (June through mid-Sept. 3 per month) and Greece.

Car Rental: Hertz, via Mazzini, 1 (tel. 606 50). Fri. 2pm-Mon. 9am L120,000, with unlimited mileage. Open Mon.-Fri. 8am-noon and 3-7pm, Sat. 8am-12:30pm.

Swimming Pool: Piscina Communale "Bruno Bianchi," riva Gulli, 3 (tel. 30 60 24), along the waterfront. Indoor.

Public Baths: In front of the train station. Showers L4000. Open Mon.-Tues. and Thurs.-Sat. 8am-6pm, Sun. 8am-noon.

Laundromat: via Ginnastica, 36 (tel. 74 18 34). Open Mon.-Thurs. 7:30am-1:30pm, Fri. 7:30am-1:30pm and 4-7pm.

Hospital: For **medical emergency,** tel. 77 63. For **ambulance,** tel. 688 88.

Police: Questura, via Teatro Romano (tel. 603 11), off corso Italia.

Accommodations

Pensione Venezia, via Genova, 23 (tel. 684 80), off riva Tre Novembre. Run by a pleasant family. Spacious and pristine. Singles L18,000. Doubles L25,000. Triples L33,000. Showers L1000.

Pensione Centro, via Roma, 13 (tel. 644 08), 1 block before the canal. From the station, take via Ghega. Immaculate rooms with high ceilings, a pretty pink den, and Smurf posters. English spoken. Singles L15,000. Doubles L26,000. Showers (in morning only) L2000.

Pensione San Nicolò, via San Nicolò, 2 (tel. 645 45), off riva Tre Novembre. Rarely available singles L14,000. Doubles L24,000. Showers L2000.

Camping

The nearest **campgrounds** are in Opicina, a suburb on the rocky Carso overlooking the city, and Sistiana, a cliffside perch five minutes from decent beaches.

Buses leave for Sistiana every hour (L1500), but hitchhiking is quicker and easier: The road to Sistiana begins alongside the train station. **Camping Marepineta** (tel. (040) 29 92 64), along the coast, provides beachside luxury. (L8000-10,000 per tent and/or car, L4500-5500 per person. Hot water, electricity, and a bar included. Open May-Sept.) Alongside the campground is a pretty little 2-kilometer trail billed as the **Rilke Sentiere** after Rilke, who lived in **Duino,** the village at the other end of the trail. (Consult Ingeborg Hoesterey for more information on this and other German lyricists.) Duino guards the exotic old ruins of a **castle.**

Trains travel from p. Oberdan in Trieste to Opicina, a sparsely beautiful place to camp for those not umbilicaly attached to the beach. **Camping Obelisco** (tel. (040) 21 16 55), near the huge obelisk visible from the coast, charges L1500 to 2500 per tent and L2500 to L3000 per person.

Food

Many dishes in Trieste's restaurants have an Eastern European edge (usually Hungarian) and are loaded with paprika. The city is renowned for its fish; try *sardoni in savor* (large sardines marinated in oil and garlic). Monday is a non-day in Trieste, as many shops and restaurants close down. To fend for yourself, visit one of the several supermarkets on via Carducci. The **market** sells great produce and horrid clothes in p. Ponterosso, by the canal. (Open Tues.-Sat. 8am-7pm.)

Pizzeria Barattolo, p. San Antonio, 2 (tel. 614 80), along the canal. Amazing pizza (L3000-6000), also a bar, and *tavola calda* offerings. Open Tues.-Sun. 8am-1am.

Hostaria El Gaucho, viale XX Settembre, 59 (tel. 57 77 44), past the Teatro Politeama. Revitalize your over-pasta-fed taste buds with a Mexican *comida.* Tacos L8000. Rice with corn, shrimp, and more L4500. Service 10%. Open Mon.-Sat. noon-2pm and 7pm-2am.

Paninoteca Da Livio, via della Ginnastica, 3/B, inland off via Carducci. Small shop but monster *panini* (L2000-4000), dozens of brands of beer, and hordes of comrades. Open Mon.-Sat. 8:30am-3pm and 5-10pm.

Mini Pub, via della Ginnastica, 46A, off via Carducci. A bit of a hike. Anglothematic—lots of wood, low lights—without the pretensions. A focus on the essentials: beer, beer, and *more beer!* (L1500-2500). *Panini* about L3000. Open Wed.-Mon. noon-2pm and 7-11pm.

La Massaia Gastronomica, on via Carducci at via Ginnastica. A take-out gourmet deli. Sublime but reasonable. Most dishes L1500-3000 per *etto.* Open Tues.-Sat. 8am-2pm and 4-7:30pm, Sun. 8am-1pm.

Sights

Nineteenth-century Viennese urban planners mutilated a large chunk of Trieste to create borgo Teresiano, a district of straight avenues bordering the waterfront and the canal. Facing the canal from the south is the district's one beautiful church, the Serbian Orthodox **San Spirideone.** Cyrillic lettering and powder-blue domes testify to the city's diverse past. Unfortunately, the church is imprisoned within a steel barricade, so you'll probably have to admire it from the outside. Some eclectic nineteenth-century Viennese architecture makes the area intriguing; the **Municipio** at the head of **piazza dell' Unità d'Italia,** a monument to the limits of ambition, sags under the weight of its own heavy architectural ornamentation and oversized tower. The *piazza* is the largest in Italy; in its corner stands an allegorical fountain with statues representing the four continents. The surreal effect is completed by the eerie old stone warehouses rotting slowly along the waterfront toward the station. The area turns spooky after dark.

The fifteenth-century Venetian **Fortress of San Giusto,** named after the city's patron saint, presides over **Capitoline Hill,** the city's historic center. You can take bus #24 (L600) from the station to the last stop at the fortress, and ascend the hill by climbing the monumental Scala Dei Giganti (over 250 steps), rising from p. Goldini. From the walls of the fortress you'll have a fantastic view of everything for miles around. Facing the sea from the west tower, you can see downtown Trieste to your right and Yugoslavia to your left. Within the walls is a huge outdoor theater where film festivals are held in the summer—an amusing way to improve your Italian. Directly below are the remains of the old Roman city center, and across the street is the restored **Cathedral of San Giusto.** Its irregular plan is due to its origins as two churches built simultaneously from the fifth to the eleventh centuries, one to San Giusto, the other to Santa Maria Assunta. Go inside to admire two splendid mosaics in the chapels directly to the left and right of the altar. The wild piece of statuary tucked up against the Roman *piazza* exemplifies Fascist taste. (The building now serves as the administrative headquarters of the provincial tourist offices).

Continue down the other side of the hill past the *duomo* to the eclectic **Museo di Storia ed Arte e Orto Lapidario** (Museum of History and Art and Rock Garden; tel. 725 316) in p. Cattedrale, with prehistoric material from the Giulia region, Greek and Roman sculpture, and Egyptian antiquities. The museum's most treasured pieces are a rhyton (goblet), sculpted in the shape of a deer's head, and a bronze wine-vessel, both from Tarentum (5th century B.C.E.). (Open Tues.-Sun. 9am-1pm. Admission L1000, students with ID L500.)

Below the museum lies the **Teatro Romano.** Walk toward via Donota, which is the continuation of via Cattedrale and via Monache, and you'll be able to wander around the *teatro* and see the beautiful Chiesa di San Giovanni from the street. You can take minibus #24 from the station, but the walk is preferable to the bus ride and inspiring at sunset. Descending the hill towards the *teatro,* you end up only a few short blocks from p. Unità d'Italia.

A delightful collection of drawings and paintings by Tiepolo, Veneziano, and others has recently been moved from the Capitoline Hill to the **Museo Sartorio,** largo

Papa Giovanni XXIII (tel. 30 14 79), a few minutes from the center and most easily reached by walking along the quays. (Open Tues.-Sun. 9am-1pm.)

Entertainment

The regular opera season of the **Teatro Verdi** extends from November to April, but a six-week operetta season is held July and August. Get tickets (L20,000-35,000) at p. Verdi, 1 (tel. 63 19 48), or make reservations at Bigletteria Centrale, Galleria Protti, 2, 34121 Trieste (tel. 683 11). There are frequent performances of music and dance in the castle during the summer, when the **Teatro Romano** stages works by Plautus and Euripides as well as modern authors.

Italian fashion is high on the shopping lists of Yugoslavs and Austrians, who make daytrips to nearby Trieste to buy Italian goods. Opportunistic capitalists have packed the streets with cheap buys: corso Italia, via Roma, via Carducci, and viale XX Settembre.

Caffé Tommaseo, in p. Tommaseo along the canal, and **Caffé San Marco,** on via Battisti, cling to the city's turn-of-the-century cafe culture. The *passegiata* is liveliest along viale XX Settembre. Youths exhausted from the evening's show-and-tell reward themselves with pasta-shaped ice cream at **Gelateria Zampoli** along the corso. (Open Tues.-Sun. 8am-midnight.)

Near Trieste

West of Trieste you can sunbathe along the rocky coast and visit the **Castello Miramare,** the elegant castle of Hapsburg Emperor Franz Joseph of Austria. Spread on a high promontory overlooking the sea, Miramare was built between 1855 and 1860 and is easily visible from the Capitoline Hill in Trieste (see above). The villa is bathed in colored lights on Tuesday, Thursday, and Saturday nights in summer. (Open Tues.-Sat. 9:30am-1pm and 2:30-6pm. Admission L3500. Parks and gardens open daily 8am-7pm.) Psychedelic sound and light shows enliven the park of the castle in July and August (L5000); the 9:30pm show on Tuesdays is in English. Take bus #6 west from the north side of the train station to Barcola, then change to #36 (a ½-hr. trip). There exist plenty of places to hop off for a swim on the way to the villa.

For cosmic **camping,** take bus #36 for about 10 minutes until it starts to leave the coast. Get off and find viale Miramare, 325. Opposite this building is a roofed-over platform used for swimming and diving. At night it is deserted, and travelers sack out here, with a solid roof over their heads, the waves at their feet, cold water and showers, and invisibility from the road. It's a snug spot during the thunder-showers that often strike at night. About 15km from Trieste is the spectacular Grotta Gigante, the world's largest accessible cave. Despite the superlatives used to describe the site, it has yet to be infested by tourists. (Open April-Sept. 9am-noon and 2-7pm; Nov.-Feb. 10am-noon and 2:30-4:30pm; March and Oct. 9am-noon and 2-5pm.)

From just south of Trieste, Yugoslavia's **Istrian Peninsula** extends out into the Adriatic. Boats leave for Istria daily at 8am from Trieste's Bersaglieri wharf (2 blocks beyond p. Unità d'Italia, on the right side of the wharf coming from the street). Most of the Istrian towns are under four hours away by boat. The small and well-preserved harbor town of **Poreč** (boats April-June 8 Thurs.-Sat., June 9-Sept. 15 Tues.-Sat.; 2½ hr.; L10,500) has an impressive sixteenth-century basilica. The resort **Rovinj** (boats April-June 8 Sat.-Sun, June 9-Sept. 15 Fri.-Sun.; 3½ hr.; L11,500) harbors a beach and secluded nudist campground. From nearby Obula Pino Budicia, another ferry leaves for **Crveni Otok,** which hosts the nicest beaches in the region and an excellent campground. The last stop, on the southern tip of Istria, is the old Roman city of **Pula,** which has an incredibly intact amphitheater and a good archeological museum. In summer, all return ferries leave the respective towns after 2pm on the same day of the trip from Trieste and arrive back at Bersaglieri between 7 and 9pm. (For more information, see Ferries or Travel Agency under Practical Information, or call the Yugoslavian travel agency **Rompass** at (0038) 677 21 01.

Aquileia and Grado

In its heyday (200 B.C.E to 452 C.E.), Aquileia flourished as the Roman capital of the northern Adriatic region. Later the city rose as a patriarchal seat, successfully defying the Popes until it faded into obscurity in the High Renaissance. Today, Aquileia is one of the country's most pristine treasure chests of Roman remains and early Christian art, and though on first impression it may appear deserted, there still remain about 3000 hospitable inhabitants. Buses leave hourly (every 10 min., L800) from the train station Cevignano on the Venice-Trieste rail line. The town is also an hour's bus excursion from Udine.

The helpful **tourist office** (open unreliably April-Oct. daily 9am-noon and 3:30-6pm) and the **basilica** lie on opposite sides of p. Capitolo, ½ block from the bus stop. The Roman fourth-century mosaic floor covers 700 square meters with geometric designs and realistic bestial depictions. In the crypt beneath the altar are soulful, twelfth-century frescoes, especially the *Deposition* to the right of the altar. (Open daily 7am-8pm. Admission L200.) The **Cripta degli Scavi,** entered by a small door to the left of the main portal, is remarkable for its three levels of mosaics: some from a pavement contemporary with that of the basilica, others from a Roman house (near the entrance), and others from another basilica altogether. (Open Mon. 9am-2pm, Tues.-Sat. 9am-6:30pm, Sun. 9am-1pm.)

The most spectacular ruins in town are the massive limestone blocks of the **Roman harbor,** now left behind by the receding waters. Scattered nearby are excavations of the impressive public buildings of the Roman stronghold: the forum, the amphitheater, the baths, and the mausoleum. The **archeological museum** on via Roma (tel. 910 16) has an impressive collection of Roman sculpture, mosaics, glass, and other artifacts found in the area. (Open Tues.-Sat. 9am-6:30pm, Sun. 9am-1pm and 3-6:30pm. Admission L3000.) To see every last mosaic in town, go to the **Museo Paleocristiano** (tel. 911 31), near the campground. (Open Tues.-Sat. 9am-6:30pm, Sun. 9am-1pm and 3-6:30pm. Free.)

Camping Aquileia, via Gemina, 10 (tel. (0431) 910 42 in summer; 910 37 in winter) is a shady spot with a swimming pool near the forum. Walk to the right behind the basilica and down the cypress-lined alley to shack up there for L3500 per person and L5000 per site. (Open May 15-Sept. 15.) **Albergo Roma,** via Roma, 28 (tel. (0431) 910 08), past the archeological museum, offers the least expensive rooms in town. (Singles L21,000. Doubles L40,500. Sept. to mid-June singles L18,000; doubles L34,000.)

If you wondered about the dearth of tourists in Aquileia, get back on the bus for about 10km and you'll find out where they all are.

Grado, an ancient island outpost of Aquileia, is today a booming beach resort. In summer, the ferry from Trieste (1½ hr., L3800) to Yugoslavia's Istrian Peninsula stops here at 9:30am on its way to Istria and then at 5:30pm on its way back. (June 9-Sept. 15 Tues. and Fri.-Sun.; see Ferries under Trieste.)

Grado's **tourist office** is at viale Dante, 72 (tel. (0431) 800 35), near the entrance to the beach. (Open daily 8am-1pm and 4-7pm.) Grado is serious about its tourist industry: The few reasonably priced *pensioni* often require full pension. Try **Alla Laguna,** via Manzoni, 24 (tel. (0431) 803 41), where full pension is L41,000 (obligatory mid-June to Sept.) Singles are L15,000; doubles L26,500.

Lignano-Sabbiadoro

Twenty years ago Lignano-Sabbiadoro was empty save for a spectacular 9-kilometer beach. Today, its astute tourist board has been so industrious that in season, the once picturesque city is overrun by tourists, and the strand crowded with parasols and pedal boats. Go to Lignano to sunbathe and swim, but not to pick up local culture—it's non-existent. Most visitors are Austrian, and the town is virtually bilingual.

Orientation and Practical Information

The resort is actually a peninsula, with Lignano-Sabbiadoro at the eastern end and Lignano-Pineta and Lignano-Riviera farther west. The frequent trains on the Venice-Trieste line will deposit you at the town of **Latisana.** When you walk out of its station, go straight 2 blocks and on your left you will find the Bar Rossitto, where you can buy an SGEA ticket to Lignano (every hr.; 25 min.; L1800, round-trip L3200).

Azienda Autonoma di Turismo: In Sabbiadoro, via Latisana, 42 (tel. 718 21). In **Pineta,** via dei Pini, 53 (tel. 42 70 09). Zealous and efficient. Good free map. An essential stop for accommodations in high season. Open June-Aug. daily 9am-7pm; Sept.-May Mon.-Fri. 8am-2pm.

Post Office: In Sabbiadoro, viale Gorizia, 37. Open Mon.-Fri. 8:10am-6:15pm, Sat. 8:10am-1pm. In Pineta, p. Rosa dei Venti. Open Mon.-Fri. 8am-2pm, Sat. 8am-12:30pm. **Postal code:** 33054.

Telephones: SIP, In Sabbiadoro, via Codroipo, 9. In Pineta, raggio dell' Ostra, 8. Both open daily 8am-midnight. Public telephones in bars and hotels are marked on the tourist office's map, which is posted around town. **Telephone code:** 0431.

Bus Station: Ferrari SGEA (tel. 713 73) and city buses leave from viale Gorizia, 28. From Lignano, there is frequent bus service to Udine (L3300). **ATVO** buses leave from via Verona, 10 (tel. 700 69). To Milan (3 per day, L28,000) and Verona (3 per day, L19,000). Round-trip bus-boat excursion to Venice (1 per day, 3 hr., L14,000).

Bike Rental: Graziella, via Friuli, 16 (no phone). L1500 per ½-hr., L5000 per 2 hr., L8,000 per day. Hourly rate available only on weekends. Tandems L3000 per ½-hr., L5000 per hr. Motorcycles too. Leave an important document as deposit. Open May-Sept. daily 8:30am-midnight.

Free Showers: Along the beach outside.

First Aid: parco San Giovanni Bosco, 20/A, on the beach in Sabbiadoro.

Police: viale Europa, 26 (tel. 700 21).

Accommodations

Forget arriving unannounced in Lignano from August 1-20. If you do, arrive at the tourist office before 10am to swoop down on cancelations.

In off-season (May-June and Sept.), the weather is beautiful and mild, and Lignano is one of the cheapest beach resorts in the world. Most places offer much better deals if you take full or half-pension and stay at least three days. The city virtually closes down in winter.

Pensione Amalfi, via Udine, 80 (tel. 715 33), 1 block east of the town center. Both this place and the next one are large, impersonal, and cheap. Close to the beach. Singles L18,000. Doubles L31,000. In off-season: Singles L16,000; doubles L28,000. Showers L2000. Open May 15-Sept. 15.

Albergo Graziosa, via Latisana, 70 (tel. 716 88), 2 blocks east of the tourist office. Neat, attractive, and modern. A step up in both price and atmosphere. Price goes down L2000 after the 1st night. Singles L19,000. Doubles L33,800. In off-season: Singles L18,000; doubles L32,000. Showers included. Pleasant breakfast L2000. Open May-Sept.

Pensione Ornella, via Adriatica, 11 (tel. 712 62), off viale Venezia, about 5 blocks east of the tourist office. Airy and spotless. Singles L25,000. Doubles L42,000. In off-season: Singles L20,000; doubles L32,000. Breakfast and bath included. Open May-Sept.

Camping

Camping is not a bad deal in the off-season or if you're planning to stay at least three days with a group of two or more people. Each of the campgrounds has an absurdly complicated price system. Those listed below are approximate high-season prices. All rates include showers.

Camping Sabbiadoro, via Sabbiadoro, 8 (tel. 714 55), about halfway to L. Pineta. The most expensive and centrally located. L10,500 per site, L6500 per person. 4-person bungalows L36,000-85,000. Open May-Sept.

Camping Pino Mare, Lignano Rivera (tel. 42 85 12 or 42 84 54), on the beach. At the far eastern end of the peninsula, closest to Latisana. L6500 per person, L5100 per tent. Bungalows L35,000 (3 people), L46,000 (for 4); in off-season L17,000 (for 3), L23,000 (for 4). Open May 10-Sept. 20.

Food and Entertainment

Food prices here, even for groceries, are like balloons—inflated. Inexpensive alternatives to pizza and sandwiches are the numerous *tavole calde* and *gastronomie* catering to beachgoers—better than your average beach vendor and less pricey than your average sit-down meal.

Discos and travel agencies threaten to take over every last building in Lignano. The former have hefty cover charges of L10,000-15,000 (less on weeknights). Try dancing on the beach at the **Terrazza a Mare** in a funky, otherworldly building. The travel agencies offer surprisingly cheap "day-and-night tours," whirlwind expeditions into Friulia, Yugoslavia, and Venice. Also look into the officially subsidized boat-and-bus tours of Friulia (L18,000) at the tourist office, as well as their *free* boat-trips on Mondays.

For further amusement, visit the **Luna Park** (fair) on via Centrale next to the big garage, or **Aqua Splash,** "the biggest park of watergames in Europe," on viale Europa.

Udine

Those who venture here will congratulate themselves on their unorthodox itinerary: Udine is an unexpectedly captivating town. Not quite as Austrian as the bilingual cities to the north, not quite as central European as Trieste 70km to the east, and not typically Italian, Udine is *Friuli* (that is, Friulian). The local dialect owes something to Serbo-Croatian and to German, but is legitimately independent.

The city has had a much calmer history than nearby Trieste; it was the seat of the Roman Catholic Patriarch of Aquileia from 1238 to 1751, conquered by the Venetians, ceded to the Austrians in the late eighteenth century, and finally joined the young Italian nation in 1866. The disastrous earthquake Udine suffered in 1976 induced amazing harmony—everything is either new or recently renovated.

Orientation and Practical Information

Udine is about 1½ hours by train from both Venice and Trieste; trains run in both directions about once every two hours. The train and bus stations are a couple of hundred meters from each other and are both on viale Europa Unità in the southern part of town. Bus #1 runs from viale Europa Unità straight up to the center of town. You can also make the 15-minute walk. From the station, go right around the bus station and take via Aquileia under the arches to the center of town. When you hit via Piave, about 5 blocks up the road, a right turn will take you directly to the tourist office.

Azienda Autonoma di Turismo: via Piave, 27 (tel. 29 59 72). From p. Libertà, take via Veneto 3 blocks, and turn left. Wonderful maps and information on both the city and province. Open Mon.-Fri. 8:30am-1pm and 2:30-6pm, Sat. 8:30am-1pm.

Student Travel: Turismo Universitario, via Aquileia, 50 (tel. 211 55), off the main road between the train station and downtown. Don't let the shabby alley intimidate. Ad hoc, but very friendly. Open Sept.-July Mon.-Fri. 4:30-7pm.

Post Office: via V. Veneto, 42 (tel. 50 19 93). A splendiferous office. Open Mon.-Sat. 8:15am-7:40pm. Fermo Posta (L2500 per letter) and stamps through the left door at desk #9. **Postal code:** 33100.

Telephones: SIP, via Piave, 17 (tel. 27 81), a few doors down from the tourist office. Open daily 9am-9pm. **Telephone code:** 0432.

Train Station: viale Europa Unità (tel. 20 89 69). To Venice (26 per day, 2 hr., L6900), Trieste (16 per day, 70 min.-2 hr., L4400), Palmanova, the place with the nifty medieval walls (12 per day, ½ hr., round-trip L1800), and Vienna (4 per day, 7 hr., L48,500).

Buses: viale Europa Unità (tel. 20 39 41), 1 block to the right of the train station as you exit. Comprehensive and efficient service throughout Friuli-Venezia Giulia. To Trieste (9 per day, 1 hr., L3300), Venice (2 hr., L5700 if you take the 7am or 3pm bus; 1½ hr., L8000 if you leave at 11:25pm), Lignano (5 per day, 1 hr., L3300), and Cividale (8 per day, ½ hr., L1400).

Mountaineering: The bulletin board of the Società Alpina Friuliana is under the arcades of the city hall, at the base of via Mercato Vecchio. Information on upcoming trips and skiing. The English-speaking director of the Società Guide can be reached at home (tel. 66 02 77).

Swimming Pool: Piscina Comunale, via Ampezzo, 4 (tel. 269 67), to the northwest. Open mid-Sept. through May and mid-June through Aug. Mon.-Sat. 2-7pm, Sun. 10am-noon and 2-7pm. Admission L2000, children L1000.

Day Hotel: Centro Estetico Diurno, viale Europa Unita, 31 (tel. 29 28 00), 1 block from the train station to the right as you exit. Showers L5000, baths L7000. Saunas L20,000. Open Mon.-Sat. 8am-7:30pm.

Hospital: Ospedale Civile, p. S. Maria d. Misercordia (tel. 49 91). Take bus #1 north to the last stop. **Ambulance:** Tel. 451 55.

Police: Questura, via della Prefettura, 16 (tel. 50 28 41).

Accommodations

First the good news: The large map outside the train station is clearly marked with the locations of Udine's hotels, and some are steals. The bad news: Workers have probably taken the best spots long ago. (Campers should see Camping under Trieste.)

Albergo Manin, via Manin, 5 (tel. 50 11 46). Finely furnished rooms in a spotless old building. Just off the main *piazza* and cheap for a group of at least 2. Singles L19,000. Doubles L32,000. Groups L15,000 per person. Showers included. Often full Aug.-Sept.

Da Arturo, via Pracchiuso, 75 (tel. 20 52 62), a bit out of the center on a street off p. I. Maggio. Clean and functional. Popular with workers. Most windows boast a splendid view of a hallway. Single L12,000. Doubles L24,000. Showers included. Open Aug.-July 15.

Albergo Piccolo Friuli, via Magrini, 9 (tel. 29 08 17), just before the Museo D'Arti Populari. Tale via Cavour west to via G. Muratti. A luxury hotel, with private bath, TV, and refrigerated bar in room. All in a refurbished old building. Singles L26,200. Doubles L42,000.

Albergo Clocchiatti, via Cividale, 29 (tel. 50 50 47), 5 min. from Da Arturo straight across p. Oberdan. Beautiful, well-kept rooms—feels like a Swiss chalet. Singles L20,000, with bath L25,000. Doubles L30,000, with bath L35,000.

Food

A pastiche of earthy Italian, Austrian, and Slovene, Udinese cuisine tends more toward the hearty than the *haute.* A typical regional specialty is *brovada e muselo,* a stew made of marinated turnips and boiled sausage.

For those arriving famished in Udine, **Al Tutto Buono,** a *pizzeria/gastronomia/*deli extraordinaire, is just a few steps from the station at via Roma, 52-58. (Open Tues. and Thurs.-Sat. 8am-1pm and 4-7:30pm, Mon. and Wed. 8am-1pm.) Don't miss the great *pasticceria* next door for bread and dessert. The restaurant in the station is also better than most for an inexpensive, warm sit-down meal (L13,000).

Get your ice cream at **Gelateria Panciera** (tel. 20 47 49), under the northern arcades of city hall, where a mere L600 buys you a delectable scoop. (Open Dec.-Oct. Sat.-Thurs. 8am-midnight.) On Thursdays visit the **open-air market** on via Riccordo di Giusto, off via Aquiela, and on Saturdays on via Liruti, past p. 1° Maggio. (Both open 8am-noon.) A supermarket (COOP) lies on via Europa Unità at Aquileia. (Open Tues. and Thurs.-Sat. 8:30am-1pm and 4:15-7:30pm, Mon. and Wed. 8:30am-1pm.)

Da Arturo, via Pracchiuso, 75 (see Accommodations). A scrumptious, reasonable neighborhood *trattoria.* L13,000 *menù* includes *primo, secondo,* and *contorno.* Open Aug. 15-July 15 Tues.-Sun. noon-2pm and 7-10pm.

Spaghetti House, via Zara, 11 (tel. 29 12 25). Use the entrance on via Cividale next to Albergo Clocchiati after 11pm. Over 20 different types of spaghetti doled out generously (L4000-6000). Also a fun place for late-night ice cream. Open Tues.-Sun. noon-3pm and 5:30pm-2am.

Moretti Stazione, via Roma, 60 (tel. 29 38 97), opposite the station. Decent hot sandwiches (L1500) and pizza (L3000). Open Wed.-Mon. 7am-midnight.

Sights and Entertainment

The free booklet *Udine: Eight Itineraries* is a great guide to the city. If you can read Italian, also ask about the booklet *Vedifriuli,* a guide to all of Friulia.

The center of Udine, at the foot of the hill, is **piazza della Libertà,** an elegant green *piazza.* Along its higher side runs the graceful **Arcade of San Giovanni,** built in 1523. The clock tower that surmounts the arcade is itself topped with two bronze Moors who strike the hours. These figures, like the two symbolic columns of Venice in the *piazza,* were erected in towns that the Venetian Republic conquered. Across the *piazza* in Udine stands the delicate, Venetian style **Loggia del Lionello** (*c.* 1450), constructed as a focal point for civic functions.

The rugged **Arco Bollani** (1566, designed by Palladio), in the corner near the clock tower, lets you through the walls that enclose the **Chiesa Di Santa Maria** and the **castello** of the Venetian governors. On the left, the dignified **Portico Lippomano** (1487) was named for the governor who commissioned it. The small Venetian fountains that line the road have quenched the public thirst since the sixteenth century. The church contains some interesting frescoes but is more notable for its beautiful setting; the park has a stupendous view and is ideal for mellowing or a picnic. The castle itself has been closed since the 1976 earthquake.

Back in p. del Duomo, just 50m from the more hectic p. Libertà, stands the fine Roman-Gothic *duomo,* with several Tiepolos inside (the 1st, 2nd, and 4th altars on the right side). There is a small **museum** in the squat brick baptistery *campanile,* which comprises two chapels with fourteenth-century frescoes by Vitale da Bologna, among others. (Open Wed., Thurs., and Sat. 9am-noon. Free.) Udine has been called the city of Tiepolo, and some of this baroque painter's finest works adorn the **Oratorio della Purità,** just across from the *duomo.* The *Assumption* frescoed on the ceiling (1759) and the *Immaculate Conception* of the altarpiece represent Tiepolo's world of light, air, and awe. (Ask the cathedral sacristan to let you in. L500 tip expected.)

A large sample of earlier Tiepolo frescoes lies in the **Palazzo Arcivescovile** (tel. 50 20 29), in p. Patriarcato at the head of via Ungheria. Here, in 1726-30, Tiepolo executed a large series of scenes from the Old Testament. (Open Mon.-Fri. 9am-noon. Free.)

For a breath of fresh air and some simpler aesthetic pleasures, walk a few blocks south from p. Libertà along via Stringher to the **Chiesa di San Francesco,** just off p. XX Settembre. This architectural gem of the early Renaissance is considered Udine's most beautiful church.

There are also a number of interesting provincial museums, including an excellent **Gallery of Modern Art,** p. P. Diacono (tel. 29 58 91), on the ring road that circles the old city. Your convoluted trek to the museum will be rewarded with works by De Kooning and Liechtenstein, graphics by Chagall and Picasso, and exhibits of every major twentieth-century Italian artist. (Open Tues.-Sat. 9:30am-12:30pm and 3-6pm, Sun. 9:30am-12:30pm. Admission L2000, with student ID L1000.)

The tourist office compiles two booklets of concerts and other events titled *Events* and *La Locantina.* In July and August, open-air performances of the **Estate Teatrale** take place in the the Giardino del Torso, near p. Garibaldi. (Tickets L6000-10,000, on sale at the *giardini.* Shows start at 9:30pm.) The misnamed **Settembre Udinese** is an outdoor series of free musical concerts held mostly during October. From June to August, **La Contarena** (tel. 29 46 22), the most happening cafe on p. della Libertà, serenades its guests and the whole square with live singing and violin playing. For L1800 you can sip a *cappuccino* outside. (Open Tues.-Sun. 8am-4am.)

Near Udine

Fifteen kilometers east of Udine, in the river valley of the Natisone, lies the hamlet **Cividale.** Though sleepy today, the town was the center of this entire region in Roman times and again under the Lombards and Franks, when "Civitas Austria" was the capital of the Veneto-Illyria region. Eight trains depart daily from Udine to Cividale (½ hr., round-trip L1700; see Buses under Practical Information). The **tourist office** is at largo Boiano, 4 (tel. 73 13 98), near the p. del Duomo. (Open Mon.-Sat. 8am-1pm and 3:30-5:30pm.)

The otherwise undistinguished ***duomo*** contains the wonderfully carved **Altar of Ratchis** and **Baptistery of Callisto,** both from the eighth century. Ask the sacristan to open the treasury and show you the Great Sword, used every year at Epiphany to bless the congregation. (Open daily 9am-noon and 3:30-6:30pm. Free.) Also beautiful is the **Tempietto Longobardo.** Eastern influences are evident in the frescoes, choirstalls, and bas-reliefs. (Open Tues.-Sat. 9am-noon and 3-6pm, Sun. 9am-noon. Free. You may need to track down the custodian for keys.) The **Museo Archeologico** houses Roman artifacts as well as a collection of Lombard jewelry and armor; it's worth a visit. (Open Mon.-Sat. 9am-1:30pm, Sun. 9am-12:30pm. Admission L2000, seniors and children L1000.)

Palmanova, a symmetrical nine-sided Venetian fortress (1593), lies between Udine and Aquileia (12 trains per day, ½ hr., round-trip L1800). The city's **tourist office** (open Mon.-Sat. 9am-noon and 3:30-6:30pm) is in the unexceptional *museo civico* (tel. 92 91 06; open Tues.-Sun. 10am-noon).

The **Alpi Carniche** are a rugged range of mountains across northern Friuli that open only at the Passo di Monte Croce Carnico and at **Tarvisio.** Tarvisio is the northeasternmost tip of Italy, bordering Austria and Yugoslavia. There are many hiking, camping, fishing, and climbing opportunities, especially on **Lake Raibl, Lake Russine,** the **Val Canale,** and **Monte Lussari** (1789m, accessible from Valbruna). Leaf through *Sentieri di Montagna,* a guide to 20 mountain trails distributed by the tourist offices in Udine and Tarvisio (tel. 21 35 or 29 72).

CENTRAL ITALY

Emilia Romagna

Emilia Romagna's rich plains have been the source of much of Italy's wheat and dairy products for centuries. Bounded by the Po River, the Adriatic, and the eastern edge of the Appenine Mountains, the region derives its name from via Emilia, the Roman road that followed the edge of the mountains from Rimini to Piacenza. The eastern half is Romagna, the western half Emilia, and the city of Bologna separates the two.

Emilia Romagna's landscape is unusual for Italy: The colors are muted grays and browns, and the farm buildings low, square, and flat-roofed. The uninterrupted plains create an eerie sense of infinite space. The illusion of distance is magnified by the cold gray fog of winter—replaced in summer by a silver haze that makes the towns and buildings shimmer.

The region's towns were founded by the Romans as way stations along the via Emilia, but most of what dominates the terrain dates from the Middle Ages. Developing as autonomous *comuni* during this chaotic time, the towns were ruled by the great Renaissance families: the Malatesta in Rimini, the Bentivoglio in Bologna, the Farnese in Parma and Piacenza, and the d'Este in Ferrara and Modena. In the nineteenth century the Italian Socialist movement was born here, setting the scene for the area's present role as a stronghold of the Italian Communist Party.

Anonymous sculpture from the period of the independent *comuni* gives even the smallest towns artistic fame. A common subject was the Labors of the Months, usually rendered directly and naturalistically. The same spirit imbues the local architecture—cathedrals are erected with arches that seem to have grown into their place, cloisters are composed of carved columns that look like trees covered with ivy.

If Tuscany artistically outshone its neighbors to the north during the Renaissance, Emilia Romagna has recently found its own glory, giving the world such artists as the conductor Arturo Toscanini, the great tenor Luciano Pavarotti, and the giants of modern film, Antonioni and Federico Fellini.

Even those unmoved by the region's art and landscape succumb to Emilia Romagna's enchanting cuisine. You won't eat better in Italy, so plan to splurge on Parmesan cheese and sausage, Bolognese *tortellini* and *mortadella,* Ferrarese *salame,* and *grana* cheese. All pasta is excellent—try those stuffed with goodies. And don't forget the wines: Two sparkling reds are *lambrusco* from Modena and *sangiovese* from Romagna; a dry Bologna white is *trebbiano di Romagna.*

Bologna

Bologna's porticos, streets, and buildings attest to its long-standing dedication to community. Bastion of the Partito Comunista, "Red Bologna" served as the base for most progressive parties and movements until the recent fragmentation of the Italian left. As striking as the town's political color is the deep orange-red of its buildings, and the seemingly endless rows of marble and brick arcades that line the city center. Today apartments lurk over the porticos, housing large numbers of students and transients, but town elders have not allowed the old city to be exploited: Saturdays are reserved for buses and Sundays for horse-drawn carriages.

Bolognese art, less studied than the art of Florence, often seems to go out of its way to show hooked noses and wrinkles. Petrarch summarized this distinction by noting that only the learned are amazed by a Giotto, whereas virtually everyone understands a Bolognese work. Bolognese art reached its apex in the late sixteenth century, when the three Carracci (Ludovico, Agostino, and Annibale) revolted

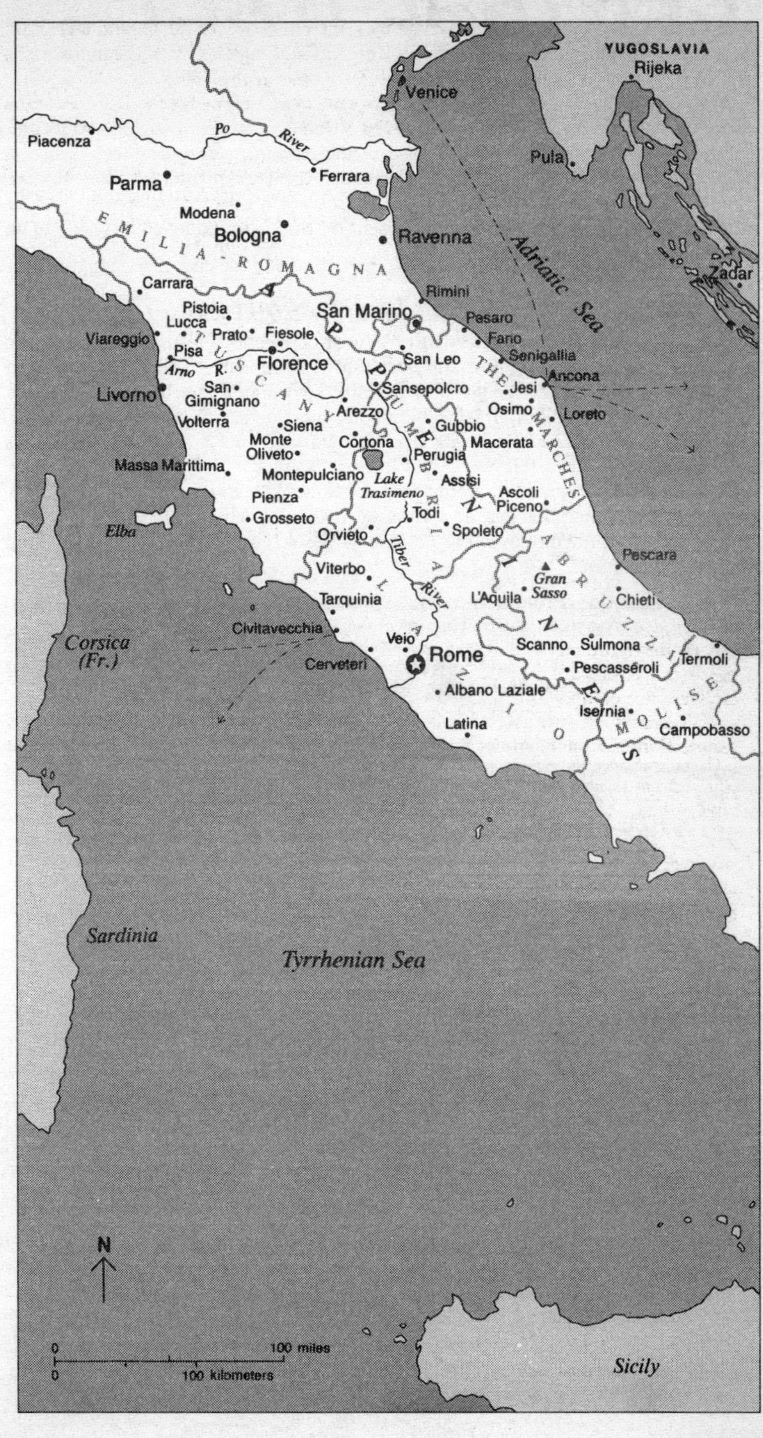
YUGOSLAVIA
Rijeka
Venice
Piacenza
Po River
Parma
Ferrara
Modena
Bologna
Ravenna
EMILIA-ROMAGNA
Adriatic Sea
Pula
Zadar
Carrara
Rimini
Pistoia
Lucca
San Marino
Pesaro
Viareggio
Prato
Fiesole
Fano
Pisa
Florence
San Leo
Senigallia
Arno R.
TUSCANY
Ancona
Livorno
San Gimignano
Sansepolcro
Jesi
Volterra
Arezzo
Osimo
Loreto
Siena
Gubbio
Monte Oliveto
Cortona
Macerata
Perugia
Massa Marittima
Montepulciano
Lake Trasimeno
Assisi
THE MARCHES
UMBRIA
APPENNINES
Pienza
Ascoli Piceno
Todi
Grosseto
Spoleto
Elba
Orvieto
ABRUZZI
Pescara
Tiber River
Viterbo
Gran Sasso
L'Aquila
Chieti
Tarquinia
LAZIO
Civitavecchia
Veio
Corsica (Fr.)
Scanno
Sulmona
Rome
Termoli
Cerveteri
Pescasseroli
Albano Laziale
Isernia
MOLISE
Latina
Campobasso
Sardinia
Tyrrhenian Sea
N
0
100 miles
0
100 kilometers
Sicily

against the controversies of mannerism by reintroducing naturalism and a grander conception of the figure. The "Carracci Revolution," together with the innovations of Caravaggio, founded the baroque style in Rome in the 1590s.

Traditionally nicknamed "Bologna La Dotta" (The Learned) as well as "Bologna La Grassa" (The Fat), the city continues to attract thousands of students to its university. Europe's oldest, it was founded in the eleventh century by legal scholars employed to settle real estate disputes between the Papacy and the Holy Roman Empire. This influx of academics sparked Bologna's urban development and its transformation from a feudal city dependent on the surrounding countryside to an independent merchant *comune.*

Orientation and Practical Information

Bologna is a major rail center with frequent connections to major Italian cities and the Adriatic coast. Almost any bus (except #38 and 39) will take you from the station, at the northern edge of town, into the center, and urban buses between these two points run all night (tickets L600 at most *tabacchi*). The center of town, however, is only a 12-minute walk from the station; walk a bit to the left across p. XX Settembre, then follow via dell'Indipendenza.

The main Italian highway, **Autostrada del Sole (A1),** comes over the Appenines just before reaching Bologna and runs northwest to Milan. Other major roads branch out from the city over the Po Valley: the A13 to Ferrara and Venice, and the A14 to Rimini.

Informazione Azienda Turistica: In the train station (tel. 24 65 41), next to the baggage depot. They'll book rooms without deposit or commission. Pick up the bimonthly brochure, *A Guest In Bologna,* for up-to-date information on sights and entertainment. Open Mon.-Sat. 9am-7pm, Sun. 9am-1pm. Hotel vacancies posted after hours. **Main office** in Palazzo Communale, in p. Maggiore (tel. 23 96 60). Information and pamphlets on other cities. Genial staff. Open Mon.-Sat. 9am-7pm, Sun. 9am-1pm.

Student Travel: Centro Turistico Studentesco (CTS), via delle Belle Arti, 20 (tel. 26 48 62). The most reliable and popular, and the only place open in late summer. ISICs. Open Mon.-Fri. 9:30am-12:30pm and 3:30-6:30pm, Sat. 9:30am-noon. **University Viaggi,** via Zamboni, 16E (tel. 22 85 84 or 23 62 55). Open Sept.-July. Both issue BIJ tickets and IYHF cards. Big discounts on sea and air travel. Arrive early morning to avoid the lines.

Currency Exchange: Banking hours Mon.-Fri. 8:20am-1:20pm and 2:30-3:30pm or 2:45-3:45pm. In a bind, change at the train station. Open 24 hours.

American Express: Renotur Viacolvento Viaggi, p. XX Settembre, 6 (tel. 22 04 77), in the same building as the bus station. Doesn't sell traveler's checks and gives you Italian cash only for card/personal check combo. Will hold mail—those without AmEx card or checks must pay L2000. Open Sept.-July.

Post Office: P. Minghetti (tel. 22 35 98), southeast of p. Maggiore. Fermo Posta at #20 in the Casellario Abbonati wing. Open Mon.-Fri. 8:15am-6:40pm, Sat. 8:15am-12:30pm. **Postal code:** 40100.

Telephones: ASST, p. VIII Agosto, 24, off via dell'Indipendenza. Open 24 hours. Also in the bus station in p. XX Settembre. Open 9:30pm-9am. **SIP,** via Fossalta, 4/E, off p. Nettuno. Open daily 8am-9:30pm. Also at the train station. Open 7am-midnight. **Telephone code:** 051.

Airport: At "Borgo Panigale" (tel. 31 15 78 or 31 22 59; for reservations 31 22 97). Take bus #91 (with or without a bar through it) on the blue, or suburban system, from the station. For European flights. Many charters are available.

Trains: Tel. 24 64 90. Open 8am-8pm. The harried staff never answers the phone. Go instead to the tourist office in p. Maggiore, where they will make free copies of any national train schedule. To Florence (every hr., 1-1½ hr., L4900), Venice (every hr., 2-2½ hr., L7800), Milano (every hr., 2½-3 hr., L10,700), and Modena (every hr., 30 min.; L2000, round-trip L3000).

Buses: Intercity buses depart from the terminal on the far side of p. XX Settembre (tel. 24 83 74). Walk left from the train station.

English Bookstore: Feltrinelli, via dei Giudei, 1/E and 6/C (tel. 26 54 76), off p. Ravegnana. Interesting travel guides at 1/E; a huge selection of English books at 6/C. Open Mon.-Fri. 9am-1pm and 3:30-7:30pm, Sat. 9am-1pm.

Laundromat: Puliget, via Tibaldi, 21 (tel. 35 78 73), north of the station. Wash L10,000 per 5kg, wash and dry L14,000. Open Aug. 24-July Mon.-Fri. 8am-12:30pm and 3-7pm.

Day Hotel: In the station (tel. 24 63 13). Showers (*semplice*) L4500, with shampoo and two towels L5500. Toilet L1000; public facilities are around the corner. Open Mon.-Sat. 6:30am-9pm, Sun. 7am-8pm.

Pharmacy: At the train station. Open 7:30am-11pm.

Hospitals: Ospedale Traumatologico, via Boltrini, 2 (tel. 22 49 63). For accidents. Otherwise **Ospedale Maggiore** (tel. 38 29 86), in the northwest part of town. **First Aid,** tel. 33 33 33.

Police: Questura, p. Galileo, 7 (tel. 27 88 46). To reach their Ufficio Stranieri (Traveler's Office), call 33 74 73 or 33 74 75.

Accommodations

Hotels in Bologna are baloney. In summer singles run about L26,000, doubles about L42,000, if you're lucky enough to find a room at all. But don't despair: Bologna has a youth hostel. It's a trek from town, but set in a relieving pastoral setting.

Ostello di San Sisto (IYHF), via Viadagota, 14 (tel. 51 92 02), in the Localita di San Sisto 6km northeast of the center of town, off via San Donato. Bus #93 (Mon.-Sat. every ½-hr., last bus at 8:15pm) runs along via San Donato outside of town. Get off after 12 min. at the 2nd stop after the rotary, and follow the signs. On Sundays and Aug. 1-24 you must take bus #19, which runs from the center of town toward the station on via Indipendenza and turns onto via Irnerio. Get off at the 1st stop after the bus leaves via San Donato, and walk the remaining 1.5km to the hostel. A charming, homey villa sitting among green pastures. Open 7-9am and 5-11:30pm. L10,000, nonmembers L12,500. Breakfast included. Dinner L8000.

Protezione della Giovane, via Santo Stefano, 45 (tel. 22 55 73), off p. Ravegana. Usually filled with students in the winter. Women only. A full pension that's no bologna: L8000-10,000 for bed, breakfast, *and* supper. Curfew 10:30pm.

Pensione Neva, via L. Serra (tel. 36 98 93). Turn left out of the station and then cross the tracks on via Matteotti. Turn left on via Tiarini and then immediately right on via Serra. A pleasant, immaculate, family-run place. Singles L18,000-25,000. Doubles L38,000.

Pensione Marconi, via Marconi, 22 (tel. 26 28 32). Bear right from the station onto via Amendola, which becomes via Marconi. Large enough to have someone at the desk all night. Spotless. Singles L26,000. Doubles L44,000, with shower L49,000.

Pensione Farini, via Farini, 13 (tel. 27 19 69), near the junction with via d'Azeglio, which runs south from p. Maggiore. Not fastidiously kept, but spacious and likely to have room. The cheapest place near p. Maggiore. Singles L24,000. Doubles L37,000, with shower L42,000. Open Sept.-July.

Pensione Ferraresi, via Livraghi, 1 (tel. 22 18 02) or **Pensione Fiorita,** via San Felice, 6 (tel. 22 95 60), both off via Ugo Bassi. Centrally located and slightly upscale. Singles L26,000. Doubles L40,000. Showers L2000.

Food

Bologna earned its nickname "La Grassa" (The Fat) for its gastronomic feats. Try the pasta above all: *tortellini,* folded around cheese or meat; *lasagna,* a Bolognese specialty; and *spaghetti alla bolognese,* with a hefty meat-and-tomato sauce. Bologna is renowned for sausages of all kinds, including, yes, bologna—ask for *mortadella.* Be sure to sample the fruit-filled Bolognese *crostata,* a flat pastry that comes in all varieties.

You will quickly notice that Bologna supports an awe-inspiring number of restaurants, *trattorie,* and *pizzerie.* Many places close in late July and August.

If you prefer to prepare your own meals, try the **Mercato Ugo Bassi,** via Ugo Bassi, 27, a large indoor market selling a wide variety of produce, cheeses, and meats. (Open Mon.-Wed. 7:15am-1pm and 5-7pm, Fri. 7am-1pm and 4:30-7:30pm, Thurs. and Sat. 7:15am-1pm.) Or you can go to Bologna's crowded outdoor market in via Pescherie Vecchie, off p. Maggiore. For more sedate shopping, check out the famous *rosticceria*/gourmet food store, **A. F. Tamburini,** around the corner at via Drapperie, 2/C. (Open Sept.-July.) **Orlavio e Sergio** is a *salumeria* (deli) at strada Maggiore, 35/A (tel. 23 85 67). Try **Frulé,** via Castiglione, 7/E, south of p. Ravegnanna, for refreshing fruitshakes called *frullati* (L1500-4000). Ask for extra *ghiaccio* (ice) if you like them freezing. (Open Mon.-Sat. 8am-2pm.)

Mensa Universitaria, via Zamboni, 25, just beyond p. Giuseppe Verdi. Filling meals, but crowded. L2300 for pasta, *secondo, contorno, vino,* and *frutta.* Technically only University of Bologna students are allowed in. Open Sept.-July Mon.-Sat. 12:30-2:30pm and 7-9pm. If no luck here, try the one up the street at p. Puntoni, 1, where via Zamboni meets via delle Belle Arti. At both, just say nothing and pay L2300 at the door. Kosher food is served by the **Mensa Studenti Ebraici,** via Gombruti, 9 (tel. 27 55 24).

CAMST, via A. Righi, 2 (tel. 23 85 67), at via Indipendenza. A *ristorante/tavola calda/rosticceria:* the same food with service, self-service, or take-out options. The selection is enormous; try the *lasagna verde. Primi* L4000-6000, *secondi* L6000-8000. Cheap wine by the glass or carafe. *Rosticceria* open 10:30am-3pm and 5:30-9pm. *Tavola calda* open 11:30am-2:30pm and 6:30-9:30pm. *Ristorante* open noon-2:30pm and 7-10pm.

Pizzeria Altero, via Indipendenza, 33 (tel. 23 47 58). A virtuoso product sold by the slice. Fight your way through the screaming mob and have a taste. *Pomodoro* (tomato) L800, *mozzarella* L1000, and *funghi* (mushroom) L1500. Open Sept.-July Mon.-Sat. 8am-midnight.

Trattoria, via Broccaindosso, 21/A, off strada Maggiore. A no-name popular with students and workers. Adequate full meals about L10,000. Open Sept.-July Mon.-Sat.

Jam Coffeeshop, via Barberia, 34 (tel. 58 51 62), at p. Malphigi just south of San Francesco. Acidic American coffee. Try to forget its price (L1800) and enjoy the coffeeshop atmosphere. An assortment of *panini and cakes L2000-5000.*

Trattoria da Danio, via S. Felice, 50 (tel. 55 52 02). A 10-min. hike up via San Felice rewards you with a large and appetizing menu. Start with *gnocchi, lasagna verde,* or one of the many classic pasta dishes. A good place to try *salsicca* such as *cotechino.* Full meals L13,000-17,000. Open Sept.-July Mon.-Sat. noon-2:30pm and 7:30-10pm.

Ristorante due Torri, via de Giudei, 6F. Service either sit-down or at the bar, the latter with only a L400 cover charge. Cheap food with character. *Primi* L3000-4000, *secondi* L5000 or less. Meat dishes L5200-7000. Open Mon.-Sat. noon-3pm only.

Ristorante Franco Rossi, via Donzelle, 1 (tel. 27 99 59), just off via dell'Indipendenza. One of the places that gives Bologna its gustatory reputation. Pasta L10,000, *secondi* from L18,000. Cover L5000. Open Mon.-Sat. 12:30-3pm and 7:30-11:30pm.

Pizzeria da Ciro, via de' Gessi, 5/C (tel. 22 69 17), a tiny dead-end street off via Parigi, between via N. Sauro and via Galleria. A secluded but convenient place with outdoor tables and a moderately-priced menu. Bolognese wait in line here. Great pizza L3000-5000, full meals L15,000. Open Sept.-July Thurs.-Tues.

Ristorante Donatello, via A. Righi, 8 (tel. 23 54 38). Full meals L18,000-24,000. Try the *tagliatelle alla vecchia bologna.* Open Sept. to mid-July Sun.-Fri. noon-2:30pm and 7:30-10pm.

Trattoria Buca San Petronio, via de Masi, 2 (tel. 22 45 43), in a wonderful location behind the basilica. A worthwhile expense, with pasta dishes L6000 and *secondi* L7500-9000. Open Fri.-Wed. noon-2:30pm.

Italy, Italy, via Indipendenza, 42. Eating chain-restaurant food in Bologna should be illegal. But the hungry can come for spaghetti (L3350) and the salad bar (L4250). Open Tues.-Thurs. and Sun. noon-midnight, Fri.-Sat. 10am-1am.

Ristorante Dal Duttòur Balanzon, via Fossalta, 45 (tel. 23 20 98), just off p. Maggiore across from the SIP phones. Rosy marble and gleaming amber wood worthy of a castle justifies the princely prices. Full meals around L25,000. Open Mon.-Sat. 11:30am-3pm and 6:30-10:30pm.

Sights

Piazza Maggiore is Bologna's crowded center and a monument to its past. The vast square is surrounded by huge buildings of various epochs. Most conspicuous is the **Basilica di San Petronio,** designed by Antonio da Vincenzo and begun in 1390. The Bolognese wanted to make their basilica (named after the city's patron saint) larger than Rome's Saint Peter's, but the Church ordered that the funds be used instead to build the nearby **Palazzo Archiginnasio.** The red-and-white (the town's heraldic colors) marble facade was completed as far as the magnificent central portal. The now-eroded marble *Virgin and Child* and the expressive Old and New Testament reliefs are by Jacopo della Quercia (1367-1438). The cavernous Gothic interior has hosted such historic events as meetings of the Council of Trent and the 1530 ceremony in which Pope Clement VII gave Italy to the German ing Charles V. Legend has it that this was also where Martin Luther became disgusted with the pomp and pageantry of the Papacy, and left to reform Germany. The chapels to the left house a few curios: The zodiacal sundial on the wall is the largest in Italy—it measures hours, days, and months when the sun shines through the ceiling opening onto the floor. The seventh chapel has a fifteenth-century Lorenzo Costa *Madonna and Saints;* next door is Parmigianino's extravagant *St. Roch* and Giovanni da Modena's imaginatively frescoed fourth chapel with allegorical scenes. The museum at the end of the nave, to the left, exhibits numerous plans for the facade and the enlargement of the church—you can see how several famous artists thought it ought to look. (Church open daily 7:30am-7pm. Museum open Fri.-Mon. and Wed. 10am-noon.)

Behind San Petronio, through one of the busiest of Bologna's porticos, is the **Palazzo Archiginnasio,** formerly a university building, covered with memorials to and crests of various notable scholars. It now houses the town library; there's an old anatomical theater upstairs, but you have to ask the *portiere* to open it up. This theater was destroyed during the bombing of 1944. Later, it was reconstructed from thousands of pieces of rubble. (Open Mon.-Sat. 9am-1:45pm. Free.)

Piazza del Nettuno adjoins p. Maggiore, with Giambologna's bronze *Neptune and Attendants* splashing in the sixteenth-century fountain. The **Palazzo Comunale** to the right of the *piazza* is a large brick block enlivened by a clock tower, a beautiful terracotta *Madonna* by Nicolò dell' Arca (1414-1494), a Menganti bronze statue of Pope Gregory XIV (the reformer of the calendar), and some Gothic windows by Bologna's favorite Renaissance architect, Fioravante Fioravanti. The *palazzo* displays on its second floor exquisite objets d'art acquired by the city. (Closed for restoration in 1988.) Fioravanti's son Aristotile had more architectural skill—in the late fifteenth century, he remodeled the Romanesque **Palazzo del Podestà,** across the *piazza,* facing San Petronio. He went on to design Moscow's Kremlin.

The via Rizzoli leads from p. Nettuno to **piazza Porta Ravegnana,** where seven streets converge in Bologna's medieval quarter. The two towers here are the emblem of Bologna. Only a dozen or so towers remain of the 200 built in the twelfth and thirteenth centuries by aristocratic Bolognese families. Legend has it that the two principal families of Bologna, the Asinelli and the Garisendi, competed to build the tallest and best-looking tower. The Garisendi plunged into the construction of their tower without suitably enforcing the foundation. It sank on one side, the upper portion fell off, and all that remains is the leaning section. The Asinelli were more cautious and built their tower to a sleek 97m. It's still standing today, though it's also 2¼m shorter. Climb the **Torre degli Asinelli** for an amazing view of the city walls and concentric streets. (Open daily 9am-6pm. Admission around L2000.)

The Strada Maggiore leads east from the two towers past the **Basilica of San Bartolomeo.** Stop here and see the exquisite *Madonna* by Guido Reni in the left transept before going to the **Church of Santa Maria dei Servi,** an amazingly intact Gothic church. The church is flanked by porticos that stand out even in the city of graceful porticos. In a left-hand chapel behind the altar hangs Cimabue's great *Madonna Enthroned.* The altar with stellar Renaissance sculpture is by Giovanni

Antonio Montorsoli, a pupil of Michelangelo. The church was constructed by Antoniodi Vincenzo, architect of San Petronio.

Via Santo Stefano leads from the two towers past the pointed arches of the portico of the **Palazzo di Mercanzia** (the customs offices of Bologna—note the guilds' coats of arms on top) and opens into the triangular **piazza Santo Stefano.** The **basilica's** four interlocking churches, all that's left of the original seven, stand here, a Romanesque group of breathtaking simplicity. The most spectacular church, the round **Chiesa del San Sepolcro,** is the center of the group. San Petronio, patron saint of Bologna, is buried here under a spiraling carved pulpit. In the courtyard behind is the Basin of Pilate—the governor supposedly absolved himself of responsibility for Christ's death in this bath-size tub. Flanking San Sepolcro is the oldest church in the group, the **Church of SS. Vitale e Agricola.** Bits of Roman temples, capitals, and columns are incorporated into its arched interior. A labyrinth of little chapels opens off the side of "Pilate's courtyard," and in the back is the dark **Church of the Trinity.** The small religious museum on the top story is worth a quick tour. (Open daily 9am-noon and 3-6pm. Admission L500.)

The **Church of San Domenico,** in p. San Domenico, is 3 blocks from p. Maggiore. From p. Maggiore, follow via dell'Archigianasio to via Farini and then via Garibaldi. San Domenico, founder of the Dominican order, is buried here. Nicolò dell' Arca earned his name from the work he did on the tomb, or "ark," of the saint. His statues challenge the Michelangelos in the tomb and the softly modeled reliefs (13-century) by Nicola Pisano. To tell whose work is whose, consult the informative schema hanging near the entrance to the chapel. Also look for the inlaid wooden choir stalls (enter through the sacristy) and Filippino Lippi's *Visit of St. Catherine* at the end of the right aisle.

Other interesting churches in Bologna include the **Church of Santa Maria in Vita** on via Clavature, off p. Maggiore, with a masterly and frenzied *Pietà* by Nicolò dell' Arca (1485). The French-flavored **Church of San Francesco,** off p. Malpighi, is one of Italy's oldest Gothic churches. Inside, the elaborate high altar was sculpted by the brothers Dalle Masegne in the late fourteenth century.

The **Church of San Giacomo Maggiore,** in p. Rossini, is a successful amalgam of the Gothic and Romanesque styles. The church was built in the late thirteenth century, when such popular church movements as the Dominican and Franciscan brotherhoods, who favored the Gothic design, were beginning to gain influence over the aristocratic clergy, adherents to the Romanesque style. The chapels enclose paintings by Caracci, Veneziano, Tibaldi, and Barocci, and a tomb sculpture by Jacopo della Quercia hangs high on the wall of the ambulatory. The adjoining Romanesque **Oratorio di Santa Cecilia** (ask the sacristan to let you through the back of the church) is covered with a calm cycle of Renaissance frescoes by Amico Aspertini. These contrast sharply with Tibaldi's. Behind, in the ambulatory, is the **Bentiroglio chapel,** commissioned by Bologna's version of the Medici of the fifteenth century. On the wall are frescoes by Lorenzo Costa, one depicting the Bentiroglio clan. On the altar is a magnificent Francesco Francia altarpiece.

The **Museo Civico Archeologico,** via Archiginnasio, 2 (tel. 23 38 49), exhibits an excellent collection of prehistoric and Etruscan remains. Innumerable Roman inscriptions and Bronze and Stone Age tools are displayed along with more artistic antiquities, such as the *pietra Zannoni,* a funeral carving from the Etruscan city unearthed in the nineteenth century at nearby Villanova di Castelnaso. The carving is the oldest Etruscan depiction of the voyage of the dead to the underworld, one of the earliest testimonies to belief in immortality. (Open Tues.-Sat. 9am-2pm, Sun. 9am-12:30pm. Admission L2500.)

The **Pinacoteca Nazionale,** via delle Belle Arti, 56 (tel. 22 37 74), is one of Italy's best galleries. Follow the progress of Bolognese artists from the primitives to the mannerists and others. Note especially Vitale da Bologna's *St. George and Dragon.* Bolognese painting may have overlooked the Renaissance but the Pinacoteca doesn't. The first section contains a Giotto altarpiece, and the Renaissance wing contains other glorious works: Raphael's *Ecstasy of Santa Cecilia,* Perugino's *Madonna in Glory,* Guido Reni's *Madonna,* and Parmigianino's *Madonna di Santa*

Margherita. There is a room of great works by the three Carracci and another with pieces by the Crespi. (Open Tues.-Sat. 9am-2pm, Sun. 9am-1pm. Admission L3000.)

The **Museo Civico Medievale e del Rinascimento** contains, besides a number of exquisite *curios,* a superb collection of sculpted tombs of medieval Bolognese professors, which typically show the professor reading to students. Note how the students doze, daydream, and gossip. Other important pieces include the huge gilt bronze statue of Pope Boniface VIII and the "Stone of Peace," which depicts the Virgin and child flanked by kneeling students, who came to terms with the *commune* in 1321 after protesting the execution of a fellow student. (The students in Bologna have been politically active since well before the '60s.) (Open Mon. and Wed.-Sat. 9am-2pm, Sun. 9am-12:30pm.)

The **Santuario della Madonna di San Luca** is a distinctive landmark outside the city on Monte della Guardia—you'll probably notice it from the train when arriving in Bologna. Built in the early 1700s by Carlo Dotti, the sanctuary houses the painting *Madonna and Child,* which is attributed to St. Luke, though it is undoubtedly the work of a twelfth-century Byzantine artist. Most notable about this site is the 4-km portico stretching from Bologna's southwest city gate, the Porta Saragozza, up the hill to the church. Six hundred sixty-five arches form the walkway, constructed between 1674 and 1793. Bus #21 or 22 will take you to the foot of the walkway, located off via Saragozza, southwest of the center.

Every Friday and Saturday from September through July (8am-2pm), a large open-air **market** takes place on the p. VIII Agosto. Clothes, shoes, tools, and more are sold cheaply from over 100 stalls.

Entertainment

Bologna, with its large university population, has recently become the center of Italy's **new wave music** scene. The city has attracted many British bands that have in turn influenced local talent. For an idea of the sound, tune into 102.2FM. For information on live concerts, check out the posters at p. G. Verdi, in the center of the university quarter. Or go by the record store **Nanucci,** at via G. Oberdan, 7/B.

La Fonte di Euterpe, via Nicolo dell'Arca, 37B (tel. 35 79 90), on the north side of the railway station. The place for blues in Bologna, with occasional live foreign acts.

Piccolo Bar (also **Black Lady**), p. G. Verdi (tel. 27 14 38), off via Zamboni. The principal student hangout, with occasional live entertainment and rock videos. Slick and funky. Thumbs up. Open Mon.-Sat. 8am-2pm.

Caffè del Teatro, via Zamboni, 26 (tel. 22 26 23), across the *piazza.* Similar to PicBar, but with fewer live acts and better sandwiches.

Charlie, vicolo Bianchetti, 4 (tel. 23 41 60), off strada Maggiore. Chic disco in a converted garage. Open Sept.-July.

Cassero di Porta, via Saragozza (tel. 43 33 95). Sponsors films and lectures on homosexuality and runs gay and lesbian discos on the weekends.

The city government sponsors a free nightly **open-air disco** in July and August—with proto-Travoltas tripping in Parco Cavaioni, on the outskirts of the city. (Action begins about 10pm.) To get to the park, take bus #52 from p. Minghetti into the hills 5km out. Once there, make friends fast, as bus service may end by 10pm. Bologna's newest nighttime summer entertainment is the city-sponsored **Bologna Sogna** (Bologna Dreams) series, which features different concerts nightly at various *palazzi* and museums around town through July and August. Admission is only L2500; if the concert is in a museum, viewing the surrounding exhibits comes gratis. Ask the tourist office for a schedule of events.

Modena

It is fitting that Modena should be the hometown of Luciano Pavarotti, operatic tenor *par excellence*. Like the Ferraris and Maseratis the city exports, Modena purrs with burgher prosperity. Conquered by the Romans in the third century B.C.E., the city owed its early prominence to its location: The region's principal road, the via Emilia, ran through the heart of town. In 1598, the Este family lost Ferrara to the Pope and the seat of their duchy was re-established in Modena. The city is best visited as an excursion from Bologna or Parma or as a stopover between the two.

Orientation and Practical Information

Modena is a half-hour from Bologna and 45 minutes from Parma on the Milan-Bologna train line. The train station is on the ring road, about 25 minutes from **piazza Grande,** Modena's central square. Buses #1, 2, and 9 (L500) run from the train station to the center of town, picking up *via Emilia,* the main street.

Modena was bisected by Venice-like canals until city planners—clueless of the tastes of future tourists—paved them over in the middle ages.

APT: via Emilia, 179, across from p. Mazzini. As helpful as one might desire. An annually updated list of hotels and a miniscule map (magnifying glass not included). Open Mon.-Fri. 9:45am-12:30pm and 3:30-6:30pm, Sat. 9:45am-12:30pm.

Student Travel: Agenzia Viaggiatori Iter, via S. Carlo, 5 (tel. 22 23 70), off via Emilia 1 block from p. Grande. **BIJ** tickets and information on student discounts. Open Mon.-Fri. 8:30am-12:30pm and 3-7pm. Closed for a week in Aug.

Post Office: via Emilia, 86 (tel. 24 20 30). Open Mon.-Fri. 8:15am-6:50pm, Sat. 8:15am-12:50pm. **Postal code:** 41100.

Telephones: SIP via Università, 23, off corso Canal Grande. Open daily 8am-9:30pm. **Telephone code:** 059.

Trains: Tel. 21 82 26; daily 8:25am-noon and 3-7pm. To Bologna (every hr., 40 min., L2000) and Parma (L2700).

Buses: via Fabriani (tel. 30 88 00), off via Monte Kosica. To Bologna (every hr., L3300), Ferrara (every hour, L4500), and dozens of small hamlets.

Bike Rental: via Sant'Agostino, 3 (tel. 24 20 92), next to the Palazzo dei Musei. L700 per day. Run by Italy's right-wing party. Open Mon.-Sat. 8am-8pm.

Swimming pools: Piscina Comunale, along via Dogali (tel. 22 37 86), in the northwest part of the city beyond the stadium. Open June to mid-Sept. daily 9am-7pm. Admission L4000, children L2800.

Hospital: Nuovo Policlinico, Tel. 36 10 24. Take bus #7 east and watch for via del Pozzo.

Police: Questura, viale Rimembrenze, 14 (tel. 22 51 72). In **emergencies,** call 21 11 11.

Accommodations and Camping

Prices run high and quality low in Modena. Singles are scarce—call a few days ahead.

Locanda Sole, via Malatesta, 45 (tel. 21 42 45), off via Emilia at p. Muratori, before the *duomo.* Clean and cool. Run by an affable young family. Singles L17,000. Doubles L31,500. Showers included.

Albergo Astoria, via Sant' Eufemia, 43 (tel. 22 55 87), parallel to and south of via Emilia, off p. Grande. Clean rooms. Singles L17,200. Doubles L31,300. Showers L3000.

Albergo Del Pozzo, via del Pozzo, 72/A (tel. 36 03 50). Follow the directions for the hospital in Practical Information. Adequate rooms with great prices. Often full. Singles L17,000. Doubles L25,500.

Camping: International Camping Modena, via Cave Ramo, 111 (tel. 33 22 52). Take bus #7 to the bus station and then #12 (without a bar through it) to within ½km of the site. L4000, children L2000. L3500 per tent. Open April-Sept.

Food

Modena rivals Bologna as one of Italy's gastronomic strongholds. Particularly famous are the city's sausages and smoked pork, among them *prosciutto, loppa, ciccioli,* and *pancetta. Gnocco* is a type of fried bread on which these meats are often served. *Tigella* is a softer version of the same. Popular pasta dishes are rich-layered *lasagne* and creamy *tortellini* and *tagliatelle.* Typical main courses include *zampone* (pig's feet), *bolliti* (boiled meats), and any type of *arrosto* (roast). Modena is Italy's great producer of balsamic vinegar, and you'll find it used generously. The best local wine is the unforgettable *lambrusco di Sorbara,* a slightly sparkling red: Chill before imbibing. Sampling local specialties is expensive; try picnicking.

Mensa Centro Storico (CORIS), via S. Geminiano, 3 (tel. 23 04 30), off via Canalino near the EPT. Excellent cafeteria food and nice outdoor tables. Decent meals about L8000. Open Sept.-July Mon.-Sat. 11:50am-2:30pm and 7-9pm.

Ghirlandina Grill, via Leodoino, 9 (tel. 23 72 55), off via Sant' Eufemia, ½ block from p. Grande. Another excellent, convenient cafeteria under L8000. Open Sept.-July Sun.-Fri. noon-2pm and 7-9pm.

Ristorante-Pizzeria l'Aragosta, via Emilia, 192 (tel. 22 22 75), on p. Muratori. Ignore the seafood and eat local specialties for about L14,000 a head, or pizza for L7000. Open Wed.-Mon. 12:30-3pm and 6:30pm-1am. Closed 2 weeks in Aug.

Italy, Italy, via del Università, off via Emilia next to the SIP telephone office. Italy's answer to McDonalds. All-you-can-eat salad bar L4500. Modena's under-25 crowd gathers here in the evenings. Open Wed.-Mon. 11am-midnight.

Sights

Built in the early twelfth century, Modena's **duomo,** in p. Grande, is one of the best-preserved Romanesque cathedrals in Italy. The lions on the south portal show a Lombard influence, but there are also some original departures from the traditional Lombard-Romanesque style. The cathedral was built under the patronage of the Marchioness Matilda of Canossa, who held a fief that included Tuscany, Parma, Ferrara, and Mantua. Matilda was an ally of the Pope, although much of her territory was loyal to the Holy Roman Emperor, especially the merchant *comune* of Modena. The stylistic innovations on the religious buildings the Marchioness sponsored were often politically inspired. Since her Ghibelline opposition was based in Lombardy, for instance, Modena's *duomo* has a trussed, rather than a Lombard vaulted, roof. Also innovative are the three parallel apses symbolizing the Holy Trinity at the right end of the horizontal axis; half-column supports are exposed on the outside of the cathedral. (*Duomo* open 8am-noon and 3:30-6pm, except during mass.)

The cathedral has several entrances, all decorated with beautiful carvings. The front doorway off the *piazza* is adorned with floral carvings that represent heaven and Christ's genealogy. Over the left and central portals are scenes from the Old Testament. Over the right entrance, carvings depict San Gimignano, Modena's patron saint, traveling in Asia. The entrance facing via Emilia is decorated by locally inspired Labors of the Months. The master sculptor Wiligelmo and his school decorated most of the *duomo*—his stylized carvings are inspired by local, Roman, biblical, and even Celtic themes. Another master sculpted the fantastically imaginative capitals on the thin columns surrounding the building. Much original work from the portals is housed in the **Museo Lapidario del Duomo,** across the street on the via Lanfranco side. (Open daily 10am-noon and 3:30-6pm, if someone is free to show you around and no mass is in progress. Free.)

Inside the *duomo,* the altar lies over the exposed crypt where San Gimignano is buried. The chancel floor is supported by pillars, which rest on Lombard lions, and is enclosed by a remarkable screen of Romanesque panels depicting the Passion. (Crypt open daily 10am-noon and 3:30-6pm.)

The 95-m **Ghirlandina Tower,** symbol of Modena, looms over the *duomo.* Built a century after the completion of the church, in the late thirteenth century, it incorporates Gothic as well as Romanesque elements. A memorial to those who died fighting the Nazis and Fascists during World War II has been added to the base. Climb the tower for a view of the flat area surrounding the tower. (Open Mon.-Sat. 9am-12:30pm and 3:30-7pm, though you must get a porter in the *municipio* (town hall) to admit you.) While you're in the *municipio,* see if you can convince a porter to show you the elegant back rooms, decorated floor-to-ceiling with Renaissance pictorials.

The **Palazzo dei Musei,** in largo Sant' Agostino at the western side of via Emilia, contains both the **Biblioteca Estense** (d'Este Library) and picture gallery. In the library is a permanent display of masterpieces including elaborate fifteenth- and sixteenth-century bindings, an early Portuguese map of the world from 1501, a 1481 copy of Dante's *Divine Comedy,* and a series of exquisitely illuminated manuscripts. Foremost is the **Bible of Borso d'Este,** partially illustrated by Taddeo Crivelli, a fifteenth-century Emilian painter, who, like a Bolognese, represented his figures realistically. (Open mid-Sept. to mid-Aug. Mon.-Sat. 10am-1pm. Free.)

The **Galleria Estense** (tel. 23 50 04), on the floor above the library, is unusually well dispersed and lit, but of uneven quality. Bernini's bust of Francesco d'Este I, who assembled much of the collection, presides from an alcove as you enter. To its right is a long gallery that begins with earthy Emilian primitives and hits its high point in Cosmè Tura's strangely expressionistic *St. Anthony of Padua.* Beyond is a remarkably strong Flemish section, highlighted by Joos van Cleve's *Virgin and Child with St. Anne.* A room of Anthonio Begarelli's elegant terra-cotta sculptures is followed by another room saturated with Dosso Dossi's eccentric conceptions. Mannerist and baroque galleries follow, with some Venetian works by Tintoretto and El Greco, as well as Velàzquez's famous portrait of Francesco I D'Este. Included are Emilian paintings ranging from Correggio's delicate *Madonna and Child* (1489-1534) to Guercino's explosive *Martyrdom of St. Peter,* to Parmigianino's peculiar elongated portraits. (Open Tues., Wed., and Fri. 9am-2pm; Thurs. and Sat. 9am-7:20pm; Sun. 9am-1pm. Admission L2000.)

From the museum, retrace your steps up via Emilia, then turn left on via Farini just after the cathedral to reach the grandiose **Palazzo Ducale.** Designed by the Roman Bartolomeo Avanzini, the huge building now houses Italy's national military academy. Note the detailing: The windows on each story differ from those above and below. The palace was begun in 1634, and the main courtyard is a baroque wonder.

Entertainment

The city sponsors frequent cultural events in the *piazze* of the historic center, as well as in various parks, churches, and theaters. Several of the city's theaters double as discos—check posters.

Winter brings **opera** to Modena's **Teatro Comunale,** corso Canal Grande, 85 (tel. 22 51 83), next to the Ghirlandina Tower. On the fourth weekend of every month, the city puts on the **Fiera Antiquaria,** a boisterous celebration of food, wine, and custom. Adventurous types may want to try talking their way into a game of *bocce,* played with miniature bowling balls along via A. Fontanelli.

When the spirit moves him, native son Luciano Pavarotti comes back to Modena to give a free concert. The event isn't advertised outside of Modena—check with the tourist office. Even so, it's always mobbed; show up three to four hours ahead of time.

Parma

Parma combines Emilia Romagna's cultural riches, cheap accommodations, and clear weather. The town concentrates the brilliant art, elegant architecture, and rich food of a large city into a small mass of narrow streets and medieval homes. After development as a medieval and Renaissance *commune,* Parma was remodeled in the early modern era by French colonialists, and today the Francophone residue is so pronounced that Parmesans can still be heard rolling the French "r." Once you tire of exploring the older streets in the center, stroll through the parks and boulevards that line the Torrente Di Parma.

Orientation and Practical Information

Downtown Parma stretches along the left bank of the river between the train station and **piazza Garibaldi,** about a kilometer apart. Perpendicular to the river runs the town's central axis, **via Mazzini,** which leads from the *torrente* to p. Garibaldi.

EPT: p. del Duomo, 5 (tel. 347 35). From the station, walk to the end of via Verdi, bear left on Bodoni, continue on via Garibaldi, and make a left onto strada Pisacane. Extremely helpful. An excellent map and very thorough food listings for Parma and its province. Will phone to check for hotel vacancies. The hostel manager can be swayed by his buddies from the tourist office to let you in. Open May-Sept. Mon.-Fri. 9am-12:30pm and 3:30-6:30pm, Sat. 9am-12:30pm; Oct.-April Mon.-Fri. 9am-12:30pm and 3-6pm, Sat. 9am-12:30pm.

Student Travel: Centro Turistico Studentesco e Giovanile, borgo Pipa, 2 (tel. 252 62). Budget travel information. Open Mon., Thurs., Fri. 6:30-8pm. Branch office, via N. Sauro, 4, off strada Farini. Open Sun.-Fri. 4-7pm.

Currency Exchange: Credito Romagnolo, via Mazzini, 6. A bank on the main drag where money can be withdrawn with a VISA card. Open Mon.-Fri. 8:20am-1:20pm and 3-4pm, Sat. 8:20-11:20am. Also at the **train station.**

Post Office: At strada Pisacane and strada Cavour, near the *duomo.* Open Mon.-Fri. 8:15am-6:40pm, Sat. 8:15am-12:20pm. The branch at the station (directly to your left as you face the station) may be more convenient. Open Mon.-Fri. 8:15am-7:40pm, Sat. 8:15am-12:30pm. **Postal code:** 43100.

Telephones: SIP (tel. 384 81), on the front side of the city hall, opening onto p. Garibaldi. Open daily 8am-9:30pm. From 9:30pm to 8am, go to **Hotel Milano,** viale Bottego, 9 (tel. 773 03). **Telephone code:** 0521.

Train Station: p. della Stazione (tel. 77 11 18). To Milan (20 per day; one way L6400, round-trip L10,800), Bologna (34 per day; one way L4400, round-trip L7600), and Florence (7 per day; one way L9300, round-trip L17,800). As a last resort, change money here. Open daily 7am-9pm.

Bus Station: viale P. Toschi (tel. 338 13), between Palazzo della Pilotta and the river. Much more convenient than trains to provincial towns. To Colorno (6 per day, L1300; change here for Cremona), Fontanellato (nearly every hr., L1900), Torrechiara (nearly hr., L1900), and Mantua (4 per day, L5300).

Bike Rental: At the door marked *Deposito* to your left as you leave the train station (tel. 726 87). L500 per hr., L3000 per day, with ID as deposit. Insist on a lock, and try to avoid surrendering your passport. Open Mon.-Sat. 5:30am-10:30pm; Sun. and holidays 5:30am-11pm.

English Bookstore: Feltrinelli, via della Repubblica, 2, just off p. Garibaldi. Open Mon.-Wed., Fri., and Sat. 9am-1pm and 3:30-7:30pm, Thurs. 9am-1pm.

Laundromat: borgo della Colonne, 38/B, behind S. Giovanni. If you go there, note the church (still frescoed inside) at #28, now used as a garage. Open (flexibly) Sept.-July Mon.-Sat. 9am-noon and 3-7pm.

Hospital: via Gramsci, 14 (tel. 967 20), across the river beyond the Ducal Palace.

Police: Questura, borgo della Posta (tel. 388 88).

Accommodations

No problems here—there are plenty of inexpensive fourth-class hotels and *locande* in Parma, as well as a fine youth hostel.

Ostello Cittadella (IYHF), via Passo Buole (tel. 58 15 46), actually inside a seventeenth-century Farnese fortress (the *cittadella*), now a public park. Take bus #9 or 10 from the *fermata* across the street and to your left as you leave the station, or bus #6 from p. Garibaldi (last bus at 8pm). No kitchen or common room. Bedrooms dimly lit. Showers absolutely luxurious. Medieval pit toilets sparkling clean. Occasional bug troops. L7500, nonmembers L10,000. Reception open all day, but lockout 9:30am-5pm. Curfew 11pm. Ring bell after 9pm. The only **campground** near Parma is also here. L4500 per person, L5000 per tent.

Casa della Giovane, via del Conservatorio, 11 (tel. 28 32 29). Take bus #1 or 8 from p. Garibaldi. The nuns will accept only female guests. Cleanliness is next to godliness here, and so is friendliness. When rooms are tight, younger women will be given preference. Doubles and triples L10,000 per person. Breakfast and showers included. Curfew 9:30pm.

Albergo Stella d'Italia, via Albertelli, 10 (tel. 28 56 24), between vie Verdi and Garibaldi, 2 blocks from the station. Cheapest rooms in town. Singles L11,500. Doubles L18,900. Showers and a key to the front door included.

Albergo Leon D'Oro, viale A. Fratti, 4 (tel. 77 31 82), off via Trento. From the station, go 2 blocks left. Functional rooms, convenient to the center. Singles L15,600. Doubles L24,000. The **Zucconi,** up the street at #14 (tel. 77 24 37), is the cheapest place in town. Rooms occupied mostly by workers who stay for weeks. Singles L9500. Doubles L15,700.

Locanda Concari, on the far side of p. S. Croce (tel. 28 58 65), next to Pizzeria Al Cozzicaro—the sign reads only "allogio." From the station, cut through the ducal park; from p. Garibaldi, walk out via M. d'Azeglio, the cross-river continuation of via Mazzini. 11 rooms in a pretty yellow building. Gregarious. More space than in the center of town. Singles L14,300. Doubles L24,500. Showers L1500. Closed part of July.

Food

Parma teems with delicious food and drink. Any pasta can be ordered covered in native *parmigiano* cheese, which is expensive but worth it. Nothing will have prepared you for the sinfully rich flavor sprinkled on your *panino.* Ham and various sausage dishes are local specialties. Drink *lambrusco* here, too. When exported, this sparkling red wine loses its natural fizz and has carbon dioxide added—you'll never have another chance at the real thing. Also be sure to try some Parma *prosciutto crudo* (ham)—Italy's best.

Via Garibaldi teems with grocery stores. For shopping in an **open-air market,** venture Wednesday and Saturday mornings into p. Ghiaia, off viale Mariotti, past Palazzo Pilotta.

Da Walter, borgo Palmia, 2/B, off strada Farini. A Gatsbyesque abundance of *panini:* about 50 different, hot and cold sandwich offerings, including all the types of *salsicce* and *prosciutto* for which the city is famous (L1800-3000). *Lambrusco* L1000 per glass. Open Mon.-Sat. 8:30am-8:30pm.

Ristorante Giardinetto, borgo S. Chiara, 10/A (tel. 355 51), off borgo G. Tommasini, which is off via della Repubblica. One of the cheapest *menù* in Italy: L5700. A safe bet is *prosciutto al forno* (baked ham). Patronized by regulars. Wine L1200 per ½-liter, water L500. Open Sept.-July Mon.-Fri. noon-2:30pm and 7-8:30pm.

Alice, via N. Sauro, 13/B, a short walk from Walter. Cross strada Farini. A 1st-class *trattoria* run by a charming couple. Food prepared in front of your eyes. Little English, but lots of good will. Full meals L15,000, wine L2500 per ½-liter. Open Mon.-Sat. noon-2:30pm and 6:30-11pm. Closed 2 weeks in Aug.

Ristorante/Pizzeria Fontana, at via S. Vitale and via N. Sauro (tel. 28 25 63), south of p. Garibaldi. Elegant but affordable. Try *pizza alla Messicana* (with tuna, L4000) or *alla Parma* (with *prosciutto crudo,* L5000). Cover L1500. Open Aug.-June Tues.-Sun.

Da Antonio, via Garibaldi, 46 (tel. 330 70), on the main drag. Melodious but mysterious menu; pick what looks best and point. *Antipasti* L2000, *primi* L4000, *secondi* L6000. Open Sun.-Fri. 7am-11pm.

Salumeria Garibaldi, via Garibaldi, 42. A great selection of deli items and *panini.* The *funghi chiodini* (marinated mushrooms) are a steal at L2500 per *etto.* Open Fri.-Wed. 8:30am-1pm and 4-7:30pm, Thurs. 8:30am-1pm.

Ceres, borgo delle Colonne, 8 (tel 377 93). From the *duomo,* follow borgo Pipa to p. D'Acquisto. A macrobiotic and natural food grocery store. Open Mon., Wed., and Fri. 9am-12:30pm and 4:30-7:30pm; Tues. 9:30am-12:30pm, 4:30-7:30pm, and 9-10:30pm; Thurs. and Sat. 9am-12:30pm.

La Filoma, via XX Marzo, 15 (tel. 342 69). You'll probably spend L35,000-40,000 with wine (unless you forgo the *secondi*), but the food is magnificent, and it's one of Parma's most famous restaurants. The *tortelli d'erbete* (ravioli with a cheese and herb stuffing) may induce you to emigrate. Open mid-Sept. to July Mon.-Sat. 12:30-2:30pm and 7:30-10:30pm.

Sights

There may be more beautiful cathedrals or more ornate baptisteries, but none surpasses the restful beauty of Parma's *duomo* and *battistero.* The **duomo,** an eleventh-century Romanesque church, is saturated with invaluable artwork. The "Sanctus" bell, cast in 1493, still hangs in the bell tower. Before going inside, walk around the church to see the *loggie* above the metamorphosing animals below. The interior retains two medieval masterpieces, the moving *Descent from the Cross* bas-relief by the master Benedetto Antelami in the south transept, and the *Episcopal Throne* supported by tiers in the apse. In the cupola is a real delight: Correggio's *Virgin* rises to a gold heaven in a swirl of white robes, pink *putti,* and blue sky; Parma's patron saints watch from cloudy box seats, and the apostles gaze from above. The impression of depth is stunning; you'll have to practically stand beneath one corner and look straight up to convince yourself the scene doesn't burst into sculpture to create its illusion, as many baroque ceilings do. (Open daily 7:30am-noon and 3-7pm. L200 to light up the cupola, L400 for the "total illumination.")

The **baptistery** is an architectural miracle resulting from the transformation of the Romanesque style into Gothic. Begun in 1196, the basic structure was completed in 1216 while ornamentation continued until the 1260s. If you look closely, you'll see the baptistery isn't symmetrical—in the Middle Ages, symmetry connoted death. The structure is a showcase for sculptures by Antelami (1177-1233), particularly *Solomon and the Queen of Sheba,* on the northwest side. There's more inside. Some of the religious scenes are by Antelami's pupils, but the bas-reliefs of the 12 months (which probably came off the *duomo* facade) are unmistakably the work of the master. The thirteenth-century frescoes above merit close attention. Their creator is unknown, but he was certainly one of the painting masters of the period. (Open April-June Tues.-Sun. 9am-noon and 3-6pm; July-Aug. Tues.-Sun. 9am-12:30pm and 3:30-7pm; Sept.-March Tues.-Sun. 9am-noon and 3-5pm. Admission a ridiculous L3000.)

Behind the *duomo,* in p. San Giovanni, is the **Church of San Giovanni Evangelista,** (tel. 390 67). Its cupola is painted with a Corregio fresco: Earthbound St. John looks up to heaven to see the rest of the apostles already with Christ. Correggio's work once covered the entire ceiling, but rebuilding in 1587 destroyed all except the cupola decoration and the fresco over the door to the right of the altar. Along the left nave over the first, second, and fourth chapels are frescoes by Correggio's mannerist contemporary, Parmigianino (1503-1540). **La spezieria** (a historic pharmacy) and a library are in the same building. (Open Tues.-Sun. 9am-7:30pm. Admission L2000.)

The gigantic complex of the **Palazzo della Pilotta** sits by the river, across via Garibaldi from the *duomo.* Constructed in 1602, the palace is the architectural expression of the authoritarian ambitions of the Farnese dukes. Parma developed from antiquity as a series of distinct nodes, or fortified clusters of buildings, controlled by religious and civic powers. The Farnese built two new nodes, the Pilotta Palace and the **citadel** (now a park), in an attempt to politically and militarily dominate the city. The palace was never completed and was partially destroyed during World War II.

The Pilotta Palace is big enough to hold several museums, the most important being the **Galleria Nazionale** (tel. 333 09). Enter the gallery through the **Farnese Theater,** built in 1615 in imitation of Palladio's Teatro Olimpico in Vicenza. In the spectacular Farnese style, this version is much larger and has a movable set. Half-destroyed by a 1944 air raid, the theater has been restored to its original appearance. A habitrail path leads into the painting gallery proper. This extraordinary collection includes both works of the Ferrarese and Parmesan schools, and miscellaneous Italian and European masterpieces. Prominently displayed works by Correggio and Parmigianino are the centerpieces of the locally produced paintings. Be sure not to miss the following paintings: *Testa di una Fanciulla* (Head of a Young Girl) by Leonardo da Vinci, all of Dosso Dossi's work, and The *Pietà* by Cima da Conegliano. In addition to these Italian works are several Holbeins, van Dyck's *Isabella of Spain,* Esteban Murillo's *Job,* several small pieces by the Breughels, and a fragment attributed to El Greco. (Open Tues.-Sun. 9am-7:30pm. Admission to both gallery and theater L5000, ages over 60 or under 18 free.)

Also in the Palazzo della Pilotta, the large **Museo Archeologico Nazionale** (tel. 337 18) houses coins, bronzes, and sculptures of Greek, Etruscan, Roman, and Egyptian origin. Roman artifacts from the nearby town of Veleia include a "food table" on which donations to a charitable foundation initiated by the Emperor Trajan are recorded. Unfortunately, visits to the museum can be made only with advance notice; contact the EPT.

Housed in some amazingly ornate Napoleonic rooms of the palazzo, the **Biblioteca Palatina** (tel. 222 17) contains rare books and prints. (Open Sept. to mid-Aug. Mon.-Sat. 8:30am-1:30pm. Free.) Annexed to it is the **Museo Bodoniano,** in honor of the nineteenth-century inventor of our everyday Bodoni typeface. Bibliophiles will relish the excellent collection of old printed books, including Bodoni's own editions. (Theoretically open Sept. to mid-Aug. Mon.-Sat. 9am-noon. Free.)

The **Camera di Correggio** (tel. 333 09) is just across the *piazza,* in the small courtyard behind the gate that opens off via M. Melloni (actually just out the back door of the post office). The room is also called the **Camera di San Paolo** because it was the dining room of the abbess of that convent. If Correggio's lively, lusty scenes of gods and *putti* are any indication, being abbess did not prevent Giovanna Piacenze, who commissioned the decoration in 1519, from indulging in life's pleasures. In fact, Giovanna's face appears over the fireplace as the goddess Diana, hunting deer. (Open daily 9am-7:30pm. Free.)

Outside the *duomo* area, Parma preserves a French flavor, dating from the years of Gallic influence in the sixteenth and eighteenth centuries and Napoleonic rule. (In modern liberated style, the city was ruled from 1814 to 1847 by Napoleon's wife, Marie-Louise.) The **Museo Glauco Lombardi,** in the Palazzo di Riserva at via Garibaldi, 15 (tel. 337 27), has a collection of period pieces devoted to Parma during the reign of Duchess Marie-Louise. (Open May-Sept. Tues.-Sat. 9:30am-12:30pm and 4-6pm, Sun. 9:30am-1pm; Oct.-April 9:30am-12:30pm and 3-5pm, Sun. 9:30am-1pm. Free.)

Unfortunately, many of the French *palazzi* were razed during the last war, but enough of the older buildings survive to convey the elegance and sophistication Stendhal described in *The Charterhouse of Parma.* Even if you haven't read this novel of ambition and intrigue set in eighteenth-century Italy, you might want to visit. The **certosa** (tel. 49 22 47) is 4km out of Parma. Take bus #10 from the stop just below Ponte Verdi, near the inter-city bus station. Or walk down via Repubblica and via Emilia, turn left on via Mantova, cross the rail tracks, and turn right on viale alla Certosa. The monastic complex was constructed in 1282 and completely rebuilt in 1673. Most of it is a school; some of the halls are covered with frescoes. Thanks to restoration, only the church is open to visitors. (Open Feb.-Oct. Mon.-Fri. 9am-noon and 3-6pm, Sat.-Sun. 9am-noon; Nov.-Jan. Mon.-Fri. 9am-noon and 2-4pm; Sat.-Sun. 9am-noon. Free.)

Retreat with a picnic to the wonderfully leafy and green baroque **Ducal Park.** (Open May-Sept. 6am-midnight; Oct.-April dawn-dusk.) The mustard-colored palace is now the police headquarters. Italians of every age and description bicycle past.

Entertainment

This birthplace of Verdi and Toscanini holds festivals of the performing and fine arts throughout the year. Of the many concert series sponsored by the **Teatro Regio,** the July music festival is particularly distinguished. Tickets to **Musica e Stella** (Music and Stars) cost L15,000. The orchestra of Emilia Romagna, named after Arturo Toscanini, often performs (tickets L8000). Inquire at the box office (tel. 79 56 78; open Mon.-Fri. 9am-12:30pm and 4:30-7pm). From June through August, the **Questa Sera Si Recita Al Castello** (Tonight We Perform at the Castle) stages dramatic readings in various nearby castles. The province of Parma is similarly fervent about festivals; even small towns actively sponsor music and drama. Write to the EPT or the Teatro Regio for detailed programs and tickets.

Near Parma

Indiscriminating penchants for crocodiled moats and more scholarly appetites for medieval and Renaissance architecture can both be sated by the villas and fantasy castles in the province of Parma. Most are private property and many are still in the hands of noble Italian families. Check with the EPT before setting out.

The older and more interesting (but also more remote) castles are south of Parma. The **Castello Di Bardi** is one of the oldest, most charming, and farthest away from Parma (65km, 2 hr., arrange visits with the warden; tel. (0525) 713 21). Four buses leave Parma for Bardi on weekdays, two on Sundays; the first bus leaves Parma at 6:35am, and the last one returns at 6:10pm. The fifteenth-century castles of **Torrechiara** (tel. 85 52 55, 10 per day, 25 min.) and **Montechiarugolo** (5 per day, ½ hr.) are much closer and are filled with paintings from the same period. (Torrechiara open April to mid-Sept. Tues.-Sun. 9:30am-noon and 3:30-7pm; mid-Sept. to March 9am-5pm. Admission L2000. Arrange visits to Montechiarugolo with the warden; tel. 65 93 43.) **Fontanello,** 21 km north of Parma (about 7 buses per day, 30 min.), has the beautifully preserved, moated **Castle of San Vitale,** which Parmigianino decorated with frescoes depicting the myth of Diana and Actaeon (tel. 82 11 88; open March 16-Oct. 15 daily 9:30am-12:30pm and 3-7pm, Oct. 16-March 15 daily 9:30am-12:30pm and 3-6pm; admission L1500). **Colorno,** around 20 km from Parma is the seventeenth- to eighteenth-century miniature Versailles of the Farnese Dukes of Parma (open by appointment; tel. (0521) 81 54 18). Both buses headed for Coltaro and those going to Mezzano Inferiore pass through Colarno (about 8 per day, 30-40 min.). Information on the other castles, villas, and abbeys in the province is available at the EPT.

Piacenza

Piacenza is the northernmost city in Emilia Romagna, combining the region's cultural heritage with neighboring Lombardy's modern prosperity. Founded as Placentia, the town first thrived as the terminus of the via Emilia, the great Roman road that ran southeast to Rimini. Although no Roman remnants survive here, Piacenza is home to several noteworthy monuments from the Middle Ages and the Renaissance. The center of town, which still follows the lines of the old Roman settlement, is dominated by an outstanding example of secular Lombard Gothic architecture, **Il Gotico,** built in 1280. This was the **Palazzo del Comune** (Town Hall) during the Communal Period (roughly 1200-1400), Piacenza's glory days as a leading member of the Lombard League. Il Gotico is remarkable for its well-preserved state, the powerful sense of depth gained through the use of a recessed nave surrounded by a massive outer portico of pointed Gothic arches, and the soaring crenelated battlements. In the *piazza* in front of Il Gotico stand two of the earliest masterpieces of baroque sculpture. The two **equestrian statues** by Francesco Mochi were cast between 1620 and 1625. The statue to the left represents Duke Alessandro Farnese (1545-1592); the one on the right, Duke Ranuccio I (1592-1622), his son. Both were rulers of Piacenza during the time when it comprised, together with Parma, the Farnese Dukedom. The **duomo** at the end of via XX Settembre is only slightly less impressive than those of Cremona and Modena. A fine Romanesque building constructed between 1122 and 1233, the cathedral has a slightly gloomy interior laid out in three naves supported by round pillars. Note the column, near the entrance, that still bears traces of its original frescoes.

The Renaissance **Church of the Madonna di Campagna** is Piacenza's other major sight. To reach the symmetrical gem, walk out of town along corso Garibaldi, which becomes via di Campagna. A. Tramello designed and built the church in the shape of a Greek cross in 1528, but the presbytery was elongated at the end of the eighteenth century. Two other churches are notable: **Sant' Antonino,** an eleventh-century Romanesque structure, and **San Sisto,** with its fine early-Renaissance interior and inlaid choir stalls (1514).

The **EPT** (tel. 293 24) is in p. dei Mercanti. If you feel like staying in Piacenza, the most convenient place is **Albergo Moderno,** via Tibini, 31 (tel. 292 96), near the station. Its friendly proprietor once lived in the U.S. (Singles L16,000. Doubles L26,000, with bath L32,000. Showers included.) The cheapest restaurant in town is the **Trattoria Due Stelle,** via Alberoni, 85 (tel. 38 40 93), at via Tibini. Tasty full meals cost about L12,000. Sample the local pasta dish *pisare e fas,* made with peas. (Open Sept.-July Mon.-Sat. noon-2:30pm and 6:30-9pm.) Piacenza's **telephone code** is 0523.

Ferrara

The Ferrara court was a paragon for northern Italian Renaissance city-states. During their rule from 1294 to 1598, the d'Este dukes patronized poets such as Ariosto and Tasso, painters such as Pisanello and Mantegna, and scholars such as Guarino. In 1492, Duke Ercole d'Este embarked upon a grandiose urban design project that more than doubled the size of the city. Today, the long streets of the Addizione Erculea, lined with deserted Renaissance *palazzi* and gardens, combine with the medieval town center to create a melancholy atmosphere—captured by Giorgio Bassani in *The Garden of the Finzi-Contini,* a novel (later made into a film by De Sica) about Ferrarese Jews at the beginning of World War II. Today, Ferrara harbors relics from its Renaissance past, not to mention relatively cheap accommodations and *trattorie.* A pleasant daytrip from Bologna or a stopover on the way to the Adriatic, Ferrara is a leisurely breath of culture on the way to the gusts of bigger cities.

Orientation and Practical Information

Ferrara lies on the train line between Bologna and Venice, with 14 connections to Ravenna per day. When you walk out of the train station, turn left along viale Constituzione to viale Cavour, which leads to the Castello Estense at the center of town (1km). Buses #1, 2, and 9 also travel this route (L500).

Informazioni Azienda Turistica, in the Palazzo Municipio (tel. 350 17), which sits in the *piazza* of the same name, 1 block from the *castello.* Exceptionally nice and insightful. Open daily 9am-1pm and 2:30-7pm.

Post Office: viale Cavour, 27 (tel. 345 04), 1 block toward the train station from the *castello.* Open Mon.-Fri. 8am-7:30pm, Sat. 8am-1pm. **Postal code:** 44100.

Telephones: SIP, largo Castello, 30 (tel. 497 91). Open 8am-8pm. From midnight to 8am, try **Hotel Ripagrande,** via Ripagrande, 21 (tel. 324 38). **Telephone code:** 0532.

Trains: Tel. 376 49; Mon.-Sat. 8:30am-noon and 3-7pm. To Bologna (33 per day, 40 min.; one-way L2500, round-trip L4200), Venezia (24 per day, 1½ hr.; L5000), Ravenna (14 per day, 1 hr.; one-way L3400, round-trip L7200).

Buses: ACFT and **GGFP,** both on corso Isonzo at the Ramparti di San Paolo (tel. 258 15), on the south side of the city. Take bus #3 from the train station. To Ferrara's beaches (12 per day, 1 hr., L4300). Buses for Modena depart from the train station (11 per day, 1½-2 hr., L4300).

Bike Rental: Fratelli Cervi, via Ripagrande (tel. 349 21).

Swimming Pool: via Porta Catena, 103 (tel. 374 08), to the northwest. Take bus #3. Open June-Sept. Tues.-Sun. 9:30am-8pm. Admission L4000, children less.

Hospital: corso Giovecca, 203 (tel. 334 71).

Police: Questura, corso Ercole I d'Este, 26 (tel. 333 33), off largo Castello.

Accommodations and Camping

Ferrara's budget accommodations make the town an attractive stopover on any Venice-Bologna jaunt.

Ostello Estense (IYHF), via Benvenuto Tisi Garofalo, 5 (tel. 210 98). Take bus #1, 2, or 9 from the station to via Ariosto, turn onto Ariosto, then turn left again onto via Cosmè Tura to the hostel. If you arrive after 8:30pm, when the buses stop running, follow the directions to viale Cavour (Ariosto is a cross street). This 50-bed, 2-room facility isn't the most comfortable or the cleanest, but it offers the cheapest beds in town. Kitchen facilities. L6200. Open in summer 7-9am (when they kick you out) and 6-11pm; in off-season 7-9am and 6-10pm. Open Feb.-Dec. 20.

Albergo San Paolo, via Pescherie Vecchie, 12 (tel. 565 65). Walk down corso Porta Reno from the *duomo,* turn left on via Carlo Mayr, and take the 1st right. This recently-renovated hotel is immaculate. Singles L15,800, with bath L20,500. Doubles L28,500, with bath L36,900.

Albergo Nazionale, corso Porta Reno, 32 (tel. 352 10), on a street that begins between the castle and the *duomo.* One of the best deals in town: wonderful location, sparkingly clean rooms. Likely to have free singles. Singles with bath L20,500. Doubles with bath L36,000.

Pensione Casa Degli Artisti, via Vittoria, 66 (tel. 353 14). Like the next two hotels listed, this is nestled in the twisting streets of Ferrara. Take bus #2 to p. Verdi, walk back down via Porta Reno, and turn left on via Ragno. Via Vittoria is the 3rd left (10 min.). Tons of spotless space and furniture that's younger than the guests. Often filled with workers. Singles L14,000. Doubles L25,000. Showers included.

Albergo Raiti, via Scienze, 13 (tel. 46 41 56), also off via Ragno. Tidy if plain rooms—the cheapest in town. Singles L13,500. Doubles L25,000. Showers included.

Albergo Delle Volte, via Capo delle Volte, 39 (tel. 336 58), just off p. Verdi across Carlo Mayr. Refreshingly clean, and just a bit more expensive at L25,000 for doubles.

Camping: Estense, via Porta Catena, 118 (tel. 527 91). Take bus #3. L2350 per person, L1180 per child. L3770 per tent.

Food

Ferrara hosts a few outstanding restaurants, though most are out of the budgetarian's price range. You can, however, sample some of the local specialties, such as *salame* and *capelletti,* at the establishments listed below and in the numerous *paninoteche* that line the city's streets. For picnics, stop by the **Mercato Comunale,** via Boccacanale di S. Stefano, just off via Garibaldi, west of the *duomo.* (Open Mon.-Wed. and Fri. 7am-1:30pm and 4-7pm, Thurs. and Sat. 7am-1:30pm.) In **piazza Travaglia** on Mondays and Fridays from 8am to noon, you can pick up an "Italians do it better" T-shirt to wrap your bread and cheese in. You might want to take your purchases to the **Parco Pareschi,** at corso Giovecca, 148 (about 10 min. away). On Thursdays in Ferrara all shops and restaurants close in the afternoons.

Mensa DLF, at the train station (tel. 265 51). Go around the station towards the luggage office. Full meals L7000, and seating under the trees. Open Mon.-Sat. 11am-3pm and 6-10pm, Sun. 7-10pm.

Il Cuocco, via Voltacasotto, 3 (tel. 476 09), off via C. Mayr. A popular mom-and-pop *trattoria.* Try the typically Ferrarese *pizzocheri* (broad flat noodles smothered in a butter, cream, potato, and sage sauce). Full meals around L17,000. Open Thurs.-Tues. noon-2:30pm and 7:30-11:30pm.

Ristorante/Pizzeria Antica Ferrara, via de' Romei, 51 (tel. 368 45), between via Mazzini and via Voltapaletto, the western continuation of via Savonarola. In a basement with white-washed ceilings. Pizza all day, cheap *tavola fredda* at lunch, reasonable dinners about L12,000. Open Sept.-July.

Bar La Favorita, via Carlo Mayr, 22 (no phone). A tiny pine-lined cubby hole, opined by local teenagers to be great for toasted sandwiches. The house specialty, "La Favorita," comes with *prosciutto crudo* and tangy, homemade mushroom sauce. *Panini* L2500-3500. Open Thurs.-Tues. 7am-1pm.

Il Mago Di Oz, via C. Mayr, 169 (tel. 261 65), a 5-min. walk from p. Verdi. Another bar/pizzeria/restaurant. Caters to a young crowd. From snacks to full meals. Open late Aug.-late July Thurs.-Tues.

Sights

The **castello** dominates Ferrara just as the d'Este family once did. Towered and turreted, the awesome brick complex stands exactly in the center of town. Corso della Giovecca lies where the moat once was, splitting the medieval part of town from the section planned by the duke's architect, Biagio Rossetti. The castle was originally built on the town wall to prevent the recurrence of popular riots such as the one in 1385. The ducal apartments began at the hanging garden facing p. del Duomo and stretched inside the *palazzo;* they were reached via the grand staircase in the rear courtyard of the building. The Salone dei Giochi and the surrounding rooms retain rich frescoes on their ceilings, the best of which are in the Loggetta degli Aranci. The wealth of the Lombardesque **Cappella di Renata di Francia** (Chapel of Renée of France) seems a bit out of place here—as Renée herself, a Protestant married to a Catholic, might have felt. In the damp prison underneath, Parisina, the wife of Duke Niccolo d'Este, was killed with her lover, the Duke's younger brother, Ugolino. This domestic tragedy beneath the castle's unrippled elegance inspired Browning to write "My Last Duchess." (Open Tues.-Sun. 9am-12:30pm and 2:30-5pm. Free. Guided tours upon request.)

The **duomo** is a hop, skip, and jump from the medieval quarter. Alongside the church under the double arcade, little shops and vendors operate much as they did in the Middle Ages; today, however, they pawn Fendi and Fiorucci logos. Altered by every noble with designs on Ferrara, the cathedral and the castle have always formed the effective center of town. The tall slender arches and terra-cotta that ornament the apse were designed by Rossetti, the town planner; the pink *campanile* covered with Estense seals and crests was designed by Leon Battista Alberti (1404-1484), the Florentine theorist whose precepts Rossetti had in mind as he worked. Notice the "fake" rose windows in the left and right portions of the facade. (Church open Mon.-Sat. 6:30am-noon and 4-7:30pm, Sun. 7:15am-1pm and 4-7:45pm.) The best pieces are now in the **Museo del Duomo** upstairs: Cosimo Tura's fifteenth-century *San Giorgio* and *Annunciation* from the Ferrarese school, and Jacopo della Quercia's *Madonna della Melagrana* is also a masterpiece. The gems of the collection are the anonymous sculptures of the "Labors of the Months" that once decorated the Porta dei Mesi (Door of the Months). (Museum open Mon.-Sat. 10am-noon and 4-6pm. Donations accepted.)

At one end of the cathedral *piazza* is the **Palazzo del Municipio.** Atop the protruding arch (designed by Alberti), Niccolo III sits on horseback, holding the reins of power. Go into **piazza del Municipio** to admire the elegant staircase with a dome over the landing, designed by Benvenuti. Back in piazza del Duomo, the **Torre dei Ribelli,** in the southwest corner of the *piazza,* incorporates remnants of some rebel nobles' houses, showing what happened to anyone who tried to get the better of the d'Este. The streets of the medieval town south of the cathedral teem with fortified houses. Also worth a glance is the arch-filled medieval quintessence of **via delle Volte,** a back alley for the *palazzi* along the now-receded Po River.

On the fringes of the city center stand the d'Este *palazzi.* Only the carved door of the **Palazzo Schifanoia,** via Scandiana, 23 (tel. 620 38), hints at the wealth of frescoes inside. The magnificent frescoes in the Saloni dei Mesi offer one of the most accurate and vivid depictions of Quattrocento courtly life in Italy. (Open daily 9am-7pm. Admission L2500, free the 2nd Sun. and Mon. of each month.) The **Palazzo Ludovico Il Moro,** via XX Settembre, 124, features a courtyard where Rossetti took Lombard decoration to its height. Inside, the **Museo Archeologico Nazionale** houses extensive finds from the Greco-Roman city of Spina and an outstanding collection of Athenian vases. (Open Tues.-Sun. 9am-4pm. Free.)

The **Palazzo dei Diamanti,** at corso Ercole I d'Este and corso Rossetti (the continuation of corso Porta Po), on the other side of town, outshines all the other ducal residences. Its name derives from the pointed-stone rustication crawling up the facade. Inside, the **Pinacoteca Nazionale** (tel. 218 31) contains the best work of the Ferrarese school. Most impressive are the *Passing of the Virgin* (1508) by Carpaccio and the incredibly overworked *Massacre of the Innocents* by Garofalo. (Open Tues.-Sat. 9am-2pm, Sun. 9am-1pm. Admission L3000.) On the ground floor, the **Galleria Civica d'Arte Moderna** often mounts special exhibits by well-known contemporary Italian and European artists. (Open daily 9:30am-1pm and 3:30-7pm.)

Down corso Porta Mare at #7 is the museum complex of **Palazzo Massari.** The most interesting museum is the original **Museo Documentario della Metafisica** (tel. 378 16), which documents, through a well-displayed slide presentation, the works of Giorgio de Chirico, Carlo Carrà, and Giorgio Morandi, three of Italy's greatest twentieth-century painters. Other museums in Palazzo Massari include the **Museo Boldini,** filled with paintings by the nineteenth-century Italian painter Giovanni Boldini; the **Museo Ferrarese dell' Ottocento,** which has a general collection of nineteenth-century Italian paintings; and the tiny **Galleria della Fotografia** and **Galleria Civica,** both of which house revolving displays of local work. (All museums in the complex open daily 9:30am-1pm and 3:30-7pm. Admission L2500, students and the 1st Sun. and Mon. of each month free.)

At #170 of the Giovecca is the **Palazzina di Marfisa d'Este,** a grand palace in miniature that has been recently restored to its former luxury. (Open daily 9am-12:30pm and 3-6pm. Admission L2000.) The walk by the **Palazzo dei Bentivoglio,** easily found at via Garibaldi, 90, is a fantastic showpiece of the mannerist liberties that eventually developed into the baroque style.

The sixteenth-century **walls** of Ferrara were designed to protect against cannons; they were low, wide, earth-and-brick works. In fact, when Michaelangelo was commissioned to build fortifications in Florence in the late 1520s, he modelled his design after Ferrara's walls. Walk down corso Ercole I d'Este, which runs the length of the Addizione to the northern walls, now tree-lined. The pervasive sense of history in Ferrara is nowhere stronger than in the **Cimitero Israelitico** (Jewish cemetery) at the end of via delle Vigne off corso Porta Mare. Here the Finzi and Contini are buried as well as most of Ferrara's flourishing nineteenth-century Jewish community. Ring the bell and the custodian will let you in. Look for the moving monument to Ferrarese Jews killed at Auschwitz.

Entertainment

In July and August, Ferrara is host to **Ferrara Estate,** a music and theater festival that brings performances of various kinds to the city's *piazze* (tickets L6000 at the tourist office). During the rest of the year, there is avant-garde theater at the **Sala Polivalente,** corso Porta Mare, 7. For more information, contact the Museo della Metafisica (tel. 378 16). Each year on the last Sunday of May, Ferrara re-creates the ancient **Palio di San Giorgio,** a footrace of kids (human), donkeys, and horses, preceded by a procession in traditional costumes.

Near Ferrara

The **Abbazia di Pomposa,** one of the oldest and most beautiful abbeys left in Italy by the Benedictine order, is one hour from Ferrara towards the coast. The oldest parts of the church date from the eighth century, but most of the structure now bears the Romanesque stamp. The carving on the facade is exceptional: The animal and vegetal intermingle in a unity later lost in the Renaissance.

Inside the church, intricate twelfth-century mosaics and stonework decorate the pavement, and fourteenth-century frescoes cover the walls of the entire nave with scenes from the Old and New Testaments and The Book of Revelation. Above, in the museum, there are well-displayed reliefs with fantastic, orientalized beasts that once decorated the church. (Free.)

The abbey is equipped with an amiable **tourist office,** 50m in front of the church within the eleventh century **Palazzo della Ragione** (the grandiose abbots' quarters). (Tel. (0533) 71 01 00. Open May-Oct. 9am-1pm and 2:30-7:30pm.) The romantic abbey also serves as the site for the **Musica Pomposa** concert series, with high-quality classical performances every Saturday and many Wednesday evenings in July and August. (Write to the Pomposa Abbey APT at via Pomposa, 4, or to the Ferrara tourist office for the 1989 brochure.)

Unfortunately, getting to the Abbey from Ferrara is difficult without a car. Only one early-morning bus makes the trip, and none returns. From the abbey, however, it is not too hard to get to **Comacchio,** 20 minutes south of Pomposa, a village with an illustrious history. One of the greatest producers of salt in the fifteenth century, Comacchio was powerful enough to rival Venice. Now the salt industry has washed away but the town remains a beautiful, melancholy place crossed by canals and ennobled by several fine baroque buildings. The **tourist office** is at via Buonafede, 12 (tel. (0533) 31 28 44); they can provide information on tours of Comacchio's lagoons, which contain ingenious fishing devices developed over the centuries. (Open daily 10am-noon and 4-7pm.) Comacchio also sponsors a number of jazz concerts and an **International Ballet Festival.** Spending the night at Comacchio is a snap; **Albergo La Pace,** overlooking a lovely canal, offers singles at L15,000 and doubles at L28,500, but you might want to take full room and board (*pensione completa*) for L40,000. The food is excellent.

Five kilometers from Comacchio is a vast strip of beach, unfortunately quite crowded in summer. Lidi di Porto Garibaldi is probably the busgetarian's best lodging bet. Three hotels are centrally located on viale dei Mille: **The Ariston, The Atlantic,** and **The Canoa** charge L16,000-20,000 for a single and L26,000-36,900 for a double. If you stay in Comacchio, however, you can avoid the crowds and easily reach the beaches by using the frequent buses. The most uncluttered beach is Lido di Spina, the farthest south. Twelve buses run daily from Ferrara's bus station, the first at 7:30am and the last back from Lido Nazione at 9:15pm. Comacchio is also convenient to and from Ravenna, with six ACFT buses making the one-hour run daily (4 on Sun., L2800; take the bus at via Tre Ponti near the large COOP store.)

Ravenna

Ravenna's moment of geopolitical superstardom came—and went—14 centuries ago, when Justinian and Theodora, rulers of the Byzantine Empire, chose Ravenna as the center of their attempt to restore order to the anarchic west. They didn't succeed, but their artistic legacy remains, and includes perhaps the most important examples of Byzantine art outside Istanbul.

Today, Ravenna is a small industrial city of about 100,000, offering the tourist a day's worth of some of the world's most beautiful mosaics, some interesting churches, the bones of Dante, and a 20-kilometer strip of crowded beach.

Orientation and Practical Information

Ravenna can be visited as a daytrip from Bologna (L7300) or Ferrara (L3800). There are frequent trains to Ferrara, where you can change for the train to Venice. Bologna is reached via Castelbolognese and Florence via Faenza. To go south along the Adriatic coast, take the Rimini line. The train station is at the east end of town in p. Farini. Viale Farini leads from the station straight into p. del Popolo and the center of town (an 8-minute walk).

Azienda Autonoma Di Turismo, via Salara, 8 (tel. 354 04), toward San Vitale, northwest of p. del Popolo. English spoken. Open daily 8am-1pm and 3-6pm.

Post Office: p. Garibaldi, 1. Open Mon.-Sat. 8am-7pm. **Postal code:** 48100.

Telephones: SIP, via Rasponi, off p. XX Settembre. Open daily 8am-9:30pm. After hours, try the **hotel** at via IV Novembre, 41. **Telephone code:** 0544.

Buses: ATR (regional) and **ATM** (municipal) buses depart for the coast and beach towns of Marina di Ravenna, Lido di Classe, etc. The ATM system is by far the easiest to use. Tickets L800—buy 2 tickets at once since they are difficult to find in the suburbs.

Public Toilets: via Pasolini, off via Cavour. Super-modern, disinfected after every use. L400.

Hospital: Santa Maria delle Croci, via S. Guaccimanni (tel. 332 12; **Ambulance:** 330 11).

Police: p. del Popolo (tel. 332 12).

Accommodations

Unfortunately, all of Ravenna's inexpensive accommodations lie near major transportation lines, and thus are quite noisy. Consider visiting from Ferrara, only an hour away by *rapido.* Staying in one of the quiet beach towns nearby is an especially attractive alternative, except during crowded July and August. Seaside camping is also available. In Ravenna proper, mid-July to mid-August is particularly tight because of the organ festival.

Ostello Dante, via A. Nicolodi, 12 (tel. 42 04 05). Take bus #1 from viale G. Pallavicini, left of the station (last bus shortly after 9pm). A large and institutional hostel in the eastern suburbs. Next to a coastal road, the women's quarters are the noisiest in Ravenna. Hot showers from 6-9pm only. The multi-lingual manager is a charm. 6-bed rooms. L7500. Sheets L1000. Showers and breakfast included. Fine dinner L7000. Bicycle rental L6000 per day. Free locks for closets with a L5000 deposit. Open March-Oct. 7am-9am and 5-11pm. Curfew 11:30pm.

Albergo Al Giaciglio, via Rocca Brancaleone, 42 (tel. 394 03). Walk along viale Farini, then right across p. Mameli. The quietest, cheapest place in town. Singles L17,000. Doubles L28,000.

Hotel Italia, viale Pallavicini (tel. 356 10), to the left as you exit the station. Congenial management, modern rooms, and quieter than you'd expect so close to the station. Singles L22,000. Doubles L35,000.

Hotel Roma, via Candiano, 26 (tel. 42 15 15), around the corner from the station to the left. Tidy and contemporary. Singles L22,000. Doubles L35,000.

Minerva, viale Maroncelli, 1 (tel. 345 49), to the right of the station. Rooms similar to but noisier than those at the Italia. Singles with bath L25,000. Doubles L33,500, with bath L38,000.

Albergo Mokadoro, via Baiona, 18 (tel. 260 03). Take bus #2 northbound (ask the driver, about 10-min., every ½-hr. until 11:30pm). 65 modern rooms on an unattractive but quiet road outside town. Singles L15,000, with bath L17,000. Doubles L26,000, with bath L28,000.

Hotel Piccolo, just down the road at via Baiona, 59 (tel. 281 39). Almost identical to the Mokadoro. Singles L17,000, with bath L23,000. Doubles L32,000, with bath L40,000.

Food

Aside from the *mense,* both of which are closed in August, there are only two restaurants in the center of Ravenna—most lurk on the outskirts. If you're staying at the hostel, you may wish to avail yourself of the L7000 dinner or L2500 plate of spaghetti. Hostelers also benefit from the adjacent bargain supermarket. (Open Mon.-Sat. 9am-noon and 3:30-6pm.) The busy **Mercato Coperto** is in p. Andrea Costa, just up via IV Novembre from p. del Popolo. Finally, the **Ca' de' Ven** (wine house) at via Corrado Ricci, 24, maintains a huge store of vintage wines produced in Emilia Romagna. (Open Tues.-Sun.)

Mensa Il Duomo Self-Service, via Oberdan, 8 (tel. 239 70), off p. del Duomo. Decent institutional meals in a new facility. L6000. Open Sept.-July Mon.-Fri. noon-2:15pm.

Ristorante Scai, p. Baracca (tel. 225 20), a 10-minute walk down boutique-lined via Cavour. *Primi* such as *gnocchi, lasagna,* and *cannelloni* L4500-5000; with a *contorno* (vegetable side dish), they make a meal. Most of the *secondi* (including the many fish dishes) go for L8500. Open Tues.-Sun.

Ristorante/Pizzeria Guidarello, via R. Gessi, 7, off p. Arcivescovado. Nice, cool, with respectable food, and quick service. Pizza L3500-5000, *primi* L3500-5500, *secondi* around L6500. Open Tues.-Sun.

Ristorante da Renato, via Mentana, 31, around the corner and a xerox of the above, but usually somewhat better food. Open Mon.-Sat. noon-2:30pm and 7-9:15pm.

Il Gelato, several locations along via Armando Diaz. Makes up for the lack of restaurants. Who needs substance, anyway?

Sights

Brilliant mosaics depicting biblical history adorn the sixteenth-century **Basilica di San Vitale.** The simple scenes of Abel's sacrifice, Abraham and Isaac, Moses' life, and above them, the Four Evangelists, are all delightfully decipherable. The courts of the Emperor Justinian and his wife Theodora stand in formal Byzantine splendor; Christ, seated in the dome, rests on a sphere of blue so vivid it hardly betrays its 1300 years. (Open daily 8:30am-7:30pm.)

The interior of the tiny **Mausoleum of Galla Placidia** is coated with the oldest and arguably most exquisite mosaics in the city. (Coin box for illumination outside.) Note the carved sarcophagi here, stone echoes of the mosaic motifs. (Open daily 8:30am-7pm. Free.)

Through the gate between San Vitale and the Mausoleum lies the sprawling **Museo Nazionale,** in the cloisters of what was once the convent attached to the church. At the entrance is a funeral stele of the Roman carpenter who built the military fleet that once anchored in the nearby port of Classe. Other rooms' floors are covered with mosaics, just in case you can't get enough. (Open Tues.-Sat. 8:30am-7pm, Sun. 8:30am-1:30pm. Admission L3000.)

The **duomo** itself is a hilarious baroque hodgepodge. Glance inside at the two sarcophagi and the charming bird-covered pulpit, gifts of early bishops. In the **Battistero Neoniano** next door are some poorly restored mosaics on the lower level and three levels of fifth-century mosaics above. Since the ground level is today significantly higher then it was 1500 years ago, you get a better view of the mosaics then the Byzantines ever did. (Church open daily 6am-noon and 2-6pm. *Battistero* open Mon.-Sat. 9am-noon and 2:30-6pm, Sun. 9am-noon. Admission L100.)

A small but precious collection of mosaics from the *duomo* is on display in the **Museo Arcivescovile,** nearby. Also exhibited are a mosaic chapel and the Throne of Maximilian, perhaps the best piece of ivory carving in the Christian world and the zenith of Ravennine sculpture. (Open mid-March to mid-Oct. Tues.-Sat. 9am-noon and 2:30-6pm, Sun. 9am-1pm; mid-Oct. to mid-March Tues.-Sat. 9am-noon and 2:30-5pm, Sun. 9am-1pm. Admission L500.) Compare the mosaics in the orthodox Battistero Neoniano (above) with those in the **Battistero degli Ariani,** on via degli Ariani off via Diaz, used by the Arians, a sect condemned as heretics for doubting the Trinity. Theologians might revel in the iconographic differences, but laymen will simply enjoy their better-preserved beauty.

Ravenna took in Dante Alighieri (1265-1321) when he was exiled from Florence, and has never let anyone forget it. The city is rather eager to capitalize on the poet's remains, which now repose next to the Church of San Francesco. Last year, for example, Ravenna sponsored a sculpture competition on themes drawn from the *Commedia,* and then exhibited the entries all summer. You can pay your respects at the humdrum sepulcher off p. dei Caduti.

The **Church of Sant' Apollinare Nuovo** has the largest mosaics in Ravenna along its nave. Underneath some scenes from the life of Christ, two splendid processions, one of virgins and one of martyrs, move up toward the altar between rows of palms on a gold background. (Open daily 8:30am-7pm. Free.)

The mosaics of Ravenna culminate in those of the **Church of Sant' Apollinare in Classe,** a sixth-century basilica outside the city. The classical style yields to the Byzantine in the figures of angels and evangelists on the mosaic-covered triumphal arch. The mosaic scene is full of lovely details, including the jewel-studded cross and the tiny birds in the field. (Open daily 8am-noon and 2-6:30pm; bus #4 leaves every 30 min. from the station.) The **Pineta di Classe,** a somewhat eerie pine grove, stretches around the church, setting off its solemn brick facade and huge circular *campanile.* The lawn makes a perfect picnic site.

Entertainment

From mid-July to mid-August, an annual **International Organ Festival** is held in San Vitale, a series of performances by top-notch artists (tickets L4000). At the **Rocca di Brancaleone,** there are open-air opera and dance performances in summer; in winter, opera and ballet are performed in the **Teatro Alighieri.** There is an annual **Dante Festival** the second week in September, with exhibits, readings, and various performances. Ravenna sponsors an excellent **Estate;** activities are concentrated in July. Obtain a schedule at the Azienda or at any EPT office in Emilia Romagna.

The **Centro Internazionale di Studi dell' Insegnamento del Mosaico (CISIM),** at Lido Adriano, gives 15-day courses in making mosaics during the summer. Applications are due by the end of May; write to the Azienda Autonoma for details.

Near Ravenna

Along the coast, several kilometers away, are Ravenna's beach towns—from Casalborsetti in the north through Marina di Ravenna and Punta Marina to Lido di Savio in the south. These towns are famous not only for their beautiful beaches but also for the pine trees that enclose them from the rear. Unfortunately, the water is murky and the industrial backdrop a little disenchanting. Bus A of the ATM network runs in a circuit from p. Farini, in front of the train station, along via Molinetto (by the hostel), to Punta Marina, Marina di Ravenna, and then back inland along via Trieste to the *piazza* (L800). If you're at the hostel, get on and off the bus at the via Molinetto stop.

There is good rod-fishing from **Marina di Ravenna's** two breakwaters, which extend 2½km into the ocean. If staying the night, try **Hotel Bristol** at viale T. de Revel, 18 (tel. 43 01 04), 4 blocks beyond the Azienda, then inland a bit. The rooms are small but relaxing. (Singles L19,000. Doubles L25,000.) For food, head to **Ristorante Bunker** at viale delle Nazioni, 177, which serves decent fish dishes for L6000-10,000. The **tourist office** is at viale delle Nazioni, 159 (tel. 43 10 17). You may wish to backtrack to **Punta Marina** and try the large **Albergo Elite** at via della Fontana, 11 (tel. 43 73 09). (Singles with bath L18,000. Doubles with bath L28,000. Open June-Sept. 15.) Farther south at **Lido di Savio,** you can have a relaxing Italian-style vacation at **Albergo Rock,** via Cesena, 12 (tel. 94 92 41). Doubles are L35,000, but take *pensione completa* at L40,000 per person; the food is amazing. (Open April-Sept.) If you prefer **camping,** your most pleasant options are the campgrounds **Pineta,** via Spallazzi (tel. 44 51 52; L2780 per person, L6000 per tent), in **Casalbor-**

setti, and **Ceroni** on via Matelda, 245 (tel. 49 41 69; L2950 per person, L5200 per tent), in **Lido di Dante.** Ask the bus driver to let you off. (Both open May-Sept.) There are numerous campgrounds, but some are enormous complexes with thousands of people.

Rimini

One face of Rimini, sporting sunglasses and a dark tan, looks toward the sea: a frenetic Miami Beach with fewer bikini tops and more *pizzerie.* Its other face gazes with Augustan nostalgia to its great past, located in the historic center farther inland—an alluring jumble of medieval streets graced with the Malatesia Temple. If the latter visage bears the noble features of Renaissance-man Leon Battista Alberti (designer of the temple), the other is a carnivalesque caricature worthy of native son Federico Fellini.

Orientation and Practical Information

Rimini is a major stop on the Bologna-Lecce rail line and is served by an airport with service to many European cities (mostly charters). Rimini is also the gateway to San Marino, the tiny, tacky mountain republic an hour to the west by bus. To get to the beach from the station on foot (10 min.), follow the signs indicating *al mare.* By bus, take #10 or 11 to head south along the main drag; tickets (L600 per hr.) can be purchased on the bus until 7pm. After that, buy them at the kiosk in front of the station or at newsstands. To reach the center of the inland town, walk along via Dante Alighieri from the station.

APT: piazzale C. Battisti, 1 (tel. 279 27), to your left as you leave the station. Organized and friendly. Open June-Sept. Mon.-Sat. 8am-8pm, Sun. 9am-1pm; Oct.-May Mon.-Sat. 8am-2pm.

Azienda di Promozione Turistica: Main office, via Matteucci, 4 (tel. 245 11). **Branch office,** piazzale dell'Indipendenza, 3 (tel. 245 11), at the sea next to the Cassa di Risparmio di Rimini. Less mobbed than the APT, so usually more helpful. Open in summer daily 8am-10pm; in off-season Mon.-Sat. 8am-2pm. **Other offices** at Bellariva, Miramare, Rivabella, Viserba, and Torre Pedrera (open Sept. 15-June).

Promozione Alberghiera: viale Vespucci (tel. 522 69), across from piazzale dell'Indipendenza. This hotel owners' association will find you a room. Open Mon.-Wed. and Fri.-Sat. 8:30am-12:30pm and 3-6:30pm, Tues. and Thurs. 8:30am-12:30pm. **Branch office,** at the train station (tel. 511 94). Open late May to mid-Sept. 8:30am-8:30pm. **Third office,** in p. Tripoli (tel. 217 62).

San Marino Information Office: piazzale C. Battisti, 1 (tel. 563 33), next to the APT. Bus schedules, shopping and accommodations information, but no postage stamps. Open April-Oct. Mon.-Fri. 8am-7pm; in off-season 8:30am-1pm and 3-6:30pm, Sat.-Sun. 2-7pm.

Student Travel: CTS, in the P. A. Viaggi office at viale Vespucci, 1 (tel 247 81). Open Mon.-Fri. 9am-1pm and 3:30-7:30pm, Sat 9am-1pm. Also **Transalpino** tickets at via Amerigo Vespucci, 11/C (tel. 265 00). Open in summer 9:30am-12:30pm and 3:30-10pm; in off-season Mon.-Fri. 9am-12:30pm and 3-7pm, Sat. 9am-12:30pm.

Post Office: corso Augusto, 8. Open Mon.-Sat. 8:20am-1:20pm and 3:05-4pm. Also at the beach, viale P. Mantegazza off viale Vespucci. Open Mon.-Fri. 8:15am-1:30pm, Sat. 8:15am-noon. **Postal code:** 47037.

Telephones: SIP, p. Ferrari, 22, in the Galleria U. Fabbri. Open daily 8am-9:30pm. At other times, try any of the many bars along the beach and near the station. **Telephone code:** 0541.

Buses: Intercity bus station, at viale Roma at p. Clementini, a few hundred meters from the station.

Car Rental: Hertz and **Avis,** both on viale Trieste, 14 and 16 (tel. 531 16), near the beach. Also offices at the airport in Miramare (Hertz tel. 37 51 08, Avis 37 07 21). Rates are nearly half what they are in the rest of the country. Less than L310,000 per week with unlimited mileage, tax and insurance included (available summer only).

Automobile Club d'Italia: viale Roma, 66 (tel. 242 75), near the station.

English Bookstores: Libreria Riminese, via IV Novembre, 46 (tel. 264 17). Decent novels. Open in summer Mon.-Sat. 8:30am-12:30pm and 4:20-8pm; in off-season Mon. and Wed.-Fri.

Red Cross: via Savonarola, 6 (tel. 266 12), near the canal.

Medical Assistance: On the beach at the end of viale Gounod, just beyond viale Pascoli. Free walk-in clinic for tourists. Open in summer daily 9:30am-noon and 3:30-7pm.

Police: corso d'Augusto, 192 (tel. 510 00).

Accommodations and Camping

Bringing a list of hotels to Rimini is as useful as taking coals to Newcastle—the city is run by innkeepers. During high season (last week in June through Aug.), your best chance of finding a room is through the accommodation services of the central offices, while during off-season, most places will be begging for your business. While there are some fine hotels in the old city, it's fun and reasonable to stay on the beach.

The **Promozione Alberghiera** runs an accommodation service. When you arrive at the train station, they will find you a room if you pay L200 "for the telephone call." Be insistent about what you can or will pay—if they are unrealistic, start making noises about going to the hostel. If you arrive after this office has closed—a very bad idea—take bus #10 or 11 to p. dell'Indipendenza. There, close to the Azienda, is a board with a city map and a list of hotels. Those whose red light has not yet been lit have room (the closer to the bottom of the list, the cheaper). To avoid these hassles, simply reserve in advance by phone. Prices per person without pension average L18,000-25,000 in high season and about half that in low season for the *locanda*-class hotels. Be warned, however, that many places require guests to take *pensione completa,* usually at an additional L25,000 per person.

Almost all of Rimini's hundreds of hotels close from October to May. The three below, all in the older part of town, don't—and neither do they require *pensione completa* in summer.

Ostello Urland (IYHF), via Flaminia, 300 (tel. 37 32 16), by the airport, 10 min. away on bus #9. L8500. Breakfast included. Curfew 11pm. Always call ahead. Open May-Sept.

Albergo dei Cavalieri, p. Cavour, 16 (tel. 248 00). An excellent, flower-filled *albergo* in the heart of the old city. Run by a wonderful family with an English-speaking daughter and their cat Camille (who's almost as warm as Camille Landau). Singles L21,400, in off-season L16,100. Doubles L33,600, in off-season L24,900. Triples L44,400, in off-season L33,600. Showers included.

Hotel Cardellini, via Dante, 50 (tel. 264 12), 100m from the train station. 63 tidy if tiny rooms with high ceilings. Singles L27,000, with bath L35,000. Doubles L42,700, with bath L55,000. Parking garage.

Albergo Malatesta, p. Malatesta, 31 (tel. 78 04 61), at the end of via Verdi. Ask for a room with a balcony. Doubles L36,000, with bath L40,000.

Camping Maximum Tel. 37 26 02 or 37 02 71. Take bus #10 to the last stop ("Miramare").

Food

Restaurants in Rimini loot the lire-pouch, especially if you order fish. You'll find the most reasonable places in the old city. Along the beach, the *tavole calde* and *pizzerie* are reasonable for light fare, but extortionate for full meals. Avoid the places sporting German and British flags. Rimini's **covered market,** between via Castelfidardo and the Tempio, is unusually clean and appetizing. (Open Mon.-Wed. and Fri.-Sat. 7:15am-1pm and 5-7:30pm, Thurs. 7:15am-1pm.)

Ristorante Kennedy, on the beach at p. Kennedy. Touristed but cheap. Saturating spaghetti L5000. Cover L1000.

Mensa Dopolavoro Ferroviario, viale Roma, 70. Go down via Dante and turn left on viale Roma. The only bargain in town, with decent food. *Primi* L2500, *secondi* L4600. Wine L1000 per ½-liter. Open Mon.-Sat. 11:30am-3pm and 6:30-9pm.

Ristorante/Pizzeria Pic Nic, via Tempio Malatestiano, 30. Delectable fare cooked on an open fire. Pizza L3500-6000, full meals L15,000. Cover L1500. Open Tues.-Sun. noon-3pm and 7pm-1am.

Bar Canosta, p. Cavour. Try the exceptional, bright orange passion-fruit *gelato.* Somewhat pricey.

Sights

Any tour of Rimini's historic center should begin with the Renaissance **Tempio Malatestiano.** Originally a Franciscan church constructed in the Gothic style, it was classicized in the 1440s and made into a monument to the ruling Sigismondo Malatesta and his fourth wife, the lovely Isotta.

Sigismondo Malatesta was excommunicated by the Papacy, burned in effigy, and damned in Rome by Pius II as a heretic guilty of "murder, violation, adultery, incest, sacrilege, perjury so dissolute that he raped his daughters and sons-in-law and as a boy often acted as the female partner in shameful loves, and later forced men to act as women." Nonetheless, he was a soldier and patriot who ruled Rimini at its height (1417-1468) and employed such artists as Piero della Francesca and Leon Battista Alberti, who designed the exterior of the new church.

Alberti modeled the front of the temple after the ancient Roman Arch of Augustus, which still stands at the gates of the city. The two front arches, which were originally intended to hold the sarcophagi of Sigismondo and Isotta, are now filled with limestone. (The dollar signs you see in the floral frieze are actually the intertwined initials of Sigismondo and Isotta.)

The spacious, single-naved interior and its wooden-trussed roof are reminiscent of a medieval Franciscan church. In the postcard and guide shop you'll find Piero della Francesca's famous portrait of Sigismondo Malatesta kneeling before his name-saint. In the chapel to the left of the card shop hangs a looming Giotto Crucifix. The sprightly sculptures and reliefs found in almost every chapel are the creations of Agostino di Duccio. (Open April-Sept. daily 7am-noon and 3-7pm; Oct.-March irregular hours.)

A short distance from the temple is the **piazza Tre Martiri** (named after three partisans hanged by the Fascists in 1944), the ramshackle, noisy city center that also marks the site of the ancient Roman forum. The forum's columns now serve as porticos for the two eastern buildings. The most important reminder of Rimini's former glory, however, is the **Arch of Augustus,** at the end of corso d'Augusto. The oldest Roman triumphal arch (27 B.C.E.), its combination of arch, column, and medallion inspired the design for the Malatesta Temple.

A short walk across the river from the ancient Ponte di Tiberio (the 3rd right off viale Tiberio) brings you to an unassuming neighborhood square and the **Church of San Giuliano.** This small Renaissance structure shelters the last work of the great Venetian master, Paolo Veronese, *The Martyrdom of St. Julian* (1558).

Rimini's old medieval center and favorite hangout, **piazza Cavour,** contains one of the oddest collections of buildings in Italy. Three municipal *palazzi* line the north side of the square, all in the robust "no-nonsense" style of Bologna. The tall Renaissance arcade of the **Palazzo Garampi** contrasts with the adjoining fortresslike **Palazzo dell' Arengo** (1207) and the smaller **Palazzo del Podestà** (1334). Between the first two buildings is an Italian version of Brussels' famous *le pisseur,* elaborated in a full baroque setting. Adding a lighter touch to the vista, the pink brick **Teatro Comunale** (1857) completes a second side to the square, minus its auditorium, which was bombed during World War II. On the third side of the square, in the jumble of shops, bars, and offices, is the refined Renaissance entrance to the **fish market** (*pescheria*). Four stone dolphins in the corners of the market once filled the small canals (still visible under the benches) with water used to clean the fish. In addition, two curious sculptures pose in the center of the *piazza:* an eccentric, moss-encrusted fountain (1543), engraved with an inscription recalling the presence of Leonardo da Vinci, and a sumptuously garbed Pope Paul V (1614), sitting in a chair bearing ferocious eagles and a bas-relief of Rimini on the back.

Other sights include the old fortress, **Rocca Malatestiana** (closed for restoration in 1988), built by Sigismondo between 1437 and 1446 (behind the Communal Theater); the **Church of Sant' Agostino** with its great cycle of Riminese-Gothic frescoes in its choir; and the lush, almost theatrical baroque interior of the **Church of the Servi.** The **Museo Civico,** via Gambalunga, 27, houses a collection of Roman mosaics and early Italian paintings, highlighted by Giovanni Bellini's *Dead Christ with Four Angels.* (Museum open in summer Tues.-Sun. 8:30am-1pm and 3:30-8:30pm; in off-season Mon.-Sat. 8am-1pm.)

Entertainment

Fashion-conscious teenieboppers join the *passeggiata* nightly on **piazza Indipendenza** and **viale Regina** to see and be seen. There are hundreds of discotheques to choose from. For a list of the latest and greatest, pick up a copy of *Kursaal* at the tourist office—though sexist, it's a free and complete weekly guide to Rimini's beach and disco culture. Rimini has instituted a new service for carless disco-goers: The **Blue Line** is a bus (L1500) that leaves from the "Night Office," a yellow double-decker bus stationed in p. Kennedy, and runs all night (9pm-5am) to all the clubs.

Beginning in mid-June and continuing through the summer, the **Sagra Musicale Malatestiana** brings international artists and companies to Rimini. Pick up a schedule at the tourist office. Folk groups from all over Italy perform at the *quartiere fieristico* (almost daily at 9:30pm, free).

Near Rimini

San Marino, the "smallest and oldest republic in the world," is a tourist trap to be avoided. From its reconstructed Disneyesque medieval buildings to the cutesy green-and-red uniforms of its toy soldiers, San Marino glares as much as the thousands of postcards and assorted tourist junk that line its torturously picturesque streets. If, however, you're a true tourist, take one of **Filli Benedettini's** buses from p. Tripoli (June-Sept. 15 per day, L1800, check for times at the San Marino Tourist Office). If you want to stay for any length of time here, pick up the exhaustive *San Marino Practical Guide* at the tourist office. Hotels in the republic are out of the budget range, but you can camp at **Camping della Murata,** via del Serrone, 594 (tel. (0541) 99 12 99), 1½km out of town. (L3000 per person, L2000 per tent.)

You're much better off going to **San Leo,** which combines an interesting collection of historical buildings with a spectacular setting—you can even see San Marino from the roadway. The walls and cylindrical towers of the fortress, now the emblem of the city, were designed in the fifteenth century by Francesco di Giorgio Martini. The oldest building is the beautiful Pieve, dating from the ninth century and in miraculously good condition. The twelth-century *duomo* nearby is a harmonious blend of Romanesque and Gothic. Two buses per day, one in the morning and one in the afternoon, leave from the Rimini train station for the 70-minute trip to San Leo. Or venture several miles farther down the coast to the hallowed beach resort of **Igea Marina.**

Tuscany (Toscana)

If Italy's provinces had astrological signs, Tuscany would be libra: It is in every respect the fulcrum between north and south. The sun broils its olive orchards in summer, but is never as hot as in the torrid south; cypresses and pines give the region a greenness to cool the dry ochres, but the foliage is never as lush as in the north. The people also embody this equilibrium; friendly and generous, they exude more

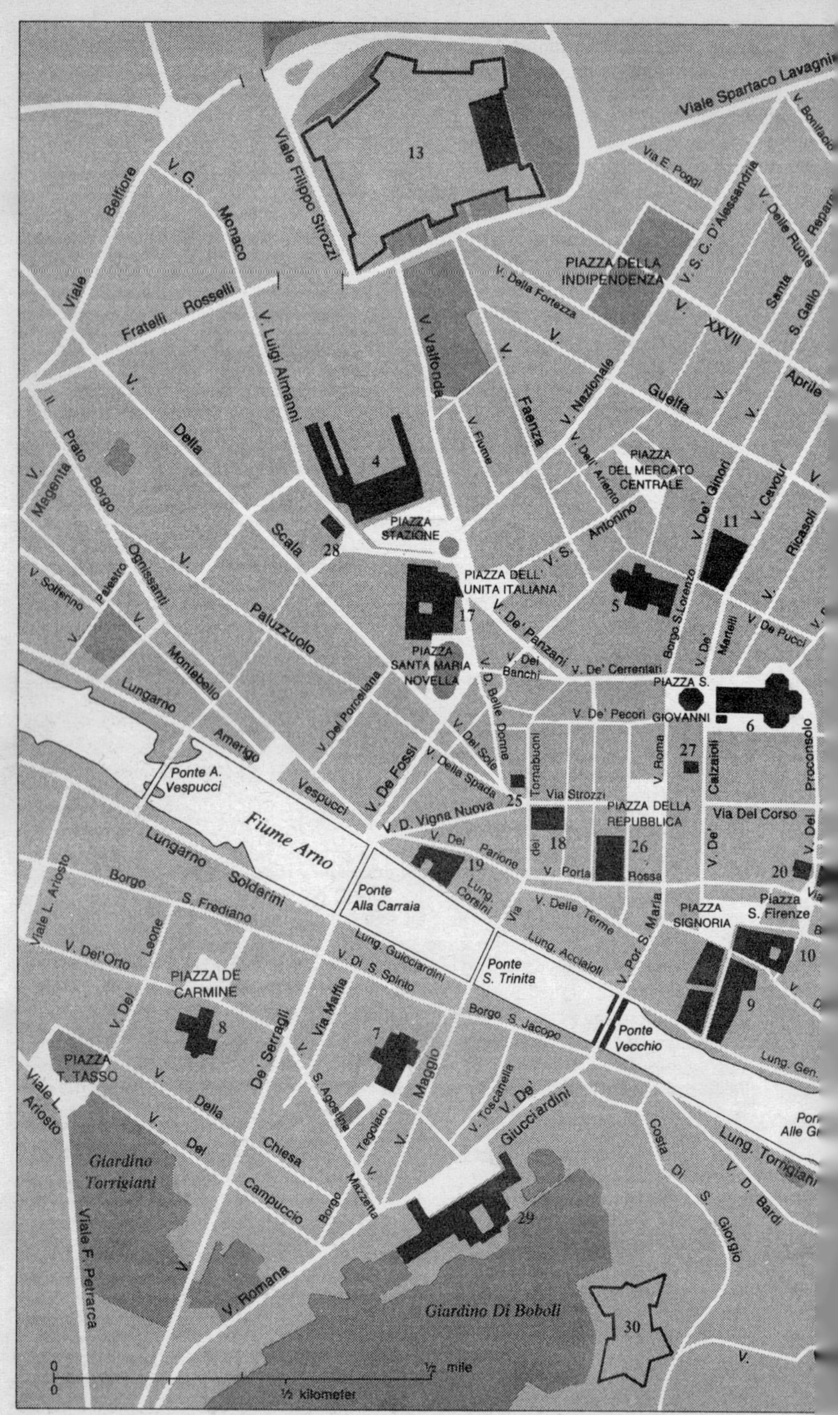
Viale Spartaco Lavagnini
13
Viale Filippo Strozzi
V. G. Monaco
Viale Belfiore
Viale Fratelli Rosselli
PIAZZA DELLA INDIPENDENZA
V. Della Fortezza
V. Luigi Alamanni
V. Valfonda
V. Faenza
V. Nazionale
V. XXVII Aprile
V. Guelfa
V. Della Scala
4
PIAZZA STAZIONE
28
PIAZZA DEL MERCATO CENTRALE
V. Dell' Ariento
V. S. Antonino
PIAZZA DELL' UNITA ITALIANA
17
5
11
V. De' Ginori
V. Cavour
V. Ricasoli
PIAZZA SANTA MARIA NOVELLA
V. De' Panzani
V. De' Cerretani
PIAZZA S. GIOVANNI
6
V. De' Pecori
27
Via Strozzi
25
PIAZZA DELLA REPUBBLICA
Via Del Corso
18
26
19
20
Fiume Arno
Ponte A. Vespucci
Ponte Alla Carraia
Ponte S. Trinita
Ponte Vecchio
PIAZZA SIGNORIA
Piazza S. Firenze
10
9
PIAZZA DE CARMINE
8
7
PIAZZA T. TASSO
Giardino Torrigiani
Giardino Di Boboli
29
30
V. Romana
Viale F. Petrarca
½ mile
½ kilometer

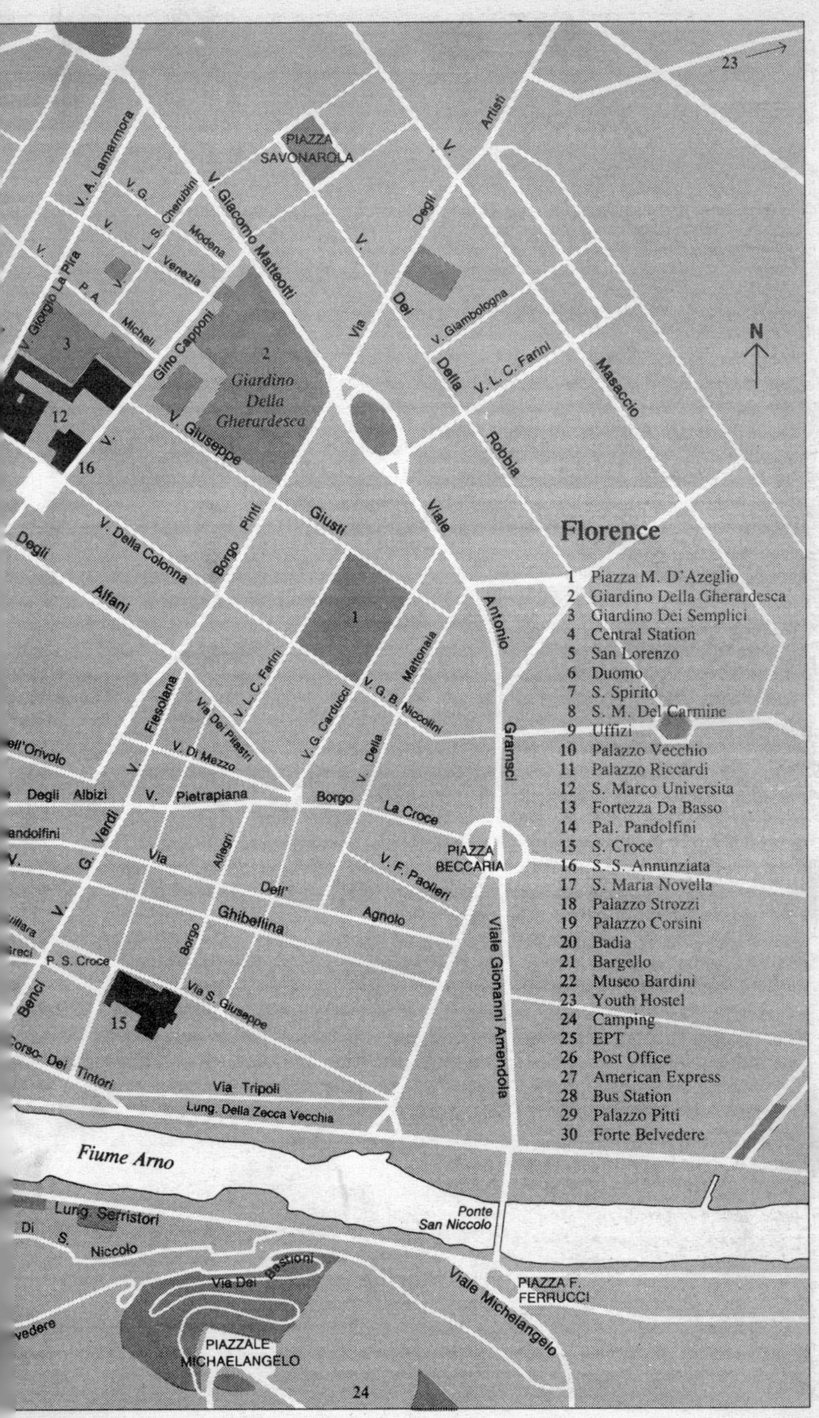
Florence
1 Piazza M. D'Azeglio
2 Giardino Della Gherardesca
3 Giardino Dei Semplici
4 Central Station
5 San Lorenzo
6 Duomo
7 S. Spirito
8 S. M. Del Carmine
9 Uffizi
10 Palazzo Vecchio
11 Palazzo Riccardi
12 S. Marco Universita
13 Fortezza Da Basso
14 Pal. Pandolfini
15 S. Croce
16 S. S. Annunziata
17 S. Maria Novella
18 Palazzo Strozzi
19 Palazzo Corsini
20 Badia
21 Bargello
22 Museo Bardini
23 Youth Hostel
24 Camping
25 EPT
26 Post Office
27 American Express
28 Bus Station
29 Palazzo Pitti
30 Forte Belvedere
N
PIAZZA SAVONAROLA
V. Giacomo Matteotti
Giardino Della Gherardesca
Viale Antonio Gramsci
PIAZZA BECCARIA
Viale Giovanni Amendola
Fiume Arno
Ponte San Niccolo
PIAZZA F. FERRUCCI
Viale Michelangelo
PIAZZALE MICHAELANGELO
Lung. Serristori
Lung. Della Zecca Vecchia
Via Tripoli
Borgo La Croce
Via Ghibellina
Borgo Pinti
V. Giuseppe Giusti
V. Della Colonna
Degli Alfani
Via S. Giuseppe
Corso Dei Tintori
Via Dei Bastioni

warmth than the northerners, but seem reserved when compared to the Sicilians or Neapolitans. Nature endowed the region with gently rolling, sun-kissed farmland, and Tuscans complemented this fortune with artistic patrimony and economic prosperity. The Tuscan landscape forms the classic background of much of Italian painting, and Tuscan, the language of Dante, Petrarch, and Machiavelli, is today's textbook Italian.

The region includes a variety of landscapes—the rocky, forested Apuan Alps; the cosmopolitan coast; and the marshy Maremma near Lazio—but is renowned for its hilly, fertile interior. The land here has been cultivated for thousands of years, and looks it. Fields of grapevines flow down gentle slopes overlooking a sea of sunflowers below.

Tuscany's pastoral beauty contrasts sharply with its violent history. This blessed region has encouraged continuous settlement and competition for land ever since the Etruscans first developed the area in the eighth century B.C.E. The Romans annexed the region, which they called Tuscia, in 351 B.C.E. It remained a unified state even after the fall of the Empire, ruled by a series of Frankish vassals of Charlemagne. Eventually, most of the cities took advantage of the territorial struggles between popes and emperors to declare their independence as city-states or communes. This period was characterized by nearly constant war, and cities rushed to fortify their ramparts, building the towers, fortresses, and city walls distinctly preserved today in towns such as Lucca, San Gimignano, and Siena. A typical commune was ruled by a city council in which two major social groups were represented—the *magnati* (the nobles) and the *popolani* (the *nouveau riche*).

In the latter half of the fourteenth century, the *popolani* gradually ousted the *magnati* from power. The biggest coup was realized by the Florentine Medici, a family of bankers who rose to power by manipulating local financial interests and carried out political intrigues to their own—and ultimately Florence's—advantage. Under the Medici, Florence grew in wealth and power and was at last able to overtake rival city-states, including Siena, Lucca, and Pisa. The height of Medici rule came under Cosimo I (1389-1464) and his grandson Lorenzo Il Magnifico (1449-1492), who, in typical *nouveau riche* fashion, sought to legitimize their newly acquired wealth by pouring a part of it into the arts.

Though periodically ousted by the French and those Florentines loyal to the Republican cause, the Medici became increasingly powerful and decadent, ultimately precipitating a decline in culture and a ruined economy. Disenfranchised by the French and the Austrians, Tuscany played its part in the unification of Italy, with Florence serving as capital until Rome was captured from the papacy in 1870. Despite damage suffered during World War II, Tuscany today is economically robust and is an intellectual and cultural center.

An extensive and convenient transportation system makes it easy to tour Tuscany's lovely countryside. The state railroad serves all major towns and many smaller ones, though Tuscany's numerous hill towns are perhaps better reached by bus (since the nearest train stations are usually several kilometers away in the valley below). Hitching is also not difficult throughout Tuscany.

Youth hostels abound in Tuscany, and hotel rooms are affordable, except in a few small towns such as Volterra, where competition is scarce. Tuscany is popular with tourists; especially in Florence, Siena, Pisa, and on the island of Elba, reservations are advisable in summer. Camping is possible at the region's many lakes, mountains, and coastal resorts.

Eating well in Tuscany without spending a fortune is not difficult with hearty *ribollita* (bean and cabbage stew), *cocciucco* (seafood stew), and the delicious meatless *panzanella* (bread, tomatoes, and vegetables) and *fiori di zucca fritti* (fried zucchini flowers). Meat specialties include *coniglio* (rabbit), *trippa* (tripe), and the famous, and very costly, *bistecca alla fiorentina.* The wonderful local green-black olive oil is unfortunately very rare now, thanks to the 1985 frost.

Tuscany's gastronomic triumph, however, is its wine. The region's most renowned wine is *chianti,* from the area around Florence and Siena; *chianti classico* is the highest quality—look for the *gallo nero* (black rooster) label on the neck. Tuscany's renowned red wine, however, is the more expensive *brunello di Montalcino,* an excellent dry red from a town south of Siena. *Vino Nobile di Montepulciano* is another full-bodied red from the same area. The region's best white is the luscious *vernaccia di San Gimignano.* A unique Tuscan wine is *vin santo,* a sweet, sherry-like wine made from grapes hung in lofts to dry for several months before being crushed; drink it as Tuscans do—with a plateful of *cantuccini di prato* (crispy almond cookies) for dipping.

Florence (Firenze)

Florence was the epicenter of the Renaissance. Michelangelo, Machiavelli, and the Medici called it home. Fueled by an innovative banking system, the city catapulted from a medieval wool and silk trade into a bastion of political experimentation and artistic rebirth.

Fifteenth-century figures quickly made comparisons with ancient Rome, and, in fervent moments, dubbed the city a new and more secular Jerusalem. There was no doubt that providence—as well as the Muses—had smiled on Flornece. Leonardo Bruni, the great fifteenth-century humanist and chancellor of Florence, made sure the perfection of the city's internal organization matched the perfection of its geographical placement: Equidistant from both the Mediterranean and the Adriatic, Florence could at the same time enjoy easy access to the sea and a secure inland position amidst the fertile countryside.

Today the city is a living museum, if not a brothel of culture. Despite the continual flood of tourists, Florence reduces even the most experienced travelers to a state of wonder. More remains of the city's incomparable heritage than stones and paint—the lively and indomitable spirit of the city has survived the centuries too. To get a better feel for the city's genuine atmosphere, step away from the usual tourist turf. Eat in an outlying *trattoria,* or visit a small church on the edge of town.

Irving Stone's imaginative *The Agony and the Ecstasy* and the recently published novel *The Notebook of Gismondo Cavaletti* will help you know the Florence of a different time. For a non-fiction account of Florence's golden age, take a look at Jacob Burckhardt's classic, *The Civilization of the Renaissance in Italy.*

Orientation

Florence lies in the heart of Italy, easily accessible by train from Milan, Bologna, Venice, and Rome. Most trains arrive at **Santa Maria Novella Station** (often posted as Firenze S.M.N.), in the center of town, though some *locali* and *diretti* stop only at **Campo di Marte Station** on the east side. (See Train Stations under Practical Information.) From p. della Stazione, it is a short walk on via de' Panzani (which in 2 blocks becomes via de' Cerretani) to the center of Florence, the area bordered by the *duomo* in the north, the river Arno in the south, and the Bargello and Palazzo Strozzi in the east and west. This area is known as the old city and is characterized by cobblestone streets and grand old *palazzi.*

Major arteries radiate out of **piazza S. Giovanni/piazza Duomo** (borgo S. Lorenzo to p. San Lorenzo, via dei Servi to p. SS. Annunziata, via del Proconsolo to the Badia and Bargello); the city's major thoroughfare, **via dei Calzaioli,** runs from here to p. Signoria. **Piazza Signoria,** in turn, is just around the corner from the Ponte Vecchio, which spans the Arno to the district called the **Oltrarno.** South of via dei Calzaioli lies **piazza della Repubblica,** the largest open space in the city, and near it runs **via Tornabuoni,** a major route to the river at Ponte Santa Trinità. Beyond the old city sprawls a vast and ugly suburbia.

For guidance through Florence's often confusing center, pick up a free map either inside the station from the booth marked *Informazione Turistiche Alberghiere* or just outside at the red and white tourist booth. A more detailed map is the *Nicola Vincitorio Pianta Generale,* the one with a red, white, and black cover (L3500 at most newsstands).

Artistic and historical relics are scattered throughout Florence. Few places are too distant to be reached by foot, but if the pedestrian traffic oppresses you, don't hesitate to hop onto one of the prompt and comfortable city ATAF buses. (See Buses under Practical Information.)

Florence's streets are numbered in red and black sequences. Red numbers indicate commercial establishments, while black numbers denote residential addresses (including most sights and hotels). Here, as in Florentine publications, black addresses will appear as a numeral only, while red addresses will appear as a number followed by an "r." In general, street numbers on streets parallel to the Arno start upstream and increase as you go downstream; at right angles to the river, they increase as the street moves away from it.

Practical Information

There are numerous guides and listings to aid travelers in Florence, but many are unhelpful and outdated. At the tourist offices, specifically request pamphlets for budget travelers. Peruse the local entertainment glossies at the newsstands, such as the monthly *Firenze Spettacolo* (L1500) and *Firenze La Sera* (L2500).

As in the rest of Italy, most establishments close for two to four hours in the afternoon. In addition to the major Italian holidays (see Festivals and Holidays in the General Introduction), Florence celebrates its patron San Giovanni on June 24. As on all major holidays, everything but the occasional bar will close—so join in the festivities (see Entertainment below).

Azienda Autonoma di Turismo: via Tornabuoni, 15 (tel. 21 65 44), up 1 flight of stairs. From the station, walk across p. Unità and along via de' Panzani; take the 2nd right onto via Rondinelli, which becomes via Tornabuoni. The staff occasionally takes a moment from their coffee to assist one of the tourists milling about the counter. Good map and lots of free pamphlets. Open Mon.-Sat. 9am-1pm.

EPT: via A. Manzoni, 16 (tel. 247 81 41), a bit out of the way. Information on all of Tuscany, and then some. No accommodations service, but it handles complaints about hotels. Will provide tourist information, but is largely administrative. Supposedly open Mon.-Fri. 8:30am-1:30pm and 4-6:30pm, Sat. 8:30am-1:30pm.

Other Tourist Offices: At the red and white **Informazione Turistica** booth at the train station (exit by track #16). Great place to pick up a map and a hotel guide (*Elenco degli alberghi*) if you bypass the station accommodation service (see below). Booths usually staffed by students who are far friendlier than their professional counterparts. Open in summer daily 9am-9pm. Also at via Santa Monaca, 2. Convenient if you're staying at one of the nearby hostels. Staffed by helpful university students with up-to-date information. Open in summer Mon.-Fri. 8-11am and 4-7pm. Several seasonal tourist information offices may also be open in summer, notably around the *duomo,* p. Repubblica, p. Cattedrale, and the Palazzo Vecchio, although locations change yearly.

Accommodations Service: ACISJF, At the train station 50m down track #16 (tel. 29 46 35). An undiscovered resource. Provides a budget accommodations list and will make reservations without commission. Open Sept.-July Mon.-Sat. 10am-12:30pm and 1-4pm. **Informazioni Turistiche Alberghiere,** at the train station by track #10 (tel. 28 28 93). Give them a price range and they will get you a room, though perhaps not the best value and probably near the station. Come in person; no booking by phone. You pay 1st night's rent plus a L1500-1800 commission. If you arrive early in the day or speak some Italian, you're probably better off striking out on your own. Open daily mid-April to mid-Nov. 8am-9:30pm; mid-Nov. to mid-April 9am-6:30pm.

Student Travel: Centro Turistico Studentesco e Giovanile (CTSG), via dei Ginori, 11r (tel. 26 35 70), near San Lorenzo. BIJ tickets, charter flights, and discounts on ferries to Greece and Spain. No accommodations service and long lines. Open Mon.-Fri. 9:30am-1pm and 4-7pm, Sat. 9am-12:30pm. **International Student Club: Amici di Ale,** via San Giovanni, 28r (tel. 22 02 72), in Oltrano. A nominal membership fee (3500 per day, L6000 per year) entitles you to cheap bike rental, discounted laundry facilities, guided excursions, fully equipped gym . . . and parties. Decent prices, good beer, *great* student scene.

Consulates: U.S., lungarno Vespucci, 38 (tel. 29 82 76), at via Palestro near the station. Open Mon.-Fri. 8:30am-noon and 2-4pm. **U.K.,** lungarno Corsini, 2 (tel. 28 41 33). Open Mon.-Fri. 9:30am-12:30pm and 2:30-4:30pm. After hours leave a message on the answering machine. Citizens of **Canada, Australia,** and **New Zealand** should contact their consulates in Rome.

Currency Exchange: The best exchange rates can be found at the local banks. Open Mon.-Fri. 8:20am-1:20pm and 2:45-3:45pm. A small but growing number of banks (notably branches of **Cassa di Risparmio di Firenze**) are open Sat. afternoon. **Esercizio Promozione Turismo,** via Condotta, 42r (tel. 29 45 51), near p. Signoria, exchanges money at official rates after banks close and on holidays (commission at least L2000). Open Mon.-Sat. 10am-7pm and Sun. 10am-6pm. Also has an extensive selection of maps, guides, and Italian literature in translation. Go to **Ufficio Informazione,** in the station, only as a last resort. Open daily 7:20am-1:20pm and 2:35-8pm.

American Express: via Guciardini, 49r (tel. 27 87 51). Cashes personal checks for cardholders. Mail service upstairs (L2000 to check for noncustomers, L1000 to leave a message). Does not accept wired money. Open Mon.-Fri. 9am-6pm, Sat. 9am-1pm.

Post Office: via Pellicceria (tel. 21 61 22), off p. della Repubblica. Stamps at windows #21 and 22; Fermo Posta at windows #23 and 24 (L250 per letter). To send packages, go around to the back of the building and enter at via de' Sassetti, 4. Open Mon.-Fri. 8:15am-7pm, Sat. 8:15am-noon. **Telegram** office in front half of building open 24 hours. **Phone books** available Mon.-Sat. 8am-11pm. **Postal code:** 50100.

Telephones: ASST, via Pellicceria, at the post office. Also at via Cavour, 21r. Both open 24 hours. **SIP,** in the train station near track #5. Lines usually shorter than at ASST. One booth available for international calls to most European countries and the U.S. No traveler's checks accepted. Open daily 7:30am-9:30pm. **Telephone code:** 055.

Airport: Galileo Galilei Airport (tel. (050) 401 32), at Pisa. Take the airport express (1 hr.; one way L4900, round-trip L8400) from the Florence train station (daily 6:15am-7pm every 1-2 hr.). In Florence, call 27 88 for flight information.

Train Stations: Santa Maria Novella Station, near the center of town. Information office (tel. 27 87 85) open daily 7am-9pm. Hourly service to Venice (3½ hr., one way L12,700, round-trip L20,600), Rome (3 hr., L20,000), Milan (3½ hr., L20,000), and Bologna (1 hr., one way L4700, round-trip L8000). Almost all trains arrive here except some locals and a few trains to and from Rome, which use **Campo di Marte Station,** on the east side of town. Bus #19 connects the 2 stations approximately every 20 min. (24 hours).

Buses: City buses (ATAF), p. del duomo, 57r (tel. 21 23 01). Tickets (L600 or L700 for 70 min.) must be bought before boarding and are available at the train station or at *tabacchi* throughout the city. Many riders board without a ticket; before you follow suit, consider the L18,000 fine. The only bus route map in existence is posted at the ATAF booth in the railway station. **SITA,** via Santa Caterina da Siena, 15r (tel. 21 14 87), southwest of the station. Frequent buses to Siena, Volterra, and Arezzo. **CAT,** via Fiume, 2 (tel. 28 34 00), near the station. Buy tickets at via Nazionale, 4, for points within Tuscany. **LAZZI,** via della Stazione, 1-6r (tel. 21 51 54). Frequent service to Lucca (L5800), Pisa (L7600), Prato (L1800), and Pistoia (L3000). **LAZZI Eurolines,** via Mercadante, 2 (tel. 29 88 41). Service to Scandinavia (only L208,000 to Stockholm, "the Venice of the North"), Austria, Hungary, and Spain, as well as to Rome and Naples.

Taxi: Tel. 47 98 or 43 90.

Car Rental: Hertz, via Fininguerra, 11 (tel. 28 22 60). Open Mon.-Sat. 7am-8pm, Sun. 8:30am-1pm and 5-8pm. **Avis,** Borgo Ognissanti, 128r (tel. 21 36 29). Open Mon.-Sat. 8am-8pm, Sun. 8am-1pm and 5-8pm. **Inter-Rent,** via Il Prato, 1r (tel. 21 86 65). Open Mon.-Sat. 8am-1pm and 2-8pm, Sun. and holidays 8am-1pm. All are in the Borgo Ognissanti area southwest of the station. To rent a car, you must be at least 21 and have driven at least a year. No international driver's license is necessary. Rates are varied and complicated, so shop around. English spoken.

Moped Rental: Program, Borgo Ognissanti, 135r (tel. 26 27 24). Piaggio Si' (1-seater) L25,000 per day, L130,000 per week. Piaggio Vespa 125 (2-seater) L55,000 per day with 100 free km or L250,000 per week. Also rents by the month. Open Mon.-Sat. 8:30am-1pm and 3-8pm.

Bicycle Rental: Outside the train station at the beginning of via Alamani (tel. 21 33 07). L6000 per 3 hr., L15,000 per day. Document with photo required as deposit. Open daily 4:30am-midnight.

Hitching: For the A-1 north to Bologna and Milan, or the A-11 northwest to the Riviera and Genoa, take bus #29, 30, or 35 from the station to the feeder near Peretola. For the A-1 south to Rome and the extension to Siena, take bus #31 or 32 from the station to exit 23, Firenze Sud.

Lost Property: Oggetti Ritrovati, via Circondaria, 19 (tel. 36 79 43; for towed cars 35 15 62). Take bus #23 (A, B, or C) from the station to reclaim lost property. Open Mon.-Wed. and Fri.-Sat. 9am-noon.

English Bookstores: Paperback Exchange, via Fiesolana, 31r (tel. 247 81 54). The answer to a traveling bookworm's prayer. Florence reading list available. Open March 15-Nov. 15 Mon.-Sat. 9am-1pm and 3:30-7:30pm; Nov. 16-March 14 Tues.-Sat. 9am-1pm and 3:30-7:30pm. **Seeber,** via Tornabuoni, 68r (tel. 21 56 97). The widest selection of new books. Open same hours as above except closed for 2 weeks in mid-Aug. Both these stores carry *Let's Go.* **BM Bookshop,** Borgo Ognissanti, 4r (tel. 29 45 75), near the Excelsior Hotel. Belongs to the American Booksellers Association. Open daily 9am-1pm and 3:30-7:30pm. **Ideabooks,** via della Spada, 24r. Specializes in art books. Open Tues.-Sun. 9:30am-2pm and 3:30-7:30pm, Mon. 3:30-7:30pm.

Laundromats: via XXVII Aprile, at via Reparata near the hostels and train station. All usually charge over L10,000 per 5kg. One of the cheaper deals (L9000 per 5kg) is **Lavanderia Manfredi,** via S. Antonio, 66r (tel. 28 79 20), across from the Mercato Centrale.

Public Toilets: Some of the most convenient are upstairs in the Mercato Centrale, in the Palazzo Vecchio, in the Palazzo Pitti, and in the underground passage leading to the train station. All cost L150-200.

Public Baths: Albergo Diurno, just outside the train station exit near track #16. Showers L4000, soap and towel L1700, toilets L1500. Also has a bar, manicurist, and barber. Open Mon.-Wed. and Fri.-Sat. 6am-8pm, Sun. 6am-1pm. **Bagno S. Agostino,** via S. Agostino, 8 (tel. 28 44 82), off p. Santo Spirito. Baths L2000, towel and soap L1000. Open Tues. and Thurs. 3:30-7:30pm, Sat. 8:30am-12:30pm and 3:30-7:30pm.

Swimming pools: Try **Bellariva,** lungarno Columbo, 6 (tel. 67 75 21). Bus #14 from the station or a 15-min. walk upstream along the Arno. Popular. Open June-Sept. daily 10am-6pm. FREE. Also on Florence's east side is the **Costoli** covered pool in the huge sports complex at Campo di Marte (tel. 67 57 44). Take bus #17 from p. Unità toward the *duomo.* A clean Olympic-sized pool with separate diving and kiddie pools. Arrive early. Open daily 10am-6pm. Admission June-Sept. L4500, children L1000, ages over 60 free.

All-Night Pharmacies: Farmacia Comunale, at the train station by track #16 (tel. 26 34 35). **Molteni,** via Calzaioli, 7r (tel. 26 34 90). **Taverna,** p. S. Giovanni, 20r (tel. 21 13 43). All open 24 hours.

First Aid: Misericordia, p. del Duomo, 20 (tel. 21 22 22). A time-honored Florentine institution, they will send an ambulance. **Tourist Medical Service,** via Lorenzo il Magnifico, 59 (tel. 47 54 11). A group of general practitioners and specialists with someone always on call. A list of English-speaking doctors is available from the U.S. consulate.

Police: Questura (*Ufficio Stranieri,* for foreigners), via Zara, 2 (tel. 497 71). English-speaking personnel should be available 9am-2pm.

Accommodations

Despite the hordes of tourists and students who inundate Florence every year, you should have little problem finding a place to stay. Reservations (*prenotazioni*) are wise, especially if you plan to visit Florence at Easter or between June and August. The vast majority of *pensioni* prefer to receive reservations in the form of a letter with at least one night's deposit. Hotels start filling unclaimed spaces at about 2pm.

If you have not secured a place in advance, begin looking early—many of the best places fill by noon. If you arrive much later, it may be best to try the free **ACISJF** accommodations service in the train station (see Practical Information). If the prices they quote are far out of line, tell them you are willing to share a room.

Be warned that some *pensioni* exploit the high-season tourist stream by overcharging. Maximum prices are posted on the back of every door—make sure you're not paying more. The price for a triple, if not posted, should be no more than 35% the price of a double. If you have a complaint, do not hesitate to go to the EPT on via Manzoni. Although it is illegal for hotels to require you to take breakfast for another L5000, many attempt to do so in the high season. Beware that some places will extort as much as L2500-3000 for a shower—sometimes just a cool trickle.

Sleeping in Florence's train stations, streets, or parks is a poor idea. The police strongly object to people who unroll sleeping bags in public places. Le Cascinè, the large parks just downriver from the city center, are notorious local centers of prostitution. If you plan to sleep outdoors, consult the list of officially designated campgrounds below.

In summers past, the city has opened an **Area di Sosta,** or official, free sleeping area, outside of town. "Lodging" usually means roof-covered plots of ground on open-air, sleeping-bag sites. Ask at the red and white information booth at the station (near the exit by track #16).

Hostels

Ostello della Gioventù Europa Villa Camerata (IYHF), viale Augusto Righi, 2-4 (tel. 60 14 51), northeast of town. Leave the station by track #5, then take bus #17B (20-30 min.). You can also take this bus from p. del Duomo. In a great old building with *loggia* and gardens. Tidy and popular if far away—eating in this neighborhood may pose a problem (though there is a snack bar). Members only, L12,000. Sheets and breakfast included. Reception open Mon.-Fri. 9am-1pm and 3-7pm. Dinner L8000. Check-out 9am. Curfew midnight. Open in summer 2-11:30pm; in off-season 4-10:30pm. In summer, hostel fills by 2:30pm. Reserve by letter only.

Ostello Santa Monaca, via S. Monaca, 6 (tel. 26 83 38 or 29 67 04), across the river. The street that runs along the left of the church across from the station takes you to p. S. Maria Novella. Take bus #36 or 37 from here to the 1st stop across the river or make the 10-min. walk: Take via de' Fossi (which leaves the *piazza* directly across from the church) straight to the river. Cross the Ponte Alla Carraia and go straight ahead on via de' Serragli. Via S. Monaca is on the right. A popular hostel with spacious, spotless rooms, a lively atmosphere, kitchen privileges, a free trickle of hot water, a free valuables check, and a sympathetic staff. The disadvantages are equally impressive, including occasional crowds and noise. Wake-up music blares at 8am; lights go out at 11:30pm; and it's impossible to leave before 7am. L12,000. Sheets L2000. A sign-up sheet is posted 9:30am-1pm, with as many spaces as there are beds available. No reservations. Hostel and office open 8-9:30am and 4-11:30pm.

Pensionato Pio X-Artigianelli, via dei Serragli, 106 (tel. 22 50 44). Follow the directions to the Santa Monaca, but take the bus to the 2nd stop across the river. Much quieter, no daytime lock-out, gregarious management, and only 4 or 5 beds per room. L10,000. Showers included. Reservations discouraged. Arrive early. If the *completo* sign is up, ask anyhow since they sometimes forget to take it down. Curfew midnight. Check-out 10am. 2-day min. Open July-Sept.

Suore Oblate dello Spirito Santo, via Nazionale, 8 (tel. 29 82 02), near the station. Women only. 30 beds in huge rooms with sparkling modern bathrooms and a secure atmosphere. Run by pleasant nuns. Doubles L25,000 per person. Triples and quads L20,000 per person. L2000 less without breakfast. Open July-Oct. 15 24 hours. Curfew 11:30pm. Phone reservations accepted.

Istituto Gould, via dei Serragli, 49 (tel. 21 25 76), near the Ostello Santa Monaca. A small, friendly, hostelstyle setup. 32 beds in newly remodeled rooms make this perhaps the best deal in town. Unfortunately, it's impossible to leave on weekends as they keep your passport while you keep their key. Doubles L18,000 per person. Quads L16,000 per person. Showers included. Arrivals outside office hours only with reservations. Rooms are scarce during the academic year, especially in spring. Reserve 3-4 months in advance with deposit.

Near the Station

As you leave the station, a left turn onto via Nazionale will plunge you into a neighborhood of seedy hotels swarming with American travelers. If you can't avoid this quarter, walk away from the heart of the zone. Here along **via Nazionale, via Faenza, via Fiume, via Guelfa,** and nearby streets, cheap establishments abound—often several to a building. Hotel quality and owner friendliness vary greatly, though everywhere the *completo* (full) signs appear by late morning in June, July, and August. Listings follow in order of proximity to the station, not in order of quality. Note that prices have risen considerably here and may continue to do so.

Hotel Desirée, via Fiume, 20 (tel. 26 23 82). Don't let the exterior fool you—this hotel contains spacious, elegant, top-floor rooms, many with tiled floors and balconies. Singles L35,000, with bath L45,000. Doubles L60,000, with bath L76,500. Shower and breakfast included.

Pensione Merlini, via Faenza, 56 (tel. 21 28 48). The best in this building, with well-furnished rooms and shiny bathrooms. Ask for one of the rooms overlooking the quiet garden. Singles L22,500. Doubles L35,000, with bath 41,500. Breakfast L6000.

Pensione Azzi, via Faenza, 56 (tel. 21 38 06), on the 1st floor. Elegant dining room and terrace, color TV in breakfast room, and 24-hour bar. Doubles L50,000. There is a suite of 3 doubles where women can stay for L20,000 per person. Shower and breakfast included.

Pensione Anna, via Faenza, 56 (tel. 29 83 22). Its helpful and friendly owner will make your stay pleasant. Doubles L53,000. Shower and breakfast included. Curfew 1am.

Pensioni Armonia and **Paola,** via Faenza, 56 (tel. 21 11 46 and 21 36 82, respectively). Clean, adequate rooms. Armonia charges L19,000 per person. Breakfast L4000. Group rates available. Curfew midnight. Paola's owner speaks English. Doubles L25,000 per person. Triples L21,000 per person. Quads L19,000 per person. Shower and breakfast (in your room) included. No curfew.

Hotel Apollo and **Tony's Inn,** via Faenza, 77 (tel. 28 41 19 and 21 79 75, respectively). Now combined under the dynamic direction of Italian-Canadian Rose Zarb and husband Antonio Lelli, who together speak myriad languages. Each of the 20 rooms is unique and most have large private baths. Singles with bath L36,500. Doubles with bath L58,500. Breakfast included. Curfew midnight.

Locanda Giovanna, via Faenza, 69 (tel. 26 13 53). An endearingly talkative older couple presides over these 7 small but well-kept rooms on an upper floor. Singles L24,000. Doubles L38,000. Showers included. Curfew midnight, but they'll give you a key. Reservations with deposit only.

Locanda Nella, via Faenza, 69 (tel. 28 42 56). 7 large, clean rooms with desks, mirrors, and a garden view. Singles L22,500. Doubles L33,000. Showers L2000.

Pensione Daniel, via Nazionale, 22 (tel. 21 72 93), near p. dell' Indipendenza. Small and a bit dark, but one of the best deals in town. The walls are painted over every Easter in pinks, yellows, and blues reminiscent of a Fra Angelico fresco. Doubles L24,000. Triples and quads L12,000 per person. Showers L1500. Breakfast L3000, in summer only. Curfew 12:30am. Reservations with deposit only.

Ausonia e Rimini, via Nazionale, 24 (tel. 49 65 47), next door to Daniel. Breakfast room has TV and a bar. English spoken. Singles L22,500, with bath L28,000. Doubles L43,000, with bath L53,500. Hearty breakfast included. 5% discount to *Let's Go* users; Jan.-March 10%.

Pensione Mary, p. Indipendenza, 5 (tel. 49 63 10). Lovely rooms off a leafy square. Ask for 1 of the 4 in the back with a glorious view of the Duomo and the Forte Belvedere. Professional, pleasant management. Singles L22,500, with bath L28,000. Doubles L33,000, with bath L41,500. Breakfast L6000.

Hotel San Lorenzo, via Rosina, 4 (tel. 28 49 25), just off Mercato Centrale. Spotless rooms with classic '70s furniture. Singles L29,000, with bath L36,000. Doubles L42,000, with bath L54,000. Showers included. Breakfast L6500.

Piazza Santa Maria Novella and Environs

If you stand in front of the station, you will be staring directly at the back of the church of Santa Maria Novella; just beyond it lie numerous hidden budget establishments, excellent alternatives to tramping to via Nazionale and via Faenza. Particularly lucky souls even get a view of the pigeon-filled *piazza.*

Pensione La Mia Casa, p. Santa Maria Novella, 23 (tel. 21 30 61). A touch of disorder adds to the charm of the 15 popular rooms in this antique-filled, 17th-century palace. The owner is helpful and speaks some English. The bar/breakfast room with reasonably priced drinks and a color TV overlooks the *piazza.* Singles L21,000. Doubles L31,000, with bath L40,000. Showers included. Breakfast L5000. Curfew midnight. Phone reservations held until 3pm.

Soggiorno Iris, p. Santa Maria Novella, 22 (tel. 29 67 35), 2 doors down from La Mia Casa. Reasonable rooms and a warm management that speaks some English. Singles L22,500. Doubles L32,500. Triples L43,900. Shower L2000, but if you stay several days the charge is dropped. Curfew midnight.

Albergo Universo, p. Santa Maria Novella, 20 (tel. 21 14 84). Unspectacular, impersonal, and a little expensive—but 54 clean rooms. Some English spoken. Singles (some closet-sized) L28,000. Doubles L45,000, with bath L53,500. Shower and breakfast included.

Locanda La Romagnola and **Soggiorno Gigliola,** via della Scala, 40 (tel. 21 15 97). The best deal among a whole string of *pensioni* that line via della Scala between the station and p. S. Maria Novella. Leave the station by track #5, walk across the street, and turn right onto via della Scala after 1 short block. 43 rooms, some recently renovated. Friendly, simple, and likely to have rooms. Singles L22,500, with bath L28,000. Doubles L33,000, with bath L41,500. Showers L2000. Curfew midnight. Phone reservations sometimes accepted.

Pensione Montreal, via della Scala, 43 (tel. 26 23 31); **Pensione Margareth,** via della Scala, 25 (tel. 21 01 38); and **Pensione La Scala,** via della Scala, 21 (tel. 21 26 29). There are more exciting places to stay than these three, which line the right side of the street between the station and p. S. Maria Novella, but all are tidy. Singles L22,000-25,000, with bath L29,000. Doubles L33,000, with bath 41,000.

Near the University Quarter

Pensione Colomba, via Cavour, 21 (tel. 26 31 39), near p. San Marco. Sunny, with modern wooden furniture. British Rebecca will give you information on the hippest places in Florence. Singles L22,500. Doubles L33,000, with bath L41,000. Showers included. Breakfast L7000.

Albergo Sampaoli, via S. Gallo, 14 (tel. 28 48 34), 3 blocks from p. dell' Indipendenza by the *mensa.* One of the nicest women in Florence happily presides over a newly renovated and enlarged establishment (14 light-filled rooms), home to a few university students. Singles L25,000. Doubles L33,000, with bath L45,000. Showers L2500. No reservations.

Hotel Rudy, via San Gallo, 51 (tel. 47 55 19), 1 block from p. San Marco. Serene and clean in quaint antique surroundings. Singles L26,000, with bath L28,000. Doubles L40,000, with bath L42,000. Showers included. Curfew 1am. Reservations with deposit only.

Old City (Near the Duomo)

Many establishments along the most ancient streets are not flooded by the daily tide of arrivals from the station, so they bloat less quickly and provide a more authentic atmosphere. Each of the following lies within a 10- to 20-minute walk of the station.

Soggiorno Brunori, via del Proconsolo, 5 (tel. 26 36 48), parallel to via Calzaioli off p. del Duomo. This beautiful and convenient building harbors 9 fine rooms. Extremely helpful owners. Doubles L33,000, with bath L41,500. Triples L48,000, with bath L60,000. Quads L60,000, with bath L74,000. Unlimited use of common shower L1000-2000. Curfew midnight.

Maria Luisa de' Medici, via del Corso, 1 (tel. 28 00 48), on a narrow road closed to car traffic off p. della Repubblica. Each elegant room is adorned with a Medici portrait and funky, high-modernist furniture. Eccentric and wonderful English-speaking management. Doubles L54,000. Triples L27,000 per person, with bath L29,000. Showers and abundant breakfast included. Curfew 1am.

★**Hotel Colore,** via dei Calzaioli, 13 (tel. 21 03 01), off p. Duomo. Small, clean rooms and small prices in a central location. Singles L22,500. Doubles L33,000. **Locanda Aldini** (tel. 21 47 52), 1 floor down, has more spacious rooms. Singles L22,500. Doubles with bath L40,000. Showers L3000.

Soggiorno Bavaria, borgo degli Albizi, 26 (tel. 234 03 13). From p. della Repubblica walk straight up Il Corso, which becomes borgo Albizi; Bavaria is on the left. Genial management. Dark but quiet. Singles L28,500. Doubles L45,000, with bath L53,000. Showers included. Discount for *Let's Go* users 5%; Nov.-March 10%.

Locanda Orchidea, borgo degli Albizi, 11 (tel. 248 03 46), up the street. An Italian woman and her British husband manage 7 large rooms (some with garden views) in an historic setting—Dante's wife was born here. Singles L24,000. Doubles L37,000. Showers L2000.

Albergo Firenze, p. Donati, 4 (tel. 21 42 03 or 26 83 01), just off Il Corso. Central location. Singles L24,500. Doubles L37,000. Breakfast L6000.

Pensione Maxim, via di Medici, 4 (tel. 21 74 74), between p. della Repubblica and via de Calzaiuoli. Reasonable and convenient. Doubles L46,000, with bath L56,500. Triples L66,000, with bath L78,500. Shower and breakfast included. Flexible curfew 1:30am.

Old City (Near the River)

Narrow streets and small establishments with around half a dozen rooms are the rule here. Expect to ring some doorbells and climb some stairs.

Pensione Davanzati, via Porta Rossa, 15 (tel. 28 34 14), just off via Tornabuoni. Excellent location and prices. 10 sunny but small rooms—one great room with a terrace. Some English spoken. Singles L22,500. Doubles L33,000, with bath L42,000. Showers L2000. Breakfast L6000.

Albergo Archibuseri, vicolo Marzio, 1 (tel. 28 24 80). Stand at the foot of the Ponte Vecchio facing the Duomo, and look to your right across p. del Pesce for the building labeled "Pensione Hermitage." 7 rooms. No-nonsense proprietor. Singles L22,500. Doubles L34,000. Showers L2500. Curfew midnight.

Soggiorno Cestelli, borgo SS. Apostoli, 25 (tel. 21 42 13), 1 block from the river between the Ponte Vecchio and Ponte Sta. Trinità. 7 stately rooms. Singles L21,500. Doubles L31,500, with bath L40,000. Breakfast L6000. Showers included.

Pensione Rigatti, lungarno Diaz, 2 (tel. 21 30 22), on the river at Ponte alle Grazie. The elegant salons, Old Master paintings, lush garden, and impeccable standards in this *palazzo* that once belonged to the Alberti family merit busting your budget. The soft-spoken proprietor speaks English. Singles L39,500, with shower L48,000. Doubles L63,000, with bath L75,500. Shower and breakfast included. Curfew 1am. Reserve up to 6 months ahead.

Pensione Esperanza, via dell' Inferno, 3 (tel. 21 37 73). From via del Parione between p. Goldoni and via Tornabuoni, go through the arch called Volta della Vecchia, turn left on via del Purgatorio, then immediately turn right. Great prices for some dark rooms with older furniture. Singles L19,000. Doubles L30,000. Showers L2000. Curfew 1am.

In the Oltrarno

Pensioni in the Oltrarno, across the river, often overlook the river, gardens, or *piazze,* and are a bit quieter and more spacious. The following are 15 to 25 minutes by foot from the station.

Pensione La Scaletta, via Guicciardini, 13 (tel. 28 30 28), across the Ponte Vecchio towards the Pitti Palace. Fine rooms with phones, friendly management, and gorgeous views from the rooftop terraces. Singles with bath L48,500. Doubles L64,000, with bath L76,500. Shower and breakfast included. Phones in each room.

Pensione Sorelle Bandini, p. Santo Spirito, 9 (tel. 21 53 08). Old world elegance and amicable people on the top floor of a large *palazzo.* Beautiful sun-filled *loggia.* Often booked by groups, but worth trying. English spoken. Doubles L49,500, with bath L58,000. Shower and breakfast included.

Camping

The **campground Italiani e Stranieri** at viale Michelangelo, 80 (tel. 681 19 77), near p. Michelangelo, offers a spectacular view of Florence but is extremely crowded. Take red or black bus #13 from the station (15 min., last bus 11:55pm). They offer fantastic facilities, including a well-stocked food store and bar. They may post a *completo* sign or tell you the same by phone, but if you show up without a vehicle they will often let you in. (L4300 per person, L5000 per tent, L2800 per car, L1400 per motorcycle. Open April to mid-Oct. 6am-midnight.) Florence's other campground is at the **Villa Cameratu,** viale A. Righi, 2/A (tel. 61 03 00), outside the IYHF youth hostel on the #17B bus route (catch the bus at the train station or at p. del Duomo). (L3800 per person, L3850 per small tent, L5000 per large tent. Open April-Oct. 7:30am-1pm and 3-9pm; if it's closed, stake your site and come back later.) Outside the city in nearby Fiesole, try **Camping Panoramico,** via Peramonda, 1 (tel. 59 90 69), for a steep L6650 per person and L4500 per tent. Among the array of bungalows also available, a two-person unit costs L38,000, with bath L48,000. Take bus #7 from the station to Fiesole (last buses 11:25pm and 12:30am, L600).

Food

Florence's lofty culture has been matched over the centuries by its high cusine. Local specialties include *bistecca alla fiorentina,* a variation on thick sirloin steak, each inch more succulent and expensive than the last. Cheaper specialties include *minestra di fagioli* (a delicious white bean and pasta soup), *ribollita* (a hearty soup made with black cabbage, bread, and beans), *trippa alla fiorentina* (tripe cooked in a tomato cheese sauce), and *árista* (Florentine-style roast pork). The best local cheese is *pecorino,* made from sheep's milk. Wine is another Florentine staple, and the local *chianti* is superb. Real *chianti classico,* the highest quality *chianti,* has a black rooster on the neck label and is known as *gallo nero.* Many other famous wines such as *Ricasoli,* have no black rooster because they fall outside the official chianti zone, but may be just as good. While most restaurants serve nice house wines, bottled wine bought in a store is a more economical way to sample the local grape. A liter of house wine typically costs L4000-5000 in Florence's *trattorie,* while stores sell bottles of delicious wine, even *chianti classico,* for as little as L2000.

Good alternatives for lunch are the plentiful *rosticcerie,* which cook up all kinds of roast meat, pasta, and vegetable dishes to take out, and the similar *gastronomie,* which sell mostly cold prepared dishes and salads. If you manage to work up an appetite for tripe, try the cheap and filling *panino con lampredotto,* a tripe sandwich, which can be bought for L1500-2000 at food wagons throughout the city. In the past, the Franciscans have offered lunches to the destitute and to students for L6000 in **Casa di San Francesco** at p. SS. Annunziata, 2 (tel. 21 88 27). The **Mercato Centrale,** between via Nazionale and the back of San Lorenzo, offers fresh produce and meats. Whole swordfish, rabbits, and tripe are something to look at even if you're not planning to buy. (Open June-Sept. Mon-Sat. 8am-1pm; Oct.-May Mon.-Sat. 6:30am-1pm and 4-8:30pm.)

Near the Station and University Quarter

Trattoria Da Za-Za, p. Mercato Centrale, 26r (tel. 21 54 11). Excellent food in a place with character and quite a few Italians. Meals from L14,000. Open Aug. 20-July Mon.-Sat. noon-2:30pm and 7-10pm.

Trattoria da Mario, via Rosina, 2r (tel. 21 85 50), 2 doors from the above. Packed with Florentine workers at lunch, and for good reason. Hearty food and neighborhood atmosphere. *Primi* L3000-4000, *secondi* L4000-6500, *contorni* L2000. Cover L800. Open Sept.-July Mon.-Sat. 7am-5pm at the bar, noon-3pm for lunch.

Pepe Verde, p. Mercato Centrale, 17-18r (tel. 28 39 06). A new favorite with young Florentines, featuring a bar, an outside cafe, and an indoor dining room. *Primi* L4000-5000, *secondi* L7000-10,000. Open Wed.-Mon. noon-3pm and 7-10:30pm. Closed 10 days in Aug.

Trattoria, via Palazzuolo, 69r, a bit past the Space Electronic disco. The cheapest meal in town. People stand in line at this no-name for superb meals under L10,000. Open Sept.-July Sun.-Fri. 11am-3pm and 7pm-midnight. Get there early, but if the line's too long go to **Trattoria da Giorgio,** down the street at #100r, for a similar deal and a more Italian atmosphere.

La Colisèe, via Cavour, 52r (tel. 21 36 85), a great spot for lunch, a snack, or a light dinner. Creative cold cuisine. Salmon and herb sandwhich L2000. Great salads, drinks, pastry, and *gelato.* Open Sept.-July Mon.-Sat. 7am-midnight; in summer until 10pm.

Almanacco (Centro Vegetariano Fiorentino), via delle Ruote, 30r (tel. 47 50 30). Quiet atmosphere and delicious vegetarian dishes. Meals L12,000. Open Sept.-July Tues.-Fri. 1-3pm and 8-10:30pm, Sat.-Sun. 8-10:30pm.

Baccus, via Borgo Ognissanti, 45r (tel. 23 37 14), diagonally across from the church of the Ognissanti. One of the more fashionable spots in Florence, featuring innovative dishes and a high-tech interior. Reasonable prices. Excellent pasta dishes L6000-10,000. Try the *chiocciolini Sri Lanka,* shells with a curry, corn, and prosciutto sauce (L6900). Open Mon.-Sat. 7:30pm-midnight. Make reservations.

Old City (Near the Duomo)

Trattoria Le Mossacce, via del Proconsolo, 55r (tel. 29 43 61), between the Duomo and Bargello. Excellent food at affordable prices. Full of Florentines, a rarity in the center of town.

Menù L15,000; a la carte just a bit more. Always packed. Open Aug. 20-July Mon.-Fri. noon-3pm and 7-10pm.

Pizzeria-Ristorante I Ghibellini, p. S. Pier Maggíore, 8 (tel. 21 44 24), off borgo degli Albizi. A crowded food factory popular mainly with tourists. Outdoor tables on a quiet *piazza.* Rarely a line. Limited *menù* L15,000, a la carte about L6000 more. Pizza L3500-6000. Open Thurs.-Tues. noon-4pm and 7pm-12:30am.

Osteria, via Matteo Palmieri, 37r, next door to Ghibellini. Depending on the special, their fabulously cheap L11,000 *menù* with everything down to the coffee can be a great deal. Open Wed.-Mon. 12:30-3pm and 7-11 or 12pm.

Friggitoria, volta San Piero, 5, across the *piazza* from Osteria and I Ghibellini. Get a hamburger (L2500, with spinach L3000) or another cheap dish at the stand. Top it all off with *gelato* afterwards. Open Mon.-Sat. 8am-9pm.

Ristorante della Comunità Israelica, via Farini, 4 (tel. 24 18 90), next to the synagogue. Kosher food at about L15,000 for a full meal. Open Mon.-Fri. noon-2pm and 7-9pm.

Old City (Near the River)

La Maremmana, via dei Macci, 77r (tel. 24 12 26). A time-honored combination: simple, generous, and affordable. *Menùs* L11,000, L14,000, and L18,000. Tablecloths, cut flowers, pasta, and *secondi* with side dishes, a fruit dessert, and wine included. Look for the scrumptious *antipasto* buffet. Justifiably busy. Open Sept.-July Mon.-Sat. 12:30-3pm and 7:30-10:30pm.

Acqua al Due, via dell' Acqua, 2 (tel. 28 41 70), behind the Bargello. Florentine specialties in a cozy, air-conditioned place popular with young Italians. Indulge at L25,000 for a 3-course meal. Open Tues.-Sun. noon-3pm and 7:30pm-1am.

Acquerello, via Ghibellini, 156r (tel. 234 05 54). A definite splurge in a pseudo-Memphis decor. *Spaghetti acquerello* (flaming spaghetti) for 2 L14,000. Rice with champagne and truffles L10,000 in season—this is a dining experience to savor. Full meals L35,000-40,000. Make dinner reservations. Open Wed.-Mon. noon-2:30pm and 7:30pm-midnight.

I Che C'è C'è, via dei Magalotti, 11r (tel. 26 28 67), off via d'Anguillara near p. Firenze. An honored standby for Florentines largely undiscovered by tourists. Try the *risotto al grànchio* (rice with crab) or the *spaghetti alle vongole* (with clams), both L5000. Full meals L20,000. Open Tues.-Sun. 12:15-2:30pm and 7:30-10:30pm.

Trattoria Santa Croce, Borgo Santa Croce, 31r (tel. 24 49 01), in front of the church of Santa Croce. The place to go for an excellent lunch in a snazzy environment. Fantastic homemade pasta dishes L5000-6000. Complete *menù* L13,000. Open Mon.-Sat. noon-3pm.

Trattoria Mario, via di Meri, 74, 2 blocks east of Palazzo Vecchio. Not to be confused with "da Mario" at via Rosina. *Menù* L10,000, but make sure you ask about what's included. No menu—just look and point. Open Tues.-Sun. noon-9:30pm.

In the Oltrarno

Trattoria Casalinga, via Michelozzi, 9r (tel. 21 86 24), between S. Spirito and via Maggio. Delicious full meals L12,000-13,000. Crowded, so your meal is likely to be quick. Dishes change daily (look for the *piatti del giorno*) in this homestyle, family-operated spot. Open Mon.-Fri. 11:45am-2:30pm and 7-9:30pm.

I Tarocchi, via dei Renai, 14r (tel. 21 78 50). A good place for a sit-down meal of pizza or spaghetti (L5000-6000). A wide variety of pasta (including 5 *tortellini* dishes), plus omelettes and hamburgers. Long wooden benches and plenty of food. Florence's 1st *pizzeria* and still the best. Get there before 9pm to beat the rush. Open Tues.-Sun. 7pm-1am.

Il Fornaio, via Guicciardini, 3r, across the Ponte Vecchio, with chain restaurants around town. A great selection of sandwiches and fresh-baked items can make a gratifying lunch (L5000). Open Mon.-Tues. and Thurs.-Sat. 8am-2pm and 4:30-7:30pm, Sun. and Wed. 8am-2pm.

No dinner in this ice cream capital of the world would be complete without a visit to at least one of its *gelaterie.* Look for a sign reading *produzione propria* to ensure the *gelato* is homemade.

Vivoli's, via della Stinche, 7 (tel. 29 23 34), behind the Bargello. The star of Florentine *gelaterie.* Open Sept.-July.

Perché No?, via Tavolini, 19r (tel. 29 89 69), off via Calzaioli. Equally marvelous. An array of orgasmic flavors in a snappy neon setting. Open Wed.-Mon. 8am-1pm.

Bar Gelateria l'Oasi, volta S. Piero, 11, 3 doors down from **Friggitoria** (above). Great place to top off your dinner with wine, coffee, and *gelato* (L1000). Open Thurs.-Tues. 7am-1:30am.

Festival del Gelato, via del Corso, 75r (tel. 29 43 86). 75 flavors. It's difficult to decide which is more colorful: the neon lights or the ice cream. Dinky-sized cups L1000 and L2000; the *grande* L2500. Open daily 10:30am-2pm.

Il Triangolo delle Bermude, via Nazionale, 61r. Delicious and unusual flavors include rose, whiskey, and peanut. Open Tues.-Sun. 8am-midnight.

Ricchi, p. S. Spirito, 9r (tel. 21 58 64), in the Oltrarno. Open daily 1pm-1am.

Sights

> *Florence! One of the only places in Europe where I understood that underneath my revolt, a consent was lying dormant.*
>
> —*Albert Camus*

It takes quite a city to pacify an existentialist. The same ponderous romance that enchanted intellectuals from Camus to Dickens can overwhelm the first-time visitor. Pick up the xeroxed museum listings at the Azienda for the most complete and up-to-date information on those places that have either changed their hours or closed for restoration. One note of caution: When in churches, bear in mind they are not museums, but places of worship demanding deference, particularly during services.

As you compile your itinerary, sifting through the complicated hours kept by churches, museums, and chapels, keep in mind that many of the most popular sights—the Duomo, the Uffizi, the Accademia, and the Bargello—are subject to extreme overcrowding in the summer. Arrive early.

The Duomo

Henry James described the Duomo as "the image of some mighty hillside enameled with blooming flowers." Others have called it "the Cathedral in pajamas." Whatever its resemblance, the walls of inlaid marble and the enormous red-tiled dome are the symbol of Florence. Climax of the Republic's fourteenth-century building campaign, the Duomo embodies the faults of civic pride as well as its virtues. Arnolfo da Cambio began the church (1296-1310) in a style more ornate and Gothic than later builders liked—you can see where the simpler mode took over on the outside of the nave, near the facade. The process of building the church was democratic to an extreme: Brunelleschi, the great Renaissance architect and engineer, was given the commission for the cupola on the condition that his arch-rival Lorenzo Ghiberti (1378-1456) be co-director. The collective approach worked well with the notable exception of the facade, which was the subject of continuous artistic competitions and commissions. The present neo-Gothic solution was the result of the 1871 contest.

Inside, the works of art are almost lost in the structure's hall-like nave. The fresco in the left aisle illustrating Dante's *Divine Comedy* pays tribute to the poet who was forced to flee Florence after backing the losing side in the struggle between the Guelphs and the Ghibellines. Nearby is a fresco of an equestrian statue of the English *condottiere* mercenary general John Hawkwood. Hawkwood was promised a memorial statue in the Duomo and the ever-frugal republic delivered only a fresco.

Construction of the cathedral's crossing was begun even though its builders had no idea how to construct a dome large enough to span it. Filippo Brunelleschi came up with the solution: a double-shelled dome built with interlocking bricks that would support itself as it was built. The first monumental dome raised since antiquity, it combined Tuscan tradition and classical forms. Alberti described the dome as "large enough to shelter all of Tuscany within its shadow . . . and of a construction that perhaps not even the ancients knew or understood"—the ultimate compliment in a period awed by the genius of Greece and Rome. Michelangelo paid tribute to its harmonious proportions in a ditty he composed upon receiving the commission for the dome of St. Peter's: "*Io farò la sorella,/Già più gran ma non più bella.*" (I'm going to make its sister,/Bigger, yes, but not more beautiful.)

Climb up to the lantern for a great view from the external gallery. (Duomo open daily 7am-noon and 2:30-6pm. Last entrance 5:30pm. Free. Lantern (tel. 21 32 29) open Mon.-Sat. 8:30am-12:30pm and 2:30-5pm. Last entrance 4:30pm. Admission L3000.)

Most of the Duomo's sculpture has been placed in the **Museo dell' Opera di S. Maria del Fiore** (tel. 21 32 29), directly behind the Duomo at p. del Duomo, 9. Just up the first flight of stairs is a late *Pietà* by Michelangelo (the more famous one is in Saint Peter's in Rome). Frustrated by his own work, the sculptor intentionally damaged the figure; soon thereafter, the master's pupil touched up the work, leaving parts of Mary Magdalen's head with visible "scars" and removing a leg. There are other masterpieces: Donatello's elegant *cantoria* (high up on the wall) and his *St. Mary Magdalen,* a tortured, naked figure, entirely draped in her own hair; Andrea Pisano's powerfully expressive bas-reliefs depicting various fields of human activity; and a silver altar by Michelozzo, Pollaiolo, and Verrocchio. (Open March-Oct. Mon.-Sat. 9am-8pm, Sun. 10am-1pm; in off-season Mon.-Sat. 9am-6pm, Sun. 10am-1pm. Admission L3000, Sun. free.)

In one sense, the most important dome in p. del Duomo is the little octagonal vault of the **baptistery.** Dedicated to St. John the Baptist, patron saint of Florence, the building predates the year 1000. Florentines have long clung to the belief that the baptistery was an ancient Roman building, a legacy and proof of their city's classical past.

The commission to execute the famous bronze doors of the baptistery was among the most important in Florence. In 1330, Andrea Pisano (1270-1349) was imported from Pisa, and Venetian foundry-workers were brought in to do the first set of doors, now on the south side (toward the river). Set in a rigidly geometric framework, the scenes contain only the bare essentials of gesture and setting; the few figures stand out in gold against the dark bronze. The next time around, in 1401, Lorenzo Ghiberti was chosen over rival Brunelleschi. (The competition pieces, panels depicting the sacrifice of Abraham, now hang in the Bargello.)

Ghiberti's doors, on the north side away from the river, start with Pisano's framework, but add detail, movement, and classical draperies. His work was so admired that the last set of doors was ordered from him as soon as he finished the first, in 1425. The **"Gates of Paradise,"** as Michelangelo reportedly called them, are nothing like the two earlier portals. Originally intended to stand as the third set of doors on the north side, they so impressed the Florentines that they were switched with the second doors and placed in the position they now hold facing the cathedral. Ghiberti took all the Renaissance pictorial innovations—receding landscapes, architectural settings, and classical allusions—and turned them into a gilt three-dimensional painting. In the center of the door frame at the top of the second row of panels is a bust of Ghiberti and his son Vittorio (right), who did all the door frames. Upon entering the cavernous interior, note the mosaic of the Last Judgement in the cupola (in part by Cimabue)—the devils beneath Christ's feet and the intricate tortures of Hell are imaginings worthy of Dante, who himself was baptized here. (Open daily 9am-12:30pm and 2:30-5:30pm. Free.)

Next to the duomo stands the **campanile.** Andrea Pisano completed two stories and Francesco Talenti (1325-1364) topped it off. The bright colors unify the tower, despite the visible changes in style. The original reliefs by Pisano and the statues of prophets by Donatello rest now in the **Museo dell 'Opera del Duomo.** (Open in summer 9am-7pm; in off-season 9am-5pm. Last entrance 40 min. before closing. Admission L3000.)

Just behind the Duomo, at via dell' Oriulo, 4, is the **Museo Firenze Com' Era** (Florence As It Was; tel. 21 73 05), a rich and fascinating historical and topographical collection. (Open Mon.-Wed. and Fri.-Sat. 9am-2pm, Sun. 9am-1pm. Admission L1000.)

Around the Signoria

From p. del Duomo, a walk along via dei Calzaioli, one of the city's oldest streets, will lead you to p. Signoria. **Via dei Calzaioli,** laid out as part of the original Roman *castrum* (camp), today bustles with crowds, chic stores, ice cream shops, and vendors who spread their wares in the evening. At the far end, the area around the Palazzo della Signoria, today known as the **Palazzo Vecchio** (tel. 276 84 65), forms the civic center of Florence. The fortresslike *palazzo* was built in the late thirteenth century to replace the Bargello as the seat of the commune's government; its interior apartments were designed as living quarters for the seven members of the *signoria* (council) during their rotating, one-month terms in office. By the time of Medici rule, the building's style, symbolic of communal government, had become somewhat ironic. Abandoning the Medici secret of success—cloaking despotism in the form of republicanism—Cosimo, the Medici duke, moved across the river to the even better fortified and more palatial Pitti Palace.

The courtyard, rebuilt by Michelozzo in 1444 and decorated by Vasari in 1565 to please a Medici bride, contains a copy of Verrocchio's charming fifteenth-century *putto* fountain and several stone lions (the heraldic symbol of the city). Michelangelo and Leonardo da Vinci were commissioned to paint either wall of the **Salone dei Cinquecento** up Vasari's sweeping stairs, with frescoes; this is where the Grand Council of the Republic met. Although they did not get around to painting the frescoes, their drawings for them, the *Battle of Cascina* and the *Battle of Anghiari,* were intensely studied by all the young Florentine artists and copied for mass production by engravers. Michelangelo's *Victory* now rests in the center niche and commemorative frescoes cover the rest of the room. The little **Studio of Francesco I,** built by Vasari, is a treasure house of mannerist art. The other rooms contain a few prize bronzes, such as Giambologna's little devil, the real Verrocchio *Putto,* and many mannerist frescoes. The best of the art is collected in the **Mezzanino.** Here are Bronzino's portrait of the poet Laura Battiferi and Giambologna's *Hercules and the Hydra.* (Open Mon.-Fri. 9am-7pm, Sun. 8am-1pm. Admission a scandalous L6000.)

A vast space by medieval standards, **piazza della Signoria** was created during the fourteenth century by destroying the house-towers belonging to the Uberti clan after they had lost a political skirmish. For a long time, no subsequent power wanted to own or even build on the place. They did burn Savonarola, the charismatic political leader and religious prophet, in the middle; a plaque marks the spot. Symbolic sculpture clusters around the front of the *palazzo:* Donatello's *Judith and Holofernes,* Michelangelo's *David* (only copies are on display today), and Bandinelli's *Hercules.* Duke Cosimo de' Medici added Bartolomeo Ammanati's Neptune fountain on the corner and the equestrian statue of himself by Giambologna in the middle of the far side of the *piazza.* The Neptune statue occasioned the following rhyme at the expense of the sixteenth-century sculptor: *Ammanati, Ammanati, quanti marmi hai rovinati* (Ammanati Ammanati, how many blocks of marble you've ruined).

The array of sculpture continues under the **Loggia dei Lanzi** on the corner. Built as a space for civic speakers, the graceful fourteenth-century *loggia* gradually became a sculpture gallery under the Medici dukes, as their appreciation of art began to exceed that of free speech. Forgotten—or disproven—was Matteo Villani's approving comment that *loggie* were a form of architecture befitting a free commune, not tyranny.

The **Uffizi** (offices) form a double row behind the *loggia.* The *palazzi* were designed by Vasari in 1554, when Duke Cosimo wanted to consolidate the various institutions of the administration under his control. The street is a sophisticated piece of urban political design, framing the tower of Palazzo Vecchio at one end and the Medici Forte Belvedere across the Arno at the other. Giambologna's bust of Cosimo oversees the entire complex at the Arno end. Vasari incorporated a secret corridor between Palazzo Vecchio and the Medici's Palazzo Pitti in the structure;

now reopened, it runs through the Uffizi and over Ponte Vecchio and houses more art, including a special collection of artists' self-portraits. (Corridor open Wed., Fri., and Sun. by appointment at 9:30am; call 21 83 41 to see if there is space on the guided tour. Admission included in the L5000 Uffizi fee.)

The **Uffizi Gallery** contains one of the world's greatest collections of paintings. The holdings span the thirteenth through seventeenth centuries; if you have time, choose a few per visit and then return. Botticelli's *Annunciation,* opposite the elevators by the coat-check, is just a prelude of what's to come. The Print and Drawings Rooms on the mezzanine often have superlative exhibits. The Gallery proper begins with the triple majesty of Cimabue's, Duccio's, and Giotto's *Maestàs,* which illustrate the accelerated changes taking place in painting at the turn of the thirteenth and fourteenth centuries. In the next room, the delicate lines of Simone Martini's *Annunciation* from the fourteenth century stand out among the Sienese works. Compare Gentile da Fabriano's *Adoration of the Magi* with that of his early fifteenth-century contemporary, Lorenzo Monaco—one flamboyant, one restrained. Suddenly you find yourself in the powerfully charged atmosphere of the early Florentine Renaissance with Masaccio and Masolino's *Virgin and Child with St. Anne* and Domenico Veneziano's *Madonna Enthroned and Saints,* a vivid expression of religious emotion. Paolo Uccello's *Battle of San Romano,* one third of a series that hung in Lorenzo de Medici's bedroom (the other two parts are in Paris and London), marshals color in its geometric horses. In the center of the room Piero della Francesca's bluntly realistic portraits of *Federico da Montefeltro* and his wife, *Battista Sforza,* stare at each other in a cool manner befitting the Renaissance aristocrats they portray, while Filippo Lippi's capricious and amusing ecclesiastical paintings hang in the next room.

Botticelli's *Primavera, Birth of Venus, Madonna della Melagrana,* and *Pallas and the Centaur,* all in one room, are even more splendid after their recent restoration. The *Birth of Venus* may have been inspired by a classical statue of the goddess, the Medici *Venus* (in room #18 here); Botticelli placed her on a seashell in accordance with the classical tradition that she was born from the foam of the sea. The Botticelli *Adoration of the Magi* hangs nearby, filled with Medici portraits: Cosino is the oldest king, in the act of offering; Lorenzo il Magnifico is to the left in the dark tunic; Giuliano kneels in the center. Botticelli included himself, looking challengingly at the viewer from the right edge. The *Adoration* paintings by van der Goes (1440-1482) and Ghirlandaio (1449-1494) are beautifully detailed but do not match the composition of da Vinci's unfinished *Adoration* or radiant *Annunciation.* Next comes the *Tribuna,* designed by Buontalenti in the 1580s, a pleasure dome of mannerist art and antique masterpieces from the Medici collection, including many aristocratic portraits by Bronzino, Pontormo's posthumous portrait of *Cosimo di Medici,* Salviati's sultry *Charity,* and the famous antique Medici *Venus Pudica.* The collection continues with Dürer (an entire roomful), Holbein, Cranach, Pontormo, Bronzino, Mantegna, Correggio, and Bellini—a heady mix.

On the other side, the staircase near the corner leads to Vasari's corridor and another selection of incredible masterpieces. Michelangelo's *Holy Family,* his only easel painting, and Raphael's *Madonna of the Finch* and famous portrait of *Pope Leo X* start the galleries here. Titian's *Venus of Urbino,* which set the female ideal for a whole age, appears in the next room, followed by Parmigianino's affectedly graceful mannerist masterpiece, *Madonna of the Long Neck.* Paolo Veronese's lavish compositions follow, accompanied by Tintoretto's brilliant colors, and Barocci's magisterial proto-baroque statement, the *Madonna del Popolo.* Rubens's energetic triumphal pictures for Maria de' Medici and Philip IV, as well as his sensitive portrait of his wife, Isabella Brandt, fill another room. The collection closes with several Caravaggios, including his *Sacrifice of Isaac* and *Bacchus,* and two Rembrandt self-portraits, one young, one old. (Open Tues.-Sat. 9am-7pm, Sun. 9am-1pm. Admission L5000.)

After skipping by 400 years of the world's greatest canvases, hop over to the nearby **Ponte Vecchio,** which has spanned the Arno's narrowest point since Roman times, surviving floods, wars, and rebuilding. The Medici, in an effort to "improve" the area, kicked out the butchers and tanners, whose shops lined the bridge in the 1500s, and installed the goldsmiths and diamond-carvers whose descendants remain today. The commander in charge of the German army's retreat across the river in 1944 could not bear to blow it up, as directed, and blew up the buildings on either side instead to make the bridge impassable. Today, the peddlers and artisans who line the bridge by day make way for street musicians at night.

Around the Bargello

The heart of medieval Florence lies between the Duomo and the Signoria around the Bargello, a fortress that served as the prison and was once the residence of the chief magistrate (the *podestà*) and later that of the chief of police. Now the **Museo Nazionale** (tel. 21 08 01), the fortress contains superior Florentine sculpture. The forbidding exterior hides a lovely courtyard with an elegant staircase. Several early Michelangelos are on the ground floor: his first unfinished *David;* a debauched *Bacchus;* and a handsome bust of *Brutus,* Michealangelo's most outspoken republican statement. Also in this gallery is Giambologna's *Mercury,* miraculously poised on top of a puff of air blown by an angel beneath him. The *loggia* upstairs is inhabited by Giambologna's bronze animals, made for a Medici garden grotto. Donatellos are in the Great Hall opening off the right—the lean, boyish *David* and the *Marzocco* are the most famous. On the wall to the right are the *Sacrifices of Abraham* executed by Ghiberti and Brunelleschi for the 1401 baptistery door competition. (Open Tues.-Sat. 9am-2pm, Sun. 9am-1pm. Admission L3000.)

The **Badia,** just across via del Proconsolo from the Bargello, was the church of medieval Florence's richest monastery. Filippino Lippi's *Apparition of the Virgin to St. Bernard,* on the left as you enter, is one of the most famous paintings of the late fifteenth century. Around the corner in via S. Margherita is the **Casa di Dante** (tel. 28 33 43), the reconstructed house of Dante Alighieri's family. (Open Thurs.-Sat. and Mon.-Tues. 9:30am-12:30pm and 3:30-6:30pm, Sun. 9:30am-12:30pm. Free.) The small museum outlines the poet's life, but you get a better idea of a fourteenth-century dwelling at **Palazzo Salviati,** a few blocks away on via della Vigna Vecchia at via dell' Isola delle Stinche.

Equidistant from the Duomo and the Signoria is the intriguing **Orsanmichele,** via dei Calzainoli (tel. 28 47 15), a combination of the sacred and secular aspects of Florentine life. Built in 1337, it is the only example still standing of the Florentine Gothic architectural style. Originally built as a granary and *loggia,* and later converted into a church, Orsanmichele today combines secular and spiritual concerns in the statues along its facade, representations of the patron saints of the major craft guilds. The collection includes Ghiberti's *St. John the Baptist* and Verrocchio's *Doubting Thomas* on the via Calzaioli facade, Donatello's *St. Mark* and two della Robbia terra-cottas on the via Lamberti side. (His Saint George is only a copy; the original is in the Bargello.) Nanni di Banco's *Sant' Eligius* graces the northwest corner. Inside, the miraculous *Virgin* painted by Bernardo Daddi (1280-1350) is encased in a fabulous tabernacle designed by Andrea Orcagna, and there are stained-glass windows dating from 1410, when the religious treasures had become so prized that the *loggia* was walled up to form an oratory, and the grain trade for which the building had originally been constructed was moved elsewhere. Temporary exhibits are shown in the *saloni* on the top floor; go see whatever is there, if only for the view over the city. (Open daily 7am-noon and 2-7pm. Free.)

Markets, Palazzi, and Santa Maria Novella

Florence financed its golden age with nuggets from all over Europe. In the early 1420s 72 banks operated in Florence, most in the area around the **Mercato Nuovo** and **via Tornabuoni.** Birthplace of capitalism, the city made money in trade and reinvested it in land and the manufacture of wool and silk. The Mercato Nuovo arcades, constructed in 1547, housed the silk and gold trade. Pietro Tacca's ferocious statue called the *Porcellino* (Piglet) was added some 50 years later. Starkly neoclassical **piazza della Repubblica** replaced the Mercato Vecchio (old market) in 1890, sadly disposing of one of the city's most historic quarters. Today, the inscription, "*Antico centro della città, da secolare squalore, a vita nuova restituito*" (the ancient center of the city, squalid for centuries, restored to new life), seems ironic, emblematic of another, more determinedly progressive age. The statue in the center, on the corner near the UPIM store, is a replacement for Donatello's statue of *Abundance,* which once surveyed the square. Here are several of the city's most popular cafes, and an active crowd of passersby until late in the evening.

With their profits, Florentine bankers and merchants built grander houses than any the city had ever seen before. The great Quattrocento boom had its roots in the construction of the Palazzo Davanzati, via Porta Rossa, 13. Today the *palazzo* has been refinished to show life as the affluent fifteenth-century merchant lived it, and is called the **Museo della Casa Fiorentina Antica** (tel. 21 65 18; open for guided tours in Italian only, Tues.-Sat. hourly 9am-2pm, Sun. 9am-1pm; admission L3000).

The relative modesty of the Palazzo Davanzati soon gave way to the stately *palazzi,* such as the Strozzi and Rucellai, clearly envisioned by their builders as personal and dynastic monuments. The **Palazzo Strozzi** (tel. 21 59 90), on via Tornabuoni at via Strozzi, begun in 1489, is perhaps the most august palace and is open for visits. Inside, you will appreciate its gargantuan scale—its three stories parallel a modern, nine-story office building. (Open Mon., Wed., and Fri. 4-7pm. Free.) The **Palazzo Rucellai,** via della Vigina Nuova, 46r, was designed by Leon Battista Alberti in the 1450s and is renowned for its facade. Its newly renovated interior now houses the **Alinari Museum of Photographic History** (tel. 21 33 70), with temporary exhibits from the treasure trove of the Alinari photo archives. (Open Sun.-Thurs. 9am-1pm and 3-8pm, Fri.-Sat. 9am-1pm and 3-10:30pm. Admission L3000.)

Many builders of earlier *palazzi* also commissioned a family chapel in the **Church of Santa Trinità** on via Tornabuoni to house their bones and save their souls in the best company. The fourth chapel on the right houses remains of a fresco cycle of the life of the Virgin and on the altar a magnificent *Annunciation* by Lorenzo Monaco. The Sassetti chapel in the right arm of the transept is entirely frescoed with scenes from the life of St. Francis by Domenico Ghirlandaio. The famous altarpiece of the *Adoration of the Shepherds,* also by Ghirlandaio, is a copy; the original is in the Uffizi.

The **Church of Ognissanti,** near the river on Borgo Ognissanti between Ponte Vespucci and Ponte alla Carraia, was built in the twelth century and reconstructded in the seventeenth. The simple interior, with one nave and a transept, houses valuable art pieces. The second altar on the right has a fresco of the Madonna of Mercy, an early work by Ghirlandiao. Halfway up the nave on a pillar on the right is a fresco by Botticello of St. Augustine; across the nave is Ghirlandaio's less forceful *St. Jerome.* Next door to the church in the *cenacolo* (the former refectory) is Ghirlandaio's famous *Last Supper.*

The very wealthy merchants had their chapels in the **Church of Santa Maria Novella** (tel. 21 01 13), near the station. Giovanni Rucellai commissioned Alberti to design the top half of the facade and had a chapel built inside. The Strozzi also have two chapels here, one at the right end of the transept, the other at the left end, both with splendid frescoes. The church was covered with frescoes before the Medici commissioned Vasari to paint others in their honor, and had most of the other walls whitewashed so their rivals would not be remembered. Fortunately Vasari respected Masaccio's powerful *Trinity,* possibly the earliest painting to use mathematical perspective, and he preserved it about halfway up the nave on the left. The choir contains Ghirlandaio's most important frescoes, a pair of cycles depicting the lives of the Virgin and Saint John the Baptist. Among the numerous pupils who assisted the master was the young Michelangelo. In the adjoining Strozzi chapel to the right, Filippino Lippi's frescoes have been preserved. (Open daily 7-11:30am and 3:30-5pm.) Next door, be sure to visit the cloister to see Paolo Uccello's frescoes, including *The Flood* and *The Sacrifice of Noah.* Even more fascinating is the adjoining so-called **Spanish Chapel** (tel. 28 21 87), with the important fourteenth-century frescoes of Andrea di Bonaiuto. Commissioned to portray the history of the Dominican order, he produced a stunning allegory of the life of the Church; in one fresco you can see the black-and-white dogs (*domini* *canes*—Dominicans, or dogs of the Lord in Latin) chasing the Church's persecutors. (Open Mon.-Thurs. and Sat. 9am-4pm, Sun. 8am-1pm. Admission L3000.)

Around San Lorenzo

The Medici staked out an entire portion of the city north of the Duomo in which to build their own church, the **Basilica of San Lorenzo,** and the Palazzo Medici (also known as the Palazzo Medici-Riccardi after its subsequent occupants). San Lorenzo was begun in 1419 following plans by Brunelleschi. The Medici lent the city the necessary funds to build the church and in return were given control over its design. Their coat of arms, with its six red balls, is carved all over the nave; their tombs fill the two sacristies and the Cappella dei Principi behind the altar. (Cosimo's is strategically placed in front of the high altar, thus making the entire church his personal mausoleum.) The Medici-commissioned Laurentian Library is attached to the side of the church. Michaelangelo never got around to constructing the facade he had designed for the church, and it stands bare to the present day. The rough brick, however, seems consistent with the rusticated **Palazzo Medici,** diagonally across the *piazza.* Inside San Lorenzo, Desiderio da Settignano's delicate marble tabernacle (against the right wall) stands behind Donatello's two bronze pulpits. At the end of the left transept is the **Old Sacristy,** the calm gray stone structure designed by Brunelleschi and filled with Donatello's sculpture. The graceful *Annunciation* altarpiece by Filippo Lippi is tucked away in the other corner of the left transept. Next door, the **Biblioteca Mediceo-Laurenziana** (tel. 21 07 60) illustrates Michelangelo's virtuoso architectural ability, and shows the license he took with the classical architectural vocabulary. (Open Mon.-Sat. 9am-5pm. Free. Entrance to the left as you face the basilica's main facade.)

To reach the **Cappelle dei Medici** (tel. 21 32 06), you must go outside and walk around the church through the market to the back entrance on p. Madonna degli Aldobrandini. Intended as a grand mausoleum, the **Cappella dei Principi** (Princes' Chapel) imitates the baptistery. Except for the operatic gilded portraits of the Medici dukes, the decor is oppressive, a rare moment of the baroque in Florence. Michelangelo's **New Sacristy** (1524), containing the tombs of Lorenzo and Giuliano de' Medici, seems stark by contrast, reflecting the architect's study of Brunelleschi. The architecture may be more effective than the sculpture, however—a large part of the intended program was never completed. Lorenzo, his face cast in shadow, has a grave and pensive nature; on his sarcophagus are the somber figures of *Twilight* (male) and *Dawn* (female). Giuliano is portrayed as a man of action, and his tomb is surmounted by the resolutely contrasting figures of *Night* (female) and *Day* (male). The sculptural treatment of the female figures is especially intriguing; their unnatural look may derive from Michelangelo's refusal to work from female models. (Open Tues.-Sat. 9am-2pm, Sun. 9am-1pm. Admission L4350.)

According to art historians, Brunelleschi proposed a sumptuous design for the **Palazzo Medici** (tel. 276 01), but the pragmatic merchant Cosimo decided against it. With its arched window frames and the "kneeling" windows on the southwest corner, Michelozzo's *palazzo* is quite impressive, and set the trend in palace styles. The entrance is at via Cavour, 1; inside, the private chapel is covered with Benozzo Gozzoli's ornate, fifteenth-century, tapestry-like murals of the three Magi (including portraits of the Medici and their family). Luca Giordano's seventeenth-century frescoes on the ceiling of an upstairs room try to apotheosize the Medici, and the result is hilariously overblown. (Open Mon.-Tues. and Thurs.-Sat. 9am-12:30pm and 3-5pm, Sun. 9am-noon. Free.) At via Faenza, 42, behind San Lorenzo, the convent refectory, **Cenacolo di Foligno** (tel. 28 69 82), houses Perugino's *Last Supper.* If imitation is the sincerest form of flattery, San Lorenzo is one huge tribute to the famous designers of Italy.

Around Piazza Santissima Annunziata

The complex of religious buildings encircling p. Santissima Annunziata emanates serenity. The *loggia* of the **Spedale degli Innocenti** (on the right), designed by Brunelleschi and built in the 1420s, was copied on the other side by Antonio da Sangallo a century later. The visual unity so pleased contemporary tastes that the *loggia* was continued across the facade of the church in 1601. The statue of Ferdinando de' Medici stands over the *piazza* in a position intentionally reminiscent of that of Marcus Aurelius in Rome's Campidoglio. At #12, the **Galleria dello Spedale degli Innocenti** (tel. 24 77 95) contains the lovely *Madonna e Angelo* by Botticelli and Ghirlandaio's *Epiphany.* (Open in summer Mon.-Tues. and Thurs.-Sat. 9am-7pm, Sun. 8am-1pm; in off-season Mon.-Tues. and Thurs.-Sat. 9am-2pm, Sun. 8am-1pm. Admission L2000.)

The atrium in front of the **Church of Santissima Annunziata,** called the Chiostrino dei Voti, is full of great murals, mostly by Andrea del Sarto, with two early mannerist additions: the *Visitation* by Pontormo and the *Assumption* by Rosso. Inside the rococo church, look at the round choir designed by Alberti, who is buried in the church. Giambologna and his pupils designed the central chapel for his own grave. From the left transcept, enter the cloister. Directly above the door is Andrea del Sarto's gentle *Madonna del Sacco.* Several other important sixteenth-century artists are buried in the **Cappella di San Luca,** off the cloister. (Open daily 7am-12:30pm and 4-7pm.) The **Museo Archeologico** (tel. 247 86 41), nearby at via della Colonna, 36, contains much of the Medici collection of antiques, sculpture, and vases. The sculptures include the Etruscan *Chimera,* the *Idolino,* and the Etruscan *Actor.* (Open Tues.-Sat. 9am-2pm, Sun. 9am-1pm. Admission L3000.)

The **Church of San Marco** (tel. 21 07 41) belongs to the Dominican order and is not especially captivating. However, its museum, to the right of the church, is blessed with the major, miraculous works of Fra Angelico. Directly to the right upon entering, a large room contains some of the angelic painter's major works, including the altarpiece formerly on the high altar of the church, the *San Marco altarpiece.* Across the cloister in the chapter room is a huge muralled *Crucifixion* by Fra Angelico. Mount the stairs to see his magnificent *Annunciation* at the top. Here, in the dormitory, each cell contains a Fra Angelico fresco as well, painted in flat colors and sparse forms so as to facilitate the monks' meditation on the scene. Michelozzo's library, Saronarola's cell, and Cosimo di Medici's personal cell are all worth a peek. (Open Tues.-Sat. 9am-2pm, Sun. 9am-1pm. Admission L3000.)

The **Accademia** (tel. 21 43 75) lies between the two churches at via Ricasoli, 60. Almost all of the museum is closed, but the collection itself is not. Michelangelo's triumphant *David,* brought from p. Signoria in 1873 after 400 years as a symbol of Florentine fortitude, stands in self-assured perfection under the rotunda designed to accommodate him. Michelangelo's *Prisoners* struggle in the arcade to push out of the stone. (Open Tues.-Sat. 9am-2pm, Sun. 9am-1pm. Admission L4000.) Almost as stunning as the *David* is the line to get in to see him in summer. The situation is worst on Sunday and Tuesday, but the line usually thins around noon. Early birds should try showing up shortly after 8am.

From p. SS. Annunziata, take bus #6 (get off at via Andrea del Sarto) to the **Cenacolo di San Salvi** (tel. 67 75 70), an abbey refectory that houses Andrea del Sarto's stupendous *Last Supper* (1519). Visitors are allowed only with a prior appointment, so apply to the Sopraintendenza ai Beni Artistici e Storici, via della Ninna, 5 (tel. 21 83 41; open Tues.-Sat. 9am-2pm, Sun. 9am-1pm; admission L2000).

Around Santa Croce

The Franciscans built the **Church of Santa Croce** as far as possible from San Marco and their Dominican rivals. It is by far the most splendid church in the city, rather ironic considering ascetic Franciscan ideals. On the right of the altar, the **Peruzzi** and **Bardi Chapels** were both decorated by Giotto and his school, and vie with each other in the slightly different media of tempera mural (Peruzzi) and fresco (Bardi). The latter technique is more durable and accounts for the Bardi Chapel's better state of preservation. Explore all the chapels because most have a minor masterpiece hidden somewhere. Among the famous Florentines buried here are Michelangelo, who rests at the beginning of the right aisle in a tomb designed by Vasari, and the humanist Leonardo Bruni, shown holding his precious *History of Florence* on a tomb designed by Bernardo Rossellino. On the same wall is Dante's empty sarcophagus. Although the Florentines, who banished him, repented and begged for his remains to be returned, the people of Ravenna, the city in which he died, cling stubbornly to them. A bit closer to the altar lies the political philosopher Machiavelli, and in the right aisle is the tomb of the Pisan Galileo. (Open daily 7am-12:30pm and 3-6:30pm.)

The Gothic splendor of Sante Croce provides contrasts fascinatingly with the brittle architecture of Brunelleschi's small **Pazzi Chapel,** at the end of the cloister next to the church. This is an excellent example of the innovations of early Renaissance architecture. Look at the lovely second cloister and the **Museo dell' Opera di Croce** (tel. 24 46 19; through the *loggia* in front of the Pazzi Chapel), the latter still recovering from the disastrous 1966 flood that left many works, including the great Cimabue *Crucifixion,* in a tragic state. The one-time refectory contains Taddeo Gaddi's wonderfully imaginative fresco of *The Tree of the Cross;* beneath it, in the *Last Supper,* Christ and the disciples surround a long table just as monks once did in this very room. Also in the museum is Donatello's gilt bronze *St. Louis,* originally in the central niche of the facade of Orsanmichele. (Open March-Sept. Thurs.-Tues. 9am-12:30pm and 3-6:30pm; Oct.-Feb. 9am-12:30pm and 3-5pm. Admission to both L2000. Enter to your left as you leave Santa Croce.)

From the museum, follow via dell' Oriolo 2 blocks past p. Saluemini and make a right on via Buonarotti to reach the **Casa Buonarotti,** via Ghibellina, 70 (tel. 24 17 52), which houses the expected Michelangelo memorabilia as well as two important early works, *The Madonna of the Steps* and *The Battle of the Centaurs.* Both are in the first rooms to the left of the landing on the second floor. These panels were executed when he was about 16 years old, and show his transition from bas-relief to full sculpture. (Open Wed.-Mon. 9am-1pm. Admission L4000.)

A few streets north of via Ghibellina at via Farini, 4, and via Pilastri stands the beautiful **Synagogue of Florence** (tel. 24 52 52; sometimes listed as the Museo del Tempio Israelitico). Built between 1872 and 1874 by the architects Micheli and Treves for the Spanish Jewish community, the sfardic temple is decked out in a modified Moorish style, decorated with elaborate geometrical designs. (Open May-Sept. Sun. and Thurs. 9am-1pm, Mon. and Wed. 2-5pm; Oct.-April Sun.-Mon. and Wed. 10am-1pm. Free, with frequent informative tours. Men should cover their heads and women should dress modestly.)

In the Oltrarno

Historically disdained by urban Florentines, the far side of the Arno remains a lively, no-nonsense quarter. The main streets, particularly via Maggio, harbor some of the priciest art and antique dealers in town, and the side streets are full of furniture repairers and restorers. Even in high season, when most Florentines avoid public places, piazza Santo Spirito bustles with its workaday business, delightfully unaffected.

One of the most powerful and moving fresco styles anywhere can be found in the Brancacci Chapel in the **Church of Santa Maria del Carmine** (tel. 21 23 31), a few blocks west of p. Santo Spirito. Adorned with frescoes by Masaccio with the help of Masolino and later additions by Filippino Lippi, the *Expulsion from Paradise* portrays the agonizing tragedy of the Fall. Beside it is *The Tribute Money,* a composition entirely by Masaccio, whose three-dimensional treatment of space touched off a revolution in painting. Light up all the frescoes here—they will light up your imagination.

As Brunelleschi designed it, the **Church of Santo Spirito** would have been one of the most exciting pieces of sacred architecture ever. He envisioned a four-aisled nave encircled by hollow chapels, which the exterior would reveal as a series of convex bumps. Brunelleschi died when the project was only partially completed, and the plans were adjusted to make the building more conventional. Nonetheless, it remains a masterpiece of Renaissance harmony, similar to but far less busy than San Lorenzo. (Open daily 7am-noon and 3:30-6pm.) The **Cenacolo di Santo Spirito** (tel. 28 70 43), next door at #29 (turn right as you exit the church), contains one of Florence's largest *Crucifixion* murals in the only surviving room of the former Augustinian convent. (Open Tues.-Sat. 9am-2pm, Sun. 8am-1pm. Admission L1000, Sun. free.)

Luca Pitti, a *nouveau-riche* banker of the fifteenth century, built his *palazzo* east of Santo Spirito, against the Boboli hill. The Medici acquired the *palazzo* and the hill in the sixteenth century and enlarged the building tremendously. The courtyard was redesigned by Ammanati; the motif of columns captured in the rusticated blocks is an architectural expression of the sixteenth-century preoccupation with the theme of nature versus art. The **Pitti Palace** now houses no less than five museums. Three reflect the imperial lifestyle. The **Museo degli Argenti,** on the ground floor, exhibits the Medici treasure; the newly renovated **Royal Apartments** above preserve furnishings from the period when the Pitti Palace was the residence of the Royal House of Savoy; and the **Museum of Coaches** displays their carriages. The **Galleria Palatina** (tel. 21 03 23), one of the earliest public galleries, was opened in 1833. Though the pictures are poorly displayed in the large hall, the treasures inside should still be seen. It is a veritable mine of Raphaels (most unfortunately behind glass), and also harbors works by Titian, Andrea del Sarto, Rosso, Caravaggio, and Rubens. The fifth and final museum, the **Galleria d' Arte Moderna,** houses one of the big surprises of Italian art: the Macchiaioli school, which inaugurated Italian impressionism in the nineteenth century. Fattori and Lega easily compare with Degas, Monet, and Jaccard. (Galleria Palatina, Galleria d'Arte Moderna, and Royal Apartments open Tues.-Sat. 9am-2pm, Sun. 9am-1pm. Museo degli Argenti open Wed. and Fri. 9am-2pm, Sun. 9am-1pm. Admission to the Palatina, Apartments, and Argenti L4000, to the Arte Moderna an additional L4000.)

The elaborately landscaped **Boboli Gardens** (tel. 21 34 40), behind the palace, explore another more cooperative relationship between art and nature. Perched at the top of the hill, the **Forte Belvedere** was the Medici fortress and treasury. You must go up via di Costa San Giorgio (off p. Santa Felcità, to the left after crossing the Ponte Vecchio) to reach the villa, an unusual construction with a central *loggia* designed by Ammanati. The Medici chose their defensive position well, providing themselves with a magnificent view over Florence. The exhibits held here are generally among the best in the city. (Gardens open May-Aug. daily 9am-6:30pm; March-April and Sept.-Oct. 9am-5:30pm; Nov.-Feb. 9am-4:30pm. Fort open daily 9am-8pm. Both free.)

San Miniato al Monte, one of Florence's oldest churches, perches atop its own hill, west of the Belvedere. (Take bus #13 from the station or climb the stairs from p. Michelangelo.) The inlaid marble facade with thirteenth-century mosaics is only a prelude to the spectacular pavement inside, patterned with lions, doves, and astrological signs. See the Cardinal of Portugal's chapel here (ask the sacristan to open it), where excellent architecture, painting, and sculpture rest, including some superlative della Robbia terra-cottas.

Entertainment

Most Florentine cultural magazines flit in and out of what's hot and what's not, but you can always consult the veterans, *Firenze Spettacolo* (L1500) and *Firenze La Sera* (L2500) for current entertainment information. If you are dying for a movie in English, head for the **Astro Cinema,** p. Simone near S. Croce (across from Vivoli's *gelateria*), where movies cost L6000.

Italians and foreigners alike enjoy the *passeggiata* along **via dei Calzaioli,** while locals in particular seem to frequent the cafes in **piazze Repubblica.** (If you sit outside, expect to pay twice what you would standing at the bar.) Street performers often perform on the steps of the Duomo, under the arcades of the Mercato Nuovo, and up in piazzale Michelangelo. If you'd rather leave the crowds behind, take a bus up to a hill town such as **Fiesole, Maiano,** or **Settignano,** and stroll in the evening air, enjoying the view before visiting one of the local wine shops.

Florence vies with England for the honor of having invented modern soccer (football to Brits), and every June the various *quartieri* of the city turn out in costume to play their own medieval version of the sport, known as **Calcio Storico.** The game is played in p. Signoria with a wooden ball by two teams of 27 players, and sometimes resembles a riot. Check newspapers or with the tourist office for the dates and locations of either historic or modern *calcio,* and keep in mind the *Calcio Storico* sells out about two weeks in advance. Tickets are sold at the Chiosco degli Sportivi, on via de' Anselmi (tel. 29 23 63). If you prefer to watch sports in a sociable atmosphere over beer (L2000-4000) and gourmet snacks (L3000-4000), try **Break,** via delle Terme, 17r (open 8am-midnight), or **Bierstube,** Borgo Ognissanti, 144r (open 9:30am-2:30pm and 6pm-midnight). **La Dolce Vita,** p. del Carmine, a snazzy hangout decked with monochromes in the Oltrarno, is a bit more expensive, but a good bet if you're staying in one of the hostels around via dei Serragli. (Open Sept.-July Mon.-Sat. 8am-1pm.)

For general nightlife, try **Amici di Ale,** a club on via San Giovanni (see Student Travel Information under Practical Information). Other student hotspots include **Lush Life** and **Video Diva,** at via S. Zanobi, 90 and 114; or try **Yellow Bar,** via del Proconsolo, 39. (All three open Sept.-July) For live jazz, go to the **Jazz Club,** via Nuova de' Caccini, 3, at Borgo Pinti. (Disregard the "members only" sign on the door. Open Sept. 21-July 14.) For a taste of Florence's artsy scene, go to **Last Exit,** down the street at Borgo Pinti, 17r, where videos, exhibits, and dancing come together. Go late. (Open Sept.-June.) The last two places mentioned are much more active in the winter than in June. Note that many of the discos listed below cater almost exclusively to tourists and to a few Italians who have dubious ambition with regard to foreign women.

Dancing

Space Electronic, via Palazzuolo, 37 (tel. 29 30 82), near Santa Maria Novella. Multitudes of mirrors reflect a young, international (i.e., American) crowd. Beer L6000, mixed drinks L7000. Cover with 1 drink L12,000, with a copy of *Let's Go* L10,000. Open nightly 9:30pm-1:30am, Oct.-Feb. Tues.-Sun. only. **Moonlight,** not far away at via della Scala, 89 (tel. 21 63 87), is smaller.

Yab Yum, via dei Sassetti, 5 (tel. 28 20 18), off p. della Repubblica. Italians and Americans alike will mention this name if they hear the word discotheque. Cover with 1st drink L10,000. Open Tues.-Sun. 10pm-3am. In summer, Yab Yum's business moves to **Central Park** in the Parco delle Cascinè, in front of the Hotel Michelangelo (tel. 35 67 23). Take bus #17C from the Duomo or station. Open nightly.

The Red Garter, via dei Benci, 33r (tel. 26 30 04), near Santa Croce. Beer, peanuts, banjos, and loads of Americans—occasional live music. Drinks L5000-7000, beer L5000. 1-drink minimum. Open daily 8:30pm-1am.

Tabasco Gay Club, p. S. Cecilia, 3r (tel. 21 30 00), in a tiny alleyway across p. della Signoria from the Palazzo Vecchio. Florence's most popular gay disco. Minimum age 18. Cover L10,000; Fri.-Sun. L15,000, including a drink. Open Tues.-Sun. 9:30pm-2:30am.

Festivals

The major city festivals are the Easter Sunday **Scoppio del Carro** (Explosion of the Cart), the **Festa del Patrono** (the Feast of Saint John the Baptist, the patron saint of Florence) on June 24, and the **Calcio Storico** (see Entertainment). During the Easter celebration, a firework-filled float is exploded in p. Duomo, while on the night of the Festa del Patrono, fireworks are launched over the city from p. Michelangelo. These start at about 10pm and are easily visible from along the Arno.

Music festivals enliven the summer, starting with the **Maggio Musicale** (May-June), which draws its performers from the world's foremost classical musicians. The **Estate Fiesolana** (June-Aug.) fills the Roman Theater in Fiesole with concerts, opera, theater, ballet, and movies. For information on tickets, contact the Biglietteria Centrale in the Teatro Comunale, corso Italia, 16 (tel. 21 62 53 or 277 92 36), or Universalturismo, via degli Speziali, 7r (tel. 21 72 41), off p. della Repubblica.

Finally, film flourishes in Florence. The **Florence Film Festival,** held generally in December, is justly famous. For more information contact the film festival command center at via Martini de Popolo (tel. 24 07 20).

Shopping

The Florentine sense of design is as apparent in the window displays of the shops as in the well-crafted wares. This applies to small, less expensive merchants as well as to the Fifth Avenue ambience of **via Tornabuoni,** or the goldsmiths on the **Ponte Vecchio.** Some of the best-known, *haute couture* shops are **Gucci,** via Tornabuoni, 9 (tel. 21 10 55); **Pucci,** via Pucci, 6 (tel. 29 30 61); **Ungaro,** via della Vigina Nuova, 30r (tel. 21 01 29); **Ferragamo,** via Tornabuoni, 2 (tel. 21 07 56); and its neighbor **Saint Laurent,** via Tornabuoni, 29r (tel. 28 40 40). Italy's official fashion capital, Florence makes its contribution to *alta moda* with its biannual Pitti Uomo show, the world's most important collection of menswear (held mid-Jan. and July), and its companion Pitti fashion shows. Not all Florentine *couture* is *haute,* however. If you find good quality used and antique clothing the way to go, Florence won't let you down. Try **La Belle Epogne,** volta di S. Piero, 8r (tel. 21 61 69), off p. S. Pier Maggiore, or **Lord Brummel Store,** via del Purgatorio, 26r (tel. 28 75 40), off via di Tornabuoni, where the two young owners, besides selling fine clothes, are artists: his paintings hang on the wall (also for sale) and she might play the piano for you if you're lucky.

The city's artisan traditions continue to thrive at the open markets. **San Lorenzo,** the largest, cheapest, and most tourist-oriented, sprawls for several blocks around p. San Lorenzo, offering just about anything made from leather, wool, cloth, or gold. (Open Mon.-Sat.) Prices are low, but often so are quality and honesty. If you use a credit card here, be careful the carbons are destroyed. For clothing and shoes, the market held Tuesday mornings in **Parco delle Cascinè** (take bus #17C from the station) is a better deal. Avoid the **Mercato Nuovo,** under the arcades where via Por Santa Maria becomes via Calimala. For a flea market specializing in old furniture, postcards, and bric-a-brac, visit **piazza Ciompi,** just off via Pietrapana (walk out borgo degli Albizi). Virtually undiscovered, it's one of the city's best. (Open Mon.-Sat.) Florentines may be the merchants of the world, but they are not hagglers. Bargaining is uncouth unless you feel the price is outrageous.

Books and art reproductions are some of the best souvenirs you can carry away from Florence. Famed **Alinari,** via della Vigna Nuova, 46-48r (tel. 21 89 75), stocks the world's largest selection of art reproductions and high-quality photographs, about L5000-8000 apiece. (Open Mon.-Sat. 9am-1pm and 4-8pm.) For color reproductions, Rizzoli's *Maestri del Colore* series is a bargain. **Feltrinelli,** via Cavour, 2 (tel. 29 63 20), opposite the Palazzo Medici-Riccardi, has the best selection of art books. (Open Mon.-Fri. 9am-7:30pm, Sat. 9am-1pm.) Don't miss the chance to browse at **Franco Maria Ricci,** via delle Belle Donne, 41r (tel. 28 33 12), at via del Moro near Santa Maria Novella.

Florence is perhaps best-known for its gold-, paper-, and leatherwork. Gold is most readily available in the shops along Ponte Vecchio. *Cartolerie* (stationery stores) and many gift shops carry samples of the famous *carta fiorentina,* paper goods covered in an intricate floral design. Florentine leatherwork is generally of high quality and frequently affordable. Leather shops fill the city, but piazza Santa Croce and via Por Santa Maria are particularly good places to look. A number of the smaller shops, such as **Bagman,** via dell' Alberto, 19, off via della Scala, let you peek in at the artists. Check for such opportunities in other stores too, especially in jewelry stores: Many of them sell only goods made on the premises.

Fiesole

Perched on a series of knolls 8km northeast of Florence, Fiesole makes for a delightful escape from the sprawling metropolis. Fiesole's panoramic view of the city and river basin below have made it a coveted spot for such people as the Etruscans, the Romans, and *literati* from Shelley to Dickens. Da Vinci's attraction to the town was somewhat more flighty—he experimented with flying off its hills. Today the vista is just as stunning, and a picnic lunch on the verdant Tuscan slopes an antidote to the hustle and bustle of urban life. Former inhabitants—Etruscan, Roman, medieval Italian, to name a few—have left intriguing artifacts, and the town possesses a rustic charm and serenity all its own.

Practical Information

Azienda Autonoma di Turismo: p. Mino da Fiesole, 45 (tel. 59 87 20). Open in summer Mon.-Fri. 9am-1pm and 3-6pm, Sat. 9am-1pm; in off-season Mon.-Fri. 9am-1pm and 2:30-5:30pm, Sat. 9am-1pm.

Post Office: via Gramsci, 5. Open Mon.-Fri. 8:15am-7pm, Sat. 8:15am-noon. **Postal code:** 50014.

Telephone Code: 055.

Buses: ATAF. Bus #7 runs from the Florence train station, from p. del Duomo, and from p. San Marco to its last stop at p. Mino da Fiesole every 10-15 min. during the day, less frequently at night (L600). Last bus back to Florence leaves Fiesole at 11pm. Last bus to Fiesole leaves Florence 11:45pm.

Pharmacy: p. Mino, 15. Open Mon.-Sat. 9am-1pm and 4-8pm, Sun. 9:30am-1pm and 4:30-8pm.

Hospital: Ospetale Sant Antonio, via Vecchia Fiesolana, 10 (tel. 59 91 51).

Police: Carabinieri, via Gramsci, 20 (tel. 591 36). **Vigili Urbani,** p. Mino, 23 (tel. 59 71 77).

Accommodations, Camping, and Food

There is a paucity of budget accommodations in Fiesole, and what does exist disappears in July and August. Make reservations. If you do get a room here, however, you can avoid frenetic Florence while remaining within easy striking distance.

Villa Sorriso, via Gramsci, 21 (tel. 590 27), a short walk off p. Mino da Fiesole. Simple, affordable rooms. Singles L35,000. Doubles L45,000, with bath L50,000.

Villa Baccano, via Bosconi, 4 (tel. 593 41), about 1km farther from p. Mino da Fiesole than Sorriso. Singles L21,500, with bath L27,000. Doubles L31,500, with bath L40,000.

Camping: Camping Panoramico, via Peramonda (tel. 59 90 69), 3km out of town, with a back-breaking hill to top off the journey. Bus #70 runs every ½ hr. from p. Mino da Fiesole to the base of the hill. (Last bus leaves at approximately 7pm.) Rooms with views. Decent facilities, with a store and a bar. L6650 per person, L4500 per tent, L3000 per car. Also offers tiny bungalows. Doubles L38,000, with bath L48,000. Triples L50,000, with bath L63,000. Quads L60,000, with bath L78,000.

Overpriced, tourist-oriented restaurants abound in Fiesole. Opt for one of the several markets and fruit stands on **via Gramsci.**

Pizzeria Etrusca, p. Mino, 13. Pizza L4500-8000. Filling, if not stellar pies. Open Thurs.-Tues.

Il Lordo, p. Mino, 13 (tel. 590 95). Serves a variety of sensibly priced dishes (L4000-8000) in a crowded, cavernous setting. Service rushes solo diners.

Sights and Entertainment

Directly across the p. Mino da Fiesole from the Azienda is the **Cattedrale di S. Romolo Fiesole (duomo).** Hardly recognizable due to recent construction, the *duomo* houses a number of interesting works of art. Pause upon entering to look at the colorful della Robbia terra-cotta of San Romolo on the reverse of the facade. Also note that some of the columns of the nave have antique capitals taken from ruined Greek buildings. Upstairs to the right of the altar to the Salutati Chapel lies the tomb of the bishop of the same name and his altar, both by Mino da Fiesole (1430-1484). Mino's representation of the Christ child at the Madonna's feet is one of the earliest in which the newborn Jesus appears as a real, roly-poly baby rather than a miniature adult saint. The **Bandini Museum,** behind the *duomo,* is undergoing extensive restoration and will remain closed to the public at least until early 1989. Inquire at the Azienda.

Around the block from the *duomo* is the **Teatro Romano** and its **Museo Archeologico.** The theater is in excellent condition and still hosts performances year-round, most notably the **Estate Fiesolana** festival of music, dance, drama, and film (June-Aug.). A typical Roman theater, the structure is designed to give the audience an awe-inspiring view of the surrounding countryside, presumably to ensure that the audience is entertained regardless of any failings in the show. Tickets for performances (L12,000-20,000) are available at the box office of the theater, or at City Travel, via Gramsci, 52 (tel. 59 88 81). The museum houses a well-displayed collection of artifacts from excavations in and around Fiesole, including numerous bronze vases, tools, household items, and a fine selection of Roman coins. Particularly noteworthy are the remains of a formidable bronze lioness (*circa* the 1st century B.C.E.), two beautiful alabaster urns from Volterra (*circa* 100 B.C.E.), and a transfixing marble head with a great headdress, which is possibly a marriage portrait of Vibra Sabina, wife of the Emperor Hadrian. (Open April-Sept. Tues.-Sun. 9am-7pm; Oct.-March Tues.-Sun. 10am-4pm. Admission L2500, with ISIC L1000.)

To appreciate Fiesole's spectacular spread of typical Tuscan turf, walk across the main *piazza* from the Teatro Romano to via Francesco. After a left turn, take a right into the small park offering a modest view of Fiesole and its Roman and Etruscan ruins. Return to the steeply ascending alley to find a pair of belvederes, the first facing east, the second south. Take your pick. The view of the valley that the Arno carved into the surrounding hills is unsurpassed. These slopes, recognizable by their candelabra-like larches and stiff cypresses, serve as the background in countless Renaissance paintings by Tuscan masters.

Just behind the higher belvedere is the **Church of Sant' Alessandro;** don't let its white-washed, modern facade dissuade you from entering. Within is the nave of a ninth-century basilica graced by antique Eubean (Greek) columns nade of the unique *marmo cipollina* (onion marble), and topped by delicate ionic capitals. Off the nave to the left is a chapel with recently restored fifteenth-century frescoes by Perugino. (Open daily 7am-noon and 3-6:30pm.)

The **Church of San Francesco,** farther up the slope, was first a fortress, then a convent, and finally a Franciscan monastery. Though the interior of the church has been altered somewhat, the delightful exterior, cloisters, and lovely internal courtyards remain authentic. Through the church and to the left, a tiny cloister worthy of a Buddhist monk opens onto a patch of sky. Canaries sing in a cage at one side, probably placed in this meditative spot to bring back the memory of St. Francis, who was famous for his conversations with birds. (Church open daily 7am-12:30pm and 3-7:30pm.)

If you are in the area between September and June, come on the second Sunday of the month for the **Fiesole Antiquaria,** an exhibition and sale of myriad antique objects and other curiosities. The celebration of Fiesole's patron saint, the **Fiera di San Romolo,** takes place on July 6 and is accompanied by processions, floats, and fireworks.

Prato

High-tension electrical towers march single file from Florence to Prato, symbolizing an industrial link between the two cities that has existed since 1351. Today, Prato's machine shops and textile mills have earned it the nickname "the Manchester of Tuscany." Penetrate the city's rough exterior, however, to find the capital that commissioned a number of artistic gems. Prato's manageable size and proximity to Florence (25 min. by bus or train) make it an easy daytrip, and the virtual absence of tourists ensures hotel availability even in summer.

Practical Information and Orientation

The train from Florence is only L1000, but spend the extra L800 for a CAP bus ticket (the station is on via Nazionale just off p. della Stazione), which will get you directly to Prato's **piazza del Duomo,** the center of town. (Buses run every ½ hr. on weekdays, hourly on weekends and holidays.) If arriving by train, proceed to the piazza del Duomo by crossing the bridge over the River Bisenzio. Walk straight up via Veneto, which becomes via Piave, and continue diagonally for several blocks to reach the *duomo.*

Ufficio Informazioni dell' Azienda Autonoma di Turismo: via Cairoli, 48 (tel. 241 12), across from the *cartello.* Open Mon.-Sat. 8:30am-6:30pm.

Post Office: via Archivescovo Martini, 8 (tel. 490 01). **Postal code:** 50047.

Telephone Code: 0574.

Train Information: At the station (tel. 266 17). Open 8am-noon and 3-7pm.

Bus Information: p. del Duomo, 23 (tel. 490 11). They also sell train tickets.

All-night Pharmacy: p. Mercatale, 142 (tel. 303 27).

Hospital: Guardia Medica, via del Seminario, 26 (tel. 384 38 or 422 03).

Police: Polizia Municipale, tel. 423 91.

Accommodations

Prato lodges far more business travelers than tourists, so hotels are reliably available in high season, when Florence swells with visitors.

Albergo Centrale, via Magnolfi, 15 (tel. 231 82), right off p. del Duomo. Noisy but affordable, and strong hot showers. Singles L22,000. Doubles L33,000.

Albergo Stella D'Italia, p. del. Duomo, 8 (tel. 279 10). Also somewhat loud, yet a friendly proprietor and an aura of not-too-faded elegance more than make up for this. Singles L33,000, with bath L40,500. Doubles L46,000, with bath L58,000.

Albergo Il Giglio, p. San Marco, 14 (tel. 370 49), 3 blocks from train station. Warm management, superlative rooms. Singles L32,500, with bath L39,500. Doubles L46,000, with bath L58,500.

Hotel San Marco, p. San Marco, 48 (tel. 213 21), across from Il Giglio. Large and expensive. Singles L55,000. Doubles L75,000.

Food

The piazza Mercatale hosts an **open-air market** every Wednesday and Saturday (8am-1pm). There are many "bars" serving tasty snacks from sandwiches to pizza, which will do the trick for lunch. For dinner or a heartier meal, try **Pizzeria/Bar Renato** at via Magnolfi, 30, 100m from p. del Duomo, where Renato himself will serve up delicious slices (L1000) and share fun historical facts. (Open Mon.-Sat. 7am-8pm.) A Pratese favorite is **Trattoria Lapo** in boisterous p. Mercatale, 141, which serves simple, filling meals for L11,000, including wine. (Open Mon.-Sat. until 10pm.) For dessert, the **Brasserie Bigi** in p. del Duomo has the freshest pastries and creamiest *gelato* in town. Try some *cantuccini di Prato,* crunchy cookies deservedly renowned throughout Italy and usually accompanied by a glass of *vin santo*—both available in most bars.

Sights

The **piazza del Duomo** is Prato in a nutshell: The *duomo* sits alone in one corner, while more mundane establishments such as insurance companies and perfume shops dominate the chaotic square. Yet the cathedral's Romanesque and Gothic facade, with alternating bands of green and white marble, gives the structure a harmony and elegance that transcend its surroundings. The *duomo*'s most unusual feature is the **Pergamo del Sacro Cingolo** (Pulpit of the Sacred Belt), a reproduction of which projects from the facade at its right corner. The original work resides in the Museo dell' Opera del Duomo, next door. The pulpit represents a brilliant collaborative effort by Donatello and Michelozzo. Donatello sculpted the fine bas-relief *putti,* sprightly and sensuous cherubs dancing around the smooth marble exterior, while Michelozzo contributed the delicately classical canopy and the supporting entablature. The pulpit was commissioned to honor the local legend of the *sacro cingolo,* which involves the apostle Thomas, who doubted the Assumption of the Virgin Mary. When he asked to see her tomb for proof, he found it filled with flowers; then, looking up to heaven, he saw the Virgin herself, who gave him her belt as confirmation. This gift is celebrated five days a year (Easter, May 1, August 15, September 8, and Christmas), when church dignitaries ascend to the reproduction of the pulpit and display the *sacro cingolo* to enthusiastic crowds. Other works from the cathedral that are now housed in the museum include the recently cleaned *Death of St. Jerome* by Prato's son Filippo Lippi. Be sure to stop in the courtyard and examine the columns at the far end; some have wonderfully carved capitals depicting lions and birds locked in struggle.

Inside the *duomo* are a number of artistic treasures. To the left sits the **Chapel of the Sacro Cingolo,** in which Angelo Gaddi painted scenes from the life of the Virgin. The illusionistic marble panels on the bottom register show the conceits that fourteenth-century painters had already delighted in. The Madonna and Child sculpture on the altar here is by Giovanni Pisano. Halfway up the nave on the left is another pulpit, often eclipsed in the minds of tourists by the one outside. On this one, Antonio Rossellino and Mino da Fiesole carved scenes from the lives of St. Stephen and St. John the Baptist (the patron saints of Prato and Florence, respectively), and an *Assumption with the Holy Girdle.* In the apse is a masterful fresco series by Fra Filippo Lippi, also depicting the lives of St. Stephen and St. John the Baptist. The vivid action and attention to courtly detail suggest an artistic temperament ill-suited to monastic life. In fact, Lippi eventually renounced his vows and married one of his models after she had given birth to his illegitimate son Filippino Lippi, who became a painter like his father. (*Duomo* open in summer 6:30am-noon and 4-7pm; in off-season 6:30am-noon and 3:30-6:30pm. Museo dell 'Opera del Duomo open Mon. and Wed.-Sat. 9:30am-12:30pm and 3-6:30pm, Sun. 9:30am-12:30pm. Admission L1000.)

Leaving the *duomo,* turn left onto via Mazzini and proceed to p. Comune, which is dominated by the **Palazzo Pretorio,** the executive center back when Prato was a medieval commune. Inside the *palazzo* is the **Galleria Comunale,** a small but loaded collection of painting and sculpture. On the second floor, a tastefully arranged gallery of altarpieces from the thirteenth and fourteenth centuries includes works by father and son Lippi, including a warm and humorous *Nativity with St. Vincent* by Filippo Lippi. (Open Mon.-Sat. 9am-1pm and 3-7pm. Admission L1000.)

Walk back to p. del Comune, go straight 2 blocks, and turn right to arrive at the **Church of Santa Maria delle Carceri,** built by Lorenzo de' Medici's favorite architect, Giuliano da Sangallo, between 1484 and 1492. The church embodies the Renaissance architectural paragon: the centralized, Greek-cross plan. Inside, the perfectly rounded dome and dignified Corinthian pilasters (carved in light grey *pietra santa*) announce the classical grandeur of the High Renaissance.

Next door is the **Castello dell 'Imperatore.** Built by Frederick II in the manner of his beloved Norman fortresses, this *castello* is the only one of its kind north of Puglia. From the battlements (open Tues.-Sat. 9am-noon and 3-6pm, Sun. 9am-noon), you can see Prato's two sides: the cranes and smokestacks that spread thickly to the north and east, and the tree-covered hills to the west.

Pistoia

Nestled in the Appenines, Pistoia offers the modest charm typical of small Tuscan towns. Roman in origin, the town came into its own in 1177, when it was declared a free commune and became one of the first Italian city states to publish its municipal statutes. Politically, economically, and militarily advanced, Pistoia nevertheless went into decline, enabling its powerful neighbors, Florence, Lucca, and Pisa, to dominate it in turn. With the end of Medici rule in Florence, Pistoia regained its independence.

Pistoia's claim to fame is a tool of war it perfected in the sixteenth century—the pistol. Today, the city is home to one of the world's foremost train manufacturers, which supplies many American subways, including the Washington, DC Metro. Pistoia also harbors some of life's less racy pleasures. One of Europe's foremost flower producers, the city enjoys the recreational benefits of the Appenine mountains to the north.

Pistoia is an ideal daytrip from Florence (35 min.), Lucca, or Pisa, but the city's traditional quarter, with its narrow streets and beautiful **piazza del Duomo,** may well convince you to stay a while.

Orientation and Practical Information

Pistoia is on the Florence-Viareggio line and on a secondary Florence-Bologna line. The fare from Florence is L2000; from Lucca L2500; from Pisa via Lucca L3500; and from Bologna L4900. Lazzi bus service from Florence costs L3000 and drops you off in front of the train station. The last bus back to Florence departs at 9pm. For more information, call 251 32. To get to p. del Duomo from the train station, take bus #10, 12, 26, 27, or 28, or walk along via XX Settembre, which becomes via Vannucci, via Cino, and via Buozzi before ending at via degli Orafi, where you should turn right for the *duomo* (25 min.).

EPT: Palazzo dei Vescovi, p. del Duomo (tel. 216 22). A plethora of pamphlets. Open in summer Mon.-Sat. 9:30am-12:30pm and 3:30-6:30pm, Sun. 9:30am-12:30pm; in off-season Tues.-Sat. 9:30am-12:30pm and 3:30-6:30pm.

Post Office: via Roma, 5 (tel. 222 78). Fermo Posta open Mon.-Fri. 8:30am-7pm, Sat. 8:30am-noon. **Postal code:** 51100.

Telephones: corso A. Gramsci, 96 (tel. 261 11). Open Mon.-Fri. 8:30am-12:30pm and 3-7pm, Sat. 9am-noon. Also try **Bar Commercio,** p. Leonardo da Vinci, 13. Open daily 8am-8pm. **Telephone code:** 0573.

Police: Carabinieri, Tel. 212 12.

Accommodations

Getting a reasonably priced room in town can be tricky, as *pensioni* are small and hotels often quite expensive. The EPT may be able to save you some time by phoning ahead.

Albergo Firenze, via Curtatone e Montanara, 42 (tel. 231 41), near via Buozzi at via degli Orafi. Amiable proprietor, central location, and sparse but spotless rooms make a winning combo. Singles L20,000. Doubles L31,000, with bath L35,000.

Albergo Autisti, viale Pacinotti, 93 (tel. 217 71), a 5-min. walk from p. Treviso (the 1st street off via XX Settembre). Tidy and simple rooms. Pink wallpaper and astoundingly narrow, high-ceilinged corridors. Singles L15,000. Doubles L30,000, with bath L40,000.

Albergo Appennino, via Francesco Crispi, 8 (tel. 251 87), off via Cavour. Modern and clean, but compact. Singles L33,000, with bath L48,000. Doubles L49,500, with bath L65,000.

Il Boschetto, viale Adva, 467 (tel. 344 32), in Capostrada outside Pistoia. Take bus #10 from the station or from p. Mazzini. A hassle to get to, but in a lovely setting. Quite possibly the only one-star lodging in Tuscany (if not Italy) with a swimming pool. Singles L25,000. Doubles with bath L42,000.

Food

You can count on a good meal in Pistoia, though you'll have to count your money first—you'll pay for culinary pleasure here. The **open-air market** held in p. della Sala every Wednesday and Saturday (8am-2pm) is an inexpensive, amusing alternative. Stores in this quarter sell excellent fruit and sandwiches all week long.

Trattoria da Loriano, via Dalmazia, 69 (tel. 329 37). Take via Porta al Borgo away from the center and turn right. Hearty *cucina casalinga* (homestyle cooking) at homestyle prices. Back-slapping, boisterous locals frequent the joint. *Primi* L2000-3500, *secondi* L5000-6500. Open Tues.-Sun. 8am-10pm.

Pizzeria Tonino, via C. Gramsci, 159b (tel. 333 30), behind the Palazzo Marchetti. Cosmic food at astronomical prices. Try the *spaghetti al puttaniera* (a seafood sauce with pepper and cream), or indulge with the *bistecca all fiorentino.* Complete meals L15,000-18,000. Open Tues.-Sun. noon-2:30pm and 7:30pm-midnight.

Il Magico Chiosco, corso S. Fedi, 97, next to p. Garibaldi. Pistoian youth hang out *en masse* to munch American food. For better or worse, the cheapest meal in town. Grilled hot dog L1500, grilled cheeseburger L2200. Open Tues.-Sun. 7am-2pm and 4-8pm.

Sights and Entertainment

Pistoia focuses on the **piazza del Duomo** both geographically and culturally. On the right is the broad-based, unusually squat *duomo,* **La Cattedrale di San Zeno.** Originally built in the fifth century, the church has been restructured three times; luckily, it has escaped the fate of some other Italian churches and remains beautifully simple in form and facade. The Romanesque facade is Pisan in style with three rows of *loggie* stacked one atop other. The *duomo* is dwarfed by the **campanile** to its left. Rising 67m in the air, this belltower presents a dramatic architectural mix: The mellow brown base is a Lombard watchtower—it is surmounted by three Pisan tiers of arches, a red brick roof, and a bronze spire complete with the ball and cross of the Ghibellines.

Inside the *duomo,* whose main doorway is brightened by a della Robbia tympanum, is a wealth of early Renaissance art. The most interesting piece is the ***Dossale di San Jacopo,*** an enormous silver altarpiece that rests in a chapel (usually locked) on the right wall. Ask the sacristan to illuminate the work (L1000), which took nearly 200 years of Sienese, Florentine, and Pistoian silversmithing to create. On the left in the first panel above the altar table are portraits of the prophets Jeremiah and Isaiah by the famous Renaissance sculptor and architect, Filippo Brunelleschi. (Cathedral open Mon.-Sat. 7am-noon and 4-7pm, Sun. 7am-1pm and 4-7pm except during services.)

The **baptistery** across from the *duomo* has a modest exterior, enlivened by Nino and Tommaso Pisano's *Virgin and Child* in the tympanum, a work which replicates the canonical form established by their grandfather Giovanni in his ivory *Virgin and Child* in Pisa. Inside, a striking brick ceiling soars upward in a perfect cone. The city is quite protective of this unusual design and has posted a surly guard to prevent all photos and sketches. Just behind the bell tower stands the **Palazzo Comunale.** Built in the thirteenth and fourteenth centuries, the *palazzo* has a spartan facade graced by two rows of slender mullioned windows, the Medici arms, and one curious detail: To the left of the central balcony an arm reaches out of the wall, brandishing a club above the black marble head below—a tribute to the 1115 Pistoian victory over the moorish king Musetto. Inside, the ground floor is devoted almost entirely to one of Italy's most important modern artists, Pistoia-born Marino Marini. The **Centro Marino Marini** houses numerous drawings, etchings, and sculptures by the artist. (Open Tues.-Sat. 9am-1pm and 3-7pm, Sun. 9am-1pm. Free. The *centro* is moving to the Palazzo del Tau; check with the EPT to see if it's made it by 1989.) Climbing the stairs from the courtyard you'll find two sculptures notable for their quality, if not their gaiety. The first, by Marini, stands on the first landing. Entitled *Erode* (Herod), it is a disturbing portrayal of the king holding a dead child at his side. Continue to the top of the stairs, and turn left down the hall to the assembly room; in the far corner, you'll find Agenore Fabbri's horrifying *Ancora una Pietà,* in which the agony of Christ's death is expressed in the tortured bodies of the martyr and his mother.

For earlier and less morose art, head upstairs into the **Museo Civico,** a collection of paintings from the thirteenth through nineteenth centuries. The order is roughly chronological as one ascends the three upper floors of the *palazzo.* In the first room, there is a glossy, recently restored *Madonna and Saints* by Lorenzo di Credi. The Baroque room above houses a couple of dramatic paintings by Postoia's own Giacinto Gimignani. (Open Tues.-Sat. 9am-1pm and 3-7pm, Sun. 9am-12:30pm. Admission L2500, ages under 18 and over 70 L1000.)

Exit p. del Duomo by via del Duca, continue up via dei Rossi, and the **Church of Sant' Andrea,** with a typically Pisan Romanesque facade, will appear on the left. The church proudly houses Giovanni Pisano's finest pulpit (*circa* 1310). Below the narrative panels, prophets in thc spandrels of the arches display their scrolls, and sybils seated at the corners are startled by the messages angels whisper in their ears. The sculptor saved the most impressive scene, the *Massacre of the Innocents,* for the panel most clearly visible from the nave of the church.

From here, walk down via del Carmine and via delle Pappe to reach the **Ospedale del Ceppo,** named after the tree stump in which offerings were collected. The delicate Renaissance portico of this building was closely patterned after Brunelleschi's Ospedale degli Innocenti in Florence. However, while the della Robbia terra-cottas adorning the Florentine building are quiet blue with white lunettes, here they form a multicolored frieze, so vibrant that they outshine the rest of the facade.

Exit the *Ospedale,* turn left, and a narrow street will take you through Pistoia's more residential quarters to p. San Lorenzo. The slightly dilapidated church on the left (partially obscured by the adjoining building), is the **Church of Santa Maria delle Grazie,** designed by Giorgio Vasari at a time Pistoia was the site of greater pretensions. Come to this quaint *piazza* for some peace and quiet.

At the southern end of the city, on via Cavour at via Francesco Crispi, don't miss the **Church of San Giovanni Fuorcivitas.** The left side of the building has actually become its facade, since it faces the main street. The single-naved interior is a vast, boxlike space. On the right wall stands a massive, dramatic pulpit by Fra Guglielmo da Pisa, supported by two truculent marble lions. Distinctly classical figures act out scenes from the New Testament with an oddly pleasing lack of perspective.

To view nature's wonders rather than humanity's, hop on bus #29 from the station to the surprisingly verdant and well-stocked **zoo,** 5km out of town. Big cats, birds, and reptiles of every kind provide a respite from Tuscan civilization. (Open daily 9am-7pm. Admission L6000.) For a more vigorous escape, dive into the **public swimming pool** several hundred meters up the road.

The **Luglio Pistoiese** fills the month of July with first-rate operas, ballets and concerts, sporting events, craft shows, and folklore presentations. Inquire at the EPT. The festival culminates with the **Giostra dell' Orso** (Joust of the Bear), held in p. del Duomo on or about July 25, the feast of St. James (patron saint of the city). The *Giostra* began in the fourteenth century as a bloody contest between 12 mounted knights and a bear dressed in a white-and-red-checked cloak. The 12 knights and colorful costumes remain, but the bear has been replaced by a more placid wooden dummy. Evenings can also be spent peacefully watching the *passeggiata* on via degli Orafi.

Lucca

Less cosmopolitan than Florence, more isolated than Pisa, and less artistically endowed than both, Lucca nevertheless possesses a charm and unity that eludes its larger neighbors. Once a powerful medieval city-state, Lucca has retained much from those earlier days, most notably its surrounding fortress walls, battlements, and moat. Sitting at the foot of the Appenines, the city once controlled the Via

Franca and the passage northward through the mountains. Today, though a major producer of olive oil, wine, textiles, and flowers, it preserves a delightful old world quiescence.

Orientation and Practical Information

Lucca is 30 minutes by train from Pisa (L1500), 90 minutes by train (L3900) and 70 minutes by Lazzi bus (L5800) from Florence. Frequent trains (L1300) and buses (L2300) go to Viareggio on the coast. Lazzi and CLAP buses serve nearby towns.

EPT: via Vittorio Veneto, 40 (tel. 436 39), off p. Napoleone. Information but no accommodations service. Understaffed. Open Mon.-Sat. 9am-noon and 3:30-6:30pm, Sun. 9am-noon.

Post Office: via Vallisneri (tel. 456 90), off p. del Duomo. Open Mon.-Fri. 8:15am-7pm, Sat. 8:15am-noon. **Postal code:** 55100.

Telephones: via Cenami, 15-19 (tel. 553 66), off p. San Giusto. Open Mon.-Sat. 8:45am-12:30pm and 3:30-7pm. Otherwise, try **Bar Casali,** p. S. Michele. Open 8am-10pm. **Telephone code:** 0583.

Bus Station: Lazzi, piazzale Verdi, 2 (tel. 58 48 77). To Florence (every 45 min.), Viareggio (every 55 min.), and various seaside resorts (comparable frequency).

Bicycle Rental: Casermetta S. Croce (tel. 58 78 57), northwest rampart. A bargain at L1000 per hr., L6000 per day. Open in summer daily 9am-8pm; in off-season Mon.-Sat. 10am-6pm, Sun. 9am-8pm.

Hospital: campo di Marti (tel. 818 21).

Police: Questura, viale Cavour, 38 (tel. 420 01).

Accommodations

Although a trek from town, the youth hostel is the most reliable last-minute option. Of the half-dozen one-star *alberghi,* many are fully booked by permanent residents, and from June through August, tourists swell the rest. The **CIV-EX travel agency,** via V. Veneto, 28 (tel. 567 41), provides an accommodations service.

Ostello Il Serchio (IYHF), via del Brennero (tel. 95 36 86), on the main road north from the city, 3km from the station. Take bus #7 until 7:30pm, hike, or grab a taxi (L7000). Clean, well-kept and seldom full. 90 beds at L8500 per person. Breakfast, showers, and sheets included. Uninspired dinners L7000. Curfew midnight. Reception open 6-11pm. Open March-Oct. 15.

Albergo La Pace, corte Portici, 2 (tel. 449 81), off via Calderia. Small and centrally located. Singles L17,500. Doubles L35,000. Triples L50,000.

Albergo Diana, via del Molinetto, 11 (tel. 422 02), off p. San Martino. Attractive rooms, cheerful manager. Singles L21,500. Doubles L35,000, with bath L42,000.

Hotel Cinzia, via della Dogana, 9 (tel. 413 23), 1 block from the Diana. Clean and quaint, in a quiet neighborhood right near *centro.* Singles L19,000. Doubles L31,000.

Albergo Margherita, via S. Andrea, 8 (tel. 441 46), a short walk off via Fillungo. You must walk through the restaurant to get to the decent rooms in this old *palazzo* with high ceilings. Odd proprietors. Make reservations. Singles L17,500. Doubles L33,000.

Food

Quite a few respectable, moderately priced *trattorie* exist in Lucca, and the city is also a picnicker's haven, with an abundance of *pizzicherie* (delicatessens) offering great sandwiches, fresh fruit, and veggies. The **central market** in the large building at the west side of p. del Carmine is also an option. (Open Mon.-Sat. 7am-1pm and 4-7:30pm.) An **open-air market** is held every Wednesday and Saturday (8am-1pm) in p. Anfiteatro. A well-stocked **supermarket** stands at via V. Emanuelle II, 50, off p. Napoleone.

Trattoria da Leo, via Felrighi, 1 (tel. 422 36), behind p. del Salvatore, off via degli Asili. Tastefully arranged homemade food, gregarious young waiters. Full meals L15,000. Open Mon.-Sat. noon-2:30pm and 7:30-11pm.

Ristorante da Guido, via Cesare Battisti, 28 (tel. 472 19), at via degli Angeli. Roll up your sleeves with the locals and sit down to an affordable, quality meal. Lunch menù L12,000. Dinner menùs L15,000, or drop one of the many courses for a lesser price. Open Mon.-Sat. noon-2pm and 7:30-10:30pm.

Trattoria da Giulio, via San Tommaso, 29 (tel. 559 48), off via Galli Tassi, near the northwest corner of the ramparts. 1st-class meals at 2nd-class prices (complete meals L18,000). Always a line. No menu, so bring your dictionary. Open Sept.-July Tues.-Sat.

Pizzeria Castagnacci, p. San Michele, 25. Constantly packed with locals. Tasty pizza L900 per *etto. Focaccia* L500, stuffed with cheese L1500. Open Mon.-Sat. 8am-10pm.

Sights

Piazza Napoleone is Lucca's most central square and the town's busy administrative center. For a more relaxed sampling of Lucca's charms, head down via del Duomo to **piazza San Martino** and its atmosphere of genteel nobility. Here, the ornate, asymmetrical **duomo** seems to lean against its bell-tower. The facade is a testament to Romanesque decorative ingenuity: Of the many columns arranged in rows across the facade, you won't find one designed like any other. Look for Nicola Pisano's *Deposition* and *Nativity* above the right door, and reliefs depicting St. Martin's life and the *Labors of the Months* between the doors.

Inside, the mirth of the facade gives way to somber drama. Long *logge* run along the upper part of the nave, whose columns partially hide vast, dark spaces. In a peaceful alcove in the left transept is the *Tomb of Ilaria del Caretto,* by Jacopo della Quercia, one of the most powerful works of Italian sculpture. The serenity of the fragile young Ilaria matches the extremely delicate finish of the marble. The sacristy contains the beautiful and well-preserved *Madonna and Saints* by Ghirlandaio, and Tintoretto's *Last Supper* is in the third chapel on the right. Most famous of the *duomo*'s treasures is the *Volto Santo,* a life-sized statue of Christ that Dante thought impressive enough to include in the *Inferno* (XXI). A bishop gained possession of the relic, but it was soon lost at sea. When it drifted ashore at Luni (near the Italian Riviera), the residents of Luni and Lucca both claimed ownership of the statue. It was placed on an oxcart to determine the rightful owner, and the oxen turned toward Lucca. It is now in a round chapel in the north nave, but is taken for a ride through the town every September 13 in commemoration. (Open daily March-Sept. 7am-noon and 3:30-6:30pm; Oct.-Feb. 7am-noon and 3-5:30pm.)

From the cathedral, head down via Duomo past the Church of San Giovanni to p. Napoleone. Continue up to central **piazza San Michele,** the old Roman forum, which is ringed by impressive brick *palazzi* typical of medieval Lucca. Here, the annual **Palio della Balestra,** a crossbow competition from feudal times, is held every July 12, mainly for the benefit of tourists. The **Church of San Michele in Foro** epitomizes Pisan-Lucchese architecture. A huge bronze sculpture of Archangel Michael stands at the top of the facade, guarding the slim columns and dancing animals set amid geometric designs. The right transept houses a delicate painting of four saints by Filippino Lippi.

From the *piazza,* stroll along nearby **via Fillungo,** Lucca's best-preserved medieval street. Just off p. Scarpellini rises the **Church of San Frediano,** an imposing Romanesque structure with a huge polychrome mosaic highlighting its facade (under restoration in 1988). Within, the second chapel to the right holds the *mummy of Santa Zita* (beloved Virgin of Lucca). One chapel over to the left, drop a L100 coin into the box to light up the frescoes of the *Legend of the Volto Santo* by Amico Aspertini—you will be amazed by the sparkling tiles and their intricate design.

From the church, cut across p. Anfiteatro (whose oval shape and name are vestiges of the Roman amphitheatre that used to stand there) to via A. Mondoni. A right on via Guinigi will bring you to the **Palazzo Guinigi,** a splendidly preserved complex of medieval palaces in red brick and white marble columns. From the lofty tower, crowned by flowers and small oak trees, you can catch a breathtaking view of the whole region. (Open in summer Mon.-Sat. 9am-7pm, in off-season 10am-5pm. Admission L3000, with ISIC L2000.)

The ideal conclusion to a tour of Lucca is a walk or bike ride (see Practical Information) around the city walls. The shaded, breezy path, most of which is closed to auto traffic, regularly crosses grassy parks and cool fountains along the *baluardi* (battlements) high above the grass and moat below. With every step you get a different taste of Lucca—a majestic tower, a tortuous little back street, children playing on the steps of an ancient church.

Entertainment

Lucca's calendar is loaded with superlative classical music and dance events. The musical delights of the **Estate Musicale Lucchese** stretch from July to September. The **Festival di Marlia** (late July-Aug.) features the powerful operas of Lucchese Giacomo Puccini, also showcased in the September opera season at the **Teatro Comunale del Giglio.** The **Settembre Lucchese** is a lively assortment of artistic, athletic, and folklore presentations. Get an up-to-date calendar of events *(Calendario Manifestazioni)* from the EPT.

If in Lucca on the third Saturday and Sunday of the month, go to the Piazza dell 'Arancio for the **Piazetta dell 'Arte,** an outdoor exhibition of sculpture, painting, and graphic art by Lucca's contemporary artists.

Pisa

As long as its prominent leaning landmark remains standing, Pisa will unavoidably be associated with it. But while the legendary tower and the entire **Campo dei Miracoli** (Field of Miracles) merit the better part of a day, few of the 800,000 tourists who come to gawk at the tower's questionable stability choose to discover the appeal of Pisa's less renowned quarters. Mingle a bit in the Pisa outside the tower's shadow, and leave town with a much more balanced perspective.

The city-state of Pisa once outshone Genoa and Venice as a maritime power, rivaled Padua and Perugia as a university town, and developed an architectural style as distinctive as those of Florence and Siena. Today Pisan commerce centers around tourists, relying primarily on the manufacture of plastic Leaning Tower replicas.

Orientation and Practical Information

Trains run between Pisa and Florence every half-hour (L4400). Pisa is also on the coastal line between Genoa (L8300) and Rome (L16,600), and connected by hourly shuttles to Lucca (20 min; L1500) and Livorno in the other direction (L1000). **Lazzi buses** serve the surrounding area, while **ACIT buses** link Pisa with its coastal satellites, Marina di Pisa, Tirrenia, and Livorno. The train station is on the opposite side of the Arno from the major sights, so take bus #1 to p. del Duomo (L500). On foot, take via Crispi out of p. S. Antonio (next to p. V. Emanuele), and across the river; via Roma heads to p. del Duomo.

EPT: p. Archivescovado, 8 (tel. 56 04 64), off p. del Duomo. Helpful and friendly. Open in summer Mon.-Sat. 8am-8pm; in off-season Mon.-Sat. 10am-1pm and 3-7pm. **Branches** at p. della Stazione, 11 (open in summer 8am-10pm), and at v. Lungarno Mediceo, 42 (tel. 20 35 12; open Mon.-Fri. 9am-noon).

Student Travel: CTS, via Santa Maria, 45B (tel. 454 31). Open Mon.-Fri. 9:30am-12:30pm and 4-7pm, Sat. 9:30am-12:30pm.

Currency Exchange: In the **EPT.** Open April-Oct. Mon.-Sat. 8am-1pm and 3-7pm; June-Sept. also Sun. 9am-12:30pm; Nov.-March Mon.-Sat. 8:30am-12:30pm and 3-6pm. At other times, try the train station, large hotels, or the airport (open until 7pm for exchanges).

Post Office: p. V. Emanuele, 8 (tel. 242 97), near the station. Open Mon.-Fri. 8:15am-7pm, Sat. 8:15am-1pm. **Postal code:** 56100.

Telephones: At the **rail station.** Open 24 hours. In the **EPT** office. Open Mon.-Sat. 8am-7:45pm. **Telephone code:** 050.

Airport: Charter, domestic, and a good selection of international flights. Trains make the 4-min. trip (L600) from the train station, roughly to coincide with departures.

Train Information: At the **station,** p. della Stazione (tel. 422 91), in the south end of town. Open 8:30am-8:30pm.

Buses: Lazzi, p. V. Emanuele, 11 (tel. 462 88). **APT,** p. Sant' Antonio (tel. 50 10 38), near the station.

Laundromat: Super Lava, via Mercanti, 12 (tel. 431 14), off p. S. Paolo all' Orto. Open Mon.-Fri. 7:30am-1pm and 3:30-8pm, Sat. 7:30am-1pm. Wash and dry L12,000.

Medical Emergencies: First Aid, Tel. 443 33. **Hospital,** Tel. 59 21 11. Both at via Bonanno, near p. del Duomo.

Police: Questura, via M. Lalli (tel. 50 15 13).

Accommodations

Pisa swarms with small, cheap *pensioni* and *locande,* but from early September until mid-July most are booked solid by swarms of university students. The tourist office can be helpful, but don't expect much luck; call ahead instead and reserve. There are two hostels, though neither is in Pisa proper.

Ostello Il Serchio (IYHF), via del Brennero (tel. 95 36 86), a few km from Lucca in the hamlet of Salicchi. Take bus #7 (every ½ hr. until 7:30pm; 1 hr.), or the train (½ hr.). Moderately sized, comfortable dorm rooms with hot showers and breakfast L7500. Curfew 11pm.

Ostello Santo Francesco (IYHF), in Calambrone (tel. 374 42), near Tirrenia. The 15km from Pisa are covered quickly by APT bus ("Livorno"). This newly opened hostel is located right on the beach. L11,000. Breakfast included. Dinner L8000. Membership required.

Albergo Gronchi, p. Archivescovado, 1 (tel. 56 18 23), adjacent to p. del Duomo. Perhaps the only worthwhile operation of any kind so close to the tower. Ask for a room overlooking the lush gardens in back. Fills early. Curfew midnight. Singles L17,000. Doubles L33,000.

Locanda Serena, via. D. Cavalca, 45 (tel. 244 91), near p. Dante. Dingy, but cheap and in the heart of the traditional quarter. Curfew midnight. Singles L16,500. Doubles L28,000.

Albergo Helvetia, via Don G. Boschi, 31 (tel. 412 32), off p. Arcivescovado, 2 min. from the *duomo.* Spartan rooms. Curfew midnight. Singles L23,000. Doubles L33,500, with bath L41,000.

Casa della Giovane, via F. Corridoni, 31 (tel. 227 32), a 10-min. walk from the station. Turn right as you leave. An ACISJF hostel for women only. L14,000 per person in clean and bright doubles, triples, and quads. Breakfast included. Curfew 12:30am. Reception open 7am-midnight.

Pensione Rinascente, via del Castelletto, 28 (tel. 50 24 36), just below P. dei Cavalieri. Prints of Pisa and tall ceilings grace this old *palazzo,* which lodges students during the school year. Singles around L20,000. Doubles L30,000-40,000. Call the pleasant owner, a couple of days in advance.

Locanda Galileo, via Santa Maria, 12 (tel. 406 21). 9 spacious, spotless rooms, many with frescoed ceilings. A bit noisy. Singles L23,500. Doubles L33,500. Triples L43,000. Quads and quints too. Showers included.

Albergo di Stefano, via Sant' Apollonia, 35 (tel. 263 59), parallel to via Carducci. Tomb like elevators lead to modern, tidy rooms. Quiet neighborhood. Singles L20,000. Doubles L31,000. Triples L42,000.

Albergo Leon Bianco, p. del Pozzetto, 6 (tel. 226 91), near Ponte di Mezzo. Bus #1 stops here en route to p. del Duomo. Large, but does not live up to its price. Negotiating is, however, not out of the question. Singles L28,000, with bath L35,000. Doubles L42,000, with bath L54,000.

Camping: There are two campgrounds near Pisa but they can be dreadfully hot and crowded in the summer. The closest, **Campeggio Torre Pendente,** viale delle Cascine, 86 (tel. 56 17 04), is 1km away; follow the signs from p. Manin. Over L6000 per person and over L3000 per tent. Open mid-March to mid-Oct. **Marina di Pisa,** via Litoranea (tel. 365 53), is 14km away, but situated on a private beach with a bar and restaurant. Take an **ACIT** bus to San Marina di Pisa. Open May-Sept.

Food

Beware the sleazy yet expensive *trattorie* that swallow the stream of tourists visiting the Leaning Tower. The following are each at least a five-minute walk from p. del Duomo, but worth the trouble. The **open-air market** is held in p. Vettovaglie (take via Vigina off lungarno Pacinotti), at the core of the popular quarter. Nearby are bakeries, cheese shops, and places to buy cold meat, making a picnic lunch an easy option. For a cheap snack, try the local specialty *torta di ceci* (or *cecina*), a delicious type of pizza made with chick peas and available at most *bar-pizzerie* for L700-1000 per slice.

Trattoria Gli Amici, via Luigi Bianchi, 39 (tel. 55 09 38). Amazing food, plentiful portions. If you enjoy a tart taste, the *scallopine ai limone* (L8000) is just your thing. Open Fri.-Wed. 11:30am-2:30pm and 6:30-11pm.

La Stanzina, via Cavalca, 30. This warm, quiet little pizzeria cooks ample pizzas for L5000-6000, and the *penne all' arrabbiata* are no less plentiful at L4000. Open mid-Aug. to July Tues.-Sun. noon-3pm and 6:30pm-1am.

Al Castelletto, p. San Delice, 12, at via del Castelletto. A wide selection of pizzas (L3500-8000) and sandwiches (L2500-4500). Affordable full meals, too: *primi* L3000-5000, *secondi* L5000-9000. Open Mon.-Sat. noon-2:30pm and 7-11pm.

Pizzeria il Montino, vicolo del Monte, 3, between p. San Felice and via Oberdan. Crusty, delicious pizzas (L4000) are whipped out of wood-burning ovens and immediately devoured by crowds of hungry locals. The various *fritelle* (a sort of fritter, L1000-2500) make a hot, tasty snack. Open Mon.-Sat. 9:30am-3pm and 4:30-10pm.

Trattoria da Bruno, via Luigi Bianchi, 12 (tel. 55 09 64), across from Glie Amici. Arrogantly bills itself as "famous," but serves some terrific stuff. Try the *polenta con funghi* (a rich corn-meal soup with mushrooms), and tasty squid. No bargain—full meals L21,000 and up. Open Wed.-Mon.

Ristorante 77, via S. Lorenzo, 69 (tel. 424 02), at the north end of via Oberdan by p. della Liberta. Fantastic food, moderate prices: *primi* L3000-4000, *secondi* L4000-8000. Excellent wine selection L4500-8000 per bottle. Open Thurs.-Tues. 12:30-3pm and 7:30-10:30pm.

Mensa Universitaria, via Martiri, off p. dei Cavalieri in the wierd modern building. Average institutional fare at only L2100 for a full meal. If you aren't able to buy tickets at the office, wait outside for Italian students who may have extras. Open mid-Sept. to mid-July Mon.-Fri. noon-2:30pm and 7-9pm, Sat.-Sun. noon-2:30pm.

Sights

The **piazza del Duomo** is also known as the Campo dei Miracoli (Field of Miracles). Indeed, the shining cathedral, baptistery, *camposanto,* and Leaning Tower, rising like ivory statues out of a sea of lush grass and enclosed by the ancient city wall, look something like a pop-up postcard. Despite the promise of imminent collapse, the Leaning Tower will not topple before you visit the other three monuments. (Tower open 8am-7pm.) Stretch out on the grass and study the facade of the **duomo,** a quintessential work of Pisan religious architecture. The first impression is one of simple harmony. Brilliant white columns soar in five tapered arcades, and the winged angels at the upper corners seem to pull the entire structure aloft. As your eyes accustom themselves to the dazzling whiteness, intricate details such as contorted human faces and mysterious inscriptions emerge from the harmonious ensemble.

Enter the cathedral through the detailed bronze doors by Giovanni da Bologna's school. The interior, a dark forest of Corinthian columns growing between striped walls and checkered arches, swells with painting and sculpture.

The Baroque painting adorning the walls on either aisle are rather generic, but don't miss the alterpieces of Cristofano Allori, il Passignano, Andrea del Sarto, Perino del Vaga, and others in the chapels.

Giovanni Pisano's last and longest **pulpit,** no doubt designed to compete with his father's in the baptistery of fifty years earlier, stands at one corner of the crossing. The classical statues of Hercules, St. Michael, the Lion of Nemea, the Virtues, and the Evangelists surround and support the figure of Christ. The scene facing the right-hand door of the cathedral is a combination of two episodes, one of silent joy—the *Presentation in the Temple*—and one of grieving—the *Flight into Egypt.* Michelangelo used to stop to admire this and other works by Giovanni and his father Nicola on his way to Carrara to quarry marble. Across the nave hangs a bronze lamp whose regular swinging supposedly sparked Galileo's first meditations on the motion of the pendulum in 1581. Remember that the dress code does not allow shorts, minis, or any other substantial display of skin. (Open daily 7:45am-1pm and 3-7pm; it's advisable to work your visit around mass time, 10-10:45am.)

The **baptistery,** an enormous drum of a building decorated with lacelike tracery, presents a curious combination of the Tuscan Romanesque and Gothic styles. The interior is simple and elegant, speckled by shafts of light seeping through the stained glass windows. The **pulpit** (1260) of Nicola Pisano, to the left of the baptismal font, is smaller than his son's work in the cathedral; it embodies the first concerted attempt in Tuscan art to return to the sobriety and dignity of classical antiquity, and has thus been seen as the seed of Renaissance art in Italy. For a small fee, one of the custodians will walk to the center of the octagonal floor and sing a series of notes, which echo off the dome and leave a major chord suspended in the air. (Baptistery open daily 9am-12:50pm and 3-6:50pm.)

With this note still ringing in your ears, stroll over to the **camposanto,** a long, white-walled cemetery filled with earth brought back from Mt. Calvary by the Crusaders. This museum holds many Roman sarcophagi with relief sculptures that served as sources for Nicola Pisano's baptistery pulpit. Among the flowers and tombstones are haunting frescoes by the so-called "Master of the Triumph of Death." The *camposanto*'s many other superb frescoes were ruined by Allied bombs in World War II, but the patchiness of these fearsome pieces heightens their mystery. On the left wall of the north gallery is the *Triumph of Death,* a medieval expression of the impermanence of earthly delights, attributed to Bonamico Buffalmacco. On the adjoining wall is the *Last Judgment,* in which both Mary and Christ ignore the saved and sternly scrutinize the expulsion of the weeping, fearful damned. Next in line is *Hell,* the culmination of the series. The entire fresco is a writhing mass of snakes, skewered corpses, and demons performing unspeakable punishments. In the same room are the products of less feverish imaginations. The landscape by Taddeo Gaddi is a delicate combination of Renaissance towers and pastel countryside. The huge fresco of the cosmos on the left wall portrays God sitting atop concentric rings of angels, and a fourteenth-century map of the world in the middle. (Open daily in summer 9am-12:45pm and 3-6:50pm; in off-season 9am-5pm. Admission L2000.)

Across the square from the *camposanto* is the **Museo delle Sinopie,** which displays *sinopie* (sketches preliminary to the fresco process) from the fourteenth- to fifteenth-century, discovered when restoration began after World War II. The sparse elegance of the line sketches evoke comparisons with Rembrandt's drawings. (Open daily in summer 9am-12:40pm and 3-6:40pm; in off-season 9am-12:45pm and 3-5:30pm. Admission L1000.)

The last and greatest miracle in the Campo dei Miracoli is the **Leaning Tower.** No matter how many chintzy replicas you've seen, the tower is an awe-inspiring climax to the whole sacred complex. All the buildings here took a notoriously long time to construct, but the belltower, started by Bonanno Pisano in 1174, was not completed until 1350, partly because it started leaning—which explains the different angle of the belfry. You can feel how much it has tilted (at present, 14 ft.) by taking the dizzying climb to the top; half the time you must actually walk down to get farther up the tower. The *torre* continues to slip 1-2mm each year, and in 1987 the

Italian government approved a three-year, $25 million project to halt its glacial tilt—all this amidst local suspicion that such extravagance will only hasten the tower's downfall. (Open Easter-Christmas 9am-7pm; Christmas-Easter closing time gradually shifts from 5 to 7pm. Admission a steep L4000, but the exciting hike and the great view from the top make it worth every lira; ticket sales stop 30 min. before closing.) To best enjoy the beauty, wait for the tourists and the trinket hawkers to call it a day. At sunset, the tower leans majestically against the rosy Pisan sky; at twilight, the tower's white marble takes on an unreal phosphorescent glow, growing more stunning as darkness descends.

As though the *campo*'s historical grounds and sinking cylinder were not enough *miracula* for one town, the new **Museo dell' Opera del Duano,** located behind the EPT office, displays magical artwork taken from the three buildings of the p. del Duomo. Its most significant icon is the ivory *Madonna and Crucifix* by Giovanni Pisano. Another gem of the museum is Giovanni Pisano's ivory *Madonna and Child;* the unique sway of the figure is not simply a Gothic stylization, it is the artist's graceful means of conforming to the natural curvature of the tusk from which the figure was carved. (Museum open daily in summer 8am-8pm; in off-season 9am-5pm. Admission L4000.)

The **Museo Nazionale di San Matteo,** on the Arno, should not be missed despite its distance from the Campo; among other treasures, it houses sculptures by the two Pisano brothers that once graced the *duomo,* baptistery, and *camposanto.* The *Figura Danzante* (Dancing Figure), decapitated but still cavorting, is the inspired works of Giovanni. Andrea's *Madonna del Latte* (the Nursing Madonna) displays wonderful human dignity. Among the paintings, Massacio's *St. Paul* and Giunta Pisano's two-sided crucifix stand out. Many such double-sided paintings have forced the organizers to create an unconventional, yet inviting, museum space. (Open Tues.-Sat. 8:30am-7:30pm and Sun. 8:30am-1:30pm. Admission L3000.)

Though surrounded by stately palaces, the **piazza dei Cavalieri,** designed by Giorgio Rasari when the Medici controlled Pisa in the sixteenth century, is more intriguing historically than visually. In Roman times it was the site of the forum and the center of activity in the Pisan republic. In the patchy structure of the **Palazzo dell' Orologio** may be seen the remnants of two ancient towers. In one of these, known formerly as the "tower of hunger," the Pisan government starved Count Ugolino and his sons to death, having unjustly found them guilty of treason. Dante's description of the incident (*Inferno* XXXIII) is one of his most gruesome.

Another site of note is the **Church of San Nicola,** between via S. Maria and p. Carrara. Nicola is the patron saint of Pisa: See him in the famous alterpiece of the fourth chapel on the right, breaking and deflecting the arrows that the wrath of God showers down on Pisa.

Be sure to explore Pisa's **historic district,** too. Roughly surrounding **piazza San Frediano,** the area features surpentine alleys and conveys hints of a more glorious past. Here the stuccoed walls of the old buildings are mostly painted in gold or ochre, giving the city a light, upbeat tone. Take a stroll down the **Borgo Stretto,** which turns into **via Oberdan** as you head away from the Arno. The fashion boutiques seem strangely out of place as the ancient buildings that house them jut out over the wide sidewalk, where students relax at the streetside cafes.

Entertainment

Keep an eye out for the intermittent **concerts** given in the *duomo,* where the acoustics are astounding. On **via San Zeno,** a former church holds experimental concerts attended by a motley crüe. Since they've just spent a few billion lire cleaning up Pisa's beaches, you might want to take advantage of them. It's a bit of a trick to find a few grains of sand that haven't been fenced off, but several possible spots exist between **Marina di Pisa** and **Tirrenia,** two coastal towns linked to Pisa by ACIT bus (every hr.). Also accessible by bus is the **Migliarino, S. Rossore, and Massaciuccoli Nature Park and Preserve.** Created in 1979, the *parco naturale* extends for 21,000 hectares along the coast between Viareggio and Livorno, and includes forest, marsh, lake, and beach. Not all of the park is open to the public, but the area provides ample space and facilities for pleasant strolls, light hiking, and picnic lunches. To reach Lake Massaciuccoli and the surrounding marshes, take the hourly bus from p. Vittorio Emanuele II to Tombolo, near Calambrone (and the hostel there), and then catch the hourly Livorno bus from p. San Antonio. To visit the **Presidential Estate** of S. Rossore (open Sun. only), take bus #11 from Lungarno Gambacorti (at 8:30am, noon, and 2:10pm).

Livorno

When Amerigo Vespucci set out for the New World, he left behind an insignificant settlement. But by the sixteenth century, when the city came into the mighty hands of the Medici, Livorno was on its way to becoming an important Mediterranean port. Known today primarily as a junction en route to Elba and the rest of the Tuscan archipelago, Sardinia, Corsica, Sicily, and the French Riviera, Livorno itself is remarkably tourist-free, an Italian town that offers no grand spectacle other than its own workaday hustle and bustle. This, along with the earthy cheerfulness of the Livornesi, the ample accommodations, and the tasty seafood, can make a brief stay in Livorno a surprisingly pleasant respite from the more frequented corners of the boot.

Orientation and Practical Information

A major station on the coastal rail line, Livorno is connected to Pisa (10 min., L1000), Florence (1 hr., L5400), and Piombino (1½ hr., L5700). To get to the central **piazza Grande** from the train station, take bus #1, 2, or 8. You can also make the 25-minute walk up viale Carducci, which becomes via de Larderel, through p. Repubblica, and up via Grande.

EPT: p. Cavour, 6 (tel. 331 11). Charming and helpful. Open Mon.-Fri. 6:30am-12:30pm. If you speak Italian, you can get help later in the day at **TCI,** Via Scali delle Cantine, 24 (tel. 88 03 95). Not a tourist office, but the good-natured staff has loads of information and knowledge. They also sell the excellent TCI guidebook and map series. Open Mon.-Fri. 9am-12:30pm and 3:30-7:30pm, Sat. 9am-12:30pm.

Currency Exchange: The **Dogana** (customs), p. dell' Arsenale (tel. 380 41), in the Porto Mediceo. Also the travel agents in p. Grande.

Post Office: via Cairoli, 12-16 (tel. 233 21). Open Mon.-Fri. 8:15am-7pm, Sat. 8:15am-noon. For packages open Mon.-Fri. until 5pm. **Postal code:** 57100.

Telephones: ASST, p. Grande, 14. Open Mon.-Sat. 7:15am-3:30pm. **Telephone code:** 0586.

Ferries: Toremar (tel. 86 61 13). To the islands of Gorgona (L5100), Capraia (L9900), and Portoferraio on Elba (L11,300) at least twice per day. **Corsica Ferries**(tel. 342 73) goes to Corsica (Bastia, L46,000) and **Sardinia Ferries** (tel. 310 02) to Sardinia (Olbia, L49,000), both daily in high season and about 3 times per week in off-season. **Navarma** runs the same number of boats to Bastia (L35,000, in off-season L31,000), as well as to Olbia (L39,000). All companies have offices at via Calafati, 4. Tickets for July and Aug. are very difficult to secure, and should be reserved at least 2-3 weeks in advance. Also, be sure to find out where your boat leaves; some depart from the Porto Industriale, a 30-min. bus ride away. (Take #18 from p. Grande every ½ hr., L600.)

Train Information: At the station in p. Dante (tel. 40 11 05). Open daily 8am-noon and 3-7pm.

Buses: ACIT, p. Grande. Regular service to Piombino Porto (8 per day).

Taxi: P. Grande. To Porto Industriale L16,000.

Police: Carabinieri, in **emergencies** tel. 21 21 21.

Hospital: Pronto Soccorso, tTel. 40 33 51 or 42 13 98.

Accommodations

Livorno swarms with cheap hotels—finding a roof is generally no problem even in high season. Unless you're desperate, avoid the train station and port areas and head for the center of town.

Hotel Corsica, corso Mazzini, 148 (tel. 88 21 03 or 88 22 80). Run by an endearing proprietor. Quaint furnishings. Lovely garden in back features a well-placed copy of Verrocchio's *puttino* fountain. Singles L21,000, with bath L25,000. Doubles L31,000, with bath L36,000.

Hotel Goldoni, via E. Mayer, 42 (tel. 247 05). Take via E. Rossi 1 block out of p. Cavour. Clean, modern, and central, though rooms are a bit cramped. Amiable staff. Singles with bath L25,000. Doubles with bath L36,000.

Hotel Cremona, corso Mazzini, 24 (tel. 89 96 81). Spotless rooms that rarely book up. Run by an old couple amenable to students. Singles L20,000, with bath L25,000. Doubles L31,000, with bath L36,000.

Hotel Milano, via degli Asili, 48 (tel. 88 22 71), off borgo dei Cappacunni. Quiet, family-run establishment near the port. Singles L22,000. Doubles L31,000. Showers L1500.

Albergo Italia, corso Mazzini, 120 (tel. 290 20), down the street from the Cremona. The warm welcome of the owner's white poodle and the rococo ornate rooms overcome the fly-infested lobby. Singles L15,000. Doubles L25,000. Showers included.

Food

Livorno's culinary specialties, like its livelihood, derive from the sea. An **open-air market** is held on via Buontalenti (Mon.-Sat. morning). Many bread, fruit, and vegetable stores line via G. Verdi between p. Mazzini and via Adua.

La Cantonata, corso G. Mazzini, 222 (tel. 264 42). Smiling owner dishes out huge plates of *spaghetti ai frutti di mare* (seafood spaghetti), the freshest fish, and brimming glasses of *chianti* for about L20,000 per person.

Trattoria Il Sottomarino, via dei Terrazzini, 48 (tel. 237 71), off p. della Repubblica at the end of via Pina d' Oro. Natives come from all over Tuscany just to taste their *cacciucco,* a fiery and delicious seafood stew. Delicious prices, too. Open Aug.-June.

La Barcarola, via Carducci, 63 (tel. 40 23 67), not far from the train station. Come here when Il Sottomarino's closed. Great *cacciucco* and other seafood dishes. Try the *risotto pescatore.*)

Ristorante l'Attias, via Rocasoli, 127 (tel. 234 41), at corso Mazzini. The best stand-up lunch in town. Have a *panino varia fantasia* (L3500-4000): You pick from the goodies at the bar and they'll put them into a sandwich. Have it with a ½-liter of wine (L2000). Sit-down meals about L18,000. Open Fri.-Wed. 8:30am-2:30pm and 6pm-midnight.

Pizzeria Umbra, via E. Mayer, 1, at via Maggi. The choice of the Livornesi for palatable pizza at palatable prices.

Pasticceria-Gelateria Verdi, via Verdi, 36 (tel. 89 91 48), 2 blocks from p. Cavour. An excellent selection of sweets and homemade ice cream.

Sights

Livorno's sights probably don't warrant a special trip, but if you happen to be in town, they can make for an interesting afternoon. Start at the waterfront on via San Giovanni, where the massive **Fortezza Vecchia** sprawls amid cranes and cables. Built by the powerful Marquises of Tuscany, the portly tower in the middle was the first fortification on the site in the ninth century. Later, when Pisans controlled Livorno, they built a fort around the tower. In the sixteenth century the Medici came along and surrounded the ensemble with robust brick walls to consolidate their hold on Livorno, by then the cardinal Tuscan port.

Just down the quay is piazza Micheli, distinguished by its disquieting **Monumento a Ferdinando I.** Ferdinand, the third Medici grand-duke, strikes a stiff, haughty pose atop a marble pedestal. Chained to the pedestal beneath are the statues of four slaves, which artist Pietro Tacca fashioned after inmates from a nearby prison. Livorno sparked two great highlights in Italian painting. The first is the group of nineteenth-century painters called "I Macchiaioli" (literally, "the blotters"), led by Giovanni Fattori (alias Giovanni Flori). In the **Museo Civico Giovanni Fattori** in **Villa Fabbricotti** at via della Libertà, 20, you can see their luminous proto-impressionist work. Livorno's second contribution to painting is the twentieth-century painter Amedeo Modigliani. To view his warm-toned, sensitive nudes, go to the **Museo Progressivo di Anti Contemporanea,** in beautiful **Villa Maria** at via delle Siepi, 22, a few blocks northeast of Villa Fabbricotti. (Both museums open Tues.-Wed., Fri., and Sun. 10am-1pm, Thurs. and Sat. 10am-1pm and 3-7pm; in summer 3:30-7:30pm. Admission for both L2500.)

For less cluttered surroundings and a breath of salubrious air, head down the waterfront on via Cialdini to viale Italia, which follows the shoreline for several kilometers past grassy parks and sea vistas. Livorno's chief festival, the rough-and-ready **Palio Marinaro,** is held just off this stretch of coast. Burly rowers from the different *rioni* (neighborhoods) of the city race their traditional crafts towards the old port, to the cheers of spectators cramming the banks.

San Gimignano

This hilltop village is a time-machine back to the Middle Ages; it is so well preserved and picturesque you expect to walk by feudal knights and serfs in the cobblestone streets. A delightful and convenient escape from the urban claustrophobia of Siena or Pisa, San Gimignano is packed on weekends by foreign and Italian tourists alike. During the week, however, the town provides breathing room to explore a surprising number of artistic and historical treasures and to gaze at the Tuscan landscape, with its stark rows of cypress trees and olive groves. Spend an evening, as relatively few do, and you'll be hooked.

Surrounded by ramparts, San Gimignano bristles with the tall fortress-towers of its medieval nobility. Only 15 of the original 72 stand, reminders of the factionalism and civil war that tore San Gimignano apart in years past. The rivalry between the Guelph and Ghibelline accounted for the fortress-towers common to most Tuscan city-states. The towers were status symbols as well as defense structures. When the *popolani* (higher bourgeoisie) gained power in Florence and elsewhere, one of the first things they usually did was to tear down the towers of the *magnati* (nobility). San Gimignano's 15 towers are still standing because the town lost its freedom before the *popolani* ascended to power. The city fell under Florentine rule in 1353, and has been something of a backwater ever since.

Orientation and Practical Information

San Gimignano has no train station, but **TRA-IN** buses run to Florence and Siena every one to two hours (L4400). Change buses at Poggibonsi. Poggibonsi is also the nearest rail station, 20 minutes by bus from San Gimignano. Buses arrive in San Gimignano at Porta San Giovanni and are easiest to catch when leaving the city at the other end of town, outside Porta San Matteo. Tickets are available at the APL office.

Associazione Pro Loco (APL): p. del Duomo, 1 (tel. 94 00 08). A personable manager who loves to practice his English and has reams of pamphlets. No accommodations service, but a complete list of cheap rooms in private residences. Also **changes currency** (at a poor rate) and sells bus tickets. Open Tues.-Sun. 9:30am-12:30pm and 3-6:30pm. For hotel reservations, try the **Ufficio Informazioni Turistiche,** via S. Giovanni, 125 (tel. 94 08 09). Open Mon.-Sat. 9:30am-12:30pm and 2:30-7pm, Sun. 9:30am-12:30pm.

Post Office: Behind the *duomo.* Open Mon.-Fri. 8:15am-7pm, Sat. 8:15am-noon. **Postal code:** 53037.

Telephones: At the APL office. Also at via San Matteo, 13. Open 8am-midnight. **Telephone code:** 0577.

Buses: TRA-IN buses leave from p. Martiri outside porta San Giovanni. Schedules available in the APL office.

Public Toilets: Via Arco dei Becci, 6, behind the Palazzo del Poedstà.

First Aid: Ospedale, via Folgore da San Gimignano (tel. 94 03 12).

Police: Carabinieri, tel. 94 03 13.

Accommodations

A great new hostel has saved San Gimignano from becoming an exclusive place to stay. Other alternatives to lire-lecherous hotels are rooms in private homes, with singles about L20,000 and doubles about L30,000. Get a list from the tourist office or the police station. Via Giacomo Matteotti alone has three such residences: #15 (tel. 94 10 18), #19A (tel 94 01 01), and #25 (tel. 94 05 92). For a treat, the Nencioni family at via Piandornella, 6 (tel. 94 05 46), rents a spacious apartment with a priceless panorama for L40,000 per person. Another option is to head to **La Rocca,** an accommodations service at via dei Fossi, 35A (tel. 94 03 87), just outside the walls near Parco della Rocca. The nice manager will find you a room in a private home plus provide a guide to lead you there, all for a L2500 commission. (Open daily 9am-1pm and 3-9pm.) Otherwise, go to via S. Giovanni, 95 (tel. 94 00 26), where the **Agenzia d'Affari Simona** will find you a room (commission 10%).

Ostello della Gioventù, via delle Fonti, 1 (tel. 94 19 91), at via Folgore di S. Gimignano. A fantastic place run by congenial young people. No membership required. L10,090. Breakfast and hot shower included. Reception open 7:30-9:30am and 5-11:30pm.

Ostello del Chianti, via Roma, 137 (IYHF; tel. (055) 807 70 09), in Tavernelle Val di Pesa. Quite a hike. Take the SITA bus (change at Poggibonsi, 1 hr.); check the schedule since connections are not the greatest. The hostel is splendid and the countryside beautiful. Membership required. 54 beds. L6300. Breakfast and hot showers included. Reception open 6:30-11pm.

Convento di Sant' Agostino, p. S. Agostino (tel. 94 03 83). Otherworldly cloister and divine rooms (some with cosmic views) at heavenly prices. Write to the Padre Superiore 1 month ahead for reservations in summer, but if you pop in unexpectedly, it can't hurt to ask the monk in the church gift shop. Singles L15,000. Doubles L20,000. Triples L25,000.

Ristorante Il Pino, via San Matteo, 102 (tel. 94 04 15). 2 doubles L34,000. Triple L45,000. Extra bed L10,000.

Leon Bianco, p. della Cisterna (tel. 94 12 94), in the heart of town. Contemporary and comfortable. Singles L35,700. Doubles L61,400.

Camping: Il Boschetto, at Santa Lucia (tel. 94 03 52), 2½km down the hill from Porta San Giovanni. Mon.-Sat. 11 buses per day and Sun. 9 per day run from town to the site (L500), but it's not a bad hike. Lovely location, bar, and market. L3700 per person and L1700 to pitch a small tent. L1150 per car or cycle. Hot showers included. Office open 8am-1pm, 3-8pm, and 9-11pm.

Food

Dining is costly (and 70% more for an outside table), but the **open-air market** in p. del Duomo (Thurs. and Sat. mornings) can provide a picnic on the ramparts of La Rocca (old fortress). While you're in town, be sure to try the famous *Vernaccia di San Gimignano,* one of Italy's best white wines.

Le Vecchie Mura, via Piandornella, 15. Take a right off via San Giovanni as you enter town. Restaurant, pizzeria, and self-service all in one. The medieval interior is so quaint and the food so delicious you'll forget this is one of the cheapest places in town. Pizza L4500, complete meals (wine included) L15,000. Open Wed.-Mon. noon-2:30pm and 7-9:30pm.

Pizzeria da Pietro, via N. Cannicci, 4, outside Porta San Matteo. Follow the signs. The tacky display of international flags in front notwithstanding, a simple place at moderate prices. Pizza L4000-6000, full meals L15,000-19,000. Open Tues.-Sun.

Ristorante La Stella, via S. Matteo, 75. Most of the food here comes from their own farm. Notice (and taste!) the black-green olive oil. Also delectable is the *prosciutto di San Gimignano.* Full meals L17,000-20,000. Open Thurs.-Tues. 12:15-2:30pm and 7:15-10:15pm.

Pizza Center, via XX Settembre, 4. Rustic pizza made with the freshest, chunkiest ingredients (about L1000 per slice). Try it with a glass of smooth and light *Vernaccia* (L800). Open Fri.-Wed. 4-9pm.

Sights

You will most likely enter the town through Porta San Giovanni, right off p. Martiri. Walk up along via San Giovanni, the backbone of the town, to **piazza della Cisterna,** named after the thirteenth-century cistern in its center. The square, surrounded by towers and *palazzi* of all shapes and sizes, is particularly striking at night. In the adjoining p. del Duomo, reminiscent of a giant chess board, the **Palazzo del Podestà** rises with its impressive tower built in the ochre brick so characteristic of San Gimignano. To the right is the **Palazzo del Popolo,** a gorgeous patchwork structure riddled with tunnels and intricate *loggie.* Off the right side of the *palazzo* soars the **Torre Grossa,** the highest tower in town and the only one you can ascend; it's well worth the climb. On the left are the twin towers of the Ardinghelli, thwarted by a city government injunction that no structure may be higher than the **Torre Grossa.**

Within the Palazzo del Podestà, through an enchanting courtyard covered with frescoes, is the **Sala di Dante,** so called because Dante made a speech here in 1300 as the Guelph ambassador to the city. The room is frescoed with hunting scenes and Lippo Memmi's large *Maestà,* which closely follows that by his master Simone Martini in Siena. In the **Museo Civico** on the second floor, you can view Filippino Lippi's radiant *Annunciation* (done as two separate circular paintings) and Taddeo di Bartolo's *San Gimignano altarpiece.* (Open April-Sept. daily 9:30am-12:30pm and 3:30-6:30pm; Oct.-March Tues.-Sun. 9:30am-12:30pm and 2:30-5:30pm. Admission L4000, but the ticket also allows you to enter the Chapel of Santa Fina in the *duomo,* the pharmacy museum, and the Torre Grossa.) Benozzo Gozzoli created the fabulous fresco cycle of the life of St. Augustine in the **Church of Sant' Agostino** at the other end of town. (Open in summer 8am-noon and 3-7pm; in off-season 2-5pm.) The humorous scenes of the little proto-saint being punished by his grammar teacher, as well as the touching scene of his death, reveal Gozzoli's gift for incorporating simple human emotions into his work.

The bare facade of the **duomo** hides a Romanesque interior covered with exceptional Renaissance frescoes. Start with the **Chapel of Santa Fina** off the right aisle (open same hours as the Museo). A marvel of Renaissance harmony created by Giuliano and Benedetto Maiano, it is adorned by Ghirlandaio's splendid frescoes. Other worthwhile frescoes in the church include Bartolo di Fredi's Old Testament series along the left aisle, the New Testament scenes by Barna da Siena along the right aisle, and a gut-wrenching *Inferno* by Taddeo di Bartolo, whose graphic scenes reveal a morbid imagination.

San Gimignano was also home to one of the oldest hospitals in the world. At **Una Farmacia Preindustriale in Val d'Elsa,** in the church of San Lorenzo, on via del Castello below p. della Cisterna, you can examine the pharmaceutical instruments and medicinal jugs of the Hospital and Pharmacy of Santa Fina (1253). (Open Tues.-Sun. 9:30am-12:30pm and 3:30-6:30pm. Admission included in the general L4000 ticket.)

La Rocca, the fortress, lies directly behind the *duomo.* From its ramparts there is a superb spread of the Tuscan turf, largely unchanged since San Gimignano's heyday. For **entertainment,** movies are shown in the courtyard of La Rocca, and operas and plays are performed in p. del Duomo in summer.

Volterra

In compact and cosmopolitan Tuscany, the physical isolation of the town is striking. Volterra has always been fiercely independent, frowning on the rest of the world from its rocky pedestal. The Etruscans made use of the knoll's naturally defensible position to establish Velathri, which by the fourth century B.C.E. was one of their most powerful cities. During the Middle Ages, Volterra's size diminished to one-third of the area covered by the Etruscan city, giving it the aspect of having been distilled by history into the perfectly preserved medieval town. This quality has inspired infinite poetic musings on the town's hoary mysteriousness, but today Volterra caters to weekend visitors more than poets, depending increasingly upon tourism to nurture its alabaster production and trade. Shops catering to tourists sell gaudy alabaster trinkets in the old city. Avoid the town on the weekend, however, and Volterra remains a quaint, quiet town with a spectacular hilltop setting.

Orientation and Practical Information

Although nearer to San Gimignano and Siena, Volterra is linked administratively to Pisa, from which **TRA-IN** bus service is most frequent (L5400). **SITA** buses also run from Florence (4 per day, L5700), Siena (5 per day, L4600), and San Gimignano (4 per day, L3600). There is a small rail station 9km west of town at Saline di Volterra, with sporadic trains from Pisa (L4200) and the coastal line. **APT** buses, more or less synchronized with the trains, run between Saline and Volterra (8 per day, L1500). All buses arrive and depart from p. XX Settembre, where the Caffè Jolly sells tickets and schedules.

Tourist Office: via G. Turazza, 2 (tel. 861 50), off p. dei Priori. Complete bus and train information, as well as maps and brochures. Also has **telephones.** Open Mon.-Sat. 9am-12:30pm and 3:30-6:30pm.

Post Office: p. dei Priori (tel. 869 69). Open Mon.-Fri. 8am-7pm, Sat. 8am-noon. **Postal code:** 56048.

Telephone Code: 0588.

Public Bathroom: via delle Prigioni, 3, off p. dei Priori. Decent. L300.

First Aid: Misericordia, Pronto Soccorso, p. San Giovanni (tel. 861 64).

Police: Carabinieri, tel. 860 35.

Accommodations

The youth hostel has turned Volterra from a budget traveler's nightmare into a dream. The tourist office provides an accommodations service, but you're best served by the hostel or the fine campground outside town. Also, shop windows often advertise reasonableprivate rooms.

Ostello Volterra, via del Poggetto (tel. 855 77), off via Don Minzoni across from Rampa di Castello. Simonized ceramic floors. 74 beds in a dormitory setting. Membership not required. Curfew 11:30pm. Desk open only after 6pm, but someone who will let you leave your bags is there until 10am. L10,000. Breakfast L2500.

Albergo Etruria, via Matteoti, 32 (tel. 873 77), in the center of town. Pleasant rooms. Singles L29,000, with bath L34,000. Doubles L42,000, with bath L56,000. Nov.-March. rooms L4000-7000 cheaper. Aug.-early Sept. reservations advised.

Albergo Villa Nencini, borgo Santo Stefano, 55 (tel. 863 86), outside the medieval walls through Porta San Francesco. Worth the walk and prices. Awesome views from a 16th-century building. Wine cellar and tavern serve authentic Tuscan fare. Singles L30,000, with bath L36,000. Doubles L45,000, with bath L60,000. Reservations advised.

Camping "Le Balze," farther down the road at via Mandringa, 15 (tel. 878 80). This attractive campsite has bungalows, a restaurant, and a refreshing pool, plus a view over Le Balze, where a widening chasm has gradually engulfed Etruscan necropolises, churches, and monasteries. L3500 per person plus L3500 per tent and L1000 per car. 4-person bungalow L25,000. 6-person bungalow L35,000. Open May-Sept. Reservations accepted.

Kodak
True MacHugh.
Introducing new Kodacolor Gold 100 film. The truest color, the most realistic color, the most accurate color of any print film, anywhere.
Show Your True Colors.
Kodacolor
Gold 100
© Eastman Kodak Company, 1988

CARRY-ON RELIEF.

Food

An excellent selection of Volterra's game dishes and locally produced cheeses is available at the various **alimentari** on via Guarnacci and via Gramsci. Try *salsiccia di cinghiale* (wild boar sausage) and the local *pecorino* cheese.

L'Ombra della Sera, via Gramsci, 70 (tel. 866 63), off p. XX Settembre. Great fare, *really* great prices. For an extravagant dessert, sample the delightfully rich *torta etruria,* a local version of Siena's *panforte. Primi* L3000-5000, *secondi* L4500-6500. Open Tues.-Sun. noon-3pm and 7-10pm.

La Tavernetta, via Guarnacci, 14 (tel. 876 30), near the Porta Fiorentina. Fantastic and plentiful pasta dishes (L3500-6000) which make the bland *secondi* (L7000-12,000) unnecessary. Mythological figures will spy on you from the frescoed ceiling overhead. Open daily noon-3pm and 7:30-11:30pm.

Ristorante La Grotta, via G. Turazza, 23 (tel. 864 30), off p. dei Priori. Many native game dishes, such as the *pappardelle di lepre* (hare). Complete meals L17,000-20,000. Open Thurs.-Tues. 12:15pm and 7:30-9:30pm.

Sights

The long brick walls of Volterra's **Fortezza Medicea,** a remnant from the period of Florentine domination, now used as a jail, are the first structures to come into view as one ascends to the town. Volterra's core is its **piazza dei Priori,** a medieval *piazza.* The heavy and forbidding **Palazzo dei Priori,** the oldest governmental palace in Tuscany (1208-1254), presides over the square. Across the *piazza* sits the **Palazzo Pretorio,** a series of thirteenth-century buildings and towers tightly pressed one against the other.

Behind the Palazzo dei Priori is the **duomo,** which contains some fascinating Romanesque sculpture. Halfway up the left aisle is a thirteenth-century pulpit with delightful reliefs of the Last Supper, the Visitation, and the Sacrifice of Isaac by Guglielmo Pisano. The strange and haunting capitals of the columns in the supporting zone were sculpted by Bonamico Pisano. The first chapel in the right arm of the transept houses the famed huge polychromed-wood sculpture group of the *Deposition from the Cross* (also 13th century).

Around the corner is the cathedral's **Museo d'Arte Sacra,** which houses a small but interesting collection of works by della Robbia, Pollaiolo, Rosso Fiorentino, and Giambologna. (Closed for restoration in 1988.)

Cross back over the *piazza* and take a right down via dell' Arco to see the massive, third-century B.C.E. **Etruscan arch,** one of the oldest gates of the city. Note the black stone knobs on the outside, formerly sculpted human heads.

On the other side of the p. dei Priori on via dei Sarti is the **Pinacoteca Comunale,** which has found a new home in the **Palazzo Minucci-Solaini,** an elegant building with a gracefully arcaded courtyard, probably designed by Sangallo. The highlights of this collection are in the last room on the first floor: an *Annunciation* by Luca Signorelli, and Rosso Fiorentino's frenetic and dizzying *Deposition.* (Open daily 9:30am-1pm and 3-6:30pm. Admission L2500, students L1500.)

Continue along via dei Sorti and take via di Sotto for some picturesque views of the landscape framed by the town's medieval houses, to arrive at p. XX Settembre, where lives a series of **alabaster craft shops.** At #57, watch workers at the grinding wheel, then buy some of their products at via di Sotto, 2, just off the *piazza.*

Pack a wild-boar sandwich and walk up to the nearby **Parco Archeologico.** Despite some ancient artifacts, this is somewhat of a misnomer since the Etruscan acropolis and the Roman baths are fenced off, but you can enjoy the view here while vegging on the grassy slope.

Volterra's main attraction is the **Museo Etrusco Guarnacci,** a few steps away from the park at via Don Minzoni, 15. On display are over 600 finely carved Etruscan funerary urns; the dramatic bas-reliefs represent voyages to the underworld. Also famous is the oddly elongated figurine called *l' Ombra della Sera* (the Shadow of Evening). (Open daily 9am-1pm and 3-6:30pm. Admission L4000, students L3000.)

For yet another reminder of Volterra's glorious past, follow via Guarnacci through the Porta Fiorentina and down viale Ferrucci to the surprisingly complete **Teatro Romano.** (Open daily 10am-noon and 4-7pm. Free. Closed in 1988 for restoration.

Past the *Teatro* on the edge of town is the **Church of San Francesco.** In the *capella della Pietà,* off the left aisle, a well-preserved fifteenth-century sculpture group shows the Virgin and Saint John mourning over the dead Christ; the group startlingly comes alive if you place yourself in the position from which it is meant to be seen—kneeling on the prie-dieu before it. The more famous *capella della Croce,* off the right aisle, is covered with frescoes by Cenno Cenni depicting the story of the True Cross, from its origin in the wood of the Garden of Eden's Tree of Knowledge through to its recovery as a relic in the Middle Ages.

The sights of Volterra are not, however, limited to the museums and churches. This town begs strolling; every street is more charming than the last, and the best ones have no monument anywhere near them. To walk with the locals, go to the **viale dei Ponti,** below the Fortezza Medicea, for the afternoon *passeggiata* and a vista of the valleys and mountains.

During the second week of July, the city hosts the **Volterra Teatro** drama festival in p. dei Priori, in which a different play is put on nightly 10 nights running. In August, the *piazza* becomes the scene of various concerts, mostly of contemporary music. Inquire at the tourist office.

Siena

The quintessential medieval city in Italy, Siena is the closest you'll come to experiencing the urban side of the Middle Ages in the middle of the modern age. In an area renowned for its artistic output, Siena stands out as a living masterpiece, a tribute to the care and creativity of its builders and inhabitants. Other towns constructed more significant cathedrals, built higher towers, and erected grander *palazzi,* but nowhere else does an entire town come together as harmoniously as Siena. The city spreads in medieval perfection over the red clay hills, from which the color "burnt sienna" gets its name. Great caution is taken nowadays to see that all modern buildings—outside as well as within the city walls—blend gracefully into the original cityscape; these measures distinguish Siena from other Italian cities. And indeed, twentieth-century Sienese feel themselves a breed apart: They vigorously preserve the medieval division of the city into 17 *contrade* (districts) and speak some of the purest Italian in the country.

Today it is easy to regard Siena as a little sister to Florence, but in the Middle Ages the two cities were fierce rivals. In 1230, the belligerent Florentines catapulted excrement and dead donkeys over Siena's walls in an effort to trigger a decisive plague. The rude ploy failed, and in 1260, Siena's military mastered the Florentines at the Battle of Montaperti. The sixteenth century, however, witnessed Siena's fall, along with the rest of Tuscany, under the yoke of the Medici duchy. While not as pronounced today, intercity differences still abound, and the Sienese adamantly claim to be less flamboyant than the Florentines, retaining Tuscany's medieval character and customs, such as il Palio (see Entertainment). A comparison of painting styles highlights these differences. Unlike the analytically inclined Florentines, who explored perspective and carved out the third dimension, Siena's great artists of the fourteenth century, Duccio and Simone Martini, remained closer to the Byzantine tradition, with its concern for linear gracefulness on the flat surface of the panel. The city's sensitive preservation of tradition has saved the historic center, which is closed to automobiles—for once you don't have to dodge mopeds—in order to protect the rust-red buildings from discoloration. But beware: The pigeons of Siena promote discoloration in their own way, and in the narrow alleyways surrounding the piazza Il Campo, they pose a continuous threat.

Orientation and Practical Information

Siena lies on a small **train** route off the main lines. Change at Chiusi if coming from Rome (L12,700) and the south, or at Empoli if arriving from Florence (L4900) and the north. If you come by train, cross the street and take any bus (L500, buy tickets before boarding) to p. Matteoti. Exit the *piazza* by the UPIM store and follow the numerous signs to p. Il Campo. Siena is also off the main **autostrada** network, and an extension of *superstrada* A-1 connects it to Florence. **SITA/TRA-IN** buses link Siena with Florence (roughly every hr.) and the rest of Tuscany sporadically (including Arezzo, San Gimignano, Volterra, Pienza, Montepulciano, and Massa Marittima). It is about an hour's bus ride from Florence on the express bus (L6400), faster than the train connection.

Azienda Autonoma di Turismo: p. del Campo, 55 (tel. 28 05 51). Accommodations service. Harried, but amiable and helpful. Travel agency in the same office will **exchange currency** at acceptable rates when banks are closed. Open July-Sept. daily 8:30am-1pm; Oct.-June Mon.-Sat. 4-7pm. For a daily list of rooms available in private homes, head to the Azienda office at via della Città, 43. Open July-Sept. daily 9am-12:30pm and 3:30-7pm; Oct.-June Mon.-Sat. 4-7pm. There is also a **tourist booth** in p. San Domenico, where they change money, reserve hotel rooms, distribute bus tickets, and sell city maps (L200). Open July-Sept. Mon.-Sat. 9am-1pm and 3:30-7:30pm, Sun. 9am-1pm; Oct.-June Mon.-Sat. 9am-1pm and 3:30-7:30pm.

CTGS: via Cecco Angiolieri, 25 (tel. 28 50 08), 1st floor off p. Tolomei. Student travel services. They'll help with accommodations if you're stuck. Open Mon.-Fri. 9:30am-12:30pm and 4-7pm..

Post Office: p. Matteoti, 36. Fermo posta at window #12. Open Mon.-Fri. 8:15am-7pm, Sat. 8:15am-noon. **Postal code:** 53100.

Telephones: At via dei Termini, 40. Open daily 8am-8:30pm. Also **SIP,** via Donzelle, 8. Open 7am-midnight. At other times try **Bar Cecco,** via Cavour, 222 (open 5am-1am), or **Bar Centrale,** via Cecco Angiolieri, 37 (open 6am-midnight). **Telephone code:** 0577.

Buses: SITA/TRA-IN, p. S. Domenico, 1 (tel. 22 12 21). Service to all Tuscany and Italy, including Florence (L5400), San Gimignano (L3700), Volterra (L3800), Montepulciano (L4300), and Rome (3½ hr., L12,300).

Taxi: Radio Taxi (tel. 492 22). Open June-Oct. 7am-11pm; Nov.-May 7am-9pm.

Car Rental: Eurodrive, via delle Sperandie, 23 (tel. 41 14 80). From p. Campo walk out via G. Dupré, turn right at via S. Agata (which turns into via delle Cerchia), and then make a right at the fork onto via Sperandie. L23,000 per day plus L363 per km. Great weekend deal—Fri. 5pm to Mon. 9am L39,000 plus L363 per km. Also try **Autonoleggio A.C.I.** via Vittorio Veneto, 47 (tel. 491 18). Comparable prices.

English Books: Feltrinelli, via dei Bianchi Sopra, 66. A wide range. Open Mon.-Sat. 9:30am-8pm. **Libreria Bassi,** via dei Bianchi Sopra, 4. A more limited selection. Open Mon.-Sat. 7am-1pm and 3:30-8pm.

Swimming Pool: The one with the longest hours is **Le Quattro Quercie,** via di Marciano, 31 (tel. 400 13). Take bus #1 or any other that goes to Località Cappuccini, then ask to use this private pool. L5000 per day, L3500 per morning (8am-1pm). Open June-Sept. 8am-8pm and 9pm-midnight.

Public Toilets: In p. San Domenico, across from the bus ticket office. Also between the *campo* and the *duomo* on via di Beccharia, just off via di Città.

First Aid: Ospedale, p. del Duomo, 1 (tel. 29 01 11).

Police: Questura, via del Castoro, near the *duomo.*

Accommodations and Camping

Siena has a youth hostel that's new and clean, with double rooms as well as dorms. (Couples can stay together if both have cards.) Private budget accommodations are difficult to come by in July and August, so it's best to arrive at the hostel in the morning. Singles are virtually unavailable in summer, so solo travelers may want to find a partner; try the youth hostel, or inquire at the Locanda Garibaldi.

For stays of at least a week, rooms in private homes are an attractive alternative, with singles L45,000-60,000. The Azienda has a list and will phone for you. In a pinch, students in Siena's numerous *Case dello Studente* (student residences) may offer a place to sleep.

Ostello della Gioventù "Guidoriccio" (IYHF), via Fiorentina, 17 (tel. 522 12), in Località Lo Stellino, about 2km from the center of Siena. Take bus #10 or 15 across from the station or from p. Matteoti. If coming from Florence by bus, get off at the stop just after you see the large blue sign announcing that you have entered Siena. Management won't go out of their way to do you favors. 120 beds. L10,900. Breakfast included. Dinner L7000. Card required. Curfew 11pm.

Albergo Tre Donzelle, via delle Donzelle, 5 (tel. 28 03 58), off p. Il Campo, 61. Impeccable and with classy furniture in a great location. Telephone reservations accepted. Singles (rarely available) L20,400. Doubles L33,740. Triples L45,000. Curfew 12:30am.

Casa del Pellegrino (Santuario di S. Caterina), via Camporeggio, 31 (tel. 441 77), behind San Domenico. Spotless rooms, most with stunning views of the city. Singles L22,000. Doubles L34,000. Triples and quads also available. Curfew 11pm. Deposit and reservations preferred.

Albergo Garibaldi, via G. Dupré, 18 (tel. 28 42 04), behind the Palazzo Pubblicco. Fills early. 8 cozy doubles L30,000. Curfew midnight. They also have an inexpensive **restaurant** downstairs (*menù* L14,000).

Albergho Bernini, via della Sapienza, 15 (tel. 28 90 47), below S. Domenico. 8 tiny rooms with Easter-egg colored walls. Somewhat shabby, but in a quiet, convenient location. Singles L24,400. Doubles L33,000. Curfew 12:30am.

Albergo Nuove Donzelle, via delle Donzelle, 1-3 (tel. 28 80 88), next door to Tre Donzelle. Cramped rooms. But the family is hospitable and the price is right. Curfew 12:30am. Single L18,120. Doubles L31,140. Triples L42,500. Quads L53,800. Phone reservations held until noon.

Albergo Centrale, via Calzoleria, 24 (tel. 28 03 79), off p. Tolomei. Quite a few rooms in this clean, cavernous building, so likely to have space. A trifle more expensive, but worth it for confy, large beds. Doubles L41,950. Triples L52,000. Curfew 12:30am. Reservations with deposit.

Albergo Chiusarelli, viale Curtatone, 9 (tel. 28 05 62), between p. Matteoti and San Domenico. Set in a slowly deteriorating old villa with palm trees and a garden. A respectable, reasonably-priced restaurant as well. Lovely terrace overlooks soccer stadium. Singles (very few) L24,950, with bath L36,300. Doubles with bath L54,400. Prepaid reservations preferred.

Albergo Cannon d'Oro, via Montanini, 28 (tel. 443 21), near p. Matteoti. Your last chance in the budget range. Well-decorated and well-maintained rooms. 3 singles L36,300, but ask about the tiny, sunny single on the top floor (L25,000). Doubles with bath L54,400. If they win their battle with city hall, a new wing with cheaper rooms *senza bagno* (without bath) will be added in 1989. Reservations with deposit.

Piccolo Hotel il Palio, p. del Sale, 19 (tel. 28 11 3), off via G. Garibaldi. A bit of a walk so more likely than most to have a vacancy. Decent rooms. Singles L24,950. Doubles L41,950, with bath L54,400. Curfew midnight. Buffet breakfast.

Affittacamera G. Rauch, ria del Giglio, 14, just above p. del Campo off p. Tolomei. Mount the stairs to the top. This is a last-ditch, but it might come through at overcrowded il Palio time. Not the most fragrant place, but the commodious rooms feature antique furniture and a couple have superior views. Singles L17,000. Doubles L32,000.

Camping: Colleverde, strada di Scacciapensieri, 47 (tel. 28 00 44), 2km from the center. Take bus #8 from p. Matteoti (until 10pm). About L7000 per person. Good facilities, including a store. Open April-Oct.

Food

Siena specializes sinfully rich pastries. Try the many varieties of *panforte,* a dense conglomeration of honey, almonds, and candied fruit—a sliver goes a long way. Sample the various kinds (plus a hundred different and delectable pastries) at the **Bar Pasticceria Nannini,** via dei Banchi di Sopra, 22-24. The local *chianti* is also delicious. Stop by the **Enoteca Italia** in the Fortezza Medicea, near the entrance off via Cesare Maccari, where the old dungeons have been put to less fiery use as wine cellars. Don't buy bottles here—you can do that more cheaply in any **Vini-Olii** shop—but look around. It's an oenological experience of the most educational nature. Siena's **open-air market** is held in La Lizza every Wednesday. (Open 8am-1pm.)

Ristorante Turiddo, via Diacceto, 1 (tel. 28 21 21), off p. Indipendenza. The locals' favorite for reasonably-priced meals. *Primi* L4500-6000, *secondi* L7500-9000. Open Sun.-Fri.

Il Barbero, p. Il Campo, 80-81 (tel. 28 04 93). Modern and crowded, but you can eat as much or as little as you like. From an excellent salad bar (L2500) to a 5-course meal (L15,000), this place does much to redeem self-service. Open daily noon-2:30pm and 7-10pm.

Mensa Universitaria, via Sant' Agata, 1. Tucked away in a courtyard beneath Sant' Agata you'll find the cheapest meals in town (L6000). Packed and noisy, but decent fare. Open Sept.-July. noon-2pm and 6:45-9pm; in summer shorter hours.

Osteria Le Logge, Via del Porrione, 13 (tel. 480 13), off p. Il Campo. A real hit-or-miss. The *pennne all osteria,* with basil, tomatoes, and fresh cream (L5000), and the *zuppa di funghi porcini* (L4500) are outstanding. Full meals from L16,000. If eating outside, beware of the birds. Open Mon.-Sat.

Severino Ristorante, via del Capitano, 8 (tel. 28 80 04), off p. del Duomo. Excellent fare vindicates its self-billing as a restaurant run by a "family which cooks for you." Full meals from L16,000. Open Mon.-Sat.

La Grotta del Gallo Nero, via del Porrione, 65-67 (tel. 22 04 46), down the street from p. del Campo. Fast becoming one of the most popular places in town, this restaurant serves excellent Tuscan specialties at unbeatable prices. *Primi* L3000-6000, *secondi,* L6000-9000. Delicious pizzas L3500-5000. Open daily noon-3pm and 7pm-1:30am; in winter often closed Mon. Reservations advised.

Trattoria Torre, via di Salicotto, just off the p. Il Campo. Simple, pleasing fare at simply pleasing prices. All the pasta is fresh. *Primi* L3500-4000, *secondi* L5000-7500. Open Fri.-Wed.

Il Salotto, via di Città, 20 (tel. 431 71). Spacious interior (a luxury in Siena) makes the decent pizza (L4000-6000) great. Full meals from L16,000. Open Thurs.-Tues.

Pizzeria Malborghetto, via G. Dupré, 37 (tel. 28 92 58), behind p. Il Campo. A phenomenal selection of pizzas (L3500-5000) and primi (L3000-4500). Vicious vista of the city from the terrace. Open Fri.-Wed.

Pizzeria Poppi Ivano, via Banchi di Sopra, 25 (tel. 402 07). Cheap pizza L800-1000 per slice. Open Mon.-Sat. 9:30am-1:30pm and 4-8pm.

Ristorante Il Verrocchio, logge del Papa, 2 (tel. 28 40 62). Well-prepared food in an elegant setting; many local specialties. *Primi* L3500-4500, *secondi* L8000-9000. Open Thurs.-Tues.

Gelateria Fonte Gaia, p. del Campo, 21-23. Unsurpassable ice cream in an unsurpassed location account for the high prices. Open in summer Tues.-Sun. 9:30am-1:30am; in off-season 10am-11pm.

Sights

Siena radiates from the **piazza Il Campo,** the shell-shaped, salmon-colored brick square that looks up the curve of a hill into the open theaterlike setting of the city. Designed for civic events, the paving stones of the *piazza* are divided into nine sections representative of the city's medieval "Government of Nine," and 11 streets enter the *piazza.*

Il Campo has long fascinated cultural figures. Dante described the real-life drama of Provenzan Salvani, the heroic Sienese *condottiere* who begged around Il Campo to ransom a friend. Sienese mystics like San Bernadino found the *piazza* a natural amphitheater in which to preach. Henry James, too, admired its proportional elegance. Yet Il Campo has also always been used for common fun, with the various *contrade* (districts) of Siena holding games and contests here. *Il Palio,* a horse race and Siena's biggest tourist attraction, is still held here semiannually. Horses careen around the mattress-padded oval surrounded by frenzied partisans, cheering on the horse of their favorite *contrada.*

At the highest point in Il Campo's central axis, the **Fonte Gaia** is a pool surrounded by reproductions of Jacopo della Quercia's famous carvings (1367-1438), now a favorite roost of the local pigeon population. Closing the bottom of the shell, the **Palazzo Pubblico** is perhaps the most graceful Gothic palace in Tuscany. The **Torre del Mangia** rises like a scepter on the left, nicknamed for a gluttonous watchman who was in charge of striking the hours. In front of the *palazzo,* what looks like a carved canopy supported on round arches is the **Cappella di Piazza,** built in 1378 in gratitude for the end of a plague that had carried off half of the town's population. Go into the **Cortile del Podestà,** the courtyard to the right of the *cappella,* for a look at the statue of Mangia, the Glutton.

The *palazzo*'s interior is filled with exceptional works of Sienese art, heavily influenced by Byzantine stylization. Begin with the Sala del Mappamondo, which contains the *Maestà* and *Guidoriccio da Fogliano* by Simone Martini. These two frescoes, facing each other across the vast room, demonstrate two aspects of Sienese medieval government: On the one hand, the city looked to the patron saint of the city, the Virgin, for justification and legitimacy; on the other hand, it paid great mercenary soldiers to defend the city. In the next room, the Sala della Pace, Sienese civic pride comes through in Pietro and Ambrogio Lorenzetti's murals of the *Allegories of Good and Bad Government and their Effects on Town and Country:* On the right side, in the elaborate and cerebral *Allegory of Good Government,* people dance in the streets, artisans work away happily, and vast stretches of fertile land worked by happy farmers unfurl in the horizon. On the left side, that of bad government, a gloomy, desolate landscape is populated only by thieves and sinners. The chapel next to the Sala del Mappamondo houses some excellent frescoes by Taddeo di Bartolo, and a delicate altarpiece by Sodoma. Continuing past this chapel, enter the Sala di Balia, which contains some gripping frescoes of crusade scenes and marine battles by Spinello Aretino. Through this room, the lengthy stairway to the right takes you up to the **Musee Civico** on the upper floors of the *palazzo,* which holds the original della Quercias from the fountain and some molds of his other works. Head back downstairs to the entrance, cross the courtyard, and climb the 300 narrow steps up the tower. The spectacular view of the *duomo* and the entire city is worth the effort and any claustrophobia you may have on the way up. (*Palazzo* and museum open April-Sept. Mon.-Sat. 9am-6:30pm, Sun. 9am-1pm; Oct.-March daily 9am-1:30pm. Admission L5000, students L2500. Torre del Mangia open April-Oct. Mon.-Sat. 9am-6:30pm, Sun. 9:30am-1pm; Nov.-March Mon.-Sat. 9:30am-1:30pm, Sun. 9:30am-1pm. Admission L2500.)

Siena is trisected by the intersection of **via Banchi di Sopra, via Banchi di Sotto,** and **via di Città,** just above Il Campo. Via di Città begins with the **Loggia della Mercanzia** (dedicated to trade) and continues past the towers of various medieval families to the **Palazzo Chigi-Saracini,** a magnificent Gothic structure of brick and stone, now used by the Accademia Musicale Chigiana. Turning right up via del Capitano, you pass the **Palazzo del Capitano di Giustizia**—the residence of the chief magistrates in the thirteenth century.

The **duomo,** atop one of Siena's three hills, took so long to build that it transcended two architectural epochs, from Romanesque arches to Gothic pinnacles. The lower part of the facade, carved by Giovanni Pisano from green and pink marble, is adorned with copies of Pisano's splendid statues of prophets, sybils and philosophers, who hold an intense theological debate across the expanse of the facade. (The originals are in the nearby museum.) The *duomo* was planned to be much bigger (the present cathedral would have been the transept of the new one), but lack of money and labor stopped construction after the plague. Unfortunately, parts of the inlaid marble floor are usually covered to help preserve the marble masterpieces; the ideal time to visit is August 15 through September 15, when the best works by the "Marchese d'Adamo" are uncovered. Halfway up the left aisle, just after the tourist shop, is the Piccolomini altar, a complete architectural structure designed by Andrea Bregno in 1503. At the bottom on either side are statues of St. Peter and St. Paul, two often-forgotten works by Michelangelo executed during the same years as the *David.*

A little farther down this aisle, the lavish **Libreria Piccolomini** is a feast for the eyes. It was built by Pope Pius III to house the elaborately illustrated books of his uncle, Pius II; these still adorn the walls. Above them, frescoes by Pinturicchio illustrate the life of Pius II. The library also contains the beautiful Roman statue of the *Three Graces,* recently moved back here from the museum, as well as fifteenth-century illuminated lyrical scores. (Open in summer daily 9am-7:30pm; in off-season 10am-1pm and 2:30-5pm. Admission L1500.)

Around the corner in the left transept is the chapel of St. John the Baptist, which holds Donatello's expressionistic bronze statue of the Baptist. Towards the left of the crossing is Nicola Pisano's **pulpit** (1260-1280), carved with scenes from the life of Christ and allegorical figures. In the right transept, across from the chapel of the Baptist, is the capella del Voto. The architecture and sculpture is Bernini baroque through and through, and is something of an ornate abscess in predominantly medieval and Renaissance Siena. (*Duomo* open daily April-Oct. 9am-7pm; Nov.-March 8am-5pm.)

The Museo dell' Opera Metropolitana (cathedral museum), housing all the art that formerly graced the cathedral, hides under the arches of p. Jacopo della Quereia, adjoining p. del Duomo. The first floor contains some of the foremost Gothic statuary in Italy, all by Giovanni Pisano. Upstairs is Duccio's *Maestà,* originally the screen of the cathedral's altar (the missing panels are in the U.K. and the U.S.). From the third floor, which contains some lesser Sienese works, don't miss your chance to climb up onto the wall at the end of the *piazza,* which was the intended facade of the planned colossal cathedral. From here revel in the view over the city and countryside. (Open daily in summer 9am-7:30pm; in off-season 9am-1:30pm. Admission L4000.)

The **baptistery** stands behind the *duomo* at the bottom of the church's apse. Gilt bronze bas-reliefs and statues by della Quercia, Donatello, Giovanni di Turino, and Ghiberti surround the font inside. (Open daily 9am-1pm and 3-7pm. Free.)

Siena's **Pinacoteca Nazionale,** down the street at via San Pietro, 29, features temporary exhibits in the courtyard and works by every major artist of the Sienese school: the bandwagon of Onccio followers, Simone Martini, the flying Lorenzetti brothers, Bartolo di Fredi, Sano di Pietro, Francesco di Giorgio, Sodoma, and many others. Don't miss Dürer's intimate painting of St. Jerome on the top floor. (Open Tues.-Sat. 8:30am-7pm, Sun. 8:30am-1pm. Admission L3000.)

As in most Italian towns, the Franciscans and the Dominicans set up rival basilicas in Siena at opposite ends of town. The **Church of San Domenico** contains Andrea Vanni's portrait of Saint Catherine of Siena and dramatic frescoes by Il Sodoma (1477-1549). The *cappella* also contains a macabre relic: Catherine's head. Behind the apse, a door opens onto a terrace, which commands a magnificent view of Siena. The **Church of San Francesco** houses two mournful frescoes by Pietro and Ambrogio Lorenzetti. The adjacent **Oratory of San Bernardino** (ring the bell at #22 for the doorkeeper) houses several more Sodomas.

Entertainment

The Accademia Chigiana sponsors an excellent and diverse music festival, the **Settimane Musicali Senesi,** or Siena's Musical Weeks (in late July and Aug.). There is also a **jazz festival** in July, which features internationally recognized musicians. Check the posters or the Azienda for details.

The **Palio di Siena** takes place on July 2 and August 16. As the race approaches, Siena's emotional temperature rises steadily; fights are not uncommon around il Palio time. Ten of the 17 *contrade* (no room for all in Il Campo) make elaborate traditional preparations. The morning of the contest, each horse is brought into the church of its respective *contrada* to be blessed. (If an animal behaves disrespectfully, it is taken as a good omen.) A colorful procession of heralds and flagbearers prefaces anarchy with regal pomp. The horses tear around Il Campo, unsaddled jockeys clinging to their backs. Officials pad the buildings of the *piazza* with mattresses, for many a rider has lost control and careened off the track. Packed in the center of Il Campo and hanging from the balconies of the surrounding *palazzi,* the throng becomes almost frantic with excitement.

To see il Palio, book rooms at least four months in advance—especially budget accommodations. Write the EPT (via di Città, 5) in March or April for a list of individuals and companies that let rooms. The July race starts at 7:45pm and the one in August at 7pm. You can watch in royal style from the stands for a king's price (L70,000-140,000), but even these places are hard to secure and should be reserved by writing to the Azienda Autonoma di Turismo, via di Città, 43. You can stand, however, in the "infield" of the *piazza* for free. The official word is that access to the *piazza* ceases early, but some squeeze their way in at the last moment. However, you won't get near the edge of the track unless you've staked out a place early in the day.

An alternative to the exorbitant prices of the stands and the unbearable density of the crowd in the *piazza* is to watch the historic parade through the streets in the afternoon and then go to a bar with a large television during the race. There you can absorb genuine Sienese atmosphere with an unobstructed view of the race (which takes only 80 seconds from start to finish). For the full scoop on il Palio ask at the tourist office and pick up their excellent program.

To experience the essence of the il Palio without all the tourists, go to the more purely Sienese phase of the event, the choosing of the horses, which takes place on June 29 at noon. Ten of the best horses are selected and then assigned to each *contrada* by lottery. As each assignment is announced, the members of that *contrada* rush down in an emotional frenzy from every corner of the *piazza* to claim their horse. If the horse is particularly strong, the partisans go monkey. At this event, you can sit in the stands gratis, since the Sienese are all in the *piazza* awaiting their horses.

Southern Tuscany

Monte Oliveto Maggiore

Perched on a knoll halfway between Montepulciano and Siena, the beautiful **Monastery of Monte Oliveto Maggiore** is the paragon of a wealthy Benedictine monastery, functioning today much as it did during the Middle Ages. Its picturesque isolation has saved it from being reduced to a museum, but it also makes it challenging to reach without a car. The hilltop was first settled in 1313 by hermits who later embraced the Benedictine order. Most of the Gothic buildings sprouted up the following century.

The real treasures of Monte Oliveto Maggiore are in the **Chiostro Grande.** On the wall of this large cloister, to the right as you exit from the church, begins a cycle of frescoes depicting the life of St. Benedict. Nine of the 36 panels were done by the meticulous Luca Signorelli from 1497 to 1498, and the remainder were completed by Il Sodoma during the following decade.

The **Chiesa Abbazia,** just off the Chiostro Grande, though thoroughly renovated in the eighteenth century, contains some treasures from disparate eras, most notably the wood-inlaid, sixteenth-century stalls lining the nave and the modern stained-glass work. (Abbey open in summer daily 9:15am-12:30pm and 3-7pm; in off-season 9:15am-12:30pm and 3-5:30pm. Ring if the door is closed.)

It is evident from the fresco cycle that early Benedictine life involved hard labor and also some carnal indulgences. Today the monks are still hard at work and can be seen going about their duties, both sacred and mundane. They make their own wine, honey, olive oil, and a strange herb liquor called *Flora di Monte Oliveto;* there is a small shop within the abbey.

These monks are part of a diminishing order, for Monte Oliveto is one of the few grandiose monasteries in Italy that clings to its 1400-year-old traditions. If you find these mysterious medieval organizations intriguing, or if you just care to indulge in wonderful vistas and striking artwork in a remote setting, consider making the pilgrimage. **Rooms** are available for visiting students and are best reserved by writing. (Write the Abbazia di Monte Oliveto Maggiore, 53020 Siena.) On shorter notice, telephone the abbey (tel. (0577) 70 70 17), where, unfortunately, no one speaks English. Space is often difficult to secure on Saturdays. Singles are approximately L15,000, doubles L25,000 (no meals included). Free **camping** in the lovely area surrounding the abbey is also possible, though level spots are few and far between. At the entrance to the abbey grounds, in the old tower and gate house, is a **restaurant** serving a variety of foods (sandwiches L1500-2500, pizza L4000-6000, full meals around L15,000). They also operate a *bar-pasticceria,* which sells basic necessities (e.g., toiletries and batteries), as well as drinks.

A bus runs at inconvenient hours from Siena to **Chiusure,** 2km from Monte Oliveto (leaves at 2pm, returns at 7am, Mon.-Sat., round-trip L5100). It's easier to take one of the frequent TRA-IN buses bound for Montalcino to the town of **Buonconvento** (on the Siena-Rome highway) and then hitch the 9km of country road toward **Asciano,** 7km from Monte Oliveto on the Siena-Chimi line. (Traffic to the monastery is particularly plentiful on Sundays, when you are most likely to find a fellow pilgrim in a benevolent mood.) Another option is to take the train to Asciano and then hitch; but be prepared to walk, as traffic borders on nonexistent.

San Galgano

An abbey with an entirely different spirit is San Galgano, the church with a sky-roof. In the thirteenth century the Cistercian abbey was one of the richest and most powerful in Tuscany. Its monks served as judges for the communes of Siena and Volterra, helped construct the *duomo* of Siena, and gave numerous bishops—and even a few saints—to the Church. In the fifteenth century, however, the abbey began to decline, and by the mid-sixteenth century the church had fallen into ruins.

Its very dilapidation makes San Galgano an unforgettable sight: Nature has been kind to the massive old building, the foremost specimen of Cistercian Gothic architecture in Italy, and has removed the top completely without harming the majestic pillars within. Thick green grass grows in the nave, and moss fills in missing patches of fresco. Through the numerous Gothic windows and rosettes, once filled with stained glass, distant hills and the sky are now visible.

Unfortunately, San Galgano's mysterious uniqueness has attracted numerous visitors (including the Soviet film director Andrei Tarkovsky, who used the setting in his recent film *Nostalgia*), breaking its mystical spell. If at all possible, visit at sunrise or early morning or at dusk on a weeknight. With a little timing and luck, you will share San Galgano with only the swallows.

Three **buses** per day link San Galgano with both Siena and Massa Marittima (2 on Sun.). To ensure solitude at San Galgano, spend the night in the hamlet of **Palazzetto,** 2½km to the west. The bar (tel. 75 01 60) operates an *alimentari* open all day and a good restaurant with a *menù* for L15,000. (Open Aug.-June daily 7am-1pm and 3:30-8pm.) Under the same management as the bar, tiny **Il Palazzetto** (8 rooms, often full on weekends) offers clean singles for L14,500, with bath L18,000; doubles for L24,000, with bath L29,000. Hitching between San Galgano and Palazzetto should pose little problem.

Massa Marittima

No pearly white sands smother the coast of Massa Marittima, a mining town since Etruscan times. In fact, it takes a particularly clear day to catch a glimpse of the sea, some 18km away at Follonica. Despite its misleading name (it had some beachfront property thousands of years ago when the entire Maremma district was covered by the sea), the town's small *centro storico* retains the air of an undisturbed, walled village, and especially if you are an art-lover, is well worth a day's visit.

Piazza Garibaldi, the center of town, is dominated by a thirteenth-century *duomo* with a marvelous Pisan-Romanesque facade. The steep stairs leading up to the church are a work of art in themselves; at the corner, they converge like a fan into a flat wall. Behind the high altar in the choir is the *Arca di San Cerbone,* the tomb of the city's patron saint (1324). If you look closely at the sharply-cut bas-reliefs, which tell the story of the saint's life, you will detect chips of colored paint in the deeper incisions—the entire piece was originally polychrome and not the gleaming white we see today. In the chapel to the left of the high altar is a transfixing *Madonna delle Grazie,* attributed by many to Duccio. A series of eleventh-century bas-reliefs decorate the inside wall of the facade. The simian faces of the apostles and the primitive narrative expression of the reliefs are haunting products of the Middle Ages. (Open daily 8am-noon and 3-7pm.)

Next to the cathedral is the medieval **Palazzo del Podestà,** which recently became the **Museo Civico.** Its first floor contains a collection of relics glorifying Massa's role in the Risorgimento, along with some Etruscan and Roman coins and vases. Upstairs is Ambrogio Lorenzetti's *Maestà.* (Open April-Oct. Tues.-Sun. 10am-12:30pm and 3:30-7pm; Nov.-March Tues.-Sun. 9-11am and 3-4pm. Admission to Pinacoteca alone L1000, to the ground floor collections L2500, and to everything, including the mining museum L5000.) The lobby of the museum doubles as a **tourist office.**

From p. Garibaldi, go up steep but charming via Moncini to the upper part of town. As you pass through the fortress wall at the top of the street, you will see a huge, soaring arch bridging the wall and the campanile. To the left is a small park; go through it and above you will be rewarded with a bird's-eye view of the surrounding terrain and the lower part of town, including the *duomo.* On a relatively clear day, you can glimpse the twinkling blue sea 18km away in Follonica.

Follow the signs to reach the **Museo della Miniera.** Originally a mine, it was converted to a bomb shelter during World War II and recently opened as a museum displaying all the machinery and techniques used to excavate the area's mineral deposits. (Open Tues.-Sun. for guided tours in Italian at 10:10am, 11am, 11:50am, 3:40pm, 4:30pm, 5:20pm, and 6:20pm. Admission L2500.) Try to visit Massa on the Sunday following May 20 or the second Sunday of August to catch the **Balestro del Girifalco.** This lively procession in medieval costume culminates in a suspenseful crossbow match between the *terzieri* (three sections) of the town. You might find this more pleasant to watch than Siena's famed Palio since it attracts far fewer foreigners.

The only hotel in the town's center is the **Hotel Cris,** via Cappellini, 3 (tel. (0556) 90 23 05), off via Roma near p. Cavour. Singles cost L19,000, doubles L30,000. A family-run restaurant is downstairs.

For a truly memorable meal, head to **Trattoria Da Alberto,** via Parenti, 35 (tel. (0556) 90 20 93). Excellent service under grapevines in an outdoor garden brings you delectable Tuscan food—the *farfalle di salmone* (L6500) and the *cinghiale alle bosciaole* (wild boar, L8000) will keep you coming back. Full meals start at L16,000.

TRA-IN buses leave from via Ximenes outside the walls behind the *duomo* daily for Siena at 8:30am and 5:30pm (1½ hr., L5100). Buy tickets from the friendly travel agency **Massa Veternensis,** p. Garibaldi, 18 (tel. 90 20 62; open daily 8am-1pm and 3:30-7:30pm). **Ferrovia Massa-Follonica buses** link Massa to Follonica (every 45 min., 20 min., L1800). Buy tickets at the office behind the AGIP station on p. Mazzini (tel. 90 20 16). Two buses per day link Massa with Piombino and the ferry to Elba (L3600).

Montalcino

Tucked away in the wavy green knolls south of Siena sits the medieval hill town of Montalcino. Best known for its heavenly red wine (*brunello di Montalcino*), the town lacks the important sights that draw tourists. Removed from the beaten track, Montalcino is quiet and genuine—the perfect place to get to know a Tuscan village and savor some superb views.

Caught in the centuries-long struggle between Florence and Siena, Montalcino ultimately became a Sienese stronghold; indeed, for four years after the fall of Siena, from 1555 to 1559, it was known as "The Republic of Siena in Montalcino." The town today retains much of its medieval physiognomy, as well as its alliance with Siena. The city walls still stand, along with the remains of the town's original 19 fortified towers. Montalcino's **Rocca,** or fortress, stands intact in the southeast corner of town, still sheltering the flag of the Sienese exiles. Inside the fortress is a peaceful, sylvan courtyard, and medieval choral music often wafts through the ancient stones. For L1200 you can climb into its fourteenth-century walls, chambers, and turrets, from which there is a stunning view of the exquisite landscape. (If you speak Italian, chat with the manager of the wine shop downstairs, and he might let you wander onto the ramparts for free.) On the way down, stop at the small *enoteca* in the *fortezza*'s cavernous main room; try the tasty sandwiches (L1500-2500) as you sample the excellent local wines. (Rocca open Tues.-Sun. 9am-1pm and 2-8pm.)

Walking north through the town brings you to a number of medieval monuments, notably the **Palazzo Comunale,** a severe stone edifice in central p. del. Popolo. Above this *piazza,* off p. Garibaldi, stands the **Church of Sant' Agostino,** a curious blend of Gothic and Romanesque architecture, rich in frescoes by fourteenth-century artists from Siena. Near the church are the attached **Civic and Diocesan Museums.** The Diocesan contains fine Sienese paintings, including a few altarpieces by Bartolo di Fredi and a heart-warming panel by Luca di Tommè, in which the Virgin and Child gently tickle each other. (Open July-Aug. daily 9am-1pm and 3-7pm; in off-season Tues.-Sun. 10am-noon and 3-5pm.)

Montalcino's main sight lies some 9km away down a serpentine country road (buses run Mon.-Sat. 3-4 per day, 2 on Sun.; L400). Built in the twelfth century on the remains of a ninth-century church said to be founded by Charlemagne, the **Abbazia di Sant' Antimo** is one of Italy's most beautiful Romanesque churches. (Open daily 10:30am-12:30pm and 3-6pm, but the monk caretaker often leaves early.)

The most compelling reason to visit Montalcino, however, is its world-class wine. Though bottles can be a bit costly (the best deals can be found at the Coop market off p. del Popolo), several bars and *enoteche* in town allow you to sample the many-faceted, full-bodied wine (L2500-3000 per glass). To really gain an appreciation for the local vineyards, head 5km down the road to Sant' Antino to the **Fattoria dei Barbi** (tel. (0577) 84 82 77). (*Cantina* open Mon.-Sat. 9:30am-noon and 2-5:30pm, Sun. 2-6pm.) When the *brunello* puts you in a mood to blow three days' food budget for a fine meal at the winery, the *taverna*'s outstanding and sizeable servings will satisfy you with full meals for L20,000. (Open Thurs.-Tues. 12:30-2:30pm and 7-9:30pm.) Traffic is light on the road out of Montalcino, but enough oenology buffs drive out to make hitching viable.

Rooms are scarce and expensive in Montalcino, so try to find a room in a private home. The **Tourist Office Pro Loco** at via Mazzini, 33, can help. (Usually open Sept.-May.) Try **Affita camere Idolina** at via Mazzini, 2 (tel. 84 86 34), to see if one of their four large and comfortable rooms is available. (Doubles L40,000.) Otherwise, the **Albergo Giardino,** p. Cavour, 2 (tel. 84 82 57), will give you a modern room. (Singles L26,000. Doubles L40,000, with bath L55,000.)

Montalcino is best seen as a daytrip from Siena. **TRA-IN** buses make the one-hour trip daily (L3600). If coming from Pienza or Montepulciano, change buses at Torrenieri. Visit in mid-July, when the town conducts a **Teatro** festival.

Pienza

Pienza was built virtually overnight, as the brainstorm of one man—Aeneas Silvius Piccolomini. After becoming Pope Pius II in 1458, he satisfied a humanist dream and transformed his native hamlet into a tiny utopia that the inhabitants subsequently renamed Pienza in his honor. The approach of the commissioned architect, Bernardo Rossellino, called for a group of monumental structures to be erected around a *piazza:* one cathedral, one papal *palazzo,* one town hall, and one town well. Completed between 1459 and 1462, the mini-city exemplifies the Tuscan Renaissance style. In fact, piazza Pio II is in such classical "good taste" that it is almost boring; you yearn for some element of disorder in the facade of the **cathedral,** whose exterior could be a textbook example of Italian Renaissance architectural principles. The luminous interior rivets visitors with the Renaissance perfection of masters such as Vecchietta and Giovanni di Paulo. Nature slowly destroys the artistic harmony, though; huge cracks cleave the walls from floor to ceiling. (Open daily 8am-1pm and 3-8pm.)

Palazzo Piccolomini, to the right of the *piazza* as you face the church, was modeled after the Palazzo Rucellai in Florence. The impressive front is an indication of the *palazzo*'s social purpose. Within, various collections of weapons and medals come from the pope's personal possessions. (Open Tues.-Sun. 10am-12:30pm and 4-7pm; in off-season Tues.-Sun. 10am-12:30pm and 4-5pm. Admission L2000.) The **Palazzo Pubblico,** facing the cathedral, incorporates the requisite *loggia* on the ground floor and a crenelated clock tower. Inside is the resourceful **tourist office.** (Open daily April-Nov. 9:30am-12:30pm and 4-7pm; Dec. 24-Jan. 6 3:30-6:30pm; at other times hope for the best—they keep no fixed hours.) The most pleasing bit of the *piazza* ensemble is the well, a piece of urban furniture that looks surprisingly like an ashtray. To the left as you face the cathedral is the cathedral **museum,** which contains, among many fascinating liturgical knick-knacks, the cape worn by Pius II, brocaded in gold and silk. A fourteenth-century textile made in England, the *Opus Anglicanum* is a masterpiece of Gothic art. (Open March-Oct. Wed.-Mon. 10am-1pm and 4-6pm; Nov.-Feb. Wed.-Mon 10am-1pm and 2-4pm. Admission L1000.)

If you're game for an invigorating pilgrimage rewarding you with great vistas, go to p. Dante Alighieri and take viale Santa Caterina about 500m down to the church of the same name. Turn left down the dirt road and right on a paved road to reach the **Piere di San Vito,** where Pius II was baptized. The key to this melancholy church dating from the eleventh to the thirteenth centuries is available at the house next door. August and September bring the "Meeting with a Master of Art" display to the chamber, featuring work by a contemporary artist. Come to town on the first Sunday of September for the **Fiera del Cacio,** when Pienza celebrates the local delicacy *pecorino* (sheep's cheese) by recreating the medieval marketplace. The day before (Saturday) features the **Sabbato Serenata,** when a philanderer clad in traditional threads serenades a matron perched in a window of the Palazzo Piccolomini with old Tuscan folk songs.

The three "penthouse" rooms at the **Il Corsignano** hotel on via della Modonnina (tel. (0578) 74 85 01), at the western entrance to town, are the best values in Pienza—doubles are L40,000, with a balcony and panorama to boot. (The "real" hotel charges L27,500 for singles and L45,000 for doubles, without the balcony.) The tiny, clean rooms above the **Ristorante dal Falco,** on p. Dante Alighieri, are less expensive: Singles cost L20,000, with bath L25,000; doubles L35,000, with bath L40,000. **Trattoria Poggialini,** corso Il Rosselino, 8, on old Pienza's main street, offers fine, filling meals for under L14,000 (open mid-July through June Tues.-Sun.), but you may wish to gorge yourself on the delicious, fresh country specialties available in any of Pienza's many enticing *alimentari* (watch the price-tags, though). Craft shops here are equally irresistible. For leather products, head for the shop near the end of via Bernardo Rossellino—follow the sound of the classical music. Pottery is available at **Ceramiche della Mezzaluna,** at the foot of the stairs to the right of the *duomo.*

TRA-IN buses run between Pienza and Siena four times per day, but only two run after 7am (Mon.-Sat., L4300). Pienza is best seen as a daytrip from Montepulciano, from which seven buses run per day at more civilized hours (L1400).

Montepulciano

This stately town celebrated its heyday in the sixteenth and seventeenth centuries and has changed little since. Stretched along the crest of a hill, the town has had no space or desire for modern expansion. Renaissance *palazzi* abound, and as you climb up the cobblestone streets, vistas of the neighboring knolls sprout on either side. Montepulciano is a pre-adolescent in the tourist industry.

The cordial and meticulous **tourist office,** via Ricci, 9 (tel. (0578) 71 69 35), off p. Grande, offers maps and directories listing hotels and restaurants. Especially helpful is the booklet *Montepulciano—Perla del Cinquecento,* in English and French. Though conservative on the sight descriptions, it contains loads of useful information, including a list of private homes that rent rooms—check before you trek, however, as information is subject to change. (Open Tues.-Fri. 10am-1pm and 4-7pm, Sat. 10am-1pm and 3-7:30pm, Sun. 10:30am-1pm and 4-6pm.)

TRA-IN buses run to Montepulciano from Siena, Florence, Pienza, and Chiusi on the Florence-Rome line. Montepulciano is a somewhat difficult daytrip from Siena, since only four buses run per day (Mon.-Sat., 2 hr., L5100). Connections to Chiusi are much more frequent (every hr., 1 hr., L1800), so you may want to visit as a stopover on the Siena-Rome route. There is also a Montepulciano station on the Siena-Chiusi line, but it's 11km from town and only eight buses per day make the run.

Accommodations

Cheap rooms are as scarce as traces of the twentieth century in Montepulciano.

Ristorante Cittino, vicolo della via Nuova, 2 (tel. 75 73 35), off via di Voltaia nel Corso. The best place in town for both chow and lodging. Clean, homey singles L14,000, doubles L26,000. The restaurant serves superb homecooked food. Full meals L14,000. Try the *pici* (fat spaghetti) in meat sauce, a local pasta specialty. Open July to mid-June.

Il Marzocco, p. Savonarola, 18 (tel. 757 26), the 1st square as you walk up via Gracciano. Established in 1850, this hotel has learned the art of the trade. Pricier, but relaxing and classy. Request a room with a terrace and view. Billiard room, small library, comfortable TV den, and an excellent restaurant. Singles L22,000, with bath L28,000. Doubles L40,000, with bath L50,000.

Affitacamere "Brilli," p. Don Minzoni, 10 (tel. 71 69 72), next to the bus station. Genial elderly couple offers clean, cheap rooms. Singles L20,000. Doubles L30,000.

Meublé Il Riccio, via Talosa, 21 (tel. 75 77 13), off p. Grande. Indulge in the mosaic-filled courtyard, lovely outdoor terrace with a view of the skyline, comfortable TV lounge, and immaculate rooms. Singles L35,000. Doubles L45,000.

Food

Montepulciano bursts with excellent, affordable restaurants. Ristorante Cittino is one of the best deals (see Accommodations). There are **mini-markets** all along the Corso and a larger **supermarket** in p. Savonarola at the bottom of the Corso, as well as an **open-air market** every Thursday (8am-1pm) in p. Sant' Agnese.

Trattoria Diva, via Gracciano nel Corso, 92 (tel. 71 69 51). The locals' favorite, so expect a wait to be seated, but the fare is fair reward for the trouble. Full meals from L17,000. Open Wed.-Mon.

Da Bruno, via dell' Opio nel Corso, 30 (tel. 75 82 29). Excellent pizza L4000, *pici* L2000, and ravioli and lasagna L3000. Complete your meal to the tune of a myna bird chattering away in the corner. Open Tues.-Sun. 12:30-3pm and 7:30-9:30pm.

Rosticceria di "Voltaia," via di Voltaia nel Corso, 86, down the street. Tasty homecooked dishes to eat in or take out. Full meals from L10,000, somewhat cheaper to go. Open daily.

Sights

Montepulciano prospered in the sixteenth and seventeenth centuries, and its streets are replete with grandiose *palazzi.* The exquisite details of Renaissance and baroque architecture can be found in every nook of the brick, marble, and stucco of Montepulciano's buildings.

The town's main vein, known simply as the **Corso,** is divided into four parts: via di Gracciano nel Corso, via di Voltaia nel Corso, via dell' Opio nel Corso, and via del Poliziano nel Corso. The lowest quarter of the street (via di Gracciano) is lined with impressive *palazzi.* On your right at #91 is the stately **Palazzo Avignonesi,** attributed to Vignola. The lionheads on either side of the door echo the lion on top of the **Marzocco Column,** in front of the *palazzo.* The lion, heraldic symbol of Florence, replaced the she-wolf of Siena in this spot when Florence took the city in 1511. A little farther up on the other side of the street at #70 rises the asymmetrical yet classical facade of **Palazzo Cocconi,** attributed to the highly influential Antonio da Sangallo the Elder (1455-1534). Right across the street at #73 is the fascinating **Palazzo Bucelli,** whose frontal base is inset with Roman and Etruscan reliefs, urn slabs, and inscriptions collected by the eighteenth-century proprietor, Pietro Bucelli.

Continue up the street to p. Michelozzo, dominated by the **Church of Sant' Agostino.** The lower part of the facade demonstrates the masterful classicism of Michelozzo. The second level is the work of a more curious mind: The architect here has "quoted" the Gothic style without letting you believe for a minute that this is anything other than a mannerist diversion. For some lighthearted spirituality, visit the "Presepio" (Bethlehem) off the nave in a separate chapel: Drop a coin and watch a hilariously kitch nativity scene of sculpted figures come to life with colored lights and Christmas music.

Back on the Corso, which soon becomes via di Voltaia nel Corso, at #21, you will find the U-shaped **Palazzo Cerrini.** This plan's "external courtyard" in front of the building is common in country villas but rare in urban residences, and here serves a double purpose as a symbol of the family's grandeur and as a magnanimous "civic" gesture in that the clan made their private space public.

Continue walking up the Corso and you will find one anonymous architectural marvel after another, each with its own idiosyncrasies. You can either slither slowly around or mount the steep alleys to the right to get to **piazza Grande,** ringed by the unfinished *duomo,* the Palazzo Tarugi, the Palazzo Cantucci, and the fourteenth-century Palazzo Comunale, younger sibling of the Palazzo Vecchio in Florence. The *duomo* is unpretentious with its simple stone and brick exterior; its facade was never finished. Within the *duomo* are a number of excellent Renaissance sculptures (one attributed to Michelozzo) and a stirring *Assumption* by Taddeo di Bartolo, in a triptych above the altar. The austere, gray-white **Palazzo Communale** took nearly a century to build, finally completed in the mid-1400s by Michelozzo. The *palazzo*'s tower affords a view of the countryside, and on a clear day, you can see from Siena's towers in the north to the snowcapped Gran Sasso mountains in the south. Beware the narrow and unprotected staircase. (Open Mon.-Sat. 9am-1pm.) The remaining two *palazzi* were both designed by Antonio Sangallo the Elder. The elegant white facade of **Palazzo de' Nobili-Tarugi** faces the *duomo.* Two arches on the bottom left allow one to enter a deep vaulted *loggia* that cuts through the entire corner of the building; this is another example of the opening of the private domain for public use. Another communal gesture was the furnishing of benches for civilians to sit on, as in the **Palazzo Contucci,** directly across from the Palazzo Communale.

Sangallo's consummate architectural feat is the **Church of San Biagio,** outside the town walls. If you go out Porta Collazzi, you can look down on it and enjoy its perfect and natural setting. Walk the steep ½-km down the hill to appreciate up close the balance of its centralized plan and the gracefulness of its details. Stand directly under the dome and clap your hands to hear the remarkable acoustic effects.

Montepulciano is best known for its garnet-colored *vino noble,* a full-bodied wine. The **Contucci** cellars, in the Palazzo Contucci (tel. 75 00 06), off p. Grande, are maintained by the enthusiastic caretaker, whose tour of the facilities conveys the passion that goes into the production of a top-notch wine. (Open Mon.-Sat. 9:30am-1pm and 3:30-6pm.)

Visit Montepulciano the last Sunday in August to see the raucous **Bravio** (Barrel Race), held to commemorate eight *contrados* (military units) who fended off the Florentines and Sienese.

Elba

The third largest Italian island after Sicily and Sardinia, Elba is queen of the Tuscan Archipelago, a series of islands stretching up the coast. With its turquoise water and mountainous terrain, Elba's beauty cannot be exaggerated. Its sunshine is slightly less reliable than the rest of the islands in the Mediterranean, but you can enjoy the spectacular sight of clouds nestling among rugged slopes clothed with cool, green pinewoods. Elba was first populated by the Etruscans, who mined the island's iron. Since then it has changed hands many times (once going to the exiled Napoleon) and is currently dominated by German families on holiday. Try to visit in off-season, since over one million tourists flock to this tiny island in August, making accommodations (and solitude) impossible to find.

Getting There

The cheapest way to reach Elba is by ferry (*traghetto*) from Piombino Marittima (also called Piombino Porto) to Portoferraio, Elba's largest city. Trains on the Genoa-Rome line stop at Campiglia Marittima, whence a tiny commuter train leaves for the ferries in Piombino Marittima (make sure to wait for the *port* of Piombino stop). Because of Elba's popularity as a weekend trip, many major cities operate special train-ferry services that are synchronized to make the various connections and arrive at Portoferraio in the minimum possible time. Florence, for example, runs the *Freccia d'Elba* (the Elban Arrow), which leaves around 6:30am and arrives in Portoferraio some four hours later. Check local train stations for details. Two companies, **Toremar** and **Navarma,** together run about 18 boats per day (1 hr., last boat at 10pm, L3800-4000). The **hydrofoil** covers the same distance in half the time at double the price (4 per day, ½ hr., L7900). Toremar also runs a boat from Livorno that makes the trip daily via the islands of Gorgona and Capraia (4 hr., L11,900). From June 16 to September 30, this boat goes straight to Livorno in three hours for the same price. Some boats go to ports other than Portoferraio, so check schedules carefully. In summer, jet-setters can fly in from Pisa for a miserly L87,000. The daily flight takes a half-hour. Both Toremar (tel. (0565) 311 00) and Navarma (tel. 397 75) are at piazzale Premuda, 13, in Piombino.

Getting Around

On Elba, **ATL** buses regularly connect the major cities of Portoferraio, Marina di Campo, Procchio, and Porto Azzurro (about 15 per day), but frequency to other destinations varies, so pick up the bus schedule from the station or the tourist information offices. Pending demand, ATL also organizes eight-hour **tours** of the island in July and August. Popular **boat excursions** also cover various parts of the coast; ask a travel agent for details. Renting a **moped** is a fast, fun, and independent means of touring the island. However, beware the winding roads and expensive prices.

Practical Information (Portoferraio)

Azienda Autonoma di Turismo, calata Italia, 26 (tel. 926 71), on the 1st floor, directly across from the ferry landing. Go up the stairway between Hotel Massimo and the Aethal tour office, turn left at the landing, and continue up another short flight of stairs. Information on accommodations (especially campsites), a map, bus schedule, and brochure. Open in summer Mon.-Sat. 8am-1pm and 3-6pm; in off-season 9am-1pm and 4-6pm. Also a **tourist information booth** on viale Elba. Open daily 8am-8pm.

Accommodations Service: Associazione Albergatori, calata Italia, 21 (tel. 927 54). Better for room-finding, and helpful with campgrounds. No commission. Open in summer Mon.-Sat. 9am-12:30pm and 3:30-7pm; in off-season 8:30am-12:30pm and 3-6pm.

Post Office: p. Hutre, off p. della Repubblica. Open Mon.-Fri. 8am-7pm, Sat. 8am-noon. **Postal code:** 57037.

Telephones: SIP, calata Italia, across viale Elba from Hotel Massimo. Open daily 8am-10pm. In Marina di Campo, try **Pietre Bigiotteria,** via Roma, 41. Open Mon.-Sat. 9am-12:30pm and 3:30-7pm, Sun. 9am-noon. **Telephone code:** 0565.

Buses: ATL, viale Elba, 20 (tel. 923 92). Open daily 9am-1:30pm and 4-9:30pm. **Baggage check** next door. Open daily 8am-12:30pm and 2:30-7pm. Don't trust them with your valuables.

Ferries: Toremar, calata Italia, 22 (tel. 91 80 80). To Piombino (L3800). **Navarma,** viale Elba, 4 (tel. 91 81 01). To Piombino (L4000). Book **hydrofoil** tickets at the **Toremar Aliscafi** booth on the waterfront in front of the main Toremar office. Open daily 4-8pm.

Moped and Bike Rental: Alle Ghiaie, via Cairoli, 26 (tel. 926 66). Bikes L7000 per afternoon, L13,000 per day. Mopeds L6000 per hr., L15,000 per afternoon, L25,000 per day. Deposit L50,000. Open April-Oct.

English Books: Il Libraio, calata Mazzini, 9 (tel. 91 71 35). Small selection of paperbacks.

Public Toilets: via Garibaldi, 13, down the street from the post office, across from p. della Repubblica. Open daily 8am-noon and 3-7pm.

Hospital: Ospedale Civile Elbano, Tel. 91 74 21.

Police: via Garibaldi (tel. 920 06).

Accommodations

Elba hosts 200 hotels of varying categories and numerous campsites, yet there is no hostel and room anywhere is nigh impossible to come by in July and August. Book in advance if you can. There is an office in Piombino that can give you a list of hotels, and any free time waiting for a ferry can be spent phoning hotels. In Portoferraio, the tourist information booth and office will do what they can. Remember that campsites fill as well, and the police vigilantly check the beach for impromptu campers.

Mini-apartamenti and more primitive bungalows, available everywhere, are an excellent option if you're planning to stay a week or more. There are usually four beds in one or two rooms with cooking facilities. The accommodations service or the tourist office can help you find one. Residences run L60,000-150,000 per day, while bungalows are cheaper at L40,000-75,000.

Portoferraio is Elba's major port, and it has more charm, bus connections, and reasonably-priced rooms than any other place on the island.

Le Ghiaie, via De Gasperi (tel. 91 51 78), on Ghiaie beach beyond the public gardens. If you can get a room, it's an unbeatable value. Doubles with bath L37,000.

Albergo L'Ape Elbana, salita Cosimo de Medici, 1 (tel. 922 45), off p. Repubblica in the Centro Storico. Family-run. Capacious, airy rooms. The restaurant on the ground floor is decent. A fantastic view of the harbor from the annex. Singles L30,000. Doubles L48,000. Triples L55,000. In off-season prices somewhat lower.

Hotel Nobel, via Manganaro, 72 (tel. 91 52 17), a 5-min. walk from the port in an uninspiring part of town. Modern rooms. Singles L22,000, with bath L29,000. Doubles L38,000, with bath L47,000.

Hotel Il Faro, via Cairoli, 18 (tel. 923 64), down the street from Le Ghiaie. Go up the stairs to the left of Hotel Crystal. Slightly unconventional. Rooms sparse but spotless, and within shouting distance from the beach. For keys and reservations, go to the management at Ristorante Le Sirene across the public gardens toward the beach. Singles L25,000. Doubles L37,000.

Camping

With its varied verdant terrain, Elba is a camper's paradise. It can be as expensive, however, as a decent hotel. The southeastern coast is the place for beach-going campers, as numerous campsites pepper the seaside. The western shoreline is mercifully less crowded in July and August, and from Marciana Marina to Marina di Campo, it is punctuated by charming little, white-powder beaches. In the interior of the western mass, hiking trails wind through craggy, tree-covered hills. There

NO POSTAGE NECESSARY IF MAILED IN THE UNITED STATES

BUSINESS REPLY CARD

FIRST CLASS PERMIT NO. 14826 WASHINGTON, D.C.

POSTAGE WILL BE PAID BY ADDRESSEE

Travel Assistance International
by Europ Assistance Worldwide Services, Inc.
1333 F Street, NW, Suite 300
Washington, D.C. 20077

PLEASE follow these instructions carefully. Incomplete applications will be returned. Failure to follow directions causes needless processing delays.

Application for International Student Identity Card enclose: 1) Dated proof of current student status (copy of transcript or letter from registrar stating that you are currently a full-time student). The proof should be from a registered educational institution and CLEARLY indicate that you are currently a full-time student. 2) One small picture (1 1/2″ x 2″) signed on the reverse side. Applicants must be at least 12 years old.

Application for the Youth International Educational Exchange Card enclose: 1) Proof of birthdate (copy of birth certificate or passport). Applicants must be under 26. 2) One small picture (1 1/2″ x 2″) signed on the reverse side. 3) Passport number_______ 4) sex: M F

Last Name____
First Name_______________________ Middle Initial________

US addresses only. We do not send mail overseas.
Street____
City__________________ State_______ Zip Code__________
Home Phone (area code)_______________________________
Date of Birth___________________ Citizenship:_____________
School/College______________________________________
Date of Departure___________________________________

☐ **CHECK HERE** for more information on Travel Gear, charter flights, car rental, Britrail and France Vacances passes, travel guides and maps.

PLEASE ALLOW AT LEAST 3 WEEKS FOR DELIVERY (unless Rush Service)

are few official campsites on the western half of the island, however, and the police will oust unofficial campers. The Italian government ranks campgrounds on a three-star system and sets maximum prices accordingly. A one-star campground can charge L5900 per person and L6400 per tent; a two-star, L7150 per person, L7700 per tent; and a three-star, L7700 per person, L8200 per tent. Cars warrant a maximum L2200 surcharge. A list of campgrounds can be obtained from the tourist office.

Portoferraio Area: Enfola (tel. 91 53 90) is 6km from town on the shore, with a helpful manager and a beautiful location. Take the ATL bus for Viticcio. L7950 per person, L4800 per tent.

Rosselba Le Palme (tel. 96 61 01), at Ottone, 10km from town. The largest in the area, and well equipped, with comparable prices. A bit cheaper is **La Sorgente** (tel. 91 71 39), 5km from town and 50m from the sea. Also try **Camping Aquavivia,** (tel. 80 63 06), 4km from town on Enfola Rd. and close to the beach. L7100 per person, L7500 per tent.

The South (Capoliveri/Lancona area): Among the many family-run campsites that hug the shore, the following are the more reliable. **Stella del Mare,** Tel. 96 40 07. Take the bus for Lacona or Porto Azzurro, and ask the driver to drop you at the Bivio Lacona, from where it's a short walk to the campsite. L7950 per person, L8450 per tent. **Tallinucci** (tel. 96 40 69) costs the same, and the personable manager will happily accept arrivals until 11pm. Near Porto Azzurro is **Arrighi** (tel. 955 68), a bit out of the way but usually less crowded. Take the Cavo bus and get off at the Bivio di Barba Rossa. L6200 per person, L5800 per small tent.

The Northeast: Sole e Mare (tel. 96 10 59) is truly secluded—you must walk 4½km up an unpaved road after the bus gets you to Bagnaia. Receives campers until 10:30pm. L7800 per person, L4400 per tent; much cheaper in off-season.

Food

Mix and match your meal at the **open-air market** every Friday morning in p. Repubblica. Also near p. Repubblica lies a well-stocked **mini-market** via Mercato, 88. (Open Tues. and Thurs.-Sat. 7am-1pm and 5-8pm, Mon. and Wed. 7am-1pm.)

Ristorante Albatros, salita Cosinio di Medici, 16, off p. Repubblica. Seaweed murals and terraced outdoor seating enhance the tasty food. Pizzas L3500-5000. Full meals L15,000. Open 11am-2:30pm and 7:30-10pm.

Trattoria da Lido, salita del Falcone, 2 (tel. 926 50), off p. Cavour. Super selection and service. The *spaghetti alle vongole* (with clams, L6500) is outstanding. Open Tues.-Sun.

Sights

Portoferraio is a miracle: a town that thrives on neon-clad tourists while preserving a personality all its own. An evening walk around the old port on calata Mazzini and calata Matteotti brings this dichotomy to light. Elbans, seemingly oblivious to the tourists, sip espresso and chat in the open-air *caffès.* Follow the natives' example, and watch the lights on boats and nearby buildings dance in the waves of the harbor.

Elba is primarily a cozy island of oceanside langour, but hardy Francophiles can find Napoleonic memorabilia in two places. The first, and by far the more interesting, is the **Villa dei Mulini,** the Emperor's house in Portoferraio. It can be reached by climbing to the top of the hill in the Centro Storico, the quaint old town on the promontory extending out from the modern port. The villa contains personal effects of Napoleon, of his generals, and of his sister Pauline Borghese. (Open Mon.-Sat. 9am-1:30pm, Sun. 9am-12:30pm. Admission L3000.)

During his 10 months on the island, Napoleon was King of Elba. Shortly before his departure, his sister procured what is known as the **Villa San Martino,** about 6km away by city bus #1 from Portoferraio, as their country residence. On a hill overlooking the ocean, the villa is notable mostly for its view. The central room is painted with scenes from Napoleon's Egyptian campaign. A plastic shield protects the section of the wall where he scribbled "Napoleon is happy everywhere." (Open same hours and same admission as at Villa dei Mulini.)

For a taste of an earlier Elba (and a spectacular view of the town and the Portoferraio bay), hike up the hill behind the Centro Storico and turn left on cosimo del Falcone to reach the **Fortezze Medicee.** Built by Cosimo I de Medici in 1548, these buildings put Portoferraio on the map. Once marking a strategic outpost of the Medici-ruled Duchy of Tuscany, the larger **Forte Falcone** now features, besides the vista from the ramparts, a couple of kiddie parks and a grove of fragrant fig trees, as well as a fascinating demonstration of how the natural rock was formed to fit the walls of the fortress above it. (Open daily 8:30am-7pm. Admission L1000.)

Despite the Napoleonic relics, Elba is most venerated (even by the French) for its coastline. Both beaches in Portoferraio, **Le Ghiaie** and **Le Viste,** are pebbly, but the latter more picturesque. Steps lead down to it near the Villa dei Mulini. Sandy beaches are nearby at **La Biodola** and **Procchio,** where the rocky ocean bottom leaves the blue water sediment-free and pellucid. Procchio is home to the **Elba Windsurfing School,** whose headquarters are on the beach at the **Hotel La Perla** (tel. 90 74 01). The calm seas here make it an ideal place to learn this sport. Other great beaches lie on the south coast at **Marina di Campo, Cavoli, Seccheto, Fetovaia,** and **Lacona,** the last of which has the most frequent bus service. In Marine di Campo, **Hotel Lido** at via Mascagni, 29 (tel. 970 40), offers pleasant rooms near the beach. (Singles L26,000. Doubles L35,000.)

If it's a clear day and you don't feel like swimming, take a bus to Marciana and the cable car up to **Monte Capanne** (1018m). From here, there's a splendid view of the whole island. (Open daily 10am-noon and 2:30-6pm, wind permitting. Round-trip L8500.)

Entertainment

Porteferraio has seen a number of discos come and go in recent years, but two die-hard establishments, **Norman's Club** (tel. 96 99 43) and **Il 64,** still survive outside Marina di Campo (17km from Porteferraio). Unfortunately, buses stop running long before the dancing begins.

Arezzo

Arezzo is the birthplace of many great minds—the poet Petrarch, the humanist Leonardo Bruni, the acerbic journalist Pietro Aretino, the artist and historian Giorgio Vasari, and Guido d'Arezzo, who created modern musical notation. Yet many moved on to greener pastures and more cosmopolitan settings. Petrarch left for the papal court in Avignon; Bruni became the intellectual leader and chancellor of Florence; Aretino went to the court in Venice; Guido headed for Ferrara; and though Vasari had a house here, he spent little time in it. Tourists who travel to these cities to appreciate the work of Aretine artists often completely bypass Arezzo itself. However, the city has a small medieval quarter that is remarkably tranquil, and local son Piero della Francesca stayed home long enough to paint one of the most moving fresco cycles in Italy. Stop to savor Arezzo's "small-town" appeal on your way between bustling Florence and Rome.

Orientation and Practical Information

Arezzo lies on the Florence-Rome train line, about an hour from Florence (L4400). Buses connect it with nearby hill towns, including Cortona (LFI, L2400) and Sansepolcro (CAT, L2700). A morning bus runs to Siena (Mon.-Sat. at 7am, L4600), returning to Arezzo later in the afternoon.

Arezzo's historic center is within easy walking distance of the train station. **Via Guido Monaco** becomes progressively steeper and its buildings less modern as it ascends to the medieval and Renaissance old town, where via Cesalpino and corso Italia continue to the crowning Florentine **Fortezza Medicea** at the summit. If you're staying only for the day and don't want to lug your pack up the hill, leave it at the **baggage deposit,** just to the left as you leave the station (L800).

EPT: p. Risorgimento, 116 (tel. 239 52), on the 2nd floor. Take the 1st right off via Guido Monaco after p. della Repubblica. Accommodations service. Understaffed but helpful. Be sure to pick up a free poster. Open Mon.-Fri. 9am-noon and 4-6pm, Sat. 9am-noon.

CTS: 1 floor below the EPT (tel. 35 06 70). An amiable young staff with information on international flights and rail tickets with youth and student discounts. For CTS or FIYTO cardholders only, but you can buy the cards on the spot. Open Mon.-Fri. 9am-1pm and 4-7:30pm, Sat. 9am-1pm.

Post Office: via Guido Monaco, 34, above p. Guido Monaco. Open Mon.-Fri. 8:30am-7:30pm, Sat. 8:30am-noon. **Postal code:** 52100.

Telephones: SIP, p. Guido Monaco, 2, in the shopping arcade. Open daily 8am-midnight. Also at via Margaritone, just off via Niccolo Aretino near the Archeological Museum. Open Mon.-Sat. 9am-12:30pm and 3:30-6:45pm. **Telephone code:** 0575.

Train Station: p. della Repubblica. Information office (tel. 226 63) open daily 8am-noon and 2-6pm.

Bus Station: viale Piero della Francesca (tel. 38 26 44), in front of the train station. Open Mon.-Sat. 6:15am-8:35pm, Sun. 9:10-11:15am and 3:20-7:15pm.

Public Toilets: in p. Grande. Open Thurs.-Tues.

Hospital: via Fonte Veneziana (tel. 35 67 57; at nights and Sun. 35 18 00).

Police: Questura, off via Fra' Guittone, near the train station.

Accommodations

The hotels of Arezzo bloat during the Fiera Antiquaria (Antique Fair) on the first weekend of every month. Reservations are also necessary during the last four days of August during the **Concorso Polifonico Guido d'Arezzo,** a vocal competition. Otherwise, you should have little trouble finding a room. A new youth hostel on via Francesco Redi, beyond the Ospedale Civile, was scheduled to open in October, 1988. Check with the EPT.

Albergo Milano, via Madonna del Prato, 83 (tel. 268 36), near the EPT. Simple and comfortable. Singles L18,000, with bath L23,000. Doubles L28,000, with bath L35,000. Triples L35,000, with bath L40,000. Quads L45,000, with bath L54,000. Showers included.

Albergo Michelangelo, viale Michelangelo, 26 (tel. 206 73). Turn right as you leave the station. Spotless, spacious rooms, but avoid the rooms overlooking the busy street. Singles L18,000. Doubles L28,000, with bath L35,000.

Cecco, corso Italia, 215 (tel. 209 86). Turn right as you leave the station, then take a left at the 1st set of lights. Large and likely to have space. Singles L24,000, with bath L33,000. Doubles L38,000, with bath L51,000.

Food

The **supermarket** (Santaprisca) at via Guido Monaco, 84, is convenient and inexpensive. (Open Sun.-Fri. 8am-1pm and 4:30-8pm, Sat. 8am-1pm.) **Open-air markets** are held Tuesday, Thursday, and Saturday in p. S. Agostino. For your bread, go to **Forno Pane e Salute,** corso Italia, 11, next to Santa Maria della Piere.

La Scaletta, p. del Popolo, 11 (tel. 35 37 34), next to the post office. Quite possibly the best value in Tuscany. The earthy proprietor takes pride in serving dishes so tasty you won't want to eat elsewhere. Try the *scallopa gorgonzola* (L7000). Pizzas L3000-5000. Full meals from L14,000. Open Fri.-Wed. 12:15-3:15pm and 7pm-1am.

La Piazzetta, p. Risorgimento, 16, a block away from Albergo Milano and in front of the EPT. Fashionable young customers; tasteful, modern decor; and fantastic food at reasonable prices. Try the *tagliatelle ai funghi porcini* (flat pasta in a wild mushroom cream sauce, L5000). Open Thurs.-Tues. 12:30-3pm and 7:30-11pm.

Self-Service MCL, via Mazzini, 6, off corso Italia. Uninspiring fare, but the price is right. Full meals from L9000. Open Mon.-Sat. and the 1st Sun. of the month noon-3pm.

La Tavernetta, via M. Del Prato, 74 (tel. 263 25), at via Roma off p. Guido Monaco. Tasty food. Packed with locals. Pizza L3000-5000. Full meals from L15,000. Open Tues.-Sun.

Bistrot Vecchia Posta, via Cavour, 98/100 (tel. 35 49 87). Sophisticated decor, chic clientele. Stick to the pizza (L4000-6000). Open Thurs.-Tues. 7:30pm-1am.

Ristorante La Tagliatella, viale Giotto, 45. From p. Guido Monaco, follow via Roma as it becomes via F. Crispi and then viale Giotto. A bit out of the way and not cheap, but one of the nicest restaurants in town. Dinner about L17,000.

Gelateria "New Flower," via Roma, 14 (tel. 30 02 66). *Gelato* to rival any in Florence, at half the price and triple the portion. Open Wed.-Mon.

Sights and Seasonal Events

The **Church of San Francesco** is the spiritual and physical center of Arezzo. The simplicity of this fourteenth-century structure—all the more rustic because its facade was left unfinished—guards Piero della Francesca's (1416-1492) famous fresco cycle, the *Legend of the Cross.* The frescoes are undergoing extensive restoration, however, and may not be fully visible for another three years. The stained glass in the church is the work of the French master Guillaume de Marcillat (1467-1529), who came to Italy to work at the Vatican and ended up settling in Arezzo. (Open daily 7am-noon and 2:30-7pm.)

Contrast this Franciscan art with the decoration of the rival Dominican order on the other side of town. The **Church of San Domenico** contains a superb Cimabue crucifix (1265), Spinello Aretino's vaguely Byzantine *Annunciation* in the chapel to the right of the altar, and the Marcillat rose window over the door. (Open in summer 7am-noon and 3:30-7pm; in off-season 7am-noon and 3:30-6pm.)

Down from the church on via XX Settembre is **Vasari's house,** the gaudiest sight in Arezzo. Filled with heroic frescoes, the house should be visited just to see the lengths to which decorative art can go. (Open Mon.-Sat. 9am-7pm, Sun. 9am-1:30pm. Free.)

A right turn on via Domenico and an uphill climb on p. di Murello will bring you to the ***duomo,*** a big, barnlike Gothic structure. The altar is a wildly complex assembly of fourteenth-century local carving. Also noteworthy are the placid *Maddalena* by Piero della Francesca (turn on the lightswitch on the pillar in front of it), the tomb of Arezzo's bishop (Lord Guido Tarlati), and Andrea della Robbia's terra-cotta *Madonna del Conforto* (to the left of the nave), not to mention the excellent Marcillat stained-glass windows. (Open daily 7am-noon and 3:30-7:30pm.)

Backtracking down corso Italia, you will see the Pisan-Romanesque **Church of Santa Maria della Pieve,** Arezzo's most important architectural monument, on the left. The soaring bell tower is nicknamed "the tower of a hundred holes" for the Romanesque windows that pierce the prismlike structure on all sides. The windows were designed to reduce the immense weight exerted on the fragile supporting wall. The interior features a great variety of shadowy forms—massive pillars supporting arcades and half-domes—that seem to focus attention on the raised altar in the back. Above the altar is a resplendent Pietro Lorenzetti polyptych, with a highly individualized Madonna and Child and four saints against a smoky gold background. (Open daily in summer 7:30am-1pm and 3-7pm; in off-season 8am-1pm and 2:30-6pm.)

Behind the Pieve is **piazza Grande,** surrounded by a chronological sequence of Arezzo's best architecture. Next to the impressive arches of the Pieve's backside, the **Palazzo della Fraternità dei Laici** mixes the Renaissance and Gothic styles. In the lunette is a famous relief of the *Madonna della Misericordia* by Bernardo Rossellino, in which she is shown sheltering the members of the confraternity under her mantle. Along the highest side of the *piazza* stands the grandiose **Palazzo delle Logge,** designed by Vasari. The *botteghe* under its portico follow the ancient Roman model. A reconstruction of the Petrone rises at the *piazza*'s high point, a column where criminals were exhibited and proclamations read; at the lower point is the requisite fountain, placed there because water refused to go any higher.

Surrounded by a tower and medieval houses, piazza Grande is the ideal setting for the **Giostra del Saracino,** a medieval joust performed the first Sunday in September. (To meet demand and increase revenues, the Giostra has also been held on summer Sundays the past 2 years, 1 year in June and the next in Aug.) "Knights" representing each of the four quarters of the town charge with lowered lance at a wooden effigy of the Saracen "Buratto, King of India." If they hit him in the middle of his shield, they win; if they miss, the figure spins and whacks them in the back with his heavy whip. Feasting and processions accompany the event, and the winning *quartiere* carries off the prize, a golden lance. The **Fiera Antiquaria** on the first Sunday of every month fills p. Grande and the surrounding medieval street with interesting antiques and hyperactive dealers. The last week of August brings scores of polyphonic vocalists from all over Europe for the **Concorso Polifonico.** For nighttime entertainment devoid of foreign patrons, try **Il Principe,** on viale Michelangelo beyond corso Italia, and **Le Roi,** on via Della down the block from the EPT.

Sansepolcro

Sansepolcro harbors myriad Piero della Francesca paintings. Otherwise, it is a pleasant but sleepy central Italian town. It is only an hour (L2700) by CAT bus from Arezzo (also accessible by train on the Terni-Perugia line). Its **Museo Civico** houses some of Piero's most powerful works. On the wall of the main chamber is a *Resurrection* painted while he was a city council member in Sansepolcro. Across the room is another della Francesca masterpiece, the *Madonna della Misericordia* (Madonna of Mercy) polyptych. It was commissioned by a local charitable society, whose members kneel in worship at the Virgin's feet, protected by her cape. The panels below are obviously by students. Nevertheless, the *Noli mi Tangere* scene is most touching. Among the other works is an impressive *Crucifixion* by Luca Signorelli, a student of della Francesca.

The museum also contains an interesting collection of engravings by Cherubino Alberti; an altarpiece by Matteo di Giovanni (missing its center panel); and a mannerist *St. Quentin* by Pontormo, who makes impalement look sensual. For a respite from the Renaissance, visit the second floor's two small rooms, dedicated to prehistoric artifacts. Don't miss the small *Venus* figure, linked to fertility rites. (Museum open daily 9:30am-1pm and 2:30-6pm. Admission L3000.) For artistic pilgrims, **Piero della Francesca's birthplace** is just up from the museum at via Aggiunti, 71.

After the Museo Civico, there is little to see or do in a town whose primary industrial product is macaroni. Its whitewashed ***duomo,*** on via Matteoti, has the distinction of being one of the few Italian cathedrals in which all the artworks are neatly labeled.

CAT buses (tel. (0575) 73 35 83) will drop you on via G. Marconi at via Aggiunti, from which signs point the way down via Aggiunti to the *museo.* The last bus back to Arezzo leaves at 8pm. Should night fall or hunger strike, try the **Albergo Fiorentino,** via Luca Pacioli, 60 (tel. 760 33), 2 blocks from the Museo Civico. Singles are L16,000, with bath L22,000. Doubles are L28,000, with bath L43,000. Showers are an exorbitant L3500. It's an efficient, comfortable establishment with huge towels and a touch of class. **Trattoria Ricci,** via della Fraternità, off p. Torre di Berta, serves simple, satiating meals for L14,000. (Open Wed.-Mon.). Also, **Ristorante Da Ventura,** via Aggiunti, 30 (tel. 765 60), serves outstanding pasta dishes (L5000-7000) in a refined setting. (Open Tues.-Sun.)

Probably the only time worth spending the night here is the second Sunday in September, when the **Palio della Balestra** is held. The competition between archers of Gubbio and Sansepolcro is well worth an overnight stay to join in the revelry. During the two weeks preceding the Palio, the **Festival delle Nazioni di Musica da Camera** focuses on the chamber music of a particular guest nation.

Another important stop on any Piero della Francesca odyssey is the tiny chapel halfway between Arezzo and Sansepolcro, just outside the town of **Monterchi.** Twenty-four kilometers outside of Arezzo on highway 73, there is a fork in the road, and just up the right fork (highway 221), in the midst of the fabulous Tuscan-Umbrian countryside, is the chapel. Within is the unusual *Madonna del Parto,*

Piero's rendition of the Madonna still pregnant with Child. The fresco depicts a divine force, which leads the peasant mothers of the area to seek the blessing of the Madonna del Parto just before their time comes to give birth. (Open daily 10am-12:30pm and 3-7pm.) There is a stop of the Arezzo-Sansepolcro bus nearby, but be sure there's another bus to your final destination before getting off.

Cortona

People with artistic treasures, medieval ambience, and panoramas, Cortona is the quintessential hill town, able to satisfy frustrated mountain-climbers and ravenous culture-vultures alike. Although dominated by the Florentines since 1409, Cortona has retained its medieval, Umbrian character. Built on a ridge of Monte Sant' Egidio, the town tumbles down from the summit's Fortezza Medicea into the tree-laden banks below. The site has little room for expansion, and, as a result, most Cortonese workers commute the 5km to the industries in **Camucia,** in the valley below, allowing the upper town to remain much as it has been for the last 400 years.

Unfortunately, Cortona has been discovered by numerous foreign students speaking in a Southern drawl, most attached to a University of Georgia art program. Many shops post Dear American Friends notices, entreating the students to gain an appreciation for Italian customs and culture. And the market displays a 5-foot loaf of bread inscribed "Cortona-Athens" (Georgia).

Orientation and Practical Information

Even the fastest Rome-Florence **trains** stop at Terontola-Cortona, 11km from the city, and *locale* will drop you off 6km closer at Camucia-Cortona; train fare to Terontola is L9800 from Rome, L6400 from Florence, and L1800 from Arezzo. Both stations are connected to p. Garibaldi by **LFI buses** (L1200 from Terontola, L800 from Camucia), which also run to and from Arezzo, the easiest city from which to see Cortona as a daytrip (L2400).

Azienda Autonoma di Turismo, via Nazionale, 72 (tel. 60 30 56). Open Mon.-Sat. 8:30am-12:30pm and 3-6pm. Friendly and helpful. A bit Americanized.

Post Office: p. della Repubblica. Open Mon.-Fri. 8:15am-7pm, Sat. 8:15am-noon. **Postal code:** 52044.

Telephones: Bar Signorelli, via Nazionale, 2, off p. della Repubblica. Open Feb.-Dec. Tues.-Sun. 8am-10pm. **Bar Banchelli,** via Nazionale, 64 (tel. 60 31 79). Open Tues.-Sun. 7am-1pm and 2:30-10pm. **SIP,** via Guelfa, off p. della Repubblica. Open daily 8am-midnight. **Telephone code:** 0575.

Train Information: Terontola, Tel. 670 34. **Camucia,** Tel. 60 30 18.

Bus Information: LFI, via Nazionale, 73 (tel. 60 45 76).

Police: Carabinieri, via Dardano, 9 (tel. 60 30 06).

First Aid: Serrizio Guardia Medica Turistica, via Roma, 3 (tel. 60 18 17). For emergencies. Open 8am-8pm. At other hours, call 628 93.

Hospital: via Maffei (tel. 629 41).

Swimming Pool: 7km away at Sodo (tel. 60 13 74). Take the bus for Arezzo and ask the driver to let you off at the *piscina.* Open daily 10am-11pm. Admission L4000, including a terrific water slide.

Accommodations

The superb hostel and decently priced *alberghi* in Cortona should have plenty of space, but if you arrive in Camucia after the last bus up to town (9pm), there is an excellent alternative. The warm proprietress at the **Albergo Firenze** (tel. 60 32 10), 2 blocks up via Regina Elena from the train station, will make you feel right at home in her newly-renovated hotel. (Singles L16,000, with bath L21,000. Doubles L27,000, with bath, L35,000.)

Ostello San Marco (IYHF), via Maffei, 57 (tel. 60 13 92), a healthy hike uphill from p. Garibaldi. Walk up via S. Margarita, then around and left on via Maffei. A cool, spotless hostel with a friendly manager. Up to 15 beds per room. The double is open to couples if both have an IYHF card. Laundry facilities. Rarely full. Beds L8500. Sheets and breakfast included. Lunch or dinner in the handsome dining room L8000. Curfew 11:30pm. Reception open until 1pm and after 6:30pm. Open mid-March through Oct.

Albergo Italia, via Ghibellina, 5 (tel. 60 32 64), off p. Vittorio Emanuele. Plenty of tidy pads with high ceilings, some with firm beds, some with views. Singles L18,000. Doubles L29,000, with bath L36,000. Showers included.

Albergo Athens, via San Antonio (tel. 60 30 08). Take the 1st right beyond and above the youth hostel, turn right again on tiny vicolo Borghi, turn left (no name), continue until this street ends, go left on via Berretini, and finally take the 1st right onto via San Antonio. Capacious, tidy rooms, but, unfortunately, the Athens refers to Georgia, and the place is booked solid with summer students July-Aug. Singles L17,000, with bath L21,000. Doubles L31,000, with bath L36,000. Open April-Sept.

Food

Perhaps due to competition for the palates of the large foreign contingency, a number of *trattorie* feature a reasonable *menù*. The best local wine is the smooth *bianco vergine di Valdichiana*. True penny-pinchers can buy a bottle (L2500) and do all their shopping at the **Supermercato Duemila,** via Nazionale, 10. (Open daily 8am-1pm and 4-8pm.) On Saturday, p. della Repubblica explodes into a great **open-air market.** For a full list of culinary options with tourist menu prices in Cortona and its environs, pick up a copy of the thorough *Cortona In Cucina* at the tourist office.

Trattoria dell' Amico, via Dardano, 12 (tel. 60 41 92). Gregarious owner serves up great pasta at great prices. Try the *spaghetti al pesto* (L4500) or the *penne alle gorgonzola* (L4200). For a *secondo,* sample the wonderful *salsice al vino* (L3200). Full meals L14,000. Open in summer daily; in winter Tues.-Sun.

Pizzeria-Ristorante Zerolandia, via Ghibellina, 3 (tel. 60 36 38). The best pizza in town L2500-4000. The *simpatico* young owner has covered the walls with pictures of David Bowie and Renato Zero, the Italian transvestite rock singer after whom the restaurant is named. Excellent full meals (try the *spaghetti al fumo*) L11,000. Superb antipasto plate L8000. *Menù* L13,000. Open Thurs.-Tues. 8am-midnight.

Trattoria la Grotta, p. Baldelli, 3, off p. della Repubblica. Reputation for delectable fare. Sample the *gnocchi alla ricotta e spinaci* (ricotta and spinach balls in tomato and meat sauce). Menù L15,000. Open Wed.-Mon.

Bar Unica, via Nazionale, 26. Decent eats. Staff remains remarkably good-natured in the face of the American onslaught. Hot dogs L2300, hamburgers L2800, pizzas L4000. Sit outside and watch the *passeggiata.*

Sights

On the way to the center of Cortona are two spectacular vistas. The first is on the approach from the valley. The citadel springs out from the mountainside, with its *fortezza* atop the ridge, and encircling medieval walls below. The second panorama is from p. Garibaldi, at the entrance to the old town, and is of Lake Trasimeno and the hills beyond.

Proceed up **via Nazionale,** the only level street in Cortona, to p. della Repubblica. Immediately opposite is the thirteenth-century **Palazzo del Comune,** with its clock tower and monumental staircase. **Palazzo Casali,** to the right, dominates the piazza Signorelli. For centuries, this imposing edifice was known as the **Palazzo Pretorio** (Prefect's Palace), but recently it was renamed after the Casali family, who ruled Cortona from its founding until the Florentine takeover. Only courtyard walls, with their coats-of-arms, and the outside right wall remain from the original thirteenth-century *palazzo.* The Renaissance facade was added in the early sixteenth century, along with the delightful interlocking staircase in the courtyard.

The upper set of steps leads to the **Museo dell' Accademia Etrusca.** Only two of the museum's 12 rooms are devoted to Etruscan objects. In the first gallery is a circular bronze chandelier from the fifth century B.C.E., mounted in a glass case suspended from the ceiling. With 16 voluminous cups for burning oil, it weighs 58kg when empty. A rare example of intricate Etruscan stone carving, the *lampadario* was discovered by a local farmer plowing his field. The same room contains a curious *Janus,* shown as a full figure rather than the usual bust. (Open April-Sept. Tues.-Sun. 10am-1pm and 4-7pm; Oct.-March Tues.-Sun. 9am-1pm and 3-5pm. Admission L3000, Thurs. free.)

To the right and downhill from the Palazzo Casali is **piazza del Duomo.** Far more remarkable than the much-remodeled cathedral is the **Museo Diocesano** opposite. This two-room museum, strung together by a monumental staircase of Vasari's design, can hold its own with almost any museum in Tuscany. In the gallery on the left, you are confronted by Christ's pathetic face in Pietro Lorenzitti's fresco of *The Way to Calvary.* This room also holds a famous *Lentation* and many other paintings by Luca Signorelli, Cortona's most celebrated contribution to the Renaissance. Fra Angelico rivals in the next room with his infinitely delicate *Annunciation.* Everything about this painting is deliberate: the Virgin's answer to Gabriel ("Behold the servant of the Lord . . . ") is even written upside down, since the message is intended to be read by someone overhead. (Open April-Sept. Tues.-Sun. 9am-1pm and 3-6:30pm; Oct.-March 9am-1pm and 3-5pm. Admission L3000.) Perhaps the best example of Signorelli's work is his depiction of *Christ Deposed,* which resides in the sixteenth-century **Church of San Niccolò,** up the hill beyond the youth hostel. Ring the bell if the church isn't open, and after the kind woman shows you the painting ask her to switch on the nifty mechanism that turns the panel around so you can see Signorelli's *Madonna and Saints* on the other side.

When the afternoon calm descends on Cortona, head up to the **Fortezza Medicea** for a splendid view and refreshing breeze. Take the stairlike via San Cristoforo, which winds between tall cypresses up the hill from the small church of the same name. You will pass the remains of Etruscan and medieval city walls, the site of an ancient temple dedicated to Mars, and a stone explaining how Santa Margherita there cured a sick person for the first time. At the top is the tree-filled fortress, built on the remains of an Etruscan fortification. (Open Tues.-Sun. 10am-1pm and 4-7pm.) Enjoy a picnic lunch in this lush and peaceful area. Cortona pours down the hillside beneath you, while in the distance float Lake Trasimeno and Mt. Amiata.

Another worthwhile excursion is to the Renaissance **Church of Madonna del Calcinaio,** designed by Francesco di Giorgio Martini, about 2km down the road near Camucia. The soft grey *pietra serena* stone is beautifully carved in the interior, and with the white walls as backdrop, creates a cool tonality. Unfortunately this soft stone did not hold up on the exterior and is badly weathered. Don't miss the simple perfection of the only remaining stained glass window in the church. (Generally closed from noon to 3:30pm.)

Entertainment

The Cortonese boast with justification of their foods and wines. Of the numerous gastronomic festivals throughout the year, the most important and exciting is the **Sagra della Bistecca,** held August 14 and 15. The whole town pours into the public gardens, where long tables and enormous charcoal grills have been set up, to feast upon the superb local beefsteak hot off the grill and wash it down with the wonderful local wines. Cortonese consider these the best two days of the year, and they carry on the chowing and merrymaking well into the night.

At other times of year, the public gardens are lovely and quiet, the ideal spot to sit and people-watch, or to join them in the *passeggiata* along the so-called *parterre.* The park is also a great place to jog and, in summer, movies in Italian are screened here. For dancing, try **Casina dei Tigli,** also along the *parterre,* or go to the local hot spot **Tuchulcha,** a disco right on p. Garibaldi (tel. 627 67; cover and 1st drink L5000).

Rome

Rome the Empire, in the sweeping words of Edward Gibbon, "comprehended the fairest part of the Earth and the most civilized part of mankind." Today, Rome's glory is not dimmed. To the oft-asked question, "*Bella Roma, no?*" there is still only one answer.

The Eternal City has been home and playground to Caesars, popes, and artists who have sought to memorialize themselves. Augustus boasted that he found Rome a city of brick and left it one of marble, but his work was only the beginning. The Forum and Palantine may evoke the spirit of the ancients, but the shadows of medieval nobles lurk around Palazzo Cenci, and scarlet-robed prelates still roam the halls of St. Peter's.

Romans live and revel in their city rather than let it become a museum. There are concerts in the classical ruins; movies and soccer games are projected onto vast screens in the majestic *piazze;* people hang laundry on priceless monuments and place hats on Bernini statues. Efforts to set aside certain buildings as "sights" have often detracted from their grandeur. The alternative to planned preservation—chance plus public sentiment plus occasional private patronage—has proven fruitful in Rome. Livy ended his *Early History of Rome* with the words, "in general, the layout of Rome is more like a squatter's settlement than a properly planned city." Two thousand years of squatting by the luminaries of European history and culture later, Rome is still a splendid, sprawling circus.

Getting In and Out of Rome

International flights touch down at **Leonardo da Vinci Airport** (tel. 601 21), referred to as **Fiumicino** for the city in which it is located. This modern, well-equipped facility operates most services: money exchange, baggage check, etc. From here, take the blue Acotral bus to **Stazione Termini.** Buses arrive from and depart for the airport at via G. Giolitti, 36, on the west side of Termini (6:30am-9pm every 15 min., 9:30pm-6:30am every ½-hr.; 45 min.; L5000). Most charter and domestic flights arrive at **Ciampino** (tel. 46 94 or 60 02 51), a dowdy military airport. From here take the Acotral bus to the Anagnina stop of subway line A (7am-11pm every hr. on the hr.; 30 min.; L1000). Line A takes you to Termini, the Spanish Steps, or the Vatican.

Stazione Termini, as its name suggests, is the terminus of all train and subway lines and the focal point for all transportation in Rome. Virtually a city unto itself, Termini offers information booths, currency exchange offices, baggage services, restaurants, bars, day hotels, barbershops, telephone offices, gift shops, and even an aquarium. (See also Practical Information.) Overnight trains that do not start or finish their journey in the city often bypass Termini and stop instead at the various stations on the fringe of town. All of these are connected by bus and/or train to Termini.

Those entering Rome by car approach the city center by way of the **Grando Raccordo Anulare,** the beltway that encircles Rome. You can take any of several exits off this ring road into the city. If you are coming from the north, enter the city on **via Flaminia, via Salaria,** or **via Nomentana.** At all costs avoid **via Cassia,** whose ancient two-chariot lanes can't cope with modern-day traffic. **Via Tiburtina** to the east is even worse. Rather than try any of the narrow roads on the eastern side (unless it's very late or very early), go around on the Grande Raccordo to **via del Mare** to the south, which connects Rome to **Lido di Ostia.** When leaving the city by car,

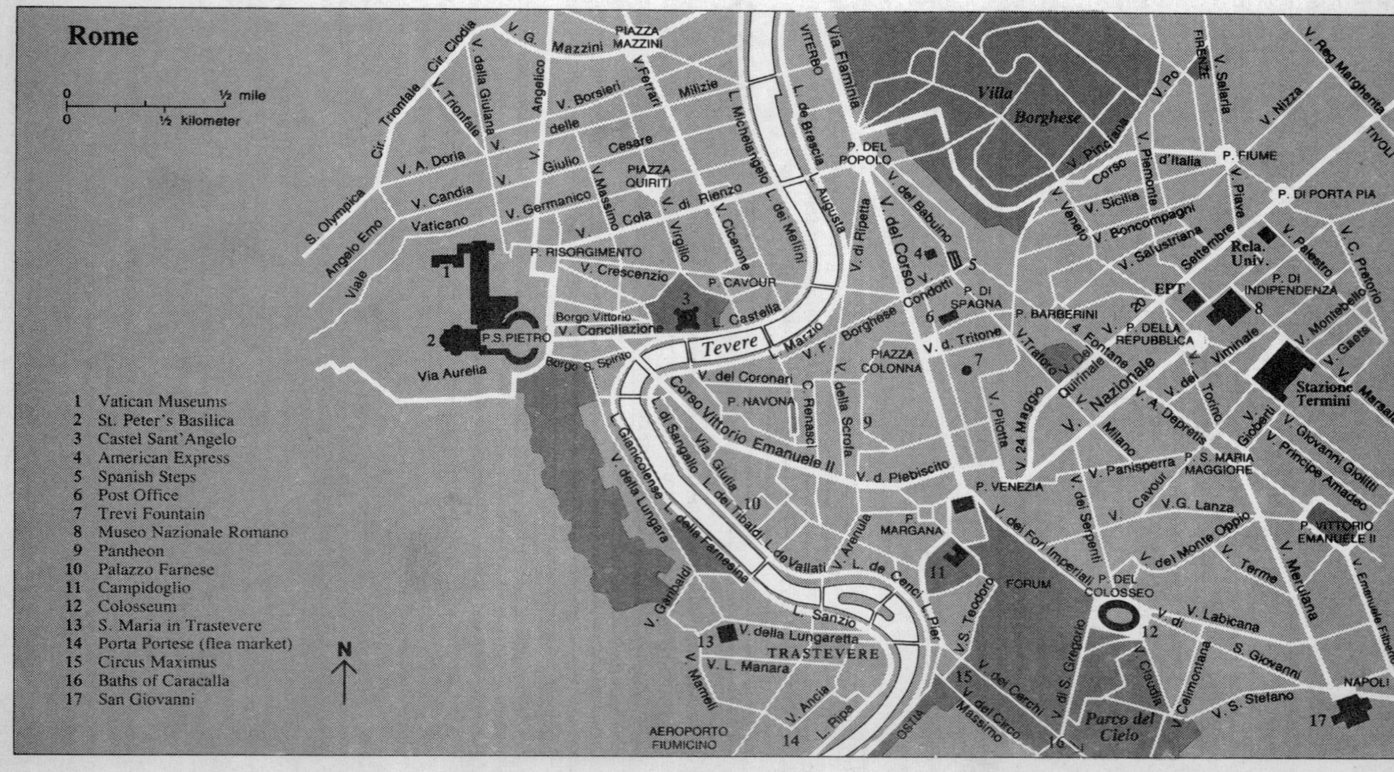
Rome
0 ½ mile
0 ½ kilometer
1 Vatican Museums
2 St. Peter's Basilica
3 Castel Sant'Angelo
4 American Express
5 Spanish Steps
6 Post Office
7 Trevi Fountain
8 Museo Nazionale Romano
9 Pantheon
10 Palazzo Farnese
11 Campidoglio
12 Colosseum
13 S. Maria in Trastevere
14 Porta Portese (flea market)
15 Circus Maximus
16 Baths of Caracalla
17 San Giovanni
N
Tevere
Villa Borghese
TRASTEVERE
Stazione Termini
P.S.PIETRO
P. DEL POPOLO
P. VENEZIA
P. DEL COLOSSEO
P. DELLA REPUBBLICA
PIAZZA MAZZINI
PIAZZA QUIRITI
P. RISORGIMENTO
P. CAVOUR
P. NAVONA
PIAZZA COLONNA
P. DI SPAGNA
P. BARBERINI
P. FIUME
P. DI PORTA PIA
P. DI INDIPENDENZA
P. S. MARIA MAGGIORE
P. VITTORIO EMANUELE II
P. MARGANA
FORUM
EPT
Rela. Univ.
AEROPORTO FIUMICINO
OSTIA
NAPOLI
TIVOLI
FIRENZE
VITERBO
Via Flaminia
V. del Corso
V. Nazionale
Corso Vittorio Emanuele II
V. Conciliazione
Via Aurelia
Parco del Cielo

don't attempt to follow the green Autostrade per Firenze signs through the center of town; they are vaguely marked, and you will encounter heavy traffic. Instead, get on the Grande Raccordo quickly and follow it around; it's longer but faster. From the south, **via del Mare** and **via Pontina** are the most direct connections from the coastal road from Naples. From the Adriatic coast, take **via Appia Nuova** or **via Tuscolana** off the southeastern quadrant of the Raccordo.

Since Italian railways are inexpensive and convenient, **hitchhiking** doesn't make much sense but is possible. To head north toward Florence, take bus #319 to p. Vescovio and then #135 onto via Salaria. Get off as near the entrance to the *autostrada* as possible—it's illegal to hitch on the *autostrada* itself. To go south toward Naples, take subway line A to Anagnina (the last stop) on via Tuscolana right at the entrance to the *autostrada.*

Orientation

Rome gives priority to coffee and lunch breaks, the *pennicchella* (the infamous midafternoon siesta), and extended holidays. All schedules and timetables lead to frustration; simply go with the flow. Most shops and offices are open weekdays from 9am to 1pm and 4 to 8pm; in winter 3:30 to 7:30pm. Just about everything closes down on Sunday, on Saturday afternoon in summer, and on Monday morning in winter, except a few "bars" (cafes) and restaurants. Food shops close early on Thursday. Churches usually open with the first mass of the day at 6 or 7am and remain open until 12:30pm. If no mass is planned, each church follows the divine caprices of its curate. (You'll find that no 2 sources of information ever agree on opening hours.) Many churches reopen at 4pm for a couple of hours. Most museums and monuments close at 1:30 or 2pm. Plan your day carefully: Get an early start, spend your mornings in museums, and, if you haven't succumbed to the *pennicchella,* save the afternoons for sights that don't observe siestas (e.g., the Forum, the Colosseum, *piazze,* fountains, or the major basilicas affiliated with the Vatican).

Rome shuts down in the beginning of August and is deserted except for tourists by August 15, which is Ferragosto, the big summer holiday for Italians. Though most of the museums and sights remain open, most offices and restaurants close down completely. You won't starve during this period, however, thanks to a humanitarian law that prevents bread shops from closing more than one day at a time.

Layout of Rome

The city is a cartographer's nightmare: a jumble of staircases, winding streets, *piazze,* and parks that defy both gravity and geography. Nonetheless, it is possible to conquer this city. In fact, the historical center is small enough to explore mostly on foot. The tourist office and most hotels hand out a free map that includes bus and subway routes but lacks an index and somehow manages to make distances look shorter than they are. If stuck, try to find a copy of *Tutto Città,* an indexed pamphlet of maps of the city, complete with all bus routes and most useful phone numbers. It is printed by **Agenzia SEAT,** via Agri, 2/A (tel. 849 41), as an addendum to Rome's yellow pages. Though not for sale, most offices, *tabacchi,* hotels, and *pensioni* have one you can look at. Another useful street atlas is *Roma a Tavole,* an exhaustively indexed book with easy-to-read maps; it is available at bookstores and newsstands for L8000. *Tourist Guide: Rome and Latium,* at tourist offices, offers compact and well-designed maps of the city and the surrounding province, as well as informative guides to walking tours.

No longer defined by the Seven Hills, Rome sprawls over a large area between the hills of the **Castelli Romani** and the beach at **Ostia.** Even so, the old city is fairly compact and navigable. From Termini, the **Città Universitaria** and a few good restaurants are to the east, but everything you'll want to visit is to the west. To the northwest, around **piazza di Spagna** and **via Veneto,** are sumptuous shops. **Piazza del Popolo, piazza Barberini, piazza San Silvestro,** and **Fontana di Trevi**

(Trevi Fountain) are all close at hand. Above is Rome's largest park, the **Villa Borghese.** To the southwest are the **Forum, Palantine,** and **Colosseum,** and below them the **Protestant cemetery.** Directly to the west is the **Old City** itself, winding around the **Pantheon, piazza Navona,** and **Campo dei Fiori.** Finally, on the western banks of the Tiber River are the self-contained palaces of **Vatican City** and the colorful quarter of **Trastevere** to the south. Almost all the sights lie within these rough boundaries. The **Catacombs** are just outside the city walls, accessible by bus.

Transportation

Every visitor to Rome can play the intrepid explorer, treading boldly across *terra incognita* and chancing upon a majestic *piazza* or the lofty spire of a lovely church. The streets are steep, however, and the city hot and humid in summer. The public transportation system is efficient and cheap (L700 per ride), though congested during rush hours. Beware that the great majority of thefts in Rome occur unnoticed on crowded city buses.

ATAC (tel. 46 95), the city bus line, sells bus maps in English (L1000) at their headquarters at via Volturno, 65, and at the ATAC information booth in the center of p. dei Cinquecento in front of Termini. Bus routes are also marked in blue on the maps distributed by the EPT. If you plan to use buses frequently, consider purchasing a *biglietto settimanale* (L10,000) at the ATAC booth in front of Termini: It allows you unlimited bus travel for eight days. Also available are half-day passes good from 5:30am to 2pm or 2pm to midnight (L1000) and a full-day bus and subway pass (L2800). Regular tickets must be purchased at *tabacchi* or kiosks before boarding and then machine-punched on the bus. Only about half a dozen inspectors roam the city, but if one catches you without a ticket, there is a strict L10,000 fine.

Some useful routes are #64, which runs from Termini to the Vatican (and is popular among pickpockets); #170 from Termini to Trastevere; and #492 from Termini to Villa Borghese and Ottaviano. Buses #60, 61, and 62 run down via XX Settembre past the area near the Spanish Steps on their way to Trastevere, p. San Silvestro, and the Vatican. Infrequent night buses run after normal service shuts down around midnight; look for the *servizio notturno* signs, which list the route and scheduled times. Key *servizio notturno* routes include #30 from the Vatican and Trastevere to the Colosseum and the area within a 10-minute walk south of Termini; #60 from via Veneto through corso Vittorio Emanuele to Trastevere; and #78 from the Vatican to Termini. Consult the ATAC map for the frequency of this service. These buses are completely safe and have conductors who will sell you a ticket.

ATAC also offers a no-frills, three-hour circuit of the city, leaving from p. dei Cinquecento (April-Sept. daily at 3:30pm, Oct.-March Sat.-Sun. and holidays at 2:30pm; L6000). They provide a map and some explanation in Italian and quasi-English, whirling you around the city for a comprehensive peek. This can be a comfortable way of orienting yourself. You can also jump on bus #30, a trolley, and follow it along viale Trastevere, across the Tiber to piazza Risorgimento. On its regular route the bus passes almost all of Rome's important sites.

The new **subway's** two lines, whisking you speedily across town, intersect at Termini and can be reached by descending the stairs at the station. Line A, the cleaner of the two, runs from Ottaviano in the northwest near the Vatican to Anagnina in the southeast, and line B runs from Termini to Laurentini in the area of EUR, to the south. Important stops on line A are piazza della Repubblica, piazza Barberini, piazza di Spagna, and Ottaviano, near the Vatican. Important stops on line B are the Colosseum and *Piramide* (for trains to the beach). For the most part, the subway is safe. Bear in mind, however, that the majority of Rome's sights are a trek from any of the rather dispersed subway stops. Remember, too, that the metro runs *only* from 5:40am to 11:30pm. Subway tickets (L700) can be bought at newsstands, *tabacchi,* or machines in the stations that accept L50, L100, and L500 coins. All stations are equipped with machines that change L1000 bills. Note as well that while they share tracks with the subway, trains to Ostia and the Lido beach are *not* part of the system. Tickets for these trains cost L700 and must be purchased at a separate booth at Termini.

Finally, if you are out after midnight and no *servizio notturno* bus is near at hand, **taxis** are a viable option. On call 24 hours, they can be flagged down in the streets.

Practical Information

Ente Provinciale per il Turismo (EPT): In the Termini Station (tel. 475 00 78 or 46 54 61), between aisles #1 and 2. Open daily 9am-7pm. **Central office,** via Parigi, 5 (tel. 46 37 48). Walk straight from the station on viale L. Einaudi until you arrive at p. della Repubblica. Cross the *piazza* and turn right on via G. Gomita, which becomes via Parigi. Open Mon.-Sat. 8:30am-7pm. The 10-min. walk to the central office from the station is strongly recommended as there are interminable lines at the Termini booth. Both offices provide maps and the excellent brochures *Young Rome* and *Qui Roma,* which contain important telephone numbers, accommodations listings, sample tourist itineraries, and shopping and entertainment options. The *Carnet di Roma e del Lazio* lists (in Italian and English) the month's museum exhibits, concerts, and festivals in the region. If you will be traveling in the region around Rome, also ask for *Alberghi di Roma e Provincia,* which lists all hotels and *pensioni* registered with the EPT. Both places will try to help you find a room, but all places listed below will be booked in summer. Make reservations.

Ente Nazionale Italiano per il Turismo (ENIT): via Marghera, 2/6 (tel. 497 12 82). This national tourist office does not offer information on Rome, but distributes brochures and hotel listings for all of Italy's regions and important cities. Open Mon.-Fri. 9am-1pm, Wed. 4-6pm.

Vatican Information Office, p. San Pietro (tel. 698 44 66), by the Arch of the Bells, to the left of the *piazza* as you face the basilica. Pick up a free copy of the *Plan of the Vatican City and of St. Peter's Church,* which includes maps and information on hours and tours. **Tours** are offered of the otherwise inaccessible Vatican Gardens (Tues, Fri., and Sat. at 10am. Admission L900) and combining the gardens and the Sistine Chapel (March-April and June-Oct. Mon. and Thurs. at 10am. L18,000). To attend a **papal audience,** apply in writing to the **Prefettura della Casa Pontificia,** 00120 Città del Vaticano, or go to the office by the bronze door of St. Peter's Mon.-Tues. 9am-1pm (tel. 69 82). The papal audiences are held Wed. at 11am when he is in Rome, 10am when he's at his summer estate south of Rome in Castel Gandolfo. Information office open Mon.-Sat. 8:30am-1pm and 2-6:30pm.

Compagnia Italiana di Turismo (CIT): p. della Repubblica, 64 (tel. 479 44 11). A national travel agency that can book and provide information on discount train tickets and tours. Open Mon.-Fri. 6:30am-8pm, Sat.-Sun. 7:30am-3:30pm. Also in Termini (tel. 475 14 36 or 46 16 78). Open Mon.-Fri. 9am-1pm and 2:30-6pm. Office at the station also **exchanges money.**

Centro Turistico Studentesco (CTS): via Genova, 16 (tel. 44 67 91), off via Nazionale, which veers off p. della Repubblica. Information on ISIC and YIEE cards, non-student plane, train, boat, and bus discounts, in addition to a free map and the brochure *Young Rome.* An accommodations service (including out-of-town reservations). A bulletin board with notices from people seeking and offering rides, companionship, special services, etc. Open Mon.-Fri. 9am-1pm and 4-7pm, Sat. 9am-1pm. **Branch offices** at via Appia Nuova, 434 (tel. 785 79 06), in the southwestern part of the city, and via Banchi Vecchi, 138 (tel. 654 78 83), west of p. Navona near p. di Chiesa Nuova. Open Mon.-Fri. 9:30am-1pm and 4-7pm, Sat. 9:30am-1pm.

Italian Youth Hostels Association (AIG): via Carlo Poma, 2 (tel. 359 92 95 or 38 59 43), off p. Mazzini and via Brofferio, north of the Vatican. No beds here but plenty of advice and lists of hostels throughout Italy. IYH cards L15,000. Open Mon.-Sat. 8am-2pm.

Embassies: U.S., via Vittorio Veneto, 119A (tel. 467 41). Consular and passport services Mon.-Fri. 8:30am-5:15pm. **Canada,** via Zara, 30 (tel. 844 18 41). Consular and passport services Sept. 3-July 17 Mon.-Fri. 10am-noon and 2-4pm; July 18-Sept. 2 Mon.-Fri. 10am-2pm. **U.K.,** via XX Settembre, 80/A (tel. 475 54 41). Consular and passport services Sept. 3-July 17 Mon.-Fri. 9:30am-12:30pm and 2-4pm; July 18-Sept. 2 8am-1pm. **Australia,** via Alessandria, 215 (tel. 83 27 21). Consular and passport services Mon.-Thurs. 9am-noon and 1:30-4pm, Fri. 9am-noon. **New Zealand,** via Zara, 28 (tel. 844 86 59). Consular and passport services Sept.-June Mon.-Fri. 8:30am-12:45pm and 1:45-5pm; July-Aug. Mon. and Thurs. 8am-5pm, Tues.-Wed. and Fri. 8am-2pm. All embassies maintain a 24-hour referral service in case of emergency.

Currency Exchange: Numismatica Internazionale, p. dei Cinquecento, 57/58, outside the train station on the left side of the *piazza* as you face away from the station. No commission. Open Mon.-Sat. 8am-7pm.

American Express: p. di Spagna, 38 (tel. 676 41; for lost or stolen cards 54 79 81; for lost or stolen checks toll-free 167 87 20 00). Chaotic at times, but fairly efficient. Mail pick-up free with AmEx card or traveler's checks, otherwise L1500. Mail is held for 30 days, after which it can be forwarded to another address by surface mail for a L4500 fee upon arrival, or by airmail with prepaid postage. Messages can be left in the office in a stamped envelope for L1000. There's no need to change checks here, as you can get the same rate, also without commission, at any of the small *cambio* stores all over the city, where there are also shorter lines. Open Mon.-Fri. 9am-5pm, Sat. 9am-noon.

Post Office: Main Office, p. San Silvestro, 28 (tel. 67 71), near p. di Spagna off via del Tritone. Stamps at booths #22 and 23. Fermo Posta at booths #58 and 60 (L250 per letter). Open Mon.-Fri. 8:30am-8pm, Sat 8:30am-noon. **Telegrams** can be sent from p. San Silvestro, 18, next door. Open 24 hours. Unsealed packages under 1kg (500g for Australia) can be mailed from San Silvestro; otherwise they must be mailed from **p. dei Caprettari,** near the Pantheon. Open Mon.-Fri. 8:30am-3:30pm. Parcels sealed with tape or glue will be charged at the higher letter rate. A 2nd parcel office is on **via della Terme;** the entrance is on via Viminale. Open Mon.-Fri. 8:30am-6pm. Stamps (*francobolli*) are available at most *tabacchi.* Letters within Europe L650, post cards L500. Overseas letters L1050, postcards L850. **Vatican Post Office,** p. San Pietro. Service that is several days quicker and somewhat more reliable. Open Mon.-Fri. 8:30am-7pm, Sat. 8:30am-6pm. No Fermo posta. Will mail packages up to 1kg. **DHL Worldwide,** via Labicana, 78b (tel. 724 21), southwest of Termini near the Colosseum. Will deliver packages overnight anywhere in the U.S., Canada, or Europe (L40,000). Open Mon.-Fri. 9am-5:30pm. **Postal code:** 00100.

Telephones: ASST, p. San Silvestro (tel. 679 61 91), next to the main post office. Open Mon.-Sat. 8am-11:30pm, Sun. 9am-8:30pm. Agonizing lines. Americans can use AT&T calling cards by dialing 111 99 39 05 55. Also 2 offices at Termini (tel. 474 56 89 or 474 57 13), one on the ground level and one downstairs. Either one or both open 24 hours. **SIP,** corso V. Emanuele, 201, near p. Navona. Open 8am-9pm. Also in the Villa Borgese parking lot. Open same hours. For general telephone information, dial 12. For collect calls in Europe, dial 15. For intercontinental collect calls, dial 170. **Telephone code:** 06.

Train Station: Stazione Termini (tel. 47 75; for reservations 110; for *direzione* 48 48 19). Continually busy phone lines open daily 7am-10:40pm. Information in many languages, money exchange until late (don't rely on it Sun. evenings), and luggage storage (open 7:20am-8:40pm, L1100 per piece per day). Food here is expensive. Sleeping here is also expensive—it could cost you your life. Open 24 hours. 7 smaller stations in the suburbs.

Trains: Trip times given are for *diretto* trains, unless otherwise indicated. To **Florence** on the Naples-Milan, Rome-Verona, or Rome-Trieste lines (3½ hr., L15,600). To **Venice** 9 per day on the Rome-Trieste line (7½ hr., L28,000). If you plan to visit Florence and then Venice within 3 days of one another, you need only buy 1 ticket for Venice. To **Naples** on the Rome-Naples, Rome-Campobasso-Naples, Rome-Bari, and Rome-Syracuse lines (2½ hr., L10,700). **To Greece:** Take the train to Brindisi, whence ferries leave for Greece. 2 direct trains per day at 1:05pm (*rapido,* arriving 8:54pm), 9:05pm (*rapido,* arriving 7:53am). Also one at 10:25pm July 2-Sept. 10 (*rapido,* arriving 9:55am). Otherwise, take one of 2 trains to Bari, switching trains there for Brindisi at 7:15am (*rapido,* arriving Brindisi at 2:05pm) and at 9:05am (arriving Brindisi at 5:02pm). Train fare L34,100, plus L6900 surcharge for *rapido.* Information and tickets for boats from Brindisi are available at **Hellenic Mediterranean Lines,** via Umbria, 21 (tel. 474 01 41; open Mon.-Fri. 9am-1pm and 2-6pm). Boats leave from Brindisi daily at 10:30pm; in summer several times per day. See also Brindisi Practical Information.

Transalpino: p. Esquilino, 8A (tel. 475 10 75 or 475 10 64). 40-50% youth discounts on international train tickets. Open Mon.-Fri. 9am-7pm, Sat. 9am-1pm. Also at a booth in Termini aisle #6 (tel. 460 536). Open daily 8:30am-9:30pm.

Regional Buses: Acotral, via Ostiense, 131 (tel. 575 31), or via Portanaccio, 25 (tel. 57 98). These offices are far from the city center and there is no guarantee of finding an English speaker. EPT or CIT can provide all necessary information and directions. Stops located throughout the city.

City Buses: ATAC, via Volturno, 65 (tel. 46 95). Bus maps L1000. Also at the booth near Termini in p. dei Cinquecento. Both open daily 7:15am-7:15pm.

Taxi: On 24-hour radio call, and can be flagged down on the street. Fare L2800 plus L266 per minute. L500 per piece of luggage. L3000 surcharge 10pm-7am. No charge per number of passengers. Taxicab companies include La Capitale (tel. 49 94), Cooperativa Radio Taxi Romana (tel. 35 70), and Cosmos (tel. 84 33). Always be sure your taxi-driver is official, otherwise you will be overcharged.

Car Rental: Avis, p. dell' Esquilino, 38A (tel. 470 12 16). Open Mon.-Fri. 8am-1pm and 4:20-7pm, Sat. 8am-1pm. **Hertz,** via Sallustiana, 28 (tel. 54 79 91). Open Mon.-Sat. 7am-8pm, Sun. 7am-1:30pm and 5-7:30pm. **Maggiore,** p. della Repubblica, 57/58 (tel. 475 50 37). Open Mon.-Fri. 8:30am-1pm and 2:30-7pm, Sat. 8:30am-1pm. **Budget,** via Sistina, 24/B (tel. 48 48 10 or 46 19 05). **Europcar,** via Lombardia, 7 (tel. 54 90 42 26). **Prestige,** via Marco Aurelio, 47/B (tel. 73 25 42). Open Mon.-Sat. 8am-8pm, Sun. 8am-1pm and 3-8pm. Avis and Hertz may be more dependable but the others are cheaper. Prestige quotes the lowest rates at L168,000 plus L410 per km. The most economic cars are L300,000-500,000 per week with unlimited mileage. However, nonresidents of Italy are eligible for discounts of up to 60%. It is best to reserve from home. Rates do not include insurance and Italy's steep 18% tax. Moreover, all agencies require either a credit card or a minimum deposit of L200,000 in cash. You must be at least 21 years of age with a valid international driver's license. Avis, Hertz, Maggiore, and Europcar all operate booths on the east side of Termini.

Guided Sightseeing Tours: For those on a tight schedule, a hasty but complete air-conditioned bus tour of the city's principal sights might do the trick. **Carrani Tours,** via V.E. Orlando (tel. 46 05 10), off p. della Repubblica, is the oldest and most reliable firm in the city and offers 40% discounts to students. Tours leave daily at 9am—they will pick you up at your hotel at 8:15am free of charge—and last 3 hours. Four different tours are offered, each hitting different sights. (Students L17,200). Also offers a number of bus tours from Rome to other cities in Italy (L28,000). **Pioneer Line,** via Filippo Turati, 43 (tel. 73 42 34), offers the most complete tour of St. Peter's and the Vatican Museums (L43,000, students L25,800, including admission to the museums). They also offer a comprehensive, 1-day tour of the entire city (L58,000, students L34,800). Buses leave at 9am daily—they will pick you up at your hotel at 8:15am (free).

Scooter-Bike Rental: Scooters for Rent, via della Purificazione, 13/14 (tel. 46 54 85), off p. Barberini. Bikes L15,000 per day. Vespas and motorcycles L30,000-65,000 per day. Rates go down the longer you rent. Deposit L200-600. Minimum age 16 for Vespa models, 21 for motorcycles; valid driver's license required for both. Open daily 9am-7:30pm.

Lost Property: Oggeti Rinvenuti, via Nicolò Bettoni, 1 (tel. 581 60 40). Open 9am-noon. Also try Termini aisle #1 (tel. 473 06 82) or the **Ufficio Stranieri** (see below). For objects lost on city buses, contact ATAC, via Volturno, 65 (tel. 46 95).

English Language Bookstores: Economy Book and Video Center, via Torino, 136 (tel. 474 68 77), off via Nazionale, which runs off p. della Repubblica. New and old books. Will buy books, too. Also at p. di Spagna. Open July-Sept. Mon.-Fri. 9:30am-7:30pm, Sat. 9:30am-1:30pm; Oct.-June Mon. 3:30-7:30pm, Tues.-Sat. 9:30am-7:30pm. **American Book Shop,** via della Vite, 57 (tel. 679 52 22). Lots of new hardbacks and books on Italy. Open July-Aug. Mon.-Fri. 9am-1pm and 4-8pm, Sat. 9am-1pm; Sept.-June Mon. 3:30-7:30pm, Tues.-Sat. 9am-1pm and 3:30-7:30pm. **The Lion Bookshop,** via del Babuino, 181 (tel. 678 96 29), near p. del Popolo. Good for literature. Open June-July Mon.-Fri. 9am-1pm and 3:30-7:30pm, Sat. 9am-1pm; Sept.-May Mon. 3:30-7:30pm, Tues.-Sat. 9am-1pm and 3:30-7:30pm. **Open Door Bookshop,** via della Lungaretta (tel. 589 64 78). New and used literature, music, and art books. Open July-Sept. Mon.-Sat. 10am-1:30pm and 4-8pm; Oct.-June Mon. 4-8pm, Tues.-Sat. 10am-1:30pm and 4-8pm.

English Language Libraries: USIS (United States Information Service), via Veneto, 119A (tel. 467 41), off p. Barberini. Mostly non-fiction and magazines. Only Rome residents can take books out. Open Sept.-July Mon.-Tues. and Thurs.-Fri. 1:30-5:30pm, Wed. 1:30-7pm. **British Council Library,** via Quattro Fontane, 20 (tel. 475 66 41), on the street that runs between p. Barberini and via Nazionale. Lots of fiction. Also films and lectures. Borrowing privileges with membership only (1-yr. membership L25,000). Open Sept. 6-July 9 Mon.-Fri. 10am-1pm and 2-6pm. **Centro Studi Americani,** via Michelangelo Caetani, 32 (tel. 654 16 13), off p. Mattei in a large *palazzo* on the 2nd floor. Borrowing allowed with deposit. Open Sept.-June 26 Mon.-Tues. and Thurs.-Fri. 9:30am-5pm, Wed. 3-7pm; June 27-July 26 Mon., Wed., and Fri. 8:30am-2:30pm, Tues. and Thurs. 10am-6pm.

Laundromats: Lavaservice, via Montebello, 11 (tel. 474 55 03), east of Termini. Not self-service. Make sure that laundries don't put your clothes in more washers than you need. Open Mon.-Fri. 9am-7pm, Sat. 9am-1pm. **Laundry,** via dei Serpenti, 131 (tel. 46 33 95), 1½ blocks off via Cavour, near the Colosseum. Open Mon.-Fri. 8am-1pm and 3-7:30pm. **Lavasecco a gettone, p. campo dei Fiori, 38 (tel. 678 90 96). Open Sept. to mid-Aug. Mon.-Fri. 9am-7:30pm. Also at via Castelfidardo, 29, near Termini. Open Mon.-Fri. 9:30am-1pm and 3:30-7:30pm, Sat. 9:30am-1pm. Laundromats charge by weight: L9000-10,000 for a minimum load of 3-4kg.**

Public Baths: Albergo Diurno Stazione Termini (tel. 475 57 76), underground in the station. Showers L6000. Towels L1000. Soap L500. Open daily 6:40am-8:40pm.

Swimming Pools: Piscina delle Rose, viale America, 20 (tel. 592 67 17). Take subway line B to the EUR Marconi stop. An outdoor pool. Morning swim L5500 (Sun. L6500), afternoon swim L6500 (Sun. L8000). Open May 28-Sept. 4 daily 9am-12:30pm and 2-7pm.

Beaches: The closest beach to Rome is **Lido di Ostia,** 28km away. Not especially clean, it is an adequate seaside resort nonetheless. Take subway line B from Termini to the Piramide stop and switch trains for the beach (6am-10:30pm every 15 min., 45 min.; L700 for the metro, L700 for the train). Buy both tickets at Termini.

Crisis Hotline: Samaritans, Chiesa di San Silvestro, p. San Silvestro (tel. 678 92 27). English-speaking. Phones answered 4:30-10:30pm; at other times, leave a message.

Pharmacies: Inside **Termini** (tel. 46 07 66). Open Sept.-July 7am-11pm. **All-Night pharmacy: Farmacia Internazionale Antonucci,** p. Barberini, 49 (tel. 46 29 96), between the train station and the Spanish Steps. Take bus #60, 61, or 62. **Late-Night Pharmacies:** Tel. 19 21 for recorded listings in Italian.

V.D. Clinic: San Gallicano, via dei Fratte di Trastevere, 34 (tel. 581 37 41 or 58 48 31). Small free clinic operated by nuns. Open Mon.-Fri. 8-10am.

Hospitals: Salvator Mundi, viale delle Mura Gianicolensi, 67 (tel. 58 60 41). Expensive private clinic. You are guaranteed English-speaking doctors. **Policlinico Umberto I,** viale de Policlinico, 55 (tel. 49 23 41). A free, public facility close to the train station. **Policlinico A. Gemelli,** largo A. Gemelli, 8 (tel. 330 51 for administration, 338 69 22 for information). A university complex farther from the town center.

Medical Emergency: Red Cross (tel. 51 00). An ambulance service that cannot guarantee that you will be delivered to an English-speaking hospital. All hospitals, however, have staff members conversant in English.

Police: Ufficio Stranieri (Foreigners' Dept.), at the Police Headquarters (*Questura*), via S. Vitale, 15 (tel. 46 86), on the street entrance marked via Genova. English spoken. Report thefts here. Ufficio Stranieri also maintains a **lost and found.** Open 24 hours.

Accommodations

In summer, Rome splits at the seams with backpackers, students, and camera-toters. Fortunately, Rome offers a vast array of rooms, ranging from the one-star pensioni to *locande* (unrated hotels) to *alberghi* (hotels; some, 5-star luxury affairs). The best bargains fill quickly; make reservations well in advance. Some places require a first-night deposit; others only a telephone call. If you are unable to reserve, get here early in the morning. Prices vary substantially with the time of year and with the thickness of your accent. Always try to bargain down a price; most establishments have at least one person nearby who speaks some English, and a proprietor's willingness to bargain over rooms and rates increases in proportion to the length of your stay, the number of vacancies, and the size of your group. Make sure you are not charged more than the price the hotel is required to post on the front door of your room.

The EPT tourist offices (see Practical Information) will scrounge to find you a room. Go to the main office for the most help. The **Centro Turistico Studentesco e Giovanile (CTS),** via Genova, 16 (tel. 47 99 31), will also sometimes help you find a place. The **Protezione della Giovane** (tel. 475 15 94) maintains an office in the train station and will assist women in finding convent accommodations and moderately priced rooms. (The office is staffed when someone is available.)

Whatever you do, steer clear of the many "official"-looking people crawling all over Termini and offering to help you find a place. They will likely direct you to a run-down location where you may pay 50% more than the going rate. Authentic tourism officials carry photographic identification issued by the EPT.

If the queue at the tourist office extends to infinity, check your bags at the station and investigate the streets around Termini. It's not hard to find a *pensione.* Several establishments often operate in a single building. If you are hanging around for more than one night, it is best to steer clear of establishments in the dirty, crowded, and inconvenient train station area.

It is illegal and ill-advised to attempt to "camp out" in the public places of Rome. Though violent crime is surprisingly rare, dozing tourists invite trouble.

Hotels and Pensioni

East of Termini

The area to your right as you leave Termini offers a miscellany of cheap rooms. Although run-down, it is not particularly dangerous; all that remains of what used to be a Red Light District are two struggling porn theaters and the prostitution at the Diocletian Baths, a couple of blocks away. Don't despair at the labyrinthine nature of the district: Facing away from the station, follow via Marsala left and it will lead into via Volturno; as you walk northwest along via Volturno, via Gaeta, via Calatafimi, and then via Montebello will all intersect; take via Gaeta to get to the streets running parallel to via Volturno (via Palestro and via Castelfidaro).

Pensione Papà Germano, via Calatafimi, 14A (tel. 48 69 19), off via Volturno. Clean rooms, great showers, and some of the lowest prices in Rome have made Mamma and Papà Germano, the genial young couple running the place, something of a legend among backpackers. English spoken. Singles L18,000. Doubles L34,000, with bath L42,000. Triples L14,000 per person. Nov.-March triples L12,000 per person, L3000-7000 reductions in all other rooms. Phone reservations accepted a day in advance. The proprietor will help you find a room if the hotel is already booked (with commission).

Pensione Lachea, via San Martino della Battaglia, 11 (tel. 495 72 56). Follow via Solferino, which becomes via San Martino, off via Marsala. A warm-hearted owner and plenty of comfort make the bargain prices secondary. Singles L20,000. Doubles 30,000. Triples 45,000.

Pensione Katty, via Palestro, 35 (tel. 404 12 16), on the 3rd floor. Rooms less than elegant, but tidy and habitable. Price is the lure. Triples L12,000 per person. Doubles L26,000. Curfew midnight. **Locanda Marini** (tel. 404 13 80), next door, is listed in Frommer's, but we won't hold it against the place. Adequate rooms L10,000 per person. Doubles L28,000. They often charge L3000 per shower.

Pensione Cervia, via Palestro, 55 (tel. 404 13 77). Affable management. Meticulously maintained, though the facilities themselves are somewhat aged. Singles L18,000. Large doubles L30,000. Multi-bedded rooms L15,000 per person. Phone reservations recommended, but there's no guarantee the room will be held after noon without a deposit. Curfew 2am.

Pensione Restivo (tel 49 21 72), on the 3rd floor, edges out its competitor downstairs by offering rooms that are spotless and more pleasant. Excellent beds. Gregarious management. The older woman doesn't speak English and prefers dialect to Italian. Doubles L32,000. Triples L45,000.

Petit Hotel Asmara, via Castelfidardo, 31 (tel. 474 28 94), on the 3rd floor. The prices here approach unaffordable, but the rooms and hallways are commodious and clean. English spoken. L20,000 per person. Singles L22,000. Doubles L35,000, with bath L45,000. **Pensione Blanda** (tel. 494 13 78), on the 4th floor, is tidy and reasonable.

Pensione Ercoli, via Collina, 48 (tel. 474 54 54), on the 3rd floor. A 15-min. walk from the station: Take via Goito from p. Indipendenza, cross via XX Settembre onto via Piave, then take your 1st left on via Flavia, which leads to via Collina. In a much safer area than the other choices around Termini. The young, English-speaking management is personable and enjoys students. Rooms and bathrooms in perfect order. Singles L20,000. Doubles L30,000, with shower L34,000. Breakfast L5000. **Pensione Tizi** (tel. 474 32 66), 1 floor below, is equally pleasant, but could use a bit of restoration. Singles L20,500. Doubles L30,000, with shower L34,000. Breakfast L5000.

Pensione Monaco, via Flavia, 84 (tel. 474 43 35), around the corner from Ercoli. Spacious and orderly rooms and a strict midnight curfew behind double-locked doors. Humdrum atmosphere, but an inspirational bargain. Singles L19,000. Doubles L29,000. Triples L39,150. Breakfast L5500. Daily shower permitted.

Pensione Blanda, via Castelfidardo, 31 (tel. 46 47 56), on the 4th floor. A homey decor. Beware that the owners' child is a human alarm clock. Singles L20,000. Doubles L30,000. Triples L42,000.

Pensione Danubio, via Palestro, 34 (tel. 404 13 05). The ideal retreat for those with lingering lire. Tranquil surroundings. English management. Singles L25,000. Doubles L42,000, with shower L47,000. Triples L60,000. Hall showers L1500 per 8 min. Breakfast included. They'll do your wash for you (L8000), and an iron is available. Flexible midnight curfew.

Pensione Cristallo, via Montebello, 114 (tel. 404 13 29), on the 2nd floor. One of many *pensioni* in this building crammed with low-priced rooms. But a cut above the rest: high ceilings, carpeting, and glass light fixtures. Single L22,000. Doubles L35,000.

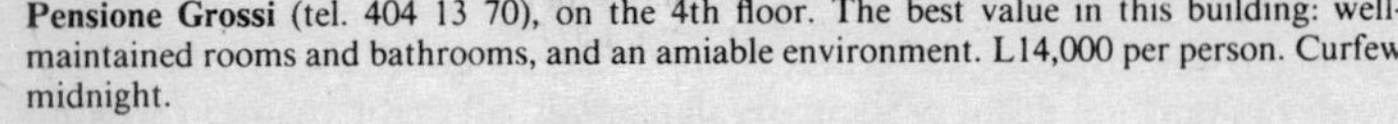

Pensione Grossi (tel. 404 13 70), on the 4th floor. The best value in this building: well-maintained rooms and bathrooms, and an amiable environment. L14,000 per person. Curfew midnight.

Pensione Cina, via Montebello, 114 (tel. 404 13 79), on the 4th floor. Run by an odd man. Tiny rooms L12,000 per person. Doubles L30,000. Curfew 1am.

Pensione Manita (tel. 404 13 77), on the 3rd floor. The epitome of mayhem: boarding house environment with as many as 5 people per room. L13,000 per person; Nov.-March L1000 less. Small doubles L28,000.

West of Termini

The area to your left as you leave the station is busier and noisier than the area to the right, but it offers a comparable selection of affordable accommodations. To avoid confusion among the crisscrossing streets, remember that via Principe Amadeo runs parallel with the west side of the station 2 blocks over and can be reached by taking any of the side streets that intersect via Giovanni Giolitti outside the west exit of the station. Note that the closer you get to piazza V. Emanuele, the seedier the area becomes at night.

Hotel Pezzotti, via Principe Amadeo, 79a (tel. 73 46 33), on the 2nd floor. Go in the entrance to the left as you enter the courtyard. The best choice on this *albergo*-happy street. Jolly Signor Pezzotti loves sharing his decent rooms with delighted tourists. Singles L20,000. Doubles L16,500 per person. Showers included. Breakfast L5000.

Pensione di Rienzo, via Principe Amadeo, 79a (tel. 73 69 56), on the 1st floor, and **Pensione Cotorillo** (tel. 731 60 64), on the 5th floor. Both in the same building as Pezzotti—enter through the door to the right as you enter the courtyard. This dynamic duo of *albergi* is second only to their neighbor across the courtyard. English spoken at both. Di Renzo's bathrooms smell sweeter than *gelato.* Singles L22,200. Doubles L34,500. Breakfast L5000. Cotorillo is slightly nicer. Singles L24,000. Doubles L32,000. Breakfast L6000. Showers included.

Pensione Morgana, via Turati, 37 (tel. 73 48 74), on a street parallel to via Principe Amadeo. 3 young Roman brothers offer over 60 different rooms that are worth every red lire of their slightly higher prices. Safe. The rooms on the upper levels are least expensive. Free storage during daytrips. English spoken and preferred. Singles L35,000-45,000. Doubles L40,000-60,000, with bath L50,000-70,000. 35% more per additional person. Showers included. Credit cards accepted. The doorman at Morgana has also just opened a *pensione* next door—spanking-new rooms with fresh paint and shining fixtures. L15,000-20,000 per person. Call the Morgana and ask for Luigi Romano.

Pensione Tony, via Principe Amadeo, 79/D (tel. 73 69 94), on the 5th floor. Immaculate rooms with genial management. English spoken. Flexible curfew midnight. Singles L25,000. Doubles L35,000, with shower L40,000. Showers free.

Pensione Eureka/Arrivederci p. della Repubblica, 49 (tel. 475 58 06). Agreeable, and the statues and murals in the entry make you feel right at Rome. English-speaking management. Singles L24,000, with shower L27,000. Doubles L41,000, with shower L46,500. Breakfast included. Curfew 1am.

Pensione Weltzer (tel. 475 19 94), on the 5th floor. Although this place has a German name, Mamma Clara, the cranky though affectionate *padrone* runs it 100% Italian style. The 5 rooms tend toward the disorderly, but are cozy. Doubles L23,000. Breakfast L3500. Curfew midnight.

Pensione Terni, via Principe Amadeo, 62 (tel. 474 54 28), on the 1st floor through the entryway to the left. Light wood and bright colors make this place agreeable. Immigrants frequently occupy the rooms for long periods. Doubles L35,000. Curfew midnight. Reservations with deposit. **Pensione Fiorini** (tel. 46 50 65), on the 5th floor through the entryway to the right in the same building. Rooms that wallow in the midst of dismal gray wallpaper. Comfortable beds. Singles L25,000. Doubles L36,000, with bath L45,000. Showers included. Breakfast L4500. Elevator L10. Curfew midnight.

The Everest, via Cavour, 47 (tel. 46 16 29), on the 2nd floor. Outside of the floral wallpaper that hits you in the entry, the place is an uninspiring bargain. Singles L19,800. Doubles L30,000, with shower L35,000. Triples L39,000. Breakfast included.

Pensione Chèrie, via Cavour, 238 (tel. 474 17 89), at largo Visconti Venosta across from via Cavour subway stop. A tail-wagging dog welcomes you to one of the cleanest and friendliest bargains in the city. Reserve early. 6 have balconies with impressive views. English spoken. Doubles L45,000, with shower, L50,000, with bath, L52,000. Triples L70,000, with bath or shower, L75,000. Breakfast included. Bargaining is encouraged.

Hotel San Paolo, via Panisperna, 95 (tel. 474 52 13), at via Caprareccia. Signor Reuben, the elderly owner, doesn't mind that his place is named for a saint, or that his rooms have uneven floors and unsightly decorations. All are clean, and Mr. R. is a gracious host conversant in English and Yiddish. Singles L18,000-20,000. Doubles L28,000, with bath L38,000. Curfew midnight.

Near the Spanish Steps

The chic shopping district around Piazza di Spagna harbors refined buildings, gurgling fountains, and luxurious promenades. Inexpensive accommodations are rare, and the zone suffers from a paucity of grocery stores and restaurants.

Pensione Fiorella, via del Babuino, 196 (tel. 361 05 97), off p. di Spagna before p. del Popolo. Only the strict 1am curfew detracts from this tiny place with courteous management. Some English spoken. Singles L24,500. Doubles L43,000. Breakfast included.

Pensione Irene, via del Lavatore, 37 (tel. 679 11 31), off p. di Trevi south of p. di Spagna. It's on an enchanting side street a coin's throw away from the famous fountain, but the innards of this *pensione* are somewhat less noteworthy. Little fresh air seeps into the rooms, and no hot water seeps into the showers in summer. Nonetheless, a steal in this area. English spoken. Singles L15,500. Doubles L26,000. Triples L38,000. Showers L2500.

Pensione Parlamento, via delle Convertite, 5 (tel. 678 78 80), off v. del Corso on the street leading to p. San Silvestro. Carpeting, high ceilings, and velvet couches make these rooms the cream of the budget crop. Unfortunately, management plans a massive rate hike soon. Singles L33,000. Doubles L44,000, with shower L54,000, with bath L60,000. Triples L64,000, with shower L74,000, with bath L80,000. Breakfast L6000.

Pensione Doge, via due Macelli, 106 (tel. 678 00 38), off p. Mignanelli to the right of p. di Spagna, facing the steps, on the 4th floor. The cats sacked out in the hallways add to the eccentric olive and blue interior design. Clean and comfortable. Singles L40,000. Doubles with bath L70,000. Triples with bath L97,500. Breakfast included.

Pensione Erdarelli, via due Macelli, 28 (tel. 679 12 65), across from Doge. Expensive, but telephones in rooms, a television lounge, and optional A/C (L12,000). Pleasant breakfast lounge. Singles L37,800, with bath L46,000. Doubles L67,600, with bath L78,500. Breakfast included. Reservations with deposit.

Pensione Manfredi, via Margutta, 61 (tel. 679 47 35), just off p. di Spagna. Take via Aliberti off via del Babuino. On a quiet, posh street. Although this 3rd floor, family-run *pensione* is beginning to show signs of wear, there's a fully-stocked fridge in each room (you pay for what you consume, of course). English spoken. Doubles L57,000, with shower L69,000, with full bath L80,000. Triples L74,000, with shower L94,000, with full bath L110,000. Breakfast included.

Around Piazza Navona

Possibly the best base for the adventuresome traveler is Vecchia Roma (Old Rome), the demonstrative and impromptu area that surrounds piazza Navona.

Albergo Sole, via del Biscione, 76 (tel. 654 08 73). Take via dei Baullari off corso V. Emanuele. Inattentive management and general chaos—embodies the psychotic piazza Navona area. Parking lot. English spoken. Singles L18,000-22,000, with bath L27,000. Doubles L34,000-37,000, with bath L50,000.

Albergo Della Lunetta, p. del Paradiso, 68 (tel. 656 10 80), around the corner from Albergo Sole. An indifferent management presides over these clean if mediocre habitations. Singles L19,200, with bath L31,500. Doubles L34,500, with bath L52,800. Make reservations with deposit far in advance.

Pensione Sinatti, via del Seminario, 87 (tel. 679 49 35). Take via di Torre Argentina north and follow it all the way to p. Rotonda; the hotel is to your right as you stand with your back to the Pantheon. Gracious management in an ideal location, though the lackluster rooms are something of a let down. English spoken. Singles L22,000. Doubles L38,000. Breakfast L3000.

Pensione Primavera, p. San Pantaleo, 3 (tel. 654 31 09), off corso V. Emanuele south of p. Navona. Small, clean rooms, all in slight disrepair. Considerable noise in rooms facing the *piazza.* English spoken. Doubles L46,000. Triples L69,000. Showers L2000. Breakfast included (if you specify that you don't want breakfast, the price will shrink L5000).

Petit Hotel Arenula, v. Santa Maria de' Calderari, 47 (tel. 687 94 54). Take v. Arenula from largo Torre Argentina and turn left at p. Cairoli. The amiable management does its best to keep this comfortable place spotless, but the rain has stubbornly left its mark on some of the rooms' ceilings and walls. Telephones in every room; phone booth for international calls. English spoken. Singles L20,000, with shower L23,000, with full bath L28,000. Doubles L30,000, with shower L34,000, with full bath L47,000.

Pensione Navona, via dei Sediari, 8 (tel. 686 42 03). Take via de' Canestrari off p. Navona and cross over corso del Rinascimento. The sociable English-speaking family makes the place your home for the duration of your stay. Singles L30,500. Doubles L53,000, with bath L60,000. L24,500 per additional person. Breakfast included.

Albergo Abruzzi, p. della Rotonda, 69 (tel. 679 20 21), smack-dab in front of the Pantheon. Tidy rooms, but the mattresses are about as comfy as the Colosseum steps. Professional but impersonal management. Prices vary with room size. Singles L24,000-29,500. Doubles L43,000-52,000. Triples L58,000-70,000. Reserve at least 1 month in advance with deposit in summer.

Across the River

The *pensioni* on the other side of the Tiber lie primarily in two areas: **Ottaviano,** near the Vatican, attractive for its proximity to the numerous sights in the area of St. Peter's, and **Trastevere,** down the river, a popular district for nighttime hedonism. Bus #64 from p. del Cinquecento and 81 from corso Cavour at S. Maria Maggiore, as well as subway line A, all run to Ottaviano. Buses #75 from p. Indipendenza, 60 from via XX Settembre, and 170 from p. del Cinquecento all run from near Termini to Trastevere.

Pensione Ottaviano, via Ottaviano, 6 (tel. 38 39 56), off p. del Risorgimento just east of p. S. Pietro. The sharp, congenial owner recruits arriving backpackers at the train station into his hostel-style *pensione.* A glance at the crowded rooms with 4-6 bunks each will explain why he has to make the effort. Nevertheless, a personable and safe place, conveniently located, and cheap at L15,000 per bed. English spoken.

Hotel Amalia, v. Germanico, 66 (tel. 31 45 19). From p. del Risorgimento, take the 1st left off via Ottaviano. Immaculate if not inspirational; telephones in the rooms. English spoken. Singles L23,500. Doubles L40,000. Triples L54,000. Quartet of sacks L70,000. Breakfast L5000.

Pensione Zurigo, via Germanico, 198 (tel. 35 01 39). From p. del Risorgimento, take a right off via Ottaviano. This spic-and-span, spacious place runs like clock-work thanks to a management that even monitors its downstairs lobby with a TV camera. A television lounge with piano and an elevator that doesn't require coins. Doubles L42,000, with shower L52,000. L16,000 per additional person. Breakfast L3500. **Pensione Nautilus** (tel. 31 55 49), downstairs, has the exact same management and exactly the same prices, though the rooms are slightly more modern. English spoken. Make reservations for stays longer than 1 week.

Residence Guiggioli (tel. 31 52 09), in the same building as Zurigo and Nautilus. A tiny place administered by an older woman and her tame pooch. If you chance upon one of the 5 rooms, you're in for a real treat. The matrimonial suite is commodious, with a lovely, antique mahogany dresser and private bath for L52,000. Doubles without bath L40,000. L15,000 per additional person. Full breakfast L8000.

Pensione Alimandi, via Tunisi, 8 (tel. 679 93 43). Take the steps off viale Vaticano down onto via Sebastiano Veniero, and go straight—literally feet away from the Vatican Museum. A gorgeous place, with a beautiful garden patio on the 1st floor and a terrace on the roof. Telephones in every room. TV lounge with electric piano. Bar with reasonably-priced drinks. Filled with sociable students. The beds are cots, however, and showers shared with 10 others. Singles L28,000. Doubles L33,000, with bath L65,000. Triples L77,000, with bath L90,000. Curfew 1am. Reservation essential.

Pensione Silla, via Silla, 3 (tel. 35 19 22), off via Germanico. Large, primitive rooms are clean, but show signs of wear. Singles L25,000. Doubles L48,000. Triples L65,000, with bath 95,000. Breakfast L8000.

Pensione Manara, via Luciano Manara, 25 (tel. 589 07 19). Take a right off viale Trastevere onto via delle Fratte di Trastevere straight to via Luciano Manara. Well furnished and in the middle of the Trastevere area action, but cluttered atmosphere. English spoken. Doubles L32,000. Triples L42,500. Showers L3000.

Pensione Esty, viale Trastevere, 108 (tel. 589 12 01), about ½km down viale Trastevere from p. Sonnino. Somewhat removed from the rowdy heart of Trastevere. Rooms are tidy, if lacking in character. Affable, English-speaking management. Singles L24,000. Doubles L36,000. Triples L48,000.

Institutional and Student Accommodations

Staying in institutions is not the ticket to a raucous time in Rome. Both the IYHF and the various religious organizations institute curfews that keep you locked away from Rome at its best; you won't save enough money to make this worthwhile.

Ostello del Foro Italico (IYHF), viale delle Olimpiadi, 61 (tel. 396 47 09). Take bus #492 to the last stop and then #32. Inconveniently located and institutional. 350 beds. 3-night maximum (extensions granted when vacancies exist). Lockers are provided, though management takes no responsibility for valuables. L11,000. Breakfast and shower included. Open 2-11pm. Lockout 9am. IYHF card required and can be purchased at the desk. To reserve, write to AIG, lungotevere Maresciallo Cadorna, 31, 00194 Rome (tel. 396 00 09).

YWCA, via Cesare Balbo, 4 (tel. 46 04 60), off via Torino, west of Termini. Women only. Beds in simple, safe rooms. No bargain: Singles L26,000. Doubles L40,000. Triples L51,000. Breakfast and shower included. Curfew midnight. Oct.-July lunch L10,000.

University Housing: In recent summers, **AIG,** the Italian Youth Hostel organization, has inaugurated an experimental program in conjunction with Rome's universities to provide housing for tourists in vacated student quarters (late July to mid-Sept.). The centers are via Cesare de Lollis, 24/B, and viale del Ministro degli Affari Esteri, 6. Bed and breakfast L12,500 per person. 1-week maximum. Contact the EPT at Termini or at via Parigi, 5 (tel. 46 37 48), or AIG, via Carlo Poma, 2 (tel. 369 92 95).

Religious Institutions: Convents, monasteries, and religious houses. Unless you have a personal reason for seeking such accommodations, it is unadvisable, as rooms often exceed L20,000 per night and strict curfews incarcerate you at 11pm. **Protezione della Giovane** at Termini (tel. 475 15 94; open erratic hours) can make arrangements. A letter of introduction from your own priest, pastor, or rabbi (on letterhead) might facilitate matters.

Camping

Admittedly, most travelers don't come to Rome for the wilderness, but if you arrive with sleeping bag under arm, options do exist. The closest and best campground is **Flaminio,** via Flaminia (tel. 327 90 06), 8km away. From Termini, take line A to Stazione Flaminio, and then bus #202, 204, or 205. (L7700 per person, L3200 per tent. Cars L3200, motorcycles L1300.) **Capitol Campground,** via di Castelfusano (tel. 566 27 20), in Ostia, Antica, is 3km from the ruins and offers a swimming pool and tennis courts. Take the train to Ostia Antica and walk the remaining 3km, or take the train to Lido Centro and bus #5 to the site. (L5000 per person, L2500 per tent. Cars L1900, motorcycles L1350.) Closer to Rome (11½km away) is **Nomentano,** via della Cesarina (tel. 610 02 96), at via Nomentana. Take bus #36 from Termini and switch to #337 at p. Sempione. (L6300 per person, L3200 per tent. Cars L3200, motorcycles L1400.)

Food

Meals in Rome are lengthy affairs, continuing for hours on end as each course is savored with uncharacteristic temperance. Corks fly off the local *Castelli Romani* wines, and a crispy *bruschetta,* a toasted piece of bread usually garnished with a little oil, garlic, and herbs, begins the meal. Later the pasta arrives, done either *alla*

Carbonara (with bacon and egg) or *all' Amatriciana* (with bacon, white wine, tomato, and pepper). Popular main courses are *saltimbocca* (slices of ham and veal cooked together) and *coda alla vaccinara* (stewed oxtail with vegetables). After hours of lingering, fruit and *espressos* are served. The final blow is a potent shot of *sambuca* (anise liqueur)—try it flaming with the traditional coffee beans floating on top.

When time fails, or when your empty stomach and empty wallet call for home-cooking, go to *alimentari* **for basic groceries,** *panetterie* for breads, cheeses, and basic processed meats, and *salsamentarie,* which combine the offerings of the other two stores. Rome's major supermarket chains, **SMA** and **GS,** don't operate stores near the city center. (Food stores open roughly Mon.-Fri. 8am-1pm and 5:30-8pm, Sat. 8am-1pm.) For the freshest provisions in the most vibrant atmosphere, visit the various **outdoor markets** especially the one in p. Vittorio Emanuele, not far from Termini. 'Za is sold in slices by weight at any place that brandishes the *pizza rustica* sign. An *etto* (100g) is perfect for a snack-attack. The rudimentary pizza sold in these shops, however, does not compare with the real variety made by hand at wood-burning oven pizzerias. A well-prepared pizza is light and crispy, served piping hot by the master craftsman, the *pizzailo* (pizza maker) himself. Other favorite Roman snacks are the *suppli al telefono,* a tasty, deep-fried rice ball with melted mozzarella in the middle, named for the long, telephone-chord-like strands that the mozzarella makes as you pull the treat away from your mouth, and *baccalà,* deep-fried cod fillets.

When dining out, simple *trattorie* do the trick for a sit-down meal. Stay away from the area near the train station and the places that print menus in English and solicit zealously—their cunning is more impressive than their cooking. Most ostensible "bargain" restaurants (offering dirt-cheap fixed-price menus) are actually second-rate snares for tourists. They serve nothing resembling Italian cuisine; their cooks, in fact, are often Arab immigrants. Instead of chowing near the station, hop on bus #71 for 10 minutes to reach the district of **San Lorenzo,** or head out on bus #27 to the area known as **Testaccio,** on the eastern banks of the Tiber. These are the last untouristed restaurant districts in Rome. Here establishment can't afford to rely on transient clientele—if they dare serve anything but the best food or charge unfair prices, they will be out of business in a snap. In the city center, hiding on the side streets of old Rome, are a number of excellent, affordable places. Try the areas around piazza Navona and Trastevere. The best places fill up immediately, so set out early to avoid the rush.

San Lorenzo

A quick bus ride west of Termini, San Lorenzo is in the midst of the *Città Universitaria.* Many unpretentious trattorias and pizzerias offer hearty and economical meals for the university students here in an atmosphere that encourages conversation.

Pizzeria L'Economica, via Tiburtina, 44 (tel. 495 66 69), on the main road of the bus route. The name says it all. The large family who runs this place also cooks up some of the most vicious 'za around, baking it in the wood-burning oven (from L2400 per *etto*). Or try the antipasto dish for an incredible L3500. Mineral water L700 per ½-liter. Open Sept.-July Mon.-Sat. 6:30-11pm.

Trattoria da Paolo, via dei Sapelli, 8 (tel. 49 17 96). Take via Porta L'Abicana off via Tiburtina and then take your 3rd left. A small, traditional *trattoria* that hasn't changed a bit since its doors first opened 50 years ago. The 90-year-old grandmother of the family still hand-rolls *pappardelle* pasta for an unbelievably low L4500. Other pastas L4000. *Spezzatino* (skewered meat) L5000. Wine L2000 per liter. The students and neighborhood rustics keep spirits high. Open Sept.-July Mon.-Sat. noon-3pm and 7-11pm.

La Tanasarda, via Tiburtina, 116 (tel. 49 35 50). Personable Sardinians run from table to table, piling plates high with wonderful delicacies. All meals start with a free basket of Sardinian *carta di musica,* paper thin, crisp bread. Romans rave about the *gnocchetti sardi* (twirled pasta with meat sauce) and the *ravioli sardi* (Sardinian ravioli filled with flavored ricotta).

The *cascio di tacchino al forno* (roast turkey leg) keeps forks, knives, and mouths in constant motion (L4000). Cover L1000. Open Sept.-July Mon.-Sat. noon-3:30pm and 7-11pm.

Pizzeria il Maratoneta, via dei Sardi, 20 (tel. 49 00 27), off via Tiburtina. 4 young marathon runners bake pizzas to titillate even the most discriminating tongue (L4000-5500). Their *Pizza Mare Monte* (Sea and Mountain pizza) is gorgeous—half is covered with tomatoes and marinated seafood, half piled high with tomatoes, mozzarella, mushrooms, eggplant, onion, zucchini, and peppers (L5500). Open Mon.-Sat. 6pm-12:15am.

Near the Station

There is no reason to inflict the gastronomic nightmare of the Termini restaurants on yourself. Locals avoid the restaurants here like the plague. Still, some places do better than others.

Trattoria L'Archetto, via Filippo Turati, 104/106 (tel. 73 03 18). Take via Manin off via Giolitti, then make the 1st left on via Turati and follow it down 300m. The honest, rustic family running this lovely new place have not yet learned that you can't serve fantastic food for a low price. Their provincial specialty is *taccumelle,* wonderful, square-shaped pasta with a zingy sauce of tomato, mushroom, and sausage (L5000). Also try *scamorza alla griglia,* fresh grilled scamorza cheese (L5000). Filling fixed menu L10,000. Wine L3000 per liter. Cover L1300, service 13%. Open Mon.-Sat. noon-3pm and 6:30-11pm.

Osteria con Cucina de Andreis Luciano, via Giovanni Amendola, 73-75 (tel. 46 16 40). Take via Cavour west from p. dei Cinquecento; via Giovanni Amendola is the 1st intersecting street. One of the few places whose silverware rarely touches the lips of tourists. The unglamorous place serves earthy, cheap, and generous portions to the workmen who crowd it in the afternoon. Standard pasta dishes L2300-2800. Go for the huge marinated half-chicken (L5000) or *pollo e pepperoni* (chicken and peppers, L3700). For those without a workman's appetite, half-sized portions can be ordered for half-price plus L300. Wines L2000 per liter. Bread L500. Open Mon.-Fri. 11:30am-3pm and 7-9pm, Sat. 11:30am-5pm.

Bottigliera Reali, via Servio Tullio, 8 (tel. 474 55 24). Take via Goito from p. Indipendenza to via XX Settembre. After a left on Settembre, take the 1st right. Small, personal, and very inviting. Len's favorite. Unpretentious, it offers a different home-cooked meal every day for very few lire. Pasta dish L3800. Hearty soup L3000. Fresh fish or meat L7000. Wine L3000 per liter. Cover L1200. Open Sept.-July Mon.-Fri. noon-3pm and 7:30-10:30pm, Sat. noon-3pm.

Fiaschetteria Marini, via R. Cadorna, 7/11 (tel. 474 55 34). Near Bottiglieria Reali, off via Collina. Sit back and savor any of the numerous wines they offer (L3200-3600 per liter) to accompany their abundant lunches. Excellent *Pasta e Ceci* (bean soup, L2500). Also try the *Baccalà al Gratin con Patate* (fish and potato stew, L6000). Cover L1000. Open Mon.-Fri. 12:30-8pm for drinks and snacks, Mon.-Sat. 12:30-2:30pm for meals.

Ristorante da Nazzareno, via Magenta, 35 (tel. 495 92 11), at via Marghera, which runs off via Marsala. Huge and impersonal, but classy: tablecloths and sparkling glass. The best choice near Termini. The L14,000 menù skimps on nothing, beverage included. If you just want pasta, try *tagliolini alla nazzareno* (3-color noodles with white meat and vegetable sauce, L5000). *Secondi* L4500-9000. Cover L1500, service 12%. Open Thurs.-Tues. noon-4pm and 7-10:30pm.

Restaurant Monte Arci, via Castelfidardo, 33 (tel. 474 48 90). Take via Solferino past p. Indipendenza off the east side of the station and then take the 1st left past the *piazza.* Jolly waiters and genuine Italian food make this dive respectable. Adequate L15,000 tourist menù and inspirational a la carte items (cover L1500), such as *linguine al pesto* with basil, garlic, and pignola nuts (L5500). Indulge in a wood-oven-baked pizza at night (L4500-7500). Open Thurs.-Tues. noon-3pm and 7-11:30pm.

Gran Sasso Vino e Cucina, via Petrarca, 13 (tel. 73 30 41). Take via Cairoli off via G. Giolitti west of the station and follow it all the way to via Emanuele Filiberto. Via Petrarca runs off the other side of the street. At L8000 for pasta, meat, vegetable, and fruit, you can't go wrong. The *menù* changes daily, but there's always a variety of options. Try the *spaghetti alla matriciana.* Avoid the expensive a la carte items, which are accompanied by a L2000 cover. *Castelli Romani* house wine L2000 per liter. Open Sept.-mid-Aug. Mon.-Sat. 11am-3pm and 5:30-11pm.

Le Caveau Birreria, via Conte Verde, 6 (tel. 731 02 66). Follow via Giovanni Giolitti along the train station until you hit via Cairoli. It intersects via Conte Verde about 600m down. This rambunctious hideout seethes with happy Roman youth. Lots of loud music and 24 types of pizza cooked in the blazing, wood-burning oven (L3500-6000). Try the plentiful *pizza* *caveau,* with mushroom, sausage, and artichoke hearts (L6000). Excellent grilled dishes cooked in front of your eyes. Try a *Spiedino Caveau,* grilled, skewered meat (L5000). Excellent beers L2000-3000. Open Tues.-Sun. 6:30pm-1am.

Piazza Navona

This is a fine area for unspoiled and inexpensive little *trattorie.* Stay away from the main *piazze* where the restaurants tend to exploit the witless tourist, and venture into the alleys for eats truer to native standards. Via Governo Vecchio and the intersecting streets offer some particularly homey *trattorie* and pizzerie.

Fiaschetteria da Alfredo, via Banchi Nuovi, 14 (tel. 686 37 34). Take via del Governo Vecchio to via Banchi Nuovi, and follow this street almost to its end. Small and easy to miss. One of the last vestiges of traditional Rome. Papà Alfredo and his lovely wife go to their vineyards in the country to press the wine they serve at the old marble tables (L4000 per liter). The menu boasts a new face daily. Pasta about L4000. Meat dishes L8000. Bread L1000. Open Sept.-July Mon.-Fri. noon-3:30pm and 8pm-midnight.

L'Insalata Ricca, largo di Chiavari, 85 (tel. 65 36 56), off corso V. Emanuele near p. S. Andrea della Valle. Funky modern art, imaginative dishes, and an off-beat character challenge the traditional *trattoria,* but neighborly service and savory food bring it down to earth. Try the crepe with ricotta and spinach (L5000), or attack their namesake *insalata ricca,* a robust salad with everything on it (L4500, smaller portion L3000). No smoking: Doodle on the white paper table cloths instead. Cover L1200. Open late Aug.-early July. Thurs.-Tues. 12:30-3pm and 6:45-11pm.

Ristorante der Pallaro, largo del Pallaro, 15 (tel. 654 14 88), down the street from L'Insalata Ricca. Italian food prepared with *anima* (soul). Dole out a worthwhile L18,000 for an all-out full-course meal, including wine and dessert. No choices—you get whatever they're inspired to make. Pleasant outdoor tables. Open Sept.-July Tues.-Sun. 8pm-1am.

Pizzeria Baffetto, via Governo Vecchio, 114 (tel. 656 16 17). Take via di Pasquino off the southwest corner of p. Navona, and follow it to via Governo Vecchio and its intersection with via Sora. This unrefined *pizzeria* has made Baffetto a household word among Romans. The pizza *gigante* (the largest) can sate even the most ravenous appetite. *Pizza Margherita* (with mozzarella and tomato) L3500-4500. *Pizza Capricciosa* (the one most everyone orders—with sausage, mushrooms, egg, artichoke hearts, prosciutto, tomato, and mozzarella) L5500-6500. Cover L500. Open Sept.-July Mon.-Sat. 6:30pm-1am.

Pizzeria Monte Carlo, vicolo Savelli, 11-13 (tel. 686 18 77), off via Governo Vecchio, near Baffetto. If not for tradition, this sleek new *pizzeria* would certainly give Baffetto a run for its money. The atmosphere is definitely more pleasant and the pies arguably as good and cheaper (from L3000). Or give their antipasto-buffet a go (L5000). Beer L1500. Cover L500. Open Sept.-July Tues.-Sun. 7pm-1am.

Pizza Corallo, via del Corallo, 10-11 (tel. 654 77 03), off via Governo Vecchio. A unique breed of pizza, served in a chic setting of arches and stucco. Wild combinations such as *focacce con scamorza e rughetta,* a strapping pizza with the pungent tastes of scamorza cheese and the rughetta herb (L7500). Other equally creative inventions L5000-8000. Also try the *bruschetta alla acciughe,* toasted bread with oil, spices, and anchovies (L2000). Several fancy pasta and rice dishes as well. Steer clear of the expensive main dishes and wines. Cover L1000. Open Tues.-Sun. 7pm-1am.

Filetti di Baccalà, largo dei Librari. Take via dè Giubbonari off p. Campo dei Fiori. Be careful not to miss this busy little establishment in a miniature *piazza* beneath a lovely church. The ideal spot for informal antipasto and wine, this self-service favorite makes the best *filetti di baccalà* (deep fried cod fillet, L2500). Wine L3000 per liter. Squeeze in at one of the outdoor tables. Open Sept.-July Mon.-Sat. 5:30-11pm.

Hostaria la Capannina, p. delle Coppelle, 8 (tel. 654 39 21), near the Pantheon. Take via della Rosetta off the northwest corner of p. della Rotonda, following it to via della Maddalena, and then take a left at via delle Coppelle. An amiable place with decent food, interesting locals, and its share of tourists. Full meals around L23,000. Seafood dishes are the specialty: Try the *rigatoni primavera* (macaroni served cold with tomato, tuna fish, and olive oil, L7000) or the tasty *risotto alla crema di scampi* (rice with shrimp sauce, L8000). Wine L5000-6000 per liter. Cover L1500, service 10%. Sit at the outdoor tables in the tranquil *piazza.* Open late Sept.-early Aug. Tues.-Sun. 9am-4pm and 7pm-midnight.

Near the Spanish Steps

Most restaurants in this flashy district are elegant, excellent, and expensive, or atrocious and still expensive. Before entering the *McDonalds* at piazza di Spagna, stop, look at the Big Mac wrappers on the Spanish Steps, and reconsider.

Pizzeria Al Leoncino, via del Leoncino, 28 (tel. 687 63 06), at via dell 'Arancio. Take via Condotti from p. di Spagna, cross via del Corso, and take via del Leoncino off via Tomacelli. The Italian answer to McDonalds. Fast, inexpensive, and informal. However, the traditional, hand-prepared Italian pizzas are baked right in front of you in a wood-burning oven. Bubbling-hot pizza L4000-6000. Beer L1500. Open Sept.-July Thurs.-Tues. 6pm-midnight.

Al Piccolo Arancio, vicolo Scanderbeg, 112 (tel. 678 61 39), near the Trevi Fountain in an alley off via del Lavatore, which runs off p. di Trevi. The sign says "Osteria." The 2 young brothers who own the place and do all the cooking are Italian-Americans trained by their Italian uncle. Try the homemade *ravioli di pesce,* stuffed with seafood (available Tues. and Fri., L6000), and the *tonnarelli alla rughetta* (pasta with raw tomato, saffron, and rughetta herb, L5000). The *filetto alle cinque herbe* is the favorite meat dish (L10,500). Always packed, so arrive early. Cover L1500. Open Sept.-July Tues.-Sun. 1-4pm and 6:30pm-1am.

Osteria Carlino, via Antonio Canova, 27 (tel. 360 72 56), off via Ripetta, which runs off p. del Popolo. The atmosphere is ephemeral at best, but the *tortellini* are out of this world at L4000. Large portions. *Secondi* L7000-8000. Cover L1800. Open Sept.-July Mon.-Sat. 7:30pm-11pm.

Centro Macrobiotico Italiano, via della Vite, 14 (tel. 679 24 09), on the 3rd floor. Take via della Propaganda off p. Mignanelli, which is next to p. di Spagna, then take your 2nd right onto via della Vite. Members only, but tourists are allowed one meal with a L2000 surcharge and a passport. Choose from the many exotic daily specials offered at the cafeteriastyle counter (around L3000 per dish). Yogurt shakes L1900, carrot juice L1800, and natural ice cream L3200. Stock up on health food supplies in the store. Open Sept.-June Mon.-Fri. 10am-7:30pm, Sat. 10am-3pm; July Mon.-Fri. only.

Trattoria da Settimio all' Arancio, via dell' Arancio, 50 (tel. 687 61 19), around the corner from Pizzeria al Leoncino. Come for dinner, when the better chef is here and you can order excellent 3-course meals for L22,000-25,000. Try the *ossobuco* (braised veal knuckle in a flavorful sauce) or *abbacchio* (roast lamb—especially good in the spring). The huge vegetable portions are fresh and only L3000. Cover L2000. Open Mon.-Sat. 1-4pm and 9pm-1am. Closed 2 weeks in mid-Aug.

Margutta, via Margutta, 119 (tel. 678 60 33), off via del Babuino. Costly vegetarian restaurant that emulates the earthy Californian appeal. L25,000 gets you a healthy, hearty 3-course meal prepared with style, though the L12,000 buffet plate with all sorts of sauteed and marinated vegetable and pasta will probably make you just as happy. Beverages are expensive. Beer L8000. Open Sept.-July Mon.-Sat. 1-3pm and 7-11pm.

Trattoria La Buca di Ripetta, via di Ripetta, 36 (tel. 361 93 91), 2 blocks from p. del Popolo. A tourist's air-conditioned sanctuary serving sanctifying fare. The *piatta del giorno* (daily specials) never fail. Pasta L6000, *secondi* L8000-10,000. Cover L2000. Wine L6000 per liter. One of the few places open Sun. for lunch. Dress nicely. Open Sept.-July Tues.-Sat. 12:15-3pm and 7:30-11pm, Sun. 12:15-3pm.

The Vatican, Trastevere, and Testaccio

Across the Tiber, the dining possibilities fall into three districts. The area around the Vatican teems with flagrant tourist traps. Save your appetite and take the next bus down the river to Trastevere, the hub of the city's finest and most expensive restaurants as well as its most endearing and economical *trattorie,* attracting the many and diverse to its crowded streets at night. Catch an evening in one of its numerous outdoor *pizzerias;* you won't have experienced Rome without a Trastevere pizza on an open-air patio. Farther south, back on the other side of the Tiber, lies the oldest area of Rome, known as Testaccio and reached by bus #27 from Termini or bus #92 from p. Venezia. This untouristed area is a stronghold of Roman tradition. Especially in the Mattatoio neighborhood, around the old slaughter houses, you will find the only restaurants that serve unadulterated Roman delicacies. The *coda alla vaccinara* (oxtail) must be sampled. Also take a stab at the *rigatoni con pajata* (noodles with tomato sauce and lamb intestines—delicious; the intestines just look like other noodles), *animelle alla griglia* (grilled calf's veins—tasty when slightly chewy), and *fegato* (plain ole liver). The less exotic dishes are also cooked with care.

Hostaria dei Bastioni, via Leone IV, 29 (tel. 31 93 78), off p. del Risorgimento near the Vatican Museum. A heaven-sent restaurant well hidden in an elegant underground space. The seafood specialties are a real catch. *Risotto alla pescatora* (rice with seafood) L4500, *Fettucine alla bastione* (with cream seafood sauce) L4500. Fresh fish dishes L10,000-12,000. Wine L3,000-4000 per carafe. Cover L1500, service 10%. Open Mon.-Sat. noon-3pm and 7-11:30pm.

La Griglietta, via Germanico, 170 (tel. 35 06 33), off via Ottaviano. Expensive. An Italian clientele attacks grilled specialties like *spiedino del buongustaio* (6 types of skewered meat, L9000). *Penne ai quattro formaggi* (with 4-cheese sauce) is the favorite pasta dish (L6000). At night pizza comes piping-hot out of the wood-fire oven for L6000-7000. Cover L2000, service 15%. Open Mon.-Sat. noon-4pm and 7:30pm-midnight. Closed 2 weeks in Aug.

Pizzeria Ivo, via di San Francesca a Ripa, 157/158 (tel. 581 70 82). Take via delle Fratte di Trastevere off viale Trastevere. A legend. Ivo's, with its jam-packed outdoor tables and spacious but also thronged interior, is the ultimate, electrifying Trastevere experience. The best pizza on the Tiber's west bank (L4500-8000). Expect to wait. Cover L1000. Open Sept.-July Wed.-Mon. 7pm-1am.

Mario's, via del Moro, 53 (tel. 580 38 09). Take via della Lungaretta off viale Trastevere, and turn right at p. di San Appolonia. No sign outside. A L10,000 *menù,* including drink, makes this place a veritable steal. Pasta is consistently phenomenal; meat dishes are not. The cavernous and unkempt interior enhance your dining experience. Open Sept. to mid-Aug. Mon.-Sat. noon-4pm and 7pm-midnight.

Birreria della Scala, p. della Scala, 58/60. Take via della Lungaretta off p. Sonnino; follow it past p. di Santa Maria onto via della Paglia and turn right at p. di S. Egidio. Packed and pulsating with live music 8-10pm every night, and a never-ending menu offering 26 types of pasta (L4000-5000) and notorious mixed drinks at the bar (L4500-5000). The hub of Trastevere's social scene. Open Thurs.-Tues. 8pm-2am.

Da Giovanni, via della Lungara, 41 (tel. 656 15 14). Take via della Scala onto via della Lungara, and follow it about ½km until right before the Mazzini Bridge. Alternatively, take one of the many buses that run along the Lungotevere. Out of the way, but well worth the trip. A family-run *trattoria:* simple but superior meals about L12,000. Try the homemade *fettucine* (L3600). Large wine selection (L2500-12,000 per liter). Food always fresh and carefully prepared. Cover L800. Open Sept.-July Tues.-Sun. 7:30-10:30pm.

Pizzeria Panattoni, viale Trastevere, 53-59 (tel. 580 09 19), in the heart of Trastevere. Called the "L'Obitorio" ("the Morgue") by the locals for its marble tables, but also because people are just dying to eat here. Easily the largest, loudest, and most crowded *pizzeria* in all of Trastevere. Also the most inexpensive and informal. Pizzas L4500-6000. Wine L3400-3800 per liter. Come on Saturday night and watch them crank out 50 pizzas in 5 min. Open Thurs.-Tues. 6pm-1am. Closed 10 days in Aug.

Trattoria Turiddo, via Galvani, 64 (tel. 57 45 04 47), in the Mattatoio district of Testaccio. Take bus #27 from Termini or take subway line A to Piramide, exiting onto via Marmorato and following until it intersects with via Galvani. Locals come here to chow the food they grew up on: *rigatoni con pajata* (with tomato and lamb intestine, L5000), *coda alla vaccinara* (stewed ox-tail, L9000), *animelle alla griglia* (grilled calf's veins, L8000). All taste better than they sound. Standard Roman specialties available too. Cover L1500. Open Sept. 21-Aug. Mon.-Wed. and Fri.-Sat. 1-3pm and 7-11pm., Sun. 1-3pm.

Trattoria al Vecchio Mattatoio, p. O. Giustanini, 2 (tel. 574 13 82), just around the corner. A genuine, gutsy Roman eatery. Try their *tonnarelli sugo coda* (thick spaghetti with tomato oxtail sauce, L5000) and the *arrosto misto di frattaglie* (a mixed grill of liver, intestine, veins, and back muscles, L9000). Swallow it with some extra-strong wine (L4000-5000 per liter). Cover L2000, service 12%. Open Sept.-July Wed.-Sun. 1-3pm and 7:30-11pm., Mon. 1-3pm.

Trattoria da Bucantino, via Luca della Robbia, 84/86 (tel. 57 48 86). Take via Vanvitelli off via Marmorata and then take your 1st left. A wonderful little Testaccio tavern without a tourist in sight. Indigenous pasta delights like *bucatini all' amatriciana* (L5500). Wrestle with their meaty *coda alla vaccinara* (L8000). Vegetable dishes L3000. Wine L3500-4000 per liter. Cover L1800. Open Aug. 26-July 24 Tues.-Sun. noon-2:30pm and 7:30-11pm.

Snacks and Desserts

If you have a sweet tooth, Rome will be your ruin. The glazed pastries adorning the myriad bakery windows will stop you in your tracks, and the hundreds of enticing, rainbow-colored flavors of the world-famous Italian *gelato* make every cone the most difficult choice of your life. The following are some of the superlative places to satisfy your cravings.

Giolitti, via degli Uffici del Vicario, 40 (tel. 679 42 06), near the Pantheon off via della Maddelena. A Roman institution; renowned for the best ice cream in Italy. Cones start at L1500. 3 flavors per cone—the choices will send you reeling. The selection of baked goods is delectable but expensive. Open Tues.-Sun. 9am-2am.

Fassi Palazzo del Freddo, via Principe Eugenio, 65/67 (tel. 73 78 04), on a street off p. Vittorio Emanuele, west of Termini. This huge, century-old *gelato* factory is a monument to the scrumptious treat. Many will contend that the *gelato* here beats Giolitti's hands down. You'll have to try both and choose for yourself. Cones L1500-3000. Open Tues.-Fri. 3pm-midnight, Sat.-Sun. 10am-2am.

Gelateria della Palma, via della Maddalena, 20 (tel. 654 07 62), off p. della Rotonda. Decent ice cream, but the decor borders on glamorous. Cups L2500-4000. Cones L2000-3000. Open June-Aug. daily 8am-2am; Sept.-May Thurs.-Tues. 8am-2am.

Gelateria Trevi di A. Cercere, via del Lavatore 84/85 (tel. 679 20 60), near the Trevi Fountain. This is the small, family-run *gelateria* of yesteryear, whose fare puts the glitzy *gelateria* down the street to shame. Make sure one of the flavors you choose is *zabajone sillabub,* the house special. Small cones L1500. Open Fri.-Wed. 11am-1am.

Bernasconi, largo di Torre Argentina, 1 (tel. 654 81 41), near corso V. Emanuele. A marvelous, air-conditioned pastry shop. Point out your favorite cream-filled, chocolate-glazed, or candied treat (L1800 each). Open Tues.-Sun. 7:30am-11pm. **Branch** in p. Colonna.

Pascucci, via Torre Argentina, 20 (tel. 656 48 16), off corso V. Emanuele, east of p. Navona. The 6 noisy blenders on the bar have given this place a name throughout the republic; they grind up fresh fruit into colorful, frothy *frulatti* drinks (L1600-1800). Ask for extra ice. Open Sept.-Aug. Tues.-Sat. 7am-midnight.

Caffè Sant' Eustachio, p. S. Eustachio, 82 (tel. 656 13 09), in the *piazza* just southwest of the Pantheon. Take via Monterone off corso V. Emanuele. Rome's coffee empire. Sit out on the *piazza* and nurse a steaming cappucino (L2500). Open Sept.-July Tues.-Sun. 8:20am-1am. For down-to-earth Italian coffee, visit **Caffè Tazza D'Oro,** nearby at via degli Orfani, 84/86 (tel. 679 27 68). Caffè Tazza has no place to sit but pours the best brew around. Open Mon.-Sat. 7am-8:30pm. Try the *granita di cafe con panne* (a mixture of iced coffee and whipped cream) at either establishment for L1500.

Enoteca il Piccolo, via del Governo Vecchio, 74/75 (tel. 654 17 46). A cozy bar lined with wine bottles and round marble tables, serving fizzy drinks. The *Sangria ai Frutti di Bosco,* a deep burgundy punch loaded with fresh wild berries, sits well with the regulars (L7000 per large mug). *Fragolino* is a sparkling strawberry champagne (L5000 per glass). Open May-Sept. daily 5:30pm-2am; Oct.-April Wed.-Mon.

Bar Tre Scalini, f. Navona, 28. The *tartufo* ice cream cup will send your tastebuds into orbit (L3500, sit-down L7000). Open Thurs.-Tues. 8am-1am.

Sights

It is said that one can arrive at Rome's huge Porta Portese Sunday market with the most eccentric wants—from a pair of gold nail clippers to a small *putti* reproduction—and leave satisfied. Rome similarly overflows with options for every *gusto.* As the saying goes, *Roma, non basta una vita*—"one life is not enough for Rome." In fact, the greatest challenge is deciding where to begin.

Before embarking on your Roman adventure, know that you should be careful on the crowded city buses, as they are favorite stake-outs for pickpockets (especially #64). Beware of the *zingarelli,* or **gypsy children:** These pint-sized pilferers approach tourists, usually with a newspaper draped over an arm, and as they nudge the paper against you, their little hands wander into pockets and purses.

Delinquency aside, one last caveat applies: When choosing a neighborhood to explore, make certain that its major sites will be open. This is especially critical on Monday, when, with the exception of the Vatican, all of Rome's museums are closed.

Piazza Rotonda

One of the few classical buildings left largely undamaged by the Catholic Church's millennia-long war on pagan monuments, the **Pantheon** stands as a bittersweet reminder of Rome the Empire, dominating its tiny *piazza.* The inscription across the portico explains that Marcus Agrippa, three times consul, erected the building in 27 B.C.E. It was completely rebuilt by Hadrian, who preserved Agrippa's name on the frieze, and later repaired by the Emperors Septimius Severus and Caracalla. Recent sandblasting cleared away much plant overgrowth and years of dirt, revealing the impressive columns and original bronze doors. The proportion and harmony of the interior are breathtaking; nowhere else in Rome do the accomplishments of a civilization dead some 1500 years speak so eloquently. The only source of light is the central hole of the famous cupola—an unprecedented, and for a long time inimitable, structural feat.

The Pantheon served originally as a temple to all the Roman gods—*pan* (all), *theos* (gods). The first Christian emperors tried to close it, but popular opposition proved too strong; the popes compromised and made it into a church. Later on in the Middle Ages, it functioned as a fortress and even a fish market. The Pantheon remained such an important center of civic life that when Pope Urban VII Barberini (1590) took the bronze beams from the portico to make the *baldacchino* (canopy over the altar) for Saint Peter's, the popular response was "*Quod non fecerunt barbari fecit Barberini*" (What the barbarians didn't do, Barberini did). Raphael and the first two kings of Italy chose to be buried here; their tombs can be seen along the sides of the interior. (Open Tues.-Sat. 9am-2pm, Sun. and holidays 9am-1pm. Free.)

As you leave, look at the baroque fountain by Giacomo della Porta (1537-1604). The Egyptian obelisk on top was added in the eighteenth century, when obelisks were in fashion. With the Pantheon behind you, go right and back around the Pantheon to reach **piazza Minerva.** Here, Bernini's winsome elephant statue supports an obelisk that overshadows the unassuming **Church of Santa Maria sopra Minerva.** The stained-glass windows of the church cast a soft radiance on the single Gothic interior in Rome, and the ceiling is celestial. The **Caraffa Chapel,** full of frescoes by Filippo Lippi (1457-1504), is back to the right, while Michelangelo's famous sculpture of *Christ Bearing the Cross* is to the left of the altar as you enter. (Bring L100 coins to illuminate the chapels.) The fifteenth-century artist Fra Angelico is buried in the church's north transept behind a bronze fence. The epitaph was composed by Pope Nicholas V, an oddity in a city where popes are usually commemorated by artists, not the other way around. (Church open daily 7am-noon and 4-7pm.)

Opposite the apse of the church, about a ½ block away, is the **Collegio Romano,** the former site of the Jesuit College. On the left behind the building, **piazza di Sant' Ignazio,** with its pale orange facades and delicate window frames and balcony railings, reveals the subtle, decorative style of rococo architecture. The Jesuit **Church of Sant' Ignazio di Loyola,** by contrast, demonstrates the artistic magnificence of the baroque era. Its sumptuous interior celebrates the sainthood of the founder of the Jesuit movement. The master work of the church is Padre Andrea Pozzo's *trompe l'oeil* ceiling painting, the *Triumph of St. Ignatius.* Notice in particular how the painting seems to project the walls of the church far beyond their actual boundaries. (Church open daily 7:30am-12:30pm and 4-7:15pm.)

The **Galleria Doria Pamphili,** in the *palazzo* of the same name at p. del Collegio Romano, 1A (tel. 679 43 65), houses what many consider the most important surviving Roman patrician art collection. The gallery has treasures from the sixteenth through eighteenth centuries: Caravaggio's *Flight into Egypt* and Bellini's *Madonna,* as well as Rubens's *Portrait of a Franciscan* and Velásquez's *Portrait of Innocent X.* The private apartments contain some of the best paintings: Fra Filippo Lippi's *Annunciation* and Memling's *Deposition.* (Open Tues. and Fri.-Sun. 10am-1pm. Admission L2000. Guided tour of private apartments an additional L2000.) Across from Palazzo Doria is **piazza Venezia,** not so much a *piazza* as a deadly, wide-open stretch of asphalt where all the frustrated Mario Andrettis of Rome try to hit fourth gear before reentering Rome's narrow and crowded streets. **Palazzo Venezia,** the first great Roman Renaissance *palazzo* and one-time papal residence, dominates the *piazza.* During his regime, Mussolini occupied the building and delivered some of his most famous speeches from the balcony overlooking the *piazza.* The arches of the portico in the courtyard and the arched facade of the **Church of San Marco** (facing the Campidoglio) exemplify the Renaissance appropriation of antiquity. The **Museo Palazzo Venezia** (tel. 679 88 65) maintains a dull permanent collection of papal objets d'art but often hosts exciting exhibits announced by banners flying outside the building. (Open Tues.-Sat. 9am-2pm, Sun. and holidays 9am-1pm. Admission L4000.)

Piazza Navona

Piazza Navona has sacrificed beauty to popularity and is now more lively than lyrical. Indeed, you must come very early or very late to appreciate the serene harmony of the *piazza*'s arrangement. The stadium of Domitian once stood here, against whose walls later grew houses and streets. In the *piazza*'s circus, Christian martyrs once met their fate. According to seventeenth-century paintings, the *piazza* was sometimes turned into a large pool by blocking off the ends and flooding it. Those with carriages drove around in the water, those without splashed on foot. Today the *piazza* swarms with sidewalk artists, people basking on stone benches, strolling couples, and playing children. At night, the *piazza* hops with activity; you can drink L4000 cups of coffee at the expensive cafes or have your fortune read on the street that leads out of the *piazza* toward corso V. Emanuele.

Three Bernini fountains spout life into piazza Navona. In the center, the magnificent **Fountain of the Four Rivers** represents the Nile, Ganges, Danube, and Rio della Plata, all identified by representative fauna and flora. (The obelisk is a later addition.) An apocryphal story holds that Bernini designed the Nile and Plata statues, which seem to shield their eyes defensively with their arms, to express a revulsion for the **Church of Sant' Agnese** opposite, designed by Bernini's great rival, Borromini.

At the southern end of piazza Navona, via di Pasquino passes behind the triangular Palazzo Braschi, now the **Museo di Roma,** p. San Pantaleo, 10 (tel. 687 58 80). The museum offers various exhibits of artists who worked in Rome, and its magnificent staircase alone merits a visit. The museum frequently mounts special exhibitions and is therefore often closed to rearrange the collection. (Open Mon., Wed., and Fri.-Sat. 9am-2pm, Tues. and Thurs. 9am-2pm and 5-8pm, Sun. 9am-1pm. Admission L4000.)

The damaged torso of a classical statue stands against the back corner of Palazzo Braschi and is all that remains of the poor chap **Pasquino,** a graffitied spokesman for Rome ever since Cardinal Caraffa put him here in 1501. Early activists affixed satirical comments against city authorities, the pope, and other targets to Pasquino's base for all to read, making the statue a communal bitchboard. You may still find some graffiti on Pasquino, although present authorities have successfully kept him clean.

Via del Governo Vecchio, lined with antique shops in fifteenth-century *palazzi,* leads out of p. Pasquino and eventually to **piazza dell' Orologio.** Borromini's lithesome clock tower rises here on the corner of the Philippine **Chiesa Nuova Convent,** which holds two paintings by Rubens. The **Oratorio** next door provides another example of Borromini's work.

East of p. Navona, across corso del Rinascimento, stands **Palazzo Madama,** seat of the Italian Senate since 1871. If you happen to come by when the Senate is in session (and only then), you may enter the gallery above and witness the infamous Italian politicians in action. The **Church of San Luigi dei Francesi,** around the corner on the left, is the French national church. Of the three paintings in the Chapel of Saint Matthew (on the back, left-hand side), Caravaggio's *The Vocation of St. Matthew,* will particularly enthrall you with its dramatic lighting and impressive figures. (Church open Fri.-Wed. 7:30am-12:30pm and 3:30-7pm, Thurs. 7:30am-12:30pm.) When you come out on corso del Rinascimento behind San Luigi, turn left to reach the **Palazzo della Sapienza,** whose spiral cupola can be seen from kilometers away. Within the deceptively plain front door of **Sant' Ivo's Church** (1660) emerges Borromini's glorious creation of curved, extending lines. (Open Sept.-May Sun. 10am-noon.)

Campo dei Fiori

Across corso V. Emanuele from p. Navona, wonderful little campo dei Fiori is a haphazard clearing in the middle of a dense medieval quarter. "Campo dei Fiori" means "Field of the Flowers," a name whose promise is fulfilled by the landscape of a bright and colorful market each morning. The *campo* is also surrounded by some of Rome's most venerable shops, like the **Bottiglieria** (a wine shop) on its long side. In the past, however, the area was the site of countless executions. It is fitting that in the center of the *piazza,* a statue of one victim, Giordano Bruno (1548-1600), rises above the bustle, arms folded over his book. Scientifically and philosophically ahead of his age, Bruno was burned in 1600 for believing that life existed elsewhere in the universe. His heretical spirit still haunts the square; Rome's remaining flower children gather at the end of the *piazza* by the Cinema Farnese.

The streets around the *campo* are some of the most picturesque in Rome and warrant a few hours of aimless wandering. Here, in the middle of a city of three million, you can turn a corner and hear nothing but the slow trickle of a fountain. Rome's charm is, indeed, that it is simply Italy's biggest village.

An imposing stone coat of arms identifies the **Cancelleria,** an early Renaissance *palazzo* just outside the *campo* in the direction that Bruno faces in piazza della Cancelleria. Designed in 1485, the impressive *palazzo* has clearly been appreciated by various popes and cardinals, who have appended their insignia to it. Today, the Cancelleria is the seat of the three Tribunals of the Vatican. The architect remains anonymous, but the unprecedented size and style of the building have often been attributed to Bramante. The courtyard, a three-story arched *loggia* on Doric columns, is certainly in line with Bramante's mastery, which restored the adjoining **Church of San Lorenzo in Damaso.** (No admittance beyond the courtyard of the Cancelleria. Church open daily 7am-noon and 5-8pm.)

Heading up to corso V. Emanuele and then following it right for a long block, you will come to the **Church of Sant' Andrea della Valle,** claiming the second largest cupola in Rome, designed by Carlo Maderno (1556-1629). Puccini's opera *Tosca* begins in this church, continues in p. Farnese, and ends at the Castel Sant' Angelo, across the river at the end of corso V. Emanuele.

Piazza Farnese

Several streets lead from campo dei Fiori toward the Tiber into piazza Farnese. The square is dominated by the huge **Palazzo Farnese,** which was begun in 1514 and marks the apex of the Renaissance *palazzo*-building fad. Pope Paul III (1534-1549), alias Alessandro Farnese, commissioned the best architects of his day to plan his dream: Antonio da Sangallo, Michelangelo, and Giacomo della Porta. (Unfortunately, the pope selected architects so advanced in their careers that they died while working for him.) Although Sangallo's facade and entrance passage are remarkable, the most impressive parts of the building are Michelangelo's elaborate cornice and courtyard. Today, the French Embassy rents the *palazzo* at the token rate of one lira per 99 years (palace not open to the public). In the sixteenth and early seventeenth centuries, the Farnese family hosted great spectacles in the square. The two huge tubs that today compose the fountains were brought from the Baths of Caracalla to serve as "royal boxes" from which members of the patrician family could view the spectacles. While in the square, take a quick look at the **Church of San Brigida,** whose ornate portal curiously upstages its *palazzo*-like facade.

The elaborate facade of **Palazzo Spada,** a short distance down vicolo dei Venti in piazza Capo di Ferro, contrasts stunningly with the Palazzo Farnese. Spada's interior courtyard bears even more intricate ornamentation, and dozens of nude statues line the walls. The **Galleria Spada,** p. Capodiferro, 3 (tel. 686 11 58), on the upper floors of the *palazzo* (accessible from the back of the courtyard), contains some paintings that will excite even the most discriminating art lover, imparting new appreciation for seventeenth-century artists like Guido Reni (note his *Judith* and portrait of Cardinal Spada). Paintings are numbered, not captioned—to identify them you must buy a catalog. (Open Tues.-Fri. 9am-2pm, Sat.-Sun. 9am-1pm. Admission L2000.)

Piazza Mattei

Although you'll inevitably pass through **Largo Argentina** several times, it is not a proper *piazza*—the walled-off excavations and the busy traffic make this an inhospitable intersection. As you wait for a bus, look at the ruins of Roman Republican temples in the center for an idea of what underlies most of the present city at that level.

The intersection defines four areas: the Pantheon, directly north; piazza Navona, to the northwest; campo dei Fiori, to the southwest; and piazza Mattei, directly south. In this last area, graceful sixteenth-century **Fontana delle Tartarughe** (Turtle Fountain) by Taddeo Landini marks the center of the ghetto, the quarter where Jews were constrained to live from the sixteenth to the nineteenth century. There are no less than five *palazzi* Mattei in the surrounding area, traditionally controlled by the noble Mattei family. Heading out of the *piazza* toward the river along via Sant' Ambrogio, you'll come onto via Portico d'Ottavia. Several houses on this street date from medieval times. Note in particular the inscription on the building at via Portico d'Ottavia, 1, which includes the patriotic invocation *Ave Roma.*

The Roman ruins at the end of the street are the **Portico d' Ottavia** and **Teatro di Marcello.** The church installed inside the portico, **Sant' Angelo in Pescheria,** is named for Rome's fish market, which operated there from the twelfth to nineteenth centuries. The theater, begun by Julius and finished by Augustus, was transformed into a fortified *palazzo* by various Roman families from the twelfth century on. Artists rediscovered the impressive antique structure three centuries later; its ruined arches appear in Piranesi prints and Heemskirk drawings. (No admittance to either the theater or the portico.)

In a city overrun with Catholic iconography and classical designs, the **Sinagoga Ashkenazita** (Synagogue of Rome, tel. 656 46 48) defiantly proclaims its unique heritage. Built from 1874 to 1904 after the emancipation of the Italian Jews following Italian unification, the synagogue incorporates Persian and Babylonian architectural devices. The synagogue also houses a museum whose collection includes ceremonial objects from the seventeenth-century Jewish community. Unfortunately, a recent terrorist bombing has left both the synagogue and its museum temporarily closed for repair. A less violent, equally biting affront to the synagogue is made at the **Church of San Gregorio** (facing the synagogue on the south), whose facade carries a Hebrew and Latin inscription admonishing the Jews to convert to Catholicism.

At the end of via del Teatro di Marcello, 2 blocks to the left of the theater as you face the Tiber, is the **Church of Santa Maria in Cosmedin,** erected on the site of an ancient temple in the sixth century. The twelfth-century portico holds the famous *Bocca della Verità* (Mouth of Truth), originally a drain cover in the shape of a huge face with an open mouth—the mask of a river god. The Mouth of Truth, it was said, would close on the hand of a liar, cutting off the fingers. You may remember Gregory Peck and Audrey Hepburn frolicking here in the movie *Roman*

Holiday. The building is an excellent example of an early medieval Roman church incorporating both Imperial Roman and early Christian styles, although its nineteenth-century restoration may have dampened its original charm. (Portico open daily 9am-5pm. Church open daily 9am-1pm and 3-5pm.)

Returning to via Portico d'Ottavia, retrace your steps up via Catalana, past the synagogue, and note the **Palazzo Cenci** at the end of the street. Popular legend and Shelley's play associate the little **Chapel of San Tommaso** (at the top of Monte Cenci next to the *palazzo*) with repulsive Francesco Cenci, who decorated it in preparation for the burial of his two children, whom he planned to kill. His murderous intentions were undermined after he raped his daughter Beatrice; she, with the aid of her brother and mother, killed their father instead. Although the three were condemned to death on September 11, 1599, an annual mass is still held for them on that day in the chapel.

In the other direction from p. Mattei lies **via delle Botteghe Oscure,** off via Caetani. At its intersection with via Aracoeli lie the headquarters of the Partito Communista Italiano. The PCI is near the headquarters of another organization that has guided the course of European history and continues to influence the Catholic world—the Society of Jesus. The construction of **Il Gesú,** the Jesuits' principal church in Rome, began in 1568 under Vignola (1507-1573) for Alessandro Farnese. The facade and plan by della Porta became the prototype for churches built during the Counter-Reformation. The glory of this most important missionary church is accentuated by its grandiose decorations, especially Baccicia's fresco *The Triumph of Jesus* in the vault of the nave. Also look for the Chapel of Sant' Ignazio di Loyola, dedicated to the founder of the order, who lies buried under the altar. (Open daily 6am-12:30pm and 4:15-7:30pm.)

Campidoglio

A flight of stairs lures you upward from p. d' Aracoeli (to the right and rear of p. di Venezia as you face the grandiose monument to Vittorio Emmanuele) as you approach the **Capitoline Hill,** smallest of Rome's Seven Hills. The political and religious center of the ancient empire, it has been the seat of the city's civic government since the eleventh century. The **Palazzo Senatorio** is today the office of the Mayor of Rome. At the base of the hill, from in front of the two Egyptian lions (ancient Roman imports converted into baroque fountains), you have a choice of three paths up the hill. To the left, the steep, brick medieval staircase leads to the Church of Santa Maria d' Aracoeli; to the right lies the curved road of via dell Tre Pile (built in 1692); in the center, Michelangelo's magnificent staircase, the *cordonata,* has a central ramp of gradual escalation, finished in the mid-1500s.

If you go up the *cordonata,* notice the statue of Cola di Rienzo, leader of a popular revolt in 1347 that sought to re-establish a Roman republic. Farther to your left under the trees is a cage which, until recently, held a live she-wolf in commemoration of the one that suckled Romulus and Remus, the mythical founders of Rome. At the top, the space opens out into a *piazza* bordered by the matching **Palazzo dei Conservatori** (to the right) and **Palazzo Nuovo** (to the left), and the **Palazzo dei Senatori** in the rear. A statue of Marcus Aurelius on horseback used to grace the center, but both Marcus and his steed have succumbed to Roman pollution and were removed for restoration. The equestrian bronze was revered through the Middle Ages as it was believed to represent the Christian Emperor Constantine. The statue had also been immortalized by a legend that the end of the world would be announced on the day all the gilding flaked off the horse. When Pope Paul III commissioned Michaelangelo to improve the neglected Campidoglio in 1536, the artist managed to work within the papal dictum that the statue be transferred here from the Vatican, making the statue the focal point of his symmetrical plan. He also put a new front on the Palazzo dei Conservatori and built the Palazzo Nuovo opposite, for balance. His design was realized slowly after his death; the Palazzo Nuovo was completed only in 1655.

Today, the two palaces of the **piazza del Campidoglio** house the treasures of the **Musei Capitolini** (tel. 671 01), the world's oldest museum. This collection of classical sculpture was begun by Pope Sextus IV (1471-1484). The collection is not well labeled, but the least expensive guide is only L8000. In the Palazzo Nuovo, be sure to find the dramatic *Dying Gaul,* the third century B.C.E. Roman copy of a statue commemorating a Pergamum victory over the Gauls, and the bronzes of the *Old and Young Centaurs,* one weeping because he is old, the other because he is young. In the courtyard of the Palazzo dei Conservatori, the fragments of a colossus of Constantine speak, like Ozymandias, of shattered glory. Among the statues in the rooms above stand the delicate *Boy with a Thorn* and the famous Etruscan *Capitoline Wolf.* Romulus and Remus were added to the wolf only during the Renaissance, to represent more vividly the ancestral myth of Rome. The new wing of the museum, divided into the **Museo Nuovo** and the **Braccio Nuovo,** houses statues from the Temple of Jove that stood on this site (you can see fragments of the temple in the courtyard). The Greek statues *Apollo Shooting* and *Athena* are the best of the group. On the top floor, the **pinacoteca** (picture gallery) contains some excellent fifteenth-century paintings by Bellini, Titian, Lotto, Pietro da Cortona, and others, but Caravaggio's *Fortune Teller* outshines them all. (Open Wed. and Fri. 9am-1:30pm, Tues. and Thurs. 9am-1:30pm and 5-8pm, Sat. 9am-1:30pm and 8-11pm, Sun. 9am-1pm. Admission to both the Palazzo Nuovo and the Palazzo dei Conservatori L4000, last Sun. of the month free.) The new wing is closed for restoration in 1989.

Up Capitoline Hill's medieval staircase, in the **Church of Santa Maria d' Aracoeli,** a masterly fresco cycle by Pinturicchio (1454-1513) covers the first chapel on the right as you enter. The chapel in the back on the left houses the *Bambino,* a revered wooden image representing the Christ child. (Open daily 7am-noon and 3:30pm-sunset.) Piazza del Campidoglio hosts a series of concerts in July by the Accademia di S. Cecilia. Inquire at via Vittoria, 6 (tel. 678 07 42), or at the wooden ticket booth at the foot of the Campidoglio steps.

Back down the stairs, from the terrace on the right side behind Palazzo Senatorio, you get a spectacular view over the Forum, especially at night. Original Roman flagstones pave the downhill road on this side. From below, the Roman base of the Palazzo Senatorio inserts itself neatly into the ruins of the Temples of Vespasian and Concord, which lie on that side of via del Foro Romano along the hill. The other side of the *palazzo* commands a less spectacular view over the imperial forums. From here, a double flight of stairs leads to the **Mamertine Prison,** now consecrated as **San Pietro in Carcere** to commemorate St. Peter's imprisonment here. Inside a plaque lists the other early Christian martyrs, including St. Paul, who fell into the fetters of Mamertine. (Open May-Sept. Wed.-Mon. 9am-5pm; Oct.-April Wed.-Mon. 9am-4pm. Donation requested.)

Forum and Palatine

Originally nothing more than a marshy valley, the area now occupying the Forum eventually became a market, and later Rome's chief public and civic square. Here the butcher shops and fish markets mingled with the area's many temples and government buildings. Most of the emperors left their marks on the Forum, adding monuments and statues or restoring existing buildings. Excavation of the Forum began in 1803 and has not yet been completed. Even two-and-a-half centuries after the first structures of the Forum had their debut, it is possible to visualize life amid these now broken buildings.

The entrance to the Forum on via dei Fori Imperiali (now closed to traffic on Sun.) lies about halfway along via Sacra, the processional street that runs through the Forum from the **Arch of Tiberius,** in the west, to the **Arch of Titus,** in the east. (Forum grounds open Mon. and Wed.-Sat. 9am-sunset, Sun. 9am-1pm. Admission L5000. For information on the renovation/excavation status of particular monuments call the Sopraintendenza Archeologica di Roma at tel. 679 03 03.)

On your right as you enter is the **Basilica Aemilia,** an Augustan edifice burned by the Gauls when they sacked Rome in 410 C.E. What marble remained was removed to adorn Renaissance constructions. The open space in front of the basilica is the original Forum, which, as a meeting place, was kept free of buildings. All civic ceremonies and religious festivals occurred here until new centers of activity arose during the Imperial period. **Via Sacra,** the oldest street in Rome, runs through the Forum, lined on both sides by important sanctuaries. At the eastern end of the Forum stands the **Temple of Julius Caesar,** dedicated by Augustus on the spot where his predecessor's body was cremated.

The brick building at the end of the Basilica Aemilia is the **Curia,** meeting place of the ancient Roman senate. The present structure, built by the Emperor Diocletian in 303 C.E., owes its survival to its sanctification as St. Hadrian's Church in the seventh century. The assembly met in the *comitium,* the space in front of the Curia, until Julius Caesar moved the gathering point to campo Marzio, present-day campo dei Fiori. The so-called **Tomb of Romulus,** an ancient temple, lies below this *piazza.* The **Arch of Septimius Severus** nearby is a well-proportioned Roman triumphal arch, originally dedicated to Septimius and his two sons. Later, however, one of the sons proved unworthy of such an honor, and was killed by his brother; his name had to be chopped out. To the left of the arch, marking one end of the Forum proper, are the *rostra* (podiums for public speakers), named for the ships' prows (*rostra*) that ornamented the front, originally won as prizes of war. Behind the *rostra,* the **Umbilicus Urbis** (symbolic center of ancient Rome) adjoins the pre-Roman **Altar of Vulcan,** probably the oldest continually used temple in the Forum (now located under some aluminum sheeting). From the altar, you can enjoy a view of the Capitoline Hill and the **tabularium,** or depository of the Senate archives, which lies under the Palazzo Senatorio and is currently being excavated. The eight columns halfway up the hill (under scaffolding in 1988) mark the porch of the **Temple of Saturn,** inaugurated in 500 B.C.E. and one of the most revered sanctuaries in Republican Rome.

Julius Caesar's **Basilica Giulia** bounds the south side of the Forum. Justice was administered in its central hall, and business conducted in the colonnaded porticos. Via Sacra runs in front of the building. The Column of Phocas in front of the basilica honors the man who seized the throne of Byzantium and awarded the Pantheon to Pope Boniface IV. At the east end of the Basilica Giulia, the **Temple of Castor and Pollux** commemorates the heavenly twins who descended to earth to help the Romans defeat neighboring enemies on the shores of Lake Regilles in 496 B.C.E.

Via Sacra continues through what was the **Arch of Augustus** and then passes between the Regia (the pontiff's office) and the restored, circular **Temple of Vesta,** honoring the goddess of fire. The Vestal Virgins lived in this elaborate structure, whose ruins extend behind the temple, and were responsible for keeping the fire in the center of this temple lit day and night. As long as they obeyed the rule of virginity, the Vestals were among the most powerful and respected women in ancient Rome. Those who strayed, however, were buried alive. Statues of the more famous virgins surround the courtyard of their house; one base, with the name scraped off and the statue gone, commemorates an upstart who eloped with her lover. North of the Regia, the **Temple of Antonius and Faustina** displays an elegant frieze. East of the temple is the **ancient necropolis,** the cemetery of the original inhabitants of the area, dating from before the traditional founding of Rome (753 B.C.E.). The bronze doors of the nearby **Temple of Romulus** (son of Maxentius) survive from the fourth century C.E.

The **Basilica of Maxentius and Constantine,** coming next along via Sacra, is the largest monument in the Forum and one of the most important existing examples of Roman architecture, inspiring numerous Renaissance constructions, possibly even Michelangelo's cupola for St. Peter's. Nearby on via Sacra is the **Antiquarium of the Forum,** housing objects uncovered during excavations. (Open Mon. and Wed.-Sun. 9:30am-12:30pm with admittance every ½-hr. Free.) Finally, dominating the east end of the Forum, the **Arch of Titus** commemorates the victory of Titus and his son Vespasian over the Kingdom of Judea in 70 C.E. The famed relief of the Romans carrying a seven-branched candelabra is on the inside of the arch.

Here at the end of via Sacra, you can turn to your right and ascend the **Palatine hill,** the site where Romulus supposedly founded Rome. The hill served as a residential area during the days of the Republic. Today its grassy environs and imperial palaces are a relaxing escape from the Forum's marble starkness. The **Clivus Palatinus,** main road of the Palatine, leads up to the **Farnese Gardens,** built over the site of the Palace of Tiberius. The **Casa di Livia** at the southern end of the gardens may have been Augustus Caesar's house, an elegant dwelling that preserves traces of frescoes on its walls. Ongoing excavation is uncovering the rest of Augustus's early imperial residence, which seems to have been a modest building compared to the immense structures that constituted the **palace complex** built for Emperor Domitian (81-96 C.E.), covering the rest of the hill. The palace is composed of three discrete parts: the official palace, or *Domus Flavius,* the imperial residence or *Domus Augustana,* and the stadium. Look for the curious central courtyard of the *Domus Flavius* with its octagonal basin. The unpopular Domitian was said to have lined the walls of this courtyard with polished stone so that he could observe the reflections of any potential assailant. The throne room of the palace is north of the peristyle and flanked by a basilica and a room for public ceremonies. To the south is the **Triclinium,** or banquet hall. East of the official palace was the private residence of the emperor. As you wander through the labyrinth of brick ruins, notice the layout of the multi-storied palace around central courts. The fragmented pavement in some of the rooms exposes the ingenious system of central heating produced by an underground stove. Nearby, the **Antiquarium of the Palatine** displays objects uncovered in excavations. (Closed in 1988.) The **Circus Maximus** lies along the south side of the Palatine. (You can see it from the hill, but to get in, you'll have to leave by the Forum exit and walk back to it.) Even the starting and finishing mark for the chariot races once held here still exists at the westernmost end.

Across the street from the Forum are the **Fori Imperiali,** a conglomeration of late imperial monuments and *piazze* built during the last days of the Republic, partly in response to the increasing congestion in the Roman Forum. In the 1930s, the aspiring emperor Mussolini paved via dell' Impero (street of the Empire), now known as via dei Fori Imperiali, over much of the imperial fora, desiring an impressive thoroughfare for his military parades. Today only about 1/5 of the original fora area remains visible. Of that which remains, the **Forum of Trajan** is the most impressive. Its famous column (under scaffolding since 1981) commemorates Emperor Trajan's conquest of the Dacians, denizens of present-day Romania. **Trajan's Market,** a semicircular shopping mall of 150 individual stores covered in Roman brick, often holds decent art exhibits. (Forum and market open Tues.-Sat. 10am-5pm, Sun. 9am-1pm. L1500. Entrance on via IV Novembre, 94.) The Forums of Caesar and Nerva are open the same hours as Trajan's Forum, but are best appreciated from street level. Augustus's Forum, entered at via Campo Carleo off p. del Grillo, is better viewed from above at via Alessandria, where you can see the remains of the Temple to Mars Ultor. (Open April-Sept. Tues.-Sat. 9am-1pm and 3-6pm, Sun. 9am-1pm; Oct.-March Tues.-Sat. 10am-5pm, Sun. 9am-1pm.)

When standing amid the ruins of the Forum, a glance northward will take in a seemingly classical tower surmounted by a winged chariot. This is the rear view of the **Vittoriano** (1885-1911), piazza Venezia's bombastic monument to King Vittore Emannuele II and the Italian unification. Fans of modern Italian history will appreciate the **Institute for The History of the Italian Risorgimento** and the **Central Museum of the Risorgimento,** which display exhibits from Italy's World War I effort. (Both open Wed., Fri., and Sun. 10am-1pm.) To get a close look at the Vittoriano, walk to the hilltop along via dei Fori Imperali.

Colosseum

The universal symbol of Rome, the Colosseum inspires much greater awe in its life-size manifestation than on the countless postcards and travel brochures it adorns. Finished by the Emperor Titus in 80 C.E., it seated 50,000 spectators. During the Middle Ages and the Renaissance, bits of its travertine stone were incorporated into the structure of Palazzo Venezia, the Cancelleria, and Saint Peter's. Not until Benedict XIV (1740-1758) consecrated the Colosseum in the memory of martyred Christians did the destruction stop. The Venerable Bede (672-735) remarked that "as long as the Colosseum stands, Rome stands; when the Colosseum falls, Rome will fall; but when Rome falls, it will be the end of the world." Ominously enough, travertine has been seen falling during recent rainstorms. (Colosseum open Oct.-April daily 9am-sunset; May-Sept. 9am-7pm. Free. The climb to the upper levels, however, costs L3000 and is allowed until 1 hr. before closing. Restoration work may limit your ascent to the 1st of the Colosseum's 3 upper levels.)

On one side of the Colosseum, the **Arch of Constantine** (315 C.E.) triumphs over all triumphal arches in its sheer majesty. On the other side, the incredible **Domus Aurea** (Golden House of Nero) extends up the Colle Oppio (Oppio Hill). Construction soon after Nero's death left the emperor's vast dwelling buried beneath a mound of dirt. It was not rediscovered until the Renaissance, when the vast rooms were taken to be grottoes. The exceptionally well-preserved rooms and halls, especially the Octagonal Room, give a vivid sense of a Roman palace's interior. Many artists, Raphael among them, copied the interior decorations, and *grottesche* (grotesques) came to be the fad on *palazzo* walls. (Entrance at via Labicana. Open Tues.-Sun. 9am-1pm.)

North of the Domus Aurea on the Esquiline Hill, off via Cavour, rises the **Church of San Pietro in Vincoli** (St. Peter in Chains). Utterly nondescript, the church houses Michelangelo's unfinished tomb of Julius II with its famous statue of Moses. The anomalous goat horns protruding from Moses' head arise from a mistranslation of the Hebrew Bible. When Moses emerged from Sinai with the Ten Commandments, according to scripture, "rays" (similar to "horns" in Hebrew) shone from his brow. The tomb was never completed due to arrangements between Michelangelo and the pope and the petty jealousies of Julius's successors. Flanking the Moses statue are Leah and Rachel, who represent the active and the contemplative life. Under the altar of the church, the chains of St. Peter are exhibited. (Open daily 6:30am-12:30pm and 3:30-7pm. Take L100 coins to illuminate the statue of Moses.)

The **Church of San Clemente,** an early Christian structure of several layers, stands 1½ blocks east of the Colosseum along via San Giovanni in Laterano. A Mithraic temple (related to the Eastern cult popular in the late Roman empire) lies beneath two ancient Roman basilicas and a twelfth-century church that changed greatly with Domenico Fontana's addition of baroque stucco. The upper church's artistic gems include a medieval mosaic of *The Triumph of the Cross* in the apse, and Masolino's moving frescoes in the **Chapel of Santa Caterina.** The frescoes on the lower levels, however, are less impressive. (Lower church open Mon.-Sat. 9am-noon and 3:30-6:30pm, Sun. 10am-noon and 3:30-6:30pm. Admission L1000.)

The grandiose **Church of San Giovanni in Laterano** is farther east of the Colosseum at the end of via San Giovanni in Laterano, in the *piazza* of the same name. This is the cathedral of the diocese of Rome, and the end of the traditional pilgrimage route from Saint Peter's. The huge church, accorded the same rights of extraterritoriality as the Vatican, is used by the pope for Mass on certain feast days. On Corpus Christi, a triumphal procession including the college of Cardinals, the Swiss Guard, and hundreds of Italian girl scouts leads the Pontiff back towards the Vatican after the service. The church has been rebuilt many times. In its present form it is largely the work of Borromini, but the imposing facade is by Alessandro Galilei. San Giovanni houses a vast complex of important religious monuments (the tabernacle, for example, contains the heads of Saints Peter and Paul). Be sure to examine the remarkable sixteenth-century wooden ceiling, the baptistery, and the cloisters. (Open daily 7am-7pm. Dress code vigorously enforced.) Also worth a gander is the **Scala Sancta.** To the right and in front of the cathedral, this building houses what are believed to be the stairs used by Jesus in Pilate's house in Jerusalem. Pilgrims are granted an indulgence for ascending the 28 well-worn steps on their knees; if you prefer to walk, avoid entering behind a devotee. (Open daily 6am-12:30pm and 3:30-7pm. Also vigorously enforces dress code.)

From San Giovanni, a 15-minute walk down via di Amba Aradam and via Druso leads to the **Terme di Caracalla** (Baths of Caracalla), the best-preserved of Rome's imperial baths. (Open Tues.-Sun. 9am-5pm. Admission L3000.) An additional 10-minute walk along the walls of the city on viale Giotto brings you to the cryptic **Piramide di Caio Cestio.** Nearby, at via Caio Cestio, 6, you will find the entrance to the **Protestant Cemetery** (tel. 57 19 00), a beautifully maintained burial site for non-Catholics. Here, in the shadow of the pyramid lies John Keats, beside his friend Joseph Severn. The tombstone itself never mentions the writer by name; it merely commemorates a "Young English Poet" and records, "Here lies one whose name is writ in water." Near the austere tomb, you'll find a snub-nosed bust of Keats and even some eulogistic verse. On the other side of the small cemetery, Shelley is buried, beside his piratical friend, Trelawny, under a simple plaque hailing him as *Cor Cordium* (Heart of Hearts). Goethe's son, Axel Munthe, and Richard Dana (author of *Two Years Before the Mast*), are all also buried here. (Open April-Sept. daily 8-11:30am and 3:20-5:30pm; Oct.-March 8-11:30am and 2:20-4:30pm. Donation of L500 requested.)

Piazza Barberini

Indifferent to the modern hum around its square, Bernini's baroque **Triton Fountain,** with its well-muscled figurehead, blows its perfect stream of water high into the stirring air of piazza Barberini. This spout marks the fulcrum of baroque Rome. Twisting north is the opulent stretch of **via Veneto**, which has seen its *dolce vita* replaced by a flood of wealthy entertainment-seekers, airline offices, and embassies. It offers its best right away—the Bernini "Bee Fountain," buzzing the same honey-producing motif that graces the aristocratic Barberini family's coat-of-arms. Farther up via Veneto, the decor of the **Cappuccin Crypt** (beneath the **Church of Santa Maria della Concezione**) is a particularly grisly work of art. The walls are decorated with the skulls and bones of former friars, as a perpetual reminder to the monks of their own mortality. (Crypt open daily 9am-noon and 3-6pm. Donation requested.)

In the other direction, just up via delle Quattro Fontane, the sumptuous **Palazzo Barberini,** at via delle Quattro Fontane, 13, houses the **Galleria Nazionale d' Arte Antica** (tel. 475 01 84), a national gallery of paintings with a superb collection spanning the thirteenth to eighteenth centuries. Of the earlier works, note Filippo Lippi's *Annunciation and Donors* and Piero di Cosimo's riveting *La Maddalena.* Holbein's *Portrait of Henry VIII* is here, as are several excellent canvases by Titian, Tintoretto, Caravaggio (including his gruesome *Judith and Holofernes*), El Greco, and Poussin. The most startling aspect of the collection, however, is the entrance hall, whose ceiling radiates with Pietro da Cortona's *Triumph of Divine Providence* celebrating the papacy of Urban VIII and his family, the Barberinis. The family apartments on the second story are worth a look, though they are anticlimactic after the extraordinary collection on the first floor. In addition to preserving the rooms of the *palazzo* as they were during the height of the Barberini family's influence, these galleries display period ceramics, silver, and a collection of gorgeous gowns. The gallery collection is unusually well-labeled; if you understand any Italian, you should have no problems identifying the displays. (Open Tues.-Sun. 9:15am-7pm. During renovation visits to the apartments are allowed every hour on the hour. Admission to both galleries and apartments L3000.)

Along with the four fountains that give it its name, the juncture of via delle Quattro Fontane with via XX Settembre is the site of the small and unique **Church of San Carlino alle Quattro Fontane.** This Borrominian gem, designed to fit inside one of the pilasters of Saint Peter's, features a perfectly proportioned dome and cloister. (If the interior is closed, ring at the convent next door.) Wherever Borromini is, Bernini is not hard to find. The simple facade of **Sant' Andrea al Quirinale** masks a domed, elliptical interior. (Open Wed.-Mon. 8am-noon and 3:45-7pm.)

Piazza del Quirinale, at the end of via del Quirnale running from via XX Settembre, occupies the summit of the highest of Rome's seven hills. The **Palazzo del Quirinale** is the official residence of the president of the Italian Republic. The **Palazzo della Consulta** on the right is home to the Italian Supreme Court for Constitutional matters. (No admittance to either building.) In the middle of the *piazza* are the famous representations of Castor and Pollux, the *Dioscuri.* The two statues were separated in the eighteenth-century to accommodate the obelisk between them.

Returning on via del Quirinale past San Carlino, you come to the **Church of Santa Maria della Vittoria,** which houses Bernini's *Saint Teresa in Ecstasy.* Note the *trompe l'oeil* effects of the balcony scene overlooking the ecstasy in the Cornaro chapel, executed by Bernini's students. The half-hidden figure on the far left is said to be a portrait of Bernini. (Open daily 6:30am-noon and 4:30-7:30pm.)

Following via della Consulta south from the *piazza* to via Nazionale, you can trek east or hop on any of the buses headed to p. della Repubblica, site of the **Church of Santa Maria degli Angeli.** Built by Michelangelo in 1566, the church is a structural imitation of the *tepidarium* (warm room) of the Baths of Diocletian, done to honor the Christian slaves who built the ancient site. Around the corner on via delle Terme di Diocleziano is the **Museo Nazionale Romano delle Terme** (tel. 46 05 30), which combines sculptures and antiquities found in Rome since 1870 with several important patrician collections. Don't miss the Sala dei Capolavori (Room of Masterpieces) and the so-called Ludovisi throne, a Greek statue dating from the fifth century B.C.E. Upstairs, the frescoes from the Villa di Livia at Prima Porta, a town north of Rome, are still remarkably vivid. Due to reconstruction, only a quarter of the exhibits were open in 1988. (Open Tues.-Sat. 9am-2pm, Sun. 9am-1pm. Admission L4000.)

As you leave the museum, bear right toward Termini. When you reach via Cavour, follow it to the **Church of Santa Maria Maggiore,** one of the seven pilgrimage churches of Rome. As if the exterior weren't impressive enough, two chapels inside, the **Cappella Sistina** (almost a church in itself) and the matching **Cappella Paolina** across the nave, vie in decorative sumptuousness. Two elegant colonnades enhance the nave, and its coffered ceiling glows with gold leaf reputedly brought from America by Columbus. From the obelisk in the back of the church you can look straight past the Quattro Fontane to the obelisk in front of the **Church of Santa Trinità dei Monti** at the top of the Spanish Steps. (Church open daily 7am-7pm. Dress code stringently enforced.)

Piazza di Spagna (Spanish Steps)

Designed by an Italian, paid for by the French, named for the Spaniards, occupied most ferociously by the Britons, and now plagued by Americans and *McDonalds,* the Spanish Steps are, not surprisingly, the area toward which most foreigners gravitate. The Spanish Steps and piazza di Spagna take their names from the Spanish Embassy, located since 1647 in the other triangle of the hourglass-shaped *piazza.* Piazza di Spagna possesses all the requisite elements of a *piazza,* but you have to look for them. The fountain at the foot of the steps was designed in the shape of a boat by Bernini's father, supposedly after he witnessed a boat wash up in the *piazza* after a flooding of the Tiber. The *piazza*'s obelisk is at the top of the stairs, in front of the **Church of Santa Trinità dei Monti.** Despite a simple design by Carlo Maderno, the church's rosy facade offers a worthy climax to the stairs' grand curves, not to mention a sweeping view over the city. The Zuccari brothers who frescoed Santa Trinità in the sixteenth century thought enough of the site to want to stay; their *palazzetto* at the corner of the *piazza* on via Sistina has one of the most imaginative facades in the city.

Wreathed in flowers and peppered with tourists, the *piazza* has always attracted artists. Stendhal, Balzac, Wagner, and Liszt all stayed near here; Henry James and the Brownings lived at different times on via Bocca di Leone, a small side street in the area, and, above via Frattina, 50, amid the glitter and glamor of chic boutiques, you'll see a plaque commemorating James Joyce's former residence. Another small plaque on the side of the house to the right of the Spanish Steps commemorates the place where Keats died in 1821. The second floor of the house at p. di Spagna, 26, is now the charming **Keats-Shelley Memorial Museum** (tel. 68 42 35). You can scrutinize a lock of Keats's hair, an urn containing Shelley's bones, and even some curious drawings by Keats. Byron is honored here too because he once lived at p. di Spagna, 66. The library contains an extensive collection of books about the works and lives of Keats, Shelley, and Byron, as well as originals of some of their works. (The museum was closed for restoration in 1988.)

Today, more young tourists than artists frequent these steps, whose magnetism attracts dirty feet, water bottles, hamburger wrappers, and battered guitars from all corners of the world. Women beware—every eligible man in Rome wanders here at nightfall. Another word of caution: don't buy drugs in this area. The best thing that can happen is to be busted by one of the many uniformed or undercover cops.

Along viale Trinità dei Monti on the other side of Santa Trinità, the **Villa Medici** now houses the **Accademia di Francia** (tel. 676 12 56). Founded in 1666 to give young French artists a chance to come to Rome (Berlioz and Debussy were among the scheme's beneficiaries), the organization now keeps the building in mint condition and arranges excellent exhibits (mainly the work of French artists). Behind the villa's severe Tuscan front lies a beautiful garden and an elaborate back facade. The park harbors semi-ruined towers and romantic walks. (Academy open Nov. to mid-July Wed. and Sat.-Sun. 10am-1pm. Admission L2000 by guided tour only. The villa is closed to the public except during exhibits. Admission varies.) The **Pincio,** a public park of formal style, extends up the hill beyond the villa. At the top, you'll enjoy a panorama of piazza del Popolo and Rome from p. Napoleone.

Back on the *piazza* exist two renowned eating establishments. Immediately to the right of the steps as you descend is **Babington's Tea Room,** which has catered to the English community since 1896 (open Fri.-Wed. 8am-9pm). Older still is **Antico Caffè Greco,** at via Condotti, 86, crowded with memorabilia from the days in which Goethe, Liszt, Byron, and even Buffalo Bill dilly-dallyed here. (Open Mon.-Fri. 8am-8:30pm, Sat. 8am-2pm.)

The streets between p. di Spagna and via del Corso are the most elegant in Rome, gleaming with glass, glamor, and beautiful people. **Via Condotti** and **via Frattina** are littered with boutiques, **via Borgogna** sparkles with jewelry stores, **via della Croce** tempts with exquisite edibles, and **via del Babuino** and **via Margutta** supply the art scene.

Piazza del Popolo

Piazza del Popolo, the northern entrance to the city, was the first sight that greeted nineteenth-century travelers who arrived in Rome through the Porta del Popolo. The "people's square," as its name suggests, is a favorite site for communal antics. After a victory by one of the city's soccer teams the *piazza* explodes with music and merriment.

Despite the occasional fanaticism of its visitors, the *piazza* itself is serenely symmetrical; as you walk around, you will see buildings in one quadrant beautifully echoing those in another. One of Guiseppe Valadier's masterpieces, the *piazza* was built between 1816 and 1824 with two encircling walls and a central obelisk. Tucked away on the north side of the *piazza* near the Porta del Popolo, the small and deceptively simple **Church of Santa Maria del Popolo** contains two iridescent canvases by Caravaggio in the chapel to the left of the altar: the *Conversion of Saint Paul* and the *Crucifixion of Saint Peter.* The paintings steal the show from the **Chigi Chapel** designed by Raphael; notice the Pinturicchio frescoes as well. (Open daily 8am-12:30pm and 4-7pm.)

Via di Ripetta, twin street to via del Babuino, leads out of p. del Popolo toward the Tiber. The huge brick mound of the **Mausoleum of Augustus** and the glass-encased **Ara Pacis,** the ninth century B.C.E. monumental altar erected in honor of Augustus, stand approximately where via di Ripetta meets the river. Both ancient monuments warrant a walk around—the former from a distance for its overall effect and the latter close up for details. (Ara Pacis open Tues.-Sat. 9am-1:30pm and 3:30-5:30pm, Sun. 9am-1pm. Admission L1500.)

Farther south, on via del Corso, the street opens onto **piazza Colonna,** named after the **Column of Marcus Aurelius** (covered for restoration), which towers over the square. Long the center of the city, piazza Colonna is home to two major actors in Italian politics. **Palazzo Chigi,** directly on the *piazza,* is the official residence of the prime minister (it's hosted many denizens in recent years). The convex, almost polygonal building to its right, designed by Bernini, is **Palazzo di Montecitorio,** seat of the power house of the Italian legislature, the **Chamber of Deputies.** (No admittance to either building.) Facing via del Corso is the office of the newspaper *Il Tempo.* On the side of the building, pedestrians gather to read pages from the latest edition (displayed in the windows). Those with a hearty appetite for art can visit the **Galleria Colonna** (tel. 679 43 62) in the *palazzo* across via del Corso from the *piazza.* Yet another patrician collection, the museum includes works by Van Dyck, Tintoretto, Poussin, Rubens, and Reni. (Open Sept.-July Sat. 9am-1pm. Admission L3500.)

As you walk east along via Sabina, the air thickens with dampness and carries the sounds of water. The **Fontana di Trevi**—so named because this is where three streets (*tre vie*) converge—takes up most of the tiny *piazza,* and Nicola Salvi's (1697-1751) rocks and figures mount the *palazzo* behind. The water for the fountain comes from the Acqua Vergine aqueduct, which also supplies the spouts in p. Navona, p. di Spagna, and p. Farnese. The aqueduct name derives from the maiden who allegedly pointed out the spring to thirsty Roman soldiers. She appears in one of the bas-reliefs above the basin. Completed in 1762, the present fountain is a grandiose elaboration on an earlier basin. It depicts the chariot of Neptune conducted by two Tritons. A stale tradition of unknown origin suggests that travelers who throw a coin into the fountain will return to Rome. These days the city government collects the proceeds generated by wishful tourists each week. "Three coins in the fountain . . . ."

Trastevere

Trastevere is Rome's quirky quarter, hidden away across the Tiber just under the Vatican's nose. It has pungency and flair, and its tiny, meandering streets are lively and picturesque. It was here that Oriental merchants and Jews once settled, and here that dialect poetry flourished. Some of Trastevere's inhabitants boast that they have never crossed the river into Rome, and nearly all of its residents will tell you that this is the most vivacious and idiosyncratic area in the city. Trastevere seems hardly tarnished by the demands of brassy commercialism, and its *piazza* encourages you to stay up all night just watching the moon.

Take bus #170 from Termini to viale Trastevere, an area packed with ice cream parlors and movie houses. Away from the river, at the end of via della Lungaretta, is the **Church of Santa Maria in Trastevere,** in the *piazza* of the same name. Supposedly consecrated in 222 C.E., this may be the oldest church in Rome. Its facade was added in the twelfth century. The thirteenth-century mosaics on the facade are only a prelude to those within. (Open daily 8am-noon and 4-7pm.)

Returning toward the river, via della Lungaretta leads into p. Sidney-Sonnino at viale Trastevere. Here, behind some trees hides the **Torre degli Anguillara,** the only medieval town tower left of those that blanketed the area. The street continues to the Tiber, ending near one of the bridges that cross to the **Isola Tiberina,** the island in the river. There has been a hospital on the island since 291 B.C.E., and there is still one in operation. The ancient Romans made the island into a replica of the ship of Asclepius, who, according to legend, sailed up the Tiber to Rome. From farther down the banks of the Tevere at p. Castellani, via di Vascellari leads up to the **Church of Santa Cecilia in Trastevere.** Although the church has been substantially altered, the twelfth-century portico and Romanesque bell tower still stand intact, with a lovely altar inside. Don't miss the *Statua di Santa Cecilia* by

Stefano Maderno (1576-1636), and be sure to go down through the pseudo-Byzantine crypt to see the ruins below. (Open daily 10am-noon and 4-6pm.)

Adorned by busts of obscure nineteenth-century Italian heroes, the **Gianicolo Hill,** Rome's Lover's Lane, overlooks Trastevere from the northwest. To get to the summit take via della Scala from Santa Maria in Trastevere to via Garibaldi. Atop the hill sits the **Church of San Pietro in Montorio,** on the spot once believed to be the site of St. Peter's crucifixion. The church itself boasts nothing spectacular, but in the courtyard next door squats Bramante's tiny **Tempietto,** a classical monument in miniature, with every detail designed in harmony. From the front of the Tempietto you have a vista of all Rome. The roof of the Pantheon, Bramante's inspiration, lies straight ahead.

At the foot of the Gianicolo at via della Lungara, 10 (on the left as you descend via Garibaldi), is the **Palazzo Corsini** (tel. 654 23 23), home to the Corsini collection of the **Galleria Nazionale d' Arte Antica** (the rest of the collection is in the Palazzo Barberini). Covering the thirteenth through eighteenth centuries, the museum contains works by Fra Angelico, Breughel, Van Dyck, Titian, and Poussin, and several excellent examples of early seventeenth-century chiaroscuro paintings. (Open Tues.-Fri. 9am-7pm, Sat. and Mon. 9am-2pm, Sun. 9am-1pm. Admission L3000.)

Across the street, the **Villa Farnesina** (tel. 65 08 31) houses several rooms frescoed by Raphael, Giulio Romano (1492-1546), and assistants. The *Fables of Psyche* that ring the ceiling are voluptuous and visually stunning. Raphael's *Galatea,* in the left-hand room, demonstrates why Vasari called him "*Maestro del Colorito.*" Il Sodoma's *Marriage of Alexander and Roxana* on the first floor and Peruzzi's *trompe l'oeil* perspective room next to it attest to the excellence of the artists who worked here. The museum also hosts frequent temporary collections. (Open Mon.-Sat. 9am-1pm.)

Vatican City

Occupying 108.5 urban acres entirely within Italy's capital, the State of Vatican City is the last temporal toehold of a Catholic Church that once wheeled and dealed as a mighty European power. Under the Lateran Treaty of 1929, the Pope remains supreme monarch of his tiny theocracy, exercising all legislative, judicial, and executive powers over the 300 souls who hold Vatican citizenship. The state maintains its own army in the form of the Swiss Guards, all descended from sixteenth-century mercenaries hired by Pope Julius II, and whose uniforms were designed by Michelangelo. The state also prints its own commemorative coins and operates an independent postal service whose efficiency far surpasses that of the national system. The official means of exchange within the city is, however, Italian currency.

From the baroque office complex known as the Curia, the priestly hierarchy governs the spiritual lives of hundreds of millions of Catholics around the world. From the resplendent style of dress of this Catholic officialdom to the echoing choirs and brazen processions, to the unparalleled wealth of its artistic treasury, the tiny state's grand mission, of "truth, justice, and peace . . . salvation for mankind," is most majestically undertaken. Spend some time examining the city's surrounding ninth-century wall—replete with arrow slots for the pontifical archers—or hunt in the cluttered hallways of the Vatican Museums for the only known portrait of Pericles, the fifth-century-B.C.E. Athenian demagogue who built the Parthenon and plunged his city into the disastrous Peloponnesian War. Or venture into Michelangelo's world-renowned Sistine Chapel.

No visitors can enter St. Peter's in shorts and no women in skirts above the knees or in sleeveless dresses. Photography is also officially banned.

Begin your visit at the **Information Office** (tel. 698 44 66), in p. San Pietro by the Arch of the Bells, on the left of the *piazza* as you face the basilica. To attend a **papal audience** or a special ceremony in St. Peter's, you must apply in writing to the Prefettura della Casa Pontificia, 00120 Citta del Vaticano (tel. 69 82; office by the Bronze Door, open Mon.-Sat. 9am-1pm). Public audiences are usually held

Wednesdays at 11am when the Pope is in Rome, at 10am when he's at his summer estate south of Rome in Castel Gandolfo.

Though outside the borders of the modern Vatican City, the **Castel Sant' Angelo** (tel. 656 42 27) for centuries provided popes with a last-ditch refuge and a secure fortress in which to imprison heretics (the rivaling Cenci, the irreverent Giordano Bruno, and the alleged spy Benvenuto Cellini among them). Emperor Hadrian built the structure as his mausoleum in 135 C.E., and though it has undergone frequent alteration in years since, many original features remain, including its square base. Much of Puccini's *La Tosca* is set within the walls of this ancient castle. A tour reveals an array of ancient weapons and artillery, as well as memorabilia from the days when it was used as a prison, though the walk through may be disappointing to those who are not fortress buffs. (Open Tues.-Sat. 9am-1pm, Sun. 9am-noon. Admission L3000.) Angels line the lovely **Ponte Sant' Angelo,** the bridge leading to the castle, whose sculptures were done by Bernini's pupils to his specifications. Here is the starting point for the traditional pilgrimage route from St. Peter's to the Basilica of San Giovanni in Laterno on the other side of Rome.

The ingenious design of Bernini's elliptical **piazza San Pietro** creates a mesmerizing setting for its majestic freight. If you stand on the round dark stones in front of each of the *piazza*'s twin fountains, a glance at the colonnade will show you how perfectly Bernini calculated his design—the three rows of columns lose their respective depth, reducing to a single one.

St. Peter's Cathedral sits upon the reputed site of its eponym's tomb, and a Christian structure of some kind has stood here since Emperor Constantine made Christianity the Roman state religion in the fourth century C.E. In 1452, with Constantine's original brick basilica showing its age, Pope Niccolo V commissioned Rossellino to rebuild it. Work didn't begin until 1506, however, and continued at the leisurely pace typical of Italian bureaucracy until today; a parade of brilliant technicians—including Sangallo, Raphael, and Michelangelo—directed the work. The facade and final shape of the building (a Latin cross) were designed by its last architect, Carlo Maderno. In 1626 Pope Urban VIII consecrated the building, and the Vatican officially reopened for business.

The overwhelming interior of the basilica measures 186m by 137m along the transepts. Metal lettering on the floor in the nave indicates the lengths of the principal churches of the world, which pale in comparison to the size of St. Peter's. Just inside, note the round red stone in the pavement by the door, where Charlemagne was crowned Holy Roman Emperor in 800 C.E. To the right, Michelangelo's sorrowful **Pietà,** which he sculpted at age 25, now sits gracefully behind bullet-proof glass—in 1978, a fanatic attacked the famous sculpture with an axe, breaking off the left hand of the Madonna. A medieval statue of St. Peter poses just before the crossing on the right, his bronze foot worn smooth by the kisses of the faithful. The entrances to the grottoes, which are full of saints' and popes' tombs, are under the four huge saint statues. Michelangelo's soaring **cupola,** a taller, rougher replica of the one in the Pantheon, floods the entire church with light. Beneath this architectural wonder sits the *baldacchino,* Bernini's bronze masterpiece. Not so much a canopy as a sculpture, its twisted columns support a bronze cloth covered with cupids. The altar itself, in a notable example of religious recycling, was made of bronze taken from the Pantheon. Ascend the cupola to see how Michelangelo designed it in two shells, each with a slightly different curve. From St. Peter's lantern, you get an excellent perspective of the flat and hazy Roman skyline. The climb is somewhat strenuous, but worth the effort. (Dome open same hours as basilica, but may be closed when the Pope is in the basilica, often Wed. mornings. Admission L2000, half-ascending elevator L500.) Mass occurs several times per day at St. Peter's, with a particularly beautiful vespers service Sunday at 5pm.

At the other extreme of the *piazza,* you can descend to the **necropolis** on the level below the grottoes. A double row of mausoleums dating from the first century C.E. lie under the basilica. Archeologists believe they have located St. Peter's tomb here. Since the area is still being excavated, only small, pre-arranged groups are allowed to visit. (Free.) Apply to the Ufficio Scavi (excavation office), beneath the Arco della Campana to the left of the basilica.

The historical-artistic museum, or **Treasury** (entrance under the Pius VII monument on the left side of the church near the altar), contains a collection of vestments, reliquaries, missals, crucifixes, and other sacred paraphernalia. (Open April-Sept. 9am-6:30pm; Oct.-March 9am-2:30pm. Admission L2000.)

A 10-minute walk (or a L1000 bus ride—no service Wed. and Sun.—that affords glimpses of the Vatican gardens) will take you out of p. San Pietro and around the walls to the **Vatican Museums** (tel. 69 82). Because the many exhibits are often uncataloged, get an official guide book (L8000). (Most museums open Easter week and July-Sept. Mon.-Fri. 9am-5pm, Sat. 9am-2pm; in off-season Mon.-Sat. 9am-2pm. Last entrance 1 hr. before closing. Admission L8000, with YIEEC or ISIC L5000, children under 1m tall free, last Sun. of the month 9am-2pm free.)

A complete museum visit takes you through the Egyptian Museum to the classical sculpture of the Chiaramonti Gallery and the Braccio Nuovo (new wing). The most famous works of classical sculpture are in the **Pio-Clementine Museum.** To conciliate the Council of Trent in 1550, private parts left by the less inhibited ancients were removed from art. Here, in the Belvedere Court, stands the *Apollo Belvedere* and the evocative *Laocoon* group. The latter depicts the Trojan priest Laocoon and his two sons struggling in terror to free themselves from the snakes set upon them by Athena.

Upon quitting the Pio-Clementine Museum, head to the **Etruscan Museum,** a floor above, one of the best such exhibits. The remarkable **Raphael Stanze** (Raphael Rooms), at the end of the hall, were painted by the master early in the sixteenth century, at the beginning of his career in Rome. The first room, Stanza dell' Incendio, features the *Fire in the Borgo,* illustrating a fire in 847 C.E. that was miraculously extinguished as Pope Leo IV made the sign of the cross. The Stanza della Segnatura contains the famous *School of Athens,* in which Raphael meshed features of his contemporaries with those of great philosophers: Plato, in the center, resembles da Vinci; Euclid, explaining geometry on the ground, has Bramante's face; and the second person from the right, in three-quarter profile, is Raphael himself. Notice that the seated figure of Heraclitus in the foreground does not quite fit into the composition—the story has it that Raphael inserted Michelangelo, who is represented here, into the painting after he had been allowed into the Sistine Chapel and verified Michelangelo's genius.

Off the *stanze* lies the tiny **Chapel of Beato Angelico,** featuring two radiant fresco cycles by Fra Angelico depicting the lives of San Lorenzo and Santo Stefano. Before entering the chapel (you cannot do so afterwards), descend to the **Borgia Rooms** and the **Gallery of Modern Religious Art.** The first six rooms were Alexander VI's papal apartments, impressively frescoed by Pinturicchio and others.

The Vatican Museums, as you might expect, are geared to be a preamble to the **Sistine Chapel.** One of the few places in the museum outfitted with benches, this sacred chamber frequently overflows with weary, camera-laden tourists who have trudged through the rest of the museum primarily to see Michelangelo's ceiling. Unfortunately, the combination of these loitering crowds with the extensive and unsightly scaffolding that accompanies the chapel's restoration can make this room seem more like an overly-decorated lobby than the artistic marvel it is. Disregard the din and take note of the frescoes on the sides that predate Michelangelo's work. On the left events from the life of Moses are depicted; on the right, the life of Jesus. Significant works include Botticelli's (1444-1510) *Burning Bush,* Signorelli's (1441-1523) *Moses Consigning the Staff to Joshua,* and Perugino's (1446-1523) *Consignment of the Keys.*

It is Michelangelo's spectacular ceiling, however, that imbues the chapel with magnificence. The figures in the eight scenes of the Creation, come close to sculpture in their robustness. Perhaps the most pregnant moment is that captured in the *Creation of Adam.* The famous touching fingers are the dominant image of the Creation. Sibyl, prophets, and angels surround the central panels, holding mysterious signs in their larger-than-life hands and ineffable truths on their reticent faces. Art historians worldwide question the wisdom of the Sistine Chapel's newest face—a turn from dark and shadowed to bright and pastel—effected by restorations that will last into the 1990s. Despite the power of the ceiling, you will be unprepared for Michelangelo's *Last Judgement.* Its visual chaos captures the dramatic helplessness of the Day of Wrath. At Jesus' feet, St. Bartholomew holds up his flayed skin, on which Michelangelo appears to have painted his own agonized features. Like many other works predating the Council of Trent, the painting was censored by the addition of underpants to the heretofore nude bodies.

Although the Sistine Chapel is a hard act to follow, it's worth your time to visit the **Pinacoteca,** near the cafeteria and exit. Here are Filippo Lippi's *Coronation of the Virgin,* Titian's *Madonna of the Frari,* Bellini's *Pietà,* and da Vinci's *St. Jerome.* Da Vinci's painting looks oddly patched; before its discovery, it had been cut into two pieces, one of which was used as a coffer lid, the other as a stool cover in a shoemaker's shop. Best of all, however, is Raphael's *Transfiguration,* a work of striking dimension, color, and detail.

Finally, four interesting galleries are housed in several buildings erected in the 1970s. The **Gregorian Museum of Pagan Antiquities** adds to an already flowing collection of classical sculpture. The **Pio Christian Museum of Antiquities** houses relics of the early Christians. The **Ethnological Missionary Museum** presents some religious cultures from the non-Christian world, and the **Historical Museum** contains a collection of papal carriages and cars (these last two museums are open only Wed. and Sat.).

Villa Borghese

The Villa Borghese is Rome's centrally located park, occupying a large area north of via Veneto. To get there, take bus #492 from Termini. Ironically, the park's attractions are less natural than cultural. Though spacious and quiet, the grass is barren and unkempt, but there are three interesting museums. The central monument is the exquisite **Museo Borghese** (tel. 85 85 77), once a private house in which the eccentric Pauline Bonaparte, sister of the Emperor, lived. On the ground floor, the museum displays a fine collection of statues; two works by Bernini are showcased, *Apollo and Daphne* and *Rape of Proserpina.* Upstairs are paintings by Rubens, Botticelli, Titian, and Raphael, among others. Of special note are Bernini's self-portraits, some paintings by the critic Vasari, and Cranach's astonishingly ugly *Venus and Amore.* Pull out a L5000 note from your pocket and compare it to the original di Messina portrait. Perhaps best of all are Caravaggio's rude, tangled portraits, and the unlovely earthiness of the faces depicted. (The museum will be undergoing restoration in 1989 and only the ground floor will be open. Visits will be limited to groups of 25, leaving every 50 min. Tues.-Sat. 9am-1:10pm, Sun. 9am-12:10pm. Free while under reconstruction.)

Also in the Villa Borghese is the **Museo Etrusco** (tel. 360 19 51), housed in the Villa Giulia, a vast collection of Etruscan art from the area north of Rome. The Etruscan and Greek pottery, weapons, jewelry, cooking utensils, and toiletries from burial grounds are exquisite and elegant. Look carefully at the smaller bronzes: Modern sculptors like Giacometti owe their inspiration in part to the shapes of the tiny bronze warriors of Todi. (Open June-Sept. Tues. and Thurs.-Sat. 9am-2pm, Wed. 9am-6pm, Sun. 9am-1pm; Oct.-May Tues.-Sat. 9am-2pm, Sun. 9am-1pm. Admission L4000.)

The **Galleria Nazionale d'Arte Moderna** (tel. 80 27 51) is also in the park. The imposing building is finer than its holdings, but the place serves as a crash course in recent Italian painting. The most striking works here, however, are by foreigners—Klimt, Degas, Monet, and Pollock. Don't miss the beautiful garden tucked inside the museum, the lyrical sculpture garden, and the riotous, state-of-the-art optical illusions and video flashes on the second floor. (Open Tues.-Sat. 9am-2pm, Sun. 9am-1pm. Admission L4000.) If by now you've swallowed all the culture you can take, try renting a **rowboat** for a lazy afternoon on Villa Borghese's beautiful lake (rentals daily 9am-noon and 2pm-sunset; L1500 per person per 20 min., minimum of 2 persons). For a walk on the wild side, take a jaunt through the **Giardino Zoologico** (tel. 87 05 64), the Villa's zoo. (Open daily 8:30am-1 hr. before sunset. Admission L5000.) For a taste of contemporary Roman culture, hang around at night for a very different zoo.

Catacombs

Just outside the city proper, the remarkable catacombs are multi-story apartment houses of the dead stretching through tunnel after tunnel for up to 15 miles and on as many as five different levels. Of the 51 around Rome, five are open to the public, and of these the best are the Catacombs of San Sebastiano, San Callisto, and S. Domitilla, next door to one another on via Appia Antica south of the city. Take bus #118 from via Claudia near the Colosseum (20 min.). All of the Roman catacombs are shrouded in unanswered questions; every authority has an explanation as to their use, and how the Christians, persecuted and suppressed in Rome, could find the time, freedom, or opportunity to construct these subterranean chambers is baffling. The best days to visit the catacombs are Friday through Monday, when the standard three are open.

San Sebastiano is the most impressive of the sites. It is famous for being the temporary home of the bodies of Peter and Paul (or so the ancient graffiti on the wall suggests). The tunnels here are eerily decorated with animal mosaics, rotting skulls, and fantastic symbols of early Christian iconography, still clearly discernible on the walls. (Open Fri.-Wed. 8:30am-noon and 2:30-5pm. Admission L3000.) A five-minute walk away (follow the signs), **San Callisto** is the largest of the catacombs in Rome, stretching for almost 22km of winding subterranean paths, but it is less well preserved and less revealing. (Open Thurs.-Tues. 8:30am-noon and 2:30pm-sunset. Admission L3000.) **Santa Domitilla,** beyond and behind San Callisto, is most famous for its paintings—one of Christ and the apostles dates from the third century and is still intact—and its collection of inscriptions from tombstones and sarcophagi. (Open Wed.-Mon. 8:30am-noon and 2:30-5pm. Admission L3000.) In all three catacombs, visitors can follow a guided tour in the language of their choice (every 20 min., free with admission). Unfortunately, the informative nature of the tours and the actual route followed varies significantly depending on the tour guide. S. Domitilla, however, receives very few visitors, so you're almost assured of a personalized tour. If you are feeling particularly energetic, combine a visit to the catacombs with a walk down the old Appian Way. The **Tomb of Caecilia Metella,** the Circus of Maxentius, and Romulus' tomb are all within 1km of San Sebastiano. Another 1 or 2km farther is the most ancient section of the road, dotted with tombs and steles in rustic surroundings. Be forewarned that you will have to walk back to San Sebastiano as the bus turns off the Appian Way shortly after the catacombs.

If you wish to see another burial place, visit the **Church of Sant' Agnese Fuori le Mum,** northwest of the city center at via Nomentana, 349. (Take bus #38 from Termini.) Perhaps the best-preserved in Rome, the catacombs here contain skeletons of the Saint's Christian compatriots, offering an eerie welcome. Before descending into the catacombs, look above the apse for the extraordinary mosaic of Saint Agnes with two popes. (Open Sept.-July daily 9am-12:30pm and 3:30-6pm. Guided tours of catacombs L3000.) More fourth-century mosaics await in the **Church of Santa Costanza** next door. Originally built in the fourth century as a mausoleum for the saintly daughter of Constantine I, it was transformed into a baptistery and, in the thirteenth century, a church.

EUR

Rome is famous for monuments that harken back to ancient empires. South of the city stands a monument to a Roman empire that, thanks to history, never was. The neighborhood is called **EUR,** an Italian acronym for Universal Exposition of Rome, the 1942 World's Fair that Mussolini intended to be a showcase of Fascist achievements. The outbreak of World War II led to the cancelation of the fair, and wartime demands on manpower and material ensured that EUR would never complete its goal of extending Rome to the sea. Nonetheless, several principal buildings were erected, and postwar development has seen the area grow into a sterile, modern neighborhood of government buildings and retail shops. Devoid of beauty or urban vibrancy, EUR lies conveniently at the EUR-Marconi stop off subway line B. To the south is a relatively pleasant park bounded by an artificial lake. To the north is **via Cristoforo Colombo,** EUR's main street. Proceed to **viale Europa,** the liveliest street in the area, which offers unspectacular boutiques and a few cafes. The **Museo Preistorico ed Etnografico "L. Pigorini",** at viale Lincoln, 1 (tel. 591 07 02), off via C. Colombo, houses an anthropological collection focusing on prehistoric Latium. (Open Tues.-Sat. 9am-2pm, Sun. 9am-1pm. Admission L3000.) In the same building, through the entrance at p. Marconi, 10, is the **Museo dell' Alto Medioevo** (Museum of the Early Middle Ages; tel. 592 58 06), whose collection includes artifacts dating from the Dark Ages after the fall of Rome in 476 C.E. (Open same hours. Free.) Up the street is **piazza Marconi,** more a highway interchange than a Roman *piazza,* its 1959 modernist obelisk notwithstanding. Next, **piazza del Nazioni Unite** stands at the heart of the EUR ideal: Imposing modern buildings decorated with spare columns attempt to meld ancient empire with empire-to-come. At the east end of viale della Civiletà d. Lavoro stands the **Palace of Congress,** but the awkward **Palace of the Civilization of Labor,** at the west end of the street, serves as EUR's definitive symbol. Designed by Marcello Piacentini in 1938, it anticipates the post-modernist architecture of such designers as Louis Kahn by wrapping arch-like windows around the building, intending to evoke Roman ruins. Hideous statuary and monumental staircases hold expressionless faces and muscular bodies. If your taste for Fascist art isn't sated by a trip to EUR, visit Mussolini's **Foro Italico,** a 1932 sporting palace not to be confused with the **Foro Romano** near the Colosseum. Take bus #1 from p. del Popolo.

Entertainment

Roman entertainment tends to be communal and public: Concerts and operas harmonize under the stars, street fairs burst in narrow alleyways, and crowds congregate in every *piazza.* Consequently, clubs are not an integral part of Roman social life, and those that exist tend to close, if not for the summer, at least for August. Few places open during the week, and fewer still specify when their summer holiday will be. Try calling ahead before you set out—there's usually someone around weekend evenings after 8pm.

The excellent "Roma Cinema" and "Roma Teatri" sections in the newspaper *La Repubblica* (L900) give descriptions, dates, and prices for concerts, nightclubs, films, theater, and other events. The Saturday edition of the newspaper contains the magazine insert, *Trova Roma,* a weekly guide with articles and listings. Unfortunately, it's available only in Italian, though the listing are not too difficult too understand. Each month one of the tourist offices (Comune di Roma) prints *Il Taccuino,* a long and colorful sheet listing and describing the upcoming month's concerts, films, exhibitions, theater, and opera presentations, sporting events, and lectures. Also ask at the EPT for their *Carnet di Roma e del Lazio,* a monthly listing in English and Italian of monuments, special exhibits, lectures, and events (primarily opera and classical music concerts). The most comprehensive entertainment guide is *This Week in Rome,* a bilingual monthly (L4000), with sections on bars, discos, and shopping.

Rome adores summer and holds myriad celebrations. The **Festa de Noantri** comes to Trastevere for 10 days during the last two weeks in July; at night, the streets are the scene of Dionysian carousing. Festivals also explode in different *piazze;* any local will tell you where to discover acrobats, fire-eaters, or rock musicians on any given day. In p. della Repubblica, there's often a Vegas-style crooner, while in p. Navona you're more likely to run across the last vestiges of the flower generation. Follow your eyes and ears. Around June 20-24, the **Festa di San Giovanni** at San Giovanni in Laterano features a wonderful banquet where the specialties are stewed snails (*lumache*) and roast pork. The **Festa de San Lorenzo** goes on from July 17-21 on the streets of Rome's most traditional and vibrant quarter. From mid-July through early September **Estate all' Isola Tiberina** brings theater, music, and acts of all kinds to the island in the Tiber. During the first three weeks in July, the river is illuminated with the sights and sounds of **Tevere Expo,** an annual national exhibition featuring industrial products, crafts, and foods of the various regions of Italy. In general, civic authorities try to counter the image of Rome in summer as an urban wasteland by organizing a series of events under the rubric of **L'Estate Romana.**

Off-season events include Christmas-time manger scenes (*presepi*) in p. Navona, p. di Spagna, and various churches. Epiphany is celebrated in p. Navona the night of January 5-6, bringing to a climax the post-Christmas toy fair. On January 17, the pet owners of Rome celebrate **Saint Anthony's Feast Day** by gathering with their pets at the **Church of Sant' Eusebio,** p. Vittorio, for the traditional blessing. The patron saint of animals draws quite a menagerie. Shrove Tuesday is the day for the pre-lenten **Carnival** in the city's *piazze.* March 19 is the **Festa di San Guiseppe** in the Trionfale district of the city northwest of Vatican City. *Bignè* (cream puffs) are customarily served. **Holy Week** is replete with events such as the Good Friday procession of the Cross from the Colosseum to Palatine and the Pope's Easter Sunday *Urbi et Orbi* blessing in nearly 50 languages. April's spring festival features the **flower show** at p. di Spagna with the azaleas in full bloom on the Spanish Steps. Spring and autumn feature **Fiera d' Arte,** an art fair in via Margutta.

In late June and early July, there is an annual festival in storybook **Spoleto,** and you should seriously consider making a daytrip to enjoy this exuberant event. By day, you can take breathtaking walks around the town (passing churches, perched on desolate hilltops), sip *frullati,* and mingle with dancers, singers, and local painters. By night you can enjoy outstanding entertainment: Plays, operas, concerts in churches, free Marx Brothers movies, and a hundred other delights. Tickets for the celebrations cost only L15,000-20,000. By train, Spoleto is two hours and L5000 from Rome. On weekends during the festival special late trains will return you to Rome after performances; double-check the schedule beforehand, or consider spending the night in Spoleto (see Spoleto).

Music

The music never stops in Rome—keep your eyes open for posters and scan the newspapers. Concerts are held either at the **Foro Italico** (tel. 396 67 33), **Stadio Flaminio** (tel. 39 12 39), or at **Palazzo dello Sport** (tel. 592 52 05) and **Palazzo della Civiltà del Lavoro,** both at EUR. Tickets for rock concerts, held primarily at Palazzo dello Sport, start at L10,000. The acoustics are abominable and it's always jammed, but excellent groups perform. For tickets to, and information on, contemporary music events, visit the **ORBIS** agency, at p. d'Esquilino (tel. 475 14 03), near S. Maria Maggiore. (Open Mon.-Fri. 10am-1pm and 4-7pm, Sat. 10am-1pm.)

You should also try to see an opera on the spectacular stage of the **Terme di Caracalla** in July or August (tel. 46 17 55). Productions are lavish with elaborate sets and large casts, including horses, in exotic dress. Performances last from 9pm to 1am, and special buses (L1200) take you to various destinations in the city afterwards (1200). Decent unreserved seats cost L16,000, while numbered seats go for L36,000-51,000. From November through May, operas are performed at the **Teatro dell' Opera,** at p. Beniamino Gigli (tel. 46 17 55), near via Viminale. Tickets go on sale two days before performances.

Classical concerts are held mainly in winter at the **Accademia di Santa Cecilia,** via della Conciliazione, 4 (tel. 654 10 44), and the **Accademia Filarmonica,** via Flaminia, 118 (tel. 360 17 02). These are generally first-rate and cost L8000 and up. Other places hosting classical performances include the **Auditorio del Gonfalone,** via del Gonfalone, 321a (tel. 65 59 52), the **Istituzione Universitaria dei Concerti,** via Fracassini, 46 (tel. 361 00 51), and many churches. Tickets generally don't go on sale until the evening before or the morning of the performances, yet sell out within a few hours. Get there early.

In summer the **Accademia Nazionale di Santa Cecilia** (tel. 654 10 44) performs in July at p. del Campidoglio, with frequent guest appearances by world-renowned soloists. The **Rome Festival Orchestra** performs regularly in June and July at p. Collegio Romana (tel. 38 15 50 or 359 81 96). The **Villa Medici** (tel. 676 12 71) holds its own festival in early July.

The following clubs offer music nightly in less venerable surroundings. They generally don't charge cover, but drinks can cost L5000-12,000.

Yes Brasil, via S. Francesco a Ripa, 103 (tel. 581 62 69), in Trastevere. Foot-stomping live Brazilian music in crowded quarters. The favorite hang-out of young Romans. Open Mon.-Sat. 6am-2am. Music 10pm-midnight.

Clarabella, piazza S. Cosimato, 39, in Trastevere. Spacious, with lively South American music. Open daily 9pm-2am.

Mississippi Jazz Club, borgo Angelico, 16 (tel. 654 03 48), in p. Risorgimento. Open mid-Aug. to mid-July Tues.-Sun. 9pm-1am.

El Trauco, via Forte dell' Olio (tel. 589 59 28), in Trastevere. Open Sept.-July Fri.-Sat. night.

Folkstudio, via Sacchi (tel. 589 23 74). A small and relatively inexpensive club in Trastevere. Young musicians from Italy, Europe, and elsewhere, with as diverse an audience. Open Oct.-June.

Mambo, via dei Fienaroli, 30 (tel. 589 71 96). A piano bar in Trastevere. A wide variety of music. Drinks from L10,000. Open Tues.-Sun. 11pm-5am.

Basin Street Jazz Band, via Aurora, 27 (tel. 48 35 86). Drinks and snacks as well as jazz. Open Sept.-June.

Melvin's Pub, via Politeama, 8 (tel. 581 33 00). Beer and cocktails to accompany the music of Roman bands. Open Aug. to mid-July Fri.-Sat. 10pm-4am.

Due to a dearth of disco-going females, women can enter most places gratis. Men, however, must pay upwards of L15,000 to get in. If you're a *ragazza,* or a *ragazzo* who feels like disposing of lots of lire, here are some city favorites.

Acropolis, via Giovanni Schiapparelli, 29/31 (tel. 87 05 04), via Luciani in the northeast part of the city. The first choice among Romans. Rap music predominates in the early evening, but there's more ingratiating music after midnight. Cover for males L20,000 (1st drink included), women free. Weds. and Sun. couples L10,000. Shoes and appropriate dress required. Open Tues.-Sun. 10pm-6am.

Executive Club, via S. Saba, 11/A (tel. 578 20 22), near Piramide. Attracts large jeans-and-sneakers crowds, and well-rounded selection of dance music. Cover for males L20,000 (1st drink included), women free. Open Tues.-Sun. 10pm-6am.

Veleno, via Sardegna, 27 (tel. 49 35 83), off via Veneto north of p. Barberini. Something of a spectacle: men, women, questionables, dogs, and cats. Cover L20,000 (1st drink included). Open Tues.-Sun. 10pm-4am.

Notorious, via S. Nicola da Tolentino, 22 (tel. 474 68 88), off p. Barberini. Elegant vogue. Dress up in your finest threads and get ready for an Italian fashion show. Cover L25,000 (1st drink included). Semi-formal dress required. Open Tues.-Sun. 10pm-4am.

Gay Nightlife

The places listed below cater only, unfortunately, to gay men.

Angelo Azzuro, via Cardinal Merry del Val, 13 (tel. 580 04 72). Forthright atmosphere. Open Tues.-Sun. 11pm-5am.

L'Alibi, via Monte Testaccio, 44 (tel. 578 23 43), in the Testaccio district. Elegant and diverse, but slightly removed from the town center.

Easy Going, via della Purificazione, 9 (tel. 474 55 78), off p. Barberihi. Cheaper than the rest, but rather sleazy. Many patrons in fairly phenomenal drag. Mon.-Fri. no cover, L8000 per drink; Sat. cover L15,000 (1st drink free). Open Mon.-Sat. 10pm-4am.

Cinema and Other Activities

First-run cinemas in Rome tend to charge about L6000 and, though the movies are often American, they're invariably dubbed. However, "cineclubs" and "essais" show the best and most recent foreign films, old goodies, and an assortment of motley favorites in the original language. Tickets usually cost L5000. The only cinema that shows undubbed American movies is the **Pasquino,** tucked away at vicolo del Piede, 19/A (tel. 580 36 22), in Trastevere. (Take via della Lungaretta to p. S. Maria in Trastevere and turn right at the end of the *piazza.*) Their program changes every few days and tickets cost L3000 (open Sept.-July). Check to see what's showing at the following:

Filmstudio 1 and 2, via d'Orti d'Alibert, 1C (tel. 65 73 78), in Trastevere, off via della Hungara. A club, so you'll have to pay a small membership fee. New, prize-winning films. Tickets L6000.

Farnese, campo dei Fiori (tel. 656 43 95). Foreign movies galore. The center of anti-establishment Rome. Tickets L5000.

For other activities, scan the newspapers, which often include off-beat alternatives, such as the **Square Dance Club** (tel. 366 48 16), and **Shakespeare and Company,** via Tor di Millina, 10/11 (tel. 623 65 07), a bookshop where people meet to discuss twentieth-century literature in English and Italian.

Sports

If you are in Rome between September and May, you might enjoy a **soccer** game at the **Stadio Olimpico.** Rome's two teams are Roma and Lazio. Roma is the favored of the two teams, and is in the most competitive *serie A* league, though Lazio turned some heads in the 1987-88 season by dominating their *serie B* league and earning a spot for the upcoming season in the celebrated *serie A* as well. If one of the two teams is playing *in casa* (at home), you'll witness enthusiasm (and often violence) reminiscent of that in the Colosseum two millenia ago. The stadium is at the **Foro Italico** (tel. 396 67 33). Tickets average L10,000-80,000. Your best bet at tickets is to try and see Lazio as Roma can be interminably sold out.

Horse-lovers will enjoy the **Concorso Ippico Internazionale** (International Horse Show) held at p. di Siena in May. Go to the **Tor di Valle Racecourse** out on via Appia Nuova (tel. 799 00 25) for the **International Tennis Championship of Italy,** held here at the beginning of May. All the stellar players attend. Tickets for these events are available through the ORBIS agency.

Shopping

Held every Sunday from early morning until 1pm, the **flea market** begins at Porta Portese and stretches 4km to the Trastevere rail station, featuring fake antiques, junk clothing, bits of stolen bicycles, roach clips, cars, illegally cut tapes, and other such oddities. You can easily get your wallet stolen in the bargain so watch it carefully. Traders come here from as far away as Naples to set up their stands in the dark; serious shoppers should arrive very early as well. If you want the bazaar experience (crowds, food, slamdancing, and so on), wait until about 11am. During the week, tamer markets can be found daily at piazza V. Emanuele and on via Sannio near Porta San Giovanni, both open until 1pm. There are periodic market fairs on via dell' Orso north of p. Navona, and on *via Coronari,* just northwest of p. Navona.

Rome's **boutiques** sell just about everything in the way of good clothes, at prices lower than in the States. Knitwear is an excellent buy, as are shoes. Shops are generally open around 9am to 1pm and 4 to 8pm. June through August they close on Saturday afternoons, while September through May they close Monday mornings. In the area around p. di Spagna, **Tagliacozzo** and **Anticoli,** next to each other at via Gambero, 38 and 36, offer the best buys in sweaters. The funkiest shoes in town (at surprisingly good prices) are sold by **Santini and Dominici,** at via del Corso, 14.

The Romans, always talented in the art of display, have made **window-shopping** a great pleasure. Be wary of large signs saying *saldi,* which indicate a "sale," but often mean little more than a sales pitch. The most elegant and expensive shopping in Rome centers around p. di Spagna, especially along via Condotti, via Babuino, and via Borgognona. Here you will find the world-famous Italian fashion names, like **Giorgio Armani,** at via del Babuino, 102 (tel. 679 37 77), and **Valentino,** for men at via Condotti (tel. 678 36 56), for women at via Bocca di Leone, 15/18 (tel. 679 58 72). A true window-shopping tour includes a visit to the king of handbags, **Gucci,** at via Condotti, 8 (tel. 678 93 40), and via Condotti, 77 (tel. 679 61 47). If all the glitz, glamour, and exorbitant prices have left you dumbfounded, escape to the city's more modest shopping quarters. Try the area around via Ottaviano, near the Vatican, especially along via Cola di Rienzo, or around p. Bologna, at the end of the #61 or 62 bus route. These have many of the same medium-range boutiques found in the city center, with clothes at considerably reduced prices. Via Nazionale and via del Corso also contain numerous moderately priced shops but suffer from considerable automobile congestion. For a more agreeable budget shopping experience, try the winding side streets off campo del Fiori.

Near Rome

The Roman countryside is a far cry from the hustle and bustle of the city. **Frascati,** a nearby town, is justly famed for its local white wine. To get there, take the blue Acotral bus from the Subaugusta stop on subway line A (every ½ hr., L1300). The ride takes you through ugly modern suburbs, making your arrival at Frascati all the more rewarding. Get off at p. Marconi, whose monument commemorates Italy's World War II dead, including those who fell fighting for Fascism. The diturbing posters and graffiti, put up by the present-day neo-Fascist party in towns in this region commemorate the dead in another way.

Just above the *piazza* stands the **Villa Aldobrandini,** one of the great patrician estates of the Renaissance that dot the region, and one of the few open to the public. The mansion was built in 1598 by Giacomo della Porta, but it was not completed until the addition of the monumental entrance by Bizzaccherri in the eighteenth century. The park that surrounds the mansion features interesting fountains and statues. (Open Tues.-Sat. 9am-1pm. Apply to the Azienda di Soggiorno for admission.)

A few blocks to the northeast of p. Marconi is piazza San Pietro, where the seventeenth-century ***duomo*** and a pleasant eighteenth-century fountain by Fontana stand. As you walk about the town, cool off with a cone of coconut gelato from the Gelateria Bar Belvederi, off p. Marconi (L1000-2000).

Three miles uphill from Frascati are the ruins of **Tusculum** (2000 ft.), a Roman resort town. The climb offers beautiful panoramas, but the steep grade of the road makes hitchhiking the best way to travel the hill. The ruins are a great Picnic spot. Cruise down the other side of the hill to **Grottaferrata,** 3km from Frascati. Follow via Cavour past a modern shopping mall to the town's Romanesque **abbey,** founded by St. Niles in 1004. The abbey, inhabited by Greek Orthodox monks, was built as a castle on the ruins of an ancient Roman villa; its turreted exterior wall looks like a giant chessman. Sadly, scaffolding partially obscures the buildings. (Open 9am-noon and 2-6pm. Free.)

The town's rustic pizza is served at via Maggio, 3, off p. Cavour; head down via XX Settembre or via Cicerone for cheap *trattorie.* Keep an eye open for a *vino-produzione propria* (good local wine sold here) sign. You can catch the bus back to Rome at the other end of via Cavour until 9pm (L1250).

Lazio

Rome often vindicates Hobbes' definition of life in the state of nature—"nasty, brutish, and short." The best antidote is a trip to the restful sanctuaries in Lazio, the Roman hinterland. Lazio's famous sights—Tivoli, with its gardens and the villas of Hadrian and D'Este, and Ostia Antica, Rome's ancient port—are best toured as a series of excursions by travelers based in the capital. Transportation between Lazio and Rome is convenient. **Hitchhiking** is fairly dependable; just take a city bus onto the *via* leading toward your destination. **Trains** leave from the Laziali section of Termini, and one private line serves Viterbo from the Roma-Nord Station in p. Flaminio. ACOTRAL **buses** depart from via Lepanto outside the A-line subway stop (tel. 57 98).

Lazio, the birthplace of Roman civilization, is often referred to by its classical name, Latium. Between the Tyrrhenian coastline and the foothills of the Abruzzese Appenines, the region extends north and south of Rome. Referred to as "Campagna," it is a glory of sun and soft zephyrs sandwiched between two marshes. Historically, Latium was a respite from the gloom of these formerly malarial marshes. Painters and writers (e.g., Goethe in his *Italian Journey*) have reveled in the light of this volcanic plain. Ravines and deep, hill-ringed lakes provide a backdrop to the all-pervasive golden hue. The ancient Latins, Etruscans, Romans, and subsequent civilizations have all appreciated the fertility and beauty of this area. The earliest settlements in Lazio were in the Castelli Romani or Colli Albani (Alban Hills). The natural security of the Colli Albani encouraged the first settlers to inhabit the caves, and the easily-quarried tufa made excellent building material—structures appeared as early as the Iron Age. The small hill villages near Viterbo (thought to be pre-Etruscan) are still partly built of tufa and partly dug from it.

The Etruscans controlled Latium and Etruria for four hundred years before the rise of Rome, but their cities were conquered and buried and their language defunct by the time of Caligula. The tombs at Tarquinia, Cerveteri, and Veio contain the art of a proud, hedonistic people.

Although the boundaries of Rome were set one hundred miles from the city center, the Romans accorded Latium and its citizens special privileges, the *ius Latinum.* But Roman exploitation of the Campagna for state purposes caused the towns to decline and the population to become impoverished. In the second century C.E., the Campagna was partly reclaimed by wealthy Romans who built summer villas in the area. Hadrian's villa was the largest and most impressive. Renaissance popes and Roman nobles also took to villa-building in the Campagna.

Tivoli is Italy's park *par excellence,* terraced down a cliff in front of the **Villa d'Este,** a sixteenth-century social showpiece built by Cardinal Ippolito d'Este. Although the house's dark rooms full of paintings and busy murals are not intriguing in themselves, they radiate tranquility and afford grand views over the well-tended gardens. Along the avenue of One Hundred Fountains, you'll see a profusion of perfectly maintained flowerbeds. Explore the avenues, each of which offers some new burst of waterfall, carved fountain, or cavern iridescent with aquatic phantasmas. (Open June-Aug. Tues.-Sun. 9am-6:45pm; Nov.-Jan. 9am-4pm; in off-season open until 8pm. Admission a steep L5000.)

On the other side of town is the **Villa Gregoriana,** where the water of the Aniene River falls 500 ft. to create a series of beautiful waterfalls. Much scruffier than the Villa d'Este, this is a place more for nature hikes than quiet promenades. The main waterfall is the **Grande Cascata,** but the smaller ones are equally impressive. The waterfalls keep the park cool even on the hottest summer days. (Open Tues.-Sun. 9:30am to 1 hr. before sunset. Admission L750.) Downhill from the two villas are **Pinocchio,** via Palatina, 23, and **L'Orso Bianco,** via della Missione, 106. Your nose won't grow when you rave about the homemade ice cream here. (Both open Tues.-Sat. 8am-1pm and 3:30-9pm.)

Tivoli lies about an hour east of Rome and is served by an ACOTRAL bus every 20 minutes from 5:30am to midnight (L1800), leaving from via Gaeta, 1 block west of via Volturno near p. dei Cinquecento. You can get off at the next-to-last stop (Tivoli), see the Villa d'Este, walk to the Villa Gregoriana, and catch the return bus from there.

Ten minutes away from Tivoli by car (and accessible by the Rome-Tivoli bus, which leaves you at Bixio Adriana on the main road about a mile from its entrance, L1700) is the **Villa Adriana.** Here the Emperor Hadrian built a miniature version of all the buildings that had impressed him during his imperial travels in Europe and the Near East. The ruins that remain today are extensive and merit an hour or two. The buildings of the **Billa dell'Isola** and the **Canopo** deserve special notice; their juxtaposition of white marble and red brick against the turquoise water of the little lakes is striking. (Open Tues.-Sun. 9am to 1 hr. before sunset. Admission L4000.)

Ostia Antica

Ostia Antica is a prototype of the classical Roman city, regarded by many as the equal of the more famous Pompeii. The city was founded in the fourth century B.C.E. and reached its height after the Emperor Claudius developed Ostia into a Roman naval base in the first century C.E. Settled at the point where the Tiber joins the sea, Ostia was strategic for both defense and trade, and only entered into decline in the fourth century C.E., when Constantine expanded the port at the present site of Fiumicino. Some 60,000 people from all parts of the empire lived here, along with Roman soldiers and slaves. With the barbarian invasions of the fifth century, the port fell into disuse. In the 800s, Pope Gregory IV reestablished a town on the site, so that the Romans could obtain the necessary supplies to defeat the Goths, who had destroyed the port of Rome. Since 1909, Ostia has attracted archeologists from all corners. Slowly they uncover the essential public avenues and institutions, as well as private homes.

Ostia is a lovely place for a walk. You can pack a lunch and siesta on the cool steps of the Roman theater or temple. Part of Ostia's beauty is how effortless it is to imagine, in those silent chambers, the buzz of life. Plaques with the original writing turn up around overgrown corners, and you may find yourself reading "SALUTI CAESARIS AUGUST" with a chill.

To reach Ostia, take the Lido train from the Piramide stop on metro line B (every ½ hr.; 20 min.; L700, if you buy a through ticket in Rome, round-trip only L1000). Upon arrival, walk across the overpass and continue straight to the "T" intersection; make a left and follow the signs to the entrance. (Site open Tues.-Sun. 9am to 1 hr. before sunset. Admission L5000, including museum.)

Ostia's main road, **Decumano Massimo,** runs through the middle of the city from the Porta Romana, curving round to the Porta Marina, which once opened onto the now-receded sea.

Traveling down the Decumano Massimo from Porta Romana, you pass the important buildings. Tombs from different periods cluster to the left near the gate. The **Baths of the Cisiarii,** on the far side of the warehouses (to the right of the road), hold several fascinating mosaics, one with scenes of life in Ostia. Often, you can kick away the gravel covering the black-and-white floor tiles to reveal an extension of the visible mosaic. The marine mosaics in the **Baths of Neptune** are most spectacular; be sure to find the one illustrating the courtship of Neptune and Amphitrite. For an excellent view of the gymnasium, climb the stairs on the side. At the top, looking away from the baths, you can see the **Roman theater,** built under Augustus but completely redone in the days of Septimius Severus. Restored in 1827, the theater is now used for classical plays. Behind the theater, **piazzale delle Corporazioni** housed the offices of the commercial associations that did business in Ostia. Their trademarks remain on the mosaic floors outside each store, identifying merchants from across the ancient world.

Ostia's **museum,** near the parking on the north side of the site, displays a diverse and delightful collection of artifacts recovered from the excavation. (Open Tues.-Sun. 9am-1pm.) Here objects from all strata of life are exhibited, from triumphant statues of the Emperor Trajan to cooking utensils. Be sure to investigate the well-preserved sarcophagi in Room IX.

As in Rome, Ostia's **Capitolium** and **Forum** stand right in the center of town. A civic center and elegant showcase for Ostia—as well as its principal temple, the second-century Capitolium was probably intended to evoke the Capitol in Rome, judging from its elevation and shape (note 2 two columns and the enclosure behind). Across from the Capitolium are the Forum and the best **baths** in the city. Nearby, a small first-century temple dedicated to Rome and Augustus houses a statue of the goddess Roma, the only extant personification of the city besides the statue on Rome's Capitoline Hill. The third-century **Tempio Rotondo,** on vicolo del Pino, is a miniature Pantheon with an anthropocentric tilt: It is dedicated to the cult of all the emperors, rather than all the gods. Such a hubristic structure would have been inconceivable before the fall of the Republic and the imposition of the Empire. Across from it stands the **Curia,** or Senate House, where the city council met.

The residential areas of Ostia exemplify all classes of Roman housing, from the *insula* (apartment block) to the *domus-villa* (detached house). The shops and public facilities—bakeries, baths, and wells—indicate that Roman life was communal. Instead of owning an oven, for example, each family brought its meal to the communal oven. The roof and interior walls of some structures still stand, giving you a sense of how cramped the buildings were. To the right of the main road, you'll find stone ledges on the exteriors of some houses, which, like those in Italy today, held flowers and religious icons.

In the southwest corner of the site, far from the center of town and the civic institutions, stands Ostia's first-century **synagogue,** considered the most ancient Jewish temple in the West. Discovered in 1961, the Corinthian-columned structure blends with the ruins of other classical buildings, but the presence of Hebrew letters, renderings of menorah, and other Jewish symbols allowed archeologists to identify the building. Reproductions of some artifacts recovered from the site are displayed at the museum in Rome's central synagogue (see Piazza Mattei under Sights in Rome). The synagogue was maintained through the fourth century, until Ostia's end.

Rome's hideous beach, **Lido di Ostia,** is only a short walk from the site. You can combine it with a visit to Ostia Antica, or ride the Lido train directly to the end of the line. The best place to go swimming near Rome is beautiful and clean **Lake Bracciano,** Rome's reservoir. You can take a train from Termini to Bracciano (Rome-Viterbo line) and the impressive **Orsini-Odescalchi Castle** (open Thurs., Sat., and holidays 9am-noon and 3-6pm). Walk down the hill to the lake, and continue right until you find an appealing beach.

Viterbo

Heavy Allied bombing crumbled ramparts, and reconstruction has been slow. As a result, you will step from the station into traffic, rubble, and the forbidding entrance to a walled city tinctured black. But don't be deterred: The vestiges of Viterbo's eminence warrant at least a whistle stop, after which you can hop, skip, and jump to lush countryside and Bamarzo's endearing little lodge.

Viterbo began as an Etruscan center but was most important as a papal refuge from Frederick Barbarossa's seige on Rome in the twelfth century. In the next century, the real architectural splurge began as Viterbo became a Guelph stronghold in the aristocrats' civil war. It was here that the torturous (literally) process of papal elections first took shape. The *capitano* (city dictator) locked the cardinals in their palace until they chose a new pope. Incentives to prevent indecision included taking the roof off the conference room so that the cold might spur the lagging priests, and stopping deliveries of food. Today, Viterbo serves as an induction point for young men newly drafted into the Italian military.

Orientation and Practical Information

Viterbo is best reached by bus. From Rome, take metro line A to the Lepanto stop, transferring to the blue bus to Viterbo (1¾ hr., L5900). Buses also run to Orvieto (3 per day, 1½ hr.), Civitavecchia (4 per day, 80 min., L3200), and Tarquinia (5 per day, 45 min., L2900), together with other cities in Etruria. Trains travel from Roma Termini (2½ hr., L6700) and Civitavecchia (2 hr.). Left of the bus and train stations is via le Raniero Capocci. This street divides the city into old and new sectors. To get to the old city, turn left from v. Capocci and make your first right onto via San Bonaventura. Descend the first little flight of stairs on your left and you're headed straight for ancient piazza Verdi.

EPT: p. dei Caduti, 16 (tel. 22 61 61). The usual supply of pamphlets and maps, but no guarantee of an English-speaking clerk. Open in summer Mon.-Sat. 8am-2pm and 4-7pm; in off-season 8am-2pm and 3-6pm. Also a **booth** in Loggia di San Tommaso, p. della Morte—aptly named for this city.

Azienda di Turismo: p. Verdi, 4 (tel. 347 76). No English, but a helpful wall map, a thick booklet on the whole area, accommodations listing, and a staff that cares. Open daily 8am-1:40pm. After hours, try the **branch office** at p. Cavour, 1 (tel. 85 63 84).

Post Office: via F. Ascenzi. Open Mon.-Fri. 8am-1pm, Sat. 8am-noon. Also p. della Rocca. Open Mon.-Fri. 2-7pm. **Postal code:** 01100.

Telephones: SIP, via Calabresi, 7. Open Mon.-Fri. 8:30am-12:30pm and 3-6pm, Sat. 9am-noon. **Telephone code:** 0761.

Train Station: Both stations are about 10 min. out of town—one to the south on via San Biele, one to the north on viale Trento. Both have trains to Rome; only the latter has connections to Florence.

Bus Station: Buses arrive at an outdoor stop on viale Trento, at viale Trieste. Tickets must be bought at the combination movie theater/snack bar at viale Trento, 1. Buses almost every hr. to Civitavecchia (1½ hr.), Tarquinia (1 hr.), Capranola, and Bolsena. Last bus for Rome leaves at 6:30pm.

Hospital: via S. Lorenzo, 101 (tel. 22 38 23).

Police: Questura, Località Pietra Re (tel. 319 51).

Accommodations

In July and August hotels are rarely full. Four or five times per year, however, Viterbo's three *caserne* (barracks) summon Italians from all over the country for military service. At these times a room is a rarity.

Albergo Milano, via della Cava, 54 (tel. 307 05), off p. della Rocca. Outside the old town center, but near stazione Porta Fiorentina. Friendly management. Singles L17,400. Doubles L37,050. Triples L50,000.

Albergo Antico Angelo, via Orologio Vecchio, 1 (tel. 370 04), just off p. delle Erbe. An excellent location. Contemporary bathrooms. Curfew 10:30pm in winter. Singles L22,000, with bath L24,000. Doubles L33,200, with bath L43,200.

Albergo Tuscia, via Cairoli, 41 (tel. 22 33 77), off p. dei Caduti 6 min. from bus station. A big, modern hotel with telephones for international calls. Congenial management. Singles L22,000, with bath L24,000. Doubles L33,200, with bath L43,200.

Albergo Roma, via della Cava, 26 (tel. 319 09). Likely to have room, at least. No running water after 11pm. Singles L18,250. Doubles L38,850.

Suore Adoratici del Sangue di Cristo, vialeIV Novembre, 15 (tel. 346 57), off p. Francesco Crispi just outside Porta della Verità. Run by nuns. For women only. A boarding house with 22 rooms. Clean, but somewhat restrictive. Singles L22,000 per night. Full board L33,000. Curfew 10pm.

S. Giovanni Maestro Pie Venerini, largo Rosa Venerini, 1 (tel. 330 35). Like the establishment listed above, except this one's only for men only.

Camping

The nearest campgrounds are on the immaculate beach of lovely **Lago di Bolsena,** some 30km north. Each of the lakeside towns has a castle or church. The campgrounds most accessible by public transportation are those in Bolsena itself: **Il Lago,** via Cadorna (tel. 981 91; open through Sept.), and **Pineta,** via A. Diaz (no phone; open April-Oct.). There are prettier sites near Bolsena off the Cassia in the towns of Capodimonte and Montefiascone: **Cappellatta** (tel. 985 43), 3½km from Bolsena (open through Sept.), **Romantic Chez Vous** (tel. 982 03), 4km from Bolsena (open April-Sept.), and **San Lazzaro,** 1km from Capodimonte.

Food

Local specialties include the exotic looking *lombriche* (earthworm) pasta and a chestnut soup known as the *zuppa di mosciarelle.* Try the red wine *greghetto* and Viterbo's native *sambuca,* a sweet anise-flavored liqueur. One of the most celebrated local wines exults in the effervescent name *Est! Est!! Est!!!,* which are the first words of the epitaph on the grave of a German traveler who died of drink while on a journey to Rome.

Trattoria Tre Re, via Macel Gattesco, 3 (tel. 346 19), off the p. delle Erbe. Excellent, finely prepared food. Marvelous *menù* L17,000. Open Fri.-Wed.

Ristorante il Richiastro, via della Marrocca, 18 (tel. 22 36 09), off p. D. Alighieri. The best fare and classiest atmosphere in town. Choose between a table in the secluded garden and one in the stately old *salotto.* Unforgettable meals from L28,000. Open Thurs.-Sun. noon-2:30pm and 7-10pm; Mon.-Wed. by reservation only.

Taverna dell' Orologio Vecchio, on the street of the same name (tel. 357 43). A small place with delectable *ravioli alla ricotta. Menù* L12,000. Open Wed.-Mon.

La Fattoria di Ferento, strada Ombrone, 5 (tel. 41 60 43). Delicious homemade pasta—try *gnocchi* (L5000). Open Wed.-Mon.

Taverna del Padrino, via della Cava, 22. Tasty pizzas and a lively atmosphere. Popular with Italian conscripts. Pizza L2000-7500. Cover L1500. Open Wed.-Mon. noon-2:30pm and 7pm-midnight.

Sights

At the southern end of town is the medieval quarter's administrative center, **piazza del Plebescito.** The medallion-covered building with the tall clock tower is the Palazzo del Popolo, across from which is the Palazzo della Prefettura. Large stone lions, the symbol of Viterbo, protect both. Between them stands the **Palazzo Comunale,** a sprawling Renaissance edifice. The lovely courtyard within is a late addition. The odd frescoes in the **Sala Regia** are one of the few extant cycles glorifying local events with elements from local mythology. Painted in 1592, they depict the history of Viterbo, using a mixture of Christian, classical, Etruscan, and medieval legends to enhance history. (Open 9am-1pm. Admission L3000.) Go upstairs in the courtyard and ask in the office to the right at the top of the stairs to have the Royal Room opened. Outside Sant' Angelo is a late Roman sarcophagus erected in 1138. According to the inscription, it contains the body of ineffably beautiful and virtuous Galiana. When she refused to marry an amorous baron, he besieged the city, promising to spare the city if she came to the wall. As soon as Galiana appeared, the baron struck her with an arrow, thereby ensuring her fidelity.

Via San Lorenzo, which winds its way from p. del Plebescito into Viterbo's medieval heart, is lined with interesting *palazzi.* The fifteenth-century **Palazzo Farnese,** #101, is recognizable by the *fleur-de-lis* over its side windows. Its plain walls enclose an intimate courtyard graced with a balcony and lovely stairway. The street ends in p. San Lorenzo, the religious center and first-inhabited nucleus of the city. On the left is the heavy-set little **Casa Pagnotta,** a gem of fifteenth-century architecture. The **cathedral,** straight ahead, has an ordinary facade but exciting bell tower: The pairs of slender, arched windows climb to a sharp peak, in Sienese style. The most conspicuous building in Viterbo, the **Palazzo Papale** fills the far end of the *piazza* with an enormous, dark mass, topped by a row of toothlike merlons. From the airy terrace beneath the *loggia* is a bird's-eye view of a complex of early Christian churches. This has been the site of three papal conclaves, including one in which the roof was ripped off to freeze and starve the clergy. Marks on the roof show where it was detached. (Open Mon.-Sat. 10am-12:30pm. Free.)

The most intact part of medieval Viterbo is the *quartiere* of **San Pellegrino,** through which via San Pellegrino winds its halting way. The churches and towers seem to block the path completely, and the sky is a strip of blue between the dark stone walls. At one point the street widens into piazzetta San Pellegrino, a dense amalgam of archways, towers, and potted plants that captures the essence of the Middle Ages.

On your way to the **Church of Santa Maria della Verità** and the adjoining **Museo Civico,** you will pass the **Fontana Grande,** the largest and most original of Viterbo's many fountains, built in the shape of a vast Greek cross. World War II bombing destroyed most of the frescoes in the church, but the remaining bits of Lorenzo da Viterbo's *Marriage of the Virgin* gives you an idea of fifteenth-century Viterban painting. (Church open 9am-noon and 3-5pm.) Two beautiful paintings in the museum are Sebastiano del Piombo's *Pietà* and *Scourging.* Dramatic is Salvator Rosa's *Incredulità di San Tommaso,* in which a skeptical Thomas forcefully probes Christ's open wound with his finger. The museum's collection of Etruscan artifacts is displayed around a gracious cloister that dates from the thirteenth and fourteenth centuries. (Museum open April-Sept. 8am-1:30pm and 3:30-6pm. Admission L2000, Sun. free.)

The **Basilica of San Francesco** at the northern end of the city contains the tombs of two popes who died in Viterbo: Adrian V (1276, whom Dante put in hell with the misers) and Clement IV (1265-68). Both mausoleums are composed of exemplary thirteenth-century sculpture, the former attributed to Arnolfo di Cambio.

The oddest sight in Viterbo is the **Sanctuary of Santa Rosa,** a huge and hideous neoclassical temple (1908). The saint's body, sanctified for its refusal to rot, lies inside a metal urn from which it grins gruesomely.

Entertainment

At 9pm on September 3, the people of Viterbo honor Santa Rosa. One hundred stout bearers carry through the illuminated labyrinth of streets the *Macchina di Santa Rosa,* a towering construction of iron, wood, and papier mâché about 100 ft. high. Weighing about four tons, the *Machina* spirals high into the air like a giant wedding cake with the saint at its pinnacle. This procession, similar to the one in Gabbio, requires a show of faith through superhuman execution. The bearers of the tributary must not only lug it around town, but then sprint uphill to the Church of Santa Rosa. Many people have been killed in this ceremony honoring the incorruptible dead; in 1814 the Macchina fell on the *facchini* (the bearers), and in 1968 it had to be abandoned in the street because it was too heavy. For a grandstand seat, contact the EPT.

In 1172 the Viterbese destroyed their ancient rival **Ferento,** and today use the Roman amphitheater there for musical and dramatic performances in July. A local bus will take you 8km of the way to the city, from where you must walk 1½km up the road to the right. Throughout June, the **Festival Barocco** brings excellent classical music to Viterbo's churches. Ask at the EPT for tickets (L8000) and schedules.

Near Viterbo: Villa Lante and Bomarzo

The hot summers of Rome have always driven folk to the mountains or the seaside. Consequently, a *castello* or villa crowns almost every attractive hill in Lazio, built as a summer residence for a Roman prince, cardinal, or pope. (The pope still has his at Castel Gondolfo.) **Villa Lante,** in the picturesque town of **Bagnaia** just outside Viterbo, is a particularly enjoyable example of the grandiose villas that were in vogue among sixteenth-century church hierarchy.

The twin mansions of Villa Lante were built some 20 years apart for two different cardinals, but the complex works as a symmetrical whole. Enter the park of the villa at the end of the right-hand street. Immediately in front of you, one of the park's many fountains combines the formality of a sculpted horse with the drollery of aquarian *putti* blowing shells. The star-and-mountains held up by the "Four Moors" around the central fountain on the lower terrace stand for Pope Sixtus V (1585-1590). Most of the estate is now a public park, and you can wander among the fountains and along the avenues as you please. To enter the gardens immediately adjacent to the villa, however, you must ring at the gatehouse on the left as you enter and wait for a keeper to take you in. You cannot visit the interiors of the two villas without the permission of the Sopraintendenza Monumenti del Lazio, via Cavalletti, 2, Rome (tel. 678 47 96). In the *loggia* of the earlier villa (the one near the park's entrance), you can see frescoes illustrating the other villas designed by Vignola for cardinals. The Villa Lante is by far the grandest.

The terraced hill behind the villas retains the movement characteristic of an Italian Renaissance garden. Water rushes down the hill through a sequence of fountains, performing an elaborate dance before disappearing underground. The other gardens are stylized replicas of the wild: tangled and thorny. (Villa Lante open Tues.-Sun. 9am-5pm. You'll have to wait for a group to form so the guide can take you around. Park open June 9am-7pm; July-Aug. 9am-7:30pm; Sept. 9am-6pm; in spring and fall 9am-5pm; in winter 9am-4pm. Admission L3500.)

Bagnaia is on the Roma-Nord **train** line between Viterbo and Rome, about three hours from Rome and 15 minutes from Viterbo. **Bus** #6 leaves Viterbo from p. Verdi every hour for Bagnaia. You will find two decently-priced restaurants in Bagnaia: **Biscetti** and **Checcarello;** complete meals run about L17,000.

A little farther along the same road is a pleasure garden of a different sort: the **Parco dei Mostri** (Park of the Monsters; open 9am-8pm; L5000). Buses depart from Viterbo (6 per day, L1000) and drop you off 1km from the park, 3km from the farmhouse *pensione* just outside the town. In this park in Bomarzo, a surreal wilderness of grotesque forms mocks overdone aristocratic sculpture gardens of the time (e.g. Villa Lante). The eccentric Count Pietro Francesco Orsini commissioned this sixteenth-century park to deflate the lofty notions of his contemporaries. A walk through the mossy paths here is anything but calming. You stroll into the mouths of snarling beasts and past one giant ripping another apart limb by limb. Around the bend is a fanciful house intentionally built to lean. The ubiquitous distorted perspective makes the ground touch the sky and a lovely woman metamorphose into a monster. A small zoo in the park houses such animals as an ass, deer, pony, and peacock.

Straight up the hill from the park is another one of Orsini's playthings, the **Palazzo Orsini.** (Open 9am-1pm. Free.) From its windows and terraces you'll get great views of the Tiber Valley.

Bomarzo's only lodging may also once have been Orsini's. The **Club Agrituristico** is a converted sixteenth-century hunting lodge that overlooks horse pastures and vineyards. Its new owners moved from Rome to this idyll, in which they've set up two lovely rooms (L17,000 per person). They offer horseback riding (L10,000 per hr.), their own organic produce, camping (L4000 per person), and kitchen facilities. Call ahead and they'll pick you up at the bus stop (tel. (0761) 42 44 66).

Etruria

Though they dominated central Italy from the seventh to the third centuries B.C.E., and left vestiges of a flourishing culture, the Etruscans remain a mystery. They baffled even the ancient Romans, who demolished the confederation of 15 city-states and replaced the ruling empire. Claudius was one of the only Romans who could decipher Etruscan. We cannot do the same today, and their perplexing inscriptions go unread. Nor do we know the origin of the Etruscans. One theory holds they were a part native Italic and part Greek or Asian people. Until 1988, scholars assumed the Etruscan civilization was exclusive to the peninsula and that it predated the development of Roman cities. New archeological finds outside Rome, however, indicate that the two cultures existed concurrently.

What is known of the Etruscans has been dug up with difficulty from a few ruins; most of which are tombs, replete with art objects and frescoes but barren of information about the political or economic organization of Etruria. Rome took over and absorbed the civilization so completely that even the religious capital of the city-states cannot be located exactly.

Lazio is richest in Etruscan archeological sites and art. The best-excavated tombs are those at Cerveteri and Tarquinia, both easy daytrips from Viterbo or Rome. The Apollo Sanctuary at Veio is all that's left of the largest Etruscan city. All the movable objects found at these sites have been taken to various museums—the Villa Giulia museum, the Museo Nazionale Etrusco, in Tarquinia, and the Vatican Museum.

Cerveteri

You can appreciate the unique architecture of Etruscan tombs in Cerveteri. The **necropolises** that extended around Etruscan towns were designed to imitate contemporary settlements. A main street branches off into minor thoroughfares and *piazze,* and the tombs, laid out on either side of the street, are carved from the rock to imitate round houses. The interiors have household furnishings of rock and are supplied with all the objects of daily life. The ghost town encompasses large residences, including the Tomb of the Shields and Chairs; smaller houses such as the Tomb of the Alcove (note the carved-out matrimonial bed); and even row houses along the main street.

A bus runs to Cerveteri from Rome at via Lepanto (metro line A to Lepanto). The trip takes about 80 minutes (L3000). From the village, it's another kilometer to the necropolis on the road leading west; follow the signs. (Open May-Sept. daily 9am-7pm; Oct.-April Tues.-Sat. 10am-4pm, Sun. 11am-4pm. Admission L3000. Maps L500.) For a private visit with the Etruscan dead, take any of the footpaths that start near the *trattoria* on the road to the necropolis. They lead to some tombs that few people visit. A flashlight may come in handy. (Free.)

Civitavecchia

Due to its advantageously deep port, Civitavecchia has passed through a number of hands. Emperor Trojan's were the first (108 B.C.E.), followed by the Byzantines in the sixth century, the popes in the eighth, the Saracens in the next, and the French most recently in the eighteenth. Today, the city offers cheap boat connections to Sardinia. A few hours layover here can be filled with a pleasant, flower-lined walk by the water; the museum; and the good-sized downtown.

Civitavecchia is an important stop on the coastal **rail** line, accessible from Rome (1½ hr., L4200) and Pisa (2½ hr., L11,600). Tarquinia, the fascinating Etruscan capital, is only 12 minutes away by train (L1000). To get from the train station to the port, turn right on viale Garibaldi, which follows the shore. On the way is the **Azienda Autonoma Soggiorno** at #42 (tel. (0766) 253 48; open Mon.-Sat. 8:30am-12:30pm and 3:30-7pm).

The **Ferrovie dello Stato** runs the cheapest boats to Sardinia, leaving Civitavecchia twice per day (at 9:30am and 9:30pm) and arriving in Golfo Aranci, 18km from Olbia 8½ hr., deck class L10,700). Ferries also serve Olbia (7 hr., L33,000) and Cagliari (13 hr., L20,500) once per day. Ferries are synchronized with train connections to Rome, Genova, and Pisa on the mainland, and Cagliari, Sassari, and Olbia in Sardinia. **Tirrenia lines** runs bigger, more expensive, and less punctual overnight boats to Arbatax and Cagliari (all at 11pm).

The **post office** is at via Giordano Bruno, 11 (open Mon.-Sat. 8am-8:45pm). **Telephones** are in the same building and also across the street at #8, Bar Europa.

Accommodations in Civitavecchia are difficult to come by during the week. On weekend nights, however, cheap rooms abound. Unfortunately, most are to the left of the train station as you leave, removed from the port and town. The most convenient is **Albergo Miramare,** viale della Repubblica, 6 (tel. 261 67), on the waterfront between the port and the train station, which offers adequate but unspectacular lodgings. (Singles L18,000, with bath L20,000. Doubles L30,000, with bath L35,000.) Also try the **Roma Nord** on via Montegrappa (tel. 227 70). (Singles L12,000. Doubles L15,000.) Avoid the numerous *pizzerie* near the port. Instead, head for **Pizzeria da Baffone,** viale Garibaldi, 34 (tel. 252 35), where they cook their pizzas (L4500-7000) in wood-burning ovens. **Pizzeria la Tana,** via Traiana, 28, just behind the Teatro Traiana, offers even cheaper pizza (L4000-4500) and simple, full meals (L7000). **Trattoria alla Lupa,** right on the port, offers ample portions of spicy-hot Lazio favorites for about L13,000. To pack shipboard meals, try the *alimentari* across from the train station and the **Standa** supermarket on viale Garibaldi (both open Mon.-Wed. and Sat. 9am-1pm and 4:30-8:30pm, Thurs. 9am-1pm). Better yet, venture into the abundant open-air **market** on **via Doria,** running parallel to corso Centrocelle. You'll never eat figs so cheaply again.

Determined archeology buffs will go up largo Plebescito to the **Museo Nazionale Archeologico,** which houses a small collection of Roman sculptures, highlighted by a muscular torso of Apollo and some exquisite gold jewlery. The collection's more curious pieces include disembodied genitalia. (Open daily 9am-2pm. Free.)

Tarquinia

An important Etruscan capital, Tarquinia is renowned for its Etruscan art and for the many necropolises painted with scenes from the after-life that dot the countryside west of town. The Romans built on what survived the Etruscans, leaving aqueducts and stone foundations. Romans continue to come here for the beach 4km downhill and the serene medieval core. Most of them, however, come with campers. Without one, you will have trouble finding cheap lodging and may have to resort to the beach campground. Tarquinia is best as a daytrip—the beach is small beans. The site is a popular local stop on the Rome-Grosseto line, and buses run from the station and beaches ("Tarquinia Lido") into town every 30 minutes until 9:10pm. Buses also link the town with Viterbo (1 hr., L2900) and Rome (8 per day, 2 hr., L5500). The Rome bus leaves from via Lepanto, not p. Flaminio, as the EPT brochure says. For information on all of Southern Etruria (the province of Viterbo), inquire in Viterbo at the **Azienda Autonoma di Turismo,** p. Cavour, 1 (tel. (0766) 85 63 84), or at the **EPT,** p. dei Caduti, 16 (tel. 347 95). The cheapest hotel in hilltop Tarquinia is **Hotel San Marco,** p. Cavour, 18 (tel. 85 71 90), which offers commodious, confy rooms. (Singles L27,000. Doubles L39,450.) In Tarquinia Lido, 2km from where the train stops, **Albergo Miramare,** viale dei Tirreni, 36 (tel. 880 20), has beautiful doubles for only L35,000. Camp at **Tuscia** (tel. 882 94), an excellent site. It has a *pizzeria* and market, clean bathrooms, and a separate grove for tents (L5100 per person, L5800 per tent, L46,000 per 4-person bungalow). Take the bus from Tarquinia or from the train station (3km), and get off at the last stop along the beach.

Eating in Tarquinia is cheap and enjoyable. An absolute must for lunch or dinner is **Trattoria da Elena,** under the *cucina e pizzeria* sign at via M. Garibaldi, 12, at via Felice Cavallotti. This nondescript establishment cooks monumental plates of spaghetti (L3000-4000) and pizzas loaded down with toppings (L4700). Also scrumptious, despite its incongruous name, is **Pizzeria Der Etrusker,** down via Mazzini from p. Cavour. The best place for ice cream is the **Bar Gelateria Diana,** via Umberto, 38, inside Porta Romana, where the mobs of locals attest to the tastiness of the homemade *gelati.*

Buses from other cities and from the train station arrive in the **Barriera San Giusto** outside the medieval ramparts. The **tourist office** here (tel. 85 63 84; open

Mon.-Sat. 8:30am-12:30pm and 3:30-7pm) provides a wealth of information and bus schedules. Just a stone's throw away in adjoining p. Cavour is the **Museo Nazionale,** one of the best collections of Etruscan art outside of Rome, housed in the huge Gothic-Renaissance **Palazzo Vitelleschi.** Just inside the entrance are the sepulchral monuments of many of the important Tarquinian families. The reclining terracotta figures have an uncanny tranquility. On the second floor is the museum's mascot, the splendid Etruscan sculpture of the noble *Winged Horses* (4th century B.C.E.). The impressive array of Greek ceramics includes a vase shaped like a woman's head and a huge cup depicting the assembly of the gods. The Egyptian vase found in an Etruscan tomb reveals the broad extent of Etruscan trade. Also on the second floor are several reconstructed tombs; the frescoes here demonstrate the refinement of Etruscan culture. (Open Tues.-Sat. 9am-2pm, Sun. 9am-1pm. Admission L3000.)

The same ticket admits you to the **Necropolis,** Tarquinia's main attraction. Guided tours can be arranged with the museum staff, but they take time to arrange and can be superficial. Take the bus from the Barriera San Giusto (any that go to the "cimitero" stop), or better yet, walk (15 min. from the museum). Take via Umberto from p. Cavour all the way past the city walls to round p. Europa; then take a left onto via IV Novembre, which becomes via delle Croci and leads directly to the necropolis. Of the several thousand tombs that lie beneath the rolling hillsides to the east of town, only a handful have been excavated. (Due to their sensitivity to air and moisture, a paltry four to six are open on a given day.) All of the tombs are splendid works of art, decorated with paintings that are unbelievably fresh despite their age. Some race with dolphins, birds, and colors—testaments to Etruscan *joie de vivre.* Others are more mournful; demons and grotesque forms betray the ambivalence with which Etruscans faced death. The people buried in these tombs collaborated with the artist on the design. (Tombs open Tues.-Sun. 9am-7pm).

Tarquinia Lido is a typical tawdry beach. Crowded and noisy, it is not without charm. You can rent horses from **Noleggio Cavali,** on Strada Saline. Follow the sign for Galoppatoio. (L10,000 per ½-hr., L15,000 per hr.) They also rent bicycles and 2-person bicycle carriages. Also try **Noleggio,** via delle Sirene, 15 (tel. 887 17; L5000 per ½-hr., L7000 per hr.). The only other diversion in this beach town is the carnival amusement park on via Porte Clementino.

Veio

The Sanctuary at Veio is the only set of Etruscan ruins really easy to visit—just take bus #201 to **Isola Farnese** from Rome's p. Ponte Milvio (8 per day; L1000). A tiny feudal hamlet, Isola Farnese surrounds Castello Ferraioli and belongs to the Farnese clan. Before the bus goes up to the *castello,* it passes a small dirt road marked "Veio." The path descends to a waterfall where a tiny bridge crosses the rushing stream. On the other side, the path on the right leads up to a large stone gate, the entrance to the excavations. The left path leads to a *trattoria* and the middle one to fields ideal for a picnic. From here, the original Roman road paved with broad stones winds to the top, where the temples stood.

Umbria

Here, in Italy's heart of green, streams lace lush hills where farmers still grow grapes, corn, and peaches on isolated slopes. The vestiges of traditional farmhouses in the local pink stone dot the undulating countryside. All this pink and green, however, stops at the rugged ramparts of the secluded medieval hill towns. These rival fortresses accommodated the Romans and the Holy Roman Empire for centuries, and thus were only able to develop as free communes in the Middle Ages. One luminary who shined during this time was the wide-eyed St. Francis of Assisi. He threw his piety down the Umbrian hills and rediscovered it in nature. It is said, too, that

Dante was thinking of Umbria when he described the pleasant valley on the slopes of Mount Purgatory where souls rest on their way to salvation. The Roman poets Plautus and Propertius were born here, and the well-known verse of the nineteenth-century poet Giosuè Carducci was inspired by the scenery. Umbrian painting was influenced by the landscape as well, although it was also shaped by the courts that commissioned it. The odd marriage of the mannered and the mystical in the works of Perugino is the best example of this combination of influences. You'll find the artistic juices still flowing feverishly; each summer, many of the hill towns sponsor free nightly musical concerts in the resounding halls of their churches.

The Umbrians were a peaceful tribe driven into the hills by the Etruscans about 500 B.C.E.; Pliny refers to them in his *Natural History* as the oldest tribe in Italy. Their spoken language evolved from the Italic dialect of Oscan, while their script reached back through Etruscan times to the Greek alphabet. The Iguvinae Tables, ritual texts now in the town museum of Gubbio, are the longest extant record of the language. The Umbrians didn't resist the Roman expansion into their territory, which began about 300 B.C.E.; they didn't oppose the construction of Roman roads through their land (via Flaminia is still being used); nor did they help Hannibal, as did most of the other subordinate ethnic groups in the Italian peninsula.

Neutrality was not, however, isolation; Umbrian towns showcase riveting Romanesque and Gothic architecture (the Renaissance never stirred these hill towns), including the double-decker basilica of St. Francis at Assisi, the public square in Todi, and the cathedrals in Orvieto and Spoleto. Artists tended to favor one city apiece, so you can town-hop from Perugino in Perugia to Giotto in Assisi, from Pinturicchio in Spello to Signorelli in Orvieto.

Getting around Umbria is not as difficult as it may seem. The Italian State Railways (F.S.) link the major towns except Gubbio and Todi, which can be reached by bus from Perugia. To villages, buses are preferable as they drop you off in the center of town and not at the bottom of a steep hill. (Remember that service is reduced on Sundays.) Because of the light traffic, hitching may be difficult, though passing drivers will usually stop.

Lodgings in Umbria are scarce and expensive, although there are youth hostels in Perugia, Assisi, and Foligno. The only real trouble spots are Todi and Spoleto. There are numerous campsites near the hill towns (Spoleto, Perugia, Assisi, Foligno) and in the wild (at Passignano on Lake Trasimeno, or Castiglione across the shore). Thermal springs, clear streams, Etruscan ruins, and lush valleys make this an attractive option.

It's possible to feast cheaply in Umbria, particularly in the larger cities. Specialties include *porchetta* (roast suckling pig), the black truffles from Valnerina, and the local sausages. The olive oil is dark green and delicious; the best local wines are white, most notably the dry, straw-colored *orvieto* from the region's southwest corner. Umbria's sweets are justly famous, and though the Perugina chocolates from the region's capital are now shipped all over the world, nowhere is a *bacio* so wonderful and fresh.

Perugia

Perugia, Umbria's capital, compromises between being a bustling, noisy city and a sleepy country town. The city follows the hilltop-fortress plan of Umbrian urban design, with a medieval walled city atop a knoll overlooking a valley. Two universities (one for Italians, the other for foreigners) bring to its streets an international crowd, exotic crafts, and numerous cultural events. The cobblestone ways of the medieval city twist through a labyrinth of arches, tunnels, bridges, and stairways. Robust palaces line corso Vannucci, the city's main street, housing fine collections of medieval and Renaissance Umbrian art. Low-priced accommodations and food, as well as its central location, make Perugia an excellent base for exploring Umbria.

Orientation and Practical Information

Perugia is serviced by **F.S. rail** connections to Assisi (25 min., L1500), Foligno (40 min., L2500), Spoleto (1 hr. 10 min., L3800), Orvieto (1 hr. 45 min., L5500), and Rome (3 hr., L11,700) to the south; Passignano sul Trasimeno (30 min., L2500), Arezzo (1 hr. 20 min., L4000), and Florence (2 hr. 30 min, L8300) to the north. Trains also run every hour in summer to Terontola (40 min., L2800), where a bus will take you to Cortona. All leave from the main train station, **Fontivegge,** in p. V. Veneto. Trains from the **Sant' Anna** station in p. Bellucci connect with the **Perugia P. San Giovanni** station, from which a private railway serves Sansepolcro to the north and Todi to the south.

ASP buses leave regularly for Gubbio, Todi, Assisi, Spoleto, and other Umbrian towns, as well as to Urbino, Rome, and Florence, from the station in p. dei Partigiani. This *piazza* is a 5-minute walk from p. Italia—just follow the signs. City buses #26, 27, and 36 frequently connect the train station with p. Italia (20 min., L500). Complete train and bus schedules are available at the tourist office.

Azienda di Promozione Turistica: corso Vannucci, 94A (tel. 233 27). The doorway is at a right angle to the Standa shop. Accommodations service and travel information, but few maps and brochures. Add a few turns for everyone on the map. Open Mon.-Sat. 8:30am-1:30pm and 4-7pm, Sun. 9am-1pm.

CTGS: via del Roscetto, 21 (tel. 616 95). Student center with offices for travel and accommodations. Open Mon.-Fri. 9:30am-1pm and 4-7:30pm, Sat. 9:30am-1pm.

CIT: corso Vannucci, 2 (tel. 260 61).

Post Office: p. Matteotti. Fermo Posta. Open Mon.-Fri. 8am-7:30pm, Sat. 8am-2pm. **Postal code:** 06100.

Telephones: ASST, next to the post office in p. Matteotti. Open 7am-midnight. **SIP,** by the Tre Archi at via Marconi, 21. Open 8am-9:30pm. **Telephone code:** 075.

Train Information: Ferrovia Statale (State Railway Station), at p. V. Veneto (tel. 709 80). Open 8am-noon and 3-7pm. **Ferrovia Centrale Umbra,** largo Cacciatori delle Alpi, 8 (tel. 239 47), near the bottom of the *scala mobile.* Service to Sansepolcro, Città di Castello, Todi, and Terni. Information and sales of international rail tickets.

Car Rental: Paolini Paoletti, p. Dante, 28, behind the *duomo.*

Scooter Rental: Easy Bike, via G. Marconi, 27. Mon.-Fri. L30,000 per day, Sat.-Sun. L40,000 per day.

English Language Bookstores: Liberia Filosofi, via dei Filosofi, 18/20 (tel. 304 73). Take bus CS from via XIV Settembre. Out of the way, but a good selection ranging from last year's best-sellers to Faulkner and Eliot. The entire line of Penguin paperbacks (L6000-35,000). Open Mon.-Sat. 9am-1pm and 4-8pm.

Università per gli Stranieri: Palazzo Gallenga, p. Fortebraccio, 4 (tel. 643 44 or 643 45). Now in its 66th year, the university offers courses in Italian language and culture for foreigners. The university also has a student dining hall (replete with pinball machines, L100) frequented by a youthful crowd. A good place to meet other travelers, although a gourmet experience it ain't. Check the bulletin boards for free musical events. Open April-Dec.

Laundromat: Lavanderia Moderna, via Fabretti, 19, around the corner from the foreigners' university. L3000 per kg. Open 9am-12:30pm and 4-6pm.

Swimming Pool: p. Colombata (tel. 651 60), near S. Colombata. Open in summer daily noon-7:30pm; in off-season Mon.-Fri. 8:30am-12:30pm, Sat. 3-8pm. Admission L5000.

Hospital: Ospedali Riuniti-Policlinico, via Bonacci Brunamonti (tel. 60 81). **Emergencies** (*pronto soccorso*): Tel. 613 41.

Police: Questura, p. dei Partigiani. **Emergencies,** Tel. 113.

Accommodations and Camping

Perugia swells with cheap housing. The tourist office should be able to find a room for you, but if not try asking around the university. Students with rooms in the **Casa**

dello Studente may be willing to let you crash. Beware that Perugia shuts down tight after 1am. If you must rough it in town, try the park at the far end of corso Vannucci.

Centro Internazionale Accoglienza per Giovani, via Bontempi, 13 (tel. 228 80). From p. Danti, walk away from the *duomo* into p. Piccinino, and take the right fork, which is via Bontempi. The *centro* is a few doors down on the right. A clean hostel popular with Italian students as well as foreigners. Kitchen, TV room, and a spacious balcony that overlooks verdant slopes. The single-sex rooms have high ceilings, night tables, and firm bunks, but they can be packed with as many as 20 people. L9000. Sheets L2000. Showers included. Lock-out 9:30am-4pm. Strict curfew midnight. Open early Jan.-late Dec. 4-week maximum; July-Aug. often shorter. Reservations are a must during the Jazz Festival in June.

Pensione Paola, via della Canapina, 5 (tel. 238 16). From the train station, take bus #40, 41, or 51, and get off near via della Canapina, across from a large municipal parking lot. Walk up the stairs after the lot; the *pensione* is on the right. From the center of town, follow the signs for the Hotel Umbria off corso Vannucci, go past the Umbria down the steps in the passageway; at its end, turn right, and follow the 2nd set of steps down almost to the parking lot. The *pensione* is on your left. A charming place with big, beautifully furnished rooms and personable management. Singles L20,000. Doubles L30,000. Breakfast L2000. Reservations recommended.

Albergo Anna, via del Priori, 48 (tel. 663 04), off corso Vannucci. 4 flights up to clean and cool rooms. Singles L20,000. Doubles L26,000, with bath L30,000.

Albergo Eden, via Cesare Caporali, 9 (tel. 281 02). "Doubles" crowd 2 twin beds. Walk through the family's den, where the TV plays *Leave it to Beaver* in Italian. Singles L20,000. Doubles L25,000.

Albergo Etruria, via della Luna, 21 (tel. 237 30). This *pensione* sits at the precipitous end of an alleyway; the proprietress will show you through an unusual medieval sitting room, where her canaries chirp incessantly. The rooms have less character than the twelfth-century vaulted entrance. Singles L20,000. Doubles L27,000. Showers L3500.

Pensione Lory, corso Vannucci, 10 (tel. 242 66). Walk up 4 floors through an open-air stairway. The beds are lumpy. One advantage here are no dark alleys you must cross. Singles L20,000. Doubles L30,000, with bath L40,000.

Camping: Paradis d'Ete, 5km away on via del Mercatoin Trinita-Fontana (tel. 796 17). Standard facilities, plus hot showers and a *bar-tavola calda.* L4500 per person, L5000 per tent. Open July-Sept.

Food

Perugia's wealth derives from its edibles, and it is easy to taste why. Renowned for chocolate, the city also offers a variety of delectable breads and pastries; be sure to sample the *pane al formaggio* (cheese bread) and the *mele a cartoccio* (a sinful Italian version of apple pie). Both are available at **Ceccarini,** p. Matteotti, 16, or at the **Co.Fa.Pa** bakery two doors down at #14 (open Fri.-Wed. 7:30am-1pm). Ceccarini also offers an assortment of freshly baked whole grain products. Ask for *pane integrale* and choose from a number of differently sized and concocted loafs. To experience the local confectionery, such as *baci* (a combination of chocolate, nuts, and honey), go to the **Bar Ferrari,** corso Vannucci, 43. If you prefer your chocolate cold, head to the student-infested **Gelateria 2000,** via Luigi Bonazzi, 3, off p. della Repubblica, or **Gelateria Veneta,** corso Vannucci, 20. Both offer excellent *gelato* at about half what you'd pay in Rome—cones run L1500-3000.

Rosticcerie such as the one on top of scaletta S. Ercolano serve tasty food primarily to take out (though tables are often available). On Tuesday and Saturday an **open-air market** is held in the morning, and on other days, the covered market in p. Matteotti offers plenty of fruit, vegetables, and nuts (open 8am-1pm). The entrance is below street level.

Trattoria La Botte, via Volte della Pace, 31 (tel. 22 67 79), a small passageway off via Botempi, beyond p. Danti. A fun atmosphere and respectable *menùs* for L6500. ½-liter of wine or 1 liter of mineral water L1500. Open Mon.-Sat. noon-2:15pm and 7:30-10pm.

Pizzeria Medio Evo, via Baldo (tel. 207 64), through the arch off p. della Repubblica in the center of town. Decent fare. All diners are required to share tables. Pizza L4500-6500. *Menù* L13,500. Open Wed.-Mon. noon-2:30pm and 7pm-midnight.

Tavola Calda, p. Danti, 16. Fine fast food *all' italiana.* Cafeteria-style. Meals from L10,000. Pizza L1200 per slice, sandwiches L2000, and a decent *rosticceria.* Open Sun.-Fri. noon-3pm and 7-9pm.

Trattoria Fratelli Brizi, via Fabretti, 75, around the corner and a few blocks down from the foreigners' university, past the Porta Etrusca. A pleasant atmosphere, modern decor, and well prepared food. Pasta L4000, *secondi* L7000. *Menù* L14,000.

Tavola Calda Nanni, via S. Ercolano, 2 (tel. 291 91), off a quiet street parallel to corso Vannucci. L9000 buys an excellent pizza, fresh bread, and a carafe of house wine. The *pizzeria* up the street at #44 serves palatable pizza by the slice (L1200) and *calzoni* stuffed with cheese and sausage (L2000). Both open Mon.-Sat.

Ristorante dal Mi' Cocco, corso Garibaldi, 12 (tel. 625 11). Great selection of Umbrian specialties, listed on a menu written in Umbrian dialect. *Menù* L18,000. Open noon-2:30pm and 7-10pm.

Ristorante del Sole, via Oberdan, 28 (tel. 650 31), beyond p. Matteotti. One of the best in town; local specialties and a terrific wine list in an elegant atmosphere. Good views. Full meals L24,000-26,000. Open Sun.-Fri. noon-2:30pm and 7-10pm.

Frisby, via Bonazzi, next to Hotel Fortuna. For burger and fries withdrawal, except mozarella instead of Kraft. Meals around L4000.

Sights

Sigismondi once called the Perugini "the most warlike of the people of Italy." One look at the **Palazzo dei Priori** confirms this assertion. The blockish palace dominates p. IV Novembre and stretches far down corso Vannucci, with its long rows of mullioned windows and toothlike crenelation. You can still visit the richly frescoed **Sala dei Notari** and the panelled **Collegio della Mercanzia,** but save most of your time for the **Galleria Nazionale dell' Umbria** (tel. 203 16) on the floors above. This immense collection contains fine works by Duccio, Beato Angelico, and Piero della Francesca, but shines mostly for its Umbrian art. Particularly impressive are the works of Pietro Vannucci, alias Perugino, the town's most famous artist. Restoration is continuous but most of the paintings are on view and the disturbance minimal. (Open Tues.-Sat. 9am-2pm, Sun. 9am-1pm. Admission L4000.)

Next door in the **Collegio del Cambio** (tel. 613 79), Perugino demonstrated what a talented artist could do with even a mundane commission. The personages in his Council Chamber frescoes are unique. Each is delicately detailed and the whole is suffused with the gentle softness that Perugino passed on to his greatest pupil, Raphael. The latter is said to have collaborated on the *Prophets and Sibyls.* Notice also Perugino's self-portrait on the left wall. In the small chapel adjacent to the Council Chamber hang paintings of scenes from the life of John the Baptist by Giannicola di Paolo (1519). (Open Tues.-Sat. 9am-12:30pm and 2:30-5:30pm. Admission L2000.)

Head back to p. IV Novembre for a closer look at the **Fontana Maggiore,** designed by native son Fra' Bevignate and decorated by Nicola and Giovanni Pisano. The bas-reliefs covering the majestic double basin gracefully depict scenes from religious and Roman history, as well as allegories of the months and sciences (lower basin) and the saints and other historical figures (upper basin). Unfortunately, this local treasure was vandalized by spray-painting tourists several years ago, forcing the city to erect a fence around the fountain. At noon, an old man in a beret comes here with big buckets of feed, which he scatters to the delight of thousands of pigeons.

Across from the Palazzo dei Priori is Perugia's austere Gothic ***duomo.*** Its spacious interior and numerous works of art were off-limits after the 1983 earth tremors, and have only recently been reopened to the public. The renovation work continues inside, however, filling the western half of the church (around the altar) with metal scaffolding. Until the construction work is completed, the many churches around the city's old Etruscan walls remain more interesting. Follow via dei Priori, which begins behind the palace, to the jewel-like **Oratory of San Bernadino,** near the end of via dei Priori. Built between 1457 and 1461 in early Renaissance style, its vibrant facade is embellished with finely carved reliefs and sculpture. Inside, a third-century Roman sarcophagus forms the altar. The **Church of Sant' Angelo,** the city's oldest, sits at the end of a little byway off medieval corso Garibaldi. Built in the fifth century, the church has a circular interior whose columns come from various ancient buildings. At the opposite end of town, near via Cavour, stands the imposing **Church of San Domenico,** the largest in Umbria. Its huge Gothic window dramatically contrasts with the sobriety of its Renaissance interior. Don't miss the magnificently carved **Tomb of Pope Benedict XI,** finished in 1325, in the chapel to the right of the high altar. Next to the church and occupying an old Dominican convent is the **Museo Archeologico Nazionale dell' Umbria.** Its collection is notable not only for its Etruscan and Roman artifacts but also for its prehistoric objects. (Open Tues.-Sat. 9am-2pm, Sun. 9am-1pm. Admission L3000.) Continue on corso Cavour, past the Porta Romana, and you'll come to the **Church of San Pietro.** The church maintains its original tenth-century basilica form: A double arcade of closely spaced columns leads to the choir. A door at the back of the choir opens onto a small terrace with a fabulous view (be careful not to lock yourself out). (Churches open 9am-noon and 3:30-7pm.)

Returning to corso Vannucci, take a stroll down the broad avenue, stopping for a coffee or *gelato* in one of its classy bars. At the far end of the *corso,* beyond bustling p. Italia, are the **Giardini Carducci,** well-maintained public gardens. From the garden wall, there is a broad vista of the Umbrian countryside: Each high point sports its castle or ancient church, as it has for many centuries. Go around the gardens, down via Marzia, to see the **Rocca Paolina,** the sixteenth-century fortress built by Sangallo, and its odd juxtaposition of Italian antiquity and dubious modern art. The **Porta Marzia,** the Etruscan gate in the city wall, opens onto via Baglioni Sotteranea. This street within the fortress is lined with fifteenth-century houses that were buried when the gardens were built on top. (Open Tues.-Sat. 8am-2pm, Sun. 9am-1pm. Free.) If you make a left at the gate, you can follow the city wall from the outside, where many an Umbrian warrior trembled to tread.

Entertainment

Perugia's main annual event is its **Umbria Jazz Festival,** which brings a series of performances by well-known musicians for 10 days in July to the region. Chuck Mangione, Bobby McFerrin (*Be happy!*), and Carlos Santana all appeared at the 1988 festival. Ticket prices range from L5000 to L25,000. Some events are free. For information, contact the Azienda. Tickets can be purchased in advance at the Negozio Ceccherini, p. della Repubblica, 65, or in Florence at Contempo on via dei Neri.

The **Teatro in Piazza,** a collection of many different events, is held in July and August. In September there is a **Festival of Sacred Music,** with concerts performed in the various churches of the city.

The bulletin boards in Palazzo Gallenga are a good source of information on films in English and other events that the university sponsors (also a good place to meet other students). The gentle Perugia evenings can be filled with the *passeggiata* on corso Vannucci or the crowds on the steps in p. IV Novembre. The most popular place for drinks is **La Terraza,** p. Matteoti, 19.

Near Perugia

Resting 30km west of Perugia, placid **Lake Trasimeno** is Italy's fourth largest fresh-water body. Wind whistles through olive trees while fishers mend their nets in the hamlets along the shore. Things have not always been so peaceful, however. In 217 B.C.E., the Carthaginian army under Hannibal, having recently crossed the Alps, elephants and all, soundly defeated the Romans on the plain north of the lake.

The gods gave the Romans plenty of warning: The legionary standards were stuck fast in the earth and had to be dug out; the commander fell from his horse as the army set forth; and the sacred chickens carried along for divine guidance refused to eat. The villages of Ossaia (place of bones) and Sanguineto (the bloody one) were named in honor of the 16,000 Roman legionnaires who died in that battle.

In the summer, landlocked Umbria becomes stiflingly hot, and splashing in the relatively clean waters of Trasimeno can be pleasant. Luckily, getting there is no problem. **Trains** on the Foligno-Terontola line (serving Perugia) stop at **Passignano** on the north shore, the easiest point of access to the lake. In addition, many of the nonexpress Rome-Florence trains pass through **Castiglione del Lago,** just west of the lake. Near this spot is the **Azienda Autonoma del Trasimeno,** via Firenze, Castiglione del Lago (tel. 95 32 29). Both Castiglione and Passignano send frequent **ferries** (L2900 and L2700 round-trip, respectively) to **Isola Maggiore,** the largest of the three islands.

Isola Maggiore is an ideal spot for a day on the water, but bring a picnic lunch. The two restaurants on the island have a captive audience and charge accordingly. The one hotel, **Albergo Sauro** (tel. 84 61 68), is similarly overpriced with singles for L24,000 and doubles for L34,000. Unofficial **camping** is possible anywhere flat, just off the path charting the perimeter of the island. The **telephone code** for the area is 075.

The towns bordering the lake offer little of interest to tourists except a few decrepit castles. Most have fine campsites, however, with small beaches nearby, and many have reasonably priced *pensioni.* Most beaches are on the Castiglione del Lago side of the lake.

For a change of pace in museum-fare and a bit of bacchanalia, take one the seven buses making the 30-minute trip south to **Torgianio.** The **Museo del Vino,** via Garibaldi, has a unique collection of ancient wines. (Open daily 9am-noon and 3-7pm. Admission L2000.)

Assisi

The name hisses on the tongue like a sigh breathed low over the centuries. It is the sigh of the peace-loving St. Francis who was born here and survives in a devoted Franciscan community. The friars stroll the narrow, steep streets wearing the black frock of their patron . . . and the Birkenstocks of their time. They will proudly guide you around the elaborate basilica, telling in admiring tones of Francis's contributions to the Catholic faith. They will also sit meditatively, watching the birds tracing shadows on Assisi's pink stone. St. Francis once gave a sermon to the local birds and it seems they've nested here permanently. Their swarms join the swarms of daytime tourists in this popular hillside town. Assisi's church art has special force because it memorializes a life that has inspired so many. Assisi also offers ample chance to wander the woods and wildflowers that first soared the saint's spirits.

Orientation and Practical Information

Assisi is on the Foligno-Terontola rail line, about 30 minutes and L1500 from Perugia. At Terontola you can change for Florence (L10,000); at Foligno for Rome (L10,000) or Ancona (L7500) on the Adriatic. Buses link the station below the town near the Basilica of Santa Maria degli Angeli with the town proper, some 5km up the hill (every ½ hr., L500). **ASP** buses also connect Assisi with Perugia, Foligno, and Ascoli Piceno (in Le Marche), leaving from p. di Santa Chiara, near the town center. There is also one bus per day to Rome, and two to Florence; these depart from p. San Pietro.

Azienda di Promozione Turistica: p. del Comune, 12 (tel. 81 25 34). Information and accommodations service. Helpful. Pick up a schedule of musical events. Open April-Oct. daily 9am-

1pm and 4-7pm; Nov.-March Mon.-Sat. 9am-noon and 3:30-6:30pm. Beware: The tourist office in p. Santa Chiara is actually a travel agency.

Post Office: p. del Comune. Open Mon.-Fri. 8am-7pm, Sat. 8am-6:30pm. **Postal code:** 06081.

Telephones: SIP, p. del Comune. One of the most beautiful phone booths in the world. Open in summer daily 8am-8pm; in off-season 8am-7pm. **Bar Patasce,** corso Mazzini, 11a. For *scatti* and collect calls. Open Fri.-Wed. 8am-1pm and 3-9pm. **Telephone code:** 075.

Taxi: Tel. 81 26 06 or 81 26 00. Terribly expensive.

Swimming Pool: Centro Turistico Sportivo, via S. Benedetto. Take the bus from p. del Comune. Open June-Oct. daily 10am-7pm. Entrance fee L3500.

First Aid: Ospedale, on the outskirts (tel. 81 22 53). Take a city bus from p. del Comune. **Emergencies** (*pronto soccorso*), Tel. 81 28 24.

Police: Carabinieri, p. Matteotti, 3 (tel. 81 22 39).

Accommodations

In order to experience the nightly concerts in the churches, it is necessary to stay in or near expensive Assisi. Reservations are crucial around Easter, and strongly recommended for the Festa Calendimaggio (early May) and in August. There are two ways to limit your lire-expenditure when snoozing in Assisi. If you walk the few kilometers uphill to the hamlet of **Fontemaggio** along the road to Eremo delle Carceri, you will find a non-IYHF youth hostel and a camping ground (tel. 81 36 36). It has spic-and-span, single-sex rooms that each sleep 10. The showers are hot, and there is a large market next door. (L8500 per night, sheets L1200.) If you prefer to be in town, the tourist office has a list of **religious institutions.** These are peaceful and cheap (about L1200 per person), but are often difficult to find and shut down around 11pm.

Locanda Anfiteatro Romano, via Anfiteatro, 4 (tel. 81 30 25), a 5-min. walk up via S. Rofino from p. Commune, past the arch in the courtyard. It lies off p. Matteotti (a parking lot) and behind the *duomo.* A large restaurant with modern rooms in a picturesque section of town. Romantic views from rooms of the theater and castle. Singles L20,000. Doubles L26,000, with bath L30,000. Showers included. Breakfast L4000.

Camere, Rosa Maria, Rivolgersi, 19 (tel. 84 27 45), in the same area as the hotel above. Take a left in p. Matteotti at the signs for Fontemaggio. A small place run in a woman's home. Cozy, clean singles L15,000. Doubles L27,000.

Albergo La Rocca, via di Porta Perlici, 27 (tel. 81 22 84). Get off at p. Santa Chiara, follow the signs to the *duomo,* and then ask for further directions. A great choice, away from the crowds. Commodious, attractive rooms. Restaurant with a vista. Singles L20,000. Doubles L26,000, with bath L34,000. Showers L3000.

Ancajani, via Ancajani, 16 (tel. 81 24 72), off via Pennacchi. Immaculate rooms in a beautiful medieval building run by nuns. Singles L21,000, with bath L24,000. Doubles L27,000, with bath L34,000.

Hotel Sole, corso Mazzini, 35 (tel. 81 23 73), near p. del Comune. Pleasant rooms only 5 min. away from the basilica. Generally has rooms July-Aug. Reserve by mail only. Singles L24,000, with bath L30,000. Doubles L34,000, with bath L40,600.

Guesthouse of the Franciscan Sisters of St. Anthony's, via G. Alessi, 10 (tel. 81 25 42). The American sisters treat you like family and offer up their slightly wild gardens. No room for asceticism here. Singles and doubles with bath L80,000 per person. Breakfast included.

Fra. Bernardino, San Musseo, by the church of San Damiono. Run by a Californian woman. Room and meditation in exhange for at least a week's stay and some housework.

Food

Pious Assisi offers a sinful assortment of nutbreads and pastries. The bakery at p. del Comune, 32, has the widest selection, but the **Pasticceria S. Monica,** nearby at via Portica, 4, has more palatable prices. The *bricciata umbria,* a strudel-like pastry with a hint of cherries, is particularly scrumptious. For a snack, try a *por-*

chetta sandwich, carved from a whole roast pig at one of the stands near the market by S. Rufino. The ice cream is icy and creamy at the **Bar da Orfea,** where you can enjoy a view of Assisi and the surrounding countryside from an airy porch. Walk from p. Commune down via S. Gabriele dell Addolorata for fresh produce stands. The most charming bars with the best views are those that line **Camino Veccio,** parallel to via S. Franesco.

Il Pozzo Romano, via Sant' Agnese, off p. Santa Clara. The local favorite for pizza (L5000-8000). A huge selection of imported and domestic beers. Open noon-2:30pm and 6pm-1am.

Pallotta, via S. Rufino, 4, near p. del Comune. Extremely pleasant, family-run. Try their specialty, *strangozzi alla pallotta* for a unique pasta experience (L5000). Uninteresting *menù turistico* L17,000. Open Wed.-Mon.

Pizzeria Otello, behind the Chiesa Nuova. Cheap for Assisi; you can manage with L6000-10,000.

Ristorante-Pizzeria, via Italia, 34. A favorite of tourists and locals alike. Arrive early to beat the rush. Full meals L17,000, pizza L5000. Open Tues.-Sun.

Girarrosto la Fortezza, vicolo della Fortezza, 2B, near p. del Comune. Excellent fare under a vaulted ceiling. Try *faraona alla fortezza* (guinea hen). Full meals L17,000-30,000. Open Fri.-Wed.

Rosticceria-Tavola Calda Al Camino Vecchio, via S. Giacomo, 7, near the basilica. Family-run. Delicious food and plenty of it. Full meals L15,000-18,000.

Trattoria Da Elide, via Patrono d'Italia, 40, on the road near Santa Maria degli Angeli. A local hangout. Great chow at reasonable prices; full meals L15,000-20,000.

Sights

In Assisi, the glories of Saint Francis endure in the churches named for him and follower St. Clare, and in the serene, lush nature that awed him.

The **Basilica di San Francesco** is a double-decker feat of devotion and artistic prowess. When construction began in the middle thirteenth century, the Franciscan order protested against such a grandiose construction. Francis adhered to a stark asceticism; the grandiose church was an impious monument to wealth and vanity. As a solution, Brother Elia, then vicar of the order, insisted that a double church be erected—the lower level built around the saint's crypt, the upper as a church for services. The subdued art in the lower church memorializes Francis' unassuming life. The glittering upper church pays tribute to his sainthood and consecration. Cut into the green lawn outside is the word "Pax"—Peace. This two-fold structure subsequently inspired a new Franciscan architecture. Mass in English is held Sundays at 8:30am.

The entrance into the front of the church is an overwhelming experience—shafts of light angle sharply across the sky-blue ceiling, and the walls blaze with Giotto's *Life of Saint Francis* fresco series. Giotto's early genius is evident in his illustration of Francis's turbulent path to sainthood, which starts on the right wall near the altar and runs clockwise. In the first scene a teenaged Francis, in courtly dress, is surprised by a poor man who prophesies his future greatness. In the next Saint Francis has traded the city's luxury for a bare mountain retreat. Three scenes later the saint has already passed through the mystical agony of the "Dark Night," and strips himself of the clothes his father had bought him, signifying a break with his former life. The final stage of his approach to God occurs in the nineteenth frame, where Saint Francis receives the stigmata. Cimabue's frescoes in the transepts and apse have deteriorated so much they look like photograph negatives.

Bring a fistful of L100s into the lower church to illuminate the spectacular frescoes and sculptures that hide in the shadows. Pietro Lorenzetti adorned the left transept with an outstanding *Crucifixion, Last Supper,* and *Madonna and Saints.* Above the altar are four sumptuous allegorical frescoes formerly attributed to Giotto, now thought to be the work of the so-called "Maestro delle Vele," Cimabue's magnificent *Madonna and Child, Angels,* and *Saint Francis* are in the right transept. Perhaps the best of all are Simone Martini's frescoes in the first chapel off the left wall. A door in the right side of the apse leads down to a room where some of Saint Francis's riches are kept: the humble tunic he wore, his sandals, and the implements he used to mortify the flesh. (Open in summer daily 8am-7pm; in off-season 8am-12:30pm and 2-8pm. Closed to tourists Sun. morning and on holy days.)

Don't bypass the modern, well-lit **Museo-Tesoro della Basilica,** with its graceful, thirteenth-century French *Madonna and Child* made of ivory; seventeenth-century Murano glass-work; and a fragment of the Holy Cross. (Open April-Oct. Tues.-Sun. 9:30am-12:30pm and 2-6pm. Admission L3000.)

Via San Francesco, which starts in front of the Upper Church, is lined with medieval buildings, interspersed with sixteenth-century additions—note especially the **Pilgrim oratory,** frescoed inside and out. Along this street, you will notice boarded-up portals from which desperate Assisians would flee when attacked. Via San Francesco, perhaps to service its stressed population, boasts Italy's first public asylum. The thirteenth century building stands at the corner of via Fontebella. At the end of the street is the former town forum in p. del Comune. Here, bits of Roman Assisi alternate with buildings of the thirteenth-century commune. The **Temple of Minerva,** with its compressed front (the steps continue between the columns), stands next to the Romanesque **Torre** and **Palazzo del Comune,** on the uphill side. This latter building contains the **Pinacoteca,** housing Umbrian Renaissance art. (Open in summer Tues.-Sat. 9am-noon and 4-7pm, Sun. 9am-noon; in off-season Tues.-Sat. 9am-noon and 3-6pm, Sun. 9am-noon. Admission L1000.) The post office now stands on the site of the church in which Saint Francis gained his first follower. He read to his friend Bernardo da Quintavalle from the Gospels: "Whosoever will come after me, let him deny himself, and take up his cross and follow me." Bernard divested of all his riches and chose Francis's ascetic way of life.

Steep via San Rufino climbs up from p. del Comune between closely packed old houses, opening suddenly onto p. San Rufino and revealing the squat ***duomo,*** with its massive bell tower. The restored interior lacks the facade's verve, so continue uphill to the **Rocca Maggiore** (take the stepped street opposite the *duomo*). The well-preserved castle affords a vicious vista. From this height, all the cathedrals appear lined up for comparison. (Open in summer 9am-noon and 2-6pm; in off-season hours vary. Admission L2000.) Head down along via della Rocca, and you'll come out among more ruins of Roman Assisi: The **Anfiteatro** (in via dell' Anfiteatro) and the **Teatro** (in a garden in via del Torrione). The fort and the Roman remains contrast sharply with the rest of gentle, church-filled Franciscan Assisi. The pink-and-white **Basilica of Santa Chiara** stands at the other end of Assisi, on the site of the ancient basilica where Saint Francis attended school. (Open Mon.-Sat. 9am-noon and 2-7pm.) The small Byzantine crucifix, which supposedly revealed to the saint his mission, is displayed within. The body of Saint Clare lies in the crypt, and a black-veiled nun explains the saint's personal effects kept nearby. The **Oratorio di San Francesco Piccolino,** in the upper part of vicolo di Sant' Antonio, is supposedly the stable where he was born, and the **Chiesa Nuova** nearby marks the site of his family's home.

To sample Assisi's natural wealth, take the route to the **Eremo delle Carceri** but instead of following the paved road outside the arch, turn left through a grove of trees. You will pass a shaded picnic ground and then ascend the mountain.

Entertainment

Assisi's religious festivals are occasions for feasting and processions. **Easter Week** in Assisi is an especially long dramatic performance: On Holy Thursday, a mystery play based on the Deposition from the Cross is acted out, and there are traditional processions around town on Good Friday and Easter Sunday.

May is welcomed with the **Festa di Calendimaggio,** or May Day, a time for dressing up and eating out. The whole town is decked out in banners, and there is a large and noisy music contest between the various quarters of the town.

Classical concerts and organ recitals are held about once or twice per week from April to October in the various churches. During July and the beginning of August, the **Festa Musica Pro** features internationally known musicians and opera singers. The programs are often held in one of the basilicas or in the Teatro Metastasio. For details, look for posters or ask at the tourist office.

Near Assisi

In the immediate vicinity of town sit several churches associated with Saint Francis and Saint Clare, founder of the Poor Clares, the female order of the Franciscan movement. If you arrive in Assisi by train, you will see the huge **Basilica di Santa Maria degli Angeli.** The basilica itself shelters the **Porziuncola,** the first center of the Franciscan order. The chapel was originally in a forest nearby. In order to overcome temptation, Saint Francis is said to have thrown himself on thorny rosebushes in the garden just outside the basilica, thus coloring the leaves forever red with blood. The chapel became more popular when Saint Francis instituted the annual **Festa del Perdono** (Aug. 2), during which an indulgence was (and is) awarded to all who come to the church. When he died in the adjacent infirmary, now **Coppella del Transito,** the site began to attract throngs of pilgrims, and a whole ring of chapels sprang up.

By far the most memorable and inspiring sight near Assisi is the **Eremo delle Carceri** (Carceri Hermitage), about an hour's walk away, in the forest high above the town. Pass through the Porta San Francesco below the basilica and follow via Marconi. At the crossroads take the left road, which passes by the Seminario Regionale Umbro. The site of Saint Francis's retreats, this placid area better conveys the spirit of Saint Francis than the opulent basilica. Inside the hermitage is the small cell where he slept, and outside, set in the forest, is the simple stone altar where he preached to the birds. There are also a number of trails where you can walk in silence through the woods, reading Saint Francis's works or simply meditating. (Hermitage open daily in summer 6:30am-8pm; in off-season until 5pm.)

The **Convent of Saint Damian** is a 15-minute stroll down the steep road outside Porta Nuova. It was here that the crucifix told Saint Francis of his calling, and here that the saint wrote the *Canticle of the Creatures.* Inside the chapel are some fine fourteenth-century frescoes as well as a rivetting woodcarving of Christ. (Open daily 10am-6pm.)

Gubbio

Never did a reving Vespa or racing Fiat seem as incongruous as in this little Umbrian hill town. Their sudden bursts reverberate inside a maze of stone walls and ochre houses with orange-tiled roofs and then slowly fade, leaving Gubbio again the "city of silence." This is a strange nickname for a scrappy town whose history has rarely been silent. Gubbio has fought them all, beginning with its revolts against Rome, then the barbarian Lombards in the sixth century, Perugia in the twelth, the Ghibellines and Guelphs in the thirteenth, and Napoleon in the nineteenth. While Gubbio sharpened its bayonettes, it also practiced quill and brush, becoming one of Umbria's cultural capitals. The Montefeltro dukes of Urbino conquered the town in 1384 and nurtured artistic impulses. As a result, Gubbio claims Italy's first novelist, Bosone Novello Raffaelli, as well as a tradition of ceramics.

Orientation and Practical Information

There are no trains to Gubbio itself; the nearest station is at Fossato di Vico, 19km away on the Rome-Ancona line (L5400 from Ancona, L11,300 from Rome). Buses connect Gubbio from the station for L2600 (Mon.-Sat. 10 per day, 6 on Sun.). **ASP** buses cover the countryside between Gubbio and Perugia 10 times per day (1 hr., L4000). It's convenient to leave in the morning and return by dinner.

Azienda Autonoma di Turismo: corso Garibaldi, 6 (tel. 927 36 93), in p. Oderisi next door to the local Communist Party headquarters. Open April-Oct. Mon.-Sat. 8:30am-1:30pm and 3-7pm, Sun. 9:30am-12:30pm; Nov.-March Mon.-Sat. 8:30am-1:30pm and 3-6pm, Sun. 9:30am-12:30pm.

Post Office: via Cairoli, 11. Open Mon.-Sat. 8:15am-1pm. **Postal code:** 06024.

Telephones: via della Repubblica, 13, near the bridge. Open daily in summer 9am-1pm and 4-7pm; in off-season 9am-1pm and 3:30-6:30pm. **Telephone code:** 075.

Bus and Train Information: via della Repubblica, 13-15 (tel. 927 15 44). Open Mon.-Sat. 9am-1pm and 4-7pm. Also sells tickets.

Police: Carabinieri, via Matteotti (tel. 927 37 31).

First Aid: Ospedale, p. Quaranta Martiri, 14 (tel. 927 11 22). **Emergencies** (*pronto soccorso*), Tel. 927 35 00.

Accommodations

Gubbio is a delightful daytrip, but the salubrious silence might tempt you to stay overnight. High season in Gubbio runs from late April all the way to September; reservations are strongly advised during this time, especially in July and August. Get a list of hotels from the tourist office and hold the managers to the published prices.

Locanda Galletti, via Piccardi, 3 (tel. 927 42 47), off p. Quaranta Martiri. Cheapest place in town. Small and photogenic on the edge of medieval Gubbio. Hospitable homespun proprietress. Single L15,000. Doubles L30,000, with bath L34,000.

Albergo dei Consoli, via dei Consoli, 59 (tel. 927 33 35), 100m from p. della Signoria in a lovely location. Single L24,000. Doubles with bath L40,000. Open March-Jan.

Pensione Grotta dell' Angelo, via Gioia, 47 (tel. 927 17 47), off via Cairoli. The nice owners offer nice rooms in a nice setting. Nice singles L24,000, with bath L30,000. Nice doubles with bath L40,000. A nice restaurant, with a nice garden terrace and wine cellar. Full meals from L17,000.

Hotel Gattapone, via G. Ansidei, 6 (tel. 927 24 89), off via della Repubblica. Another splendid location in a cheery medieval building. Singles L25,000. Doubles L40,000. Bath included.

Hotel Oderisi, via Mazzatinti, 2 (tel. 927 37 47), off p. Quaranta Martiri. In a modern building—big and bland. Singles L24,000, with bath L30,000. Doubles L34,000, with bath L40,000.

Food

Gubbio is well stocked for the lunchtime traveler. However, be wary of expensive meals in painfully quaint settings. A sure bet is the cornucopia of fresh produce across from the bus station. A stellar snack spot is the Giardini Pensili outside the **Palazzo dei Consoli.** Here you can imbibe royally in the nobles' own courtyard. If, however, the lire lurk low, there is a free-flowing fountain on the corner of de Consoli and S. Giuliano.

Pizzeria il Bargello, via dei Consoli, 37, in a little *piazza* down the road from p. della Signoria. Outstanding pizza L4000-7000. Full meals from L16,000. A tranquil location across from a mossy fountain.

Trattoria Fiorella, corso Garibaldi, 86. Centrally located. Complete meals including sherry, wine, *primi, secondi,* fruit, and coffee L23,000. Excellent food in a family atmosphere. Open Tues.-Sun.

Trattoria San Martino, via dei Consoli, 8, near p. Bruno. Outstanding food in a pleasant outdoor setting; the *paglia e fieno* (pasta with cream, peas, and ham) is a memorable culinary experience. Meals around L17,000. Open Wed.-Mon.

San Francesco e il Lupo, via Cairoli off corso Garibaldi, near the Azienda. A homey place with filling, tasty meals (L17,000). Open mid-July through June.

Pizzeria, via Cairoli, 6B, opposite the post office. A good place for a quick, cheap, stand-up meal. Pizza of all varieties (L1000 per slice). Open last week of July through June.

Sights

As tranquil as Gubbio seems, the first sight that greets you as you get off the bus is a pompous Fascist monument, erected in 1927. A grim and muscle-bound soldier stands guard, testimony to a terrible martial vision.

Though full of medieval winding alleyways and bizarre conglomerations of buildings, the overall street plan in Gubbio is simple, a holdover from the level-headed Romans. Roughly in the center of this web is **piazza della Signoria,** the civic headquarters of Gubbio, set on a shelf of the hill on which the town is built. After looking over the edge at the town below, turn to your right to view the **Palazzo dei Consoli,** one of Italy's most graceful public buildings. The pre-Renaissance palace is built of white stone, and its rows of windows and arcades are harmonious without seeming contrived. Within is the **Museo Civico,** a quirky mix of stone sculpture and old coins featuring the puzzling *Tavole Eugubine.* Discovered in 1444, these seven bronze tablets (3rd to 1st centuries B.C.E.) are the main source of our knowledge of the Umbrian language. Written in almost undecipherable tongue, the tablets are a priceless ritual text that spells out the social and political organization of early Umbrian society. The stately rooms upstairs house the **Pinacoteca Comunale,** a rather random collection of paintings, wooden crucifixes, and sumptuous furniture of the fourteenth century. From the back room pass into the *loggia* for the best view of Gubbio's idiosyncratic medieval structure. (Open May-Sept. daily 9am-12:30pm and 3:30-6pm; Oct.-April daily 9am-1pm and 3-5pm. Admission L2000, L500 group discount.) Across the *piazza* stands the **Palazzo Pretorio.** Built along with the Palazzo dei Consoli by the fourteenth-century architect Gattapone, this palace is today the seat of civic administration.

The **Palazzo Ducale** and the ***duomo*** face each other at the top of the town. The *palazzo* was built for Federico da Montefeltro along the lines of the Duke's larger palace in Urbino. The *duomo* is an unassuming pink Gothic building with fine stained-glass windows (late 12th century) and a series of simple, lovely frescoes along the left nave. (Open Tues.-Sat. 9am-2pm, Sun. 9am-1pm.)

As you come back down to p. della Signoria along via Ducale, note the huge barrels tucked in a basement under the *duomo:* Wine casks over 3½m high abound. Continuing along via dei Consoli you end up in front of the **Bargello** (medieval police headquarters) and its fountain. This thirteenth-century structure is just one of the many well-preserved medieval buildings that are still in use. Others nearby include the thirteenth-century **Palazzo del Capitano del Popolo,** on the street of the same name, and the fifteenth-century **Palazzo Beni,** on via Cavour. Wind your way downhill along the narrow streets that run parallel to the *torrente* Camignano. The strange brick arches that span the stream and the stacked rows of ancient houses make this quarter charmingly medieval. When you arrive in p. Quaranta Martiri, the **Church of San Francesco** is on the right. In the left apse is the splendid *Vita della Madonna* (Life of the Madonna), a fifteenth-century fresco series by Ottaviano Nelli, Gubbio's most famous painter. Across the *piazza* is the **weaver's *loggia*** (closed in 1988), under whose arcades the fourteenth-century wool weavers stretched their cloth in the shade so that it would shrink evenly.

Besides wool, Gubbio's main industry in the Middle Ages was ceramics. Some particularly fine examples are preserved in the Palazzo dei Consoli Museum. Pottery is still made in Gubbio in many of the same places and in much the same manner. Potters throw and sell their wares in small shops lining the streets. A particularly pleasant spot is the **Antica Fabbrica Artigiana** at via San Giuliano, 3 (near the Bargello), a cavernous old palace filled with interesting pottery and antiques.

During lunch, when all the museums close, take the chairlift (*funivia*), shaped like a bird cage, to the peak of **Monte Ingino** for a splendid view and a great picnic spot (one way L1800, round-trip L3000). While you're there, visit the **Basilica** and **Monastery of San Ubaldo,** the local patron saint. The basilica houses the three *ceri* carried in the May 15 race (see Entertainment). It is also home to the half-decayed body of San Ubaldo, stretched out in a glass case. If you take the half-hour walk up the mountain, turn left after the second small church. You'll find a short path through the woods to a peaceful clearing. This spot on the mountain's edge makes an excellent place for musing, picnicking, or unofficial camping. On your way back to the center of town, stop at the **Church of Santa Maria Nuova** near the funicular station. The church contains a lyrical fifteenth-century fresco by Ottaviano Nelli. Get the custodian at via Dante, 66, to let you in.

From p. Quaranta Martiri, it is a short walk up via Matteotti to the **Roman amphitheater** (1st century C.E.), enormous and surprisingly intact. To visit the quiet, grassy interior, ring at the custodian's house nearby.

Entertainment

The city's two most celebrated events, both in May, are the source of great revelry. The **Corsa dei Ceri,** one of Italy's most noted processions, takes place on the 15th. The three *ceri,* hourglass-shaped wooden towers, are brought to p. della Signoria from the basilica of San Ubaldo. They are surmounted by colorfully dressed statues of San Ubaldo (in whose honor the festival is held), San Giorgio, and Sant' Antonio Abate. After 12 hours of flag-twirling and elaborate traditional preparations, the squads of husky *ceraioli* (*ceri* carriers)—quite a sight—heft the heavy objects onto their shoulders and set off up Monte Ingino at a dead run clad in Renaissance-type tights and tutus. Making occasional pit stops for alcoholic encouragement, they eventually reach the basilica of San Ubaldo, where the *ceri* are deposited until the following May.

During the **Palio della Balestra,** held on the last Sunday in May, archers from Gubbio and nearby Sansepolcro gather in p. della Signoria for the return match of a crossbow contest held in Sansepolcro the previous September. If Gubbio wins, an animated parade ensues. (Gubbio's major industry these days is the production of toy crossbows for *balestra*-happy tourists.) From mid-July to mid-August, classical and **Shakespearean plays** are performed in the Roman theater. (Information and tickets available from the tourist office.)

Spoleto

Spoleto during its arts festival is like a dignified old lady donning a miniskirt and spiked heels. The twists and turns of its medieval alleys yield to abstract sculptures of bronze and plastic. Posters ostentatiously decorate the firm stone walls, lightening Spoleto's grey with the bright hues of contemporary art. Though the festival proper runs only about a month in late June and early July, much of the art hangs around for the rest of the summer. The Calder statue you see as you exit the train station is Spoleto's to keep. Above it, you will see the curves of the old town—one whose serenity attracted Saint Francis. Be forewarned that the festival's offerings make Spoleto a popular and expensive summer spot.

Orientation and Practical Information

Spoleto is a local stop on the busy Rome-Ancona line and is easily accessible from both (2 hr. from Rome via Orte, L7500; 2½ hr. from Ancona, L8000). Transport from Perugia is also easy, with more than 10 trains per day (1 hr. 10 min., L4000). Spoleto's train station (tel. 485 16) is on via Trento e Trieste in the lower part of town. Frequent bus service (L500) connects it to the old city (get off at p. della Libertà). Several of the lines take such a circuitous route, though, that you may find it easier to walk up the hill. There are two buses per day (Spoletina) to Perugia and Assisi, and other bus connections are available to Florence, Rome, Urbino, and Rimini. Buses leave from p. della Libertà and p. Garibaldi, except those bound for Rimini, which leave only on weekends from a stand near the API gas station on via Flaminia. Buses from Rome leave from p. della Repubblica in front of Termini.

All these routes are covered more frequently by trains connecting with Assisi at Foglino or Treni. Perugia is the transfer point for Todi and Gubbio.

Azienda di Promozione Turistica: p. della Libertà, 7 (tel. 281 11). A warm and savvy office with an excellent map. Open in summer daily 9am-1pm and 4-8pm; in off-season 9am-1pm and 4-7pm.

Currency Exchange: corso Mazzini, 5. You will see several. **Casa di Risparimo** has the longest hours. Open 9am-1pm and 3:30-8:30pm.

Post Office: p. della Libertà, 12 (tel. 403 73). Open Mon.-Sat. 8am-12:30pm and 3-7:30pm. **Postal code:** 06049.

Telephones: SIP, Bar Mancini, corso Mazzini, 72 (tel. 331 93). Open daily 7am-9pm. **Telephone code:** 0743.

Pharmacy: corso Mazzini, 40 (tel. 497 03). Open Mon.-Sat. 8am-2pm and 3:30-7pm.

First Aid: Ospedale, via Loreto, 3 (tel. 60 11), outside Porta Loreto.

Police: Carabinieri, via Cerquiglia, 36 (tel. 490 44).

Accommodations and Camping

The nearest **IYHF youth hostel** is in Foligno (see Perugia Accommodations), 26km up the track (L1700). It is difficult to find a room in Spoleto during festival time; from mid-June to mid-July reserve at least a month in advance.

Pensione Aurora, via dell' Apollinare, 4 (tel. 281 15), just off p. della Libertà. Spacious, spotless rooms. Ask for one in the back, with a view of the countryside. Extremely popular. Singles with bath L20,000. Doubles with bath L34,000.

Pensione dell' Angelo, via Arco di Druso, 25 (tel. 321 85), off p. dell Mercato in the old town. Clean rooms, but lots of noise from the restaurant below. Doubles L26,000.

Locanda Fracassa, vicolo dei Focaroli, 15 (tel. 211 77), near p. Garibaldi. Convenient to the train station in the *città bassa* (lower city), but in the poorest section of town, a bit removed from the festival and the medieval city. Only 6 rooms. Singles L20,000. Doubles L26,000. Triples L38,000. Quads L50,000. Showers L2500.

Camping Monteluco (tel. 281 58), behind the church of San Pietro, a 15-min. walk from p. della Libertà. Take viale G. Matteotti out to the tennis courts, then to the left across the highway. On the far side of the highway, take via S. Pietro to the church, to the left, and up the hill. A short distance past the church a dirt path branches to the right, leading directly to the campsite. Pleasant and shaded. Horses on the hill jangle their bells. In-house cafe. L3800 per person, L4300 per tent. Open May-Sept.

Camping il Girasole (tel. 513 35), next to a vast sunflower field (hence the name) near the small town of Petragnano, outside Spoleto. Buses connect it with the train station hourly. Quiet, with plenty of shade and hot showers. L3600 per person, L4000 per tent, and L6500 to rent a 2-person tent.

Food

There is a lively open-air market in **piazza del Mercato** Monday through Saturday from 8:30am to 1pm. Try the roast pork sandwiches (L1700). At other times, take a walk down via Salore Veccia for less expensive fruit and produce than that sold in the square.

Ristorante Economico, via San Carlo, 7. Take via Matteotti away from p. della Libertà, turn left after the park, then right on via San Carlo. Run by the city government. Full meals L12,000. Limited selection, but decent fare.

Trattoria, p. del Mercato, 29. Delectable food, adequate servings, and outside seating. Run by a charming, loquacious group of women. *Menù* L10,000, but with drinks, service, and cover closer to L15,000.

Trattoria del Panciolle, largo Muzio Clemente, 4 (tel. 455 98), off via del Duomo. Considerably more refined meals L15,000-18,000, and mouth-watering cheeses. Some tables outside in the shady, gracefully sloping *piazza.*

Ristorante Sabatini, corso G. Mazzini, 52 (tel. 372 33), near p. della Libertà. Spoleto's finest traditional restaurant, with an ample list of Umbrian specialties (the *stringiozze,* a typically Spoletan pasta, rages) and a choice of wood-paneled interior or leafy garden. Iris's favorite. Excellent full meals from L20,000. Open Tues.-Sun.

Casa del Frullato, via Mazzini, 75. Some of the best fruit shakes in Umbria, including some made with tropical fruits. *Frullati* L2000-4000. Open Tues.-Sun. 10:30am-1pm and 4:30pm-midnight; in off-season 10:30am-1pm and 2:30-10pm.

Un Pinto Macrobiotica, via di Porta Fuga, 45. Complete with natural foods and jazz, this is Spoleto's scintilla of granola landocolonish yuppiedom. Open 10am-1pm and 5-8pm.

Sights

Spoleto offers art and architecture in town and lush forests in the hills to the east and south. Opt for the culture in the morning, and enjoy a hike or a picnic in the afternoon, when the museums and churches are closed.

At the eastern edge of town sits Spoleto's monumental ***duomo.*** Note how it faces a flight of stairs theatrically dropping into the *piazza.* The *duomo* is Romanesque, built partially remodeled in the twelfth century and then augmented with a portico (1491) and late Renaissance interior (1644). An utter amalgam, its soaring bell tower was cobbled together with fragments of Roman structures. The facade is animated by eight rose windows, the largest of which is decorated by the four symbols of the evangelists. Between them glitters a restored Byzantine mosaic (1207). The robust Renaissance portal below gives the church an air of solemnity.

The interior shares this seriousness, thanks to a rather heavy-handed renovation in the seventeenth century; still, there are a number of excellent frescoes. Off the right nave is a chapel containing some worn yet expressive figures by Pinturicchio, and Carracci's generous *Madonna and Saints* adorns the right transept. Filling the domed apse are the brilliantly colored scenes from the life of the virgin by Fra' Filippo Lippi. Look for Lippi and his assistants among the mourners at the *Virgin's Death.* Lippi himself habitates the south transept of the church, in a tomb commissioned by Lorenzo the Magnificent and decorated by the artist's son, Filippino Lippi.

Across from the *duomo* is the **archeological museum.** (Open 9am-1pm.) **Santa Eufemia** lacks both the *duomo*'s stature and frescoes, and poor Eufemia never amounted to much in the eyes of the Vatican. The church named for her, however, was built with Umbria's first matroneum or "womens' balconies." (Open 8am-8pm.)

Spoleto's many ruins testify to its prominence in Roman times. The **theater** (visible from p. della Libertà) was built in the first century C.E., just outside the Roman walls. The **Arco Romano** at the top of via Bronzino marked the entrance to the town, and farther along, the **Arco di Druso** marked the entrance to the forum (now p. del Mercato). Stroll through the streets around the square to catch a glimpse of the numerous artisans' shops as well as of carved corners, stairs, and arches. In nearby via de Visale there is a restored **Roman house.** (Open Wed.-Mon. 9am-noon and 3-6pm. Admission L2000.) At the other end of town are the remains of the **amphitheater.** (You must apply to the superintendent in the municipal building above the Roman house to gain entrance. Free.) Most of the Roman buildings have been recycled and the stones used to build churches, including **San Salvatore** (2½km from the town center), one of the earliest Christian churches in Italy, which retains some of its original fifth-century architecture. (Open June-Sept. 7am-7pm; Oct.-May 7am-6pm.) An architectural feat that does no glory to the Romans is the **Porta del Fugo.** Its arch reads: "Annibal Caesis Ad Trasymenum Romanis . . . ," for it was through this arch that Hannibal passed after failing to conquer Spoleto.

Much of the amphitheater went to make the **papal fortress,** or **Rocca,** which sits on the hillside far above Spoleto. The fortress, until recently a prison, was used during the war to confine Slavic and Italian political prisoners; in 1943 the prisoners staged a dramatic escape to join the partisans in the Umbrian hills. They didn't have far to run; the Rocca itself lies in sylvan hills. (Open Wed.-Mon. 10am-7:30pm. Admission L2000.) Follow the walk that curves around the fortress for panoramic views of Spoleto and the countryside. Farther on, you will reach one of the region's most stunning architectural achievements, the **Ponte delle Torri.** The 80-meter-high bridge and aqueduct, built in the fourteenth century on Roman foundations, spans the channel of the river Tessino, visible far below. On the far bank rise the craggy medieval towers for which the bridge was named.

On the far side of the bridge, there is a fork in the road. To the left, the road runs past elegant villas and ancient churches on its way up Monteluco, Spoleto's "mountain of the sacred grove." An invigorating one-and-a-half-hour climb will bring you to the **Franciscan Sanctuary of Monteluco,** once the refuge of Saint Francis and San Bernadino da Siena. (Open 8am-1pm and 4-8pm. Buses leave p. della Libertà for Monteluco every hr.)

The right fork leads over less steep grades. A five-minute stroll brings you to the Romanesque **Church of San Pietro,** whose tan facade is an amazing work of the medieval imagination. A menagerie of bas-relief animals cavort among cosmological diagrams and scenes from popular fables. Note the wolf wearing a monk's cowl and holding a book to the right of the door. Beyond the bestiary, on the ground from where the bizarre animals leapt, are Sarenic style mosaics laid in the fifth and thirteenth centuries.

Entertainment

The **Festival dei Due Mondi** (Festival of the Two Worlds) held between mid-June and mid-July was the brainchild of Italian composer Gian Carlo Menotti, and has become one of Italy's most important cultural events. (The "other world" is in Charleston, South Carolina, where a twin festival is held.) The festival features numerous high quality concerts, operas, and ballets, with performances by well-known Italian and international artists. Film screenings, shows of the latest in modern art, and local craft displays also abound. Tickets for festival events range from L8000 to L90,000 (a few are free) and must be purchased well in advance. (They are available from travel agents in most large cities or by mail. Send a check or money order for the amount plus 8% made out to Associazione Festival dei Due Mondi, via Margutta, 17, Roma 00187.) Before the Due Mondi (April-June), there is a series of organ concerts in the various churches. The opera season, which includes a number of modern and experimental works, begins in September.

Todi

An ancient legend tells of an eagle that led the founders of Todi to the site of the city. The mythical link with the eagle, now recorded in the city's coat of arms, is appropriate, considering the tiny medieval town's perch on a rocky hill. Cool mountain zephyrs blow through the narrow, steep streets between age-darkened houses and tiny wells, and breaks in the city walls reveal glimpses of the surrounding countryside. Todi's history resembles those of other Umbrian towns. Unlike its more expansive neighbors, however, Todi remained small in size and influence. Its fame is limited to an unusually graceful central square and to one of Italy's earliest poets, Izcopone da Todi.

Orientation and Practical Information

Todi is best accessed by day from Perugia (8 buses per day, L3000). Buses also connect with Terni and Rome. The private **Ferrovia Centrale Umbra** (Central Umbrian Railway) provides infrequent service to Todi from Perugia, via Spoleto and Terni. City buses meet each incoming train and take passengers the 3-kilometers from the station up to the town center.

Ufficio Informazioni Turistiche: p. V. Emanuele (tel. 88 31 58), under the stairs of Palazzo del Capitano. A professional operation with a wealth of information. Open in summer Mon.-Sat. 9am-1pm and 3:30-6:30pm, Sun. 9:30am-12:30pm and 4-6:30pm; in off-season Mon.-Sat. 9am-1pm and 3:30-6:30pm, Sun. 9:30am-12:30pm.

Post Office: p. Garibaldi (tel. 88 22 02). Open Mon.-Fri. 8:15am-6:40pm, Sat. 8am-noon. **Postal code:** 06059.

Telephones: SIP, at the Ufficio Informazioni Turistiche. **Telephone code:** 075.

Swimming Pool: Piscina Comunale, via della Consolazione. Also the **Piscina di Ponte Naia** in the lower town (take the station bus). Both open in summer daily 8am-7pm.

Hospital: Ospedale degli Infermi, via Matteotti (tel. 88 34 47).

Police: Carabinieri, via Borgo Ulpiana (tel. 88 23 23).

Accommodations

Hotels in Todi are expensive and scarce. Reservations are advisable in July and necessary in August. The only reasonably priced places to stay are the **Hotel Cavour** at corso Cavour, 12 (tel. 88 24 17), with singles for L24,400, with bath L29,750 and doubles for L34,400, with bath L46,600; and **Hotel Zodiaco,** inconveniently located on via del Crocefisso, outside Porta Romana. The latter involves a rather steep climb to the center of town and offers comparable prices.

Food

Ristorante Cavour, via Cavour, 21-23 (tel. 88 24 91). Tasty and filling meals L17,000. Excellent pizza about L5000. Try to get a seat in the cool medieval dungeon. Open Thurs.-Tues. until 9:30pm for meals, midnight for pizza.

Pizzeria, p. Bartolomeo d'Alviano, off corso Cavour. Pizza only L1000 per slice. An interesting selection of *rosticceria* fare (try the fried zucchini flowers). Open Thurs.-Tues. until 8pm.

Ristorante Umbria, via del Teatro Antiquo, 15, behind the Palazzo del Popolo. This is *the* place to sample Umbrian specialties, but be prepared to part with about L28,000. If it's a nice night, you can watch the sun set over the Tiber Valley from the terrace. Try *tagliatelle todine.* Open Wed.-Mon.

Sights

Piazza del Popolo (officially piazza V. Emanuele) is a majestic ensemble of glowering palaces and the somber *duomo,* whose air of authority is only slightly diminished by the municipal parking lot in its center. This *piazza* has been Todi's focal point since Roman times. It also serves as Todi's high point, in altitude and in architectural achievement. The **Palazzo del Capitano** (1290) stretches its cavernous portico across the east end of the *piazza,* with peaked Gothic windows on the second floor to lend sparkle to the imposing facade. The **Pinacoteca Civica** (open Tues.-Fri. 9am-noon and 3-6:30pm, Sat. 9am-12:30pm, Sun. 10am-noon; admission L2000) is on the fourth floor, but more interesting is the **Sala del Capitano del Popolo** at the top of the exterior marble staircase. The immense hall is covered with interesting frescoes, and has huge arches stretching across the ceiling like barrel hoops. The adjoining building is the **Palazzo del Popolo** (begun in 1213), crowned with a saw-toothed row of merlons. Diagonally across is the **Palazzo dei Priori** (1297-1337), whose tower and facade preserve their medieval gloom despite the rows of Renaissance windows carved out in the early sixteenth century.

Directly across the *piazza* is the rosy-faced ***duomo,*** planted solidly atop a flight of broad stone stairs. The central rose window and arched doorway command attention with their intricate decoration and carefully balanced placement. Inside, Romanesque columns with beautiful capitals support a plain wall pierced by slender windows. The delicate Gothic side arcade added in the 1300s shelters an unusual altarpiece where the Madonna's head, treated as high relief, emerges out of the flat surface of a painting. A terrifying scene of the Last Judgment (16th century) occupies the church's west wall. Ask the sacristan to light up the twelfth-century crypt for you (L200).

Neighboring **piazza Garibaldi** opens to a superb vista. To the right stands the Renaissance **Palazzo Alma** with a sadly deteriorated facade, but still beautiful for its rusticated stone corners. Returning to p. del Popolo, take via Mazzini to the angular **Church of San Fortunato.** Built by the Franciscans between the thirteenth and fifteenth centuries, the church has Romanesque portals and a Gothic interior. Between the first and second columns to the right of the door, the story of the sacrifice of Isaac is narrated.

To the right of San Fortunato, a path bends uphill toward **La Rocca,** a ruined fourteenth-century castle. Once Todi's key lookout, it now oversees the local playground. Next to the castle, a zigzagging path, appropriately named **viale della Serpentina,** leads to a breathtaking belvedere constructed on the remains of an old Roman wall. To the right, below the Tiber valley, you can see the solitary **Church of Santa Maria della Consolazione,** an exquisite work of Renaissance architecture, perhaps designed by Bramante himself. The love of forms composed of simple shapes so typical of the period finds a particularly harmonious expression here, with a half-sphere and quarter-spheres rising from a central cube. The church's refined white interior shelters a baroque polychrome altar.

The **Mostra Nazionale dell' Artigianto** (National Exhibit of Crafts) occurs in August and September, and for some years there has also been a national exhibit of antique and modern woodwork in April, as Todi is home to some of the best carpenters in Italy.

Orvieto

Set atop a volcanic plateau, the medieval fortress town of Orvieto lies removed from the rolling, fertile farmlands of southern Umbria. As a papal refuge from the Middle Ages through the Renaissance, the town had its part in European history. In the thirteenth century, while Thomas Aquinas taught in the local academies, the city served as the center for the planning of Crusades. While in Orvieto on the run from an inhospitable Rome in 1528, Pope Clement VIII rejected King Henry VIII's petition to annul his marriage to Catherine of Aragon, spelling a dim future both for Catherine and Catholicism in England. Today the townsfolk concern themselves with tourism and the fine local wine, *Orvieta classico.* Thankfully, they remain obsessed with the singular task that has dominated Orvieto's life since 1290: worshipful attention to the town's striking *duomo.*

Orientation and Practical Information

Orvieto lies midway on the Rome-Florence line. It's possible to leave Florence in the morning, spend a few hours exploring Orvieto, and be in Rome that evening, or vice versa (though this can be risky without hotel reservations in Florence). Be sure to buy a through ticket (Florence-Rome L17,000). The city is also an hour from Perugia. From the train station, take bus #1 (L500) to p. d. Capitano del Popolo, then walk along via Constituente to via Duomo, following it to the town center.

Azienda di Promozione Turistica: p. del Duomo, 24 (tel. 417 72). Accommodations service and a treasure chest of free information; be sure to get the incredibly complete pamphlet on hotels and restaurants, sights and practical information. Open in summer Mon.-Sat. 9am-1pm and 3-7pm, Sun. 10am-1pm and 4-7pm; in off-season Mon.-Sat. 9am-1pm and 3-7pm, Sun. 9am-1pm.

Post Office: via Cesare Nebbia, which begins between corso Cavour, 114 and 112. Open Mon.-Fri. 8:15am-7:30pm, Sat. 8:15am-1:20pm. **Postal code:** 05018.

Telephones: Bar Valentino, p. Fracassini, 11, between corso Cavour, 127 and 129. Open Sat.-Thurs. 8am-8:30pm. **Telephone code:** 0763.

Buses: ACOTRAL, p. XXIX Marzo. 7 per day to Viterbo. **ACT** (tel. 536 36 or 595 41), main stop in p. Marconi with others in p. XXIX Marzo and p. Cahen. 1 per day to Perugia at 5:50am (better by train). You can also catch the local bus to the train station here. The tourist office provides complete schedules.

Hospital: p. del Duomo (tel. 420 71).

Police: p. della Repubblica (tel. 400 88).

Accommodations and Camping

There are no great bargains in Orvieto, but rooms are easy to come by. The city strictly enforces its established hotel prices, so if anyone tries to overcharge you, complain to the tourist office. There is also a fine campground nearby.

Da Fiora, via Magalotti, 22 (tel. 411 19), just off p. della Republica. The forward Fiora offers several modest but spotless doubles with bath for L20,000-30,000. This is the best indoor deal in town.

Albergo Antico Zoppo, via Marabbottini Valente, 2 (tel. 403 70), off p. Fracassini. Newly redone and looks it; clean with contemporary furnishings. Singles L24,000. Doubles L34,000, with bath L40,000. Showers included. Curfew 11pm.

Albergo Posta, via L. Signorelli, 18 (tel. 419 09), near the Torre del Moro, between corso Cavour and p. I. Scalza. The location couldn't be better. A lush garden and pleasant lobby. Singles L24,000. Doubles with twin beds L34,000, with bath L40,000.

Hotel Duomo, via Maurizio, 7 (tel. 418 87), down the steps to the left of the cathedral, in a good location. Tidy, with white lace curtains. Singles L20,000. Doubles L34,000, with bath L40,000. Triples available. Showers L2000.

Albergo Corso, corso Cavour, 343 (tel. 420 20), near p. Cahen. A little out of the way. Singles with bath L30,000. Doubles with bath L40,000.

Camping Orvieto, on Lake Corbara some 12km from the center of town. Take the bus to Civitella. Fantastic swimming pool and other amenities. L5000 per person, L4350 per tent. Also rents rooms. Singles L17,000. Doubles L22,000. Open Easter-Sept.

Food

Though most of the fixings will fix you for broke, two things will please your pocketbook: cheap wine and one exceptional and exceptionally cheap restaurant.

Trattoria da Fiora, via Magalotti, 22, just off p. della Republica. Everything you always pictured in an Italian restaurant, complete with music and mama. Generous plates of pasta L2200, innovative *secondi* L4000. *Menù turistico* L9000.

Cooperativa CRAMST, via Lorenzo Maitani (tel. 433 02), off the front side of p. del Duomo. Follow the large signs. A restaurant, self-service, and *pizzeria* all rolled into one. Popular with locals. Outdoor tables on a quiet *piazza.* Pizza and wine L7000, full meals L13,000. Open Mon.-Sat. 8am-10pm.

Trattoria da Anna, p. Corsica, 4-5 (tel. 410 98), behind p. del Popolo. Hearty homecooked meals just L13,000; try a bottle of *Orvieta classico* (L4000). Open Sat.-Thurs.

Tavola Calda, corso Cavour, 100 (tel. 430 25). This self-service place is not big on atmosphere, but L12,000 will buy you an abundant fixed-price meal with drinks. Open Tues.-Sun.

Trattoria Giardino, corso Cavour, 443 (tel. 416 28), just off p. Cahen. Indulge with L17,000-21,000 meals. Pizza L4000-6000. Open Mon.-Sat.

Sights, Entertainment, and Seasonal Events

The bus from the train station deposits you in p. Capitano del Popolo, whose thirteenth-century **Palazzo del Capitano del Popolo** is decorated with the standard motif of Romanesque Orvieto architecture: a checkerboard band surrounding its windows. If you walk for 10 minutes through the town's winding streets, whose shops get more and more touristy, you will be rewarded with an incredible vision filling the horizon and obliterating the crass knicknacks of the tourist trade from your consciousness.

Indeed, the first glance of Orvieto's ***duomo*** is designed to be overwhelming. Like a giant pop-up book, the *duomo* dominates everything around it, its elaborate and fanciful facade held up by a seemingly spare and unrelated church building behind it. This elaborate facade of intertwining spires, mosaics, and sculptures dazzles and enraptures. You'll need the diagram from the tourist office to decipher all that's going on here. The bottom level features exquisitely carved bas-reliefs of the Creation and Old Testament prophecies, and a final panel of the New Testament's Last Judgement; the bronze and marble sculptures (1325-1964) emphasize the Christian pantheon of saints. But it is the fabulous mosaics that give a daylong show of interplaying light and shadow on the facade; in recognition of this, a row of benches was built opposite the facade in p. del Duomo, so that mesmerized visitors could simply sit and look. It took more than 33 architects, 90 mosaic artisans, 152 sculptors, and 68 painters working for longer than three centuries to complete the *duomo,* and the work continues. (The bronze doors were installed in 1970.)

The interior also offers treasures and mysteries to delight the eye. Observe that all the columns within the structure are octagonal, save the fourth column on the left, which is square. The *duomo*'s **organ,** built in 1580, is the second largest in Italy, its 5500 pipes generating a fittingly impressive sound (the largest is in Palermo). Luca Signorelli's violently dramatic **Apocalypse frescoes,** in the New Chapel off the right transept, were begun by Fra Angelico in 1447 and supposed to be completed by Perugino, but the city tired of waiting and commissioned Signorelli to finish the project.

On the left wall is the *Preaching of the Antichrist.* The prominent Renaissance dandy in the shimmering crimson costume to the left of the anti-Christ is the painting's patron; behind the bald man to the patron's left is the red-hatted poet Dante. The woman with the outstretched hand on the other side is Signorelli's mistress; she is seen as a prostitute engaged in the lowest act imaginable to a good Catholic of the day: taking money from a Jew (shown holding a stereotypic moneybag). Behind the prostitute stand images of Columbus, Petrarch, Cesare Borgia, and again Dante, along with other luminaries of the fifteenth and early sixteenth centuries, and far off in the corner, Signorelli and Fra Angelico, in black, stand watching the proceedings. On the opposite wall, muscular humans and skeletons pull themselves out of the earth in the uncanny *Resurrection of the Dead.* Beside it is ***Inferno,*** with Signorelli (a blue devil) and his mistress in an impassioned embrace below the ugly action.

In the left-hand chapel are late medieval religious and narrative paintings. (*Duomo* open in summer daily 7am-1pm and 2:30-8pm; offf-season 7am-1pm and 2:30-6pm. Free, but bring plenty of L200 coins to illuminate the paintings.)

The austere thirteenth-century **Palazzo dei Papi** (Palace of the Popes) sits in the right-hand shadow of the *duomo.* This site, where Clement VII turned down Henry VIII's annulment petition, now houses the **Museo dell' Opera del Duomo,** with a collection of religious articles. (Open May-Aug. Tues.-Sun. 9am-12:30pm and 3-6pm; Sept.-April 9am-12:30pm and 2:30-5pm. Admission L3000.) Behind it is the newly-expanded **Museo Archeologico Nazionale,** housing a significant set of artifacts from the area's ancient Etruscan civilization. (Open Mon.-Sat. 9am-1pm and 3-7pm, Sun. 9am-1pm. Free.) From 1351 to today, the little Moor atop the **Torre del Maurizio** (a 19th-century anachronism to the left of the *duomo*) has served as the time clock for workmen, striking the bell at starting and quitting times.

Returning toward p. Capitano del Popolo, turn left on corso Cavour for a trip through Orvieto's **medieval quarter.** No singular monuments here, but that's the charm.

On the eastern edge of town, down a steep trail off p. Cahen, is the **Pozzo di San Patrizio** (Saint Patrick's Well). Having fled war-torn Rome for the safety of Orvieto, Pope Clement VII wanted to ensure that the town did not run out of water during a siege, and in 1527 commissioned Antonio da Sangello the Younger to design the well. This staircased shaft seems more like a dungeon than a palace, but it's worth the L4000 (with student ID L2000) admission just to escape the hot Umbrian afternoon into the well's clammy coolness. (Open daily 9am-7pm.)

On the hill above is the **Fortezza,** where a fragrant sculpture garden and lofty trees crown battlements that overlook the variegated Umbrian landscape.

On August 15 all Orvieto celebrates the **Festa della Palombella.** Small wooden structures filled with fireworks are set up in front of the *duomo* and the Church of San Francesco, and are connected by a metal wire. On the stroke of noon, the San Francesco fireworks are set off, and a white metal dove shoots across the wire to ignite the explosives before the *duomo.* Lovely **concerts** are held in the *duomo* during the evenings in August. If you're around in early June, don't miss the **Procession of Corpus Domini,** a solemn parade carrying the reliquary of the Miracle of Bolsena.

Marches (Marche)

The undulating hills and punctuated mountain peaks of the Marches taper slowly into the Adriatic Sea. Patches of wheat, maize, fodder, and olives stretch along numerous valleys and the coastal plain above Ancona. Originally inhabited by the Gauls and Picenes (a native people), the area later became a Roman domain. It received its present name in the tenth century, when it was a border province of the Byzantine Empire; in the twelfth and thirteenth centuries powerful families such as the Montefeltros and Malatestas ruled, enriching the region with sumptuous churches and palaces.

Since World War II a crowded strip of international beach resorts has sprung up beside the old medieval and Renaissance cities that dot the Marches's magnificent shoreline. Even the nicer resort beaches swarm with lounge-chairs and parasols, usually arranged in impeccably straight rows. Luckily, a 20-meter strip of "free" beach is left along the shore. The beaches are occupied primarily by Germans in summer, who turn the coast into a series of little Munichs-by-the-sea. Senigallia and Fano have more or less retained their original Italian, family-oriented charm, but in general the secluded beach is an endangered species on the Adriatic Riviera.

You can divide your time between the coast and the region's two hilltop gems—the magnificent medieval-Renaissance towns of Urbino and Ascoli Piceno, both less than 90 minutes from the coast. The Marches are easy to reach by rail. There are direct trains from Rome to Ancona (4½ hr., L14,600), and it's usually not hard to find vacation buses headed to Urbino, Ascoli Piceno, or the coast from Tuscany and Umbria. The region is also served by the Milan-Lecce coastal line.

Pesaro

Located where the lush Foglia Valley opens onto the sea, Pesaro's beaches aren't nearly as crowded as those at Rimini to the north, and the town itself is quiet and inviting. Not the least of the city's attractions is its proximity to the magnificent city of Urbino, less than an hour away. Pesaro's most famous son is the operatic composer Gioacchino Rossini (1792-1868), famous for *The Barber of Seville, Cinderella,* and *William Tell,* a personal favorite of Tonto and the Lone Ranger.

Orientation and Practical Information

Pesaro lies on the main train route along the Adriatic coast to Brindisi and Lecce. From Rome, though, you must take a train toward Ancona (6 or 7 per day), then change at Falconara to one of the frequent *locale* to Pesaro. The center of the old city is the **piazza del Popolo.** Walk right from the station onto viale del Risorgimento and then continue on via Branca (5 min.). To reach p. Libertà and the beach, take bus #1, 2, 6, 7, or 11 to viale Trento (summer only; L500).

EPT, via Mazzolari, 4 (tel. 302 58), off via Rossini near p. del Popolo. Gregarious. Open Mon.-Fri. 8am-2pm. More convenient is the **tourist office** at the train station, which runs an accommodations service. Open daily 9am-noon and 4-7pm. **Azienda Autonoma de**

Turismo, p. della Libertà (tel. 693 41), on the beach. Will help you find a room. Open in summer daily 8:30am-1:30pm and 3-7:30pm.

Post Office: p. del Popolo, at the beginning of via Rossini. Open Mon.-Fri. 8:15am-8pm, Sat. 8:15am-1:30pm. **Postal code:** 61100.

Telephones: SIP, p. Matteotti, behind the AGIP station. Open daily 8am-8:30pm. At night, go to **Hotel Elvezia,** viale Fiume, 67, about ½km from the center off viale Vittoria. **Telephone code:** 0721.

Buses: p. Matteotti, down via S. Francesco from p. del Popolo. Buses #1, 2, 4, 5, 6, 7, 9, and 11 stop at p. Matteotti. To Fano, Ancona, Arezzo, Urbino (8 per day, L1600), and other towns.

First Aid: Tel. 314 44.

Police: Carabinieri, p. Cinelli, 6 (tel. 339 91).

Accommodations

Pesaro harbors over one hundred hotels and *pensioni,* so you should have little trouble finding a place to stay, though things can get tight in July and August. The Azienda will book a room for you free. Since prices are high here, you might consider camping or the youth hostel.

Ostello Ardizio (IYHF), at Fosso Sejore (tel. 557 98), 6km from town. Take the AMANUP bus toward Fano from p. Matteotti (6:30am-10pm every ½-hr., L400). Quality hostel located in a serene area close to the beach. Fastidiously kept. L8500. Breakfast included. Meals L6000.

Pensione Ristorante Arianna, via Mascagni, 84 (tel. 319 27), 100m from the beach. Standard rooms, excellent food. Boring but clean. Singles with bath L31,000; in off-season L42,000. Doubles with bath L40,000; in off-season L30,000. Restaurant open 7:30-9:30am, 12:30-1:30pm, and 7:30-8:30pm.

Pensione Aurora, viale Trieste, 147 (tel. 619 12), near the beach. 3-day minimum. Full pension required. L35,000-42,000 per person. Open May-Oct.

Camping

Camping Panorama (tel. 20 81 45), 7km north of Pesaro on the *strada panoramica* to Gabicce Mare. Take bus #1 to the end; from there it's a 20-minute uphill walk or an easy hitch. A path leads to a quiet beach. L4700 per person, L8500 per tent; in off-season L3500 and L6600. Open May-Sept.

Campo Norina (tel. 557 92), 5km south of the city center on the beach at Fossosejore. Take the bus for Fano from p. Matteotti (L500). L5200 per person, L8700 per tent; in off-season L4000 and L6900. Bungalows L25,5000; in off-season L21,500. Open April-Oct. 15.

Camping Marinella (tel. 557 95) near the Norina. Take the bus for Fano to Fossosejore. L5100 per person, L8100 per tent; in off-season L3800 and L6400. Bungalows about L6000 per person. Open April-Sept.

Food

Pesaro's **public market** is at via G. Branca, 5, off p. del Popolo behind the post office (open Mon.-Sat. 7:30am-1:30pm). Booths in the market sell hot *piadini* (round unleavened bread) with *prosciutto, formaggio,* or spinach for about L2000.

Mensa Arco della Ginera, via della Ginera, 3, near Musei Civici. Self-service with a *menù* (L6800) and a small bottle of wine (L400). Popular with *centro* workers. Open Mon.-Fri. 12:30-2:30pm.

Harnold's, p. Lazzarini, close to Teatro Rossini. Italian fast-food. The music they play has Rossini rolling in his grave, but it's excused by the satisfying L2500 *panini.* Open Thurs.-Tues. 11:30am-2am.

Pasticceria Germano, via Collenuccio, 12, near the EPT. Tasty *gelato* in a great people-watching location. Open Tues.-Sun. until late.

Sights

The **piazza del Popolo,** Pesaro's main square, wakes up daily to the clinks of bicycles. The *piazza* is enhanced by the robust arcade and cherubed window frames of the fifteenth-century **Ducal Palace,** home of Pesaro's medieval tyrants, the Della Rovere family (arrange visits with the Azienda). For the real grace and life of Pesaro, go to **corso XI Settembre** and its side streets. Narrow passages with overhanging roofs pass by open arcades and sculptured doorways. **Via Toschi Mosca** is especially picturesque. On this street, the **Musei Civici** houses a superb collection of Italian ceramics and primitives. (Open April-Sept. Tues.-Sat. 9:30am-12:30pm and 4-6:45pm, Sun. 9:30am-12:30pm; Oct.-March Tues.-Sat. 8:30am-1:30pm, Sun. 9:30am-12:30pm. Admission L2000, ages under 18 or over 60 free.) The archeological museum, the **Museo Olivierano,** nearby at via Mazza, 97, exhibits finds from a nearby necropolis (8th-6th centuries B.C.E.). To see the artifacts, you must inquire at the library upstairs. The birthplace of Rossini, known as the "Swan of Pesaro," at **via Rossini,** 34, now houses a museum dedicated to the composer. Appropriately enough, this rather eccentric and generous personality was born February 29 and died on Friday the 13th.

Unfortunately, most of Pesaro's fine Gothic churches have been adulterated by excessive baroque ornamentation. You can see the exterior of one just off p. del Popolo, on via Branca. Unfortunately, these elegant gothic structures now house modern offices. The **Church of Sant' Agostino,** on corso XI Settembre, has beautiful, late fifteenth- and early sixteenth-century wooden choir stalls inlaid with still-lifes, landscapes, and city scenes, including a representation of Pesaro's ducal palace, and a decorative portal as well. Designed by Girolamo Genga, the **Church of Saint John the Baptist,** on via Passeri, was built in the sixteenth century. The Renaissance critic Vasari considered it the "most splendid temple" of the area. Genga blended smooth Renaissance lines with baroque flourishes. The **Stigmata Chapel** inside contains frescoes of the Four Virtues. For a resplendent example of art nouveau architecture, head toward the beach; just before p. della Libertà on the left, nineteenth-century **Villino Raggeri** revels in icing-like stucco work.

Entertainment

The evening *passeggiata* takes place along viale Trieste and p. della Libertà. Popular watering holes are **Bistro,** viale Trieste, 281, under Hotel Cruiser, and **Big Ben,** via Sabbatini, 14, between Palazzo Ducale and Conservatorio Rossini, a pub with Italian food.

Pesaro hosts a **Mostra Internazionale del Nuovo Cinema** (International Festival of New Films) the first or second week in June. Rossini left his fortune to found the music school, Conservatorio di Musica G. Rossini, which sponsors events throughout the year. Contact the conservatory at the p. Olivieri for a schedule. The annual **Rossini Opera Festival** is usually held in late August and early September. Contact the tourist office for dates.

Whenever you arrive, ask the Azienda for their *Calendario Manifestazioni,* a comprehensive calendar of the month's concerts, festivals, shows, and sporting events.

Near Pesaro

Just 11½km south of Pesaro, **Fano** boasts both a fine pebble beach popular with families and an old town whose winding streets and small *piazze* accommodate little monuments of every age. The best place to stay near Fano is the Pesaro Youth Hostel (see above), and sunbathing is the thing to do. **Torrette,** 5km south of Fano, is a long beach without the usual beach umbrellas and bathing cabins. North of Pesaro, the prospects are grim—at **Gabicce Mare** there is more plastic than sand on the beach. In Fano, note **piazza XX Settembre,** with its cluster of historic sites, including the **Fontana della Fortuna** (Fountain of Good Fortune, 1576), whose lovely nude figure *Fortune* turns with the blowing wind, and the ethereal, idealized paintings of Perugino in the **Church of Santa Maria Nuova.** Fano's **tourist office,** near the train station at viale Battisti, 10 (tel. (0721) 825 34), is helpful and provides an excellent guide and map. (Open June-Sept. Mon.-Sat. 8am-1pm and 4-7pm, Sun. 8:30am-12:30pm; in off-season Mon.-Sat. only.) AMAF buses from p. Matteotti reach Fano in 15 minutes (6am-10pm every ½-hr.).

Ten kilometers north and inland of Pesaro is the perfectly preserved castle of **Gradara,** the quondam fortress of the Malatestas and the Sforzas. Dante incorporated one of the castle's legends into his *Inferno.* Gradara is accessible by AMANUP bus from p. Matteotti (6 per day, 20 min.). Ask at the Pesaro tourist office for the brochure *Itinerari Turistici,* describing daytrips to Fano and Gradara.

Urbino

If you visit only one city in the Marches—one city, in fact, in all of Italy—make it Urbino. Under the aegis of Federico Duke of Montefeltro (1444-1482), a great humanist and patron, the city became a model of cosmopolitan sophistication during the Renaissance; it is no wonder that Baldassare Castiglione decided to set the urbane dialogues of his book *The Courtier* in Urbino's Palazzo Ducale. Today, Urbino remains a mecca of culture and hosts, besides a university, countless resources for musicians, artists and graphic designers from around the globe.

Urbino's fairytale skyline has changed little in the last 500 years. While many cities are shaped by tourists, Urbino would be amorphous without its ubiquitous students, who sustain the introspective spirit of native sons Raphael and Bramante. Urbino can be a daytrip from the nearby beach resorts, or vice versa.

Orientation and Practical Information

While it is possible to take the train to Urbino from Pesaro, the **SAPUM bus** is cheap, frequent, and direct, running from p. Matteotti or from in front of the station (8-10 per day, L1500). Two **BUCCI buses** link Urbino with Fossato di Vico on the Rome-Ancona train line, and two buses per day run to Rome and Ancona. Occasional buses through Arezzo, San Sepolcro, Gubbio, Perugia, and Spoleto make it possible to incorporate Urbino into a tour of Tuscany and Umbria.

After winding up steep hills, the bus will deposit you at borgo Mercatale, above which stands the beautiful city center. A short, uphill walk (the 1st of many in Urbino) gets you to **piazza Repubblica,** the city's hub.

Azienda Autonoma di Turismo: p. Duca Federico, 35 (tel. 24 41). Hands out a list of hotels. Open in summer Mon.-Sat. 8:30am-7pm; in winter 8:30am-2pm.

Buses: Departures from borgo Mercatale. Timetable posted at the beginning of corso Garibaldi, near p. della Repubblica, or ask the Azienda.

Post Office: via Bramante, 22, near Raphael's house. Open Mon.-Fri. 8:30am-7:20pm, Sat. 8:30am-1pm. **Postal code:** 61029.

Telephones: SIP, p. Rinascimento, 4. Open Mon.-Sat. 8:30am-1pm and 3-9pm, Sun. 3-9pm. **Telephone code:** 0722.

Public Toilets: Albergo Diurno, via C. Battisti, 2, just off p. della Repubblica. Sparkling clean. L200. Open daily 7am-noon and 2-7:30pm. Also on via San Domenico, off p. Duca Federico.

Hospital: via B. da Motefeltro (tel. 32 93 51, 32 81 21, or 32 81 22), to the north of the city, out of p. Roma.

Police: Vigili Urbani, p. della Repubblica, 3 (tel. 26 45 or 32 04 91).

Accommodations and Camping

Since it is a town of day transients, cheap lodging is rare in Urbino. Try one of the many places advertising *affitacamere,* inexpensive, modern rentals normally targeted at Urbino's university students and located 2km outside town. **Trattoria Leone,** in p. della Repubblica, and signposts around **via Budassi** are sources of *af-*

fitacamere information. For longer stays, write to the Università degli Studi, calle dei Cappuccini.

Albergo Italia, corso Garibaldi, 52 (tel. 27 01), off p. della Repubblica, near palazzo Ducale. A charming hotel with affable management. A patio, great view, and elevator. Many university students live in the 48 rooms here. Singles about L25,000, with bath L31,000. Doubles L33,000, with bath L42,000; in off-season L2000-5000 less. Showers included.

Hotel Panoramic, via Nazionale, 192 (tel. 26 00), downhill from town (12-min.). From p. della Repubblica, take via Battisti outside the city walls and then bear right. Turn left onto the main road and then left again at the big intersection. The hotel is up a driveway on the right. Comfortable lodging, but off the beaten track. Your best bet for a room in summer. Doubles L30,000, in off-season L25,000.

Pensione Feltria, via Guido da Montefeltro, 18 (tel. 32 81 78). Follow the directions to the Panoramic, but bear right at the final intersection (look for the sign). Similar rooms and prices.

Camping Pineta (tel. 47 10), in the *località* of Cesane, 30km from the station. L4200 per person, L8700 per tent; in off-season L4000 and L7400. Open Easter to mid-Sept.

Food

Many fun bars and eateries ranging from *paninoteche* to *gelaterie* and burgers lurk in the vicinity of p. della Repubblica.

Ristorante Ragno D'Oro, p. Roma (tel. 22 22), at the top of via Raffaello. Quality home-cooking on an outdoor patio. Try any of their fantastic pasta dishes (L4500), and don't miss Urbino's best *cresce sfogliate* (an Urbino specialty: a flaky, flat bread filled with various meats, vegetables, or cheeses, L3000-5000). Open May-Sept. daily noon-3pm and 7-midnight.

Self Service, off p. Duca Federico. Despite the tacky sign, the food is delicious.

Pizzeria Le Tre Piante, via Foro Posterula, 1, off via Budassi. Popular with foreign students. Beautiful view from the outside tables. Pizza dinners L4000-6000, others from L13,000.

Il Girarrosto, p. S. Francesco, 3, off via Raffaello. Full meals from L14,000, but you can usually get a plate of food and a glass of wine at the bar for about L5000. Open Sat.-Thurs. noon-2:45pm and 7:30pm-midnight.

Ristorante Taverna La Fornarina, via Mazzini, 14. Come here to blow your budget. Elegant and delectable. Around L25,000. Open Tues.-Sun. noon-2:30pm and 7:30-10:30pm.

Sights

Urbino's most remarkable monument is the majestic **Palazzo Ducale** (Ducal Palace), a Renaissance architectural masterpiece. Its fairytale facade is renowned for the unique design, attributed to Luciano Laurana; two tall, slender towers enclose three central, stacked balconies. It can best be seen from the Fortezza Albornoz. The entrance to the palace is on p. Duca Federico. The interior **courtyard** is the quintessence of Renaissance harmony and proportion. To the left, a monumental staircase takes you to the private apartments of the Duke, which now house the **National Gallery of the Marches.** Grandiose vaulted rooms retain their original aquamarine and gold decoration. Some treasures are Berruguete's *Federico e Guidobaldo da Montefeltro,* Raphael's *Portrait of a Lady,* Paolo Uccello's *Profanation of the Host,* and Piero della Francesca's *Flagellation* and *Madonna of Senigallia.* The Renaissance concern for perspective and clarity is taken to a lifeless extreme in the famous painting, *The Ideal City.* By contrast, the paintings of Federico Barocci upstairs come alive with the dynamic forms and mercurial light of the earliest baroque. The most intriguing room of the palace is the Duke's study, where stunning inlays depict both Virgil and various squirrels. Nearby, a circular stairway leads down to Cappella del Perdono and the Tempietto delle Muse, where the Christian and pagan components of the Renaissance ideal exist together. The chapel was used as a repository for the holy relics accumulated by the Duke. Eleven wooden panels representing Apollo, Minerva, and the nine muses at one time covered the walls of the temple, but all 11 have been removed (8 of them are currently in Florence's

Galleria Corsini). The chapel and the temple are exactly the same size and are both beneath the Duke's study. (Open Tues.-Sat. 9am-7pm, Sun. 9am-1pm, Mon. 9am-2pm. Admission L4000.)

At the end of via Barocci lies the fourteenth-century **Oratorio di San Giovanni Battista,** decorated with colorful international Gothic frescoes by Lorenzo and Giacomo Salimbeni; they represent events from the life of St. John. If you speak Italian, the *custode* can give you a wonderful explanation of how fresco painters used lamb's blood when drawing their sketches. (Open daily 10am-noon and 3-5pm. Admission L1000.) **Raphael's house,** via Raffaello, 57, is now a delightful museum with period furnishings. His earliest work, a fresco entitled *Madonna e Bambino,* hangs in the *sala.* (Open Mon.-Sat. 9am-1pm and 3-7pm, Sun. 9am-1pm. Admission 3000.) The **Fortezza Albornoz** (turn left at the end of via Raffaello and look for the red Communist party flag) is a fourteenth-century structure surrounded by a grassy public garden. This spot pleads for a picnic, as the view of the Ducal Palace and Urbino from here is unsurpassed. (Open daily 10am-1pm and 4-7pm. Free.)

Entertainment

Urbino's piazzale della Repubblica is a veritable modeling stage for local youth in their avant-garde threads. Take a walk down this fashion ramp and then stroll (or climb) the serpentine streets at dusk.

If you seek more active entertainment, Urbino features two discotheques that cater to the large student population. **Club 83,** via Nuova, 4, is big and airy (cover L5000). At **Scorpio,** via Nazionale, 73 Ibis, on the way to Pesaro, the scene is more new wave (also L5000). A cheaper alternative, and more popular with students (especially in winter), is the **University ACLI,** on via Santa Chiona, a bar with music and small crowds. You might also try to head out to the **Collegi Universitani,** a huge modern complex with a cheap *mensa* (L1000) for Urbino students only, and a bar that's affordable and always busy. All this begins in August, when the Italian university summer session convenes.

Senigallia

Senigallia is a sedate beach resort without the frantic sun-tanning scene common on the Adriatic. The town offers an uncrowded beach, lovely strands to the south, and, despite its lack of hustle and bustle, an intriguing historic center. It is affectionately called "*La Spiaggia di Velluto*" (the Velvet Beach) because of its immaculate, pale sand. Although well-touristed, the town is almost sleepy in summer; the beach is occupied by a family crowd, complete with floats, picnic baskets, and occasionally riotous offspring.

Orientation and Practical Information

The railroad tracks divide the town roughly into two: the old town with its fountains and Renaissance *palazzi,* and the modern, tidy beachfront.

Azienda Autonoma di Turismo: p. Morandi, 2 (tel. 79 22 725), halfway between the station and the beach. More American than Italian: ugly but efficient. Pick up the booklet *Estate 89* and a good map. Open April-Sept. Mon.-Sun. 8am-2pm and 4-7pm; Oct.-March Mon.-Fri. 8am-2pm.

Post Office: via Armellini, 7. Open Mon.-Fri. 8:30am-7:30pm, Sat. 8am-1pm. **Postal code:** 60019.

Telephones: SIP, p. Girolamo Simonelli. **Telephone code:** 071.

Buses: Informazioni Biglietteria Autostazione, via Montenegro (tel. 605 39), next to the stadium. All buses stop at the station and at the Portici Ercolani. Daily to Ancona, Pesaro, Jesi, Fano, Rome, Urbino, and Milan.

Hospital: On via Cellini at via Rossini (tel. 635 55).

First Aid On The Beach: Across from the Hotel Ritz and next to the Hotel Bologna. Open July-Aug. daily 9am-1pm and 3-7pm.

Accommodations

Senigallia's 12-kilometer strip of beach billows with *pensioni* and hotels. Before searching for accommodations, however, go to the Azienda, and let them make inquiries for you. Most hotels on the beach are true *pensioni* and require a minimum three-day stay. In July and August be sure to make reservations. If you arrive at the end of May, in June (except the last week), or in September, you will have the pick of the crop.

Locanda Bice, viale Leopardi, 105 (tel. 629 51), in the center of town. Colorful and one of the most inexpensive places in town, but only a few rooms. Singles L20,000. Doubles L30,000. Showers included.

Pensione Azzurra, via La Spezia, 1 (tel. 625 04), 1 block from the beach. Modern rooms. Singles L25,000, in off-season L20,000. Doubles L36,000, in off-season L31,000. Reserve Dec.-Jan. for July-Aug.

Pensione Ivana, via Istria, 2 (tel. 628 66), ½ block from the beach. A small but comfortable place, extremely popular July-Aug. Reserve way in advance. Doubles L36,000. *Pensione completa* L40,000 per person.

Camping

There are more than 20 campgrounds along the beach. High-season (May-Sept.) prices run about L4000 per person plus L8000 per tent; low-season prices are L3000 and L5000, respectively. The beaches and waves along the campgrounds are generally better than in Senigallia itself. A complete list is available at the Azienda; always call ahead.

Summerland, via Podesti, 236 (tel. 691 69). 4-person bungalows L55,000, in off-season L35,000. **Helios,** lungomare Italia, 3B (tel. 66 51 63), in nearby Marzocca. Also offers 4-person bungalows L60,000, in off-season L38,000.

Spiaggia Di Velluto, close to town on lungomare Da Vinci (tel. 648 73). L4500 per person, in off-season L2500. Small tent L6300, large L8900.

Liana, a bit farther down lungomare Da Vinci than Spiaggia Di Velluto (tel. 628 81). L4800 per person; in off-season 40% less. 5-person tent L9000. Parking L3000.

Food

Most of the pizza places along the beach are adequate and inexpensive. Get supplies for a beach picnic from **Supermarket Sidis Discount,** across from the train station. There is also a fish and vegetable **market** at the Foro Annonario, in the old town (open Mon.-Sat. 8am-1pm).

La Taverna, via Bandiera, 55 (tel. 638 09), at via Arsilli. Fantastic food and prices in a youthful environment. Try any one of their generous pasta dishes (L5000) and top it off with a plate of figs and *prosciatto* (L5000). Open in summer daily 11am-2:30pm and 7:30-10:30pm; in off-season Mon.-Sat.

Italian Fast Food, across from Hotel City on the beach. Decent sandwiches L2000-4000. Open daily 10am-2pm and 5pm-2am.

Il Desco, via Pisacane, 32. Excellent food in a room with a vaulted ceiling. Full meals from L16,000. Open Fri.-Wed.

Unpunto Macrobiotico, via Arsilli, 37. Come here to stock up on macrobiotic goodies or savor their small tea room. Open in summer 8:30am-12:30pm and 5-8pm; in off-season 9am-1pm and 4:30-7:30pm.

Sights

The tiny old center can be seen in half a day. Start from the **Portici Ercolani,** long stone arcades that grace the south side of the Misa River. These enclose an undulating walkway in chiaroscuro that once housed the "Free Fair of Senigallia," one of the most important in the Mediterranean. Behind the Portici Ercolani on the via Gherardi is the superb sixteenth-century **Church of the Cross.** Its smoldering golden interior of intricate jewellike details provides the perfect baroque setting for Federico Barocci's *Transport of Christ to the Sepulchre* (1592).

At via Commercianti, 20, off p. Simoncelli, you will find the ancient synagogue, the sole visible reminder of the old **Jewish ghetto.** Senigallia's once large Jewish population came here through the efforts of the Duke of Urbino, who offered housing and quasi-citizenship to anyone willing to live in a city that had been wiped out by a disastrous medieval plague.

Via Marzi opens onto the **piazza del Duca,** a mangy square dominated by a large fountain. On one side of the square is the **Palazzetto Baviera.** The modest exterior bears some remarkably intricate and animated fifteenth-century stucco decorations illustrating scenes from the Bible and antiquity, done by Federico Brandani of Urbino. (Open Mon.-Sat. 10am-noon.) The fortress you see across the way is the **Rocca Roveresca** (1480), a fine example of Renaissance military architecture. (Open June to mid-Sept. Mon.-Sat. 9am-1pm and 5-10pm, Sun. 9am-1pm; mid-Sept. to May Mon.-Sat. 9am-1pm and 3-7pm, Sun. 9am-1pm.)

Entertainment

Get the booklet *Estate 89* from the Azienda: It lists the three or four shows, films, and concerts performed *nightly* for free.

There's life after sunset in Senigallia. Discos abound near the beach area; try **Snoopy, California Studios, Number One,** or **Life Club.** Most places charge a L6000-8000 admission, which gets you your first drink—drinks average L2000-4000. Women are often admitted free. If you want to do the *passeggiata* in style, consider renting a four-wheeled bicycle buggy from the shop by the Baltic Hotel for L6500 per hour. Heed the prohibition against taking these contraptions onto the state highway—the *carabinieri* take a dim view of this.

Senigallia hosts the **International Meeting of Young Pianists** in the last week of August, and the **International Competition for Pianists** during the first 10 days of September.

Ancona

Ancona resembles a machine, churning boats in and out. The capital of the Marches, it owes its prosperity to its large and ugly industrial port, one of the busiest in the Adriatic. The ancient town, with a Romanesque cathedral, is picturesque, but the main attraction here is the ferry service linking Ancona to Yugoslavia, Greece, and Turkey.

Ferry Information

Once in Ancona, the easiest way to get complete and accurate schedules is to visit the Stazione Marittima, on the waterfront just off p. Kennedy (bus #1 runs to and from the station). All the ferry lines operate ticket and information booths. The helpful **information office,** in the green traincar parked outside, sells Interrail tickets and gives free guided tours of Ancona twice per day. (Open Mon.-Fri. 8am-2pm and 4-10pm, Sat. 8am-2:30pm and 3:30-10pm.) An **arrivals/departures board** for the upcoming week hangs just to the left inside the main entrance.

Most travel agents can provide up-to-date schedules, but ferries are fickle, so it's better to call and check on dates and prices. Some lines will make you purchase an airline-type seat until these are filled, and will only then sell the cheaper deck-class tickets. Most lines will give discounts (up to 50%) for round-trip tickets. The prices listed below are the cheapest regularly available fares. From July to August, it's wise to make reservations.

Adriatica: Tel. 20 49 15. To Split at 11:30pm on the 1st, 11th, and 21st of each month Jan.-May 26, plus every Sat. at 10pm April 2-June 25 and Sept. 17-Nov. 12 (L60,000-82,000). To Dubrovnik every Tues. at 4pm June-Sept. 27 (L67,000-92,000).

Jadrolinija: Tel. 20 20 34. To Zadar at 11pm Tues., Fri., and Sat. June and Sept., plus Tues.-Wed. and Fri.-Sun. at 8am in July (L45,000-61,000). To Split (continuing to the islands of Hvar and Korčula) every Sun. at 11:30pm June and Jan., plus every Wed. at 11:30pm July-Aug. (L64,000-81,000).

Karageorgis: Tel. 20 22 23. To Patras Mon. at midnight, Wed. at 1pm, Fri.-Sat. at 9pm (L54,000-72,000).

Marlines: Tel. 500 62. The *Princess M.* leaves Fri. at midnight for Igoumenitsa, Patras, Heraklion (L48,000-62,000), and Kusadasi in Turkey (L124,000). Another ship leaves for Igoumenitsa and Patras Sat. at 10pm, Wed. at 1pm, Sun. at 8pm, and Thurs. at 1pm.

Strintzis: Tel. 20 42 47. To Corfu, Igoumenitsa, and Patras Mon. at 9pm, Tues. and Thurs. at 11pm, Sat. at 9pm, and Sun. at 11pm (L48,000-62,000).

Orientation and Practical Information

Ancona is an important rail junction on the Bologna-Lecce line and is served also by trains from Rome (4¾ hr.). The center of town, p. Roma, is a 10-minute ride on bus #1 from the train station (L500—buy the ticket before getting on the bus).

EPT: In the train station (tel. 417 03). Open Mon.-Fri. 8am-1pm and 4-7pm, Sat. 8am-1pm.

Post Office: viale della Vittoria, 2. Open Mon.-Sat. 8:30am-7:30pm. **Postal code:** 60100.

Telephones: SIP, corso Stamira, 50, off p. Roma. Open daily 8am-9:30pm. At other hours, try **Albergo Roma e Pace,** via Leopardi. **ASST,** p. Rosselli, in front of the station. For intercontinental calls. Open daily 7am-midnight. **Telephone code:** 071.

Buses: Departures from p. Cavour and the train station. Timetables posted at p. Cavour.

Car Rental: Avis, via Marconi, 17 (tel. 503 69). From L265,000 per week with unlimited mileage. Free drop-off anywhere in mainland Italy.

Public Toilets: p. Stamira.

Hospital: Tel. 59 61.

Police: Tel. 288 88.

Accommodations

About half the city's hotels are in the *piazza* in front of the train station. In summer, there are always people crashing at the Stazione Marittima, waiting for ferries.

Pensione Orazi, via Curtatone, 2 (tel. 20 11 82). Walk up via San Martino from p. Cavour, and make the 1st right after via Simeoni. Look for the sign on via San Martino. What a deal! Spotless singles L15,000. Doubles L25,000. There aren't many, so call ahead.

Pensione Garden, viale della Vittoria (tel. 283 74), 1 block from p. Cavour in the center of town. Take bus #1 to the beginning of viale della Vittoria. Cramped singles L20,000. Doubles L28,000. Showers included.

Pensione Centrale, via Marsala, 10 (tel. 543 88), near corso Stamira, on the 4th floor. Fine rooms with high ceilings and a gentle manager. Singles L19,000. Doubles L28,000, with bath L39,000. Showers L2000.

Pensione Astor, 142 (tel. 287 76), near p. Cavour, on the 3rd floor. Not cheery, but decent. Singles L28,000. Doubles L28,000.

Albergo Fiore, p. Rosselli, 24 (tel. 433 90). The nicest in the train station area. Singles L18,000. Doubles L30,000. The **Italia,** at #9 (tel. 426 07), has a friendly manager and singles for L22,5000, with bath L30,000. Doubles L34,000, with bath L49,000.

Food

Several inexpensive restaurants are anchored in Ancona. Regional specialties include *brodetto* (fish stew), *vinisgrassi* (lasagna with chicken livers and white sauce), and *pizza al formaggio* (cheese bread). Pack a meal for your ferry ride at the cheerfully old-fashioned **Mercato Pubblico** (across from corso Mazzini, 130), where you'll find fruits, veggies, cheeses, and meats. (Open in summer Mon.-Sat. 7:30am-12:45pm and 5:15-7:30pm, in off-season Mon.-Sat. 7:30am-12:45pm and 4:30-7pm.)

Trattoria Vittoria, corso Mazzini, 109, at p. Cavour. Delectable eats. Fixed-price *menù* L11,000. Open daily.

Osteria del Pozzo, via Bonda, a tiny passage off p. Plebiscito. A great find. Popular, affordable, and cheery. Full spaghetti meals L5900. Open Mon.-Sat. noon-2:30pm and 7:30-10pm.

Pizzeria Trattoria La Partonepa, across from the station in p. Rosselli. The only view you'll get is of passing cars and buses, but the breeze is nice. *Menù* L14,000.

Sights

Piazzale del Duomo, atop **Monte Guasco,** is an excellent place to view the land and sea and gain an understanding of the port's importance to Ancona's livelihood. Climb up via Papa Giovanni XXIII, or take bus #11 from the bottom of the hill in p. Cavour. If you decide to walk, you'll get a close view of the beautiful **Scalone Nappi,** a stairway street in lush surroundings. (Follow the left-hand steps at the point where the street forks; there are only 244 steps instead of 267, and the vista is more magnificent.) From the top, you can watch the immense ship-building factories directly in front of you, the city of Ancona to your left, and the beautiful sea stretching to Yugoslavia on your right; the grounds themselves are spoiled somewhat by trash and broken beer bottles. In p. del Duomo you'll find the **Cathedral of San Ciriaco.** Erected between the eleventh and thirteenth centuries on the site of an old Roman temple, this massive Romanesque church combines a variety of forms: rounded apses, a tall rectangular nave, lower side aisles, and a crowning dome and lantern. A staircase leads down to where the body of St. Ciriacus lies in full garb (entrance from the side). (Open daily 9-10:30am and noon-6pm.)

Via Pizzecolli, the charming main street of the old quarter reached from via Giovanni XXIII, passes the superb Venetian-Gothic doorway of the **Church of San Francesco delle Scale** (St. Francis of the Steps) before entering the courtyard of the **Government Palace** and **piazza Plebiscito.**

Just up the street from the Loggia dei Mercati (Merchants' Gallery), across the street, is the **Church of Santa Maria della Piazza,** with a facade overcharged with blind arches and sculptures in Romanesque bestiary ornamentation.

Ancora boasts outstanding museums. The **Museo Archeologico Nazionale delle Marche,** on via Ferretti above via Pizzeotti, has just thrown its doors open again after 16 years of impeccable restoration in the wake of the 1972 earthquakes. A life-sized group in gilt bronze of two Roman emperors on horseback captivates beyond interpretation. Ancona's painting gallery, the **Galleria Commale Francesco Podesti,** is in the sixteenth-century **Palazzo Bosdari** at via Pizzecolli, 17. They have just finished extensive conservation work on their prize possession, Titian's *Apparition of the Virgin,* and they now display it with unmistakable pride in the full glory of its original colors. Also worth noting are the tiny and intricately detailed Venetian *Madonna and Child* by Crivelli (1430-1495), the airy and graceful religious scenes of Andrea Lilli (1555-1610), and Andrea del Sarto. Don't miss the eerie and almost oriental thirteenth-century Tuscan sculpture. (Open Tues.-Sat. 10am-7pm, Sun. 9am-1pm. Admission L2000.) Evenings in Ancona are spent strolling on the wonderful, tree-lined esplanade from corso Garibaldi, past piazzale Cavour (where the statue of Italy's hero is now forced to rebuff dozens of pigeons), to viale della Vittoria.

Ascoli Piceno

Ascoli Piceno, like Urbino, combines a strong medieval and Renaissance flavor with a beautiful natural setting. Two rivers flowing through gorges filled with cascading greenery flank the old city. Beachgoers can easily alternate exploration of the town's churches, palaces, and woody hillsides with days at resorts in nearby San Benedetto del Tronto or Grottamare.

Orientation and Practical Information

Ascoli is about one hour by bus or train from San Benedetto del Tronto, which is one hour from Ancona on the Bologna-Lecce train line. Buses (Contravat) leave San Benedetto del Tronto for Ascoli about every 45 minutes. Buses also leave Ascoli every two hours for Pescara (ARPA), once per day (Mon.-Fri.) to Perugia, and three times per day to Rome from p. Serafino Orlini (L15,800).

EPT: corso Mazzini, 229 (tel. 51 11 5), on the 1st floor. Open Mon.-Fri. 8am-1:30pm and 4-5:30pm, Sat. 8am-12:30pm.

Azienda Autonoma di Turismo: via del Trivio, 1 (tel. 530 45 or 632 88). Open in winter Mon.-Sat. 8:30am-1:30pm and 3-6pm. From June to Aug., go to the helpful **Ufficio Informazione,** p. del Popolo, 17 (tel. 552 50). Open April 15-Oct. 15 9am-12:30pm and 3-7:30pm.

Post Office: via F. Crispi, off corso Mazzini. Open Mon.-Sat. 8am-8pm. **Postal code:** 63100. **Telephone Code:** 0736.

Buses: All leave from viale de' Gasperi (behind the cathedral) except Amadio, which leaves from viale Indipendenza. Timetable at **Agenzia Viaggi Brunozzi,** corso Trento e Trieste, 54/56 (tel. 504 60).

Accommodations

Without the inviting youth hostel, the situation here would be desperate. About twice per year the hostel is saturated with groups, so call ahead before you arrive.

Ostello de' Longobardi (IYHF), via Soderini, 26 (tel. 500 07), near the center of town off via delle Torre. A lot of charm, but occasional mice and not-so-clean bathrooms. But how much can you expect from a twelfth-century travertine *palazzo?* They say it's haunted by ghosts, and if that isn't enough to hold your attention, the medieval decor, complete with swords and creaky doors, should. Ask to climb the tower for a panoramic view. Run by a friendly family. Hot showers and kitchen privileges. L7000.

Albergo Piceno, via Minucia, 10 (tel. 525 53), near the cathedral and the bus stop. If your first priority is a shower. Singles with bath L24,000. Doubles with bath L45,000. Often full, so call ahead.

Pensione Pavoni, via Navicella del Tronto, 1351b (tel. 475 01), 4km from town. Singles L24,000. Doubles 42,000. Bath included.

Food

Offsetting the dearth of cheap lodgings, the restaurants here are inexpensive—an excellent meal should run you about L800. There's also a lovely **open-air market** in the loggia dei Mercanti (open Mon.-Sat. mornings).

Trattoria da Giovanna, rua dei Marcolini, 3, a tiny alley off p. Arringo. Large amounts of delicious food, including thick, juicy steaks, fresh fruit, and large, 1-liter drinks. Fixed-priced *menù* L8500. Signora Giovanna Sebastiana acts as a friendly mother to the young, mostly male crowd. Open Mon.-Sat. noon-2:30pm and 7:30-10:30pm.

Vino e Cucina, via del Trivio, 43, in back of p. del Popolo. In a pleasant location, serving scrumptious meals at skimpy prices. *Menù* L8000. Open Tues.-Sun. noon-2:30pm and 7:30-11pm.

Cantina dell' Arte, rua della Lupa, 5, behind the post office. Similar food and prices as Giovanna, but less popular and less genial. Open Mon.-Sat.

Ristorante Nuovo Picchio, via Cesare Batristi, 11 (tel. 510 51), near p. de Popola. Elegant dining. Full meals about L16,000.

Sights

Piazza del Popolo (People's Square) is the historic center of town and an oasis in this busy city. It's deceptively tranquil until dusk moves in and Ascoli Piceno's youth pours into the *piazza* for a couple of hours of mutual admiration. Simple, almost toylike Renaissance porticos from the early 1500s enclose the square on two sides. On the third is the thirteenth-century **Palazzo dei Capitani del Popolo,** whose massive portal and statue of Pope Paul III date from 1548. The *piazza* acts as a forecourt for the picturesque eastern end of the **Church of St. Francis** (13th-16th centuries). The simple facade boasts a Venetian-style central portal supported by two wonderfully expressive lions. Its spacious, three-aisled interior conceals a fourteenth-century wooden crucifix, the only art object saved from a disastrous fire in the *piazza* in 1535. (Churches open 8am-noon and 12:30-3:30pm.)

Abutting the church to the south, the gracious **Loggia dei Mercanti** (Merchant's Gallery, 1509-1513), now a favorite meeting place for the town's "elders," leads to corso Mazzini and the thirteenth-century **Church of St. Augustine.**

Via delle Torri passes the austere stone houses of the old quarter before ending at the thirteenth-century **Church of Saint Peter the Martyr** and tiny via di Solestà. This street, one of the oldest in the city, leads to the single-arched **Ponte di Solestà,** one of the four tallest Roman bridges in Europe. The small Romanesque **Church of SS. Vincenzo e Anastasio** (11th century, enlarged 13th-14th centuries) stands in p. Venidio Basso (reached from via Trebbiani). Its curious, paneled facade was once decorated with sparkling frescoes. The low *campanile,* divided by two arched windows and topped by a conical spire, is typical of the city's medieval churches.

On the other side of town, the city's massive travertine **cathedral** (facade 1539, west end from the 1400s) stands at the eastern end of monumental **piazza Arringo.** In its Cappella del Sacramento (Chapel of the Sacrament) an intricately framed polyptych of the *Virgin and Saints* (Carlo Crivelli, 1473) is displayed above a fourteenth-century silver altar. Next to the cathedral is the compact twelfth-century **baptistery,** decorated with a *loggia* of blind arches. The city's picture collection hangs amid red velvet curtains and pink walls in the **Palazzo Comunale** (southern flank of the *piazza*). It includes works by Crivelli, Titian, Van Dyck, and Ribera. There is also some amusing nineteenth-century sculpture, such as Del Gobbo's *Paolo e Francesca.* Also on the *piazza,* there's a **Museo Archeologico** with some fine iron and bronze artifacts and Roman sculptures. Its finest asset, however, is the hall of mosaics. (Open in summer Mon.-Sat. 9:30am-1:30pm and 4:30-7:30pm, Sun. 4:30-7:30pm. Free.)

Try to visit Ascoli Piceno the first Sunday in August, when the **Tournament of Quintana** invades the town with medieval pageantry. The tournament, which features armed jousting, and the evening procession to p. del Popolo are the highlights of the four-day festival of Sant' Emidio, the city's patron.

The **carnival** in February is one of the best in Italy. Masks, costumes, parades, and, generally, the funky flip-side reigns on the Tuesday, Thursday, and especially the Sunday preceding Ash Wednesday. Although the event is not mobbed by tourists, it's wise to call a week ahead to make hotel reservations.

Abruzzo

The very word Abruzzo rings harsh and unhemmed. Snowcapped mountains, a harsh climate, and a sparse population make it a rugged region. But there is nothing rugged about Abruzzo's hamlets. Their civility, captured in palaces and concerts in the park, contrasts with the rough terrain encircling them. A few hours from Rome, this region offers respite for the weary and challenge for the restless. Skiers, hikers, bird-watchers, and people-watchers will all find their niche in Abruzzo. L'Aquila, the region's capital, has a stupendous collection of medieval art, and is an ideal starting point for exploring the majestic Gran Sasso (the highest of the Appenines). A short distance away is smaller, sweet Sulmona with its motley architecture and world-famous candy stores. Occupying a large chunk of land to the south is the National Park of Abruzzo, the wildest natural region left in Italy. Avoid Abruzzo's Adriatic seacoast, a jungle of *pizzerie* and beach umbrellas, unless you are catching a boat to Yugoslavia (see Pescara). In Abruzzo, use the efficient ARPA bus service, as the rail system is painfully circuitous.

Pescara

Because of convenient connections to Rome, Naples, Venice, and Split, Yugoslavia, Pescara is a junction for many travelers. The beach, though clean, is a 20-kilometer-long string of resort hotels. Inland, the city doesn't improve: It's overcrowded, overpriced, and ungainly. Once a key Roman port called Aterno, Pescara got its present name after the fall of the Roman empire, when it reverted to a simple fishing village. It now seeks to regain its lost prominence as a hotspot on what its tourist officials refer to as the "Adriatic Riviera."

Orientation and Practical Information

Pescara is four hours from Rome by direct train (L12,400), but only about three hours by ARPA bus (L13,000; direct buses L24,000, leaving Pescara at 9:30am and 10am). Pescara is also on the Bologna-Lecce train line, and is a center for ARPA connections to the small inland towns of Abruzzo. The new station of mirrored windows and slick interior is an architectural nightmare but a traveler's dream. Connections are frequent and well-displayed (tel. 37 81 72). When you leave the station, corso Umberto lies straight ahead, and it's five minutes to the beach.

Azienda di Turismo: 22, p. Salotto (tel. 37 81 10), off corso Umberto toward the water from the train station. Tourist officials willingly answer guests' questions but admit there isn't much to Pescara besides the beaches. Open Mon.-Sat. 8:30am-1:30pm and 4:30-8:30pm, Sun. 10am-noon and 5-7:30pm.

Post Office: corso V. Emanuele, 106. Open Mon.-Fri. 8:15am-8pm, Sat. 8:15am-1pm. **Postal code:** 65100.

Telephones: SIP, via Trieste, 35, 1 block from corso V. Emanuele. Open daily 7am-9:30pm. **ASST,** corso Umberto, 21, near the train station. Open 24 hours. **Telephone code:** 085.

Buses: ARPA buses leave from p. Stazione, where schedules are posted.

Ferries: Adriatica Lines, at Banchina Sud, Porto Canale (tel. 652 47). To Split, Yugoslavia (8 hr.). July-Sept. 10 Mon.-Thurs. at noon and Fri. at 10pm (L79,000). April-June 29 and Sept. 12 to Nov. 13 Mon. and Wed. at 11pm and Fri. at noon (L67,000). If all seats are filled, you can go deck class for 10% less.

Accommodations and Camping

The *pensioni* nearest the train station and several blocks from the water are the only affordable sleeps. Even these are pricey and saturate quickly from June through August.

Hotel Roma, via Piave, 142 (tel. 421 16 57). From the station make a left on via Emanuelle and then a right. Affable manager. Simple doubles L20,000.

Pensioni Angelina, corso Umberto, 23 (tel. 402 00). Convenient to train station. Noisy but adequate 2nd floor rooms with double beds. Singles L20,000. Doubles L30,000. Triples, L40,000.

Hotel Alba, via Forti, 14 (tel. 38 91 45), off via Emanuelle. More upscale. Singles L18,500. Doubles L33,500.

Camping: Internazionale, via Cristoforo Colombo (tel. 656 53), by the water. Take bus #10 from the train station. July 11-Aug. L5200 per person, L3900 per tent; in off-season L4500 and L3000.

Food

Local specialties include two liqueurs: *Aurum,* made from grapes, and *centerba toro,* a strong concoction distilled from 100 herbs. The favorite sweet, *parrozzo,* consists of chocolate and almonds. Stop by any of the *pasticcerie* near corso Umberto for a taste test. Plan on going gourmet in Pescara. Despite the flourishing tourist trade, there are a handful of excellent, decently-priced restaurants. Also, a cooperative food market is held in a warehouse—turn left off via Margherita on via Marco Minghetti (open Mon.-Sat. 9am-11:30pm). You'll find everything from cheese and fruits to towels and comic books—all amazingly affordable.

Da Nello, p. Sacro Cuore, 35, off corso Umberto. The constant crowds say it all. *Menù turistico* L10,000. Open daily 11am-11pm.

Ristorante China Hai-Bin, via Riviera Nord (tel. 318 28), on the beach north of corso Umberto. Run by an immigrant Chinese family, this is the *real* thing. Entrees L5000. Open daily 8am-12:30am.

Sights and Entertainment

Pescara's attractions are on the beach. To get there, walk straight down corso Umberto or take bus #2 or 2c from the station. At nightfall, most people entertain themselves with the lively *passeggiata.* In mid-July the town hosts the **Pescara Jazz Festival** at the open-air theater Teatro D'Annunzio, on the waterfront. Some big names perform here every year, including Herbie Hancock and Dizzie Gillespie in 1988 (tickets L8000-12,000). Jazz also often jams during the week at the **Happy Time** club, signposted off corso Umberto. The nearest museum of any standing is 9km away in Chieti on via IV Novembre. (Open Tues.-Sun. 9am-1pm.) Pescara itself boasts only the house of native son and poet D'Annuzo, **Casa D'Annuzo,** via Manthone. (Open daily 9am-1:30pm and 4-9:30pm.)

L'Aquila

On a plateau amidst the imposing Gran Sasso Mountains, L'Aquila is a busy commercial center, peppered with remnants of its rich past. The city is known especially for the curious preponderance of the number ninety-nine: Exactly 99 churches, 99 *piazzi,* and 99 fountains grace its streets. Every night, in fact, at 9pm the civic tower rings 99 times. Besides housing medieval treasures in the National Museum of the Abruzzo, L'Aquila serves as a departure point for the wilds of Abruzzo.

Orientation and Practical Information

The quickest way to L'Aquila is by frequent bus service (ARPA and OGNIVIA buses leave from p. della Repubblica in Rome, L7000). L'Aquila lies on a spur off the main Rome-Pescara rail line, and trains generally take twice as long as buses. ARPA buses also run from Pescara eight times per day (L6200). The city's historic district revolves around **piazza del Duomo.** Modern city life culminates in the commercial district at the end of **corso Vittorio Emanuele.**

EPT: p. Santa Maria Paganica, 5 (tel. 251 49). Turn right on via Garibaldi from the bus station. Ask for their map of the Gran Sasso Mountains. Try to get there before 2pm, when the savvy employees are in. Open Mon.-Fri. 8am-2pm and 4-6pm, Sat. 8am-2pm.

Azienda di Turismo: via XX Settembre, 8 (tel. 223 06), on the other side of town from the bus station. Helpful. Open Mon.-Sat. 9am-1pm and 4-6:45pm.

Club Alpino Italiano: via XX Settembre, 15 (tel. 243 42), across from the Azienda. The best maps, books, and information on local trails and refuges, though you'll be lucky if you find an English speaker. Open Mon.-Sat. 6:30-8:30pm.

Post Office: p. del Duomo (tel. 616 41). Open Mon.-Sat. 8:15am-7:30pm. Fermo Posta until 6pm. **Postal code:** 67100.

Telephones: via XX Settembre, 75. Open daily 8:30am-9:30pm. At night, try **Albergo Leon d'Oro,** via Dragonetti, 6, off p. del Duomo. **Telephone code:** 0682.

Train Station: At p. della Stazione (tel. 204 97), on the outskirts of town. Take bus #1, 3, or 3/5 from outside the station to the center of town, or hike up viale XXV Aprile about 3km and make a right on via Roma.

Buses: Tickets and schedules at corso V. Emanuele, 49. Open Mon.-Fri. 9am-1pm and 4-6:30pm, Sat. 9am-1pm. Buses leave from Porta Paganica, where a small ticket and information stand sits (tel. 694 64). Open Mon.-Fri. 9am-1pm and 4-6:30pm, Sat. 9am-1pm.

Red Cross (First Aid): Tel. 223 33.

Police: Questura, via Strinella, 2 (tel. 220 46).

Accommodations

Albergo Italia, corso V. Emanuele, 79 (tel. 205 66). Compared with the other choices, it's elegant. Sitting room and courtyard, too. Singles L18,500, with shower L23,000. L8000 per additional person, with shower L11,000.

Albergo Aurora, via Cimino (tel. 220 53), off p. del Duomo. Large rooms and in the midst of things. Singles L18,000. L12,000 per additional person. Showers included.

Albergo Centrale, via Simonetto, 3 (tel. 225 53), in an alley off via V. Emanuele. The well-kept bathrooms and convenient location compensate for the dark atmosphere. Singles L18,000. Doubles L23,000. No showers.

Locanda Orazi, via Roma, 175 (tel. 695 45). A 10-minute walk to the center of town. Most inconvenient but cheap. Adequate singles L14,500. Doubles 19,500. Don't get charged more than the listed price.

Food

L'Aquila drips with *torrone,* a chocolate-covered nougat made of honey and almonds. The best and most renowned of the *torrone* makers is **Fratelli Nurzia,** corso Frederico II, 50, which sells the candy directly from its factory near p. del Duomo. There is an open market held every morning in the same *piazza.* Concoct your own meal of fruit, bread, and cold cuts bought from **Supermercato Standa,** via Indipendenza, 6, off p. del Duomo under the Standa department store.

Trattoria San Biagio, p. S. Biagio, 4 (tel. 221 39), down via Sasso from p. del Duomo. The local favorite. You will be satisfied with any choice you make, but especially the *minestre mediterraneo,* a soup of minced rice and vegetables (L5000), and the *mozzarella e prosciutto allo spiedo,* roasted gobs of fresh mozzarella with ham (L5700). Ask the prices before ordering daily specials. Wines L2000-4000. Cover L1500. Service 10%. Open Mon.-Sat. 11:30am-3:30pm and 6:30pm until the crowd leaves.

Trattoria Stella Alpina, via Crispomonti, 15 (tel. 201 90), off p. del Duomo. Serves regional dishes like *agnello* (lamb) and *spaghetti alla chitarra* (pasta cut with a guitarlike instrument). *Menù* L12,500. Cover L1000. Open Sat.-Thurs. 9am-3:30pm and 6-11pm.

Ristorante Renato, via Indipendenza, 9 (tel. 255 96), near p. del Duomo. Tight and smoky. The quality merits the higher price. *Orechiette con broccoletti,* a pasta dish with broccoli (L5000), and *agnello ai ferri,* grilled lamb (L10,500), are house specialties. Local wines L2000. Cover L1500. Open Mon.-Sat. noon-3:30pm and 6-10:30pm.

Bar Tropical, via Delle Aquile, 22, off Principe Umberto. An alternative to the bars in the arcade. Their exotic fruit drinks have a devoted following. Open daily noon-midnight.

Sights

L'Aquila's ***castello*** is in the pleasant park at the end of corso V. Emanuele. In the sixteenth century the Spanish built this hilltop fortress to defend against rebellious townspeople. Its thick walls now house the truly outstanding **National Museum of Abruzzi,** which focuses on the early art of Abruzzo. Many of the rooms have long corridors that provide natural lighting and panoramic views. The museum's extensive medieval collection of sacred art includes delicately carved wooden doors from a twelfth-century church, which illustrate scenes from the New Testament; a magnificent fifteenth-century, silver-plated processional cross made by local silversmiths and decorated with bells; and a multicolored wooden statue of San Sebastiano made by L'Aquila's greatest sculptor, Silvestro dell' Aquila. The paleontological section contains a fossilized wooly mammoth found near the town and a fine collection of Abruzzese pottery in characteristic black and yellow. (Open Tues.-Sat. 9am-2pm, Sun. 9am-3pm. Admission L3000.) In the evenings, the path around the fortress's moat becomes a ***passagietta.***

Off corso V. Emanuele, on via di San Bernardino, is the **Basilica of San Bernardino.** The facade (1527) consists of three rows of cornices, each supported by four sets of twin columns. You'll notice that the columns democratically vary between the Doric, Ionic, and Corinthian styles (what else would one expect from the ancient Greeks?). Inside, the basilica is baroque. It shelters the body of St. Bernadine, carried here from Siena in 1472. His mausoleum of sculpted white marble lies in the fifth chapel on the right. To get a better view of the facade, descend the steps in front of the church and view it from a distance. (Open 7am-noon and 4-7pm.) A short walk down via Fortebraccio will bring you to the **Church of Santa Maria di Collemaggio.** Begun in 1272 at the insistence of a local hermit who later became Pope Celestine V, the church has a unique facade that closely resembles an elaborately decorated handball court. This squarish facade was the prototype for later Abruzzese ecclesiastical architecture. Widely separated, pointed arches divide the interior into three separate aisles. The stripping away of baroque embellishments several years ago and the earlier loss of medieval frescoes account for the church's lack of ornamentation, save the striking white limestone Renaissance **Tomb of San Celestino** lying in the chapel to the right of the high altar. If you're lucky enough to be here on August 29, walk through the church's main door, and according to tradition, you will be pardoned of your sins. Every year on this day, important political figures from all parts of Italy march in procession to the door, in hopes of attaining absolution.

Walk down via Sassa for a short tour of L'Aquila's minor architecture. Stop at #56, Palazzetto Franchi (near the post office), which encloses a graceful Renaissance courtyard, somewhat unusual for its double *loggia* (now partially sealed). Note the unique ram's head capitals and the fireplacelike decoration on the landing. For a real surprise, walk to the courtyard of #29A and ring the doorbell on the side. Mysteriously, the door opens and a clear voice says, "*Avanti!*" This is the **Church and Convent of Beata Antonia,** run by cloistered nuns who must never be seen. Say you want to see the *affresco* (fresco), and magically, you are confronted by a magnificent fifteenth-century version of the crucifixion filling an entire wall. At the end of the road sits charming **Church of San Pietro di Sassa,** the oldest in L'Aquila.

Before leaving L'Aquila, make a pilgrimage to the thirteenth-century **Fontana delle 99 Cannelle** (Fountain of the 99 Spouts), near the train station in Porta Rivera. A symbol of the city, each of the fountain's distinct stone faces spews a steady stream of water of unknown source; they have not ceased since the fountain's construction in 1292.

From November to May, the **Società Aquilana dei Concerti** holds classical concerts in the *castello.* Also of interest are the recitals at the **Festival of Classical Guitar,** in August. For ticket and schedule information, apply to the Azienda.

In winter, L'Aquila is the skijump to central Italy's best snow sport resorts, notably **Campo Felice.** Weekly lift tickets cost L53,000; *settimana bianca* (white week) packages are more economical. These deals include room, board, and lift tickets. Write to the Azienda for information.

Near L'Aquila

The area around L'Aquila will delight explorers who seek forays off the beaten track. Knolls and peaks of all sizes conceal medieval walled cities, ancient churches and monasteries, and spectacular ruined fortresses. East of the city lie the extraordinary ruins of the **Rocca Calascio,** one of the world's most sophisticated pieces of military architecture in the fifteenth century. It is surrounded by the medieval towns of **Santo Stefano di Sessanio** and **Castel del Monte,** as well as the ninth-century **Oratorio di San Pelligrino** in the town of Bominaco. Just north of L'Aquila, the town of **Assergi** contains a beautiful twelfth-century abbey, **Santa Maria Assunta.** To L'Aquila's west there are extensive Roman archeological sites at **Amiternum** and the large, glacial **Lago di Campotosto.** ARPA buses service most of these sights.

Twelve kilometers above L'Aquila stands the **Gran Sasso D'Italia,** the snow-capped ridge that divides Abruzzo from Le Marche. It offers hiking opportunities to mountaineers of all levels. The first step is to procure a map marked *Wanderkarte* or *carta topografica per escursionisti,* available at newsstands and bookshops. Make sure it includes the *sentieri* (trails marked by difficulty) and *rifugi* (hikers' inns costing L8000-14,000 per night). Always call these refuges before setting out, and bring food as prices tend to rise with the altitude. Club Alpino Italiano (see L'Aquila Practical Information) offers the most up-to-date alpine advice. The accommodations booklet available free at L'Aquila's EPT contains an invaluable list of Abruzzo refuges.

One of the easiest ways to experience the mountains is to begin at **Campo Imperatore** (2126m), at the foot of the **Corno Grande,** the zenith of the range. In ski season, you can take the **funivia** (cable car) at Fonte Cerretco (tel. 60 61 43). In summer, you'll have to hitch as there is no bus and the *funivia* does not run. You can also make daytrips from a lower altitude. Take bus #6 or 6s bus to Assergi. Get off after passing through the town and over the *autostrada.* You will see paths threading to the right and up into the summits. Consult your map, get local advice about excursions, and decide on one that matches your time and will. An ascent of the peak takes at least seven hours; it's convenient to stay at the **Rifugio Duca Degli Abruzzi** (tel. (06) 654 34 24), near the top of the *funivia,* and get an early start.

Sulmona

"Sulmo Mihi Patria est" ("Sulmona is my country"), boasted its most famous son, the poet Ovid (43 B.C.E.-17 C.E.). His statue stands in **piazza XX Settembre,** his eyes fixed on the ledge of mountains that give Sulmona such bearing. This town grows on you; its streets and sunny *piazzas* possess a distinct sweetness, mostly due to its overabundance of candy stores, but also to the gregariousness of its residents. Sulmona has been the home of *confetti* candy since the fifteenth century. These sugar-coated almonds are exported worldwide and thrown typically at weddings (thus the name).

Sulmona's main thoroughfare is **corso Ovidio,** connected to the train station by bus A. At one end of the *corso* is a park. Next comes the **Church and Palace of SS. Annunziata.** This complex is Sulmona's architectural showpiece and one of Abruzzo's most beautiful structures. A broad terrace embellished with wrought-iron lampposts hosts four centuries of architecture; an extravagant baroque church stands next to a delicate medieval-Renaissance *palazzo.* The integrated forms include the Gothic doorway to the left and the adjacent triple-arched window, both dating from the 1300s. The first four sculptures in front of the *palazzo, Doctors of the Church,* were added in 1415; the Renaissance central doorway and windows above date from 1483; and the right-hand doorway and window were built in 1522.

The *palazzo* now houses a small museum. (Open Mon.-Sat. 10am-12:30pm and 4:30-7pm, Sun. 9am-12:30pm.)

Sulmona can easily be reached from L'Aquila (1½ hr.), Rome (3 hr.), Pescara (2 hr.), and Avezzano (1¼ hr.) by ARPA bus or train. For information on faster, more expensive buses, call 522 58. The **telephone code** is 0864. The **post office** is behind the bank in p. Garibaldi. (Open Mon.-Fri. 8:15am-7pm.

Directly beyond the church and palace on corso Ovidio is **piazza XX Settembre,** the meeting place of Sulmona's pleasure-seekers and people-watchers. In the middle of corso Ovidio is giant **Piazza Garibaldi.** Framed by the surrounding mountain ranges, the *piazza* is the size of four soccer fields. Since 1300, water has flowed from the Gothic aqueduct, at the *piazza*'s entrance, to the Renaissance **Fontana del Vecchio.** If you stare up at the pediment on the church in the *piazza* closest to the mountains, a row of sculpted faces will stare back down at you. Also at the end of corso Ovidio, on p. del Carmine, is the **Church of San Francesco della Scarpa** (St. Francis of the Shoe). The odd name probably derives from the Franciscan friars's habit of wearing shoes when clogs were in vogue. Due to several destructive earthquakes, only a grandiose twelfth-century portico remains of the church.

The **Azienda di Turismo,** via Roma, 21 (tel. 532 76), off corso Ovidio, is usually open Monday through Saturday from 9am to 1pm, but hours are flexible. The **Albergo Italia,** p. S. Tommasi, 3 (tel. 523 08), off p. XX Settembre, offers rooms overlooking the dome of the chiesa della SS. Annunziata and the mountains. It is much classier than its prices suggest. (Singles L16,000, with bath L26,000. Doubles L26,000, with bath L33,000.) Around the corner at via Paniflo Marara, 16, **Albergo Stella** (526 53) offers shabbier doubles with bath for L30,000. At **Trattoria de Clara,** via Ciofano, 39 (tel. 512 77), off corso Ovidio, you can eat well at garden tables for L14,000. (Open Fri.-Wed. noon-3pm and 6:30-10pm, Sun. noon-7pm.) **Ristorante Stella,** beneath the hotel, offers a decent four-course meal for L12,000. Those with a sweet tooth will die for this town. **G. Di Carlo and Figlio,** via Ovidio, 185, does booming business in *confetti.* (Open daily 9am-1pm and 5-9pm.) At via Ovidio, 229, **Art Regato** sports chocolate in all incarnations. While at the train station, visit the city's renowned candy factory, the **Fabbrica Confetti Torrone William Di Carlo,** p. Vittime Civile di Guerra, 3.

National Park of Abruzzo (Parco Nazionale d'Abruzzo)

Situated in the southwest corner of the region, the National Park of Abruzzo is a huge wildlife preserve perfect for hiking and camping. With its various campsites and its easy accessibility by bus, the park is a great place to relax for a few days, away from churches, *piazze,* and museums.

Orientation and Practical Information

The park's administration center is **Pescasseroli,** which, like most towns in the preserve, is on ARPA's Avezzano-**Castel di Sangro** bus line (6 per day). **Avezzano** (on the Rome-Pescara train line) is 1½ hours from Pescasseroli (L3400), 1½ hours from Rome (L5400), and 2½ hours from Pescara (L6900). There is also an ARPA bus which links L'Aquila with Avezzano hourly (50 min., L3600). **Castel di Sangro** (on the Sulmona-Carpinone train line) is 1 hour from Pescasseroli (L3200). In July and August an ARPA bus leaves p. Esedra in Rome for Pescasseroli daily (7am) and returns to Rome in the evening (7:30pm, L8000). For the exact times of the Avezzano-Pescasseroli-Castel di Sangro buses, call ARPA in Avezzano at (0863) 462 20. The information below refers to Pescasseroli:

Ufficio di Zona del Parco: off p. Sant' Antonio (tel. 919 55), at the bus stop. Information on camping, refuges, and excursions. Park map L6000. Open daily 9am-noon and 3-7pm.

Azienda di Turismo: via Piave (tel. 914 61). Information on accommodations and transportation. More helpful than the Ufficio di Zona. Open daily 9am-1pm and 4:30-6:30pm.

Telephone Code: Pescasseroli and Avezzano, 0863; Civitella Alfedena, Castel Di Sangro, and Pescocostanzo, 0864.

Accommodations, Camping, and Food

The unattractive town of **Avezzano** is commended only by its location on both the Rome-Pescara rail line and at one end of the main bus route though the National Park. If you must stay, try the **Creati** (tel. 451 47) with singles for L16,000 and doubles for L24,000 (all rooms with private bath). Most restaurants in Avezzano are prohibitively expensive, with the possible exception of the **Ristorante Vanucci,** via Montello, 7 near the train station. (Full meals L15,000. Open Sat.-Thurs. 1-3pm and 7:30-9:30pm.)

You don't really enter the park until you begin the scenic ascent on the bus ride from Avezzano to Pescasseroli, a touristed but still pleasant little mountain town with tidy houses and firewood stacked on the streets. Most reasonably priced accommodations in town do not offer single rooms, but solo travelers can gamble with the unreliable list of *affitacamere,* available at the Azienda di Turismo. The **Ostella Del Lupo,** via Collachi (tel. 915 34), is 2km out of town and charges L10,000 per person in comfortable but crowded quad rooms. To get there, walk down viale S. Lucia off p. S. Antonio and turn right along viale Colle Dell'Oro. Follow the signs from there. Much closer to the center of town is the **Locanda Al Costello** (tel. 913 57), across from the Park Office, with clean doubles for L21,000, with bath and shower L26,000. This *locanda* often offers solitary travelers reduced rates. There are four campgrounds within 21km of town; the best is **Campeggio dell' Orso,** by the river on the Opi road.

The hands-down favorite for eating in Pescasseroli is the **Pizzeria Ristorante Picchio,** via Lungo Sangro (tel. 914 50), down the street from the Azienda. Flavorful *funghi sott' olio* (mushrooms in olive oil) is L2500; *tortelloni* is L4500. A liter of *vino rosso* costs L4000. (Cover L1000. Open Thurs.-Tues. noon-3pm and 7-11:30pm.)

ARPA buses follow the winding road through the park to the village of **Opi** (5km). Two kilometers past the village, on the bus route, is the campsite **Vecchio Mulino** (L3000 per person, L3000 per tent). At the turn-off to Camosciara there is an **information center** for foreign visitors. (Open July 10-Aug. Mon.-Sat. 9am-1pm and 2-5pm.)

Ten kilometers past Opi the bus reaches the village of **Villetta Barrea;** the turn-off to Civitella Alfederia leads to the **Pinas Nigra Campsite** after 200m. Rates are L2500 per person, L2000 per tent; the site is large and pleasant, bordered by the River Sangro. In **Civitella Alfedena,** there is a **hostel** (tel. (0864) 891 66), charging L9000 per person. The ice-cold **Banea Lake** cuts majestically into the mountains, stretching 7km between Villetta Barrea and the next village of **Barrea.** The **Colle Ciglio** campsite, on the banks of the lake, is 500m above town on the way to Alfedena, 10km southeast of Barrea.

The town of **Alfedena,** 1km from its train station, features interesting archeological sites. Its **tourist offices** (tel. 873 94), in the main square, offer information on the Roman **acropolis** and **necropolis.** Stay at **Locanda Petrarca** (tel. 871 77; singles L4800, doubles L8000) or **Leon D'Oro** (tel. 871 21; singles L11,000, with bath L14,000; doubles L21,000, with bath 26,000). **Alimentari Crispi,** off the main square, makes *panini* (sandwiches) for L1000-2000. A track leads from Alfedena to **Lago Montagna Spaccata** (3km away), where the brave can swim in the freezing mountain water.

Excursions

If you plan to hike, keep in mind that this mountainous region is not well-developed and trails are poorly marked. Begin by purchasing a trail map (L6000) from the Ufficio di Zona in Pescasseroli. The clear and detailed map points out where the different animals protected in the preserve (brown bears, chamois, deer, wolves, and eagles) are most likely to be found. Most of the interesting trails wind their way up into the valleys south of the main road. From Pescasseroli, one very picturesque climb is the 2½-hour hike to **Valico di Monte Tranquillo** (Monte Tranquillo Pass—1673m). Take Trail #C3, which starts at the southern end of town, up through the green Valle Mancina past the Rifugio della Difesa. Keep climbing and you'll eventually reach the pass, which has an impressive view of the mountain peaks to the north. Another beautiful hike is through the **Valle Fondillo.** To reach it, take a bus to the road that leads south just after the town of Opi (it's at kilometer #51; ask the driver). At the end of this road, trail #F2 guides you on a pleasant stroll up to the *Valico Passagio dell' Orso* (1672m—2½ hr. to the top). If you prefer more rugged terrain, **La Camosciara** is the area for you. To get there, take the bus to Casone Antonucci, just west of the town of Villetta Barrea (at kilometer #55-56). A paved road leads south for about 3km to p. Camosciara. From here, it is a strenuous one-hour hike to the **Rifugio della Liscia** (1650m), at the foot of the rocky peaks.

In winter, this area has excellent skiing. Package deals on **settimane bianche** (white weeks) can run as low as L300,000 for room, board, and lift tickets. For more information about skiing and other excursions in the National Park, contact the Azienda di Turismo in Pescasseroli.

Molise

Molise forms a cultural wedge between central and southern Italy. The Moliseans are ambivalent in their sentiments: Ask them about Italy's most neglected aspect and they'll point down to the dry southern-style turf. In the next minute, they'll speak derisively of that uncivilized region below, fretted with Mafia and other assorted bandits. Molise's mountainous area is mostly poor and provincial, containing some of Italy's last unpolluted wilderness. Bears, wolves, and boars still roam the woods, trying to avoid assimilation into the local cuisine, which includes *soppressate* (smoked boar sausage). One warning: Don't plan on zipping through this region. Public transportation is infrequent and the most beautiful spots are difficult to reach.

Termoli, on the Adriatic coast, is, in many ways, a typical Italian resort. A 3-hour train ride from Pescara on the Milan-Lecce line (L4600) and a 5-hour ride from Naples (L14,200), its beach is an endless sandy expanse and its waters lusciously lucid. Even amidst the throngs of visitors in summer, Termoli retains its unique medieval tradition. The **Borgo Vecchio** (Old Neighborhood), the town's historic centerpiece, can be reached from the train station by walking down corso Umberto I and taking the first left onto corso Nazionale. The **Castello Svevo,** overlooking the water in the Borgo Vecchio, was built in 1247 by Frederik II of Sweden and is the focal point of the annual festival **Sagra del Tortellino,** held on August 15. Also celebrated every August is the **Festa di San Basso,** when the local fishermen parade in honor of the city's patron saint. The **Sagra del Pesce** occurs the last Sunday in August, when fresh fish is cooked in large outdoor caldrons. Termoli's **cathedral,** built in the Pisan-Puglian Romanesque style, stands directly behind the castle. (Open daily 7:30am-6:30pm.)

On your way to Borgo Vecchio, stop at Termoli's best bargain restaurant, **Gatto Verdi,** corso Nazionale, 59 (tel. 2736). The daily *menù* is L10,000. (Open Mon.-Sat. noon-2pm and 6-11:15pm.) The **Ristorante-Pizzeria Generale Custer,** via Duomo, 40 (tel. 3709), in the Borgo Vecchio, makes a decorous *pizza Generale Custer,* with salmon, smoked fish, and *prosciutto* for L7000. Cover is L1500. (Open Mon.-Sat. 12:30-4pm and 7:30-11pm.) **Pensione Villa Ida,** via M. Milano, 27 (tel. 26 66), to the left of the train station toward the beach, is a remarkable value. (Singles

L18,000. Doubles L33,000, with bath L37,000.) If you're feeling liberal with your lire, try the **Gardenia,** via Tremiti (tel. 854 41). (Singles L15,000. Doubles L20,000.) Termoli's only campground is 3km out of town on the strand. Take the "Al Mare" bus that leaves on the hour (9am-9pm) from the station. **Cala Saracena** (tel. 521 93) is wellkept and on a private beach. Unfortunately, it borders both a highway and train tracks. (L5800 per person, L6900 per tent; in off-season L4600 and L5600.) The **post office** is located on corso Milano, 18. (Open 8:10am-6:35pm. Fermo Posta 8:15am-1pm.) Termoli's **Agenzia di Turismo,** at p. M. Bega (tel. 27 54), offers no useful literature, but they are more than willing to talk. Bus and train schedules for the region hang on the windows. (Open Mon.-Sat. 8am-1pm.)

Molise's interior cities are currently being colonized by northern Italian businesses and are thus full of high-rise construction. **Campobasso,** the region's capital, is a two-hour train ride from Termoli (1 hr. by bus) and a four-hour train ride from Sulmona or Naples. Its two sights are the fifteenth-century **Castello Monforte,** overlooking the city and the crude stone Romanesque **Church of San Giorgio.** Don't be surprised by the hundreds of Carabinieri (national police) walking the streets. Campobasso is home to the national Carabinieri school, as well as one of the country's high-security prisons. The **EPT** office, p. della Vittoria, 14 (tel. 956 62), may be helpful in getting information on lodging and directions to the provincial hill towns. To get there, follow via Cavour from the station, take the third right on via C. Gazzani and the second left on corso Vittorio Emanuele II. (Open Mon.-Fri. 9am-1pm.) If by some misadventure you must spend the night here, you'll find that the only inexpensive hotel is **Albergo Bellevedere,** via Colle delle Api, 32 (tel. 627 24). (Singles L18,000, with bath L21,000. Doubles with bath L33,000.) There are decent cheap eats at the **Trattoria Lanese,** via Heraculaneam, 17, across from the prison. Full meals are less than L13,000. Dine to the measured pace of guards on duty.

Isernia, 90 minutes from Campobasso or Naples, is a small boomtown set among undulating knolls, perfect for leisurely hiking. The city is believed to be one of the oldest in Europe, thanks to the 1979 discovery of primitive stone tools used by *Homo aeserniensis,* a human genus believed to have migrated from Africa one million years ago. There is a small **archeological museum,** 1½km from the train station down corso Garibaldi, which displays some of these tools as well as fossils of elephant, bison, bear, and rhino. (Open Mon.-Fri. 8:30am-1:30pm. Free guided tours.) Once you're in the area of the museum, you can't miss a trip to the spectacular church of **SS. Cosima e Damiano,** set atop a hill just to the southeast of the city proper. Before making the hike up to the church, unbend at **Il Vecchio Mulino** (tel. 595 17). Set alongside a racing mountain stream, it serves a meal of local specialties for under L15,000. (Open Mon.-Sat. 1:30-10:30pm.)

The **EPT** is at via Mario Farinacci, 11, off corso Garibaldi on the 8th floor. As in most towns where tourists are desired but rare, EPT services are eager and helpful. **Hotel Sayonara,** via G. Berta, 132 (tel. 509 92; walk straight from the rail station, take the 3rd right 4 blocks down), is an extremely comfortable and modern hotel. (Singles L15,000, with bath L21,000. Doubles with bath L34,500.)

Many small towns connect by bus with Isernia. **Capracotta,** situated amid green pastures and pine forests; **Pietrabbondante,** with its Roman ruins; **Carpinone,** with the well-preserved Castello del Caldora; and **Agnone,** famous for its bell factory that has been chiming since the Middle Ages, are all off-beat places to visit. For hikers and nature lovers, the under-recognized **Mainarde Mountain Range,** one of Italy's largest, can be reached by taking the bus to the town of Scapoli for under L3000; the EPT has bus schedules.

SOUTHERN ITALY

Campania

Under the shadow of Mount Vesuvius, the fertile crescent of Campania stretches out along the Bay of Naples. A magnificent natural setting, sunny climate, extraordinary historic sights, and warm people make Campania a popular region.

The area's history has long been that of Naples, its capital and major port. Because of its strategic location, Naples has been coveted ever since it was established as a Greek colony, Neapolis (New City), around 600 B.C.E. Greek Naples was conquered by the Romans in 327 B.C.E., and it became a favorite residence of emperors (Nero made his theatrical debut here) and literary personages, including Virgil, largely because of its insistence on retaining the Greek language and customs. Homer, in fact, traced much of Odysseus's journey through the cliffs, islands, and waterways of southern Italy. A Byzantine dukedom in the seventh century and later part of Norman Sicily, Naples reached the zenith of its medieval prosperity when Charles I of Anjou made it his capital in 1266. Along with his Angevin and Aragonese successors, Charles expanded the city's size and embellished it with palaces and churches. The Spanish Hapsburgs (1502-1704) were followed by Bourbons, Bonapartes, and finally the Savoys, when Campania became part of the unified Italian nation in 1860.

One caveat: The south has a reputuation for crime. Take extra care in parking your car or stowing your backpack, and tighten your moneybelt a notch.

Naples (Napoli)

Gesticulations and dialects fly as fast as strawberries and seafood across the stands at a Neapolitan market, embodying the cultural informality that is Naples. Nowhere else in Italy is the difference between North and South more pronounced than in Naples. Many Neapolitans feel a cultural and communal bond that separates them from the rest of Italy and, like most southern Italians, identify more with a clan than a modern nation-state. They resent authority (refusing to recognize one-way streets or pedestrians' right of way) but adore foreigners. Naples is home to unwavering fatalists, living amidst poverty relieved only by an intensely personal religion and numerous local festivals. Rich museums, grand palaces, and a proud populace define the city far better than the unseen Mafia.

Orientation and Practical Information

Naples is composed of several *piazze* and quarters, each with its own atmosphere. Immense **piazza Garibaldi,** on the eastern side of Naples, contains both the central train station and the major city bus terminal. Broad, tree-lined corso Umberto I leads from p. Garibaldi southwest, ending at piazza Bovio, where via Depretis branches to the south, leading to piazza Municipio and nearby piazza del Plebiscito, an area of stately buildings and statues. Between p. Municipio and p. del Plebiscito on the water lies **Molo Beverello** and the Stazione Marittima, the principal point of departure for ferries to Capri, Ischia, Procida, and Sorrento. Turn north from p. del Plebiscito and go up via Toledo (also called via Roma) to reach **piazza Dante,** the **University District,** and **Spacca Napoli** (look for the 3 spires). The straight, narrow streets of historic Spacca Napoli (via Benedetto Croce, via San Biagio dei Librai, via Tribunali, and via San Gregorio Armeno), lined with battered palaces and churches, follow the ancient Roman layout. To the west, at the foot of the hills, are the **Santa Lucia** and **Mergellina** sections, with their celebrated bayside walks of via Partenope and via Caracciolo. Farther west are the most scenic areas in Naples: the waterfront **via Posillipo** and **via Petrarca.** The **Vomero** district in the hills above the city commands a view of double-peaked Mount Vesuvio to the east, historic Naples below, and the Campi Flegrei (Phlegraean Fields) to the west. The Vomero is the least touristed section of the city and can be reached by funicular.

EPT Tourist Information: At the central train station (tel. 26 87 79). Occasionally helpful, but a royal mess. Rarely open regular hours and swarms with soliciting hotel owners. The employees send tourists to hotels run by friends. On the other hand, the office is extremely knowledgeable about practical matters (ferry and train schedules, etc.) and offers several useful brochures. Pick up the helpful but general map of the city and the indispensible guide *Qui Napoli* (Here Naples), with everything from train schedules to entertainment listings. Also get a copy of *Napoli-Top,* a monthly entertainment guide. For more specific information on arts and entertainment, check out the *Posto Unico,* a poster hanging on the wall with a current calendar of theaters, restaurants, and clubs. English supposedly spoken. Open Mon.-Sat. 8:30am-8pm, Sun. 8:30am-2pm. **Main office,** via Partenope, 10/A (tel. 40 62 89). Take tram #1 or 2 or bus #150. Open Mon.-Fri. 8:30am-2:30pm and Sat. 8:30am-noon. Also at Stazione Mergellina (tel. 761 21 02) and the airport (tel. 780 57 61). Open irregular hours.

Azienda di Turismo: Palazzo Reale (tel. 41 87 44). Take bus #106 or 150. Fairly large office, but largely administrative. Open Mon.-Fri. 8:30am-2:30pm. **Information office,** p. Gesù Nuovo (tel. 552 33 28). Take bus #185 up via Roma towards p. Dante, get off at via Capitelli, and follow it to the *piazza*—right in front of the Chiesa del Gesù Nuovo. The most helpful and professional office in the city. Unbiased advice on accommodations and tourism. Open Mon.-Sat. 9am-3pm. **Information booth,** p. Garibaldi, outside the train station. Offers little. Open Mon.-Sat. 9am-2pm. Other offices at Castel dell' Ovo (tel. 41 14 61) and at the hydrofoil port at Mergellina (tel. 66 08 16). Both open June-Sept. Same hours as office at p. Garibaldi.

Italian Youth Hostel Organization (Associazione Alberghi della Gioventù): p. Carità, 40 (tel. 552 00 84), near the central post office. An excellent resource for information on youth hostels and special IYHF plane, train, and ferry discounts. Open Mon.-Fri. 9am-1pm and 4-7pm, Sat. 9am-1pm.

Centro Turistico Studentesco e Giovanile (CTS): via Gasperi, 35 (tel. 552 00 74), off via Depretis near p. Municipio. Student travel information, ISIC and FIYTO cards, and booking service. Open Mon.-Fri. 9am-1pm and 4-7pm, Sat. 9am-1pm.

Travel Agencies: CIT, p. Municipio, 72 (tel. 554 54 26). The city's most complete travel agency. Train, plane, and ferry reservations (except those to Greece). Open Mon.-Fri. 9am-1pm and 4-7pm. For ferry reservations to Greece, go to **Travel and Holidays,** via Santa Lucia, 141 (tel. 41 41 29). Take bus #150 from p. Garibaldi. Both agencies open Mon.-Fri. 9am-1pm and 4-7pm. Sat 9am-1pm.

Consulates: U.S., p. della Repubblica (tel. 66 09 66; phone lines open 24 hours), at the western end of the Villa Communale. Take any of the buses or trains that run along the waterfront. Passport and consular services Mon.-Fri. 8am-noon and 2-4pm. A large reference library on the 4th floor. Library open Mon., Wed., and Fri. 8am-1pm; Tues. and Thurs. 2-5pm. **U.K.,** via Francesco Crispi, 122 (tel. 20 92 27), off p. Amedeo. Passport and consular services mid-Sept. to June Mon.-Fri. 9am-12:30pm and 3-5:30pm; July to mid-Sept. Mon.-Fri. 8:30am-1pm. All other English speakers should contact their consulates in Rome.

Currency Exchange: All banks in Naples charge a fairly high service charge (usually L3000). For the most efficient transactions, go to one of the banks' main offices. **Banca Nazionale del Lavoro,** p. Garibaldi, 6/8 (tel. 26 68 33), in the *piazza* outside the train station. Open Mon.-Fri. 8:30am-1:20pm. Also exchange in the Stazione Centrale (*cambio*). The longest hours, but less favorable rates. Open daily 7am-9pm.

American Express: Ashiba Travel, p. Municipio, 1 (tel. 551 53 03). Naples' official American Express representative. Holds mail 3 months for free and replaces lost cards and checks. Open Mon.-Fri. 9am-1pm and 3:30-7:30pm, Sat. 9am-1pm. To replace checks and in their other monetary matters, AmEx works with the **Bank of Rome,** via Verdi, 31 (tel. 552 42 78), right around the corner. Open Mon.-Fri. 9am-1:20pm and 2:45-3:45pm.

Post Office: p. Matteotti (tel. 552 14 56), off via Diaz, which runs off corso Umberto I at its end. One of the few well-organized services in Naples. Fermo Posta L250 per letter retrieved. Offers special *CAI post* service (Posta Celere), which delivers packages anywhere in the world in 3 days at a base rate of L50,000. Open Mon.-Fri. 8:30am-7:30pm, Sat. 8:30am-noon. Also at Galleria Umberto. Open same hours. **Postal code:** 80100.

Adriatic Sea
N
Tremiti Is.
Termoli
Rodi Garganico
Vieste
Gargano Massif
Lucera
Foggia
Manfredonia
Troia
Trani
Barletta
Bari
Benevento
Caserta
Ariano
Melfi
Bitonto
Monopoli
Naples
Pozzuoli
Vesuvius
Ischia
Pompeii
Herculaneum
Altamura
Alberobello
Brindisi
Salerno
Potenza
Eboli
Matera
Francavilla
Mesagne
Manduria
Capri
Sorrento
Amalfi
Paestum
Agropoli
Taranto
Metaponto
Lecce
Otranto
Gallipoli
Sapri
Praia a Mare
Gulf of Taranto
Rossano
A P P E N N I N E S
CAMPANIA
BASILICATA
PUGLIA
CALABRIA
Tyrrhenian Sea
Sila Massif
Cosenza
Crotone
Catanzaro
Lipari Island
Messina
Milazzo
Bagnara
Scilla
Locri
Reggio di Calabria
Strait of Messina
SICILY
Ionian Sea
Catania
0
100 miles
0
100 kilometers
Mediterranean Sea

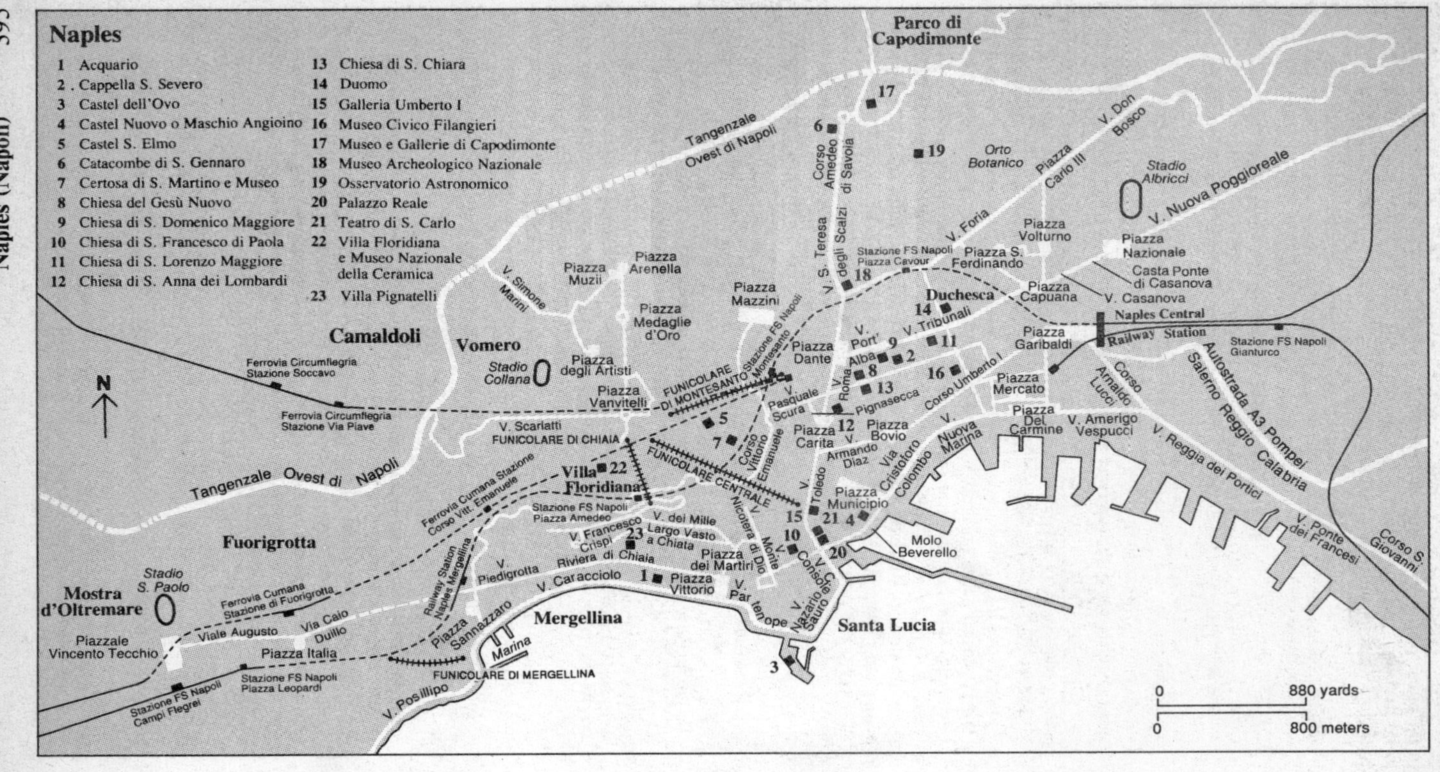
Naples
1 Acquario
2 Cappella S. Severo
3 Castel dell'Ovo
4 Castel Nuovo o Maschio Angioino
5 Castel S. Elmo
6 Catacombe di S. Gennaro
7 Certosa di S. Martino e Museo
8 Chiesa del Gesù Nuovo
9 Chiesa di S. Domenico Maggiore
10 Chiesa di S. Francesco di Paola
11 Chiesa di S. Lorenzo Maggiore
12 Chiesa di S. Anna dei Lombardi
13 Chiesa di S. Chiara
14 Duomo
15 Galleria Umberto I
16 Museo Civico Filangieri
17 Museo e Gallerie di Capodimonte
18 Museo Archeologico Nazionale
19 Osservatorio Astronomico
20 Palazzo Reale
21 Teatro di S. Carlo
22 Villa Floridiana e Museo Nazionale della Ceramica
23 Villa Pignatelli
Parco di Capodimonte
Camaldoli
Vomero
Fuorigrotta
Mostra d'Oltremare
Mergellina
Santa Lucia
Duchesca
N
Tangenzale Ovest di Napoli
Naples Central Railway Station
Railway Station Naples Mergellina
Autostrada A3 Pompei Salerno Reggio Calabria
FUNICOLARE DI MONTESANTO
FUNICOLARE DI CHIAIA
FUNICOLARE CENTRALE
FUNICOLARE DI MERGELLINA
Villa Floridiana
Piazza Dante
Piazza Garibaldi
Piazza Municipio
Piazza Nazionale
Stadio Albricci
Stadio Collana
Stadio S. Paolo
Molo Beverello
Orto Botanico
0 880 yards
0 800 meters

Telephones: ASST, at Stazione Centrale. No collect calls. Open 24 hours. **SIP,** at Galleria Umberto. Open Mon.-Sat. 8am-9:30pm. Also at via Depretis, 40, on the street off p. Bovio at the end of corso Umberto, heading south towards p. Municipio. Open 24 hours. The via Depretis office has the shortest lines. **Telephone code:** 081.

Airport: Aeroporto Capodichino, viale Umberto Maddalena (tel. 116; for departures 780 32 35; for arrivals 780 30 49), northwest of the city. Take bus #14 from p. Garibaldi in the city center. Connections to all major Italian and European cities. **Alitalia** works through **Ati Travel,** via Medina, 41/42 (tel. 542 53 33).

Train Information: Tel. 26 46 44. Lines usually busy—it will take several calls to get through. Ticket prices and schedules in English and Italian. Also **information booths** at the Stazione Centrale, but be prepared to queue up. For urgent train information, go to one of the train officials at the track with a red-banded shirt. Telephone service and information booths open daily 7:30am-10pm.

Taxi: Tel. 36 44 44 or 36 43 40. A rollercoaster ride. Fare L2300 plus L100 per 118m or 30 seconds. Sun. and holidays L1000 supplement; 10pm-7am L1700 supplement. L400 per piece of baggage. You must pay double for taxis to the airport. Take only taxis with meters.

Car Rental: Maggiore-Avis, at Stazione Centrale (tel. 28 40 41), next to EPT. Open Mon.-Fri. 8am-1pm and 3-7:30pm, Sat. 8:30am-1pm and 4-6pm. **Hertz,** p. Garibaldi, 69 (tel. 20 62 28). Open Mon.-Fri. 8am-8pm, Sat. 8am-1pm.

International Bookstore: Universal Books, Rione Sirignano, 1 (tel. 66 32 17), near Villa Comunale. Books in English and other languages. Open Mon.-Fri. 9am-1pm and 4-7pm, Sat. 9am-1pm.

Pharmacy: At Stazione Centrale (tel. 268 81). Open Mon.-Sat. 8am-8pm. Pharmacies alternate to provide nighttime service. Call 192 for the 24-hour recording of nighttime pharmacies (in Italian).

Medical Services: Tel. 752 06 96 for an ambulance. Guardia Medica Permanente, tel. 751 31 77, in the Municipio building for medical assistance at night or during holidays.

Police: Tel. 79 41 11. English speakers always available. For problems, go to the *ufficio stranieri* (foreigner's office) at the Questura, via Medina, 75, at via Diaz. **Emergencies:** Tel. 113.

Transportation

Located on the southern Tyrrhenian coast, 200km southeast of Rome, Naples is southern Italy's transportation hub. Frequent **trains** connect the Stazione Centrale to Italy's major cities, including Milan (7 hr., L38,900), Rome (3 hr., L10,700), and Syracuse (10 hr., L32,800). Trains also connect Naples to the port city of Brindisi on the Rome-Lecce line for ferries to Greece (6½ hr., L21,900). **Ferries** run from Naples's Molo Beverello to several destinations, most notably the islands of Capri, Ischia, and Procida. Eurailpasses are not valid on these ferries. Other key ferries:

Naples-Lipari Islands, Sicily: Siremar Lines, via Depretis, 78 (tel. 551 21 12). Mon.-Tues. and Thurs.-Sat. at 9pm to Stromboli (8 hr., L37,000), Lipari (12 hr., L42,000), and Vulcano (13 hr., L42,500).

Naples-Palermo: Tirrenia Lines, Stazione Marittima, porto (tel. 551 21 81). Daily at 8:30pm (10½ hr., L40,500).

Naples-Cagliari: Tirrenia. Oct.-May Tues. and Thurs.; June-Oct. Tues., Thurs., and Sun. at 5:30pm (16 hr., L56,300).

Naples-Reggio Calabria-Catania-Syracuse-Malta: Tirrenia. From Naples Thurs. at 8:30pm. To Reggio (10 hr.), Catania (15 hr.), and Syracuse (18 hr.); L40,000 for all three. To Malta (25 hr., L111,700 plus a L15,000 port-tax upon leaving Malta).

Bay of Naples Tour-Boat: The Loveboat (tel. 575 15 32) offers 1-hr. tours of the bay. From via Caracciolo harbor—take tram #1 or 4 to the port, near the U.S. consulate. July-Sept. daily at 6pm, 7pm, and 8pm. Adults L4000, children under 10 L1000.

The city offers a cornucopia of public transportation: bus, tram, subway, funicular, and a high-speed suburban rail line (Ferrovia Circumvesuviana). The fare on all inner-city transport is L600. Half-day passes (6am-2pm or 2-11pm), valid on all buses, trams, and furniculars, but not the subway (L1000; can be purchased throughout the city). Bus service, especially in the morning and late afternoon, is a disgrace. People have been known to fall out of or be crushed inside overcrowded buses. To cover long distances (especially from Mergellina to the station), use the efficient and cool subway or tram #4. The most useful lines are:

Buses #150 and 106: From p. Garibaldi to the center of the city, p. Municipio, and to the bay (Riviera di Chiaia) and Mergellina (for the youth hostel and Pozzuoli).

Buses CS and CD: From p. Garibaldi to p. Cavour (CD) or via Pessina (CS, for the Museo Archeologico Nazionale), and to p. Dante for the restaurants in the area.

Bus #185: the most direct route to p. Dante from p. Garibaldi (for the hotels and restaurants in the area).

Trams #1 and 4: A picturesque and practical way to get from the station to Mergellina. Stops right at the Molo Beverello port (for boats to Capri, Ischia, and Procida). Trams stop in front of the Garibaldi statue near Stazione Centrale.

Metropolitana: The subway system from the train station to points west: p. Cavour (Museo Nazionale), p. Amadeo (funicular to Vomero), and finally (emerging from underground) Mergellina, and Pozzuoli. Go to platform #4, 1 floor underground, at Stazione Centrale.

Ferrovia Circumvesuviana: The fastest way to get to Herculaneum, Pompeii, and Sorrento. 1 floor underground at the train station.

Funicolare Centrale: The most frequently used of the 3 cable railways to Vomero, connecting the lower city to the hills and S. Martino. Leaves from p. Duca D'Aosta, next to the Galleria Umberto on via Toledo.

Hitching to other cities from Naples is dangerous, *especially* for women. If you are forced to hitch, the most strategic spot is a good distance before the entrance to the *autostrada.* (Hitching on the *autostrada* itself is strictly prohibited.) To get there from the Stazione Centrale, follow corso Arnaldo Lucci from the southwest corner of p. Garibaldi to via Reggia di Portici, 300m from the *autostrada* entrance to all points south. To go to points north, you must take red bus #14 to get to the other entrance of the *autostrada.*

Accommodations

Hotel hunting in Naples can be disconcerting. When you arrive at the central train station, hotel-hawkers pretending to be tourist officials will try to lure you to one of the dingy hotels that give them a commission. Officials working the tourist booth at the station are also nepotistically biased. It's best to choose for yourself. Cheap hotels are a cinch to find. The most inexpensive hotels and *pensioni* are concentrated around **piazza Garibaldi** by the train station. This area is sleazy and seems thousands of miles from the sea, but hosts a variety of hotels near the historic center of town. There are some better alternatives in the area around the **university,** between p. Dante and the *duomo.* Hotels here cater primarily to students and offer well-furnished, immaculate rooms at low prices, though vacancies decrease when school is in session. The area of **Mergellina,** at the far end of the bay (served by subway and trolley), commands outstanding views of Vesuvius and Capri, but is more expensive. The pricey hostel is also located in this area.

In Naples especially, you should consider paying more for added comfort, security, and respectability. Always agree on the price before you unpack your bags, and be alert to hidden shower charges, obligatory breakfasts, and the like. When selecting a place to stay, check for double-locked doors and door buzzers. If you have a legitimate complaint against your hotel, call the EPT's special number: 41 98 88. They will connect you with someone who speaks English and who will address your grievance. For information on **camping** near Naples, see Near Naples below.

Ostello Salita Della Grotta (IYHF), salita della Grotta, 23 (tel. 761 23 46). Take the Metropolitana to Mergellina and make two sharp rights onto via Piedigrotta. Follow the *via* underneath an overpass, but do not go through the tunnel. Look for signs on the right pointing to the secluded hostel, not far from the waterfront. The safest and most secure budget lodgings in Naples. Well-maintained 2-, 4-, and 6-person pads, all with baths. The cafeteria downstairs serves full meals for L7000. Beds L11,000, nonmembers L13,500. Breakfast included. IYHF card L15,000. Check-out 9am. Curfew 11:30pm. July-Aug. 3-day maximum.

Near piazza Garibaldi

Albergo Zara, via Firenze, 81 (tel. 28 71 25). From the train station, make a right onto corso Novaro, then make the 1st left. Some of these clean rooms have peeling neoclassical ceilings. Cozy TV room. Singles L18,000. Large doubles L30,000, with shower L35,000. Breakfast L3500.

Hotel Eliseo, via Mancini, 33 (tel. 20 69 65), on the street off the back of Garibaldi's statue in p. Garibaldi. A tidy new *albergho* run by a cheery Chilean. Not accustomed to working with tourists and located in a dirty and dangerous market area. Lots of Africans and Arabs. Well-kept singles L12,200. Doubles L22,800, with sparkling bath L30,500.

Hotel Prati, via Rosaroll, 4 (tel. 26 88 98). Take via Garibaldi, off p. Garibaldi, to p. Principe Umberto. A full-fledged hotel with well-decorated rooms complete with telephones, wooden dressers, and tiled bathrooms. English spoken. Special prices for *Let's Go* users: Doubles with bath L50,000. L19,000 per additional person. Breakfast included. Full meals L15,000. Color TV in room L2500. Credit cards accepted.

Hotel Mexico, via Rosaroll, 13 (tel. 26 65 54), across from the Prati. The newest deluxe hotel in Naples also offers a special price to *Let's Go* readers. All rooms feature phones, radios, color TVs, fridge-bars, wall-to-wall carpeting, and sparkling bathrooms (with built-in hair dryers). English spoken. Doubles L49,500. L15,000 per additional person. Credit cards accepted.

Near Piazza Dante and Vomero

Take bus #185, CS, or CD from the train station to the bargain rooms around p. Dante. Though the hectic byways of this area are favorite stake-outs for Neapolitan motorbike purse bandits, it makes a central base for cautious tourists. To get to safe and more serene Vomero, get off any of the buses toward p. Dante at via Roma, near Gialleria Umberto, and take the funicular up.

Soggiorno Imperia, p. Miraglia, 386 (tel. 45 93 47). From p. Dante, walk eastward through the arch to the left of the clock tower. Continue on via S. Pietro a Maiella, to the right of Pizzeria Bellini. Continue walking through a small *piazza.* At the end, look for two large green doors on the right side of the narrow street. A 4-floor climb to rooms without sinks or bathrooms. But fairly large and bright rooms; young, helpful management accustomed to working with students; free showers (though short on hot water); a sink and washboard for laundry; and a refrigerator. English spoken. Discounts for stays of three or more days. Singles L12,000. Doubles L25,000. Triples L36,000. Call a day or two in advance July-Aug. and at Easter.

Allogio Fiamma, via Francesco del Guidice, 13 (tel. 45 91 87). Walking from the Imperia, turn right, then take the 2nd left onto via Guidice. Look for the red and white sign. If the Imperia is full, come here. Less respectable and faded. However, big, well-furnished rooms. Doubles L25,000. L11,000 per extra person. Shower included.

Pensione Margherita, v. Cimarosa, 29 (tel. 37 70 44), in the elegant Vomero area. Outside the central funicular station. A fancy hotel that offers the lowest prices in this posh district. Pleasant breakfast room with fancy paintings, color TV, and oriental rugs. English spoken. Singles L26,000. Doubles L41,000. Triples L65,000. Showers L4000 (soap and towel included). Obligatory breakfast L5000. Curfew midnight.

Near Mergellina

Hotel Crispi, via Francesco Biordani, 2 (tel. 66 48 04). Walk all the way up corso V. Emanuele from the Mergellina metro stop and take a right. Alternatively, take bus C4 from p. Garibaldi, getting off at nearby via M. Schipa. Spartan and safe rooms, some with views of Mergellina and Santa Lucia. Doubles L30,000. Triples L50,000. Curfew midnight. Reserve by mail.

Hotel Bella Napoli, via F. Caracciolo, 10 (tel. 66 38 11), on the Mergellina waterfront in the direction of Santa Lucia. An unbelievable bargain. The L45,000 doubles (L20,000 per additional person), come equipped with full bath, color TV with remote control, and great views of the *piazza.* Prices can be bargained down in winter. English spoken. Curfew 1am.

Pensione Muller, via Mergellina, 7 (tel. 66 90 56). Descend the street from the Mergellina metro stop towards the water. Enter through the side steet around the corner. Neat rooms, many with balconies overlooking the port. Doubles L40,000, with bath L50,000. Triples L52,000, with bath L64,000. Breakfast L5000. Drive a hard bargain.

Pensione Ausonia, via Caracciolo, 11 (tel. 66 22 68), down the street from the Bella Napoli. Go to the right in the courtyard through the entrance. Immaculate, airy rooms decorated with a nautical motif. English spoken. Doubles L45,000, with bath L64,000. Triples with bath L75,000. Breakfast included.

Food

Pasta, now an Italian staple, was first boiled in the pots of Neapolitan kitchens. Today, Naple's most famous pasta dishes are the savoury *spaghetti alle vongole* (with clams) and *alle cozze* (with mussels); both are served in their shells atop the pasta. *Spaghetti alla Marinara* (with a simple tomato and garlic sauce) is the pauper's favorite. Pasta aside, however, the Neapolitan creation that pleases stomachs worldwide, though never quite faithfully reproduced, is pizza. Pizza-making is an art here; the *pizzaiolos* (pizza-chefs) begin their apprenticeships as tots and perfect their craft over a lifetime. The unique combination of the skill of the *pizzaiolo,* the sweet local tomatoes, fresh mozzarella cheese, and Neapolitan water for the extra-light dough all make for an exquisite pie. The oldest and most unadulterated *pizzeria* is **Antica Pizzeria da Michele,** via cesare Sersale, 1/3 (tel. 553 92 04), off corso Umberto I not far from the train station. They make only the two original types of pizza here, *Marinara* (with tomato, garlic, oregano, and oil, L2500) and *Margherita* (with tomato and mozzarella cheese, L3000). (Open Sept.-July Mon.-Sat. 10am-10:30pm.)

The pearl of Neapolitan cuisine is its seafood, which comes in all incarnations. *Zuppa di cozze* or *cozze al limone* are delicious ways to enjoy the mussels of the gulf. There are *vongole* of all varieties, including razor clams and their more expensive cousin, the oyster. *Aragosta* (crayfish) are sweeter than lobster, and *polipi* (octopus) is one of the cheapest sources of protein around. Most good restaurants do not serve seafood on Mondays because the fish markets are closed. The city's most notable wines are *lacrima christi,* to accompany the city's great seafood, and the red *gragnano.*

Naple's most beloved pastry is the *sfoglia tella,* filled with sweetened ricotta cheese, orange rind, and candied fruit. It comes in two forms, *riccia,* the original, flakey-crusted variety and *frolla,* a softer, crumbly counterpart. The city's renowned *sfoglia tella* producer is **Attanasio,** vico Ferrovia, 2/4 (tel. 28 56 75), a 65-year-old bakery off via Milano near the train station. It sells both varieties, piping hot, for L900 each. (Open Tues.-Sun. 7:30am-8:30pm).

Neapolitan markets are a great way to eat cheap. On **via Soprammuro,** off p. Garibaldi, create your own repast from the grab bag of food options that the Neapolitan street market provides. (Active Mon.-Sat. 8am-1:30pm.) You can even buy live, slender, tasty eels here.

Near Piazza Garibaldi

Tourist-ridden, expensive, and mediocre restaurants dominate p. Garibaldi itself. Fortunately, high-quality low-cost meals lurk on the side streets off the *piazza.* Some of these areas become seedy at night, so eat early.

Osteria San Pasquale, via Ferrara, 97 (tel. 554 53 99), the 3rd right off corso Novara, which runs off p. Garibaldi. A small hangout lined with large barrels containing their great table wine (L1600-2000). Come here for a real Neapolitan meal cooked in the open kitchen. Try the *polipo in cassuola* (octopus with tomato and peppers, L3500). Open Mon.-Sat. noon-8pm.

Pizzeria Trianon da Ciro, via Pietro Colletta, 44/46 (tel. 553 94 26), near Antica Pizzeria da Michele. From p. Garibaldi, take corso Umberto, make a right 200m down on via Vincenzo Calenda, then a left at the 1st *piazza.* With old marble tables and wood-burning ovens, this ancient *pizzeria* is almost as famous as da Michele down the street, and often preferred for its larger selection. Untraditional choices like *8-gusti,* a pizza divided into 8 differently flavored sections (L7000). Beer or coke L1300. Service 15%. Open Mon.-Sat. 10am-3pm and 5-11pm.

Avellinese da Peppino, via Silvio Spaventa, 31/35 (tel. 28 38 97). From the train station, take the 3rd left on p. Garibaldi. In a safe, well-lit area. Locals and tourists dine in harmony at the outdoor tables, attracted by the tasty seafood dishes and a friendly owner. *Antipasto di mare* is an enticing mixture of all kinds of local shellfish (L4500). They also make the best *spaghetti alle vongole* (L4500). Cover L800, service 10%. Open Sun.-Fri. 11:30am-midnight.

O'Luciano, p. San Francesco, 63/65 (tel. 20 47 73), on the left side of the adjacent *piazza.* Take corso Garibaldi as far as via Cesare Rosaroll. Generations of Neapolitans have chowed here on *zuppa di cozze* (mussels in broth, L5000) and a *Nastro azzurro* (Neapolitan beer, L1000 per small bottle). Also famed for its *brodo di Polipo* (octopus broth steaming in large vats outside the kitchen, L1000). Located in an unnerving area at night. Service 10%. Open Thurs.-Tues. 11am-3am.

Trattoria da Maria, via Genova, 115, the 2nd right off corso Novara. No sign. In a city where tradition, simplicity, and hospitality come first, Papà Riccio and his family have kept their small and unrefined *trattoria* true to the Neapolitan style. Try the *penne sciuè sciuè* (with fresh tomato, basil, and mozzarella cheese, L3000). The local favorite is *bucatini alla puttanesca* (pasta with tomatoes, olives, and capers, L3000). Local wines L2000. Open Sept.-July Mon.-Fri. noon-3:30pm and 6:30-10pm.

Trattoria Clara, via Pavia, 6, a hole in the wall off via Genova. Hot and smokey, its only decor is a goldfish in a jar, but you can really stretch your lire here. Hearty, 3-course meals L9000, ½-liter house wine included. Open Mon.-Sat. noon-4pm and 7-10pm.

Near Piazza Dante

The historic center around piazza Dante, serviced by buses #185 and CD, shelters some of the city's most delightful *trattorie* and *pizzerie* on its narrow, winding streets. Many are favorite hangouts of the local university students. Via dei Tribunali shelters some of the cheapest eats.

La Campagnola, p. del Nilo, 22 (tel. 20 71 86). From p. Dante, facing the clock tower, walk through the archway on the left side of the building, follow via S. Pietro a Maiella past Miraglia onto via Tribunali, and take a right on via Nilo. The quintessential Neapolitan *trattoria.* The chow cooked in the open kitchen is tops and the prices rock-bottom. Huge salads L3000. Fresh *pasta con fruttie di mare* (with seafood) L3500. The renowned *provola alla brace* (roasted cheese) L3000. House wine L2000 per liter. Open Tues.-Fri. and Sun. noon-midnight, Sat. noon-3pm.

Vini e Olii, via dei Tribunali, 376, just down the street from the Soggiorno Imperia *pensione.* The elderly women cook to the chirping sounds of their pet canaries for only five tables, so they prepare their fare with care. Pasta L2000-3000. Fresh fish L3500. Salad L1500. Wine L2000. Open Sept.-July Mon.-Sat. noon-3pm.

Pizzeria Port' Alba, via Port' Alba, 18 (tel. 45 97 13), inside the Port' Alba arch on the left side of the p. Dante clock tower. Established in 1830, this is Naples's oldest *pizzeria.* The *pizza port' Alba* is a masterpiece, split into four quarters, one with shrimp and calamari, one with tomato and mozzarella, one with capers and anchovies, and one with mushrooms; and in the center a little surprise (L6500). Also good restaurant food. Cover for pizza L700, for restaurant L1000. Service 15%. Open Wed.-Mon. 9am-1am.

Pizzeria Sorbillo, via Tribunali, 35. The chef inherited this tiny joint and grew up making the pie. The lowest-price pizza in the area (from L2000). Try the *pizza a Filetto* in summer, made with fresh plum tomatoes, basil, prosciutto, mushrooms, and mozzarella (L4000). Beer L1000 per small bottle. Service 10%. Open Mon.-Sat. 11am-11pm.

Gelateria della Scimmia, p. della Carità, 4 (tel. 552 02 72). Follow via Roma south from p. Dante until you come to a large *piazza.* The bronze monkey that hangs in the storefront has come to symbolize superior ice cream and desserts. Try the *formetta,* an ice cream sandwich made with thin crispy wafers (L1500). Cones L1200-3000. Open Thurs.-Tues. 10am-midnight.

Piazza Amedeo and Mergellia

Piazza Amedeo, located on the city's subway line, is a favorite hangout of Naples's chic youth. Along its scenic avenues, just north of the Villa Communale park, you will find several *nouveau mode* cafes and pubs. Restaurant prices are high, but search the streets for great snack-bars.

Osteria Canterbury, via Ascensione, 6 (tel. 41 35 84). Take via Vittoria Colonna off p. Amedeo, make the 1st right down a flight of stairs, then turn right and immediately left.

The best affordable meals in the area. A bowl of large olives and a *sangria* are served free with every meal. A full-course *pranzo* will save you money, but it is only served in the afternoon (L10,000). In the evening, go with the *penne di casa Canterbury* (pasta with eggplant, cheese, and tomato sauce, L6000). For dessert, try the homemade *tiramisù,* a rich chocolate custard (L3000). Cover L2000. Open Mon.-Sat. 1-3:30pm and 8:30pm-midnight.

Pizzeria Trianon da Ciro, Parco Margherita, 27 (tel. 41 46 78). A favorite hangout of the young. Modern interior. Superendifolous pizzas (L3000-6000). Cover 1500. Open daily 11:30am-3:30pm and 6:30pm-2am.

Caffè Marciapiede, via S. Teresa a Chiaja, 41B, on a street popular with strollers and parallel to via Colonna. A ritzy cafe with stone floors and soft lights. Assorted fancy sandwiches L1600. Filling lunches served noon-4pm (L5000). Try one of their great salads, like *insalata fresca* (L4500). *Prosecco del marciapiede* wine L1500 per glass. Open Mon.-Sat. 7am-midnight.

Mergellina, southwest of p. Amedeo on the waterfront, is accessible by tram #1 or by subway. It's an excellent area for informal but hearty Neapolitan dining. **Piazza Sannazzaro,** in the heart of Mergellina, is famous for its many *trattorie* which serve up the beloved local *zuppa di cozze* at outdoor tables. Via Piedigrotta and the surrounding streets also offer affordable alternatives.

Antica Trattoria al Vicoletto, via Camillo Cucca, 52 (tel. 66 14 24). From the exit of the metro stop, walk straight across the street, bearing left onto via Piedigrotta. Follow it about 300m until you see the sign, then turn left into the narrow alley. The food here is *puro, genuino,* and *economico!* An incredible full-course meal L12,000 (served during the day only, July-Sept. during the evening too). Choose from 4 types of homemade pasta, 4 meat or fish specialties, and any of a number of antipastos. Open Sept.-July Mon.-Sat. noon-3pm and 8pm-midnight.

Pizzeria da Pasqualino, p. Sannazzaro, 79 (tel. 68 15 24). Lots of outdoor tables and amazing pizza (L3000-6000). Also terrific seafood and fried snacks. The *cozze impepata* (mussels in pepper broth, L4000) will put spring in your step. Wine from L3000 per liter. Service and cover included. Open Wed.-Mon. 10am-midnight.

Birreria Gloria, p. Sannazzaro, 70b (tel. 68 01 13). A nifty little joint that pours out onto the *piazza.* Try *spaghetti ai frutti di mare* (L6000) or the popular *zuppa di cozze* (L4000). Wine L3000 per liter. Cover L1000, service 15%. Open Tues.-Sun. 11am-midnight.

Remy Gelo, via F. Galiani, 29/A (tel. 66 73 04). Take via Giordano Bruno off p. Sannazzaro until you come to p. Torretta. Off the piazza in the direction of the water. Naples's 1st choice ice cream, with over 90 flavors. Cones L1000-3000. Open Tues.-Fri. 9am-11pm., Sat. and Sun. 9am-midnight.

Vomero

A cable car up to Vomero will bring you into the city's most hopping spot and favorite dining area. Restaurants are generally pricier, but there are a couple *trattorie* from yesteryear on **via Bernini** and **via Kerbaker.**

Trattoria da Sica, via Bernini, 17 (tel. 37 75 20). An unmarred, family-run *trattoria.* Decorated with black-and-white photos, marble, and stone floors. Traditional Neapolitan fare like *vermicelli all puttanesca* (pasta with tomatoes, olives, and capers, L3500) and *pasta e fagioli* (pasta and bean soup, L3000). Terrific wines from L3000 per liter. Cover L1000, service 12%. Open Oct.-Aug. Fri.-Wed. noon-3:30pm and 8pm-midnight.

Pizzeria Gorizia, via Bernini, 29-31 (tel. 24 22 48). Like the *trattoria* next door, Gorizia, the oldest *pizzeria* in Vomero, is timeless. Same great pizza (L4000-6000) and pasta they munched here 50 years ago. Try the *pizza alla gorizia* (with fresh artichoke) L6000. *Gnocchi con mozzarella* (potato dumplings with tomato-and-cheese sauce, L4000) is the best pasta choice. Open Sept.-July Thurs.-Tues. noon-3pm and 7pm-midnight.

Osteria Donna Teresa, via Kerbaker, 58 (tel. 37 70 70). Wonderful, homey place. Most dishes less than L4500. The *pasta al forno* (baked pasta, L4000) is excellent. Wines L1500-2000 per liter. Cover L500. Open Mon.-Sat. noon-2pm and 4pm-midnight.

Cucina Casareccia, via Kerbaker, 124 (tel. 37 71 24). Enter around the corner at p. Durante, 1. A sweet place run by a grandmotherly woman. Excellent house wines L2000 per liter. Try *spezzatino* (rolled, stuffed meat, L4500). Open Mon.-Sat. noon-4pm and 7-11pm.

Sights

Don't be deceived by the unpleasant scene that greets you as you leave the train station. **Piazza Garibaldi,** locally known as the "Zona Vasta," is a confusing mish-mash of hotels, small bars, parked cars, buses, vendors, and black-market dealers. Branching off the *piazza* is **corso Umberto,** an impressive boulevard lined with beautiful, cast-iron street lamps and nineteenth-century buildings which is Naples's main artery. A couple of detours lead off the *corso,* into the interesting side alleys of old Naples. Off to the north, **via Sant' Agostino alla Zecca** leads to the dilapidated eighteenth-century church of the same name. The dramatic interior features a mighty Christ sharing a cloud with Saint Augustine. (Church open daily 8am-12:30pm and 4:30-7pm.)

Corso Umberto ends at the seventeenth-century **Fountain of Neptune** with a view of the ponderous **Castel Nuovo,** located behind p. Municipio. The castle was originally built in the thirteenth century by Charles of Anjou to replace the waterfront Castel dell'Ovo, which was too susceptible to foreign attack. The castle was later restored by King Alfonso I of Aragon and others. The remarkable double-tiered **Laurana Arch** (1467) adorning the entrance has a finely modeled central panel showing King Alfonso in his chariot, surrounded by his court. It is one of the earliest examples of Renaissance sculpture in the city, built to commemorate Alfonso's arrival in Naples in 1443. In the courtyard, the elegant Renaissance portal at the entrance to the fourteenth-century Chapel of Santa Barbara is surmounted by a Madonna and a flamboyant Gothic rose window. The castle proper houses the offices of the city government and is closed to the public. Continue away from the station past p. Municipio to **piazza del Plebiscito,** the most decorative and harmonious square in the city, dominated by the neoclassical **Church of San Francesco di Paola** (1817-1846), erected by Ferdinando I in fulfillment of a vow sworn for the recovery of his kingdom from the Bonapartes. Like many buildings of the early nineteenth century, it was modeled after the Pantheon in Rome. The dome, raised high on a drum, overpowers everything in the square; it even gave birth to two baby domes on either side. The effect of the building and square, however, was saved by a trick learned from Bernini's piazza San Pietro in Rome—the portico extends into a curving colonnade, giving the illusion of more space. The interior is impressive but feels more like a Supreme Court chamber than a church. (Open daily 8am-12:30pm and 4:30-7pm.)

In front of the church stand two equestrian statues, one of Charles III (Don Carlos) and the other of Ferdinando I. The buildings flanking them are the eighteenth-century Palazzo Salerno and the Palazzo della Prefettura (1815). The plain, three-story facade of the **Palazzo Reale,** erected from 1600 to 1602 and enlarged in the eighteenth century, is a perfect foil for the swelling forms of the San Francesco church. In the series of niches below the facade, the fierce statues (late 19th-century) represent the eight dynasties that ruled Naples. From the courtyard, you enter the huge Staircase of Honor, decorated with grained marble panels. Its fifteenth-century bas-reliefs depict the battle between Ferdinand of Aragon and René of Anjou. (A cannonball is still embedded in the middle panel on the left.) Above, on the second floor, are the royal apartments that constitute the **Palazzo Reale Museum** (open Tues.-Sat. 9am-2pm, Sun. 9am-1pm; admission L3000) and the charming eighteenth-century **Court Theater.** Next to the palace is the **Teatro San Carlo** (1737; tel. 797 21 11), the most distinguished opera theater in Italy after Milan's La Scala. Its gray and white front, with Ionic columns and bas-reliefs, comes from an 1816 rebuilding. (Open Tues.-Sat. 8:30-10am and 1:30-4pm, Sun. 8:30am-1pm, and Mon. 8:30am-4pm.) The neighboring **Galleria Umberto,** a four-story facade of shops and offices constructed between 1887 and 1890 (10 years after Milan's), is a skillfull combination of glass and iron, one of those wonderful late-Victorian marriages of technology and art.

Spaccanapoli (Historic Naples)

Via Roma, a favorite street among Neapolitans, begins off to the side of p. del Plebiscito at the small and busy p. Trieste e Trento and runs through the heart of the city's historic district. The Spanish built the street and gave it its original name, via Toledo, and are responsible for the small checkerboard of streets that climb the hill to the west. At the corner of the *piazza,* the **Church of San Ferdinando** (1622) is typically Jesuit, with a single wide aisle (better for preaching). The lectern, fonts, and chairs are decorated with the emblem of the king of Spain. The ceiling painting over the nave, *The Glory of Saint Ignatius,* seems much smaller than its 37-meter length. A Ribera painting of San Antonio is hidden away in the sacristy. (Church open daily 8am-12:30pm and 4:30-7pm.)

From here, a walk south to p. Carità brings you to the **Church of Sant' Anna dei Lombardi** (under restoration in 1988), a venerable museum of Renaissance sculpture and a refreshing respite from the city's baroque excesses. Its most noted sculpture and perhaps the most popular one in Naples is the realistic *Pietà* (1492) by G. Mazzoni, in the chapel at the end of the right transept. A group of seven life-sized, terra-cotta sculptures in lamentation surrounds the dead Christ. In the Piccolomini Chapel, to the left of the entrance, is the beautiful monument to Maria d'Aragona by Antonio Rossellino and Benedetto da Maiano. Opposite the church, **piazza Gesù Nuovo** stands as a great symbol of Naples's architectural diversity. On one side of the *piazza* is the **Church of Il Gesù Nuovo.** Erected from 1584 to 1601, its dazzling facade is adorned with diamonds and is actually part of a fifteenth-century Renaissance palace. The interior is spacious and light with colored marbles and typically florid Neapolitan frescoes. (Churches open daily 7:15am-1pm and 4-7:15pm.)

On the other side of the square is the **Church of Santa Chiara,** one of the principal monuments of medieval Naples. Constructed in the early fourteenth century, it was rebuilt in a stripped Gothic style. The large, single-aisled interior without an apse is famous for its medieval sarcophagi and tombs, many decorated with beautiful Gothic canopies. In the back of the church is the **Cloister of the Clarisse.** To reach it, leave from the left side of the church and walk down the side alley around to the front. A departure from the customary intimacy and delicacy of a medieval cloister, this huge, overgrown garden has two alleys of trellises decorated with majolica tiles depicting rural and town scenes, carnivals, and myths. (Church open daily 7:15am-noon and 4:30-7:45pm. Cloister open daily 9am-12:30pm and 4:30-7:45pm.) Continuing up via Roma past p. Dante and onto via Pessina, you will soon arrive at the **Museo Archeologico Nazionale** (tel. 44 01 66). It is worth the trip to Naples just to see Europe's most important archeological museum, whose collection includes the treasures of Pompeii and Herculaneum. You may want to pick up an English guidebook at the museum's souvenir shop (L6000), since few pieces are adequately labeled. To get directly to the museum, take the subway to p. Cavour. Alternatively, take buses CS, CD, or any other going up via Toledo and get off at p. Museo. The museum occupies a huge red building that was first a military barracks (1585) and then the seat of a university (1616-1777).

Dominating the Great Masters Gallery on the ground floor are the *Farnese Hercules* and the *Farnese Bull* (actually a group of four figures and animals), the largest surviving sculpture from antiquity, carved out of a single block of marble. The back hall exhibits some powerfully realistic portrait busts. Among them are Socrates, with his pug nose, swollen face, and balding head, and Seneca, with his protruding tongue and loose folds of skin. Another highlight is the *Tyrant Killers,* two menacing larger-than-life statues that confront you as you enter the gallery to the right of the museum entrance.

The real treasures, however, are upstairs. The mosaics from Pompeii, on the mezzanine, are striking in their subtlety. Don't miss the large *Mosaic of Alexander,* which portrays an extremely young, wide-eyed, and fearless Alexander routing a terrified army of Persians. The *Medea* poignantly captures the anguish of the mythical sorceress as she debates taking the lives of her own children. The *Portrait of a Woman* depicts a curiously modern-looking aristocrat of Pompeii, with perfectly coiffed hair, pearl necklace, and elaborate earrings. (Museum open July-Sept. Tues.-Sat. 9am-7pm, Sun. 9am-1pm; Oct.-June Tues.-Sat. 9am-2pm, Sun. 9am-1pm. Admission L4000, ages under 18 or over 60 free.)

The **Church of San Domenico Maggiore** forms one side of a small *piazza* of the same name located off via Toledo between p. Carità and p. Dante. A fourteenth-century church with a nineteenth-century Gothic interior, San Domenico is a combination of the two styles; the pointed arches and windows and the groin-vaulted side aisles are Gothic, but the color and texture of the decor are strictly Neapolitan baroque. The thirteenth-century painting that spoke to Saint Thomas Aquinas, who lived in the church's adjoining monastery, is in the Chapel of the Crucifix. To the painting's question, "Well hast thou written me, Thomas. What would'st thou have as a reward?" Saint Thomas replied, "None other than thee." In the chapel to the left of the high altar is a copy of Caravaggio's *The Flagellations.* (The original is now at Naples's Capodimonte museum.) The small **Church of Sant' Angelo a Nilo,** across from San Domenico, was named after the ancient statue erected here by the Alexandrian colony. It has beautiful fifteenth-century carved wooden doors and the sepulchre of Cardinal Rinaldo Brancaccio, in which the talents of the Florentine artists Donatello, Michelozzo, and Portigiana were combined. (Both churches open daily 8am-12:30pm and 4:30-7pm.)

Without a doubt, Naples's best kept secret is the **Cappella San Severo,** which hides on via De Sanctis, a small side street just north of p. San Domenico Maggiore. The chapel, now a private museum, features the *Cristo Velato* (*Veiled Christ*) by Guiseppe Sammartino, painted in 1753. Sammartino's remarkable, ultra-thin marble veil, erafted with impeccable detail, clings like a wet cloth to the wounded, prostrate body of Christ, continuing to fool viewers. To the right of the altar in a group titled *Disillusion,* in which a man extricates himself from marble netting with the encouragement of a seated angel. The altar shows cherubs opening up the empty tomb below a representation of the Deposition, all sculpted from a single block of marble. On the opposite end of the chapel above the entrance, Cecco di Sangro, a builder of the church, is shown leaving his tomb, sword in hand. Descend the stairs through a door to the right and you will meet up with two grizzly sixteenth-century corpses displayed in glass showcases. Their veins and arteries were mysteriously kept completely intact by a medieval elixir. (Open Mon.-Sat. 10am-1:30pm, Sun. 11am-1:30pm. Admission L2000.)

Via Benedetto Croce, via San Biagio dei Librai, and via Vicaria Vecchia all converge from east to west, following the course of the old Roman Decumanus Maximus (the route they follow, referred to as Spaccanapoli by Neapolitans, actually changes its name 6 times in little more than a mile). This is the heart of the old city, a narrow way enclosed by tall tenements and *palazzi.* On via San Biagio dei Librai alone, lie #121, the Renaissance **Palazzo Sant' Angelo;** #114, **Monte di Pietà** (Banco di Napoli); and #37, **Palazzo Marigliano.** The street continues, widening at intervals to accommodate a church or monument. Via San Biagio ends at via dei Duomo, where you'll find the eighteenth-century **Church of San Giorgio Maggiore.** In its vestibule are the antique columns and walls of a primitive Paleo-Christian structure. Diagonally across from the church is the beautiful Renaissance **Palazzo Cuomo** (1464-90). You can enter most of these private palaces from Monday through Friday (roughly 9am-1pm). In and around Spaccanapoli, you will stumble upon the venerable shops of Naples's traditional artisans. Off the *piazza* of the church of San Domenico Maggiore is **Calace Strumenti Musicali,** vico S. Domenico Maggiore, 9, where mandolins, guitars, and other intstruments are still crafted by hand with the dexterity passed from master to apprentice over generations. **Scultura Sacra Lebro,** v. San Gregorio Armano, 41, is a family operation and one of the last to produce hand-carved and painted religious statues. The most endearing shop in Old Naples is the tiny **Ospedale delle Bambole** (doll hospital), via S. Biagio dei Librai, 81, near via Duomo. The mirthful shopkeeper is perfectly suited for the rejuvenation of injured toy dolls for teary-eyed Neapolitan children.

(Open Oct.-July Mon.-Fri. 10:30am-1:30pm and 4:30-8pm, Sat. 10:30-1pm; Aug.-Sept. Mon.-Fri 10:30am-1:30pm and 4:30-8pm.)

Unlike the cathedrals of other Italian cities, Naples's ***duomo*** is squeezed into a side street. Its huge, spacious interior is all the more majestic as a result. Dating from the end of the thirteenth century, the church was once a fifth-century Paleo-Christian basilica. The facade, late nineteenth-century neo-Gothic, retains its original doors; the middle one is particularly ornate. The Gothic outlines of the pointed arches in the interior are covered with a baroque veneer (except for the two chapels on either side of the high altar, which retain their original form and are decorated with 14th-century frescoes). Halfway down the left side is the entrance to the **Church of Santa Restituta,** the first Christian basilica of Naples. It was built in the fourth century and conserves its ancient forms in the nave's columns and in a fifth-century baptistery, whose primitive font is dug out of the floor (entrance to baptistery at the end of the right aisle). Also of note is the early fourteenth-century mosaic of the Madonna with two saints (6th chapel off the left aisle). Protected by a beautiful seventeenth-century bronze grille is the baroque **Chapel of San Gennaro.** Relics of Saint Januarius are said to have stopped lava from Mount Vesuvius at the gates of the city. A silver reliquary is hidden behind the high altar, holding the head of the saint and two vials of his congealed blood. According to legend, disaster will strike the city if the blood fails to liquefy at appointed times (the 1st Sat. of May, September 19, and December 16). On leaving the cathedral, note how the adjacent buildings rest on arcades to give the church more space. During masses, the cathedral is enriched with music, incense, candles, and brightly frocked priests. (Cathedral open daily 8am-1pm and 5-7:30pm.)

Piazza Capuana, between the *duomo* and p. Garibaldi, is the center of an interesting section of old Naples. Two ponderous towers frame one of the most beautiful Renaissance archways in Italy, the **Porta Capuana.** On one side of the *piazza,* the elegant Renaissance **Church of Santa Caterina a Formiello** (1519) matches the gray stone and white stucco of the gateway. (Closed for restoration in 1988.) Via Carbonara is a characteristic main street of a Neapolitan quarter. Its neighborhood church is called by two names (officially **San Giovanni a Carbonara,** but locally known as **Santa Sofia**); its *piazza* kicks with soccer games; and the nearby narrow side streets abound with tall buildings, hanging laundry, and people leaning out of windows or sitting on small wooden chairs.

Santa Lucia and Mergellina

Walk along the bay in the late afternoon and early evening to see the sun set and the Villa Comunale fill with evening strollers. Via Sauro in the Santa Lucia section is the traditional place to watch sunsets. The twelfth-century **Castel dell'Ovo** (Egg Castle; open for exhibits only), a massive Norman structure of yellow brick and incongruously converging angles, stands on the promontory of the port of Santa Lucia, dividing the bay into two parts. To the west is the **Villa Comunale,** a waterfront park dotted with sycamores and palms and graced by sculpture, fountains, and an aquarium. The **aquarium** (tel. 40 62 22), the oldest in Europe, features a collection of 200 species of fish and submarine fauna native to the Bay of Naples. (Open Tues.-Sat. 9am-5pm, Sun. 10am-7pm. Admission L1000, students L700, ages under 6 L500.)

A snapshot streetcar runs along the Riviera di Chiaia, where at stop #200 you'll find the **Villa Pignatelli,** one of the few verdant villa grounds left in the city. There the **Museo Principe di Aragona Pignatelli Cortes** (tel. 66 96 75) is housed in a beautiful neoclassical mansion with a collection of eighteenth- and nineteenth-century porcelain, furniture, and paintings. (Open Tues.-Sat. 9am-2pm, Sun. 9am-1pm. Admission L2000.)

At the foot of the hills of Posillipo is Mergellina, which affords the most celebrated view in Naples and a small port for boats leaving to the islands. Via Mergellina ends with a stairway to a terrace offering a panorama of the bay.

Vomero and the Hills

The breezy calm of the hillside residential district of Vomero provides respite from Naples. A full morning, or perhaps two, should be reserved for visiting Vomero's important historical sights, the Villa Floridiana and the Monastery of Saint Martin. Funiculars to the top of this leafy area leave from via Toledo across from the Galleria, from p. Amadeo, and from p. Montesanto.

The **Villa Floridiana** (entrance at via Cimarosa, 77) crowns a knoll notable for its camellias, its pine trees, and its terrace overlooking the bay. The villa itself, a graceful white mansion in the neoclassical style (1817-1819), houses the **Duca di Martina Museum** (tel. 37 93 15), which contains porcelain, ivory, china, pottery, and a small group of seventeenth-century Neapolitan paintings. (Open Tues.-Sat. 9am-2pm, Sun. 9am-1pm. Admission L2000. The landscaped grounds are open 9am-1 hr. before sunset. A picnic paradise.)

The huge Carthusian **Certosa di S. Martino** (Monastery of St. Martin) rises from a spur of the Vomero hill near Castel Sant' Elmo. Though erected in the fourteenth century, it was remodeled during the Renaissance and baroque periods. It is now the seat of the **Museo Nazionale di San Martino** (tel. 37 70 05), which consists of weighty rooms documenting the art, history, and life of Naples from the sixteenth century to the present. In the monk's chancel, there is a medley of Neapolitan baroque marbles, stucco, statues, and paintings. From a balcony off gallery 25, you can see the deep, narrow notches of the streets of the old city. (Open Tues.-Sat. 9am-2pm, Sun. 9am-1pm. Admission L3000.)

The **Museo e Gallerie di Capodimonte** is housed in a restored eighteenth-century royal palace set in the sylvan hills north of the National Museum. Its collection ranges from masterpieces to kitsch; the former are on the second floor, the latter on the first. Note particularly Massacio's *Crucifixion* with a golden-haired Mary Magdalene (room #6); Filippino Lippi's *Annunciation and Saints,* conveying a poetic stillness with Florence in the background (room #7); Raphael's portrait of Pope Leo X and two cardinals, brilliant with the many reds of robes, chairs, and tables, and his drawing of *Moses* (room #12); Michelangelo's stunning drawing of *Three Soldiers* (room #12); and two superb Breughels—*The Allegory of the Blind* and *The Misanthrope* (room #20). (Open July-Sept. Tues.-Sat. 9am-7pm, Sun. 9am-1pm; Oct.-June Tues.-Sat. 9am-2pm, Sun. 9am-1pm. Admission L4000.) Take bus #110 or 127 from Stazione Centrale, #22 or 23 from p. del Plebiscito, or #160 or 161 from p. Dante.

Near the Galleria di Capodimonte, on via di Capodimonte, are the **Catacombe di San Gennaro,** dating from as far back as the second century and noted for their early Christian chapels, many of which are decorated with frescoes. (Open for prearranged visits Fri.-Sun. at 9:30am, 10:15am, 11am, and 11:45am. Admission L3000.)

Entertainment

The monthly *Qui Napoli* (*Here's Naples*) and the weekly poster *Posto Unico,* both available at the tourist office, offer excellent information on events in Naples. Most of the information in *Qui Napoli* is translated into English, and there are brief descriptions of the city's major sites. The *Posto Unico* provides lists of films, discos, and clubs. The free monthly guide *Napoli-Top,* available at tourist offices, restaurants, and hotels, offers added information.

In July, **Luglio Musicale a Capodimonte,** a series of free concerts on Thursdays and Sundays at 8pm, fills the air outside the Museo di Capodimonte with music by top-notch performers.

Naples is at its liveliest during its many religious festivals. The festival of **Piedigrotta** on September 7 and of **San Gennaro,** the patron saint of Naples, on September 19, both explode with music, dance, and food. The festival of **Madonna del Carmine,** held on July 16 at p. del Carmine at the southern end of corso Garibaldi, is accompanied by fireworks at the Fra' Nuvolo tower. During Christmas, hundreds of creches decorate the city. Also noteworthy are the sepulchre decorations during Easter and the grand "Easter Parade" in the center of town.

Naples is quiet at night, except for the Sunday evening *passeggiata,* when the Villa Comunale along the bay bulges with Italians taking in the cool air. The young elite show off their new threads around **piazza Amedeo.** And there are via Posillipo for those who savor the smell of the sea and via Petrarca for a romantic stroll (accessible by bus #C21 at p. Plebiscito). Throughout the year, the Azienda offers free folk music concerts with typical Neapolitan and Italian songs. The concerts are given Tuesday to Sunday from 9 to 10:45pm. The site of the concerts changes regularly; inquire at the EPT.

Nighttime hotspots frequented by university students include **Casablanca,** via Petrarca, 101 (tel. 769 48 82); **Chez Moi,** parco Margherita, 13 (tel. 40 75 26; take the Metropolitana to p. Amadeo); and **My Way** (alluding to the theme song of Italy's native son Frank Sinatra), via Cappella Vecchia (tel. 42 20 83; take bus #150 to p. Vittoria). All three feature dancing on Friday and on weekends from 10pm and charge a L10,000-15,000 cover. (All closed in August.) **The Shaker Club,** via N. Sauro, 24 (tel. 41 67 75; take bus #150 to via Partenope), caters to the older crowd with a more refined nightclub atmosphere. Gay men and women can socialize at **Bagatto,** via Partenope (close to the Hotel Royal) and **Jimmy Club,** via Manzoni, 28 (take bus C21 from p. del Plebiscito). The Villa Communale is a gathering spot for gay people at night, as well as the **Bar Marotta** in p. Vittoria.

Shopping

Located throughout the city, especially in the **Duchesca** region off via Mancini near p. Garibaldi and the **Pignasecca** region off p. Carità, street markets offer belts, radios, shoes and other inexpensive handicrafts. Never buy electronic products here, and cling tightly to your valuables on the crowded streets. (Markets are generally open Mon.-Sat. 9am-sunset; many close at 2pm Tues.)

If, on the other hand, you feel more comfortable just window-shopping at the fancy stores, the main shopping districts center around **corso Umberto I; via Roma** (via Toledo); **via Chiaia,** near p. Trieste e Trento; and **via dei Mille,** in the Santa Lucia region. The most modern and expensive shopping district is in the hills of Vomero along **via Scarlatti** and **via Luca Giordano,** perpendicular to each other. Two affordable clothes chains that sell the most contemporary Italian casual wear are **Whiscky & Coca** and **Omonimo.**

Near Naples

Campi Flegrei (Phlegraean Fields)

The Bay of Naples was originally a strategic trading port for the Greeks, who associated its westerly peninsula with the fiery underworld. The volcanic lakes and bubbling mud baths of the Phlegraean (Burning) Fields did not phase the Greeks or Romans, however; both decorated the area with imposing monuments.

The best base from which to explore the Campi Flegrei is **Pozzuoli,** west of Naples on the coast, serviced by subway from Naples's Stazione Centrale and by the Ferrovia Cumana train from Montesanto in Naples (just southwest of p. Dante). From Naples, visiting all the sights in this area will take a full day since they are all far apart. There are numerous signs to the sights and those who feel more secure with a map in hand can look for signs directing them to the useful **Azienda di Turismo,** via Domitiana, 3 (tel. 867 14 81), off p. Capo Mazza. (English spoken. Open Mon.-Fri. 9am-2pm and 4-6:30pm, Sat. 9am-1pm.) Pozzuoli's **Anifeteatro Flavio** (69-79 C.E.) is a large and well-preserved example of a Roman ampitheater. (Open daily 9am-2 hr. before sunset. Admission L2000.) From the Metropolitana station, turn right onto via Solfatara; turn right again on via Anifiteatro and follow it to the entrance. Visitors can enter the amphitheater and peer into the pit that housed animals for use during the games. As many sections of the amphitheater are closed for safety reasons, half an hour should suffice to view it thoroughly. **Tempio di Serapide** was not a temple at all, but an ancient city market that just happened to enclose a statue of the god Serapia. Geological activity has caused the entire structure to sink, and with its puddles of water and eerie, half-submerged pillars, the site looks like a miniature Atlantis risen from the sea. On via Solfatara, directly to the right of the Metropolitana station, you can take any of the city buses going uphill to get to the **Solfatara Crater.** (Open 9am-1 hr. before sunset. Admission L3000.) It is also an easy 20-minute walk from the train station. Tread along the thick ashen lining of the still-active crater and smell the sulfur. Some of the ground is still so hot that you cannot touch it with your hand.

From any of the SEPSA bus stops located throughout Pozzuoli or by way of the Ferrovia Cumana, you can take a 20-minute ride to **Baia** (L600), notable for the Roman baths that have recently been excavated there and for its history as a hedonist's hotspot. A bit to the north is **Lake Averno,** a ghostly place that Homer and Virgil described in their epics as the entrance to Hades. From the Baia area, you can take a bus (L600 on the Napoli-Torre Gaveta line) or the Ferrovia Cumana train line to **Cumae,** perhaps the most impressive site in the Campi Flegrei. (Open Tues.-Sun. 9am-2 hrs. before sunset. Admission L2000.) Cumae was one of the earliest Greek colonies (founded in the 8th century B.C.E.), and for a time controlled both Pozzuoli and Naples. Its highlight is **Antro della Sibilla,** a long gallery built for the Cumaean Sibyl. In this great hallway, excavated in 1932, devotees awaited the Sibyl's prophecies. The Cumaean ruins are spread out and require at least an hour's visit.

For the cheapest rooms in the city of Pozzuoli, **Martusciello,** via Emporio, 6 (tel. 867 17 02), above the restaurant of the same name and located near the ports, offers spotless, spacious doubles with bath for L30,000. Seaside Pozzuoli floods with outdoor seafood restaurants. **Trattoria da Gigetta,** via Roma, 45 (tel. 867 15 61), is a charming little joint on the water next to the Villa Communale that serves delicious *risotto all pescatore* (rice with seafood sauce, L6000) and wonderful *pizza alla pescatore* (L5000). (Cover L1000, service 15%. Open Thurs.-Tues. noon-11pm.) **Trattoria da Don Antonio,** via Magazzino, 20 (tel. 867 39 41), off the port in shabby, but ebullient surroundings, cooks the cheapest chow in town, offering a full meal of fresh seafood with drink included for L15,000. (Open Sept.-July Mon.-Sat. 12:30-4pm and 7-11pm.)

The beaches and countryside of the area are fabulous. Many visitors unofficially camp near the sea or by one of the many volcanic lakes. There are several sites with facilities in the area; if there are only two or three of you, this is a safer proposition. **Vulcano Solfatara,** via Solfatara, 161 (tel. 867 34 13; open April-Oct.15), offers sites next to the crater for L5400 per person, L2900 per 2-person tent, L4300 per large tent; June 11-Sept.9 L6200 per person, L3000 per 2-person tent, L5000 per large tent. The **Automobile Club d'Italia,** p. Tecchio, 49/D, in Naples (tel. 61 10 44), provides information on camping.

Caserta

Caserta, 45 minutes from Naples by train (the 1st leaves from Stazione Centrale at 7:15am; L2000) claims as its main attraction the fabulous **Palazzo Reale** (Royal Palace). The gigantic palace with its magnificent gardens was built between 1752 and 1774 by Luigi Vanvittelli for Charles di Borbone. The building contains 1200 rooms, 1790 windows, and 34 flights of stairs. The southern wing of the first floor alone is sufficient to house a museum. (Open Tues.-Sat. 9am-2pm, Sun. 9am-1pm. Admission L3000.) Bring a picnic lunch as there are no restaurants nearby. (Gardens open daily 9am-sunset. Free.)

After the palace, walk around the haunting medieval town of **Caserta Vecchia,** a short bus ride to the east. The cathedral, built in Romanesque-Puglian style, dates from 1153 and shows distinctive Middle Eastern influence.

Benevento

The countryside of Benevento is enchanting and well worth a visit. Although it's best if you have your own wheels, there are also direct bus connections and trains (the 1st of the hourly trains departs at 7:22am, 2 hr., L4900). Try exploring the village of **Montesarchio,** with its fifteenth-century castle, or **Sant' Agata dei Goti,** with its Romanesque cathedral. Benevento's quiet, unhurried atmosphere is itself a delightful contrast to Naples. Visit **Trajan's Arch,** constructed in 114 C.E. and decorated with fine bas-reliefs, and the huge Roman theater (2nd century B.C.E.), one of the largest in Italy. Before returning to Naples, try Benevento's *Strega* (Witch) liqueur—it will leave you spellbound.

Pompeii and Herculaneum (Ercolano)

Vicious Mount Vesuvius's towering flames, black clouds, and seething lava meant sudden death for the prosperous, riotous Roman city of **Pompeii** in 79 C.E. The eruption left the city—its tall temples, aristocratic houses, massive theatres, and all—submerged in 30 feet of volcanic ash. Archeological findings indicate that Pompeii was inhabited as early as the eighth century B.C.E. and that during the seventh century B.C.E., it came under the influence of Greeks and Etruscans, who established it as a commercial center. By the second century B.C.E., Pompeii was a fully developed Italian city with (thanks to its trade connections) a strongly Hellenized culture. Conquered by the Romans in 80 B.C.E., the city further developed commercially and culturally. Successive layers of ash, dust, pebbles, lava, and rock from the sudden eruption preserved not only the buildings but also its inhabitants. The nearby excavated city of Herculaneum was first discovered when farmers in the early eighteenth century began digging for wells. Soon after, the analysis of ancient texts revealed another, larger city nearby—Pompeii. Covered with soft material (in contrast to the hard tufa stone over Herculaneum), Pompeii was quickly unearthed and resuscitated. Today, Pompeii and partially excavated Herculaneum are stunning displays of the ancient world.

The **circumvesuviana** rail line from underground at Naples's Stazione Centrale is the quickest route to Pompeii from Naples. There is a less frequent state train that leaves from the main track at the station, stopping at Pompeii on the route to Salerno (7 per day 7:10am-1:15pm). On the *circumvesuviana,* there are two ways to get to the ruins. The most frequently used route is on the Naples-Sorrento line, letting you off at the Pompeii-Villa dei Misteri stop, just ouside the west entry. An alternative is to take the train from Naples to Poggiomarino-Sarno, hopping off at the Pompeii (*not* Pompeii Valle) stop. Then walk straight from the station, take a right across your first *piazza,* and head about 300m down via Roma to the east entrance. If you take the state railway, get off at the Pompeii stop, head straight from the station all the way down via Sacra, and take a left at the far end of the *piazza* in front of the church, following via Roma to the east entrance. (Both entrances open 9am-1 hr. before sunset. Admission L5000.)

The **Azienda di Turismo,** via Sacra, 1 (tel. 863 10 41), across from p. Barolo Longo on the way to the east entrance) offers free maps as well as the useful pamphlet *Notizario Turistico Regionale,* with tons o' practical information. There is another Azienda office near the west entrance on via Villa dei Misteri (tel. 861 09 13), to the right of the *circumvesuviana* stop. (Both open Mon.-Sat. 9am-1pm; July-Aug. longer hours.) On your first visit, concentrate on the major sites, which can be encompassed in two walks.

As you enter from the east entrance, the **Grande Palestra** (Great Gymnasium) will be on your left. The large structure, enclosed on three sides by a colonnade and shady pine trees, was used by Pompeiian youths for gymnastic exercises and competitions.

The **amphitheater** across from the gymnasium, built in 80 B.C.E., is the oldest in existence. Originally seating 15,000, it has been remarkably preserved and offers a view of Pompeii and the mountain behind. Next to the gymnasium, the **House of Loreius Tiburtinus** preserves the essentials of a Roman garden—long rectangular pools sheltered with trellises and formal paintings. Walking toward the Forum, which is near the west or "sea" entrance, you'll pass the **teatro grande,** constructed in the Hellenistic Age (200-150 B.C.E.) in a hollow of a hill. In July, August, and September classical concerts with big-name performers are featured here, usually on Friday, Saturday, and Sunday nights at 9pm (L10,000-30,000). Parallel to the stage to the left is the much smaller *teatro piccolo* built later during the Roman times and used especially for concerts, pantomime, and ballet. Just north of the theater is the **Temple of Isis,** eloquent testimony to the importance of the cult of the Egyptian fertility goddess at Pompeii. Going north from the temple, you will reach **via dell' Abbondanza,** Pompeii's main street (1km long) and part of the city's Greek ckeckerboard road system.

From via dell' Abbondanza, you can backtrack towards the east entrance and turn off to the **Casa di Menandro.** Named after Menander, the Greek poet whose fresco was found in the courtyard, the house is one of the largest and most intact in the city. The entrance leads to an atrium with a pool that was used to catch rain water from the ceiling opening. Around the atrium are bedrooms, and in the corner a small shrine for a household god. On the left is a fresco depicting the Trojan War. The small room at the far wall of the court houses two little beds, an *excedra* (bench in a niche) with a hunting scene, and a yellow fresco of Menander.

Heading west on via dell' Abbondanza towards the Forum, you will reach the **Terme Stabiane** (public baths), which are entered through another *palestra.* The east side was for men and included a dressing room, cold baths (*frigidaria*), warm baths (*tepidaria*), and hot or steam baths (*caldaria*).

In this ancient city, the world's oldest profession found its stomping grounds one street over in the Red Light District of **Vico del Lupanare.** At the top of this street is the small **bordello,** consisting of several bed-stalls. Each of the stalls has a pornographic painting above it depicting the sexual specialty of the women who inhabited it.

Via dell' Abbondanza ends at the **Forum,** the commercial, governmental, and religious center of the city, framed by a wonderful view of Vesuvio. The **basilica** (law courts), which runs along the south side of the Forum, was the largest building in Pompeii and retains parts of its impressive dais in the southeast corner. Three temples also graced the Forum. On the northern side is the **Temple of Jupiter.** The **Temple of Apollo,** next to the basilica, rests on a high structure almost hidden from the rest of the city (unlike a Greek temple, which usually crowns a hill). The stone in the middle was used as a sacrificial altar. In the **Temple of Vespasian,** on the western side, the altarpiece has a delicate frieze showing the preparation for a sacrifice.

In showcases along the western side of the Forum, there are plaster casts of some of the victims of the great eruption, such as those of a crouching pregnant woman and a running boy. These were made by pouring plastic into the cavities formed by the hardening ash around the decomposing bodies. A detailed cast of a dog in a contorted position suggests that the inhabitants were suffocated by the gases of the eruption rather than swallowed up by its ashen discharge.

Just north of the Forum, you can rest in the cafeteria (go up to its roof for the only aerial view of Pompeii) before starting on a second walk to the northwest corner of the site and out to the Villa dei Misteri. Walk up to the massive **Casa del Fauno,** which is in front of the **Casa dei Vettii.** The Casa dei Vettii contains Pompeii's most remarkable frescoes, all done in the latest of Pompeii's styles, consisting of fantastic architectural visions with perspective gone wild. For a chuckle, follow the halls to the right to a tiny room where everyone is snapping photographs. This room, which is unlocked for adults only, contains a two-and-a-half-foot-tall marble statue of a naked man proudly displaying his colossal member—almost as large as he is; frescoes in other parts of the *casa* feature equally pornographic braggadocio. A more amorous theme runs through the frieze of Cupids decorating the large *triclinium,* where symposia and dinners were held. Next to it is a smaller *triclinium* containing some of the most intact examples of this late style of Roman painting.

A short walk away from the Casa dei Vettii is the **Villa dei Misteri.** A renowned cycle of paintings depicting the ritual of initiating brides is in a room directly to the right of the entrance.

Unless you wish to tour Pompeii extensively, there is no reason to stay overnight in its uninteresting modern city. The cheapest alternative is to stay at one of the three campsites, all located near the ruins. Unfortunately, all are somewhat ruined themselves. Some have comfortable bungalows with bathrooms, however. **Camping Zeus** (tel. 861 53 20) is right outside the Villa dei Misteri *circumvesuviana* stop and has a swimming pool and restaurant (L5000 per person, L2000 per tent; 2-person bungalows L40,000, for 3 people L45,000). Not far away, on via Plinio, the main road that runs from the ruins, are the other two campsites, located right next to one another. **Camping Pompeii** (tel. 862 78 82), the better of the two, is under the same ownership as Zeus, charges the same prices, and offers the same attractive bungalows. You can sack on the floor of its indoor lobby for L4000 per night. **Camping Spartacus** (tel. 861 49 01) charges L6000 per person, L3500 per tent; Sept.-June L4000 per person, L2500 per tent. Cramped, two-person bungalows cost L30,000 and four-person bungalows L40,000. All sites are desperate for customers, so you can usually bargain them down at least 25%.

Dozens of restaurants line via Roma outside the gates to the ruins, but most are too concerned with capitalizing on the flow of tourists to pay any attention to their cooking. However, **Zi Catarina** via Roma, 16-22, offers fancy, air-conditioned bliss, tasty pizza from L3500, and a delightful plate of *linguine imperial,* topped with loads of fresh seafood for L9000. (Open Wed.-Mon. noon-11pm.) **La Vinicola,** via Roma, 29, has a nice outdoor courtyard and abundant *gnocchi con mozzarella* (potato dumplings with tomato and cheese, L4000). Also try the *zuppa di cozze* for L3500. (Cover L1000, service 15%. Open Sat.-Thurs. noon-4pm and 7pm-midnight.) For the best deal, go hungry to **La Tavolaccia,** p. Bartololongo, 18. Take via Marianna de Fusco off via Roma near the church and look for the red, white, and blue Tavola Calda Self-Service sign. A full meal of bread, pasta, a meat dish, a vegetable, and a beer costs L8000. (Open Aug.-June Wed.-Mon. 11:30am-midnight.)

Closer to Naples, **Ercolano (Herculaneum)** is scenically situated on the sea with Vesuvio in the background. Take any *circumvesuviana* train toward Pompeii from Naples's central train station to the Ercolano stop (15 min., L600). If you finish your tour of Pompeii early, you may consider stopping here on the way back to Naples for a quick tour of this smaller set of ruins. The **ticket office** for the ruins is 500m down the hill from the station. (Open daily 9am-1hr. before sunset. Visitors may remain until a half-hour before sunset. Admission L5000.) The neatly organized and excavated Herculaneum, no more than one-third the physical size of Pompeii, is so intact as to elude the term "ruins." Once a wealthy residential and intellectual center used primarily as a transit station on the Roman coast road, Herculaneum does not evoke the same sense of tragedy as Pompeii since most of its inhabitants escaped the terrors of Vesuvius in time. Today, the city provides an unadulterated sense of the private life of the ancient people. In a much less disorienting (and less crowded) tour than in Pompeii, you can wind your way through the 15 or so houses and baths that are now open to the public. Practically all of them are locked and are shown to you by a guard, on request; since there are invariably more houses than guards, you are apt to find many places closed without anyone in sight. The best thing to do is rush in every time you see a small crowd about to go through some door, as it makes no difference which house you see first. There are no large buildings or temples to grab your imagination here, but the houses, with their remarkably fresh interior decoration, are similarly inspiring. Two thousand-year-old frescoes, furniture, mosaics, small sculptures, and even wood paneling seem as fresh as the day they were made. Before entering, consider purchasing the *Amadeo-Maiuri* guide to Herculaneum, the most comprehensive of the books on the ruins, available in the bar across the street from the ruins (L7000). From the Ercolano stop, it's also possible to take a blue bus to **Mount Vesuvius** (round-trip L1200), still the only active volcano on the mainland of Europe. Rest assured, it's now dormant. You can climb to the top (1 hr.), but you must be accompanied by a guide, for which you must pay an additional L3000. The views from the summit are spectacular, however, and worth the climb. (4 buses daily from the

Ercolano stop to Mt. Vesuvius April-Sept. at 7:30am, 9:25am, 1:30pm, and 5pm; Oct.-March 3 buses daily at 8am, 11:20am, and 2:30pm.)

Islands

Lingering languidly in the Bay of Naples, the pleasure islands of **Capri, Ischia,** and **Procida** beckon the haggard traveler.

Large ferries (*traghetti*) and hydrofoils (*aliscafi*) leave daily from Naples's **Molo Beverello** at the end of p. Municipio. (Take bus #150 or tram #1 or 4 from Naples's *stazione centrale.*) **Caremar,** Molo Beverello, Naples (tel. 551 53 84), is the main line that services the islands, while **Navigazione Libera del Golfo (NGL),** Molo Beverello, Naples (tel. 552 07 63), offers slightly lower prices, but less comfortable boats. Avoid purchasing a round-trip ticket as you are subject to the whims of a single company for the duration. Eight ferries leave for Capri between 6:40am (Sun. 7am) and 7:40pm every two to three hours (L4600). The last boat returning to Naples leaves at 7:20pm. Ferries to Ischia have the same prices and similar schedules, leaving Naples from 6:30am (Sun. 7:05am) to 7:30pm, with a late ferry (via Procida) at 11pm. Direct ferries to Procida run between the same hours but less frequently (5 per day, L3900). There is also service between Ischia and Procida (L1700), Capri and Sorrento (L2800), Ischia and Sorrento (L8000), and Ischia and Pozzuoli (L3100). Hydrofoils for all islands leave from the Mergellina Marina more frequently, but cost about twice as much. Between the end of September and June, ferries run about half as often.

Capri

The fantasy commences with the ferry's dramatic approach to the stately island, with its rugged cliffs and shimmering, azure water. Capri, the bay of Naples's jewel, is as mythical to the masses of tourists huddled on its shores as it was to the Roman emperors who chose it over all other locations for their indulgent vacations. Augustus couldn't get enough of his beloved Caprese, and his successor Tiberius spent his last 10 years here in wild debauchery. The island consists of two large rock formations, **Monte Tiberio** (334m), sheltering the jam-packed, extravagant town of Capri to the west, in the valley on the way to the steep **Monte Solaro** (589m), which hides the smaller, more pleasant, and more affordable town of Anacapri.

Orientation and Practical Information

Most ferries dock at the Marina Grande on the north side of the island, from which you can take the **funicular** to the town of Capri (6:35am-9:15pm every 15 min., L1300). Buses leave from town to all other points on the island. Anacapri can be reached by a winding, uphill bus ride from the center of Capri (6:30am-1:40am every 15 min., L1300) or directly from Marina Grande less frequently (L1300).

Azienda di Turismo: At the end of the dock at Marina Grande (tel. 837 06 34). Also in p. Umberto I (tel. 837 06 86), where the funicular stops. Both open July-Aug. 8am-8pm; in off-season Mon.-Sat. 9am-1pm and 3:30-6:45pm. In Anacapri, there is an information office at via G. Orlandi, 19/A (tel. 837 15 24), off the main *piazza.* Open April-Oct. Mon.-Sat. 9am-1pm and 3:30-6:45pm; Nov.-March irregularly Mon.-Sat. 9am-2pm. These offices provide a vague map, an updated list of hotels, and ferry and bus schedules.

Currency Exchange: Cambio, via Roma, across from the main bus stop in Cambio. No commission. Open March 15-Nov. 15 daily 9am-9pm. Also at p. Vittoria, 2, in the center of Anacapri. No commission. Open March 15-Nov. 20 daily 8:30am-7:30pm.

Post Office: Central office in Capri on via Roma (tel. 837 72 40), a couple of blocks downhill from p. Umberto. Open Mon.-Fri. 8:15am-6:30pm, Sat. 8:15am-12:10pm. Also a branch in Anacapri at viale de Tommaso, 4 (tel. 837 10 15). Open Mon.-Fri. 8:15am-1:30pm, Sat. 8:15am-12:10pm. **Postal code:** 80073.

Telephones: SIP, behind the funicular stop in Capri. Open daily June-Sept. 9am-1pm and 3-10:45pm; Oct.-May 9am-1pm and 3-8pm. Public phones in Anacapri at the **Emporio Gargiulo,** via Giuseppe Orlandi, 63, the main street. Open Mon.-Sat. 8am-1pm and 5-9pm, Sun. 10am-1pm. **Telephone code:** 081.

Buses: In Capri, buses depart from via Roma for Anacapri, Marina Piccola, and points in between. In Anacapri, buses depart from p. Barile off via G. Orlandi for Grotta Azzurra and points in the vicinity. Also a direct bus line between Marina Grande and Anacapri. Buses cost an astounding L1300 per ride. Consider renting a motor scooter in Sorrento and bringing it over on the Sorrento ferry. (See Sorrento Practical Information below.)

Baggage Storage: At the Caremar ticket office, across from the Marina Grande dock. L1800-5100 per bag, depending on its size. Open daily 8am-7pm.

Hospital: Ospedale Capilupi, via Provinciale Anacapri (tel. 837 00 14 or 837 87 62), between Capri and Anacapri. For minor medical assistance, call the Guardia Medica in Capri (tel. 837 00 54).

Police, via Roma (tel. 837 72 45). Will connect you with an English speaker.

Accommodations

Hordes of vacationers make it difficult to find a room extemporaneously in July and August. You will have much better luck finding a place in the less popular but no less ingratiating town of Anacapri than in Capri. Many of the cheaper hotels on the island close during the off-season. If you are not visiting in high season, haggle with the hotel owners. **Camping** is strictly forbidden, and during the summer police increase surveillance of the beaches and will fine. Beware: At Marina Grande port, gangs of hotel employees will accost you and attempt to deceitfully lure you to their overpriced hotels.

In the Town of Capri

Pensione Quattro Stagioni, via Marina Piccola, 1 (tel. 837 00 41). From p. Umberto at the top of the funicular walk downhill on via Roma. Turn left at the 3-pronged fork in the road, and look for the 1st house on the left. Comfy disorder. Hot but clean rooms with sensational views, and an outgoing, English-speaking owner. Singles L15,000. Doubles L40,000, with bath L50,000. Breakfast L8000 (July.-Aug. required). Agree on prices before unpacking. Open March 15-Nov.

Albergo La Tosca, via D. Birago, 5 (tel. 837 09 89). Walk up the stairs at p. Umberto at the exit of the funicular and through the 2nd alley on the left, via Padre S. Cimino. Follow the twisting path, taking a right on via Valentino and a left where the street ends; follow the signs for Hotel Villa Margherita. Spacious rooms, some with knock-out views. Singles L23,000. Doubles with bath L45,000. Breakfast included.

Pensione Villa Bianca, via Belvedere Cesina, 9 (tel. 837 80 16), a short hike from the top of the funicular. Go left through a narrow passageway to via Longano, and continue to the end, then take a right on via Sopramonte. In a quiet section of Capri. Capacious, tidy pads with views. Owners speak excellent English. Singles L37,000. Doubles L62,000-65,000. Triples L89,000. All with baths. Breakfast of eggs and juice and use of kitchen with refrigerator included. Open March-Oct.

Albergo Stella Maris, via Roma, 27 (tel. 837 04 52), in the town center across from the bus terminal. Spotless, spacious rooms, but lacking the paradisiacal isolation of Capri's more remote hotels. Doubles L50,000, with bath L75,000.

Anacapri

Villa Eva, via La Fabbrica, 8 (tel. 837 20 40). Set high among the gardens and trees in the deep interior of Anacapri, this place is something special. The wonderful isolation, however, makes it difficult to reach. From the port at Marina Grande, take the direct bus to Anacapri and get off at p. Vittoria. From here, telephone Villa Eva and they will pick you up. You can walk by getting off 3 stops later and following the series of signs down numerous winding roads. Once you enter this secluded sanctuary, it will be difficult to say good-bye to warm-hearted Mamma Eva and her bearded husband Vincenzo. L15,000 per person in tidy, tasteful rooms with baths. Breakfast L6000. Telephone a few days in advance and again on the day of your arrival to confirm your reservations.

Hotel Villa Filomena, via Caprile, 4 (tel. 837 14 50). From p. Vittoria in Anacapri center, follow via De Tommaso all the way down. Not bad, but no competition for Villa Eva. Prices are the best on the island, and the rooms are clean and commodious. Singles L15,000. Doubles L24,000, with bath L30,000. L11,000 per additional bed.

Hotel Caesar Augustus, via Giuseppe Orlandi, 4 (tel. 837 14 21), on the main bus route right before the town center. The rusty remains of a grand luxury hotel from yesteryear. Woebegone rooms with aristocratic views an egalitarian L25,000 per person. Breakfast and bath included. If the hotel is full (on the weekends and in August), they will stick you in an interior room without views or in their annex. English spoken. Private bus service from the port L1300. Open Easter-Oct.

Food

Capresian fare is as glorious as the vistas from the island's highest cliffs. The *ravioli alla caprese* is hand-stuffed with the tastiest of local cheeses. Their local *mozzarella* is delicious eaten alone, or with tomatoes, oil, and oregano in a dish known as *insalata caprese.* Don't miss the *torta di Mandorla* (chocolate almond cake).

Restaurant and bar prices in the town of Capri will make you gasp—its best to buy food from one of the small groceries on the island. **Salumeria Capri,** via Roma, 30, offers the lowest prices and largest selection. Salami and prosciutto cost L1800 per *etto* (enough for a couple sandwiches), and a liter bottle of local Tiberio wine costs L1800. Their *panino caprese* (tomato, mozzarella, and basil sandwich) is a real hero for L2000. (Open June-Oct. daily 8am-midnight; Nov.-May Mon.-Fri. 8am-8pm, Sat. 8am-1pm.) A jaunt over to Anacapri will bring you back to the world of approachable restaurants.

In the Town of Capri

La Cantina del Marchese, via Tiberio, 7 (tel. 837 08 57). From p. Umberto I, follow via delle Botteghe into via Fuorlovado, which leads up, up, up to via Tiberio (15 min.). No effort is needed, however, to savor their homemade cheeses and salami (L6000-8000 for a large plate), or their hearty *spaghetti della Cantina* (with olives, capers, tomato, and anchovies, L5000). Excellent hand-cooked pizzas at night L3000-8000. House wine L6000 per liter. Open July-Sept. daily noon-3pm and 7pm-midnight; Oct.-June Fri.-Wed.

Ristorante Da Giorgio, via Roma, 34 (tel. 837 08 90), next to the bus terminal. Quality, scenic dining at a higher price. Zesty, hand-prepared *ravioli Caprese* L6500. Their pizza is a cheaper, but equally pleasing alternative for L4500-6500. Wine L7000 per liter. Cover L2000. Open June-Aug. daily noon-2:30pm and 6:30-11pm; April-May and Sept.-Dec. Fri.-Wed.

Anacapri

Trattoria il Solitario, via G. Orlandi, 54 (tel. 837 13 82), off p. Vittoria. Great cheap food in an amazing, ivy-covered hideaway. Chirp along with the colorful birds in the dining area to the tune of the *ravioli Caprese* (L6000). Salads L2500. Wine L5000 per bottle. Cover L1000. Open June 20-Sept. 20 daily 12:15-3pm and 7pm-midnight; Sept. 21-June 19 Tues.-Sun.

Ristorante il Cucciolo, via della Fabbrica, 52 (tel. 837 19 17), near the bus stop for the Damecuta ruins on the road to the Blue Grotto. Full meals with drink L15,000—easily the best bargain on the island. Meticulously prepared dishes complemented by a view of distant Naples. Avoid a la carte; you will pay twice as much. Open March 10-Oct. 18 Fri.-Wed. noon-3pm and 7pm-midnight.

Trattoria Materita, via G. Orlandi, 140 (tel. 837 12 42). Follow via Orlandi from p. Vittoria until you come to via Boffe. With a German waiter, an Indian cook, and a local Neapolitan pizza chef, this place promotes international peace. The *spaghetti sciuè sciuè* (with spicy tomato and basil sauce) promotes gustatory satisfaction (L5000), but the greatest attraction is *pizza Saltimbocca,* the pizza chef's flying saucer-shaped invention stuffed with ricotta, ham, mozzarella, and secret spices (L6000). For dessert, don't miss the *Tiramisù di Lello e Anna,* a hearty homemade pudding cake (L3500). Cover L1000. Open June 23-Sept. daily noon-3pm and 7pm-midnight; Oct.-June 22 Wed.-Mon.

Sights

To appreciate Capri's Mediterranean beauty from on high, take via Longano from p. Umberto in Capri center and then make the hike up to the left on via Tiberio to **Villa Jovis** (1 hr.). This is Emperor Tiberius's ruined but still magnificent pleasure palace. Legend has it that Tiberius threw his enemies off the sheer rocks. We advise walking down. (Open daily 9am-1 hr. before sunset. Admission L2000.) Descending by the path, a short detour takes you to the **Arco Naturale,** the arch of rock on the east end of the island. On a clear day you can see as far as Paestum through the weathered arch.

Toward the southern edge of the town of Capri lies the **Certosa,** a fourteenth-century Carthusian monastery. The Gothic chapel has been somewhat disturbed by the eighteenth-century baroque frescoes, but remains unruffled and angular. (Open Tues.-Sun. 8am-2pm. Free.) The nearby **Giardini di Augusto** (Gardens of Augustus) are not noted for their horticultural beauty; instead, a superb series of belvederes, stacked on top of one another, make the visit worthwhile. In one corner of the gardens a small statue is dedicated to Lenin, who fled to Capri after the abortive St. Petersburg uprising of 1905. (Gorky and Chaliapin also stayed here.) The garden's terraces offer the best view of the **faraglioni,** the twin rock pinnacles sprouting from the ocean that have become the symbol of Capri.

Literally "over Capri," **Anacapri** is a less visited but more beautiful sample of island living. From p. Vittoria in Anacapri, you can take a 10-minute chairlift (round-trip L5500) to the top of **Monte Solaro.** (Open 9:30am-2 hr. before sunset.) The view from the top is terrific: On a clear day, it is possible to see the Apennines to the east and the mountains of Calabria to the south. You can hike to the top of a trail beginning on via Solaro. Another reason to visit Anacapri is the **Villa San Michele.** (Open daily 9am-1 hr. before sunset. Admission L3000.) Built earlier this century on the site of another villa of Emperor Tiberius, it was the lifelong work of the Swedish author and physician Axel Munthe. The villa is filled with classical sculptures; many were retrieved from Capri's sea bottom where they were hurled when Tiberius died by the ghosts of those he had hurled down the cliffs. Particularly notable is a Medusa's head on the wall of Munthe's study. Should you fall in love with the villa, as many have, be sure to pick up a copy of Munthe's delightful memoir *The Story of San Michele* (L10,400 at the entrance). While in Anacapri center, also visit the **Church of San Michele,** located off via S. Nicola, which runs off via G. Orlandi. It has a magnificently designed eighteenth-century tile floor depicting paradise on earth. Walk up to the upper balcony to get the full effect. (Open April-Oct. Mon.-Sat. 10am-6pm, Sun. 10am-2pm. Admission L1000.) From Anacapri center, take a bus to the **faro,** Italy's second tallest lighthouse.

Capri's most famous attraction, the **Grotta Azzurra** (Blue Grotto) was also known to the Romans, and has become the island's most fearsome tourist trap. A motorboat from Marina Grande, barely 2km away, costs L5400 round-trip (Sun. L4900), leaving regularly from 9am to 2 hr. before sunset. You are then transferred unceremoniously to rowboats for a tour of the grotto (L6750). The "captains" take you through at such thundering speed that your eyes scarcely have time to adjust to the remarkable blue glow, best seen in the early evening. You can save the money from the initial motorboat ride by taking a bus from Anacapri to the cliff just above the grotto (every 10 min., L1300). Many visitors dive into the clear water of the grotto. It's advisable to do this early in the morning or in the early evening, when the rowboats are not running. During the day rowboat pilots are certain to harass you. Although a swim here will be unforgettable, don't go alone or if the surf is heavy. Swimming in caves is extremely hazardous. For a chance to soak in some scenery, take any of the frequent buses to **Marina Piccola,** (every 15 min., L1300), Capri's most beautiful seaside area, located on its southern coast. Though the beach is a glorified pile of rocks, you can revel in the pellucid water and immense lava stone.

Ischia

Ischia is the largest of the islands in the Bay of Naples, and though lacking the glamor and romance of Capri, it tenders the pleasures of island living with a lower price tag. Volcanic in origin, the island is noted for its hot springs and therapeutic radioactive mud baths. Since Ischia is a favorite destination of German sun-seekers, most Italian restaurant and hotel proprietors speak a fair amount of German, though very little English. Ischia's main towns are **Ischia Porto,** the area surrounding the major port; **Cassamicciola Terme,** an expensive spa with an overcrowded beach; **Lacco Ameno,** not much of anything; **Forio,** with many *pensioni;* and the popular **San Francesco beach.** The most superior is **Maronte,** on the south side of the island (serviced by bus #5 from the main port every 20 min.; take a boat-taxi to the secluded beach from the last stop, L2000) and **Citara** to the west, a larger, more frequented beach with giant rocks nearby that some people swim to and dive from. The **Castle of Ischia,** a group of ruined fifteenth-century edifices, stands on an islet just east of Ischia Porto. Boats to Ischia run daily from Naples (6:10am-11pm every 2 hr., Sun. 7:05am-11pm; L4600) and Pozzuoli (4 per day, 9:45am-7:30pm; L3900).

Accommodations, Camping, and Food

The **Azienda di Turismo** at the Scalo Porto Salvo in Ischia Porto (tel. 99 11 46; open Mon.-Sat. 8:30am-8pm, Sun. 9am-noon) will help you find lodgings, although by late July and August rooms are hard to come by without reservations at least three months in advance. Most hotels have no singles, and since rooms are in such high demand, hotel owners may not rent rooms for less than a week. The longer you plan to stay, the better your chances of getting a room will be. Prices plummet after September until May. **Buses** to destinations all over the island depart from Ischia Porto and are labelled with their destinations. The main towns of Cassamicciola Terme, Lacco Ameno, Forio, and Sant' Angelo are serviced on the principle bus route #1, which leaves approximately every half-hour during the day and less frequently at night. (Tickets L900-1100, depending on distance.) From June 15 to Sept. 30, you can travel the island by way of the **Metro del Mare** (tel. 99 19 90), a boat shuttle running from Ischia Porto to the various beach localities on the island and on nearby Procida. (Departures at 8am, 8:50am, 10:20am, 11:30am, 4pm, and 4:50pm. Tickets L1500-L3000, depending on destination.)

Ischia Porto

Hotel Macri, via Jasolino, 96 (tel. 99 26 03), near the port off the street that runs along the water. The cheapest rooms in summer because they don't require meals. The rooms are respectable, but the hotel is located in the least pleasing area of the island, close to the ferries and far from the amazing beaches. Singles with bath L26,000. Doubles with bath L40,600. Sept.-June singles with bath L23,400; doubles with bath L36,400.

Il Crostolo, via B. Cossa, 32 (tel. 99 10 94). Follow the street that runs past the bus terminal. The 10-min. walk to the hotel provides a panoramic view of the port, though you can see little from the rooms themselves. Doubles with bath L50,000.

Cassamicciola Terme

Pensione Quisisana, p. Bagni, 35 (tel. 99 45 20). Take bus #3 from the port to the sweet *piazza* where its located. Tiny, family-run establishment with plenty of comfort. A 10-min. walk from the beach. July-Aug. obligatory pension L42,000 per person. In off-season half-pension L35,000 per person. All rooms have full baths. Curfew midnight. Open May-Oct.

Forio

Pensione Villa Franca, strada statale Lacco, 155 (tel. 98 74 20). Take bus #1 from Ischia Port, getting off at the stop for the San Francesco beach. On the main street on which the bus travels. Rudimentary but well-kept rooms, with a lovely patio and swimming pool. A 15-min. walk from the beach. English spoken. The homecooked meals make the L48,000 obligatory full pension in July and Aug. worthwhile. In off-season full pension L45,000. Open April-Oct.

Residence Villa Tina, via Strada Statale Forio, 136 (tel. 99 77 82). Farther along the main bus route from Villa Franca and ½km from the water. The best choice in Ischia. Sparkling 4-person and 6-person apartments with kitchens, bathrooms, and outdoor terraces. June-Sept. L25,000 per person; Oct.-May L20,000 per person.

Camping: Two delightful campsites are located at Ischia port. The better of the two is **Camping Internazionale,** via M. Mazella (tel. 99 14 49), a 15-min. walk from the port. Take via Alfredo de Luca from via del Porto and bear right onto via M. Mazzella at p. degli Eroe. Note that there are 2 via Mazzellas—Michelle and Leonardo—running parallel. Lush foliage and tranquil surroundings. L7500 per person, L5800 per tent, L3100 per small tent; in off-season L6500 per person, L4500 per tent. Immaculate 2-person bungalows with bath L44,000, L14,000 per additional person; in off-season L34,000, L12,000 per additional person. Open April 22-Oct. 10. **Eurocamping dei Pini,** via delle Ginestre, 28 (tel. 98 20 69), is only a 10-min. walk from the port. Take via del Porto onto via Alfredo de Luca walking uphill and taking a right on via delle Terme where you will see the arrow indicating Camping. July-Sept. L6500 per person, L5900 per tent, L3100 per small tent. In off-season L6500 per person. L4800 per tent, L2700 per small tent. 2-person bungalows with bath L34,000, L12,000 per additional person; July-Aug. L40,000, L16,000 per additional person. The tent site is more senic than the bungalow site. Open Easter and June-Sept.

There are several ways to beat the high cost of eating out. Take a left as you get off the ferry and walk to the first intersection to get to **Da Ciccio,** via Porto, 1 (tel. 99 13 14), with a wide variety of dishes under L5000. Cover in the dining area is L500. (Open daily 8am-1am.) Follow via Roma off via Porto for several blocks for a more dignified meal at **Trattoria Greco,** via Roma, 41 (tel. 99 11 87). Eat at one of the marble tables near the kitchen to avoid paying the cover and the service charges. A plate of *gnocchi* here saturates in superior style (L3500). Pizza is L2500-4500. (Cover L1500, service 15%. Open daily June-Sept.; Oct.-May Tues.-Sun. 12:30-3:30pm and 7pm-midnight.)

Procida

A provincial island of fisherfolk and farmers, Procida proudly perfers to remain a spectator as its neighboring islands become summertime countryclubs. Though crowds also clammer to Procida, they don't hold on long enough to soil its untarnished beaches. The island can be reached from Naples by one of four daily, 1½-hour ferries (the first at 9:20am; L3900). Ferries also leave from Pozzuoli and Ischia. The 14-kilometer coast, volcanic in origin, has three principle beaches: *spiggia chiaia, spiaggia ciraccio,* and *chiaiolella.* Buses do not directly service many parts of the island, but the island is only 4km wide and taxis do run from the port (tel. 896 87 85). Buses can, however, take you to **Chiaolella** (L500), where you can cross over the footbridge to the wonderful little islet of **Vivara,** now preserved as a wildlife sanctuary. **Angolo di Paradiso,** via Salette (tel. 896 76 57), on Ciraccio beach, serves excellent, inexpensive dishes in beachside surroundings. *Spaghetti alla scarpara* is a fried spaghetti dish with myriad spices (L3000), and their *coniglio alla Procidana* (local rabbit) will make you hop for joy (L7000). (Cover L1500, service 10%. Open May-Sept. daily 1-4pm and 7-10:30pm.) Of the three hotels, only the **Riviera,** via G. Da Procida, 36 (tel. 896 71 97), is affordable. (Open April-Sept. Singles L30,000. Doubles L50,000. Bath and breakfast included. July-Aug. full pension L58,000-63,000.) The campsite **Graziella,** at via Salette (tel. (081) 896 77 47), right on the beach, is reached by taking the island bus from the port to p. Urno and walking ½km to Spiaggia Ciraccio. It lacks in facilities, but is peaceful. (L4000 per person, L4000 per tent; July-Aug. L5000 per person, L5000 per tent. Open May-Aug.)

Sorrento

Homer's Odysseus and crew shielded their ears from the beautiful song of the Sirens, who inhabited Sorrento's peninsula. If the Sirens stil exist, chances are they chant in English and German to camera-clad foreigners. Despite the lack of Italian *anima,* travelers still animate Sorrento with good reason. Unrivalled in physical attractiveness, it is a haven of relatively inexpensive hotels and restaurants, and an easy place from which to explore the islands or the Amalfi coast.

Orientation and Practical Information

One of the best reasons to begin your tour of the Campania region in Sorrento is that it is the only city near the Amalfi coast and the islands where you can rent a **motorbike,** the ideal way to see the mountainous coast and Capri. If you're not comfortable shifting gears, choose an automatic moped over the more powerful Vespa scooters—the Italian drivers and winding mountain roads will occupy your attention. Do not ride these machines with a backpack, as doing so raises your center of gravity perilously. **Ciro's,** via degli Aranci, 93B/C (tel. 878 25 22), on the street running behind the station, is the superior rental firm in the city. They speak English and will kindly help organize your travels. (Mopeds L23,000 per day. Scooters L34,000 per day. Tax 18%. Gas not included. Must be at least 18 to rent a scooter, 14 for mopeds.) They also rent **cars** at L75,000 per day, with unlimited mileage. You must be at least 21 and have an international driver's license. (Open daily 8am-1pm and 2-9pm.)

Azienda di Turismo, via L. De Maio, 35 (tel. 878 11 15), off p. Antonino, behind p. Tasso heading towards the water. A large, well-run, English-speaking office with maps, hotel listings (and reservations within the city), and information on cultural events. Open Mon.-Sat. 8:30am-2:30pm and 5-8pm.

Post Office: corso Italia, 210T-U, near p. A. Lauro. Open Mon.-Sat. 8:15am-7:30pm. **Postal code:** 80067.

Telephones: SIP, p. Tasso, at via Correale under the church on the far side. Open daily 9am-1pm and 4-9:30pm. **Telephone code:** 081.

Buses: SITA, from the *circumvesuviana* station to Positano and Amalfi (6:35am-10:10pm every 1-2 hr.).

Ferries: The most direct and cheapest route to Capri. Descend the stairs at p. Tasso to find the companies that run to Capri. **Caremar** (tel. 878 12 82) is the cheapest. Boats leave daily at 8am, 10am, 2:45pm, 5:45pm, and 7:45pm. Tickets L2800. Several hydrofoils run daily to Capri (L5500) and Naples (L5500).

Hospital: Ospedale S. Maria Misericordia, corso Italia (tel. 878 34 96). English speakers on hand. Also emergency pharmaceuticals.

Police: p. Antonino, 15/16 (tel. 878 11 10). Ask for the English-speaking foreigners office (*ufficio stranieri*).

Accommodations and Camping

Sorrento offers a surprising array of comfortable, cheap rooms, making it the ideal base for exploration of Campania. In the summer, and especially in August, availability wanes as the optimal offerings are lost to reservations made months before.

Ostello Surriento (IYHF), via Capasso, 5 (tel. 878 17 83). From the train station, make a right onto corso Italia and look for via Capasso across the street. Amiable, savvy young management; wild decorations; and a location near the waterfront redeem the primitive 6-, 10-, and 14-person rooms (22- and 42-person rooms for women). The free shower may be warm if you wake up early. Doesn't require hostel card when business is slow. Beds L7000. Breakfast L1500, dinner L7000. Lockout 9:30am-5pm. Loose curfew 11:30pm. Open March-Oct.

Hotel Linda, via degli Aranci, 125 (tel. 878 29 16), behind the train station. Though located in a barren area, the fresh rooms are comfortable. Affable management. Room service available. English spoken. Doubles L30,000, with bath L35,000. Breakfast L4000. English spoken. Reservations with deposit.

Hotel City, corso Italia, 221 (tel. 877 22 10), on the main street that heads toward p. Tasso from the train station. A colorful, art-filled place with a genial owner. English spoken. Comfortable but humble doubles with bath (some with garden patios) L30,000-35,000. Singles available Sept.-June L20,000-25,000. Breakfast L3000. Reserve at least 2 months in advance for Aug.

Hotel Nice, corso Italia, 257 (tel. 878 16 50), in the direction of the train station from Hotel City. Clean rooms. Only the prices are truly nice. Doubles L24,000, L36,000 with bath.

Hotel Rivoli, via S. M. delle Grazie, 16 (tel. 878 17 09), off p. Antonio, which is right behind p. Tusso. A small, central place consisting of clean, no-frills doubles, L30,000. L12,000 per additional person.

Pensione Mara, via Rota, 5 (tel. 878 36 65). Turn right on corso Italia from the train station, take via Capasso past the youth hostel, and then make your 1st right. Immaculate and beautifully located. English spoken. Singles L15,000. Doubles L35,000. Bath included. July-Aug. obligatory half-pension L40,000 per person. Reserve with deposit early.

Hotel Loreley, via A. Califano, 2 (tel. 878 15 08). Take via Capasso past the youth hostel all the way to the waterfront. Elevated prices for elevated rooms with elevated views over cliffs and sea. English spoken. Oct.-May doubles with bath L50,000; June-Sept. L52,000. July-Aug. 10-day minimum stay. Reserve at least 3 months in advance for July-Aug.

Hotel Savoia, via Fuorimura, 50 (tel. 878 25 11), on the street off the right hand of the statue in p. Tasso. In a barren area of town, but rooms with phones and fresh towels. Your best bet if you're coming in the summer without reservations. Amiable, English-speaking management. Small singles with bath L25,000. Doubles with bath L45,000. Breakfast L5000. Oct.-March. reduced prices.

Camping: The cheapest place is **Nube d'Argento,** via Capo, 21 (tel. 878 13 44). From the train station, follow corso Italia past p. Tasso until it becomes via Capo. L9000 per person, L6900 per tent. Sept.-June L6000 per person, L6000 per tent. Another campground right on the beach is **Villaggio Verde,** via Cesaro, 12 (tel. 878 32 58), a 10-min. walk from the town center off via degli Aranci. L6700 per person, L6700 per tent. Sept.-June L5000 per person, L5000 per tent. 2-person bungalows with kitchen and bath L50,000. For an inexpensive site outside of the city, take the *circumvesuviana* train 12km to the Seiano stop and then take one of the regular buses to the port to **Campeggio Sant' Antonio,** via Marina d'Equa (tel. 879 92 61). It is right on the water and shaded by almond and orange trees. July and Aug. L7000 per person and tent. March 15-July 1 and Sept. to Oct. 15 L6000 per person and tent. 4-person bungalows with bath, kitchen, and fridge July-Aug. L60,000. March 15-July 1 and Sept.-Oct. 15 L40,000.

Food

Traditionally, Sorrento is famous for its *gnocchi,* plump potato dumplings smothered in a zesty tomato and cheese sauce. Also popular are the *canneloni,* stuffed and rolled strips of pasta with tomato sauce. Regretfully, few of the affordable restaurants in Sorrento offer local fare, opting instead to cater to the Germans with *Würstel* and to the English with fish and chips. But you can always hop on the *circumvesuviana* train line to hit some of the local hangouts in the province.

Outside the City

Gigini Pizza a Metro, via Nicotera, 11, Vico Equense (tel. 879 84 24), 10-minute train ride from Sorrento. Take the *circumvesuviana* to the Vico Equense stop, go left as you exit the station, and follow the winding road uphill to its end at p. Umberto I. Finally, take a left on via Roma and another left on via Nicotera. This is unofficially the world's largest *pizzeria,* a massive 2-story facility with monstrous wood-burning ovens that cook *pizza a metro* (meter-long pizza). A delighful meter will feed at least 5 starving tourists, so save your appetite for a hundred centimeters of *pizza margherita* (with fresh tomato and mozzarella, L22,000) or *quattro stagioni* (cheese, prosciutto, mushroom, and tomato, L24,000). Chug ½-liter of beer (L2500). Cover L1000, service 13%. Open daily noon-1am.

Mastù Rocco, corso Italia, 97, Sant' Agnello (tel. 878 24 42). Take the *circumvesuviana* to Sant' Agnello and turn left at the main street, following it about 150m around the 1st bend. If you thought the traditional, family-run *trattoria* was obsolete in Sorrento, old Rocco and his spirited wife will prove you wrong. Full-course lunch with drink L10,000 served under the vine-covered terrace in back. Try *penne alla Sorrentina* (pasta with fresh tomato, peppers, basil, and mozzarella, L3000). Open Tues.-Sun. noon-4pm.

In the City

Pizzeria da Gigino, via degli Archi, 15 (tel. 870 19 27). Follow corso Italia off p. Tasso, and take your 1st right. Personable and moderately priced. Eat well for about L14,000. Pasta dishes L4000-8000, mixed fried fish L7500, pizza L4000-5000, and wine L3500 per liter. Open June-Sept. daily 11:30am-2:30pm and 6-11:30pm; Oct.-May Wed.-Mon. 11:30am-2:30pm and 6-11:30pm.

L'Antica Trattoria, via Reginaldo Giuliani, 33 (tel. 807 10 82), the 2nd right off corso Italia after via degli Archi. Genuine Italian dining in classy environs. Lengthy menu includes *cannelloni alla Sorrentina* (L4500). Open daily 10am-3pm and 7pm-1am.

Ristorante e Pizzeria Giardiniello, via Accademia, 7 (tel. 878 46 16). Take a left off via Giuliani after the Shaker Bar. This large, open-air establishment is true to Italian standards. They serve an excellent *linguine al cartoccio* (pasta with seafood, served in a foil wrap, L8000). Don't miss their pizza specialties. *Vino di Sorrento* L3000 per bottle. Cover L1000. Open June-Sept. daily 11:30am-midnight; Oct.-May Tues.-Sun.

Sights and Entertainment

Rather than a cauldron of culture, Sorrento is an ideal place for haggard travelers to kick back and relax.

The **Punta di Sorrento** is a lovely place for a sunset swim. Walk down the Ruderia Romana off via Capo; after 400m, it turns into a footpath that leads to the water, bypassing the ruins of a medieval fortress. A bit farther, southwest of the city, is the **Villa di Pollio,** a lovely public park featuring ruins, a fantastic swimming hole, and relatively untouristed serenity. To get there, take a bus to Capo di Sorrento, and then walk 12 min. past the stop.

The town hosts several interesting events throughout the year, including an elaborate procession on Good Friday and an International Film Festival in October. Classical music concerts are performed about every other night throughout July and August at the outdoor atrium of the **Chiostro di San Francesco,** near Villa Communale on the water. (Showtime 9:15pm. Admission L16,000, students under 26 L10,000.) From November to March, the Sorrento Tourist Board offers a free entertainment program that includes movies, concerts, local folklore exhibits and guided tours of town. The area around placid p. Tasso becomes Sorrento's hotspot after dark. **Tiffany,** strada Sant' Antonino, 6, offers live music nightly. Make sure to catch a performance by Carmello, the top-notch Neapolitan singer. (Open 9pm-3am.) The **Fauno Notte Club,** in p. Tasso (tel. 878 10 21), features the *tarantella,* a traditional dance show, every night from February to November at 9pm, as well as disco-dancing after the show. (Cover L18,000; 1st drink included.)

Amalfi Coast

The Amalfi Coast, the mountainous peninsula that separates the Gulf of Naples from the Gulf of Salerno, sports some spectacular scenery. A limestone range marked by deep gorges and fantastically shaped rocks, the coast is traversed by a narrow, dizzying road high up on an escarpment with unequaled views of the coastline. Lemon groves, grape vines, olive trees, almonds, camelias, and oleanders flourish in the fertile soil, tempering the harshness of the coast's steep and imposing crags.

The coast is accessible from Sorrento, Salerno (from where SITA buses run every 2 hr.), or from the Meta stop on the *circumvesuviana* train from Naples. You will revere the bus drivers after this voyage; they manage the serpentine roads with aplomb. The entire trip from Sorrento to Salerno takes 2½ hours (L3500). The most exhilirating way to see the coast is on a rented motorbike (see Sorrento Practical Information). Take pleasure in breaking up this magnificent trip by spending a few nights at the small cliff towns that dot the coast. Hitching between towns may also be fruitful. Simply post yourself along Strada Nazionale, the coastal road along which the clifftop towns are strung like beads. Stand in the crook of any of the great bends in the road, and wave excitedly at the cars as they slow down to turn.

Positano, a hillside town that looks as if it's about to slide into the sea, is a little less than an hour from Sorrento (L1100). From the SITA bus stop at Chiesa Nuova, you can either walk down the winding *scalinatella* (stairway) to the village, or take the bus, which runs every half-hour (L500). This, the over-touristed fashion capital of the coast, began as a fishing settlement at the base of the steep cliffs on which it now perches precariously. It was once a favorite haunt of John Steinbeck, who remarked that it could never be ruined by an influx of tourists: "In the first place there is no room." The charter buses that regularly deposit visitors into the town's overpriced boutiques contradict him. The Positanese vistas still remain cosmic, especially when you look back at the town as you depart in the direction of Sorrento and at night when the Positano cliff is an orchestra of sparkling lights. The **Church of Santa Maria Assunta** is the town's primary sight, located near the last bus stop. It houses a stunning Byzantine Black Madonna dating from the thirteenth century.

If you can't bear to leave, try one of the many *pensioni* in the area. (Reserve early in the crowded summer.) **Villa Maria Luisa,** via Fornillo, 40 (tel. 87 50 23), near Fornillo beach, leases rooms with baths that offer splendid views and relaxing terraces. (L20,000-22,000 per person. Breakfast included. July 15-Sept. obligatory half-pension.) **LaBougainville,** via C. Colombo, 25 (tel. 87 50 47), off the *piazza* at the last bus stop in Positano, is set among plush Positano boutiques and run by a kind woman. (Singles L33,000. Doubles L45,000. Both with baths and many with seaside balconies.) Fifty meters uphill is **La Tavolozza,** via C. Columbo, 10 (tel. 87 50 40), with superior vistas from its hilltop location. (Doubles with bath L50,000-55,000.) Food prices are as steep as the cliffs here, but **O'Capurale,** Marina di Positano (tel. 87 53 74), cooks heaping plates of *bucatini alla caporalessa* (baked pasta with eggplant and cheese) for L5000 and other pasta specialties, and serves it at outdoor tables facing the beach. Main dishes are L7000-9000. Wine is L5000 per liter. (Cover L1500, service 10%. Open March-Oct. daily 12:30-3:30pm and 7:30-11pm.)

Take the bus from the top of Positano or hike the 45-minute trail to **Monte Pertuso.** On the way, stop at the locals' favorite eternal spring of fresh water, at the site of a small madonna. Monte Pertuso, a high cliff pierced by a large *pertuso* (hole) that creates curious optical effects against the sky, towers over the beautiful hamlet of **Praiano,** which is quickly becoming one of the most fashionable spots on the coast. One way to take advantage of the rapturous panorama is to stay at the excellent campsite-hotel **Tranquilità** (tel. 87 40 84), on the road to Amalfi. Rooms overlook a garden, and campgrounds are beveled into the steep cliffs, providing unobstructed views of the surrounding caves, gorges, and sea. (L8000 per person, July-Aug. L10,000. Bungalows with bath and often terrace L20,000. Breakfast L4000.) Right above is the equally scenic, open-air **Ristorante Continental,** which offers exquisite full meals for L10,000. Ravello wine is L4000 per bottle. (Open daily noon-3pm and 8pm-midnight. Hotel and restaurant both open March-Nov.)

For a real taste of Amalfi coast opulence, Praiano's luxury hotel, **Tramonto d'Oro** (tel. (089) 87 40 08), built on the coastal cliffs down the road toward Sorrento, offers its comfortable, windowless rooms with baths for L20,000-25,000 per person, use of roof-top pool included. Rooms with a view cost three times as much. **Trattoria San Gennaro da Vittoria,** next door, cooks tasty *gnocchi alla Sorrentina* (L3500) and *zuppadi di cozze* (mussel soup, L5000). Local wine is L2500 per bottle. (Cover L1000. Open daily noon-midnight.)

Amalfi

This once-favored Edwardian resort immediately enchants. Just sit along Lungomare dei Cavalieri and watch the horse-drawn carts pass by, sip coffee in the intimate *piazza* in front of the cathedral, or stroll the beautiful bayside promenades. Although Amalfi is small today, it was once the oldest of the four medieval maritime republics, a city of over 100,000 that challenged Genoa and Pisa for control of the Mediterranean.

Practical Information

Azienda di Turismo: corso Romano, 26 (tel. 87 11 07), near the water and the bus stop. Walk in the direction of Salerno from the bus stop. Maps and some assistance in finding lodgings, but not exuberant. Open Mon.-Sat. 9am-1pm and 4:30-7pm.

Post Office: corso Roma, 29, on the road running along the waterfront. Open Mon.-Fri. 8:15am-2pm, Sat. 9am-noon. **Postal code:** 84011.

Telephones: Bar Della Valle, via Pietro Capuana, off via Mansone I heading uphill. Open daily 8am-1pm and 3-10pm. **Telephone code:** 089.

Police: via Fiume (tel. 87 10 22).

Accommodations

The largest town on the "Divine Coast," Amalfi is the only one not totally dependent on tourism industry. As a result, some high-quality, reasonably-priced accommodations exist. They are often full in July and August, so reserve at least one month in advance. Possibly the best option for backpackers is in the tiny beachside village of Atrani, a 20-minute walk from Amalfi, at the friendly, family-run **A Scalinatella,** p. Umberto I (tel. 87 14 92), at the town's main *piazza.* From the center of Amalfi, walk along the main waterfront road leading toward Salerno. Just before you arrive at the tunnel, descend the public stairs that pass through the Ristorante Zaccaria to the water and take a left through the arch at the bottom. The bus from Amalfi to Ravello or Salerno also stops at Atrani (L600). One of the tiniest towns in all Europe, Atrani is a convenient escape from crowded Amalfi. A Scalinatella's hostel-type rooms for 2, 4, and 6 people are excellent. The sociable owners make living easy, offering free use of common kitchens, bathrooms equipped with washboards, and use of washing machines (L2500 per load). They also offer free tourist information and baggage storage. (Sept.-July L10,000 per person, plus L2500 if you stay 1-2 days without your own bedding. Aug. L15,000 per person.)

Pensione Proto, Salita dei Curiali, 4 (tel. 87 10 13), on a tiny alley that runs off via Genova (also called via Lorenzo D'Amalfi), 34. Comfy but rickety rooms. English spoken. Oct.-May L16,500 per person, with bath L18,000. June-Sept. L19,000 per person, with bath L20,000. July-Aug. obligatory breakfast (L3000) and dinner (L10,000).

Hotel Amalfi, via dei Pastai, 3 (tel. 87 24 40), to the left off via Genova as you go uphill. Mary Ellen's favorite: Immaculate rooms, attentive management, and attractive outdoor roof terraces make this Amalfi's best. English spoken. June-Sept. only doubles L65,000, breakfast included. Oct.-May singles with bath L30,000. Doubles with baths. June-Sept. L40,000.

Hotel Vittoria, Salita Truglio, 5 (tel. 87 10 57), next to Hotel Amalfi. Comfortable doubles with baths. June-Sept. L40,000, with breakfast L42,000. Oct.-May L30,000, with breakfast L35,000. Curfew midnight.

Hotel Lidomare, via Piccolomini, 9 (tel. 87 13 32), through the passageway off via Genova across from the *duomo.* Take a quick left up the flight of stairs, and then go up another set of stairs through the arch on the far-right side of the *piazza.* A posh and immaculate small hotel with a lovely antique lounge equipped with color TV and a mahogany piano. Run by two sweet women. Ask for an inexpensive room. Doubles with bath from L50,000. Breakfast included. A/C L5000. Aug. obligatory half-pension L58,000 per person.

Food

To counter the low-quality, high-priced outlets that feed on the charter busloads, the **supermarket** at via Lorenzo d'Amalfi, 32, the street that runs by the *duomo,* will fill you up with cold cuts (about L1500-3000 per *etto*) and *passolini,* a regional specialty of plump raisins wrapped in inedible lemon leaves (L800). Also pick up a bottle of Ravello wine for about L1200 per bottle. (Open Mon.-Sat. 8am-1:30pm and 4:30-9:30pm, Sun. 8am-1pm; in off-season Mon.-Sat. only.)

Bar Il Tarì, via P. Capuano, 9 (tel. 87 18 32), on the street that via Genova runs into going uphill. This tiny, modest place serves fancy food cooked in its expensive restaurant next door for more casual prices. The *gnocchi* (potato pasta) are hand-made and heavenly (L3000). Several daily specials. Wine L4000 per liter. Open June-Oct. daily 10am-3pm and 7-11:30pm; Nov.-May Wed.-Mon.

Ristorante al Mulino, valle dei Mulini (tel. 87 22 23). Follow via Genova uphill about 800m. A calm, outdoor eating terrace. Full meals L12,000. The *spaghetti alle vongole* (with clams) makes a great 1st course. Piping-hot pizzas at night L2500-5000. Cover L1000, service 10%. Open June-Sept. daily; Oct.-May Tues.-Sun. noon-midnight.

Trattoria-Pizzeria de Maria, via Genova, 14 (tel. 87 18 80), on the main road leading uphill past the *duomo.* The one *trattoria* in Amalfi with character. The owner bounces from table to table, serving up his tasty *spaghetti scuiè scuiè* (with garlic, oil, parsley, peppers, and a touch of tomato, L4000) and aromatic *pollo alla Griglia* (chicken roasted in the open, wood-burning oven, L6000). Cover L1500, service 15%. Open June-Sept. daily; Oct.-May Sat.-Thurs. noon-3:30pm and 7pm-midnight.

Trattoria La Perla, salita Truglio, 3 (tel. 87 14 40), next to Hotel Vittoria. Classy food in classy surroundings. Terrific homemade *cannelloni Amalfitana* (pasta stuffed with veal and spices, L4000) and bounteous *spaghetti al Profumo di Mare* (with seafood, L6500). Superior full meals L14,000. *Sammarco vino* from Ravello L5000 per bottle. Cover L1500. Open June-Sept. daily; Oct.-May Wed.-Mon. noon-3:30pm and 7pm-midnight.

Sights

The major monument in town is the ***duomo,*** off via Mansone I, at the top of a long flight of stairs overlooking p. Duomo. Rebuilt in the nineteenth century according to the original medieval plan, the cathedral's brilliant facade of varied geometric designs is startling, and the *campanile* in Norman-Saracen style adds to the dramatic effect of the mountains and monasteries in the background. The handsome interior has unusually narrow bays that add to its elegance. Downstairs, the crypt houses the remains of Sant' Andrea (all except his head, which the Pope gave to Saint Andrew's church in Patras, Greece) and a bronze statue of the apostle. The statue is the work of a student of Michelangelo, while the two smaller statues on either side are attributed to Bernini's father (cathedral open daily 7am-1:30pm and 3-8pm. Appropriate dress required.) To the left of the church is the **Chiostro Paradiso** (the Cloister of Paradise), a thirteenth-century cemetery that has become a graveyard for miscellaneous column fragments, broken statues, and sarcophagi. Its Arabic arches create a romantic mood for piano and vocal concerts on Friday or Saturday nights from July to September. Tickets cost L5000. (Cloister open daily 9am-1:30pm and 3-8pm. Admission L1000.)

If you didn't see the Blue Grotto in Capri, visit the **Grotto dello Smeraldo** (Emerald Grotto), 4km from Amalfi on the road to Sorrento. Some believe this grotto to be even more breathtaking than its azure counterpart. Sunlight (best 10:30am-3pm) reflects up from below the emerald water to reveal deep gorges and rock formations on the grotto floor. You can also see a lovely submerged manger scene, constructed underwater by the RAI Italian television network in the 1960s as part of their Christmas celebration. Take the SITA bus from Amalfi toward Sorrento to get to the elevator that takes you down to the grotto from the road. The cost of the elevator and the boat into the grotto is L4000. More scenic are the motor boats that leave from the docks in Amalfi. (In summer boats leave whenever a group is formed. L6000 per person, plus L4000 for the transfer boat going into the grotto.) Grotto open June to September 8:30am-5pm. Swimming is prohibited.

A spectacle worth making special arrangements to see is the **Regatta of the Four Ancient Maritime Republics,** held by the states of Amalfi, Pisa, Genoa, and Venice. The contest, complete with galleons, rotates annually between the four cities. Throughout the summer, you can make a spectacle of yourself at the **Disco Marinella,** via Lungomare dei Cavallieri, 1 (tel. 87 10 43), a small disco set on the Amalfi waterfront. (Open June-Oct. daily 10pm-1:30am. Cover L10,000, includes 1st drink.)

Near Amalfi

From Amalfi, the first excursion you can make is to **Atrani,** a shimmering little town of 1200 inhabitants, situated on a lovely beach. Come here for a swim and stroll in its petit *piazza.* It is a 20-minute walk from Amalfi, or one bus stop on the route to Ravello or Salerno.

A quick bus ride from Amalfi will take you to the cliffside aristocratic town of **Ravello** (buses leave hourly 7am-10pm). Planted trees and flowers, small churches, and winding byways enhance the already spectacular setting of Ravello's **Villa Rufolo,** perched 360m above the sea. This eleventh-century country estate was built by a wealthy Ravellian family but later housed several popes, Charles of Anjou, and the expatriate composer Wagner. You enter through a medieval tower with a beautiful Norman-Saracen vault and four statues symbolizing the seasons. Continue on to the famous Moorish cloister, overgrown with flowers and greenery, whose rich polychrome decoration retains its original splendor. Beyond, a fragrant terrace overlooks the jagged coast and calm Tyrrhenian. (Enter from p. Vescovado, where the bus stops. Open June-Sept. 9:30am-1pm and 3-7pm, Oct.-May 9:30am-1pm and 2-5pm. Admission L1000.)

Ravello's **cathedral,** recently stripped of its baroque accoutrements, has a simple nave arcade of antique columns that sets off two fantastic pulpits, one large enough to be a separate building. Both are covered with marble, mosaics, and depictions of strange animals. A small niche to the right of the high altar contains a reliquary with the skull of Santa Barbara. To the left of the altar is the chapel of San Pantaleone, patron of the town, whose "unleakable" blood is preserved in a cracked vessel. The nearby **Villa Cimbrone** warrants an afternoon's visit. Based on a medieval design, the villa was actually built early in this century. (Open daily 8am-sunset. Admission L2000.)

Ravello's **classical music festival,** held in the last week of June, hosts internationally renowned musicians. Concerts resound in the gardens of Villa Rufulo and in the cathedral. Tickets cost L5000 and L10,000. The **Azienda,** p. Vescovada, 13 (tel. 87 10 14; open Tues.-Sat. 8am-7pm, Sun.-Mon. 8am-1pm), provides helpful information on this and other events and sights in the city.

Ravello churns out some of southern Italy's best wines. The three famous marks, *Sammarco, Gran Caruso,* and *Episcopio* pour into glasses over the globe. You can pick up a few bottles of *Sammarco* (L2500) at the vineyard's warehouse, **Casa Vinicola Ettore Sammarco,** via Civita, 9, at the SITA bus stop 3½km from Amalfi on the road to Ravello. (Open daily 8am-1pm and 3-7pm.)

The city of **Scala** faces Ravello to the northwest, dominatng the coast 400m above sea-level. Take any of the buses from Amalfi (7am-9pm) or from Ravello (10:30am-9:30pm). The still air, the ebbing mist, and the glimmer of the sea behind the cliffs of Ravello below, make Scala's photogenic panorama the consummate Amalfi coast vision. Savor the views over a table at **Ristorante-Pizzeria Belvedere,** via V. D'Amata (tel. 85 73 96), in the Campidoglio area of Scala, 1km uphill from the bus stop. The huge plates of *pasta al sugo di pesce* (with fresh seafood, L7500) confirm that you are in heaven. (Cover L1500, service 10%. Open June-Sept. daily; Oct.-May Thurs.-Tues. noon-3pm and 7pm-midnight.)

Minori, a half-hour walk east of Ravello (or 1 stop by bus), houses an interesting first-century **Roman Villa** with a small antiquarium inside displaying pottery, ceramics, and tools dating from the first to third century C.E. (The villa is located below the Minori bus stop. Open daily 9am-sunset. Free.) The villa also contains an open-air theater that presents ballet, concerts, and theater in July, August, and the beginning of September. For information and a program contact the **Pro Loco,** p. Umberto, Minori (tel. (089) 87 76 07).

Toward Salerno you will pass **Maiori,** a modern beach city, and **Vietri sul Mare,** a simpler and older village with small, quiet beaches and pricey hotels. For a list of accommodations in Maiori contact the Azienda, via Lungomare, Maiori (tel. (089) 87 74 52). For information about Vietri sul Mare, contact the Pro Loco (tel. (089) 21 15 48).

Salerno

Home to Europe's first medical school, Salerno was the city where medieval patients received the latest drugs and surgical techniques. Today, no spoonful of sugar is needed to help down a dose of Amalfi coast beaches and inexpensive hotels. Salerno is still a university town and retains an intellectual snobbery that sets it apart. There isn't much to see in the city proper, but the extensive bus and train networks facilitate transit to all of the Amalfi coast and the archeological sites of Pompeii and Paestum.

Practical Information

EPT: p. Ferrovia (tel. 23 14 32), to the right as you leave the train station. Maps and pamphlets on the Amalfi coast. Excellent guide to Salerno's *alberghi* with map, bus schedule, and entertainment listings. The helpful employees speak English. Open Mon.-Sat. 8:30am-8:30pm.

Azienda Autonomia di Soggiorno e Turismo, p. Amendolo, 8 (tel. 22 47 44), by the water. West on corso Garibaldi from the train station for 1km until it becomes via Roma. Come here for the scoop on Salerno itself. Open Mon.-Sat. 9am-2pm and 5-8pm.

Post Office: corso Garibaldi, 203, at via dei Principati. Open Mon.-Sat. 8:30am-7:30pm. **Postal code:** 84100.

Telephones: SIP, corso Garibaldi, 31, set in from the street to the left as you leave the train station. Crowded in summer. Open daily 8am-9:30pm. **Telephone code:** 089.

Train Station: In p. Ferrovia (tel. 23 14 15), behind p. Vittorio Veneto. Salerno's 2 main streets, corso V. Emanuele and corso Garibaldi, lead west from the station toward the old part of town. Trains depart regularly 5am-11pm to Pompeii (40 min., L1500) and Naples (1 hr., L3200). Also several trains to Paestum on the Salerno-Reggio-Calabria line (45 min., L2000).

Buses: SITA buses (tel. 22 66 04) leave from outside the SITA information office at corso Garibaldi, 117. Information office open Mon.-Sat. 8am-1pm and 4:30pm-8pm. To Naples (6am-9pm every 10-15 min., L3000), Amalfi (6am-10:30pm every 20-60 min., L1500), and Sorrento (6am-7pm 9 buses per day, L3500) with stops at the Amalfi coastal towns of Praino (L2000) and Positano (L2500). Buses run less frequently on Sun. **ATAC** (tel. 22 58 99) city bus #4 leaves regularly from outside the train station to Pompeii (5:55am-9:55pm every 20 min. per day, L1500). Several bus lines run from p. Concordia, near the train station on the waterfront, to Paestum (direction "Sapri," L2000).

Police: Tel. 23 18 19. **Emergency:** Tel. 113.

Accommodations

For such a comfortable, well-situated city, Salerno is surprisingly short on hotels. The few existing establishments fill rapidly in late July and August, so arrive early in the morning to secure a place.

Ostello della Gioventù "Irno" (IYHF), lungomare Marconi, 34 (tel. 23 72 34), 1km south along the sea from the train station. Take bus #4, 6, or 8. Three unexciting 8-person rooms. Members only, L6000. Showers included. Lockout 9am-5pm. Curfew June-Sept. 11:30pm; Oct.-May 10:30pm.

Albergo Santa Rosa, corso V. Emanuele (tel. 22 53 46), off the *piazza* in front of the train station. Clean, bright, and a bargain. English spoken. Singles L17,500. Doubles L28,000. Triples L37,800. Showers included. Curfew midnight.

Albergo Cinzia, corso V. Emanuele, 74 (tel. 23 27 73), down the street from Santa Rosa. Pronounced "Chintzy-AH," and with good reason. The cheapest hotel in the city. Doubles L22,000.

Albergo Italia, corso V. Emanuele, 84 (tel. 22 66 53). Another cheap-o hotel. The rooms are as blah as the indifferent management. Singles L15,000. Doubles L25,000. Showers included.

Albergo Amorelli, via A. M. De Luca, 6 (tel. 23 14 13). Take corso V. Emanuele about 800m west from the train station to via De Luca, across from the Banca Commerciale D'Italia. Decent rooms. Singles L14,000. Doubles L22,000.

Food

Salerno lays claim to no particular dish, but emulates the culinary genius of the entire campania region, serving delightful specialties like *pasta e fagioli* (pasta and bean soup), and all sorts of seafood-based offerings such as the beloved *spaghetti alle vongole* (with clams).

Mensa Universitaria, via L. Cacciature, 27-37, north of the train station by the stadium. From corso V. Emanuele heading away from the train statin, take a right on via Diaz or via Papio to via Volpe, and turn right; via Volpe becomes via Nizza. When you arrive at the square by the stadium, turn right onto via Michele Conforti, then left. Show your student ID for large meals at only L3000. Open Sept.-July daily 12:15-2:45pm and 6:45-8:30pm.

Pizzeria del Vicolo della Neve, vicolo della Neve, 24 (tel. 42 57 05). Take the side street that intersects with via Roma before #160. In the old city, this piece of Salernitan history hasn't changed since it opened 500 years ago. Try their tasty traditional dishes like *baccalà in cassuola* (salted fish with tomatoes, oregano, and oil, L6000) or *giambotta* (a mix of potatoes, eggplant, and peppers, L4000). Cover L2000, service 12%. Open Thurs.-Tues. 8pm-3am.

Self-Service Papio, via Papio, 33. Take a right off corso V. Emanuele, about 450m away from the train station. Cafeteria-style dining with high-quality, made-to-order specialties. Menu changes daily, but you'll always have a choice of 3 pasta dishes (L2500) and 7 main courses (L4500). Wine L800 per glass. Open Mon.-Sat. noon-3:30pm.

Trattoria Rosalia, via degli Orti, 22 (tel. 22 96 71), off corso V. Emanuele after via Diaz. Delicious pasta. For L500, they will significantly increase the tonnage of your dish. Their specialty is seafood, so start with *spaghetti ai fruitti di mare* (with seafood, L5500). Other pastas L3000-4500. *Menù* with drink L12,000. Cover L1000, service 10%. Open Sept.-July Mon.-Sat. noon-4pm and 7pm-midnight.

La Trappola, via Roma, 170 (tel. 23 78 37), near the Azienda. The happy Neapolitan owner loves to ramble in broken English while he serves up huge plates of *penne alla trappola* (pasta with tomato, eggplant, basil, and cheese, L3500), and unfathomably inexpensive *polipi alla luciana* (octopus with tomato, garlic, parsley, and pepper, L3500). *Ravello vino* L3500 per bottle. Cover L1500, service 10%. Open Wed.-Mon. noon-3:30pm and 6:30pm-2am.

Sights

For Salerno's best view, walk along the city's lush, tree-lined waterfront promenade—the **Lungomare.** Taking via Molo Manfredi off of the Villa Comunale at the western end of via Roma, you can stroll onto the seawall that extends into the bay, from where you can revel in the splendorous Amalfi coast and the sights and sounds of the nearby fishing harbor. Unfortunately, Salerno's sea is filthy. To swim, go to the closest town on the Amalfi coast, the hamlet of **Vietri sul Mare** (take the SITA bus towards Sorrento; 15 min.), or to any of the coast's other towns.

For a more commanding view of Salerno's majestic vicinity, take bus #19 from Teatro Verdi, west of Villa Comunale, to the medieval **Castello di Arechi,** dating from the eighth century C.E. (Open daily 9am-1pm and 3-6pm. Free.) Back down at city level, visit Salerno's medieval quarter. Walk along corso V. Emanuele until it fades into narrow via dei Mercanti, literally "the street of shopkeepers." There are bargains to be found in the leather and antique stores. The medieval city was quite famous in its day, as capital of the Norman empire before Palermo (1077-1127) and home of Europe's oldest medical school. So old, in fact, was the medical school that codices dating from 846 C.E. were already calling it ancient. Watched over by a twelfth-century Norman tower, the **cathedral,** built between 1076 and 1085 by order of the Norman leader Robert Guiscard, is dedicated to Salerno's patron saint, San Matteo. An ancient pool lies in the center of its colorful atrium, complementing the Roman sarcophagi that were converted into medieval tombs. The bronze doors of the central portal (1099) lead inside, where the paschal (Easter) candelabra complement two splendid twelfth-century pulpits laden with mosaics. The revered tooth of San Matteo can be seen in a reliquary in the crypt. (Cathedral open daily 9:30am-12:30pm and 4-7pm.)

Entertainment

Salerno is an outdoors city, so don't miss the Sunday evening *passeggiata* when the *lungomare* swarms with people strolling, eating ice cream, and swinging on porch chairs. During June, July, and August, an **arts festival** is held, featuring free concerts and drama in the atrium of the cathedral and at the city's stadium. Salerno also hosts an **international film festival** in October at Cinema Capitol in the center of the city (tickets L6000).

The area around Salerno features some intense discos reminiscent of Tokyo. From June to September, the nighttime hotspot is the renowned **Fuenti** (tel. 21 09 33) in the small locality of Cetara, 4km west of Salerno. Uniquely situated on the coastal cliffs, it features three full floors of open-air dancing. (Open Sat.-Sun. 10pm-4am. Cover L15,000, 1st drink included.) In the winter, Salerno hops at **Living,** via Gelsi Rossi (tel. 39 92 01), just northeast of the train station in the city center. Huge video screens and blinking lights create funky images. (Open Oct.-May Thurs.-Fri. 8:30pm-2am, Sat. 9:30pm-3am, and Sun. 6:30pm-3am. Thurs.-Fri. free, Sat.-Sun. cover L13,000, 1st drink included.)

Paestum

Paestum's ruins bask in an open field amid flowers and wild grasses. Founded in the seventh century B.C.E. as Poseidonia by a group of Greek colonists from Sibari (near Crotona on the Ionian Sea), Paestum quickly became a flourishing commercial center enjoying an expansive trade with the Etruscans and the fecund lands to the north. Conquered in the fourth century B.C.E. by native Italians, it was revived under Roman rule with the addition of baths, forums, and amphitheaters. Decline began when completion of the Appian Way allowed Rome to bypass the Adriatic with trade routes that passed through the Tyrrhenian Sea. Recurrent malaria bouts and Saracen raids during the ninth century hastened the city's demise, leaving Paestum the ghost town it is today.

Visit the site early in the morning, when the stillness is broken only by an occasional passing car. Though the temples do not open until 9am, you can easily view them from behind the fence around the grounds. (Museum open Tues.-Sun. 9am-2pm. Temple grounds open daily until 2 hr. before sunset. Admission to both site and museum L3000.) Hotels and restaurants lie to the north and south of the site. It's most convenient, however, to stay in Salerno, which is only an hour away and is connected by frequent bus and train service. Buses on the Salerno-Sapri line leave from p. Concordia, near the Salerno train station, about every half-hour (1st bus leaves at 5:45am); trains run about every two hours. The last bus back to Salerno is at 8:10pm; the last train 9:30pm. Both bus and train cost about L2000. The best guidebook is Nunzio Daniele's *Paestum: Hypothesis and Reality.*

The three major temples lie along the ancient road called the **via Sacra.** The **basilica** (6th century B.C.E.) dedicated to Hera is thought to be the oldest temple in Paestum. Its archaic form indicates an early stage of aesthetic development: The temple is extremely wide (9 columns across—even the Parthenon is only 6), the tapering of its columns so extreme it creates a bulbous shape and makes the temple's outer colonnade seem to lean outward on both sides.

The neighboring **Temple of Neptune** (450 B.C.E.) is the largest, most intact Doric structure in the city. Its proportion of six columns by 14 columns creates a long, graceful shape. In contrast to the basilica, a slight upward curving of the temple floor corrects the optical illusion that the columns sag outwards. The basilica's inner room is divided into two narrow aisles by a single row of columns (3 of which still stand), while the Temple of Neptune has three aisles created by two rows of superimposed columns. Sit on the far wall of the basilica looking towards Neptune for a remarkable view of the forest of columns. In front of the temples are the remians of large altars, a large block of limestone in front of the basilica, and two basins (the small one Roman and the other Greek).

At the opposite end of the grounds, past the forum and amphitheater, is the small **Temple of Ceres** (*c.* 500 B.C.E.), whose Ionic capitals now stand in the museum. Sacrificial altars rest in front of the temple and to the right is a lone votive column.

The **museum** (tel. (0828) 81 10 23), outside the temple grounds on the other side of via Aquila, has a fascinating collection of sculpture, architectural fragments, terra-cottas, and unusual tomb paintings that come from Paestum and excavations in the nearby plain of Sele. Some highlights include the 34 metopes (6th century B.C.E.), which illustrate Greek myths, including those of Sisyphus and Heracles; the large bust of a fertility goddess; and architectural fragments of temple cornices still bearing traces of their original bright colors.

In July and August Paestum hosts an international festival of music, drama, and dance. For a program and information, write or visit the **Azienda di Turismo,** on via Aquila (tel. (0828) 81 10 16; open Mon.-Sat. 8am-2pm).

There is a popular beach in Paestum about 2km east of the temples that is much more inviting than the grimy sands of Salerno. There are several campsites on the beach. **FLIC** (tel. (0828) 81 12 91) offers spots with electricity and running water for L6250 (July-Aug. L10,800) plus L1400 per person (July-Aug. L3500). Nearby is **Mare Pineta** (tel. (0828) 81 10 86), which charges L7000 per tent (July-Aug. L9000) and L3500 per person (July-Aug. L4500). Both sites are open from June to September.

The best seashore on the coast is at **Palinuro,** about 60km south of Paestum and accessible by train from the nearby city of Pisciotta (on the Salerno-Reggio di Calabria line), from where you can take one of the frequent buses to the beach. Small Palinuro is big on reasonable accommodations and campsites. Contact the **EPT** in Salerno.

Apulia (Puglia)

Puglia has long been a place of beginnings and endings. The **Appian Way** terminated at the port of Brindisi, a perpetual point of cultural fusion. Carriages heavy with the region's wealth of wine, wheat, and olives rumbled to a halt there and loaded ships for export in the harbor, where they mingled with overseas vessels. Puglia's ports crackled with exchange of all sorts—cargo, crusaders, and conquerers. From the north came the Normans, from the south and east the Saracens, Greeks, and Byzantines. Throughout the area, whitewashed houses with rounded arches bespeak the influence of the East. Coastal towns from Vieste to Bari combine this soft domesticity with fanciful Norman castles and cathedrals: an architectural nexus of two worlds.

Puglia remains a gateway between two worlds, now northern Italians exploring the south, and vice versa though the split between the two territories narrows increasingly, many northerners consider Puglia and what lies below entirely foreign.

Puglia is as accessible to contemporary tourists as it was to ancient invaders. Direct rail lines run from Naples to Bari and from Bologna to Lecce. Although the sterility of Foggia and Brindisi in part justify the lack of a tourist deluge, the magnificent beaches, grottoes, cathedrals, and wilderness (especially of the Gargano) warrant wandering here.

Foggia

"Location, location, location"—the age-old real estate adage—applies well to Foggia. The city itself has little to offer other than a convenient siutation on two major rail lines: Bologna-Lecce and Naples-Bari. Foggia is thus an excellent base for exploring Gangano and northern Puglia, and for daytrips to the medieval towns of Lucera and Troia.

Practical Information

EPT: via Emilio Perrone, 17 (tel. 236 50), inconveniently located off p. Puglia. From the station, follow viale XXIV Maggio past p. Cavour, then take the 3rd left on via D. Cirillo to via Bari. Or take bus MD. Genial. Almost no information about Foggia; instead, information on the Tremiti Islands, Vieste, and Gargano. Open Mon.-Sat. 8am-2pm.

Post Office: viale XXIV Maggio, 30 (tel. 240 01), about 3 blocks straight from the station. Open Mon.-Fri. 8:15am-2pm, Sat. 8:15am-noon. **Postal code:** 71100.

Telephones: (SIP), via Conte Appiano, 14-18, near p. Cavour. Open daily 8am-9pm. At other times, try **Hotel Europa,** via Monfalcone, 52. **Telephone code:** 0881.

Buses: SITA, p. V. Veneto, in front of the train station. To Vieste (4 per day, 3 hr., L5500) and Monte Sant'Angelo (every 2 hr., 1½ hr., L3400). **ATAF** to Troia (every ½-hr., 45 min., L1900). **Ferrovie dello Stato** to Lucera (every hr., 30 min., L1700).

Accommodations

Foggia has not been tempered for tourism, but finding an inexpensive room shoudln't be difficult. Most of the cheaper *pensioni* are conveniently located near the station, particularly on **via Monfalcone,** 2 blocks up from p. Veneto, perpendicular to viale XXIV Maggio.

Albergo Centrale, corso Cairoli, 5 (tel. 718 62). From the station, follow viale XXIV Maggio to p. Cavour, then turn right on via Lanza to corso Cairoli, which branches off to the left. From the entrance, this place looks like it's either coming up or going down. Rooms tidy, sheets wonderfully fresh, and bath capacious. Singles L15,000. Doubles L30,000.

Hotel Bologna, via Monfalcone, 53 (tel. 213 41). Standard rooms with showers. Singles L15,000. Doubles L30,000.

Hotel Asi, via Monfalcone, 1 (tel. 233 27). Large and decent, with red-carpet hotel reception. Singles L20,000, with bath L23,000. Doubles L38,000, with bath L43,000.

Albergo Venezia, via Piave, 40 (tel. 709 03), 1 block past via Monfalcone, off viale XXIV Maggio. Somewhat unkept. Singles with bath L20,000. Doubles L26,000, with bath L34,000.

Food

Trattoria Santa Lucia, via Trieste, 57, 1 block from Hotel Bologna. Loving service and delicious meals. *Pasto completo* includes *primo, secondo,* beverage, fruit, vegetable, cover, and service (L13,500). Try the *troccoli,* homemade pasta, or *spaghetti alla sfiziosa.* Open Mon.-Sat. noon-3:30pm and 6:30-11pm.

Sorrento Cucina Casalinga, via Trieste, 37, near the Santa Lucia. A great little find. *Menù* L10,000. Try *pasta e ceci* and *frittura di pesce.* Open Sun.-Fri. noon-4pm and 7-10pm.

Ristorante del Cacciatore, via Pietro Mascagni, 12, off the end of corso V. Emanuele. Delicious homemade *tagliatelle verdi* (spinach noodles) L5000. Most main dishes L8500-9500. *Menù* L14,000, including L1500 cover and 10% service. Open Mon.-Sat. noon-3pm and 7:30-10pm.

Ristorante Ton Fen, via Piave, 60, off viale XXIV Muggio. An elegant Chinese restaurant lacking only fortune cookies. Entrees L5000. Open daily noon-11pm.

Sights

The historic interest in Foggia is the **cathedral,** now embellished by an overscaled baroque tower dating from 1731. Bombardment during World War II revealed an interesting Pisan-style arcade along the church's lower flanks, which probably dates from a fourteenth-century restoration. The church, originally constructed in 1155, retains its original Romanesque crypt supported by short columns with delicately decorated capitals. From p. Cavour, take a right onto via Lanza then another right at p. Umberto Giordano onto corso V. Emanuele. The open *loggia* at p. de Sanctis, 88, across from the cathedral, and a few remaining pilasters on nearby via Arpi are all that's left of the Renaissance city.

Foggia's ancient past is well documented at the newly renovated **Civic Museum,** off the end of via Zara on via della Repubblica. Here, vases, ceramics, figurines, and coins are displayed from the two nearby archeological sites of Arpi and Sipontum. On the outside walls of the museum are three curious arches: one a Romanesque doorway with carved eagles from the thirteenth-century palace of Frederick II; another a rebuilt Renaissance arch from a nearby *palazzo* destroyed during the war; and the center arch, a piece of medieval city wall. (Open Mon.-Tues. and Thurs.-Sat. 9am-1pm, Wed. 9am-1pm and 5-7pm.) Take a detour to the left on via San Eligio to the unusual baroque **Church of Calvary** (1693), set in a mall behind five little domed structures and seen through a baroque gateway.

Near Foggia: Lucera

Thirty minutes from Foggia, **Lucera** is located on a high plateau, and its enormous castle dominates the region for miles. The old city, with its courtyards, narrow dusty streets, and Byzantine arches, reverberates with past Arab hegemony in the region.

The **cathedral,** one of the great architectural creations of medieval Puglia, was erected by Charles II of Anjou in the late 1300s. The facade is spartan, with two antique marble columns supporting a Gothic canopy. This church is best seen from behind, where the jagged planar surfaces of the nave and the polygonal belfry create a stark cubist effect. Stand in p. Salandra for the full impact. If you're interested in pursuing the Lombard-French style further, inspect the nearby fourteenth-century **Church of San Francesco,** which houses fine Gothic and baroque frescoes. (Both cathedral and church open daily 8am-noon and 5-8pm.)

Behind the cathedral is the **Civic Museum.** A guide will whisk you through Roman coins, Arab pottery, antique marble, relics from the reign of Roman Emperor Frederick II (1220-1250), the *Marine Venus* (a Roman copy of a Greek statue), a beautiful Roman mosaic, and other artifacts excavated in Lucera. (Open May-Sept. Mon. and Wed.-Thurs. 9am-2pm, Tues. and Fri. 9am-2pm and 5-7pm, Sat.-Sun. 9am-1pm; Oct.-April Mon.-Fri. 9am-2pm and 4-6pm, Sat.-Sun. 9am-1pm. Admission L1000.) The medieval ***castello*** (castle), built by Frederick II in 1230, is roughly pentagonal. The complex is more than 1km in circumference and is topped with 24 towers, almost all impressively intact. The castle commands a fine view of the fertile plain below, known as the Tavoliere (chessboard). (Castle open Tues.-Sun. same hours as museum. Free.)

The **Anfiteatro Romano,** dating back to the first century B.C.E., sits at the foot of the hills in the eastern end of the city. Its terraced stands, now covered with underbrush, were dug like rice paddies into the hillside.

Of the two hotels in Lucera, the better is **Albergo Al Passetto,** p. del Popolo, 28 (tel. 94 11 24), a pleasant place built into the old city wall. (Singles L20,000. Doubles L35,000. Bath included.) This hotel also serves adequate meals from L11,000. Slightly more expensive is **Hotel Gioia,** nearby at viale Ferrovia, 15 (tel. 94 52 07; singles L24,000, doubles with bath L45,000). This establishment also houses an eatery, with full meals about L17,000. (Open daily in summer.) On the way to the castle, you can stop at the **Bar Monaco,** via Federico, 24, for a *semifreddi* (homemade ice cream dipped in chocolate, L1200) or a giant *cassata* (L3300).

Gargano

After the flatness of the Foggia plain, the varied beauty of the **Gargano Massif** comes as a pleasant surprise. The southern half is barren and rocky, its isolation broken by an occasional hill town. Farther inland, at an elevation of 800m, is the Foresta Umbra, a dense patch of giant beech and oak trees. On the northern coast is a 65-kilometer-long beach. Dunes enclose two lakes from which a flat, fertile plain extends away from the water to the base of limestone cliffs. Sea pines and small picturesque villages hidden on rocky shores decorate the eastern coast.

Gargano was once a large island off the coast. Over thousands of years, the sediment from its river built a land bridge to the mainland. Gargano is still in some ways a world unto itself, where old men riding sidesaddle on donkeys watch youngsters speed by on scooters, and where the Italian sounds more like Greek.

Not very interesting itself, **Manfredonia** serves as a good base for exploring the southern coast and the interior of the promontory. The town's main diversion is a popular mile-long sandy strand. At one end is Manfredonia's industrial sector, which includes a riveting shipbuilding trade. From Foggia, you can reach Manfredonia either by taking a **SITA** bus, which leaves every 2 hours until 5:25pm, or by hopping on one of the many **Ferrovie Dello Stato** trains. The **tourist office,** via Manfredi, 26 (tel. 219 98), off p. Marconi, offers up-to-date bus and boat information. Walk to the right from the train station on viale Aldo Moro (10 min.). (Open Mon.-Sat. 8am-2pm.)

Albergo San Michele, via degli Orti, 10 (tel. (0884) 219 53), off p. Marconi, has pleasant singles for L16,000 and doubles for L25,000. Next door, **Albergo Santa Maria** (tel. 224 65) offers spotless and antiseptic green singles for L15,000, doubles L30,000. **Albergo Santa Maria delle Grazie,** p. Salvo Nacquisto, 5 (tel. (0884) 224 65), offers dingier rooms without bath. (Singles L18,000. Doubles L25,000.) **Trattoria Dallo Scellerato,** via Palatella, 3/5, one street past via degli Orti, serves filling meals for about L8,000 (service 10%).

Three kilometers southwest of Manfredonia is **Siponto,** a city of ancient origin that was abandoned after a twelfth-century earthquake and plague. The sole survivor is the remarkable **Church of Santa Maria di Siponto,** which stands alone in a grove of pines amidst small pre-Roman ruins. Built during the eleventh century in Puglian-Romanesque style, the church's blind arcade shows strong Pisan influence, while the square plan and cupola show the church's Byzantine inspiration. Siponto is the next-to-last stop on the Foggia-Manfredonia train line.

The most impressive town in the Gargano interior is **Monte Sant'Angelo,** northeast of Manfredonia, which glances down at land and sea from a narrow, 240-meter-high precipice. Monte Sant'Angelo is an ancient town where folk dressed in black climb narrow alleyways lined with whitewashed houses. Long strings of garlic hang against doors where eyelet curtains flutter in the sunlight. In the evening, old women sell fresh oregano and chick peas on streets that only a few hours earlier entertained only the church bells. The town is most famous for its **Santuario di San Michele** (Saint Michael's Sanctuary), an important pilgrimage site in Italy. The sanctuary is built over the caverns where, according to tradition, the archangel Michael left his red cloak after appearing to some shepherds. Down a few flights of steps, the **grotto** is entered through handsome eleventh-century bronze doors wrought with scenes from the Old and New Testaments. Inside, a Gothic vestibule (1273) opens into a dripping cavern. Over the high altar a life-size alabaster statue of San Michele (16th century) lies encased in a silver-plated box. Behind the altar, covered by a wooden canopy and supported by four antique columns, is a small fountain (actually an opening in the rocks) said to have miraculous powers at certain times of the day. (Open daily 8am-noon and 3-8pm.)

Directly across from the upper entrance of San Michele is the **Tomba di Rotari** (Tomb of Rotharis), actually a twelfth- or thirteenth-century baptistery next to the ruined church of San Pietro. Look for the charming relief of the Passion above the doorway; the capitals inside are sculpted with biblical scenes.

The desolate ruins of the **Norman castle** retain powerfully fortified walls that offer a fine view of the countryside and town. Walk down via Verdi past the stone church and tower of San Benedetto—the road leads to a lookout (2nd right after the Municipio) with a panoramic vista of Manfredonia and the sea. Most Manefredonians, however, concern themselves more with the soccer stadium next door.

The only place to stay in Manefredonia is **Albergo Moderno** (tel. 613 31), where homey singles go for L12,000, doubles L24,000. **SITA** buses leave Foggia about every two hours for Manfredonia, whence you can take the bus to Monte Sant'Angelo (½ hr., L1100). Three buses per day (Mon.-Sat.) run directly from Foggia to Monte Sant'Angelo (1½ hr.).

Farther north is the beautiful **Foresta Umbra** (Shady Forest). The forest, comprised mainly of beech, pine, and oak, is extraordinarily peaceful (except on Sun., when it becomes a picnic area for Foggian families on their weekend outing). Where the roads from Monte Sant'Angelo, Vieste, and Vico del Gargano intersect in the center of the forest, there is a small lake, a deer preserve, and an information office. The most accessible hikes begin within the first kilometer on the road to Vieste and last about two hours. Unfortunately, the isolated Foresta Umbra is difficult to reach by public transport. **SITA** buses leave Monte Sant'Angelo daily at 1:10pm and take one hour to reach the intersection in the middle of the forest on their way to Vico del Gargano near the northern coast 40km away. For information, call the **Centro Visitatori** in Monte Sant' Angelo (tel. 637 83). Problem: The bus that brings you here won't take you back. Hitching in this area is slow, but dependable; the Vico-Monte Sant' Angelo road is busy enough, but the road to Vieste (30km away) has traffic only on Sundays, the worst day to visit the forest since it is packed with tourists.

Vieste

Vieste sits on the tip of a sun-burnt Roman nose called the Gargano promontory. Protruding nosily into the calm Adriatic, this charming town captures the hearts of (too) many Italians and Germans every summer. What makes Vieste more than just a pretty patch of sun and sand is its situation on the peninsula. It rises in a cluster of whitewashed houses alongside terraced stairways. Below are inlets and coves and infinite stretches of silken beach. The town meets its yearly invasion with a spread of hotels and campsites. Luckily, these provisions are removed from the strand and thus are not intrusive.

Along with Peschici (23km northwest), Vieste is the most convenient base for exploring Gargano's spectacular coastline, or for making a daytrip to the Tremiti Islands.

Orientation and Practical Information

There are two ways of getting to Vieste, both remarkably picturesque. If you are coming from the north on the Bologna-Lecce line, get off at San Severo, where you can catch the Ferrovie del Gargano **train** to Peschici; a bus continues to Vieste (whole trip 3 hr.). A direct Ferrovie del Gargano **bus** from San Severo to Vieste leaves daily at 12:15pm (3½ hr.). **SITA** buses (6 per day) run from the south to Vieste on a twisting, bone-jarring road from Foggia via Manfredonia (3 hr., L5600).

Azienda di Turismo: p. V. Emanuele II, 1 (tel. 788 06). From the bus stop, walk up viale XXIV Maggio, which becomes corso L. Fazzini, to p. V. Emanuele II. Ask directions frequently, as the signs are misleading. English spoken and affable. Decent map of the city. Open Mon.-Sat. 8am-8pm.

Post Office: via V. Veneto, next to the public gardens. Open Mon.-Fri. 8:15am-6:40pm, Sat. 8:15am-12:20pm. **Postal code:** 71019.

Telephone Code: 0884.

Buses: Schedules are posted outside the town hall (*municipio*). **Ferrovia del Gargano,** Tel. (0882) 214 15. **SITA,** Tel. (0881) 731 17.

Ferries: To the Tremiti Islands daily. **Adriatica's** ferry *Daunia* stops in Vieste at 10:05am on the way to the islands (3 hr. 20 min., L10,000). **Faraglione** leaves directly from the port at 9:15am (2 hr., L15,000). Tickets for both lines must be purchased in advance at **Gargano Viaggi,** p. Roma, 7 (tel. 785 01), off corso L. Fazzini. (Open July-Aug. Mon.-Sat. 9am-lpm and 5-8pm; in off-season Mon.-Sat. only.)

Bike/Moped Rental: Calabrese Noleggio, viale XXIV Maggio, 23 (tel. 782 05). Bicycles L9000 per 4 hr. Tandems L17,000 per day. Mopeds L27,000 per day. Open daily 8:30am-1:30pm and 3-9pm.

Foreign Newspapers: Across from the post office on via V. Veneto.

Police: Carabinieri, Tel. 750 10.

Accommodations

Vieste is a summer resort without budget provisions. If you plan to visit between mid-July and August, be sure to make reservations and refuel your lire-pouch.

Albergo Riviera, via IV Novembre, 2 (tel. 750 00), just off via V. Veneto. Fastidiously kept and airy. Singles L20,000. Doubles L35,000.

Albergo Lido, via Pellico, 1 (tel. 767 09). Head for the beach from the bus station and you will soon see signs. Modern and comfortable. Doubles L54,000. Aug. 29-July 14 small but cozy singles L22,000; doubles L34,000. All rooms with showers.

Pensione San Giorgio, via Madonna della Libera (tel. 786 18), 3 blocks before via Pellico. In June tidy, contemporary doubles L32,000, singles L25,000. Full pension in July L50,000, Aug. L60,000, and Sept. L45,000. In off-season prices lower. All rooms with showers.

Pensione Giacla, on Lungomare Europa north beach (tel. 765 93). Commodious doubles with bath and balcony L45,000, in off-season L35,000.

Camping: More than 80 campsites line the beaches north and south of the city. **Apeneste,** in town on the southern beach, is off lungomare E. Mattei. L4500 per person, L4000 per small tent, 14,800 per large tent; July-Aug. 20 L5000 per person, L4500 per small tent, L5300 per large tent. Open June-Sept. The next site on this beach is **Lunik** (tel. 774 59). Set among olive trees behind a restaurant, this is a cozy, family-run establishment. The owner learned his English as a prisoner of war in England. L6000 per person, L1000 per tent. **Casablanca** is next. Primitive and a bit grimy, but small and secluded. L5000 per person, L3000 per tent. Tent rental L7000. **Arcobaleno** (tel. 775 45), 2km down lungomare E. Mattei, also on the southern beach has a tennis court and private beach. L3500 per person, L8000 per tent; July L3,500 per person, L800 per tent; and Aug. 1-20 L5500 per person, L10,000 per tent. On the northern beach, 1km from town is camping **Baia degli Aranci** (tel. 765 91), on lungomare Europa. A large site set in pine trees and orange and olive groves. L3800 per person, L6400 per tent; July 11-Aug. 22 L5800 per person, L9100 per tent.

Food

Wander around the old town, where basements and stuccoed corners hide restaurants. There are large produce and wine markets by the bus station and across town by the water. At night the candy vendors sell fare that will give you cavities with just a glance.

Ristorante Padre Pio, via Santa Denittis, 7 (tel. 689 40), off via Naccarti on the waterfront. One of the most reasonably-priced sit-down places in Vieste. Pasta dishes about L5000, meats L7000. Local wine L3000 per liter. Cover L1500, service 10%. Open daily noon-4pm and 6-11:30pm.

Ristorante Bella Napoli, via Naccarati, 31 (tel. 771 33), between the promontories on the water. Stellar pizzas L2500-5000, served only at night. *Spaghetti alle aglio, olio, e pepperoncino* L3200, *Piatto di cozze* (mussels) L5000. Wine L3000 per liter. Cover L500. Open daily noon-2:30pm and 6pm-midnight.

Ristorante Box 19, via S. Maria di Merino, 19 (tel. 752 29), off corso L. Fazzini, near lungomare Europa. The town favorite. All pasta dishes L4000-5000. Try the *melanzane ripieni* (stuffed eggplant) L6500. Wine L3000 per liter. Open daily noon-3:30pm and 7pm-midnight.

Pizzeria, via Gorizia, 5, off via Merino. Pizza baked in sheets. Fight your way past the eager beavers for a huge piece of *pizza alla Viestana* or *pizza di patate* (potato pizza). Open daily 5:30pm-midnight.

Tavola Calda Mambo, corso Fazzini, 25, near the water. Bourgeois at its best: high-class food at low-class prices. *Orechiette al forno* (with sauce of eggplant, tomato, basil, and cheese) L4000, *pesce misto* (mixed fish) L6000. Local wine L2000 per liter. Open May-Sept. Tues.-Sun. 10am-midnight.

Sights and Entertainment

In southern Vieste at the end of via G. Battisti, you'll find the well-preserved old town. The *castello* (castle) rises from its summit and offers a tremendous view of the *costa garganica.* Nearby is the ***duomo,*** notable for its ancient pillars and sensitive restoration. The massive flow of people of Vieste's popular *passeggiata* concentrates around the **Giardini Pubblici V. Veneto** (also called Villa Comunale) and **corso Lorenzo Fazzini.** Stop by Bar Pierrot on via V. Venetto. Two rotund men play traditional music outside. The best **shopping** at night is on corso Fazzini, where dozens of stands sell all kinds of jewelry, leather goods, and even Peruvian ceramics. Of Vieste's three splendid **beaches,** the southern beach parallel to lungomare E. Mattei is the nicest. A few spots on the coastline are owned by big hotels, but there's always enough space for everyone. Throughout this area, the water is gorgeous and so pellucid the sandy bottom can be seen hundreds of feet out. You can also join the locals who dive off the rocks at the end of Vieste's two promontories.

From Vieste, there is a 2½-hour motorboat excursion to the local **grottoes,** and especially to the intriguing **Grotta Campana** (Bell Grotto). This is the best way to see the famed Gargano coastline. Boats depart in summer daily at 8:30am definitely, 2:30pm if enough people show (L12,000, ages under 12 L6000).

Near Vieste

Along the coast north of Vieste **Peschici,** an old city with labyrinthine streets, and **Rodi Garganico,** a seaside resort with ferries to the Tremiti Islands. South of Vieste are **Pugnochiuso** and **Mattinata,** a city known as the "white butterfly" for its unique shape and coloring. You may want to stay in **Peschici,** where the pace is somewhat slower and the prices lower than in Vieste. The village is perched on a hill overlooking a gorgeous bay. **Pensione Graziella,** corso Garibaldi (tel. 940 33), offers full pension for L42,000, but is booked solid during July and August. Doubles without pension cost L25,000 but are not available in July and August. From Peschici, you can hike or hitch east to any one of the luxurious coves lying between San Nicola and Vieste.

Tremiti Islands (Isole Tremiti)

Where the Adriatic is murky, these islets transform it to a crystaline green, where the water lies in monotonous lines, these islands channel it into inviting coves. And ancient monasteries make the islands interesting even apart from the sun and surf opportunities. Because many a foot lands on their shores, however, services on the Tremitis cost an arm and a leg (ones you may have just tanned). Bring your own provisions and a sleep sack. Because of their proximity to the mainland, they are easily enjoyed as daytrips from Vieste, Termoli, or several other points. From June 13 to September 13, **ferries** run from Termoli. (Daily at 9am, L6000; at 11am and 6pm, L6700. Boats return at 5:30pm.) From June 1 to September 13, ferries also run from Manfredonia (daily at 8am, L15,400), Vieste (daily at 10:05am, L10,600), Peschici (daily at 11:10am, L7200), and Rodi Garganico (daily at 11:55am, L5800). Ferries from Manfredonia, Vieste, Peschici, and Rodi Garganico arrive at 1:25pm, and from Termoli at 10:45am. Ferries run less frequently during other times of the year (April 14-May 16 and Sept. 15-29). **Hydrofoils** also link some of these cities with the islands (Peschici, Rodi Garganico, and Termoli), but are more expensive (from Peschici L13,700, from Rodi Garganico L11,400, from Termoli L13,100). Hydrofoils also link Ortona and Vasto daily with the islets (May 30-July 3 and Aug. 31-Sept. 27 Ortona at 8am and Vasto at 9am; July 4-Aug. 30 Ortona at 7:30am and Vasto at 8am; L13,000 from Ortona, L9,200 from Vasto). **San Lucia Lines** runs the cheapest boats from Termoli. They are located on the port Bar del Porto 2707 (tel. 48 59). For more comprehensive but expensive service, contact **Adriatica/Intercontinental Navigazione** in Manfredonia at Ditta Antonio Galli e Figlio, corso Manfredi, 4-6 (tel. (0884) 228 88); in Vieste at Gargano Viaggi, p. Roma, 7 (tel. (0884) 785 01); in Termoli at Intercontinental, corso Umberto I, 93 (tel. (0875) 24 29); in Peschici at Elvira Massa, corso Garibaldi, 49 (tel. (0884) 940 74); in Rodi

Garganico at Soc. Fratelli Delle Fave de' Manonghia, via Trieste, 6 (tel. (0884) 950 31); and in Vasto at Massacesi, p. Diomede, 3 (tel. (0873) 51 61 80).

All boats will deposit you at the port of **San Nicola,** one of the 3 main islands, where you will immediately be assailed by a loudspeaker announcing departures for boat tours of the isle San Domino and its grottoes. The excursion is nothing spectacular and barely worth the L9000. You can deposit bags at the port (L1500) while you explore. Climb up the ancient ramp behind the port on San Nicola and enter the fifteenth-century *castello,* notable for its panoramic view. The **Church of Santa Maria** is so ancient it was *rebuilt* in 1045. Originally part of a ninth-century abbey, the structure incorporates details from almost every architectural period through the Renaissance, and the interior houses a fine eleventh-century mosaic floor. The whole complex, however, appears to be in a state of perpetual repair. San Nicola's shoreline is rocky, making swimming difficult. If you're somewhat adventurous, however, you can take the little trail to the left-hand side of the port as you face the sea. This path brings you to some rocks (rarely frequented by tourists), where nude bathing is common.

San Domino, the largest of the Tremitis, is accessible by boat from San Nicola (L1500). The island has small sandy beaches, plus a host of restaurants and accommodations. To reach the bathing paradise along the island's eastern coast, follow the signs off the main road to town to "Villagio Internazionale." This will lead you to the northern tip of the island, where you can head south until you find a *cala* (cove) you like. Alternatively, follow the step path to the left of the port. If you keep bearing left on paths through the pines, you'll come upon some rocky paths to the sea and sand.

Pitching tents is strictly forbidden on all the islands, but **Punta del Diamante** (tel. (0882) 66 30 34), on San Domino, rents prefabricated aluminum tents (L20,000-44,000 per person, breakfast included). Because pines blanket the island, it is possible to find a clearing for a sleep sack on the sly. A pair of affordable *pensioni* sits atop the hill across from **Bar Diomede.** This excellent place overlooks the sea in one of the classier parts of Tremiti. **Pensione Giovanna** (tel. 66 32 13) offers doubles with bath and balcony for L40,000. If you're alone and there's a vacancy, the accommodating proprietress will give you the room for L20,000. Next door and almost identical is **Pensione La Bussola.** To get here from the port, follow the gnarly knoll to the left and hook left at the Hotel Paradiso. Most other accommodations require full pension in summer. **Pensione Rosanna** (tel. 66 30 37), up the steep hill to the left of the port, requires full pension only from July 1 through August. (L60,000 in July, L65,000 in Aug.) The rest of the year, singles are L22,000-25,000 and doubles L38,000-40,000. (Open April-Sept.) **Albergo Villa Olimpia** (tel. (0882) 66 30 46), to the left on the way to the island's center, offers singles for L27,000-33,000 and doubles L48,000-50,000, both without bath (full pension L58,000). **La Nassa** (tel. 66 30 75), in the center of town, charges L20,000 per person (July 10-Aug. obligatory full pension L57,000). *Affittacamere,* private rooms rented out to visitors in summer, have private bathrooms (L20,000-25,000 per person). Needless to say, you should reserve early. All supplies must be brought in by ship, so restaurants serve up enormous bills. Bring your own provisions and save, or go to one of the *alimentari* in the center. Even these are expensive, however. **Da Michele** will make you a huge sandwich for L2400. (Open 8am-7pm.) The **telephone code** on San Domino is 0882.

Bari

Bari has a facade and a flip-side. On the exterior, the city is the proud capital of Puglia, the seat of its largest university, and the center for theater and art. It is typified by the broad expanse of corso Cavour, where people peruse the posh shops of the most modern Puglian city. The other Bari is a poverty-stricken old city where drying clothes flutter over narrow alleys and public fountains are used as showers. To see the sites and wring from Bari all that it has to offer, you'll encounter both.

Orientation and Practical Information

Bari lies on rail lines from Rome (3 per day, 8 hr., L24,500, last at 10pm) and Milan (11 per day, 13 hr., L41,000, last at 11pm). Trains connect Bari with all of Puglia's larger towns: Foggia (1½ hr., L6400), Taranto (2 hr., L7100), Brindisi (2 hr., L5900), and Lecce (2½ hr., L7300). The station also maintains the **Ferrovie del Sud-Est** (to Castellana Grotte, Alberobello, and Martina Franca), on the last track of the central station, and the **Bari-Nord** (to Bitonto and Barletta) and the **Ferrovie Calabro-Lucane** (to Matera in Basilicata), both on the western side of the square.

Bari is Italy's principal embarkation point for **ferries** to Yugoslavia and sends several boats per week to Greece from June through September. **Adriatica,** c/o Agestea s.r.l. Agenzia Marittima, via Roberto da Bari, 133 (tel. (080) 33 03 60; box #6 at the port), serves Dubrovnik (May 30-Oct. 11 Mon.-Fri. daily; in off-season 3 per month; 8 hr.; L45,000, July-Aug. L63,000), Split (Jan. 5-May 25 and Oct. 5-Dec. 25, 3 per month, 10 hr., L51,000), and Zadar (May 30-Oct. 11, every Sun.; 22 hr.; L55,000, July-Aug. L78,000). Greece is served by **Ventouris Ferries,** c/o Pan Travel, via XXIV Maggio, 40 (tel. (080) 21 05 04; box #9-10 at the port), which runs 2 to 3 times per week April 15 to October 30. Ferries run to Corfu and Igoumenitsa (11-12½ hr.; L55,000, students L45,000; high season L65,000, students L55,000). **Eurail** and **InterRail** holders are eligible for a 30% discount. These ferries continue to Patras, charging an extra L5000.

Important: You must check in at the Stazione Marittima 2 hours before departure time.

EPT: p. Aldo Moro, 33A (tel. 22 53 27), to the right as you leave the station. Maps of Puglia, including individual maps of Bari, Taranto, Foggia, Brindisi, and Lecce. The young woman speaks perfect English and is eager to help. Open Mon.-Fri. 8:30am-1pm and 4:30-7:30pm, Sat. 9-11am.

CTS: via Dante, 111 (tel. 23 27 16). From the station, walk 1 block past p. Umberto and to the left. Information on student discount travel. Open Mon.-Fri. 9:30am-1pm and 4:30-7pm, Sat 9:30am-1pm.

Transalpino tickets: Il Baricentro, corso Cavour, 48 (tel. 54 42 92), near Teatro Petruzzelli. Open Mon.-Fri. 9am-1pm and 4-8pm, Sat. 9am-1pm.

Currency Exchange: At the Information Desk at the F.S. **train station** when banks are closed. Also at the **Automobile Club Italiano** at the ferry terminal, but only when boats are arriving or departing.

Post Office: p. Battisti, behind the university. From p. Umberto, take a left on via Crisanzio, then the 1st right on via Cairoli. Open Mon.-Fri. 8:20am-8:30pm, Sat. 8:20am-1pm. **Postal code:** 70100.

Telephones: SIP, via Oriani, near the *castello.* Open daily 8am-9pm. **ASST,** outside the station. Open daily 7am-10pm. ASST is better for international calls. **Telephone Code:** 080.

Laundromat: Lavanderia Americana, via Cardassi, 39, off corso Cavour. Token-operated. L11,000 per load. No dryers. Water supply most reliable in the morning. Open Mon.-Fri. 9am-1pm and 5:30-8pm, Sat.9am-1pm.

Pharmacy: Lojacando, corso Cavour, 47 (tel. 21 26 15). Open daily 5pm-1pm.

Medical Emergency: Ospedale Regionale Consorziale, via Dalmazia (tel. 22 15 14).

Police Carabinieri, Tel. 33 05 33.

Accommodations

Finding an inexpensive room in Bari is like pulling teeth, since many *pensioni* have their mouths full with *strattati,* homeless dependents of the state. Ask the EPT to check around for you. Though the following locations are not intimidating by day, they can be unnerving at night. Lone women, in particular, may have trouble finding a comfortable sleep.

Ostello del Levante (IYHF), via Nicola Massaro, 33 (tel. 32 02 82), inconveniently located in Palese Marina. Take bus #1 from the Teatro Petruzzelli on corso Cavour (5:30am-11pm every 20 min., 40 min., L600). Follow the hostel sign on strada Fontanelle to the sea. Filled with down-and-outers and gruesome mosquitoes. The "soup kitchen" serves overpriced lunch and dinner (L8000). L8500, nonmembers L11,000. Breakfast included. Open 7-9am and 6-11:30pm. IYHF cards sold (L20,000).

Pensione Darinka, via Calefati, 15A, off corso Cavour. From p. Umberto, walk down via Fargiro and turn right. Safe and pleasant. Doubles L28,000, but the proprietress will let them as singles for L25,000.

Del Corso, corso V. Emanuele, 30 (tel. 21 61 00). Walk down via Sparano from p. Umberto, and turn left on corso V. Emanuele. The lighted streets make for a relatively safe walk home at night. Clean and capacious. Doubles L30,000.

Allogio Redentore, via Crisanzio, 135 (tel. 23 79 38), off p. Umberto. A gloomy entrance hall, but the rooms are well kept. Lots of commotion and noise. Singles L20,000. Doubles L30,000.

Pensione Romeo, via Crisanzio, 12 (tel. 23 72 63), near p. Umberto, a short walk from the train station. Be aware that the prices here differ from those the EPT quotes. Singles L25,000. Doubles L30,000, with bath L48,000. Showers included. In the same building **Pensione Giulia** (tel. 21 66 30) offers singles for L22,000. Doubles L35,000, with bath L45,000. Showers included. Both have tidy pads. Some are windowless; you will be told this keeps out the hot sun.

Locanda Florini, via Imbriani, 69. Make a right on via Dante Alighieri and keep going. Small rooms. Dark building. Singles L11,000. Doubles L22,000. Showers L3000. Poor water supply. If the proprietress has no vacancy, she may send you upstairs to **Pensione Serene.** Siren would be a more appropriate name, given the noise. Nicer rooms than Florini's, but some have no windows. Singles L15,000. Doubles L30,000.

Food

Near both the sea and rich grazing land, Bari's dishes consist primarily of seafood and lamb (*agnello*). Many pasta dishes are accompanied by zesty seafood sauces such as *ciambotto,* made of fish, olive oil, onions, and tomatoes. Another local specialty is *agnello alla squero,* lamb cooked on a spit. Ricotta cheese, made with sheep's milk, is Bari's Kraft. *Tielle di cozze,* mussels in layers of rice, cheese, onions, and potatoes, is a remnant of Spain's seventeenth-century domination of the region.

Vini e Cucina, strada Vallisa, 23, in the old city. Follow corso Cavour to p. del Ferrarese. Looks like a dungeon, but a charming one at that. Try to make it for lunch when locals crowd in. Full meals with house wine L8500. Open Mon.-Sat. noon-3pm and 6-10pm.

Osteria delle Travi, largo Chiurlia, 12, at the end of via Sparano. Turn left through the arches at the entrance to the old city. Regional specialties galore. Full meals only L9000. The *orechiette con Braciola* is homemade pasta with horsemeat (sorry, Mr. Ed, but it's actually quite good). Try *braciola* (filet of horsemeat) for a *secondo.* By far the most popular joint in town. Open Tues.-Sun. 12:30-3pm and 7-10:30pm.

Zio Matteo, via Carulli, 87. From p. Umberto, follow via Carulli 800m toward the water. Full meals (antipasto through fruit) L11,000, prosciutto and mozzarella antipasto only L1000, pasta L2800-3000, meat and fish L3000-3500, wine L800 per ½-liter. Cover L1000, service included. Open Mon.-Sat. noon-5pm.

Taverna Verde, largo Adua, 18/19 (tel. 54 03 09), on the *lungomare* between Molo San Nicola and La Rotunda, at the end of corso Cavour. Black-tie service and elegant meals for ripped-jean prices. *Orechiette alla barese* (the regional pasta speciality) L3500, *involtini alla sasalinga* (a delicious stuffed meat dish) L5500. Local wine L3000 per liter. Cover L1500, service 15%. Open Tues.-Sun. noon-3pm and 8pm-midnight.

Pizzeria Osteria, via Giuseppe Bozzi, 86, on the water. Outdoor seating, specializes in **pizza del mare** (seafood pizza). Cover L1000. Open Mon.-Sat. noon-11pm.

Sights

Sundry activities along corso Cavour, the broad, sunny, tree-lined boulevard of the new city, make it a good starting point. The oval-domed, rusty-red **Teatro**

Petruzzelli (1903), an opera house rivalling those of Milan and Naples, dominates the south side of the street.

Across corso V. Emanuele bustles the workaday world of the **old city.** At the entrance to the city is **piazza del Ferrarese,** named after a colony of Ferrara merchants who lived here in the seventeenth century; it is now the site of a colorful morning market. **Piazza Mercantile** lies under the open porch and clock tower of the **Sedile,** the medieval meeting place of the Council of Nobles. Fraudulent debtors were tied to the Column of Justice (far right of square), as a reminder that even in commercial Bari, honesty remained the best policy. Before leaving the square, climb the stairs at p. Mercantile, 1, to a public terrace with a view of the small fishing harbor and corso Cavour.

From p. Mercantile, follow via Palazzo di Città to the **Church of San Nicola,** built in the twelfth century to hold the remains of Saint Nicholas of Santa Claus fame, also renowned for resurrecting three children who were cut up by a nasty butcher and put into a bottle of brine. The church's spartan appearance befits a fortress; in fact, the tower on the right comes from a Byzantine castle originally occupying the site. The central door exemplifies the motley sources of the Puglian-Romanesque style: Saracen in the arabesques and symbolic figures around the door, classical in the rosettes of the cornice, Byzantine in the solemn angels surrounding the arches, and Lombard in the crude animal carvings of the bases. The interior reveals an overwhelming seventeenth-century baroque ceiling depicting episodes of San Nicola's life. (Beware of surprise precipitation from the birds that have made the church their home.) The crypt, with its interesting windows of translucent marble, houses the remains of Saint Nicholas beside a beautiful silver reliquary.

From the church it is a short walk to Bari's Puglian-Romanesque **cathedral.** Passing down **strada del Carmine,** you'll be greeted by the intimate life of the old streets: narrow alleys lined with small whitewashed houses and thronged with children, vendors, and women dressed in black. Begun at the end of the twelfth century during the peaceful years of Norman rule, the cathedral has a typically austere Gothic facade, modified somewhat by the baroque decoration around the doors. The cathedral's interior is a fine example of Romanesque architecture, with a choir and chapel that protrude gently from the smooth beauty of the nave. The timber ceiling, a tell tale sign of pre-Gothic construction, complements the cathedral's columns and arches and contrasts with the ornate baroque ceiling of the Church of San Nicola.

On the outskirts of the old city, not far from the cathedral, the **castello** evokes the grandeur and power of three different periods. The castle proper and its four keeps are of Byzantine-Norman origin, rearranged by Frederick II (1230-1240) into a trapezoid with two of the towers still standing in the interior. In the north, toward the sea, a pointed door and beautiful mullioned windows derive from the thirteenth century. The bulwarks and angular keeps that jut outward were added in the sixteenth century. A bridge over an empty moat leads to the courtyard separating the outer walls from Frederick's palace, and a gracious lobby announces the great court of the palace itself. Much of the castle is closed for the excavation of a recently discovered Roman city on the site. (Open Mon.-Sat. 9am-1:30pm and 3:30-7:30pm, Sun. 9am-1pm. Admission L2000.)

Beyond the castle is a seawalk, leading past the ferry port to a small fishing harbor and eventually to the **Molo San Nicola** (San Nicola's Wharf). Every May 8th, a procession of boats carrying the image of San Nicola leaves the pier and sets out to sea, where the villagers pay homage to the icon. The gray-and-white towered building in the distance, the **Palazzo della Provincia,** lung. N. Sauro (tel. 33 44 45), houses the **Pinacoteca Provinciale** on its top floor. This museum owns paintings by Veronese, Tintoretto, and Bellini, including the latter's *San Pietro Martire.* Sword in heart, knife in head, the painting's hero is coolness incarnate. The museum also displays medieval sculpture, an exemplary wooden crucifix from the thirteenth century, and icons. You will make the guard's day if you ask to see the works of Francesco Netti, Bari's greatest artist and Italy's only impressive impressionist painter. (Museum open Tues.-Sat. 9am-1pm and 5-8pm, Sun. 10am-1pm. Free.)

Crammed into the first floor of the palazzo Ateneo in **Bari University,** at p. Umberto, is an archeology museum containing Greek and Puglian pottery, bronzes, some prehistoric objects, armor, a rich collection of native ceramics, Greek figurines, and ornamental objects of gold, silver, and ivory. (Open Tues.-Sun. 9am-2pm. Free.)

Entertainment

Bari ranks with Naples as a cultural nucleus in southern Italy. The two-month opera season at the **Teatro Petruzzelli** (tel. 21 81 32) begins in January, along with a concert season at the **Teatro Piccinni.** The **auditorium,** via Cimarusti, holds concerts year-round. For more information, inquire at the EPT and consult the Bari Sera section of *La Gazzetta del Mezzogiorno* (the local newspaper), or get a copy of *Ecco Bari,* the Azienda's entertainment guide. Another bastion of information is Giani (Jonny) Roman in the **Palazzo Di Cita;** he knows offhand of every event in the city. The concert and opera seasons slow down in summer, but occasional productions are held in the *castello.*

The great commercial event of the year, the **Levante Fair,** lasts for ten days in mid-September. The largest fair in southern Italy, it displays goods from all over the world (both agricultural and industrial) in the huge fairgrounds by the municipal stadium, off lungomare Starita. For nighttime fun in the summer, take your dancing shoes to **L'Ousi del Picchio Club,** via Le Prov. Ceglie, 37 (tel. 35 39 29), 4km from the city in the district of Loseto. Take bus #4 from corso Cavour. (Open May 20-Sept. 20 Tues.-Sun. 8pm-2am. Admission with 1 drink L8000.) Gay people can try the **Lively Club,** outside the city in the district of Noicattaro, inaccessible by public transportation.

Near Bari

Bitonto

For a potent dose of Puglian-Romanesque architecture, take the half-hour train ride from the Bari-Nord station to Bitonto. In the city's medieval quarter stands Puglia's most beautiful **cathedral,** almost untouched by remodeling or renovation. Constructed between the twelfth and thirteenth centuries out of a mellow golden stone, the church has a compact form enhanced by majestic side arches. The main portal of the church's facade is enlivened by sculptured lions, griffins, and bas-relief New Testament scenes.

Inside, windows illuminate a finely carved wooden ceiling that is a late nineteenth-century reproduction of the original design. The splendid pulpit at the end of the nave (1299) bears a charming panel of Frederick II and his family. The **crypt** (if not open, contact the sacristan in early morning or late afternoon, small tip expected) floats on 30 columns said to have come from a Roman temple. Their capitals were the gifts of 30 members of the city's medieval nobility.

The rest of medieval Bitonto, somewhat battered and forlorn, boasts several interesting buildings, including the Gothic **Church of San Francesco d'Assisi** (1286) and the **Palazzo Sylos Labini,** whose Catalan-Gothic doorway leads to an elaborate Renaissance courtyard.

To get to Bitonto, take the hourly train from Bari's **Ferrovia Bari Nord Station,** adjacent to the main station (½ hr.). When you arrive, a 1-km walk down via Matteotti and a right turn will deposit you in the medieval quarter. The three hotels in town are expensive and unpleasant, so make Bitonto a daytrip.

Trulli District

In the **Valley of Itoia,** between Bari and Taranto, cluster hundreds of unusual, conical-shaped dwellings, known as *trulli.* Two or three hundred years old, the mortarless structures utilize a prehistoric design of stacking concentric stone circles of decreasing radii and "icing the cake" with a limestone cap. The prehistoric versions probably stored grain or religious relics, but as the agricultural revolution plowed through and the surf of serfdom rolled in, the *trulli* became the residences they are today. The most impressive *trulli* clusters line the narrow streets of **Alberobello.** You can see other *trulli* sprinkled among fields of flowers in the surrounding **Itria Valley** by taking the train to Martina Franca. The *trulli* stand out against a backdrop of green vineyards, red earth, and golden wheat. Most inhabitants are more than willing to show their immaculate homes.

Although the city of **Martina Franca** itself doesn't have many *trulli,* it is one of the most charming "old cities" in all Puglia. From the train station, make your way up the hill to p. Roma, where you can pick up a map at the **Azienda** at #37 (tel. (080) 70 57 02; open Mon.-Fri. 9am-12:30pm and 4:30-7:30pm, Sat. 9am-12:30pm). Follow viale della Stazione uphill to viale Alessandro. Then continue downhill, turning left onto busy corso Italia. Turn left at green p. XX Settembre and walk through the archway; the Azienda is on the right. Nearby is the grandiose **Ducal Palace** (1669), with its more than 300 rooms, most of which are now offices. To tour the few remaining rooms open to the public, take the left-hand stairs to the third floor. (Open Mon.-Sat. 9am-1pm and 5-7pm. Free.) Be sure not to miss the **Church of San Martino** (18th century) with its fanciful baroque facade in p. Plebiscito. From viale de Gaspari, there is an excellent span of the Itria Valley and its *trulli.* An unofficial **youth hostel** 7km away in Locando San Paolo (tel. (080) 71 50 52) offers dorm rooms of four, six, and eight beds for L12,000 per night, L35,000 for full pension. To get there, take a Ferrovie del Sud-Est bus, which leaves from p. Crispi off via Taranto for Taranto to Locando San Paolo. There are no cheap hotels here. Your best bet is **Hotel da Luigi,** via Taranto (tel. 90 13 24), 1km from the train station. From the train station, turn right onto viale della Stazione, right again when you come to viale dei Lecce, and right once more onto via Taranto. (Singles with bath L22,250. Doubles with bath L42,350.) For a meal that shines, try **La Tavernetta,** corso V. Emanuele (tel. 60 63 23), off p. Roma. Homemade *orechiette al sugo* is L5000, main dishes L8000-12,000, local wine L2500 per liter, cover L1500, and service 15%. (Open Tues.-Sun. noon-3pm and 7:30pm-midnight.)

Martina Franca's **Festival della Valle d'Itria** brings an interesting series of concerts and opera to the city between July 23 and August 8. Tickets for the event are costly, however, ranging L5000-30,000. During the first weekend in July, the **Festa di San Martino** awakens the town to the sounds of outdoor concerts and parades.

Alberobello and Martina Franca are 20 minutes apart on the Bari-Taranto train lines of the Ferrovie del Sud-Est, about 45 minutes from Taranto and 1½ hours from Bari. (Trains leave 7:15am-9:30pm every 2-3 hr.) Frequent bus service from Ferrovie del Sud-Est connects Martina Franca with Taranto's p. del Castello (11 per day, L1800). Also on the Sud-Est rail from Bari to Alberobello, is **Castellana Grotte,** home of Italy's finest caverns. From the train station, follow the Grotte signs. They are 2km away; hitching is easy. You enter from an enormous pit called *La Grave,* which, despite its beauty, was used as a garbage dump until the rest of the caverns were discovered in 1938. The real masterpiece lies at the end of the tunnel—the *Caverna Bianca* (White Cavern), a sea of stalactites and stalagmites. Complete tours (1¾ hr., L9500) are scheduled about every hour from 8:30am to 12:30pm and at 3pm, 4pm, 5:30pm and 6:30pm (less frequently in winter). Partial tours (40 min., L5000) do not include the *Caverna Bianca,* and are given at 9am, 10am, 11am, 1pm, 3:30pm, 4:30pm, 6pm and 7pm.

Trani

Trani and Barletta, both on the coast north of Bari, prospered as free ports in the fourteenth and fifteenth centuries. Of the two, Trani is the more captivating. Its *ordinameta maris,* a maritime commercial code enacted in 1063, is the Mediterranean's oldest recorded evidence of commerce. The city's well-preserved medieval quarter evokes the time of Trani's ascendancy. On the quarter's edge the Romanesque cathedral stand alone. Trani also boasts a castle and an endless stretch of rocky beach. From the train station, walk down via Cavour to the lovely p. della Repubblica, site of an **ASST** (tel. (0883) 432 95). Knowledgeable staff distribute pamphlets and maps. (Open Mon.-Fri. 8:30am-12:30pm and 4-6pm, Sat. 8:30am-12:30pm.) Continuing down via Cavour to p. Plebiscito, you will reach the flourishing **public gardens,** with pleasant portside vistas. A small fishing harbor separates the gardens from the eleventh-century **cathedral,** which rises on a promontory overlooking the sea. The patron of this cathedral is Nicholas the Pilgrim, a diehard religious fanatic who spoke only two words, repeated mercilessly: *"Kyrie Eleison"* (Lord, have mercy). The cathedral's tall *campanile* offsets the austere facade; it is decorated with a small rose window. The miniature panels of saints and biblical scenes on the bronze front doors are the works of Barisano da Trani. Inside, a lattice-work of light filters through the leaded windows onto the gray stone walls. The primary crypt of San Nicola Pellegrino is one of the world's largest, measuring 24m by 11½m by 5½m. From here you can descend to the other crypt, known as the **Church of Santa Maria,** whose marble columns came from ancient buildings. (Cathedral open 7am-noon and 3-7pm.)

Down the waterfront from the cathedral is the **Castello Suevo** (1249), now undergoing a face-lift. An old-world flavor still prevails along the harbor and **via Ognissanti,** which runs parallel to the harbor. Here workshops (mostly of antique furniture restorers) exist beside medieval palaces and churches. The **Palazzo Caccetta** (1451-56) at via Ognissanti, 5, features a late Gothic doorway and delicately traced pointed windows.

Trani's medieval Jewish community endures in street names (via La Giudea, via Sinagoga, via Mosè di Trani) as well as two small **churches** (Santa Maria Scuolanove, Sant' Anna) that were synagogues before the sixteenth century. The latter, on via La Giudea off via Prologo across from the Palazzo Caccetta, was built in 1247 and preserves a Hebrew inscription on a marble plaque inside.

In summer, the AAST organizes a number of musical and cultural activities nightly at p. Quercia. If you're in Trani during the first weekend in August, be sure to see the festivities of the **Festa di San Nicola Pellegrino.**

A low-priced and convenient hotel in Trani is **Albergo Lucy,** p. Plebiscito, 11 (tel. 410 22), near the public gardens. Its huge doubles with bath cost L44,000, plus L10,000 for kitchen use. **Trattoria Emanuele,** by the port at Supportico Della Corca, 2, serves full meals for L15,000. Pasta dishes cost around L3500. (Cover L2000. Open Thurs.-Tues. noon-4pm and 6pm-midnight.) Parrots greet you at the entrance. **La Fattoria,** via Cavour, 102, sells wonderful *focaccio,* pizza bread with tomatoes, oregano, and cheese (L300 per slice). (Open Mon.-Fri. 7am-1pm and 5:30-9pm Sat. 7am-1pm.)

Barletta

Barletta is a little city with a big sense of fun. Its star attraction resembles an enormous toy—an ancient gargantuan statue whose knees meet childrens' eyes. Another amusing draw is Barletta's pageant on the last Sunday in July. The city reenacts the 1503 **Disfida** (Challenge), when 13 Italian knights handily defeated 13 Frenchman in bloody battle. In case you miss the action, visit the **Cantina della Disfida,** a small museum that displays furniture and artifacts of the epoch. (Open Tues.-Sat. 9am-1pm and 4-6pm, Sun. 9am-1pm. Free.) There are serious structures here, too, including some interesting Romanesque churches and an outstanding collection of paintings by Giuseppe de Nittis, one of Italy's great nineteenth-century artists. To reach all of Barletta's sites, walk straight from the station and turn right on via Garibaldi.

The twelfth-century **Church of San Sepolcro** (Holy Sepulchre) sits at the center of town on corso V. Emanuele at corso Garibaldi. The facade conserves remnants of an original entry porch, a pointed doorway, and two blind arches. Almost the only decoration remaining in the recently restored church interior is the large, thirteenth-century baptismal font to the left of the entrance, and the tender, sixteenth-century Byzantine-style Madonna at the end of the right aisle. (Open 8am-1pm and 5-8pm.) On a low podium next to the church stands the awesome 5-meter-high **Colosso.** This fourth-century bronze statue from Constantinople represents a Byzantine emperor, possibly Valentinian I, holding a cross and globe that symbolize the two realms of his power. After the Venetians recovered the statue in the thirteenth century, a shipwreck sent it to Barletta's shore. It was then dismembered by a group of friars who melted its bronze limbs for use as church bells. The limbs you see now were fashioned by a fifteenth-century sculptor, commissioned to make-over the *colosso.*

Corso Garibaldi leads you to the winding alleys of the old city and to Barletta's gray **cathedral.** Erected in 1150 in Romanesque form, but enlarged centuries later in the Gothic style, the church is memorable for its curious nave, which sports instead of a transept an outward bulge that meets the choir directly. *La Madonna della Disfida* (1587) graces the chapel behind the main altar. The cathedral was closed for restoration in 1988. Also closed was the **Castello Svevo** next door. The city plans to move its museum into the castle by 1989. (Open Mon.-Fri. 8am-12:40pm and 4-8pm.) For a view of the *duomo* and castle from the sea, walk along the pier. Barletta has one of the few beaches in the area. Squeezed between two blocks of industry, however, it is not picturesque.

The **Museo e Pinacoteca Comunali** (City Museum and Art Gallery), in via Cavour at corso Garibaldi, houses archeological material, including the only known bust of Holy Roman Emperor Frederick II and marvelous paintings by Giuseppe de Nittis. De Nittis combined impressionist techniques with the more finely modeled portraiture of the Neapolitan school. His paintings chronicle the gluttonous world of the nineteenth century *haute bourgeoisie.* (Open Tues.-Sun. 9am-1pm. Free.)

The **tourist office** on via Gabbiani, 4, near p. Caduti in Guerra, on corso Garibaldi, has good maps of the city and region. (Open Mon.-Sat. 8am-2pm.) The **Pensione Prezioso,** via Teatini, 11 (tel. 320 06), at p. del Plebiscito, has tidy, comfy singles for L20,000, with bath L24,000. Doubles with bath go for L34,000. (Showers included.) Call ahead in summer. **Hotel Centrale,** corso Garibaldi, 35 (tel. 332 95), offers clean, cheerful rooms with tiny windows. Singles run L19,000, with bath L22,000. Doubles run L34,000, with bath L40,000. For eats, try the **Bella Napoli,** across from the museum at corso Garibaldi, 129. The food and service are superb, though expensive: full meals L17,000, cover L1500, service 20%. (Open daily noon-3pm and 7pm-midnight.) More economical is **Pizzeria dei Saraceni,** p. del Plebiscito, 65, with complete meals for L10,000. Try their tasty *pizza al Saraceni* (with ham, artichokes, olives, capers, etc.) for L3500. (Cover L1000, service 15%. Open daily 11am-12:30am.) **Ondaverde,** via Giuseppe dei Nettis, 13, off p. Caduti in Guerra, serves a fast-food *menù* for L10,000. (Open daily 1-3pm and 7pm-midnight.)

Barletta is 15 minutes north of Trani on either the Bologna-Lecce or Bari-Norde train lines (L800 from Trani).

History-buffs should make the jaunt to **Canne della Battaglia** (the ancient Cannae), only 12km from Barletta on the Barletta-Spinazzola train line (round-trip L3700). It is here that Hannibal devised a new strategy to defeat the Romans in 216 B.C.E. Under his command, the Carthaginians first attacked and then retreated rapidly, drawing the unsuspecting Roman army between their flanks. In the ensuing struggle, 50,000 Romans were massacred, possibly the worst defeat in Roman history.

Brindisi

The Brindisi most visitors see is the distant view over the the stern of a ship departing for the Greek isles. Somehow you expect more than backpackers at the terminus of the Appian Way, Rome's historic stepping stone to the eastern world. A closer look at the town reveals low, nondescript buildings; straight, tree-lined streets; a harbor bordered by industrial debris; and swarms of travelers in transit. Still, Brindisi does not deserve the curses heaped upon it by transients. It is certainly more pleasant than its Greek counterpart Patras. Brindisi's sights—a prototypically

Puglian castle, an intact old town, and folk from around the globe—fill a layover well.

Ferry Information

Brindisi is the major embarkation point for ferries from Italy to Greece (see Bari Practical Information). There is regular service to **Corfu** (8½-9½ hr.), **Igoumenitsa** (10½-11½ hr.), **Patras** (15-20 hr.), **Cefalonia** (Adriatic lines, 16½ hr.), and **Paxi** and **Ithaca** (Lonis lines, 12 hr. and 15½ hr., respectively). From Patras, there is bus service (4 hr., 1000dr—about $7) and train service (railpasses valid) to Athens. Ask about stopping over in Corfu if you have a ticket to Patras.

Arrive in Brindisi well before your departure time. On most lines, if you don't check in at least two hours before departure, you lose your reservation. Allow plenty of time for late trains and the 1-km walk from the train station to the maritime station. From mid-July to mid-August, you may consider making reservations before you get to Brindisi. There are so many lines running at this time, however, that you can almost always pick up a reservation at the last minute. Escape the lines at the portside ticket booths by purchasing your ticket at one of the many travel agencies on the way to the port from the train station. Here you will pay the obligatory port tax (L6000), and the office will give you a boarding card, which you must have stamped at the police station on the first floor of the maritime station.

Fares and discounts

In 1988, the average, lowest regular rates were as follows: To Corfu or Igoumenitsa, deck-class L50,000 (students L40,000), from the third week of July through the second week of August L80,000 (students L70,000). To Cefalonia, Paxi, Ithaca, or Patras L55,000 (students L45,000), in high season L75,000 (students L60,000). Deck class is fine in summer—sleeping horizontally outside is more comfortable than spending the night in an airline-type seat in a smoke-filled room. Be sure to bring warm clothes and a sleeping bag. Bicycles travel free, and motorcycles are approximately L30,000-40,000, in off-season L20,000.

There are plenty of ways to reduce these figures. Most lines offer discounts to those 26 and under, and to ISIC-holders. All fares increase by up to 40% from late July to early August. **Eurailpass** holders get free deck passage on Adriatica Lines and Hellenic Mediterranean Lines (space available basis—you could get bumped by a paying passenger), but must pay a L14,000 supplement from June 10 through September (this includes the port tax). Some lines cut 30% off the regular fare for **InterRail** holders. Often the discount is valid only if you buy the ticket in Brindisi. Finally, there are group (usually 10 people minimum) reductions for approximately 10% on one-way and 20% on round-trip tickets. In 1988 **Fragline** offered the lowest fares. The following is a list of the vital statistics of the ferry companies in operation as of July 1988.

Adriatica, Stazione Marittima, 2nd floor (tel. 238 25). One of the largest and most expensive lines, unless you have a Eurailpass. Service to Patras and Corfu/Igoumenitsa year-round. Daily trips June 10-Sept.

Hellenic Mediterranean Lines, corso Garibaldi, 8 (tel. 285 31). Same service and similar prices as Adriatica. March-Dec.

Fragline, corso Garibaldi, 88 (tel. 265 02). Cheapest fares. Daily service to Corfu, Igoumenitsa, and Patras. March 20-Oct.

Adriatic Ferries, c/o Pattimare, p. E. Dionisi, 11 (tel. 265 48). Daily service to Corfu, Igoumenitsa, and Patras June 24-Sept. 12. Also to Cefalonia July 7-Aug. 19.

Ionis, c/o Pattimare p. E. Dionisi, 11 (tel. 265 48). Service every other day to Corfu, Paxi, Ithaca, Cefalonia, and Patras. June 2-June 21 and July-Sept. 13.

Practical Information

EPT: Lungomare Regina Margherita, 12 (tel. 219 44), at the dock to the left of the *stazione marittima,* 1 block to the side of the grassy p. Vittorio Emanuele. English spoken. Open 8:30am-12:30pm and 4:30-7pm. **Information desk:** at p. Cairoli, on the way to the port from the train station, and at the *stazione marittima* (2nd floor). Both open Mon.-Sat. 9am-2pm and 3:30-8:30pm. All offer the latest ferry information, but go to the one on the lungomare for information on sites.

Azienda di Turismo, via Rubini, 19 (tel. 210 91), off corso Garibaldi after p. del Popolo. Mostly administrative, but it stocks tons of pamphlets and maps. Open Mon-Fri. 8am-2pm.

Transalpino tickets: Agenzia di Viaggi Hellitalia, via del Mare, 4 (tel. 22 29 88), facing the maritime station. Open Mon.-Fri. 8:30am-1pm and 4-8pm, Sat. 8:30am-1pm.

Currency Exchange: At the **Cambio** in the *stazione marittima.* Closest to the port. Will exchange U.S. dollars for Greek drachmae. Open Mon.-Sat. 9am-noon and 5-9pm. Several others, with lousy rates, line corso Garibaldi. Also exchange on board some ferries.

Post Office: p. della Vittoria, near the intersection of corso Umberto and corso Garibaldi. Open Mon.-Sat. 8:15am-8pm. **Postal code:** 72100.

Telephones: SIP, via XX Settembre, 6, to the left on your way from the station to the port, near Hotel Villa Bianca and Albergo Venezia. Full service on international calls. Open daily 9am-1pm and 3:30-6:30pm. At other times, **Albergo Corso,** corso Roma, 88. **Telephone code:** 0831.

Showers and Toilets: Lungomare Regina Marghenta, 11, on the water by the tourist office. Fastidiously-kept facilities. Open daily 6am-10pm. Free.

Hospital: Ospedale Di Suma, p. Antonio (tel. 20 42).

Police: Carabinieri, Tel. 209 91.

Accommodations

Not many people hit the sack in Brindisi. If they do, it's usually on a train station bench. As a result, the selection is unimpressive.

Ostello della Gioventù Casale, via Brandi, 4 (tel. 41 31 00), 2km away on the coast of the lagoon opposite the port. Take bus #3 or 4 two blocks in front of the train station, and ask the driver to drop you off at the hostel. A first-rate hostel. No smoking in the bedrooms. L8500. Membership not required. Breakfast included. Curfew 11pm, but latecomers off the train are welcome. Dinner L8000. Open 5pm-8:30am.

Locanda Doria, via Fulvia, 38 (tel. 264 53). Three lefts and a right could serve you right: Turn left as you leave the train station, left again on via Appia, right on via Arione, then left on via Fulvia. The best choice if there's room. Cozy and cheap, but somewhat inconvenient—about 1km from the train station as you leave the port. L10,000 per person.

Albergo Venezia, via Pisanelli, 6 (tel. 254 11), off via S. Lorenzo da Brindisi. In the same neighborhood as the Bianca, near the marketplace. Safe and family-run, but no atmosphere. Pay in advance. Singles L20,000. Doubles L30,000.

Hotel Royal, p. Cairoli, 5 (tel. 285 47). Recently renovated rooms are small and unimaginative but sanitary. Some have no windows. Singles L18,000. Shared rooms L15,000 per person. American breakfast L2500. Showers included.

Food

Avoid the hagglers on corso Garibaldi, who feed on those waiting for ferries. A wonderful **open-air market,** off corso Umberto on via Battisti, sells fresh fruit by the tons. (Open Mon.-Sat. 7am-1pm.) In Brindisi, as in most of Puglia, pizza is called *focacce,* made in huge sheets, and sold by weight. **Jolly Pizzeria,** off the market at via Ferrante, 12, makes delicious *focaccine* (pizza babies) for L1000, but their specialty is a tasty but greasy *prosciutella ripiena,* a large tart filled with a doughy cheese, ham, and tomato (L13,000). (Open Mon.-Sat. 7am-3pm and 5-11pm.) *Focaccio* from the market area *alimentaris* will cost you half as much as those in the tourist-trap showcases. Try the no-name shop at via Pisanelli, 22.

Osteria Splugen, vico di Raimondo, near Albergo Venezia by the marketplace. You will feel at home here in the dumpy little TV room with a cheery woman serving the food. Limited variety but a full meal (from *primo* to *frutta*) L10,500, and a vegetarian dinner (cheese substituted for meat) L8500. Open Sun.-Fri. noon-10pm.

Spaghetti House Osteria Cucina Casalinga, via Mazzini, 57, parallel to corso Umberto, not far from the station. Lots of delicious fare. Full meals L6000-10,000. Cover L500. Open Mon.-Sat. 9am-9pm.

Trattoria L'Angoletto, via Pergola, 3, near the port, off corso Garibaldi to your right as you face the sea. If you are swept in the stream of people running toward the port, come here. Dinner of spaghetti, pizza, salad, and mineral water L8500. Pizza L4000-7000. Cover L1500 (except for students). Open Thurs.-Tues. 9am-11pm.

Ristorante Shangai, largo Concordia, 9, in the old town off p. della Vittoria. Go exotic, opt for the Orient: entrees about L5000. Open Mon.-Sat. noon-3pm and 7-11pm. Sun. 4-9:30pm.

Sights

Stand with your back to the port and to the right on the stairs facing the water will lie the only remaining Terminal Columns of the **Appian way.** If you look closely, you'll find a marble capital graced with Jove, Neptune, Mars, and eight tritons. Directly across the water, on the other side of the port, rises another pillar. This modern counterpart to the Roman relic is a monument to the Italian sailor. The **Marinaio d'Italia** takes the shape of an oversized rudder, 175 ft. high and surrounded by a vast seaside park. You can easily hop over on one of the **Casale** ferries that leave every 10 minutes from Banghina Montenegro, opposite via Montenegro (round-trip L200).

Back in Brindisi, wander through the nooks and crannies of the old town. Just above the Appian Way column, you'll stumble across the ruins of the Roman house in which Virgil supposedly died on his way home from Greece. Piazza Duomo showpieces the *duomo* itself (twelfth-century, rebuilt in the eighteenth century), where Frederick II made a bride of Jerusalem's Yolande,and the **Palazzo Balsamo** (fourteenth-century), which offers a perfect example of the Puglian accretion of Byzantine, Romanesque, and Gothic.

If you follow the water for 2km or take the Casale ferry (same as above), you'll come to Brindisi's pride, the **Santa Maria del Casale,** a multicolored, elaborately adorned building harking back to Byzantine structures, but also incorporating Gothic ornamentation. It was built by Prince Phillip of neighboring Taranto, who enlisted his countryman Rinaldo da Taranto to paint an impressive Last Judgement fresco. As for entertainment—if you're lucky you won't be here long enough to seek it—Brindisi honors its tourists with a "tourist festival" on the port the last weekend of July.

Lecce

Lecce is to the baroque as Florence is to the Renaissance. Under the influence of the Spanish court, and with the backing of the clergy and commercial class, the architects and artisans of Lecce designed and built palaces, churches, and gateways in the most elaborate baroque style. Cornices curl around columns, draperies drip with *putti,* balconies resemble fruitbowls, and windowsills flower stalls.

Lupiae, as Lecce was known to the Romans, was where Octavian learned of the assassination of his greatuncle, Julius Caesar. Now, with a student and artist community, Lecce dons a bohemian air. In comparison to other Puglian cities, Lecce is worldly, and worlds apart in its unusual beauty.

Lecce serves as a good starting point for a trip down the Salento Peninsula, Italy's high heel, where you'll find a spectacular coastline of limestone cliffs worn into fantastic shapes. Small Turkish- and Greek-looking towns dot the peninsula, and in some places you'll hear a dialect similar to Greek.

Orientation and Practical Information

Lecce lies some 35km south and inland of Brindisi, accessible by an hour-long train ride nine times per day (L2200). To get to the center from the train station, walk down viale Quarta and turn right onto the broad via Gallipoli. Turn left at viale Otranto and continue to the end. Just past the castle on your left is piazze S. Oronzo and the EPT office. Immense Portale Napoli can be reached by following via Umberto I from p. S. Oronzo to via Principi di Savoia, then turning left.

EPT: p. S. Oronzo (tel. 464 58), in the beautiful Palazetto del Sedile next to the amphitheater. Busy but helpful. Maps, pamphlets, and hotel listings, mostly in Italian. Open Mon.-Fri. 9am-1pm and 5:30-7:30pm, Sat. 9am-1pm.

CTS: via Folomeneo, 1, at via Pialmieri. A student travel service. Air and rail information, tickets, and discounts. Open Mon.-Fri. 8:30am-1pm and 5-8:30pm, Sat. 8:30am-1pm.

Post Office: via F. Cavallotti, 4, at the end of viale Otranto next to a large indoor market. Open Mon.-Sat. 8:15am-8pm. **Postal code:** 73100.

Telephones: SIP, on via S. Nicola at viale degli Studenti, outside Portale Napoli. Open daily 8:15am-8:30pm. **Telephone code:** 0832.

Train Station: Both the **F.S.** (for the north) and the provincial **Ferrovie del Sud-Est** (for the Salento Peninsula) in p. Stazione, about 1km from the town center.

Bus Station: via Adua, parallel to via Taranto. Connections to the Salento Peninsula. **Sud-Est,** via A. Boito. Connections to other areas in Puglia.

Hospital: Ospedale Vito Fazzi, p. Bottazzi (tel. 64 20 31).

Police: Carabinieri, via Lupiae. Tel. 21 21 21.

Accommodations and Camping

An affordable, decent pad, especially a single, is rare here.

Ostello della Gioventù Adriatico (non-IYHF) (tel. 65 00 26), 12km from Lecce on the beach of San Cataldo. Take the bus toward San Cataldo from Villa Comunale (near p. S. Oronzo), Porta Rudiae, or viale Brindisi (July-Aug. every hr. on the hr.; in off-season 4 per day). L7000 per person. Open May-Sept.

Pensione Carmen, via V. Morelli, 13 (tel. 464 08). From viale Quarta, turn left on viale Gallipoli, then right on via Lombardia. Not far from the train station, but you're bound to get lost trying to find it, and trying to find some kindness from the proprietress. Doubles with bath L30,000.

Hotel Cappello, via Montenegrappa, 4, to the left of the station. The gregarious manager has a few rooms with half-bathrooms, which he'll let for lower rates. Well-fitted rooms facing the train tracks. Singles L22,500. Doubles L30,000.

Allogio Faggiano, via Cavour, 4 (tel. 428 54). Walking toward the post office on via Otranto, take a left on via L. Simone and then another left. The building looks older than the city's baroque churches. Doubles L25,000. Showers included.

Camping: The best spot for camping near Lecce is the secluded **Camping Torre Rinalda** (tel. 65 21 61), 3km from the beach in the zone of Litoranea. To get to the site from Lecce, take bus #18 to Litoranea. L4000 per person, L3000 per small tent, and L5000 per large tent. July 16-Aug. 30 L5500 per person, L4000 per small tent, L6500 per large tent. Open May-Sept. 15.

Camping Pinimar (tel. 428 43), 12km northeast of Lecce at Marina di Frigole. Seven buses depart from Lecce's Villa Comunale (at 6:30am, 7:40am, 10am, 12:10pm, 1:50pm, 3pm, and 5pm). A good option. L4400 per person, L3900 per small tent, L4500 per medium tent, and L6500 per large tent. Use of kitchette L2200.

Solicara Camping Club (tel. 65 60 64), 9km from Lecce, near the Marina di Torre Chianca. Easily reached by bus. L3500 per person, L3500 per tent, L2500 per small tent. Use of lighting L1500.

Food

The massive **indoor market,** next to the post office, will keep you wellstocked with apples, oranges and other fresh foods. (Open Mon.-Fri. 5am-2pm, Sat. 5am-2pm and 4-8pm.) For dessert, visit **Il Fornaio,** p. S. Olonzo, 23, across from the EPT, and ask for a few *pasticiotti,* a cream-filled cupcake. They also make fabulous *pizzo* bread, filled with olives, tomatoes, and onions. (Open Mon.-Wed. and Fri.-Sat. 7:45am-1:30pm and 4:30-8:30pm, Thurs. 7:45am-1:30pm.)

Ristorante-Pizzeria da Claudio, via Cavour, 11, 1 block down from Soggiorno Faggiano. Fabulous *tortellini* L2300-3500. Complete dinner L11,000. Pasta from L3500. Meat dishes L5000-7000. Pizzas L3500-7000. Also an excellent house red wine, L3000 per liter. Cover L1000, service 10%. Open Thurs.-Tues. noon-2:30pm and 7-10pm.

Trattoria Lu Turcinieddhu, via Duca degli Abruzzi (tel. 205 13), off via Cairoli. Don't try to pronounce the name—sit back and enjoy the *orecchiette alla casalinga* or any of the other pastas (L4500). *Calamari arrosto,* (roast squid) L6000. Pizza served at night. Cover L1500. Open Fri.-Wed. noon-3pm and 7-11:30pm.

Trattoria-Pizzeria La Stalla, viale Taranto, 15, near Portale Napoli. Dazzling pizza (L2000-3000), but a banal dining room. Pasta dishes L3000. Main dishes L5000-8000. Good *Torrequarto* wine L3500 per liter. Cover L500, service 15%. Open Thurs.-Tues. noon-4pm and 7:30pm-midnight.

La Capannina, via Cairoli, 13 (tel. 241 59), 700m from the station. Unusual, delicious dishes. *Fave e cicorie* (pasta with beans) L3500. *Lumachine* (snails prepared with onions, oil, and wine) L8000. *Vino Primo Fiore* L2000 per liter. Cover L1000, service 15%. Open Tues.-Sun. noon-3pm and 7-11:30pm.

Perla D'Oriente, via Francesco de Marconi, 14. This under-recognized Chinese restaurant is located on the second floor with tables on the balcony. Open daily noon-3:30pm and 7-11pm.

Kenzia Bar, via Palmieri, 31. The classiest bar in these parts. Bucks the Italian tradition by welcoming you to sit down with your drink. Mixed drinks L2500-4000.

Sights and Entertainment

In Lecce, the omnipresent baroque teases the eye relentlessly. After your initial disappointment with the city's drab outskirts, head for the **Church of Saint Irene** (1591-1639), off p. Oronzo, a fine example not only of Roman baroque, but also of the more florid Lecce style. You will be delighted by the marvelous complex of **piazza del Duomo,** a short distance away on via V. Emanuele. In front is the **cathedral,** rebuilt between 1659 and 1670 by Giuseppe Zimbalo, the architect of many of Lecce's most celebrated buildings. On his elaborate two-story frontispiece, tacked on as a side entrance, even the decoration has decoration. The interior dates mostly from the eighteenth century, except for a couple of typical Leccese altars. (Open 8-11am and 4:30-7:30pm.)

To the right of the cathedral (the 1st building as you enter the square) is the **seminary** (1709) by G. Cino, a pupil of Zimbalo. Cino was also wellversed in flamboyant architecture, here stopping just short of debauchery with the help of a little bilateral symmetry. The solid center portal keeps the windows in line—their frames swirl like icing on a cake.

The **Palazzo Vescovile** (Bishop's Palace), distinguished by its open portico, has been remodeled several times since its original construction in 1632. The porticos held shops in the days when an annual fair took place in the *piazza.* The final element of the *piazza,* the ***campanile*** (1682) exhibits a restrained elegance and provides a necessary vertical accent.

A walk down via G. Libertini takes you to the **Porta Rudiae** (1703) and past the unfinished baroque facade of the **Church of Santa Teresa;** the simple Renaissance facade of the **Church of Sant' Anna;** and, at the end of the street, the bizarrely complicated **Church of the Rosary,** Zimbalo's last work.

No amount of extravagant architecture quite prepares one for the **Church of Santa Croce** (1548-1646), the supreme expression of Leccese baroque and the city's prized possession. Fantastic figures of monsters and caryatids adorn the facade, along with a great rose window that resembles an upside-down wedding cake. Instead of surfaces lavished with sculpture and painting as in many baroque buildings, two simple rows of Corinthian columns support plain white walls within the church. A wonderfully animated altar (1614) by F. A. Zimbalo, Giuseppe's papa, adorns the chapel to the left of the apse. (The exterior was wrapped in scaffolding in 1988. Open 9am-1pm and 5:30-7:30pm.)

To the left of Santa Croce lies the **Palazzo del Governo.** Zimbalo designed the lower half of the facade while Cino worked on the upper portion. Diagonally across the street, the **Palazzo Adorni** is a Florentine-style palace with a secret, enclosed garden in the back. (Both open daily 8am-1pm.) From here vie Umberto and Principe di Savoia take you to the **Arco di Trionfo,** erected in 1548 in honor of Charles V, whose coat of arms is reproduced on the front. Located in an ancient cemetery beyond the Arco di Trionfo is the **Church of SS. Nicolo e Cataldo.** Founded in 1180 by the Normans and modified in 1716 by Cino, the church still shows Arab-influenced design, especially in the portal. Small mausoleums of every conceivable style cluster around narrow paths in the cemetery next door.

Little is left of Lecce's Roman city except the **amphitheater,** which seems just part of the scenery at **piazza Sant' Oronzo.** The **Column of Sant' Oronzo,** which rises high above the *piazza* next to the amphitheater, is one of two that once marked the end of the Appian Way in Brindisi.

Still more baroque churches await your visit. The **Church of Santa Chiara** (1694) lies at the end of p. V. Emanuele. Attributed to Cino, this church houses fine Leccese baroque altars. **Via Arte della Cartapesta,** socalled because it was once a center for the making of papier-mâché figures of saints, runs to the left of the church. The **Church of Carmine,** whose whimsical facade (1717) was Cino's last work, is in perfect contrast with the plain facade of the **Church of the Gesù** (1579), and is an ultimate expression of Leccese baroque.

On viale Gallipoli toward the station, you'll find the **Museo Provinciale,** anything but provincial. It houses an interesting collection of bronze statuettes, inscriptions, vases, and rare fourth-century B.C.E. fish plates. In the *pinacoteca* on the third floor is a stunning thirteenth-century gospel cover inlaid with gold and blue and white enamel. (Open Mon.-Fri. 9am-1:30pm and 3:30-7:30pm, Sun. and holidays 9am-1:30pm. Admission L1000, Sun. free.)

This subdued city comes alive in July and August with cultural activities. The EPT sponsors three programs in summer: the **Estate Musicale Leccese,** a festival of music and dance; the **Sud Nord Express,** which features international acting companies; and **Visioni Barocche,** a series of popular international films. The **Liros Society** (tel. 270 07) holds three days of music, dance, and drama during the first weekend in July at p. Duomo.

Near Lecce: Salento Peninsula

While in Lecce, take the time to visit one of the many medieval fortresses and castles scattered throughout the **Salento Peninsula.** Any tourist office in Puglia can profide a map showing their locations. The castle closest to Lecce (7 miles away on the road to Struda) is **Acaia,** a forgotten ruin overgrown by weeds. Huge vaultings, remnants of mosaics, narrow staircases, and a desolate courtyard compel medieval fantasies. Climb to the top for a view of the sea and countryside. (3 buses per day leave for Acaia from the via Adua station in Lecce.)

Other places in the Salento Peninsula are somewhat inaccessible by public transportation. The **Ferrovie del Sud-Est,** a private railway, serves most of the larger communities (Gallipoli, Otranto, Gagliano), but is slow and infrequent. You might take the train to one of the larger towns by the sea and then use the EPT map to guide you in hitching.

Otranto is the best starting point for a tour of the Adriatic Coast (a 1-hr. train ride, L2700; change at Maglie). An ancient city of Greek origin and the easternmost point of habitation in Italy, Otranto was once the capital of Byzantine territory in

Puglia. As such, it was a chief embarkation point for the East during the Crusades. Today, the village of whitewashed houses hugs a sea wall leagues away from baroque Lecce. The cathedral retains an eleventh-century mosaic pavement of the Tree of Life that extends the entire length of the nave. The crypt also houses 42 columns—all of varying marbles deriving from Greek, Roman, and Arab structures. In the Chapel of the Martyrs are the remains of 560 victims of a 1480 Turkish raid on the town. The exterior has changed greatly since the eleventh century and now bears an elaborate baroque portal from the eighteenth century and a fine Gothic rose window. The treasure of the city is the little Byzantine **Church of San Pietro,** hidden away in an enclosed square. Built between the tenth and eleventh centuries in the shape of a Greek cross, it showcases a brooding interior decorated with frescoes.

Otranto's **Azienda di Turismo** is on lungomare Kennedy (tel. (0836) 814 36). If you plan to stay, try **Il Gabbiano** (tel. (0836) 812 51), which offers singles for L25,000 and doubles for L42,000 (both with bath and breakfast). **Albergo Ester,** via Giovanni XXIII, 19 (tel. (0836) 841 69), near the Aragonese castle, offers doubles with bath for L40,000. (reserve in Aug.). A dilapidated **ferry** runs from Otranto to Corfu and Igoumenitsa, operated by **Roana Lines;** it might be safer to swim. (Boats leave Jan. 3-Jun. 14 and Sept. 14-Sept. 28 Mon., Wed., and Sat. at 11pm; Jun. 15-Sept. 14 Mon.-Fri. at 10:30pm.) Fares average L35,000-42,000 (students L30,000-35,000), but they jump to L65,000 (students L55,000) from July 27 through August. Information and reservations can be obtained from the *stazione marittima* (tel. (0836) 810 05).

A few miles north of Otranto is **Torre dell' Orso,** a lido lying at the end of a beautiful inlet surrounded by pinewoods. A smiling Madonna sits at the **Grotta della Poesia**, a small pool of clear water enclosed by low cliffs and a natural bridge.

The coast south of Otranto is more rugged, bordered by limestone cliffs and dotted with flat-roofed homes. **Santa Cesàrea Terme** is the important resort in the area, famous for its thermal springs and spectacular location. On a terrace, it overlooks cliffs plunging down to the sea. Just south of here (6km) is the marine cave **Zinzulusa Grotto,** filled with stalactites and stalagmites (called *zinzuli* in the local dialect). Two Ferrovie del Sud-Est buses per day run to Santa Cesàrea Terme from via Adua in Lecce.

To explore the peninsula's **Ionic Coast,** start at **Gallipoli** (1 hr. from Lecce by frequent train or bus, L3000). Named "beautiful city" by the Greeks, it has traditionally been a port for trade in olive oil and wine. Its old city, located on an island, is distinctly Greek in appearance. Pastel houses enclose narrow winding streets and lead to the seaside promenade that has replaced the city's ancient walls. Running along Gallipoli's northern coast are two picturesque beaches, **Santa Maria al Bagno** and **Santa Caterina.** Close to town and south of Gallipoli are some quiet spots among the beaches (admission around L500). **Lido San Giovanni,** on the beach road, harbors pebbly sand and pellucid water. Gallipoli's extremely modest **EPT,** corso Roma, 225, is located next to p. Fontana Greca. (Open Mon.-Fri. 10am-noon and 5-7pm.) Continue up corso Roma over the bridge and into the old town. On the left at corso Roma, 3 is an indoor fruit market. (Open 7am-1:30pm and 5-8pm.) Across the street in p. Imbriani is the **post office.** (Open Mon.-Fri. 8:30am-1pm.)

Unfortunately, Gallipoli offers no bargain lodgings. The best you'll find is **Pensione Sirocco,** via Urso, 49 (tel. 47 39 27). Walk straight from the station, turn right on corso Roma, and then take the first left. Newly renovated, the doubles have their own baths and electric fans. (L35,000 for one person, L40,000 for two.) Camping, however, is feasible: **Camping Vecchia Torre** (tel. (0833) 47 60 46) and **Baia di Gallipoli** (tel. (0832) 495 26) are both about 3km from town. Baia di Gallipoli, 800m from the beach, offers 6-person bungalows for L90,000, 3-person tents for L18,000, and free use of their swimming pool, tennis courts, and disco. (Open June-Sept.) For a meal, try **Pizzeria Sally,** viale Bari, which whips up generous pizzas for L5000-6000.

Unless you have a foot fetish, there's no reason to travel to the tip of Italy's heel (1½ hr. by train from Lecce to Gagliano, then a short bus ride to the shore). **Leuca** is a nondescript beach resort—only the **Cape of Santa Maria di Leuca,** a conspicuous white limestone cliff that separates the Adriatic from the Ionian Sea, is marginally noteworthy.

Taranto

High insteps are deemed a sign of nobility. They are also the part of a footprint that disappears in the sand. Taranto, located at the top of the boot's arch, exudes a noble air but washes away quickly from the shores of memory. Its extensive archeological museum and seaside promenade comprise the city's sites. Taranto is primarily a port town of sailors in starched white uniforms and great brooding cargo ships that creep to shore.

Orientation and Practical Information

Taranto is on the Naples-Brindisi train line and is also connected by train with Rome (8½ hr.), Naples (6 hr.), Brindisi (1½ hr.), and Bari (1½ hr.).

The city is divided into three parts: the **port area** to the north, where the train station is located; the **old city,** a small island across ponte di Porta Napoli from the station; and the **new city,** to the southeast across the *canale navigabile,* which houses the majority of hotels, restaurants, and offices. Take bus #8 or ½ from the train station.

EPT: corso Umberto, 113 (tel. 21 23 3), in the new city. Take bus #8 from the station; get off 3 stops after the 2nd bridge. Make a left on via D. Acclavio, and follow it to corso Umberto; the office is across corso Umberto on the corner. Well-equipped, genial. English spoken. A good map and lots of help with accommodations. Open Mon.-Fri. 8:30am-1pm and 5:30-7pm, Sat. 10am-noon.

Post Office: lungomare Vittorio Emanuele, a few blocks up from the beginning of the street at the *canale navigabile.* Open Mon.-Sat. 9am-1pm and 5:30-8:30pm. **Postal code:** 74100.

Telephones: SIP, lungomare V. Emanuele, 20, near the post office. Open 8am-9:30pm. At other times, try **Albergo Imperiale,** via Pitagora, 94. **Telephone code:** 099.

Train Station: In p. Duca d'Aosta for both **F.S.** and **Ferrovie del Sud-Est.** To Martina Franca (9 per day, 45 min., L1800), Alberobello via Martina Franca (L2500, 20 min. from Martina Franca), and Castellana Grotte via Martina Franca (L3700, 1 hr. from Martina Franca).

Buses: AMAT city bus tickets cost L500 and are bought at *tabacchi* before you get on. **Ferrovie Autobus del Sud-Est** (tel. 280 72) buses to Martina Franca (7am-9pm 11 per day, 1 hr., L1700) and Bari (4 per day, 2 hr., L5800) leave from p. Castello (in the old city, just across from the *canale navigabile*); buses to Lecce (4 per day, 2 hr., L4200) leave from via Magnaghi (in the northeastern outskirts of the new city).

Hospital: SS. Annunziata, via Bruno (tel. 944 01).

Police: Carabinieri Tel. 112.

Accommodations and Camping

Finding inexpensive accommodations in Taranto is not smooth sailing; your best bet is the new city. The cheap hotels around the port are often full and always dangerous. Since accommodations are spread out over a wide area, it's a good idea to phone ahead or to seek assistance from the EPT.

Ostello per i Giovani, Strada Statale 172 dei Trulli (tel. (080) 71 50 52), in Lanzo. Quite far; take the Ferrovie del Sud-Est bus from p. Castello for Martina Franca, and get off at Loc. San Paolo (50 min.). In the middle of nowhere, yet right on the *autostrada.* Hot showers. Curfew midnight. 4, 6, or 8 beds per room. L10,000 per person. Lunch or dinner L12,000. Full pension L34,000. Call ahead.

Albergo Aquila d'Oro, via Margherita, 8 (tel. 204 72), across the bridge in the new city. Drab rooms, but well situated and cheap. Smiling management and endless hot water supply. Singles L15,000. Doubles L26,000, with bath L32,000. Showers L2000.

Pensione Rivera, via Campania, 203 (tel. 33 88 90), on the outskirts of town. Take the "Circolare Rossa" bus from via Regina Margherita, get off at via Campania (15 min.), and walk toward the water. Contemporary, comfortable rooms in a residential area safe for women. Call ahead. Singles L16,000. Doubles L27,000. Showers L2500.

Albergo Pisani, via Cavour, 43 (tel. 240 87), just over the bridge to the new city, off p. Garibaldi. The brightest, newest place in town. Rooms encircle an atrium. Singles and doubles L20,000.

Albergo Sorrentino, p. Fontana, 7 (tel. 40 74 56). Walk down viale Duca d'Aosta from the train station until you cross a small bridge into the old city. Family-run, with capacious rooms. Because of its seedy location by the port, not for women. Singles L15,000. Doubles L25,000, with bath L35,000. Showers free.

Albergo Ariston, p. Fontana, 15 (tel. 45 75 63), near the Sorrentino. Well-kept rooms, many of which look out onto the sea. Unfortunately, many long-term clients. Not for women. Singles L15,000. Doubles L25,000. Showers included.

Camping: Sun Bay Campsite at Lido Bruno is 10km away on the beach. Some of the "Circolare Rossa/Nera" buses (C/N or C/R) go there from the beginning of via d'Aquino; ask the driver. July-Aug. L5200 per person, L3900-7400 per tent; in off-season L3900 per person, L3200-6000 per tent.

Food

Sea-soaked Taranto swarms with seafood. Try *cozze* (mussels in basil and olive oil), a traditional dish. Inexpensive restaurants flood the new city, and the *menù turistico* is often a catch here, frequently as varied as the regular menu.

Ristorante G. Basile, via Pitagora, 76, across from the Giardini Pubblici, 1 street up from corso Umberto. An excellent value—pleasant atmosphere, prompt service, and delicious food. Try *fritto misto* (fried prawns and squid), *risotto ai funghi* (rice with mushrooms), or *melanzane ripiene di carne* (eggplant). *Menù turistico* L11,000. Open Sun.-Fri.

La Grande Birreria, via Regina Margherita, 43 (tel. 211 54), in the new city off corso Umberto near the 2nd bridge. A happening place with lots of space to enjoy the respectable self-service food. *Primi* L3000-4000, *secondi* L4000-5000, fruit L1200, *contorni* L1500. Food served at the large tables costs twice as much. Open Sat.-Thurs. noon-3pm and 7-11:30pm.

Birreria Amstel, via D'Aquino, 27, in the new city, parallel to corso Umberto off p. Immacolata. Tasty *risotto alla marinara* (rice with seafood) L5500. *Fritto misto di pesce* (fried fish) L6500. If you eat in the *tavola calda,* you will save L1000 per dish and be spared the cover. Splendid pizzas in the evening L2500-5000. Full-choice *menù turistico* L15,000. Wine L3000 per liter. Cover L1500. Open Aug.-June Thurs.-Tues. 12:30-2:30pm and 7-11:30pm.

Trattoria al Sabbione, via Acclavio, 32, off corso Umberto near the EPT. Family-run place run with your tastebuds in mind. *Pasto completo* (L8000) is the best bet. Ask for the *pasta e fagioli* (pasta with beans). Open Mon.-Sat. noon-3pm and 7-9:30pm.

Ristorante Orologio, p. Fontane, 61-62 (tel. 40 76 31), after the bridge into the old city. Religious wall-hangings and high ceilings. The food itself is heavenly. Without a doubt, the best *menù turistico* in the city. Choose whatever dishes you want from its huge seafood menu—*primo, secondo, contorno,* fruit, and wine all included—L16,000. Open Mon.-Sat. noon-3pm and 6-10:30pm.

Sights

Other than the cathedral and the superb National Museum, not much remains of the city's past glory. Nonetheless, there's a graciousness about the waterside and main square. Visit the tree-lined **lungomare Vittorio Emanuele** in the new city for a far-reaching view over the Mar Grande. Enclosing the outer harbor, the islands of **San Pietro** and **San Paolo** are also within sight, close to the horizon line, between Rondinella Point to the right and Capo San Vito with the lighthouse to the left. Both are military outposts, however, and can be visited only with permission. The **Villa Peripato** (or *giardini pubblici*), a lush garden on the other side of the city, opens to a terrace overlooking the Mar Piccolo and the Italian naval base.

The **old city** entices visitors to wander its dark byways. Keep an eye on your pocketbook. It is home to a remarkable **cathedral** built in the tenth century and rebuilt in 1713. The church was originally a Greek cross; the Latin arm was added in 1170, creating the present basilica shape. The Byzantine exterior walls and cupola are still visible at the sides of the church. Under the chancel is the crypt, supported by stocky columns and decorated with twelfth-century Byzantine frescoes. Compare this structure with Taranto's other prominent cathedral in the eastern part of the new city. Designed by the renowned architect Gio Ponti, it is modern Gothic and in the shape of a sail. Another welcome relief to the solemnity of the old town is the riotous decoration of the **San Cataldo Chapel** (end of the right aisle), whose multi-colored, intricate marble designs exemplify the Lecce baroque influence.

The finest testimony to Taranto's former importance—besides its Aragonese castle, occupied by the military and closed to the public—is the excellent **National Museum,** corso Umberto, 41, at corso Cavour. This museum holds the finest examples of Magna Grecian art in Italy. The collection, excavated mostly from the city's necropolis, includes sculpture and mosaics, imported and local pottery, jewelry, terracotta figures, coins, and prehistoric materials. Look for the sarcophagus cut from a single block of stone and enclosing the skeleton of a young athlete whose magnificent white teeth are still intact; sculpted heads bearing large dangling gold earrings and tiaras; and a truly extraordinary golden diadem decorated with exquisite flowers made of gold, precious gems, and enamels. (Open June 15-Oct. 14 Tues.-Sat. 9am-2pm and 3:30-7:30pm, Sun.-Mon. 9am-2pm; in off-season Mon.-Sat. 9am-2pm, Sun. 9am-1pm. Admission L3000.)

In summer, an ACTT city bus makes stops along the lungomare (8:15am-7:30pm 10 per day) and will take you to the most beautiful **beach** in the area, **Lido Silvana.** Other beaches in the area, such as **Lido Gandoli, Mon Reve,** and **Carneto,** are more crowded with Italians.

Entertainment

Taranto has one of southern Italy's liveliest *passeggiata.* Every night from about 6 to 8pm, the entire stretch of **via d'Aquino** becomes mobbed. Action concentrates especially around **piazza della Vittoria.**

Taranto's **Holy Week festival** is famous throughout Italy. In a ceremony with medieval Spanish roots, men dress up in long white robes with pointed hoods and masks and parade with a cart through the streets, on a pilgrimage to the Holy Sepulchres that are set up in Taranto's churches. The festivities begin on the Sunday before Easter. Two processions occur Thursday (at 3pm and midnight) and one on Good Friday (at 5pm). The Procession of Our Lady of Sorrows leaves at midnight from the Church of San Domenico. A large train of people crosses the city, walking for 12 hours into Good Friday. A local noble organized this pageant around the turn of the seventeenth century.

On May 10, the city celebrates the **Festa di San Cataldo** with a procession of boats that escorts the statue of San Cataldo around the harbor. As it passes the Aragonese Castle, the castle lights up in a beautiful firework display.

Basilicata

Squeezed into the peninsula's instep between Puglia, Campania, and Calabria, Basilicata is Italy's poorest and least known province. Mountainous and isolated, backward Basilicata was long shunned. While its neighbors flourished during the agricultural revolution, it stagnated. Small farmers struggled to harvest corn and wheat, but the hillsides eroded and left them empty-handed.

In recent decades, loads of lire have gone to the rehabilitation of the region, and it is no longer the aching, motionless land of the past. Still, however, nature abuses Basilicata, striking it often with earthquakes. In 1980, the great quake that razed Naples had its epicenter here. One would expect the Greek gods to better treat this region, one of the Greeks' most prized colonies. Between 900 and 500 B.C.E., "Lucania" was part of Magna Grecia. Metaponto and Heraclea comprised the western ports in a sea circuit that extended all the way east into Turkey. Rome lured the Lucanians under its aegis and there they stayed until the Lombards conquered the region in the sixth century.

The capital Potenza has few potent offerings, but the cultural stronghold Matera harbors some interesting, esoteric structures. The **Sassi** are abandoned rock dwellings dating from the Paleolithic Age. In the ninth century, the caves sheltered persecuted monks. Today, they house artists (and an occasional movie crew) attracted by the primitive sparsity. The southern coast bordering the Gulf of Taranto consists of sandy beaches and ancient Greek ruins.

Basilicata is cut by two major train lines: the Taranto-Reggio di Calabria line, which stops at Metaponto for a bus connection to Matera, and the Taranto-Naples line, which stops at Potenza and Ferrandina, where buses connect to Matera. A direct Ferrovie Calabro-Lucane train links Bari with Matera.

Matera

Matera is at once Italy's newest metropolis and the world's second oldest residence. From the Stone Age to 1957, most inhabitants lived in ancient niches carved into the valley walls. These *sassi* were abandoned by the rustic denizens when cranes and bulldozers transformed the silent expanse into a hip, modern city. Today Basilicata's younger crowd fills the prehistoric caves with the throb of rock music.

Orientation and Practical Information

Matera is a difficult city to reach by public transportation. There are only eight **SITA** buses per day from Metaponto's train station (7am-6:30pm, 6 buses in winter 7am-5:30pm; L2300) and 2 from Potenza (at 5am and 2pm, L4700). Six **Ferrovie Calabro-Lucane** buses leave from Ferrandina's train station on the Potenza-Taranto line (6:30am-10:20pm, L2000). **Trains** also leave every 1-2 hours from Bari's central train station on the Calabro-Lucane line (6:50am-10:57pm, L3200). Most service is drastically reduced on Sundays and holidays. Matera is the only sizable city *not* served by the national FS rail system. Therefore, transportation rides heavily on buses. **Hitching** from Metaponto is feasible. Station yourself past the archeological site at the AGIP gas station. On a sunny day, stand at the beach street exit (100m in front of the train station); it's best to wait around 3pm, when Materese return home from the strand.

EPT: p. Vittorio Veneto, 19 (tel. 21 24 88). Follow via Roma down from the bus station. Not quite accustomed to the rigors of the tourist trade, but getting there. Maps and a pamphlet. English spoken. Also a new office near the *sassi* at p. San Pietro Caveoso (tel. 22 26 02). Both open July-Aug. Mon.-Fri. 8am-2pm and 3-8pm, Sat. 8am-2pm; in off-season, Mon.-Sat. 8am-2pm.

Post Office: via del Corso, off p. V. Veneto. Open Mon.-Fri. 8am-8pm, Sat. 8am-1:30pm. **Postal code:** 75100.

Telephones: SIP, via del Corso, 5 (tel. 221 08). Open daily 8am-9pm. At night, try **Antonoleggio Tommaso,** vico XX Settembre. Open 9pm-8am. **Telephone code:** 0835.

Buses and Trains: At P. Matteoti. **Ferrovie Calabro-Lucane** bus for Ferrandina, **SITA** buses for Metaponto and Potenza, **Ferrovia Calabro-Lucane** train for Bari. **SITA information** at p. Matteoti, 3 (tel. 21 22 44).

Police: Carabinieri, Tel. 21 21 21.

Accommodations

This accommodating city is regretfully short on accommodations. There are only three inexpensive hotels.

Albergo Roma, via Roma, 62 (tel. 21 27 01), downhill from the bus station in p. Matteotti. A pleasant place to stay—friendly, clean, and conveniently located. The owner distributes maps of the city (so you can avoid the EPT). Fills up fast during festival period (late June-early July). Singles L12,500. Doubles L19,000, with bath L22,000.

Albergo Italia, via D. Ridola, 5 (tel. 21 11 95), at via del Corso. Request one of the rooms that overlook the *sassi.* Singles L20,800, with bath L27,300. Doubles L36,000, with bath L43,700. Showers included.

Albergo Moderno, via dei Sariis, 11 (tel. 21 23 36). Continue downhill from Albergo Roma to via Lucana, turn left, then take the 3rd left. Rooms not spotless. Probable vacancy. Singles L12,500. Doubles L18,600. Showers included.

Food

Matera's fare is simple, but two dishes, typical of the farming region, are unusual: *favetta con cicore* (a soup of beans, celery, chicory, and croutons, all mixed in olive oil) and *frittata di spaghetti* (a pasta dish mixed with anchovies, eggs, bread crumbs, garlic, and oil). Don't leave Matera without trying *pane di grano duro,* a bread famous for its high-quality wheat. **Panificio Perrone,** via dei Sariis, 6, across from Albergo Moderno, sells large, fluffy loaves (L1350 per kg). They also sell tasty *biscotti al vino,* cookies baked with wine (L6000 per kg). (Open Mon.-Wed. and Fri.-Sat. 8am-2pm and 4-8pm, Thurs. 8am-2pm.) Create your own meal cheaply at the **market** between via Lucana and via A. Persio, near p. V. Veneto. (Open Mon.-Sat. 7am-1pm.) A warning for vegetarians and dieters: much of the food in the area is cooked with lard.

Osteria Paternoster, via Lombardi, 3. Descend the stairs next to the Libreria Cifarelli in p. V. Veneto. Subterranean and cool. Inexpensive family-style fare. *Pasto completo (primo, secondo,* ¼-liter of wine, service, and cover) L10,000. Open July-Aug. daily 11:30am-4pm and 6-10pm; in off-season Mon.-Sat. only.

Trattoria Cucina Casalinga, via Lucana, 46, off via Roma. Matera's best restaurant. Order the *orechiette al Materana,* noodles with a sauce of tomatoes, eggplant, zucchini, and basil (L6000). Their specialty is *involtino al Materana,* a veal dish (L8000). Local wine L3000 per liter. Cover L1500. Open July-Aug. daily noon-3pm and 8-10:30pm; in off-season Mon.-Sat. only.

Taverna Vecchia Matera, via B. Buozzi, 136. Inside a Paleolithic cave in *sasso caveoso. Menù* L16,000. Go wild for this price (*primo, secondo,* vegetable, fruit, and wine). The best dishes are *orechiette alle contadina* (with meat sauce) and *agnello a artigiano* (lamb with onions and tomato). Actor Richard Gere allegedly ate here daily when filming the movie *King David.* Open daily 8am-2pm and 6pm-midnight.

Il Cantinone, via S. Biagio, 13, off p. V. Veneto. An airy, mellow hangout. Self-service food. *Orechiette al tegamino,* baked pasta with meat and cheese (L4500). Regional specialties on request. Pizza L2800-5000. Vast selection of beer L1300-4000 per bottle. Open daily 7pm-midnight.

Sights

Before venturing to the *sassi,* take a quick look around the churches at the city's fringes. Walking up via San Biagio away from p. Vittorio Veneto, you will come first to the **Church of San Giovanni Battista** (St. John the Baptist). This thirteenth-century building is outstanding for its decorative portal. The interior is pure Gothic: Arches, vaults, and columns create a beautiful, compact, medieval interior. By backtracking through p. V. Veneto onto via del Corso, you will come to the baroque **Church of San Francesco,** dedicated to Saint Francis of Assisi, and completely rebuilt in the seventeenth century. The **cathedral** in p. del Duomo, at the end of via Duomo and in the heart of the *sassi* zone, is one of the finest of those formidable structures built in the Puglian-Romanesque style. Erected between 1268 and 1270, the church sports the typical features of that period: a tall nave, projected moldings, rose windows, and richly carved doorways. The sixteenth-century **Cappella dell' Annunziata,** (the last chapel on the left before the transept), is especially stunning. (Hit the lights on the left as you enter.) Also notice at the end of the transept, the sixteenth-century stone nativity, seemingly modelled on the region's caves and those who lived there.

From here, you can begin your tour of the amazing *sassi* in the two valleys **Sasso Caveoso** and **Sasso Barisano.** The *sassi* are of obscure origin; the crudest are prehistoric niches in the natural rock, some occupied 2000 years ago. The later *sassi and streets were built from cut stone. Although the sassi* were almost completely evacuated after the new city was erected, young couples are creatively restoring the ancient homes. Knock on some doors and ask to take a look around; most will consent to a peek. After viewing the Sasso Barisano from the square, walk through the arch down to **via Madonna delle Virtù,** also called the Strada Panoramica dei Sassi. Across the gorgeous canyon formed by the **Gravina River,** you can see prehistoric caves. Among these are sixth-century **chiese rupestri** (rock churches), many of which have remnants of Byzantine frescoes from the twelfth to sixteenth centuries. If you follow via Madonna delle Virtù south (to the right), you will eventually come to the **Churches of San Pietro Caveoso** and **Santa Maria d' Idris,** and farther down to the **Church of Santa Lucia alla Malve.** Although the Church of San Pietro Caveoso is closed to the public, the two other churches feature beautiful eleventh-century Byzantine frescoes dug right into the tufa of the caves. (Both open June-Sept. 8am-1pm and 2-8pm.) To enter them at other times of the year, contact Sopraintendenza ai Beni Artistici e Storicie, p. Pascoli, 1 (tel. 22 27 41).

As you roam the Sasso Caveoso, you're likely to be approached by young children who get their spending money by giving tours of *sassi.* Take one up on the offer (tip L1000-2000); even if you don't know a word of Italian, you'll get to see places that would be difficult to spot otherwise. Your guide will show you tombs, excavations, and Byzantine frescoes; take you deep inside some of the dwellings to demonstrate how cool they remain in the summer and warm in winter; and reveal the king and queen's quarters. These kids also have agreements with every vendor in the *sassi,* so don't be surprised if your "tour" includes detours to a few souvenir stands. (The shopkeepers here are, however, extremely courteous.)

Via Buozzi winds through the Sasso Caveoso to p. Pascoli and the **Pinacoteca d' Errico** (in the newer part of the city overlooking the *sassi*), which exhibits a group of seventeenth- and eighteenth-century paintings. Call the *sopraintendenza* for permission to visit. Down the street, in the direction of p. V. Veneto, the **Museo Nazionale Domenico Ridola,** via Ridola, 24 (tel. 21 12 39), off via Lucana outside the *sassi,* houses an excellent, boldly-displayed prehistoric and early classical collection, all in a former seventeenth-century monastery. (Open Tues.-Sun 9am-2pm. Free.)

Entertainment

Matera's big moment comes in the **Festival of Santa Maria della Bruna,** held during the last week of June. This celebration harks back to 1380, when it was a religious event. Now, almost wholly secular, it culminates on July 2, when a procession of shepherds leaves the *duomo* at dawn. They are followed at dusk by the "carro" or cart holding a Madonna. Two families work on the cart for four months, attesting to the Materan expertise in woodworking and papier mâché. The ornate cart rumbles along via XX Settembre, which is kindled like an amusement park with thousands of small lights while warriors in medieval costume and clergy on horseback solemnly march alongside. At one point, everyone goes monkey in an event known as "The Tearing of the Cart," in which the cart holding the Madonna is ripped to pieces by people anxious for precious relics, after the Madonna statue and other valuables have been removed to tower quarters.

Continuing for the rest of the month of July is the **Festival Internazionale Luglio Materano,** which holds cultural events at 9pm every evening. Most are held in the open air and are free. Contact the administrative office of Matera's EPT, via Viti de Marco, 9 (tel. 21 24 88), for programs. All of Matera's 150,000 townspeople seem to make a show along p. Vittorio Veneto for the mighty *passegiata.*

Metaponto

Lumped together under the name Metaponto are a popular beach resort, a lonely train station, and scattered archeological ruins, all several kilometers apart.

If you can tear yourself away from the water, check out the impressive Greek ruins. Follow the road that leads away from the station for about 3km, and then turn right onto the coastal highway for Taranto. From this crossing, it's 2km more (an easy hitch) to the **Tavole Palatine**—the ruins of the Greek temple of Hera. The famous Greek mathematician Pythagoras is supposed to have taught here until his death in 479 B.C.E. The ruins, 15 standing columns and part of the flooring and entablature, have been called Tavole Palatine since the Crusades when *paladini* (nobles) gathered here before leaving for the Holy Land. Metapontum was founded in 773 B.C.E. by the Greek inhabitants of Sybaris, a people known for their hedonism. The city suited Pythagoras, who fled here after being expelled from Crotone. The adjacent **Antiquarium** displays maps and aerial photos that explain the development of the city, and Greek artifacts from the area, including some well-preserved decorative elements from the temple. (Open Oct.-March. Tues.-Sat. 9am-noon and 2-5pm; April.-Sept. Tues.-Sat. 9am-1pm and 3:30-6:30pm.)

At the end of a pleasant country road (the 2nd right off the road leading away from the train station), you'll find the scanty ruins of the Doric **Temple of Apollo Licius** and the remains of a **Greek theater** (25-min. walk). The theater was the first to be constructed from a mound of dirt and encircled by containing walls rather than dug out of a hillside. To reach the clear water and fine sand of Metaponto's **beach,** take the first right off the road that leads away from the train station. From here, it is a short 2-km walk or a simple hitch. Metaponto's streets are lined with flowering trees that sway in the steady wind. Concessions cover only part of the beach; much of it is undeveloped and borders grassy dunes. There are only two lodging options. **Hotel Oasi,** via Olimpia (tel. 74 19 30), off via Ionio (the 1st street off the main road to the beach, 2km from the station) requires full pension at L38,000 per person. A luxurious alternative and the only one for single travelers is the **Hotel Kennedy,** viale Jonio (tel. 74 19 60), on the right just at the turnoff from the station. If you hold them to the listed prices, you can get a gorgeous single with balcony for L21,000. Doubles are L34,000.

Camping is probably the best idea if you plan to hang out at Metaponto's beaches for a couple of days. One of the nicest of the campgrounds that line the main beach road is **Camping Magna Grecia,** via Lido, 1 (tel. 74 18 55), ½km from the strand, which charges L4500 per person and L4500 per tent. (July 1-Aug. 23 L5000 per person, L5500 per tent.) Located at the edge of a pine forest, Magna Grecia is a veritable amusement park with tennis courts, swimming pool, game rooms, snack bars, and a disco. The campground closest to the beach is **Camping Internazionale,** via Nareide (tel. 74 19 16), whose rates are L4000 per person, L3500 per large tent, and L3000 per small tent. (July and Aug. L4800 per person, L4300 per large tent, and L3800 per small tent.) This campsite is less spacious but pleasant and sylvan.

Metaponto is an important **rail** junction on the Taranto-Reggio line (50 min. from the former, L2200) with a connection to Naples by way of Potenza. **Bus** service connects the Metaponto station with Matera (7am-6:30pm 8 per day, in winter 7am-5:30pm 6 per day; L2100). The **EPT office** on viale delle Sirene (tel. 74 19 33) is open daily (July-Sept. 8am-2pm and 3-8pm). The official here speaks excellent English and is a Basilicata native. There is only one **bank,** in the center of town (open Mon.-Fri. 8am-1pm). Metaponto's **telephone code** is 0835.

Calabria

Calabria is Italy's last foothold before it lunges for Sicily. An agricultural region, it is split by plush green valleys and sprinkled with fishing villages. Though surrounded by water—the Ionian and Tyrrhenian Seas and the Strait of Messina—water rarely blesses the dry, Calabrian ground that needs it most. That farms in the region grow so verdant is due to endless irrigation. In contrast to fecund Sicily, water was so scarce only 30 years ago that pharmacies sold it to desperate farmers. "Cultural" ties, however, draw the two regions together—the Sicilian Mafia expands into Calabria, where the fearsome mob is called the *'ndrangheta.* As in Sicily, the conniving clan's activities have obstructed public works and clipped development. These and other setbacks have sent shiploads of Calabrian hopefuls to America in this century.

Calabria shares the hot-potato history of most of southern Italy. Beginning with the ancient Greeks, hordes of foreign invaders such as the Byzantines, Saracens, Normans, and Aragonese tossed around this land and left their indelible marks on buildings and on a population of diverse ancestral lineages.

Of the region's four important cities, only two warrant your time and energy. Cosenza has a picturesque old town and an interesting Romanesque cathedral—set in the heart of the Sila Massif, a great granite plateau (1100-1700m) running between Catanzaro and Cosenza. Magnificent pine and oak forests, emerald-green lakes, and carpets of flowers beautify the Sila in summer, while steep mountains and steady snowfall make for perfect skiing in the winter. Near the southern tip of Calabria is Reggio di Calabria, a city with a superb archeological museum that houses the recently discovered *Bronze Warriors of Riace*—two extraordinary Greek statues. Instead of spending your time in Calabria's other two major cities, polluted Crotone and vapid Catanzaro, venture north along the sandy beaches of the Calabrian Riviera. Be sure to stop at Rossano and Gerace, two under-recognized towns that have preserved numerous Byzantine monuments.

Public transportation in Calabria is far more likely to cause you difficulty than the *'ndrangheta*'s cement boots. Don't expect to cover large distances quickly.

Cosenza

This little town is divided into old and new sections by the Busento River. Cosenza's major asset is its location; it's a perfect base for exploring the Sila Massif, a breathtaking, unspoiled chain of mountains.

Orientation and Practical Information

The new, multi-million-dollar train station lies outside the city on the *superstrada,* Trains every half-hour service Paola on the Rome-Reggio Calabria coastal line (L3200). Trains also run from Metaponto, changing at Sibari (L7300). To get to town from the new train station, take bus #5 to the old station (5:20am-11pm, L500). **Corso Mazzini,** one of the main thoroughfares, runs parallel to the tracks, 2 blocks in front of the old station. Once on corso Mazzini, with your back to the train station, turn left for the old town, right for the bus station and SIP.

Tourist Offices: via Tagliamento, 15 (tel. 278 21), off corso Mazzini. An administrative office. Open Mon.-Fri. 8am-2pm. **Public information** office inconveniently located in p. Rossi (tel. 39 05 95). From p. Fera near the bus station, follow via Simonetta to viale della Repubblica, then bear right on via p. Rossi. The tourist office is across the rotary at the beginning of the *autostrada.* Maps, hotel listings, and some information on the Sila, but no English spoken. Open Mon.-Fri. 8am-1:30pm and 2-8pm, Sun. 8am-1:30pm.

Post Office: via V. Veneto, at the end of via Piave. Open Mon.-Sat. 8:15am-7:30pm. **Postal code:** 87100.

Telephones: SIP, via dell'Autostazione, above the bus station. Open daily 8:10am-8pm. At other times, try **Croce Bianca,** via Beato Angelo D'Acri, 29. **Telephone code:** 0984.

New Train Station: via Pompilla (tel. 39 19 62), on Superstrada SS 107.

Bus Station: off p. Fera (tel. 282 76), at the opposite end of corso Mazzini from the train station. **Ferrovie dello Stato** and **Ferrovie Calabro-Lucane.** Schedules are posted at each gate

(#5 for Catanzaro, #14 for the Western Coast). Adequate snackbar open 24 hours. Buses run infrequently on Sun. and holidays.

Hospital: Ospedale Civile dell'Annunziata, Tel. 72 91.

Police: Carabinieri, In emergencies tel. 21 21 21.

Accommodations and Camping

The small beans Cosenza has to offer in affordable accommodations sprout near the old train station.

Albergo Bruno, corso Mazzini, 27 (tel. 738 89). Run by a hospitable woman who will tailor rooms to fit 1-4 people. Homey. Shared bathroom with tub. Singles L15,000. Doubles L25,000.

Hotel Exelsior, p. Matteoti, 14 (tel. 743 83), facing the old train station. Aged and with a ragged red carpet that expected better. Singles L24,000, with bath L30,000. Doubles L36,000, with bath L40,000.

Locanda Santelli, viale Trieste, 8 (tel. 732 63). If you can ignore the barbed wire and electronically locked main door, you will find an almost habitable cell; by far the cheapest alternative for single travelers. Singles L12,500. Doubles L21,500. Showers L3000.

Camping: The best camping in the area is at the Sila Massif (see Near Cosenza) and in the seaside town of Scalea (6:35am-6pm 4 buses per day, 1¼ hr.). Two sites on Scalea's Tyrrhenian waterfront are **Camping il Gabbiano** (tel. (0985) 205 63) and **Campeggio Moby Dick** (tel. (0985) 202 78).

Food

The fare here, as in much of Calabria, is spiced deliciously with hot peppers. The few restaurants in the ancient city are cheaper and more colorful than those in the modern. Try the famed *gelato* over the bridge at Coni Zorro. The produce market is behind the bus station.

Trattoria Peppino, p. Crispi, 3/4, near the old station. The younger crowd gathers here; the price is right and the food abundant. *Menù* with beverage L10,000. Assorted pasta dishes L4000, meat dishes L5500. Cover L1500. Open Mon.-Sat. noon-3pm and 7-9:30pm.

Trattoria Italia, viale Trieste, 92 (tel. 733 97). Excellent, family-run restaurant decorated with foliage and ancient artifacts. *Menù* L15,000. The best *primo* is *gnocchi alla tamarra* (with chunks of pepperoni sausage). For the *secondi,* try the *trota silana ai ferri* (grilled trout) or *pesca spada* (swordfish). Open Mon.-Sat. 11:30am-3:30pm and 6:30-10pm.

L'Archibugie, via Biscardi, 3, off via Mazzini toward bus station. A fast-food cafeteria in Wonderland. Tables and chairs are designed from stained tree stumps. Pasta dishes L2500, sausage or chicken L3000, and stuffed eggplant L2000. Cover L500. Open Tues.-Sun. 11am-3:30pm and 6-10:30pm.

Pizzeria Tavola Calda, corso Telesio, 214, over the Mario Martire bridge in the old city. Tiny restaurant, tiny brick oven, giant *pizza grande* (L3000). Stand-up or take-out orders only. Open Mon.-Fri. 9am-12:30pm and 5-8:30pm, Sat. 9am-12:30pm.

Sights

Everything of interest in Cosenza is across the murky **Busento River** in the old town. In the fifth century, King Alaric of the Goths headed for Calabria after sacking Rome, but he died of malaria soon afterward in Cosenza. The despondent tribe buried its leader, clad in his armor and mounted on his horse, beneath the mud of the river bed. Several fruitless digs have been performed in hope of discovering Alaric's hidden treasures.

After crossing the river, turn left onto corso Telesio, and make the gradual climb uphill to the **cathedral.** Keep your head up while walking, for there is no telling what will be disposed of from the medieval windows. Despite the excess of garbage, these dark, winding streets are as intriguing as the cathedral itself. When the cathedral was finished in 1222, Frederick II donated what is today the city's most prized possession—the tiny, ornate **Byzantine Cross.** The colorful jewel (204mm by 264mm) is adorned on the obverse with a Christ figure accompanied by the mourning Madonna on the left arm, the supplicating St. John the Evangelist on the right, and the archangel St. Michael above. In 1988, the cross was in Florence undergoing restoration. At the top of the hill is p. XV Marzo and the **Museo Civico,** with an impressive collection of prehistoric bronzes. (Open Mon.-Sat. 9am-1pm. Free.) Next to the museum sits the ninth-century **Teatro Rendano,** completely rebuilt after its destruction in World War II. The theater reverberates with opera from January to April. From p. XV Marzo, you can make the climb to the twelfth-century **Norman Castle** and its spectacular view. (The castle's doorman will grant admission, especially in mornings.) Relax in the olive grove nearby—a perfect place for a picnic. While descending the hill, the unimpressive **Church of San Francesco d' Assisi** will appear on your left.

Near Cosenza: Sila Massif

If you've journeyed all the way to Cosenza, chances are you've come to visit the **Sila Massif.** La Sila constitutes 2000 square kilometers of uninterrupted natural beauty spread among three main sectors: La Greca, the traditional area to the north; la Grande, the central area with Camigliatello and San Giovanni in Fiore; and la Piccola, a coastal area that contains Lago Ampolino. These three areas together constitute one of the last mountain chains in Italy still covered with virgin forest. However, summer homes, hotels, and restaurants are ever more prevalent, and a new super-highway now cuts through la Sila.

La Sila's two main villages, **Camigliatello Silano** and **San Giovanni in Fiore,** can both be reached easily from Cosenza (7 buses per day, 45 min., L1700; 3 Calabro-Lucane trains per day, 1½ hr., L1500). The train route is definitely the more scenic. It is best to explore the area from Camigliatello, a wonderful little alpine town with clean streets and chateaux. Before trekking into the wilderness, confer with the somewhat disorganized hiking experts at **Pro Loco,** on via del Turismo (tel. 97 80 91), off via Roma in Camigliatello. They sell a useful trail map of the Sila for L1000. (Theoretically open daily 9am-12:30pm and 3-8pm.)

From Camigliatello, there are two interesting hikes. Following the signs, you can walk (1½ hr.) or hitch down to **Lago Cecita,** one of the area's three beautiful lakes. Take any of the dirt roads that bear left after the small pine forest and you will eventually reach the shore. A more demanding and confusing hike is the 2½-hour climb to the top of **Monte Botte Donato** (1930m), the highest peak in la Sila. To get there, follow the highway back toward Cosenza for about 4km and take the left turn at the *Fago del Soldato* intersection. While climbing, bear left and you will eventually come to a ski-lift—climb under it until you reach an unmarked road. Turn left onto the road and continue climbing until you reach the summit. From the peak of Monte Botte Donato, on a clear day, you can see both the Tyrrhenian and Ionian Seas. The less adventurous can visit the nearby pine forest located close to Camigliatello; pack a picnic at any of the grocery stores on via Roma. (**Alimentari F. Scrivano,** at #186, stocks a wide selection of wines and cold cuts. (Open Mon.-Sat. 7am-1pm and 4-9pm.) To reach the woods, take the path starting at the Cultura Residence sign, ½km along the highway to Cosenza. Continue walking until you see the trees. **Da Sa Sà,** via Roma, 12, rents bicycles for L3000 per hour. Another way to see the Sila is to continue on the little train from Camigliatello to San Giovanni (2 per day, 40 min., L1500). The view from the train is splendid. You'll see Alpine plateaus covered with pine and oak forests, and countless green fields laced by rushing mountain streams. You can return to Camigliatello by either train or bus (the bus is more frequent—20 min., L1400).

Amazing **skiing** conditions bring downhill diehards from Christmas until the Ides of March. Camigliatello's **Tasso Ski Trail,** on Monte Curcio, is about 3km from town, and the lift up costs L1800 per trip (L22,000 per day). You can rent skis and boots at **Da Sa Sà** for L16,000 per day. Camigliatello's **Albergo Tana del Lupo,** on via Federici (tel. (0984) 97 83 17), about 700m off via Roma, offers pine-scented singles for L20,000, doubles L35,000, with bath L40,000. (July-Sept. and Dec.-March obligatory full pension L65,000.) During high season, **Hotel Mancuso,** via del Turismo (tel. 97 80 02), requires only half-pension (L43,500), but also offers a more economical full pension (L53,000). The **Baita,** on via Roma (tel. 97 81 97), has less elegant singles with bath (L25,000), doubles with bath (L45,000), and mandatory full pension in high-season (L50,000).

The closest campsite to Camigliatello is **La Fattoria** (tel. (0984) 97 83 64), about 3km from Camigliatello on the road to Lago Cecita. The nicer **Villagio Lago Arvo** (tel. (0984) 99 70 60) sits on the banks of the Lago Arvo Lake in Lorica, 37km from Camigliatello. Take the bus or train toward San Giovanni in Fiore and get off at Silvana Mansio, a 15-kilometer hitch from Lorica.

Western Coast

Aging fortresses on the bluffs offset the displeasing effect of the rows of apartment buildings lining the coast. The beaches on the Tyrrhenian stretch for miles, but you should be selective. Going as far south as Pizzo means rocky terrain and tourist crowds. The northern, more picturesque region hugs the coast between Praia a Mare and Sangineto. White beaches and the towering rocks of inland mountains meet here to form a majestic landscape. Most trains to or from Naples or Reggio stop at **Praia a Mare.** The street leading away from the train station will take you directly to the beach: If you can handle the masses here, you can not only enjoy the pellucid blue water of the Tyrrhenian sea, but also a view of the **Isola di Dino**—an island where, according to legend, Ulysses sojourned. If you plan to spend the night in Praia a Mare, try the **Pensione la Piedigrotta,** on via N. Mairorana.

From Praia a Mare, any local train headed toward Reggio Calabria will take you to the western coast's other seaside villages: **Scalea, Cirella, Diamante,** and **Sangineto** (with its ruins of an ancient castle). **Paola** is another coastal town that makes a convenient stopover, especially if you're on your way to Cosenza. To reach the shoreline, take a right turn immediately outside the train station. While a right under the trestle will lead you to the beach, a left followed by another left deposits you at **Albergo Elena,** via San Leonardo, 8 (tel. (0982) 21 40; singles L14,000, with bath L18,000; doubles L27,000, with bath L33,000; full pension L40,000, with bath L45,000). Reserve early for August.

Reggio di Calabria

Totally rebuilt after the 1908 earthquake, Reggio has little character. The lido area is only a slight improvement over the port and no more inviting. Reggio's sole gift to Calabria is its exceptional National Museum. Here, at the edge of the Roman homeland, bronze figures flaunt ideal proportions and flawless craftsmanship. Otherwise, try to escape to the countryside, where orange, lemon, and olive groves as well as flower fields cultivated by the perfume industry reveal the sensuous side of Italian life. Less than 35km north along a coastal road (from which you can view Sicily, the sea, and the volcanic Aeolian Islands), lies the tiny village of Scilla. The rocks on which Scilla rests stretch out into the sea; the ships in Homer's *Odyssey* perished on them after escaping the turbulent currents of the gulf.

Ferries

Reggio lies at the end of two train lines: Rome-Reggio and Metaponto-Reggio. The city's port harbors ferries to Sicily and Malta, but the fastest route to these islands is via the trains that pass through the nearby city of **Villa San Giovanni. Ferrovie dello Stato** ferries (tel. (0965) 981 23) accept all InterRail, Eurail, and kilometric tickets. **SNAV** hydrofoils (tel. 295 68) and **Tirrenia** ferries, via B. Bozzi, 31 (tel. 920 32), also serve Reggio's port.

San Giovanni-Messina: Ferrovie departs 3:20am-10:05pm (22 per day, 35 min., L600). **Caronte** also runs the route.

Reggio-Messina: Ferrovie departs 6:55am-9:55pm (10 per day, 50 min., L800). **SNAV** departs Mon.-Fri. 7:15am-10:20pm (18 per day) and Sat. (12 per day, 20 min., L4000).

Reggio-Vulcano (Lipari Islands): SNAV hydrofoil departs June 15-Sept. 15 (3 per day, 2 hr., L25,000).

Reggio-Catania: Tirrenia departs Tues., Fri., and Sun. at 8:30am (3 hr. 15 min., L10,400).

Reggio-Syracuse: Tirrenia departs Tues., Fri., and Sun. at 8:30am (6 hr. 45 min., L10,400).

Reggio-Malta: Tirrenia departs Tues., Fri., and Sun. at 8:30am (11 hr.; Oct.-May L55,000; June-Sept. L66,300).

Practical Information

Most traveling within Reggio will be along the strip of **corso Garibaldi,** well traversed by city bus (L500). It is only about 1½km from Reggio Lido to Reggio Centrale.

Tourist Information: APT, booth at the central train station (tel. 271 20). Open irregularly Mon.-Sat. 8am-2pm and 2:30-8pm. The **main information office,** corso Garibaldi, 329 (tel. 920 12), is also helpful and more convenient to the Lido train station. Open Mon.-Fri. 8am-8pm, Sat. 8am-1pm and 2-7pm. Two other booths with similar hours at the airport (tel. 32 02 91) and at via Roma, 3 (tel. 211 71).

CTS: Azienda Viaggi Rossana, corso Garibaldi, 238 (tel. 286 27). Student travel information and service. Open Mon.-Fri. 9am-1pm and 4:30-7:30pm, Sat. 9am-1pm.

Post Office: via Miraglia, 14, near p. Italia. Open Mon.-Fri. 8am-7pm, Sat. 8am-2pm. **Postal code:** 89100.

Telephones: SIP, corso Garibaldi, 200m past the Azienda toward the port. Open daily 8am-8pm. **Telephone code:** 0965.

Train Stations: Centrale, p. Garibaldi at the southern end of town near inexpensive accommodations. **Lido,** at the northern end of via Zerbi near the museum, port, and beaches. Most trains stop at both stations. Night train service to Milan (12 per day, L48,000), Rome (8 per day, L34,000), Florence (10 per day, L44,500), Venice (L50,000), and Naples (6 per day, L23,000).

Hospital: via Melacrino (tel. 200 10).

Police: Carabinieri Tel. 21 21 21.

Accommodations and Camping

A room in Reggio means digging deep into the pocketbook, unless you venture to the hostel in nearby Scilla.

Ostello Principessa Paola del Belgio (IYHF), via Nazionale, 2 (tel. 75 40 33), at Scilla (45 min. by train, 7 per day; by bus, 11 per day). In an old castle overlooking the sea. A 10-min. walk from the beach. L6000 per night in advance. Lockout 9am-5pm. Open April-Sept.

Albergo San Giorgio, via Gaeta, 9 (tel. 994 64), near the central train station, off corso Garibaldi before the bridge as you walk away from the port. Clean, safe, with genial management. Somber rooms. Singles L25,000, with bath L30,000. Doubles L37,000, with bath L47,000. Showers included.

Albergo Noel, via Zerbi, 13 (tel. 33 00 44), across from Stazione Lido. Another good choice with more availability. Small singles L25,000, with bath L30,000. Doubles L32,000, with bath L40,000. Showers included.

Callea, via Verona, 2 (tel. 941 54), 2 blocks uphill from the archeological museum. This creepy, foul-smelling place is not a good choice for women. Singles L15,000. Doubles L30,000. Showers L2000.

Albergo Saturnia, via Caprera, 5 (tel. 210 12), near Stazione Centrale. Cramped, noisy rooms in an unpleasant atmosphere. Broken windows. Often full. Singles L15,000. Doubles L20,000. Showers L2500.

Albergo Abruzzo (tel. 238 62), across the hall from Albergo Saturnia. Run by two elderly women. Disheveled rooms. Usually full. Singles with bath L26,000. Doubles with bath L34,000.

Camping: Campeggio degli Ulivi, località Eremo Botte (tel. 919 13). A 10-minute bus ride from the central station on #7 or 8. In a hillside park overlooking the city and sea, it offers the best deal in town: 4-person bungalows with bath and refrigerator L37,000. 2-room suites L42,000. Camping L3500 per person, L6000-10,000 per tent.

Food

Reggio's kitchens feel most at home with *spaghetti alla Calabrese* (noodles dressed in a potent pimento sauce), *capicolli* ham, and other meats spiced with local hot peppers. Reggio's large and active **market** lies at p. del Popolo, off via Amendola near the port. (Open Mon.-Sat. 6am-1:30pm.)

Trattoria del Villeggiante, via Tripepi, 1 (tel. 990 01), at the northern end of town up the street from the market. A happy little establishment that specializes in do-it-yourself dinners—give them your price, and they will kindly design your meal. A la carte specialties include *pesce spada* (swordfish, L6000). *Menù* L10,000. Cover L1000. Open Mon.-Sat. noon-4pm and 7-11pm.

Rusty Pizzeria, p. De Nava, 7 (tel. 200 12), next to the museum. Stand at a counter or sit on low benches to eat the thick pizza. Zesty 'za and beer less than L5000. Pizza L6000-7000 per kg. Beer and soft drinks L1200. The restaurant next door serves whole pizzas (L3500-4000), spaghetti with mushroom, pepper, or shrimp (L5000), and *involtini* (rolled meat, L4000). Cover L1000. No wine served. Open Thurs.-Tues. noon-2pm and 6pm-midnight.

Ristorante al Bronzi, via III Settembre, 1 (tel. 214 52), off via Zerbi, on the road towards corso Garibaldi from Stazione Lido. The flashing light outside screams, "We speak English!" Luckily, the food speaks Italian. Full meals L16,000. Savor the *maccheroncini della Nonna* with its hot eggplant and tomato sauce. Wine L2000 per glass. Open Sat.-Thurs. 12:30-3pm and 7:30-11pm.

La Comida, via N. Furnari, 63 (tel. 59 39 98). Follow corso Garibaldi to the river, go left up the hill, cross the 2nd bridge onto viale Calabria, and take the 1st right. Far away from the main part of town, but Reggio's best pizzeria. Take-out pizzas L2000-2900. Open Fri.-Wed. 8pm-midnight.

La Pignata, via D. Tripepi, 122 (tel. 278 41), off corso Garibaldi near the SIP. An elegant pizzeria-restaurant, with carved wooden ceilings and leather seats. *Pizza polifemo* (with mussels) L4500. *Maccheroni calabresi* L6000. All meals, including pizzas, come with a tasty appetizer of *bruschetta,* pieces of hard bread topped with a spicy red sauce. Cover at pizzeria L1000, at restaurant L1500. Open Thurs.-Tues. noon-2:45pm and 7:30-11pm.

Sights and Entertainment

If not for the sea, this dreary city of narrow streets and low concrete buildings would have little livelihood. The **lungomare,** a pleasant park strip overlooking the water and the rugged Sicilian coast, and its beach are Reggio's only scenic offerings.

The unimpressive ruins along its route—remnants of a Roman bath and some pieces of Greek wall by the post office—do not properly preface the top-rated **Museo Nazionale,** p. De Nava, on corso Garibaldi near the Stazione Lido, which documents Magna Grecia civilization from excavations in Calabria. Note especially a set of dramatic tablets from the fifth and sixth centuries B.C.E. illustrating the story of Persephone and other mythological groupings: *Castor and Pollux* and *Achilles and Agamemnon.* The bas-reliefs are extremely refined and expressive. Upstairs is a fine picture gallery that houses works by southern artists, including Antonello da Messina. The two masterpieces of the museum, however, are the extraordinary **Bronzi di Riace** (Bronze Warriors of Riace)—two large Greek statues found off the coast of Riace, Calabria, in 1972. These overwhelming statues were miraculously preserved for over 2000 years in the gentle waters of the Ionian. After painstaking restoration, these works were identified as Greek originals and dated at the middle of the fifth century B.C.E., the Golden Age of Greek sculpture. (Open Tues.-Sat. 9am-1:30pm and 3:30-7pm, Sun. and Mon. 9am-12:30pm. Admission L3000.)

Reggio is more inviting as the sun sets and corso Garibaldi fills for the evening *passeggiata*. For a night of entertainment, **Papillon,** via II Settembre, 55/57 (tel. 981 95), trips the light fantastic nightly in summer (L8000). Run to **L'Oasi** (tel. 484 59) to soak in rays along the beachside, in the Pentimele zone of Reggio. Admission (L28,000) includes a cabin with shower, tennis courts, swimming pool, and an evening of disco. You can sit on its flower-lined beach for free. A full meal in the lovely restaurant is an extra L8500. Reggio's **Feste di Settembre** causes a yearly ruckus with folklore exhibitions, concerts, and religious ceremonies. From March 21 to June 21 the town hosts a popular bicycle race.

Near Reggio

Scilla and Bagnara Calabra are two fishing villages each about 45 minutes from Reggio along the Tyrrhenian coast (see the hostel listing under Reggio accommodations). The picturesque hamlet and beach resort of **Scilla** sits above the famous rock behind which, according to Homer, a female monster with six heads, 12 feet, and a voice like a yelping puppy hid before devouring entire ships newly escaped from the harrowing whirlpool of Charybdis. Try to avoid Scilla on Sundays, when half of Calabria drains onto its small rocky beach. A 10-minute walk from the beach will take you to an enjoyable locals' cafe with a superb view, **Paper Ros** (tel. 75 42 62) opens its doors daily from 8:30am to 2am. The town is best at night, after the daytrippers have left and yellow lights illuminate the square-jawed castle.

A Scilla splurge will carry you up to **Virtigine,** p. San Rocco, 14, for a drink. The outdoor seats overlook the castle. (Open daily 7:30pm-midnight.)

Bagnara Calabra, 8km north of Scilla, is a small town nestled among cliffs and grottoes. Swordfishing boats bob offshore, their tall lookout towers reaching skyward. The road north of town commands a view of the town, Sicily, and the Lipari Islands. If you feel like visiting the mountains rather than the sea, try the pine- and birch-covered **Aspromonte,** a mountain chain that occupies the southernmost tip of the Italian peninsula. To reach the center of the area, take one of the nine daily blue buses (#127 or 128) in front of Reggio's central train station to **Gamberie** (L1800), where you will enjoy a marvelous view of Sicily and the straits of Messina from the heights of Puntone di Scirocco (1660m), accessible by chairlift.

Calabrian Riviera

The long stretch of silken beaches (sadly interrupted by several oil refineries) from Reggio di Calabria to Lido di Metaponto is a hotspot for Italians and Germans, but is rarely frequented by Americans. Of the numerous beaches along this stretch, reached by train along the Reggio-Catanzaro line, **Soverato** (2½ hr. from Reggio, L8000) and **Capo Rizzuto** (4½ hr., L11,900) are among the most expansive and scenic. If you are staying in Reggio, however, and have only a little time to explore the area, you might consider visiting the lovely, nearby beaches at **Bova Marina** and **Bovalino,** which are reached easily by train (L2400 and L4400, respectively).

Locri (2 hr. by train from Reggio, L4500) is a sleepy modern town with an endless, smooth beach, plenty of tennis courts, and some disappointing Roman ruins. Originally founded by the Greeks in 673 B.C.E., the town was subsequently conquered by the Romans in 205 B.C.E. and completely destroyed by the Saracens in the seventh century. Unfortunately, little remains from its past. If clouds interfere with your sun-worshipping plans in Locri, you might consider walking or hitching to the excavation site 3½km south of the town. On the grounds there is an **Antiquarium,** which houses some architectural fragments and a few coins. (Open in summer Mon. 9am-1pm, Tues.-Sat. 9am-1pm and 4:30-7:30pm.) The National Museum in Reggio houses many of the best pieces from the excavation.

If you plan to spend the night in Locri, try the **Ristorante and Albergo Orientale,** on via Tripoli, 31 (tel. (0964) 202 61). From the train station, walk away from the sea 4 blocks to a major thoroughfare, then turn right; the Orientale is on a street to the left, another 4 blocks away. The place almost always has space, and its somewhat eccentric owner (a veteran of the Spanish Civil War) earnestly entreats you to stay in the well-kept if aging hotel. (Singles L9000. Doubles L18,000.) For an inferno of flavor and spice, the **Trattoria Manglaviti,** via Roma, 116, cooks up a L10,000 *menù* for elder locals who have been dealing and drinking here for years. (Open daily 10am-11pm.)

Although Locri itself is disappointing, only 10km inland is **Gerace,** a lovely medieval town perched on a cliff high above the colorful Calabrian countryside. Buses to Gerace leave from the *piazza* in front of the Locri train station (Mon.-Sat. 7am-5:30pm 6 per day, L900). Gerace lives and breathes medieval architecture, with the heartbeat throbbing at the **cathedral,** Calabria's largest. When you enter you'll immediately notice the structure's imperial crypt, supported by 26 ancient columns from Locri. From the crypt, climb the stairs up into a wonderful Romanesque interior characterized by the finest basilica proportions. The arcades, which separate the cathedral's three naves, are composed of overlapping double arches resting on ancient columns made from granite or marble. Outside, to the left of the entrance, is an exquisitely detailed Gothic portal. Another extraordinary portal graces the **Church of San Francesco** (1252), down the street and to the right of the cathedral entrance. Its geometric design reveals Byzantine influence. Gerace only has one hotel (**Dei Monti;** tel. 35 61 16) and it'll rob your moneybelt, so make it a daytrip. For information about Gerace and Locri, consult the **EPT** office in Locri, via Fiume, 1 (tel. (0964) 296 00; open July-Aug. Mon.-Sat. 8am-8pm, Sun. 8am-noon; in off-season Mon.-Fri. 8am-2pm.)

About 40km north of Locri is the small coastal town of **Monasterace Marina** (on the train line to Catanzaro, L2000). From the train station here you can catch a bus to **Stilo,** a snapshot hilltop village that houses the famous church, **La Cattolica.** This tenth-century Byzantine structure has a unique square floor-plan and five drum-shaped towers. (To enter, ask for the woman with the key.) Another interesting church can be found in **Rossano,** about 45km northwest of Ciro Marina. Although the train station called "Rossano" is actually 5km down the hill from the main village, there is frequent bus service shuttling passengers between station and town (L500). To visit Rossano's magnificent Byzantine **Church of San Marco,** you may pick up a local "tour guide"—any of the children or elderly men hanging around the main square will help you in exchange for a few thousand lire. Built in approximately 1000 C.E., San Marco is a small, originally square-shaped church with five drum-shaped domes and three apses—considered, along with La Cattolica at Stilo, Calabria's most important Byzantine monument. The interior, recently restored, is a conglomeration of symmetrical arches and vaults, which create an oriental ambience. Worn-down remains of frescoes and pieces of the original altar interrupt the stark white walls.

After you visit San Marco, your guide will probably accompany you to the cathedral and the little **Museo Diocesano,** which has more to see per square meter than most museums in Italy. Be sure to examine the fifth-century *Codex Purpureus,* a 188-page manuscript containing the Gospels of St. Mark and St. Matthew. Although there is a total of 16 illustrated sheets, only two are on display. In the manuscript illustration of *The Last Supper,* all the figures are lying down and eating out of a simple platter, true to ancient Middle Eastern custom. The accompanying Greek text flaunts exquisite calligraphy. The manuscript was originally produced somewhere in the Middle East before it was brought to Rossano by fleeing monks. The museum also contains fine oil paintings and a few fifteenth-century Gregorian chant-books. (Open daily 9am-noon and 4-6pm. Free.)

Although there are a few cheap hotels in Rossano, you'll do better in the town of **Trebisacce,** 40 minutes away by train along the coast. **Albergo Noia,** via Duca di Genova, 185 (tel. (0981) 513 21), offers singles for L15,000, with bath L18,000. Doubles cost L25,000, with bath L28,000. (July-Aug. obligatory full pension

L43,000 or half-pension L32,000.) The owner enjoys foreigners. If it's full (as is likely in Aug.), try the **Albergo Parnaso,** via A. Lutri (tel. (0981) 511 97), with singles for L20,000 and doubles for L32,000, all with bath. They also serve well-prepared and modestly priced meals (L12,000). Try the *penne all' arrabbiata* (pasta in hot sauce).

SARDINIA (SARDEGNA)

"Not a bit like the rest of Italy . . . ," declared D.H. Lawrence about Sardinia, inspired by its harsh, mountainous terrain and ardent rusticity. While these persist in the untamed interior, the concrete beehive condominiums and tourist amenities (and prices) of the twentieth century have long since sprouted on the coast. In the major cities, people dress as classily, drive as recklessly, and have the same passion for *gelato* as the "continentals." They do, however, speak a beautifully clear Italian that puts most Romans to shame.

Nonetheless, an old Sardinian legend expresses a sense of inferiority: When God finished making the world, he had a handful of dirt left over, which he threw down into the Mediterranean Sea and stepped on, creating Sardinia. Some curious landscaping took place over 3500 years ago; the island is dotted with over 7000 *nuraghi,* cone-shaped stone huts. Little is known of their former inhabitants except that they were not indigenous and were most concerned with defense.

Only decades ago, *padroni* (landlords) still held the land, and poor farmers toiled under a system akin to serfdom. Under the growing influence of the Italian Communist Party (both its founder, Antonio Gramsci, and its late Secretary General, Enrico Berlinguer, were Sards), much of the land is now owned by those who work it, but large sections of Sardinia's scenic coastline remain in the hands of foreign speculators. Since Sardinian attempts at industrialization have failed, conscious efforts have been made to expand the tourist industry. Despite a massive campaign launched on the continent to promote Sardinia's vacation attractiveness, however, many of the island's attractions are nigh impossible to access without the aid of a rental car. If nowhere else on this wild island, visit the cities Alghero and Cagliari, even if it costs you an arm and a leg; both will be worth every missing member.

Getting There

Because tourism is a political issue for separatists in Sardinia, be prepared for strikes. If you travel by ferry between June and September, for example, buy your ticket at least two weeks in advance, preferably from the company office. If you get it through a travel agent, check frequently with the company office—service disruptions and schedule changes are not uncommon. Prices listed below are for *posto ponte* (deck class). *Poltrone* (reserved reclining chairs) and first- and second-class cabins are also available. **Tirrenia** operates the most ferries and offers the cheapest fares, but also, sometimes, the longest delays. Tirrenia is represented in the U. S. by **Extra Value Travel,** 683 S. Collier Blvd., Marco Island, FL 33937 (tel. (800) 255-2847; in FL (813) 394-3384).

Note: Departure dates change frequently. The following information was gathered in July 1988.

Civitavecchia-Olbia: Daily at 11pm (7 hr., L10,600). July-Aug. book 2 weeks in advance. There is also a **Ferrovie dello Stato** connection to Golfo Aranci, near Olbia (4 per day, 8 hr., *poltrone* L16,400).

Civitavecchia-Cagliari: Daily at 8:30pm from Civitavecchia. Daily at 6pm from Cagliari. (13½ hr., L23,300.)

Civitavecchia-Arbatax: Fri. at 8:30pm from Civitavecchia. Sun. at midnight from Arbatax. (Service briefly suspended in 1988—call early to verify departure times. 9 hr., L16,600.)

Genoa-Cagliari: Tues., Thurs., and Sat. at 6pm from Genoa. Mon., Wed., and Fri. at 6pm from Cagliari. (19 hr., L40,000.)

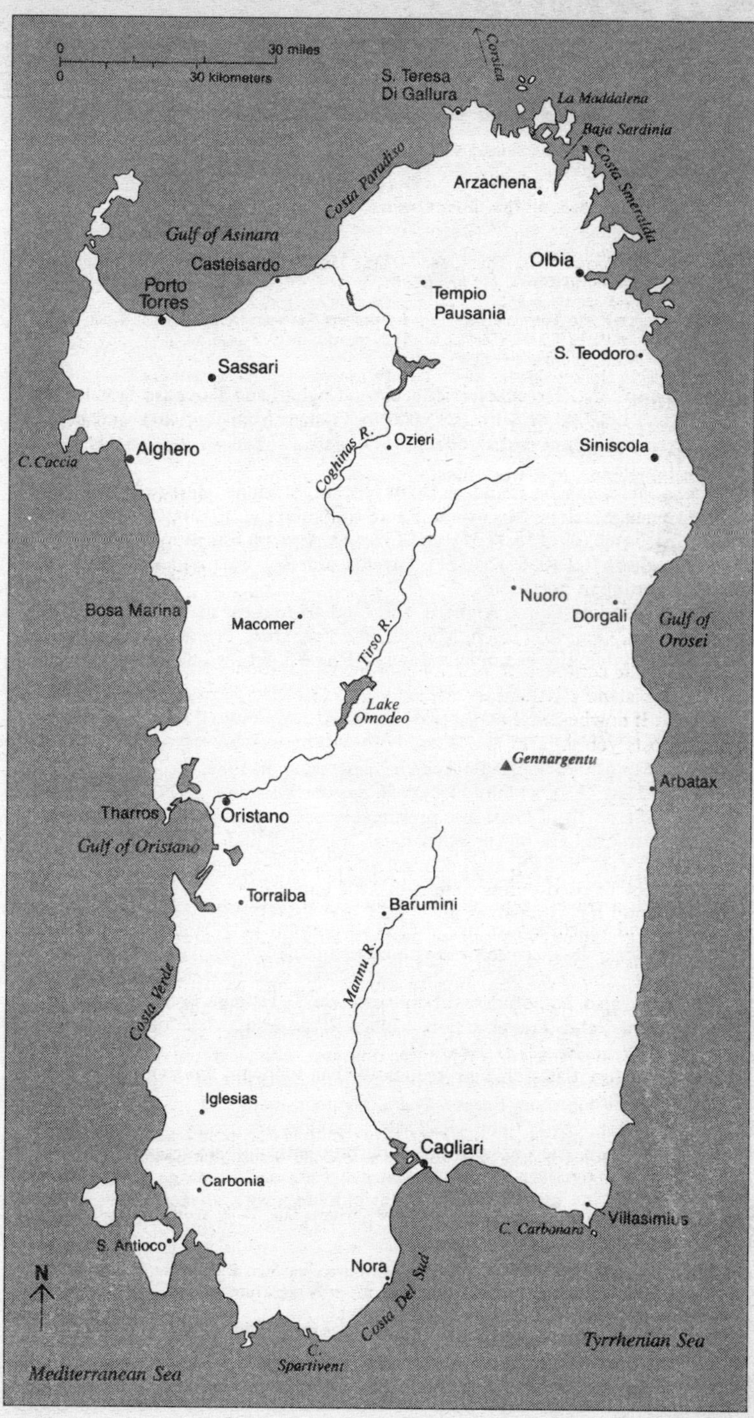
0 30 miles
0 30 kilometers
Corsica
S. Teresa Di Gallura
La Maddalena
Baja Sardinia
Costa Smeralda
Costa Paradiso
Arzachena
Gulf of Asinara
Castelsardo
Porto Torres
Olbia
Tempio Pausania
S. Teodoro
Sassari
Coghinas R.
Ozieri
Alghero
C. Caccia
Siniscola
Bosa Marina
Macomer
Nuoro
Dorgali
Gulf of Orosei
Tirso R.
Lake Omodeo
Gennargentu
Arbatax
Tharros
Oristano
Gulf of Oristano
Torralba
Barumini
Mannu R.
Costa Verde
Iglesias
Cagliari
Carbonia
Villasimius
C. Carbonara
S. Antioco
Nora
Costa Del Sud
N
C. Spartivent
Tyrrhenian Sea
Mediterranean Sea

Genoa-Porto Torres: Daily at 8pm from Genoa. Daily at 7pm from Porto Torres. (12½ hr., L26,600.)

Genoa-Arbatax: Tues. and Sat. at 6:30pm from Genoa. Wed. and Sun. at 2pm from Arbatax. (Service briefly suspended in 1988—call early to verify departure times. 18 hr., L26,600.)

Naples-Cagliari: Tues. and Sun. at 6:30pm from Naples. Mon. and Fri. at 5:30pm from Cagliari. (15 hr., L20,000.)

Palermo-Cagliari: Sun. at 7pm from Cagliari. Mon. at 7pm from Palermo. (12½ hr., L18,000.)

Livorno-Porto Torres: Tues., Thurs., and Sat. at 8:45pm from Livorno. Sat., Wed., and Fri. at 8:30pm from Porto Torres. (12 hr., L28,000.)

Tolone, France-Porto Torres: April-Aug. 1-4 per week at 8pm from Jolone. 1-4 per week at 3:30pm from Porto Torres. (Service briefly suspended in 1988—call early to verify departure times. 14 hr., *poltrone* L76,000.)

You can also catch **Tirrenia** ferries between Cagliari and Tunis via Trapani every Tues. (21 hr., L80,000 or 8 hr., L15,000 to Trapani from Cagliari), and between Santa Teresa di Gallura and Bonifacio (in Corsica, France) several times per day (1 hr., L10,000).

Tirrenia offices can be found in **Civitavecchia,** Stazione Marittima (tel. (0766) 288 01); **Genoa,** Stazione Marittima, Ponte Colombo (tel. (010) 269 81); **Palermo,** via Roma, 385 (tel. (091) 58 57 33); and **Livorno,** Agenzia Marittima Carlo Laviosa, Scali D'Azeglio, 6 (tel. (0586) 350 51). Tirrenia addresses are listed in *Let's Go* under individual Sardinian port cities.

Airplanes also link Olbia, Alghero, and Cagliari to most major Italian cities, as well as to Paris, Geneva, Zurich, Munich, and Frankfurt. Prices are steep, but discounts are available: For example, a Cagliari-Rome flight for L82,000, with student ID L58,000.

Transportation

Public transportation in Sardinia can be frustrating. In 1988, the inexpensive **Italian State Railway (FS),** which links Olbia, Sassari, Oristano, and Cagliari, was utterly unreliable north of Oristano, presumably because of construction or repair. Travel south to Cagliari, on the other hand, was rapid and convenient. Other Sardinian railways (**FCS, SFS,** etc.) connect smaller towns, but are exceedingly slow and should not be used unless time is of little concern.

The two main bus companies are ARST and PANI. **ARST** operates extensive service, linking almost every village on the island to the nearest big town. Their service is oriented toward local residents; the bus stops at every cluster of houses and tends to leave for the provinces in the evening and return to the cities in the morning. In smaller towns, ask locals to find out where the bus stops. Buses soon become hideously overcrowded, so try to get on at the first stop. Service is fairly slow but quite inexpensive. **PANI,** by contrast, connects only the major cities—Cagliari, Sassari, Oristano, and Nuoro. Many buses are nonstop, and you must buy tickets before boarding. Buses travel along main roads and are comfortable and fast, but a bit more costly than ARST. Both services are prompt but tend to leave between 5 and 7am, the next bus not departing until mid-afternoon.

The easiest way to cover the island is by car. Rent one in a large town. **Hitching** is best around resorts, although natives stay close to town and vacationers are wary of picking up strangers. Thumbing can be dangerous—women, especially, are warned against it, even in pairs.

Accommodations and Food

Virtually all growth in Sardinia's rapidly expanding vacation industry has been in the luxury price range. Most cities do not offer a wide selection of moderately priced accommodations. Sassari and Cagliari are exceptions; in other cities, you can usually find centrally located *locande* with clean but shabby singles for about

L17,000. Consult the local tourist office, and ask for the reliable and comprehensive *Annuario Alberghi,* which lists prices for all hotels, *pensioni,* and official campsites on the island. Rooms are scarce in August—many travelers sack out in a train station or on a secluded beach. The four **youth hostels** are an inexpensive, but undependable alternative, as they are often full in August and sometimes shut down unexpectedly. All are on the beach, with airy, though crowded, rooms. If you have a car or motorcycle, it's best to camp. **Camping** outside official campsites is illegal, but discreetly practiced nonetheless.

Sardinia's cuisine takes after the terrain from which it is derived—it's rustic and far from refined. Sards whip up tasty and hearty dishes, such as *sa fregula* (pasta in broth with saffron—a spice rarely used on the mainland), *malloreddus* (dumpling with saffron), or *culurgiones* (ravioli stuffed with cheese and beetroots, covered with tomato sauce, lamb, and sausage). The best dishes are in the pastoral tradition: grilled pigs or goats, *cordula* (lamb entrails), or pig cooked in lamb's stomach. Fish and shellfish (even on pizza) abound on the island and are bound to titillate your tongue in a novel way. Unfortunately, it's hard to find these typically Sardinian dishes except in expensive restaurants. For the cheapest meals, eat at *pizzerie, rosticcerie,* or *tavola calde,* or prepare your own meals (most hostels have facilities). Shepherd's bread, fresh goat and sheep cheese, and fruit are delicious staples. If you're not squeamish, try pulling sea urchins off rocks (be careful—they sting if crushed). Scoop out the inside and you'll have a poor person's caviar. Sardinian pastry makes an outstanding breakfast or snack. *Pane frattau* is thin bread covered with eggs, cheese, and tomato sauce; *sebada* is delicious dough filled with cheese, sugar, and honey. Sardinia's wines are not fully appreciated: Try *vernaccia d'Oristano* (with a heady almond aftertaste) with fish, or a robust *cannonau di Sardegna* with meat.

Olbia

Olbia is the Liverpool of Sardinia—your basic uninviting, uninspiring port town. While not particularly seedy, Olbia boasts no music-making insects or other indigenous interests, and thus serves best as a stopover on your way to the Costa Smeralda and other more intriguing spots.

Practical Information

Azienda di Turismo: via Catello Piro, 1 (tel. 214 53), off corso Umberto. Excellent map of the town. Be sure to pick up the *Annuario Alberghi,* a great help in finding accommodations, as well as a list of campgrounds and youth hostels on the island. Open May-Sept. Mon.-Sat. 8:30am-1pm and 4-7pm, Sun. 8:30am-noon; Oct.-April Mon.-Fri. 8:30am-1pm and 4-6pm, Sat. 8:30am-noon.

Post Office: via Acquedotto (tel. 222 51), 2 blocks off p. Matteoti. Open Mon.-Sat. 8:15am-7:15pm. **Postal code:** 07026.

Telephone Code: 0789.

Train Station: via Pala, off corso Umberto by the bus station.

Bus Station: ARST, at the far end of corso Umberto, 168 (tel. 211 97). To Nuoro (4 per day, L6000), Arzachena (10 per day, L1500), and Santa Teresa di Gallura (5 per day, L3300). Schedule posted in the station.

Ferries: Tirrenia, corso Umberto, 17 (tel. 226 88, for bookings 246 91). Service to Civitavecchia and Genoa. Open Mon.-Sat. 8:30am-1:30pm and 4:30-6pm. Be sure to check in at the crowded Tirrenia office at the port 1½ hr. in advance—strikes and schedule changes are common. Port office open Mon.-Sat. 4:45-11pm, Sun. 6:45-11pm. **Linea dei Golfi** (tel. 221 26) runs to Piambino and has an office at the port. **Sardina Ferries,** corso Umberto, 4 (tel. 252 00), runs to Livorno.

Car Rental: Smeralda Express, via Catello Piro, 9 (tel. 255 12).

Hospital: Ospedale Civile, via Aldo Moro (tel. 585 95 or 586 31).

Police: Carabinieri, Tel. 212 21 or 233 20.

Accommodations and Food

Albergo Minerva, via Mazzini, 6 (tel. 211 90). Friendly management, sparkling clean rooms, but mattresses sag. Singles L21,800, with bath L29,100. Doubles L36,400, with bath L46,800.

Albergo Galluria, via corso Umberto (tel. 246 48). On a busy street, but the low prices make up for the noise. Singles L25,000, with bath L32,000. Doubles L39,400, with bath L50,400.

Albergo Mastino, via A. Vespucci, 4-5 (tel. 213 20 and 211 30). With bar and restaurant. Come here as a last resort; rooms look older than Olbia. Singles with bath L25,000. Doubles with bath L40,000.

While dining in Olbia is not outrageously expensive, it isn't particularly cheap either. Try the **Mercato Civico** on via Acquedetto (open Mon.-Sat. 7:30am-1pm and 4:30-8pm) for real bargains, or the **Standa Supermarket** at corso Umberto, 156 (open Mon.-Sat. 9am-1pm and 4-8pm).

Pizzeria Al Ciclope, via Acquedetto, 24, within shouting distance of the post office. Take-out cheese pizza L800. No drinks served. Open daily 11am-4pm and 5-9pm.

Ristorante Pausania, via Cavour, 10 (tel. 216 75), off p. Matteoti. A touch of elegance at a moderate price. Full meals from L16,000.

Frisby, via corso Umberto at via Porto Romano. Olbia's version of McDonalds; try the Frisburger (L4000).

Gelateria "Slip Slap," at via Mazzini and via Olbia (tel. 260 40), off corso Umberto. The amazing *gelato* is the best thing Olbia has to offer.

Sights and Near Olbia

Nearly all traces of Olbia's Greek, Roman, and medieval past have disappeared. The only noteworthy sight in town is the **Church of San Simplicio,** behind the railroad station. The twelfth-century Pisan structure is impressive and beautiful, with a strangely pleasing asymmetrical facade in white-gray granite.

Short excursions from Olbia include trips to the *nuraghi* at **S' Abe** (6km away) on the road to Castello Pedrese, and the "giants' tombs" of **Su Monte.** If you take the bus to Nuoro, shortly out of Olbia you'll pass the surrealistic **Isola Tavolara,** an immense prism of rock sticking 1500 feet out of the sea. Five buses each day run to **San Teodoro,** 30 km from Olbia, where there is a long, luxurious beach with cornflower blue water. It's worthwhile despite the large number of tourists in July and August. Ask at the bus station about the buses that run toward the beach, otherwise you'll have a 45-minute walk. If the sun and surf entice you to stay, try the **Albergho L'Esagono** on via Cala d'Ambra (tel. 86 57 83), with singles at L21,200 and doubles at L32,000, all with bath. Just down the road is the **Cala D'Ambra**campground (tel. 865 60) with decent facilities (L3500 per person, L5000 per tent).

About 22km farther, just before Siniscola, is the little hill town of **Posada.** Above the town, the **Castello della Fava** commands a magnificent view of the surrounding valley and ocean. The locals' expressions as you walk by will remind you that you're an outsider.

Emerald Coast (Costa Smeralda)

Once upon a time, the windy, craggy, irregular coastline above Olbia was nothing but a series of poor fishing villages. Then, in 1962, a group of foreign investors led by the Aga Khan developed the area into the posh and pricey Emerald Coast. Today, the fine sand beaches and irresistible azure waters are obscured by an expanse of luxury hotels, restaurants, and shops. Prices for accommodations and food are outrageous, and the alert police force actively discourages unofficial camping.

Crowds are sizable year-round, and unbearable in July and August. It is impossible to find a room anywhere on the coast in August: Book ahead or bring a sleeping bag.

Arzachena

A bland town of pastel stucco, swallow's nests, and a potent dose of reinforced concrete, Arzachena is notable mainly for its nearby gulf. The town is a central stop on the northern coast, halfway between Olbia and Santa Teresa di Galura on the ARST bus route, one hour from each (11 per day from Olbia, L1500). There is no reason to pause here, as it's quite landlocked and offers very little of interest. If you must, the **Azienda di Turismo** has an office on via Risorgimento (tel. 826 24; open May-Sept. 8am-1:30pm and 4-9pm; Oct.-April 3-7:15pm). Catch all buses 2 blocks down the hill behind the *azienda* in front of the Bar Smeralda.

Palau and La Maddalena

The most relieving sight in Palau is that of cars lined up to board the ferry to La Maddalena—the town could not be more congested in summer. The rather unhelpful **Tourist office** is at via Nazionale, 94 (tel. 70 95 90; open May-Sept. Mon.-Sat. 8am-1pm and 4-7pm). If you're stuck in Palau, the **Hotel Serra** (tel. 70 95 19) offers singles with bath for L25,000, doubles with bath for L40,000, but don't count on any vacancies in summer.

Palau's main attraction is as a departure point to the outlying islands. For about L25,000, boats will take you on a daytrip to three of the more remote islands—**S. Maria, Budelli,** and **Spargi**—in the stunning Maddalene archipelago (operates May-Oct., inquire next to the Tirrenia ticket office at the port). More conventional itineraries follow the continual ferries to the beautiful islands of La Maddalena and Caprera (L750). Arrive early as excursions sell out quickly.

In addition to being a major port of call for the U.S. Navy, **La Maddalena** is one enormous campground innundated by visitors. A panoramic road encircles the island, passing small fishing harbors, tourist villages, and splendid beaches—**Baja Trinità** is especially wonderful. Many travelers sleep unnoticed on the rocks between the harbor and the campground, or in the forest. Be aware, however, that this is illegal. Non-campers can stay at **Locanda da Raffaele** at La Ricciolina (tel. 73 87 59), which has doubles for L29,000. The **tourist office** is at via XX Settembre, 24 (tel. 73 63 21). The restaurants on the islands and at Palau are expensive. Try **Pizzeria Del Mar 2,** to the right just off via Nazionale on the way to the Azienda: Crispy pizzas L4000-6000. Cover 20%, service included.

Many visitors to **Caprera** sleep in the official campsites or the numberous deserted beaches. The first dirt road on the right after you cross the bridge leads to a pleasant area on a small bay. While on Caprera, visit **Garibaldi's home** and resting place. Recently restored, it houses an impressive array of artifacts relating to Italy's unification. Rent a sailboat at the **Centro Velico Caprera** on Punta Coda (tel. 777 91). The **travel agency** 1 block from the port next to the paltry **market,** rents vehicles of all sorts. (Bicycles L12,000, mopeds L25,000. Open daily 9am-6pm.) There is also excruciatingly slow **train** service from Palau to Sassari (2 per day, 4 hr., L7300).

Santa Teresa di Gallura

Perched on Sardinia's northwest tip, Santa Teresa di Gallura is a pleasant and not-too-touristed coastal resort. Summer evenings in the central piazza V. Emanuele bring out the mainland hordes, who by day swarm the spectacular beaches. From the beach **Rena Bianca,** Corsica looms in the horizon.

If you've tired of Rena Bianca (which, can get over-crowded), a dirt path leads away from the beach up the hill. At the fork, the lower path leads to **Isola Municca,** an attractive little island. The higher trail twists between wonderful granite formations and offers stupendous views of Corsica and Capo Testa, especially in the morning. Follow the hill to reach the isthmus connecting **Capo Testa** with the mainland.

Otherwise, go back into town and take via Capo Testa (3km). There are beaches on both sides of the isthmus—check which way the wind is blowing and choose the leeward side. From Capo Testa's lighthouse, you can walk down to an isolated series of scenic coves. Little paths lead south through spectacular ancient Roman and granite quarries. **Cala Grande,** directly under the highest peak on the cape, is beautiful and often a site for nude bathing.

Santa Teresa's **azienda,** p. V. Emanuele, 24 (tel. (0789) 75 41 27), can help you find accommodations. (Open May-Sept. daily 8:30am-1pm and 4-8pm; Oct.-April Mon.-Sat. 8:30am-1pm and 4-8pm.) From Santa Teresa, daily **ferries** sail to Bonifacio in Corsica (1 hr., L10,000; French visa required). Both Tirrenia (tel. 75 41 56) and Navarma (tel. 75 52 80) staff offices at the tiny port. If you wish to cross into French waters yourself, rent a sailboat or motorboat from **Circolo Nautico Capo Testa** on the isthmus (open June-Sept.). Or stay landbound and rent a horse at **Centro Ippico Ruoni** (tel. 75 15 90), 5km out of town in Ruoni. ARST buses travel to Olbia (5 per day, 1½ hr., L3300) and Sassari (2 per day, 3 hr., L5800). They leave from via Eleonara D'Arborea, adjacent to the post office off via Nazionale.

Accommodations, Camping, and Food

Cheap hotels are often full in July, *always* in August. Ask the *azienda* for help. Avoid staying in any hotel that insists on full pension.

Da Cecco, via Po (tel. 75 42 20). Walk 2 blocks on via XX Settembre, behind p. V. Emanuele, and then turn right. Wonderful management, modern rooms, and great showers. Singles L26,600, doubles L35,400.

Pensione Scano, via Lazio, 4 (tel. 75 44 47), off via Capo Testa. Tiny, clean singles L13,000, doubles L26,000. Often requires full pensione (L44,000 per person), but plead your case.

Canne al Vento, via Nazionale, 23 (tel. 75 42 19), near the bus stop. Small and far from the beach, but *pensione* not obligatory. Singles L17,000, with bath L22,700. Doubles L27,000, with bath L34,000.

Hotel Bellavista, via Sonnino, 8 (tel. 75 41 62), at the edge of town overlooking Rena Bianca. Comfortable rooms, great views, but *pensione* can be a problem (L56,800 per person). Singles L14,800, with bath L23,300. Doubles L34,400. Open May 1-Oct. 15.

Camping: Gallura, 3km south of town on the road to Castelsardo (tel. (0374) 60 19 97). Small market. L3500 per person, L4800 per tent. Open June 15-Sept. 15.

Most restaurants in town are astronomically expensive. The **supermarket,** via Nazionale, 24 (open Mon.-Sat. 8am-1pm and 5-8:30pm), is a wise alternative.

Papa Satan, via la Marmora, 18. Look for the sign off via Nazionale. Futuristic patio in back. Devilishly good pizzas (L4300-8000), tasty but expensive full meals. Try the *spaghetti alle cozze* (L5500). Open 12:30-2:30pm and 7pm-12:30am.

Panino's Shop, via XX Settembre, off p. V. Emanuele. Standard fast food, but the hamburger and chickburger (L2500) are surprisingly good and filling.

If the boogie bug bites in Santa Teresa, try the **Corallora Club,** above Rena Bianca (tel. 75 46 74), or **Marina Acquarius,** in the port (tel. 75 50 44); both pack 'em in late into the summer's eve.

Nuoro

In Nuoro, the jagged terrain of Sardinia's interior clashes with increasingly urban tendencies; here the merging of modern and traditional has detracted from the beauty of both. Few and conspicuous are the peasants clad in the traditional magpie black dresses and trousers. Similarly, cement apartment complexes stick out like thumbs against the rugged Sardinian countryside. Despite its designation as the capital of its namesake province, Nuoro lacks noticeably in activities and interests. The city serves well, however, as a convenient base for expeditions into the mountains and to the magnificent beaches around Cala Gonone.

Practical Information

EPT: p. Italia, 9 (tel. 300 83). English-speaking and helpful. Ask for the map, which is, unfortunately, not reflective of local topography. Generally open June-Oct. Mon.-Fri. 8am-2pm, Sat. 9am-1pm and 3-7pm, and Sun. 9am-1pm; Nov.-May Mon.-Tues. 8am-2pm and 3-6pm, Wed.-Tues. 8am-2pm.

Post Office: p. Crispi, 8 (tel. 302 78), off via Dante. Open Mon.-Sat. 8:15am-7:40pm. **Postal Code:** 08100.

Telephones: SIP, via Brigata Sassari, 6, at p. Italia 1 block from the EPT. Open daily 8am-8pm. **Telephone Code:** 0784.

Train Station: p. Berlinguer (tel. 301 15), off via Lamarmora near p. Sardegna.

Bus Stations: PANI, via Brigata Sassari (tel. 368 56), a few blocks from p. Italia. Daily service to Sassari (L9200), Oristano (L7000), and Cagliari (L13,300). **ARST,** at the foot of p. V. Emanuele (tel. 322 01). Buses to Olbia, Dorgali, and other small towns.

Car Rental: Autonoleggio Maggiore, via Convento, 32 (tel. 304 61).

Accommodations and Food

Inexpensive establishments are few and far between in Nuoro. Only one bona fide budget hotel exists in town, and the youth hostel and campground are miles out.

Da Giovanni, via IV Novembre, 7 (tel. 305 62), up from the Chiesa Delle Grazie at the beginning of corso G. Garibaldi. Musty but neat rooms. Showers exist in name only. Singles L15,000, doubles L25,000.

Il Portico, via Mannu (tel. 375 35), near the end of p. V. Emanuele. A definite step up. Singles L21,700, with shower L25,000. Doubles L34,000, with shower L38,000.

Hotel Grillo, via Mons. Melas, 14 (tel. 386 78). From the ARST station, take a right on via Giovanni XXIII, left 1 block on via Manzoni, then take the first left. Wonderful manager, not-so-wonderful prices. Singles with bath L36,400. Doubles with bath L52,000.

Cheap restaurants are scarce. Try the well-hidden **supermarket** at via Giovanni XXIII, off V. Manzoni. (Open Sun.-Fri. 8am-12:45pm and 5:30-7:15pm, Sat. 8am-12:45pm.) For fresh fruit, cheese, and meat, explore the enclosed **market** at p. Mameli, 20, also off V. Manzoni. (Open Mon.-Sat. 7am-1pm and 4:30-7pm.)

Rosticceria Bonamici, p. Mameli, 6, behind the ARST station. Great *panini fettini* filled with grilled beef L2500.

Pizzeria Del Diavolo, corso G. Gareibaldi, 134, near del Popolo. A variety of sinfully good pizzas (cheese L1400). Huge tank harboring tiny fish. Open Mon.-Sat. 9:30am-1pm and 5-9pm.

Tomasbar, via XX Settembre, 9, near p. del Popolo. For an evening *caffe espresso* (L700) or sandwich.

Sights and Seasonal Events

As the nineteenth-century ***duomo*** is less than impressive (open daily 8am-noon), the only worthwhile visit in town is the **Museo della Vita e delle Tradizioni Popolari Sarde** (Museum of Sardinian Life and Popular Traditions), via Mereu, 56. Following the sign in p. Santa Maria della Neve in front of the cathedral. On display are the spectacular traditional costumes of the island, each deriving from a different village. The museum also houses old guns, canteens, and jewelry, all finely crafted and well-displayed. (Open Tues.-Sat. 9am-1pm and 3-7pm, Sun. 9am-1pm. Free.) Nuoro's more primitive side emerges during the **Sagra del Rendetore,** celebrated primarily the last two Sundays of August and highlighted by a parade of very energetic men wearing skins and grotesque wooden masks.

Near Nuoro

For a picnic, take the bus from p. V. Emanuele up to **Monte Ortobene** (12 per day, L850). On top of the mountain lies a shady park, as well as a large bronze statue of Christ the Redeemer. From the bus stop on top of Monte Ortobene, walk 20m down the road to gain a breathtaking vista of colossal white **Monte Corrasi,** dwarfing the town of **Oliena** below. An easy (and expensive) way to become acquainted with Sardinia's wilderness is to join **Sardegna De Scoprire's** guided forays into the rugged Supramonte mountain range, south of Olbia (L40,000 per day, minimum 6 people). Ask at the flowershop at via Dante, 29 (tel. 304 00), below p. Italia.

Just over one hour east of Nuoro by ARST bus (8 per day through Dorgali, L2300) lies **Cala Gonone,** the gateway to a number of spectacular beaches and caves.

The beaches at Cala Gonone are pebbly and crowded. A walk or hitch down the dirt road along the coast leads to some less-populated, sandier beaches. Boats leave 5 times per day (more often in July and Aug.; L7750) for the stunning **Grotta del Bue Marino** (Cave of the Marine Ox), one of the last haunts of the elusive monk seal, a cold-water vestige from the days of the Mediterranean Ice Age. The seals rarely appear during the day, however, and the cave itself is the main attraction. Nearly 1 km of its more than 5km expanse of caverns, stalagmites, and lakes, is illuminated. Only the stampeding crowd and the locked gate to the glowing grotto mar this work of nature. The surrounding water is so clear that the bottom is visible more than 200m out. Just down the coast is the huge, splendid beach of **Cala Luna,** where the water is clearer than glass. Encircled by marshes and caverns, the beach is accessible only by boat (L7400, combined grotto-Cala Luna ticket L15,150). There are also sporadic boat trips to the more remote and equally breathtaking beaches of **Cala Sisine** (L12,700) and **Cala Mariolu** (L14,800). From Nuoro it's possible to make both trips the same day; in summer, buses return from Cala Gonone (above the city park, buy your ticket in Nuoro or at the port) at 6:30pm and 8pm.

Cala Gonone offers an abundance of budget-priced rooms, even in August. The **Piccolo Hotel,** via Colomba, 32 (tel. 932 32), above the Fronteddu market on the main drag, has eight tiny but clean singles for L22,000, doubles with bath L32,000. **Albergo Gabbiano** in the port offers singles for L18,900, doubles L26,500. **Pensione La Ginestre,** on via Gustui (tel. 931 27), lies above the campground on the left of the main road just before town. It's a friendly place with a cascade of flowers. Singles are L20,800, with bath L27,600; doubles L32,000, with bath L38,600. A large, expensive campground on via Collodi (tel. 931 65), across from the city park (where camping is expressly forbidden), charges L6100 per person, L9200 per tent. (Open April 1-Sept. 30.)

Public transportation limits exploration of the numerous hill towns south of Nuoro, where Sardinian traditions and hospitality remain unaffected by coastal tourism. ARST bus service runs round-trips at ungodly hours. One remote town well-worth visiting and easily accessible from Nuoro is **Orgòsolo,** a pleasant 40-minute ride through rolling, ochre-colored countryside punctuated by vineyards. Orgòsolo's "sights" are colorful 1960s **murals,** a series of leftist, and nationalist paintings covering walls on corso Repubblica, the town's main street. Note the ironic anomalies, such as a scene of the locals transforming city hall into a *casa del popolo* painted atop the town's own *municipio,* or of violent American imperialism adjacent to via John Kennedy. If you choose to spend the night, the **Petit Hotel,** via Mannu, 9 (tel. (0784) 40 20 09), off corso Repubblica, offers comfortable rooms and prices (singles L15,000, doubles L20,000). If you miss the last bus back to Nuoro and are tempted to hitch after dark, think again—*bandito* activity is not a myth in the countryside.

Porto Torres

There is little to say for a town whose most scenic spot is a tiny park next to the main bus stop. Once the ancient Roman harbor of Turris Libyssonis, the area has become a major petrochemical center and an important ferry terminal for boats to and from Civitavecchia, Genoa, and Toulon (France). The Porto Torres tourist brochure's only boast is that the growth rate has been negative since 1982, averaging −35%. Do as Caesar would have done: Come, see, and leave quickly.

Orientation and Practical Information

Whether you have stepped off an ARST bus from Sassari or Alghero, or a ship from more distant horizons, you will find yourself at the port. The train, timed to meet incoming ferries, also leaves from a stretch of track right by the water.

As you stand with your back to the water, straight ahead is **corso Vittorio Emanuele II,** the main street, which leads from the port to the church of San Garino. Follow the craggy coastline to your left for a splendid view.

Azienda di Turismo: In the Aragonese tower by the port (no phone). English-speaking and helpful. Handy map. Open June-Sept. Mon.-Sat. 8am-8pm, Sun. 8am-2pm.

Currency Exchange: Banks and travel agencies on corso V. Emanuele II and in the port.

Post Office: via Ponte Romano, 77 (tel. 51 47 77). Ope Mon.-Fri. 8:10am-6:15pm, Sat. 8am-12:45pm. **Postal code:** 07046.

Telephones: Bar at via Sassari, 61 (tel. 50 15 21), down from the church of San Gavino. Open Mon.-Sat. 8am-noon and 3-7pm, Sun. and holidays 8am-noon. **Telephone code:** 079.

Train Station: Via Ponte Romano (tel. 51 46 36), in front of the port. Trains stop in the middle of the street.

Bus Station: None, but the main *fermata* is by the train station, across from the port. **ARST** buses run to and from Sassari incessantly (Mon.-Sat. 48 per day, Sun. 22 per day; L1000) and Alghero (6 per day, L2000). For service to Stintino, walk 2 blocks from the port to p. Umberto, where you can also catch the bus to Sassari. It's best to purchase tickets in advance at the **Bar Acciazo** on corso V. Emanuele II, halfway between the port and p. Umberto (look for the big pink sign).

Ferries: Tirrenia, Stazione Marittima in the port (tel. 51 41 07).

Taxi: p. XX Settembre (tel. 51 04 39), in front of the souvenir shop.

Car Rental: Mureddo, via Mare, 8 (tel. 51 01 81, after hours 27 46 29), across from the port. Fiat Panda 126 with unlimited mileage L430,000 per week, plus 18% tax and (highly advisable) insurance. Must be age 18. 20% discount with *Let's Go.* Open daily 8:10am-1pm and 4:15-7pm.

Basketball Court: In front of *Municipio* in p. Umberto. For the addict in need of shooting some hoop.

Medical Emergency: Ospedale Civile, via De Nicola, 14 (tel. 22 05 00), in Sassari.

First Aid: Pronto Soccorso, via Delle Terme, 5 (tel. 51 03 92).

Accommodations and Food

There's no need to stay or munch in Porto Torres with more reasonable Sassari only 30 minutes away by bus. Prices for rooms (when available) are high; the **IYHF youth hostel** is tiny; and the windows of restaurants on the main street are plastered with outrageous "tourist menus." Stock up for sea and land expeditions at **Turris-market,** via Pacinotti, 1, at via Sacchi beyond San Gavino. (Open Tues.-Sat. 8:15am-12:45pm and 5:30-8pm, Mon. 8:15am-12:45pm.) Try **Pizzeria il Drago,** via Ponte Romano, 54, or **Trattoria maria,** via Principessa, 20.

Ostello dei Gioventu Balai (IYHF), via Balai (tel. 50 27 61). Walk 2km from the port along the costal road to Castelsardo, or take the local bus which leaves every 30 min. from the *fermata* in front of the port. Adjacent to a nice beach. Often full in summer, so call ahead. Reception open 6-11pm. L7500 per person. Dinner L7000. Open April-Oct.

Albergo Royal, via S. Satta (tel. 50 22 78). From corso V. Emanuele II, walk uphill several blocks on via Petronia. Clean and pleasant, with 5-star bathrooms. Singles L18,100, with bath 22,100. Doubles L28,200, with bath L36,800.

Albergo Da Elisa, via Mare, 2 (tel. 51 48 72), across from the port. Convenience for a price. Singles with bath L22,100. Doubles with bath L36,300.

Sights

According to experts, the ruins of a Roman bath (**Terme Centrali**) next to the train station are some of the most important Roman remains in Sardinia, but to the untrained eye, they look like marble rubble. Townspeople, themselves uncertain, named them "Il Palazzo del Re Barbaro" (Palace of the Barbarian King). On the other hand, the seven marble arches that span the narrow **Turitano River** nearby are recognizable as part of a **Roman bridge.**

Porto Torres's only real sight is the **Church of San Gavino,** masterpiece of Sardinian architecture. It was built in the eleventh century in the Pisan style, with a second apse in front replacing the formal facade. The interior shelters a double row of 28 antique columns, a raised choir, and a wooden truss ceiling. Outside, courtyards enclosed by tiny dilapidated houses with external staircases provide a picturesque, antique setting. Comic relief is supplied by a little mounted warrior, who strains against an imaginary opponent at the top of a pillar.

Near Porto Torres

Stintino, 24km northwest of Porto Torres on the Capo del Falcone, was until recently a quaint fishing village, a pleasant refuge from the distant smokestacks of Porto Torres. Today it is a prototypical victim of the tourist onslaught. The winter population (746) increases almost 30-fold in summer. Much of Stintino's transformation can be attributed to the stunning beauty of **Spiaggia di Pelosa,** a beach 4km outside town, whose sparkling turquoise waters glisten against the bone-dry **Isola Asinara.** Avoid the beach on weekends. An easy, 500-meter wade across thigh-deep water leads to a tiny islet featuring an eighteenth-century Aragonese tower. Buses service Stintino from Porto Torres (1 per day, 30 min., L1800) and Sassari (4 per day, 1 hr., L2800.) Don't miss the last bus, as impromptu camping is nigh impossible (some try to avoid detection behind the *torre*). If you're desperate, try **Albergho Silvestrino** (tel. 52 30 07), where singles run L23,800 and doubles with bath L44,300.

Sassari

Sardinia's second-largest city sits atop a limestone plateau in the north, where its medieval founders sought refuge from the war and malaria epidemics on the coast. Today Sassari is an important petrochemical center, and modern suburbs surround the compact medieval nucleus, overflowing the plateau and seeping far to the north and west. Besides having the distinction of living in Italy's largest province (Sassan—7520 sq. km), inhabitants here enjoy the highest standard of living on Sardinia.

Orientation and Practical Information

Luckily, you can afford to ignore the modern city and confine your movements to the area around the cathedral in the Old Town. All roads radiate from the newly restored **piazza d'Italia.** As you stand facing the Banco di Napoli in the *piazza,* **via Roma** (and the **PANI station**) is on your left; **emiciclo Garibaldi** (and the **ARST station**), with the university and Public Gardens behind it, is straight ahead; the leafy **piazza Castello,** behind it the main shopping street (corso Vittorio Emanuele), and the train station, are on your right. The towns of Alghero and Porto Torres are located conveniently 37km southwest and 18.5km northwest, respectively. The only larger city on the island, Cagliari, is 208km to the south, linked to Sassari by a road complete in 1829.

Azienda di Turismo: via Molescott (tel. 23 13 31 or 23 35 34), in p. Italia, on the left side of the provincial building. Reams of brochures and a friendly staff. Open Mon.-Sat. 8am-8pm. Note: In 1988 this office was closed; services were run out of the administration building at via Brigata Sassari, 19 (same tel. as above).

Student Travel Office: CTS, via E. Costa, 48 (tel. 23 45 85). Open Mon.-Fri. 10:30am-1pm and 3:30-7:30pm, Sat. 10:30am-1pm.

Currency Exchange: In the train station. Open daily 7am-9pm.

Post Office: via Brigata Sassari, 13, off p. Castello. Open Mon.-Sat. 8:15am-7:40pm. **Postal code:** 07100.

Telephones: SIP, viale Italia, 7A. Open daily 8am-9pm. (Sassari boasts more public telephones per person than any city in Italy.) **Telephone code:** 079.

Airport: 28km south, near Alghera Fertilia. Free ARST buses leave for airport from station 80 min. before departures.

Train Station: p. Stazione (tel. 26 03 62), 1 block from p. Sant. Antonio. To Olbia (5 per day, L5900), Oristano (4 per day, 2¾ hr., L8300), Cagliari (4 per day, 3½ hr., L12,700), Porto Torres (8 per day, 20 min., L1000), and Palau (2 per day, 4 hr., L7300).

Bus stations: PANI, via Bellieni, 25 (tel. 23 69 83 or 23 47 82), off via Roma, 1 block from p. d'Italia. To Cagliari (at 6am and 2:15pm, 3 hr., L16,200; direct at 2pm, 1¾ hr., L9200), Nuoro (2½ hr., L7300), and Oristano (3 per day, 2¼ hr., L8000). **ARST,** emiciclo Garibaldi, 23 (tel. 23 14 49), services most local routes. **SFS,** next door at #26 (tel. 24 13 01), runs buses to Alghero (9 per day, 90 min., L2300).

All-night Pharmacy: Simon, via Brigata Sassari, 2 (tel. 23 32 38).

Medical Emergency: Ospedale Civile, via E. DeNicola (tel. 22 05 00). **First Aid:** Tel. 22 06 21.

Police: Tel. 23 23 43.

Accommodations

Cheap rooms in Sassari evaporate in July and August. With the torrent of tourists and business people, finding a room that is both cheap *and* pleasant is no mean feat.

Pensione Famiglia, viale Umberto, 65 (tel. 23 95 43). Rooms with zany dimensions, comfy mattresses, and hot showers. Front door locked midnight-7am. Doubles L17,200.

Albergo Gallura, viccolo San Leonardo, 9 (tel. 23 87 13), off corso V. Emanuele behind UPIM store. Well-run place in the middle of town—but vacancy is rare. Singles with bath L16,500. Doubles with bath L30,000.

Food

A wide selection of *pizzerie* line **corso V. Emanuele.** Any student ID allows you to eat at the **University Mensa,** via Padre Manzella, 2, off p. A. Gramsci. Decent, filling meals L2500-3500. The *alimentare* at via Brigata Sassari, 56, off via E. Costa, sells staples. (Open Mon.-Sat. 8am-1pm and 5-8pm.) The large, enclosed **market** is located in p. Mercato, down via Rosello from via Vittorio Emanuele. (Open Mon.-Sat. 8am-1pm and 4:30-8pm.) The **Standa Supermarket** is on viale Italia, at the Sardegna. (Open Mon.-Fri. 8:45am-1pm and 4:30-8:15pm, Sat. 9am-1pm.)

Pizzeria al Corso, corso V. Emanuele, 148 (tel. 23 42 10). Perhaps the island's best pizzas, loaded with cheese and toasted to perfection in a wood-burning oven (L3000-6000). The *cappricciosa,* with ham, olives, artichoke hearts, and mushrooms, is a cosmic experience (L5000). Delightfully strong house wine. Open Tues.-Sun. 9:30am-1pm and 6:30-11pm.

Ristorante Marini, p. d'Italia, 10. Large, grilled hamburger on a fresh roll L2200. Open Mon.-Sat. 10:15am-4:30pm and 7:30-11:15pm.

Sights and Seasonal Events

The **Museo Giovanni Antonio Sanna,** via Roma, 64, has reconstructed *nuraghi* for the archeologist, gripping Sardinian paintings for the art historian, traditional costumes to fascinate any anthropologist, and a lush garden for the horticulturist and culture-weary. The graceful Roman statues and mosaics are also a treat, but perhaps best of all is the droning, rhythmic Sardinian music played in the ethnographic section. (Open Tues.-Sat. 9am-2pm, Sun. 9am-1pm, 2nd Wed. of each month 4:30-7:30pm. Admission L3000, ages under 18 and over 60 free.) The **Cathedral of San Niccolò,** originally a thirteenth-century Romanesque structure, it gained a Spanish Colonial baroque facade in the seventeenth century. The facade is so intricately decorated, and it provides such relief from the surrounding grayness, Elio Vittorini once called it "an immense flower of stone." The **Church of Santa Maria di Betlem** (Saint Mary of Bethlehem), near the train station, is another hybrid: Its fourteenth-century Gothic vaults shelter elegant baroque altars, and the adjacent cloister preserves a medieval fountain with bronze spigots.

The **Sardinian Cavalcade,** held on the second-to-last Sunday in May, is one of Sardinia's most notable folk festivals. The festivities involve a morning procession of costumes, an afternoon *Palio* (horserace), and an evening song and dance show. Additionally, adjusting to modernity has introduced the tradition of celebrating the start of the tourist season.

I Candelieri, the festival of the candlesticks, is celebrated on Assumption Day (August 14), when giant replicas of adorned candlesticks are paraded through the streets. The festival dates back to the sixteenth century, when people believed that the plague was a result of their not having offered enough candles to the Virgin Mary.

Near Sassari

Castelsardo's striking location high above a promontory jutting into the sea and its proximity to sandy beaches make it a popular junction along Sardinia's northern coast (the Costa Paradiso). Only 34km northwest of Sassari, it is also a convenient daytrip (9 ARST buses per day, L1800). The hilltop town doesn't have much in the way of culture except for a late Gothic **cathedral** (tastelessly replastered in a drab coating) that shelters an impressive fifteenth-century painting of the *Madonna with Angels.* The **castle** (open daily 8am-8pm) at the top of the hill provides a great view of the coast to the north. The town has taken its names over time from the three sovereign owners of the castle—until 1520 Castello Aragonese; until 1769 Castello Genovese; and now Castello Sardo. Small gray houses line the tiny streets and are picturesque when lit at night.

There are no rooms in the old town. Try **Pensione Pinna,** via Lungomare Anglona, 7 (tel. (079) 47 01 68), across the street from the harbor. (Singles L16,100, with bath L22,900. Doubles L30,200, with bath L35,400.) For a tasty, satisfying lunch, try one of the *foccacina* (L2500) at **Pizzeria Number One,** p. La Pianetta, 33.

Just 30km south of Sassari are some easily accessible, representative *nuraghi*—most notably **Nuraghi Santu Antine** at **Torralba.** Some of the most interesting prehistoric architecture in the western Mediterranean hides just off the road. Early genius is evident in the beautiful spiral stairs and passageways carved out of huge stones. The central tower dates from the ninth century B.C.E. and the fortifications surrounding it from the seventh. (Site open daily 9am to 1 hr. before dusk. Free.) The Torralba train station (Cagliari-Sassari line) lies 1km from the monument, and PANI and ARST buses run to the town (4km from the site). This is a must— especially if you can't make the site at Barumini (see Near Cagliari).

Alghero

For a place originally labelled "L'Aleguerium" due to the vast quantities of seaweed cluttering its shores, Alghero has come a long way. Cobblestone streets and brilliant flowers now introduce a magnificent expanse of ocean. The most charming town in Sardinia, Alghero was transformed by the Genovese in the eleventh century from an insignificant fishing village into a major trading post, and then repopulated with Catalans from Spain in 1353. Many natives still speak the melodious Catalan language, a number of restaurants serve *paella,* many of the *piazze* are called *placas,* and streets have names such as via Barcelonetta. Luckily, the influx of tourists in recent years has not interfered with the rhythms of the original fishing village; at sunset, you can still watch fishing folk load their small craft with ice for the catch. In addition, the Alghero administration has begun a campaign to restore the old city. If the gods grant you only one stop on Sardinia, pray that it's here.

Orientation and Practical Information

To get to and from Alghero by public transport usually requires going through Sassari. Alghero is one hour from Sassari by ARST bus (5 per day, L2300), SFS bus (10 per day, L2300), and by train (10 per day, L1800). ARST buses also run directly to Porto Torres (4 per day, 50 min., L2600).

Azienda di Turismo: p. Porta Terra, 9 (tel. 97 90 54), near the bus stop. Walk toward the old city from the park. English spoken. Provides a useful map, list of accommodations, bus and train schedules. Open daily May-Sept. Mon.-Sat. 8am-8pm; Oct.-April Mon.-Sat. 8am-2pm.

Currency Exchange: Guarda Giulio, via XX Settembre, 18, near the center. Open Mon.-Fri. 8:30am-12:30pm and 3:30-6pm, Sat. 8:30am-12:30pm.

Post Office: via Carducci, 29. Open Mon.-Sat. 10am-7:30pm and 10am-1:20pm for *fermo posta.* **Branch Office** at via Colombano, 44, near the tourist office. Open Mon.-Fri. 8:10am-1:15pm, Sat. 8am-12:45pm. **Postal code:** 07041.

Telephones: In a bar at p. Municipio, 1. No *gettoni* (tokens) necessary. **Telephone code:** 079.

Train Station: At via Don Minzoni and via Fleming, in the northern part of the city. Take the bus at the *fermata* 1 block north of the tourist office. There is also a tiny and more convenient terminal beyond the main station on via Garibaldi, adjacent to the port.

Bus Station: ARST and **SFS** buses depart from via Catalogna, by the park. Purchase ARST tickets on board, SFS tickets at kiosks or cafes.

Taxi: p. Porta Terra, across from tourist office.

Moped and Bicycle Rental: Noleggio di Tilocca Tomaso, via la Marmora, 39 (tel. 97 65 92). Bikes L10,000 per day. Mopeds L20,000 per day. Open Mon.-Sat. 8:30am-1pm and 4-8:30pm, Sun. 8:30am-noon. **Velosport,** via V. Veneto, 90 (tel. 97 71 82). Similar prices and a much larger stock. They also rent scooters. Open Mon.-Sat. 9am-1pm and 4:30-8:30pm.

Hospital: Ospedale Civile, Regione la Pietraia (tel. 95 10 96), a few blocks north of the main train station.

Accommodations

There are good values to be had, but not in July and August. Singles are particularly difficult to find. Don't expect much help from the *azienda.* If all else fails, **Masia Margherita** at via Angelo Roth, 12 (tel. 97 53 93) will have a room in a private house for about L15,000 per single (more in high season) and L30,000 per double with shower. Unfortunately, campgrounds near Alghero are all and expensive.

Ostello dei Giuliani (IYHF), via Zara, 3 (tel. 93 03 53), 7km from Alghero in Fertilia. Yellow AF city buses make the trip every hour from via La Marmora (15 min., L500). ARST buses around the corner also go there. L6000 per person, including linen. Showers L800. Breakfast L1300. Scrumptious lunches and dinners L8000. Curfew midnight. *Always* reserved to capacity in July and August. Call ahead to see about cancelations. Open April 15-Oct. 15.

Hotel Sardegna, via S. Agostino, 1 (tel. 97 52 47). Take via La Marmora away from the port. A modern, clean place with helpful management. Curfew midnight. Few singles L11,900, with bath L13,600. Doubles L21,000, with bath L23,300.

Locanda Catalana, via Catalogna, 5 (tel. 95 24 40), 1 block from bus stop. Modest rooms. Singles L16,000. Doubles L26,500.

Pensione Normandie, via E. Mattei, 6 (tel. 97 53 02), a 10-min. walk from the port. From via Cagliari (which turns into via Giovanni XXIII), turn right on via E. Mattei. Adequate rooms in friendly, family-run place. Singles L14,100. Doubles L23,000.

Hotel San Francesco, via A. Machin, 2 (tel. 97 92 58). From the tourist office, follow via Simon along the old city boundary, and take the 2nd right. Tranquil, comfortable rooms in the church cloister. Occasional concerts. Reserve ahead in summer. Singles L17,700. Doubles L31,800.

Hotel Milano, lungomare Valencia, 16 (tel. 97 95 31). Follow the sea away from the old town for 10 min. Nice rooms and powerful showers for a price; availability more likely than elsewhere. Singles L25,000. Doubles L37,000. Open April 20-Oct. 20.

Camping: La Mariposa, via Lido (tel. 95 03 60), 3km away on the Alghero-Fertilia road—near the beach. Packed in summer. L9000 per person. Open April-Sept. **Calik,** 6km away, before the bridge into Fertilia (tel. 93 01 11). Large, crowded, and just as much a strain on your wallet.

Food

Reasonably priced restaurants are rare in Alghero. Eat cheaply by shopping at the **market** by the park at the bus stop; enter from via Cagliari or via lo Fasso (open Tues.-Sat. 7am-1pm). Every Wednesday, crowds engulf the **open-air market** on via XX Settembre (open 8am-1pm). Down the street, the **Standa Supermarket,** via XX Settembre, 3, allows indoor, less claustrophobic shopping.

Pizzeria, vicolo Adami, 17. Venture down via Roma from the *azienda.* This 1-table pizzeria is in the small *piazza* on the left. Small cheese pizza L1500. Open daily 6-10pm.

Pizzeria Bastò, via Mazzini, 83, at via La Marmora. Another 1-table joint. Friendly owner cooks 'za with a passion (L900-3500). A local favorite. Open in summer Thurs.-Tues. noon-2:30pm and 6-10pm; in off-season Thurs.-Tues. 6-10pm.

Tavola Calda di Meloni Bruno, via Mazzini, 69, a couple doors down from Bastò. Average but filling *menù* L9500, including wine. A rare gastronomical bargain in Alghero. Open daily 8am-3:30pm and 5:30-9:30pm.

Sights and Entertainment

Wander at leisure through the **Old City,** creeping down every little alleyway, entering every church, inspecting every architectural curiosity (Alghero puts the "arch" back into "architecture"), and surfacing at times to walk around the ancient walls and view the shimmering sea beyond. From p. Sulis, via Carlo Alberto takes you to the fourteenth-century **Church of San Francesco,** whose heavy neo-classical facade conceals a gracious Gothic presbytery. In July and August, classical music concerts reverberate through the cloisters three times per week (L5000, with student ID L3500). On nearby via Principe Umberto, a perfectly medieval street, is the **Casa Doria,** at #7, with its beautiful sixteenth-century front, built by the powerful Doria clan from Genoa that founded Alghero. Down the street you can see the most interesting view of the cathedral—the back. Redone in the nineteenth century, the church retains its striking Gothic choirs and bell tower.

For a look at what's prowling around the waters (besides the tourists), visit the **Mare Nostrum Aquarium,** via XX Settembre, 1 (tel. 97 83 33), across from the old city. The aquarium is home to the local fish and reptile population, along with some not-so-local carnivores: **piranhas.** Several sharks in the collection might make you think twice about taking a dip at nearby beaches. (Open June-Sept. daily 9:30am-1:30pm and 4:30-11:30pm; Oct.-May Mon.-Fri. 10am-1pm and 5-11pm, Sat.-Sun. 4-9pm. Admission L5000, with ISIC L3000.)

Alghero hosts myriad seasonal events, including Catalan music and folk performances; ask as the *azienda.* Alghero's **Campionato Italiano Triathlon** in early June brings athletes and spectators from all points on the boot.

Near Alghero

Grotte di Nettuno is an eerie cavern of daggerlike stalactites and mushrooming stalagmites, a vast natural wonder not to be missed. Some athletic ability is required to stumble through, and even leaving the boat is a bit of unexpected exercise. The grotto is near the edge of Cape Caccia, which juts out majestically from Porto Conte (25km by land from Alghero, 15km by sea). (Groups are admitted every hour May-Sept. 8am-7pm; Oct.-April 8am-2pm. Admission L5000.) Boats leave Alghero's Bastione della Madalena at 9am, 10am, 3pm, and 4pm (round-trip 3 hr., L10,000). The SFS bus combs the beautiful coast (leaving at 9:15am and 2:50pm, returning at 1pm and 6:55pm; 50 min.; one-way L1300). Mopeds can reach the *grotte* in 30 minutes. Once there, you must walk down an enervating 671 steps that plunge between massive white cliffs and under wheeling gulls all the way down to the sea. After the tour, you'll have an hour to recuperate from the climb. If you're moped-mobile, stop at the beaches of Porto Conte and the exquisite Capo Caccia, as well as the **Nuraghe of Palmavera** (10km out of Alghero), where an intriguing central tower dates from 1100 B.C.E. If you've rented a moped for the full day, ride 10km towards Porto Torres to the **Necropolis of Anghelu Ruju,** a complex of 38 tombs from about 300 B.C.E.

The coastal road south of Alghero merits a hitched ride. The road, recently reopened after massive landslides, also passes through one of the last habitats of the Griffon vulture, a bird of impressive wingspan that can be seen soaring overhead. Shortly before **Bosa,** 45km south of Alghero, several outstanding beaches are a short climb down the hillside away from town. A bus returns to Alghero (via an interior route) at 5:30pm. The beaches, **Spiaggia di San Giovanni**and **Spiaggia di Marta Pia,** are north of town and can be reached by following the sea away from Alghero. You will find lots of clear water, if also many tourists. The **Spiaggia Le Bombarde,** close to Fertilia (and the hostel), is less crowded, but is receding rapidly into the sea. A determined walk to **Torre del Lazzaretto** (farther along the shore) will be more rewarding. The AP city buses serve Porte Corte and the beaches.

Oristano

At the center of Sardinia's most productive farming regions, Oristano sustains a quiet life removed from the island's other cities and the demands of foreign visitors. Thirty-thousand inhabitants strong, it is the only town of any consequence along the stretch of coast between Alghero and Cagliari. It's also a convenient base for visiting the ancient port of Tharros.

Practical Information

EPT: via Cagliari, 278 (tel. 731 91), 6th floor, near p. Mannu across from the ARST station. Eager to please, with plenty of information on both the town and region. Open Mon. and Thurs.-Fri. 8am-2pm, Tues.-Wed. 8am-2pm and 4-7pm. **Pro Loco,** vico Umberto, 15 (tel. 706 21), off via de Castro, between p. Roma and p. Eleonora. This independent tourist office has information only on Oristano. Open Mon.-Fri. 9-11:30am and 5-8pm, Sat. 8:30-11:30am.

Post Office: via Mariano IV, 10. Open Mon.-Fri. 8am-2pm, Sat. 8am-noon. **Postal code:** 09170.

Telephones: SIP, p. Eleonora, 40, opposite the Church of San Francesco. Open Mon.-Fri. 8:30am-12:30pm and 3-7pm, Sat. 8:30am-12:30pm. **Telephone code:** 0783.

Train Station: p. Ungheria (tel. 722 70), about 1km from town center. Trains to Sassari and Olbia (3-4 hr.) and to Cagliari (1-2 hr.).

Bus Stations: PANI, via Lombardia, 26 (tel. 21 23 27). To Cagliari (3 per day, 1½hr., L6400), Nuoro (3 per day, 2 hr., L7000), and Sassari (3 per day, 2¼hr., L8000). **ARST,** via Cagliari. Connects local routes, as well as running 2 slower and cheaper buses to Cagliari (at 7:15am and 2:15pm, 2¼ hr., L5300).

English Books: In the back room of the *libreria,* corso Umberto, 19. One shelf with classics and decent mysteries.

Medical Emergency: Tel. 782 22. **Main hospital,** via Fondazione Rockefeller (tel. 742 61).

First Aid: Tel. 743 33.

Accommodations and Camping

There is nothing resembling a one-star hotel in Oristano, and the youth hostel was closed in the summer of 1988 because of political turmoil. Your best bet is to camp 7km west of town in Torre Grande.

Ostello Eleonora d'Arborea (IYHF), via dei Pescatori, 31 (tel. 220 97), in Torre Grande next to a nice beach. In summer, ARST buses run every 30 min. (last bus 8:30pm, L800). Follow the unpaved road across from the bus stop for 2 blocks. 2 crowded rooms with 34 beds. L6200 per person. Breakfast L1300. Lunch or dinner L7000. Showers L800. Lockout 3-5pm. Curfew 11pm. Closed in 1988, and bleak prospects for 1989.

Piccolo Hotel, via Martignano, 19 (tel. 715 00), in the mazelike *centro storico.* From p. Eleonara, walk in the direction the statue faces; take a right, an immediate left, a third right, and then a left. Tidy, tiny rooms, several with massive balconies. Helpful management. Singles L20,000, with bath L22,900. Doubles with bath L39,800.

Hotel Amiscora, viale S. Martino, 13 (tel. 725 03), 1 block beyond p. Mannu. Modern, with A/C, at hefty rates. Singles L27,200. Doubles L47,300.

Camping: Torre Grande, via Stella Mare (tel. 220 08), 100m out of Torre Grande on the road to Oristano. Facilities galore, but packed in summer. L3600 per person, L3800 per tent. Open May-Oct.

Food

To compensate for the expensive accommodations, hit the **market** at via Mariano IV, 2 blocks from p. Roma. (Open Mon.-Fri. 7am-1pm and 4-7pm, Sat. 7am-1pm.) The **Standa Supermarket** is at the corner of via A. Diaz and via XX Settembre. (Open Mon.-Fri. 8:30am-1pm and 4:30-8pm, Sat. 9am-1pm.)

Pizzeria Zio Nino, via Figola, 10, near p. Roma. A lonely take-away with tasty offerings. Large slices L1100-1500, full pizzas L2200-3700. Open Tues.-Sun. 5:30-9:30pm.

Arborea, p. Roma, 15 (tel. 703 63). Boisterous locals dine under huge murals depicting key events in Sardinian history. Try the outstanding *spaghetti alle arselle* (scallops, L5000) or the filling and delicious *antipasto mare* (L6500). Full meals a budget-blasting binge at L13,500. Open Tues.-Sun. 12:30-2:30pm and 7-9:30pm.

Sights and Entertainment

The center of town is **piazza Roma,** dominated by the thirteenth-century **Tower of Saint Christopher.** The *piazza* and adjoining **corso Umberto** explode with youthful Oristanese for several hours of the early evening in summer. The city's **Antiquarium** houses a fine collection of nuraghic bronzes and ceramics, Punic glassware, and Roman artifacts, but has been closed for two years. The museum is scheduled to reopen at a new location on via Parpaglia, off p. Roma.

The pastel **Church of San Francesco** (1838) stands nearby at the end of via de Castro, at p. Eleonora. It is modeled after the Pantheon and houses several fine works of art. In the sacristy, the sixteenth-century polyptych of *Saint Francis Receiving the Stigmata* and the fourteenth-century statue of a bishop of Nino Pisano deserve special notice. The main sanctuary contains a wooden crucifix from the fourteenth-century Spanish school (left altar) and a balustrade formed from fragments of an eleventh-century pulpit (right transept).

A statue in p. Eleonora by the *municipio* commemorates **Eleonora d'Arborea,** Sardinia's Joan of Arc. This local heroine was a fourteenth-century princess who successfully contested the power of the Spanish House of Aragon. She is remembered for drafting the *Carta de Logu* (Code of Laws) in 1395, determining the Sardinian legal system for almost 500 years and memorializing the ancient Sardinian language in which it was written. The tradition of a woman in power continues in Oristano—the current governor of the province is the only woman to hold such an office in all of Italy.

Down via Eleonara from p. Eleonara is the **duomo,** a delightful amalgamation of thirteenth-century design and eighteenth-century additions. From the outside, the octagonal bell tower stands out distinctly. Inside are chandeliers, tapestries, paintings on all sides, and even a little stained glass. The vivid colors of the dome's interior create a particularly pleasing effect. Another outstanding church is **Santa Giusta,** 3km out of town on the road to Cagliari. A thirteenth-century stone building, its severe facade is enlivened only by a curious panel above the doorway, portraying small animals eating their prey. This church is perhaps the finest on the island.

Oristano holds a number of interesting festivals. On the last Sunday of **Carnevale** (Feb. 5 in 1989) and the following Tuesday (Mardi Gras—Feb. 7 in 1989), Oristano celebrates the **Sartiglia,** a traditional sixteenth-century race in which horsemen try to pierce six-inch metal stars with their swords as they gallop down the street. The masked *componidori* orchestrate the mysterious ritual, which aims to placate the gods and bring blessings upon the year's harvest. On July 6 and 7, **Ardia** (60km and a 1-hr. bus ride away) sponsors a frenzied horse race in which chaotic groups circle a church seven times to commemorate Emperor Constantine's victory at the Milivan Bridge in 312 C.E.

Near Oristano

Twenty kilometers west of Oristano are the ruins of the ancient Phoenician port of **Tharros.** Much of the city remains submerged under water, but recent excavations have revealed Punic fortifications, a Roman temple dedicated to Demeter, a Paleochristian baptistery, and a Punic shrine. The beaches here are also classically beautiful. To reach Tharros, take an ARST bus (40 min.; one way L1300, round-trip L2200) to San Giovanni di Sinis (in summer daily at 8am, noon, 2pm, and 6:50pm; last bus returns at 8:05pm). On the way to Tharros you'll pass two interesting churches: **San Salvatore,** built above a pagan temple whose Roman deities (Venus, Cupid, Hercules) are still seen on an underground wall, and **San Giovanni in Sinis,** a part-pagan, part-Christian structure dating from the fifth century. If you pause in San Salvatore, you might do a double take. During the 1960s the town was converted into a Mexican-American "Old West" village to serve as the backdrop for several Italian movies.

About 35km south of Oristano, the **Costa Verde,** nearly 40km of sandy coves and scintillating ocean, remains virtually untouched by the tourism that plagues much of Sardinia. In fact, apart from the two coastal towns of Porto Palma and Marina di Arbus (where there is a rudimentary campsite), there are few denizens to speak of. ARST buses can take you part of the way to Arbus (*not* Marina di Arbus) at 8:10am and 2pm, but from there, you must undertake a difficult hitch.

Barumini, near the famous **Nuraghi of Su Nuraxi** (see Near Cagliari) is somewhat accessible from Oristano on your way south to Cagliari. Ask at the EPT for the ARST connections—it's tricky.

Cagliari

Cagliari captures the superlatives as far as Sardinian cities go; it is the capital, the largest metropolis, the chief and most pleasant port, and one of the two most worthwhile places to visit on the island (Alghero's the other one). The city also boasts some improbable and delightful surprises: Roman ruins, Spanish churches, medieval bastions, exquisite beaches, and a large pink flamingo population (especially in winter). Despite all its assets, Cagliari makes no pretensions to sophistication, and besides having an unusually amiable harbor, it harbors all the amenities and budget accommodations imaginable. Furthermore, it is a perfect base for daytrips to the nuraghic ruins near Barumini, the Phoenician- Roman city of Nora, and the sandy beaches of the Costa del Sud.

Orientation and Practical Information

The main drag is **via Roma,** which runs along the harbor, framed on one side by p. Matteotti (and the train and ARST stations), on the other by p. Deffenu (and the PANI station and Tirrenia docks). Behind via Roma cluster the city's main streets, hotels, restaurants, and shops. And behind them, on a hill commanding a great view of the city and sea, is the **castello,** the historic center of town where churches, ruins, narrow streets, and forbidding towers evoke the days of Pisan rule.

Azienda di Turismo, p. Matteotti, 9 (tel. 66 92 55 or 66 49 23). Wonderfully helpful and pleasant. Information on all corners of Sardinia. Open daily June-Sept. 8am-8pm; Oct.-May 8am-2pm.

Student Travel: CTS, via Cesare Balbo, 4 (tel. 48 82 60). Very informative.

Associazione Italiana Studenti Sardi: via Farina, 43 (tel. 66 84 13). Travel information.

American Express: Sartourist, p. Deffenu, 14 (tel. 65 29 71). Assistance with car rental and hotel reservations. Open Mon.-Sat. 9am-1pm and 4-8pm, Sat. 9am-1pm.

Post Office: p. del Carmine (tel. 65 82 57), near p. Matteotti. **Fermo posta** L250 per letter. Open Mon.-Sat. 7:20am-8:30pm, but some services close at 1 or 1:30pm. **Postal code:** 09100.

Telephones: ASST, via G. M. Angioy, off p. Matteotti. An efficient, comfortable office. Open 24 hours for international calls. **SIP,** via Cima, 9, off via G. Mannu. Open daily 8am-10pm. **Telephone code:** 070.

Airport: In the village of **Elmas** (tel. 24 01 11, 24 00 46, or 24 01 69). Before each flight, ARST buses run between the airport and the city terminal in p. Matteotti (20-min., free).

Train Stations: Ferrovie dello Stato, p. Matteotti (tel. 65 62 93). To Olbia (7 per day, L14,100), Porto Torres (2 per day, L13,700), Sassari (6 per day, L12,700), and Oristano (6 per day, L4900). **Ferrovie Complimentarie della Sardegna,** p. della Repubblica (tel. 49 13 04).

Bus Stations: PANI, p. Darsena, 4 (tel. 65 23 26). Nonstop service to Sassari at 7am and 2:15pm (L16,200). Office open Mon.-Sat. 9am-2pm and 5-7pm, Sun. 1-2pm and 5:15-6:15pm. **ARST,** p. Matteoti, 6 (tel. 65 72 36). Good for local routes.

Ferry Office: Tirrenia, via Campidano, 1 (tel. 66 60 65), at the end of the via Roma arcade. Crowded and unpleasant. Open Mon.-Fri. 9am-12:45pm and 4:30-7pm, Sat. 9am-noon. Also open 1 hr. before ships leave.

Car Rental: Ruvioli, via dei Mille, 11 (tel. 65 89 55). Best deal is 1 week with unlimited mileage for L375,400, plus 18% tax and optional (advisable) insurance. Minimum age 21.

English Books: La Bancarella, via Roma, 169. A selection of classic and recent paperbacks. Open Mon.-Fri. 9am-12:30pm and 4-7pm; Sat. 9am-12:30pm.

Flea Market: Sun. morning at the **Bastione di San Remy** (Terrazza Umberto). A blast: used clothes, toys, and assorted junk.

Hospital: via Ospedale (tel. 65 76 71). **First Aid:** Tel. 65 69 71.

Police: Questura, via Amat, 9 (tel. 49 22 01).

Accommodations

Cagliari crawls with inexpensive pads, but there is competition year-round: University students from September until mid-July, and tourists from July to mid-September. Still, there are so many rooms you will eventually find one; try the

American Express office or the tourist office in p. Matteotti for help. If you are staying at a small *allogio,* make sure you find out the curfew.

Allogio Firenze, corso V. Emanuele, 50 (tel. 65 36 78). Corso V. Emanuele is parallel to via Roma and 4 blocks from p. Matteotti. Clean, pleasant rooms in a classy atmosphere, but often full in summer. Harsh 3-story ascent. Singles L9100. Doubles L14,800.

Allogio Olimpio, corso V. Emanuele, 145 (tel. 65 89 15). Large, immaculate rooms. Proprietress settles you right in. Singles L9100. Doubles L15,800. Showers L900. Curfew midnight.

Locanda la Perla, via Sardegna, 18B (tel. 66 94 46), on the 1st road parallel to via Roma, near p. Matteotti. Singles L9100. Doubles L20,000. Showers L1000. Curfew midnight.

Locanda Las Palmas, via Sardegna, 14 (tel. 65 16 79), next to La Perla. Spruce and well-run. Microscopic singles L10,000. Doubles L16,700. Triples L22,500. Showers L2000.

Locanda Castello, largo Carlo Felice, 26 (tel. 66 56 15). Largo C. Felice is perpendicular to via Roma and begins in p. Matteotti. Ideal location and friendly management, but weak showers. 5 dingy rooms. Doubles L16,000.

Allogio Micheletti, via Crispi, 13 (tel. 65 09 46). Via Crispi is the western continuation of via Sardegna. Immense and likely to have vacancy. Singles L9000. Doubles L18,100.

Albergo Centrale, via Sardegna, 4 (tel. 65 47 83), by la Perla. Singles L10,000. Doubles L18,100. Showers L1000.

Albergo Flora, via Sassari, 43 (tel. 65 82 19), 2 blocks from p. Matteotti. A bit grimy, but one of the 30 rooms is bound to be free. Singles L17,600. Doubles L29,700.

Institutia Maria Ausiliatrice, via XXVIII Febbraio (tel. 49 18 39). Catch bus #1 or M from via Roma. Women only. An odd, out-of-the-way place. About L5000 per person.

Food

For cheap food, go to via dei Mille (off via Roma), where several *pizzerie* and *trattorie* serve lots of carbohydrates in not the cleanest or most aromatic atmosphere. Via Sardegna and via Cavour, the first two streets parallel to via Roma, offer more refined food and surroundings for only a few thousand lire more. The Azienda distributes a helpful list of all restaurants in the city or province that provide a tourist *menù* for under L15,000.

Trattoria Gennargentu, via Sardegna, 60 (tel. 65 82 47). Heaping plates of lasagna and *gnocchi,* tasty shish-kebab, and savory squid—this place has it all, including a cozy atmosphere and warming house wines. Complete meals a worthwhile L12,000. Open Mon.-Sat.

Gastronomia/Rosticceria Azuni, via Azuni, 5 (tel. 66 24 01). Large and satisfying *menù turistico* includes dessert and a beer for L9500. Gregarious owner-chef also offers local dishes made of pigs' feet, and scrumptious homemade pasta (L2500). Open daily.

Trattoria Congera, via Sardegna, 37 (tel. 66 78 15). A mainstay on the "Sardegna strip." Mounds of decent munch at moderate prices. Try the *spaghetti alla carbonara* (L4000) or indulge in the complete *menù* (L12,000). Open Mon.-Sat.

La Cantina, via dei Mille, 3. A cavernous interior and fast-food offerings and prices. Stuff yourself for less than L4000. Open Mon.-Sat. 10:15am-11pm.

Basilio, via Satta, 112 (tel. 48 03 30), tucked away on a side street. From p. Deffenu, go uphill on via XX Settembre, continue on via Sonnino, and turn right 3 blocks later on via Grazia Deledda—via Satta is on the left. Complete dinners for L15,000. Try *burrida,* an indigenous local fish served with diced walnuts. Open Mon.-Sat.

Caffè Genovese, p. Constituzione, 10-11. An elegant, old-fashioned cafe, great for coffee and ice cream (L1500).

Economarket, via Angioy, 56, 3 blocks off via Roma. A well-stocked supermarket close to the port. Open Mon.-Fri. 8am-1pm and 5-8pm.

Sights and Seasonal Events

The conspicuous pink towers of the **Bastione di San Remy** mark the division between the modern port and the densely packed medieval quarter on the hill above. Climb the stairway to the terrace for a spectacular view of the Golfo degli Angeli, the marshes to the west, and the mountains that surround Cagliari. Up the skinny steps behind the *bastione* lies medieval Cagliari, where narrow balconies overflow with flowers and outdated music seeps down from the upper stories. More narrow streets lead uphill to the **duomo,** a charming mixture of Pisan geometry and baroque flourish. The exterior, with its simple outline, serried rows of columns, and squat bell tower, is pure Pisan; the interior, tutti-frutti marble and ornate metal work, epitomizes baroque. The pulpits at the entrance, depicting scenes from the New Testament, and the four lions at the base of the high altar are the work of Guglielmo, and derive from the cathedral at Pisa. Before leaving, look over the cathedral's lower sanctuary, emblazoned with colorful marble inlays and animated miniatures of Sardinian saints.

The age-blackened **Torre di San Pancrazio** sits just up the hill on p. Indipendenza. It is hard to believe that this former bulwark in the Pisan defensive walls was erected without the help of the cranes that are now being used to restore it. In the shadow of the tower is the **Museo Archeologico,** a wonderful sampling of Cagliari's long and varied past. Native, prehistoric figurines stand side by side with elegant Greek statues, and sparkling Phoenician jewelry is reflected by the surface of Roman vases. Perhaps most impressive are the broad-shouldered warriors and pot-bellied gods, crafted in bronzed stone by the people of the mysterious nuraghic civilization. In the garden, littered with fascinating bits of mosaic and funerary stele, a cool sea breeze wafts an occasional boat whistle from the port far below. (Open in summer Tues.-Sat. 9am-2pm and 2:30-6:30pm, Sun. 9am-1pm; in off-season Tues.-Sat. 9am-2pm and Sun. 9am-1pm. Admission L4000.)

Pass under the Torre di San Pancrazio to **Arsenale,** with its lofty towers and startling views of the city, and then stroll through the well-visited public gardens at the end of viale R. Elena. To the left of the **city museum,** a contemporary Sardinian gallery (open June-Sept. Tues.-Sat. 9am-1pm and 5-8pm; Oct.-May 9am-1pm and 4-7pm), is an uphill, rocky road winding left. Catch your breath and admire the view here before forging ahead to viale Buon Cammino and the **Roman Amphitheater,** the most significant Roman ruin in Sardinia. It was constructed in the second century C.E. out of a natural depression in the rock. Wild animals for the spectacles were caged in ditches still visible under the stage. Continue down viale Fra Ignazio da Laconi, past the botanical gardens, to the **Church of San Michele.** The grandiose baroque facade prefaces an interior cluttered with color and ornamentation.

A small pagan temple also from the Roman era was incorporated into the sixth-century **Church of San Saturno.** This, one of the oldest Christian churches in Sardinia, was built in the shape of a Greek cross with a dome to mark the site where Saturnus was martyred during the reign of Diocletian. It now stands closed and rather forlornly in an empty lot in San Cosimo near via Sonnino.

During the first four days of May, Sardinians flock to Cagliari for the **Festival of Sant' Efisio,** faithfully honoring a vow made 300 years ago to the man who saved the island from the plague. A costumed procession, on horseback and foot, escorts his effigy from the capital down the coast to the small church that bears his name.

From July to September, the city runs amuck with an arts festival; the Roman Amphitheater comes alive with classic plays; and outdoor movies are shown at the Marina Piccola, off Spiaggia del Poetto (take Bus P). Get the schedule from the Azienda. Bus P also runs every 20 minutes from p. Matteotti to the **beach,** packed with locals.

Near Cagliari

Nora, said to be the oldest city in Sardinia, was settled by the Phoenicians (circa 850 B.C.E.), who coveted its strategic position at the end of a high, narrow peninsula. The town prospered, becoming in time a Roman stronghold. But its luck faltered with the onslaught of pirate raids, and by the eighth century, Nora had been completely abandoned. The site is fascinating for its motley ruins—from Phoenician temples to a sixteenth-century Spanish watchtower—and its rugged location. Strong winds whip across the ancient walls, and the high ground next to the watchtower commands a sweeping view of the sea. Leisurely exploration of the ruins can be combined with a swim at the nearby beach. (Open daily in summer 9am-8pm; in off-season 9am-5pm. Admission L4000.) ARST buses make the uninspiring run to Pula every hour (30 min., round-trip L1500-2600). From Pula, it's a pleasant 4km walk to Nora; follow corso V. Emanuele, turn left when it ends, and follow the signs. Strongly consider hitching once out of Nora.

Barumini, an agricultural bastion in the rolling countryside 60km north of Cagliari, is 1km west of the **Nuraghi of Su Nuraxi.** (Open daily 8am-dusk; in off-season 9am-4pm.) These ruins are the best-preserved complex of nuraghi in Sardinia. Set atop a hill that commands a broad vista of the treeless plain below, the village is constructed of huge, rough-hewn blocks in an intricate layout, vividly illustrating the defensive nature of this civilization.

The only direct bus from Cagliari to Barumini is the daily ARST run at 2:10pm (1½ hr., L3500).

To return, take the FCS bus at 6:20pm (L1300) to San Luri. Once in San Luri, ask for the FS train station, where you catch the commuter train to Cagliari at 7:10pm (L2500). The Azienda can clarify this route.

East of Cagliari, a scenic coastal road winds above once-pristine coastline that has been commercially developed all the way down to Villasimius on Sardinia's southeastern tip. Five buses per day ply this beaten track. To get a taste of the undeveloped beauty that has become increasingly scarce in Sardinia, head for the **Costa del Sud,** which begins about 50km southwest of Cagliari. A small road follows the shore, with paths branching down to the coves. No industry exists here to taint the azure water, and no campground to clutter the windswept shore.

Good news for all who love roughing it in beautiful isolation: The absence of business or tourist facilities makes ARST bus service minimal at best. Only a few buses per day run to Chia (1 hr., L2500), on the Costa del Sud's eastern edge. Even fewer continue on to Teulada (1½ hr., L3300), an inland town only 8km from the more isolated western end.

The tiny village of **Uta** (20km west of Cagliari) shelters the **Church of Santa Maria,** one of Sardinia's most notable Romanesque buildings. Built around 1140, the church is a deft amalgam of French and Pisan architectural styles on the outside. Within, slender columns march down three simple naves in classical severity. Nine ARST buses per day (L1300, round-trip L2200) depart for Uta.

San Separate (19km northwest of Cagliari) is a small agricultural center that since the early 1960s has boasted walls and fences decorated with huge murals in the vein of the great Mexican muralists Rivera and Orozco. The earlier wall paintings are inspired by the Sardinian Communist party, a populist radical movement with considerable clout on the island. ARST buses leave Cagliari for San Separate every two hours (L1000, round-trip L1700). **C. S. Elia** and **Il Poetto** (4km and 5km southeast of the city, respectively) are huge beaches with fine sand. The latter stretches 10km from the mountainous Sella del Diavolo (Devil's Saddle) to the Margine Rosso (Red Bluff); behind it are the **Raft Ponds of Molentargius,** a flamingo hang-out. This place used to be extraordinary, but now half of Cagliari flocks in every Sunday, and it's getting grubby. See it on a weekday. City bus P leaves from via Roma (ticket must be bought beforehand at a newsstand). If you want to stay here, try **Locanda Garibaldi,** via Lipari, 11 (tel. 37 29 25), with singles L10,000, doubles, L20,000.

SICILY (SICILIA)

Strategically located and endowed with rich volcanic soil, the largest Mediterranean island bears witness to its epic past with a breathtaking array of ruins ranging from an eighth-century B.C.E. Phonecian village to an eighteenth-century Bourbon *palazzi.*

When Sicily was part of Magna Graecia, the military power of Syracuse was rivaled only by that of Athens. In the ninth century, the island became a Muslim outpost second in importance only to Spain. It later served as the seat of the Norman court, one of the most enlightened in medieval Europe, and then became a valuable pawn of Renaissance dynasties. Centuries of foreign domination led to a fierce Sicilian spirit. After World War II, a growing separatist movement called for the end of northern European rule, offering the island to America as the 49th state. The crusade was stifled (and its leaders were assassinated) by a combination of powers—the Italian army, the Communists, and the powerful Cosa Nostra ("Our Thing," as the Mafia is literally called). Brought to public light in recent years by its involvement in drug trafficking and sundry extralegal activities, the Mafia is responsible for Sicily's underground economy, but remains virtually invisible to the foreign tourist.

To Giuseppe Lampedusa, Sicily was a "landscape which knows no mean between sensuous sag and hellish drought; which is never petty, never ordinary, never relaxed . . . ." Time and again Sicilians have been reminded of the destructive forces lurking beneath their island's surface, as earthquakes and eruptions of Mount Etna, Europe's largest active volcano, have destroyed people and land. At the base of Mount Etna, Catania, leveled numerous times by the mountain in its backyard, is proof of the Sicilians' staying power. Chic and wealthy Taormina, stunningly propped against the mountain's slopes, is evidence of the benefits of such a precarious position. The major cities along Sicily's irregular coastal plane—Messina, the raucous capital of Palermo, and Trapani—are interspersed with farmlands planted with olives, grapes, and almonds. The luxurious appearance of the coast contrasts with the barren and impoverished hinterland. Here you'll see fields of lemon and lime trees, as well as cultivated *ficliomolia* (prickly pears), which also grow wild along the train tracks and rock bluffs. Sicily's countless monuments from the great ages of Western civilization have earned it the nickname "the archeological museum of Europe."

For a traditional tour of Sicily, stick close to the coast; for a tour of traditional Sicily, venture into the heartland. Only in the interior does the beautiful choreography of Sicilian life remain unspoiled by the tourist swarms.

A note about the climate: In summer Sicily swelters for weeks at a time (35-45°C). The burning African *scirocco* winds can scorch your vacation any time in July and August. In addition, haze and random fires often obscure vistas in the summer months. Spring and autumn are ideal for a visit to the island.

Getting There and Getting Around

There are flights from all major Italian cities to Palermo and Catania (see Palermo and Catania Practical Information). The cheapest way to reach Sicily is by train and ferry to Messina (from Rome to Reggio di Calabria L34,100). (Stay on the train for a free trip across the strait.) **Tirrenia,** the largest private ferry service in Italy, is the most extensive and reliable, though you should still expect considerable delays. **Gozo Channel** is the least expensive option for passage to and from Malta, and **Grandi-Traghetti** offers better off-season rates to Palermo from Genova and Livorno. Listings are for Tirrenia lines unless otherwise stated.

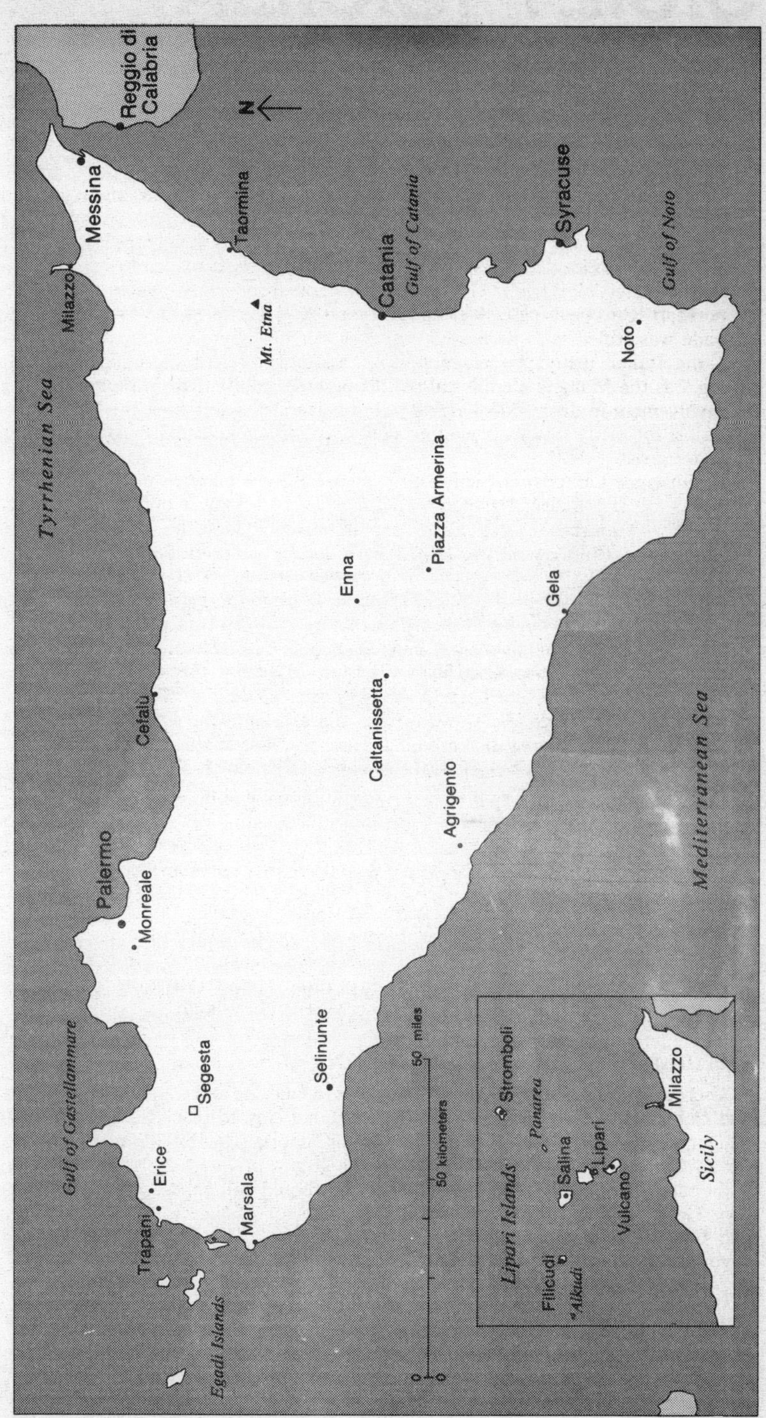

Reggio di Calabria
N
Messina
Milazzo
Taormina
Mt. Etna
Catania
Gulf of Catania
Syracuse
Gulf of Noto
Noto
Tyrrhenian Sea
Piazza Armerina
Enna
Gela
Caltanissetta
Cefalu
Agrigento
Mediterranean Sea
Palermo
Monreale
Gulf of Castellammare
Segesta
Selinunte
Erice
Trapani
Marsala
Egadi Islands
0
50 miles
0
50 kilometers
Lipari Islands
Stromboli
Panarea
Salina
Lipari
Vulcano
Filicudi
Alicudi
Milazzo
Sicily

Reggio di Calabria-Messina (¾ hr.): 12 per day on the state railroad ferry 5am-10pm (L1000). To cut this senic 50-min. crossing to 20 min., take the *aliscafo* from the same terminal at the Reggio port (L3700).

Villa San Giovanni-Messina: 22 per day on the state railroad ferry 3:20am-10:05pm (L800).

Genoa-Palermo (22 hr.): **Grandi-Traghetti Lines** departs Sept. 18-June 25 Wed. at 11pm and Sat. at noon; June 26-Sept. 17 Mon. at 6pm, Wed. at midnight, and Sat. at 11am. *Poltrona* (armchair) L72,000 (July 25-Aug. 10 L92,000; Oct.-June 14 L62,000). **Tirrenia Lines** departs Tues., Thurs., and Sat.-Sun. at 1pm. Deck seats L63,000. *Poltrona* L78,600 (Oct.-May L72,200).

Naples-Palermo (10½ hr.): 1 per day at 8:30pm. Deck seats L35,000. *Poltrona* L43,800 (Oct.-May L40,100).

Cagliari-Palermo (14 hr.): Fri. at 7pm. Deck seats L20,000. *Poltrona* L24,900 (Oct.-May L22,800).

Livorno-Palermo (18 hr.): **Grandi-Traghetti** departs Tues. and Thurs. at 6pm and Sat. at 5pm. *Poltrona* L70,000 (July 23-Aug. 10 L90,000; Oct.-June 17 L60,000). Deck seats L63,000, available only if all other classes are filled.

Naples-Catania (15 hr.): Thurs. at 8:30pm. Deck seats L35,000. *Poltrona* L43,800, in off-season L40,100.

Reggio di Calabria-Catania-Syracuse: To Syracuse Tues., Fri., and Sun. at 8:30am (3¼ hr.). A bargain. Deck fare to either port L12,000. *Poltrona* L17,200; in off-season L15,900.

Malta-Syracuse-Catania: Mon., Wed., and Sat. at 8:45am (5¼ hr. to Syracuse, 9 hr. to Catania). Deck fare L59,000; in off-season L50,000. Also to Catania via the **Gozo Channel** April 3-June 27 Fri. at 11:30pm (L38,000, round-trip L72,000); July 2-Sept. 26 Wed., Fri., and Sun. at 11:30pm (L48,000, round-trip L88,000). Student discount L2000.

Cagliari-Trapani (10 hr.): From June-Sept. leaving Cagliari Tues. at 7pm, Trapani Thurs. at 9pm; in off-season leaving Cagliari Mon. at 7pm and Trapani Wed. at 9pm. Another bargain: deck fare L20,000, *poltrona* L24,900; Oct.-May deck L20,000, *poltrona* L22,800.

La Goulette (Tunisia)-Trapani (8 hr.): The cheapest route between Africa and Europe, except for the ferry service between Spain and Morocco. June-Sept. Wed. at 8pm, Oct.-May. Tues. at 8pm. June-Sept. *poltrona* L74,200; Oct.-May deck L56,000, *poltrona* L61,800.

Trains along Sicily's coastlines belie their reputation for tardiness with acceptable if steamy service. Do not, however, trust any rail schedule for the interior or to Agrigento; the lines are undergoing electrification, and the wait is very long. Buses are more efficient and cooler, if more expensive, alternatives to most Sicilian destinations.

Check in every city and with every driver for the bus schedules to your next destination; there is no central authority for any of the island's numerous coach companies.

Hitchhiking is difficult on long hauls, due to the celerity of Sicily's *autostrada* drivers (no one slows down). Stand near the turn-off to roads for short, specific trips. Single women should not hitchhike in Sicily. Period.

Messina

Take the "-ina" off Messina and what have you got? The "Port of Sicily" lives up to its functional billing with an utterly unattractive, industrial harbor. It seems the Fates have conspired to ruin historical Messina: In 1908 an earthquake killed 80,000, levelled the coast, arrested the activity of the nearby whirlpool Charybdis (of *Odyssey* fame), and forced the rebuilding of the old town into an uninspired urban grid pattern. Just as reconstruction was close to completion, the massive Allied bombings of 1943 razed the city again. The combined effect of the two disasters has been aesthetically fatal. Aside from a few gems, namely the twice-restored ***duomo*** and the Museo Nazionale, Messina's sights are small beans in comparison to what lies beyond in Sicily; admire Messina for its determination—but admire it hastily. Proceed onward to the treasures of the west and south of the island.

Orientation and Practical Information

Both trains and ferries stop at the **Central Station,** located at the joint of the sickle-shaped harbor at piazza della Repubblica. Hydrofoils dock 1km north on corso Vittorio Emanuele II, which becomes via della Libertà before it passes the **Museo Nazionale** (Civic National Museum), 3km north. From the station, via Primo Settembre runs directly to the **duomo,** while via Tommaso Cannizzaro leads through the center of town, and at piazza Cairoli, heads towards the university. Local buses (L500) often run from p. della Repubblica into town. Trains leave regularly for Palermo (5 hr., L11,700) with stops at Milazzo (50 min., L2000) and Cefalù (3½ hr., L9400); for Syracuse (3 hr., L9300) with a stop at Taormina (40 min., L2500); for Rome (9 per day, 11 hr., L34,100); and for Milan (4 per day, 15½ hr., L47,100). **SAIS** buses (tel. 77 19 14) leave the train station regularly from 5:40am to 8:30pm for Taormina (1½ hr., L3400) and Catania (3 hr., L6600). **Giuntabus** (tel. 77 37 82) leaves regularly from viale S. Martino at via Terranova (take via del Vespro directly in front of the station to viale S. Martino, then turn left 1 block) for Milazzo (L4000). Hydrofoils (tel. 36 40 44) leave daily from June 15 to September 15 for the Lípari Islands (3 per day, 2 hr., L24,500).

APT: Outside the Central Station to the right in p. della Repubblica (tel. 77 29 44), also at p. Cairoli, 45 (tel. 293 35 41). Affable, English-speaking, and complete with a blind bard. Copious materials and English maps. Both offices open Mon.-Sat. 9am-1pm.

Post Office: At p. Antonello, off corso Cavour near the cathedral. Perhaps Italy's only outdoor post office. Open Mon.-Sat. 8:30am-6:40pm. **Postal Code:** 98100.

Telephones (ASST): On your right from the train station. Open daily 8am-9:30pm. **SIP,** via G. Natoli, 59, left off via T. Cannizzaro. Open 8am-8pm. **Telephone code:** 090.

Lost and Found: Tel. 77 37 52.

Pharmacy: Logocando, corso Garibaldi, 69 (tel. 77 20 18). Open Mon.-Fri. 8:30am-1pm and 4:30-8pm. Check listings outside any pharmacy for the rotating 24-hour service.

Police: Carabinieri, Tel. 112.

Hospital: Ospedale Piemonte, viale Europa (tel. 22 21).

Accommodations and Camping

Singles are sparse in Messina, as they are either grabbed in the morning by traveling business people or occupied by itinerant workers. In summer call a day in advance, or at least the morning of the day you arrive. You'll probably have the easiest time finding a room on the weekends. Italian-speaking women should inquire about the summer exchanges offered by the university's *Casa della Studentessa* (tel. 71 63 03)—it erratically provides accommodations gratis. Many smaller establishments are wary of foreigners with backpacks; it's best to leave your bags at the station when searching.

Albergo Roma, p. Duomo, 3 (tel. 77 55 66), near the cathedral. Large, clean, but archaic. The senior management knows the city inside out, and the price is a steal. Singles L9000. Doubles L18000. Showers L1000.

Albergo Mirage, via N. Scotto, 1 (tel. 293 83 44), 100m to the left from the train station. Affordable rooms with tremendous ceilings. In the darkest corner of town, so not the best choice for women. Fills up quickly. Singles L15,000. Doubles L30,000, with bath L34,000. Showers L2000.

Hotel Monza, viale San Martino, 63 (tel. 77 37 75), at via T. Cannizzaro. Treat yourself. A jungle of plants in the lobby welcomes you to comfortable, tranquil (though warm) rooms. Singles L25,800, with bath L29,800. Doubles L47,300, with bath L54,000.

Camere La Bussola, via Dei Mille, 89 (no phone), off via T. Cannizzarro after p. Carioli. Don't be intimidated by the heavy gate; inside are agreeable rooms run by an agreeable manager. Singles L20,000. All others L15,000 per person.

Camping: Bus #28 will take you to **Il Peloritano** (tel. 84 40 57). L2500 per person, small tent L1800. Open May-Oct.

Food

Many inexpensive restaurants and *trattorie* line via Risorgimento, off via T. Cannizzarro, and the university area around piazza del Popolo. In summer, try the specialty *pescespada* (swordfish), direct from the Straits of Messina.

University Mensa, via C. Battisti, 251. Follow via T. Cannizzaro from the station, then turn left on via Battisti. A *Casa dello Studente* sign in front, but enter in back and buy a L850 ticket. Anyone remotely resembling a student gets in for a complete meal (pasta, cold cuts or cheese, bread, fruit, and drink). Hang around at night to watch a soccer game on TV with the rowdy young crowd. Open Mon.-Sat. 11:30am-2:30pm and 6:30-8:30pm.

Trattoria Etnea, via Porta Imperiale, 38 (tel. 71 07 07), off p. del Popolo near the mensa. Disorderly, but the food will set the taste buds whirling with glee. Start with their unique *Spaghetti alla Siciliana,* with eggplant, tomato, and meat sauce (L2500), followed by *Pesce Stocco Messinese* (fish with tomatoes, olives, potatoes, and celery, L4500). Local wine L2000 per liter. Open noon-3:30pm and 7-11pm.

L'Angolo del Ristoro, via Risorgimento, 85, at v. 27 Luglio. Self-service. Always packed with students at night. Luscious lasagna (L3000 per *etto*) and pizza (L2500-4500). Open Sat.-Thurs. 10:30am-2:30pm and 5:30-11:30pm.

Sights

The turf of Messina's history has been broken continually by earthquakes; unfortunately, its monument sites are therefore speckled with only occasional fragments. Two remarkable reconstructions are the medieval *duomo* (closed noon-4pm) and the tiny Norman **Church of SS. Annunziata dei Catalani** (open for services only), eleventh- and twelfth-century structures, respectively. The stark Romanesque walls, which lead to an imposing image of Christ the Pantocrator, offer striking contrast to the intricate wooden ceiling inside. Outside, compare the *duomo*'s lavish original main portal to the more demure Arabic-influenced sidings of SS. Annunziata.

The piazza Duomo's grace and simplicity compound the sense of loss over Messina's catastrophic fate. From the steps of the *duomo,* the *piazza* offers a rare view of the nearby knolls.In front of the church is the vivacious **Fontana di Orione** (1547, by Michelangelo's pupil Angelo Montorsoli), which when unveiled caused outrage with its sultry show of skin. A twentieth-century addition to the *piazza,* the **campanile** houses one of the world's largest astronomical clocks (1933). Female figurines take turns banging the bells at quarter hours, and at noon a mechanical procession of animals, angels, and legendary figures acts out the local legend of the Madonna della Lettera, patron saint of the city. (Festivals in her honor take place June 3 and Aug. 13-15, the latter a 500,000-strong procession called **Ferragosto Messinese**).

The Civic National Museum, founded in 1806 with five private collections, became a state museum in 1914 when it was transformed into a repository for the works of art, furnishings, and valuables recovered from churches and civic buildings after the 1908 earthquake. Today it includes a wonderful collection of Renaissance and Baroque masters: *The Polyptych of the Rosary* (1473) by Antonello da Messina, a stellar southern Italian painter; an Andrea della Robbia terra cotta of the Virgin and Child; a sixteenth-century *Pietà* by the Flemish mannerist Colyn de Coter; and two Caravaggio masterpieces, *The Adoration of the Shepherds* (1604) and the *Resurrection of Lazarus* (1609). Take bus #8 from the station or p. Duomo (20 min.); walk part of the way back to view the harbor's *zankle* form and the colorful fishermen selling their wares by the roadside. (Museum open Tues., Thurs., and Sat. 9am-1:30pm and 3-6pm, Wed., Fri., and Sun.-Mon. 9am-1:30pm. Admission L2000.)

Two principal beaches scatter their sands near Messina: **Mortelle** (bus #8 or 28) is on the Tyrrhenian Sea, while **Santa Margherita** (bus #9) is on the Ionian Sea with rocks, more room, and icy water. Near Messina, the **Tindari** park in the Patti district harbors archeological sites, including a Greek theater, Roman walls, and an interesting Antiquarium. (Open daily 9am-1 hr. before sunset. Free.) Take a train to Oliveri, then a bus to Tindari. A gorgeous sandy beach lies at **Marina di Patti,** 3km from town. A bus and a very slow train run the route.

Lípari Islands (Isole Eolie)

Few foreigners have discovered what Italians rightfully consider one of the most breathtaking parts of their country. The Lípari or **Aeolian Islands,** an archipelago of seven islands of volcanic origin, lie off the Sicilian coast north of Milazzo (1 hr. west of Messina). Believed by the ancient Greeks to be the home of Aeolus, God of the Winds, the islands appear as mirages floating over the clear water on hot summer days. Food and accommodations hit the money pouch harder here than in the rest of Sicily, and in August prices really skyrocket and most hotels bulge to capacity (make reservations on the main islands no later than May). However, if you stay on the campgrounds or in the hostel and cook for yourself, you can stay cheaply on the islands, even by mainland standards. Of the three most frequented islands, visit Lípari for its well-equipped tourist center, castle, and museum; Vulcano for its bubbling mud baths and billowing sulfurous crater; and Stromboli for its lush vegetation and restless volcano.

Getting There

The principal and least expensive embarkation point for the islands is the coastal city of **Milazzo,** on the Messina-Palermo train line (1 hr. from Messina, L2000; 4 hr. from Palermo, L9800) and on **Giuntabus** routes (19 per day from Messina 5:45am-7pm, 4 on Sun., 45 min., L4000; also daily from Catania airport June-Sept., L18,000). Both ferries and hydrofoils depart from Milazzo's port. Ferries leave much less frequently from **Naples'** Molo Beverello port. Hydrofoils (about twice the price of ferries) run regularly in late July and August from **Messina, Cefalù, Palermo,** and **Reggio Calabria.** Due to frequent strikes and fluctuating departure times, the only sure way to travel through the islands is to pick up a schedule for each transport company at the booths that dot every port.

Ferries

Siremar (tel. (090) 928 32 42 in Milazzo) and **Navigazione Generale Insulare** (tel. 928 34 15) run reliable ferries out of Milazzo. Siremar also services several smaller islands and Naples (tel. (081) 551 21 13 in Naples). Frequencies listed are for the period from June through September. Prices are the same for both lines.

Milazzo-Lípari: 2 hr., L5600. **Siremar:** 6:30am-6:30pm 6 per day. **NGI:** 6:15am-10pm 3 per day.

Milazzo-Vulcano: 1½ hr., L5300. Same frequencies as to Lípari.

Milazzo-Stromboli: 5½ hr., L10,600. **Siremar:** 1:30-2:30pm 1 per day. **NGI:** Fri. at 6:15am.

Lípari-Stromboli: 3 hr., L6800. **Siremar:** 10am-2:45pm 2 per day. **NGI:** Fri. at 8:45am.

Lípari-Filicudi: 2½ hr., L5600. **Siremar:** Mon., Wed., Fri., and Sun. at 8:50am.

Naples-Stromboli: 8 hr., L36,500. **Lípari:** 12 hr., L41,300. Mon.-Tues., and Thurs.-Sat. at 9pm from the Movo Beverello port. **Hydrofoils (Aliscafi)**

Aside from Siremar, the two best hydrofoil companies are **Covemar** (tel. 928 20 23 in Milazzo), located in the **Delfo Viaggi** office in Milazzo, and **SNAV** (tel. 928 45 09 in Milazzo, 77 75 in Messina). Hydrofoils run at least twice as often as ferries, for twice the price, and in half the time. Catch one of the 15 daily *aliscafi* to Vulcano for a meager L2400. From July 10 to September 15, SNAV runs from Messina (3 per day, L24,500), Reggio Calabria (3 per day, L26,000), Cefalù (3 per week, L30,000), Palermo (Mon.-Sat., L45,000), and Naples (1 per day, L84,000).

The **telephone code** for the islands is 090 (you most pay extra for calls between the islands). The **postal code** for Lípari is 98055, for Canneto-Lípari 98052, and for the rest of the islands 98050.

Lípari

Lípari, the largest of the islands, shelters a picturesque town by the same name. Its pastel-colored houses hug a small promontory crowned by the walls of a medieval *castello,* once the site of an ancient Greek acropolis. Canneto, 3km away, boasts the best beach on the island, **Spiagga Bianca,** a charcoal-colored mixture of fine sand and pebbles.

Orientation and Practical Information

Lined with souvenir shops and overpriced cafes, **corso Vittorio Emanuele** rises from the ferry dock up one side of the castle. **Via Garibaldi** ascends from the hydrofoil docks on the other side, passing by steep stairs that lead directly to the hostel. Lípari is liberal with its lunch-hour ; the town virtually shuts down daily from 1 to 4pm.

Tourist Office: Azienda Autonomia di Soggiorno e Turismo, corso V. Emanuele, 253 (tel. 981 14 10), directly in front of the ferry dock. Soon this office will move up the street. Especially helpful in finding accommodations and planning trips to other islands. English spoken. Open Mon.-Thurs. 8am-2:30pm and 4:30-7:30pm, Fri.-Sat. 8am-2:30pm.

Currency Exchange: Bank on corso V. Emanuele, 1 block from the port. Open Mon.-Fri. 8:30am-1pm.

Post Office: corso V. Emanuele, 207, 1 block up from the tourist offce. Fermo Posta. Open Mon.-Fri. 8:10am-6:30pm, Sat. 8-11:20am.

Telephones: SIP, in Boutique Patrizia, corso V. Emanuele, 252, the 1st store off the port. Open Mon.-Sat. 9am-noon and 5-11pm, Sun. 9am-noon. Also in the Hotel Augustus, v. Ausonia, the 1st right on corso V. Emanuele. Open daily 9am-1pm and 4-11pm.

Pharmacy: corso V. Emanuele, 128 (tel. 98 15 83). English-speaking doctor.

Medical Emergency: Tel. 98 11 15 55. Hospital, Tel. 981 10 10.

Police: Carabinieri, Tel. 981 13 33.

Accommodations and Camping

The tourist office will arrange stays in *affitacamere* (private rooms and apartments). You can rent a spacious apartment with kitchen facilities for about L15,000 per person per day (L22,000 in Aug.). Most require at least a one-week stay in summer. Try to come during the beautiful days in fall and spring, when prices sink to under L10,000 per person.

City of Lípari

Ostello Lípari (IYHF), via Castello, 17 (tel. 981 15 40), within the walls of a fortress, next to the cathedral. The hostel has a courtyard with shaded tables and blooming trees. The 120 beds are often full July-Aug., so make reservations. L6600. Cold showers (after 6pm) and sheets included. Kitchen facilities. Breakfast L2000, complete lunch L8000, dinner L10,000 (book lunch and dinner in the morning). Management has a quick temper. Open March-Oct. daily 7-9am, noon-2pm, and 6-11pm. Requires IYHF card only when reaching capacity.

Locanda Salina, via Garibaldi, 18 (tel. 981 23 32), near the hydrofoil port. Beautiful rooms overlook the water. Reserve several days in advance for June, months before for August. Singles L13,000. Doubles L24,000. Showers included. Breakfast L2500.

Albergo Europeo, corso V. Emanuele, 98 (tel. 981 15 89). Shabby, olive-green rooms with sinks. Reserve early for June-Aug. Singles L17,900, with bath L22,000. Doubles L29,300, with bath L34,400. Showers L1500. Breakfast L3000.

Cassarà Vittorio, vico Sparviero, 15 (tel. 981 15 23). Go to the owner's clothes store at via Garibaldi, 78. Small rooms but a magnificent terrace overlooking the island. L12,000 per person (July-Aug. from L15,000). No private baths. Kitchen use L2000 a day.

Puglisi Antonino, vico Odissea (tel. 981 14 92). Even tinier. Usually requires a 1-week minimum stay. Inquire at the fruit store at corso V. Emanuele, 150, 5 blocks away. L15,000 per person; July-Aug. L16,000. Full in Aug.

Camping: Baia Unci (tel. 981 19 09), 2km from Lípari at the entrance to the hamlet of Canneto. Miniscule and tightly spaced, this tree-shaded site has amiable management and a cheap self-service restaurant (roasted swordfish a bargain at L8000). L6000 per person, tent included. Open April-Oct. 15. Restaurant open Mon.-Sat. noon-2pm and 7-10pm.

Although freelance camping is a no-no on the islands' beaches, visitors have been known to inconscipuously pitch a tent.

Food

Try any dish with the island's famous *caperi* (capers), and accompany it with the indigenous ambrosia, *Malvasia* wine. The **Supermercato d'Anieri Bartolo,** corso V. Emanuele, 212, provides staples. (Open Mon.-Sat. 8:30am-1pm and 4:30-9:30pm.) One cheap, tasty option is the pizza served by the bakeries at corso V. Emanuele, 210, or via Garibaldi, 34. They charge by weight, but L3500 should buy enough to bulge anyone's belly.

U Zu Bob, corso V. Emanuele, 214 (tel. 981 22 80), across from the tourist information office, near the ferry port. Run by 2 Lípari natives who spent 30 years in Australia. One of the island's best values. The *spaghetti du "Zu Bob"* bathes in a sauce of capers, olives, and anchovies (L5500). Superlatives will abound after a bite of the *Pizza a Liprota,* piled with tomatoes, capers, sliced potato, onions, and anchovies (L6000). Eat at the bar indoors to escape the flies and the 20% outdoor service charge. Open daily 10:30am-2:30pm and 6:30pm-midnight.

A Sfiziusa, via Roma, 27-33 (tel. 981 12 16), past the hydrofoil port. A typical tourist spot, but decent prices. *Menù* L12,000, pasta dishes L3200-4000, meat and fish dishes L7000-10,000. *Vino locale* L5000 per liter. Cover L1000, service 13%. Open in summer daily 11:30am-3pm and 7pm-midnight; in off-season Sat.-Thurs.

Self-Service Marina Corta, via Garibaldi, 12 (tel. 981 24 62). Portions are small. You may also lose your spaghetti among the oddly striped walls and subterranean plants. Elegantly prepared food. Pasta and other *primi* L3500, excellent stuffed eggplant L3500, fish dishes L6000-7500. Wine L1000 per glass. Open July 15-Aug. daily 11am-3pm and 5pm-1am; in off-season Sat.-Sun.

Sights and Entertainment

The medieval **castello** crowns the promontory of the town of Lípari. Within the fortress stand four churches and a **cathedral.** The latter contains an eighteenth-century silver statue of San Bartolomeo (above the high altar) and a sixteenth-century Madonna (in the right transept). The ruins opposite the cathedral in the *parco archeologico* reveal layers of civilization that go back as far as 1700 B.C.E. Many of the artifacts decorate the excellent **Museo Archeologico Eoliano,** which occupies the two buildings flanking the cathedral. Inside the museum is the *serione geologico-vulcanologica,* tracing the volcanic history of the islands. Exhibits are labeled in Italian, but the models of the islands are fascinating and require no explanation. (Open Mon.-Fri. 9am-2pm, Sun. 9am-1pm.) A charming neoclassical amphitheater inside the fortress hosts events in the July **Festival delle Isole Eolie.**

As the sun sets on the island and the zephrys roll in from the sea, stroll over to the **Turmalin Club,** outside the castle walls, for some open-air disco dancing. (Open July-Aug. daily 10am-2am. Cover L8000.) In a farewell to its summer tourist season, Lípari goes crazy with festivities, a colorful procession, and fireworks on August 24—the day of the cathedral's patron saint, Saint Bartholomew.

To freewheel across the island, rent bikes (L10,000 per 8 hr.) or mopeds (L30,000 per day) from **Christian Noleggio,** via F. Crispi, 92 (tel. 981 19 04), or **Foti Roberto,** via F. Crispi, 31 (tel. 981 23 52), both on the main road from the ferry dock. (Both open Easter-Oct. 15 daily 8:30am-7pm.) The two compete fiercely, so drive a hard bargain.

Near Lípari

One way to explore Lípari Island is to take the local bus north to the coastal village of **Canneto,** or in the opposite direction to the lookout point at **Quattrocchi** (Four Eyes). A large pumice industry detracts from the northern shoreline, but on clear days the road offers spectacular views of the islands **Salina, Panarea,** and **Stromboli** (round-trip bus fare L4000, only L1000 less than renting a moped for a fast 1-hr. trip). To get to the **Spiaggia Bianca** (White Beach), north of Canneto, take the waterfront road to the No Camping sign, then climb the stairs of via Spranello and walk between the abandoned houses for a quarter mile. This beach, now ironically a charcoal grey, was covered with a soft layer of white dust, waste from Lípari's pumice industry, before a 1981 tropical storm and committed environmentalists combined to wash the natural hazard into the sea. The beach is the island's spot for topless (and sometimes bottomless) sunbathing. In the crystal clear waters off the beach, you might find polished, ebony-colored obsidian. From Canneto center, explore the secluded sandy coves flanking Spiaggia Bianca by renting one of the rafts, kayaks, or canoes that line the beach at via M. Garibaldi. Prices range L6000-L7000 per hour, and L25,000-L35,000 per day. Buses leave the Esso station at Lípari's ferry port for Canneto 9 times per day (16 in July and Sept.; 21 in Aug.; L900). **Quattrocchi,** named for its view of the four headlands that lie off the island's coast, offers a panorama of Lípari's *castello* and Vulcano island. You can walk 4km uphill to the Quattrocchi Belvedere from Lípari, or take the bus and hook up with it again on its way down 20 to 30 minutes later. The route ends at **Quattropani** (one way L1200), a hamlet with a vista over Salina. The **Thermal Baths** at **San Calogero** (on the west side of the island opposite Lípari) were famous during Roman times. The salty sulphate-bicarbonate waters are 54°C. Take the bus to Quattropani and then walk ½km to the baths at a "lake" where you can sit in the bubbling mud or water. Some baths estimated to be over 6500 years old were discovered here recently. Boats leave from the hydrofoil port in Lípari and run tours around the island and to neighboring islands. The best excursions are run by the **Società Navigazione Basso Tirreno** (tel. 981 25 92), which offers tours of Lípari (Mon., Wed., and Sat. at 9:30am, returning at 6pm; L20,000); Alicudi and Filicudi (Tues. and Fri. at 9am, returning at 7pm; L40,000); and Stromboli (Mon., Wed.-Thurs. and Sat.-Sun. at 3pm, returning at 11pm—witness the fire shooting out of the crater at night; L30,000). They also provide convenient transport to Vulcano (3-4 per day, one way L2000).

Vulcano

The pungent smell of sulfur and gurgling mud puddles lend credence to concerns that Vulcano may cataclysmically explode within the next 20 years. For the time being, the great crater lies inactive at the island's center. Easy access from Lípari makes Vulcano an excellent daytrip—the potent fumes make a longer stay advisable only for those with iron stomachs.

Orientation and Practical Information

Ferries and hydrofoils dock at the eastern **Porto Levante. Sabbie Nere** (Black Sands), the only smooth beach on the Aeolian Islands lies across the peninsula in the Porto Ponente. From the dock via Piano curves to the left and via Provinciale to the right, intersecting via Porto Levante (which becomes via Porto Ponente to the right). To get to the **Great Crater** from the port, follow via Piano for 100m to the foot of a cobbled path that begins the climb to the crater at the flying bird statues. Further up via Piano there is a **post office** (open Mon.-Fri. 8:05am-1:30pm, Sat. 8:05am-11:20pm). For **medical emergencies,** dial 985 22 20; for **police,** call the carabinieri at 985 21 10.

Accommodations and Food

Luckily, Vulcano's camping facilities lie far from the sulfur pits; most of its hotels are, however, not so fortunate. The unexciting but comfortable **Togo Bungalows,** located at the far end of via Levante (tel. 985 21 28), are an economical option. Small, four-person bungalows with stoves are available for L10,000 per person; there are lockers for valuables. **Casa Sipione,** via Levante, 55 (tel. 985 20 34), is one of the nicest places in southern Italy—a long, white ranchhouse run by an amiable couple who treat guests like family. Follow the road to Porto Ponetite, and bear left at the top of the hill onto a tree-shaded street. The nine-room Casa is down the path next to the church. (Singles with bath L18,300. Doubles with bath L35,000. Open June-Sept. Reservations highly recommended.) The **Rojas Hotel** (tel. 985 20 80), located behind the thermal baths at Porto Levante, offers singles (L27,000) and half-pension (L57,000, L52,000 per person in doubles). Make reservations in June for August, when prices rise L10,000. The largest and most conveniently located campground is **Campeggio Togo Togo** (tel. 985 23 03), 800m from the port in the Vulcanello area behind the Sabbie Nere beach. Its rather rudimentary facilities cost L5000-6000 (July-Aug. L6000 per tent; in off-season free).

The general store **Agostino** is located on via Favoloro, which turns into via Provinciale after via Levante.

Fanned by sulfurous fumes, the **Ristorante Mare Caldo** (tel. 985 20 80), in the Rojas Hotel, runs self-service (*primi* L4000, *secondi* L6000-9000) and offers a *menù turistico* (L10,000) that is popular among Italian tourists. (Open June-Sept. daily 11:30am-3pm and 8:30-11pm.) A nameless pizzeria has opened up across from Agostino, serving zesty pies from L5000 and salads at L3000. (Open June-Sept. daily 12:30-3pm and 7:30pm-2am. Cover L1000.) The only really cosmic eating experience on the islands is the **Trattoria del Cratere** (tel. 985 20 45), near the entrance to the path to the crater. Its *Rigatoni del Cratere* and aromatic grilled swordfish (L12,000) can be savored with excellent imported beer for only L1500. Italians generally gravitate towards the *menù* for L16,000. (Open daily 12:30-3pm and 8-10pm.)

Sights and Entertainment

Once on Vulcano, the one-hour hike to the crater along the snaking footpath (see Practical Information) should be your first resolve. The climb is least straining before 11am or in late afternoon. Don't be deceived by the stone pavement at the start of the path. After about 100m, rugged terrain prevails. From the rim of the crater, you can see all seven of the main islands on a clear day. The crater itself reeks of sulfur and is dotted with active pockets of billowing smoke. Although inactive since 1890, the volcano is far from dormant. Walking toward Vulcanello, you come quickly to the **Laghetto di Fanghi** (mud pool), a feeder trough of hot, sulfurous mud for hundreds of folks spreading the allegedly therapeutic goop over their bodies. If you have no varicose veins to smoothe out or if you don't dig mud, wade in the nearby waters of the **Aquacalda.** Here, underwater volcanic outlets make the sea percolate like a jacuzzi. For cooler enjoyment, visit the crowded beach and crystal-clear waters of Sabbie Nere. **Società Navigazione Basso Tirreno** schedules two-hour boat excursions at 10:30am and 2pm (L10,000). Get off the boat and get down at **Pyro Pyro Disco** (tel. 985 21 13) or the more popular **Rocce Rosse** (tel. 985 21 44; both open June-Sept; cover L10,000). Free minibuses leave for both establishments from Porto Levante from 10pm to 1am.

Stromboli

Rising to a startling height and emitting cauliflower-shaped clouds of smoke, Stromboli is the most dramatic of the islands. Small eruptions occur approximately four times per hour. Once a major shipping port, the island's shores swarm today with more than nautical vessels. An up-and-coming international tourist attraction, Stromboli's hotel and restaurant prices are now about as lofty as the island's summit. Camping on the volcano and buying food in the main supermarket, however, will limit your lira output.

Just as the mythic home of Hephaestus, the smithy god, dominates Stromboli, so the **Church of San Vincento** crowns the main town of Ficogrande, which also harbors a black sand and pebble beach. From the ferry and hydrofoil dock via Roma leads up the hill past stores and restaurants to the church; via Filzi leads from the scenic piazza Vincenzo across to via Nunziante, which descends past more food joints to the **tourist office** (tel. 986 23). The helpful local official is conversant in English and can provide useful information on accommodations (open June 15-Sept. 15 Mon.-Sat. 9:30am-12:30pm and 5-8pm). An alternate route to the Azienda is via Marina, along the waterfront, which doubles as the best route to the volcano. Wary about hiking on hot turf? Go with one of the island's three authorized guides: Nino, Prospero, or Antonio (service offered April-Oct., L15,000 per person with a minimum of 10 people). Trips leave daily from Ficogrande at the stairs of v. Nunziante at 5 to 6pm, returning from 11pm to midnight. Despite large warning signs, an unguided ascent to the summit (927m) is *not* illegal—the dangers of heat exhaustion and twisted ankles are braved by approximately 100 people every night. An experienced hiker can make a round-trip in 3½ hours; others should allow three hours for the ascent, two for the descent. Deposit heavy bags in one of Ficogrande's bars, and take sturdy shoes, a flashlight, warm clothes for the exposed summit, and *at least* two liters of water per person. Plan to reach the summit at dusk to catch the brilliant red lava rivers against the night sky. The trail to the volcano's mouth divides into three segments. First, take via Marina past the Azienda, bearing right at the large warning sign ½km down the road. Past the garbage dump the rocky road leads up to a white house labeled "Regina Marina," where the trail cuts a clean swath left through ten-foot-high reeds. Next, follow any path up the switchbacks, taking all shortcuts except those marked "No". Halfway up the slope is the island's best view of the tremendous **Sciara del Fuoco** ("Trail of Fire") streaming down the mountain into the sea, and a glimpse of the crater. Finally, the trail becomes a scramble up volcanic rock and ash, where it pays to follow the red-and-white-striped rock markings. At the top ridge heed the warning signs: Several years ago a photographer fell to her death in search of a closer shot. The climb, however, is worth any blood, sweat, and tears. Europe's most active volcano belches forth a thundering shower of molten boulders every 10 minutes to the cheers of onlookers. For an overnight trip, bring a sturdy food bag (there are occasional rats), plastic to place between you and the wet sand, warm clothing, and foul weather gear, as the peak experiences wet, frigid fogs.

In July and August, **Libera Navigazione Stromboli** (tel. 98 61 35) runs two boat trips from Ficogrande: One to view the molten crimson trail of the **Sciara del Fuoco** (at 10pm, L10,000); the other around Stromboli and **Strombolicchio,** the slender lighthouse-capped basalt island off Ficogrande (2 per day, L15,000).

Hotels on Stromboli are booked solid in August by the previous winter. In other months, check via Roma for occasional bargains. **Pensione Roma** (tel. 98 60 88), above the Bar Roma, is five minutes from the ferry dock. The rooms are cool and comfortable. (L15,000 per person. Shower included. Open March-Oct.) Farther past the church is **Locanda Stella,** via Filzi, 14 (tel. 986 20), where two senior women rent warm (temperature and atmosphere) doubles and triples. (L20,000 per person. Showers included. In Aug. obligatory half-pension L45,000.) The best affordable hotel on the island is the beautiful **Miramare,** via Nunziante, 3 (tel. 98 60 47), directly behind the Azienda. Shrouded in foliage and sporting a terrace overlooking the beach, it is a delightful indulgence. (Singles L23,000. Doubles L43,500. Baths, showers, and breakfast included. In Aug. obligatory half-pension L55,000.)

Private residences offer rooms during the off-season for well under L10,000 per person. Check with Stromboli's Azienda.

The lowest food prices in town are at the **Duval Market,** halfway to the church on via Roma. (Open daily 8:30am-1pm and 5-9pm.) Lower down on via Roma is the *rosticceria* **Scibilia;** La Trattola sign hangs outside. Half a roast chicken is L5000, pizza runs L2000 per *etto,* and *aranchini* (mixed rice and meat balls) costs only L1500. (Open daily 10am-1pm and 5-9pm.) On a breezy terrace overlooking the sea is **La Lampara,** on via Filzi between the church and via Nunziante. Grilled swordfish (L10,000) and the myriad pizzas (L5000-8000) satisfy immensely. (Cover L1000. Open May-Oct. daily 12:30-3pm and 7pm-midnight.) After the tiring trek to the crater, stop in at **Il Gabbiano,** via Nunziante above the Azienda, to rest weary feet and fill deserving stomachs. The young, personable staff serves a wicked *spaghetti alla vongole* (spaghetti with seafood) for L8000, and a large beer is L2000. (Open for dining April-Oct. daily 12:30-3pm and 7-10pm.) **Il Gabbiano** doubles as a free disco in summer, vying for dancing dynamos only with the outdoor **La Nassa** (cover L5000 with 1 drink), located on via Marina towards the ferry dock. (Both open July-Sept. 10pm-2am.)

Stromboli's **post office** lies on via Roma (open Mon.-Fri. 8:05am-1:30pm, Sat. 8:05-11:20am). The **tourist office** (tel. 986 23), on the beach at Ficogrande, provides information on ferries and accommodations (open June 15-Sept. 15 Mon.-Sat. 9:30am-1pm and 5-8pm). The island's only bank is next to the Gabbiano restaurant at Ficogrande (open June-Sept. Mon.-Fri. 8:30am-1:30pm). For **medical emergencies** call 98 60 97 or go to the Guarda Medica on the Ficogrande side of the church; for **police,** call 98 60 98.

Other Islands

Escape the the crowds on Lípari, Vulcano, and Stromboli, and visit the other four islands, harboring more peaceful rural delights.

Salina, the second largest island, is a verdant paradise offering relaxation and some of the best *Malvasia* wine (available at Malfa, on the north coast). It also features the famous rock formations Semaforo di Pollara and Punta Lingua. **Pensione Mamma Santina,** via Sanità, 26 (tel. 984 30 54), offers doubles with bath for L30,000 from Oct. to May. (July-Sept. obligatory half-pension L48,000.) **Villa Orchidea,** via Roma (tel. 984 40 79), in Malfa, lets doubles with bath for L45,000 (July-Aug. obligatory half-pension L50,000). At Rinella, **Camping Tre Pini** (tel. 984 21 55) charges L6000 per person, including tent and use of facilities. (Open June-Sept.) Ferries run daily to the island's two main ports, **Rinella** (L3150) and **S. Marina Salina** (L2250) from Lípari from June to September.

Filicudi, west of Lípari, hosts an array of volcanic rock formations and the enchanting **Grotta del Bue Marino** (Grotto of the Sea Ox). **Capo Graziano** includes a prehistoric village. **Alicudi,** little more than a speck in the sea, is the westernmost of the Aeolian islands. Wild and untouristed, here exists absolute solitude. Filicudi and Alicudi have one hotel each. On Filicudi it's the expensive **Albergo Phenicusa** (tel. 984 41 85), with singles at L33,000 and doubles at L51,000, bath included. However, at least L4000 slips off these rates during off-season. (Open May-Sept.) Although full pension is advisable because these islands are so isolated, it can prove expensive since they import most food. At the Phenicusa, full pension averages L60,000-80,000. Alicudi is home to the much more modest **Albergo Ericusa** (tel. 981 23 70), which requires half-pension at L32,000; full pension runs L54,000. (Open June 15-Sept. 10.) Ferries run daily in summer to Filicudi (L5600) and Alicudi (L10,500) from Lípari.

Panarea, a small island between Lípari and Stromboli, is renowned for its pellucid waters (and, therefore, scuba diving), as well as its striking natural rock sculptures. **Punto Milazzese,** on the southern tip of the island, is the site of a Bronze Age prehistoric village, while the opposite end sports a sulfurous fumarole. Much less frequented than the larger islands, Panarea is still booked by April for the month of August. In June, July, and September, try the **Locanda Stella Maris** (tel. 98 31 63), at the ferry dock in S. Pietro (June-July L20,000 per person, half-pension L46,000; August obligatory half-pension L51,000. 2 doubles share a bath. Showers included. Open Easter-Sept.) Up the street next to the SNAV office is the **Pensione O Palma** (tel. 98 31 55), with one single and several doubles. (L20,000 per person, more in Aug.) Farther up past the post office is **Gaetaro Roda** (tel. 98 30 06), which offers the cheapest August rates for doubles. (June-July and Sept. L20,000 per person; Aug. L25,000 per person. Bath and showers included.) On the right of the ticket office is the **Trattoria Francesco** (tel. 98 30 23), a restaurant and pension with a fantastic view of the harbor. (June-July and Sept. L20,000 per person. Breakfast and showers included.) Panarea is reached daily by Siremar and NGI ferries (L3400) and hydrofoil.

Cefalù

Named for the head-shaped promontory (now called the Rocca) that stares down upon the sleepy fishing village, Cefalù remains a treasure trove of Arab, Norman, and medieval architecture. A rediscovery of the city's charm and beautiful beaches, however, has begun to transform it into a favored getaway. Caught unawares by the onslaught of vacationers, Cefalù offers only limited accommodations, all of which swell in August. Visit Cefalù as a daytrip from Palermo, only one hour away by train (L3500), or as a stopover between Messina and Palermo. You can easily tour the town in half a day and still have time for a swim at the long sandy beach.

Practical Information

Azienda Autonoma di Soggiorno e Turismo: Corso Ruggero, 77 (tel. 210 50), in the old city. From the train station turn right onto via A. Moro, which first becomes via Matteotti then corso Ruggero (10 min.). English-speaking staff helps with accommodations and hands out 2 helpful maps of the city. Open Mon.-Fri. 8am-2pm and 4:30-7:30pm, Sat. 8am-2pm. Also at the **train station.** English spoken. Open in summer Mon.-Sat. 8am-8pm, Sun. 8am-2pm.

Post Office: Off via Matteotti, 43, on the way to the Azienda. Open Mon.-Fri. 8am-7pm, Sat. 8-11:20am. **Postal code:** 90015.

Telephones: SIP, via Roma, 2 blocks left of v. Moro in an ugly modern building marked "Generali." Open Mon.-Tue. and Thurs.-Fri. 9am-1pm and 4-7:30pm, Wed. 9am-1pm. **Telephone Code:** 0921.

Buses: Sais. To Palermo (2 per day, 1 hr., L3700), Castelbuono, and Geraci. **SPISA,** via Umberto I, 28, in front of Bar Musotto. Serves local towns for under L1300. Take v. A. Moro from the train station to the 1st intersection, and go right 1 block on via Mazzini.

Hospital: Via A. Moro (tel. 211 18). Nighttime medical emergency (tel. 236 23).

Accommodations, Camping, and Food

Cefalù's pristine waterfront is devoid of crass resort hotels, but that means no hope in August for noncampers without reservations.

Pensione delle Rose, via Gibilmanna (tel. 218 85). Turn right on via A. Moro from the station to the 1st stoplight, right up the hill, right at the *pensione* sign, and right up the tree-lined stairs. After 4 rights, you can't go wrong: airy rooms with a German flavor and a spectacular spread of the town. June-Sept. singles L20,000; doubles L36,000, with bath L46,000. Oct.-May singles L19,000; doubles L31,000, with bath L41,000. Showers included.

Riva del Sola, via Lungomare, 25 (tel. 212 30 or 219 84), behind the octagonal restaurant on the beach. Ask for the *dipendenzia,* not the hotel, for simple doubles with a communal bath at L40,000 in season. Showers included. Aug. reservations accepted through July.

Locanda Cangelosi, via Umberto I, 28 (tel. 215 00 91), down the street from the SPISA bus stop. The cheapest in town. Triples L10,000 per person (the family management mixes and matches). No hot water.

Camping: Costa Ponente Internazionale (tel. 200 85), 3km west at locando contrada Ogliastrillo (a 45-min. walk or a short ride on the Cefalù-Lasari bus). Swimming pool and tennis court. July-Aug. L4600 per person, L4000 per small tent, L5000 per large tent; in off-season L3700 per person, L3200 per small tent. Nearby, **Camping Sanfilippo** (tel. 201 84) charges L4000 per person, L3000 per small tent, L5000 per large tent. Also try **Magurà** (tel. 211 38), accessible by bus to Ferla.

The affordable restaurants cluster around corso Ruggero and via V. Emanuele.

Arkade Grill, via Vanni, 9 (tel. 218 56). Follow via Moro from the station as it becomes via Matteotti and corso Ruggero, then take the 4th left. Extra thick *pasta con sarde* (with sardines) L3500, Tunisian *mergez* (sausage) L5000. Or combine the 2 nationalities with *pizza tunisina. Menù* L12,000. Wine L3500. Cover L1000. Open in summer daily noon-4pm and 7-11:30pm; in off-season Fri.-Wed.

Pizzeria Da Nino, via Lungomare, 11 (tel. 225 82). Super views, prices, and location. Pizzas cooked in the old-fashioned, wood-burning stove (L2500-6000). Complete *menù* L14,000.

Wine L4000 per liter. Cover L15,000. Open in summer Wed.-Mon. noon-3:15pm and 7:30pm-midnight.

Sights and Entertainment

Cefalù's austere Norman **cathedral** (1133-1148) is a stunning monument, ever for Sicily. Roger II purportedly ordered its construction in fulfillment of a vow made during a shipwreck off the coast. The church's powerful facade has two handsome, belligerent towers. Inside, tall columns support elegant horseshoe arches, an example of the Saracen influence on Norman architecture in Sicily. The mosaics of the tribune are Byzantine at its best. (Open daily 9am-noon and 3:30-7pm. No shorts.)

Opposite the cathedral, down via Mandralisca, the private **Museo Mandralisca** houses a fine collection of paintings, Greek ceramics, Arab pottery, antique money, and Antonello da Messina's *Ritratto di Ignoto* (Portrait of an Unknown Man, 1470-1472), the face on most Sicilian travel brochures. (Open daily 9am-noon and 3:30-6:30pm. Admission L1000.) On the way to Cefalù's fine sandy beach, at via V. Emanuele, 57, a sixteenth-century **lavatorio medioevale** (medieval laundromat) will appear—a series of waterpools tucked away in a hidden courtyard.

For a bird's-eye view of the city, make the one-hour trek up the Rocca by way of the Salita Saraceni, which begins near p. Garibaldi off corso Umberto I. On the mountain, walkways lined with ancient stone walls lead to the **Temple of Diana,** dating back to the fourth century B.C.E., used first for sea-cult worship and later as a defensive outpost.

Dance under the stars at the popular outdoor disco **Tropical,** 1km down via Lungomare, or savor the cafe's creamy *gelato.* (Open June-Sept. daily 10:30pm-3am.) From July to September, Cefalù hosts the **Incontri d'Estate,** a brouhaha of music, dance, and theater. The **Festa di San Salvatore,** held from August 4 to 6, honors Cefalù's patron saint with fireworks and marching bands.

Palermo

A sprawling commercial center, Palermo is the capital of Sicily and the international stronghold of the Mafia. Gossip and crime vie for the right of way on frenetic boulevards, and the resulting sins occur amdist centuries of Catholic architecture. First Phoenician, then Roman and Byzantine, Palermo achieved its heyday under Saracen rule (831-1072) and in the Norman aftermath (1072-1194). Enjoying unusual good will and tolerance, the city became a junction for trade between East and West and the intellectual bastion of southern Italy. Palermo's Golden Age endures in a unique style of architecture called the Norman-Saracen: Massive Norman buildings are decorated with intricate Arab designs. Ravaged by the rough hands of time, bombarded in World War II, and only now gaining attention as a national treasure, the city's historic district is little touristed and most fascinating.

Orientation and Practical Information

Palermo and its crescent-shaped harbor lie at the end of a fertile basin called the **Conca d'Oro.** Its most distinguishing natural feature is **Monte Pellegrino,** a 610-m limestone mass that encloses the harbor to the north and separates the city from its beautiful beach, **Mondello.** A maze of alleys and courtyards, the cramped old town of Palermo runs along **via Roma** as you leave the train station. It is divided into equal quadrants by **corso Vittorio Emanuele,** running from the sea to the western mountains, and **via Maqueda,** running north-south through the city. Slip behind the main streets to see the innards of historic Palermo. The contrast with the spacious and sterile grids west of piazza Castelnuovo in the new sectors of the city is phenomenal. For abundant food markets, turn right off via Roma several blocks away from the station. Via Roma and via Maqueda offer a cornucopia of goods to shoppers. Everything in Palermo except restaurants closes from noon to 3pm and then again around 8pm.

APT: P. Castelnuovo, 34 (tel. 58 38 47), 2km north of the train station. Take a bus that goes west from the station (#7 (red) or 46), and get off in front of Teatro Politeama. Well informed and helpful. Maps give a skeletal view of the city. Open Mon.-Fri. 8am-8pm, Sat. 8am-2pm. Also at p. San Sepolcro (tel. 616 13 61), off via Maqueda near the Quattro Canti (open Mon.-Sat. 8am-2pm); the airport (tel. 59 16 98; open Mon.-Sat. 8am-8pm); and the train station (open Mon.-Sat. 8am-8pm).

CTS Student Travel: Via Garzilli, 28g (tel. 33 22 09). Take via Maqueda to where it becomes viale della Libertà, then turn left onto via Messina. A harried yet efficient office. Open Mon.-Fri. 9am-1pm and 4-7:30pm, Sat. 9am-1pm.

U.S. Consulate: Via G.B. Vaccarini, 1 (tel. 34 35 32; after hours 322 77 77). Take bus #14 or 15. Open Mon.-Fri. 8:30am-12:30pm and 3-5pm. Emergencies only.

American Express: G. Ruggieri, via E. Amari, 40 (tel. 58 71 44). Follow via E. Amari from p. Politeama toward the water. Open Mon.-Fri. 9am-1pm and 4-7pm, Sat. 9am-1pm.

Post Office: Via Roma (tel. 32 08 15), by the Museo Archeologico. Open Mon.-Fri. 8:10am-7:30pm, Sat. 8:30am-1:30pm. Fermo Posta at window #15. **Postal code:** 90100.

Telephones: ASST, Via Lincoln, across from the train station. Open 24 hours. Also **SIP,** via Ppe. d. Belmonte, 1st right off via R. Settimo before the Politeama Garibaldi. A brass and pine office. Open daily 8am-8pm. **Telephone code:** 091.

Airport: Cinisi-Punta Raisi (tel. 59 16 90), 31km west of Palermo. 15 public buses connect the airport to p. Politeama (5:40am-9:30pm, L3600). Taxis charge at least L35,000 for the same route.

Alitalia: Viale della Libertà, 39 (tel. 601 92 111), at via Messina. 30% discount for those under 21 flying within Italy. Daily to Rome (L135,000), Milan (L209,500), Genoa (L191,000), and Naples (L104,500). Open Mon.-Sat. 9am-5pm.

Train Station: P. G. Cesare (tel. 616 18 06), on the eastern side of town. To Milan (22 hr., L48,800), Rome (15 hr., L42,200), and Naples (13 hr., L35,700).

Buses: City buses (AMAT; tel. 22 23 98) cost L600—buy tickets from *tabacchi* (correct change only). The main station is in front of the train station. **Filli Camilleri-Argento** (tel. (0922) 390 84) runs buses to Agrigento (2-3 per day, 2¼ hr., L8000) from via Balsamo on the right of the train station. **Autoservizi Segesta,** via Balsamo, 26 (tel. 28 60 39), has 19 departures per day direct to Trapani (1¾ hr., L7000). **Sais** buses leave from via Balsamo, 16 (tel. 616 60 28), to Cefalù (Mon.-Sat. 6 per day, 1 hr., L4300), Catania (16 per day, 2½ hr., L12,700), and Syracuse (Mon.-Sat. 5 per day, 4 hr., L16,800).

Ferries: Tirrenia, via Roma, 385 (tel. 33 33 00). Open 8:30am-1pm and 3-5pm. **Grandi-Traghetti,** via M. Stabile, 53 (tel. 58 78 32). Open Sun.-Fri. 8:30am-5pm. (See Sicily, Getting There and Getting Around.)

Gay Men's Resource Center: Arei-Gay, via Trapani, 3 (tel. 32 49 17 or 32 49 18). Information on events. Open Mon.-Fri. 9:30-11:30pm.

Late-Night Pharmacy: Lo Cascio, via Roma, 1 (tel. 616 21 17), near the train station. Open Sun.-Fri. 5:30pm-1pm, Sat. 8pm-9am.

Hospital: Civico Regional e Generale, via Carrabia (tel. 59 21 22). **Medical Emergency,** Tel. 32 18 60.

Police: Tel. 112 or 113.

Palermitans are notorious for rudeness towards visitors to their city; be as inconspicuous as possible. Leave large bags and valuables at your hotel; women should abstain from flashy jewelry. Keep wallets in moneybelts or neck pouches, *not* in front pockets or handbags. Palermo is home to highly adept pickpockets and motorcycling bag-snatchers. Be aware of your surroundings and belongings at all times.

Accommodations and Camping

Finding a decent and inexpensive place to stay is as easy as pie in Palermo. A surfeit of *alberghi* clusters on **via Roma** and **via Maqueda,** and hotel prices are lower here than in any other Italian city. The Centro Universitario Sportivo Italiano plans to open a youth hostel here, but don't hold your breath. All of Palermo suffers from severe water-pressure problems, and showers are little more than trickles.

Albergo Universo, p. Chiesa Cocchieri, 4 (tel. 616 52 32). Take via Divisi off via Roma until it becomes via Aragona toward the water. 1 block after p. Rivoluzione, turn right onto via Alloro then walk 2 blocks; the Universo is on the left. Call ahead before searching for this homey *albergo.* Run by a large and affable family. Not in the safest of areas. Singles L10,000. Doubles L18,000. Showers L2000.

Albergo Odeon, via E. Amari, 140 (tel. 33 27 78), next to the Teatro Politeama. Take any bus headed up via Roma from the train station (use the bus island farthest from the station). Request one of the balcony rooms, or you will find things tight. Singles L14,000, with bath L18,000. Doubles L25,000, with bath L30,000.

Pensione Di Fiore, via Roma, 391 (tel. 58 80 36). Quiet, ample rooms with lumpy mattresses. Safe for women. Singles L18,000. Doubles L26,000. Showers included.

Pensione Rizzico, via M. Stabile, 139 (tel. 33 24 34), off via Roma near p. Castelnuovo. Lots of domestic hubbub keeps the burglars away. Singles L14,000. Doubles L25,000. Full pension L39,000.

Pensione Sud, via Maqueda, 8 (tel. 28 36 81). Capacious rooms and a caring owner who will probably lower the price if you look hesitant. Singles L16,000. Doubles L26,000. Showers L2000. Also try **Locanda Eden** (tel. 23 74 55), on the same floor as Sud, but reached by the other stairway. Singles L10,000. Doubles L15,000. Showers L2000. Or, for larger and more attractive rooms, descend 1 flight to **Albergo Vittoria** (tel. 616 24 57). Singles L17,000. Doubles with toilets L30,000. Showers L2000.

Albergo Orientale, via Maqueda, 26 (tel. 616 57 27). Motherly proprietor. Another good choice for women. Situated on one side of a magnificent Renaissance *palazzo.* Painted murals on the ceiling of the TV room. The commodious rooms are rather dreary. Singles L18,000. Doubles L28,000, with bath L34,000. Showers included.

Albergo Rosalia Conca d'Oro, via Santa Rosalia, 7 (tel. 616 45 43). Turn left off via Roma as you leave the station. Run by an older couple who provide helpful advice, free city maps, and, sometimes, free tickets to special beaches at Mondello. Singles L18,000. Doubles L28,000. Showers included.

Albergo Pretoria, via Maqueda, 124 (tel. 33 10 68), in a remodeled seventeenth-century *palazzo.* Spacious rooms and charming management make this popular with students. TV lounge and hot showers. Singles L15,000, with bath L19,000. Doubles L28,000, with bath L33,000. Showers included.

Albergo Milton, via Roma, 188 (tel. 33 12 82). Tidy rooms, aromatic bathrooms. For old-fashioned entertainment go downstairs to the 2nd floor *billiardi* to shoot some pool (L4000 per hr.), play ping pong, or sample the videogames. Singles L15,000. Doubles L20,000. Showers L2000.

Albergo Alessandra, via Divisi, 99 (tel. 616 70 09), off via Maqueda. Abundant quarters with beautifully decorated ceilings. A high-quality *albergo* with moderate prices. Singles L17,000, with bath L20,000. Doubles L30,000, with bath L32,000. Showers L2000. **Albergo Sicilia** (tel. 28 44 60), 1 floor below, offers similar rooms at higher prices. Singles L19,000, with bath L23,000. Doubles with bath L35,000.

Camping: Trinacria, via Barcarello (tel. 53 05 90), at Sferracavallo by the sea. Take bus #28 from Teatro Massimo. L6700 per person. Tent included. 4-bed bungalows L50,000. Also at Sferracavallo, but a step down is **Club dell'Ulivo,** via Pegaso (tel. 58 43 92). L5000 per person. Tent included.

Food

Palermo is famous for its *pasta con le sarde* (with sardines and fennel) and *rigatoni alla palermitana* (sauce of meat and peas). The best *piscine* platter is swordfish, either plain (*pesce spada*) or rolled and stuffed (*involtini di pesce spada*). Eggplant exists in all forms here: cold in a tasty sauce, deep-fried in sandwiches, or in a dish called *capanata di melanzana,* stewed with onions, celery, green olives, and capers. For snacks, *arancine,* fattening balls of fried dough filled with rice and meat, *panelle,* fried dumplings made from chick pea flour, and *calzoni* are all cheap and omnipresent. For breakfast, try anything in a *pasticceria:* The Palermitans die for *brioches,* gelato stuffed between a sliced sweet roll, topped with whipped cream (about L1500).

Osteria Lo Bianco, via E. Amari, 104 (tel. 58 58 16), off via Roma near p. Custelnuovo. Local crowds wipe the sweat off their brows between each delectable bite. Excellent *pasta con sarde al forno* L3000, *pesce spada* L7000. Wine L2000 per liter. For the best meal of your day, try the *menù* (L10,000). Open Mon.-Sat. noon-3pm and 7-11pm.

Il Cotto e il Crudo, p. Marina, 45 (tel. 28 62 61). From via Roma, head toward the water on corso V. Emanuele, then right on via dei Bottai. Petite and peaceful. Palermitans prize the place. Try the *riso alle alghe* (rice with seaweed and motley goodies, L6000), *gazpacho* (L4000), and *goulash* (L7000). Cover L1000, service 10%. Open Wed.-Mon. noon-3pm and 6:30-10pm.

Hostaria al Duar 2, via E. Amari, 92 (tel. 32 16 78), near the Teatro Politeama. Italian and Middle Eastern cuisine. *Spaghetti allo chef* (with parsley, capers, and basil) L3000, *involtini siciliani* (meat with a spicy cheese and ham stuffing) L6000. Sample Tunisia by trying the *completo Tunisino* (L11,000), fruit and drink included. Open Thurs.-Tues. noon-3:30pm and 6-11:30pm.

Antica Foccacceria S. Francesco, via A. Paternostro, 58, off corso V. Emanuele across from the Church of S. Francesco. A 120-year-old pizzeria: dark wood, cast iron, and aged silence. Pizza about L2000 per slice. Indigenous *sfincione* (mini-pizza topped with onions) is appetizing and saturating for L1600. Their specialty is *pane ca' meusa,* a small sandwich of ricotta and marinated tripe for L1600. Beer L2500. Open Tues.-Sun. 7am-midnight.

Hotel Patria, via Alloro, 104 (tel. 616 11 36). Take via Paternostro off corso V. Emanuele until the Hotel Patria sign jumps into view. A city treasure: Delicious food in a spacious, old courtyard. Try the *spaghetti ala pesce spada* (superb swordfish sauce) L6000, *secondi* L7000-9000. Cover L1500, service 10%. Open Fri.-Wed. noon-3pm and 7:30pm-midnight.

Trattoria dei Vespri, p. Sta. Croce dei Vespri, 6/A (tel. 28 20 19). Turn off via Roma onto via Dicesa dei Giudici at the large Tarantino sign, then walk 1 *piazza* past the church of Sta. Anna. Also coveted for its titillating, outdoor fare. Pasta L4000 and the town's best *pescespada arrosto* L8000. Cover L1500, service 10%. Open Wed.-Mon. noon-3pm and 8pm-midnight.

Osteria da Toto, via dei Coltellieri, 5, near the church of S. Domenico. Descend the steps at via Roma, 203. All the hawkers in the surrounding market take out here. Simply good food in a simple setting, and an owner who really takes care of you. Pasta L3000, *secondi* L5000. Open for lunch only.

L'Uccelleria, via Volturno, 108 (tel. 58 23 31), behind Teatro Massimo. There's nothing more pleasant than sitting in this little poster-covered room and being served great chow by an experienced Palermitan. No menu—just the meal of the day for L9000. Open Mon.-Sat. 1-3:30pm.

Self-Service Ferrara, p. Guilio Cesare, 46, to the left as you leave the train station. The best of the quick-eating places near the station. A huge selection of ready-made foods, including pizzas (L2500-4000). Open Wed.-Mon. 11am-midnight.

Bar Fiore, via Principe di Belmonte, 84 (tel. 33 25 39), off via Roma near the Teatro Politeama. Frank, the owner, claims the house specialty is cordiality, and he's not kidding. Relax at their outdoor tables with a *maccheroni* or salad (both L3000). Superlative *brioches* (L1200, with whipped cream L1500). Open daily 6am-10pm.

Undoubtedly the best *gelato* around can be found at **Recupero,** fronted by outdoor tables on via Malaspina in the new city. Take bus #34 from near the Politeama Theater, or walk and work up an appetite.

Sights

Palermo is today in an incredible state of disrepair. In the past several years, efforts have begun to clean, rebuild, and reopen structures like the magnificent Teatro Massimo, closed due to water damage for the past 15 years. The bizarre sight of half-crumbled, soot-blackened sixteenth-century *palazzi* startles visitors accustomed to the cleaner historic districts of northern Italy. Peek into random courtyards in your path to find the *cortiles* for which the city is famous. They include a palm tree, fountain, and stone in exuberant baroque style. Visit the ones at Corso

V. Emanuele, 452 (across from the duomo); the sylvan interior of via Maqueda, 83 (halfway between the duomo and the train station); and the arches of via Paternostro, 48 (off corso V. Emanuele). For a glimpse of Palermo's ravaged splendor, climb the red marble staircase at via Maqueda, 26, across from the Orfeo cinema, to the tremendous balustrade on the top floor. (Tell the doorman you are an architecture student if he asks.)

From Quattro Canti to San Giovanni degli Eremiti

The intersection of corso V. Emanuele and via Maqueda forms the **Quattro Canti,** four corners with statues representing a season, a king of Spain, and a patron saint of the city. The Canti—undergoing restoration—date from the early seventeenth century, when Sicily was under Spanish rule. A few steps away in **piazza Pretoria** sits a lavish fountain (1555-1575) intended for a Florentine villa. Its score of nude figures shocked Palermitans when it was unveiled, hence its nickname, "the fountain of shame." Flanking the *piazza* are the sixteenth-century **Palazzo del Municipio** and the splendid baroque **Church of Santa Caterina** (1566-1596).

Across via Maqueda from p. Pretoria, you'll find the most magnificent of Palermo's baroque churches, the **Church of San Guiseppe dei Teatini** (1612). This church is decorated profusely, but the monolithic gray columns save the interior from excess. Don't miss such details as the upside-down angels supporting the fonts at the entrance, or the frieze of children playing musical instruments on the wall on the south transept. (Church closed for reconstruction in 1988.)

A few steps down via Maqueda and to the right, **piazza Bellini** embraces the **Church of San Cataldo** (1160), a Norman building whose red domes and arches give it the air of a mosque. **La Martorana,** or more properly, Santa Maria dell'Ammiraglio (built for an admiral of the Norman king Roger II), shares San Cataldo's platform. Seventeenth-century baroque additions all but conceal its twelfth-century structure. On the western interior wall of La Martorana are the extensively restored mosaics from the original building. (Open Mon.-Sat. 8:30am-1pm and 3:30-7pm, Sun. 8:30am-1pm.)

Via Ponticello, across via Maqueda from p. Bellini, winds through a crowded neighborhood to **Il Gesù** (or Casa Professa, 1564-1363). Its ochre stucco facade conceals a dazzling, multi-colored marble interior and an almost fluorescent depiction of the Last Judgment. Standing in Il Gesù's courtyard, you can see traces of American bombing during World War II; the **Quartiere dell'Albergheria,** the inner core of the city, never quite recovered from the war's destruction.

Farther along via Ponticello, **piazza Ballaro** combines a lively market with a view of the seventeenth-century **Church of the Carmine.** This area, replete with narrow streets and hidden gardens, warrants delving into.

Venturing off the Quattro Canti onto **via V. Emanuele,** you will pass the dilapidated *palazzi* of the **piazza Bologni** and a spindly statue of Charles V (1630), before confronting the exotic exuberance of Palermo's **cathedral,** an utterly eclectic building. Erected in 1185 by the Normans, it absorbed relics from every architectural style from the thirteenth through eighteenth centuries. Walk around to the east end of the cathedral to see the intertwined arches and multi-colored inlay of the three apses and two towers from the original twelfth-century construction. Inside, the chapels on the left contain six royal tombs (4 canopied and 2 set in the wall) of Norman kings and Hohenstaufen emperors dating from the twelfth to fourteenth centuries. The *tesoro* (treasury), to the right of the apse, contains a dazzling array of sacerdotal vestments from the sixteenth and seventeenth centuries as well as episcopal rings, chalices, and croziers. (Open daily 7am-noon and 4-6pm.) Take bus #4, 27, or 38.

Set behind a tropical garden across from the church, the **Palazzo dei Normanni** contains the **Cappella Palatina** (1132-40). Built by Roger II, it, is also a fantastic fusion of styles—a carved wooden stalactite ceiling, a cycle of golden Byzantine mosaics, and geometric marble walls. In the apse, Christ looms large above a nineteenth-century mosaic of the Virgin. Before leaving, visit the **Sala di Ruggiero** (King Roger's Hall; 1 floor above the Palatina), a room adorned with mosaics of animal and botanical motifs. Because the *palazzo* is now the seat of the Sicilian Parliament, you must wait at the desk for an escort. (Palace open Mon. and Fri.-Sat. 9am-12:30pm. Chapel open Mon.-Tues. and Thurs.-Sat. 9am-1pm and 3-5:30pm, Wed. 9am-1pm, Sun. 9-10am, 11-11:30am, and 12:15-1pm.)

Walk back to via V. Emanuele to see the **Porta Nuova,** a huge gate topped by a pyramidal roof. The gate was erected to commemorate Charles V's triumphal entrance in 1535, but modified in 1668 with the rugged figures that now embellish the entrance arch.

Perhaps the most romantic spot in Palermo is the garden and cloister of the **Church of San Giovanni degli Eremiti** (St. John of the Hermits), via dei Benedettini, 3, visible from the palace grounds. Built in 1132, its nave is divided in two, each side topped by a red dome and ending in a row of three apses also crowned by domes. (Open Mon.-Sat. 9am-7pm, Sun. 8:30am-2pm.) Take bus #27, 34, or 38.

From the Church of San Francesco to the Villa Giulia

The churches and palaces east of via Roma towards the old port (la Cala) lie in a maze of tiny, serpentine streets. The church of **San Francesco d'Assisi,** via Paternostro, off via V. Emanuele, could be Palermo's most significant ecclesiastical structure. An intricate rose window and a zig-zag design on the outside, the church's restored Gothic interior was augmented by side chapels in the fourteenth and fifteenth centuries, adorned by Renaissance and baroque ornamentation. The triumphal arch of the fourth chapel to the left (1468), one of the earliest important Renaissance works in Sicily, contrasts sharply with the explosive baroque chapel to the right of the high altar. (San Francesco may be undergoing restoration in 1989.) The **Oratory of San Lorenzo,** a few doors down, was decorated by the master of stucco, Giacomo Serpotta (1656-1732). This mono-colored stucco has a hard finish that appears from a distance to be carved stone. Note the beautifully wrought male figures high on the wall and the 10 sumptuous statues of *The Virtues.* Caravaggio's last known work, *The Nativity* (1609), was stolen from the altar in 1969, hence the seven locks on the oratory door. (Usually open 9am-1pm. L1000 is expected at the end of your tour.) Take bus #5.

The **Giardino Garibaldi,** a park several blocks east on via V. Emanuele, is replete with royal palms, fig trees, and giant banyans. The boa-like aerial roots of the banyans make the area more like a zoo of prehistoric creatures than a city square. Interesting though dilapidated buildings surround the square; check out the **Museo delle Marionette,** in the Palazzo Fatta, a puppet museum with a wonderful collection (open Mon.-Sat. 10am-1pm and 5-7pm, Sun. 10am-1pm; puppet shows Sat. at 5:30pm), and **Palazzo Chiramonte,** p. Marina, 60. Take bus #8 or 24. The palace (finished 1380) remains a paradigmatic medieval Sicilian *palazzo*—look for the three Gothic windows and the colorful Saracen limestone decoration. From the nearby **Church of Santa Maria della Catena** you can see the small inlet of **la Cala,** once the old harbor and now a fishing port. Via V. Emanuele ends at the war-scarred remains of the **Porta Felice** (begun in 1582). You can see how large the medieval-Renaissance city was by looking back at the Porta Nuova in the distance. Once a fashionable seaside drive, the **Foro Italico** is now a tacky boardwalk strip. The part-Gothic, part-Renaissance **Palazzo Abatellis** (1495) houses one of Sicily's superb Regional Galleries. Upstairs, an entire room is devoted to painter Antonello da Messina (1430-1479), Sicily's number-one son. Works by Leandro Bassano (1557-1622), Vincenzo da Pavia, and Leonard Macaluss round out the Sicilian crew. (Open Wed. and Fri.-Sat. 9am-1:30pm, Tues. and Thurs. 9am-1:30pm and 3-4:30pm, Sun. and holidays 9am-12:30pm. Admission L2000.) Take bus #3 or 24.

To the south, down Foro Umberto, which becomes via Ponte di Mare, **Villa Giulia** has a dilapidated garden, which, despite atrophy, has a little something for everyone: band shells, playgrounds, menagerie, sculpture and floral gardens, cenotaphs, and a small amusement park.

From the Church of San Matteo to the Museo Archeologico

Most of Palermo's other noteworthy sights lie along **via Roma,** north of via V. Emanuele. The **Church of San Matteo** (via V. Emanuele), a baroque church of 1663, harbors an ornate marble interior and four statues by Serpotta in the pilasters of the dome. (Open daily 8am-noon and 4-7pm.) Near the intersection of via Roma and via V. Emanuele is the **Church of Sant' Antonio,** raised on a platform, constructed in the twelfth century, and revamped in the fourteenth and nineteenth centuries. You can still see the original structure in the square frame and the columns of the chancel. To the left of the church, the **Bocceria Vecchia,** an alley descending to the middle of the ancient market of Palermo, is the most hopping place in town.

The **Church of San Domenico** fronts the *piazza* of the same name on via Roma. Rebuilt in 1640, the church is Sicily's Pantheon, containing tombs and cenotaphs of distinguished, if not interesting, citizens. The **Oratorio del Rosario,** behind San Domenico on via Bambini (ring at #16), houses a famous altarpiece by Van Dyck, *Madonna of the Rosary with Saint Dominique and the Patroness of Palermo* (1628). The painting shows a child conceived during a plague holding his nose. Saint Faustus's decaying skull decorates the rear altar. (Usually open 9am-1pm.)

The **Church of Santa Città,** on via Squarcialupo, was damaged during the war, causing its severe exterior, but a rosary showers the interior with baroque color and texture. The marble arches on the east wall of the choir and the sarcophagus in the second chapel on the left remain from the original Renaissance structure. To get there, descend one of the small streets off via Roma across from the main post office. The **Oratorio di Santa Zita,** (open 9am-noon and 4-6pm, behind the church (ring at via Valverde, 3), is decorated with more of Serpotta's *Virtues,* reliefs of New Testament scenes, and, on the short wall near the entrance, a depiction of the Battle of Lepanto where Cervantes lost an arm. Note the mother-of-pearl inlaid benches. (Open 9am-noon and 4-6pm.) Take black or red bus #34.

The **Museo Archeologico,** at p. Olivella, 4, occupies a seventeenth-century convent and displays a motley collection in two beautiful courtyards. Unfortunately, it is undergoing renovation, and its priceless collection of metopes from Selinunte are all packed away. See the building for its *cortiles,* and pick up an English language picture book for the admission price, especially if journeying on to Selinunte. In the bronze collection is the Ram of Syracuse (Greek, 3rd century B.C.E.), renowned for its lifelike quality. (Open Mon., Wed.-Thurs., and Sat. 9am-1:30pm., Tues. and Fri. 9am-1:30pm and 3-5pm, Sun. 9am-12:30pm. Admission L2000.)

Other Sights

Across via Maqueda from the Archeological Museum, the **Teatro Massimo,** constructed between 1875 and 1897 in a robust neoclassical style, is the largest indoor stage in Europe after the Paris Opera House. The Massimo is currently closed and will be for a while as $8½ million is poured into its reconstruction. The exiled opera and symphony perform in the **Politeama Garibaldi** (farther up via Maqueda, which becomes via Ruggiero Settima), a huge circular theater built in 1874, with a triumphal arch entrance crowned by a bronze chariot and four horses. The theater also houses the **Galleria d' Arte Moderna.** (Theater runs: Jan.-late May and mid-July to Aug. Tickets from L10,000. Gallery open Wed. and Fri.-Sun. 9am-1pm, Tues. and Thurs. 9am-1pm and 4:30-7:30pm. Admission L500.)

The **Convento dei Cappuccini** attracts attention with its catacombs; 8000 ghoulish bodies inhabit long subterranean corridors, some mummified by unusual processes, others slowly rotting. (Open daily 9am-noon and 3-5pm. Donation L1000.) Take bus #27 from p. Castelnuovo.

Monte Pellegrino, an isolated mass of limestone rising from the sea, is Palermo's renowned natural landmark, separating the city from the beach at Mondello. Near its summit, the **Santuario di Santa Rosalia** marks the site where Rosalia, a young Norman princess, sought ascetic seclusion. Her bones were discovered in 1624 and brought to Palermo, where they magically cured the city of a raging plague. The present sanctuary is built over the cave where she performed her ablutions. Its trickling waters are said to have miraculous powers. The summit of Pellegrino (a ½-hr. climb from the sanctuary) offers a gorgeous view of Palermo, Conca d' Oro, and on a crystal clear day, the Lípari Islands and Mount Etna. Take bus #12 from p. XIII Vittime to the sanctuary.

Parco della Favorita, Palermo's enormous park, was created in 1799 by the Bourbon king Ferdinand III. This huge greensward at the western base of Monte Pellegrino looks enticing on a city map but is disappointing in reality (and dangerous at night). Next to the Chinese Palace, the **Museo Etnografico Pitrè** displays relics from the life and customs of the Sicilian people. (Open Mon.-Thurs. and Sat. 8:30am-1pm and 3-5pm, Fri. 3-5pm, Sun. 9am-12:30pm and 3-5pm. Admission L1000. Free puppet show daily at 4pm.) Take bus #14 or 15.

Entertainment and Seasonal Events

The major summer event is at the **Teatro del Parco di Villa Castelnuovo.** From the first week in July through the first in August, an international festival of ballet, jazz, and classical music takes place in a seaside open-air theater. For tickets and information, contact the **Politeama Garibaldi,** p. Settimo (tel. 58 43 34; open Tues.-Sat. 10am-1pm and 5-7pm), across from the tourist office, or write the APT office for a program. The **Festa di Santa Rosalia,** held from July 10 to 15, gives the city reason to shed its usual sobriety and go on a binge of music and merriment.

Palermo's quiet *passeggiata* centers on the large open area in front of the Teatro Politeama. Otherwise, the streets are fairly empty after 8pm. This is because, in summer at least, everyone's at the lido of **Mondello.** To join them, take bus #14 or 15 from via della Libertà near the Teatro Politeama, and ask to get off at Mondello Paese (L600). In summer, express bus #6 ("Bello") also runs to Mondello, beginning at the train station and stopping along via della Libertà (30 min.). On this peninsula jutting into the Mediterranean, crowds of young Palermitans mill about sampling seafood from the waterfront stalls (a complete dinner can come to a meager L5000), sipping coffee, and exchanging glances. Mondello Paese is almost the only place where young Palermitan women appear at night. Another hotspot, frequented by a posher crowd, is **Villa Boscogrande,** a gorgeous *palazzo* where director Luchino Visconti filmed *The Leopard,* now featuring both bar and disco. Take bus #28 from via della Libertà.

Sferracavallo is a roomier but rockier beach (bus #28 from via della Libertà), and **Addaura** entertains the young Palermitan jet-set crowd in summer (bus #3 from the train station or via della Libertà).

The cheapest accommodations at Mondello are in the **Villa Resi,** via Reg. Elena, 23 (tel. 45 01 34). Doubles are L35,000.

Near Palermo: Monreale

About 10km southwest of Palermo, the golden city of Monreale and its magnificent Norman-Saracen **cathedral** inspired Jacques Cartier to name his Canadian city, with a bit of braggadocio, Montreal. The interior of the cathedral is one of the most rococo in Italy, but it has also been a *trattoria* for termites since 1807. Pest control specialists continue their battle to protect the fragile, wooden dome from these hungry insects. Unpalatable to the little timber-eaters, the mosaics here have made Monreale the home of the Italian government Mosaic Institute. You can "read" Genesis, Exodus, and episodes from the New Testament as you follow the mosaics around the church; start in the upper right-hand corner of the inner nave (L100 to light up mosaics). The huge net around the ceiling protects onlookers from falling wood and stone—the termites are messy eaters. Outside, circle around back to see the intricate arches and multi-colored inlays. The cloister (admission L2000) is renowned for the capitals of its colonnade. Considered to be the richest collection of Sicilian sculpture, the capitals run the gamut of styles: Greco-Roman, Romanesque, Gothic, and various combinations. In the corner by the lesser colonnade and its fountain, look for the capital depicting William II offering the Cathedral of Monreale to the Virgin. The mosaic inlay and spiral carving of the twin columns supporting the capitals lend a Moorish atmosphere to the scene. (Cathedral open Mon.-Sat. 7:30am-noon and 3-6:30pm, Sun. 7am-12:30pm. Cloister open Mon.-Sat. 9am-7pm., Sun. 9am-1pm. Admission L2000.) Take bus #9 from via Lincoln across from the station to the left, or #8/9, which leaves every 30 minutes from via Paola Bolsamo, near the train station in Palermo. **Tourist Information** (tel. 41 01 81) is in the building to the left of the church.

Sate your hunger at **Taverna del Pavone** (tel. 41 22 53), off p. G. Matteoti directly up the street from the duomo. Try *maccheroni del pavone* (with meat, tomato, mushroom, and olives, L7000) or pizza (L3000-5000)—to be downed with one of 40 types of beer (L3000). (Cover L1500, service 12%. Open Tues.-Sun. 1-3pm and 7pm-midnight.) The **Salamone** food store, via Roma, 41, will provide not only a quick nutrition fix, but also a quick history fix from its knowledgeable owner. (Open Mon.-Sat. 8am-1:30pm and 5-8pm.)

Trapani

Best seen from a bus window leaving town, Trapani reeks with a sulfurous odor, emanating from a fouled sewer system and open fish markets. The city's only attraction is its location; it is the perfect base from which to explore neighboring islands, beaches, Greek temple sites, and Erice, a photogenic hill town. A couple of hours is more than enough time here; spend your layover in historic Trapani, where African and European influences mingle among abandoned baroque churches.

Ferries

Ferries and hydrofoils leave Trapani for the Egadi Islands (Levanzo, Favignana, and Marettimo). Tickets for both are available from **Siremar,** via Ammiraglio Staiti, 61 (tel. 405 15; open Mon.-Fri. 6:30am-1:30pm and 3:30-6:30pm, Sat. 6:30am-1:30pm and 3:30-4:30pm, Sun. 6:30am-3pm), for only ferries from **Traghetti delle Isole,** via Ammiraglio Staiti, 15 (tel. 217 54; open Mon.-Fri. 9am-1pm and 4-7pm, Sat. 9am-noon), and for only hydrofoils from **Alivit,** molo Sanità (tel. 240 73). The following departure times are for mid-June through mid-September only. The prices are the same on all lines. (See Sicily Getting There and Getting Around for ferries to Cagliari, Sardinia, and La Goulette, Tunisia.)

Trapani-Favignana: 6 per day (7am-4:15pm, 50 min., L2700). 15 hydrofoils per day (7am-7:15pm, 25 min., L5500).

Trapani-Levanzo: 4-6 per day (7am-4:15pm, 1½ hr., L2700). 15 hydrofoils per day (7am-7:15pm, 15 min., L5500).

Trapani-Marettimo: Ferries depart Mon. and Wed. at 9:15am and noon, Tues. and Fri. at 9:15am, Sat. at 9:15am and 10:30am, Sun. at 8:30am (2½ hr., L6000). Hydrofoils depart daily at 8:15am, 3:30pm, and 5pm (1¼ hr., L12,600).

Trapani-Pantelleria: Ferries depart Thurs.-Tues. at 9am and midnight, Wed. at 9am (4½ hr., L22,500). SNAV hydrofoils (tel. 240 14) depart Sun., Tues., and Fri. at 8am (L30,000).

Orientation and Practical Information

Trapani is 2¾ hours from Palermo by train (L6400). An express bus makes the trip in two hours, leaving from via Paolo Balsamo, 16, near the train station, in Palermo, to p. Garibaldi in Trapani (L8000). The port offers no facilities for checking luggage; leave bags at the train station (baggage consignment open 24 hours; L800 per piece). The old town lies directly in front of the *stazione;* the new town and Erice are behind.

Tourist Office: p. Saturno (tel. 290 00). Take via Osorio from the Mobil sign, turn left at its end, and then right onto corso Italia all the way to the *piazzetta.* An erudite man with armfuls of handouts. English spoken. Open Mon.-Sat. 8am-8pm, Sun. 9am-noon and 3-6pm.

Information booth at airport. Open daily 1-9pm. To see one of Trapani's finest homes, go to the **APT main office,** via Vito Sorba (tel. 270 77), 4 blocks behind the station to the right. Open Mon.-Sat. 8:30am-1pm.

Post Office: p. V. Veneto, up via Osorio and then right on via XXX Gennaio. Open Mon.-Sat. 8:30am-7pm. **Postal code:** 91100.

Telephones: SIP, via Scontrino, near the station. Open daily 8am-7:30pm. **Telephone code:** 0923.

Airport: V. Florio (tel. 84 12 22), outside the city in Birgi. Buses leave 1 hr. before flight time from outside **Salvo Viaggi,** corso Italia, 52/56 (tel. 238 18), the official Alitalia agent.

Buses: AST buses to Erice leave p. Malta, around the left corner of the train station. Mon.-Sat. 6:45am-7pm 10 per day, Sun. 9am-6:15pm 5 per day. One way L1800, round-trip L2600. Catch the return bus in Erice on via C.A. Pepoli 7:30am-7:55pm. For information, call 200 66.

Hospital: Ospedale S. Antonio Abate, via Cosenza (tel. 629 44).

Police: Carabinieri, via Orlandini, 19 (tel. 271 22).

Accommodations and Camping

Rooms fill up in the evening, so decide quickly if you must snooze here. Hotels are much better and only slightly more expensive in the beach resort **San Vito lo Capt,** accessible by bus from p. Malta (8 per day, 1 hr., round-trip L4900). Soon (here that means some time before the turn of the century), a hostel will crop up in Erice, on viale delle Pinete (tel. 86 91 44).

Pensione Messina, corso V. Emanuele, 71 (tel. 211 98), on the busy main street. Spacious rooms, firm beds, but only cold water in the rooms. Lively family management and an even livelier pink bathroom. Singles L10,000. Doubles L20,000. Showers L2000.

Pensione Maccotta, via degli Argentieri, 4 (tel. 284 18), behind the EPT office on p. Saturno. Quiet location, airy rooms. Singles L13,000. Doubles L24,000. Showers L3000.

Hotel Sole, p. Umberto I, 3 (tel. 220 35), to the right as you leave the train station. Large, with some exceptional rooms (complete with ceiling murals), and fresh bathrooms. Spoiled only by the crabby proprietress. Singles L16,000. Doubles L26,500. Showers L3500.

Hotel Vittoria, via Francesco Crispi, 4 (tel. 272 44). Turn right onto via Crispi from the train station, and walk across the arboreal via Fardella. A slice above the others in bed quality and tidiness. Single L20,500, with bath L29,000. Doubles L36,000, with bath L48,000. Showers included.

Sabbia d'Oro, via Santuario, 49 (tel. 97 25 08), on the beachfront in Capo San Vito. Impeccable, great location, and a bargain for the area. Singles L18,200. Doubles L28,200. Bath and showers included.

Camping

Capo San Vito and **Casteldamare del Golfo,** on the opposite side of the cape (2 buses per day at 12:30pm and 2:30pm, 1½ hr., round-trip L5600), host most of the nearby campsites.

Near Capo San Vito: Camping La Fata, via P. Mattarella (tel. 97 26 11), and **Camping Soleado,** via della Secca (tel. 97 21 66). Both charge L3500 per person, L3300 per small tent, L5000 per large tent. **Camping El Bahira** (tel. 97 25 77), 2km before Capo S. Vito in Salinella, on the water, charges higher prices for its better location and facilities. L7200 per person, L6000 per small tent, L10,300 per large tent. All open June-Sept.

Near Casteldamare del Golfo: Baia di Guidaloca (tel. 59 60 22), **Lu Baruni** (tel. 391 33), **Nausicaa** (tel. 315 18), and the cheapest, **Ciauli** (tel. 390 49), which charges L4000 per person, L3500 per small tent, L5500 per large tent. The other sites charge about L1000 more. All open June-Sept., except Lu Baruni, which is open year-round.

Food

Beat the *menù* market and go to the **open-air market,** in p. Mercato di Pesce at the end of via Torrearsa. (Open Mon.-Sat. 8am-2pm.) On the way from the train station to the port, pick up essentials at the **Schic Market,** via Osori, 52. (Open July-Aug. 15 Mon.-Thurs. 8am-2pm; Aug. 15-Aug. 30 Mon.-Fri. 8am-8pm; Sept.-June Mon.-Sat. 8am-8pm.)

Mensa Ferrovieri, at the train station. This employees' cafeteria is also open to tourists. Run by a woman who makes all dishes to order, it is one of Trapani's few saving graces. Full meals (bread, pasta, meat, salad and a drink—beer or wine) L7600. Gregarious regulars. Open daily 11am-3pm and 6-10pm.

Casablanca, via S. Francesco d'Assisi, 69 (tel. 200 50), near the port at via Serisso. More soothing than Bogart's resonant voice. A bubbling fountain, a large ceiling fan, and soft classical music. Work on a plate of *farfalle allo spada* (pasta with swordfish and a bite of mint, L6000). Try the great *crêpe caprese* (stuffed with tomatoes, basil, and mozzarella, L5000). Wine L3000 per liter. Cover L1000. Open Tues.-Sun. noon-3pm and 7:30pm-midnight.

Itrabinis, largo Porta Galli, 4. From the station, take via Osorio past the Mobil sign, turn left at the end onto via XXX Gennaio, and take the last right before the water. A new, groovy Italo-Tunisian affair with groovy prices. Try the *couscus primo* with meat or fish (L3500), or go exotic with *spaghetti itrabinis* (piping hot with pepperoni, garlic, and hot peppers, L5000). Cover L1500. Open Thurs.-Tues. 1-8pm.

Pizzeria Mediterranea, corso V. Emanuele, 195 (tel. 47 17 16). One of the few places left on Sicily that still makes Sicilian pizza. *Pizza rianata* (L3500) consists of whole tomatoes, garlic, oregano, anchovies, and sharp *pecorino* cheese. It just don't get any better dan dis. Beer L3000 per mug. Service 15%. Open Fri.-Wed. 5pm-midnight.

Sights and Entertainment

You can cover Trapani's major sights in a pleasant two-hour walk. Start with **via Giudecca,** off via XXX Gennaio, once the principal street of the old Jewish ghetto and now one of the most impoverished areas in the city. At #43 you can see a sixteenth-century *palazzo* tucked away amid small houses. Farther off corso Italia, the Gothic-Renaissance **Church of Santa Maria** has a beautiful marble baldachin (1521) sheltering a della Robbia terra-cotta. **Piazzetta Saturno** is the most charming square in the city. On one side rises the facade of the former **Church of Sant' Agostino** (14th century), which preserves a Gothic portal and rose window. The **Fountain of Saturn,** a triple-tiered basin supported by sirens, is from the late sixteenth century.

The main street of the old city, **corso Vittorio Emanuele,** is around the corner and is lined by elaborate facades: The seventeenth-century pink **Municipio** houses temporary art exhibits on its main floor; the **Collegio** church (1636) has an eighteenth-century carved walnut cupboard; and the **cathedral** has a striking green-tiled dome and pink stucco walls (facade 1635, portico 1740). Down a small street to the left on via Giglio, the wonderful little baroque church **Chiesa del Purgatorio** has a free-standing sculpture and a small emerald dome outside, and a group of wooden statues inside. This collection, called *Misteri* (The Mysteries), is carried in procession around the town on Good Friday.

Viale Regina Elena runs along the port, commanding a view of the small harbor and the Egadi Islands. **Viale Duca d' Aosta,** used as a place to repair and dry fishing nets, leads to the tip of the city, known as the **Torre di Ligny.**

To return to corso V. Emanuele from the Torre di Ligny, take via Libertà past the fish market to **via Garibaldi,** the most handsome street in the city. A broad flight of steps to the right brings you to the **Church of San Domenico,** which features a rose window, an early fresco by the entrance, and a fourteenth-century wooden crucifix. Via Garibaldi continues past the pink, twisted columns of the **Church of San Giuseppe** and the 1695 **Church of SS. Itria.**

Farther out in the new section of town is the **Museo Nazionale Popoli.** (It's a grueling walk; take bus #1, 10, or 11, L500.) The museum's magnificent baroque interior staircase leads to a collection of sculpture, painting, objects carved out of coral, and folk-art figurines. (Open Fri.-Tues. 9am-1:30pm, Wed.-Thurs. 9am-1:30pm and 4-6:30pm. Admission L2000. Sun. free.)

Trapani sponsors a festival of opera, ballet, and drama, **Luglio Musicale Trapanese** (tel. (0923) 229 34), which attracts international companies. It takes place in an open-air theater in the city park, the Villa Margherita, during the last three weeks in July. (Shows begin at 9pm. Tickets from L11,000.) **Settimana dell' Egadi,** in late May, greets the new crop of tourists with music, food, and archeological tours. Moan and groan to the music of the **Processione dei Misteri** on Good Friday at the church of San Domenico. Swaying townsfolk, bemasked and becolored, carry eight brass replicas of biblical scenes on an eerie march through the dark streets of the city.

Near Trapani

Perched 750m above Trapani, **Erice** was one of Sicily's renowned divine locations throughout ancient times. Mythic home to successive goddesses of fecundity (first the Elymnian Astarte, then the Greek Aphrodite, and finally the Roman Venus), the town has engendered few new structures since its medieval plan. Aside from the unsightly TV antennae bordering the ancient walls, Erice is quintessentially quaint. As hotel prices tend not to be quaint, it makes an excellent daytrip from Trapani or Capo San Vito. Once you get on the single road up the hill (follow the arrows at the far end of via G.B. Fardella), Erice is an easy hitch. The bus from Trapani takes about 45 minutes to make the 18-kilometer climb and leaves from p. Malta (Mon.-Sat. 10 per day, last at 7pm; Sun. 5 per day, last at 6:15pm). The cheapest place to stay in Erice is the **Edelweiss,** cortile p. Vincenzo (tel. 86 91 58). Singles are L28,500; doubles L46,000, all with bath. For otherworldly pizza (L4000-6000), try **Da Mario/La Vetta,** via G. Fontara, 5 (tel. 86 94 04), off p. Umberto I. They also make *panini* to order (L1500-2000). (Open daily 9am-midnight.)

If you don't make it your base in the northwest, at least set aside a day to visit the gentle shores of **San Vito lo Capo.** A raucous family fanfare from April to September, it is a major resort for northern Italians, but somehow remains both a bargain and an immaculate beach all summer. Buses from the Trapani *autostazione* at p. Malta leave 8 times per day (7am-8pm, 1¼ hr., roundtrip L4500). The last bus back to Trapani leaves at 9:30pm.

Western Coast

Egadi Islands (Isole Egadi)

If ever lucubrating in the wee hours you have thought of deserted islands with grottoes, coral reefs, and crystalline waters licking its shores, the Egadi will amaze you. The archipelago (Favignana, Levanzo, and the more distant and cleaner Marehimo) once supported a huge tuna industry, whose remains darken the harbor of Favignana and the tiny islet of Formica; they were also exploited for their tufa, or vulcanic rock, and thus some areas resemble miniature Grand Canyons. In addition, patches of the islands were bombed during WWII, never to be repaired. Despite all this, the islands swim in the cleanest, clearest water in all Italy, and have yet to know the din of tourist hordes. All three can be reached by frequent ferries and hydrofoils out of Trapani. (See Trapani Ferries.)

Favigna sports a traditional beach, the **Lido Burrone,** 3km across the island from the main harbor. Either hitch or rent a bike from **Noleggio Biciclette Isidoro,** via Mazzini, 40 (tel. 92 16 67), or **Biciclette Frrresche,** via Vittorio Emanuele (tel. 92 16 35). Signs for both shops are prominently displayed at the dock, and rentals run about L5000 per day. Bike to one of Italy's hidden treasures, an old quarry by the sea called the **Bue Marino** (Sea Ox). Follow the paved road around the left side of the island, heading towards Calarussa, but continue past the turnoff until the road becomes dirt. After a winding descent, the road runs directly into cliffs leading to the sea. Some travelers find the caves here perfect for unofficial camping, but the island also hosts three large campgrounds. **Camping Egàd** (tel. 92 15 55) lures you with its shuttle van which meets every ferry and hydrofoil. (Elaborate facilities for L4500 per person, L4000 per small tent.) **Miramare** (tel. 92 31 30) charges the same for similar facilities. Both are open June through September. cheapest is **Camping Quattro Rose** (tel. 92 12 23; L3500 per person, L3300 per small tent; open April-Sept.). The island's single hotel, the **Egadi,** via C. Colombo, 17 (tel. 92 12 32), off the main *piazza,* is booked weeks in advance during July and August. From late September until early June, singles are L16,000, with bath L22,500. Doubles are L26,500, with bath L33,000. Half-pension is required in high season for L46,000, but you decide the menu. The cheapest food on the island is the well-stocked **San Paola Alimartari,** on via Mazzini.

Levanzo has a rocky coastline similar to Favignana's; as it was less damaged in the war, it is less ragged in appearance. Notable for archeologists and devotees of prehistoric graffitti is the **Cava del Genovese,** about an hour north of the main port by foot. The island has one hotel, the **Paradiso,** on via Calvario (tel. 92 40 80). (Singles L15,400, with bath L19,200. Doubles L24,000, with bath L29,000.)

Marehimo is the pristine paradise of the trio, with beautiful bays, colorful reefs, and snapshot houses of whitewashed tufa. To stay overnight, simply ask around at the port for a villager offering rooms (L10,000-15,000).

Pantelleria

Floating between Sicily and Africa, this wild volcanic island is covered with rocks and cliffs, leaving it with something akin to a lunar landscape. The vineyards on the terraced slopes produce a famous wine and the raisins are the size of plums. Ferries and hydrofoils connect the island daily with Trapani (see Trapani Ferries), but it unfortunately costs less by plane. **Alitalia** flights leave Trapani daily at 7am and 2:05pm, and Pantelleria for the return trip at 9am and 4:15pm. With the 50% tourist discount, the price for this half-hour flight is an amazing L14,500.

The cheapest place to stay here is the **Miryam,** corso Umberto I (tel. 91 13 74), with singles for L20,500 (with bath L29,000) and doubles for L36,500 (with bath L48,000). The **Agadir,** via Catania (tel. 91 11 00), has singles for L29,000 and doubles for L48,400, all with bath. There is no campground on Pantelleria and freelancers are heavily fined.

Segesta

One of the best-kept secrets of the archeological world is the Greek temple at Segesta. Glimpsing the temple in its solitary splendor is an ecstasy as wild as the deep gorges below. Italian film director Lina Wertmuller used the temple to great effect in her film *Blood Feud.* Approaching it from the train station can be equally satisfying, with snippets of the temple and a view of the ancient theater crowning the hill on the left. The two ruins are the sole remains of the once flourishing city of a native Sicilian people. This fifth-century temple was never finished, however: It has no inner walls or roof and the columns are unfluted. According to Thucydides's *Peloponnesian Wars,* the trickery of the Segestans condemned Athens to the fatal defeat to Selinunte in the battle of Syracuse. From mid-July until the first week of August during odd-numbered years, classical plays are performed in the ancient theater. Special buses leave p. Politeama in Palermo (1¾ hr. before showtime) and p. Marina in Trapani (1 hr. before showtime). Tickets are L10,000 from any travel agent in Palermo or Trapani. The theater, commanding a spectacular vista of the surrounding farmlands stretching out to the northern coast, is a 20-minute walk up the road from the bar. Allow at least 2½ hours to explore the ruins on foot. Only two trains daily from Palermo and three from Trapani stop at Segesta's bombed-out, unmanned, pink station (Palimo-Segesta L4200, Tropani-Segesta L3600).

Marsala

Marsala occupies the extreme western point of Sicily on the promontory of Cape Lilibero. An ugly commercial center famous for its wine, the city was founded by the Phoenicians and renamed Mars-al-Allah (Port of God) by the Muslims. Garibaldi landed here on May 11, 1860 to start the expedition which freed Sicily from foreign domination. Speaking of landing, Marsala suffered heavy bombing during WWII, and concrete bunkers still pock the modern town. Although the city is best as a springboard to the unique and mysterious **Moxia,** Marsala's two museums are intriguing in themselves.

In **piazza della Repubblica** stand the eighteenth-century Palazzo Comunale and the grandiose, unfinished baroque **cathedral.** A variety of sculpture from the sixteenth-century school of Gagini, including the fine statue of Saint Thomas the Apostle, decorates the church's vast interior. Behind the cathedral at via Garraffa, 57, is the **Museo Degli Arazzi,** which contains Philip II's eight elaborate sixteenth-century tapestries illustrating Titus's war against the Jews. Nary a soul comes to see these magisterial hangings, so a polite request will get you a guided tour from the enthusiastic keeper. (Open Mon.-Sat. 9am-1pm and 4-6pm. Free.) The **Museo Lilibeo,** at the end of viale N. Sauro off p. della Vittoria, houses a 35-meter Phoenician warship believed to have been sunk during the Battle of the Egadi Islands, which ended the First Punic War in 241 B.C.E. (Open 9am-1:30pm and sometimes 4-7pm. Free.) Another document of Marsala's ancient past is the nearby **Insula Romana** (Roman House), accessible from viale V. Veneto, one of the few buildings excavated in the vast archeological zone. It dates from the third century C.E. and has some fine mosaics. (Open upon request at the Museo Lilibeo.) The small **Church of San Giovanni** (at the opposite end of the archeological zone of viale Sauro) covers Grotta della Sibilla, where the Cumaean Sibyl is said to have proclaimed her oracles through a medium of water.

Marsala is a half-hour by train from Trapani (L1800) and 3 hours from Palermo. Connections to Selinunte and Agrigento are infrequent and slow; a bus from p. del Popolo is the best option. The **Pro Loco** information office is at via Garibaldi, 45 (tel. 95 80 97), off via XI Maggio. (Open Mon.-Sat. 8am-8pm, Sunday 9am-noon.) There is a **post office** up the street at via Garibaldi, 3-7. (Open Mon.-Sat. 8:10am-1:20pm.) **Trattoria al Fanaletto,** via Crispi, 53 (tel. 95 84 24), one street down from the train station off via Roma, bastes its *scallopina al marsala* (L5000) with Marsala wine, which you can savor without the veal for L4000 per liter. (Cover L1000. Open daily 12:30-3pm and 7-11pm.) The cheapest hotel in town is the **Garden,** via Gambini, 36 (tel. 98 23 20), near the train station. Singles L20,500, with bath L29,000. Doubles L36,500, with bath L48,000.)

San Pantaleo (ancient Moxia or Motya) was the scene of a monumental naval battle when the Syracusan tyrant Dionysius annihilated the Carthaginian Himilco in 397 B.C.E. with the aid of a new invention, the catapult. The near-deserted islet lies 8km north of Marsala, across a thin strait traversed hourly by a scrawny boat (Mon.-Sat. 9am-7pm, L2500). Remains of the original, child-sacrificing Phonecian inhabitants are plentiful, from the ritual altar to the dry dock on the other side of the tiny island. Most unusual is the sixth-century B.C.E. underwater road that runs between the old necropolis on Moxia and Trapani's airport. Many of the island's archeological finds are on display in the tiny museum at the port. Only seven people live on the island year-round; two archeologists commute daily.

From Trapani, take a bus from via Malta to Marsala, but make sure to tell the driver where you are headed and get off at Granatello. From there, walk towards San Leonardo, bearing left at the train tracks then following the signs (1 hr.; fill your daypack with lunch and water). The trip from Marsala is easier, as there are hourly buses (#14, and occasionally a #4, L600), from p. del Popolo. For information, tel. (6923) 95 95 98.

Selinunte

A mound of ruins on a magnificient plateau overlooking the Mediterranean, Selinunte (from the Greek *Selinus,* the wild celery that once grew in the valley) is impressive for its sheer size and desolation. Composed mainly of a trio of temples to the east (the only one standing was reconstructed in 1958), and an acropolis across the valley to the west (again restructured 1925-7), these piles of rubble testify to Selinunte's glory as an ally of Syracuse in the sixth century B.C.E. Battles a century later against the Carthaginians did much to ravage the city's monuments, and numerous later earthquakes exacerbated the mess. Most intact is the lone north-south main street on the far side of the acropolis, where you can pick chips of ancient pottery out of the dirt. (Open 8am-sunset. Admission L2000.) Getting to Selinunte is a hassle. From Palermo, Trapani, or Marsala, take the bus or train to Castelveltrano. Buses leave for Selinunte from Castelveltrano's train station five times per day (½ hr., L900). From Trapani allow 3½ hours travel time, from Palermo 4½ hours.

Nearby Marinella (telephone code 0924) is a fairly cheap mini-resort town, with silken beaches and gentle breezes. There is a **SIP** in the Bar Amigos near the bus depot (the old train station), and the **Supermercato Selinuntese** is a true bargain. Follow the white signs to via S.S. Otto, 5 (tel. 462 38; open Mon.-Sat. 8am-1:30pm and 4-11pm). The hotel **Lido Azzurro,** via Marco Polo, 98 (tel. 460 57), has a polyglot management who will watch daytrippers' bags while they dip in the sea across the road. (Singles L16,000, with bath L21,500. Doubles L26,500, with bath L33,000.) The **Costa d'Avorio** is at via Stazione, 10 (tel. 460 11). (Singles L15,000, with bath L19,000. Doubles L24,000, with bath L30,000.) Nearby is **Camping il Maggiolino** (tel. 460 44), offering a piece of turf for L3500 per person, L3300 per small tent.

Agrigento

The ancient Greeks named it Akragas, the Romans Agrigentum, and the Arabs Kerkent, but you may call it a polluted tourist convention. Have patience. Despite the brown haze pumped across the city's magnificient marine vista by Porto Empedocle's refinery, and despite the English reverberating through the streets and temples, Agrigento belongs on any complete Sicilian itinerary. It is best known for the Valley of the Temples, an ancient city with over 20 Greek temples, of which the most splendid is the Temple of Concordia, one of the best-preserved Doric temples in the world. The modern city surrounds a labrynthine medieval quarter. At night (May-Sept. until 11:30pm; in off-season until 10:30pm), the temples are lit against a starry sky. Mounted on a 3km, treeless ridge that overlooks the distant sea, their Doric columns create an unforgettable vision.

Orientation and Practical Information

To preserve your mental health, do not take a train to or from Agrigento. Every line is undergoing electrification, which means that the 100-kilometer trip to Enna, for example, takes seven hours. Sundry buses gather at the autostation in p. Roselli, off via Cicerone and up the hill from the train station. From Selinunte, take the 6:20am, 8:20am, or 2:30pm bus to Ribara (1 hr., L2500), then walk down a block to catch another to Agrigento (1 hr., L3600). For information, call **Fratelli Camilleri and Argento** (tel. (0922) 390 84). **Cuffaro** (tel. (0922) 91 63 49) runs buses from Palermo's via Lincoln Station (2¼ hr., L7000) and from Catania's p. Bellini station (2¾ hr., L12,000).

Agrigento lingers at the midpoint of Sicily's southern coast. The medieval and modern cities are bisected by the transportation terminals and a park in p. Moro.

City Tourist Information Office: p. A. Moro, 5 (tel. 204 54), in the Banco di Sicilia building up from the train station. Useful map. If you arrive in July, ask about cultural events at the Valley of the Temples. English spoken. Open Mon.-Sat. 8:30am-2pm and 5:30-7:30pm.

Post Office: p. V. Emanuele. Open Mon.-Fri. 8:10am-7:30pm, Sat. 8-11am. Fermo Posta. **Postal code:** 92100.

Telephones: via Alcide de Gaspari, 21, off viale S. Vito (up the steps). Open daily 8am-8pm. **Telephone code:** 0922.

Ferries: Siremar runs ferries out of nearby Porto Empedocle (L1100 by bus) to the Pelagie Islands of **Linosa** (L26,900) and **Lampedusa** (L33,000). April-Oct. 15 daily at midnight; Oct. 16-May 30 Mon.-Sat. at midnight—arriving between 5:30am and 8:15am at the islands. Return boats leave Lampedusa at 10:15am.

Hospital: Ospedale Civile San Giovanni di Dio, via Giovanni XXIII (tel. 207 55). Late night pharmacy information; tel. 100 13.

Police: Carabinieri, p. Moro (tel. 563 22).

Accommodations and Camping

Bella Napoli, p. Lena, 6 (tel. 204 35), off via Bac Bac, which leads uphill from the western end of via Atenea. Immaculate rooms, powerful showers, amiable savvy staff, and a rooftop terrace overlooking the valley. Singles L17,000, with bath L25,000. Doubles L31,000, with bath L37,000. Showers included.

Concordia, via S. Francesco, 11 (tel. 59 62 66). Take via Pirandello from the bottom of p. Moro. A modern hotel, with fresh rooms and bathrooms, but on the dirty market street. Singles L16,000, with bath L22,000. Doubles L31,000, with bath L38,000.

Albergo Gorizia, via Bocciere, 39 (tel. 201 05), between via Atenea, 283 and 285, a 10-min. walk from p. V. Emanuele. At least it's cheap. Singles L13,000. Doubles L20,000. Showers L2500.

Camping: Internazionale San Leone at S. Leone (tel. 461 21). Take bus #9 or the "San Leone" bus to the beach and go to the left. L4500 per person, L5000 per 2-person tent. Sleeping bag only (no tent) L5500 per person. **Camping Nettuno** (tel. 462 68), 6km from Agrigento, past S. Leone on bus #9. Less green and less comfortable than San Leone, but cheaper. L3500 per person, L3000 per tent. Both sites open April-Oct.

Food

Walk down the steps from p. Marconi to the soccer field for a market of both edibles and non-edibles. (Open Mon.-Sat. 9am-early afternoon.) For cheaper prices but less atmosphere, try the **Standa,** in Agrigento's tallest building, at via Gioeni, 41. (Open Tues.-Sat. 9am-1pm and 4:30-8:30pm, Mon. 4:30-8:30pm.) Inexpensive, informal *trattorie* line **via Atenea.**

Paninoteca Manhattan, salita M. Angeli, 9, up the steps to the right off via Atenea near p. Moro. Creative Italian sandwiches with American names. The Rockefeller combines tuna, pepper, lettuce, *insalata russa,* tabasco, and a healthy dose of whiskey (L3300). Or design your own. Innumerable brands of beer (L1000-4000). Open Mon.-Sat. 8:30am-3pm and 5:30pm-midnight.

Self-Service Taglialavoro, up the street from p. Aldo Moro. Huge selection of ready-made, carefully-prepared dishes. Pasta L2400, *cannelloni* smothered in cheese L4000, *pollo alla cacciatora* L4000. Delectable pizza served after 7pm (L1800-3500). Open daily 7am-11pm.

Trattoria Atenea, via Ficani, 32, the 2nd right off via Atenea from p. Moro. Don't be scared by the ominous We speak English and Nous parlons Français signs—this is an authentic *trattoria,* from the questionable decoration down to the slightly soiled tablecloths. 3-course lunch with beverage L10,000. Complete dinner (without the pasta course) L7000. *Calamari* or *gamberi* L6000. Wine L2500 per liter. Open Mon.-Sat. noon-3:30pm and 7-11pm.

Trattoria Black Horse, via Celauro, 8, off via Atenea on a carpeted side street. An interesting, family-run establishment. The best food in town, but small portions. *Tronchetto dello chef* (L4500) is the specialty: a thick lasagna packed with peas, ham, and meat sauce. Wine L4000. Cover L1000, service 15%. Open Mon.-Sat. noon-3:30pm and 7-11pm.

Sights and Entertainment

The most interesting building of the medieval city is the small, eleventh-century Norman **Church of Santa Maria dei Greci,** occupying the site of a fifth-century B.C.E. Doric temple at the end of via Atenea off p. Sinatra. A Gothic portal bearing the insignia of a Spanish noble family on its keystone leads to a three-aisled interior whose central apse incorporates stones from the original Greek temple. Part of the wooden Norman ceiling remains, as well as some fourteenth-century Byzantine frescoes. Look for the astonishing secret tunnel, which you can enter from the courtyard. It preserves the six stumps and stylobate (the platform beneath the columns) of the ancient temple. (If closed, call 255 62 for the custodian; L1500 tip expected.)

Via Girolamo, which roughly flanks via Atenea, takes you past the former Consulate of the British Empire (#63), replete with lions and royal insignia, to **Santo Spirito,** a complex chapel, chapter house, and refectory (now used as a library) founded by Cistercian nuns at the end of the thirteenth century. The church has beautiful stuccos (1693-1695) by Serpotta, illustrating scenes from Christ's life, and a fifteenth-century Byzantine wooden ceiling. To enter ring the bell on the church door. (Closed for restoration in 1988.) For more Serpotta stuccos, take a walk down via S. Spirito and via Foder to the **Chiesa del Purgatorio** (Church of the Purgatory), which houses eight elegant statues representing the Virtues. To the left of the church, underneath a sleeping lion, is the entrance to underground channels and reservoirs built by the Greeks in the fifth century B.C.E. (Open daily 7:30am-12:30pm.)

To get to the **Valle dei Templi** (Valley of the Temples), take bus #10 from the train station (last bus back at 9:50pm; L500). When you arrive at the site, go first to the **Museo Nazionale Archeologico di San Nicola,** where you can orient yourself with the maps and photos of the site. The museum has a notable collection of artifacts, especially vases from Agrigento and the rest of central Sicily. (Open June-Sept. Tues.-Sun. 9:30am-1:30pm and 3:30-5pm; Oct.-May Tues.-Sat. 9:30am-1:30pm. Free.) Visit the adjacent **Church of San Nicola,** once the site of a Greek sanctuary and now a small thirteenth-century Romanesque-Gothic church preserving a magnificent Roman Sarcophagus of Phaedra (2nd chapel on the right) that was inspired by Greek models. (Open sunrise-sunset.)

The **Hellenistic-Roman Quarter** gives you an excellent idea of the old city's organization, with its four roads and a complex of buildings sloping down in a series of terraces. Take a short walk down the hill to the parking lot and turn left. The **Tempio di Ercole** (Hercules), the first you encounter as you enter the complex, is the oldest of the temples (6th century B.C.E.).

Uphill from the Temple of Hercules is the **Tempio della Concordia,** the most intact Greek temple in the world next to the Temple of Theseus in Athens. The four-sided, free-standing colonnade gives a living quality to the building, accentuated by the changing shadows. The temple was erected in the mid-fifth century B.C.E. out of a volcanic rock now faded golden. It owes its remarkable preservation to early resanctification as a Christian church, San Gregorio del Rape ("of the Turnip"), which protected it from the "anti-pagan" hooliganism that destroyed the other temples. You can still see the niches in the interior walls that were created for Christian worship.

The next temple spiraling proudly in the distance is the **Tempio di Giunone** (Juno), which also dates from the fifth century B.C.E. and is a weathered version of the Tempio della Concordia. The sacrificial altar still exists on the eastern side, and on the west is an ancient cistern. The red stains of fire on some of the columns bear witness to the Carthaginian destruction of the city in 406-405 B.C.E.

Walk back down the hill to the parking lot and cross the road to visit the other set of ruins. The first site here is the **Tempio dell' Olimpico Giove** (Jupiter), believed to be one of the largest Greek temples ever constructed, though there isn't much left today. Its 18-meter columns were supported by 38 figures each 8m high, with arms raised above for additional support. Much of the temple's stone was carted away in the eighteenth century to build a jetty at nearby Porto Empedocle, so only rubble remains. The four columns supporting an entablature are all that's left of the fifth-century B.C.E. **Tempio di Castore e Polluce** (Castor and Pollux).

Back in town, *literati* make pilgrimages to the birthplace of playwright **Luigi Pirandello,** in p. Chaos (named for Pirandello's most famous work). Take bus #8 to this small museum of books and notes, honored by his gravestone in the backyard. (Open Mon.-Sat. 9am-noon. Free.) From late July through early August, the **Settimana Pirandelliana** (tel. (0922) 235 61) features plays by Pirandello and his contemporaries (tickets L5000-7000).

The first Sunday of February is the **Almond Blossom Festival,** an international folklore event in the Valley of the Temples. In early July, townsfolk throw bread at an effigy of St. Calogero, in thanks for curing the city of a deadly yeast epidemic. **San Leone,** 4km from Agrigento (bus #9 or 10), hops to the gossip of a beachside *passeggiata* and to the tunes of **Discoteca Aster** (tel. 423 66; free). Buses stop running at 9:30pm, but rides are easy to finagle.

Syracuse (Siracusa)

Sicily's great Grecian city, Syracuse glows with the classical romance of Rome, charms with the petite aspect of Venice, and harbors the climate of a vacation island. Cicero proclaimed "There is not a day without sunshine in Syracuse." Much of what is now considered Greek culture actually originated here; for example, it was home to Epicarus, the originator of theatrical comedy, and to Archimedes, the great third century B.C.E. mathematician and physicist.

Attracted to its splendid harbor and natural spring water, the Corinthians claimed the soil in 734 B.C.E., but the city reached its pinnacle in the fifth and fourth centuries B.C.E., largely as a result of its ascension to Sicilian dominance under the tyrant Gelon and his successor and brother Hieron I. Syracuse escaped a jealous Athenian attempt to capture the city, decimating the fleet in one of the great naval battles of ancient history (413 B.C.E.). Two centuries later the city was sacked by Rome, and then flowed into mainstream Sicilian history, changing hands among the Arabs, Normans, Angevins, Aragons, Savoys, Austrians, and Bourbons. Today the city exhibits some extraordinary reminders of its yesteryear glory, including the celebrated Greek theater set in a large and verdant archeological park. Ortigia, linked to the mainland by two small bridges, is an island of narrow streets, saltwater breezes, and glistening buildings.

Orientation and Practical Information

Syracuse rests on the southeastern corner of Sicily, 55km south of Catania. **Tirrenia,** via Mazzini, 5 (tel. 669 56; open 9am-noon and 3-6pm), runs weekly **ferries** to Naples (Wed. at 3:30pm from Molo San Antonio, arriving in Naples Thurs. at 9:30am, L40,100), and ferries to Reggio di Calabria (Mon., Wed., and Sat. at 3:30pm, arriving at Reggio di Calabria at 10pm, L15,900). Ferries also leave for **Malta** (Sun., Tues., and Fri. at 4:30pm, arriving at Vittoriosa at 9:30pm; June-Sept. L61,700, Oct.-May L54,800). Reservations for the catamaran to Malta (Wed. and Fri. at 9:35am and 9:35pm, 2 hr.) can be made at **G. Bozzanca** travel agency, corso G. Matteotti, 88-92 (tel. 671 22), on the corner of the Apollo Temple.

Azienda di Turismo: via Maestranza, 33 (tel. 669 32), in the old city (Island of Ortigia), near p. Archimede. A blessing with maps and accommodations. English spoken. Open Mon.-Sat. 9am-1pm and 3-7pm. Also at the train station (tel. 662 22). Open Mon.-Sat. 9am-8pm, Sun. 9am-1pm and 3-7pm.

EPT: via San Sebastiano, 43 (tel. 677 10), across from the Catacombs of San Giovanni. Open Mon.-Sat. 9am-6pm. Come here for information on the province, not the city. Also EPT information at the archeological park (tel. 605 10). Open July-Aug. daily 8am-8pm; in off-season Mon.-Sat. 8am-2pm and 3-6pm.

Post Office: p. delle Poste, in the old city near the bridge. Fermo Posta. Open Mon.-Fri. 8am-8pm, Sat. 8am-1pm. **Postal code:** 96100.

Telephones: SIP, via Brenta, 33, behind the train station. Open daily 8am-8pm. At other times, try **Bar Tamanaco** p. Marconi, 19. **Telephone code:** 0931.

Train Station: Midway between the old city and the archeological park. To Catania (1½ hr., L4400), Taormina (2 hr., L6900), Messina (3 hr., L9300), and Palermo (5 hr., L15,600).

Buses: SAIS buses leave from via Trieste, 28 (tel. 667 10), in Ortigia. To Catania (8 per day, 1½ hr., L4100), Palermo (4 per day, 4 hr., L15,000), and Enna (at 1pm, 3 hr., L9800). **AST** buses leave from p. delle Poste in front of the post office (tel. 656 89). To Catania (15 per day, L4100), Noto (12 per day, 45 min., L2400), and Piazza Amerina (at 5:25am, 3 hr., L5800). **City buses** cost L600.

Hospital: via Testaferrata (tel. 685 55). Late-night *Guardia Medica,* tel. 44 24 35.

Police: Carabinieri, via S. Sebastiano (tel. 21 21 21).

Accommodations and Camping

Albergo per la Gioventù, via Epipoli, 45 (tel. 71 11 18), near the Castello Eurialo about 8km from Syracuse. Take bus #9, 10, or 11 from the Temple of Apollo or Foro Siracusano, the park on corso Umberto, to Belvedere. L10,000. Showers L1000. Breakfast L4000. Lunch or dinner L15,000.

Hotel Centrale, corso Umberto, 141 (tel. 605 28). Walk to the left of the train station, and make the 1st right. Firm beds in tidy, airy rooms. Singles L12,500. Doubles L23,500. Showers included. Bath in the hall.

Pensione Pantheon, via Foro Siracusano, 22 (tel. 229 85), off corso Umberto. Clean and cheery. Soft beds. Tiled floors sparkle. Singles L16,000, with bath L18,000. Doubles L27,000, with bath L30,000. Showers included.

Gran Bretagna, via Savoia, 21 (tel. 687 65), off L. go XXV Luglio across the bridge in Ortigia. A timeworn but charming hotel. Many of the differently-shaped rooms have a view of the sea, some with huge 19th-century frescoes as well. Singles L22,000, with bath L26,000. Doubles L38,000, with bath L45,000. Breakfast included. Showers L2000.

Pensione Bel-Sit, via Oglio, 5 (tel. 602 45). Take via Tirso off corso Gelone. Its stark, modern rooms are well maintained by an affable owner. Singles L16,000, with bath L18,000. Doubles L22,000. Showers L1000.

Camping: Agriturist (tel. 72 12 24) has sites away from the beach, 4km from Syracuse. Walk left from the train station, and take bus #34 or 35 from Foro Siracusano on corso Umberto. L3500 per person, L3700 per small tent, L5900 per large tent, L4500 per open-air camper. Take bus #34 16km farther along the coast to **Fontane Bianche** (tel. 79 03 33), which has sites near the beach. L4500 per person, L4500 per tent, L7000 per large tent, L5000 for sleep-sackers. Open April-Oct.

Food

Meals under L15,000 are a joke in Syracuse. Pizza is about the only budget option, besides the **market** on via Trento, near the Temple of Apollo. (Open Mon.-Sat. 7am-early afternoon.) For staples, try the **Supermercato Fratti Linguanti,** corso Umberto, 137, underneath the Hotel Centrale. (Open Mon.-Tues. and Thurs.-Sat. 7am-1pm and 3-8pm, Wed. 7am-1pm.)

Natoli, via G. Di Natale, 10 (tel. 607 88), on the way to the archeological park off corso Gelone. A wonderful surprise—an affordable, sit-down restaurant. Pasta L2500-3500. Succulent *calamari* L6000. Wine L2000 per liter. Cover L1500. Open Tues.-Sun. noon-2:30pm and 7-10pm.

Spaghetteria do Scugghiu, via Sciná, 11, off p. Archimede. 22 delicious types of pasta, all for L4000. Solely Syracusan crowd. Cover L1000. Open Tues.-Sun. noon-3pm and 6-11pm.

Self-Service Santuario, p. della Vittoria, 14, near the Santuario della Madonna at the end of via M. Carabelli. A tasteful cafeteria that serves restaurant-quality meals. *Lasagna* L2500, *merluzzo in barca* (cod stuffed with eggplant and sauce) L3500, and fried chicken L3500. Open daily noon-3pm.

Pizzeria Ierone, via Ierone, 32/36, off Largo Empedocle. Great *tavola calda Arancine* (L1000-4000). *Pizza Ierone* is piled with sundry seafood (L5000). Avoid the cover (L500) by ordering take-out. *Portopallo* wine L3000 per liter. Open Thurs.-Tues. noon-midnight.

Trattoria Cenalogo, via del Consiglio, 10 (tel. 650 99). From p. del Duomo, walk north down via Landolina and turn right. *Spaghetti al pomodoro* L3000, *calamari* L8000. Wine L5000 per liter. Cover L1000, service 15%. Open Thurs.-Tues. noon-2:30pm and 7-10:30pm.

Sights

The historic sights are concentrated in two areas a couple of kilometers apart: the enclosed **archeological park** and the Island of Ortigia.

Archeological Park

The larger monuments, including the Greek theater and the famous Paradise Quarry, are clustered in the park. (Open Mon.-Sat. 9am-2 hr. before sunset, Sun. 9am-1pm. Admission L2000.) The **Greek theater,** scooped out of solid rock at the beginning of the fifth century B.C.E., is the largest known Greek theater in existence. The *cavea,* or auditorium, originally had 59 rows of seats (now 42) in nine wedges, seating 15,000 people. The three divisions of the theater are still visible: the *cavea,* the semi-circular orchestra pit, and the rectangular stage, which had a two-story permanent set with niches and colonnades. Halfway up the *cavea,* around an ambulatory, inscriptions in large Greek letters show the names of persons or gods to whom wedges of seats were dedicated.

The most refreshing part of the park is the flowery area in front of the chalk cliffs, outside of the entrance to the Greek theater, known as the **Paradise Quarry.** It consists of two large grottoes: the **Orecchio di Dionisio** (Ear of Dionysius) and the **Grotta dei Cordari** (Cordmakers' Cave). The former is an artificial grotto of cathedral-like proportions (65m long, 5-11m wide, 23m high). Its name is derived from its resemblance to a giant earlobe and its exceptional acoustics—supposedly its echo allowed Dionysius, tyrant of Syracuse, to overhear conversations of prisoners confined in a lower room. The other grotto, that of the Cordmakers, is a layered cavern supported by huge piers hewn from the rock. (Grotta dei Cordari was closed for renovation in 1988.)

Near the park is the huge **Roman amphitheater,** constructed in the second century C.E. and used for gladiatorial sports. Partially hollowed out of the hillside, the theater is not as open and airy as the Greek theater. Next to the amphitheater is the huge **Altar of Hieron II** (241-215 B.C.E.), which was used for public sacrifices. It is the largest altar known: 198m long and 23m wide. Only the lower part, cut out of the living rock, remains; the upper part, which was made of blocks, was crated off by the Spanish in the sixteenth century for building material. The long flat surface is used today as a stage for dance and theater. For ticket and program information, contact the Bozzanca Travel Agency, corso Matteotti, 88 (tel. 671 22), the EPT, or the Azienda di Turismo.

The **Catacombe di San Giovanni,** a few blocks away down viale Teocrito, are extensive catacombs dug from 315 to 360 C.E. From the main gallery radiate five secondary corridors ending in circular chapels, some painted with frescoes. Outside the catacombs are the ruins of a building said to be the first Christian church in Sicily. Below the ruins lies the fourth-century crypt of San Marciano. (Catacombs closed for restoration in 1988). The new **Museum Landolino** is a marvel of archeological museum design, located down viale Teocrito from the park. Inside are a statuette of an earth mother suckling two babes (6th century B.C.E.); the *Venere Anadiomene* ("arising from the sea"), a first-century B.C.E. Roman copy of a Greek statue; a small torso of Ephebus (500-490 B.C.E.); statues of youths (*kouri*); a small statue of the young Hercules (late 4th century B.C.E.); and a mask of a fanged Gorgon (mid-6th century B.C.E.), which once adorned the front of the Temple of Athena in Cela to ward off evil spirits. (Open Tues.-Sun. 9am-2pm. Last entrance at 1pm. Admission L2000, ages under 18 or over 60 free.)

Ortygia

The impressive ruins of two Greek temples and some charming Gothic and Renaissance churches and palaces mix among the picturesque side streets of the **Island of Ortigia.** The first ancient structure you come to when you cross the bridge to the island are the ruins of the **Temple of Apollo.** This is the oldest Doric temple in Sicily, erected around 565 B.C.E. All that remain are two columns supporting a piece of entablature and parts of the *cella* wall, showing traces of the subsequent Byzantine church.

Up corso Matteotti to the right, **piazza Archimede,** the principal square of the old city, has remnants of several interesting buildings: Palazzo Lanzo (#27), a fifteenth-century building with some original Gothic fenestration; and a beautiful Catalan fourteenth-century staircase in the courtyard (#6). Right off #8, a small passageway leads to a fantastic external view of the **Palazzo Montalto** (1397), the fanciest of the Gothic palaces in town, with triple light windows set in Arab-decorated pointed arches. From here, backtrack to p. Archimede and walk up vie Roma and Minerva to p. del Duomo. The ***duomo*** is one of the most extraordinary buildings in Italy. More than 1300 years separate the eighteenth-century baroque facade from the attached fifth-century B.C.E. Temple of Athena, each speaking eloquently of its own history, yet combining to form a harmonious medley of classical architecture.

The **Temple of Athena,** admired by Cicero, was converted to a three-aisled Christian basilica in the seventh century. The columns were embedded in a solid wall and arches were carved out of the interior walls (as at Agrigento's Temple of Concord). Twenty-six of its original 34 columns still exist, not only on the sides but also in the entrance and in the Byzantine chapel at the end of the north aisle. The sixteenth-century wooden ceiling sports an inscription quoting a papal bill issued by Leo X in 1517 to assert the importance of the church. Also of interest are a marble font from the Catacombs of San Giovanni, supported by thirteenth-century bronze lions (1st chapel on the right) and an altar that was made from the temple's entablature.

Piazza del Duomo in front of the cathedral is lined with fragrant oleander trees and surrounded by an array of extraordinary buildings. At #24, the graceful facade of the **Palazzo Benevantano** (reconstructed in 1788) conceals an elegant serpentine balcony. In the basement of the **Municipio** (1633) are the remains of an Ionic temple, which you can stumble over in an unlit room. The restrained facade with a wrought-iron balcony introduces the church at the far end of the square, **Santa Lucia alla Badia** (1695-1703; open only during church services).

From the *piazza,* a walk down via Picherale will bring you to the ancient **Fontana Aretusa.** According to legend, the nymph Arethusa was changed into this fountain by the goddess Diana when she escaped through a tunnel from her admirer Alpheus, who was then changed into the river that feeds the fountain. (If you throw a wooden cup into the Alpheus River in Greece, it will supposedly emerge in this spring, since the waters of the two are connected through the tunnel.) Unfortunately, the fountain has lost its former grandeur. Steps lead to the **Foro Italico,** a treelined walk along the harbor.

The **Museo Nazionale di Palazzo Bellomo,** left on via Capodieci, is an engaging museum with miniature courtyards and fountains that connect to small rooms housing painting and sculpture. The masterpiece of the collection is an *Annunciation* by Antonello da Messina (1474). (Open daily 9am-1pm.)

Entertainment

During even-numbered years, **Greek classical drama** is performed in the spectacular setting of the Greek Theater during May and June. The cheapest seats cost L8000 and are available at the EPT office. July and August bring a full season of music and theater to **Ara di Ierone II,** from reggae to classical ballet. (Tickets L5000 and L10,000.) For summer culture, though, there are more varied and higher-quality selections up the coast in Catania and Taormino.

Beachcombers can bus the 18km from Syracuse to **Fontane Bianche** (bus #34, L1000), an endless, silken beach touristed by jet-setters. A smaller, less spectacular beach, more popular with the local folk, is **Arenella,** 8km from the city (bus #35, L500). To play in waters of a different sort, take a daytrip to the **Fiume** and **Fonte Ciane,** home of the world's only major papyrus groves outside of Egypt. Take AST bus #21 or 22 from in front of the post office to the Fiume Ciane bridge (15 min., L600; tell the driver where you want to go); then walk along the path up to the source.

The cafes on Ortigia stay open late and are fun to loiter in, especially along Foro V. Emanuele II. Join John Travolta wanna-bes at **Il Trabochetto,** via delle Vecchio Carceri, near p. Duomo (L10,000), or at the **Fontane Bianche,** via Mazzarò in the namesake city.

Near Syracuse: Noto

After being completely destroyed by an earthquake in 1693, Noto, 32km southwest of Syracuse, was rebuilt in baroque opulence. Golden palaces and churches, some set behind monumental staircases and others behind tropical gardens, glisten along **corso Vittorio Emanuele.** The Spanish **Palazzo Nicolaci,** on via Nicolaci, is rimmed by convoluted balcony gratings. The **APT** ofice, p. XVI Maggio (tel. 83 67 44), on corso V. Emanuele, provides a free map of the most beautiful buildings. (Open daily April-Oct. 9am-8pm; Nov.-March 8am-2pm and 4-6pm. English spoken.) **Trattoria del Carmine,** via Ducezio, 9 (tel. 83 87 05), on the first street off via S. La Rosa from p. XXVI Maggio, serves homecooked *tagliatelle capricciosa* (L3000) and *ravioli con la ricotta* (L3500). Full meals run L12,000-14,000. (Open Tues.-Sun. noon-3pm and 7-11pm.) Or try Spanish *paella* (L8000) at the more spacious **Trattoria il Giglio,** p. Municipio, 8/10 (tel. 83 86 40), near the *duomo.* Spaghetti with fish sauce is L4000, and wine is only L2000 per liter. Cover is L1000. (Open in summer daily noon-4pm and 7pm-midnight; in winter noon-4pm and 6-10pm.)

Spend an entire day in Noto if you can. SAIS and AST **buses** leave from Syracuse from 4:15am to 7:50pm (25 per day, L2400), and the last bus back leaves at 9:10pm. Noto can also be reached by the local train for Modica, which departs every hour from the central train station (L1800), but it's a 20-minute uphill walk into town from the station. Noto's one hotel, **Hotel Stella,** via F. Maiore, 40 (tel. 83 56 95), will put you up in singles for L13,000, doubles for L26,000, with bath L28,000. Showers are L2000.

Catania

It takes character for a town to name its main artery after a volcano that decimated it several times. But that's Catania: brash, optimistic, and energetic. Though the city is ancient, its present appearance dates from the time following the 1692 earthquake, when it was rebuilt on a regular plan of straight lines and embellished with sumptuous baroque buildings by the architect G. B. Vaccarini.

Orientation and Practical Information

Catania lies between Messina and Syracuse on Sicily's eastern coast. The main street, **via Etnea,** runs north from piazza del Duomo to piazza Gioeni, but there is little of interest beyond piazza Cavour. From the train station walk inland past corso Martiri della Libertà to **corso Sicilia,** bursting with banks. Buses arrive in **piazza Bellini,** off via Vittorio Emanuele; to get to the *duomo,* walk back to via V. Emanuele and take a right.

Ferries leave Catonia's port for Naples (Thurs. at 8:30pm), Reggio di Calabria (Tues., Fri., and Sun. at 8:30am), and Malta (Mon., Wed., and Sat. at 8:45am). **Tirrenia** has an office at p. Grenoble, 26 (tel. 3163 94), but the cheapest fares to Malta are at **Gozo Channel** (one-way L48,000, round-trip L88,000), whose office is at via

Anzalone, 7 (tel. 31 06 29), one flight up. (Open Mon.-Fri. 9am-12:30pm and 3-6pm, Sat. 9am-1pm.) Catania's office for the new catamaran to Malta is located in the American Express office. (See Malta Getting There.)

APT: largo Paisiello, 5 (tel. 31 21 24), off via Etnea near the post office. Open Mon.-Fri. 8:30am-1:30pm , Sat. 8:30am-1:30pm. Also at the **airport** (tel. 53 18 01). Open Mon.-Fri. 8am-2pm and 3-9pm.

CTS: viale Regina Margherita, 4/C (tel. 43 90 90). Student travel information. Open Mon.-Fri. 9am-1pm and 4-7:30pm, Sat. 9:30am-12:30pm.

American Express: L. Duca and Co. Viaggi, via Etnea, 65 (tel. 31 61 55). Book catamaran tickets to Malta here. Open Mon.-Fri. 9am-1pm and 4:30-8pm, Sat. 9am-noon.

Post Office: via Etnea, across from the Villa Bellini Gardens. Open Mon.-Sat. 8:15am-7:40pm. **Postal code:** 95100.

Telephones: SIP, via S. Euplio, 122. Take via Argentina off via Etnea to the Villa Bellini Gardens. Open daily 8am-9pm. At other times, via Antonio Longo, 56. **ASST,** p. Papa Giovanni XXII, 12, across from the train station. Open Mon.-Sat. 8am-8:30pm. **Telephone code:** 095.

Airport: Fontanarossa, Tel. 34 16 15. Take bus #24. Flights to **Rome** (7 per day, L154,500), **Milan** (5 per day, L209,500), **Genoa** (3 per day, L209,500), **Naples** (1 per day at 8:40pm, L117,000), and **Torino** (7 per day, L209,500). **Alitalia,** corso Sicilia, 115 (tel. 32 75 55). Open Mon.-Fri. 8:30am-7pm, Sat. 9am-5pm. Also two flights weekly to **Malta** (Fri. at 7:30pm and Mon. at 2:30pm, L170,000) with **Air Malta,** via Ventimiglia, 84 (tel. 32 51 83).

Train Station: p. Papa Giovanni XXII (tel. 53 16 25). To get to via Etnea from the station, take corso Martiri della Liberta to corso Sicilia. Hourly departures to Syracuse (L4400) and Messina (L4700). Also to Enna (9 per day, L4400), Agrigento (4 per day, L9800), and Palermo (3 per day, L12,200).

Bus Terminal: p. Teatro Massimo. From the *duomo,* head toward the water, and turn left off via Vittorio Emanuele II. **SAIS** (tel. 31 69 42; open 6am-9pm) runs to Messina (15 per day, 1½ hr., L6600), Taormina (13 per day, 1½ hr., L3400), Syracuse (8 per day, 1½ hr., L4000), Enna (7 per day, 1¼ hr., L6300), Palermo (4 per day, 3 hr., L12,700), and Agrigento (4 per day, 3 hr., L12,300). **AST,** p. Teatro Massimo (tel. 34 80 83; open 5am-8:30pm) offers more frequent service to Syracuse (14 per day, 1½ hr., L4000). **ETNA** will take you from the train station to p. Armerina in Enna (2 hr., L5600). All bus services are sharply reduced on Sun.

City Buses: From via Etnea, headed south, buses #29, 33, and 36 to the central train station; bus #24 to the airport; and bus #27 or D to the beach. Tickets L600, L750 per 2 hr., L1000 per 9 hr.

Port Information: Tel. 31 63 94 or 53 11 34.

Late-Night Pharmacy: Crocerossa, via Etnea, 274 (tel. 31 70 53).

Hospital: Garibaldi, p. S.M. de Gesù (tel. 33 36 17). Late-night medical **emergency:** Tel. 37 71 22.

Police: Carabinieri, Tel. 112.

Accommodations

Catania has a number of inexpensive *pensioni.* Unfortunately, many of them house long-term residents and are full in summer.

Peloro, via Paterno, 12 (tel. 32 64 90), off p. Stesicoro where corso Sicilia and via Etnea intersect. Neat rooms, though the halls are less so. Singles L7000. Doubles L12,000. Showers L2500.

Hotel Savona, via V. Emanuele, 210 (tel. 32 69 82), near p. del Duomo. The owner is courteous, the rooms large and clean, and the central location makes this the best choice for women travelers. Singles L15,000, with bath L24,900. Doubles L26,900, with bath L39,800. Showers included.

Pensione Corona, via Crociferi, 81 (tel. 32 77 08), 3 blocks west of and parallel to via Etnea. No sign outside—ring the buzzer. Terrific elderly woman in charge offers clean homey rooms.

Singles L8000. Doubles L15,000, with hot shower L20,000. Popular year-round. Call a week in advance.

Pensione Gresi, via Pacini, 28 (tel. 32 27 09), off via Etnea near Villa Bellini. Don't let the charred doors on the 1st floor discourage you; the *pensione* on the 3rd floor is spotless. Pleasant rooms. Predominantly male clientele. Singles L13,000. Doubles L24,000, with bath L28,000.

Holland International, the last building on the north side of via V. Emanuele II at the water. Walk into the courtyard and follow the signs. Some magnificent rooms with views of the harbor. Sumptuous lounge. L15,000 per person. Shower included.

Pensione Continental, p. Trento, 6 (tel. 44 77 86), off viale XX Settembre 200m north of the Villa Bellini Gardens. In a safe part of town, but in a dismal building. Clean rooms. Singles L12,000. Doubles L22,000. Hot shower L3000.

Camping: Villagio Turistico Internazionale (Catania Plaja), at lungomare Kennedy, 47 (tel. 34 08 80). Luxurious, with stove, refrigerator, and other niceties. L3650-4850 per person, L3850-5150 per small tent, L6200-8250 per large tent. 2-bed bungalows L40,800-54,400. Rates are the same at the neighboring **Europeo,** lungomare Kennedy, 91 (tel. 59 10 26). Take bus #24, 27, or D south from via Etnea.

Food

Don't leave Catania without trying the spaghetti named after Catanese composer Vincenzo Bellini's famous melody, the *Norma.* Topped with tomato sauce, eggplant, and salted ricotta cheese, it is a symphony for the tastebuds. For a peek at the crazy ways of the Catanese, go to the vivacious **fish market** south and west of p. del Duomo, and the **produce market** off via Umberto I and via Garibaldi. (Markets open Mon.-Sat. 7am-1pm.)

Pizzeria Mungibeedu, via Corrodeni, 37, off via Umberto I east of via Etnea. Delicious pizza cooked in the blazing, wood-burning stove L3500-5000. Open Sat.-Thurs. noon-3pm and 7pm-midnight.

Trattoria La Paglia, via Pardo, 23 (tel. 34 68 38), behind p. del Duomo in the middle of the fish market. Catch of the day, *spaghetti marinara,* vegetable, fruit, and wine L12,000. *Pesce spada* (swordfish) is a delicacy. Open Mon.-Sat. noon-11pm.

Ristorante Rapido, via Corridoni, 17, down the street from Mungibeedu. Speedy service, super food—the choice of Catanians. Complete lunch or dinner L9000. Try the *rigatoni alla rapido* (with meat, eggplant, and mozzarella) L3000 or the *mista di pesce arrosta* (mixed roasted fish) L4000. Wine L2000 per liter. Cover L1000, if you don't have the menù. Open Mon.-Sat. 12:30-3:30pm and 6:30-10:30pm.

Gastronomy C. Conte, via Etnea, 158. Decorated with brass, marble, and mirrors. A thoroughly international hole-in-the-wall. *Menù* L10,000. *Pizzette* and other *tavola calda* snacks L1200-1400. Counters only, so come early. Also take-out service. Open Mon.-Sat. 11:30am-9pm.

Sights

At the center of Catania's **piazza del Duomo,** Vaccarini's lava-built **Fontana dell' Elefante** (Elephant Fountain, 1736) supports an Egyptian obelisk, once a turning post from a Roman circus. Residents pledge that visitors may attain citizenship by smooching the elephant's massive tush, but the altitude of the behemoth's rear precludes any such aspirations. (Those clever Catanians.) Stand behind the fountain on the far end of the square for a good view of the **cathedral,** introduced by an open space at its side, which allows the full play of baroque regalia. The other buildings on the square (the 18th-century Palazzo Municipio on the left, the former Seminario dei Chierici on the right) incorporate an elegant white-stripe motif that contrasts with the facade. Vaccarini rebuilt the eleventh-century structure after the 1693 earthquake. Still visible from via V. Emanuele, 159, are parts of the old medieval lava stone apses. The lower half of the handsome facade is enhanced by columns taken from the nearby Roman theater.

The church interior, now with a baroque barrel-vaulted nave and domed side aisles, once looked quite different, as 1950s restoration work revealed. Stumps of the old columns were found as well as the tall pointed arches of the original three apses. The two transept chapels have exquisitely paneled Renaissance frames (1545). One of them, the Norman **Capella della Madonna** (right), preserves a beautiful Roman sarcophagus and a fifteenth-century statue of the Virgin. Back in the main altar, Catania's patron Saint Agata is depicted amongst the wooden choir stalls performing various feats (1588). Before venturing back onto the streets, look up into the sacristy for a seventeenth-century fresco depicting the 1669 destruction of Catania by lava flowing from Etna. (Cathedral open daily 8am-noon and 5-6:30pm.)

Via Crociferi, which runs 3 blocks west of and parallel to via Etnea from p. del Duomo to Villa Bellini, is packed with churches (6 on 2 streets).

Via Gesuiti, which runs off of via Crociferi at the church with an octagonal tower, climbs a hill to the **Church of San Niccolò,** the largest and most frightening in Sicily. A giant unfinished facade with amputated columns and black protuberances encloses a cavernous interior. In the chancel is the empty shell of a once sumptuous organ and the tomb of the man who built it. From the dome (sometimes open), there's a magnificent view of the city and the slopes of Etna. (Church open 8am-2pm.) Next to the church is a former **convent** (partially in restoration), one of the largest in Europe, with ornate windows and balconies. One of the two courts encloses a beautiful garden, but it's easy to miss the entrance (through an ordinary doorway), so ask where it is. Along sloping via V. Emanuele on the way to via Etnea, you pass the remains of two **Roman theaters,** whose marble was covered with lava in the 1669 eruption.

A stroll up via Etnea will reward you with several fine baroque sights. Two seventeenth-century buildings enclose **piazza dell' Università,** just north of p. Duomo. Both by Vaccarini, the **Palazzo San Giuliano** is on the right and the **Palazzo dell' Università,** with an animated nineteenth-century facade, is opposite. Next comes the vibrant **Collegiata** (1768), once a college for priests, which contrasts with the more restrained nearby **Church of San Michele.** The church organ once knew the hands of Catania's native son, the composer Bellini, whose namesake park is farther up via Etnea. **Villa Bellini** spans Mt. Etna and provides refuge from Catania's opulence and squalor. Picnicking is especially recommended on the sylvan northern side.

For insight into the man who first composed at age six, go to the **Museo Belliniano,** p. Francesco d'Assisi, west of p. del Duomo off v. Emanuele II. This little shrine of memorabilia rests within the composer's birthplace. (Open daily 9am-1:30pm. Free.)

To the south is **Castello Ursino,** the city's only medieval building not swept away by lava or crumbled by the earth's shaking. Its thirteenth-century interior will remain closed for restoration until after 1990.

Entertainment

The **Teatro Bellini** (tel. 31 20 20) opened in 1890 with a performance of the composer's opera *Norma,* and is now the city's principal theater for opera and concerts. The four-month opera season begins in the middle of January, following the three-month symphonic season. The box office is open from 6 to 8pm on performance nights, and you can usually leave your passport at the ticket window if you just want to peek inside. From July to September, the city and province host performances as part of the **Catania Musica Estate,** held at Ente Fiera (take buses #27 or D from p. del Duomo, 20 min., L600). Some events are free, others cost L5000. Schedules are plastered about town.

For less sophisticated summer fun, try **La Plaja,** a crowded silken beach (take bus #27). Farther away from the industry of Catania's port, **La Scogliera,** ½ hr. away by bus #34 from p. Duomo, is a clear bathing area beside igneous cliffs near the equally overbuilt towns of Ognina and San Giovanni Li Cuti.

Catania's most important religious festival is the **Festa della Patrona Sant' Agata** (Feb. 3-5), when wooden candles (5m high, engraved, and painted) are paraded around the city.

Near Catania

A day on the slopes of **Mount Etna** is the apex of any Sicilian jaunt. One of the world's major active volcanoes, and the largest and highest in Europe, Etna awes and humbles. Grimacing and spitting from gaseous craters, Etna's face is pock-marked with fissures and patches of yellow sulphur, but the view from its head—a cartographer's panorama of Sicily—is perfectly healthy.

The Greek poet Hesiod thought Etna to be the home of Typhon, the last monster conceived by Earth to fight the gods before the dawn of the human race. Barren women worshiped Venus on its slopes, expecting less-than-immaculate conception from the molten depths.

The trains of **Ferrovia Circumetnea** circumnavigate the volcano's base, stopping at interesting towns and natural volcanic phenomena. The train station is located at **Stazione Borgo,** via Caronda, 352/A (tel. 54 11 11), off viale Leonardo da Vinci. On Sundays in July and on Sundays and Thursdays in August and September, the *giro turistico* (L14,000, ages under 10 L7000) is good for a round-trip tour from Stazione Borgo beginning at 8:55am; reserve at corso delle Province, 13 (tel. 37 48 42). An **AST** bus leaves from in front of the central train station at 8am for Sapienza and returns at 5pm (round-trip L3800). The *funivia* (cable car) is indefinitely out of service following a minor eruption that sent molten lava down the pathway of the cable's towers and destroyed a few. From Sapienza you can hike to the top of Etna in about four hours or take a jeep from Sapienza's bus stop (L28,000 per person) to points that are only a 30-minute walk from the top.

Taormina

Taormina perches on a high terrace overlooking the sea and coastline, with Etna as a backdrop. The city has long hosted chic vacationers—in summer its winding streets are packed with beautiful people watching other beautiful people and storekeepers who know phrases in German, French, and English. Still, Taormina's magnificent setting and Greek Theatre, its proximity to various beaches, and its firm reputation as the eastern center of Sicilian culture make it a fascinating trip. Space is tight from July to September, so reserve in advance or make it a daytrip from Catania.

Orientation and Practical Information

Taormina is a 1½-hour bus ride from either Messina (L3200) or Catania (L3400). It is much less convenient to travel by train on the Messina-Syracuse line, since the train station lies on the coast 1½km below the city. Buses run from the train station every 15 to 45 minutes until 9:15pm (L1200).

Reservations for the catamaran to Malta can be made at **Naxos Travel Service,** via Naxos, 237 (tel. 516 08), in Giardini Naxos, or at their office in Taormina at corso Umberto, 206 (tel. 237 72). (Open daily 9am-1pm and 5-8pm; see Malta Getting There.)

Corso Umberto I, the main drag, runs the length of the town from gate to gate and is lined with expensive boutiques and tacky tourist shops. Innumerable side streets, for the most part stepped, lead off the *corso* into a labyrinth of houses. **Via Bagnoli Croci** (Sue Balluo Bagnoli's ancestors lived here) heads downhill to the public gardens, while via Circonvallazione, above corso Umberto, has a stepped path up to the **Castel Taormina.** Buses stop slightly below town on **via Pirandello.**

Azienda di Turismo: p. Santa Caterina (tel. 232 43), off corso Umberto at p. V. Emanuele in Palazzo Corvaia. Helpful and well organized. Will help with your accommodations search (difficult in Aug.). English spoken. A **ticket office** in the Azienda sells tickets to the many artistic events in summer; be sure to pick up a program. Open Mon.-Sat. 8am-1:30pm and 3-7:30pm.

Post Office: p. S. Antonio, at the end of corso Umberto near the hospital. Fermo Posta. Open Mon.-Sat. 8:10am-6:30pm; last day of the month closes at noon. **Postal code:** 98039.

Telephones: SIP, via San Pancrazio, 6, at the top of via Pirandello in the Avis office. Open Mon.-Sat. 8am-12:30pm and 4:30-8pm, Sun. 9am-12:30pm. **Telephone code:** 0942.

Buses: SAIS Tel. (0942) 234 94. To Mt. Etna. Departs to "Etna South" April-Oct. Tues., Thurs., and Sat. at 8am, returning at 4pm. Departs to "Etna North" at 3pm, returning at noon the following day. Round-trip L19,000. Call to reserve.

Car Rental: Avis, via San Pancrazio, 6 (tel. 230 41). Open Mon.-Sat. 8:30am-12:30pm and 4:30-8:30pm, Sun. 9:30am-12:30pm.

Moped Rental: California, via Bagnoli Croce, 86 (tel. 237 69). Scooters L18,000 per day, L110,000 per week. Vespa 2-seaters L26,000 per day, L180,000 per week. Must be 16. Open daily 9am-1pm and 4-8pm.

English Language Bookstore: Libreria Interpress, corso Umberto, 37 (tel. 249 89). Reams of new and secondhand paperbacks around L12,000.

Hospital: Ospedale Civico San Vincenzo, p. San Vincenzo (tel. 533 10).

Medical Emergency: Tel. 231 49.

Police: Carabinieri, Tel. 112.

Accommodations and Camping

Don't bother to come to Taormina in August without reservations unless you're willing to sleep illegally in the street. The following *pensioni* usually have vacancies in the off-season, but most will not accept phone reservations from late June to September. If you are determined to stay overnight in summer, go to the tourist office as early as possible. The staff will greet your request incredulously but will usually locate a room.

Villa Pompei, via Bagnoli Croci, 88 (tel. 238 12), across from the public gardens. You can smell the flowers from the rooms. Run by a sweet, caring woman. Rooms L15,000 per person. Bath included. Reservations for June-Sept. required 1 month in advance with deposit. Breakfast L5000.

Pensione Svizzera, via Pirandello, 26 (tel. 237 90). Turn right at the eastern end of corso Umberto. Between the bus station and the town center. A bit of a budget-buster, but the rose and ivy-colored building looks out over the gorgeous coastline. Spotless rooms. Polite management. Singles L25,000. Doubles L42,000. Bath and breakfast included. Open March-Nov.

Pensione Columbia, via Iallia Bassia, 11 (tel. 234 23), across from Grazia. Spotless rooms and fresh-smelling bathrooms, with one quad at a discount. Single L17,400. Doubles L32,000, with bath L35,000. Breakfast L5000. July-Aug. singles L22,000; doubles 42,000, with bath L44,000, breakfast obligatory. Reserve for summer 1 month in advance. Open irregularly in winter.

Il Leone, via Bagnoli Croci, 127 (tel. 238 78), down the street from the gardens. This modest *pensione* hides inside the beautiful, deluxe-hotel carnival. June-Sept. singles L15,000, with bath L18,000; doubles L30,000, with bath L36,000. Stay a month and the price drops to L10,000 per day. Shower and breakfast included.

Camping: Campeggio San Leo (tel. 246 58), on the cape. L2800 per person, L2100 per small tent, L4000 per large tent. **Eurocamping Marmaruca** (tel. 366 76), 5km from Taormina in the Letojanni area. L4000 per person and L3000 per tent. Both sites reached by taking a SAIS bus toward Messina (L1100).

Food

Cheap eateries are few and far between in Taormina. Even buying bread, cheese, and fruit can be expensive unless you try the **Standa** supermarket on via Apollo Arcageta, at the end of corso Umberto 1 block up from the post office. (Open July-

Aug. Mon.-Sat. 8:30am-1pm and 5-9pm, Sept.-June Mon.-Sat. 8:30am-1pm and 4:30-8:30pm). Weekday mornings there is a small **market** at via Cappuccini, which runs off via C. Patrizio at the beginning of corso Umberto.

Manitta Francesco, via Cappuccini, 8 (tel. 212 10). Family-run *pizzeria* with delicious 'za (L1000-1500 per *etto*). Open Mon.-Sat. 9am-8pm.

U Lantirnaru, via Apollo Arcageta, 14 (tel. 245 65), at the end of corso Umberto. Watch the chickens spinning in their huge wood-burning oven. Half a big bird, a large plate of French fries, bread, and a beer or soda for L9000, without the fries L7000. Open Mon. and Wed.-Sat. 9am-11pm, Sun. 9am-2pm.

Pace, p. San Pancrazio, 3 (tel. 231 84), at the end of via Pirandello. Outdoor tables, plenty of company, and a great location. You can smell the pizza for miles (L4500-7500). *Maccheroni alla cisterna* (with basil, mushrooms, and garlic) L5000. *Scallopine alla Marsala* L8000. Wine L5000 per liter. Pizza slices to go L1500. Open Wed.-Mon. noon-3pm and 7-11:30pm.

Piccolo Mondo, p. San Pancrazio, 18 (tel. 243 22), across from Pace. Its long and narrow dining hall belongs in a *piccolo mondo* (small world), but food is on a grand scale. *Pennette arrabbiante* (a spicy dish with peppers) L4500. *Piazza del piccolo mondo* (salmon, capers, olives, and onions) L7500. Other pizzas L4000-7000. Wine L6000 per liter. Open daily noon-3pm and 6pm-midnight.

Ristorante Grotta Azzurra, via Bagnoli Croci, 2 (tel. 241 63), near the public gardens. Decorations on the walls and ceilings seem to descend upon you. *Tagliatelle alla bolognese* (thick noodles, meat, and tomato sauce) L4500. *Cannelloni alla siciliana* L5000. Meat dishes L8500. Wine L7000 per liter. Open daily noon-3pm and 7-11:30pm.

Sights

Goethe thought the **Greek Theater** in Taormina commanded one of the most beautiful views in the world. Constructed in the third century B.C.E., it was rebuilt by the Romans in the second century C.E. (Open daily 9am-1 hr. before sunset. Admission L2000, ages under 18 and over 60 free.)

Just a few blocks away at the end of corso Umberto is the **Roman Odeon,** partly covered by the Church of Santa Caterina next door. At the other end of corso Umberto lies the thirteenth-century ***duomo,*** rebuilt during the Renaissance. (Open 8am-6pm.) The Gothic interior shelters some fair paintings by Messinese artists and a fine alabaster statue of the Virgin. Crowning the rock pinnacle that towers above Taormina, the ***castello*** is enjoyed most easily from a distance; the hike up the sheer rock cliffs to the top is a grueling affair.

The **public garden,** on via Croce, offers a secluded spot for appreciating Taormina's marvelous scenery and the view of Etna. Each olive tree along the promenade bears the name of a Taorminian soldier lost in World War I.

Entertainment

Throughout the summer, the city hosts **Taormina Arte,** an international festival of theater, music, and film, which goes on from July through September. Most performances are in the Greek theater and in the public gardens. (Tickets L10,000 and L20,000. Film festival seats L5000 and L10,000. For information call 211 42 or visit the outdoor offices in p. Vittorio Emanuele.) Taormina is home to a number of overpriced, uneventful discotheques. One worthwhile nightspot is **Tout Va,** via Pirandello, 70 (tel. 238 24), an open-air club with vistas, although it's a tiring half-hour trek from town. (Open in summer daily 10pm-3:30am. Cover with 1st drink L10,000.) **Le Perroquet** (tel. 248 08), on via Roma and p. S. Domenico de Guzman, is a popular gay club. (Open July 15-Sept. 15 daily. Cover L15,000.) Travel by car or *motorino* down to Naxos for more hopping discos. At the end of May, Taormina welcomes the **Raduno del Costume e del Carretto Siciliano,** a traditional parade of brightly-colored costumes and horse-drawn carriages.

Near Taormina

Beachniks should descend to the **Isola Bella** in sybaritic preparation for the evening *passeggiata.* This tiny island, last year proclaimed a national nature preserve, is accessible by a short hitch or the *funivia* (cable car) from via Pirandello in Taormina (every 15 min.; L1000, after 9pm L1500; last car up at 2am). Huge lines form for the return trip at "rush hour" from 5 to 7pm.

Up the coast is the less exotic but more silken **Lido Mazarrò,** where hotels and bars have monopolized every grain of sand.

Nearby **Giardini Naxos** was the site of the first Greek colony in Sicily (725 B.C.E.). Recent excavations in the **archeological park** have revealed the outlines of the city walls, built with huge irregular blocks of solidified lava. (Open Mon.-Sat. 9am-1 hr. before sunset, Sun. 9am-1pm. Free.) A long sandy beach, not entirely taken over by hotels, makes the city an appealing alternative to Lido Mazarrò. **Ristorante Fratelli Marano** serves tasty *spaghetti alle melanzane* (with eggplant) for L3500, but their main attraction is the pizza (L3000-L6500). (Open daily noon-3pm and 7pm-midnight.) SAIS buses leave from Taormina's bus terminal every 15 to 45 minutes (L1200, round-trip L2000).

Trips around **Mount Etna** are easily arranged from Taormina. (See Practical Information and Near Catania.)

Enna

Soaring above the poorest and only landlocked province in Sicily, Enna is an inviting, unblemished town that offers a peek into the interior and its residents. With views of Mt. Etna and the surrounding mountain ranges, it is the highest provincial capital in Italy.

Enna is known as the "navel of Sicily" since it is located smack-dab in the center; consequently, it was imbued with mythic significance in antiquity as the base of the cult of Demeter, goddess of the earth and fecundity.

Throughout its history, the town has also been a popular military base, passing from the hands of its original Sikan inhabitants to Greek, Roman, Arab, Norman, Lombard, and Bourbon rule. The only vestiges of this past are a huge medieval castle, a Lombard tower, and a curiously remodeled thirteenth-century cathedral.

Orientation and Practical Information

Enna is easily accessible by bus from Palermo (2 hr., L9000) or Catania (1¼ hr., L7000); coming up from the south requires transfers at either Caltanissetta or Gela (Mon.-Sat. 5 per day, 1 hr., L3500). Buses leave Catania from p. Bellini and Palermo from via P. Balsamo, 16. Train service from both cities is cheaper, but don't count on arriving in even double the time quoted by the railway. The train station is 5km from town and a bus runs to the terminal on viale Diaz (every 2 hr., L900). To get to the center from the train station, turn right onto corso Sicilia, and walk down to where via S. Agata branches off to the right. This runs directly into **via Roma,** Enna's main strip, which leads up to the **Castello di Lombardia** on the left, and down through the residential section of town to the right.

EPT: p. Garibaldi, 1 (tel. 211 84). Take via de Benedetto off via Roma at the yellow EPT sign. Savvy but harried staff offers loads of brochures, including a good map of Enna with a very detailed map of Sicily and the surrounding islands on the reverse. Open Mon.-Sat. 8:30am-1:30pm. If these times aren't convenient, try the **Azienda di Turismo,** p. N. Colajanni (tel. 261 19), farther up via Roma. Open Mon.-Fri. 4:30-6:30pm.

Post Office: via A. Volta, 1. Fermo Posta. Open Mon.-Sat. 8am-7:30pm. **Postal code:** 94100.

Telephones: (SIP), p. Umberto. Open daily 8am-8pm. At other times, try **Albergo Sicilia,** p. N. Colajanni. **Telephone code:** 0935.

Bus station: SAIS, viale Diaz (tel. 219 02), outside the city center. Open daily 6am-9:30pm.

Hospital: Ospedale Umberto I, Tel. 451 11; at night and on Sun. 454 09.

Police: Carabinieri, Tel. 217 77.

Accommodations

Few tourists means an undeveloped budget hotel scene, but the **Belvedere** is a newly reopened gem. If there is zilch to be found in town, take a SAIS bus to the town of **Pergusa** (Mon.-Sat. 7am-2pm, 6 per day, L700), a lakeside retreat 7km from Enna. Here you will find **La Pergola** (tel. 423 33), on the lake, and **Miralago** (tel. 362 72), both of which charge L15,800 for singles and L25,500 for doubles—all with bath. Undoubtedly the best option is pitching a tent at **Camping La Pineta,** a free campsite with cooking and bath facilities. To get to this wooded site from Pergusa's bus stop, take a right on the Autodromo di Pergusa.

Hotel Belvedere, F. Crispi (tel. 210 20). Turn left off via Roma. A reincarnation of one of Enna's grand hotels, at a fraction of the cost. Fastidiously kept rooms with stupendous views of the valley. Singles L19,000, with bath L26,400. Doubles L32,300, with bath L42,900. Showers included.

Allogio, via Trieste, 95 (tel. 217 62), off via Diaz. Turn left from the bus terminal. 4 tiny rooms without showers, but only L8000 per person.

Grande Albergo Sicilia, p. N. Colajanni, 5 (tel. 216 44), right on via Roma behind the EPT sign. Posh. Come here when there's no vacant value to be found. Singles with bath L27,500. Doubles with bath L44,600.

Food

Enna specializes in *pasta con i finochetti* (pasta with tomatoes and fresh fennel) and *pan di spagna* (a sweet, spongy cake). Enna's most famous product, however, is its *piacentino* cheese, sharp, spicy, and best sampled at the **market** on via Mercato S. Antonio, off via Roma at p. Umberto I. (Open Mon.-Sat. 6am-2pm.) **Centro Formaggi** at via Mercato S. Antonio, 33, is the other cheese connection. The cheapest prices are at **Max Market Romano,** located behind the bus station. (Open Mon.-Fri. 8am-1:30pm and 4-8pm, Sat. 8am-8:30pm.)

Ristorante Familiare, via S. Agata, 123 (tel. 236 61), in front of the Chiesa di S. Francesco. Ample portions of delicious chows prepared by one of the friendliest chefs in Sicily. If you don't speak Italian he'll take you to the kitchen for a look at your options. Pastas L3000, main dishes L5000, and heavenly red wine L2000 per liter. Cover L1000. Open Tues.-Sun. noon-3:30pm and 6-11pm.

Da Marino, viale C. Savoca, 62 (tel. 252 88). Enna's best outdoor pizza only L3000-4500. Try their "Radio Euro," with prosciutto, basil, and artichoke (L4500). Cover L1000, service 10%. Open Wed.-Mon. noon-3:30pm and 7pm-midnight.

Pigalle, via Castagna, 1 (tel. 251 56), off Vittoria Emanuele. Where all the kool kats eat their French fries with ketchup, mayonnaise, and mushrooms (L1300). More standard is the *calzone* (ham, cheese, and tomato, L1200), to be downed with a liter mug of Tuborg beer on tap (L5000). Open Fri.-Wed. noon-3pm and 5-10pm.

Sights and Entertainment

Via Roma ascends through the old city, leading first to the **cathedral.** Founded in 1307 and renovated in the sixteenth century, it has a slender baroque facade. The polygonal transepts, the apses, and the south door date from the original medieval structure. Bring a L100 coin for the excellent recording about the cathedral's history and numerous artworks. (Open daily 9am-1pm and 5-8pm.) Behind the church, the small **Museo Alessi** displays the cathedral's treasury and some Greek and Roman artifacts and medieval paintings. (Open Tues.-Sun. 9am-1pm. Free.) The second of Enna's magnificent museums is the nearby **Museo Varisano,** on p. Mazzini across from the Duomo. Aside from changing exhibits, it houses an archeological collection dating from 3000 B.C.E. (Open daily 9am-1pm. Free.)

The **Castello di Lombardia,** at the eastern end of town, was built by Frederick II on a 5000-year-old foundation to maintain control of the center of the island. Six towers of the original 20 remian. One of its three courtyards is now used as an open-air theater. The view from the terrace of its Pisana Tower is one of the most celebrated in Sicily; on a clear day you can see majestic Mount Etna to the east, the Nebrodian Mountains and the small medieval town of Calascibetta to the north, Pizzo di Cammarata (Cammarata Peak) to the west, and Lago di Pergusa to the south. Myth has it that Pluto abducted Persephone by the shores of this meteor-impressed lake as her mother Demeter helplessly looked on. Behind the castle, at the summit of the mountain, is that same Demeter's sacred ground, the **Rocca di Cerere,** with a view of the fertile fields below. Don't miss the hilarious statue outside the castle wall of Eunous, the Syrian slave who instigated one of the greatest revolts in history against the Romans in 135 B.C.E. (Castle open 9am-1pm and 3-7pm. Free.)

The **Torre di Federico II,** an octagonal lookout with finely preserved Gothic vaulting, rises 24m at the opposite edge of the city. It is now surrounded by the city's public garden. (Garden open daily 8am-8pm.) A secret tunnel, still visible from the tower's third level, once connected the tower with the Castello di Lombardia. (Access to the tower only by permission from the gatekeeper, whose house is on the grounds of the public gardens.)

In July and August, Enna holds its **Estate Ennese,** a series of concerts and performances, including some by Italy's most popular contemporary artists, in the theater at Castello di Lombardia. (Tickets L5000-10,000.) The **Autodromo di Pergusa** (tel. 256 60) hosts international Gran Premio car races from April through September. Enna's big festival is the **Festa della Madonna,** held on July 2, marked by the incessant fire crackers and the interminable eating of *mastazzoli,* an apple cookie.

Near Enna: Piazza Armerina

Piazza Armerina is a heavenly hamlet whose golden baroque buildings rise gracefully on three knolls overlooking the Ennese countryside. It neighbors **Villa Imperiale,** a Roman country house that preserves some of the finest mosaics of the ancient world.

The villa lies 5½km southwest of town. Officially known as the Villa Romana del Casale, it was probably a hunting lodge of Maximanius Heraclius, co-emperor with Diocletian under the Principate. It was built about 300 C.E. and occupied until the Arab period. Sacked in 1160 and covered by a landslide soon after, it remained undiscovered until 1916, and full-scale excavations did not begin until 1950. Catwalks provide a bird's-eye view of most of the floors.

The **mosaics,** the largest and most intact works of their kind in the world, are noted for their sumptuous color and design. In the Corridor of the Big Game Hunt, a varied landscape of hills, trees, rocks, and villas surround hunters pursuing their game while the hunted animals themselves chase smaller prey. The Room of the Ten Maidens displays a series of scantily clad young women performing gymnastics. In the the Triclinium (the large banquet hall), a muscular Hercules stands amidst nudes of *remarkable* detail!

Unfortunately, there is no bus service to the villa, but hitching is fairly easy and vans regularly shuttle tourists to the site. The best guide to the villa, *Piazza Armerina: Town of the Mosaics,* by Ignazio Nigrelli, is available at the city tourist office. (Villa open daily 9am-1 hr. before sunset. Admission L2000.)

Piazza Armerina's narrow medieval streets are pleasantly interrupted by *piazze* filled with pine, eucalyptus, poplar, and cedar trees. In the center is **piazza Garibaldi,** with several eighteenth-century buildings. The **cathedral** (1627), at the summit of the town has an imposing baroque facade (17th to 18th centuries) and a fifteenth-century Gothic-Sicilian belfry. Inside, above the high altar, a baroque tabernacle contains a Byzantine icon of the *Madonna della Vittoria,* a gift of Pope Nicholas II. It is carried in procession during the **Feast of the Assumption** on August

15. The painted crucifix and the Madonna in the chapel to the left both date from the fifteenth century.

Piazza Armerina is a 45-minute bus ride from Enna (7 per day, L3200). Buses also run directly to Palermo, Catania, and Syracuse. To reach Ragusa on the way east or south, take a bus to the petrochemical wasteland of Gela (several per day, 1 hr., L2500; ask at least 3 bus drivers hanging out in p. Gen. Cascino for the correct times). From Gela, the best option is the train (3 per day, 2 hr., L3500).

City **tourist information** is at p. Garibaldi, 1 (tel. 68 02 01; open Mon. and Sat. 8:30am-1:30pm, Tues.-Fri. 8:30am-1:30pm and 5:30-7:30pm). The town has no inexpensive accommodations, but if you're stuck, try the **Park Hotel Paradiso** (tel. 857 00) or the **Selene** (tel. 802 54), both with singles for L27,000 and doubles for L43,900, bath included. There is also a new campsite, **Campeggio** (tel. 68 05 42), located next to the restaurant and souvenir shop that sits at the turn-off to the villa, 4km outside of the town (L3000 per person, showers extra).

Ragusa

Moving with the plodding pace of an Ingmar Bergman film and populated by an abundance of friendly old veterans who fill the *piazze,* Ragusa is an all-purpose escape. If you arrive on a weekend, the town resembles the inside of a coffin—clean, neat, and dead. During the week, this scene is revived only during business hours, and occasionally on the main street, **via Roma,** at night. The city and its older downhill neighbor, **Ragusa Ibla,** more than compensate for this lack of gusto, however, with some of the most picturesque streets and vistas on the island. Located on a valley ridge and a lower hill in the middle of a barren plateau, Ragusa and Ibla offer the dedicated street-wanderer a treasure of baroque facades, tiny homes, and peace and quiet.

Orientation and Practical Information

The train and bus stations are in p. del Popolo and p. Gramsci, respectively. To reach the city center, go left through hideously fascistic p. Libertà to the Ponte Nuovo, one of the three bridges crossing the Torrente Santa Domenica. The *ponte* runs directly into via Roma, which continues across town to its abrupt end at the edge of a moonscape. **Corso Italia,** right off via Roma, leads to the stairs to Ragusa Ibla at **Santa Maria delle Scale. AST Buses** run regularly from Syracuse's post office (Mon.-Sat. 8 per day, Sun. 8am only; 3 hr.; L5000). From Enna, take the bus to Gela (2 hr., L4600) and then the train (2 hr., L3500).

APT: via Natalelli, 131 (tel. 214 21), up one flight. Turn left off via Roma at p. Libertà. No English, no maps, but otherwise helpful. Open Mon.-Sat. 8:30am-1:30pm.

Post Office: p. Matteotti, 2 blocks down corso Italia from via Roma. Fermo Posta. Open Mon.-Sat. 8:15am-7:30pm.

Telephones: (SIP), via Maiorana, on the cityside of the middle bridge. Open Mon.-Sat. 8am-7:30pm. At other times, go to the **Hotel S. Giovanni,** on the opposite side of the bridge. **Telephone code:** 0932

AST Bus Service: p. Gramsci (tel. 212 49).

Hospital and Guardia Medica: Ospedale Civile, tel. 214 10. Nighttime and holiday emergency service tel. 239 46.

Police: Carabinieri, tel. 112.

Accommodations

Tivoli, via Gabriele d'Annunzio, 60 (tel. 248 85), behind the train station. Take a right onto via Dante, cross the tracks, and then take another right on via Archimeda. The best prices in town. Singles L15,500, with bath L22,000. Doubles L26,500, with bath L32,000. Showers included.

Mediterraneo, via Roma, 189 (tel. 219 44), on the cityside of the new bridge, above the Standa. Clean, contemporary, copious rooms. Private baths are shiny new; communal baths aren't. Singles L15,100, with bath L27,100. Doubles with bath L43,700. Triples with bath L58,800. Showers included.

S. Giovanni, via Transpontino, 3 (tel. 210 13), on the station-side of the middle bridge. A quiet, tidy hotel with great beds and a hilarious TV room. Singles L21,900. Doubles L31,200, with bath L46,000. Showers included.

Camping: Ragusa's campgrounds are at Marina, 30km to the south. Tumino buses (tel. 390 51) run regularly from p. Gramsci in Ragusa to p. Duca degli Abruzzi in Marina (½ hr., round-trip L3500). **Baja del Sole** (tel. 398 44) charges L4000 per person, L4000 per tent, L5500 per person with sleeping bag. **Villa Nifosì** (tel. 391 18) charges L500 more per person and per tent, but only L5000 for a sleeping bag-er.

Food

The prominent **Standa** *supermercato* sells cheap food Tuesday to Saturday from 9am-1pm and 4-8pm and Monday afternoon. For gourmet fare, try **La Piccola Fattoria,** via S. Anna, 99 (tel. 210 69), off via Roma to the right. (Open Mon.-Sat. 9am-noon and 5-7pm.)

Pizzeria La Grotta, via Cartia, the 2nd right off via Roma at the sign. Amazing pizzas and *calzoni* (L1200), with draft beer for only L1500. Open Wed.-Mon. 10am-3pm and 6-10pm.

Lavalle, via Risorgimento, 66 (tel. 293 41). From the station take a right onto viale Sicilia, then walk downhill past the gas station. *The* place young Ragusans recommend. Tasty dishes at bargain prices. Pasta L4500. A wide variety of pizzas L3500-5000. Open Sat.-Thurs. noon-2:30pm and 6-11pm.

Caffe Trieste, corso Italia, 78, across from the post office. Superior southern Sicilian pastries L1000-1500. Open Mon.-Sat. 8am-noon and 4-10pm, Sun. 9am-noon.

Sights and Entertainment

Ragusa and Ibla shine because of their exteriors—church interiors rarely live up to their elaborate baroque facades, and many side streets endear solely because of their quaint doorways. The upper town boasts an **Archeology Museum** that lies one floor down and in back of the Standa, with interesting artifacts from the nearby Syracusan colony of Camarina. (Open Tues.-Sat. 9am-2pm, Sun. 9am-1pm.) The **Cathedral of San Giovanni Battista,** on via Roma at corso Italia, is interesting primarily due to the old men in white shirts who gather in front. On the way down to **Santa Maria delle Scale,** note one of the few fourteenth-century structures that survived the terrible earthquake of 1693. Take two small streets off via Sta. Anna: via delle Frecce and via dei Vespri. These two lanes are lined with some of Ragusa's most charming homes.

The stairs at Santa Maria offer a stellar spread of Ragusa Ibla, crowned by a monastery and the eighteenth-century dome of **San Giorgio.** Descend under the roadway to p. Repubblica (where more senior folk congregate), and you will soon come to a dirt road that circumscribes the town, passing mysterious, abandoned *palazzi* and monasteries. At the far end of the hill, ascend the steps to **corso XXX Aprile.** From here the beautifully arranged **piazza del Duomo** and **S. Giorgio** lie to the left, while the shadey **Giardino Ibleo** is downhill to the right. Bus #3 leaves from in front of the garden on the hour and half-hour back to via Roma in Ragusa (L500). The greatest feast day is August 29, when the town celebrates the **Festival of S. Giovanni.**

If Ragusa's summertime emptiness disturbs you, visit **Marina di Ragusa**—the streets are so crowded at night that walking poses a problem. Autolinee Tumino (tel. 390 51) runs 10 buses per day to Marina (last bus there Mon.-Sat. 8:15pm, Sun. 6:15pm; last bus back Mon.-Sat. 9:30pm, Sun. 10:40pm; round-trip L3500). A complete schedule is posted in the Polleria Giarrosto in Marina's p. Duca degli Abruzzi. Located in the same *piazza* is the Marina's best ice cream, **Delle Rose,** where the scoops are so big they give you *two* cones. The best pizza on the beach is **Delfino** (tel. 302 39), located beyond p. Malta on the lungomare Andrea Doria, to the left of p. Duca. Try their filling *calzone* (L4000) for a picnic on the beach. (Open Sat.-Thurs. 11am-3pm and 6-11pm.)

For an overnight stay, try the **Hotel Miramare** (tel. 390 84), to the left along lungomare Andrea Doria. (Doubles L29,500, with bath L34,000. Showers included.) Marina also sports two campsites (see Ragusa Accomodations).

MALTA

US $1 = Lm0.35	**Lm1 = US $2.85**
CDN $1 = Lm0.29	**Lm1 = CDN $3.43**
UK £1 = Lm0.59	**Lm1 = UK £1.69**
AUS $1 = Lm0.28	**Lm1 = AUS $3.56**
NZ $1 = Lm0.23	**Lm1 = NZ $4.32**

This small land of 330,000 has a titanic history. Once Europe's earliest Copper Age civilization, it is now the continent's youngest sovereign state. Variety pervades the archipelago: There are three major islands (Malta, rural Gozo, and tiny Comino); three languages (Phonecian-derived Maltese, English, and Italian); two heated political parties (97.4% of the country voted in the last national election); and a coastline ranging from Europe's largest dry dock to its clearest waters. On Malta you can have a traditional English breakfast of sausage and pies, an American lunch of hamburger and fries, and a spicy Arabic dinner that will clear your sinuses—all at the same restaurant. Five thousand years of history catalogue a legend or conquest for every hairbreadth within Malta's 121 square miles. Back in 3800 B.C.E., neolithic farmers from Sicily erected temples for the fertility-death cult; their Copper Age kids erected a slew of temples as well, and then mysteriously vanished by 2000 B.C.E. Archeological finds of the last decade suggest that Great Britain's renowned Stonehenge civilization was in fact a scion of Malta's earliest colonizers. Not until the ninth century B.C.E. did Phoenicians waft onto the islands—the first in a string of foreign rulers including Carthaginians, Romans, and Byzantines. Blessings came ashore in 60 C.E., when the shipwrecked apostle Paul converted the archipelago to Catholicism in a matter of three proselytizing months.

Malta's Roman period left an exquisite villa for posterity, but the legacy of Arab domination (9th to 11th centuries) prevails; Arabic place-names and Islamic-influenced architecture dot the areas outside the main cities. Count Roger included the archipelago in the Norman conquest of 1090, initiating a phase of European possession that ended only in 1530, when Malta was given by King Charles V of Spain to the Knights of St. John. Although charged initially with maintenance of Europe's finest Renaissance hospitals, the knights soon found themselves at the other end of the sword, battling for the integrity of Christian Europe in 1565 against a thunderous onslaught of Turkish soldiers.

Their successful defense of Malta, led by the Grandmaster Jean Purisot de la Valette (who built his namesake town in the years after this victory), is considered by the islanders to be one of two high points in the country's history. The other came in the midst of 150 years of British domination when, in World War II, the Maltese withstood over 16,000 tons of Axis bombs to earn themselves the George Cross, England's highest civilian honor. Independence stepped over the well-worn welcome mat on September 21, 1964, but Malta now eagerly woos another form of European colonization—half a million sun-searching northerners.

Despite the hedonistic tendencies of those visitors, catholicism continues to shape Maltese life, from the plastic religious statues affixed to funky green municipal buses to the rowdy patron-saint *festas* that fill the archipelago's summer calendar. Islanders are equally emphatic about their politics; the roughly equal division of population into democratic Nationalist and socialist Labor camps makes for battle-scarred elections. The pro-tourism Nationalists ended 16 years of Socialist rule in May of 1987, and Malta is now a haven for capitalist hucksters.

Surrounded by the Mediterranean, the island of Malta lies 96km south of Sicily and 290km north of Africa. The island contains the country's major cities, including Valletta, the contemporary capital; Mdina, the historic capital; and Rabat and Mosta, the Arab centers. Neolithic ruins in Ghar Dalam, Copper Age temples in

Tarxien and Hagar Qim, and the subterranean religious complex at Paola, cut from the living rock in about 2400 B.C.E., are the island's archeological lures.

The rural island of Gozo offers the awe-inspiring Ggantija temples, numerous stalagtite-saturated caves, and the islands' cleanest, silkiest beaches. Minescule Comino attracts with its Blue Lagoon, whose pellucid waters seem illuminated by an underwater sun.

For seaside and nightime entertainment, Malta is a student's paradise. Discounts abound on anything from snorkels to parasailing and the islands' superb discotheques offer free or reduced admission several times per week.

On the main island, all major towns and villages are connected by an efficient bus system that terminates service between 9 and 11pm. Like their chums in the U.K., the Maltese drive on the left side of the road, and gasoline is 35¢ per liter.

Getting There and Getting Around

Although many Italian travel agents claim that **Tirrenia** is the only ferry company that serves Malta from Italy, **Gozo Channel** runs the same routes for less. Tirrenia, 311 Republic St. (tel. 23 22 11), in Valletta, departs from most major ports in southern Italy and Sicily. Gozo Channel (tel. 60 39 64) schedules routes only through Catania in Sicily while monopolizing transport among the Maltese islands themselves. Tickets and information for Gozo Channel are available at **EMS Travel,** 65 South St. (tel. 22 78 01), to the left off Republic St. after Valletta's City Gate.

Catania-Valletta (8½ hr.): **Gozo Channel** (to Sa Maişon). Departs July 2-Sept. 26 Thurs. and Sun. at 3pm (Lm12, round-trip Lm21); April 3-June 27 Sat. at 3pm (Lm10, round-trip Lm18); students with ID 20% discount. **Tirrenia** (to Vittorioso). Departs Tues., Fri., and Sun. at 1pm (June-Sept. Lm16.70; Oct.-May Lm13.90).

Syracuse-Valletta (7 hr.): **Tirrenia** (to Vittoriosa). Departs Tues., Fri., and Sun. at 4:30pm. (June-Sept. Lm16.7; Oct.-May Lm13.9).

Naples-Valletta (25 hr.): **Tirrenia** (to Vittoriosa). Departs Thurs. at 8:30pm (June-Sept. Lm28.40; Oct.-May Lm24.10).

Reggio Calabria-Valletta (13 hr.): **Tirrenia** (to Vittoriosa). Departs Tues., Fri., and Sun. at 8:30am (June-Sept. Lm 19.30; Oct.-May Lm15.90).

Malta-Gozo: Gozo Channel (to Mġarr). 30 min. From Cirkewwa on the northern tip of Malta (take bus #45 from Valletta), April-Sept. 14 per day; Oct.-March 8 per day. From Sa Maison near Valletta July-Sept. Mon.-Wed., Fri., and Sun. at 9:30am and 5pm; in off-season Mon.-Fri. (50¢, scooters 15¢).

Malta (Marfa)-Comino: Comino Hotel (tel. 57 30 51). 5 per day (Lm1). Take bus #45 or 48 from Valletta to the hotel at Marfa.

Malta is also served by a spanking new catamaran ferry that reduces the crossing from Sicily to two or four hours, depending on your point of embarkation. Reservations should be made a day in advance at the booking agents listed for Syracuse, Catania, and Taormina (see Practical Information for those cities). In Valletta, go to any tourist office with a picture of a ship in the window. The catamaran's operators, **Virtu Rapid Ferries,** are located halfway between Valletta and Sliema in Ta' Xbiex (tash-BEESH), at the bottom of Princess Elizabeth St. (tel. 31 70 88). All departure times listed are for June through November.

Taormina (Naxos)-Valletta (4 hr.): Departs Sun.-Mon. at 10am and 10:30pm (Lm18, round-trip Lm30; ages under 22 and over 60 Lm12, round-trip Lm24; 10% reduction for families with children under 16).

Catania-Valletta (3½ hr.): Departs Tues., Thurs., and Sat. at 10:10am and 10:10pm (same fare as Taormina).

Syracuse-Valletta (2 hr.): Departs Wed. and Fri. at 9:35am and 9:35pm (same fare as Taormina).

Flights leave most frequently for the two-hour trip from Rome to Malta's **Luga Airport** (tel. 62 28 73) aboard **Air Malta** (tel. 62 33 97) and **Alitalia** (tel. 62 04 31).

Air Malta offers a one-day, one-way standby fare for students under 24 of Lm31, but the regular round-trip fare is a hefty Lm114. **British Airways** (tel. 62 22 33) offers numerous student fares to London (3½ hr.), which is also served by Air Malta (round-trip Lm114). Valletta is accessible from the airport by buses #32 and 34 (every 15 min., 10¢). Malta levies a Lm2 airport tax and a Lm14 port tax for all international travel.

Practical Information

Valletta is the capital of Malta and on the island of the same name; Gozo Island and its cardinal city lie to the west. Comino is an oversized rock stuck between these two isles. Ferries dock on either side of Valletta's imposing walls, which overlook the **Grand Harbor** to the east and the increasingly affluent communities of Ta' Xbiex, Sliema (SLEE-ma), St. Julien's, and Paceville (PATCH-e-vil) to the west. **The Strand** and **Tower Road** border the peninsula of Sliema, making ideal locales for Italian-style *passegiate,* while the hottest nightlife is found in the harbor of St. Julien's and on St. George St. in Paceville. Your first purchase on the islands should be "What's On in Malta and Gozo," a 15¢ monthly guide to everything, with maps of the major cities.

Government Tourist Information Offices: At City Gate 1 (tel. 22 77 47), in Valletta near the bus terminal. A well-stocked office with helpful workers and a decent map (better one at NSTS). Accommodations service for the desperate. Open June 16-Sept. Mon.-Sat. 8:30am-1pm and 3-6pm, Sun. 8:30am-1pm; Oct.-June 15 Mon.-Sat. 8:30am-12:30pm and 1:15-6pm, Sun. 8:30am-12:30pm. Other equally helpful offices in Sliema (tel. 331 34 09), St. Julien's (tel. 334 26 71), at Luqa Airport (tel. 22 99 15), and on Gozo at Mġarr Harbor (tel. 55 33 43). Open daily 8am-6pm.

Student Travel: National Student Travel Service (NSTS), 220 Saint Paul St. (tel. 62 66 28), in Valletta. From inside the city gate, take South St. to Castille Pl., then go left on St. Paul down the hill. A great map of the Valletta-Sliema area, student discount information, and ISIC/YIEE cards. Come here first to find out about their **Aquacenter** (tel. 34 21 78) in Sliema, where any water sport can be pursued cheaply (e.g. windsurfing Lm2 per hr.). Open May-Sept. Mon.-Fri. 9:30am-1pm and 3-6pm, Sat. 9:30am-noon; Oct.-April Mon.-Fri. 9:30am-noon and 2:30-4:30pm, Sat. 9:30am-noon.

Embassies: U.S., St. Anne's St. (tel. 62 36 53), in Fliorana down the street from the Valletta bus terminal. Open Mon.-Fri. 8am-3:30pm. **U.K.** 7 St. Anne's St. (tel. 23 31 34), across from the U.S. Embassy. Open Mon.-Fri. 8am-1pm. **Australia,** Airways House, Gaiety Ln. (tel. 33 82 01), in Sliema. Open Mon.-Fri. 8:15am-12:15pm. **Canada,** Archbishop St. (tel. 23 31 21), off Republic St. in Valletta. Open Mon.-Fri. 9am-5pm.

Currency Exchange: If taking the ferry from Italy to Malta, be sure to exchange some money before you leave. Most major banks are open Mon.-Fri. until noon and Sat. until 11:30am. **Bank of Valletta** branches on Republic St. in Valletta and at the Strand in Sliema, and **Mid-Med** branches at the city gate in Valletta and on High St. in Sliema, are open June 16-Sept. 4-7pm and Oct.-June 15 3-6pm. Both banks also have 24-hour branches at the airport.

American Express: 14 St. Zachary St. (tel. 223 21 41), in Valletta off St. John's Sq. Holds mail without charge. Open June 16-Sept. Mon.-Fri. 9am-5pm, Sat. 9am-12:30pm; Oct.-June 15 Mon.-Fri. 9am-12:30pm and 2:30-5pm, Sat. 9am-12:30pm.

Post Office: Merchant St., in Valletta. Inside the Auberge d'Italie, off South St. Open June 16-Sept. 30 Mon.-Sat. 7:30am-6pm; Oct.-June 15 daily 8am-6:30pm. Poste Restante at the **Mail Room,** Castille Pl., in Valletta. Open Mon.-Fri. 8am-8pm, Sat. 8am-7pm. Malta has no postal code.

Telephones: Telemalta Corp., at St. John Sq., across from the cathedral in Valletta. Open Mon.-Sat. 8am-6:30pm. Also on St. George St. in Paceville (open Mon.-Sat. 24 hours) and Bisazza St. in Sliema (open Mon.-Sat. 8am-9pm). No collect calls can be made from any of these offices. Public phones cost 3¢. Telephone information: Tel. 990. **Telephone code:** 356. From the island of Gozo, dial 8 first.

Buses: Main terminal (tel. 22 40 01), outside in Valletta. Fares 6-10¢. Operates 5:30am-9 or 11pm. Buses on the island of Gozo originate at the capital city of Victoria on Main Gate St., but are unreliable.

Taxis: Wembley Garage, Tel. 33 20 74. Sliema to Valletta Lm2.50, to Luqa Airport Lm4. In general, inordinately expensive.

Car Rental: Hertz, United Garage, 66 Gzira Rd. (tel. 331 46 37), in Gzira. Must be 25. Lm6 per day with unlimited mileage. Open daily 8am-8pm. In general, rental cars are difficult to obtain for July-Aug.

Moped Rental: Go to any tourist agency along Tower Rd. in Sliema for help in obtaining a moped. They will most likely call **Peter's Scooter,** 175 D'Argens Rd. (tel. 33 52 44), in Msida. Low availability July-Aug. Lm3.25 per day. 4-day minimum. Must be 18 with valid driver's license. Open Mon.-Fri. 9am-noon and 2-5:30pm, Sat. 9am-noon. On Gozo, **Victoria Garage,** 150 Main Gate St. (tel. 55 64 14), in Victoria, across from the bus terminal. Scooters Lm4 per day, bikes Lm1 per day (but useless on the terrain). Must be 18 with valid drivers' license. Open Mon.-Fri. 7:30am-noon and 2-6:30pm, Sat. 7:30am-noon and 2-5pm.

Laundromat: Square-Deal, 36 The Strand (tel. 33 00 71), in Sliema. Wash Lm1.25. Dry 10¢ per 4 min. Open Mon.-Fri. 8:30am-noon and 12:30-6pm, Sat. 9am-1pm.

Hospitals: St. Luke's, Tel. 62 12 51. On Gozo, **Craig,** Tel. 55 68 51.

Emergency: tel. 999.

Police: Tel. 22 40 01. On Gozo, Tel. 55 64 30.

Accommodations

Come August, every inch of mattress on the island is occupied, but in winter the luxury hotels forego profits to entice visitors. Malta's many English-language schools provide student housing year-round; contact the **Education Department** (tel. 22 77 47) or the Government Tourist Office for full listings.

Although there is no official **camping** on the islands, some travelers find the vast number of beaches perfectly permissible sites. **Ghajn Tuffieha Bay,** accessibile by bus #47 or 52 from Valletta, offers flat soil and a large, sandy beach. The island of **Comino** is isolated enough to make you feel like Robinson Crusoe, especially since there are no convenience stores.

Valletta Youth Hostels Association (IYHF) (tel. 22 93 61). A vicissitudinous venture that regularly changes location. In 1988 the hostel was in **Paola,** 17 Tal-Borg St., near the Mid-Med bank (buses #5, 11, or 26 from Valletta). Members only, Lm2.25. Ages under 26, Lm1.50.

Hibernia House (NSTS), Depiro St. (tel. 33 38 59), in Sliema. Take Old College St. from the Sliema waterfront to St. Ignatius Junction, then go left on Depiro St. High-quality, made-for-students rooms. Each suite has a bedroom, lounge, bathroom, and kitchenette. Linen, towels, and kitchen utensils included. May-Sept. Lm3 per person; Oct.-April Lm1.50 per person. Reserve with NSTS at least 1 month in advance for summer (see Practical Information).

Sport Hotel, Saint Georges Rd., Saint Julien's (tel. 31 25 58), on the bus route right on the Paceville line. In an ideal location, near the best restaurants and discos. Immaculate but impersonal. June 15-Sept. 15 Lm4 per person; Sept. 16-June 14 Lm3 per person. Most rooms with baths. Breakfast included. Lm1 supplement per single occupancy. 10% discount with ISIC or YIEE.

Kent Hotel, 24 St. Margaret St. (tel. 33 09 28), in Sliema off Tower Rd. on the Saint Julien line. A classy hotel decked out in china and deerhorns. June-Oct. Lm4 per person; Nov.-May Lm3.50 per person. Most rooms have baths. Breakfast included. Enjoy a 3-course meal in their lovely little dining room for Lm2.

Cumberland Hotel, 111 St. John's St. (tel. 22 77 32), downhill from the cathedral. Though managed in modern-style by an Apple computer at the front desk, this hotel smacks of Valletta's glory days under the Spanish knights. Stone arches, a shaded courtyard, and coats of arms welcome crusaders to airy rooms with bathrooms and closed balconies. Lm4.25 per person. Doubles Lm8. Bath and breakfast included.

Coronation Guest House, 10E M.A. Vassalli St. (tel. 22 76 52). Take South St. toward the Museum of Fine Arts, and descend the steps to the right before the Osborne Hotel. The fatherly owner makes guests feel at home. The spacious, spotless rooms have external baths. Dec. and April-Sept. Lm3 per person; Oct.-Nov. and Jan.-March Lm2.50 per person. Breakfast 50¢. Reserve at least 2 weeks in advance July-Aug.

Food

Maltese cuisine is a hybrid of the dishes of countries that have occupied the land through the years—particularly Britain and Italy. But the many cooks have done anything but ruin the batter here: *Timpana* combines the Italian love for pasta with the British predisposition for pies, and *minestra* soup is a stuffy minestrone. Home-grown dishes include *lampuka,* a native fish (in season late August), and *fenkatta,* rabbit served over pasta or in a stew. Malta has even developed its own junk food: *pastizzi* (flaky, greasy biscuits filled with ricotta) and *hobs-biz-zejt* (a sandwich filled with beans, tomatoes, olives, and capers). The prime local pastry is *Qaqà-tal-ghasel* (ah-tah-LAH-sel), a delicious, ring-shaped cookie filled with molasses.

As in any other hot Mediterranean country, avoid eating food that has been baking at a sidewalk stand, and stay away from pork.

For an impressive spread of the Grand Harbor, take a picnic to Valletta's Upper or Lower Barrakka Gardens. Stock up at the **Wembley Store,** 305 Republic St., directly inside the City Gate. (Open Mon.-Fri. 9am-1pm and 3-7pm, Sat. 9am-1pm.)

Agius Pastizzeria, 273 St. Paul's St., off Castille Place. Undoubtedly the best food option in town, if you don't mind standing up while you eat. Homebaked concoctions sold fresh daily. Lots of dough for little dough: huge slabs of *timpana* 15¢, *pastizzi* 4¢, *pudina* (chocolate pudding tart) 10¢. Open Mon.-Sat. 6am-8pm, Sun. 6am-noon.

General Workers' Union, South St. (tel. 62 19 66), 1 block before the Fine Arts Museum. Turn left off Republic St. directly after the City Gate. A plain but popular restaurant with cafeteria prices and heaps of food. Complete breakfast with juice, bacon, eggs, tomatoes, toast, and tea 85¢. For lunch, dive into the fish burger, an indelicate mix of fish, eggs, sausage, and cheese for 80¢. Open Mon.-Fri. 7-10am and 11:30am-2pm, Sat. 7am-1pm.

Blundell Restaurant, 121 Old Theater St., off Republic St. near the Manoel Theater. A small, undecorated room with some tables and a surplus of customers. *Timpana* 30¢, *ravjul* (ravioli) 40¢, *ross-al-forn* (baked rice) 35¢, *hobz-biz-zejt* 15¢. Open June-Sept. Mon.-Sat. 10am-2:30pm; Oct.-May Mon.-Sat. 10am-2:30pm and 6-9pm.

Jimmy's Restaurant, 52 Melita St. (tel. 202 46). Walking away from City Gate on Republic St., take a left on Melita St. just after South St. A tiny place upstairs. Jimmy and his wife will serve you excellent spaghetti with a smile (70¢). Swordfish Lm2.30, *minestra* soup 30¢. Open daily 11:30am-2:30pm and 6:30-10:30pm.

British Hotel, 38 Battery St. (tel. 22 47 30), at the end of St. John St. Terrace perches over the Grand Harbor, offering Valletta's finest dining view. *Minestra* 50¢. *Fenek* (rabbit) in white wine sauce Lm1.80. A complete meal (soup/pasta, meat/fish, cheese/fruit, ice cream, and wine and coffee) a mere Lm2.25. Open daily noon-2pm and 7-9:30pm.

Sliema-St. Julien's-Paceville

Restaurants pack the waterfront from The Strand in Sliema, past Tower Rd., and then onto Main St. in St. Julien's. Some of the best deals lurk up the hill in Paceville on Church St., Gort St., and Paceville Ave.

Il Vilaġġ, Church St. (tel. 51 13 80), Triq il-Knisja. Bright yellow tables, red seats, flourescent lights, and unusual dishes. *Pasta al villaggio,* with mushroom, spinach, and egg, Lm1.05. Large French crepes 90¢-Lm1.30. Dessert crepes 85¢-Lm1. Open July-Sept. Sun.-Fri. 6:30pm-midnight, Sat. 6:30pm-12:30am; Oct.-June Mon.-Fri. 6-11:30pm, Sat. 6pm-midnight, Sun. 11:30am-3pm and 6-11:30pm.

Kċina Restaurant, Paceville Ave. (tel. 33 17 65), off Gort St. Serves a slew of Maltese dishes in its cork-covered dining room. *Minestra* 55¢, *timpana* 90¢, *lampuki* Lm2, *fenkatta* Lm1.95. Open mid-Feb. to mid-Jan. daily 6:30-11pm.

Tá Ġorġ Restaurant, St. Georges Rd. (tel. 33 35 86), at the bottom of the hill to Paceville. Sinatra bellows in the dining hall while the kitchen rocks with Tina Turner. No matter, every dish here hits the Top 40. *Timpana* 50¢, curry rice chicken Lm1.40, stewed *fenkatta* (work around the bones) Lm1.80, fish soup 30¢. Open mid-Feb. to mid-Jan. daily 6:30-11pm.

Ta' Kolina Restaurant, 151 Tower Rd. (tel. 35 51 06), on the Sliema waterfront. Locally renowned for its island dishes. *Minestra* 75¢, spaghetti with rabbit sauce 95¢, *fenkatta* Lm2.70. Open Mon.-Sat. 6-10pm, Sun. noon-2pm and 6-10pm. Reserve on weekends.

Malta's best ice cream shop is **La Gelateria Lungomare,** ½ Windsor Terrace (tel. 31 30 22), on Tower Rd. near Ta' Kolina Restaurant. Exceptional cones of *baci* (chocolate with praline cream) are 15¢. (Open daily 8am-midnight.)

The Villages

Restaurants in Malta's smaller villages are generally a step up in quality and price. Marsascala, a snapshot bayside town on the eastern shore (bus #19), has two of the best. **Christopher's,** 29 Marina St. (tel. 82 99 53), sports a tiny room filled with wicker lamps, dried flowers, brass decor, and personal service. *Fettucine Maltaise* (with cream, goat's cheese, and sausage) is only 90¢, and *sole marquerey* (packed with mussels and shrimp in a wine sauce) will set you back Lm2.60. (Cover 15¢. Open June-Sept. Tues.-Sat. 12:30-2pm and 7:30-11pm, Mon. 7:30-11pm; Oct.-May Tues.-Sun. 12:30-2pm and 7:30-11pm.) Ask anyone where to find the **Fisherman's Rest** (tel. 82 20 49), Malta's revered seafood restaurant. Tasty spaghetti with octopus is a favorite for 80¢, or splurge with their mixed seafood platter, including swordfish, octopus, shrimp, and mussels for Lm2.95. (Open Feb.-Dec. Tues.-Sat. 12:30-2:45pm and 7:30-10:45pm, Sun. 12:30-2:45pm.)

Sights

Valletta

Malta's capital city clangs with chaos during business hours, but is hushed otherwise. Showcasing seventeenth-century balconies and rubble from the last war, it warrants sacrificing at least a day of tanning. **Republic Street** is itself a historical walking trail running the entire length of the city—from **City Gate** to **Fort St. Elmo,** the old protective fortress at the city's northeastern tip. The **War Museum,** on St. Joseph St., holds Britain's coveted George Cross, a Maltese fighter plane, and other memorabilia from World War II. One glance at the photographs of Malta's massive losses in bombing attacks revives the electrifying chill of Churchill's dictum: "No more let us falter! From Malta to Yalta! Let nobody alter!" (Open June 16-Sept. 30 daily 7:45am-2pm; in off-season 8:30am-5pm. Admission 15¢, children 7¢, students with ID free.) Old Theater St. leads back up to Republic St. and the **Grand Master's Palace** (1569), the historic residence of Malta's ruling parties—from knight to governor to parliament. Now open to the public, the palatial halls feature opulent decor, including a throne that monarchs-to-be can try on for size. (Open Mon.-Sat. 9am-1pm.) The adjacent **Armoury** opens the door to chivalric romance and sixteenth- to eighteenth-century wardrobes of precious-metal armor. Frowning upon the tourist-saturated square of the same name, **St. John's Co-Cathedral** (1573-1577), designed by Gerolamo Cassar, rebounds with a splash of color indoors—including a floor inlaid with 400 marble coats of arms. The Oratory and Museum, entered through a door to the right of the cathedral's entrance, reveals two masterful works by Caravaggio. (Church and museum open Mon.-Sat. 9am-1pm and 3-5pm, Sun. 9am-1:30pm. Museum admission 50¢.)

Dive from the height of the Renaissance into the deep, dark past at the **National Museum of Archeology,** inside the old Auberge de Provence on Republic St. A preface to the temple sites farther inland, the museum displays pottery from 4000 B.C.E. and bulbous fertility statuettes. (Open June 16-Sept. 30 daily 7:45am-2pm; in off-season 8:15am-5pm. Admission 15¢, children 7¢, students with ID free.) Make a left onto South St. at the City Gate to reach the **Auberge de Castille** (1574-1744) on Castille Pl., across from the Teatro Mansel. Designed by Cassar, the *auberge* was one of four homes for Castillian and Portuguese knights who defended the Santa Barbara bastions nearby, but now it houses the offices of Malta's prime minister. Ledges in the Upper Barrakka gardens next door afford magnificent views of the remains of sixteenth-century fortresses.

Central Malta

Bus #80 takes Valletta passengers inland to the island's cultural heart. From the bus stop at Parish Sq. in **Rabat,** a right onto St. Cataldus St. and a left at St. Agatha St. brings you to the entrances of two ancient Christian **catacombs.** Just inside the entrance to St. Paul's catacombs is a large chamber with a round stone table, where the relatives of the deceased munched hors d'oeuvres for the funeral feast. The more interesting St. Agatha's catacombs across the street sheltered St. Agatha herself from the Romans, who chased her across Sicily. (Open June 16-Sept. daily 7:45am-2pm; in off-season 8:15am-5pm. Admission 15¢, children 7¢, students with ID free.) When they finally hopped across the Mediterranean, the emperor's men founded the **Roman Villa,** now thoroughly reconstructed to the side of St. Paul's St. in Rabat. A set of stairs leads down to the Peristyle Room, an open court fully covered with mosaics and originally surrounded by 16 columns, only one of which still stands. (Open June 16-Sept. daily 7:45am-2pm; in off-season 8:15am-5pm. Admission 15¢, children 7¢, students with ID free.)

Outside the villa is the main gate to the ninth-century Saracen fortifications that define **Mdina** (Em-DEE-nah). Devoid of cars and business suits along its 300-meter main street, the old city recalls the seventeenth century with a flourish of baroque buildings and narrow alleyways. Not far up Villegaignon St. is the **new cathedral** (1697-1702), a baroque exaggeration of Valletta's banal bombast. The apse supports Mattia Preti's fresco *The Shipwreck of St. Paul,* and the **museum** in the building to the right contains a large collection of Roman and Punic coins. (Cathedral and museum open June 16-Sept. Mon.-Sat. 9am-1pm and 2-5pm; in off-season 9am-1pm and 1:30-4:30pm.) The obscure **Norman House** (1475), at the end of Villegaignon St., played house to an Aragonese family for 200 years, and it now exhibits later period furniture alongside prints of the Great Siege of 1631. Ring the buzzer at the door for a free guided tour. (Open for tours Mon., Wed., and Fri. 9am-1pm and 2-4:30pm. Free.) At the end of Villegaignon St. lies **Bastion Square,** which leads to scenic walks along the stone walls that surround the city.

To the right hides Malta's finest cake shop and cafe, **Fontanella** (tel. 67 42 64), which also enjoys a stupendous view. Try a slice of Michael's favorite lemon cake for 26¢ while your eyes wander over two-thirds of the island. (Open daily 9:30am-6pm.)

Should the staggering view of all northern Malta grab you, you should grab a humble room at **Palazzo Costanzo Guest House,** Villegaignon St. (tel. 67 63 01), inside an eighteenth-century palace. Bed and breakfast here costs Lm4 (Oct.-May Lm3).

Mosta, accessible by bus #53 from Valletta, is literally overshadowed by its main attraction, the world's third largest church dome. With an internal diameter of 130 ft., the **Mosta Dome** survived a German bomb that failed to explode after crashing through the marble shell and sliding across the floor. The bomb is now on display in the sacristy, along with a picture of the hole it left in the ceiling, to persuade any skeptics. (Church open daily 9am-noon and 3-8pm. No visitors during services, usually 6-7pm.)

Archeological Malta

Prehistoric folk immigrated from Sicily about 5000 B.C.E., producing by 2800 B.C.E. what survive as the world's oldest megalithic temples—most of them in honor of the buxom fertility statues on display in Valletta's museum.

The oldest of the old is the cave at **Ghar Dalam,** just outside the city of Birzebbugia (bus #11 from Valletta). A museum atop the cave displays prehistoric fossils plus the remains of neolithic farmers (3800 B.C.E.). Bus #11 or 26 stops in Tarxien (Tar-SHEE-in), 50m from the four reconstructed **Tarxien Temples** (2400 B.C.E.), the island's largest archeological find. Around the corner from the intact middle temple lies a net-covered chamber with original wall carvings of bull, sow, and piglet motifs. The grass that once shrouded the East Temple has recently been uprooted to reveal ancient shards of pottery—great souvenirs and about the only free merchandise on the island. (Open June 16-Sept. daily 7:45am-2pm; in off-season 8:15am-5pm. Admission 15¢, children 7¢, students with ID free.) Escape the midday heat by following Triq Hal Luqa from the bus stop to the perfectly preserved, subterranean **Hal Saflieni Hypogeum** in Paola. Amidst the labrynthine nooks of this remarkable construction, be sure to find the Oracle Room—hum into the black hole on the left wall to create thunderous reverberations throughout the complex. The pride of the hypogeum is the Holy of Holies, an arched and pillared sanctuary reached via a flight of perilously uneven steps. The bridge was not installed in the original temple, and unsuspecting intruders would fall off the last step into the pit. (Open June 16-Sept. 7:45am-2pm; in off-season 8:30am-5pm. Admission 15¢, children 7¢, students with ID free.)

Bus #35 from Valletta finishes its run at Qrendi, where a half-hour walk over two hills takes you to **Hagar Qim** (Hah-jahr-EEM) and **Mnajdra** (Im-NYE-drah). Constructed from craggy Globergina limestone, these haunting temples overlook the southern coast and the tiny offshore island of Filfla. Fertility is again pregnant here: Phallic symbols, one 7m high, compete with Rubenesque statuettes found elsewhere on the island. The temple itself was used almost exlusively as part of a death cult; inside the Oracle Room, priests sacrificed animals to the fertility gods in exchange for continuous life. (Temple open June 16-Sept. daily 7:45am-1:30pm; in off-season 8:30am-5pm. Admission 15¢, children 7¢, students with ID free.) A path leads 400m downhill to the **Menajdra Temples,** perhaps most noteworthy for their august location overlooking the sea. If you're suffering from temple torture, scramble down the steep, rocky path past Mnajdra to a silent rocky cove where you can swim alone with the tiny fish that dart through the lucid water. Or follow the signs from Hagar Qim to "Wied iz Zurrieq," where colorful water taxis (tel. 82 69 47) depart for the **Blue Grotto,** with its colorful coral, bleached sand, and idyllic blue water. (Boats leave daily. Lm3 per 1-2 persons, Lm4 per 3-4 persons, Lm5 per 5-6 persons, and Lm6 per 7-8 persons.)

Entertainment

Malta hosts some of the Mediterranean's hottest clubs—every night in summer whole sections of Paceville watch the sun rise. Partiers "in the know" (usually found along the Strand or Tower Rd.) will gladly aid a fun-seeking foreigner. All clubs charge Lm1-1.50 on weekends, and most give out complementary cards for weekday admission. In Paceville, **Styx II,** St. Augustine St., draws with its sophisticated electronics and various lounging rooms. (Mon. free with ISIC.) For outdoor dancing on the weekends, boogie down to **Ta' gianpula** in Rabat or **Numero Uno** in Ta' qali (TA-ali), both prized by the local Sliema-Paceville crowd. (Both open Fri. and Sat. 10pm-dawn. Cover Lm1-1.50.)

Gozo and Comino

On your way from Valletta to the ferry terminal at Marfa, hop off the bus at Mellieha Bay to visit the original set of rickety seaside homes used to film the movie *Popeye.* Once on the ferry, look out for the Blue Lagoon of Comino on the islet's western (Gozo) side. Scenes from this year's *Leviathan* were shot in its crystal waters.

Gozo was once the stomping grounds of the nymph Calypso, who pampered Odysseus for seven years in her luxurious cave. It may very well have been the island's busing system that prevented Odysseus from getting anywhere for so long; all buses originate from Victoria, run no more frequently than hourly to even the most popular destinations, and discontinue most service by midday. If you can't rent a vehicle from Malta, try in Gozo—mobility is key on this sleepy, rustic island. (See Practical Information.)

Victoria, the capital and main port, is crowned by a **citadel.** The main entrance to the tiny fortification leads off It-tokk Sq. in the city center. The best island view encompasses all of "Calypso's Island" from the top of Zanba St., nearer the cathedral.

To reach Xaghra (SHAH-rah) from Victoria's bus terminal, walk straight off Main Gate St., cross over the main road Republic St., and onto Xaghra Rd.; follow this street along dusty trails over an incredibly huge hill straight to the town center. A four- or five- minute walk on the road at a sharp right angle to the town church will reward you with the incredibly intact **Ggantija Temples** (Jig-AHN-tee-ha), named for legendary giants who were said to have constructed them. (Open daily 8:45am-3:15pm. Admission 15¢, children 7¢, students with ID free.)

Follow the signs from Xaghra's main square to **Ninu's Cave,** in a private house on 18a January St. In 1888, the grandfather of a current resident discovered stalagmites beneath the well, now entered through a staircase in the back room. (Open daily 8am-7pm. Tip 10¢.) On the other side of the main square, inside the house of a priest, lies an extensive stalagtite cave, the Xerri's (SHEH-ris) Grotto. The priest leads a hilarious tour of the strange rock formations, pointing out lions, wineskins, and even a "boy leaning over." (Open daily 8am-1pm and 3:30-7pm. Tip 10¢.)

To experience nature on a grander scale, don't miss **Dwejra Bay,** near the town of St. Lawrenz. Here you can swim in an inland sea (connected to the Mediterranean via a long natural tunnel), see the dramatic **Fungus Rock** and its magnificent bay, and walk out onto a sea-carved arches. Those in search of serenity should bunker down on the orange sands of **Ramla Bay** (take the road north from Xaghra). Finally, between Dwejra and Ramla sits **Ta'pinu,** a huge ornate cathedral sitting in the middle of nowhere. (From Victoria head northwest to Gharb, then follow the signs.)

To stick around Victoria a little longer, the **Guest House,** Ninu Cremona St. (tel. 55 34 20), off Republic St. near the city gardens, offers rooms with kitchen and bath for Lm2.50 (Oct.-May Lm2), breakfast included. For a cozy, sit-down meal, **Ta' Giannina,** on Republic St., 200m downhill from It-tokk Sq., has excellent *timpana* (40¢), *lampuki* (75¢), and stewed rabbit (Lm1.25). (Open daily 7:30am-3pm and 7-11pm.) In Xaghra, the **Gester Restaurant,** 8, September St. (tel. 766 21), is run by two little sisters who serve megalithic meals to rival the size of the nearby temples. *Aljotta* (fish soup) or *Kosku bitful* (bean and pasta soup) is 60¢, *lampuki* pie 75¢, and rabbit casserole Lm2.10. (Open daily 11:30am-1:30pm.)

Comino is the inverse of modern Malta—isolated and pristine. Its 8-square-kilometer surface is speckled with only two man-made structures, a seventeenth-century tower and the expensive **Comino Hotel** (tel. 57 30 51), which runs five boats daily to and from the city of Morfu on Malta. Spend the day at the **Blue Lagoon,** justly famous for the clearest waters in the archipelago, but make sure you bring plenty of food and drink, so as not to starve your wallet at the hotel restaurant.

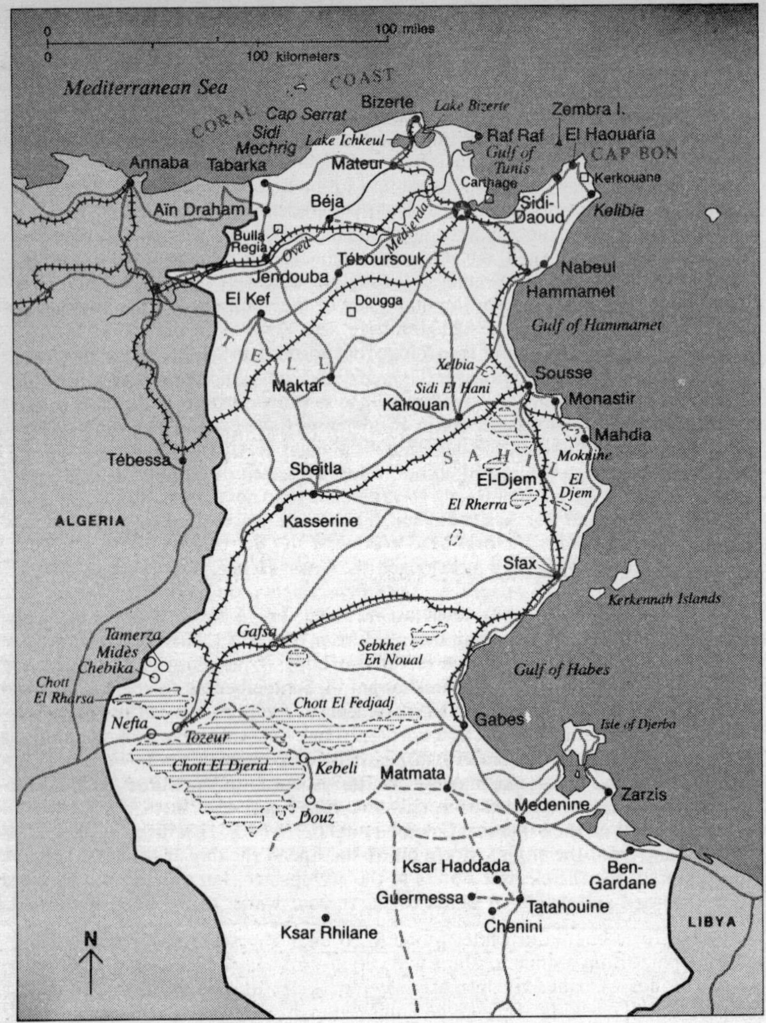

TUNISIA

US $1 = 0.862 dinar (D)	**1D = US $1.16**
CDN $1 = 0.520D	**1D = CDN $1.41**
UK £1 = 1.060D	**1D = UK £0.68**
AUS $1 = 0.690D	**1D = AUS $1.45**
NZ $1 = 0.570D	**1D = AUS $1.76**

Queen Dido of Phoenicia sailed to Carthage in the ninth century B.C.E. to found a nation "rich in wealth and harsh in the pursuit of war." Thousands of years later, Tunisia's people are far from wealthy, and little is harsh in this gentle land of vast open spaces, remote green oases, and secluded Saharan villages. However, mass tourism of the package-holiday variety dominates the Tunisian travel scene, and a visit to the larger resorts along the coast will leave you wondering where the Tunisians are. But the least bit of effort to escape the European crowds reveals a hospitable and curious people, proud of their Islamic and North African culture. Tunisia also encompasses endless, spectacular beaches and some of the world's noblest ancient ruins.

Relieved of 75 years of French colonial rule in 1956, Tunisia was for 31 years a study in the equating of one nation's identity with that of one individual. By most accounts, Habib Bourguiba, who deposed the last titular head of state in 1957 and was then declared President-for-Life, served Tunisia well. The country is a model of civic freedoms and social emancipation in the Arab world. Thirty years after stepping into office, a non-violent *coup d'état* removed Bourguiba from office; the leader was rumored to be showing increasing signs of senility. On November 7, 1987, power was given to Preseident Aine el Abidine ben Madj Hamita Ben Ali. Under President Ben Ali there is promise of economic resurgence through privatization, but many young Tunisians fear that his ardent belief in Islamic tradition will lead to a regression in recently established women's liberation policies. Bourguiba's face still adorns the currency, and his name the sign of each city's main avenue, but already a statue of the ex-leader has been torn down in Sfax, marking the onslaught of change.

Practical Information

No visa is required of U.S. citizens to enter Tunisia for up to four months, or of Canadians for up to three months. **The Tunisian National Tourist Office (ONTT)** is a good source of information, maps, and brochures. They offer a handy, pocket-sized *Tunisia Practical Guide* worth its weight in gold. Major cities also run a local tourist office called the **syndicat d'initiative.** In the U.S., write or call the **Embassy of Tunisia,** Cultural Section in Charge of Tourism, 2408 Mass. Ave. NW, Washington, DC 20008 (tel. (202) 234-6660), for maps and regional brochures. For the U.S. State Department's *Background Notes* on Tunisia, write to the Superintendent of Documents, U.S. Government Printing Office, Washington, DC 20402. The ONTT in Great Britian is at 7a, Stafford St., London W1 (tel. 629 08 58).

Money

Banks are open for exchange in summer (June 15-Sept. 15) Monday through Friday from 8 to 11am and in winter Monday through Thursday from 8 to 11:30am and 2 to 5pm, Friday from 8 to 11am and 1:30 to 4pm. During Ramadan (see Festivals and Holidays), banks are open Monday through Friday from 8 to 11:30am and 1 to 2:30pm. All ports of entry and the Tunis train station operate exchange bureaus offering standard rates and hours. A few large hotels and all airports provide exchange services outside regular hours.

The dinar (D) is divided into 1000 millimes (ml). Sums in Tunisia and in *Let's Go* are written with periods: 14.300 means 14 dinars, 300 millimes. Amounts under 5D are frequently expressed in hundreds of millimes. Change is scarce, so hang on to it, especially the precious 100ml pieces used in pay phones. Save your exchange receipts; only 30% can be reconverted.

Telephone, Telegrams, and Mail

Tunisian telephones take 100ml coins—about six to call anywhere in the country briefly. The unused balance will be returned. Dial direct using the regional area codes: Tunis and suburbs 01, Bizerte-Cap Bon region 02, Sousse-Mahdia-Monastir region 03, Sfax region 04, Gabes-Djerba region 05, Gafsa region 06, Kairouan region 07, and El Kef and the North 08. Certain rural areas can be reached only with the operator's assistance (tel. 15).

International calls may be placed from telephone offices and from major hotels. The quickest, cheapest way to call abroad is to find a phone that accepts 1D and

500ml coins, and dial direct (00 + country code + area code + phone number). Direct calls to the U.S. cost 2.400D per minute. Expect a 30-minute wait if you call collect ("en P.C.V.").

Letters to the U.S. and Canada weighing up to 20g cost 430ml; postcards are 350ml. Letters to Europe are 370ml (France 350ml); postcards are 300ml (France 250ml). Telegrams and telexes are sent from either telephone offices or post offices.

Post offices are generally open in summer (July-Sept. 15) Monday through Saturday from 8am to 1pm; in winter Monday through Friday from 8am to noon and 3 to 6pm, and Saturday from 8am to noon.

Health

The two major health problems you're likely to encounter in Tunisia are overexposure to the sun and diarrhea. The former in particular is no joke: In the interior, the midday sun is ferocious and a hat crucial. Tap **water** in Tunis and north of Gabes is allegedly potable, but it would be wise to buy inexpensive bottled water (such as Helliti or Safia *eau minerale*). Don't be lured by the treacherous, ice-cold glasses of *citronade.* Avoid produce that can't be peeled or wash it with *bottled* water. You will regret eating creamy pastries and oily food that has been standing out for a while. Beware—even when brushing your teeth—and bring a medical kit including chewable *pepto bismol* tablets. The phone numbers of all-night pharmacies and medical services in major cities are listed in the Practical Information sections. Consult your doctor, but the only vaccination presently recommended for travelers to Tunisia is a gamma globulin. Within Tunisia, vaccinations and innoculations can be obtained in Tunis at the Service Hygiène, 52, rue d'Allemagne (tel. 24 14 93), but your safest bet is vaccination at home.

Safety

In the crowded labyrinthine *souks* (market streets) of the *medina* (old city) cling to your bags, mind your pockets, and remember there is safety in numbers. The *medinas* are very dangerous after dark. The police stay out of them; they won't be sympathetic if you don't too.

Carry sums of over 10D or 15D in a moneybelt or necklace pouch. When paying for a souvenir or guide, always keep your money securely in hand until you have agreed on how much you are paying. Always pay with small bills, or, better yet, the exact amount. Beware of locals who show you around their city, and then demand a fee as a "guide." Women traveling alone in the touristed cities of the north will encounter only minor hassles if they stick to hotels and areas popular with tourists. Women venturing into the interior or the south should travel only in groups with males. Be aware that many Tunisians are angered by U.S. support of Israel and have been known to harrass U.S. citizens. Tunisia's nationwide **emergency number** is 197. (See Security and Insurance in the General Introduction.)

Language

The official language is Arabic, but all Tunisian secondary school students study French, and most people who commonly deal with tourists speak a smattering of English and German as well. French is common even in the interior.

Getting There

By Sea

The cheapest way to get to Tunisia is by boat from Italy. All connections to Italy are run by the **Tirrenia** line. (See Palermo and Trapani Practical Information.) Weather permitting, hydrofoils depart every other day from Trapani to Kelibia, east of Tunis on the Cap Bon Peninsula (53D, or L55,000). High season rates apply June through September.

Trapani-Tunis (8½ hr.): Chair L67,400, 2nd class L87,500. Departures from Trapani Wed. at 4pm, from Tunis Thurs. at 6am.

Palermo-Tunis (11 hr.): The more scenic and expensive alternative. Chair L108,000, 2nd class L113,800. Departures from Palermo Mon. at 7pm, from Tunis Tues. at 7pm.

Cagliari-Tunis, via Trapani (21 hr.): Chair L80,400, 2nd class L103,200. Departures from Cagliari Tues. at 7pm, from Tunis Wed. at 8am.

Marseille-Tunis and **Genoa-Tunis:** Run by the Compagnie Tunisienne de Navigation. Couchette on the Tunis-Marseille line one way 65D, round-trip 120D; student discount 25%. Couchette on the Tunis-Genoa line one way 47D, round-trip 82D; no student discount. Departures May-Dec. 5-14 per month.

Report for all boats leaving the port of La Goulette (a 15-min. ride on the TGM commuter train from downtown Tunis, get off at Vieille Goulette) *two hours in advance,* or you'll miss your ride. During the last two weeks of August, all boats from Tunisia are packed with migrant workers headed back to their jobs in northern Europe. Book your tickets well in advance. To buy a ferry ticket, you are required to show your bank receipt for purchase of dinar and obtain a Bons de Passage from the bank itself—a minor bureaucratic hassle, but one upon which travel agents insist. You can buy tickets from all major travel agents. In late summer crunch, it is wisest to fight it out at the crowded **Tirrenia Ticket Office** 122, rue de Yougoslavie. All boat lines are supervised by the **CTN (Compagne Tunisienne de Navigation),** which provides passenger information and ticket offices at 5, rue Dag Hammarskjold in Tunis (tel. 24 28 01); at La Goulette; at Ponte Colombo (Gare Maritime) in Genoa (tel. (01) 25 80 41); at Rione Sirignano, 2, in Naples (tel. (081) 66 03 33); and at 61, bd. des Dames in Marseille (tel. 91 91 92 20).

By Air

There are no directs flights between North America and Tunisia. North Americans should fly to Rome (see Getting There in the General Introduction) and then make their way to Tunis by plane, train, or boat. **Tunis Air** flies from most major European and North African cities and offers 50% discounts to students under 26 with ISIC, as well as a confusing array of round-trip deals. Flights to London cost 142D, but a charter company will reduce that by about 50%. Tunis Air flights to and from France are cheaper. Flights between Tunis and Marseille cost 67D. Inter-Arab fares are also quite reasonable; with student discount, Casablanca to Tunis is 88.500D and Tunis to Cairo is 108D. On domestic flights, Tunis Air offers as much as a 55% discount to students under 26. Flying to Tozeur or Djerba can save you a lot of overland delays.

By Land

The Trans-Mahgreb railway theoretically connects Tunis to Rabat with a change in Algiers. The trip from Rabat to Algiers (1470km) takes about 30 hours and costs roughly 24D, but service is in limbo because of the conflict between Algeria and Morocco over the Spanish Sahara. Service from Algiers to Tunis (950km), by contrast, is reliable, costs 20.600D, and takes 18 hours in theory. Service is not available directly through Algeria to Morocco. On the Algerian side, trains run as far as Tlemcen, on the Moroccan side as far as Oujda. Several buses run daily from Oujda to the border (1.50 Moroccan dirhams), and also daily from Tlemcen. Generally it's cheaper to fly to Tunis than to go overland, as you're required to change 1000 Algerian dinar (about 152.300D). Students are exempt from this requirement, but officials are somewhat unclear about who they will recognize as a student.

In addition to the truckers renowned for their generosity to hitchhikers, buses also cross Algeria. A good deal of tourist traffic connects Morocco with Tunisia. An especially good place to hitch out of Morocco to Tunisia is the tourist office in Oujda. In Tunis, one-month Algerian visas (required of U.S. and Canadian citizens) can be obtained at the **Algerian Embassy,** 18, rue du Niger (tel. 28 31 66). Bring four photos and 9.500D; the process takes one day. In Morocco, visas can be acquired through the **United Arab Emirates Special Mission for Algerian Affairs** (not the UAE Embassy), 82, Ankat Azrou, around the corner from the Tunisian Embassy in Rabat. (Open 9:15am-3pm.) In Rabat, visas take two days, cost 22D, and require four photos. Visas are processed more quickly at the Oujda consulate, but inquire in Rabat for an update on border regulations, mandatory currency exchange, etc.

Getting Around

Public transportation is plentiful on major routes and generally inexpensive. It comes in three forms: trains, buses, and *louages* (long-distance shared taxis). Always travel, as Tunisians do, early in the day. For example, Kairouan-Tunis buses leave at 5am, 6am, 9am, and 3:15pm—after which you'll be stranded.

Trains

A major train line runs south from Tunis to Sousse, and then splits into an eastern line through Sfax, which ends in Gabes, and a western line to Tozeur through Gafsa. Another line runs west through Jendouba to the Algerian border and splits into northwest branches ending in Bizerte and Tabarka. Although service is infrequent, these trains are pleasant and air-conditioned. Second-class prices are competitive with other forms of transport. For information, contact **Société National de Chemins de Fer Tunisienne (SNCFT)** at the train station (Gare Tunis-Ville) in place Mongi Bali on av. Carthage (tel. 24 44 40), at av. Farhat Hached. Pick up train schedules for the entire country at the information booth in the Tunis train station. Student discounts are available.

Buses

Buses are the most common form of intercity transit. They are plentiful early in the day, inexpensive, and convenient; unfortunately, they are also crowded. Always try to board at the terminal, which is usually designated the *gare routière;* this increases your chance of finding a seat and may get you onto an express (as opposed to a painfully slow local). The **Société National des Transports (SNT),** 74, av. de Carthage, Tunis, operates buses between Tunis and its suburbs. **Société du Métro-Léger du Tunis (SMLT),** av. Muhammad V, Tunis, operates the lightrail system (parts still under construction), and **Société de Transports Rural et Interurban (SNTRI),** passage Mazaguan, Tunis, operates rural, intercity, and international routes. (See Tunis Practical Information for addresses of the main bus stations.)

Louages

Louages, usually Peugeot station wagons, serve as intercity taxis. They depart as soon as they get five people with a common destination and will travel as far as the distance from Tunis to Djerba. Since no stops need be made along the way, *louages* are the quickest form of ground transport. Prices are fixed and each *louage* lists the rates. If the car doesn't fill, the policy is to charge more per head. On trunk routes, per person fares are competitive with buses and trains. Such *louages* often indicate the name of their destination on a plaque. Special requests, such as remote archeological sites, can be negotiated but usually cost more than trunk routes of equivalent distance; if the driver can't fill the car for the return voyage, the fare will be doubled. One of the major *louage* stations in Tunis is at 72, av. Farhat Hached, near the train station. Otherwise *louage* stations (defined as any spot with more than one idle vehicle) change constantly, so ask locals.

Hitchhiking

Hitchhiking is illegal but tends to be fairly easy in Tunisia for foreigners. Hitching doesn't have much of a following among natives for a number of reasons: Cars are small, locals don't make long journeys, and the *louage* tradition of renting extra room in a car is so ingrained that hitchhiking is tantamount to freeloading (some drivers may ask you to contribute). Hitch in Tunisia not to save money, since public transportation is cheap, but to save time or meet locals.

Car Rental

A private car is indispensable for touring the Sahara, where public transportation is scarce and waiting for a bus can be a heated affair. You must be at least 21 and have a valid international driver's license. *Let's Go* lists major rental agencies in Tunis, Gabes, and Houmt-Souk. Get five people together and rent a cozy two-door, four-seater with unlimited mileage, and you can cover transportation costs with 9D per day per person. The Renault 4 is the cheapest option and a reliable vehicle. You won't have to worry about scratching it up as it'll probably be a virtual wreck with doors that don't lock. Ask to inspect the car *before* you sign.

Accommodations and Camping

Tunisian accommodations come in a number of flavors. First are the beach behemoths housing the packaged-tour holiday-makers, followed by business travelers' hotels, rooming houses for itinerant workers, and finally dormitories for youth groups. The friendly little *pensions*—the budget traveler's beacon—are rare but growing in number. Remember that you are traveling in a Third World country—toilet seats and hot showers are rare.

Hostels

Tunisia has 22 Youth Centers and IYHF youth hostels, all designed to house soccer teams. They tend to be large, functional, and clean, and at 2D per night, they can salvage your budget. They are sometimes as charming as locker rooms, however, and while convenient to the local stadium, they are often far from the center of town. Some are not safe for women.

Hotels and Apartments

The ONTT classifies hotels on a zero- to four-star scale. Budget travelers should stick to the no-star (1-4D per person), one-star (5-7D per person), and two-star (8-10D per person) establishments. The ONTT provides listings of all official hotels.

In Tunis, apartments for foreigners run 200D per month and up. Check listings in *La Presse* or visit the many small *agents immobiliers* along rue Nahas Pasha or the side streets off av. Bourguiba.

Camping

Organized camping hasn't yet come of age in Tunisia, except in the south, where it may be your only alternative. Nevertheless, a handful of campgrounds have sprung up and survived. As for unofficial camping, the ONTT guide states, "You can pitch your tent where you wish on beaches and in parks after having first obtained permission from the property owner or from the nearest Police or National Guard station." In practice, it can be hard to get such permission, or even to find the right people to ask. In a pinch, most youth hostels will allow camping on their grounds for 300ml-1D per person, including use of the facilities. Public beaches are the most popular and generally the best places for freelance camping, but you shouldn't camp alone.

Food

Tunisian cooking reflects the competing foreign influences on the country. Elegant French pastry, Berber date cake, and Near Eastern *halvah* all sell in the same bakery. The staple starch is potatoes, usually cooked in a spicy tomato sauce. In all restaurants you will find *couscous,* a steamed semolina wheat preparation. *Couscous* can be topped by almost any kind of sauce. Beef and chicken are Tunisia's principal meats, typically served roasted, either plain or *en brochette. Merguez* is spicy sausage meal, often served with tomatoes and other vegetables, and one of the country's best meat dishes. *Odja* is a dish of eggs and tomato sauce with a bit of sausage, and *koucha* is a meat and potatoes mixture in a spicy red sauce. Vegetables, mostly tomatoes, cucumbers, and onions, are finely chopped in *mechouia,* Tunisia's national salad, half marinated by its generous dressing of olive oil, vinegar, pepper, and lemon juice. Fast-food stands offer *brik à l'oeuf:* eggs, potatoes, and a green vegetable served in a puff-pastry shell.

In cafes, try soothing *thé vert,* tea richly steeped with mint and heavy on the sugar. Although Islam frowns upon alcohol, beer and wine are widely served. *Celtia,* the most common brand of beer, usually costs 650ml per bottle. Tunisian red wines are heavy, but *gris de Tunisia* and *Koudiat,* both rosés, are quite good at 1.700D or 1.400D per bottle. The local liqueurs *bookha* (distilled from figs, tastes like vodka) and *thibarine* (distilled from dates) are worth a taste. Alcoholic drinking hours are generally from 3 to 10pm in summer and from 1 to 8pm in winter, and but in tourist towns you can booze around the clock. Keep in mind the probable, unpleasant consequences of non-carbonated drinks and unpeelable fruits and vegetables (see Health).

Shopping

The name of the game is hard bargaining. Asking prices are about ten times the actual value. The pleas of peddlers are especially intolerable in the *medinas.*

If you really intend to buy, avoid mingling with tour groups, and shop late in the day when salespeople will be more desperate and willing to settle for fewer dinar. Refusing, turning your back, and walking away will decrease the price substantially.

Two of the best cities to shop in are Sfax and Gabes, where tour buses haven't invaded and spoiled the vendors. Here you won't find the tourist paraphenalia that litters the *medinas* of Tunis, Hammamet, and Monastir.

History and Politics

After 31 years of enlightened autocracy under former President Habib Bourguiba, Tunisia now enters a new era under its second president ever, the more traditional Zine Ben Ali. Until Bourguiba negotiated Tunisia's independence in 1956, the area was dominated largely by various foreign powers or their proxies.

The original inhabitants of the area, such as the nomadic **Berbers,** were little affected by the **Carthaginians,** who stuck to the coast and became powerful from their prosperous trading routes around the Mediterranean. Carthage's rivalry with Rome, particularly over Sicily and Spain, led to three wars and Carthage's eventual destruction. Known only through Roman historians, the second of the three "Punic" (the Roman term for their antagonists) wars was the most spectacular. The Carthaginian general **Hannibal** led an army that included 370 elephants over the Alps, attacked the Romans from the north, and defeated them badly at Lake Trasimeno and Cannae. Hannibal was outflanked and defeated in 201 B.C.E., when Rome attacked Carthage itself. Rome remained afraid of another challenge, however, and at the emboldening urging of its stoic senator Cato, picked a fight with a weakened Carthage, attempting even to erase Carthaginian civilization by razing the city and sowing its site with salt.

Tunisia was Rome's primary African grain-producing outpost, and archeological remains indicate the colony's wealth. Like much of the Empire, it was sacked by the Vandals and reconquered by the **Byzantine Empire.** As the Arabs began to dismember Byzantium, the region was conquered in 698 C.E. and incorporated into the Abassid Empire centered in Baghdad. The four dynasties ruling Tunisia established the Islamic faith locally and built the *medinas* (old cities) at the center of present-day Tunisian urban centers.

In 1590 the **Ottoman Turks** seized the area, although they allowed the Barbary Pirates (known as the corsairs) to continue using the seaports as bases for their raids and shipping. After a century, the Ottomans relinquished control to the **Beys,** a dynasty of Turkish origin. Under these rulers, Tunisia acquired its present-day name and borders—though not much else, as the Beys concentrated mostly on decadent activities within their Bardo Palace, today the home of the National Museum, near Tunis.

While invading the country in 1881 and seizing the best land for their own settlers, the **French** did a great deal to organize and develop the country. Their definitive monument is the Tunisian civil service, one of the best in the Third World. As the effects of colonial rule became more grievous, a nationalist consciousness developed among the intelligentsia, who formed the reformist **Destour Party.** They were superseded by a new generation of young agitators who split and formed the Neo-Destour party. Tunisia's struggle for independence proved to be the least painful among the three Mahgreb countries. Bourguiba, whom the French had jailed before he escaped into exile, returned triumphantly on June 1, 1955, to negotiate Tunisia's independence, which came on **May 20, 1956.** A year later he deposed the last Bey, then the titular head of state, and became president.

Bourguiba was a pragmatist whose religion was the national development of Tunisia. Instead of settling scores with his old jailers, the French, he encouraged them to stay. A number did, to the Tunisian economy's benefit. The country's noncommittal stances on the Middle East issue cost it many Arab friends. The only initiative made to promote Arab unity was to establish ties among the Mahgreb countries. It is clear, however, that the new government wishes to obliterate the memory of the old with celerity. Even Bourguiba's birthday is no longer celebrated as a national holiday.

At the close of Bourguiba's reign, Tunisia was in financial turmoil and civil unrest abounded. Eighty-percent inflation almost brought down the house in 1984, when riots ravaged the countryside and left 100 dead in Tunis. Then the National Bank ran out of money in mid-1986. Tunisia today faces high unemployment, a wide gap between rich and poor, and a difficult recovery from a long-ruling autocratic government that was increasingly out of touch with its people. Two-thirds of Tunisia's population has been born since Bourguiba's Neo-Destour party led the country to independence, and many of the country's seven million inhabitants are ready for the inevitable change.

Festivals and Holidays

Islam is the major force shaping Tunisian life; the major celebration each year is **Ramadan,** the Muslim month of fasting that comes at different times of the Gregorian year depending on the lunar calendar. In early summer, Ramadan affects all aspects of daily life, and shops and services generally close down all afternoon. Muslims are forbidden to eat, drink, or smoke between sunrise and sunset. After sunset, streets swell with people, shops and businesses reopen, and the festivities often last until well past midnight. The end of Ramadan is marked by Id al-Fitr, a three-day celebration during which all commercial activity comes to a standstill. In rural areas and smaller towns, restaurants and cafes will be closed throughout the day.

Let's Go mentions international **cultural festivals** featuring films, music, theater, and dance in northern Tunisia on a city-by-city basis. Southern Tunisia tends to host national festivals, which invariably include camel fights as well as such less alarming forms of traditional culture as folkloric presentations and parades. The most extensive take place in Douz and Tozeur in late December and in Nefta in April. A similar spectacle is held in the north at El-Haouaria on Cap Bon in June.

Tunis

Originally the Carthaginian appendage of Thynes, Tunis rebounded from the destruction of its mother city to become a prominent outpost in Roman and Byzantine times. By the thirteenth century, Tunis had matured into a bastion of Islam. Under the Hafsid Dynasty, the city acquired a reputation for liberal ideas and progressive ways that it continues to cultivate. By North African standards, Tunis is remarkably clean and prosperous, and its inhabitants (1.5 million) sport a unique mixture of Western fashion and traditional garb. Parts of the old city are as Middle Eastern as Mecca; parts of the new are as Arabic as apple pie.

Tunis's concentric faces fail to form a unified visage. At the core is the old city or *medina,* a labyrinth of bazaars or *souks* swirling around immense mosques. Next comes a layer of French colonial buildings, remnants of an attempt to make this city the Paris of Africa. The outer ring shows the face of a Third World capital undergoing an identity crisis: Second-rate skyscrapers preside over characterless blocks of recent vintage that encroach on the slapdash shanties beyond. To the north and south, beach resorts provide a respite from the summer heat.

Orientation and Practical Information

The downtown section of the new city was laid out by the French in their beloved colonial checkerboard fashion. Major boulevards often change names after large intersections. The primary east-west axis is **avenue Habib Bourguiba,** which becomes **avenue de France** several blocks before the *medina.* This is intersected by the major north-south artery, **avenue de Carthage,** which becomes **avenue de Paris** and then **avenue de la Liberté** as it proceeds north. The former stretches from the water's edge to the *medina;* the latter extends from the southbound bus station to grassy **Belvedere Park. Avenue Habib Bourguiba** is *the* thoroughfare, attracting most of the city's major banks, travel agencies, and other services. The body of water at the end of the avenue is not the Mediterranean, but **Lac de Tunis,** an enclosed stretch of salt water. A causeway carries the electric TGM commuter train across the lake to the harbor at **La Goulette,** where the ferries dock. To get to the TGM station from the port road on the left, take a right at the castle, a left at the statue, and walk straight (10min.). The train will take you to Tunis for 180ml. The *Metro,* a newly opened above-ground trolly, connects the TGM station with the train station. The TGM line continues north to the archeological sites of Carthage, the village of Sidi Bou Said, and the beaches at La Marsa.

Tourist Office: ONTT Reception Office, place d'Afrique (tel. 25 91 33), at av. Bourguiba and av. Mohammed V. Service ranges from indifferent to incredibly rude, but this is the best place to grab brochures and the out-of-date *Tunisie Guide Pratique.* Open July 1-Sept. 15 Mon.-Sat. 7:30am-1:30pm and 4-7pm; Sept. 16-June 30 Mon.-Sat. 8:30am-1pm and 3-6pm; during Ramadan (Apr. 5-May 6) 8:30am-2:30pm and 3-6pm. For much more helpful service, try the ONTT branch offices at the **train station** (same hours), on the 2nd floor of the Tunis-Carthage **airport,** or at the **port.**

Student Travel: Many Tunisian travel agencies give 20% student discounts (keep your ISIC handy). The only purely student-oriented travel organization is **Sotutour-Stav,** 2, rue de Sparte (tel. 22 74 48), off av. de Paris. They sell ISICs and operate "vacation villages" at Hammamet, the islands of Kerkennah and Tozeur, and near Tunis.

Embassies: U.S., 144, av. de la Liberté (tel. 23 25 66 or 28 25 66). **Canada,** 3, rue Didon (tel. 28 65 77). **U.K.,** 5, place de la Victoire (tel. 24 51 00). Also the only service for citizens of Australia and New Zealand. **Egypt,** 16, rue Es-Sayouti (tel. 23 00 04), in the suburb of El Menzah. Take bus #5B or 5C from av. Bourguiba. It's economical to obtain a visa before

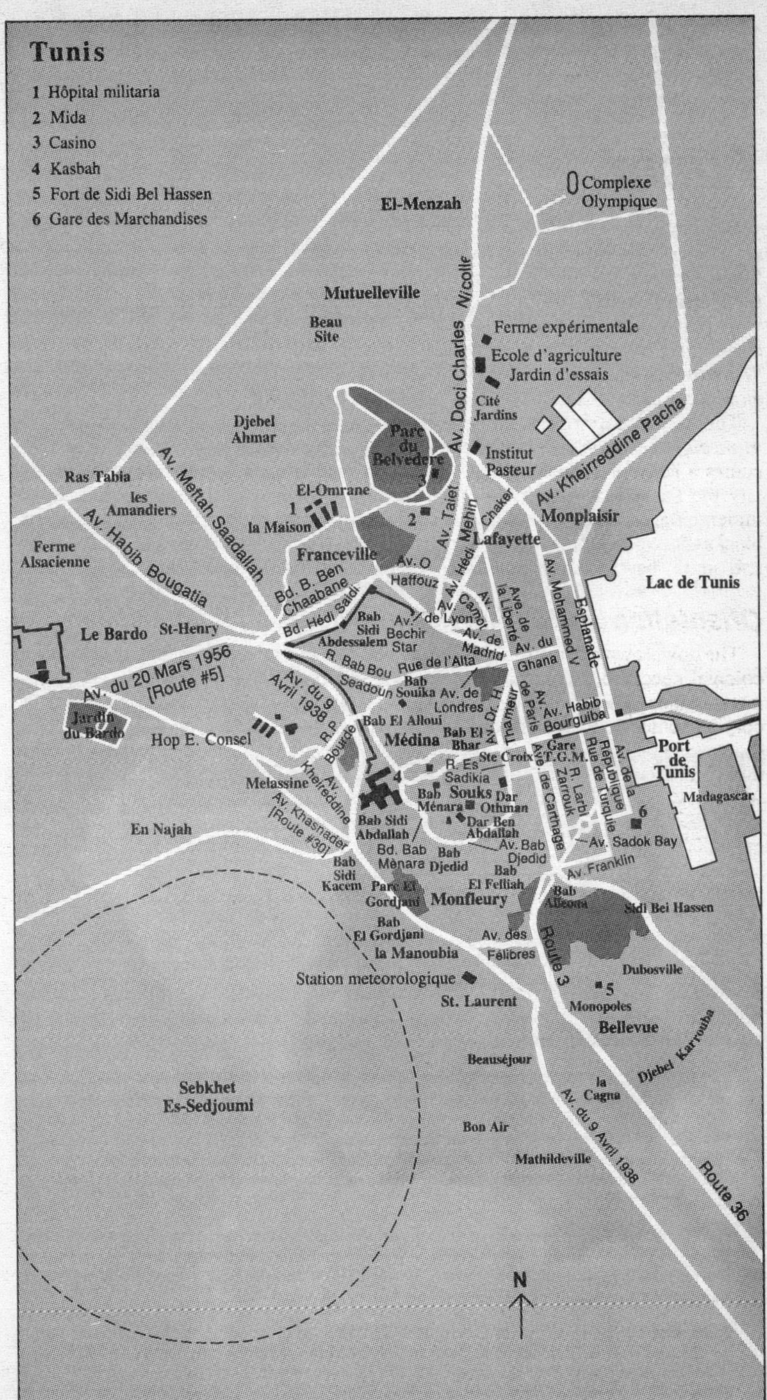
Tunis
1 Hôpital militaria
2 Mida
3 Casino
4 Kasbah
5 Fort de Sidi Bel Hassen
6 Gare des Marchandises
El-Menzah
Complexe Olympique
Mutuelleville
Beau Site
Av. Doci Charles Nicolle
Ferme expérimentale
Ecole d'agriculture
Jardin d'essais
Cité Jardins
Djebel Ahmar
Parc du Belvedere
Institut Pasteur
Av. Kheirreddine Pacha
Ras Tabia
les Amandiers
Av. Meftah Saadallah
El-Omrane
la Maison
Monplaisir
Lafayette
Ferme Alsacienne
Av. Habib Bougatia
Franceville
Av. O Haffouz
Lac de Tunis
Bd. B. Ben Chaabane
Bd. Hédi Saidi
Le Bardo
St-Henry
Bab Sidi Abdessalem
Av. de Lyon
Av. Bechir Star
Av. de Madrid
Av. du Ghana
Esplanade
Av. Mohammed V
Av. du 20 Mars 1956 [Route #5]
Av. du 9 Avril 1938
R. Bab Bou Seadoun
Rue de l'Alta
Bab Souika
Av. de Londres
Av. Habib Bourguiba
Jardin du Bardo
Hop E. Consel
Bab El Alloui
Médina
Bab El Bhar
Gare T.G.M.
Port de Tunis
Madagascar
Ste Croix
R. Es Sadikia
Melassine
Av. Kheireddine
Souks
Dar Othman
Av. Khasnader [Route #30]
Bab Sidi Abdallah
Bab Ménara
Dar Ben Abdallah
Av. Bab Djedid
Av. Sadok Bay
En Najah
Bd. Bab Mènara
Bab Djedid
Av. Franklin
Bab Sidi Kacem
Parc El Gordjani
Monfleury
Bab El Felliah
Bab Alleoua
Sidi Bel Hassen
Bab El Gordjani
la Manoubia
Av. des Félibres
Route 3
Dubosville
Station meteorologique
St. Laurent
Monopoles
Bellevue
Djebel Karrouba
Beauséjour
Sebkhet Es-Sedjoumi
la Cagna
Av. du 9 Avril 1938
Bon Air
Mathildeville
Route 36
N

entering Egypt. **Algeria,** 18, rue du Niger (tel. 28 31 66). Bring 9.500D and 4 photos for a visa. which is required of U.S., Canadian, and Australian citizens. Minimum money exchange about 1000AD.

American Express: Carthage Tours, 59, av. Habib Bourguiba (tel. 254 43 04). No banking services are available in Tunisia. Emergency check cashing for cardholders only; others can only report lost or stolen traveler's checks here. Don't expect a warm reception. Open Mon.-Fri. 8am-noon and 2:30-6pm, Sat. 8:30am-noon.

Post Office: 30, av. Charles de Gaulle, off av. de France. Limited services only in the afternoon. **Poste Restante** (150ml per letter received). Adjoining postal museum. Open Mon.-Sat. 8am-6pm.

Telephones and Telex: 29, rue Jemal Abdel Nasser, entrance around the corner from the post office. Inefficient. You may wait up to 1 hr. to make a collect call. All phones here take 1D and 500ml pieces, so you can make direct international calls (to the U.S., dial 001, area code, number). Send telegrams from here or the post office. Open 24 hours.

Telephone Code: 01.

English Books: Many stores on av. Bourguiba and av. de France have limited selections of books in English. **S.T.D.,** 5, av. de Carthage, has an assortment of amazing books in English and French. Open in summer Mon.-Sat. 8am-2:30pm; in off-season Mon.-Sat. 8am-1:30pm and 5-7:30pm. **Claire Fontaine** rue d'Alger, off av. Bourguiba, has a tiny selection. Open in summer Mon.-Sat. 8am-1:30pm; in off-season 8am-1:30pm and 4-7:30pm.

English-language Libraries: American Cultural Center, 1, av. de France, at the end of av. Bourguiba. Well-stocked lending library. Membership free, just have 2 photos taken across the street. Show your passport to enter. Open in summer Mon.-Fri. 8am-2:30pm; in winter Mon.-Fri. 9am-5:30pm, Sat. 9am-noon. The **American Community Library,** off place Pasteur, behind the U.S. A.I.D. Office, lends books to Americans on the honor system. The **British Council,** in the British Embassy at place de la Victoire, offers the same service. Membership 5D.

Foreign Newspapers: The 3 newspaper stands on the central island of av. Bourguiba carry major European newspapers and magazines, the *International Herald Tribune, Time,* and *Newsweek.* Also check the lobby of **Hotel Africa.**

Laundromats: Not a coin-operated laundromat in Tunisia, but some dry cleaners take laundry by the kilo. Avoid those charging per piece. Try **Laverie,** 15, rue d'Allemagne, across from the produce market. Wash 3D per 1-4kg, dry 900ml. Open Mon.-Sat. 7am-6pm.

Night pharmacies: 43, av. Bourguiba (tel. 25 25 07), or 20, av. de la Liberté (tel. 24 35 20).

Hospital: Hôpital Charles Nicolle, bd. du IX Avril 1938 (tel. 66 30 10).

Ambulance: Tel. 190 or 49 13 13.

Medical Emergency: Tel. 24 73 30.

Police: Tel.197. Unsympathetic and unhelpful.

Transportation

Airport: Tunis-Carthage International Airport, tel. 23 60 00. 24-hour **currency exchange.** Take bus #35 from av. Bourguiba to the airport *(aérodrome)* and back (about 320ml). Note: the TGM Aéroport stop is actually a beach named Aéroport—not the airport.

Train Station: SNCFT Tunis Ville Station, place de Barcelone (tel. 24 44 40), between rue de Hollande and av. de Carthage. Walk straight up av. de Carthage to av. Bourguiba. The new *Metro* connects this station to the TGM station. To Hammamet and Nabeul (1.160D), Sousse (2.310D), Sfax (3.750D), and Gabes (5.600D).

Commuter train: TGM, at the foot of av. Bourguiba. Carthage-La Marsa via La Goulette, Sidi Bou Said. Speedy tram service 6am-midnight. 300ml to Carthage and La Marsa, 180ml between middle stops, 100ml supplement at night.

Inter-city Buses: There are 2 main stations. **Southbound** and **Hammamet-Nabeul** (tel. 49 52 55 or 49 03 58). The SNT station is at the end of av. de Carthage across from the cemetery to the right. Walk or take municipal bus #8 from av. Bourguiba or #50 from Jemal Abdel Nasser (120ml). Taxis from av. Bourguiba cost 500ml. To Bizerte, Tabarka, and environs

("Gare Routière Nord") from the SNT station on av. du 20 Mars 1956, just beyond Bab Saadoun. Take bus #3 from av. Bourguiba.

Municipal Buses: 2 main terminals: one on av. Dr. Habib Thameur, at **Jardin Thameur,** before av. de Paris; the second next to the **TGM Tunis-Marine Station.** Buses also stop at place de Barcelone, in front of the Tunis-Ville train station and along av. Bourguiba. Fare 140ml or 220ml, depending on the distance traveled.

Harbor: La Goulette, tel. 27 53 00. Take the TGM train to Vieille Goulette, 1km from the port. Ferry tickets at any of the travel agencies along av. Bourguiba. Arrive at least 2 hr. before departure.

Taxis: Tel. 25 52 39. Always metered. 3 passengers is the usual maximum. 50% surcharge after 9pm. To the airport about 2D.

Louages: Hard to pin down. To Bizerte and Tabarka: in front of SNT station for northbound departures. To Nabeul, Hammamet, Sfax, and Bjerba: rue du Soudan, off av. de la Gare (toward the SNT station). To Kelibia and Cape Bon: near the southbound overpass at the Bab Alleoua bus station. To Jendouba and Ain Draham: Café el Hana, av. Bab Djedid.

Car Rental: Numerous agencies provide unlimited-mileage cars. The cheapest is **Top Car,** 17, av. Habib Bourguiba (tel. 24 14 62), or at the airport (box #3494, tel. 28 80 00). Renault 4s cost 110D per 3 days, 200D per week. **Hertz,** 29, av. Bourguiba (tel. 24 85 59), or at the airport (tel. 23 60 00), is more expensive but more easily serviced outside Tunis—Renault 4 120D per 3 days, 240D per week. Nearby, **Avis** and **Europcar** offer similar rates. **Garage Lafayette,** 84, av. de la Liberté (tel. 28 02 84). Fiat 127 or Autobianchi 10D per day plus 100ml per km. Beware that none of these rates includes car or passenger insurance (about 4D per day), or a contract fee (about 3D), or 14.3% tax, or gas. It is illegal for a rental car to carry more than 3 passengers plus the driver. Always have passports ready for security checks.

Biking: In this city, synonymous with death.

Accommodations and Camping

Finding a budget hotel in Tunis is no problem except in the height of summer; the problem is finding one that isn't sleazy. Women traveling alone or in groups should avoid the cheapest hotels. Men, too, should think carefully before deciding to stay in the *medina.* In late July and August, when Tunis teems with European and Algerian vacationers, start your search early in the morning; by afternoon, all the hotels will be booked. Since most of the places listed below are within 5 or 6 blocks of the train station, you might check your bags at the *gare* (500ml, open 4am-midnight) and hoof it door to door. Unfortunately, the **IYHF youth hostel** (tel. 29 56 31; members 2D) is more of a hassle than it's worth—count on a 20-minute ride on the TNCFT *Omnibus* train out to Radès, followed by a 20-minute walk. Official campgrounds are similarly inconvenient, the closest being 20 minutes farther via the *Omnibus* train to Hammam Plage.

Hotel Bristol, rue Mohamed el Aziz Taj (tel. 24 48 36), off av. de Carthage behind the Café de Paris. Clean, convenient, but cramped. A good deal. Singles 4D, doubles 6D, triples 9D, quads 11D. Showers included.

Hotel Cirta, 42, rue Charles de Gaulle (tel. 24 15 82), near the post office. One of the best deals in town. Comfy rooms, many with balconies overlooking the lively street. But even the affable manager cannot exterminate the omnipresent mosquitos. Singles 4D, doubles 6D, triples 9D. All-temperature showers 500ml.

Hotel Agriculture, 25, rue Charles de Gaulle (tel. 24 63 94), across from the Cirta, which it resembles. Decent, but less friendly than Cirta. Singles 3D. Doubles 6.500D, with bath 7.500D. Triples 10D. Quads 11D. Showers (cold in summer) 500ml.

Hotel Commodore, 17, rue d'Allemagne (tel. 24 49 41), 2nd right off av. Charles de Gaulle from av. de France. A cut above, and not much more expensive. Polished wood lobby and spotless rooms, some with shining baths. Singles 5.800D, with bath 8D. Doubles 8.500D, with bath 12D. Triples 12D, with bath 14.500D.

Victoria Hotel, 72, av. Farhat Hached (tel. 34 28 63), across from the bus stops in front of the train station. Pleasant rooms, lobby, and management. Singles 6D. Doubles 9D, with bath 10D.

Nouvel Hotel, 3, place Mongi Bali (tel. 24 33 79), across from train station. Rooms range from dumpy to cheerful and airy. Research your room individually. Singles 4D, doubles 6D, triples 8D. Showers included.

Hotel de Suisse, 5, rue de Suisse (tel. 24 38 21), in a narrow alley between rue de Hollande and rue Jamal Abdel Nasser, by the train station. Tidy and affordable, if you don't mind the cute lizards in the walls. Singles 5.400D. Doubles 7.800D, with bath 8.600D. Showers 500ml. Across the street, **Hotel Central** (tel. 24 04 33) provides mediocre rooms at unspectacular prices. English-speaking, friendly, but unsuitable for women. Doubles 6D, triples 8D, quads 10D. A mat on the roof is 2D.

Hotel Rex, 65, rue de Yougoslavie (tel. 25 73 97), at rue Ibn Khaldoun. Affable management. Breezy rooms in an ugly brown. Microscopic singles 5.500D. Capacious doubles and triples 9.500D. Showers included.

Hotel Transatlantique, 106, rue de Yougoslavie (tel. 25 81 91 or 24 06 80), at av. de Carthage. A commodious and comfortable 1-star in the center of town. Don't expect to shower here unless your pockets are loaded with gold ingots. Singles 4.650D, with bath 10D. Doubles 8.700D, with bath 11D.

Hotel de France, 8, rue Mustapha M'Barek (tel. 24 58 76), off place de la Victoire. Despite dingy hallways, this spic-and-span 1-star has the most amiable management in town. Singles 6.300D, with shower 7.500D. Doubles 7.700D, with shower 10D.

Hotel Continental, 5, rue Marseille (tel. 25 98 34), off av. Bourguiba, across from Hotel Africa. Immaculate rooms painted an upbeat blue. Noisy. Singles 5D, doubles 8D, triples 10D. Cold showers 700ml. Often full in Aug.

Hotel Grand Maghreb, 50, rue des Salines (tel. 25 98 11), off av. de Londres by Parc Habib Thameur. A pleasant place away from the onslaught of budget hotels, with a large park across the street. 3D per person in singles, doubles, or triples. Showers 800ml.

Hotel Majestic, 36, av. de Paris (tel. 24 28 48). As the name and prices indicate; a palatial marble staircase and reception hall. Welcome A/C. Singles 14.500D, doubles 22D. Bath and breakfast included. Discount with YIEE card. Be adamant if you try to get a discount with an ISIC.

Food

This is a cheap food mecca; the challenge, as in finding a room, is to find quality. The ubiquitous, stand-up *rôtisseries* and sandwich shops off av. Bourguiba and av. de la Liberté are usually rip-offs. The farther off av. Bourguiba you go, the fewer dinar you have to delve for. Budgetarians can survive on the hot snacks sold at most *pâtisseries:* mini pizzas, hot anchovy rolls, tuna rolls, and meat pies (about 250ml). Pastry shops lurk on every corner, particularly on rue Charles de Gaulle; they serve fresh-squeezed orange juice for only 200ml but drown most of their food in honey. **Chargui,** at 28 rue Charles de Gaulle (tel. 25 65 69), makes a delicious chocolate croissant (200ml) that will tide you over for lunch. For dessert, try the unique, strangely appetizing Tunisian *yagourt,* available almost everywhere.

The large **central market,** on rue Charles de Gaulle between rue d'Allemagne and av. d'Espagne, has an excellent selection. Cool off with watermelon, or munch on cheap, fresh almonds. (Open Mon.-Sat. 6am-2:30pm.) **Monoprix,** a large supermarket with stores off av. Bourguiba on rue Charles de Gaulle and on rue de la Liberté at rue du Koweit, also stocks an inexpensive selection of edibles. (Open Mon.-Sat. 8:30am-noon and 3:30-7pm, Sun. 8:30am-12:30pm.)

Men might enjoy relaxing at the numerous sidewalk cafes, but women—even in the company of men—will probably find the stares uncomfortable. A better idea is to relax in the rooftop terrace of the International Hotel with a marvelous panorama of Tunis and environs. The management's dress code has little sympathy for the backpack look—put on your best threads.

For Arabic music and belly dancing, try **M'Rabet,** in the center of the *medina* in Souk Et-Trouk (tel. 26 36 81). It's a big-time splurge (cover 4D, main dishes 3.200-7.500D), but the liveliest show in town. (Open Mon.-Sat. 8pm-midnight.) Be careful in the *medina* as you leave.

Mic Mac, at rue de Yougoslavie and Ibn Khaldoun. One of the few stand-up sandwich shops that's not a rip-off. Reasonably clean. Massive *schwarma* sandwich and fries 800ml. Open Mon.-Sat. 7am-8pm.

Restaurant Les Palmiers, 11, rue d'Egypte (tel. 28 54 07), off av. de la Liberté. Worth every second of the 10-min. walk from av. Bourguiba. Dishes are fresh, Tunisian, and served quickly. Best bread and french fries in town. *Brik à l'oeuf* 350ml, *poulet rôti* 1D, *merguez à l'oeuf* 1D, and *couscous* 1D. Open Mon.-Sat. noon-10:30pm. Closed last week of Ramadan.

Restaurant Le Poisson D'or, 27, rue Aziz Taj (tel. 25 63 38), 1 block over from av. Bourguiba. Tasty assortment of seafood and meat dishes. *Couscous Complet Tunisienne* (3D) is filling and *delicieux.*

Restaurant Neptune, 3, rue du Caire (tel. 24 45 20), across from Hotel Africa. The complete, 4-course *menù* including 1 drink is a fantastic deal (2D). Prompt service, large portions, and decent fare. A great way to taste a variety of dishes cheaply. Open daily 10:30am-10:30pm.

Restaurant Ennil, 9, rue du Caire (tel. 24 93 80). Mediocre food at reasonable prices. *Couscous au viande, macaroni au viande,* or *mermez* each 1D. *Menù* 1.500D. Open daily 10am-10:30pm. Across the street at #6, **Restaurante du Caire** serves similarly uninspired but affordable fare.

Restaurant Erriadh, 9, rue Ibn Khaldoun (tel. 24 65 16). Around the corner, the same owners run **Restaurant Abid,** 98, rue de Yougoslavie. *Biftek d'veau* and *merguez grillé a l'oeuf* each 1.500D. Open daily 11am-3pm and 7-10pm.

Restaurant El Basra, 44, av. Habib Bourguiba (tel. 24 71 06), 1 block from Hotel Africa. Pleasant outdoor setting in an alley off av. Bourguiba. *Salade tunisienne* 600ml, spicy *couscous* 2D. Service 10%.

Restaurant La Grotte, Passage #3, just off 25, av. de Paris (tel. 24 48 76). Funky interior designed to look like the inside of a grotto. Omelette and spaghetti each 1D. Crepes 0.600-1.100D.

Chez Nous, 5, rue de Marseille (tel. 24 30 43). Treat yourself to fine, expensive French food. Dinner for 2 with wine 12D plus service. *Menù* 5.500D.

Sights

For a city its size, Tunis is not particularly laden with sights, but there is never a dearth of images to muse upon, between the colorful *souks* and the hordes of gum-chewing westerners. Wander aimlessly in the vast *medina,* trek out to the outstanding Bardo Museum, and for further artistic monuments, catch the next commuter train for Sidi Bou Said and La Marsa.

The New City

The French-built New City has little to offer outside of its nightly cosmopolitan bustle. The best introduction to modern Tunis is a stroll up **avenue Habib Bourguiba,** known as the city's Champs Elysées. Including its median strip of tree-filled park, the boulevard is nearly 70m wide. The strip demonstrates the Tunisian passion for flowers—florist stalls and young boys vending jasmine blossoms line virtually its entire length. The first stretch of av. Bourguiba, from the TGM station to av. Muhammad V, borders a commercial area of little interest. **Place d'Afrique,** at the intersection of av. Muhammad V, is dominated by an equestrian statue of Bourguiba. To the right, off av. Muhammad V, are two contemporary buildings: the **Hotel du Lac,** a Western steel and glass creation resembling a pyramid set on its apex, and the new ONTT Tourist Office, a low, whitewashed block set back from the street.

Nowhere is the stamp of the French colonial period clearer than the point where av. Bourguiba proceeds from place d'Afrique, at the heart of the city. After you cross av. de Carthage on the boulevard, you will reach the **Artisanat** (a bastion of overpriced local crafts) on the left, and after it, the **National Theater.** At **place de l'Indépendence,** where av. Bourguiba comes to an abrupt halt, you may suddenly feel you are in Paris. On the left is the oversized French Embassy, a miniature Elysées palace hiding behind its elegant black iron fence. Then the street narrows suddenly and av. Bourguiba becomes av. de France. The next block on the same side forms a continuous arcade, like a grand nineteenth-century Parisian boulevard. Across the street looms the massive **cathedral,** which incorporates keyhole-shaped Islamic arches into its Gothic form. The blend is only slightly more successful than the French efforts made within the edifice to convert Tunisians to Christianity. Built in 1882, the Roman Catholic cathedral was dedicated to St. Vincent de Paul and erected with ambitious hopes. The Diocese of Africa (whose most famous son was the converted Berber St. Augustine) had been dead since the days of Byzantium, but was revived by the French for 50 years, with its seat in Tunis, before collapsing again. To get inside, walk around the block to the right. The interior houses one of the eight Mollins-Cervailles-Coll Romantic organs in the world, worth over $4.5 million. (Cathedral open daily after 3:30pm.) If you are in search of a little leafy peace, head to the **Jardin Thameur,** av. Habib Thameur. In the opposite direction, the lively shopping street of **rue Charles de Gaulle** is usually covered with a stream of pedestrians. One block down from av. de France begins the large indoor fruit, vegetable, and fish **market.**

To escape the frightening volume of travel agencies and pastry shops that line av. Bourguiba, head down av. de Paris and av. de la Liberté to **Belvedere Park,** a dot of green amidst the gray. In one part of the park is a paltry **zoo.** Children feed the deer, but the confused animals eat foil wrappers as well. (Open in summer daily 7am-7pm; in the off-season 7am-5:30pm.) Locals flock to the nearby municipal **pool.** (Open Tues.-Sun. 10am-3pm. Admission 500ml.) The hill at the center of the grounds overlooks the entire city. Sunset, however, is best enjoyed from the tower of the park's charming white, seventeenth-century **Koubba.** Signs also point to the **Museum of Modern Art,** containing works by twentieth-century Tunisian painters as well as Europeans who lived and worked in Tunisia. (Open in summer Tues.-Sat. 9:30am-1pm and 2:30-7pm; in the off-season Tues.-Sat. 9:30am-1pm and 2-4:30pm. Free.) Walk all the way to the end of av. de la Liberté, or take bus #5 or 38 from av. Bourguiba, #7 or 35 from the Jardin Thameur terminal.

Medina

In most Arab cities, the fortified, medieval old city, or *medina,* is geographically and spiritually a world apart from the nineteenth- and twentieth-century areas. This is true only of the outlying areas of Tunis's *medina,* however, as the central areas have become so infested with vulgar souvenir shops that it seems a continuation of av. Bourguiba, which leads directly toward them. The medieval *souks*—itinerant weekly markets specializing in a few wares—have become so commercialized that there is now a Souk Burger, right next to the Mustang Jeans by the mosque.

Still, the *medina* is worth a few hours, if only for its size, and if you avoid the main drags, you may be enchanted. Explore by day—in light, the *medina* is safe even for solo women, but at night, it's unsafe for anyone, and the police will be unsympathetic if you're mugged. On av. Bourguiba and by the mosque, young men claiming to be students will offer either to guide you around the sights (they will expect payment) or to accompany you to the grossly over-priced artisan shops (they will receive a commission).

If you are determined to know where you are, you can buy *Tunis la Ville et les Monuments* of the *Guides Ceres* at Claire Fontaine or STD—it maps the *medina* in exhaustive detail. It is more fun, though, to forage through the labyrinth of narrow alleys and low arches unaided.

To escape the tourist traps, take route de la Kasbah (on the right) rather than rue Djamaa ez Zitounia (on the left) from place de la Victoire. The former, like the latter, is lined with shops, but the shoppers are Tunisian. Near the mosque (left from Souk Burger), turn right and wind slowly up the Bab Souika. **Place Bab Souika,** just outside the *medina* walls but at the core of the old city, is among the most authentic spots in Tunis. Head across the street, up covered rue Halfouine, the butcher's street, past the bleeding cows' heads and goat stomachs, to the benches and stalls in front of the **mosque Sahab Tabaa**—a stronghold of Arab culture. Catch it while you can: The entire area is slated for "redevelopment" in a few years.

Those determined to "do" the medina, rather than experience it impressionistically, should start back at the Grand Mosque, in the center of the *medina,* to the left of rue Djamaa ez Zitounia. Known formally as **Djamaa ez Zitounia** (Mosque of the Olives), the Great Mosque maintains vague visiting conditions for non-Muslims—especially during the summer. Generally, you are permitted to visit the courtyard between 8am and noon (except on Fri.) if you are fully clothed. Alternatively, you can visit the terrace of one of the surrounding shops and look down into the courtyard—prayer times are quite a sight. Young men on the steps of the mosque are eager, self-appointed guides; however, their services are really not necessary. As you enter the courtyard of the mosque, a long row of carved wooden doors studded with iron stands on your left. These conceal the prayer area and the *mihrab,* which faces east toward Mecca. Opposite, you'll find the gigantic minaret, soaring over the entire *medina* from its central location. Modified in the nineteenth century, it is far more decorative than the courtyard or prayer room. The former is lined with an arcade supported by sleek pillars whose Corinthian capitals were borrowed from Roman ruins in Carthage when the Mosque was built in 723 C.E.

Alongside the mosque runs **Souk el-Attarine** (the perfumers' market), the largest and most grandiose of the *souks.* Although traditional perfume stalls still exist, many shops now sell tourist junk. From the end of Souk el-Attarine, follow Souk el-Trouk (the tailors' market) to rue Sidi Ben Zaid. On your left, you'll see the handsome seventeenth-century **Sidi Youssef Mosque,** dominated by its octagonal minaret, while on your right stands the eighteenth-century **Dar El Bay** palace, now housing the Ministry of Foreign Affairs. At the opposite end, the stylish seventeenth-century **Hammouda Pacha Mosque** awaits you with its elegant minaret and adjoining mausoleum. Walk back toward the minaret of the Grand Mosque and along its walls through the **Souk el Koumach** (also called Souk des Etoffes), a fifteenth-century passageway that specializes in women's garments. Don't miss the narrow turn-off onto **Souk el-Leffa,** the luxurious carpet *souk.* Many of the larger emporiums have beautifully tiled terraces with magnificent views overlooking the rooftops of the *souks* and the surrounding *medina.* Don't be afraid to check them out—there are no strings attached. The most famous of terraces is at the **Palais d'Orient,** the large bazaar at #58 Souk el-Leffa. Their enameled tile terrace dates from the fifteenth century and its view is featured on hundreds of postcards of Tunis. Souk el-Leffa turns into **Souk es Sekkajine,** the saddlemakers' *souk;* to your left is the turn-off for the **Sidi Bou Khrissan Museum,** a small lapidary museum. Retrace your steps, turn right onto Souk el Kouafi, and on your right will be the miniature maze of **Souk des Orfèvres—** the jewelers' neighborhood. The surrounding streets harbor artisans engraving silver, cutting stones, and making pendants and rings out of ancient coins.

As you follow **Souk de la Laine** (the wool *souk*) along the only remaining wall of the Grand Mosque, turn right to reach the eighteenth-century **Madersa es Slimaniya.** If you turn left, walk back in front of the main porch of the Grand Mosque, and straight along tiny rue el Jelloud. At #9, you can ring the doorbell and visit the small, elegant seventeenth-century **Tomb of Princess Aziza,** now a private residence. Between Souk el-Trouk and Souk el-Leffa runs **Souk el-Berka,** originally the slave market of Tunis. Now it is the home of **M'Rabet,** a famous restaurant built on the shrines of three holy men.

Other sights of interest in the *medina* lie farther from the central market area. The stately **Mosque of Sidi Mehrez,** at the far northern tip of the *medina,* deserves a visit. It can be reached by a delightful walk through completely untouristed *souks* where local residents do their shopping. From Souk el-Attarine, take Souk el-Blaghjia. You'll see the narrow, delightful **Souk du Cuivre,** the metalworkers' *souk,* forking off to the left. It rings with the sound of hammers. You can buy teapots, lamps, pipes, and hammered metal plates here directly from the artisans. At the end, turn left onto Souk el Grana, which eventually turns into Souk el Out. If you follow the covered market route, the *souks* will eventually give way to **Sidi Mehrez,** a large white mosque on the street of the same name. The seventeenth-century edifice is noted for the strong Turkish influence, with four small domes grouped around a single large central dome. (The domes are not visible from the street and entrance is forbidden; catch a glimpse from the rooftop bar of the Hotel International.) Across the street lies the fascinating **Zaouia Sidi Mehrez.** Walk straight in and turn left to find a well where women come to bathe in holy fertility water. Also a charity, the Zaouia distributes free bread and food to all comers. Just around the corner you can visit the less crowded, but also less interesting **Zaouia de Sidi Brahim.** Follow rue el Gharmatou along the wall of the Sidi Mehrez Mosque and rue el Monastiri; you'll see tiny rue Sidi Brahim on your right; the Zaouia is at #11. Enter the modest doorway and you'll discover a sumptuous polychrome tile interior surrounding the saint's coffin.

Another worthwhile excursion is a stroll over to the southern corner of the *medina.* From the Grand Mosque, follow rue Djamaa ez Zitounia, and take the first right onto Souk el Balat, which leads to rue des Teinturiers. Here you'll find the enjoyable little **Mosquée des Teinturiers**—the dyers' mosque, built in 1716. A few steps farther, signs will point the way to **Dar Ben Abdullah,** an ornate eighteenth-century palace that houses the **Museum of Traditional Arts.** If you follow rue Ben Abdullah from the courtyard of the palace, you'll eventually reach the **Souk des Teinturiers,** the dyers' colorful *souk.* Two successive right turns bring you to **Tourbet el Bey,** a palatial eighteenth-century mausoleum that houses the remains of the last ruling beys of the Husainid family. After viewing the mausoleum, meander in the charming residential quarters of the neighborhood on your own.

The Bardo Museum

While a trip to North Africa generally means escape from the endless "must-see" museums of Europe, Tunis offers no better diversion than the small Bardo Museum, home to one of the world's finest collections of ancient art. The Bardo is most renowned for its Roman mosaics; the finest works have been transported here from various archeological sites throughout the country and compensate for the uninspiring ruins at Carthage and other sites. The Bardo is housed in a nineteenth-century palace enjoyed by the Husainid Dynasty until it was deposed in 1957, although the collection itself was first organized in 1888. Converting the royal residence into a museum was no easy task, especially since some of the mosaics are half the size of a tennis court. The Bardo's redesigners wisely divided the upper two floors into a series of split-level rooms illuminated by light wells that afford unforgettable views of crucial pieces from antiquity. The Bardo's annex, guarded effectively by snarling marble lions, is the national assembly.

Unless you wish to attribute every tile and bow to every pagan deity, ignore the exhaustive guidebooks sold at the Claire Fontaine and STD bookstores; a desultory encounter can be just as memorable. The ground floor (early-Christian funeral relics) and the top floor (decorative mosaics) can defer to the treasures of the second floor (Roman sculpture and mosaics, organized by city).

On the **ground floor,** breeze from the bookshop to the cheery **Tophet Room,** full of instructions for sacrificing children to the gods. Back across the hall, the **Paleochristian Room** features brightly colored mosaic tombstones with dyspeptic icons and Latin admonitions. Room VI features the findings from **Bulla Regia,** highlighted by the fine mosaic of Perseus and Andromeda; see Bulla Regia in this book for details on this ancient Roman resort. The beautiful geometric mosaics uncovered at **Thuburbo Majus** are in Room VIII. Take refuge from the dead by floating up the staircase into the land of the immortal: Room IX, the central exhibition hall, is a Turkish confection that served as a courtyard for the bey's harem. Now it houses sculpture and mosaics excavated at **Carthage.** The **Virgilia Room,** off the far wall, displays a portrait of Virgil composing the *Aeneid,* flanked by two attending muses. On the other side of the great court, the **Hadrumetum Room** is dominated by the bony feet and hairy head of a massive Jupiter with nothing in between except his left arm (along the wall to the left). An immense mosaic from Sousse of the *Triumph of Neptune* decorates the floor. The walls above contain some of the finest pieces in the collection: three lovely, semi-circular works depicting rural houses, and a splendid fourth-century piece entitled *Mosaïque du Seigneur Julius.* Room IX houses the finds from **Dougga,** including the celebrated mosaic that depicts *Ulysses and the Sirens,* the latter quite homely and the former frightened nonetheless.

The Bardo is open Tuesday through Sunday from 9:30am to 4:30pm; during Ramadan until 4pm. (Admission 1D, students free; Fri. and Sun. afternoons 800ml. Photo permits 2D.) The museum is 4km from the downtown area. Take bus #3 from av. Bourguiba (210ml), or take bus #3 or 4 from Bab Souika east of the *medina.*

Near Tunis

Tunis's surroundings seem to exist for daytrips. The efficient TGM commuter trains make Carthage (30 min.), Sidi Bou Said (35 min.), and La Marsa (40 min.) an easy, quick ride away. The fare is 600ml round-trip to any of these destinations. The spectacular 30-km-long beach of **Raoued** begins just past Gammarth; both are accessible by municipal bus from Tunis or La Marsa. The Roman ruins at **Zaghovan** and **Thuburbo Majus,** to the southwest of the capital, are difficult to reach and not extremely rewarding.

Carthage

> *There was an ancient city (Tyrian settlers inhabited it), Carthage, opposite Italy and the far-off mouths of the Tiber, a city rich in wealth and terribly harsh in the pursuit of war. Juno is said to have loved this one city more than all lands, even preferring it to Samos.*
>
> —*Virgil, The Aeneid I* 12-16

Visitors to the modern city of Carthage are not likely to share Juno's sentiment. When the Romans set out to completely destroy Carthage in 146 B.C.E., they left nothing for posterity.

Over the last two decades, a joint project of the Tunisian government and UNESCO has unearthed bits and pieces of ancient Carthage, dating mostly from the Roman period. The ruins are scattered over a wide area that, fortunately, coincides with the six stops of the TGM rail line listed below. Successive stops are close together and the distances can be traversed easily on foot. For a brief visit, get off at the **Carthage-Hannibal** station, visit the Roman baths, and continue for as long as time or stamina permits. The nearby beaches of the Bay of Tunis offer a refreshing alternative to yet another sight.

Carthage-Salammbo: The first TGM stop takes its name from the title of a ponderous novel by Gustave Flaubert about ancient Carthage. It is here that you'll find what little remains of the powerful Punic metropolis that once ruled the Mediterranean as the ancient world's greatest naval power and second mightiest city, only to be eclipsed by Rome.

Evidence of the original Punic settlement has been discovered in the form of a cemetery. The **Tophet** (also called the **Sanctuary of Tanit**) is the site where, in periods of hardship, Carthaginians sacrificed their first-born to the bloodthirsty goddess Tanit. The Tophet contains the tombs that have been uncovered, once part of a vast cemetery devoted to the memory of the innocent victims. In theory, the sacrifice would have been most effective if the children had been offered by the city's noblest families. In practice, slave children—or, as the bones reveal, even baby sheep—were substituted. To reach the Tophet, walk straight ahead from the station—don't cross the tracks. Proceed to rue Hannibal and take a left. (Open daily in summer 7am-7pm; in off-season 8am-5pm. Admission 1D, students free. Ticket also valid at the Punic Ports.)

Carthage-Byrsa: Almost nothing remains of what *was* the world's greatest harbor, but determined archeologists have reconstructed the shape of the original **Punic Ports.** Although the setting is picturesque and beautiful gardens adorn the residences nearby (the ambassadors live here), the site itself remains as bare as the day the Romans sowed it with salt in hopes of rendering the land forever infertile. The admiral of the Carthaginian fleet had his residence in a sumptuous palace on the port's central island. Today, the spot is occupied by a small building marked "Antiquarium." The custodian will unlock it for you. Inside are detailed models of the military port during both the Punic and Roman periods; they evoke a sense of the original, circular splendor of the site. (Site open daily in summer 8am-7pm; in off-season 8am-6pm. Admission 1D, students free. Ticket also valid at the Tophet.) To reach the ports, walk toward the water from the Carthage-Byrsa station and take your third left to circle the swamp. If you've just visited the Tophet, follow rue Hannibal to the water, turn left at the sign that points right toward the **Oceanographic Museum,** then turn right and walk around the swamp. Either way, avoid the sad Oceanographic Museum, where the marine life either hangs on the walls or floats limply at the top of a tank.

Carthage-Dermech: The **National Museum of Carthage** occupies the site where an immense Roman temple once stood. The remains are scattered throughout the surrounding gardens. Join the statues for a bird's-eye view of Tunis. Inside are only a few Punic funerary steles and two sarcophagi, made from Italian Carrara marble—an indication of the city's former wealth. (Open daily in summer 7am-7pm; in off-season 8am-5pm. Admission 1D, students with ID free.) The adjoining Byzantine-Moorish-style **Cathedral of St. Louis** is a unique amalgam of Christian and Neo-Islamic architecture (closed in 1988). With its bizarre mixture of a Gothic facade, rococo interior with keyhole-shaped Islamic arches, and Indian spires, the cathedral inspires contrasting reviews. Once the seat of the Diocese of North Africa, the cathedral contains a mosaic commemorating Saint Augustine, who lived and taught on these shores. The cathedral is dedicated to King Louis of France, who in the thirteenth century had hoped to convert Tunisia to Christianity, but died shortly after arriving. Within the next few years, the cathedral and the museum will fuse to house a comprehensive exhibition on Carthaginian life. Nearby the **Hotel Reine Didon** offers panoramic views, an elegant dining room, and excellent food—for a hefty price. To reach the museum from the staion, cross the tracks and walk down on rue J. Kennedy until you see a steep flight of stairs (rue 18 Janvici) leading up the hill to the left.

Carthage-Hannibal: It is appropriate that the most substantial rubble of Carthage should be contained by the village named after the general who struck fear into the hearts of thousands of Romans. Those pressed for time should come to Hannibal directly, as Carthage's highlights are here. From the station, walk left and then toward the water to find the second-century Roman **Baths of Antonius—** the single most impressive ruin in Carthage. Once rivaling Rome's Baths of Caracalla in size, the baths were gradually destroyed by villagers who exploited the site as a quarry. A forest of Brontosaurian pediments and fallen pillars remains. The baths are buffered by a cool garden of bougainvillea and a light sea-breeze. (Open daily in summer 8am-7pm; in off-season 8am-5pm. Admission 1D, students free.)

Retrace your steps partially, cross beneath the railway tracks, and follow the signs to the **Roman City** and **Archeological Gardens** (Parc Archéologique des Villas Romains), a melange of finds including an underground Christian chapel, two Byzantine churches, and a Punic necropolis. Nearby lies the well-preserved third-century **Odéon.** Here, explore ruins free from fellow tourists, as the road is inaccessible by bus. Just beyond the city is the Theater of Carthage.

The National Museum of Carthage and the Cathedral of St. Louis (see Carthage-Dermech above) are easily reached from the Carthage-Hannibal station. Cross the tracks and walk uphill: The cathedral will appear on your left.

On the way, you will come across the battered but recognizable remnants of the Roman **amphitheater.** Another 2km to the right is the **Theater of Carthage,** a scrupulously restored stadium that provides the backdrop for the **Festival of Carthage** (July to mid-Aug.) For information, contact the tourist office in Tunis or see the schedule in *La Presse.*

Carthage-Presidence and **Carthage-Amilcar:** The last two Carthage TGM stops should also be the last two on your list. The first takes its name from the nearby **Presidential Palace,** the closely guarded waterfront residence of the President, which can be seen from the Baths of Antonius. To get to the **American Military Cemetery** from the station, cross the tracks and the field, hook around the left side of the woods, and follow the paved road. The 2,840 Americans who fell during Patton's campaigns against Rommel lie here. Closer to Carthage-Amilcar sulk the ruins of the **Basilica of St. Cyprian.**

Sidi Bou Said

Perched on the rocky promontory of Cape Carthage at the northern tip of the Bay of Tunis, the beautiful Tunisian village of Sidi Bou Said is a short train ride from downtown Tunis. A shining city on a hill, its whitewashed, cube-shaped houses and brilliant blue doorways and shutters have inspired artists from author André Gide to painter Paul Klee; they've also attracted scores of Europeans for scores of years. During summer evenings and late into Ramadan nights, the cliff-top cafes overflow with exuberance. Decorative detail is the secret to Sidi Bou Said's charm: doors studded with patterns of giant black nails, metal knockers in the shape of the Hand of Fatima, brightly painted metal window grills, and finely crafted wooden window boxes sprouting with flowers.

From the TGM station, proceed to the right and turn left at the police station. Walk up the hill along av. Docteur Habib Thameur to the magical, tiny **town square.** The **TGM** can whisk you back to Tunis until midnight. Avoid the overpriced handicraft shops along the way into town, and follow rue Sidi Bou-Fares from the main square, turn left, and hike up the hill. In front of the lighthouse, you'll be rewarded with a cosmic view of the Mediterranean. A small tip will persuade the guardian to let you climb the **lighthouse.** Alternatively, continue straight from the town square until you see the steep flight of stairs to the right. A hike down the dizzying 365 steps will take you to the little **port,** a small beach, and a few expensive restaurants and hotels. Before 10am or after 9pm, ask around the port about lending a hand on one of the fishing boats that ply the sea all night and return at dawn. The ambience is unparalleled, and, if you can spare several days, you may even get paid. (This is not, however, an advisable outing for women.) Most of the few hotels are exorbitantly priced, but one of them redeems the rest. The **Hotel Sidi Bou-Fares,** just up the hill from the main square at #15 (tel. 27 09 48), offers eight simple, spotless rooms with stone floors around a lovely garden courtyard shaded by an immense fig tree. Sit under the trees and have a cool drink and *sheeshah* (hookah pipe) while you play chess or shoot the breeze. Be sure to call ahead; a room here is a much more pleasant base of exploration than anything in Tunis. Singles are 8.500D, doubles 13.000D, and triples 18.000D.

Restaurant Chergui, just off the main square (tel. 27 11 57), is both the cheapest and one of the most appealing restaurants in town. Try the excellent *couscous poulet* for 1.200D, the *brik à l'oeuf* for 300ml, or the *tajine de fromage* (a meatless quiche) for 1.200D. All is served in a large courtyard at low, Arab-style tables. Of the expensive and trendy restaurants at the bottom of the cliff, the **Pirate** lures well-scrubbed Europeans each summer night. Stick to the well-stocked bar and the 2.500D pizza. For dessert, pick up some *bambolini,* a fried dough concoction swamped in sugar, for 120ml.

Idyllic before 10am, when the tourist buses roll in and vendors become aggressive, Sidi Bou Said really exists for the evening. As soon as the sun sets, the city's unrivalled cafes come alive. Those in the square are great for people-watching, but those with long terraces farther up the hill overlooking the sea are far more scenic. Most of these places serve freshly squeezed fruit juices, Turkish coffee, mint and nut teas, and the ubiquitous *sheeshah.* The most famous are the **Café des Nattes,** right in the main square, where the tenderest and trendiest have dreamed of glory, and the **Café Sidi Chabaane,** down the street to the left of the Restaurant Chergui, an indescribably exciting, multi-tiered place with panoramic views and delicate teas. Take the third right from the Chergui.

La Marsa, Gammarth, and Raoued

The sandy beaches of La Marsa, the rocky cliffs of Gammarth, and the seemingly infinite littoral of Raoued offer the perfect solution to the emptiness of a a hot summer afternoon when Tunis has closed up. In **La Marsa,** Europeans hang out in front of the expensive but beautiful Plaza Corniche Hotel at #32 (tel. 27 00 98), along the road to Sidi Bou Said (doubles 27.500D, breakfast included). The main beach is crowded on Sundays, when most of Tunis's population flees from the city heat. The village's main street, av. Bourguiba, starts by the train station. At #5, a shop sells foreign newspapers and magazines. A few steps farther is La Marsa's main square, **place Saf-Saf,** where you'll find the inexpensive **Restaurant du Peuple,** which serves generous portions of heavily spiced food (meat dishes 1-1.800D). Not even solo travelers will be amused by the friendliness of the flies in the restaurant, however. **Les Palmiers,** near the beach, serves delicious crepes (0.500-1.250D) at shaded, outdoor tables. Pizza is served after 7pm (1.500-2.300D). (Open 11am-midnight.) La Marsa's **Maison des Jeunes** (not a youth hostel) will let you crash on their grounds by the beach and use their shower facilities for 500ml. From the TGM station, take the main road above the beach, and take the first right at the end of the grassy terrace overlooking the beach.

Up the coast from La Marsa, the roomier and more elegant beach of **Gammarth** is lined with high-priced resort hotels. Here, the **Restaurant les Coquillages** serves main courses for about 3D in a fantastic seaside location. By week **Raoued** provides unlimited space perfect for camping and solitary beach-bumming. By weekend half of Tunis shows up and spoils the fun. Raoued is accessible by municipal bus #18 from Tunis. Take the TGM to La Marsa and hop on municipal bus #40 (220ml) to reach Gammarth and Raoued.

Cap Bon Peninsula

Across the bay from Tunis, jagged mountains jut up from the sea, marking the beginning of the Cap Bon peninsula. Stretching out like a finger pointing toward Europe, Cap Bon separates the Bay of Tunis from the Gulf of Hammamet. The Phoenicians traded with the earliest inhabitants of Cap Bon, and during the Punic era, the Romans used the peninsula to observe the movements of the Carthaginians. In the fourteenth century, Cap Bon lured waves of Andalusian refugees fleeing the re-Christianization of Spain. Today, waves of Northern Europeans seeking sun and sand engulf the towns of Hammamet and Nabeul, while in the quiet villages to the north, Kelibia El Haouaria, Sidi Daoud, and Korbous, you can experience quieter beaches and some peace of mind.

Cap Bon is easy to explore, as public transportation is excellent. Buses linking the villages of the peninsula to Tunis and each other are frequent, though sometimes packed. Unfortunately, inexpensive hotels are few and far between, forcing the budget traveler to stay in youth hostels or crash on the beach (sometimes dangerous). Outside of Hammamet and Nabeul, cheap food is abundant.

Hammamet

While the town has undoubtedly been transformed to cater to the tourists' every need, the beach has remained calm and unspoiled by the string of hotels that lines the shore. A handsome, fifteenth-century Kasbah rises out of the waves; it houses a *medina,* which is a disappointing facade of swindlers' shops. Tourist brochures boast that in years past, Gustave Flaubert, Guy de Maupassant, André Gide, Oscar Wilde, and Winston Churchill visited Hammamet. Today, the town isn't the artists' haven it used to be, but it retains a degree of harmony with its beautiful surroundings.

The **train station** (tel. 801 74) lies at the back of town, near the foot of av. Bourguiba. Trains leave Tunis for Hammamet (10 per day, 1 hr., 1.300D; change at Bir Bou Rekba), and buses (1.390D) run from Tunis's Gare Routière Sud directly to av. Habib Bourguiba, near the Kasbah in Hammamet. The **ONTT tourist office** (tel. 804 23), av. Habib Bourguiba, down the road to the right as you face the Kasbah, will give you a comprehensive hotel list, a helpful pamphlet on Cap Bon, and the *Tunisia Practical Guide.* (Open Mon.-Sat. 7:30am-1:30pm.) At 10, av. de la République, up the main street perpendicular to av. Bourguiba at the Kasbah, is a **newsstand** well stocked with foreign newspapers. Nearby is the **post office.**

The least painful of the pocket-gorging hotel lot is the **Hotel Alya,** 30, rue Ali Belhaouane (tel. 802 18), to the right as you walk away from the Kasbah up av. de la République. If they're not too crowded, the high prices can sometimes be reduced by up to 50%, especially for amiable backpacking types. The terrace upstairs offers a view of the scintillating bay, a gaudy war monument, and the sprawling town cemetery. (July-Aug. singles 12.500D, doubles 17D; April-June and Sept.-Oct. singles 9.500D, doubles 14D; Nov.-March singles 7D, doubles 10D. Bath and breakfast included.) Reservations are often necessary in summer. Less likely to have space is the somewhat cheaper **Pension Hallous,** on av. de la République (tel. 805 25) near the Kasbah. Its large, plain rooms can be noisy, but the balconies are perfect for watching the strollers below (8D per person with bath). If desperation sets in, head to the large, two-star **Hotel Sahbi** (tel. 808 07), designed primarily to receive busloads of Germans and offering spacious rooms, some with balconies. (In summer singles 10.800D, doubles 13.600D; in off-season singles 4.800D, doubles 7.600D. Breakfast included.) The only real budget accommodations in Hammamet are those at **Ideal Camping** past the Sahbi off av. de la République. Decent, centrally located grounds exist for 800ml per person, 350ml per tent. (Open year-round, curfew midnight.)

The gastronomical hot spot is actually 3km outside of the city, in tiny Bir Bou Rekba. There, **Café Relais** offers a superb *merguez* platter for only 1.500D. In Hammamet proper, the **Restaurant Populaire,** av. de la République, on a small street leading to the shopping mall, lives up to its name. It serves locals in a small, dull room. Watch people going to the large, expensive restaurants through the small doorway as you eat a cheap, filling meal, such as *spaguetti poulet* (1.200D). For true cheap eats, the **Chez Lich** sandwich stand, at the end of the waterfront square up av. Bourguiba from the Kasbah, serves a decent *merguez* concoction for 650ml.

During July and August, the **International Festival of Hammamet** takes place in the open-air theater of the Cultural Center, right on the beach about 6km west of town. Originally the palatial estate of Georges Sebastien that put the town on the map in the 1920s, the house and grounds are attractive. (Frank Lloyd Wright once called it the most beautiful house he knew.) Tickets for the performances, which feature international folk singers, are available at the door.

Nabeul

Twelve kilometers north of Hammamet, Nabeul features slightly less spectacular beaches at slightly less outrageous prices. The ceramic and tile capital of Tunisia, Nabeul sees more tourists buying vulgar pottery than Tunisians seeking to get their bathroom redone. Avoid the city at all costs on Friday mornings, when hordes of tourists are bused in for a contrived **market,** to the left of the town square as you come from Farhat Hached.

Nabeul's **bus station** (tel. 852 61) is just off av. Habib Thameur, the road to Hammamet; the **train station** (tel. 850 54) is a 5-minute walk to the right. To get to the town square, head straight up av. Thameur to av. Farhat Hached, the main ceramics street. The well-stocked, regional **ONTT tourist office,** av. Taieb M'hiri (tel. 867 37 or 868 00), is not worth the trek, though they will reward you with a map if you can find the office. Walk about 3km past the train station on av. Habib Bourguiba, turn left 1 block before the excellent beach, and turn right after another block—the office will be on the right. The **post office** is at av. Bourguiba and av. Farhat Hached. (Open Mon.-Thurs. 7:30am-12:30pm and 5-7pm, Fri.-Sat. 7:30am-1:30pm.)

Mobbed **louages** for the south and for Tunis (1.700D) leave from the intersection of av. Thameur and av. Bourguiba. They supplement buses that serve Tunis every half hour (1½ hr., 1.450D). Buses to Hammamet (12km away) leave every half hour (280ml). Red and white metered taxis charge about 2.200D for the same ride. Buses and *louages* to Kelibia and other cities in northern Cap Bon depart from the "El Mahfar"station at the far end of av. Farhat Hached, a half-block beyond the town square. If you don't feel like waiting for one of the six daily buses to Kelibia (1.160D), consider taking a local bus from El Mahtar to **Korba** (380ml) and transferring to a bus en route from Tunis (780ml).

Nabeul is blessed with a magnificently located and conscientiously managed **IYHF youth hostel** (tel. 855 47), lodged between two luxury beachside hotels. Walk away from the train station several blocks, and turn right on rue Mongi Slim, where you can wait for the local bus or walk the mile to the beach. Groups fill the crowded bunks in summer, but it's never a problem getting a mattress to camp out in the courtyard. Consider half (3.200D) or full (4.700D) pension—the food is delicious, and you'll never have to stray far from the beach (2D per night; membership not required for short stays).

Back in town, the **Pension Les Roses,** on rue Sidi Abdel Kader (tel. 855 70), off av. Farhat Hached as it winds through the tourist shops, is pleasantly pink and clean (in summer 4.500D; in winter 3D; shower 500ml). The **Hotel Les Jasmins** (tel. 853 43), 2km from the bus station down the Hammamet road, allows **camping** on their grounds for 850ml per person, 500ml per tent, showers included. They also rent **bikes** for 1.500D per hour and 6D per day, but don't despair—the beach is only 100m away.

Restaurant de la Jeunesse, 76, av. Farhat Hached, attracts a healthy mix of tourists and locals alike. Dishes average 1-2D; the *merguez grillé* is excellent at 1.600D. (Open daily 8am-11pm.) **Ideal Restaurant,** up rue Mongi Slim from the youth hostel, is a friendly, family-run place where most dishes run 1D, a tasty steak 1.800D.

Northern Cap Bon

The gem of the Cap Bon region is **Kelibia,** 58km north of Nabeul. Its magnificent fortress has changed hands more than half a dozen times since its construction in the sixth century B.C.E., towering over the plains and nearby fishing communities. Stretching north are the gorgeous sands of **El-Mansoura,** ending in the best-preserved Punic ruins in Tunisia at Kerkouane. With affordable lodgings and excellent restaurants, Kelibia is an ideal base from which to explore the peninsula.

Kelibia has two pleasant hotels which sit side by side, strategically located so the terraces of their restaurant/cafes feature views of the waterfront as well as the fortress. Keep the dome and tower on your right as you walk from the joint bus station and *louage* stop, turn left, and look for the signs. Consider stopping at the **supermarket,** visible down the road on your left before you leave town. A few blocks ahead you will find a **bus stop.** The bus that comes every 30 minutes will drop you off at the hotels, which are just past the small port. You can also take a taxi or walk about 2km to the beach and hotels. (In Aug. singles 9.900D, doubles 15.400D; otherwise singles 7.700D, doubles 11D. Breakfast included.) The **Florida** (tel. 962 48) is next door. (In summer singles 10D, doubles 18D; in winter singles 9D, doubles 16D.) **Club Natique,** a windsurfing school next to the **Ennassim** (tel. 962 45) rents sailboards for under 5D per hour. One kilometer farther, on the road to Mansourah, an **IYHF youth hostel** (tel. 961 05) offers cramped rooms for 2D per person. Between the hotels and the youth hostel, **Cafe Sidi el-Bahri,** a Moorish cafe, serves a marvelous chocolatey *café au lait* with chocolate; in the evening, you can smoke a *sheeshah* (water-pipe) and watch the fishing boats go out of the Spanish port just downhill from the cafe. Near the Bahri, on the left side of the road, is **Restaurant**

de la Plage, an inexpensive and authentic alternative to the overpriced restaurants in the Florida and Ennassim. The menu is in Arabic, but you can still read the prices. *Poulet rôti* costs 750ml. Two kilometers past the hostel, **Hotel El Mansourah** (tel. 963 15) sits right at the edge of the stunning beach. (In summer 12D per night, with breakfast, half-pension 14D, full pension 16D; in off-season 9D per night with breakfast, half-pension 11D, full pension 13D.) Room and full board is 70D per week. Make reservations early.

Windsurfing just off the beach costs 1.500D per half-hour. Freelance **camping** is tolerated at Mansourah Beach and on the deserted miles of sand farther north. Seven buses per day leave Tunis for Kelibia from the SNT station at the end of av. de Carthage (2.340D). A *louage* from Nabul costs 1.200D. Kelibia is also linked to Trapani (Sicily) by a hydrofoil (L54,000 or 47D).

The **Borj,** or fortress, towering over Kelibia and Mansourah is as amazingly intact as it is untouristed. Your senses will forgive the steep ascent when the unforgettable panorama comes into view. Little remains of its fourth-century B.C.E. walls, and most of the battlements were added by the Romans in the following centuries. During the sixteenth and seventeenth centuries, the Spanish wrested the fort from its Fatimid occupants and built the crenelations atop its walls; later it was taken by the Turks. Germans occupied the fort for three months during World War II, and when the French reconquered the area, they built a transoceanic communications center, which still provides Cap Bon with connections to Europe and the U.S. One Turkish cannon decorates the ramparts; another is marked with the seal of King George III of England. The fortress' accessibility varies, depending on who is there to greet you. Stop at the **Café El Bor** for a drink before you descend.

Excavations have revealed the original layout of an extensive Punic settlement at **Kerkouane,** 12km north of Kelibia. The city's inhabitants enjoyed an advanced civilization before abandoning it to the Romans; evidence of large homes, shops, and gathering places remain. (Open 9am-noon and 2-5pm.)

Farther north, on the tip of Cap Bon, the fishing village of **El-Haouaria** is perhaps the most interesting area on the cape. Unfortunately, the only accommodations available are the **payottes,** 2km north on the beach. These, however, are remote and slightly dangerous—especially for women. Hitch or walk out to the point of **Ras Addar,** where you can see Sicily on a clear day. Three kilometers west of El-Haouaria lies the **Cave of Bats;** a local guide can help you find the entrance. If you are interested in falconry, ask the elderly men at the downtown cafes to show off their well-trained birds. During the **falconry festival,** held around the second week in June, hunting competitions take place.

On the Tunis side of the cape stands the sleepy fishing village of **Sidi Daoud,** which only wakes up in May and June for the tuna fish *matanza;* fishers sing ancient chants and use nets several miles long to capture the migrating tuna.

Finally, only 30km from Tunis lie the rugged coastline and mineral water springs around **Korbous.** Unfortunately, the town is shockingly expensive, and you will probably have to limit yourself to a daytrip. The most beautiful spots are 3km north along the dirt track that branches west. Two buses per day leave Tunis for Korbous.

Coral Coast

Excellent daytrips from Tunis to the coastline of northern Tunisia are the old port of Bizerte, the beautiful beach at Raf Raf, and the ancient ruins of Utica. Beware, however, that roads can be bad and buses slow in the area. Beyond Bizerte and toward Tabarka lies enchanting, fertile terrain, which nearer the Algerian border turns to dense forests of cork and pine. The region has been spared the brunt of intensive tourist development and the Saharan summer heat that afflicts coastal regions farther south.

Raf Raf

Among sun-worshipers, Raf Raf is reputed to have the country's most spectacular beach. A bus leaves Tunis's Bab Saadoun station daily at 1pm to Raf Raf (1 hr., 1.430D), while 5 buses per day head to nearby Ras Djebel (1 hr., 1.370D). From the Bab Saadoun station, occasional *louages* run to Ras Djebel, and, on weekends, to Raf Raf. Several kilometers beyond the city proper, Raf Raf *plage* (beach) resembles a giant natural rendition of the Tunisian national flag: a long, graceful crescent of sand with a single tiny islet at the center of the bay. Since the area is rarely visited by Europeans, most of the riffraff of Raf Raf is Tunisian. Despite the beach's popularity, it is large enough never to overcrowd. If you retreat to the far, secluded end of the beach, beware of your belongings: Fleet-footed thieves occasionally prey on foreign tourists' preference for solitude.

Just above the beach on the main road is the **Hotel Dalia** (tel. 476 68), a pleasant place with stairwells that echo. Singles are 9D; doubles 12D; triples 18D. Freelance **camping** is tolerated on the beach, though you may want to surgically fuse your belongings to your body. You can also rent a simple straw *paillote* (3-sided hut) for 3D per day. **Restaurant la Sirene,** a 5-minute walk to the right along the beach as you face the water from the end of the main drag, serves excellent fare in a cool bamboo hut. While most seafood dishes are a hefty 3D, the tasty *poulet* is only 1.500D.

Near Raf Raf

To the south, **Ghar-el-Melh** (also known as **Porto Farina**) is a photogenic village with narrow streets and tiny stone houses set among the debris of crumbling Turkish ramparts. Unfortunately, you'll need a car to get there.

On the main Bizerte-Tunis road 33km from Tunis lies the ancient port of **Utica.** Though this was once North Africa's greatest port, what remains today is from a later period in the city's history, and consists primarily of first- to fourth-century aristocratic Roman residences. The site's museum, which houses some minor artifacts, is on your left as you arrive. Follow the cardboard sign saying "Ruines" to the **Maison de la Cascade** (House of the Fountain), so named for the fountain inside. The watchkeeper will take your 200ml amd make sure that you get to see the splendid mosaics and marble work.

Bizerte (Binzert)

Perched on Africa's northernmost point, Bizerte has long been a strategic port. As "Hippo Diarrhytus," the town was first developed by the Phoenicians, who dug the first canal linking the Mediterranean to the inland Lake Bizerte. So enamored were the French with the site and its advantageous postition for the NATO alliance that when they granted Tunisia independence in 1950, they retained residence in Bizerte. Seven years and some 1000 Tunisian military casualties later, the French withdrew.

Following the entire nation, Bizerte today undergoes a period of rapid transformation; for most visitors, however, the appeal of Bizerte's beaches, picturesque old quarters, *medina,* and stunning Cemetery of Martyrs, hasn't changed.

Orientation and Practical Information

Buses from Tunis and from the east and south arrive at the main **bus station** on the waterfront, just below the drawbridge. Another station nearby on rue d'Alger serves Ras Djebel (700ml), Raf Raf (6 per day, 860ml), Tabarka (1 per day, 3.040D), and Jendouba-El Kef (1 per day, 4.080D). The **train station** is farther south. From the main bus station, walk parallel to the water along rue de Russie and then rue de Tinja. *Louages* for Tunis (and occasionally for Ras Djebel) leave from rue du ler Mai, just off the canal and in the shadow of the drawbridge. The best way to reach Bizerte from Tunis is by bus. Buses leave every half-hour from the Bab Saadoun station for Bizerte (1½ hr., 1.500D), while the quicker *louages* leave from the station (1.600D).

Of the four trains per day to and from Tunis, two are omnibuses and take a circuitous route. A *direct-climatisé* train runs twice per day, departing from Tunis at 11:20am and 6:55pm and from Bizerte at 7:15am and 2:20pm (1½ hr., 2.400D).

The friendly but poorly informed regional **tourist office** is at 1, rue de Constantinople (tel. 327 03). From the main bus station, walk toward the bridge, turn left at the park, then turn right 1 block after the park. (Open in summer Mon.-Sat. 7:30am-1:30pm; in off-season Mon.-Sat. 8:30am-1pm and 5-7:45pm.)

On rue Moncef Bey at av. Taïeb Mehiri, a **bookstore** carries a good selection of foreign newspapers. Across the street on rue d'Espagne, the Union International de Banques is the only place that **exchanges currency** during after hours (Mon.-Fri. 5-7pm, Sat. 9am-noon). The **post** and **telephone offices** lie on av. d'Algerie, ½ block off the new town's central square.

Palais du Cycle, 50, av. Bourguiba (tel. 324 96), rents bicycles for 1D per hour.

Accommodations and Food

The resort hotels along the beach are expensive and crammed with tour bus refugees. Most cheap hotels in town fill in July and August, so arrive early.

Remel Youth Hostel (IYHF; tel. 408 04), 4km south of town on the road to Tunis. Take "Menzel Djemil" bus #8 (140ml), or the Tunis-bound bus, and ask to get off at Remel Plage. A ramshackle place with character that verges on the funky. Remel Beach, 100m away through the trees, is isolated and idyllic. 700ml. Nonmembers should have little trouble talking their way in. Cold showers 200ml. Sheets 200ml. Breakfast 400ml. Lunch or dinner 1.600D. Cooking facilities available. Open March-Jan.

Maison des Jeunes (tel. 316 08). From the bus station, walk 4 blocks across av. Bourguiba, and walk 10 min. on bd. Hassan en-Nouri; the hostel lies up a driveway to the left. A clean dormitory complex frequented by soccer teams in summer, but some beds are reserved for foreigners. 2D per night. Showers may not be available.

Hotel Zitouna, 11, place Slah-Edine Bouchoucha (tel. 314 47), 1 block from old port. From the bus station, walk 4 blocks, turn right on av. Bourguiba, and left at place Slah-Edine. Spartan, with a pleasant, well-lit interior. Rooms are tiny, sheets not the cleanest. Singles 2.500D. Doubles 4D. Showers 200ml. Dorm beds 2D (avoid these).

Hotel Continental, 29, rue 2 Mars 1934 (tel. 314 36). From the bus station, walk 2 blocks diagonally to av. d'Algeria, and make the 1st right. Larger rooms and less clean sheets than the Zitouna. Singles 4D. Doubles 6D.

Club Jalta, route de la Corniche (tel. 322 50), 2km west of the town center along the coastal road, a pleasant hike along the beach. A well-equipped resort full of German package-tour groupies in summer, but a great bargain in off-season. July-Aug. 11D per person; April-June and Sept.-Oct. 7.200D per person; Nov.-March 5D per person. Singles 2D extra in off-season; mid-season 2.500D; high season 4.500D. Rent bikes (2D per hr.) and diving equipment.

Inexpensive restaurants lurk at almost every corner. Fruit vendors abound in **place Slah-Edine,** and there is a lively **market** near the base of the old port. You will go berserk over Bizerte's plethora of ice cream shops.

Restaurant Les Etoiles, rue Ibn Khaldun and rue Habib Thameur. The painting outside depicts a cherubic waiter serving up a chicken, but this popular little place serves mostly *biftek* (1.500D).

Tip Top Restaurant, rue de la Belgique, a few blocks from the bus station at rue Moncef Bey. Excellent food, but make sure you get a price before you feast. The upper level attracts fewer flies. Meat dishes 1.500D-2D. Open daily 8am-midnight.

Patisserie de la Paix, rue 2 mars 1934 (tel. 319 58), across from Hotel Continental. Generous servings of delicious ice cream.

Sights

The charming part of the city is the celebrated **Old Port,** where the smells of rotten fish and steaming coffee surround wooden fishing boats and ancient stone ramparts. By dusk, the outdoor cafes overflow with old men playing cards and puffing on pipes. Facing the Old Port and separated by the fruit and vegetable stalls of the outdoor market, **place Slah-Edine Bouchoucha** has a small, seventeenth-century fountain, offset by the twin minarets of the Debaa and Grand Mosques. Exit through the ramparts away from the Old Port to find more cozy cafes, nestled at the foot of the massive walls of the eighteenth-century **kasbah.** Its extensive crenelated battlements are reached by a hidden staircase and offer a snapshot panorama. The **Andalusian Quarter,** with its ancient archways, winding alleys, and painted, nail-studded doors, lies just to the north. The narrow alley known as the "street of the parakeets" is lined with birdcages housing tiny yellow tykes, nervously eyeing the occasional falcon proudly perched on a block of wood. From the neighboring hilltop, the sixteenth-century **Spanish Fort,** now an open-air theater, affords a fine view of the Old City below. Also up high and in an area of new development lies the **Cimetière des Martyrs** (Cemetery of Martyrs), a grand memorial to those who died fighting the French. Walk past the scary-looking guards to enter the impressive grounds.

Sports and entertainment revolve around the three "luxury" beach hotels, **Corniche Palace, Jalta,** and **Nadhour.** Equipment rentals run quite high for waterskiing, windsurfing, and boating. The three hotels rent **horses** for a few dinars per hour (with guides). Wear long pants to pad the granite-hard saddles and sturdy shoes to keep the stirrups from cutting into your ankles. The hotels cater to the package-tour set, and the atmosphere is decidedly non-Tunisian. Nonetheless, the beaches are wide, palm-studded, and excellent. A windblown gravel road climbs up from the beach, each bend offering a fresh glimpse of the azure sea and wooded coastline; eventually you reach the summit of **Djebel Kebir** (274m), from where you can see the entire city and the coast. You can also make the ascent on foot.

Perhaps the most spectacular sight near Bizerte is **Cap Blanc,** Africa's northernmost point. To get here, follow av. de la Corniche along the beach and up the coast to the Radiophare du Cap Blanc sign, where you turn right. The rough road climbs to the top of **Djebel Nador** (288m), where the views at sunset are outstanding. Below, chalky Cap Blanc juts into the sea. To get to its tip, descend the mountain and follow the trail leading off the road. The bike ride is scenic and challenging; count on three hours round-trip.

Tabarka

Though increasingly crowded, the tranquil fishing hamlet of Tabarka remains one of the most attractive beach towns on the Coral Coast. Only a few miles from the Algerian border and far enough removed to have escaped the tourist onslaught, Tabarka's gorgeous beaches are shrouded by rolling mountains and by a sea that teems with colorful marine life. Each of the region's three industries serves to enhance the village's charm: fishing with handmade nets in brightly painted boats, stripping and exporting the cork from the surrounding forests, and crafting the red coral that abounds in the surrounding waters.

Orientation and Practical Information

The village itself is a tiny checkerboard, measuring 6 blocks across in each direction. The main artery, **avenue Habib Bourguiba,** is lined with virtually all of the city's services, including a handful of souvenir shops selling Tabarka's celebrated coral. At 33, av. Bourguiba, is the rude **tourist office.** (Open July-Aug. Mon.-Sat. 7:30am-1:30pm; Sept.-June Mon.-Sat. 8:30am-1pm and 3-5:45pm.) At the avenue's far end is the **post office,** at av. Medhdi Chaker. (Open Mon.-Thurs. 7:30am-12:30pm and 5-7pm, Fri.-Sat. 7:30am-1:30pm.) Two **bus stations** serve the same destinations (Tunis, Bizerte, Jendouba, El Kef, and Ain Draham) but at different times. One is east of place 18 Janvier on the main street, and the other is on rue du Peuple, left off av. Bourguiba near Hotel de France. Buses leave eight times per day for the four-hour trip to Tunis (3.600D) and tend to be crowded. Two buses per day run to Bizerte (3½ hr., 3.040D), and four to Ain Draham (1 hr., 500ml). Buses no longer run from Tabarka to de Calle (El Kala) on the Algerian side of the border.

Accommodations

Unfortunately, the word about Tabarka is beginning to spread. In July and August, the only two budget hotels in town often fill by 11am. Make your move for a room early in the day or make a reservation. Delightful **Hotel de France** (tel. 445 77), around the corner at the end of av. Bourguiba, offers clean and airy doubles with shower and half-pension. (July-Aug. singles 10.500D, doubles 15D; May-June and Sept. to Oct. singles 8D, doubles 10D; Nov.-April singles 5.800D, doubles 7.600D.) The hotel is filled with reminders of Habib Bourguiba's imprisonment here by the French in 1952. A marble plaque marks room #1 (now hermetically sealed), his bedroom during the ordeal. Less comfortable but much cheaper, **Hotel Corail** (tel. 944 55), up av. Bourguiba at rue Tazerka, offers musty doubles for 6D. Unfortunately, the nearby mosque makes a good snooze difficult, as it rings bells for prayer at 4am.

Food and Entertainment

Several restaurants on av. Bourguiba serve lobster, in season, for about 20D per kg. Locals frequent the restaurants along rue Farhat Hached, off av. Bourguiba near the Corail. A plate of *merguez* at **Restaurant El Hana** is 1.200D. A full meal at **Restaurant de France,** next to Hotel de France, is excellent at 3D. A bedraggled stuffed boar dominates the dining room. If you want *poulet* make a move early in the day as it sells out quickly.

In the evenings, the cafes in Tabarka are hopping. **Café Andalous,** at the end of av. Medhdi Chaker, is elaborately ornamented and serves delicious Tunisian cakes. You can dance them off at the outdoor disco in **Hotel les Mimosas,** toward the Tunis road, above the city (open in summer until 1am). The restaurant in the hotel is excellent, worth the 4D it will probably cost.

Sights and Activities

The picture-perfect hilltop **Genoese Fortress,** overlooking the port, dominates the scene. The fortress was erected in 1542, after the Spanish king Charles V presented the strategic island at the mouth of the harbor to the Genoese. The French-built causeway that connects the island to the port wasn't added until 1952. The steep climb up to the fortress is well worth the effort; notice the typically Italian lines of the walls and the decorative trim. Just before the fort on the right, the ruins of a Genoese guardhouse offer complete seclusion and cosmic sunbathing. The views from both it and the fort enchanting: The lush trees of an otherwise rocky islet contrast beautifully with the deep blue of the Mediterranean. (Open daily 8am-7pm. Free.)

Just north of the village is a group of jagged rock formations sculpted by centuries of erosion, known as the **Aiguilles** ("needles"). Walk straight from av. Bourguiba, or even better, get an unforgettable aerial view by hiking up the hill to the left of Café Andalous, past the small French Fort, then down along the road that hugs the sea. Try to come at night, when the Genoese Fortress and the Aiguilles are illuminated by spotlights.

The major attraction within the village itself is the handsome third-century **Roman Basilica,** housing an exhibition of ancient coins. To reach the basilica, walk to the end of av. Medhdi Chaker. In July and August, a **festival** takes place in Tabarka, centered around the basilica.

Tabarka's finest sights, however, are underwater. Around the tip of the Genoese Fortress, the Mediterranean teems with merou, cruising lazily among the rocks 20m below. Near the surface, hundreds of purple and black chromis swarm in shifting clouds, broken by frequent regiments of yellow-striped jacks. Great carpets of orange-red anemones fringe the scene. Somewhere between the urchin-dotted patches of sea grass and colored algae, langouste and moray eels await the dark of night. Deep beneath the sea lurks the famous reddish coral.

The **Yachting Club of Tabarka** is housed in a white building on the causeway, beneath the fortress. The center's forte is scuba diving; for 8D they'll give you all the necessary equipment and take you down. Before you rent inspect the equipment thoroughly. If you're a beginner, the week-long course is 60D; a diving certificate good for one year is 10D. A member of the World Underwater Federation (CMAS), the center will teach you the basics in its private harbor, then give you your first taste of the undersea world near a shallow rock reef. No one should miss the chance to snorkel here—no lessons necessary; just grab the tube and breathe. Across from the yachting club, the friendly, English-speaking marine store rents snorkel, mask, and flippers for 3.500D per day if you haggle. If they are out of equipment, the yachting club will rent you the same equipment for 4D per day.

Near Tabarka: Cap Serrat and Sidi Mechrig

Along the Tabarka-Bizerte highway, a pair of sand-and-rock tracks plunges into Tunisia's densest forests to emerge finally at two of the most scenic seaside locations in the country: Cap Serrat and Sidi Mechrig. Take the main road out of Tabarka past the **Ras Rejel War Cemetery,** where 500 Commonwealth soldiers from the Eighth Army lie. After 48km you'll come to a sign indicating "Sidi Mechrig" in Arabic and in faded French (watch carefully). The sandy 15-kilometer road, which is relentlessly serpentine, must be approached cautiously. Once you're past the dense pine forests and occasional villages, you'll reach the secluded but popular beach and **Hotel Sidi Mechrig.** The hotel, a very simple affair, charges less than 10D per person for half-pension. The terrace affords a vista of the remaining arches of the ancient Roman baths by the sea.

For an even cleaner and more deserted beach, you can head back to the main road, continue toward Bizerte, and take the **Cap Serrat** turn-off at Setenane. After another 10km of winding road, turn right 100m beyond the lonely food store. Stop the car before the beach if you don't want to get stuck in the sand. Once on the beach, walk left. Toward the point there is a 3-kilometer stretch of pristine white sand framed against emerald-green mountains; you'd be hard-pressed to find a better beach in all of Tunisia. Unfortunately, the price of seclusion is a lack of facilities of any kind, but some travelers sleep on the beach.

Tell

The northern interior region, known as the Tell, features the august mountains and thickly wooded forests of the Khroumirie along the Algerian border. Farther inland, ancient Roman ruins dot the vast grain fields; for five centuries Rome cultivated the Tell as its primary granary and erected colossal colonial centers.

The mountain haven, Ain Draham, is the undisputable secret paradise of Tunisia; hilly and rustic El Kef develops slowly but remains happily untrampled. The sites of Dougga and Bulla Regia are superlative as far as Roman ruins in Tunisia go, but like many of the towns, frustratingly difficult to access by bus.

Ain Draham

The Dorsale Mountains of northwestern Tunisia represent the tail end of the great Atlas range that sweeps across the Maghreb. Although the Dorsales rarely exceed 1600m, their rolling, densely wooded slopes provide the closest thing to alpine scenery in Tunisia, and, in fact, it snows in winter. Located at 800m, Ain Draham has enjoyed a reputation, formerly with French colonials, and now with affluent Tunisians, as *the* place to savor the cool mountain air.

The surrounding forests abound with trails ideal for hiking or horseback riding. There's an easy scramble up to **Col des Ruines,** the ridge opposite town (turn off 2½km along the road to Tabarka). Better still, the **Djebel Bir** (1109m), upon whose slopes Ain Draham lies, affords an inspirational view to those who make the somewhat strenuous climb.

The evergreens bear cones that sell for a whopping 20D apiece; inside the precious cones is a coveted nut used to flavor types of Tunisian tea. Although pilfering these cones will get you in trouble, slurping the cool spring water from the many spouts that dot the hillside, will make instant friends with approving locals.

Ain Draham means "spring of money," and well it should; the village is popular with the Tunisian elite. Fortunately, the **IYHF Youth Hostel** (tel. 470 87), a 10-minute walk up the hill from where the bus stop and across from where the *louages* depart, will put you up for 2D in less-than-satisfying conditions. **Hotel Beau Sejour** (tel. 470 05), on the main road, offers clean, comfortable rooms with sparkling private bathrooms. (Singles 9D. Doubles 16D. Breakfast included. 3D more in July-Aug.) Their dinner (3.500D) is excellent, with ice cream in season. The **Hotel les Chenes** (tel. 472 11), 7km south toward Jendouba, beats the places in town and charges about 10D per person, including breakfast. Excellent, affordable food abounds at the **Restaurant du Grand Maghreb,** 28, av. Bourguiba, (tel. 470 79). The spicy *brik* (300ml) and spaghetti (1D) are good choices, and you can admire the wooden handicrafts sold on the premises.

The weekly **market** in the valley is held every Monday and attracts people from the different peaks who come to purchase their weekly supplies. If you find your pocket too heavy with dinar, you can **gamble** in an innovative manner at a small arena near the bus station. Gamblers buy paper tickets, toss them into a sheep pen, a sheep is killed, and then the numbers on digested pellets found inside the carcass win any number of door prizes.

Bulla Regia

At first glance, the remote site of Bulla Reggia hardly appears worth the effort it took to get there. But disappointment soon gives way to delight; the majority of Bulla Regia's treasures lie underground. Affluent Romans of the second and third centuries built a city here, and then duplicated it underground to escape the summer heat, in the manner of the Berbers of Matmata. A seventh-century earthquake destroyed most of the exposed sections, but left the treasures below intact. Only a fraction of the underground dwellings have been excavated, but the work already done has revealed many rooms intact, some with mosaics. The site rivals Dougga as Tunisia's most spectacular Roman ruin.

The main entrance to the site stands by the extensive second-century **Baths of Julia Memma.** A glance around will reveal a large cistern and a Byzantine fortress, the most substantial monuments within view. Wander north, to the **Palais du Tresor** (Treasure House), which still has its mosaics *in situ.* A few steps farther north, you will discover the steps leading down to the most intact and evocative site, the **Palais de la Chasse** (Hunting Palace). Like the other excavations, the house is named not for its function (a private residence), but for the motif of its mosaics. An entire floor of a Roman palace remains wonderfully preserved. Corinthian columns are arranged around a central courtyard, flanked by a splendid dining room decorated with a patterned mosaic floor and built over a huge cistern. The **Palais de la Pêche** (Fishing Palace), just to the east, contains another underground floor. The major mosaics have been left in place: One depicts a hunting scene with birds, while the other presents a maritime scene. The house was a tribunal and prison; the central court contains a fountain that cooled the judge as miscreants stood before him in a semicircle.

Farther north is the **Palais d'Amphitrite,** with a magnificent mosaic portrait of the goddess Amphitrite. You can also wander over to the **Temple of Apollo** and the substantial remains of the **theater,** both near the road at the southeastern end of the site. (Site open daily 8am-6pm. Admission 1D, with student ID free. To photograph mosaics 2D. At the gate, you may hire the services of a guide who speaks functional French for about 1D.)

Near Bulla Regia

Right on the Algerian border sits the village of **Ghardimaou,** where a small **IYHF youth hostel** provides lodgings and sheets for 2D per person. Just 1½km outside the village stand the ancient ruins of **Chemtou,** a second-century B.C.E. settlement that was sacked by the Romans. Trying to hitch into Algeria from Ghardimaou is disastrous. The first village on the other side is **Souk Ahras,** 20km away, and there is almost no traffic along the road there. One train per day connects the two towns and you can hitch from there. Three trains per day pass through for Constantine and Algiers, but remember that you need a visa. Take the Jendouba train from Tunis—the last stop is Ghardimaou.

Frequent buses connect Jendouba to **Beja,** 50km down the road towards Bizerte. Located at a major transportation crossroads, the town is a convenient stopover on trans-Tunisian hauls, and has a small old quarter and Byzantine fortress with a view of the surrounding agricultural lands. A few kilometers toward Tunis on the main road is a gorgeous *oued* (depression), where miles of wildflowers thrive along the river that usually runs through the valley. Inexpensive accommodations are available at the **IYHF youth hostel** (tel. 506 21) or the **Phoenix Hotel** on av. de France (tel. 501 88).

El Kef

El Kef (also known in French as **Le Kef**) means "The Rock," an appropriate name for the impregnable ancient fortress town that presides over the surrounding plains from the summit of a craggy spur. Kef, as the locals refer to it, dates back to the Carthaginian Sicca. The town has lost much of its nineteenth-century stature as a major Tunisian center—the result is untarnished authenticity: an old *medina* with narrow cobbled alleys slithering up to the mountain and amiable townsfolk.

Orientation and Practical Information

The *medina* of El Kef lurks under the towering *kasbah,* which towers over the town. Below, the new city tumbles down the hillside into the valley. The bus and *louage* station lies in the new city, 5 minutes from the *medina*—walk up the main road, turn right, and take your second left on rue Ali Belhaoune.

Frequent *louages* supplement bus service to Jendouba (1 hr.; 1.150D, *louage* 1.350D), Tunis (4 hr.; 3.500D, *louage* 3.800D), Bizerte (2 per day, 4½ hr., 4.080D), Sousse (5 hr., 4.800D), Sfax (5 hr., 5.300D), and Gafsa (4 per day, 5 hr., 4.550D). The nearest train station is 36km away at Les Sers, connected to El Kef by frequent *louage* service.

Next to Café Dinar at place de l'Independance is a **Bureau D'Information Turistique (ASM)** (tel. 211 48) that single-handedly makes up for the rudeness and incompetence encountered in so many Tunisian tourist offices. The friendly director is an El Kef historian extraordinaire. (Open daily 8am-1pm and 5-8pm.) The town **post and telephone office** sits on rue Hedi Chaker and rue d'Alger. From the tourist office, bear left at the fork and walk 2 blocks. (Open Mon.-Sat. 8am-7pm, Sun. 9-11am.) The **Algerian consulate** is on rue Hedi Chaker.

Accommodations and Food

The town **IYHF youth hostel** (tel. 207 07), 2km down the road to Tunis, is uninspiring at best and at 2D per night no cheaper than the new **Hotel Medina** at 18, rue Farhat Hached (tel. 202 14). From place de l'Independence, walk 20m on av. Bourguiba and bear left (uphill). This hotel is a bargain at 2D per person in pleasant doubles or triples (cold showers included).

El Kef has a dearth of sit-down restaurants. If you have an iron stomach, a decent place to eat is (believe it or not) the **bus station,** whose main square is lined with a wide variety of stalls hawking spicy *casse croute,* hot *mergue,* and fresh chicken. For one dinar (and less), dishes are deliciously prepared at **Restaurant de l'Afrique,** on rue Hedi Chaker, 1 block from the main square. **Restaurant Des Amis,** on the steps to the *medina* near Hotel l'Auberge, charges similar prices.

Sights

Climb down to the *medina* from the steps starting at Hotel de la Source. These will lead you to the foot of the *kasbah* (1679), crowning the peak of El Kef's once impregnable rock and affording a fine vista of the well-irrigated plains and the bustling new town. The *kasbah* is currently under restoration, but if you wander inside, a delighted guide will give you a tour gratis. A hostel is scheduled to sprout out of the former prison cells, and in the courtyard of the big fort, an open-air theater is being built. Completion of the entire project is slated for the early '90s. Beneath the *kasbah,* the twin treasures of the *medina* stand side by side: an ancient basilica and a delightful mosque. The well-preserved fourth-century **Christian Basilica** has been known by a variety of names. The official Arabic name is Dar el-Kous; the French, who used it for services when El Kef was the base for the free French forces in World War II, call it Eglise de St-Pierre. Local villagers refer to it respectfully as Jamal el-Kebir, or Grand Mosque. During the eighth century, the basilica was converted into a mosque, making it one of the oldest in the country. The room adjoining the church was used as an agricultural bank—note the tellers' windows. (Open Tues.-Sun. Free.) Across from the basilica stands the picturesque **Mosque of Sidi Bou Makhlouf,** with its array of fluted domes and a slender, tiled octagonal minaret. Its interior is especially sumptuous. Nearby is the **Museum of Popular Arts,** at 2, rue de la Kasbah. Housed in a former mosque, the three rooms of the museum contain a surprisingly well-displayed and interesting collection of ethnography: Clothes, tents, and jewelry show how nomads lived just 50 years ago. (Open April-Sept. Tues.-Sat. 9am-noon and 3-7pm, Sun. 9am-noon; Oct.-March Tues.-Sat. 9am-4pm, Sun. 9am-noon. Admission 800ml, with student ID free.) From the museum, proceed across the square and up rue de Jendouba to the **Bab Ghdar** (Gate of Treachery), named in "honor" of the French arrival through the gate in 1881. To the left upon exiting the city and entering the forested countryside are the **Roman cisterns.** A short walk along the dirt road on the right leads to the derelict Christian **cemetery,** a reminder of the once-extensive French presence and now overrun by chickens. Below the cemetery, a path leads through the woods and back around the hill into town, passing through a similarly abandoned **Jewish cemetery.** Upon re-entering town, you'll run into a heavily-guarded **Presidential Palace** with beautifully-manicured grounds.

Up the street are a jumble of ancient ruins in the middle of town. These are second- and third-century **Roman cisterns** and **baths** from the colony of Sicca. The site is still under excavation, but the workers will let you in to see some lovely mosaics on the floors of the bath house. A lovely 4-kilometer hike wanders from Bab Ghdar through beautiful terrain to the small farming village of Sidi Mansour; ask the tourist office for directions.

Those showing symptoms of *agua* withdrawal can dive into the excellent **municipal pool,** in the park below place de l'Independance, shaded by trees and sprinkled by fountains. (Open in summer until 6pm. Admission 200ml.)

Dougga

The Roman metropolis of Dougga, the most intact ancient site in Tunisia, is everything you expected from Carthage but failed to find. From its temple to its toilets, the ancient city stands in recognizable form; indeed, it was inhabited up to a century ago, when a new town was built down the hill for the locals who, it was felt, were distracting the tourists from the ancient splendor. Perched on a high bluff (570m), overgrown with pasturelands and olive trees, and commanding a panorama of the grain fields and surrounding plains, Dougga is also the most scenically situated of Tunisia's ruined Roman cities. In the heart of the Tell region, the site is 111km southwest of Tunis, 6km from the sleepy village of Teboursouk.

Like most of its ancient neighbors, Dougga began as a Punic settlement. After the fall of Carthage in 146 B.C.E., the Romans promptly occupied the town and christened it Thugga, from which its present name derives. Under Roman rule, the city flourished as an agricultural center and was eventually promoted to the rank of a separate colony in 261 C.E. The site extends over several square miles, and a detailed tour requires the better part of a day. Fortunately, the major ruins are concentrated in a small area around the ancient forum.

The main entrance to the site leads directly to the wonderful second-century C.E. **theater.** The theater was small for a city of Dougga's importance, seating only 3500 spectators. The acoustics are excellent, and, with the aid of a few slight touches of restoration, the theater remains as functional as the day it was built. The Tunisian National Tourist Office now schedules performances of classical drama here during the **Dougga Festival,** which takes place annually in July and early August. Performances, enhanced by the theater's stunning natural backdrop, are in French and Arabic and cost 500ml-1.500D. The ONTT office in Tunis provides details.

Dominating the entire scene from its splendid pedestal, the **Capitol of Dougga** is considered by many to be the most beautiful of North Africa's ancient monuments. Erected in 166 C.E., it is the finest remnant of Roman Tunisia. Access to the sanctuary's interior is gained by a broad staircase and through a splendid portico of six towering columns crowned with Corinthian capitals. A temple dedicated to Jupiter, Juno, and Minerva, the capitol originally housed statues of the two goddesses flanking a 6-meter representation of the god. His monumental head and feet are now in the Bardo Museum, but a smaller head lolls disconcertingly where the statue once towered. The most prominent nearby structure is the third-century C.E. **Arch of Severus Alexander,** just to the west. Outside the gate, farther west, lies the **Temple of Calaestus.** The main portico of eight columns is surrounded by a handsome semicircular court. Back towards the capitol, steps descend to a main Roman street, which passes through what was once an exclusive residential neighborhood. On the left, after several minutes, are the well-preserved **Lycian Baths,** with their network of underground tunnels. Conveniently close to the baths lies the **House of Trifolium,** Dougga's largest building and originally an enormous brothel.

The pagodalike structure to the south is the **Lybico-Punic Mausoleum.** Built in the second century B.C.E. by the architect Abarish for a Numidian prince, this monument harks from the Punic period. A short walk uphill from the theater will bring you to the remains of the **Temple of Saturn,** overlooking Dougga and the surrounding plains.

The ruins of ancient **Mustis** lie right on top of the road to El Kef, 14km past the village of Nouvelle Dougga. The site makes up in charm what it lacks in grandeur. It consists of the meager remains of several Roman temples and a sixth-century Byzantine fortress, while across the road stands a tiny arch commemorating what must have been a rather modest triumph.

There is no public transportation from Teboursouk to Dougga, but the winding walk is lovely, if tiring (6km). Still, if there is any traffic, you're likely to get a lift at least one way. During July, when the theater hosts the **Dougga Festival,** special buses and cabs travel the route regularly during the afternoon and early evening. (Site open 7:30am-7:30pm. Admission 1D.) At the entrance, an urgent guide will tell you that your visit will be immeasurably poorer without his services. The opposite is true, since he'll try to extort 5D from you at the end of his tour. Unless you can agree in advance on a decent price (1-2D), shrug him off.

Teboursouk is a friendly agricultural town. The only hotel in town is two-star **Hotel Thugga** (tel. 658 00 or 657 13), a modern and comfortable establishment with cool, clean rooms around a large court and strong, hot showers. Half-pension is 8.500D, full pension 10D, and breakfast 6.500D. By car, take the road toward Tunis and Medjez el-Beb, turn left at the sign for El Kef; the hotel is 500m ahead on the right. On foot, take the small, downhill road across the street from the bus station until you reach asphalt again (5-10 min.). The **Restaurant Municipal,** next to the bus stop, serves an excellent steak (1.200D). It gets raucous on Sundays, when local farmers hit the beer and wine. From Teboursouk, buses run to El Kef (8 per day, 1 hr.) and Tunis (1¾ hr., 1,250D). *Louages* serve Beja. The last bus back to Tunis leaves at 6:30pm.

Sahil

Bulging from Tunisia's central eastern shore is a wide stretch of land known as the Sahil, or "coastal plain." Despite its seeming aridity, the area is surprisingly fecund—it receives enough condensation from the surrounding ocean to nurture endless rows of olive trees. Diversity reigns in this region: While the northern city of Sousse swells its massive *medina* with packaged-tour visitors, the southern city of Sfax has industrialized with nary a tourist in mind and boasts Tunisia's only subdued *medina.* Monastir, the coastal birthplace of former president Bourguiba, is all show and no substance, but the ancient port of Mahdia—a hop, skip, and jump down the coast—remains pristine. Inland, the holy city of Kairouan, the production center for carpets sold nationwide, shelters the Grand Mosque, which, surprisingly, is open to non-Muslims. At El Djem, a Roman coliseum embodies the grandeur of a past civilization.

Sousse

Hannibal put Sousse on the map when he transformed the small village into a major port. Now Tunisia's third largest city and the tourist stronghold of the Sahil, Sousse has a resort hotel atmosphere resembling that of Hammamet. Visitors are often struck by the contrast between the *medina*'s tangle of narrow alleyways within heavy medieval ramparts and the new city's waterfront district with its battalion of mammoth hotels, blaring discos, and countless rent-a-car agencies. Its beaches are excellent and crowded, but Sousse's lure is the sprawling residential old city and Tunisia's best-preserved *medina.*

Orientation and Practical Information

From Tunis, buses run frequently to Sousse until 5pm (2½ hr., 3.560D). The train is cheaper, faster, and more comfortable. From Kairouan, buses depart until 5pm (1½ hr., 1.540D), and *louages* continue to run until late evening (1.700D).

Down the road to the right from the train station is **place Farhat Hached,** the center of Sousse. It is here that two worlds meet as **avenue Habib Bourguiba,** the main commercial drag, collides with the entrance to the *medina. Louages* and municipal buses depart from the various parking lots surrounding the square. Most of Sousse's travel and car rental agencies, banks, and other services are either along av. Bourguiba or **avenue de la Corniche,** running parallel to the waterfront.

Tourist Offices: Syndicat d'Initiative, place Farhat Hached (tel. 223 31). Bus and train information. Tickets for the Grand Mosque and the Ribat. Open in summer daily 8am-7pm; in off-season 9am-noon and 3-6pm. **ONTT,** 1, av. Bourguiba (tel. 211 57, 211 58, or 211 59). A more helpful office. Open Mon.-Thurs. 8:30am-1pm and 3-5:45pm, Fri.-Sat. 8:30am-1:30pm. The map of the city, and especially the *medina,* is scanty at best.

Post Office: bd. Mohamed Naarouf. Approach the corner staircase and walk left 3 doors down. Open Sept.-June 8am-6pm; July-Aug. 7:30am-12:30pm and 5-7pm.

Telephone Office: 2 blocks past av. Victor Hugo. From the train station, turn left onto av. Nasser Bey. Small but helpful office. Open daily 8am-10pm.

Train Station: bd. Hassouna Ayachi, a block from place Farhat Hached. To Tunis (9 per day), Sfax (5 per day), and Gabes (2 per day). *Direct-climatisé* trains to Tunis take 2 hr.; otherwise 3 hr.

Bus Stations: av. Leopold Senghor. From place Farhat Hached, walk to the end of av. de la République and turn right. To Tunis and, on the same line, Hammamet (3 per day, 2 hr., 1.610D) and Nabeul (2½ hr., 1.640D). Also from the **port.** To Mahdia (every hour; 1½ hr.; 1.590D, *louage* 1.500D) and Monastir (every ½ hr., 340ml). Also from **Bab Djedid.** Walk to your left along the walls facing the medina from place Farhat Hached. To Kairouan (7 per day; 1½ hr.; 1.540D, *louage* 1.700D). Last bus to Tunis at 2pm; last *louages* depart early evening (3.500D).

Metro: av. Mohamed V, beside the port. To Monastir (6:10am-7:20pm every 40 min., ½ hr., 410ml). *Louages* to Monastir are plentiful and quicker (500ml).

Foreign Books: Cité du Livre, on av. Ali Bach Hamba at av. Bourguiba. No English books but a superior selection of guidebooks, maps, and foreign newspapers. Open daily 9am-11pm.

Ambulance: Tel. 197.

Police: av. Bourguiba (tel. 251 66), across from Tunis Air.

Accommodations

The hotels along the waterfront and av. de la Corniche are prohibitively expensive. For lower rates and more local color, stay within shouting distance of the *medina.* Except as noted, these hotels are generally suitable for women.

Youth Hostel (IYHF), off bd. Taib M'hiri (tel. 232 69), inconveniently 2km northwest of town. Follow the beach road or take bus #1 from place Farhat Hached. 2D. Sheets included. Lockout 9am-6pm.

Hotel Paris, rue Remparts Nord (tel. 205 64). From place Farhat Hached, bear right inside the *medina* entrance by the buses. Small but spic-and-span rooms. Upstairs terrace rooms more expensive. Genial management encourages you to join them in watching soccer on the color tube. Singles, doubles, or triples 3D per person, 2nd floor 4D per person. Hot showers 300ml.

Hotel Ahla (tel. 205 70). Great location next to the Ribat and facing the Grand Mosque. The tidy but worn rooms have sinks. Fills quickly in summer. Singles, doubles, or triples 5D per person. Extra bed 2D. Scalding showers included.

Hotel de Tunis, downwind from Hotel Paris. Disorganized, but they may have vacancies when other hotels don't. Not suitable for women. Singles 3D. Doubles 5D. Triples 6D. Showers 300ml.

Hotel Medina, 15, rue Othman Osman (tel. 217 22), behind the far wall of the Grand Mosque from the main entrance to the *medina.* A beautiful converted old mansion. Gracious manager. Singles 8D. Doubles 11D. July-Aug. surcharge 1.250D per person. Breakfast included.

Residence Messouda, av. Victor Hugo (tel. 221 77), up from the waterfront. Turn left from the train station, then right onto av. Victor Hugo. *The* choice for those interested in beach action. Immaculate and modern. Doubles with sink 8D, 3.500D per extra person. July-Aug. surcharge 2D. Communal bathrooms.

Camping: On the beach between hotels Marhaba and Marabout; check with police first.

Food

Avoid the traps that line the waterfront, av. Bourguiba, and av. de la Corniche. More reasonably-priced places can be found on the side streets off av. Bourguiba or in the *medina.* The **Monoprix** supermarket, on av. Bourguiba off place Farhat Hached, is well stocked. (Open daily 8:30am-noon and 4:30-8pm.)

Restaurant Populaire, rue de la France, 19, across from the Grand Mosque. Commodious and packed with locals. If there's no free table, just grab an empty chair. Large portions at low prices: Macaroni or *merguez* 1D. Open daily 11am-11:30pm.

Restaurant de la Jeunesse, Ali Bach Hamba St. (tel. 27 74 97), off av. Bourguiba, 1 block from place Farhat Hached. SPICY. *Poulet rôti* 1.200D, veggies with sauce 1D. Open daily 7am-11:30pm.

Restaurant National, rue El Aghalba (tel. 230 63), off Grand Mosque near the entrance to the Ribat. Excellent *poulet rôti with fries and salad 1.200D. Open daily 11am-11pm.*

Restaurant Malouf, place Farhat Hached (tel. 265 08). Expensive but excellent fare. Fantastic crepes (2D) and house brochette (2.500D). Beware the 1D bottles of water and 1.500D slivers of watermelon.

Restaurant du Port, av. Mohamed V, across from the metro. Fresh fish with salad and fries 2.500D. Open daily until 10:30pm.

Sights

The **medina** is dominated by the crenelated walls and bell-shaped watchtowers of the splendid ninth-century Aghlabite **Grand Mosque.** The indecently attired will be lent wraps. (Open daily 8am-2pm. Admission 300ml; buy tickets beforehand at the *syndicat.*) The impressive **Ribat** (fortified monastery), across from the Grand Mosque, is of the same period and is astonishingly intact. It is one of the finest relics of the long chain of Aghlabite *ribats* that once defended the North African coast from both the military and spiritual onslaught of Christianity. From the watchtower of the Ribat, you'll be able to appreciate the dramatic dimensions of the *medina* as well as a panorama of the Mediterranean. (Open in summer Tues.-Sun. 9am-noon and 3-6:30pm; in off-season Tues.-Sun. 9am-noon and 2-5:30pm. Admission 800ml.) If you walk to your right as you exit the Ribat, an alley leads to the tiny **Zaouia Zakkak,** with its delicate, Turkish-style octagonal minaret. At the opposite corner of the *medina* from the Ribat loom the ramparts of the ninth-century **Kasbah,** with its imposing **Tour Khalef,** now a lighthouse. You can climb to the top if you ask permission from one of the entrance guards. The Kasbah houses the **National Archeological Museum,** second in importance only to the Bardo in Tunis. It features a superb collection of second- and third-century Roman mosaics that adorned private residences of ancient Sousse. Particularly outstanding are the *Portrait of the Ocean Deity* and the *Triumph of Bacchus.* (Open in summer Tues.-Sun. 9am-noon and 3-6:30pm; in off-season Tues.-Sun. 9am-noon and 2-5:30pm. Admission 1D. Photo permit 2D.)

Sousse's **souks** also warrant exploration. **Rue d'Angleterre** and **rue de Paris,** the *medina*'s two souvenir arteries, run parallel to one another, originating at the Ribat and the Grand Mosque, respectively, and heading across the old city towards the museum. The *medina* in the evening is also the site of an unusual, medieval, Arabic Red Light District. For less seedy daytime entertainment, bring your own flashlights to the **catacombs,** a 1½-km trek east of the *medina.* Persecuted Christians of the third and fourth centuries carved out extensive underground galleries to house the tombs of their brethren who died in the Roman games in the arena of El Djem. From Bab el Gharbi, walk away from the *medina,* and take your first left, a right, then a left. From the museum, walk toward the large TV tower in the distance. (Catacombs open Tues.-Sun. 9am-noon and 3-6pm. Admission 1D.)

On Sundays from 7:30am to 1:30pm, the **Camel Market** is held at the fairgrounds, 2km south of town on the road to Sfax. (Take bus #5, 6, 7, 20, or 22 from place Farhat Hached.) The last camel was sold years ago, and though livestock still changes hands, everything from burned-out batteries to handwoven carpets now sells in this jungle of outdoor stalls. Each summer, from the beginning of July to mid-August, Sousse sponsors **Aoussou,** an international festival featuring nightly dance, musical, and theatrical performances by predominantly Arab artists. The tourist office posts a schedule of events. (Admission 500ml-1.500D per show.)

Kairouan

For centuries pilgrims have struggled across the desert to pay their respects at the most sacred of mosques in the Maghreb region—the **Mosque of Sidi Oqba** at Kairouan. Named for the saint who spread the word of Islam across North Africa, Kairouan is the fourth holiest city in Islam, eclipsed in importance only by the sacred triad of Mecca, Medina, and Jerusalem. Extreme religious fervor alone can account for the city's growth in the inhospitable steppe of central Tunisia. Rumor has it that seven pilgrimages to Kairouan equal one to Mecca—sufficient to absolve your sins entirely. Kairouan has the further distinction of being one of only two Islamic holy cities that admit non-Muslims (Jerusalem is the other). The city was closed to non believers until the last century, when the French forced their way inside the walls, creating a rift in Franco-Tunisian relations that has never been fully mended. According to legend, the city was founded in 670 by Sidi Oqba Ibn Nafi when a spring suddenly sprouted at his feet, revealing a precious gold chalice that had mysteriously disappeared from Mecca. The sanctity of the spot was immediately acknowledged and Kairouan flourished as the capital of the Aghlabite Empire until brutally sacked in 1057. Although it has ceded political prestige to Sousse and Mahdia, its ecclesiastical importance has only increased.

Orientation and Practical Information

Kairouan can be reached by bus from Tunis (3 hr., 2.900D) or Sousse (1½ hr., 1.540D, last bus at 5pm). *Louages* to and from Sousse (1 hr., 1.700D) run until about 8pm.

All of Kairouan's historical sights fall in and around the sprawling *medina,* while most of the town's services cluster around **avenue Habib Bourguiba,** which runs south from **Bab Ech Chouhada,** the main southern entrance to the walled city. **Place de la Victoire,** marked by a giant pedestal that once supported a statue of Habib Bourguiba, is several blocks off av. Bourguiba.

Tourist Office: place des Martyrs (tel. 217 97), facing Bab Ech Chouhada. From place de la Victoire, walk down av. Farhat Hached (to the left of the post office), then turn left. Special combined admission ticket to all the sights is available here (600ml). Ticket required for entrance to the Grand Mosque, the Mausoleum of Abou Zama, the Mausoleum of Sidi Abid Al Ghariani, and the Aghlabite Pools. Pick up a map here and ask them to mark the sights on it. Open Sat.-Thurs. 8am-5pm, Fri. 8am-noon.

Post Office: place de la Victoire. Its location on the map is incorrect. Open in summer 7:30am-1pm; in off-season 8am-1pm and 3-5:45pm.

Telephone Office, a few blocks from the post office. Take the 2nd right off av. de la Victoire. The office is on your right past the Budget Rent-A-Car.

Bus Station: At the *gare goutière,* in the eastern part of town on the route to Sousse. From the tourist office, walk right along the *medina* wall, take the 2nd right, and bear left.

Louages: Departures from the side streets off av. Bourguiba, behind the post office.

Swimming Pools: The **Hotel Continental,** near the Aghlabite Pools, and the **Hotel des Aghlabites,** near the youth hostel, will let you in for 2D and 1.500D, respectively.

Accommodations and Food

Kairouan is most economical as a daytrip from Sousse. Although budget rooms are plentiful both inside and outside the *medina,* budget fare is scarce.

Youth Hostel (IYHF), av. de Fès (tel. 203 09), near Hotel des Aghlabites. To be sure you find it, pass in front of the municipality building, to the left of av. Bourguiba, and take the circuitous route hugging the buildings on the right side. Members only. Dormitory beds with sheets 2D. Hot showers 200ml.

Hotel Sabra, rue Ali Belhaouane (tel. 202 60), next to the tourist office outside the *medina.* Comfortable and affordable. Safe. Singles 3.500D. Doubles 6D. Triples 9D. Breakfast and showers included.

Hotel Marhala (tel. 207 36), in the covered passageway of Souk el-Blaghjsa. Enter the *medina* via Bab Ech Chouhada, follow rue Ali Belhaouane until you see the entrance to the covered Souk el-Blaghjsa on your right. Actually a converted *madrasa* (Koranic school)—you sleep in what were the monks' cells. The courtyard is a bar. Unsafe for women. Singles, doubles, or triples 4D per person.

Hotel des Aghlabites, place Port de Tunis (tel. 208 80). Make a left off place de Tunis beyond Bab el Tounes to the end of the main *souk* at Bab ech Chouhada. In the heart of the *medina,* so not a wise choice for women. Simple and tidy rooms 3D per person. Showers included.

Most of the cheaper restaurants in Kairouan inflict fixed-price menus upon unsuspecting tourists. Pack a picnic lunch, including drinks. Because of the high mercury level and greedy vendors, beverages sometimes go for a whopping 500ml. (However, Cafe Sabra next to the tourist office sells soda for 140ml.) Always inquire about prices before you chow or chug. Kairouan's sweet shops feature the town's pride, *makroudh,* a rich pastry stuffed with dates and smothered in honey.

Restaurant Barrouta, behins the Barrouta. Large helpings for little money. Walk through the kitchen to get to the tables or eat outside. Most entrees 900ml-1.200D. The *macaroni-poulet* saturates nicely, and omelettes come in a wonderful spicy sauce.

Restaurant Fairouz, marked by large signs off rue Ali Belhaouane in the *medina.* A cross-cultural wonder: tasty Tunisian fare at non-Tunisian prices served with French folksongs blaring on the radio. *Poulet* with salad 2.400D. Open daily 11am-10pm.

Sights

Plan your walking tour of Kairouan around the combined ticket available at the tourist office. The sights included are the most important, and the only ones that can be entered by non-Muslims. The **Grand Mosque** (also known as the **Sidi Oqba Mosque**) is open only from 8am to 4pm (during Ramadan 8am-noon), while the other monuments are open from 8am to 6pm. As usual, you can enter the courtyard of the Grand Mosque but not the main prayer room. (Covers provided for those not in proper Muslim attire; 600ml.) Directly in front of you, the *mihrab* (prayer niche) and *minbar* (pulpit), brought from Baghdad and installed in 862, are two of the oldest examples of luster tile decoration in the world. On either side extends the prayer rooms' so-called "forest of columns," gathered from various sources. Their capitals reveal Roman, Byzantine, and Aghlabite origins. The import blocks—slats of wood introduced where the fit with borrowed capitals wasn't perfect—date from the original structure. The oldest Islamic monument in the Western world, it was erected in 688 and rebuilt in 695. Most of what you see today is ninth-century Aghlabite work that has been renovated over the centuries, resulting in an architectural hybrid. Opposite the sanctuary stands the oldest minaret in the world, built in 836. Ten minutes west of the Grand Mosque, just beyond the northern entrance to the *medina,* lie the **Aghlabite Pools,** commissioned by the son of Muhammad the Aghlabite in the ninth century. The well-conserved circular cisterns look younger than their thousand years, but the stagnant, putrid water doesn't.

The **Mausoleum of Abou Zama** is also known as the **Zaouia de Sidi Sahab,** referring to Abou Zama's role as a companion to the Prophet. Still another name for this mausoleum is **Mosquée du Barbier,** for Abou Zama always carried with him hairs of the Prophet's beard. The Zaouia is home to a religious brotherhood and its founder's tomb. Enter the courtyard and then duck through a side door into a small foyer with a carved cedar ceiling. A colonnaded corridor leads to another such foyer with an equally intricate ceiling in white stucco. The foyer leads to a second courtyard surrounded by monks' cells and saints' remains. Note the decorative tile depicting buildings, trees, and flowers, a departure from the non-pictorial tenet of Islamic art. The courtyard's ornamentation represents the apex of Islamic decorative art in Tunisia.

Head back toward the tourist office to visit **Zaouia Sidi Abid El Ghariani,** on the second right as you enter Bab ech Chouhada. It is hard to imagine a more serene resting place than this small building with its tiny courtyard of striped blue-and-white arches designed in the Moorish fashion. In a side room with a delicately carved ceiling lies the saint, doubtlessly resting in peace. Although first dedicated in 1402, the mausoleum has had many a face-lift in the past century. Up the street from the Zaouia, the **Societé Tapis-Sabra** sells its rugs in the spectacular former quarters of the pre-colonial beylile governor. Among Kairouan's numerous under-recognized mosques and holy monuments, the most noteworthy is the delicate ninth-century **Mosque of Three Doors** (Mosquée de Trois Portes).

Mergoum carpets line the walls of Kairouan's *souks.* On the third floor of a local cooperative, the **Centre Kairouanais du Tapis,** at 35, Souk des Tapis (tel. 202 23), you can watch women at work on their looms. (Open daily 7am-8pm.) A 1m by 2m rug takes more than a month to weave and includes in excess of 40,000 knots. The diamond-shaped pattern is common, symbolizing the four holy cities of Mecca, Medina, Jerusalem, and Kairouan. The *aloucha* rug signifies the Sahil's flocks of sheep, and usually comes in natural colors. Often the pattern is shaped like a *mihrab,* or prayer niche, so that the rug can be used for the ritual bows toward Mecca.

Across from the Souk des Tapis, in the narrow confines of the **Bir Barrouta,** a camel endlessly circles, pulling a fourteenth-century mechanism that extracts water from a sacred spring far below the chamber. For a small donation you can sample the refreshing water that, according to legend, flows underground from Mecca.

Kairouan draws a crowd from across Tunisia for its festive celebration of **Mouled,** the prophet Muhamed's birthday. In 1989, Mouled falls on October 23.

Near Kairouan

A new **museum** housing treasures from Kairouan is located 7km outside the city on the road to Sfax. Inquire at the tourist office for directions and information.

The Roman city of **Mactaris,** 110km west of Kairouan, next to the town of **Maktar,** boasts incredibly intact Roman baths. Adjacent to the ruins is a small **Lapidary Museum.** The hotels **Mactaris** and **Marhaba** offer beds for under 3D. Thirty kilometers north at **Seliana** is an **IYHF youth hostel** (tel. 708 71).

The Roman city of **Suffetula,** established near the end of the first century C.E., lies on the western edge of **Sbeitla** and is a premier ruin site in Tunisia. You will immediately recognize the view through the triumphal arch of the magnificent **Capitoline Temple Complex**—it's on the cover of most tourist brochures and road maps of Tunisia. The site covers a vast area, takes several hours to tour, and rivals Dougga and Bulla Regia in grandeur. (Admission is 1D. Photo permit 2D, but there are so many crumbling walls to crouch behind that some play shutterbug surreptitiously.) A small **museum** is across the road from the entrance to the ruins. Peek inside to see if more than the front two rooms are open before you pay (free with ISIC).

Sbeitla lies 115 km from Kairouan on the main road to Kasserine and can be accessed by an infrequent bus or *louage.* (The last bus to Kairouan leaves at 1:30pm.) From the bus/*louage* station, walk a few blocks down the main road (away from Kasserine), and turn left on a side street. It's a 10-minute direct shot to the ruins. Five minutes beyond the first arch is the entrance and the museum.

There are two hotels in town: the **Bakini** (tel. 652 44; singles 13D, doubles 18D, breakfast included) and the **Suffetula** (tel. 650 74 or 653 11; singles 14.200D, doubles 19.400D, breakfast included). The latter is more expensive, but one of the best deals in Tunisia: Air-conditioned rooms overlook the ruins and a swimming pool. The restaurant serves delightful dishes in peace and quiet (entrees 2-2.500D).

Monastir

Fame transformed Monastir into a monster. Since Habib Bourguiba's birth on August 3, 1903, it has evolved from a small coastal village into the nation's foremost tinsel town. Presidents-for-life are rarely noted for their modesty, and Bourguiba was no exception. Determined to carve out a slice of immortality in his hometown, he supplemented Monastir's handsome ancient monuments with a pair of equally monumental modern shrines dedicated to himself. Such lack of subtlety pervades the rest of the town too without a facade lining its *medina,* Monastir is tourist junk shops through and through. The city's historical importance as a stronghold on the Mediterranean coast, however, antedates Bourguiba's birthday by a good thousand years, and for the foreign visitor, the primary attraction remains the splendid Ribat of Harthema.

Orientation and Practical Information

You'll find the **tourist office** in the *medina* on rue de l'Indépendence (tel. 619 60), across from the Bourguiba Mosque. (Open Mon.-Sat. 7:30am-1:30pm.) They'll give you a free map, but otherwise they're useless. The **metro station** is opposite the *medina.* Walk down av. Bourguiba and turn left at the major square onto rue Trimeche to reach both the primary sights and an overdose of Bourguiba visages. From the station, trains leave for Sousse every 40 minutes (5:30am-11pm, ½ hr., 410ml), where you can connect with trains, buses, and *louages* to points all over Tunisia. From the **bus station, 1 block to the north along the** *medina* walls, buses leave for Mahdia (only in the morning) and the nearby beach at Skanes. Until late evening *louages* depart from the same location for Sousse (500ml) and Ksar Hellal (550ml), where you can transfer to a *louage* bound for Mahdia (650ml). Due to its popularity with ritzy tourists, Monastir delves deeply into the dinar. Visit the city as a daytrip from Sousse or en route to Mahdia.

Accommodations and Food

Budget accommodations in Monastir have gone the way of the passenger pigeon. The **youth hostel (IYHF),** on rue de Libye past the bus/*louage* station (tel. 612 16), costs 2D per night, but often full. (Members only.) The **Hotel Yasmin** (tel. 625 11) is the only one-star hotel in town. Though pricey (singles 11D, doubles 17D), the rooms, complete with private baths, are beautiful. The breakfast included comes with orange juice, cheese, and hot chocolate. Take route de la Falaise 1km north from the Ribat. Monastir's most authentic and economical restaurants line the waterfront.

Sights

Monastir's principal attractions are compactly located on the broad esplanade facing the main entrance to the *medina.* The circuit can be liesurely made within a few hours. Dominating the horizon are the massive stone walls of the **Ribat of Harthema,** the finest and largest of North Africa's chain of fortified monasteries when it was erected in 796. The thick walls of the fortress and its colossal interior courtyard possess a graceful austerity and were a tremendous achievement of military architecture. Outside the Ribat, the scaffolding from Hollywood filming (Zeffirelli's *Life of Christ* and Monty Python's *Life of Brian,* for starters) has only recently been dismantled. Once inside, climb the watchtower; from here you can appreciate its strategic value. A fabulous little **museum** contains artifacts ranging from coins and manuscripts to delicate Persian miniatures. (Open daily 9am-noon and 3-6:30pm. Admission 1D. Photo permit 2D.) Next to the Ribat, and dwarfed by it, sits the handsome **Grand Mosque,** erected in the eleventh century. Entrance is strictly forbidden to non-Muslims.

Fortunately, non-believers are permitted to visit the courtyard of the **Bourguiba Mosque.** If you ask at the windows along rue de l'Indépendence, you will probably be let in (except during prayer times). Otherwise, you'll have to wait for the **Syndicat d'Initiative**'s (Port de Plaisance, tel. 623 05) Saturday tour at 8:30am. Built from 1963 to 1966, the tastefully decorated mosque is an unusually successful—if occasionally gaudy—venture into Islamic revivalist architecture. Its conspicuous counterpart, the **Bourguiba Family Mausoleum,** is an uninhibited structure with gilded domes and a glossy courtyard of polished Italian Carrara marble. Some art historians consider the two modern shrines of Monastir the finest examples of Neo-Islamic architecture.

If the sand and sea by the Ribat do not suffice, 2km north of Monastir is the superb but crowded beach of **Skanes,** site of a monstrous presidential palace. Like Sousse and Mahdia, Monastir holds an **International Festival** in July and August (tickets 500ml-5D).

Mahdia

The Fatimid leader Obeid Allah was the first to realize the tremendous strategic value of the long thin peninsula of Cape Africa. Reverently known as *al-Mahdi* ("the Deliverer"), he proceeded to fortify the peninsula and found a city. Mahdia grew into an invincible bastion and flourished as the capital of the Fatimid Dynasty. Obeid Allah built the main fortress facing east toward Cairo in the hope that his rule would soon extend that far. In 968, the Fatimids gained control of Cairo and the dream was fulfilled. However, the city's glory proved short-lived. Before the century was over, Mahdia was sacked by a Christian fleet, leaving the city with a handful of impressive monuments and the memory of a heroic past. What remains is a tranquil town with an endearing *medina,* free of the telltale trappings of tourism. Winds buffet the rows of ancient stone houses, dust blows through the cobbled streets, and even the facades of its mosques bear a slightly weathered look. Mahdia lacks the polished veneer of the more popular resorts to the north, but compensates with authenticity.

Orientation and Practical Information

Rue Oubad Allah el Mehdi, the *medina*'s main drag, is narrow and charming. It originates at the massive stone gateway of the Skifa Bab Zouila and passes through place du Caire and then place Kadi Noamene, the city's three focal points. Just inside the Skifa, the **Syndicat d'Initiative** is the first building on the street. A map can be hard to come by, as the office doubles as a paint shop. **Buses** depart from the port area for Monastir, El Djem, Sousse, and Sfax. The last buses leave around 8:30pm. **Louages** are a much more convenient option to and from Mahdia, as service is frequent and competitively priced to Sousse (1.500D), Ksar Hellal (650ml), and El Djem (950ml). *Louages* leave from the Esso station next to the port, 2 blocks from the Skifa and across from the **train station. Avenue Habib Bourguiba** is the new city's main artery; along it you'll find most banks, travel agents, and, five minutes from the Skifa on the right, a **supermarket.** (Open Tues.-Sat. 8am-12:30pm and 3:15-7:30pm, Sun. 8am-12:15pm.)

Accommodations and Food

The paucity of visitors to Mandia means few options for budget accommodations, but what exists is great. Avoid arriving late in the day in summer without reservations. Mahdia's handful of restaurants cluster in the port area. Evenings in the *medina* revolve around cozy **place du Caire,** where outdoor cafe tables swell with locals.

Hotel El Jazira, rue Ibn Fourat, 36 (tel. 816 29). Walk from Skifa to place du Caire, turn left onto rue du Corrique, and walk to the water. Jazira is on your left. An incredible bargain. Clean, cozy rooms, some of which overlook the sea. Helpful management, attractive rooftop terrace. Vacancies slim in summer. Safe for women, but exercise caution crossing the *medina* at night. 2D per person. Breakfast and shower each 500ml.

Grand Hotel, on av. Bourguiba at av. Bechir Sfar (tel. 800 39). Walk 5 min. up av. Bourguiba from Skifa. Spotless rooms, some with shower. The shady courtyard in front serves as the local watering hole. 5D per person in summer; 4D in off-season. Breakfast included.

Hotel Rand, av. Taïeb M'hiri, 20 (tel. 804 48), several blocks from an excellent beach. From Skifa, walk up av. Bourguiba, bear left at the fork, and turn left at *gouvernerat* (10 min.). Spacious, spic-and-span rooms, congenial management. Singles 3D, with bath 4D. Doubles 6D, with bath 8D. Extra person 2D. Breakfast 500ml.

Camping: El Asfour, on the public beach, along the Sousse road between the El-Mehdi and Sables d'Or hotels.

Restaurant Medina, in the market building behind the large Banque de Tunisia. Spicy fare at mild prices. Amazing *brik à l'oeuf* (350ml) and *couscous au poisson* (1.200D). Open daily 8am-10pm.

Restaurant El Moez, 2nd alleyway inside the Skifa. Quiet place specializing in the day's catch. Octopus and fish dishes 1.200D.

Sights

The **Skifa Bab Zouilar** (Dark Entrance), the imposing gateway to the *medina,* is the logical place to start a tour of Mahdia. Originally, it served as the only land gate to the heavily fortified Fatimid capital. Substantially restored by the Spanish in the sixteenth century, the Skifa's walls are over 10m thick, while its long dark namesake passageway stretches over 44m. From the Skifa, walk down rue Oubad Allah el Mehdi to place du Caire, dominated by the glazed tile facade of the **Moustapha Hamza Mosque.** Mahdia's most venerable monument is a little farther toward the water at place Kadi Noamene. The **Obeidite Mosque** is Islam's oldest Fatimid mosque, and after the Grand Mosque in Kairouan, Tunisia's holiest. Obeid Allah first built the structure in 921, but a cycle of gradual deterioration and restoration has continued most recently in 1961-65. Despite major facelifting, the building's original Fatimid design has been kept intact and the long, simple lines distinguish the mosque as an incredibly harmonious structure. The arcaded courtyard conducts you to a colonnaded sanctuary. Its unadorned pillars are offset only by modest rush mats that cover the entire floor of the prayer room. At all times, visitors are restricted to the main courtyard, and extremely modest attire is required. (Inquire at the *syndicat* for the entrance hours. If they're closed, check the mosque Sat.-Thurs. in late afternoon.) Continue from the Grand Mosque along the *medina*'s waterfront, where you're likely to see young locals diving for octopus. Ahead looms the immense **Borj el-Kebir,** literally "big fort," which commands a bird's-eye view of all approaches to the city by either land or sea. The peninsula's present fortifications were erected by the Spanish toward the end of the sixteenth century. They are definitely worth a look, if only for the tranquility. (Open daily 8am-4pm. Admission 800ml.) The Borj is also home to **The Nights of Mahdia,** the equivalent of the International Festival of Sousse. It features the same shows, and tickets are sold at the gate (500ml-2.500D).

Farther along the peninsula, the **Fatimid Port** continues to harbor fishing boats over 1000 years after it was hewn out of the rocky shoreline. At the tip of windblown Cape Africa, a solitary lighthouse presides over Mahdia's sprawling cemetery. The famous underwater treasures of a sunken Roman ship were discovered off the cape in 1907 (currently on display at the Bardo Museum). After the circuit of the peninsula, continue down the coast toward Monastir and you'll come upon the **municipal beach.** Farther along the route to Sousse, the beaches remain unmarred by the debris of resort hotels that have inundated the coastline to the north. At sunset, the old stone mansions along the water's edge bathe in an orange glow.

Near Mahdia

South of Mahdia, off the road to Ksour Essaf, lies **Salakta.** Turn off at the sign and follow the road to the coast; then veer left and you'll reach **Sullecthum,** an ancient Roman seaport that engaged in lucrative trade. Though small, the **archeologi-**

cal museum houses interesting relics, including a remarkable mosaic of a lion. (A tip to the caretaker will open the museum anytime.) All around the museum, and south along the white, sandy beach, stand the ruins of the once active port.

El Djem

The colossal **amphitheater** of El Djem rises abruptly from the flat plain of the Sahil, dwarfing the uninteresting village huddled around its walls. Located along an ancient Roman road precisely halfway between Sousse and Sfax, it was once the favorite destination for citizens of Roman Africa in search of bloodthirsty entertainment. Its three tiers of seats held crowds of over 30,000, and the games of El Djem were said to rival even those of Rome. It is the world's sixth largest coliseum, and is far more intact than its famous Italian counterpart. In 1695, however, an overzealous tax collector was permitted to unleash rounds of artillery fire upon the ancient arena in order to chase out tax evaders who had installed themselves there, thus leaving the arena pock-marked. The original stepways have been reconstructed, permitting ascent from one tier to the next. From the top level, the vast plain of the Sahil stretches before you, interrupted only by the unwavering line of the asphalt highway. Underground, a tunnel extends the length of the amphitheater. (Arena open sunrise-sunset. Admission 1D.) In July and August, the coliseum is the spectacular setting of the **Festival International de Musique Symphonique.** On the road south to Sfax (10-min. walk from the amphitheater) lies the **Archeological Museum** and another, smaller amphitheater. The museum contains mosaics that once adorned the villas of the Roman city of Thydrus, the predecessor of the contemporary village. (Open Tues.-Sun. 8am-noon and 3-6pm. Admission 1D, with ISIC free. Photo permit 2D.) Behind the museum stand the ruins of a **Roman villa.** Most of the mosaics are now in the museum but those that remain conjure up images of a sumptuous lifestyle. If you are conversant in French, tip the curator and have him guide you through the ornate dining room and swimming pool.

The drab main avenue of El Djem still bears the formerly obligatory name of Bourguiba. At the opposite end from the arena, you will find El Djem's only hotel, next to the **train station: Hotel Julius** (tel. 900 44 or 904 19), with plush singles for 6.500D, doubles 11D, and triples 12D, including breakfast.

There are a few hole-in-the-wall places to eat in El Djem, but only the **Restaurant de Bonheur,** 1 block from the hotel down the road to Sfax, stands out. Avoid the undelectable *viande* dishes, but the *Poulet rôti* (1.500D) and salads (700ml) are palatable. Or request an excellent omlette (1D); it is not on the menu. The **post office** (open Mon.-Thurs. 8am-noon and 2-5pm, Fri.-Sat. 8am-12:30pm) and a **bank** are also on av. Bourguiba.

Due to its setting on the country's main north-south artery, El Djem is easily accessible. Six buses per day stop here en route to Sousse and Sfax, as well as five trains (1.590D). *Louages* to Mahdia run 950ml. Buses and *louages* depart from the square in front of Hotel Julius, across from the train station. You can leave bags safely at the train station for 500ml each.

Sfax

Tunisia's second largest city takes pride in its bustling prosperity, accomplished without anything relinquished to the tourist hordes. Although Sfax lacks notable monuments and dazzling beaches, it offers itself—an authentic modern metropolis. Amidst urban sprawl, Sfax's excellent *medina*—reputedly the oldest in Tunisia—has avoided the trinket syndrome that infects so many of the country's old quarters.

After enduring attacks by the Normans, Spaniards, and Turks, Sfax gave the French the fiercest resistance they encountered in all Tunisia when the imperialists dropped in for their seven-decade visit. The standoff produced two of the nation's most prominent nationalist leaders: Farhat Hached and Hedi Chaker. Speaking of leaders, the statue of Habib Bourguiba, once marking the town center, has been demolished, leaving only the pedestal to signify the recent downfall of Tunisia's 30-year autocracy.

Orientation and Practical Information

Avenue Habib Bourguiba, which begins at the **train station** and ends at the **port,** is the central artery. Where the statue once stood in the large square, take a right on **boulevard de la République** to head for the **medina.** On the way you will cross **boulevard Farhat Hached,** the city's other main street. **Avenue Hedi Chaker** runs in the opposite direction from the main square. The two major shopping alleys, **rue Mongi Slim** and **rue de la Grande Mosquée,** run parallel, stretching from the main entrance of Bab Diwan across the *medina* to Bab Djebli.

Tourist Office: av. Bourguiba (tel. 246 06) on place de l'Indépendence. All the Sfax you need, plus instructions on how to reach the youth hostel outside the city. Open Mon.-Sat. 7:30am-1:30pm.

Currency Exchange: Numerous banks line the main avenues, but in a pinch the Hotel Sfax will change money during off hours.

Post Office and Telephones: 5, av. de l'Armée at av. Bourguiba, 1 block from the train station. Postal service available Mon.-Sat. 8am-6pm, Sun. 9am-1pm. Phones available daily 8am-10pm.

Train Station: At one end of av. Bourguiba. To Sousse (6 per day) and Gabes (2 per day, 1st at 11:15am, 2.860D).

Ferries: At the port. Walk down av. Bourguiba away from the train station, then turn left on av. Mohammed Hedi Khefacha; a few blocks farther you will find the Bassin des Voliers where the ferries depart. To the Kerkennah Islands (6 per day in summer; the 1st leaves at 7am, the last returns at 6pm; 1½ hr.; 500ml).

Foreign Newspapers: At the kiosk in place Marbury, across av. Bourguiba and to the left of the archeological museum.

Accommodations and Food

Two of the three bargain hotels in Sfax are inside Sfax's *medina.* Although not as chaotic as the one in Tunis, this *medina* can be unnerving, especially for women. Before heading off to the Kerkennah Islands, stop at the **Monoprix** supermarket on av. Hedi Chaker to stock up on staples. (Open Mon.-Sat. 9am-12:30pm and 3:30-7:30pm, Sun. 9am-1:30pm.)

Youth Hostel (IYHF; tel. 232 07), in the suburb of Pic-Ville. 2D. Lockout 9:30am-5pm.

Medina Hotel, 53, rue Mongi Slim (tel. 203 54), the right-hand street in the *medina.* Decent rooms with comfortable beds at 3D per person.

Hotel El-Jemiaa, 89, rue Mongi Slim (tel. 213 42), farther down the street. Spartanly clean. 3D per person.

Hotel de la Paix, 17, rue Alexandre Dumas (tel. 214 36). From the train station, walk up av. Bourguiba 3 blocks and turn left. A step up in comfort and safety. 4D per person. Showers 500ml.

Restaurant Boudaya, place de la Journée de Tunis, to the left of Bab Diwan as you enter the *medina.* Hearty meals about 1.500D. Open daily 9am-10:30pm.

Restaurant Oriental, av. Hedi Chaker (tel. 219 71), near the *medina.* The china plates and ceiling fans complement the excellent food. Combine the *brochette* (2.500D), *salad Tunisienne* (1D), and *pomme frites* (700ml) to make a fabulous meal.

Sights

The **Musée des Arts and Traditions Populaires,** in the heart of the *medina* (from Bab Diwan, walk up rue Mongi Slim, turn right at rue de la Driba, and take your second left), houses intriguing costumes and household items, and its seventeenth-century interior courtyard adds to the museum's simple charm. Don't miss the calligraphy display on the top floor, where several Islamic works closely resemble Far Eastern designs. (Open Tues.-Sun. 9am-4:30pm. Admission 800ml, students free.) The **Archeological Museum,** on av. Bourguiba across from the equestrian statue of the president, harbors a small but varied collection of ruins and relics from the Sfax area. (Open Mon.-Sat. 8am-12:30pm and 3-6pm, Sun. 8am-12:30pm. Admission 500ml, with ISIC free.) After you exhaust the *medina*'s offerings, hop on a boat to the Kerkennah Islands.

Kerkennah Islands

The endless rows of date palms and eucalyptus trees on these colorful islets blend with the sounds of sun and surf to create an environment of languid leisure.

Only **Melita** and **Chergui,** the two largest members of the archipelago, are inhabited, with a causeway which dates from Roman times running between them. The population consists largely of fisherfolk who tenaciously cling to traditional ways, but who nevertheless hospitably host the occasional foreign visitor. Kerkennah's isolation has long attracted unwilling guests from Hannibal to Bourguiba for various durations of imposed exile; now, it attracts an increasing number of tourists. While the islands remain largely unspoiled, most visitors cluster around the main beach area of **Sidi Frej** and the expensive hotels that provide most of the island's services. The water is very shallow and the flat terrain barely rises 10 feet above sea level. Nevertheless, the setting is unquestionably idyllic, and Kerkennah is the perfect place to kick back.

The ferry drops you at inconsequential **Sidi Youssef** on the southern tip of Melita, and island buses will carry you the 15km across the sparsely inhabited isle to either the hotels at **Sidi Frej** (440ml), the southwestern shore of Chergui, or **Remla** (the island's largest village, 500ml), 7km farther north. The erratic buses also return to the port before each ferry, but only the hotel van (1D) meets the 1pm ferry.

The cheapest places to stay on the island are in Remla. A new **youth hostel** (IYHF; tel. (04) 811 48) stands next to a marshy stretch of water, but conveniently lies near many local fishing boats, some willing to take you along. The hostel charges 2D per night, breakfast 500ml, full meals 2D. You can **camp** in the courtyard for 700ml. From the bus stop, walk along the main road out of town, turn right at the sign for the hostel, and left again (at another sign) just short of the waterfront. The **Jazira Hotel** (tel. 810 58), in the center of town, costs a mere 2.500D per person, but its uninspiring location defeats any beach-vegetating purpose. On the beach at Sidi Frej, the **Hotel El Kastil** (tel. 812 12) offers 12 spacious bungalows for 6D per person in summer, 3D in winter. Its moderately priced restaurant serves dishes for 2-3D. The **Hotel Cercina** (tel. 812 28 or 812 62), next door, offers rooms for 10D per person in summer, 7.500D in winter, including breakfast. For another 3D, savor fresh red mullet on a full pension. Farther up the beach, **Club Kerkennah** (tel. 812 20) is an excellent deal at 14.500D for full pension, including unlimited use of the hotel's **sailboards.** The club will rent you a bike (500ml per hr.) or a sailboard (3D per hr.), or take you for a quick water-ski lesson (3.500D). Rounding out the island's offerings, the two-star **Hotel Farhat** (tel. 812 36) and **Grand Hotel** (tel. 812 66) weigh in at 17D and 20.300D respectively in summer, both nearly half that in winter. The Grand Hotel will exchange your **money** (Mon.-Thurs.).

Little remains of **Borj el Hissar,** the ancient shoreline fortifications 2km north of the hotels along a dirt road, but the walk is pleasant and the spot more secluded.

Southern Tunisia

The vast spaces, green oases, and secluded Berber villages of the Sahara will tickle anyone's fancy for emprise. The desert overpowers; its relentless heat seems to have halted even time, as the passing of centuries has left nary an imprint on much of the Sahara. Berbers still dwell in caves, Bedouins still herd camel and harvest dates, and the presence of human life is still a rare mirage in the vast ocean of sand. The diversity of the desertscape surprises most visitors. The **Great Eastern Erg** fulfills their expectations of endless rolling sand dunes. But the Sahara of Southern Tunisia has many other faces: The marshy salt flats of **Chott el Djerid,** the jagged **Ksour Mountains,** the lunar-crater landscape of Matmata, and the bursts of green oasis foliage.

For better or worse, the Tunisian South is being tamed. In summer, sardine-packed landrovers whisk Europeans from the coastal resorts to the interior. Gabes, Gafsa, and Tozeur have swelled to provide the amenities of modern life. Odysseus's land of the lotus-eaters, the island of Djerba, has become a magnet for European sun-worshipers. On the bright side, this means that you can visit the desert without much difficulty or expense. Buses and *louages* connect all major towns, and remote locations are sporadically accessible by *louage.* However, southern Tunisia's most dramatic pockets of scenery and culture lie a bit off the country's public transportation network. The lack of traffic makes **hitching** impractical off the main routes, and those interested in experiencing the heart of the desert will have to pay dearly by renting a car or abandon themselves to the guidance of one of the countless desert safari tours available through any hotel or *agence de voyages* in the south. One of the more reputable organizations, **Sahara Tours,** charges 180D per person for a six-day tour including guides, food, lodging, and transportation. Their office in Tunis is at 45, av. Bourguiba, and in Gabes at 57, av. Farhat Hached (tel. 709 30). **Car Tours,** based in Houmt-Souk on Djerba (tel. 599 86), rents large landrovers with experienced drivers for 100D per day.

Desert Survival

Summer temperatures soar in the Sahara, one of the steamiest corners of the planet. The body loses a gallon or more of liquid per day when the mercury level is this high—if you're drinking sugary beverages (even sweet juices), dilute them with water by about 50% to avoid a reaction. Alcohol and coffee cause dehydration; if you indulge, compensate with more liquid. Drink regularly, as dehydration develops rapidly. Drinking huge quantities of water after the fact, however, can be very dangerous. The desert is *not* the place to sunbathe. Breathable long sleeves, trousers, and a hat actually keep you cooler and protect you from the sun. Always keep your head covered. Whether you are driving or hiking, tote *eight liters of water per person per day;* less is adequate at higher altitudes and in winter.

If you decide to brave it in a **car,** a few caveats are in order. Make sure you don't overheat the engine, and bring food and lots of water for drinking and for the radiator. Make sure your car is equipped with a spare tire and necessary tools, and, on any trips off the major roads, a board and shovel are useful if your car gets stuck in sand. There is usually enough traffic on the roads that you don't have to worry about being stranded if you have car trouble.

Most of the routes marked on maps are navigable, but once you get off the main paved routes, conditions are horrendous. Unfortunately, a reliable road map of Tunisia does not exist. The best are the Carte Routière (available free at ONTT offices) and Michelin (sold in many bookstores); Kummerly & Frey is also trustworthy.

Stay with your vehicle if it breaks down; a car is easier to spot than a lost soul. If stranded, find whatever shade you can, drench yourself with cooled radiator water to ward off dehydration, and if you must move, do so only at night.

Gabes

An uninspiring city at the southern terminus of the rail system, Gabes is the primary gateway for journeys to the Isle of Djerba, the inland oases, and the Sahara. A cheap snooze and a budget meal is about it here, and if for some reason you are not traveling inland, try to venture into the palm groves surrounding the city for a taste of oasis life.

At the far end of av. Bourguiba, you'll find the **ONTT** (tel. 702 54; open Mon.-Sat. 7:30am-1:30pm). If arriving by train, walk 1 block away from the station and turn right on av. Farhat Hached; it's five minutes to the office. Turning left from the station will lead you several blocks to the central **telephone office and post office** (open Mon.-Sat. 8am-5pm), across the street from which is a dirt lot the *louages* call home. Two blocks farther is the bus station, where rival companies run to Djerba (7 per day, 2½ hr., 2.650D), Matmata (4 per day, 45 min., 980ml), Medenine (1¼ hr., 1.620D), Tatahouine (3 per day, 2¼ hr., 2.620D), Kebili (3 per day, 2 hr., 2.400D), and Gafsa (3 per day). *Louage* fares run slightly higher. To travel north along the coast, the train is the best option. Three air-conditioned excursions per day run all the way up to Tunis (6.900D, *direct-climatisé*). **Hertz,** 30, rue Ibn El Jazzar (tel. 709 25), near the intersection of av. Farhat Hached and av. Bourguiba, rents Renault 4s (110D per 3 days, 220D per week, not including insurance or 14.3% tax). **Avis,** on rue Tahar Sfar (tel. 702 10), offers the same sort of deal.

Accommodations

Cheap rooms abound in Gabes, but just enough summer travelers make finding a bed an occasional challenge.

Centre de Jeunesse (tel. 702 71). A **youth hostel (IYHF)** and **campground** on the northern edge of town. From av. Farhat Hached, between the train and bus stations, turn at the pharmacy onto rue Sadok Lassoued. Continue to the end of the street, then turn right and take an immediate left. The youth center is 200m ahead, on the left. Uninspiring but adequate. Members only when almost full, usually late July-Aug. Large, clean dorm rooms 2D. Well-shaded camping sites 700ml per person (tent required). Curfew 11pm.

Hotel de la Poste, av. Bourguiba (tel. 707 18), several blocks before av. Hached. Look for Café de la Poste; the hotel's right above. Huge, tidy rooms. Borderline for women. 3D per person.

Hotel Ben Nejima, 66, rue Ali Jmel (tel. 210 62), at av. Farhat Hached, to the left from the train station. Immacualte rooms with a gregarious manager who brags of his many North American friends. Conveniently located near the bus stations. Decent restaurant downstairs. Singles 4D. Doubles 8D.

Hotel Medina, rue Ali Jmel (tel. 217 21), across the street and down the block from Ben Nejima. Safe for women. Pleasant rooms. 3.700D per person. Extra beds 1.800D. Breakfast included.

Hotel Regine, 138, av. Bourguiba (tel. 720 95), near Hotel de la Poste. Spacious lobby and comfortable rooms. Singles 5.800D. Doubles 8.300D, in winter 9.300D. Triples 11.500D.

Food

Le Petit Bouef, 218, av. Bourguiba, is filled with locals eating *merguez* (1D) and meat entrees (1.200-1.500D). The restaurant below the Hotel Ben Nejima (see above) offers an excellent *brochette* (1.500D) and outdoor seating. **Restaurant de l'Oasis,** 7, av. Farhat Hached, near av. Bourguiba, is a stellar eatery. Prices are steep, the clientele mostly German, but the menu is varied and excellent. Try the heavenly *brik aux crevettes* (1.700D) or spaghetti with a spicy tomato sauce (1D).

Sights

Although there is little of interest in the city, the **market shops** off av. Bourguiba offer good deals on Berber rugs and other native crafts. Gabes's only other immediate attraction is its forest of over 300,000 palm trees leading up to the water's edge, ideal for an evening walk.

Gabes's most sacred and oldest monument is outside town: the **Mosque of Sidi Boulbaba,** overlooking a large cemetery, off the road to Medenine. A **Museum of Arts and Popular Traditions** sits next to the mosque (open Tues.-Sun. 9am-noon and 5-7pm). If you plunge through the interior of the oasis to the village of **Chenini,** down a verdant 5km stretch of road that starts at the Agil gas station, you'll find an oasisside cafe that serves as the departure point for several trails winding through the palm and pomegranate groves. Down the road toward the small white marabout dedicated to Sidi Ali el Bahouli is a pathetic **crocodile farm.** The crocodiles and alligators have been imported from the Nile and Cuba, but some of the other animals of the tiny zoo are indigenous to the local desert. (Open 7am-7pm. Admission 200ml, plus a tip for the attendant who helpfully points out the obvious crocs.) Next to the zoo, an ancient Roman dam blocks a small body of water. Behind the dam a dirt trail winds through the palms to the "cascades." Don't get too excited by the beautiful postcards: The natural body of water has since been transformed into a concrete swimming pool—part of the mini-resort complex of the **Chela Club** (tel. 704 42), located in the middle of the oasis. (Admission to pool 2D. Comfortable singles 10.500D. Doubles 14D. Breakfast included. In winter 1-2D less.) From the bungalows, continue along a round of several tracks to explore the gorge that cuts through the oasis.

A bus runs to Chenini (every hour until 6pm, 180ml) from the cafe just past the Medina Hotel on rue Haj Jilani Lahbib, the 2nd left after the central post office as you walk out of town on av. Farhat Hached. Horse-drawn carriages also lie in wait to take you to and from Chenini for an extravagant 5D.

Isle of Djerba

En route home from the Trojan War, Odysseus happened upon a peaceful desert island where the locals sipped lotus wine and lived in perpetual inebriation. Legend has it that Djerba is Homer's mythical paradise. Indeed, the island has an intoxicating effect on visitors. Its smooth, sandy surface is interrupted only by the tall, slender palm trees and the creamy-white, beehive-shaped dwellings peculiar to the island. Unfortunately, the magical lotus wine has yet to be discovered.

The beautiful northeastern coast of the island, **Sidi Mehrez,** has been transformed into the *zone touristique.* Although the mammoth hotels here charge mammoth rates, do stop to take a look; some, most notably the four-star Hotel Djerba Menzel, feature fantastic architecture.

Houmt-Souk, Djerba's largest town and transportation center, with cheaper food and accommodations, lies 10km to the west, in the center of the northern shore. From here, roads radiate west to the airport, southwest to the uninteresting port of Ajim, and southeast for 25km, past Djerba's two Jewish communities, to El Kantara, the southernmost town on the island. El Kantara is connected to Zarzis, on the mainland, by 7km of causeway (built by the Carthaginians and later upgraded by the Romans).

Buses and *louages* run between Houmt-Souk and Gabes (2½ hr.; bus 2.650D, *louage* 3.200D), Medenine (1¼ hr., louage 2.600D), and Zarzis. Less frequent buses and *louages* travel from Gabes and Medenine to Djorf, where you can catch a ferry across the narrow straits to Ajim. (Beware the plentiful jellyfish in the sea near Djorf. Ferries run 6am-8pm every ½ hr., 4-6am and 8pm-midnight every hr. 600ml per vehicle, foot passengers free.) From Ajim, you can catch a bus or hitch to Houmt-Souk. Tunis Air also flies once daily to Djerba (22D).

Houmt-Souk

Although a village by most standards, Houmt-Souk is the focal point of Djerba. It is the island's transportation hub, commercial center, and administrative capital.

The city is visually appealing: Whitewashed buildings surround a splash of color where the *souks* overflow with local crafts. The town's austere architecture stems from its many Kharijite inhabitants—members of an Islamic sect renowned for its ascetic lifestyle. Many islanders are a bit perturbed by the face-lift their community has received from an expanding ring of car rental agencies, tourist restaurants, and travel services. Although Houmt-Souk remains the most convenient base for a tour of the island, it is not the best place to sample native life.

All major services lie along av. Bourguiba, including the **tourist office** (tel. 509 15), on your left from the bus station. The map they sell for 500ml is useless. (Open in summer Mon.-Sat. 8:30am-1pm and 4-7pm; in off-season 9am-noon and 4-7pm.) The **bus and louage stations** are at the beginning of av. Bourguiba. The **post office** and accompanying **telephone office** are at its far end. (Post office open Mon.-Thurs. 8am-noon and 2:30-5:30pm, Fri.-Sat. 8am-12:30pm. Telephone office open Mon.-Sat. 7am-8pm, Sun. 8am-noon). **InterRent** offers Fiat 127s and Renault 4s with unlimited mileage for 115.800D per three days or 225D per week, not including the registration fee and a whopping 14.29% tax. (Open daily 7:30am-12:30pm and 4-7pm.) You can rent their cars at the airport (tel. 502 33) or at av. Abdelhamid el Cadhi (tel. 504 38 or 502 44), past the mosque on the way to the water. **Hertz,** past InterRent, is more expensive (about 240D per week), but can usually provide cars on short notice and allows you to return the car at any Hertz office for no extra charge. (Open daily 8am-noon and 3-6:30pm.) Next door to InterRent, **mopeds** are rented at 2D per hour or 12D per day. **Bicycles** go for 500ml per hour or 3D per day. (Open 8am-8pm.) Reservations can be made through most of Houmt-Souk's hotels. For **first aid,** call 505 28; for an **all-night pharmacy,** call 507 07.

Accommodations and Food

A night in Houmt-Souk is an experience, largely because the youth hostel and two hotels are renovated, seventeenth-century *fundugs* (resting houses for caravans).

Auberge de Jeunesse (IYHF), 11, rue Moncef Bey (tel. 506 19), 1 block off place Hedi Chaker. Walk straight on av. Bourguiba and through the *souks* on the right. Undergoing renovation in 1988, but promises to be an amazing value. Peacefully set in a 2-story *fundug.* Marred only by tacky leopard-skin sheets on the hardy beds. Genial management. Members only, 1.500D. Curfew midnight.

Marhala Touring Club, 13, rue Moncef Bey (tel. 501 46), next to the hostel. Beautifully restored *fundug,* often fully booked in summer. April-Oct. singles 3.700D, doubles 5.800D. Nov.-March singles 3.300D, doubles 5D. Breakfast included. Excellent meals 2-2.200D.

Hotel Arischa, 36, rue Mustapha Ghazi (tel. 503 84), off place de l'Eglise. Another restored *fundug* with an overgrown central courtyard and a small pool. April-Oct. singles 4.500D, doubles 7D; Nov.-March singles 4D, doubles 6D. Breakfast included.

Hotel Sables d'Or, 30, rue Mohamed Ferjani (tel. 504 23), off place Hedi Chaker. Cozy rooms with shower. Charming courtyard. Singles 4D. Doubles 8D. Triples 10.500D.

Eating out in Houmt-Souk is a bad experience as menu prices reflect the lust for loose foreign money.

Restaurant Central, 128, av. Bourguiba, next to the bus station. Tacky doesn't necessarily mean terrible: Mickey Mouse tablecloths and fake flowers preface fantastic food. The *brochette* (1.700D, beware of the hot green peppers) and the myriad omelettes (600ml) are reliable options.

Restaurant du Sportif, 147, av. Bourguiba. One of the few reasonably-priced restaurants in town. Meat dishes 1-1.700D. Open daily 10am-11pm.

Restaurant Blue Moon, place Hedi Chaker. No bargain, but probably the best of the tourist restaurants in the area. A pleasant garden in another of the town's *fundugs.* Full meals 3-4D.

Sights

Houmt-souk means **"market center,"** and on Mondays and Thursdays the villagers, along with more and more tourists, converge for the market. You can escape the aggressive merchants and overpriced bazaars by exploring the side streets, where artisans still work at embroidery or metal-engraving. Also cast a glance at the tiny white **Ghorfa Mosque,** by place Hedi Chaker, topped by a family of little domes.

The **Museum of Popular Arts and Traditions** assembles a fine collection of Djerban traditional garments, crafts, and folklore. Housed in a converted *Zaouia,* it lies on rue Abdelhamid El Kadhi, in the direction of Sidi Mahrez beach *(zone touristique).* (Open Sat.-Thurs. 9am-noon and 3-6:30pm. Admission 1D.) Most interesting, however, is the imposing, incredibly intact thirteenth-century Spanish fortress **Borj el Kebir** (also called Borj Ghazi Mustapha). The Borj guards sea-access to the port, and its ramparts offer an excellent view of both the town and water. (Open Mon.-Sat. 8am-noon and 3-6pm. Admission 800ml.) Afterwards, walk down to the port to observe the construction of wooden boats from olive trees.

For more relaxing entertainment, try a **Turkish bath** at 93, av. Bourguiba, or the one at #17, near place Hedi Chaker. (Both open to men only 6am-noon, women only 1-6pm. Bath and massage 2D.)

Hara Kebira and Hara Seghira (Er-Riadh)

The names translate into "big ghetto" and "little ghetto," respectively, and these tiny towns south of Houmt-Souk represent Djerba's centuries-old Jewish community. Local Jews proudly date their presence to the destruction of Jerusalem in the sixth century B.C.E., making them the oldest continuous Jewish community in the world. Some historians believe, however, that the first wave of Jewish immigrants left Israel only after Titus destroyed the Temple in 70 C.E. At any rate, they have peacefully coexisted for centuries with the native Djerbans, in the midst of a traditionally volatile Arab-Jewish world.

In recent decades, the community's population has dwindled to 1000 inhabitants in Hara Kebira and 300 in Hara Seghira, due to massive emigration to Israel, France, and Italy. Hara Seghira, known to most Arabs as Er-Riadh, is the site of Djerba's most handsome monument, **La Ghriba Synagogue** (The Miracle). According to local legend, a stone fell from heaven marking the site of the synagogue, and a beautiful maiden with a magic touch assisted in constructing the sanctuary. It has been vowed that when the last Jews leave Djerba to return to the homeland, the rabbi will lock the door of the temple and throw the key back up to heaven for safekeeping. The synagogue's interior sparkles with stained glass windows and enameled tiles, and features various local treasures, including parchment scrolls of one of the world's oldest existing manuscripts of the Torah. The synagogue is the object of an annual pilgrimage of Jews from all over North Africa. Visitors receive robes and yarmulkes or headwraps as they enter. (Synagogue open Sun.-Thurs. 7am-7pm, Fri. 7am-4pm. Small donation expected.) Take bus #14 from Houmt-Souk (6am-6pm, 1 per hr., 210ml). Get off at the PTT and follow the signs to the synagogue. The same bus continues to the small town of **Guellala** in the southern corner of the island, where an ancient tradition of ceramic crafts continues to thrive.

Eastern Djerba

The gorgeous beach of **Sidi Mehrez** begins 10km east of Houmt-Souk, as does an endless chain of luxury hotels. Try walking along the tongue of land that stretches from **Cape Taguermes** out to **Cape Lalla Hadria.** If you intend to indulge, try **Hotel Tanit** (tel. 571 32), a lively European enclave 20km east of Houmt-Souk on the beach. Topless bathers adorn the pool. Half-pension ranges from 20.300D for singles (in winter 9.400D) to 29D for doubles (in off-season 15.400D). Tanit and other hotels also rent **sailboards** and **horses;** both cost about 3D per hour. Just past the beautiful beach of La Seguia, **Club Sidi Ali** (tel. 570 21) will let you camp for 1D per person and 1D per tent, including use of pool and hotel facilities. The beachfront bungalows are also a decent value at 8.500D per person (in off-season 6.500D). In the neighboring village of **Aghir** is an **IYHF youth hostel and campsite** (tel. 573 66), both on the water. The hostel charges 2D per night, 500ml for breakfast, and 2D for lunch or dinner. Camping costs 700ml per person, 500ml per large tent, 300ml per small tent. (Hot showers 500ml.) The hostel is accessible from Houmt-Souk by bus #10 via Midoun or by #11 via the hotels (650ml). The last bus from Houmt-Souk leaves at 6:30pm.

Zarzis

South of Djerba, the impressive 7-km long **El Kantara** causeway connects the island to the mainland. At the opposite end, the tourist resort of Zarzis offers cheaper hotels, unimpressive beaches, and junkier tourist shops than Djerba. Though the beaches are rocky, the port is lovely and the shortage of tourists comes as a relief after Djerba. Near the bus station, **Hotel de la Station** (tel. 806 61) and **Hotel l'Olivier** (tel. 806 37) both offer repectable rooms for 3.300D per person. Next to the latter, **Le Zarzis Restaurant** whips up dependable food: *Merhez* (meat in a sauce of chick peas, onions, and green pepper) is 900ml.

Matmata

The producers of *Star Wars* thought the scenery around Matmata the perfect setting for a movie that takes place on another planet. As you descend upon the village 40km south of Gabes, you'll understand why. The landscape is decidedly extraterrestrial; lunarlike mountains, gaping craters, and desolate rolling moonscape engulf the horizon. Although the film crews packed up long ago, nature still obliges at twilight, when the ominous landscape assumes a ghoulish red glow.

At first glance, the desert surrounding Matmata appears entirely uninhabited. In few places on earth people have learned to dwell more inconspicuously. The Berber population has developed a remarkable mode of inhabitation that is rather uncomplimentarily referred to by travel guides as "troglodyte dwellings." Adapting ingeniously to the bizarre natural landscape, they have both expanded and replicated the craters that dot the landscape. A large central pit is carved out of the ground (usually about 10m deep and 10m wide), while tunnel passageways connect a constellation of adjoining chambers that provide shelter. (Luke Skywalker slept here.) These submerged pits provide cool, shady protection from the scorching sun. The present-day Berbers of Matmata have made some twentieth century concessions—their "primitive" dwellings nowadays often sprout television antennas at ground level.

Matmata's three hotels are naturally all pits. Consisting of large complexes of central pits with surrounding chambers interconnected by a network of passageways, the hotels are like giant human anthills, and are the village's major tourist attractions. Only the new youth hostel is terrestrial.

The site of the famous cantina scene in *Star Wars,* the **Marhala Touring Club Hotel** (tel. 300 15) intrigues the most of the subterranean trio. (Beds March-Oct. 2.900D per person, singles 600ml more; Nov.-Feb. 2.600D per person). An excellent lunch or dinner of *couscous, chorba* (soup), and a pastry runs 2.700D. Less authentic, but slightly more comfortable, the **Sidi Driss** (tel. 300 05) charges about the same, and **Les Berberes** (tel. 300 24), probably the least interesting of the three, is also the most likely to be filled by tour-bus throngs. (2.700D per person. Tasty 3-course dinner 1.800D.) All three hotels offer one-hour **camel rides** for 2D. The uninspiring but clean **youth hostel (IYHF)** is just to the right as you come down the hill into town (no sign). (1.500D. 2D for those traveling without the Force. Breakfast 400ml. Lunch or dinner 2D.) Avoid the cafe's 300ml sodas; small stores offer the same for 150ml.

Don't restrict your tour of Matmata to the pit-hotels. Local children will be more than delighted to show you their homes and neighbors' homes for a few hundred millimes per residence. Once inside a genuine pit-dwelling, you will find the natives hospitable though not without ulterior motives: The lady of the house will generally try to interest you in purchasing some of her embroidery or knitting. Unfortunately, tour-bus denizens have accustomed the little scoundrels to tips of 1-2D, and the children will not hesitate to call you a "Juif" (Jew) if your tip is paltry. You should pay no more than 100ml to 200ml per home.

A number of buses each day run between Matmata and Gabes (980ml), supplemented by *louage* service. Ask to confirm that your ride is going all the way to "Matmata *ancien,*" and not "Matmata *nouvelle,*" 15km short of the village.

Near Matmata

Haddej, several kilometers off the road to Gabes and 5km outside of Matmata, is best reached via buses connecting the latter two cities. This sleepy, subterranean village is a study in what Matmata must have been before mass tourism and George Lucas. **Tamerzet,** 10km to the west of Matmata, is a wonderfully preserved Berber village carved into the cliffs along the side of a mountain and commanding a dramatic view of the bleak landscape surrounding Matmata. Its stone houses are packed tightly together in defensive Berber style. If you follow the trail to the top of the town, you'll come to a cafe where you can enjoy an expensive cup of mint tea (300ml) or climb onto the roof for a look at the village below. (Get chummy with the proprietor and the price will come tumbling down.) Two buses per day run sporadically from Matmata to Tamarzet (480ml). Even if you don't make it to the village, a hike on the road is worthwhile for the dramatic landscape above. You can see more spectacular scenery along the bumpy road to **Toujane,** 23km east. Scenically perched at the edge of a cliff, the village is split in two by a deep gorge. There are no restaurants or cafes here, but children carry around small buckets with warm bottles of soft drinks for 300ml. The road continues to Medenine through more *Star Wars* landscape. However, you will probably want to forgo the direct route between Matmata and Medenine: The road is in terrible shape. Transportation between the two towns is best via the main highways through Gabes. Although twice the distance, this generally proves the more relaxing, the more expedient, and, if you're without a car, the only option.

Medenine

Medenine remains completely untouristed because it is completely uninteresting. It has one attraction, Ksar Medenine, and a weekly Friday morning market. But since Medenine is the administrative capital of the breathtaking **Ksour Mountain** province of southeastern Tunisia, it is the transportation hub of the entire region; chances are you'll get stuck here. Buses infrequently connect surrounding towns, while *louages* supplement bus service to Gabes (4 per day, 1.620D), Zarzis (1 per day, 1.350D), and Tatahouine (2 per day, 1D).

Medenine has hotels running the gamut in price and comfort and a **youth hostel** (IYHF; tel. 403 38), located about 1½km from the center of town on rue des Palmiers, the road to Djorf and Djerba. Look carefully on the left for the nondescript white building after the sign to Djorf and Djerba. A sturdy bed with sheets and clean bathroom is 2D. Other options include the **Hotel des Palmiers** on rte. de Djerba (tel. 405 92; 3- to 4-person rooms 2.500D; unsuitable for women). The **Hotel Sahara** (tel. 400 07), off av. Bourguiba on the road to Tatahouine, has amiable management and comfortable if drab rooms (6.500D per person, including breakfast). The two-star **Motel Agip** (tel. 401 51), on av. Bourguiba at the Gabes junction, has air-conditioned singles for 11.500D and doubles for 16D, including breakfast.

Ksar Medenine fascinates with its *ghorfa* dwellings—enormous, tiered, pigeonholed structures that serve as homes for the Berbers of the Ksour Mountains. Originally constructed for storing grain, over the centuries they were adapted for residential purposes as the Berbers found it advantageous to live in easily protected communities. Residential complexes of *ghorfa* chambers are called *ksars* and dot the mountains of southern Tunisia. Although Ksar Medenine is Tunisia's most famous set of *ghorfa* complexes (in the middle of town along the road to Djerba), it is not the most impressive. What remains of the original community encircles a large central courtyard with the open faces of the dwellings directly opposite one another. The tiers of chambers have mostly collapsed to two layers, but if you climb on the roofs above the courtyard, you can see some triple-level tiers among the surrounding ruins. Originally a settlement of 6000 people, Ksar Medenine is now empty except for the tourist shops and souvenir stands that thrive upon the summertime tour-bus traffic.

Near Medenine

The village of **Metameur,** only 6km from town along a paved road, is the site of more *ghorfa* dwellings. Despite its accessibility via car, foot, taxi, public bus, or thumb, few visit the site. The *ghorfas* are relatively intact, with three full tiers surviving in places. However, they have been largely evacuated by the villagers in favor of concrete modern houses. The best-preserved section was recently converted into the **Ghorfa Hotel,** where you can sleep in one of the primitive but clean chambers for 6D, including breakfast and dinner. Five buses per day (380ml) run from Medenine to Metameur, but after Metameur, the road to Toujane immediately deteriorates.

One of Tunisia's best kept secrets is **Ksar Jouama**—the most spectacular *ghorfa* complex in the Medenine area. Neither the *ksar* nor the neighboring village of Jouama is marked on most maps, but both are accessible by two daily buses along the paved road between Medenine and Beni Kheddache. The turn-off up the hill for Ksar Jouama lies just under 27km from Medenine according to the markers along the road. Now completely abandoned, the site dates from the fourteenth century and has kept miraculously well. Its peaceful hilltop setting offers a panorama of the neighboring village and environs.

The ruins of the Roman port of **Gightis** offer a possible excursion from Medenine. It is most convenient en route to or from Djerba, as the site lies just off the main road, halfway between Medenine and Djorf, where the ferry leaves for Djerba. Over the centuries, the shoreline has receded, leaving the remains of the strategic harbor far inland.

Tatahouine and Chenini

When the Russians talk about going to Siberia, the French talk about going to Tatahouine. Though experiencing the opposite climate extreme as its Russian counterpart, Tatahouine elicits the same feeling of exile and bleakness. While the *Star Wars* makers found the city's name exotic enough to give to one of their planets, Tunisia's southernmost city is only significant as a base for touring the dramatic southern edge of the Ksour mountain range. Although its semi-weekly (Mon. and Thurs.) market does attract some Berbers down from the mountains, Tatahouine remains for the most part a cheerless assortment of concrete buildings. The town was first established in this century and originally served as a convict settlement, but its recent growth is due to its importance as a military outpost near the Libyan border. Two buses per day (1D) run from Medenine, and more frequent *louages* (1.100D). Although some buses and an occasional *louage* provide access to towns along paved roads, the best way to reach more remote villages from Tatahouine is to catch a ride with villagers back home on Mondays and Thursdays after the market—especially to Douriat, Guermessa, and Chenini. You may be charged a few hundred *millimes* for the ride. On the other hand, a taxi into the countryside along the dirt roads runs about a dinar every 4-5km (negotiate with the driver). In April, a **cultural festival** features crafts and music peculiar to the Berbers who live in the *ksars* of the neighboring hills.

If you're stuck in Tatahouine for the night, stay at **La Gazelle** (tel. 600 09), an impeccable and accommodating hotel with a wonderfully air-conditioned lobby where beds are 6.500D, including breakfast. Otherwise, the only beds available are in the **Ennour,** 107, av. Bourguiba, which is dangerous for women (beds 2.500D). Still, the best accommodations are in the *ghorfa* hotel at Ksar Haddada.

The lovely cliffside Berber community of **Chenini,** 20km west of Tatahouine, is one of the country's most picturesque villages, carved into the steep, crescent-shaped cliff and crowned by an enormous ruined *ksar.* Commanding the town from its clifftop location, a white concrete mosque stands like a feudal prince over the crumbling brown mudbrick buildings below. Though at lunchtime the town's restaurant teems with tour bus folk, village life rolls on unruffled for the most part. The oilpress still turns by camel, little children play in ruined *ghorfas,* and old men sit in the shade of the mosque.

Above the buzzing activity of the village stand layer upon layer of ruined *ghorfa* dwellings, now used almost exclusively as donkey or camel stables and for grain storage. The network of honeycombed tiers is remarkably extensive; narrow trails guide you from ridge to ridge. The interiors of the abandoned dwellings can provide intermittent shade from the desert sun. Looking down from the *ksar,* you can see into many of the roofless homes of the village. The villagers have taken to ignoring the swarms of tourists who disembark, take a few snapshots, and drive away. Don't be afraid to spend the night. The village's only commercial enterprise, the **Relais Chenini Restaurant,** will let you crash for free on its grounds, but bring food in from Tatahouine, as they're only open for an expensive and crowded lunch (2.700D).

On the way back to Tatahouine, as you curve around the town, take the dirt road that branches to the right. This atrocious piste twists to the most remote mosque in Tunisia. The so-called **"underground" mosque,** 1km from Chenini, is a tiny, white-domed affair with a small leaning minaret. Its doors are always open and you can climb the minaret if you dare. The dirt road between Chenini and Tatahouine is in excellent condition. The same cannot be said, however, for the road between Chenini and Douriat, a grueling ride that should only be attempted in a sturdy vehicle. The effort, however, will be rewarded by a stark landscape, interrupted by remarkable little patches of vegetation that are the fruits of an extraordinary amount of human labor. **Douriat,** rarely visited by tourists, is encircled by pyramidal mountains. A ruined *ghorfa* village climbs up the slopes of steep rock face adjacent to the town. **Ksar Ouled Debbab,** 9km east of Douriat and 10km south of Tatahouine, features well-preserved *ghorfas* stretching in timelessness along both sides of their clifftop pedestal.

The mountain scenery is dramatic along the dirt road from Chenini to **Guermessa.** Strange-looking conical peaks with sawed-off tops, looking like squat volcanoes, pepper the landscape in all directions. This village, wholly off the trampled path, has not been jaded by tourism. Native Berber women still dress in brilliantly colored traditional garments, with large, engraved silver jewelry.

From Guermessa the dirt road continues to Ksar Haddada (see Near Medenine). The paved road that runs directly from Tatahouine to Ksar Haddada passes through the scenic town of **Ghoumrassen,** delightfully situated in the midst of a palm-studded gorge with cliff walls honeycombed by *ghorfa* dwellings, many still inhabited.

Oases

Scattered like a handful of frogs in a massive sandbox, Tunisia's oases are incomprehensible patches of green in a forbidding landscape. Nearly all have been inhabited since Roman times, and present residents make a living sheltering parched-throat travelers. While the oases differ, all give the impression of a besieged fortress:

The harsh sand resisted by the miraculous power of a tiny spring, the raging sun held at bay by the shade of the palms. And a jillion frogs, presumably former princes, hold court amongst it all.

Unfortunately, transport to the more remote and rewarding oases is difficult without a car. Driving is often complicated by the condition of the "international roadway" (the closest thing in Tunisia to a superhighway) between Kairouan and Gafsa; the road is often impassable. From Gafsa (accessed from major cities by regualr bus), there is frequent service to Tozeur and across the Chott to Kebili and Douz. *Louages* infrequently travel among all the major oasis towns. One overnight train runs each day from Tunis and Sfax, passing through Gafsa, Tozeur, and Metaloui.

Gafsa

Gafsa pales in comparison to Tunisia's other oases, but its accessibility makes it a logical starting point. Founded by the Romans as Capsa, it boasts two Roman pools, both still in use—despite the sludge. Its main claim to fame is more recent, however. Here, on January 26, 1980, a group of Libyan migrant workers attempted a coup to overthrow the Bourguiba regime. Women would be well advised not to venture here on their own, and all travelers should guard their belongings carefully.

The **tourist bureau,** place de Piscine Romaine (tel. 216 64), across from the Roman Pools, is officially open from 8am to noon, but the hours fluctuate. The **bus station** is in place Bourguiba in the center of town. All buses are first come, first serve, except for the daily air-conditioned bus to Kairouan, for which you must make reservations. Buses run to Tozeur (7 per day, 2 hr., 2.360D), Sfax (5 per day, 3 hr., 3.960D), Kairouan (3 per day, 4.840D), and Tunis. One overnight train to Tunis (8½ hr., 6.390D) leaves from the suburb of Gabes Bare, about 4km away.

The **Hotel de Tunis,** rue 11 Mars (tel. 216 60), in place Bourguiba, is run by an affable proprietor eager to practice his English; adequate rooms are 2.500D per person. The **Hotel de la Republique,** rue Ali Belhaouane (tel. 218 07), off place Bourguiba, is marked by sterile, hospital-green rooms for 3.500D per person (breakfast included, showers 500ml, single supplement 2D). The **Hotel Ennour,** rue Mohammed Kaddoum (tel. 206 20), behind place Bourguiba, offers somewhat more pleasant rooms and is safe for women. (Singles 3.500D. Doubles 6D. Triples 7D. Showers 500ml. Breakfast included.) The **Maison des Jeunes (IYHF)** (tel. 202 68) lies on the road to Tozeur. Facilities are grim, but a single bed costs 2D.

If you've ever wanted to be a part of a wild-western movie scene, visit the bar on the first floor of **Hotel Khalfallah,** where you can sip a beer (600ml) while dodging projectiles. The restaurant is less rowdy in the early evening. *Poulet roti* is 1.500D. The **Restaurant de Tunis** in place Bourguiba is not the finest, flashiest, nor friendliest, but incredibly affordable. Napkins are nailed to the wall.

On av. Bourguiba stand the ruins of the fifteenth-century **kasbah,** which can't compare with the beautiful Sahil kasbahs. Inside the walls watch the local soccer teams practicing on the gravel. The **Grand Mosque,** down the street from the kasbah, was built as a replica of the one at Kairouan. The doors are often closed, but if you're admitted, you can enjoy a fine view of the oasis surrounding the city from the minaret.

Two blocks to the west, on the other side of av. Bourguiba behind a dingy, unassuming wall, lie the **Roman Pools.** Local children climb to the top of towering palms and plunge 15m into the pellucid water.

Tamerza, Midès, and Chebika

Tunisia's most beautiful oases are nestled against the Algerian border, 80km from Gafsa. Only **Tamerza** is accessible by public transport: From Gafsa, buses travel to the mining town of Redeyef (4 per day, 1¼ hr., 2D), from which *louages* and pick-up trucks sporadically travel the remaining 33km to Tamerza (500ml). From

Tozeur, the traffic on the partially paved road to Chebika is sparse, but you can grab the torturously slow and roundabout bus to Redeyef (daily at 1:30pm, 2 hr., 2.300D) and then catch a *louage*. Arriving via the latter route, you are treated to a view of the **old village** (abandoned after the floods of 1969), framed against the verdant palms and red mountains. Tamerza is home to three waterfalls, each of which plunges about 30 ft. into a narrow valley. The falls range in temperature from tepid to ice-cold. They begin behind the **Hotel les Cascades,** perhaps the district's only hotel, which provides simple sand-floor straw bungalows for about 4.500D per person, including breakfast. Walking downstream along the mud walls of the valley, you can easily hike into the deep jagged canyon that will appear on your left.

If the hotel is closed (as it has been recently), or you just want to doze in paradise, many of Tamerza's residents will offer you a piece of their greenery for the night. Expect to pay about 1D per head, and be entertained by frogs hopping about your body as you snooze. Beware Tamerza's ubiquitous hustlers. Ask around for Mohamed Salah Taïeb, an honest and congenial host.

Backtracking toward Gafsa, you'll come to an intersection 4km outside Tamerza. If you take the unmarked leftmost of the three roads, you'll be on the way to **Midès,** an undiscovered jewel of Tunisia. Unfortunately, the road is rocky and atrocious. You can make the 6km to the oasis if you have some experience driving on sand—never slow down. Your agony will be well rewarded, despite low water levels in recent years. The **old city** dates from Roman times, and, as at Tamerza, was abandoned only after the 1969 floods. Today, only three families inhabit this outcropping of dwellings; the rest have moved to the new village. If you don't have a car, you can hire a mule and guide in Tamerza for about 5D per person for a half-day visit.

The village wall blends into the sheer cliffs of the impressive canyon that stretches behind Midès. The canyon actually winds its way through the desert clear back to Tamerza. At the western end of the ancient village an observation point commands a superb spread of the Algerian sand dunes extending west past the palms and waterfall. Halfway up the hill, behind new Midès, a red-and-white crescent flutters in the breeze at the Algerian frontier post.

Farther past Tamerza, **Chebika** clings to the side of a hill. This tiny oasis has a lush gorge with a small waterfall. Climb to the right when you reach the end of the gorge. A panorama of the desert, mountain range, and oasis will reward you. For adventure, return via the other side of the ridge and then follow the dry river bed through the narrow gorge. Hiking experience helps since the path through the gorge involves climbing down several dry waterfalls.

In Chebika there is a small cafe where soft drinks cost up to 350ml, depending on how desperate you look. The store across the road sells soft drinks for 300ml and bottled water for 500ml. The road running from Chebika to Tozeur is a rare delight in this neck of the oases.

Tozeur and Nefta

Tozeur lies on the "shores" of the **Chott el-Djerid,** a vast inland flat often covered with a few centimeters of salt water. The green palms of the oasis grow right to the edge of the huge, stagnant lake. Lying on the beach, buffeted by offshore breezes, you'll not believe you're hundreds of kilometers from the sea. The region west of the Chott, called **Bled Djerid,** is full of huge oases like Tozeur, and supports over one-and-a-half million date palms.

The Tozeur **bus station** is on av. de la Republique, off av. Bourguiba. Buses serve Nefta (5 per day, ½ hr., 500ml), Gafsa (7 per day, 2 hr., 2.360D), and Kebili (2 per day, 2 hr., 2.700D). The **louage station** is across the street. Around the corner on av. Bourguiba you'll find the friendly **Syndicat d'Initiative** (tel. 500 34; open in summer daily 7:30am-1pm, in winter 8am-noon and 3-5:45pm).

Affordable shelter abounds in Tozeur, but cheap and appealing restaurants do not. The **Auberge de Jeunesse (IYHF)** (tel. 502 35) hops in the summer. It's close to town and equipped with ping-pong tables. Women's rooms have their own bathrooms with shower; men share a common bathroom. (2D. Curfew 10pm.) Other 2D beds lie in the **Hotel Essaada,** Hart el-Houmt St. (tel. 500 97), 1 block off av. Bourguiba. Signs point the way. The street outside is noisy, however, and the hotel may be unsafe for women. Showers cost 400ml. Continue down av. Bourguiba to find a hotel a tier up in price and comfort: **Residence Warda** (tel. 505 97) on av. Aboul Kacem Chabbi right at the end of av. Bourguiba. Spotless, air-conditioned rooms are only 4D per person, including breakfast and showers (single supplement 1.500D). If your dinar supply is low, try the **campsite** at the foot of the Belvedere, where you can pitch a tent for 800ml per person. As for eating, you can join fellow tourists at the inexpensive **Restaurant El Foauiz,** across from Hotel Splendid. The **Restaurant des Amis,** across from the bus station, is less frenetic and true to its name.

In Tozeur 200 springs pour into a complex thirteenth-century irrigation system that quenches the thirst of 200,000 date palms and numerous banana, peach, fig, and pomegranate trees. A cool walk or donkey or camel ride through the vast palmerie is Edenic. Next door is the *medina,* where the 500-year-old unbaked brick walls and covered walks are decorated in rich geometric patterns. Note the white band around the waist of the women clad in traditional black, a Tozeur trademark. There is also a **folklore museum** on rue de Kairouan next to the market and town center (admission 200ml). The giant signs announcing the **Tozeur Desert Zoo** beyond the youth hostel are worth following. For 500ml you can view a rich variety of desert fauna, including foxes, scorpions, sand fish, and cobras, as well as the furry extras from movies filmed in Tunisia. (You can put your hand in a lion's mouth if that's your style.) There is a similar zoo at **Paradise Gardens,** south of town just beyond Residence Warda. (Both open daily 7am-7pm.) Visit in spring, when the most flowers are in bloom. Syrups distilled from various flowers are on sale at the entrance; an unusual, delicious glass of rose or violet juice goes for 500ml. To appreciate Tozeur's isolation, it's worth struggling up to the top of the **Belvedere,** a rock formation a few kilometers past Hotel Jerid, west on av. Aboul Kacem Chaabi.

West of Tozeur, **Nefta** is another sprawling oasis and a center of Sufism (Islamic mysticism) in Tunisia. But it's distinguished by its ratio of 350,000 palm trees to 100 religious shrines. Calmer than Tozeur, Nefta is traversed by numerous tracks that repeatedly branch off, sending tentacle like paths through the palmerie. Nefta's 17,000 inhabitants are all entitled to their own little tract of garden in the oasis. The source of the life-giving water lies in a huge rock basin, the **Corbeille.** Walk up Sahara Palace Rd. to Café de la Corbeille. From here you can either enjoy the vista or venture down into the palmerie. Two springs, one hot and sulfurous, the other cold, feed a web of shallow irrigation channels, which make the most comfortable paths for exploration. Above the *corbeille* lurks the Sahara Palace Hotel, a behemoth of modernity glowering down upon a bastion of tranquility. After working up a sweat in the *corbeille,* head to the excellent **municipal pool,** a right turn off av. Bourguiba and up several blocks on the dirt road that appears just after you cross the small bridge walking from the bus station (admission 500ml).

The more-or-less useless **Syndicat d'Initiative** (tel. 511 84), soliciting 4D personal tours, is on av. Bourguiba and at Sahara Palace Rd. (Open daily in summer 7am-7pm; in off-season 8:30am-6:30pm.) The **Marhala Touring Club Hotel** (tel. 570 27), usually booked in summer, is just outside town on the road to Algeria; it offers beautiful, tidy rooms around a central courtyard with a shallow pool. Singles are 3.600D, doubles 5.600D, and meals 2.200D. It also offers dormitory-style accommodations for 2.300D per person. **Hotel Nomades,** on the Tozeur road (tel. 570 52), has rooms with fans and private bathrooms; it makes an attempt at authenticity by placing its mattresses on the mat-covered floor. Singles are 7.500D, doubles 10D; meals 2.500D. The low-priced **Restaurant des Sources** (tel. 570 51) is on av. Bourguiba at Sahara Palace Rd. next to the *syndicat;* try the *Ojja merguez* for 1.300D.

The road across the Chott el-Djerid between Tozeur and the oasis of **Kebili** is passable from May to September. Never take your vehicle off the pavement, since water lies just below the surface of salt and spongy sand. In the middle of the lake, you'll be surrounded by a sea of white salt, pink water, and huge crystal formations in amazing shapes. In some places clumps of foliage thrive on the salty underground pools. During the summer, when the salty surface hardens, the Sotutour **Sandsailing** club sometimes sets up a tent beside the road and rents "boats" for 3.500D per hour.

Kebili and Douz

As oases go, there is little that is enticing in **Kebili,** a government administrative center, but the transportation network will probably force you to pass through. Two buses per day and infrequent *louages* cross the Chott to Tozeur (1½ hr., 2.700D). More frequent *louages* hop south to Douz (20 min., 750ml), and 3 buses per day run east to Gabes (2 hr., 2.400D). If a prisoner in Kebili for the night, the **Oasis** on the Tozeur road charges 3D per head.

South of Kebili lies the lush little oasis of **Douz** where the intense heat and humidity are unbearable from 10am to 7pm. The oasis best suits tour groups who bob around in swimming pools during the day and travel into the Sahara at night. The **Syndicat d'Initiative** (tel. 953 41) is down the main road in a cafe. Someone will always be there to snarl at you.

Back in town, 1 block behind the bus and *louage* station and to the right, is the **Hotel 20 Mars** (tel. 954 95). Stay here if you can stand the rat-size roaches native to Douz; it's only 2D per person. If not, charge into the oasis following the signs near the *syndicat* to the **Marhala Touring Club** (tel. 953 15) and the **Hotel Saharien** (tel. 953 37 or 953 39). Both have excellent pools (nonresidents can use the Marhala's for 1D), even if heavily peppered with tourists. The former offers spartan rooms for 6D per person. Half-pension is an additional 1.800D. The luxurious latter option offers singles for 9.450D (with half-pension 13D) and doubles for 15.400D (with half pension 18.700D).

Aside from the oasis, Douz has another natural attraction south of town: Sand. You can explore the rippling dunes of the Sahara on foot (good luck), or hire a camel through the *syndicat* for deeper desert exploration (2D per hr., 17D for an overnight trip including all meals). Camels and carriages leave from the lot by the *syndicat.* You can also walk to a small group of large dunes by following the road across from the *syndicat* 2km beyond the hotels. Vacant 51 weeks per year, the stadium on the town's outskirts comes to life in late December for Douz's **Festival International du Sahara,** featuring camel, horse, and *sloughie* (dog) races, as well as traditional Berber festivities. Hundreds of tourists pour in for the event, and Douz's few hotels saturate months in advance.

There is an 8am bus to Tozeur via Kebili that can save you the hassle of changing buses. In addition, a mostly paved road runs south to **Zaafrane** (2 buses per day from Douz, 300ml), less touristy and deeper in the desert. Exploration farther south is possible only if you have a car, but the roads are passable and the scenery fantastic. From Zaafrane, drive south to **Es Sabria** and **El Faouar,** where you'll find small, modern cities, beautiful palmeries, and a refreshing absence of tourists. The only food available in both towns is at one of several small grocery stores, which usually have *casse croute.*

GLOSSARY

Making Friends

Ciao.	CHOW	Hello, Goodbye.
Buon giorno.	BWON JOR-no	Good day, Hello.
Buona sera.	BWON-ah SEH-rah	Good evening.
Buona notte.	BWON-ah NOT-ay	Good night.
Arrivederci.	ah-ree-veh-DAYR-chee	So long.
Per favore.	PAYR fah-VORE-ay	Please.
Prego.	PRAY-go	You're welcome.
Molte grazie.	MOLE-tay GRAH-tsee-ay	Thank you very much.
Come va?	COM-eh vah	What's happening?
Scusi.	SKOO-zee	Excuse me.
Dov'è . . .	doe-VAY	Where is . . .
il gabinetto?	ill gah-bee-NET-oe	the bathroom?
una banca?	OO-nah BAHNK-ah	a bank?
la stazione?	lah stah-tsee-OWN-ay	the station?
l'alimentari?	lah-lee-men-TAH-ree	the grocery store?
una lavanderia a gettone?	OO-nah lah-van-dayr-EE-ah ah geh TONE-ay	a laundromat?
la spiaggia?	lah spee-AH-jah	the beach?
la chiesa?	lah key-AY-zah	the church?
il ponte?	ill PON-tay	the bridge?
l'ingresso	lin-GREH-so	the entrance?
l'uscita	loo-SHEE-tah	the exit?

Enjoying the Food

cameriere	kah-meh-ree-AYR-eh	waiter
cameriera	kah-meh-ree-AYR-ah	waitress
birra	BEER-ah	beer
vino	VEE-no	wine
acqua fresca	AH-kwah jell-LAH-tah	cold water
gelato	jay-LAH-toe	ice cream
prima colazione	PREE-mah ko-LAH-tsee-OWN-eh	breakfast
colazione	ko-LAH-tsee-OWN-eh	lunch
pranzo	PRAHN-tso	dinner
cena	CHAY-nah	supper

Et Cetera

Non parlo italiano.	nawn PAR-lo ee-tah-lee-AH-no	I don't speak Italian.
Quanto costa?	KWAHN-toe KOE-stah	How much does it cost?
Troppo caro.	TROE-poe KAH-roe	Too expensive.
bo	BOE	I don't know. (also interjectory pause—like the English "um")
L'Italia è bellissima.	lee-TAH-lee-yah AY bell-LEE-see-mah	Italy is very beautiful.

INDEX